Civil Procedure

Carolina Academic Press Context and Practice Series

Michael Hunter Schwartz
Series Editor

Administrative Law
Richard Henry Seamon

Advanced Torts
Alex B. Long and Meredith J. Duncan

Animal Law—New Perspectives on Teaching Traditional Law
Kathy Hessler, Joyce Tischler, Pamela Hart, and Sonia S. Waisman

Antitrust Law
Steven Semeraro

Civil Procedure, Second Edition
Gerald F. Hess, Theresa M. Beiner, and Scott R. Bauries

Civil Procedure for All States
Benjamin V. Madison, III

Complex Litigation
James M. Underwood

Constitutional Law, Second Edition
David Schwartz and Lori Ringhand

A Context and Practice Global Case File:
An Intersex Athlete's Constitutional Challenge,
Hastings v. USATF, IAAF, and IOC
Olivia M. Farrar

A Context and Practice Global Case File:
Rossi v. Bryce, **An International Embryo and Surrogacy Dispute**
Olivia M. Farrar

A Context and Practice Global Case File:
Thorpe v. Lightfoot, **A Mother's International Hague Petition**
for the Return of Her Child
Olivia M. Farrar

Contracts, Second Edition
Michael Hunter Schwartz and Adrian J. Walters

Criminal Law, Second Edition
Steven I. Friedland, Catherine L. Carpenter,
Kami N. Chavis, and Catherine Arcabascio

Current Issues in Constitutional Litigation, Second Edition
Sarah E. Ricks, with co-author Evelyn M. Tenenbaum

Employment Discrimination, Third Edition
Sandra F. Sperino and Jarod S. Gonzalez

Energy Law
Joshua P. Fershee

Evidence, Second Edition
Pavel Wonsowicz

International Business Transactions
Amy Deen Westbrook

International Women's Rights, Equality, and Justice
Christine M. Venter

The Lawyer's Practice
Kris Franklin

Professional Responsibility
Barbara Glesner Fines

Property Law
Alicia Kelly and Nancy Knauer

Sales, Second Edition
Edith R. Warkentine

Secured Transactions
Edith R. Warkentine and Jerome A. Grossman

Torts
Paula J. Manning

Workers' Compensation Law, Second Edition
Michael C. Duff

Your Brain and Law School
Marybeth Herald

Civil Procedure

*A Context and Practice
Casebook*

SECOND EDITION

Gerald F. Hess

PROFESSOR OF LAW EMERITUS
FOUNDER OF THE INSTITUTE FOR LAW SCHOOL TEACHING
GONZAGA UNIVERSITY SCHOOL OF LAW

Theresa M. Beiner

DEAN AND THE NADINE BAUM DISTINGUISHED PROFESSOR OF LAW
UNIVERSITY OF ARKANSAS AT LITTLE ROCK
WILLIAM H. BOWEN SCHOOL OF LAW

Scott R. Bauries

ASSOCIATE DEAN OF FACULTY RESEARCH
WILLBURT D. HAM PROFESSOR OF LAW
UNIVERSITY OF KENTUCKY COLLEGE OF LAW

CAROLINA ACADEMIC PRESS
Durham, North Carolina

ISBN   978-1-5310-0800-0
eISBN 978-1-5310-0801-7
LCCN 2019938701

Carolina Academic Press
700 Kent Street
Durham, NC 27701
Telephone (919) 489-7486
Fax (919) 493-5668
www.cap-press.com

Printed in the United States of America

Contents

Table of Principal Cases

Series Editor's Preface

Welcome to a new type of casebook. Designed by leading experts in law school teaching and learning, Context and Practice casebooks assist law professors and their students to work together to learn, minimize stress, and prepare for the rigors and joys of practicing law. **Student learning and preparation for law practice are the guiding ethics of these books.**

Why would we depart from the tried and true? Why have we abandoned the legal education model by which we were trained? Because legal education can and must improve.

In Spring 2007, the Carnegie Foundation published *Educating Lawyers: Preparation for the Practice of Law* and the Clinical Legal Education Association published *Best Practices for Legal Education*. Both works reflect in-depth efforts to assess the effectiveness of modern legal education, and both conclude that legal education, as presently practiced, falls quite short of what it can and should be. Both works criticize law professors' rigid adherence to a single teaching technique, the inadequacies of law school assessment mechanisms, and the dearth of law school instruction aimed at teaching law practice skills and inculcating professional values. Finally, the authors of both books express concern that legal education may be harming law students. Recent studies show that law students, in comparison to all other graduate students, have the highest levels of depression, anxiety and substance abuse.

The problems with traditional law school instruction begin with the textbooks law teachers use. Law professors cannot implement *Educating Lawyers* and *Best Practices* using texts designed for the traditional model of legal education. Moreover, even though our understanding of how people learn has grown exponentially in the past 100 years, no law school text to date even purports to have been designed with educational research in mind.

The Context and Practice Series is an effort to offer a genuine alternative. Grounded in learning theory and instructional design and written with *Educating Lawyers* and *Best Practices* in mind, Context and Practice casebooks make it easy for law professors to change.

I welcome reactions, criticisms, and suggestions; my e-mail address is mschwartz@pacific.edu. Knowing the author(s) of these books, I know they, too, would appreciate your input; we share a common commitment to student learning. In fact, students, if your professor cares enough about your learning to have adopted this book, I bet s/he would welcome your input, too!

Michael Hunter Schwartz, Series Designer and Editor
Consultant, Institute for Law Teaching and Learning
Dean and Professor of Law, McGeorge School of Law,
University of the Pacific

Civil Procedure

Chapter 1

Introduction and Overview

Welcome to the study of Civil Procedure. The co-authors of this book find the study of Civil Procedure both fascinating and challenging. We hope you will as well. The foundations of Civil Procedure consist of big ideas, including justice, power, efficiency, and fairness. At the same time, Civil Procedure is intensely practical, providing the mechanism to resolve millions of disputes each year though civil litigation. For many lawyers, civil litigation makes up a significant portion of their practice.

This chapter is designed to help you succeed in this course by briefly providing background information, fundamental concepts, and a context for the course in these areas:

- Section 1—Context and Practice Series Casebooks
- Section 2—Nature of Civil Procedure
- Section 3—Sources of Law
- Section 4—United States Court System
- Section 5—Characteristics of Civil Litigation
- Section 6—Alternative Dispute Resolution
- Section 7—Professionalism
- Section 8—Legal Reasoning
- Section 9—Timeline of a Civil Lawsuit.

1. Civil Procedure—A Context and Practice Casebook

This book is part of the Context and Practice casebook series. The overarching goal for the Context and Practice casebooks is to create law school textbooks that enable law professors to be more effective as teachers. The series creators are convinced that most law professors want to help their students learn; in fact, law professors frequently say that their primary goal is to teach their students to be experts at learning in the legal field.

In Spring 2007, the Carnegie Foundation's Educating Lawyers: Preparation for the Practice of Law[1] and Roy Stuckey's Best Practices for Legal Education[2] measured the

---

1. William M. Sullivan, Anne Colby, Judith Welch Wegner, Lloyd Bond, & Lee S. Shulman, Educating Lawyers: Preparation for the Profession of Law (2007).

2. Roy Stuckey & Others, Best Practices for Legal Education (2007).

effectiveness of modern legal education and concluded that legal education often falls short of what it could and should be. Both works criticized the rigid adherence to a single teaching technique and the absence of law practice and professional identity development in legal education.

Inspired by the call to action reflected in these works and by the absence of teaching materials designed in light of these studies and of the hundreds of educational studies in the instructional design field, law teaching experts from around the country envisioned a casebook series responsive to the research on teaching and learning and to the Carnegie and Stuckey studies. The result is this series. Context and Practice casebooks are designed as tools to allow law professors and their students to work together to improve students' learning and better prepare students for the rigors and joys of practicing law.

Accordingly, casebooks in the Context and Practice series:

- Emphasize active learning;
- Make it easier for professors to create multiple opportunities for practice and feedback;
- Use multiple methods of instruction;
- Focus on the application of concepts in simulated law practice contexts with a particular emphasis on problem-solving; and
- Guide students' development of professional identity.

We have structured this text into fifteen chapters. With the exception of Chapter 1 (Introduction and Overview) and Chapter 15 (Integration and Review), each chapter follows a similar format. Each chapter starts with a problem you should be able to analyze and resolve by the end of your study of that chapter. For each new body of law, we summarize or otherwise introduce the law you will be learning and, in many instances, provide a simple example. The introductions are most often followed by a series of cases, with problems and active learning exercises interspersed throughout. Many of the problems and exercises suggest you write a response, and we encourage you to do so. In class, you can expect your professor to ask you many of the questions included in this text. The chapters also include graphics designed to give you a visual sense of the concepts and the overall body of law. Finally, each chapter includes reflection questions designed to further your professional development.

2. The Nature of Civil Procedure

Civil Procedure is a subset of a vast body of American law. Although there are many ways to subdivide and characterize law in the United States, a useful division for present purposes is between criminal and civil law. A criminal lawsuit involves the state or federal government prosecuting a defendant for allegedly committing a crime, such as theft or assault. A civil lawsuit is brought by a plaintiff, such as an individual or corporation, alleging a claim, such as negligence or breach of contract, against a defendant.

Both criminal and civil law can be subdivided into substance, remedy, and procedure.

Criminal Law	Civil Law
• Substance	• Substance
• Remedy	• Remedy
• Procedure	• Procedure

In criminal law, substance includes the definition of crimes and defenses. For example, criminal law could define "burglary" as follows: "A person commits burglary by entering or remaining unlawfully in or on a residential structure with the intent to commit any theft." If the defendant is convicted of a crime, typical criminal remedies include imprisonment of the defendant and fines the defendant must pay to the government. Criminal procedure defines the process through which the government prosecutes the defendant. For example, criminal procedure determines whether the defendant remains in jail after arrest and pending trial, the defendant's right to an attorney, how to compel witnesses to appear at trial, and the manner in which the government and defendant present evidence during sentencing.

Substantive civil law determines the elements of claims and defenses. For example, the substantive law of torts, contracts, and property provide many civil claims and defenses. Likewise, the law of civil remedies prescribes the type of relief the plaintiff can recover if the defendant is found liable. Typical civil remedies include compensatory damages, which the defendant pays to the plaintiff, and injunctions, which are court orders prescribing the defendant's future behavior. Civil Procedure is an elaborate set of rules that governs how the civil litigation system resolves disputes.

A simple car accident case can illustrate civil law substance, remedy, and procedure. Assume Pat and Dell are each driving cars that collide at an intersection. Both cars are damaged and Pat and Dell are injured. Pat brings a civil lawsuit against Dell. The substantive law determines the elements of Pat's claim for negligence based on Dell's intoxication and failure to yield the right of way. Substantive law also determines whether Pat's failure to wear a seatbelt provides Dell a defense to Pat's claim. The law of remedies determines the categories of compensatory damages Pat may be entitled to recover if Dell is found to be negligent. These damages may include property damage, medical expenses, lost wages, and pain. Remedies law also governs whether Pat can recover punitive damages based on Dell's reckless behavior.

The law of Civil Procedure addresses issues regarding the civil litigation process, including:

- Can Pat sue Dell in federal or state court?
- How can Dell challenge Pat's choice of court?
- What must Pat include in the complaint to begin the lawsuit?

- How can Dell raise defenses to Pat's claims?
- How can Pat and Dell uncover facts and develop evidence from witnesses and documents?
- Are Pat or Dell entitled to a trial by jury? If so, how are jurors selected?
- What errors by parties, the judge, or jurors will give rise to a new trial?

This course will address those issues and hundreds of others that together make up the "rules of the game" for civil litigation.

The brief summary above oversimplifies the criminal/civil law distinction and the subcategories of substance, remedy, and procedure. The law is more complicated than that. For example, Dell's intoxication could give rise to a criminal prosecution by the government to punish Dell for driving while intoxicated and a civil suit initiated by Pat to recover damages caused by Dell's behavior. Likewise, as we will see in Chapter 6, the distinction between substantive law and procedural law can be quite illusive.

Exercise 1-1. The Importance of Civil Procedure

In most law schools Civil Procedure is a required course, often taught in the first year, along with other foundational courses. Try to articulate why Civil Procedure is so important in real life law practice.

---

3. Sources of Law

The United States does not have a single legal system. Instead, it has many legal systems that operate simultaneously. There is a legal system for the federal government, one for each of the fifty states, and one for each of the many Native American tribes. The primary focus in this book will be on the federal system; the secondary focus will be on state systems.

In the federal and state legal systems, law comes from four primary sources: constitutions, statutes, regulations, and judicial decisions. Each of those sources are described briefly below, along with examples of the law of Civil Procedure in the federal system.

a. Constitutions

The pinnacle of the U.S. system of law is the federal Constitution. The U.S. Constitution was drafted in 1787 and went into effect in 1789. It consists of seven articles and 27 amendments. The U.S. Constitution creates the Congress, the presidency, and the Supreme Court, identifies their respective powers, and guaranties a variety of individual rights. The Constitution is the supreme law of the land; any state or federal law in conflict with it is invalid. Each state also has its own written constitution, which forms the pinnacle of each state's system of law, but each of these state constitutions is still subordinate to the federal Constitution, along with any federal law that is consistent with it.

The U.S. Constitution establishes fundamental principles of Civil Procedure. For example, Article III creates the Supreme Court, authorizes Congress to establish other federal courts, and defines the types of cases federal courts are allowed to hear. The Seventh Amendment preserves the right to trial by jury in some, but not all, civil cases. The Fifth Amendment and Fourteenth Amendment prohibit the federal and state governments from depriving any person of "life, liberty, or property, without due process of law...." The Due Process Clauses apply to many aspects of civil litigation. And Article VI, clause II, the Supremacy Clause, establishes the supremacy of legitimate federal law over state law—the foundation of the shared system of federal-state governance that we call *federalism*.

b. Statutes

Statutes are the work of legislatures. Federal statutes are enacted by Congress, a process that requires a majority vote of the House of Representatives, a majority vote of the Senate, and approval by the president. If instead the president vetoes the bill, it becomes law only if Congress overrides the veto, which requires a 2/3 vote of each chamber. Most states follow the same general approach: to become law, a bill must pass the state legislature and then be approved by the governor.

Title 28 of the United States Code contains hundreds of statutory provisions governing Civil Procedure in federal courts. Among other statutory topics, this course will explore statutes prescribing the types of cases federal courts are allowed to hear (subject matter jurisdiction), the location of the federal courts in which the plaintiff may initiate the lawsuit (venue), mechanisms the defendant can employ to move a case from state to federal court (removal), a statutory form of action (interpleader), the enforceability of judgments from one state to the other (full faith and credit), and the selection of jurors.

c. Rules and Regulations

The federal government has a variety of executive departments (*e.g.*, the Department of Education) and administrative agencies (*e.g.*, the Environmental Protection Agency), which issue regulations designed to enforce and administer statutes. Federal departments and agencies derive their authority to issue regulations from Congress. Consequently, regulations may supplement or interpret statutes but cannot contradict statutes or exceed the scope of authority granted by Congress. At the state level, a variety of departments and agencies have similar regulatory authority.

By statute (28 U.S.C. §2072), Congress authorized the Supreme Court to prescribe rules of practice and procedure governing federal courts. Using this authority, the Supreme Court created the Federal Rules of Civil Procedure. Those rules provide detailed guidance for the initiation and processing of civil litigation in federal district courts. Large portions of this course concern the interpretation, analysis, application, and evaluation of the Federal Rules of Civil Procedure. Most states also have rules of procedure that govern civil litigation in state courts.

d. Judicial Decisions: Common Law and Equity

Courts make law. In the process of resolving disputes, both federal and state judges must interpret and apply the provisions of constitutions, statutes, and rules. In addition, state and federal judges may create legal principles in order to decide cases before them. In short, courts create law on a variety of issues on which the legislature had not spoken. This court-made law, also known as common law, has created a vast body of precedent embodied, for the most part, in the written opinions of appellate courts. American judges generally follow precedent in deciding current cases. This is partly because they see no sense in working out a fresh solution to a problem each time it recurs and partly because they are convinced — by notions of fundamental fairness — that like cases should be treated alike and that every person ought to be treated as any other would be under similar circumstances. These practical considerations give shape to the formal doctrine of "stare decisis" (Latin for "let the decision stand"), which counsels courts to follow prior decided cases where a new case presents similar facts and issues.

The notion of common law originated in England, and its fundamental ideas were brought to America by the early English settlers. Historically, what we now regard as the common law was divided into two branches: law and equity. England had two parallel court systems — one for law and one for equity. The monarch's courts dispensed law. These courts would adjudicate disputes — typically through the use of a jury — and enter judgment for one side. If the plaintiff won, the judgment would commonly order the defendant to pay a specified sum of money damages to the plaintiff. If the law was inadequate to do justice, the plaintiff could bring suit in an equity court. There, the judge, acting without a jury, might issue an order for some form of equitable relief (such as an injunction — an order to defendant to return plaintiff's property) because a legal remedy (an award of money) was not adequate under the circumstances. Today the federal and most state court systems have combined law and equity courts into a single court, yet the distinction between law and equity remains relevant. For example, the Supreme Court has interpreted the Seventh Amendment to preserve the right to a jury on "law" issues but not "equitable" issues.

A significant portion of Civil Procedure in federal courts is common law. For example, each year federal courts publish hundreds of opinions in which the judges interpret a provision of Title 28 of the United States Code or a Federal Rule of Civil Procedure. In addition, the United States Supreme Court and lower federal courts have articulated elaborate sets of legal principles to interpret and apply provisions of the U.S. Constitution. For example, an important part of this course focuses on a series of Supreme Court opinions that establish legal principles derived from the "Due Process" clauses of the Fifth and Fourteenth Amendments.

4. United States Court System

The United States judicial system has three levels of courts: trial courts, appellate courts, and the Supreme Court. Most state judicial systems have a similar three-level court structure.

a. United States District Courts

Federal trial courts are called United States District Courts. There are ninety-four district courts, one for each of the judicial districts into which the nation is divided. Each state has at least one U. S. district court; large, populous states have several. For example, California, New York, and Texas each have four districts. In contrast, states with a small population, such as Vermont, and states encompassing a small geographic area, such as New Jersey, have only one district court. In single-district states, district boundaries are coterminous with state boundaries. Whether a district court is staffed by a single judge or by many judges depends upon the population and caseload of the district.

Although state trial courts can hear most types of cases, federal district courts have limited jurisdiction. Article III of the U.S. Constitution establishes the outer limits of federal court jurisdiction. In general, federal district courts hear three classes of cases: prosecutions for federal crimes, civil claims arising under federal law, and civil claims for more than $75,000 based on state law between citizens of different states. With respect to criminal prosecutions and a small group of civil actions, the jurisdiction of the district courts is exclusive, meaning that state courts cannot hear those cases. But for the bulk of civil actions, federal district court jurisdiction is concurrent with that of state courts, so the parties may litigate their dispute in either federal court or in the courts of at least one state. Several federal trial courts have jurisdiction over particular types of cases, such as the bankruptcy courts, court of claims, and tax court.

b. United States Circuit Courts of Appeals

There are eleven numbered intermediate appellate courts, called United States Courts of Appeals, one for each of the circuits into which the nation is divided. There is one circuit court for the District of Columbia, which reviews both matters involving residents of the District and much of the federal administrative action taking place in the national capital. There is one Federal Circuit, which handles appeals primarily on tax and patent matters. Each of the numbered circuits encompasses the geographic area of several states. For example, the Court of Appeals for the Second Circuit hears appeals from federal district courts in New York, Connecticut, and Vermont. In contrast, the Court of Appeals for the Ninth Circuit hears appeals from federal district courts in nine states: Alaska, Arizona, California, Hawaii, Idaho, Montana, Nevada, Oregon, and Washington.

Each of the eleven numbered circuit courts of appeals hears appeals from all the lower federal courts within the circuit on both civil and criminal matters. In addition, each reviews the decisions of various federal agencies in cases that involve people who reside in the circuit. The circuit courts have no power to review the decisions of state courts or state administrative agencies. Most cases at the circuit court level are decided by a panel of three judges, but some important issues are heard first by a three-judge panel, and then by all of the judges of the Circuit, sitting "*en banc*."

c. The United States Supreme Court

Decisions of the courts of appeals are subject to further review in the Supreme Court of the United States. All nine justices of the Supreme Court hear every case (although a judge may recuse himself or herself because of a conflict of interest). A few cases go to the Supreme Court as a matter of right, but most only as a matter of the Supreme Court's discretion. The Court exercises its discretion sparingly, usually granting approximately 80 of the petitions for review per term, which is fewer than five percent of the petitions for review submitted to the Court. The Supreme Court is not only the highest federal court but also has power to review decisions of the highest court of each state if the decision is based on federal law, including constitutional law.

5. Characteristics of Civil Litigation

Civil litigation is an elaborate public dispute resolution system. This course will examine the complexities of the civil litigation system, explore the theories and public policy that underlie the system, evaluate the strengths and weakness of the system, and begin to prepare you to practice effectively and ethically. This section is a brief introduction to several characteristics of the civil litigation system.

a. Goals of the Civil Litigation System

What basic goals should drive the civil litigation system? Consider Federal Rule of Civil Procedure 1, which provides in part: "These rules govern the procedure in all civil actions and proceedings in the United States district courts.... They should be construed, administered, and employed by the court and the parties to secure the just, speedy, and inexpensive determination of every action and proceeding."

Exercise 1-2. Articulating and Achieving the Goals of the Civil Litigation System

1. Make a list of at least five important goals that the civil litigation system should try to achieve.

2. What can lawyers and judges do to ensure that the civil litigation system achieves those goals?

---

b. Volume and Types of Civil Cases in Federal and State Court

To get a sense of the types of civil cases that make up the dockets of federal district courts, consider these statistics from the fiscal year ending in September 2017 (http://www.uscourts.gov/statistics-reports/us-district-courts-judicial-business-2017).

- Plaintiffs filed 267,769 civil cases, including:
  - prisoner petitions—58,000
  - personal injury—54,000
  - civil rights—39,000,
  - contracts—24,000
  - social security—19,000
  - labor—18,000
  - real and personal property—12,000
  - intellectual property—11,000.
- District courts terminated 289,901 civil cases.
- District courts held 2,663 civil trials.

In contrast, during the 2015–2016 fiscal year, in the California state courts:

- Plaintiffs filed 1,270,919 civil cases
- Superior courts terminated 1,121,081 civil cases
- Superior courts held 179,835 civil trials.

(http://www.courts.ca.gov/documents/2017-Court-Statistics-Report.pdf.)

c. Adversary System

A central feature of civil litigation in the U.S. is the adversary system. The parties present their cases to a judge or jury who decides which party prevails. In the adversary system, the parties and their lawyers control many aspects of the litigation. The plaintiff decides whether to bring a civil suit. Then the parties raise claims and defenses, request remedies, investigate facts, produce evidence, present issues to the court via motions, and articulate arguments. In the traditional adversary system, the judge's role is primarily reactive—ruling on motions before and after trial, ruling on the admissibility of evidence during trial, and ultimately deciding which party prevails and the appropriate remedy. Although the judge's reactive role remains a feature of modern civil litigation, judges also manage cases by establishing schedules and deadlines to move the case along and by encouraging parties to resolve their dispute through a negotiated settlement.

A set of assumptions underlies the adversary system. First, plaintiffs will make good choices about which suits to bring for resolution in the civil litigation system.

Second, the parties and their lawyers have relatively equal abilities and resources to investigate and present their cases. Third, truth will emerge when both sides to a dispute vigorously present their cases to an unbiased decision maker.

The adversary system is not a license for parties and lawyers to engage in "win at all costs," abusive litigation tactics. The Federal Rules of Civil Procedure contain a number of provisions designed to ensure cooperation and fair play among parties and lawyers. For example, Rule 26 requires parties and lawyers to meet and develop a plan to govern discovery in the lawsuit. Rule 11 places an obligation on parties and lawyers to ensure that every paper filed in the lawsuit has a legal and factual basis and is not presented to harass other parties, cause delay, or increase the cost of litigation. Rules 26 and 37 give judges broad authority to sanction lawyers and parties who abuse or obstruct the discovery process.

Exercise 1-3. Evaluating the Adversary System

Throughout the course, as you learn about the theory and practice of civil litigation, you should evaluate and re-evaluate the adversary system. Begin that process now. What do you perceive to be the strengths and weakness of the adversary system? Identify several potential strengths and several potential weaknesses.

---

6. Alternative Dispute Resolution

Although millions of civil disputes lead to lawsuits filed in state and federal courts each year, most disputes are resolved outside of the civil litigation system. Many people resolve their disputes informally without ever consulting a lawyer. When potential clients come to lawyers seeking help in resolving conflicts, an important role for lawyers is to guide clients in selecting an appropriate mechanism for addressing the dispute. Civil litigation is one possible mechanism. Other dispute resolution mechanisms include negotiation, mediation, and arbitration (addressed in more detail in Chapter 14). To help clients make appropriate choices, lawyers must be able to explain the characteristics of each dispute resolution mechanism.

a. Civil Litigation

Four characteristics of civil litigation help define whether it is an appropriate mechanism to resolve a dispute. First, civil litigation provides a binding decision resolving the dispute. Civil lawsuits end in a judgment, enforceable through the power of the state or federal government. Second, civil litigation generally is a zero-sum game. The judge or jury decides who wins and who loses. Third, the civil litigation process can be quite lengthy. Although some civil lawsuits end within months of their filing, many take years to resolve. Fourth, civil litigation is often expensive for the parties. They pay to file the case, investigate the facts and law, and hire expert witnesses. The largest expense for most parties is attorney's fees. Under the American Rule, the parties pay their own attorney's fees, regardless of whether they win or lose the case. There are some exceptions to the American Rule, allowing prevailing parties to recover their attorney's fees from the losing parties.

b. Negotiation

People can attempt to resolve their dispute through negotiation. There is no guarantee that the negotiation will resolve the dispute—the parties may be unable to agree on a resolution. On the other hand, a negotiated settlement will rarely be a zero-sum game. The parties are free to structure the resolution to meet the needs of all parties. Parties can negotiate their disputes without lawyers or can have their lawyers participate in the negotiations. Negotiations can take place before a lawsuit is filed or during the suit. Judges often strongly encourage parties to negotiate a settlement to a lawsuit. Many lawsuits end when the parties and their lawyers negotiate a solution and dismiss the lawsuit. Negotiation plays a significant role in more formal alternative dispute resolution mechanisms including mediation (trying to reach an agreement with the assistance of a mediator) and arbitration (deciding in a negotiated contract that an arbitrator will resolve the dispute).

c. Mediation

A mediator attempts to help people resolve their disputes through communication and negotiation. The mediator does not have the power to decide the dispute or compel the parties to negotiate a solution. Instead, the mediator listens to the parties and facilitates communication among the parties, which may lead to a voluntary resolution of the dispute. Like negotiation, parties in a mediation are free to structure creative solutions that satisfy important goals of each party. Participation in mediation is often voluntary—the parties decide to engage in the mediation process. However, some state courts require that parties in civil litigation attempt to resolve the dispute via mediation before the suit continues.

d. Arbitration

Many collective bargaining agreements, commercial contracts, and consumer transactions require that the parties submit their dispute to an arbitrator. Many arbitrators have substantive expertise; for example, an arbitrator may be an expert in medical malpractice. Parties, with or without lawyers, present their cases to the arbitrator, who decides the case. Many arbitration agreements set out the process for choosing the arbitrator and the rules governing presentation of the case. Those rules are often more flexible than the rules of evidence and procedure that apply in court. Many arbitration agreements provide that the arbitrator's decision is binding. Some state courts require that the parties submit their dispute to non-binding arbitration before initiating a lawsuit.

Exercise 1-4. Selecting Dispute Resolution Mechanisms

1. Think about civil disputes you have experienced. Were any of the disputes resolved via civil litigation, arbitration, mediation, or negotiation? Did the mechanism turn out to be appropriate to effectively resolve the dispute?

2. For each of the disputes below, decide which type of dispute resolution system (arbitration, litigation, mediation, negotiated settlement) would work best. Articulate your reasons.

   a. Two married adults agree to separate but disagree about custody of their kids, ages 7 and 13.

   b. Two drivers are seriously injured in a car accident; they disagree about which of them was at fault.

   c. Labor and management disagree about how the layoff provisions of a contract should be applied as the company downsizes.

---

7. Professionalism

Lawyers are professionals. Issues of professionalism arise frequently for all lawyers involved in civil litigation. To help prepare you for practice, this book will ask you to think about professionalism issues often.

Many state and local bar associations have adopted codes of civility and professionalism. The following example from the Spokane County Bar Association is typical.

Spokane County Bar Association
Code of Professional Courtesy

As a lawyer, I recognize my first duty is to ardently and conscientiously represent my client. Yet, each lawyer also has the responsibility for making our system of justice work honorably, fairly, and efficiently. To accomplish this end, I will comply with my profession's disciplinary standards, and be guided by the following creed when dealing with clients, opposing counsel, the courts and the general public.

A. My Client:

   1. I will be loyal and sensitive to my client's needs, but I will not permit that commitment to block my ability to provide objective and candid advice.

2. I will try to achieve my client's lawful objectives as quickly and economically as possible.

3. I will advise my client that civility and courtesy are not to be equated with weakness.

4. I will abide by my client's ethical decisions regarding the client's goals, but nevertheless will advise that a willingness to engage in settlement negotiations is consistent with ardent, conscientious and effective representation.

B. Opposing Parties and their Counsel:

1. I will try to act with dignity, integrity, and courtesy in oral and written communications.

2. My word is my bond, not only with opposing counsel, but in all my dealings.

3. In litigation, I will agree with reasonable requests for extensions of time, stipulate to undisputed facts to avoid needless costs or inconvenience, and waive procedural formalities when the interests of my client will not adversely be affected.

4. I will facilitate the processing of all reasonable discovery requests.

5. I will not ask colleagues for the rescheduling of court settings or discovery proceedings unless a legitimate need exists; nor will I unreasonably withhold consent for scheduling accommodations. I will try to consult with opposing counsel before scheduling depositions, hearings, and other proceedings or meetings.

6. I will promptly respond to oral and written communications.

7. I will avoid condemning my adversary or the opposing party.

C. The Courts and Other Tribunals:

1. I will be candid with and courteous to the Court and its staff.

2. I will be punctual in attending court hearings, conferences and depositions; I recognize that tardiness is demeaning to me and to the profession.

3. I will stand to address the Court, and dress appropriately to show my respect for the Court and the law.

4. I will refrain from condemnation of the Court

D. The Public and our System of Justice:

1. I will remember that my responsibilities as a lawyer include a devotion to the public good and the improvement of the administration of justice, including the contribution of uncompensated time for those persons who cannot afford adequate legal assistance.

> 2. I will remember the need to promote the image of the profession in the eyes of the Public and be guided accordingly when considering advertising methods and content.

Exercise 1-5. Professionalism

1. What incentives do you have to comply with a code of professionalism, such as the example above?

2. What types of circumstances may make your compliance with a professionalism code particularly challenging?

8. Legal Reasoning

A course in Civil Procedure can encompass a wide variety of goals, including legal doctrine and theory, professionalism, and skills. As noted above, this course will explore four sources of Civil Procedure law—constitutions, statutes, rules, and judicial opinions—along with the theory and public policy behind that law. Further, the course will address professionalism and strategy in the context of modern civil litigation. Finally, the course will focus on analytical skills essential for the successful practice of law. This section briefly introduces two types of analytical skills that run throughout the course: case analysis and statutory analysis.

a. Case Analysis

Effective lawyers and successful law students read judicial opinions both carefully and critically. Case analysis involves identifying and summarizing essential components of the opinion. Case analysis also includes evaluation of the opinion and synthesis of a line of opinions on the same topic. As you read the cases in this text, you should pick out the various parts of the case in order to properly prepare for class. The chart below summarizes the case analysis process.

b. Statutory Analysis

Effective lawyers and successful law students also read statutes and rules both carefully and critically. The elements of statutory analysis differ somewhat from case analysis. Regardless of whether you are analyzing a statute (a provision of Title 28 of the U.S. Code) or a rule (a provision of a Federal Rule of Civil Procedure), the same five elements of analysis apply.

Chart 1-1. Case Analysis Components

Citation	*Hickman v. Taylor*, 329 U.S. 495 (1947). The citation identifies parties to the lawsuit (Hickman and Taylor), the court deciding the case (the U.S. Supreme Court), and the year the opinion was issued (1947).
Facts	Identify all of the parties to the lawsuit — the case citation often names only two of the parties. Summarize what happened to the parties that gave rise to the lawsuit to provide a real-life context for the opinion. Identify the key facts that affect the outcome of the case.
Procedural History	This is especially important in Civil Procedure. Identify the parties' claims and defenses. Note the procedural device that led to the trial court's decision, such as a motion to dismiss, a jury verdict, or a motion for a new trial. Identify the result at the trial court level and at the intermediate appellate court, if applicable. Finally, note which party appealed to the court issuing the opinion.
Issue	Set out the legal question or questions the court addresses to decide the appeal. For example, in *Hickman v. Taylor* the Court framed the issue as: "This case presents an important problem under the Federal Rules of Civil Procedure as to the extent to which a party may inquire into oral and written statements … secured by an adverse party's counsel in the course of preparation for possible litigation.…"
Holding	Give the court's answer to the question presented in the issue. For example, in *Hickman v. Taylor* the Court held that witness statements and other "work product" prepared by a lawyer in anticipation of litigation were protected from discovery by an opposing party who is unable to show a substantial need for the statements and substantial hardship in getting equivalent information through the opposing party's own investigation.
Reasoning	This often is the most important component of case analysis both in law school and in practice. The reasoning component usually includes three subparts: (1) the legal principles on which the court is relying (these principles could come from constitutions, statutes, rules, or case law); (2) application of the facts to the relevant legal principles; and (3) the policy supporting the decision (social, economic, or philosophical reasons for the decision).
Concurring and Dissenting Opinions	Why read beyond the majority opinion? Because the concurring and dissenting opinions help us understand the majority opinion. Dissenting opinions often point out weaknesses in the majority opinion, offer alternative analysis, and convey facts that the majority opinion did not mention. Further, the approach articulated in concurring and dissenting opinions may be adopted by a majority of the court in future cases. So summarize key points from the dissenting and concurring opinions.
Evaluation and Synthesis	This is the critical thinking aspect of case analysis. To evaluate the opinion and synthesize it with related opinions, ask yourself questions such as: Is the opinion logical and consistent? Is the result fair and just? Will the opinion make sound precedent? How does the opinion fit with other opinions addressing the same issues?

Statutory Interpretation Elements

- Closely read the *words* of the statutory provision at issue. Read the provision again. See if the statutory scheme has a definition section that may define key words in the provision at issue.

- Identify the statute's *purpose*. Some statutory schemes have a purpose section. For example, Federal Rule of Civil Procedure 1 identifies fundamental goals for the federal civil litigation system.

- Fit the statute in the broader statutory *scheme*. Read the statutory provisions related to the section at issue. How does the provision at issue fit with the rest of the statute? The relevant statutory scheme might include an entire title, chapter, or subchapter of the U.S. Code. The Federal Rules of Civil Procedure constitute an overall statutory scheme and a series of titles, each of which has its own mini-scheme.

- Use *legislative history*. Research how the statutory provision at issue changed over time. What do the amendments tell you about the meaning of the current version of the statute? Many statutes include legislative reports that detail the purpose of the statute. For example, helpful Advisory Committee notes accompany the Federal Rules of Civil Procedure.

- Use *cases* interpreting the statute. Many statutes have been interpreted multiple times in published opinions. In fact, many of the cases that we have included in this casebook illustrate judicial interpretations of specific statutes and rules. Once set down in an authoritative way, an interpretation of a statute or rule effectively becomes "part" of that statute or rule.

Exercise 1-6. Statutory Analysis

Assume that the Spotted Owl has been listed as an endangered species under the Endangered Species Act (ESA). It lives and breeds primarily in old growth forests in the Pacific Northwest. Your client owns 40 acres of old growth forest in Oregon, which your client would like to harvest to generate income to meet basic needs of your client's family. Does the ESA prohibit your client, a private landowner, from cutting 40 acres of old growth forests on his property?

Your research reveals the following about the ESA.

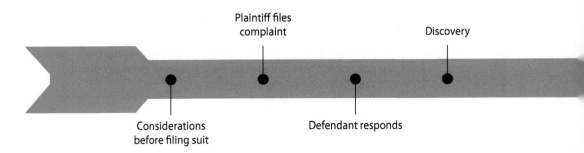

Words of the statute.

ESA section 9. "It is unlawful for any person to take any endangered species." ESA section 2. "The term 'take' means to harass, harm, pursue, hunt, shoot, wound, kill, trap, capture or collect."

Purpose of the statute.

ESA section 1. "The purposes of this chapter are to provide a means to conserve the ecosystems on which endangered species depend...."

Statutory scheme.

ESA section 4. "Concurrently with making a determination that the species is endangered, the Secretary shall designate the critical habitat of the species."

Legislative history.

The Senate Report for the ESA states: "The term 'take' is to be given the broadest possible meaning consistent with the conservation goals of the Act."

Case interpreting the statute.

Sierra Club v. Yeutter involved the U.S. Forest Service's practice of allowing clear cuts on land owned by the U.S. government. The Sierra Club sued on the grounds that the practice violated the ESA because clear cuts destroyed the critical habitat of the red cockaded woodpecker, an endangered species. The court held that the destruction of critical habitat was a "taking" in violation of the ESA.

After completing your research, you meet with your client who would like an answer to the question above. Answer the question. Explain your reasoning in a paragraph.

9. Timeline of a Civil Lawsuit

The graphic below represents a streamlined, linear view of a typical timeline for a civil lawsuit. Many lawsuits roughly follow this timeline. Civil litigation can be quite complex, however, so some lawsuits travel a more circuitous path. For purposes of this introduction to Civil Procedure, what follows is a brief description of each phase in the timeline with references to the chapters in this book where each phase is covered in detail.

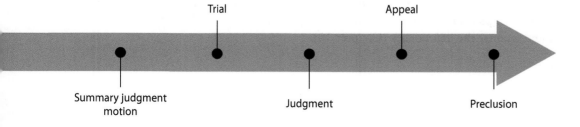

Trial · Appeal

Summary judgment motion · Judgment · Preclusion

a. Considerations before Filing Suit

When a client seeks a lawyer's help resolving a dispute, the lawyer usually engages in legal and factual investigation. Eventually, the lawyer and client will decide what type of dispute resolution mechanism may be best to address the client's dispute. Although civil litigation is one possible mechanism, some form of alternative dispute resolution may be appropriate, such as mediation or arbitration (Chapter 14).

If alternative dispute resolution is inappropriate or unsuccessful, the lawyer and client may decide to pursue civil litigation. Before initiating the suit, the lawyer will need to determine which court or courts can hear the lawsuit. This "proper court" analysis consists of subject matter jurisdiction, personal jurisdiction, and venue. Subject matter jurisdiction concerns whether a state or federal court has the power to hear the type of suit (Chapter 4). Personal jurisdiction deals with two fundamental issues: (a) basis—whether the courts of a given state have power to render a binding judgment against the defendant (Chapter 2) and (b) service—how the defendant receives proper notice of the suit (Chapter 3). Finally, venue determines which federal district courts or which courts within a state are the proper geographic location to file the suit (Chapter 5).

Choice of law issues arise before the lawsuit is filed as well. Part of the lawyer's pre-suit legal research will address the question of which law applies in the courts of the particular state where he or she files the lawsuit. Will state or federal law apply? If state law, the law of which state? Choice of law issues are addressed in Chapter 6.

b. Plaintiff Files the Complaint

The first substantive document filed in a civil lawsuit is the complaint. In the complaint, the plaintiff names the parties (plaintiffs and defendants), asserts claims, and requests remedies. The sufficiency of complaints is addressed in Chapter 7. Joinder of multiple claims and parties in one lawsuit is the subject of Chapter 8.

c. Defendant Responds

Defendants have two basic options in responding to a complaint. Defendants can raise a pre-answer motion, such as a motion to dismiss because the court lacks jurisdiction or because the plaintiff's complaint is insufficient (Chapter 10). Defendants can respond through an answer, in which the defendants respond to the allegations in the complaint, raise defenses, join additional parties, and assert claims against the plaintiff and other parties (Chapters 7 and 8). If defendants default (fail to respond to the complaint by answer or motion), the plaintiff may ask the court to enter judgment against the defendants (Chapter 10).

d. Discovery

The rules of civil procedure create an elaborate system that the parties can use to investigate facts and develop evidence (Chapter 9). Discovery devices include:

- Initial disclosures (parties identify for each other the people and documents the party may use to support its claims and defenses)
- Interrogatories (written questions from one party to another that must be answered under oath)
- Requests to produce documents and things (parties request to inspect another party's documents and things relevant to claims and defenses in the suit)
- Depositions (oral testimony given under oath by a party or non-party witness)
- Subpoenas (parties can subpoena a non-party witnesses for a deposition and can request to inspect a non-party's documents and things relevant to claims and defenses in the suit)
- Requests for admission (parties request other parties to admit the truth of statements set out in the request)
- Mental and physical exams (parties can ask the court to order another party to submit to an exam of a condition that is in controversy in the lawsuit, such as the plaintiff's injuries caused by an accident).

The discovery rules also contain robust sanctions provisions that courts can employ to police the discovery process.

e. Summary Judgment Motion

Before a lawsuit goes to trial, usually after discovery is complete, one or more of the parties may ask the court to enter summary judgment on all or part of the case. Courts grant summary judgment when there is no genuine dispute as to material facts and a party is entitled to judgment as a matter of law on an issue. Summary judgment is addressed in Chapter 10.

f. Trial

The decision maker in a civil trial may be the judge or a jury. Parties have a right to a jury trial on some, but not all, issues in civil litigation. If the case is to be decided by a jury, the judge and lawyers select a jury at the beginning of the trial. The parties then make opening statements to the jury and present their evidence. At the close of the evidence, either party may ask the judge to grant judgment as a matter of law on the grounds that no reasonable jury could decide the case for the opposing party. If the court denies that motion, the parties will make final arguments to the jury and the judge will instruct the jury on the applicable law. The jurors then deliberate and try to reach a verdict. Trial is covered in Chapter 11.

g. Judgment

If the jury reaches a verdict deciding the case, the judge will enter judgment for the prevailing party. Likewise, if the judge decides the case before trial via a motion (to dismiss or for summary judgment) the judge will enter judgment. Parties who lose at trial can make post-trial motions to undo the judgment, including a motion for judgment as a matter of law (no reasonable jury could have found for the verdict winner), for a new trial based on errors made by the judge or jury, or for relief from judgment based on newly discovered evidence or fraudulent conduct by the opposing party. Post trial motions are addressed in Chapter 11.

h. Appeal

In the federal system and in many states, the party who loses at the trial court has the right to appeal to an intermediate appellate court. Although a few decisions may be appealed even before the end of the lawsuit, in general the parties cannot appeal until the trial judge enters a final judgment. Appellate courts review errors that the appealing party identifies as the grounds for appeal. Appellate courts do not hear new evidence; instead they review the record that was developed at the trial court. Depending on the type of issue raised on appeal, the court of appeals will apply a standard of review, varying from no deference to the trial court's decision (de novo review) to upholding decisions unless the appealing party can demonstrate that the trial court abused its discretion. Appeal is the subject of Chapter 12.

i. Preclusion

A final judgment in civil litigation limits the parties in subsequent litigation. The doctrine of claim preclusion prevents the same parties from relitigating claims that were or could have been litigated in the first case. The doctrine of issue preclusion prevents a party from relitigating an issue that was litigated and decided in the first suit even if that issue is part of a different claim in a subsequent suit. Preclusion doctrines are covered in Chapter 13.

Chapter 2

Personal Jurisdiction

1. Chapter Problem

Memorandum

To: Associate
From: Mary Rogers, Partner
Re: Potential Wrongful Death Action

I received a phone call from a potential client, Sherry, who lives in Scotland. Her brother, Kevin, died in a plane crash in Scotland. The plane on which he was a passenger was manufactured by the Piper Aircraft Company in Pennsylvania. The plane was owned and operated by corporations that were organized under the laws of the United Kingdom. The four other passengers and the pilot, all of whom died in the crash, are from Scotland. In addition, a preliminary investigation into the crash revealed that there might have been a mechanical problem with the plane's propeller. Hartzell Propeller, Inc., manufactured the plane's propeller in Ohio.

Sherry contacted our office, because her Scottish attorney advised her that the laws in California are better for potential plaintiffs in tort actions like this. Therefore, if it is possible, Sherry would prefer to sue in state court in California. Please determine whether a California state court would have personal jurisdiction over Piper and Hartzell.

---

2. Introduction

For a court to issue a judgment against a particular defendant, it must have personal jurisdiction over that defendant. Personal jurisdiction refers to the power of the court to make decisions that affect a particular party. It is, along with subject matter jurisdiction (covered in Chapter 4) and venue (covered in Chapter 5), a preliminary question that all lawyers must answer before deciding where to file a lawsuit. The preceding problem is designed to help you think through the issues that arise in determining whether a court possesses personal jurisdiction. What should a court do when confronted with such a case? What is your preliminary answer to the partner's question? Why do you think this is the correct answer? The cases in this chapter will help you understand how the courts reason through a problem of personal jurisdiction.

Personal jurisdiction is just one aspect of the overall question that every lawyer must answer before filing a civil law suit: In what court can I file this lawsuit? Along with personal jurisdiction, a lawyer also must assess which court has subject matter jurisdiction over the claim (Chapter 4), and venue (Chapter 5). Personal jurisdiction and proper notice of the lawsuit are both required by the due process clauses in the Constitution. Notice is discussed in Chapter 3. Putting these concepts together to determine in which court or courts a lawyer may file a lawsuit looks something like this:

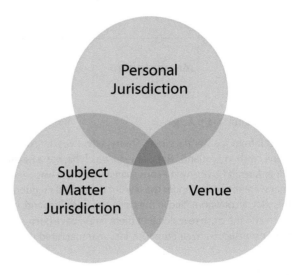

The space where these circles intersect—or, rather, the state or states where all these circles intersect—constitutes the state or states in which a lawyer can file a lawsuit. Sometimes that ends up being just one state, in which case the circles overlap.

This chapter proceeds as follows.

- Section 3 describes theoretical foundations of early personal jurisdiction law including a fundamental case in this area.

- Section 4 covers the modern theory of personal jurisdiction, including cases that mark its development through today.

- Section 5 looks at current case law on general jurisdiction, one of the bases of modern personal jurisdiction.

- Section 6 takes on personal jurisdiction in the internet age and the special problems that occur when it's easy for a defendant to reach into a state using cyberspace.

- Section 7 contains the professional development reflection for personal jurisdiction.

This chapter also provides you with opportunities to begin to develop skills that all lawyers need. The chapter begins with helping you understand how to read a case. The second case in the chapter provides tips on case reading. This chapter also introduces principles of rule reading that will become more important in succeeding chapters. One of the main skills emphasized in this chapter is case synthesis. Case synthesis refers to the process of reading a series of cases involving the same issue and putting together an overall approach to that legal issue. This is a skill that you will be honing across all subjects in law school, including in legal writing classes. In this chapter, a model synthesis will be demonstrated for you and you will have the opportunity to engage in synthesizing cases yourself. This chapter also provides you with the unique opportunity to observe how an area of law develops and changes with changing circumstances. There are few opportunities to do this in law school. Personal jurisdiction is one of those rare areas of the law where some of the earliest cases still are raised and discussed today.

3. Personal Jurisdiction Foundations

Personal jurisdiction law finds its origins in international law. Imagine that you are the monarch of a small country, Orange. One of your country's citizens, Oscar, decides to take a trip to the neighboring country of Blue to watch the Orange and Blue national soccer teams play in the World Cup. After a resounding victory by the Orange team, Oscar decides to celebrate with his fellow citizens at a bar in Blue. He gets into an argument with a citizen of Blue, Ben, who insists that the Orange national team only won because of fouls that officials ignored during the game. The argument gets heated, and Oscar hits Ben, breaking his nose. Oscar and his friends make a quick dash out of the bar and head home to Orange. Ben wants compensation from Oscar for the costs and pain associated with his broken nose. As the monarch of Orange, where would you like to see Ben sue Oscar? The argument and damage occurred while Oscar was in Blue. There likely will be witnesses there. Yet, as the monarch of Orange, would you be worried that Oscar might not receive fair treatment in the Blue courts? Why? Let's put the shoe on the other foot. What if you are a legislator from the democratic republic of Blue? Where would you want Ben to sue Oscar? Why might Ben prefer to sue Oscar in Blue? What are the disadvantages to Ben if he must sue Oscar in Orange? Do your answers to these questions change if Oscar owns a vacation home in Blue? This chapter helps you answer this fundamental question: what court has the authority to issue a judgment against a particular party (in the broken nose case, Oscar)? This is a fundamental question that all lawyers must ask in determining where to file a lawsuit. If a lawyer does not answer this question correctly, the lawsuit can be dismissed.

Personal jurisdiction is based on notions of due process from the 14th and 5th Amendments. The 14th Amendment restrains the state from taking certain actions, stating "nor shall any State deprive any person of life, liberty, or property, without due process of law." U.S. Const. Amend. XIV. In addition, the United States Supreme Court has read the United States Constitution's 5th Amendment to impose a due process requirement on federal courts. Thus, both state and federal courts must satisfy the requirements of due process when they are issuing judgments against particular parties. The term "due process" is wonderfully vague, and incorporates the concept, among others, of personal jurisdiction. Proper notice, discussed in Chapter 3, also is required as part of due process.

Because of the vague nature of the term "due process," the United States Supreme Court has issued a series of decisions over the past 130 or so years trying to define what it means in terms of a court's assertion of personal jurisdiction over defendants, and, occasionally, plaintiffs. As a student, this provides you the opportunity to see how a legal issue has developed over a period of time that includes changing circumstances. At the time the first case in this chapter was decided, much of the United States could only be reached by horseback, horse-drawn wagon, or stagecoach. By the end of the chapter, you will be reading a case that the Court decided in 2014, a time when many Americans can hop on a plane and fly across the country in a matter of hours. As you read these cases, ask yourself how changes in methods of transportation and the mobility of people might have an impact on whether or not it is consistent with due process for a court to hear a case brought against a particular defendant.

You will begin your journey in answering the question of what court has personal jurisdiction over a particular party by reading a case that is a right of passage for law students: *Pennoyer v. Neff.*

Exercise 2-1. *Pennoyer v. Neff* and Case Reading Skills

As you read *Pennoyer*, answer the questions below. These questions are designed to help you understand the key facts, reasoning, and rules that come from this case. At the end of the case, Exercise 2-2 will help you determine whether you have understood the case by asking you to apply it to new fact patterns. Reading cases is a fundamental lawyering skill that you are just beginning to learn. Dating from 1877, *Pennoyer* is a very difficult case to read and understand after the first reading. You may need to read it several times to understand it fully.

1. The *Pennoyer* case introduces many new terms. Look up the following terms in a legal dictionary in preparation for reading the case:

   a. Execution of judgment

   b. Default judgment

   c. Service of process

   d. Constructive service

   e. Attachment

   f. In rem

   g. Service by publication

    h. In personam

    i. Ex parte

    j. Full faith and credit

2. How many lawsuits are described in *Pennoyer*? What happened in the first lawsuit? Who brought the second lawsuit, and what was that plaintiff trying to accomplish?

3. What facts were most important to the outcome of *Pennoyer*?

4. Under what circumstances does a state court have authority to issue a judgment involving property?

5. Under what circumstances does a state court have authority to issue a judgment against an individual defendant?

6. How does notice factor into the Court's analysis? What problems with service by publication does the Court identify?

7. What is the difference between a judgment rendered in rem and one rendered in personam?

8. What is the *Pennoyer* Court's concept of "state sovereignty"? What role does it play in the Court's analysis?

9. How does the *Pennoyer* Court define due process?

10. What is the Court's holding in *Pennoyer*? (Note: the Court's holding is not that the first court did not have jurisdiction. The holding must answer the question of why the court did not have jurisdiction.)

Pennoyer v. Neff

95 U.S. 714 (1877)

Mr. Justice Field delivered the opinion of the court.

This is an action to recover the possession of a tract of land, of the alleged value of $15,000, situated in the State of Oregon. The plaintiff asserts title to the premises by a patent of the United States issued to him in 1866, under the act of Congress of Sept. 27, 1850, usually known as the Donation Law of Oregon. The defendant claims to have acquired the premises under a sheriff's deed, made upon a sale of the property on execution issued upon a judgment recovered against the plaintiff in one of the circuit courts of the State. The case turns upon the validity of this judgment.

It appears from the record that the judgment was rendered in February, 1866, in favor of J. H. Mitchell, for less than $300, including costs, in an action brought by him upon a demand for services as an attorney; that, at the time the action was commenced and the judgment rendered, the defendant therein, the plaintiff here, was a non-resident of the State; that he was not personally served with process, and did not appear therein; and that the judgment was entered upon his default in not answering the complaint, upon a constructive service of summons by publication.

The Code of Oregon provides for such service when an action is brought against a non-resident and absent defendant, who has property within the State. It also provides, where the action is for the recovery of money or damages, for the attachment of the property of the non-resident. And it also declares that no natural person is subject to the jurisdiction of a court of the State, "unless he appear in the court, or be found within the State, or be a resident thereof, or have property therein; and, in the last case, only to the extent of such property at the time the jurisdiction attached." Construing this latter provision to mean, that, in an action for money or damages where a defendant does not appear in the court, and is not found within the State, and is not a resident thereof, but has property therein, the jurisdiction of the court extends only over such property, the declaration expresses a principle of general, if not universal, law. The authority of every tribunal is necessarily restricted by the territorial limits of the State in which it is established. Any attempt to exercise authority beyond those limits would be deemed in every other forum, as has been said by this court, in illegitimate assumption of power, and be resisted as mere abuse. In the case against the plaintiff, the property here in controversy sold under the judgment rendered was not attached, nor in any way brought under the jurisdiction of the court. Its first connection with the case was caused by a levy of the execution. It was not, therefore, disposed of pursuant to any adjudication, but only in enforcement of a personal judgment, having no relation to the property, rendered against a non-resident without service of process upon him in the action, or his appearance therein....

... The several States of the Union are not, it is true, in every respect independent, many of the rights and powers which originally belonged to them being now vested in the government created by the Constitution. But, except as restrained and limited by that instrument, they possess and exercise the authority of independent States, and the principles of public law to which we have referred are applicable to them. One of these principles is, that every State possesses exclusive jurisdiction and sovereignty over persons and property within its territory. As a consequence, every State has the power to determine for itself the civil status and capacities of its inhabitants; to prescribe the subjects upon which they may contract, the forms and solemnities with which their contracts shall be executed, the rights and obligations arising from them, and the mode in which their validity shall be determined and their obligations enforced; and also to

This paragraph includes the power theory of jurisdiction. Can you describe it?

regulate the manner and conditions upon which property situated within such territory, both personal and real, may be acquired, enjoyed, and transferred. The other principle of public law referred to follows from the one mentioned; that is, that no State can exercise direct jurisdiction and authority over persons or property without its territory. The several States are of equal dignity and authority, and the independence of one implies the exclusion of power from all others. And so it is laid down by jurists, as an elementary principle, that the laws of one State have no operation outside of its territory, except so far as is allowed by comity; and that no tribunal established by it can extend its process beyond that territory so as to subject either persons or property to its decisions....

But as contracts made in one State may be enforceable only in another State, and property may be held by non-residents, the exercise of the jurisdiction which every State is admitted to possess over persons and property within its own territory will often affect persons and property without it. To any influence exerted in this way by a State affecting persons resident or property situated elsewhere, no objection can be justly taken; whilst any direct exertion of authority upon them, in an attempt to give ex-territorial operation to its laws, or to enforce an ex-territorial jurisdiction by its tribunals, would be deemed an encroachment upon the independence of the State in which the persons are domiciled or the property is situated, and be resisted as usurpation.

* * *

So the State, through its tribunals, may subject property situated within its limits owned by non-residents to the payment of the demand of its own citizens against them; and the exercise of this jurisdiction in no respect infringes upon the sovereignty of the State where the owners are domiciled. Every State owes protection to its own citizens; and, when non-residents deal with them, it is a legitimate and just exercise of authority to hold and appropriate any property owned by such non-residents to satisfy the claims of its citizens. It is in virtue of the State's jurisdiction over the property of the non-resident situated within its limits that its tribunals can inquire into that non-resident's obligations to its own citizens, and the inquiry can then be carried only to the extent necessary to control the disposition of the property. If the non-resident ha[s] no property in the State, there is nothing upon which the tribunals can adjudicate....

If, without personal service, judgments in personam, obtained ex parte against non-residents and absent parties, upon mere publication of process, which, in the great majority of cases, would never be seen by the parties interested, could be upheld and enforced, they would be the constant instruments of fraud and oppression. Judgments for all sorts of claims upon contracts and for torts, real or pretended, would be thus obtained, under which property would be seized, when the evidence of

The Court considers consequences in this paragraph.

the transactions upon which they were founded, if they ever had any existence, had perished.

Substituted service by publication, or in any other authorized form, may be sufficient to inform parties of the object of proceedings taken where property is once brought under the control of the court by seizure or some equivalent act. The law assumes that property is always in the possession of its owner, in person or by agent; and it proceeds upon the theory that its seizure will inform him, not only that it is taken into the custody of the court, but that he must look to any proceedings authorized by law upon such seizure for its condemnation and sale. Such service may also be sufficient in cases where the object of the action is to reach and dispose of property in the State, or of some interest therein, by enforcing a contract or a lien respecting the same, or to partition it among different owners, or, when the public is a party, to condemn and appropriate it for a public purpose. In other words, such service may answer in all actions which are substantially proceedings in rem. But where the entire object of the action is to determine the personal rights and obligations of the defendants, that is, where the suit is merely in personam, constructive service in this form upon a non-resident is ineffectual for any purpose. Process from the tribunals of one State cannot run into another State, and summon parties there domiciled to leave its territory and respond to proceedings against them. Publication of process or notice within the State where the tribunal sits cannot create any greater obligation upon the non-resident to appear. Process sent to him out of the State, and process published within it, are equally unavailing in proceedings to establish his personal liability.

The want of authority of the tribunals of a State to adjudicate upon the obligations of non-residents, where they have no property within its limits, is not denied by the court below: but the position is assumed, that, where they have property within the State, it is immaterial whether the property is in the first instance brought under the control of the court by attachment or some other equivalent act, and afterwards applied by its judgment to the satisfaction of demands against its owner; or such demands be first established in a personal action, and the property of the non-resident be afterwards seized and sold on execution. But the answer to this position has already been given in the statement, that the jurisdiction of the court to inquire into and determine his obligations at all is only incidental to its jurisdiction over the property. Its jurisdiction in that respect cannot be made to depend upon facts to be ascertained after it has tried the cause and rendered the judgment. If the judgment be previously void, it will not become valid by the subsequent discovery of property of the defendant, or by his subsequent acquisition of it. The judgment, if void when rendered, will always remain void: it cannot occupy the doubtful position of being valid if property be found, and void if there

What does it mean for a judgment to be void?

be none. Even if the position assumed were confined to cases where the non-resident defendant possessed property in the State at the commencement of the action, it would still make the validity of the proceedings and judgment depend upon the question whether, before the levy of the execution, the defendant had or had not disposed of the property. If before the levy the property should be sold, then, according to this position, the judgment would not be binding. This doctrine would introduce a new element of uncertainty in judicial proceedings. The contrary is the law: the validity of every judgment depends upon the jurisdiction of the court before it is rendered, not upon what may occur subsequently....

The force and effect of judgments rendered against non-residents without personal service of process upon them, or their voluntary appearance, have been the subject of frequent consideration in the courts of the United States and of the several States, as attempts have been made to enforce such judgments in States other than those in which they were rendered, under the provision of the Constitution requiring that "full faith and credit shall be given in each State to the public acts, records, and judicial proceedings of every other State;" and the act of Congress providing for the mode of authenticating such acts, records, and proceedings, and declaring that, when thus authenticated, "they shall have such faith and credit given to them in every court within the United States as they have by law or usage in the courts of the State from which they are or shall or taken." In the earlier cases, it was supposed that the act gave to all judgments the same effect in other States which they had by law in the State where rendered. But this view was afterwards qualified so as to make the act applicable only when the court rendering the judgment had jurisdiction of the parties and of the subject-matter, and not to preclude an inquiry into the jurisdiction of the court in which the judgment was rendered, or the right of the State itself to exercise authority over the person or the subject-matter....

Full Faith and Credit discussed here.

Be that as it may, the courts of the United States are not required to give effect to judgments of this character when any right is claimed under them. Whilst they are not foreign tribunals in their relations to the State courts, they are tribunals of a different sovereignty, exercising a distinct and independent jurisdiction, and are bound to give to the judgments of the State courts only the same faith and credit which the courts of another State are bound to give to them.

State sovereignty

Since the adoption of the Fourteenth Amendment to the Federal Constitution, the validity of such judgments may be directly questioned, and their enforcement in the State resisted, on the ground that proceedings in a court of justice to determine the personal rights and obligations of parties over whom that court has no jurisdiction do not constitute due process of law. Whatever difficulty may be experienced in giving to those terms a definition which will embrace every permissible exertion of power affecting private rights, and exclude such as is forbidden, there can be no doubt of their meaning when applied to judicial proceedings. They then mean a course of legal proceedings according to those rules and principles which have been established in our systems of jurisprudence for the protection and enforcement of private rights. To give such proceedings any validity, there must be a tribunal competent by its constitution — that is, by the law of its creation — to pass upon the subject-matter of the suit; and, if that involves merely a determination of the personal liability of the defendant, he must be brought within its jurisdiction by service of process within the State, or his voluntary appearance.

Except in cases affecting the personal status of the plaintiff, and cases in which that mode of service may be considered to have been assented to in advance, as hereinafter mentioned, the substituted service of process by publication, allowed by the law of Oregon and by similar laws in other States, where actions are brought against non-residents, is effectual only where, in connection with process against the person for commencing the action, property in the State is brought under the control of the court, and subjected to its disposition by process adapted to that purpose, or where the judgment is sought as a means of reaching such property or affecting some interest therein; in other words, where the action is in the nature of a proceeding in rem. . . .

It is true that, in a strict sense, a proceeding in rem is one taken directly against property, and has for its object the disposition of the property, without reference to the title of individual claimants; but, in a larger and more general sense, the terms are applied to actions between parties, where the direct object is to reach and dispose of property owned by them, or of some interest therein. Such are cases commenced by attachment against the property of debtors, or instituted to partition real estate, foreclose a mortgage, or enforce a lien. So far as they affect property in the State, they are substantially proceedings in rem in the broader sense which we have mentioned. . . .

It follows from the views expressed that the personal judgment recovered in the State court of Oregon against the plaintiff herein, then a non-resident of the State, was without any validity, and did not authorize a sale of the property in controversy.

Here the Court introduces caveats — what it's not holding.

To prevent any misapplication of the views expressed in this opinion, it is proper to observe that we do not mean to assert, by any thing we have said, that a State may not authorize proceedings to determine the status of one of its citizens towards a non-resident, which would be binding within the State, though made without service of process or personal notice to the non-resident. The jurisdiction which every State possesses to determine the civil status and capacities of all its inhabitants involves authority to prescribe the conditions on which proceedings affecting them may be commenced and carried on within its territory. The State, for example, has absolute right to prescribe the conditions upon which the marriage relation between its own citizens shall be created, and the causes for which it may be dissolved. One of the parties guilty of acts for which, by the law of the State, a dissolution may be granted, may have removed to a State where no dissolution is permitted. The complaining party would, therefore, fail if a divorce were sought in the State of the defendant; and if application could not be made to the tribunals of the complainant's domicile in such case, and proceedings be there instituted without personal service of process or personal notice to the offending party, the injured citizen would be without redress.

Neither do we mean to assert that a State may not require a non-resident entering into a partnership or association within its limits, or making contracts enforceable there, to appoint an agent or representative in the State to receive service of process and notice in legal proceedings instituted with respect to such partnership, association, or contracts, or to designate a place where such service may be made and notice given, and provide, upon their failure, to make such appointment or to designate such place that service may be made upon a public officer designated for that purpose, or in some other prescribed way, and that judgments rendered upon such service may not be binding upon the non-residents both within and without the State.... Nor do we doubt that a State, on creating corporations or other institutions for pecuniary or charitable purposes, may provide a mode in which their conduct may be investigated, their obligations enforced, or their charters revoked, which shall require other than personal service upon their officers or members. Parties becoming members of such corporations or institutions would hold their interest subject to the conditions prescribed by law.

In the present case, there is no feature of this kind, and, consequently, no consideration of what would be the effect of such legislation in enforcing the contract of a non-resident can arise. The question here respects only the validity of a money judgment rendered in one State, in an action upon a simple contract against the resident of another, without service of process upon him, or his appearance therein.

Notes Regarding *Pennoyer v. Neff*

1. Collateral Attack. This case involves two lawsuits. In the first, Mitchell, who was Neff's attorney at one time, sued Neff on a debt (apparently attorney's fees) Neff owed to Mitchell. Because Neff was not in the state at the time of the lawsuit, Mitchell provided notice by publishing it in a local newspaper. Likely not receiving notice, Neff did not respond to the complaint, which led to the trial court entering a default judgment against Neff. Neff later acquired title to land located in Oregon. Mitchell took his judgment against Neff and executed it against the property, which was sold to none other than Mitchell at the sale to enforce the judgment. Mitchell then conveyed the property to Pennoyer. This case is a second lawsuit brought by Neff to reclaim his property from Pennoyer. Using a second lawsuit to attack a judgment in an earlier lawsuit is called a collateral attack. Normally, if a party disagrees with a judgment against it, the proper recourse is to appeal. However, here Neff was unaware of the initial lawsuit and therefore did not have the opportunity to appeal the initial judgment against him. Thus, Neff used a second lawsuit—a collateral lawsuit—to attack the judgment in the first lawsuit.

2. Power Theory of Jurisdiction. The *Pennoyer* Court announced a basic theory of jurisdiction—often referred to as the power theory—that it continued to use for over sixty years. This theory finds its origins in international law. Think back to the hypothetical involving Oscar and Ben. Under the power theory, a state court has jurisdiction over people and things within its borders. Conversely, the state has no authority over people and things outside its borders. In rem, quasi in rem, and in personam jurisdiction, concepts discussed next, are based on this general principle.

3. Quasi In Rem. According to the *Pennoyer* Court, for the state court to have jurisdiction over Neff based on his property in Oregon, the Oregon court should have attached the property at the beginning of the lawsuit. This type of jurisdiction is known as "quasi in rem" jurisdiction. It comes in two varieties. The underlying lawsuit here did not involve the property, but instead a purported debt that Neff owed Mitchell. The only reason that the court had for asserting any authority over Neff was his ownership of property in the jurisdiction. This is an example of a quasi in rem assertion of jurisdiction where the underlying lawsuit does not directly involve the property located in the state. However, sometimes a quasi in rem case involves the underlying property, such as in an action for trespass. Thus, a quasi in rem action may or may not involve the property that forms the basis for the court's jurisdiction. The exercise before you read *Pennoyer* asked you to define in rem and in personam jurisdiction. The *Pennoyer* case further described those concepts. How does quasi in rem differ from in rem and in personam jurisdiction?

4. Notice. Had the court attached the property at the beginning of the lawsuit, this likely would have resulted in a sign being posted on the property itself, alerting its owner that the property was the subject of a court proceeding. The assumption is that a property owner does not just leave his or her property unattended. Instead, the property owner leaves someone to watch over it. Thus, a sign on the property would alert the property owner to the lawsuit in a way that simply placing a notice in a local newspaper would not. Have you ever seen a notice posted that alerted the public that a place or piece of property was subject to a court proceeding? Even today, some states require such postings, especially in unlawful detainer actions, in which a landlord is evicting a tenant who has failed to pay his or her rent. Contrast this notice with the typical legal notices you find in newspapers. Which is more likely to alert the defendant that it has been sued?

5. Questionable Attorney. Mitchell was originally Neff's lawyer. Yet, it seems that Mitchell did not act too kindly to his former client—taking his property for less than its value to extinguish a debt that was likewise worth less than the property. Professor Wendy Collins Perdue recounts Mitchell's colorful history:

> "J.H. Mitchell" was actually the Oregon alias of one John Hipple. Hipple had been a teacher in Pennsylvania who, after being forced to marry the 15-year-old student whom he had seduced, left teaching and took up law. He practiced with a partner for several years, but apparently concluded that it was time to move on to greener pastures. Thus, in 1860 Hipple headed west taking with him four thousand dollars of client money and his then current paramour, a local school teacher. They made their way to California where Hipple abandoned the teacher, ostensibly because she was sick and her medical expenses had become too burdensome, and moved on to Portland, Oregon. There, using the name John H. Mitchell, he quickly established himself as a successful lawyer ... He also remarried without bothering to divorce his first wife.

Wendy Collins Perdue, *Sin, Scandal, and Substantive Due Process: Personal Jurisdiction and* Pennoyer *Reconsidered*, 62 WASH. L. REV. 479, 482–83 (1978).

6. What happens when a court issues a judgment in the absence of personal jurisdiction? Is that judgment valid? What happened to the judgment that Mitchell obtained against Neff in the first lawsuit? Was it enforceable?

Exercise 2-2. Understanding In Rem, Quasi In Rem, and In Personam

Consider whether the particular court can assert jurisdiction over the defendant described below under the jurisdictional theories discussed in *Pennoyer*. If so, under which theory of jurisdiction—in rem, in personam, or quasi in rem—is the court's exercise of jurisdiction proper?

1. Tom and Katie live in Arkansas. They get into a car accident in Missouri. Can Katie sue Tom in Arkansas state court as a result of the injuries she received in the accident?

2. Same facts as question 1, but this time Katie sues Tom in Missouri state court. Can she do so if Tom owns a summer home on a lake in Missouri? What if Tom does not own any property in Missouri?

3. Same facts as question 1. If Katie's process server is able to serve Tom with the summons and complaint while Tom is visiting friends in Missouri, will the Missouri state court have jurisdiction over Tom?

4. Tom lives in Arkansas. Tom owns a summer home in Missouri. If the state of Missouri begins a foreclosure action because Tom has failed to pay his property taxes, may the state sue Tom in state court in Missouri?

5. Harris, a citizen of North Carolina, owed Balk, also a North Carolina citizen, $180. Epstein, a Maryland citizen, claimed that Balk owed him $344.

> While Harris was visiting Baltimore, Epstein instituted a garnishment proceeding in a Maryland court, attaching the debt Harris owed Balk. Harris was personally served with process in Maryland. Does the Maryland court have jurisdiction? Assume Harris consents to judgment against him and pays Epstein $180. Balk subsequently sues Harris in North Carolina to recover the $180. Should the North Carolina court give full faith and credit to the Maryland judgment? *See Harris v. Balk*, 198 U.S. 215 (1905) (Maryland court had jurisdiction).
>
> 6. In the Chapter Problem set out at the beginning of this chapter, would the California court have jurisdiction over Piper? Would it have jurisdiction over Hartzell? What additional facts would you need to know to answer this question?
>
> 7. A defendant in a lawsuit is served with process while flying over Arkansas on a commercial airline flight between Tennessee and Texas. Will an Arkansas state court have jurisdiction over the defendant? *See Grace v. MacArthur*, 170 F. Supp. 442 (E.D. Ark. 1959) (court had jurisdiction).

Diagramming Lawsuits

When a lawsuit becomes complex with multiple parties, diagramming who the parties are, where they are from, and what they did where can help keep track of what is going on in the lawsuit. In trying to solve Exercise 2-2(5) above, diagramming the fact pattern is helpful in keeping track of the parties. Here's one way to diagram what happened in the two cases.

The Lawsuits

Action 1: Maryland Court: Epstein (Maryland) v. Harris (North Carolina) → Harris consents and pays
judgment

Action 2: North Carolina Court: Balk (N.C.) v. Harris (N.C.)

The Debts

Harris (N.C.) owes → Balk (N.C.) owes → Epstein (Md.)

As you read the cases that follow in this and succeeding chapters, this technique can prove helpful in keeping track of cases involving multiple parties and/or lawsuits.

4. Modern Personal Jurisdiction Theory

While the power theory of jurisdiction made sense when people traveled by wagon train, modern forms of transportation, including trains, cars, and planes, transformed the manner in which people moved around the country and the world. The Court began to adapt personal jurisdiction law to accommodate some of these changes. For example, in the early twentieth century adjustments were made for cars. In the 1916 case, *Kane v. New Jersey*, 242 U.S. 160 (1916), the Court held constitutional a New Jersey law that required an out of state driver to file an instrument appointing a New Jersey agent to receive service of process in the state prior to using the state's highway. This is a form of express consent, whereby the driver agrees that the state's courts have jurisdiction over him or her in a case involving an accident that occurs while the out-of-state driver is in that state. The Court extended the concept to implied consent in *Hess v. Pawloski*, 274 U.S. 352 (1927), a case in which a Pennsylvania resident got into an accident with a Massachusetts resident while driving in Massachusetts. Massachusetts law provided that, by simply operating a car in the state, a driver consented to have the registrar as his or her attorney for all lawsuits resulting from car accidents that occurred while the non-resident was driving in Massachusetts. The law did require that the out-of-state driver receive notice of the lawsuit by registered mail.

An additional wrinkle in personal jurisdiction that the Court had to resolve was determining under what circumstances a court could assert jurisdiction over a corporation. With modern transportation came the modern corporation, which began to have business that crossed state lines. Of course, today there are corporations that conduct business in all fifty states as well as internationally. In addition, foreign corporations often conduct business in the United States. Where can a plaintiff sue such corporations? The lower courts developed a variety of theories to address jurisdiction over corporations. One of those theories—presence—is noted by the Court in the following case, *International Shoe Co. v. Washington*. Indeed, the *International Shoe* Court settled on an approach that courts continue to use (although somewhat modified) today.

Exercise 2-3. *International Shoe* and Modern Personal Jurisdiction

As you read *International Shoe*, look for answers to the following questions. These questions are designed to help you understand key facts, reasoning, and rules that come out of the case. As you read the case, consider what impact modern transportation and a national economy have had on personal jurisdiction rules.

1. *International Shoe* introduces the term special appearance. Look up the term in a legal dictionary. [Hint: You may find this under the general term "appearance."]

2. Does the Court abandon the power theory of jurisdiction? If so, with what does it replace it?

3. This case introduces the concepts of general jurisdiction and specific jurisdiction. What do these terms mean? What legal standards does the Court establish in this case for each? How do you determine which type of jurisdiction is present in a particular case?

4. Would the Washington state court have jurisdiction over International Shoe under the power theory of jurisdiction?

5. Under what theory of jurisdiction, general, specific, or both, is the Washington court's assertion of jurisdiction in this case proper?

6. What role, if any, does notice to the defendant play in the outcome of this case?

7. What actions by International Shoe provide the basis for the court's jurisdiction in this case?

8. The *International Shoe* Court adopts entirely new terminology in assessing whether jurisdiction is proper. What terms does it use? What is the nature of the shift in the Court's approach to personal jurisdiction?

9. This case introduces a common structure that courts use in organizing their decisions. Can you identify this structure? Hints about the structure of the Court's opinion are provided in the margins of the case.

10. Diagram the lawsuits involved in *International Shoe.*

International Shoe Co. v. Washington
326 U.S. 310 (1945)

Mr. Chief Justice Stone delivered the opinion of the Court.

This paragraph contains the issue.

The questions for decision are (1) whether, within the limitations of the due process clause of the Fourteenth Amendment, appellant, a Delaware corporation, has by its activities in the State of Washington rendered itself amenable to proceedings in the courts of that state to recover unpaid contributions to the state unemployment compensation fund exacted by state statutes, and (2) whether the state can exact those contributions consistently with the due process clause of the Fourteenth Amendment....

In this case notice of assessment for the years in question was personally served upon a sales solicitor employed by appellant in the State of Washington, and a copy of the notice was mailed by registered mail to appellant at its address in St. Louis, Missouri. Appellant appeared specially before the office of unemployment and moved to set aside the order and notice of assessment on the ground that the service upon appellant's salesman was not proper service upon appellant; that appellant was not a corporation of the State of Washington and was not doing business within the state; that it had no agent within the state upon whom service could be made; and that appellant is not an employer and does not furnish employment within the meaning of the statute....

Facts

The facts as found by the appeal tribunal and accepted by the state Superior Court and Supreme Court are not in dispute. Appellant is a Delaware corporation, having its principal place of business in St. Louis, Missouri, and is engaged in the manufacture and sale of shoes and other footwear. It maintains places of business in several states, other than Washington, at which its manufacturing is carried on and from which its merchandise is distributed interstate through several sales units or branches located outside the State of Washington.

Appellant has no office in Washington and makes no contracts either for sale or purchase of merchandise there. It maintains no stock of merchandise in that state and makes there no deliveries of goods in intrastate commerce. During the years from 1937 to 1940, now in question, appellant employed eleven to thirteen salesmen under direct supervision and control of sales managers located in St. Louis. These salesmen resided in Washington; their principal activities were confined to that state; and they were compensated by commissions based upon the amount of their sales. The commissions for each year totaled more than $31,000. Appellant supplies its salesmen with a line of samples, each consisting of one shoe of a pair, which they display to prospective purchasers. On occasion they rent permanent sample rooms, for exhibiting samples, in business buildings, or rent rooms in hotels or business buildings temporarily for that purpose. The cost of such rentals is reimbursed by appellant.

$31k = $439k in 2018 dollars

The authority of the salesmen is limited to exhibiting their samples and soliciting orders from prospective buyers, at prices and on terms fixed by appellant. The salesmen transmit the orders to appellant's office in St. Louis for acceptance or rejection, and when accepted the merchandise for filling the orders is shipped f.o.b. [free on board] from points outside Washington to the purchasers within the state. All the merchandise shipped into Washington is invoiced at the place of shipment from which collections are made. No salesman has authority to enter into contracts or to make collections.

More facts.

Historically the jurisdiction of courts to render judgment in personam is grounded on their de facto power over the defendant's person. Hence his presence within the territorial jurisdiction of a court was prerequisite to its rendition of a judgment personally binding him. *Pennoyer v. Neff....* [D]ue process requires only that in order to subject a defendant to a judgment in personam, if he be not present within the territory of the forum, he have certain minimum contacts with it such that the maintenance of the suit does not offend "traditional notions of fair play and substantial justice." *Milliken v. Meyer*, 311 U.S. 457, 463 (1941).

Review of the law begins here.

Since the corporate personality is a fiction, although a fiction intended to be acted upon as though it were a fact, it is clear that unlike an individual its "presence" without, as well as within, the state of its origin can be manifested only by activities carried on in its behalf by those who are authorized to act for it. To say that the corporation is so far "present" there as to satisfy due process requirements, for purposes of taxation or the maintenance of suits against it in the courts of the state, is to beg the question to be decided. For the terms "present" or "presence" are used merely to symbolize those activities of the corporation's agent within the state which courts will deem to be sufficient to satisfy the demands of due process. Those demands may be met by such contacts of the corporation with the state of the forum as make it reasonable, in the context of our federal system of government, to require the corporation to defend the particular suit which is brought there. An "estimate of the inconveniences" which would result to the corporation from a trial away from its "home" or principal place of business is relevant in this connection.

"Presence" in the state in this sense has never been doubted when the activities of the corporation there have not only been continuous and systematic, but also give rise to the liabilities sued on, even though no consent to be sued or authorization to an agent to accept service of process has been given. Conversely, it has been generally recognized that the casual presence of the corporate agent or even his conduct of single or isolated items of activities in a state in the corporation's behalf are not enough to subject it to suit on causes of action unconnected with the activities there. To require the corporation in such circumstances to defend the suit away from its home or other jurisdiction where it carries on more substantial activities has been thought to lay too great and unreasonable a burden on the corporation to comport with due process.

General jurisdiction. While it has been held in cases on which appellant relies that continuous activity of some sorts within a state is not enough to support the demand that the corporation be amenable to suits unrelated to that activity, there have been instances in which the continuous corporate operations within a state were thought so substantial and of such a nature as to justify suit against it on causes of action arising from dealings entirely distinct from those activities.

Finally, although the commission of some single or occasional acts of the corporate agent in a state sufficient to impose an obligation or liability on the corporation has not been thought to confer upon the state authority to enforce it, other such acts, because of their nature and quality and the circumstances of their commission, may be deemed sufficient to render the corporation liable to suit. True, some of the decisions holding the corporation amenable to suit have been supported by resort to the legal fiction that it has given its consent to service and suit, consent being implied from its presence in the state through the acts of its authorized agents. But more realistically it may be said that those authorized acts were of such a nature as to justify the fiction.

It is evident that the criteria by which we mark the boundary line between those activities which justify the subjection of a corporation to suit, and those which do not, cannot be simply mechanical or quantitative. The test is not merely, as has sometimes been suggested, whether the activity, which the corporation has seen fit to procure through its agents in another state, is a little more or a little less. Whether due process is satisfied must depend rather upon the quality and nature of the activity in relation to the fair and orderly administration of the laws which it was the purpose of the due process clause to insure. That clause does not contemplate that a state may make binding a judgment in personam against an individual or corporate defendant with which the state has no contacts, ties, or relations. *Cf. Pennoyer v. Neff.*

But to the extent that a corporation exercises the privilege of conducting activities within a state, it enjoys the benefits and protection of the laws of that state. The exercise of that privilege may give rise to obligations; and, so far as those obligations arise out of or are connected with the activities within the state, a procedure which requires the corporation to respond to a suit brought to enforce them can, in most instances, hardly be said to be undue.

Specific jurisdiction.

Applying these standards, the activities carried on in behalf of appellant in the State of Washington were neither irregular nor casual. They were systematic and continuous throughout the years in question. They resulted in a large volume of interstate business, in the course of which appellant received the benefits and protection of the laws of the state, including the right to resort to the courts for the enforcement of its rights. The obligation which is here sued upon arose out of those very activities. It is evident that these operations establish sufficient contacts or ties with the state of the forum to make it reasonable and just according to our traditional conception of fair play and substantial justice to permit the state to enforce the obligations which appellant has incurred there. Hence we cannot say that the maintenance of the present suit in the State of Washington involves an unreasonable or undue procedure.

Court begins applying law here.

We are likewise unable to conclude that the service of the process within the state upon an agent whose activities establish appellant's "presence" there was not sufficient notice of the suit, or that the suit was so unrelated to those activities as to make the agent an inappropriate vehicle for communicating the notice. It is enough that appellant has established such contacts with the state that the particular form of substituted service adopted there gives reasonable assurance that the notice will be actual. Nor can we say that the mailing of the notice of suit to appellant by registered mail at its home office was not reasonably calculated to apprise appellant of the suit....

Appellant having rendered itself amenable to suit upon obligations arising out of the activities of its salesmen in Washington, the state may maintain the present suit in personam to collect the tax laid upon the exercise of the privilege of employing appellant's salesmen within the state.

Conclusion

Affirmed.

Exercise 2-4. *International Shoe* Revisited

Note the structure that the Court used in deciding this case. It started with the issue; moved to the relevant facts; discussed generally the applicable law; applied that law to the facts of the case; and concluded. This is a typical approach that courts use in deciding cases. Note that it follows the general form that lawyers use to address legal issues — IRAC (Issue; Rule; Analysis; Conclusion). The Court began with the issue, announced the rule (the generally applicable law), applied it (analysis), and concluded. As a lawyer making an argument to a court, you should weave the facts into your analysis. However, often in brief writing, there is an opportunity to provide the basic facts of the case in a separate section, much like the Court has done in this case.

1. Using the IRAC approach, make the argument that the Washington state court had specific jurisdiction over *International Shoe*.

2. Based on the Court's holding and reasoning in *International Shoe*, would the following courts have jurisdiction in these cases? Under which theory — general or specific jurisdiction?

   a. Would the California court in the Chapter Problem have jurisdiction over Piper? Would it have jurisdiction over Hartzell? What additional facts might help you answer these questions?

   b. McGee was the beneficiary of a life insurance policy issued by Empire, an Arizona corporation, to Franklin, a California resident who passed away. International Life Insurance Co. ("International"), a Texas corporation, assumed Empire's obligations under the policy. International conducted business by mail with Franklin until his death. The contract was delivered to California, and Franklin sent his premium payments by placing them into the mail in California. Neither Empire nor International had an office in California. International did no business in California except for its contract with Franklin. If International refuses to pay McGee pursuant to the insurance policy, would a California court have jurisdiction over International in a lawsuit brought by McGee? *See McGee v. International Life Insurance Co.*, 355 U.S. 220 (1957) (contract with substantial connection to the state is sufficient to assert jurisdiction over defendant insurance company).

   c. Mrs. Donner, a Pennsylvania resident, established a trust in Delaware, naming a Delaware bank trustee. She later moved to Florida, where she changed the remainder beneficiaries of the trust to the children of her third daughter. She also made a will in Florida and gave most of her estate to her two other daughters. Mrs. Donner died and her two daughters named as beneficiaries in the will contested the appointment of the third daughter's children as beneficiaries of the trust, claiming the appointment was ineffective. If the corpus of the trust did not pass to Mrs. Donner's grandchildren, it would pass to her two other daughters through the will. The two daughters brought suit in Florida to invalidate the trust appointment. Does the Florida court have jurisdiction over the trustee? *See Hanson v. Denckla*, 357 U.S. 235 (1958) (unilateral actions of a third party that establish the defendant's contacts with the state are insufficient for the court to assert jurisdiction).

  d. A water heater blows up in a home in Illinois, injuring the homeowner. The accident was allegedly caused by a defective valve. The valve was manufactured by Titan in Ohio. Titan shipped the valve to American Radiator, a Pennsylvania corporation, which incorporated it into the hot water heater in Pennsylvania. That water heater exploded in Illinois. If the homeowner sued Titan and American Radiator in Illinois state court, would the Illinois court have jurisdiction over both defendants? *See Gray v. American Radiator & Standard Sanitary Corp.*, 22 Ill. 2d 432 (1966) (placing a product in the stream of commerce with the expectation that it will end up in the state establishes sufficient contacts for the assertion of jurisdiction). Try diagramming this fact pattern. It may look like this:

Plaintiff (Illinois) v. Titan (Ohio)
American Radiator (Penn.)

You could also diagram it based on the actions of the parties:

Titan (Ohio; valve) → American Radiator (Penn.; water heater) → Plaintiff (Ill.)

How would you diagram the parties in problem 2-4(c)?

Note on Long Arm Statutes

International Shoe and prior cases made it clear that it was possible for a state to assert jurisdiction over an out-of-state defendant. States enacted statutes, known as "long arm" statutes, that permitted their states' courts to "reach out and grab" an out-of-state defendant. We saw an earlier version of such statutes designed for out-of-state drivers in *Kane* and *Hess*. Modern long arm statutes are much broader. Today, many states have statutes providing that the state courts may assert jurisdiction to the limits of due process. Arkansas provides an example of such a statute.

Arkansas Code § 16-4-101(B):

Personal Jurisdiction. The courts of this state shall have personal jurisdiction of all persons, and all causes of action or claims for relief, to the maximum extent permitted by the due process of law clause of the Fourteenth Amendment of the United States Constitution.

In addition, in states that have more particular requirements for the courts to assert jurisdiction over an out-of-state defendant (for example, a statute that states that the defendant must have committed a tort in the state), many state courts of last resort have interpreted those statutes to reach to the limits of the due process clause. In these states, a lawyer need only satisfy the requirements of *International Shoe* and its progeny to determine if the state court's assertion of jurisdiction over an out-of-state defendant is proper.

Otherwise, an attorney must meet the requirements of both the state's long arm statute and due process. Kentucky provides an example of a long arm statute that does not reach to the limits of the due process clause:

Kentucky Revised Statutes § 454.210

(2) (a) A court may exercise personal jurisdiction over a person who acts directly or by an agent, as to a claim arising from the person's:

1. Transacting any business in this Commonwealth;

2. Contracting to supply services or goods in this Commonwealth;

3. Causing tortious injury by an act or omission in this Commonwealth;

4. Causing tortious injury in this Commonwealth by an act or omission outside this Commonwealth if he regularly does or solicits business, or engages in any other persistent course of conduct, or derives substantial revenue from goods used or consumed or services rendered in this Commonwealth, provided that the tortious injury occurring in this Commonwealth arises out of the doing or soliciting of business or a persistent course of conduct or derivation of substantial revenue within the Commonwealth;

5. Causing injury in this Commonwealth to any person by breach of warranty expressly or impliedly made in the sale of goods outside this Commonwealth when the seller knew such person would use, consume, or be affected by, the goods in this Commonwealth, if he also regularly does or solicits business, or engages in any other persistent course of conduct, or derives substantial revenue from goods used or consumed or services rendered in this Commonwealth;

6. Having an interest in, using, or possessing real property in this Commonwealth, providing the claim arises from the interest in, use of, or possession of the real property, provided, however, that such in personam jurisdiction shall not be imposed on a nonresident who did not himself voluntarily institute the relationship, and did not knowingly perform, or fail to perform, the act or acts upon which jurisdiction is predicated;

7. Contracting to insure any person, property, or risk located within this Commonwealth at the time of contracting;

8. Committing sexual intercourse in this state which intercourse causes the birth of a child when:

a. The father or mother or both are domiciled in this state;

b. There is a repeated pattern of intercourse between the father and mother in this state; or

c. Said intercourse is a tort or a crime in this state; or

9. Making a telephone solicitation, as defined in KRS 367.46951, into the Commonwealth.

Exercise 2-5. *Shaffer v. Heitner*

The following case involves a rather novel long arm statute. As you read *Shaffer v. Heitner*, look for answers to the questions below.

1. One of the issues left unresolved by *International Shoe* was the status of the *Pennoyer* theories of jurisdiction. How does the Court's decision in *Shaffer* affect, if at all, the following types of jurisdiction:

   a. Quasi in rem jurisdiction involving the property

   b. Quasi in rem jurisdiction not involving the property

   c. In rem

   d. In personam

   e. Consent to jurisdiction

2. *Shaffer*, like prior cases, uses new terminology. Look up the following terms in a legal dictionary in preparation for reading the case:

   a. Sequester

   b. Quash

   c. Advisory opinion

   d. Choice of law clause

   e. General appearance

3. How does the Delaware long arm statute in this case operate?

4. Do the jurisdictional principles coming out of *International Shoe* apply to individuals as well as corporations?

5. Diagram the lawsuit in *Shaffer*.

Shaffer v. Heitner

433 U.S. 186 (1977)

Mr. Justice Marshall delivered the opinion of the Court.

The controversy in this case concerns the constitutionality of a Delaware statute that allows a court of that State to take jurisdiction of a lawsuit by sequestering any property of the defendant that happens to be located in Delaware. Appellants contend that the sequestration statute as applied in this case violates the Due Process Clause of the Fourteenth Amendment both because it permits the state courts to exercise jurisdiction despite the absence of sufficient contacts among the defendants, the litigation, and the State of Delaware and because it authorizes the deprivation of defendants' property without providing adequate procedural safeguards. We find it necessary to consider only the first of these contentions.

Appellee Heitner, a nonresident of Delaware, is the owner of one share of stock in the Greyhound Corp., a business incorporated under the laws of Delaware with its principal place of business in Phoenix, Ariz. On May 22, 1974, he filed a shareholder's derivative suit in the Court of Chancery for New Castle County, Del., in which he named as defendants Greyhound, its wholly owned subsidiary Greyhound Lines, Inc., [incorporated in California with its principal place of business in Phoenix, Arizona], and 28 present or former officers or directors of one or both of the corporations. In essence, Heitner alleged that the individual defendants had violated their duties to Greyhound by causing it and its subsidiary to engage in actions that resulted in the corporations being held liable for substantial damages in a private antitrust suit and a large fine in a criminal contempt action. The activities which led to these penalties took place in Oregon. [At the same time as he filed his complaint, Heitner successfully moved, pursuant to Delaware law, to sequester Greyhound stock that the officer and director defendants owned. Delaware law provided that stock in a Delaware corporation is located in Delaware.*]

* * *

All 28 defendants were notified of the initiation of the suit by certified mail directed to their last known addresses and by publication in a New Castle County newspaper. The 21 defendants whose property was seized (hereafter referred to as appellants) responded by entering a special appearance for the purpose of moving to quash service of process and to vacate the sequestration order. They contended that the ex parte sequestration procedure did not accord them due process of law and that the property seized was not capable of attachment in Delaware. In addition, appellants asserted that under the rule of *International Shoe Co. v. Washington*, they did not have sufficient contacts with Delaware to sustain the jurisdiction of that State's courts.

* * *

The Delaware courts rejected appellants' jurisdictional challenge by noting that this suit was brought as a quasi in rem proceeding. Since quasi in rem jurisdiction is traditionally based on attachment or seizure of prop-

---

* Ed. Note. Delaware's sequestration statute provided that the court could seize the property of an out of state defendant. If a defendant did not appear, the property could be sold pursuant to the outcome of the lawsuit. However, if the defendant entered a general appearance, the defendant could petition to have the property returned. Del. Code Ann., Tit. 10, § 366(a) (1975). Thus, a defendant had to enter a general appearance to contest the sequestration of his or her stock.

erty present in the jurisdiction, not on contacts between the defendant and the State, the courts considered appellants' claimed lack of contacts with Delaware to be unimportant. This categorical analysis assumes the continued soundness of the conceptual structure founded on the century-old case of *Pennoyer v. Neff.*

* * *

The case for applying to jurisdiction in rem the same test of "fair play and substantial justice" as governs assertions of jurisdiction in personam is simple and straightforward. It is premised on recognition that "(t)he phrase, 'judicial jurisdiction over a thing', is a customary elliptical way of referring to jurisdiction over the interests of persons in a thing." RESTATE-MENT (SECOND) OF CONFLICT OF LAWS § 56, Introductory Note (1971). This recognition leads to the conclusion that in order to justify an exercise of jurisdiction in rem, the basis for jurisdiction must be sufficient to justify exercising "jurisdiction over the interests of persons in a thing." The standard for determining whether an exercise of jurisdiction over the interests of persons is consistent with the Due Process Clause is the minimum-contacts standard elucidated in *International Shoe.*

This argument, of course, does not ignore the fact that the presence of property in a State may bear on the existence of jurisdiction by providing contacts among the forum State, the defendant, and the litigation. For example, when claims to the property itself are the source of the underlying controversy between the plaintiff and the defendant, it would be unusual for the State where the property is located not to have jurisdiction. In such cases, the defendant's claim to property located in the State would normally indicate that he expected to benefit from the State's protection of his interest. The State's strong interests in assuring the marketability of property within its borders and in providing a procedure for peaceful resolution of disputes about the possession of that property would also support jurisdiction, as would the likelihood that important records and witnesses will be found in the State. The presence of property may also favor jurisdiction in cases such as suits for injury suffered on the land of an absentee owner, where the defendant's ownership of the property is conceded but the cause of action is otherwise related to rights and duties growing out of that ownership.

Presence of property

It appears, therefore, that jurisdiction over many types of actions which now are or might be brought in rem would not be affected by a holding that any assertion of state-court jurisdiction must satisfy the *International Shoe* standard. For the type of quasi in rem action typified by *Harris v. Balk* and the present case, however, accepting the proposed analysis would result in significant change. These are cases where the property which now serves as the basis for state-court jurisdiction is completely unrelated to the plaintiff's cause of action. Thus, although the presence of the de-

Quasi in Rem

fendant's property in a State might suggest the existence of other ties among the defendant, the State, and the litigation, the presence of the property alone would not support the State's jurisdiction. If those other ties did not exist, cases over which the State is now thought to have jurisdiction could not be brought in that forum.

* * *

The primary rationale for treating the presence of property as a sufficient basis for jurisdiction to adjudicate claims over which the State would not have jurisdiction if *International Shoe* applied is that a wrongdoer "should not be able to avoid payment of his obligations by the expedient of removing his assets to a place where he is not subject to an in personam suit." RESTATEMENT § 66, Comment a. This justification, however, does not explain why jurisdiction should be recognized without regard to whether the property is present in the State because of an effort to avoid the owner's obligations. Nor does it support jurisdiction to adjudicate the underlying claim. At most, it suggests that a State in which property is located should have jurisdiction to attach that property, by use of proper procedures, as security for a judgment being sought in a forum where the litigation can be maintained consistently with *International Shoe*. Moreover, we know of nothing to justify the assumption that a debtor can avoid paying his obligations by removing his property to a State in which his creditor cannot obtain personal jurisdiction over him. The Full Faith and Credit Clause, after all, makes the valid in personam judgment of one State enforceable in all other States.

It might also be suggested that allowing [quasi] in rem jurisdiction avoids the uncertainty inherent in the *International Shoe* standard and assures a plaintiff of a forum. We believe, however, that the fairness standard of *International Shoe* can be easily applied in the vast majority of cases. Moreover, when the existence of jurisdiction in a particular forum under *International Shoe* is unclear, the cost of simplifying the litigation by avoiding the jurisdictional question may be the sacrifice of "fair play and substantial justice." That cost is too high.

We are left, then, to consider the significance of the long history of jurisdiction based solely on the presence of property in a State. Although the theory that territorial power is both essential to and sufficient for jurisdiction has been undermined, we have never held that the presence of property in a State does not automatically confer jurisdiction over the owner's interest in that property. This history must be considered as supporting the proposition that jurisdiction based solely on the presence of property satisfies the demands of due process..., but it is not decisive. "[T]raditional notions of fair play and substantial justice" can be as readily offended by the perpetuation of ancient forms that are no longer justified as by the adoption of new procedures that are inconsistent with the basic values of our constitutional heritage. The fiction that an assertion of jurisdiction over property is anything but an assertion of jurisdiction over the owner of the property supports an ancient form without substantial modern justification. Its continued acceptance would serve only to allow state-court jurisdiction that is fundamentally unfair to the defendant.

We therefore conclude that all assertions of state-court jurisdiction must be evaluated according to the standards set forth in *International Shoe* and its progeny.

IV

The Delaware courts based their assertion of jurisdiction in this case solely on the statutory presence of appellants' property in Delaware. Yet that property is not the subject matter of this litigation, nor is the underlying cause of action related to the property. Appellants' holdings in Greyhound do not, therefore, provide contacts with Delaware sufficient to support the jurisdiction of that State's courts over appellants. If it exists, that jurisdiction must have some other foundation.

* * *

Appellee Heitner did not allege and does not now claim that appellants have ever set foot in Delaware. Nor does he identify any act related to his cause of action as having taken place in Delaware. Nevertheless, he contends that appellants' positions as directors and officers of a corporation chartered in Delaware provide sufficient "contacts, ties, or relations", with that State to give its courts jurisdiction over appellants in this stockholder's derivative action. This argument is based primarily on what Heitner asserts to be the strong interest of Delaware in supervising the management of a Delaware corporation. That interest is said to derive from the role of Delaware law in establishing the corporation and defining the obligations owed to it by its officers and directors. In order to protect this interest, appellee concludes, Delaware's courts must have jurisdiction over corporate fiduciaries such as appellants.

This argument is undercut by the failure of the Delaware Legislature to assert the state interest appellee finds so compelling. Delaware law bases jurisdiction, not on appellants' status as corporate fiduciaries, but rather on the presence of their property in the State.... If Delaware perceived its interest in securing jurisdiction over corporate fiduciaries to be as great as Heitner suggests, we would expect it to have enacted a statute more clearly designed to protect that interest.

Moreover, even if Heitner's assessment of the importance of Delaware's interest is accepted, his argument fails to demonstrate that Delaware is a fair forum for this litigation. The interest appellee has identified may support the application of Delaware law to resolve any controversy over appellants' actions in their capacities as officers and directors. But we have rejected the argument that if a State's law can properly be applied to a dispute, its courts necessarily have jurisdiction over the parties to that dispute....

Appellee suggests that by accepting positions as officers or directors of a Delaware corporation, appellants performed the acts required by *Hanson v. Denckla*. He notes that Delaware law provides substantial benefits to corporate officers and directors, and that these benefits were at least in part the incentive for appellants to assume their positions. It is, he says, "only fair and just" to require appellants, in return for these benefits, to respond in the State of Delaware when they are accused of misusing their power.

[T]his line of reasoning establishes only that it is appropriate for Delaware law to govern the obligations of appellants to Greyhound and its stockholders. It does not demonstrate that appellants have "purposefully avail(ed themselves) of the privilege of conducting activities within the forum State," *Hanson*, 357 U.S. 235, 253 (1958), in a way that would justify bringing them before a Delaware tribunal. Appellants have simply had nothing to do with the State of Delaware. Moreover, appellants had no reason to expect to be haled before a Delaware court. Delaware, unlike some States, has not enacted a statute that treats acceptance of a directorship as consent to jurisdiction in the State. And "(i)t strains reason ... to suggest that anyone buying securities in a corporation formed in Delaware 'impliedly consents' to subject himself to Delaware's ... jurisdiction on any cause of action." Folk A. Moyer, *Sequestration in Delaware: A Constitutional Analysis*, 73 Colum.L.Rev. 749, 785 n.10 (1973). Appellants, who were not required to acquire interests in Greyhound in order to hold their positions, did not by acquiring those interests surrender their right to be brought to judgment only in States with which they had had "minimum contacts."

The Due Process Clause "does not contemplate that a state may make binding a judgment ... against an individual or corporate defendant with which the state has no contacts, ties, or relations." [*International Shoe*, 326 U.S. at 319.]

Delaware's assertion of jurisdiction over appellants in this case is inconsistent with that constitutional limitation on state power. The judgment of the Delaware Supreme Court must, therefore, be reversed.

It is so ordered.

Mr. Justice Brennan, concurring in part and dissenting in part.

I join Parts I–III of the Court's opinion. I fully agree that the minimum-contacts analysis developed in *International Shoe* represents a far more sensible construct for the exercise of state-court jurisdiction than the patchwork of legal and factual fictions that has been generated from the decision in *Pennoyer v. Neff*. It is precisely because the inquiry into minimum contacts is now of such overriding importance, however, that I must respectfully dissent from Part IV of the Court's opinion.

I

The primary teaching of Parts I–III of today's decision is that a State, in seeking to assert jurisdiction over a person located outside its borders, may only do so on the basis of minimum contacts among the parties, the contested transaction, and the forum State....

[T]he issue of the existence of minimum contacts was never pleaded by appellee, made the subject of discovery, or ruled upon by the Delaware courts. These facts notwithstanding, the Court in Part IV reaches the minimum-contacts question and finds such contacts lacking as applied to appellants. Succinctly stated, once having properly and persuasively decided that the quasi in rem statute that Delaware admits to having enacted is invalid, the Court then proceeds to find that a minimum-contacts law that Delaware expressly denies having enacted also could not be constitutionally applied in this case.

In my view, a purer example of an advisory opinion is not to be found. True, appellants do not deny having received actual notice of the action in question. However, notice is but one ingredient of a proper assertion of state-court jurisdiction. The other is a statute authorizing the exercise of the State's judicial power along constitutionally permissible grounds which henceforth means minimum contacts. As of today, [the Delaware sequestration statute] is not such a law. Recognizing that today's decision fundamentally alters the relevant jurisdictional ground rules, I certainly would not want to rule out the possibility that Delaware's courts might decide that the legislature's overriding purpose of securing the personal appearance in state courts of defendants would best be served by reinterpreting its statute to permit state jurisdiction on the basis of constitutionally permissible contacts rather than stock ownership. Were the state courts to take this step, it would then become necessary to address the question of whether minimum contacts exist here. But in the present posture of this case, the Court's decision of this important issue is purely an abstract ruling.

My concern with the inappropriateness of the Court's action is highlighted by two other considerations. First, an inquiry into minimum contacts inevitably is highly dependent on creating a proper factual foundation detailing the contacts between the forum State and the controversy in question. Because neither the plaintiff-appellee nor the state courts viewed such an inquiry as germane in this instance, the Court today is unable to draw upon a proper factual record in reaching its conclusion; moreover, its disposition denies appellee the normal opportunity to seek discovery on the contacts issue. Second, it must be remembered that the Court's ruling is a constitutional one and necessarily will affect the reach of the jurisdictional laws of all 50 States. Ordinarily this would counsel restraint in constitutional pronouncements. Certainly it should have cautioned the Court against reaching out to decide a question that, as here, has yet to emerge from the state courts ripened for review on the federal issue.

II

Nonetheless, because the Court rules on the minimum-contacts question, I feel impelled to express my view. While evidence derived through discovery might satisfy me that minimum contacts are lacking in a given case, I am convinced that as a general rule a state forum has jurisdiction to adjudicate a shareholder derivative action centering on the conduct and policies of the directors and officers of a corporation chartered by that State. Unlike the Court, I therefore would not foreclose Delaware from asserting jurisdiction over appellants were it persuaded to do so on the basis of minimum contacts.

It is well settled that a derivative lawsuit as presented here does not inure primarily to the benefit of the named plaintiff. Rather, the primary beneficiaries are the corporation and its owners, the shareholders....

Viewed in this light, the chartering State has an unusually powerful interest in insuring the availability of a convenient forum for litigating claims involving a possible multiplicity of defendant fiduciaries and for vindicating the State's substantive policies regarding the management of its domestic corporations. I believe that our cases fairly establish that the States's valid substantive interests are important considerations in assessing whether it constitutionally may claim jurisdiction over a given cause of action.

* * *

This case is not one where, in my judgment, this preference for jurisdiction is adequately answered. Certainly nothing said by the Court persuades me that it would be unfair to subject appellants to suit in Delaware. The fact that the record does not reveal whether they "set foot" or committed "act(s) related to (the) cause of action" in Delaware ... is not decisive, for jurisdiction can be based strictly on out-of-state acts having foreseeable effects in the forum State. *E.g., McGee v. International Life Ins. Co,; Gray v. American Radiator & Standard Sanitary Corp.* I have little difficulty in applying this principle to nonresident fiduciaries whose alleged breaches of trust are said to have substantial damaging effect on the financial posture of a resident corporation. Further, I cannot understand how the existence of minimum contacts in a constitutional sense is at all affected by Delaware's failure statutorily to express an interest in controlling corporate fiduciaries. To me this simply demonstrates that Delaware did not elect to assert jurisdiction to the extent the Constitution would allow. Nor would I view as controlling or even especially meaningful Delaware's failure to exact from appellants their consent to be sued. Once we have rejected the jurisdictional framework created in *Pennoyer v. Neff*, I see no reason to rest jurisdiction on a fictional outgrowth of that system such as the existence of a consent statute, expressed or implied.

I, therefore, would approach the minimum-contacts analysis differently than does the Court. Crucial to me is the fact that appellants voluntarily associated themselves with the State of Delaware, "invoking the benefits and protections of its laws", *Hanson v. Denckla*, 357 U.S. at 253; *International Shoe Co. v. Washington*, 326 U.S. at 319, by entering into a long-term and fragile relationship with one of its domestic corporations. They thereby elected to assume powers and to undertake responsibilities wholly derived from that State's rules and regulations, and to become eligible for those benefits that Delaware law makes available to its corporations' officials. While it is possible that countervailing issues of judicial efficiency and the like might clearly favor a different forum, they do not appear on the meager record before us; and, of course, we are concerned solely with "minimum" contacts, not the "best" contacts. I thus do not believe that it is unfair to insist that appellants make themselves available to suit in a competent forum that Delaware might create for vindication of its important public policies directly pertaining to appellants' fiduciary associations with the State.

Exercise 2-6. *Shaffer v. Heitner* Revisited

1. After *Shaffer*, can a court use the following jurisdictional concepts to assert jurisdiction over an out-of-state defendant? If so, under what circumstances?

   a. Quasi in rem where the lawsuit involves the property

   b. Quasi in rem where the lawsuit does not involve the property

   c. In personam jurisdiction

   d. In rem jurisdiction

   e. Transient jurisdiction

   f. Consent to jurisdiction

2. In what ways do the majority and Justice Brennan disagree? Which justice has the better argument? What facts weigh in favor of the Delaware court's assertion of jurisdiction in this case?

3. If you were a legislator in Delaware and did not like the outcome of this case, what could you do to make certain Delaware courts would have jurisdiction over officers and directors of Delaware corporations?

4. In the following cases, explain why the court does or does not have personal jurisdiction over the defendant(s).

   a. A New York couple, Harry and Kay Robinson, bought a car in New York. The Robinsons decided to move to Arizona. On their way to Arizona, they got into a car accident in Oklahoma. They brought suit in Oklahoma state court alleging products liability. They sued the car manufacturer (Audi NSU) and its importer (Volkswagen of American, Inc.). They also sued the retail car dealership, Seaway, which was incorporated and had its principal place of business in New York. Finally, the Robinsons sued World-Wide Volkswagen Corp., a New York corporation with its principal place of business in New York. World-Wide was the regional distributor for Volkwagen and Audi, supplying cars to dealerships in New York, New Jersey, and Connecticut, including the car involved in the Robinsons' accident. Diagram the parties and actions in this case. Does the Oklahoma state court have jurisdiction over each defendant in this action after *Shaffer*? *See World-Wide Volkswagen Corp. v. Woodson*, 444 U.S. 286 (1980) (jurisdiction improper over regional distributor and local dealership).

b. A married couple separated in New York. The children remained with their father in New York, while the mother moved to California. One of the children joined the mother in California after the father bought the child a one-way ticket. The second child joined the mother in California after the mother bought the child the ticket. California's long arm statute reaches to the limits of due process. If the mother sues the father in California to modify his child support obligations, will the California court have jurisdiction over the father? *See Kulko v. Superior Court*, 436 U.S. 84 (1978) (jurisdiction improper over father who sends children out of state to live with mother in interest of family harmony).

c. Keeton, a New York resident, sued Hustler magazine, an Ohio corporation, for defamation in a federal court in New Hampshire. Hustler sold 10,000 to 15,000 copies of its magazines each month in New Hampshire. Keeton's only connection to New Hampshire was that a magazine she helped produce also was circulated there. Keeton sued in New Hampshire, because the statute of limitations on her claim under New Hampshire law had not yet run. Does the New Hampshire court have jurisdiction over Hustler? *See Keeton v. Hustler*, 465 U.S. 770 (1984) (defendant's sale of magazines in state sufficient for court to assert jurisdiction).

Note on Personal Jurisdiction in the Federal Court System

The following case, *Burger King v. Rudzewicz*, was brought in a federal trial court. Up to this point, the cases you have read have originated in the state court systems. The 14th Amendment's Due Process Clause directly applies to the actions of state courts. When trying to determine whether a state court has personal jurisdiction, the inquiry in such cases is whether the defendant has sufficient contact with the state to warrant the state court's assertion of jurisdiction over that defendant. But what if the court in which you wish to sue is a federal court? Do we ask whether the defendant has sufficient contacts with the United States as a whole?

To date, the United States Supreme Court has not definitively answered this question. However, the Federal Rules of Civil Procedure provide guidance on the circumstances under which a federal court can assert jurisdiction over a defendant.

Federal Rule of Civil Procedure 4(k): Territorial Limits of Effective Service

(1) *In General.* Serving a summons or filing a waiver of service establishes personal jurisdiction over a defendant:

(A) who is subject to the jurisdiction of a court of general jurisdiction in the state where the district court is located;

(B) who is a party joined under Rule 14 or 19 and is served within a judicial district of the United States and not more than 100 miles from where the summons was issued; or

(C) when authorized by a federal statute.

(2) *Federal Claim Outside State-Court Jurisdiction.* For a claim that arises under federal law, serving a summons or filing a waiver of service establishes personal jurisdiction over a defendant if:

(A) the defendant is not subject to jurisdiction in any state's courts of general jurisdiction; and

(B) exercising jurisdiction is consistent with the United States Constitution and laws.

Exercise 2-7. Reading Federal Rules of Civil Procedure

Rule reading is a key component of what lawyers do in determining the appropriate procedure in a given case. As introduced in Chapter 1, when reading a rule, it is important to pay close attention to the language used. Does the rule contain "and" or "or" in setting out its basic components? This rule is a bit complicated, but provides you with an opportunity to start the process of becoming an expert rule reader. After reading Rule 4(k) above, answer the following questions about the components of the rule as well as its application.

1. Rule 4(k) permits a federal court to assert jurisdiction over parties under three basic circumstances. Can you identify them? Hint: They are in part (1) of the rule.

2. In addition to the three basic circumstances under which a federal court can assert jurisdiction over a party, Rule 4(k)(2) contains a special rule for federal claims that fall outside the state courts' jurisdiction. What are the circumstances under which a court can assert jurisdiction pursuant to this subsection of the rule?

3. You wish to file the lawsuit against Piper and Hartzell described in the chapter problem in federal court. The claims Sherry wishes to assert are state law tort claims. Under Federal Rule 4(k), will a federal court in California have jurisdiction over Piper? What additional facts would you need to help you answer this question?

Exercise 2-8. *Burger King Corporation v. Rudzewicz*

Burger King Corp. v. Rudzewicz provides an excellent example of the Court's application of the principles developed in earlier case law to a new factual circumstance. As you read *Burger King*, look for answers to the following questions. The follow-up exercises in Exercise 2-9 will test whether you answered these questions correctly.

1. What is Florida's long arm statute? How does the fact pattern support the use of the applicable long arm statute?

2. In most of the prior cases, citations and references to prior case law have been edited out of the case. In this case, many of them are left in the excerpt. How does the Court use prior case law to help it reason through the legal rules that apply to this case?

3. In *Burger King*, the Court uses the term "foreseeability." What type of foreseeability is relevant to personal jurisdiction analysis?

4. The *Burger King* Court also addresses a choice of law provision in the contract. How does such a contract provision affect its jurisdictional analysis?

5. The Court describes certain actions that do not provide a basis for personal jurisdiction as "unilateral acts." How would you characterize what the Court means by this term?

6. The Court also uses the term "purposeful availment." What does it mean by this term? How did the defendant "purposefully avail" itself in this case?

7. The Court also introduces several factors that it considers to determine whether the defendant has "purposefully availed" itself of the particular forum. What are these factors?

8. This case involves a breach of contract action. What factors does the Court consider to determine whether the defendant's contacts are sufficient for the court to assert personal jurisdiction in the context of this type of claim?

9. Both the majority and the dissent in this case marshal the facts in support of and against the Florida court's assertion of personal jurisdiction over Rudzewicz. What facts do they use? How do they use the facts to support opposite arguments?

Burger King Corporation v. Rudzewicz

471 U.S. 462 (1985)

Justice Brennan delivered the opinion of the Court.

The State of Florida's long-arm statute extends jurisdiction to "[a]ny person, whether or not a citizen or resident of this state," who, *inter alia,* "[b]reach [es] a contract in this state by failing to perform acts required by the contract to be performed in this state," so long as the cause of action arises from the alleged contractual breach. Fla. Stat. §48.193(1)(g) (supp.1984). The United States District Court for the Southern District of Florida, sitting in diversity, relied on this provision in exercising personal jurisdiction over a Michigan resident who allegedly had breached a franchise agreement with a Florida corporation by failing to make required payments in Florida. The question presented is whether this exercise of long-arm jurisdiction offended "traditional conception[s] of fair play and substantial justice" embodied in the Due Process Clause of the Fourteenth Amendment. *International Shoe.*

I

A

* * *

The instant litigation grows out of Burger King's termination of one of its franchisees, and is aptly described by the franchisee as "a divorce proceeding among commercial partners." The appellee John Rudzewicz [is] a Michigan citizen and resident.... In 1978, he was approached by Brian MacShara, the son of a business acquaintance, who suggested that they jointly apply to Burger King for a franchise in the Detroit area. MacShara proposed to serve as the manager of the restaurant if Rudzewicz would put up the investment capital; in exchange, the two would evenly share the profits. Believing that MacShara's idea offered attractive investment and tax-deferral opportunities, Rudzewicz agreed to the venture.

Rudzewicz and MacShara jointly applied for a franchise to Burger King's Birmingham, Michigan, district office in the autumn of 1978. Their application was forwarded to Burger King's Miami headquarters, which entered into a preliminary agreement with them in February 1979. During the ensuing four months it was agreed that Rudzewicz and Mac-Shara would assume operation of an existing facility in Drayton Plains, Michigan. MacShara attended the prescribed management courses in Miami during this period, and the franchisees purchased $165,000 worth of restaurant equipment from Burger King's Davmor Industries division in Miami.... Rudzewicz and MacShara negotiated both with the Birmingham district office and with the Miami headquarters. With some misgivings, Rudzewicz and MacShara finally obtained limited concessions from the Miami headquarters, signed the final agreements, and commenced operations in June 1979. By signing the final agreements, Rudzewicz obligated himself personally to payments exceeding $1 million over the 20-year franchise relationship.

[The franchise eventually fell behind on its payments, and Burger King terminated the franchise agreement and ordered the defendants to vacate the premises. Burger King sued in the federal district court for southern district of Florida for breach of the franchise agreement as well as trademark infringement. Rudzewicz and MacShara entered special appearances to contest the court's jurisdiction. After losing this motion, the defendants lost at a bench trial on the merits. Rudzewicz appealed to the Court of Appeals for the 11th Circuit, which held that the district court did not have personal jurisdiction over Rudzewicz. Burger King appealed the decision to the Supreme Court of the United States.]

The Due Process Clause protects an individual's liberty interest in not being subject to the binding judgments of a forum with which he has established no meaningful "contacts, ties, or relations." *International Shoe Co. v. Washington*, 326 U.S. at 319. By requiring that individuals have "fair warning that a particular activity may subject [them] to the jurisdiction of a foreign sovereign," *Shaffer v. Heitner*, 433 U.S. 186, 218 (1977) (Stevens, J., concurring in judgment), the Due Process Clause "gives a degree of predictability to the legal system that allows potential defendants to structure their primary conduct with some minimum assurance as to where that conduct will and will not render them liable to suit," *World-Wide Volkswagen Corp. v. Woodson*, 444 U.S. 286, 297 (1980).

Where a forum seeks to assert specific jurisdiction over an out-of-state defendant who has not consented to suit there,[14] this "fair warning" requirement is satisfied if the defendant has "purposefully directed" his activities at residents of the forum, *Keeton v. Hustler Magazine, Inc.*, 645 U.S. 770, 774 (1984), and litigation results from alleged injuries that "arise out of or relate to" those activities, *Helicopteros Nacionales De Colombia, S.A. v. Hall.*, 466 U.S. 408 (1984). Thus "[t]he forum State does not exceed its powers under the Due Process Clause if it asserts personal jurisdiction over a corporation that delivers its products into the stream of commerce with the expectation that they will be purchased by consumers in the forum State" and those products subsequently injure forum consumers. *World-Wide Volkswagen*, 444 U.S. at 297–98. Similarly, a publisher who distributes magazines in a distant State may fairly be held accountable in

---

14. We have noted that, because the personal jurisdiction requirement is a waivable right, there are a "variety of legal arrangements" by which a litigant may give "express or implied consent to the personal jurisdiction of the court." For example, particularly in the commercial context, parties frequently stipulate in advance to submit their controversies for resolution within a particular jurisdiction. Where such forum-selection provisions have been obtained through "freely negotiated" agreements and are not "unreasonable and unjust," their enforcement does not offend due process.

that forum for damages resulting there from an allegedly defamatory story. *Keeton v. Hustler.* And with respect to interstate contractual obligations, we have emphasized that parties who "reach out beyond one state and create continuing relationships and obligations with citizens of another state" are subject to regulation and sanctions in the other State for the consequences of their activities. *Travelers Health Assn. v. Virginia,* 339 U.S. 643, 647 (1950). *See also McGee v. Int'l Life Ins. Co.,* 355 U.S. 220, 222–23 (1957).

* * *

Notwithstanding these considerations, the constitutional touchstone remains whether the defendant purposefully established "minimum contacts" in the forum State. *International Shoe,* 326 U.S. at 316. Although it has been argued that foreseeability of causing *injury* in another State should be sufficient to establish such contacts there when policy considerations so require, the Court has consistently held that this kind of foreseeability is not a "sufficient benchmark" for exercising personal jurisdiction. *World-Wide Volkwagon Corp.,* 444 U.S. at 295. Instead, "the foreseeability that is critical to due process analysis ... is that the defendant's conduct and connection with the forum State are such that he should reasonably anticipate being haled into court there." *Id.* at 297. In defining when it is that a potential defendant should "reasonably anticipate" out-of-state litigation, the Court frequently has drawn from the reasoning of *Hanson v. Denckla,* 357 U.S. at 253.

> "The unilateral activity of those who claim some relationship with a nonresident defendant cannot satisfy the requirement of contact with the forum State. The application of that rule will vary with the quality and nature of the defendant's activity, but it is essential in each case that there be some act by which the defendant purposefully avails itself of the privilege of conducting activities within the forum State, thus invoking the benefits and protections of its laws." *Hanson.*

This "purposeful availment" requirement ensures that a defendant will not be haled into a jurisdiction solely as a result of "random," "fortuitous," or "attenuated" contacts, *Keeton,* 465 U.S. at 774; *World-Wide Volkswagon,* 444 U.S. at 299, or of the "unilateral activity of another party or a third person," *Helicopteros,* 466 U.S. at 417. Jurisdiction is proper, however, where the contacts proximately result from actions by the defendant *himself* that create a "substantial connection" with the forum State. *McGee.,* 355 U.S. at 223.[18] Thus where the defendant "deliberately" has engaged in sig-

Margin notes: Foreseeability; Purposefully avails; Unilateral act

------

18. So long as it creates a "substantial connection" with the forum, even a single act can support jurisdiction. *McGee.* The Court has noted, however, that "some single or occasional acts" related to the forum may not be sufficient to establish jurisdiction if "their nature and quality and the circum-

nificant activities within a State, *Keeton*, 465 U.S. at 781, or has created "continuing obligations" between himself and residents of the forum, *Travelers Health Assn.*, 339 U.S. at 648, he manifestly has availed himself of the privilege of conducting business there, and because his activities are shielded by "the benefits and protections" of the forum's laws it is presumptively not unreasonable to require him to submit to the burdens of litigation in that forum as well.

Jurisdiction in these circumstances may not be avoided merely because the defendant did not *physically* enter the forum State. Although territorial presence frequently will enhance a potential defendant's affiliation with a State and reinforce the reasonable foreseeability of suit there, it is an inescapable fact of modern commercial life that a substantial amount of business is transacted solely by mail and wire communications across state lines, thus obviating the need for physical presence within a State in which business is conducted. So long as a commercial actor's efforts are "purposefully directed" toward residents of another State, we have consistently rejected the notion that an absence of physical contacts can defeat personal jurisdiction there.

Once it has been decided that a defendant purposefully established minimum contacts within the forum State, these contacts may be considered in light of other factors to determine whether the assertion of personal jurisdiction would comport with "fair play and substantial justice." *International Shoe*, 326 U.S. at 320. Thus courts in "appropriate case[s]" may evaluate "the burden on the defendant," "the forum State's interest in adjudicating the dispute," "the plaintiff's interest in obtaining convenient and effective relief," "the interstate judicial system's interest in obtaining the most efficient resolution of controversies," and the "shared interest of the several States in furthering fundamental substantive social policies." *World-Wide Volkswagon*, 444 U.S. at 292. These considerations sometimes serve to establish the reasonableness of jurisdiction upon a lesser showing of minimum contacts than would otherwise be required. On the other hand, where a defendant who purposefully has directed his activities at forum residents seeks to defeat jurisdiction, he must present a compelling case that the presence of some other considerations would render jurisdiction unreasonable. Most such considerations usually may be accommodated through means short of finding jurisdiction unconstitutional. For example, the potential clash of the forum's law with the "fundamental substantive social policies" of another State may be accommodated through application of the forum's choice-of-law rules. Similarly, a defendant

How would you characterize these factors?

---

stances of their commission" create only an "attenuated" affiliation with the forum. *International Shoe*, 362 U.S. 310, 318 (1945); *World-Wide Volkswagen*, 444 U.S. at 299. This distinction derives from the belief that, with respect to this category of "isolated" acts, the reasonable foreseeability of litigation in the forum is substantially diminished.

claiming substantial inconvenience may seek a change of venue. Nevertheless, minimum requirements inherent in the concept of "fair play and substantial justice" may defeat the reasonableness of jurisdiction even if the defendant has purposefully engaged in forum activities. *World-Wide Volkswagon*, 444 U.S. at 292. As we previously have noted, jurisdictional rules may not be employed in such a way as to make litigation "so gravely difficult and inconvenient" that a party unfairly is at a "severe disadvantage" in comparison to his opponent. *The Bremen v. Zapata Off-Shore Co.*, 407 U.S. 1, 18 (1972) (re forum-selection provisions); *McGee*, 355 U.S. at 223–24.

B

(1)

Applying these principles to the case at hand, we believe there is substantial record evidence supporting the District Court's conclusion that the assertion of personal jurisdiction over Rudzewicz in Florida for the alleged breach of his franchise agreement did not offend due process. At the outset, we note a continued division among lower courts respecting whether and to what extent a contract can constitute a "contact" for purposes of due process analysis. If the question is whether an individual's contract with an out-of-state party *alone* can automatically establish sufficient minimum contacts in the other party's home forum, we believe the answer clearly is that it cannot. The Court long ago rejected the notion that personal jurisdiction might turn on "mechanical" tests, *International Shoe*, or on "conceptualistic ... theories of the place of contracting or of performance," *Hoopeston Canning Co. v. Cullen*, 318 U.S. at 316. Instead, we have emphasized the need for a "highly realistic" approach that recognizes that a "contract" is "ordinarily but an intermediate step serving to tie up prior business negotiations with future consequences which themselves are the real object of the business transaction." *Hoopeston Canning.* It is these factors—prior negotiations and contemplated future consequences, along with the terms of the contract and the parties' actual course of dealing—that must be evaluated in determining whether the defendant purposefully established minimum contacts within the forum.

In this case, no physical ties to Florida can be attributed to Rudzewicz other than MacShara's brief training course in Miami.[22] Rudzewicz did

Analysis: Law applied to facts

Contract contacts

---

22. The Eleventh Circuit held that MacShara's presence in Florida was irrelevant to the question of Rudzewicz's minimum contacts with that forum, reasoning that "Rudzewicz and MacShara never formed a partnership" and "signed the agreements in their individual capacities." The two did jointly form a corporation through which they were seeking to conduct the franchise, however. They were required to decide which one of them would travel to Florida to satisfy the training requirements so that they could commence business, and Rudzewicz participated in the decision that MacShara would go there. We have previously noted that when commercial activities are "carried on in behalf of" an out-of-state party those activities may sometimes be ascribed to the party, *International Shoe*, at least

not maintain offices in Florida and, for all that appears from the record, has never even visited there. Yet this franchise dispute grew directly out of "a contract which had a *substantial* connection with that State." *McGee.* Eschewing the option of operating an independent local enterprise, Rudzewicz deliberately "reach[ed] out beyond" Michigan and negotiated with a Florida corporation for the purchase of a long-term franchise and the manifold benefits that would derive from affiliation with a nationwide organization. Upon approval, he entered into a carefully structured 20-year relationship that envisioned continuing and wide-reaching contacts with Burger King in Florida. In light of Rudzewicz' voluntary acceptance of the long-term and exacting regulation of his business from Burger King's Miami headquarters, the "quality and nature" of his relationship to the company in Florida can in no sense be viewed as "random," "fortuitous," or "attenuated." Rudzewicz' refusal to make the contractually required payments in Miami, and his continued use of Burger King's trademarks and confidential business information after his termination, caused foreseeable injuries to the corporation in Florida. For these reasons it was, at the very least, presumptively reasonable for Rudzewicz to be called to account there for such injuries.

The Court of Appeals concluded, however, that in light of the supervision emanating from Burger King's district office in Birmingham, Rudzewicz reasonably believed that "the Michigan office was for all intents and purposes the embodiment of Burger King" and that he therefore had no "reason to anticipate a Burger King suit outside of Michigan." This reasoning overlooks substantial record evidence indicating that Rudzewicz most certainly knew that he was affiliating himself with an enterprise based primarily in Florida. The contract documents themselves emphasize that Burger King's operations are conducted and supervised from the Miami headquarters, that all relevant notices and payments must be sent there, and that the agreements were made in and enforced from Miami. Moreover, the parties' actual course of dealing repeatedly confirmed that decision-making authority was vested in the Miami headquarters and that the district office served largely as an intermediate link between the headquarters and the franchisees. When problems arose over building design, site-development fees, rent computation, and the defaulted payments, Rudzewicz and MacShara learned that the Michigan office was powerless to resolve their disputes and could only channel their communications to Miami. Throughout these disputes, the Miami headquarters and the Michigan franchisees carried on a continuous course of direct communications by mail and by

---

where he is a "primary participan[t]" in the enterprise and has acted purposefully in directing those activities, *Calder v. Jones*, 465 U.S. at 790. Because MacShara's matriculation at Burger King University is not pivotal to the disposition of this case, we need not resolve the permissible bounds of such attribution.

telephone, and it was the Miami headquarters that made the key negotiating decisions out of which the instant litigation arose.

Moreover, we believe the Court of Appeals gave insufficient weight to provisions in the various franchise documents providing that all disputes would be governed by Florida law.... The Court of Appeals reasoned that choice-of-law provisions are irrelevant to the question of personal jurisdiction, relying on *Hanson v. Denckla* for the proposition that "the center of gravity for choice-of-law purposes does not necessarily confer the sovereign prerogative to assert jurisdiction." *Burger King Corp. v. MacShara*, 724 F.2d 1505, 1511–12 n.10 (11th Cir. 1984). This reasoning misperceives the import of the quoted proposition. The Court in *Hanson* and subsequent cases has emphasized that choice-of-law *analysis*—which focuses on all elements of a transaction, and not simply on the defendant's conduct—is distinct from minimum-contacts jurisdictional analysis—which focuses at the threshold solely on the defendant's purposeful connection to the forum. Nothing in our cases, however, suggests that a choice-of-law *provision* should be ignored in considering whether a defendant has "purposefully invoked the benefits and protections of a State's laws" for jurisdictional purposes. Although such a provision standing alone would be insufficient to confer jurisdiction, we believe that, when combined with the 20-year interdependent relationship Rudzewicz established with Burger King's Miami headquarters, it reinforced his deliberate affiliation with the forum State and the reasonable foreseeability of possible litigation there. As Judge Johnson argued in his dissent below, Rudzewicz "purposefully availed himself of the benefits and protections of Florida's laws" by entering into contracts expressly providing that those laws would govern franchise disputes. 724 F.2d, at 1513.

Choice of law clause

(2)

Nor has Rudzewicz pointed to other factors that can be said persuasively to outweigh the considerations discussed above and to establish the unconstitutionality of Florida's assertion of jurisdiction. We cannot conclude that Florida had no "legitimate interest in holding [Rudzewicz] answerable on a claim related to" the contacts he had established in that State. *Keeton v. Hustler Magazine, Inc.*, 465 U.S. at 776; *see also McGee v. International Life Insurance Co.*, 355 U.S., at 223 (noting that State frequently will have a "manifest interest in providing effective means of redress for its residents"). Moreover, although Rudzewicz has argued at some length that Michigan's Franchise Investment Law ... governs many aspects of this franchise relationship, he has not demonstrated how Michigan's acknowledged interest might possibly render jurisdiction in Florida unconstitutional. Finally, the Court of Appeals' assertion that the Florida litigation "severely impaired [Rudzewicz'] ability to call Michigan witnesses who might be essential to his defense and counterclaim," 724 F.2d at 1512–

1513, is wholly without support in the record. And even to the extent that it is inconvenient for a party who has minimum contacts with a forum to litigate there, such considerations most frequently can be accommodated through a change of venue. Although the Court has suggested that inconvenience may at some point become so substantial as to achieve constitutional magnitude, *McGee v. International Life Insurance Co.*, 355 U.S. at 223, this is not such a case.

The Court of Appeals also concluded ... that the parties' dealings involved "a characteristic disparity of bargaining power" and "elements of surprise," and that Rudzewicz "lacked fair notice" of the potential for litigation in Florida because the contractual provisions suggesting to the contrary were merely "boilerplate declarations in a lengthy printed contract." Rudzewicz presented many of these arguments to the District Court, contending that Burger King was guilty of misrepresentation, fraud, and duress; that it gave insufficient notice in its dealings with him; and that the contract was one of adhesion. After a 3-day bench trial, the District Court found that Burger King had made no misrepresentations, that Rudzewicz and MacShara "were and are experienced and sophisticated businessmen," and that "at no time" did they "ac[t] under economic duress or disadvantage imposed by" Federal Rule of Civil Procedure 52(a) requires that "[f]indings of fact shall not be set aside unless clearly erroneous," and neither Rudzewicz nor the Court of Appeals has pointed to record evidence that would support a "definite and firm conviction" that the District Court's findings are mistaken. To the contrary, Rudzewicz was represented by counsel throughout these complex transactions and ... was himself an experienced accountant "who for five months conducted negotiations with Burger King over the terms of the franchise and lease agreements, and who obligated himself personally to contracts requiring over time payments that exceeded $1 million." Rudzewicz was able to secure a modest reduction in rent and other concessions from Miami headquarters; moreover, to the extent that Burger King's terms were inflexible, Rudzewicz presumably decided that the advantages of affiliating with a national organization provided sufficient commercial benefits to offset the detriments.

III

Notwithstanding these considerations, the Court of Appeals apparently believed that it was necessary to reject jurisdiction in this case as a prophylactic measure, reasoning that an affirmance of the District Court's judgment would result in the exercise of jurisdiction over "out-of-state consumers to collect payments due on modest personal purchases" and would "sow the seeds of default judgments against franchisees owing smaller debts." 724 F.2d at 1511. We share the Court of Appeals' broader concerns and therefore reject any talismanic jurisdictional formulas.... We also have emphasized that jurisdiction may not be grounded on a contract whose terms have been obtained through "fraud, undue influence, or overweening bargaining power" and whose application would render litigation "so gravely difficult and inconvenient that [a party] will for all practical purposes be deprived of his day in court." *The Bremen v. Zapata Off-Shore Co.*, 407 U.S. at 12, 18. Just as the Due Process Clause allows flexibility in ensuring that commercial actors are not effectively "judgment proof" for the consequences of obligations they voluntarily assume in other States, *McGee*, so too does it prevent rules that would unfairly enable them to obtain default judgments against unwitting customers.

For the reasons set forth above, however, these dangers are not present in the instant case. Because Rudzewicz established a substantial and continuing relationship with Burger King's Miami headquarters, received fair notice from the contract documents and the course of dealing that he might be subject to suit in Florida, and has failed to demonstrate how jurisdiction in that forum would otherwise be fundamentally unfair, we conclude that the District Court's exercise of jurisdiction ... did not offend due process. The judgment of the Court of Appeals is accordingly reversed, and the case is remanded for further proceedings consistent with this opinion.

It is so ordered.

Justice Stevens, with whom Justice White joins, dissenting.

In my opinion there is a significant element of unfairness in requiring a franchisee to defend a case of this kind in the forum chosen by the franchisor. It is undisputed that appellee maintained no place of business in Florida, that he had no employees in that State, and that he was not licensed to do business there. Appellee did not prepare his French fries, shakes, and hamburgers in Michigan, and then deliver them into the stream of commerce "with the expectation that they [would] be purchased by consumers in" Florida. To the contrary, appellee did business only in Michigan, his business, property, and payroll taxes were payable in that State, and he sold all of his products there.

Throughout the business relationship, appellee's principal contacts with appellant were with its Michigan office. Notwithstanding its disclaimer, the Court seems ultimately to rely on nothing more than standard boilerplate language contained in various documents, to establish that appellee "'purposefully availed himself of the benefits and protections of Florida's laws.'" Such superficial analysis creates a potential for unfairness not only in negotiations between franchisors and their franchisees but, more significantly, in the resolution of the disputes that inevitably arise from time to time in such relationships.

* * *

Accordingly, I respectfully dissent.

Exercise 2-9. *Burger King* Revisited

1. The *Burger King* Court used several different concepts in addressing whether the Florida federal court had personal jurisdiction over Rudzewicz. Included in the terms it used were purposeful availment, foreseeability, unilateral act, choice of law clauses, isolated incidents, contracts with a substantial connection to the state, and a series of factors based on "fair play and substantial justice." How would you put all these concepts together into a coherent whole? In other words, what would be your approach to a problem of personal jurisdiction after this case and the ones that came before it? As described earlier in this chapter, this is an exercise in case synthesis—putting together a set of concepts taken from series of cases so that it is usable in approaching a new problem. Try putting these concepts together yourself.

2. Now that you've put the concepts together, apply them to the following fact pattern. A motorcycle rider is in an accident in California. He is injured, and his wife, who was a passenger on the motorcycle, is killed. He files a products liability action in a California state court, arguing that the motorcycle's tire, tube, and sealant were defective. The defendants include Cheng Shin Rubber Industrial Co., a Taiwanese manufacturer of the tube, and Asahi Metal Industry, Inc., a Japanese corporation that manufactured the tube's assembly valve. Asahi's sales to Cheng Shin took place in Taiwan. The goods were shipped from Japan to Taiwan. Sales to Cheng Shin were 1.24% of Asahi's income. Twenty percent of Cheng Shin's sales in the United States are in California. Some evidence in the case suggested that Cheng Shin told Asahi that some of the tubes were sold in the United States, including California. The President of Asahi, however, stated that the company did not contemplate going to court in California based on selling the fittings to a Taiwanese company. Asahi does not have any agents or employees in California. It does not advertise or solicit business in California. The defendants settled the case with respect to the motorcycle rider. Cheng Shin filed a cross-complaint against Asahi for indemnification. This is the only claim left in the case. Does the California court have jurisdiction over Asahi? Be sure to consider the "fair play and substantial justice" factors in your analysis. *See Asahi Metal Indus. Co. v. Superior Court of Cal.*, 480 U.S. 102 (1986) (In a fractured opinion, the Court concluded that the fairness factors required the case to be dismissed. Justice O'Connor's plurality opinion argued that placing a product in the stream of commerce alone was insufficient for the assertion of jurisdiction. Justice Brennan disagreed, arguing that the stream of commerce was predictable, and therefore Asahi should have known that its product would end up in the California market.).

Note on Consent to Jurisdiction

In early cases involving automobiles previously mentioned in this chapter, the Court upheld statutes that required consent to suit as a condition of driving in a state. In addition, in *International Shoe*, the Court acknowledged that states can require corporations to consent to suit in a state as a condition of doing business there. Finally, a defendant can waive personal jurisdiction by simply defending a lawsuit on its merits. Should parties be able to consent by contract to a particular jurisdiction for purposes of a future lawsuit? The contract in the *Burger King* case included a choice of law clause—a provision in the contract that required a court to apply a specific state's contract law should a dispute arise under that contract. Because a defendant can consent to jurisdiction, it has become common for parties to a contract to include a forum selection clause as well—a clause that requires any lawsuit arising under that contract to be brought in a certain forum.

The United States Supreme Court looks favorably on these clauses, although not all states do. In *Carnival Cruise Lines, Inc. v. Shute*, 499 U.S. 585 (1991), the Court enforced a forum selection clause contained in a cruise ship ticket. In that case, the plaintiffs, Eulala and Russel Shute, bought a ticket to take a seven-day cruise through a Washington travel agent, who forwarded their payment to the cruise line's headquarters in Miami, Florida. The Shutes boarded a ship in Los Angeles, California, and, while on board, Mrs. Shute was injured when she slipped on the deck during a guided tour. A forum selection clause in the ticket indicated that any disputes arising under the contract "shall be litigated" in courts in the state of Florida. *Id.* at 588. The Shutes filed their lawsuit in a federal court in the state of Washington.

In arguing that the court should not enforce the forum selection clause in the ticket, the Shutes attempted to distinguish an earlier case in which the Court had enforced a forum selection clause. *The Bremen v. Zapata Off-Shore Co.*, 407 U.S. 1 (1972), involved a dispute between two corporations. The Court enforced the agreement in that case, explaining that "such clauses are prima facie valid and should be enforced unless enforcement is shown by the resisting party to be 'unreasonable' under the circumstances." *Id.* at 10. The Shutes tried to distinguish their situation from that of *The Bremen* by arguing that the contract term in their case was unreasonable and the Florida forum would be inconvenient. Rejecting both arguments, the Court reasoned that the cruise line did not choose Florida to inconvenience the plaintiffs, but instead because that is where it was located. Further, these clauses are especially useful for this type of business, because cruise lines are likely to have customers from many different locations traveling to a variety of places. The clause also settles the forum choice with little litigation over the appropriate forum. Finally, passengers likely benefit from these clauses because they reduce the litigation costs for the cruise lines, which in turn reduces costs for passengers. *Shute*, 499 U.S. at 594.

The Court also noted that such clauses contained in form contracts "are subject to judicial scrutiny for fundamental fairness." *Id.* at 595. The Court reasoned that the Shutes' contract with Carnival was not fundamentally unfair, explaining

> In this case, there is no indication that petitioner set Florida as the forum in which disputes were to be resolved as a means of discouraging cruise passengers from pursuing legitimate claims. Any suggestion of such a bad-faith motive is belied by two facts: Petitioner has its principal place of business in Florida, and many of its cruises depart from and return to Florida ports. Similarly, there is no evidence that petitioner obtained respondents' accession to the forum clause by fraud or overreaching. Finally, respondents have conceded that they were given notice of the forum provision and, therefore, presumably retained the option of rejecting the contract with impunity. In the case before us, therefore, we conclude that the Court of Appeals erred in refusing to enforce the forum-selection clause.

499 U.S. at 595.[1] Thus, along with other forms of consent to personal jurisdiction, parties can consent through contracts.

Exercise 2-10. Modern Specific Jurisdiction Cases and International Parties: *J. McIntyre Mach., Ltd. v. Nicastro*

Up to this point, the cases you have read involved disputes involving domestic parties. How is jurisdiction assessed when one of the parties is not from the United States? Under what circumstances is it fair for a court in the United States to assert personal jurisdiction over a foreign defendant? As you read *J. McIntyre v. Nicastro*, answer the following questions:

1. What is the judgment of the Court? How does the reasoning of Justice Kennedy differ from that of Justice Breyer?

2. Does Justice Kennedy's plurality opinion invoke the power theory of jurisdiction? In what way?

3. Justice Kennedy's opinion relies heavily on the *Asahi* case, which is described in Exercise 2-9(2) above. Try to determine from the descriptions in this case what the varying Justices' opinions were in that case. What is the standard that Justice Kennedy adopts?

4. How does Justice Kennedy distinguish between a case brought in state court, like *J. McIntyre v. Nicastro*, and one that is brought in a federal court?

---

1. Congress later legislatively overruled the outcome of the *Carnival Cruise Lines* case for contracts involving passenger vessels. *See* 46 U.S.C. § 30509(a)(1).

5. How does Justice Kennedy use potential consequences of deciding the case differently in reasoning to his conclusion?

6. What facts are relevant to Justice Kennedy's decision?

7. What are Justice Ginsburg's reasons for reaching an opposite conclusion from a majority of the Court? Which side has the better argument—the majority or the dissent?

8. If you represented a foreign manufacturer, what would you advise them to do in order to avoid the jurisdiction of U.S. state courts?

9. The Court in this case refers to the petitioner and respondent as well as the plaintiff and defendant. As you read the case, determine which party has which status.

J. McIntyre Mach., Ltd. v. Nicastro

564 U.S. 873 (2011)

Justice Kennedy announced the judgment of the Court and delivered an opinion, in which Chief Justice Roberts, Justice Scalia, and Justice Thomas join.

Whether a person or entity is subject to the jurisdiction of a state court despite not having been present in the State either at the time of suit or at the time of the alleged injury, and despite not having consented to the exercise of jurisdiction, is a question that arises with great frequency in the routine course of litigation. The rules and standards for determining when a State does or does not have jurisdiction over an absent party have been unclear because of decades-old questions left open in *Asahi Metal.*

* * *

I

This case arises from a products-liability suit filed in New Jersey state court. Robert Nicastro seriously injured his hand while using a metal-shearing machine manufactured by J. McIntyre Machinery, Ltd. (J. McIntyre). The accident occurred in New Jersey, but the machine was manufactured in England, where J. McIntyre is incorporated and operates. The question here is whether the New Jersey courts have jurisdiction over J. McIntyre, notwithstanding the fact that the company at no time either marketed goods in the State or shipped them there. Nicastro was a plaintiff in the New Jersey trial court and is the respondent here; J. McIntyre was a defendant and is now the petitioner.

At oral argument in this Court, Nicastro's counsel stressed three primary facts in defense of New Jersey's assertion of jurisdiction over J. McIntyre.

First, an independent company agreed to sell J. McIntyre's machines in the United States. J. McIntyre itself did not sell its machines to buyers in this country beyond the U.S. distributor, and there is no allegation that the distributor was under J. McIntyre's control.

Second, J. McIntyre officials attended annual conventions for the scrap recycling industry to advertise J. McIntyre's machines alongside the distributor. The conventions took place in various States, but never in New Jersey.

Third, no more than four machines (the record suggests only one), including the machine that caused the injuries that are the basis for this suit, ended up in New Jersey.

In addition to these facts emphasized by petitioner, the New Jersey Supreme Court noted that J. McIntyre held both United States and European patents on its recycling technology. It also noted that the U.S. distributor "structured [its] advertising and sales efforts in accordance with" J. McIntyre's "direction and guidance whenever possible," and that "at least some of the machines were sold on consignment to" the distributor.

In light of these facts, the New Jersey Supreme Court concluded that New Jersey courts could exercise jurisdiction over petitioner without contravention of the Due Process Clause....

Both the New Jersey Supreme Court's holding and its account of what it called "[t]he stream-of-commerce doctrine of jurisdiction," were incorrect, however. This Court's *Asahi* decision may be responsible in part for that court's error regarding the stream of commerce, and this case presents an opportunity to provide greater clarity.

II

The Due Process Clause protects an individual's right to be deprived of life, liberty, or property only by the exercise of lawful power....

A court may subject a defendant to judgment only when the defendant has sufficient contacts with the sovereign "such that the maintenance of the suit does not offend 'traditional notions of fair play and substantial justice.'" *International Shoe.* Freeform notions of fundamental fairness divorced from traditional practice cannot transform a judgment rendered in the absence of authority into law. As a general rule, the sovereign's exercise of power requires some act by which the defendant "purposefully avails itself of the privilege of conducting activities within the forum State, thus invoking the benefits and protections of its laws," *Hanson*, 357 U.S. at 253, though in some cases, as with an intentional tort, the defendant might well fall within the State's authority by reason of his attempt to obstruct its laws. In products-liability cases like this one, it is the defendant's purposeful availment that makes jurisdiction consistent with "traditional notions of fair play and substantial justice."

A person may submit to a State's authority in a number of ways. There is, of course, explicit consent. Presence within a State at the time suit commences through service of process is another example. Citizenship or domicile — or, by analogy, incorporation or principal place of business for corporations — also indicates general submission to a State's powers. Each of these examples reveals circumstances, or a course of conduct, from which it is proper to infer an intention to benefit from and thus an intention to submit to the laws of the forum State. These examples support exercise of the general jurisdiction of the State's courts and allow the State to resolve both matters that originate within the State and those based on activities and events elsewhere. By contrast, those who live or operate primarily outside a State have a due process right not to be subjected to judgment in its courts as a general matter.

There is also a more limited form of submission to a State's authority for disputes that "arise out of or are connected with the activities within the state." *International Shoe.*, 326 U.S. at 319. Where a defendant "purposefully avails itself of the privilege of conducting activities within the forum State, thus invoking the benefits and protections of its laws," *Hanson,* 357 U.S. at 253, it submits to the judicial power of an otherwise foreign sovereign to the extent that power is exercised in connection with the defendant's activities touching on the State. In other words, submission through contact with and activity directed at a sovereign may justify specific jurisdiction "in a suit arising out of or related to the defendant's contacts with the forum." *Helicopteros.*, 466 U.S. at 414 n.8.

The imprecision arising from *Asahi* for the most part, results from its statement of the relation between jurisdiction and the "stream of commerce." The stream of commerce, like other metaphors, has its deficiencies as well as its utility. It refers to the movement of goods from manufacturers through distributors to consumers, yet beyond that descriptive purpose its meaning is far from exact. This Court has stated that a defendant's placing goods into the stream of commerce "with the expectation that they will be purchased by consumers within the forum State" may indicate purposeful availment. *World-Wide Volkswagen,* 444 U.S. at 298. But that statement does not amend the general rule of personal jurisdiction. It merely observes that a defendant may in an appropriate case be subject to jurisdiction without entering the forum — itself an unexceptional proposition — as where manufacturers or distributors "seek to serve" a given State's market. *Id.* at 295. The principal inquiry in cases of this sort is whether the defendant's activities manifest an intention to submit to the power of a sovereign. In other words, the defendant must "purposefully avai[l] itself of the privilege of conducting activities within the forum State, thus invoking the benefits and protections of its laws." *Hanson*, 357 U.S. at 253. Sometimes a defendant does so by sending its goods rather than its agents. The defendant's transmission of goods permits the exercise of jurisdiction only where the defendant can be said to have targeted the forum; as a general rule, it is not enough that the defendant might have predicted that its goods will reach the forum State.

In *Asahi* an opinion by Justice Brennan for four Justices outlined a different approach. It discarded the central concept of sovereign authority in favor of considerations of fairness and foreseeability. As that concurrence contended, "jurisdiction premised on the placement of a product into the stream of commerce [without more] is consistent with the Due Process Clause," for "[a]s long as a participant in this process is aware that the final product is being marketed in the forum State, the possibility of a lawsuit there cannot come as a surprise." *Asahi*, 480 U.S. at 117. It was the premise of the concurring opinion that the defendant's ability to anticipate suit renders the assertion of jurisdiction fair. In this way, the opinion made foreseeability the touchstone of jurisdiction.

The standard set forth in Justice Brennan's concurrence was rejected in an opinion written by Justice O'Connor; but the relevant part of that opinion, too, commanded the assent of only four Justices, not a majority of the Court. That opinion stated: "The 'substantial connection' between the defendant and the forum State necessary for a finding of minimum contacts must come about by an action of the defendant purposefully directed toward the forum State. The placement of a product into the stream of commerce, without more, is not an act of the defendant purposefully directed toward the forum State." *Id.* at 112.

Since *Asahi* was decided, the courts have sought to reconcile the competing opinions. But Justice Brennan's concurrence, advocating a rule based on general notions of fairness and foreseeability, is inconsistent with the premises of lawful judicial power. This Court's precedents make clear that it is the defendant's actions, not his expectations, that empower a State's courts to subject him to judgment.

* * *

Two principles are implicit in the foregoing. First, personal jurisdiction requires a forum-by-forum, or sovereign-by-sovereign, analysis. The question is whether a defendant has followed a course of conduct directed at the society or economy existing within the jurisdiction of a given sovereign, so that the sovereign has the power to subject the defendant to judgment concerning that conduct. Personal jurisdiction, of course, restricts "judicial power not as a matter of sovereignty, but as a matter of individual liberty," for due process protects the individual's right to be subject only to lawful power. *Insurance Corp.*, 456 U.S. at 702. But whether a judicial judgment is lawful depends on whether the sovereign has authority to render it.

The second principle is a corollary of the first. Because the United States is a distinct sovereign, a defendant may in principle be subject to the jurisdiction of the courts of the United States but not of any particular State. This is consistent with the premises and unique genius of our Constitution. Ours is "a legal system unprecedented in form and design, establishing two orders of government, each with its own direct relationship, its own privity, its own set of mutual rights and obligations to the people who sustain it and are governed by it." *U.S. Term Limits, Inc. v. Thornton*, 514 U.S. 779, 838 (1995) (Kennedy, J., concurring). For jurisdiction, a litigant may have the requisite relationship with the United States Government but not with the government of any individual State. That would be an exceptional case, however. If the defendant is a domestic domiciliary, the courts of its home State are available and can exercise general jurisdiction. And if another State were to assert jurisdiction in an inappropriate case, it would upset the federal balance, which posits that each State has a sovereignty that is not subject to unlawful intrusion by other States. Furthermore, foreign corporations will often target or concentrate on particular States, subjecting them to specific jurisdiction in those forums.

It must be remembered, however, that although this case and *Asahi* both involve foreign manufacturers, the undesirable consequences of Justice Brennan's approach are no less significant for domestic producers. The owner of a small Florida farm might sell crops to a large nearby distributor, for example, who might then distribute them to grocers across the country. If foreseeability were the controlling criterion, the farmer could be sued in Alaska or any number of other States' courts without ever leaving town. And the issue of foreseeability may itself be contested so that significant expenses are incurred just on the preliminary issue of jurisdiction. Jurisdictional rules should avoid these costs whenever possible.

The conclusion that the authority to subject a defendant to judgment depends on purposeful availment, consistent with Justice O'Connor's opinion in *Asahi* does not by itself resolve many difficult questions of jurisdiction that will arise in particular cases. The defendant's conduct and the economic realities of the market the defendant seeks to serve will differ across cases, and judicial exposition will, in common-law fashion, clarify the contours of that principle.

III

In this case, petitioner directed marketing and sales efforts at the United States. It may be that, assuming it were otherwise empowered to legislate on the subject, the Congress could authorize the exercise of jurisdiction in appropriate courts. That circumstance is not presented in this case, however, and it is neither necessary nor appropriate to address here any constitutional concerns that might be attendant to that exercise of power. Nor is it necessary to determine what substantive law might apply were Congress to authorize jurisdiction in a federal court in New Jersey. A sovereign's legislative authority to regulate conduct may present considerations different from those presented by its authority to subject a defendant to judgment in its courts. Here the question concerns the authority of a New Jersey state court to exercise jurisdiction, so it is petitioner's purposeful contacts with New Jersey, not with the United States, that alone are relevant.

Respondent has not established that J. McIntyre engaged in conduct purposefully directed at New Jersey. Recall that respondent's claim of jurisdiction centers on three facts: The distributor agreed to sell J. McIntyre's machines in the United States; J. McIntyre officials attended trade shows in several States but not in New Jersey; and up to four machines ended up in New Jersey. The British manufacturer had no office in New Jersey; it neither paid taxes nor owned property there; and it neither advertised in, nor sent any employees to, the State. Indeed, after discovery the trial court found that the "defendant does not have a single contact with New Jersey short of the machine in question ending up in this state." These facts may reveal an intent to serve the U.S. market, but they do not show that J. McIntyre purposefully availed itself of the New Jersey market.

It is notable that the New Jersey Supreme Court appears to agree, for it could "not find that J. McIntyre had a presence or minimum contacts in this State — in any jurisprudential sense — that would justify a New Jersey court to exercise jurisdiction in this case." The court nonetheless held that petitioner could be sued in New Jersey based on a "stream-of-commerce theory of jurisdiction." As discussed, however, the stream-of-commerce metaphor cannot supersede either the mandate of the Due Process Clause or the limits on judicial authority that Clause ensures. The New Jersey Supreme Court also cited "significant policy reasons" to justify its holding, including the State's "strong interest in protecting its citizens from defective products." That interest is doubtless strong, but the Constitution commands restraint before discarding liberty in the name of expediency.

* * *

Due process protects petitioner's right to be subject only to lawful authority. At no time did petitioner engage in any activities in New Jersey that reveal an intent to invoke or benefit from the protection of its laws. New Jersey is without power to adjudge the rights and liabilities of J. McIntyre, and its exercise of jurisdiction would violate due process. The contrary judgment of the New Jersey Supreme Court is

Reversed.*

---

* [Ed. note.] Justice Breyer, with whom Justice Alito joined, wrote a decision concurring in the

Justice Ginsburg, with whom Justice Sotomayor and Justice Kagan join, dissenting.

A foreign industrialist seeks to develop a market in the United States for machines it manufactures. It hopes to derive substantial revenue from sales it makes to United States purchasers. Where in the United States buyers reside does not matter to this manufacturer. Its goal is simply to sell as much as it can, wherever it can. It excludes no region or State from the market it wishes to reach. But, all things considered, it prefers to avoid products liability litigation in the United States. To that end, it engages a U.S. distributor to ship its machines stateside. Has it succeeded in escaping personal jurisdiction in a State where one of its products is sold and causes injury or even death to a local user?

Under this Court's pathmarking precedent in *International Shoe* and subsequent decisions, one would expect the answer to be unequivocally, "No." But instead, six Justices of this Court, in divergent opinions, tell us that the manufacturer has avoided the jurisdiction of our state courts, except perhaps in States where its products are sold in sizeable quantities. Inconceivable as it may have seemed yesterday, the splintered majority today "turn[s] the clock back to the days before modern long-arm statutes when a manufacturer, to avoid being haled into court where a user is injured, need only Pilate-like wash its hands of a product by having independent distributors market it." Weintraub, *A Map Out of the Personal Jurisdiction Labyrinth*, 28 U.C. Davis L. Rev. 531, 555 (1995).

I

[Justice Ginsburg began her dissent by reviewing in detail the facts suggesting that the court had jurisdiction.]

* * *

In sum, McIntyre UK's regular attendance and exhibitions at ISRI conventions was surely a purposeful step to reach customers for its products "anywhere in the United States." At least as purposeful was McIntyre UK's engagement of McIntyre America as the conduit for sales of McIntyre UK's machines to buyers "throughout the United States." Given McIntyre UK's endeavors to reach and profit from the United States market as a whole, Nicastro's suit, I would hold, has been brought in a forum entirely

---

judgment. Justice Breyer reasoned that, while commerce was becoming increasingly global, the case did not present a situation that warranted prescribing a broad new rule. Instead, prior Court precedent established that jurisdiction could not be premised on a single isolated sale like the sale of the machine in this case. Relying on both Justice O'Connor's opinion in *Asahi* and the majority in *World-Wide Volkswagen*, Justice Breyer reasoned that this defendant did not engage in a regular flow of commerce into New Jersey. Nor did the argument that the defendant should have reasonably foreseen that its product could end up in New Jersey support jurisdiction here. Minimum contacts is defendant-focused; not chattel-focused. While he acknowledged that the Court will need to take on cases that implicate modern concerns, such as the internet, this is not such a case.

appropriate for the adjudication of his claim. He alleges that McIntyre UK's shear machine was defectively designed or manufactured and, as a result, caused injury to him at his workplace. The machine arrived in Nicastro's New Jersey workplace not randomly or fortuitously, but as a result of the U.S. connections and distribution system that McIntyre UK deliberately arranged.[3] On what sensible view of the allocation of adjudicatory authority could the place of Nicastro's injury within the United States be deemed off limits for his products liability claim against a foreign manufacturer who targeted the United States (including all the States that constitute the Nation) as the territory it sought to develop?

* * *

III

This case is illustrative of marketing arrangements for sales in the United States common in today's commercial world. A foreign-country manufacturer engages a U.S. company to promote and distribute the manufacturer's products, not in any particular State, but anywhere and everywhere in the United States the distributor can attract purchasers. The product proves defective and injures a user in the State where the user lives or works. Often, as here, the manufacturer will have liability insurance covering personal injuries caused by its products.

* * *

McIntyre UK dealt with the United States as a single market. Like most foreign manufacturers, it was concerned not with the prospect of suit in State X as opposed to State Y, but rather with its subjection to suit anywhere in the United States. If McIntyre UK is answerable in the United States at all, is it not "perfectly appropriate to permit the exercise of that jurisdiction ... at the place of injury"?

In sum, McIntyre UK, by engaging McIntyre America to promote and sell its machines in the United States, "purposefully availed itself" of the United States market nationwide, not a market in a single State or a discrete collection of States. McIntyre UK thereby availed itself of the market of all States in which its products were sold by its exclusive distributor. "Th[e] 'purposeful availment' requirement," this Court has explained,

---

3. McIntyre UK resisted Nicastro's efforts to determine whether other McIntyre machines had been sold to New Jersey customers. McIntyre did allow that McIntyre America "may have resold products it purchased from [McIntyre UK] to a buyer in New Jersey," but said it kept no record of the ultimate destination of machines it shipped to its distributor. A private investigator engaged by Nicastro found at least one McIntyre UK machine, of unspecified type, in use in New Jersey. But McIntyre UK objected that the investigator's report was "unsworn and based upon hearsay." Moreover, McIntyre UK maintained, no evidence showed that the machine the investigator found in New Jersey had been "sold into [that State]."

simply "ensures that a defendant will not be haled into a jurisdiction solely as a result of 'random,' 'fortuitous,' or 'attenuated' contacts." *Burger King*, 471 U.S. at 475. Adjudicatory authority is appropriately exercised where "actions by the defendant *himself*" give rise to the affiliation with the forum. *Id.* How could McIntyre UK not have intended, by its actions targeting a national market, to sell products in the fourth largest destination for imports among all States of the United States and the largest scrap metal market?

Courts, both state and federal, confronting facts similar to those here, have rightly rejected the conclusion that a manufacturer selling its products across the USA may evade jurisdiction in any and all States, including the State where its defective product is distributed and causes injury. They have held, instead, that it would undermine principles of fundamental fairness to insulate the foreign manufacturer from accountability in court at the place within the United States where the manufacturer's products caused injury.

V

* * *

For the reasons stated, I would hold McIntyre UK answerable in New Jersey for the harm Nicastro suffered at his workplace in that State using McIntyre UK's shearing machine. While I dissent from the Court's judgment, I take heart that the plurality opinion does not speak for the Court, for that opinion would take a giant step away from the "notions of fair play and substantial justice" underlying *International Shoe*.

Exercise 2-11. *Nicastro* Revisited

1. If you represented a foreign manufacturer that wanted to sell its products in the United States, what advice would you provide it about how to market and distribute its products in the United States to avoid having to defend lawsuits here?

2. Given the outcome and reasoning of the *Nicastro* Court, would the courts have jurisdiction over the defendant in the following fact patterns?

   a. The plaintiff gets into a car accident in New York when she loses control over the car she is driving allegedly because of the car's faulty braking system. She sues the foreign manufacturer in New York state court under products liability laws. Will the New York court have jurisdiction if the foreign car manufacturer sells cars through a wholly owned subsidiary in the United States that is organized under Delaware law and has its principal place of business in New York?

b. Will the New York state court have jurisdiction if the foreign car manufacturer sells cars directly in the United States?

c. Will the New York state court have jurisdiction if the foreign car manufacturer's cars are sold through an independent car importer that is
   organized under the laws of Delaware and has its principal place of
   business in New York?

Note on *Bristol-Myers Squibb Co. v. Superior Court* and "Arising Out of or Relating to" the Defendant's Contact with the Forum

In *Bristol-Myers Squibb Co. v. Superior Court*, ___ U.S. ___, 137 S. Ct. 1773 (2017),
the Supreme Court of the United States discussed what it means for a claim to "arise
out of or relate" to the defendant's activities in the state in the context of a "mass action," an action in which a large number of plaintiffs sue without using a class action.
A group of five hundred plus plaintiffs, some of whom lived in California but several
hundred of whom lived in other states, sued Bristol-Myers Squibb in California state
court alleging a variety of tort claims related to using the drug Plavix. Bristol-Myers
Squibb challenged the state court's jurisdiction, arguing that the court did not have
jurisdiction over the nonresident plaintiffs' claims because they did not arise out of
or relate to the company's activities in the state. The Supreme Court of California
ruled that the state court did have jurisdiction over the case, using a "sliding scale
approach" to specific jurisdiction, whereby "the more wide ranging the defendant's
forum contacts, the more readily is shown a connection between the forum contacts
and the claim." *Id.* at 1778 (quoting 1 Cal. 5th 783, 806 (2016)). According to the
California Supreme Court, this standard was met because the claims of the California
plaintiffs were similar to those of the out-of-state plaintiffs.

The Supreme Court disagreed with this approach to specific jurisdiction, reasoning
that such a "sliding scale" approach "resembles a loose and spurious form of general
jurisdiction." 137 S. Ct. at 1781. Specific jurisdiction, instead, requires a link between
the state and the nonresidents' claims. Here, no such link existed. The Court emphasized
that personal jurisdiction implicates federalism and sovereignty concerns as well as
fairness to the defendant. As the Court explained, "What is needed—and what is missing here—is a connection between the forum and the specific claim at issue." *Id.* The
Court distinguished *Keeton v. Hustler Magazine, Inc.*, 465 U.S. 770 (1984), a defamation
case in which a nonresident plaintiff sued in the courts of New Hampshire based on
an article published there as well as throughout the United States. The Court argued
that in *Keeton*, the Court reasoned that "'[f]alse statements of fact harm both the
subject of the falsehood and the readers of the statement,'" which distinguished the
case from Bristol-Myers Squibb, in which there was no harm committed in California
or to California residents based on the nonresidents' claims. *Id.* at 1782 (quoting *Keeton*,
465 U.S. at 776). The Court reserved judgment on whether the Fifth Amendment imposes a similar restriction on the exercise of federal court jurisdiction. *Id.* at 1783–84.

Justice Sotomayor, as is becoming her habit in personal jurisdiction cases, dissented, arguing that Bristol-Myers Squibb's advertising and distribution of the drug involved in the lawsuit was nationwide and consistent across the United States. *Id.* at 1784 (Sotomayor, J., dissenting). The claims of the California plaintiffs and nonresidents plaintiffs therefore were "materially identical." *Id.* at 1785. Disagreeing with the majority's emphasis on federalism, Justice Sotomayor instead emphasized "fair play and substantial justice" considerations coming out of *International Shoe.* Justice Sotomayor argued that this case makes it difficult for plaintiffs to bring one lawsuit involving the same claims when they are from multiple states. This is often a more efficient form of litigation for cases involving small claims. What values are served by breaking up this litigation and forcing groups of plaintiffs to sue in different states when the cases involve the same fact pattern and similar, if not identical, claims against the same defendant?

5. General Jurisdiction

The cases that you have read since *International Shoe* all involve cases of specific jurisdiction. Recall that *International Shoe* also contemplated that there might be a defendant whose "continuous corporate operations within a state were thought so substantial and of such a nature as to justify suit against it on a cause of action arising from dealings entirely distinct from those activities." *International Shoe.* Many courts used a "continuous and systematic" contact standard to assess whether general jurisdiction was appropriate. Thus, if the defendant's contacts were sufficiently continuous and systematic, a state's courts could assert jurisdiction over that defendant in any case, including cases in which the dispute did not arise out of the defendant's contact with the forum state. So, for example, if a person from Tennessee were vacationing in North Carolina and slipped and fell at a local North Carolina Wal-Mart store, that Tennessee resident could return home to Tennessee and sue Wal-Mart in Tennessee under the general jurisdiction theory. Wal-Mart has a sufficient number of stores in Tennessee that its contacts with that state are continuous and systematic. Therefore, even though the accident occurred in a North Carolina Wal-Mart, a Tennessee court could assert jurisdiction in a case against Wal-Mart involving that claim because of Wal-Mart's continuous and systematic contacts with Tennessee.

The United States Supreme Court has not had much opportunity to consider the parameters of general jurisdiction. However, in three cases that are described in *Daimler*, the Supreme Court considered whether personal jurisdiction in cases involving foreign corporations was proper. Those cases include *Perkins v. Benguet*, 342 U.S. 437 (1952), *Helicopertos Nacionales de Colombia, S.A. v. Hall*, 466 U.S. 408 (1984), and *Goodyear Dunlop Tires Operations, S.A. v. Brown*, 564 U.S. 915 (2011). One of the questions that lingered after *Burger King* and *Asahi* was whether the fairness factors developed in those cases applied in cases involving general jurisdiction. *Daimler* provided an opportunity for the Court to address this question.

Exercise 2-12. General Jurisdiction in *Daimler v. Bauman*

In *Daimler*, the plaintiffs sued a foreign corporation for actions that took place outside the United States, adding another wrinkle to the analysis. As you read *Daimler*, find the answers to the following questions.

1. The Court in *Daimler* relies heavily on the decisions in *Perkins*, *Helicopteros*, and *Goodyear Dunlop*. From the description provided by the *Daimler* Court, what were the facts of *Perkins*, *Helicopteros*, and *Goodyear Dunlop*? What were the Court's holdings in *Perkins*, *Helicopteros*, and *Goodyear Dunlop*?

2. The *Daimler* Court discusses its general jurisdiction analysis from *International Shoe*. Is the Court's interpretation of that analysis consistent with your understanding from reading *International Shoe*? If not, in what ways does it differ?

3. What standard does the Court use to assess whether a state may assert general jurisdiction over the defendant in this case?

4. Justice Sotomayor agrees with the majority's outcome but disagrees with its analysis in reaching it. How does Justice Sotomayor's approach to general jurisdiction differ from that of the majority?

Daimler AG v. Bauman

571 U.S. 117 (2014)

Justice Ginsburg delivered the opinion of the Court.

This case concerns the authority of a court in the United States to entertain a claim brought by foreign plaintiffs against a foreign defendant based on events occurring entirely outside the United States. The litigation commenced in 2004, when twenty-two Argentinian residents filed a complaint in the United States District Court for the Northern District of California against DaimlerChrysler Aktiengesellschaft (Daimler), a German public stock company, headquartered in Stuttgart, that manufactures Mercedes-Benz vehicles in Germany. The complaint alleged that during Argentina's 1976–1983 "Dirty War," Daimler's Argentinian subsidiary, Mercedes-Benz Argentina (MB Argentina) collaborated with state security forces to kidnap, detain, torture, and kill certain MB Argentina workers, among them, plaintiffs or persons closely related to plaintiffs. Damages for the alleged human-rights violations were sought from Daimler under the laws of the United States, California, and Argentina. Jurisdiction over the lawsuit was predicated on the California contacts of Mercedes-Benz USA, LLC (MBUSA), a subsidiary of Daimler incorporated in Delaware with its principal place of business in New Jersey. MBUSA distributes Daimler-manufactured vehicles to independent dealerships throughout the United States, including California.

The question presented is whether the Due Process Clause of the Fourteenth Amendment precludes the District Court from exercising jurisdiction over Daimler in this case, given the absence of any California connection to the atrocities, perpetrators, or victims described in the complaint. Plaintiffs invoked the court's general or all-purpose jurisdiction. California, they urge, is a place where Daimler may be sued on any and all claims against it, wherever in the world the claims may arise. For example, as plaintiffs' counsel affirmed, under the proffered jurisdictional theory, if a Daimler-manufactured vehicle overturned in Poland, injuring a Polish driver and passenger, the injured parties could maintain a design defect suit in California. Exercises of personal jurisdiction so exorbitant, we hold, are barred by due process constraints on the assertion of adjudicatory authority.

In *Goodyear Dunlop Tires Operations, S.A. v. Brown*, 564 U.S. 915, 131 S. Ct. 2846 (2011), we addressed the distinction between general or all-purpose jurisdiction, and specific or conduct-linked jurisdiction. As to the former, we held that a court may assert jurisdiction over a foreign corporation "to hear any and all claims against [it]" only when the corporation's affiliations with the State in which suit is brought are so constant and pervasive "as to render [it] essentially at home in the forum State." *Id.* at ___, 131 S. Ct. at 2851. Instructed by *Goodyear*, we conclude Daimler is not "at home" in California, and cannot be sued there for injuries plaintiffs attribute to MB Argentina's conduct in Argentina.

I

* * *

Daimler moved to dismiss the action for want of personal jurisdiction. Opposing the motion, plaintiffs submitted declarations and exhibits purporting to demonstrate the presence of Daimler itself in California. Alternatively, plaintiffs maintained that jurisdiction over Daimler could be founded on the California contacts of MBUSA, a distinct corporate entity that, according to plaintiffs, should be treated as Daimler's agent for jurisdictional purposes.

MBUSA, an indirect subsidiary of Daimler, is a Delaware limited liability corporation. MBUSA serves as Daimler's exclusive importer and distributor in the United States, purchasing Mercedes-Benz automobiles from Daimler in Germany, then importing those vehicles, and ultimately distributing them to independent dealerships located throughout the Nation. Although MBUSA's principal place of business is in New Jersey, MBUSA has multiple California-based facilities, including a regional office in Costa Mesa, a Vehicle Preparation Center in Carson, and a Classic Center in Irvine. According to the record developed below, MBUSA is the largest supplier of luxury vehicles to the California market. In particular, over 10% of all sales of new vehicles in the United States take place in California, and MBUSA's California sales account for 2.4% of Daimler's worldwide sales.

The relationship between Daimler and MBUSA is delineated in a General Distributor Agreement, which sets forth requirements for MBUSA's distribution of Mercedes-Benz vehicles in the United States. That agreement established MBUSA as an "independent contracto[r]" that "buy[s] and sell[s] [vehicles] ... as an independent business for [its] own account."

* * *

We granted certiorari to decide whether, consistent with the Due Process Clause of the Fourteenth Amendment, Daimler is amenable to suit in California courts for claims involving only foreign plaintiffs and conduct occurring entirely abroad.

II

Federal courts ordinarily follow state law in determining the bounds of their jurisdiction over persons. Fed. Rule Civ. Pro. 4(k)(1)(A). Under California's long-arm statute, California state courts may exercise personal jurisdiction "on any basis not inconsistent with the Constitution of this state or of the United States." California's long-arm statute allows the exercise of personal jurisdiction to the full extent permissible under the U.S. Constitution. We therefore inquire whether the Ninth Circuit's holding [that personal jurisdiction was proper] comports with the limits imposed by federal due process.

III

In *Pennoyer v. Neff*, decided shortly after the enactment of the Fourteenth Amendment, the Court held that a tribunal's jurisdiction over persons reaches no farther than the geographic bounds of the forum. In time, however, that strict territorial approach yielded to a less rigid understanding, spurred by "changes in the technology of transportation and communication, and the tremendous growth of interstate business activity." *Burnham v. Superior Court of Cal.*, 495 U.S. 604, 617 (1990) (opinion of Scalia, J.).

"The canonical opinion in this area remains *International Shoe*, in which we held that a State may authorize its courts to exercise personal jurisdiction over an out-of-state defendant if the defendant has 'certain minimum contacts with [the State] such that the maintenance of the suit does not offend "traditional notions of fair play and substantial justice."'" *Goodyear*, 564 U.S. at ___, 131 S. Ct. at 2853 (quoting *International Shoe*, 326 U.S. at 316). Following *International Shoe* "the relationship among the defendant, the forum, and the litigation, rather than the mutually exclusive sovereignty of the States on which the rules of *Pennoyer* rest, became the central concern of the inquiry into personal jurisdiction." *Shaffer*, 433 U.S. at 204.

International Shoe's conception of "fair play and substantial justice" presaged the development of two categories of personal jurisdiction. The first category is represented by *International Shoe* itself, a case in which the in-state activities of the corporate defendant "ha[d] not only been continuous and systematic, but also g[a]ve rise to the liabilities sued on." 326 U.S. at 317. *International Shoe* recognized, as well, that "the commission of some single or occasional acts of the corporate agent in a state" may sometimes be enough to subject the corporation to jurisdiction in that State's tribunals with respect to suits relating to that in-state activity. *Id.* at 318. Adjudicatory authority of this order, in which the suit "aris[es] out of or relate[s] to the defendant's contacts with the forum," *Helicopteros*, is today called "specific jurisdiction." *See Goodyear*, 564 U.S. at ___, 131 S. Ct. at 2851; *Helicopteros*, 466 U.S. at 414 n.9.

International Shoe distinguished between, on the one hand, exercises of specific jurisdiction, as just described, and on the other, situations where a foreign corporation's "continuous corporate operations within a state [are] so substantial and of such a nature as to justify suit against it on causes of action arising from dealings entirely distinct from those activities." 326 U.S. at 318. As we have since explained, "[a] court may assert general jurisdiction over foreign (sister-state or foreign-country) corporations to hear any and all claims against them when their affiliations with the State are so 'continuous and systematic' as to render them essentially at home in the forum State." *Goodyear*, 564 U.S. ___, 131 S. Ct. at 2851; *Helicopteros*, 466 U.S. at 414 n.9.

* * *

Our post-*International Shoe* opinions on general jurisdiction, by comparison, are few. "[The Court's] 1952 decision in *Perkins v. Benguet Consol. Mining Co.* remains the textbook case of general jurisdiction appropriately exercised over a foreign corporation that has not consented to suit in the forum." *Goodyear*, 564 U.S. at ___, 131 S. Ct. at 2856. The defendant in *Perkins*, Benguet, was a company incorporated under the laws of the Philippines, where it operated gold and silver mines. Benguet ceased its mining operations during the Japanese occupation of the Philippines in World War II; its president moved to Ohio, where he kept an office, maintained the company's files, and oversaw the company's activities. *Perkins v. Benguet Consol. Mining Co.*, 342 U.S. 437, 448 (1952). The plaintiff, an Ohio resident, sued Benguet on a claim that neither arose in Ohio nor related to the corporation's activities in that State. We held that the Ohio courts could exercise general jurisdiction over Benguet without offending due process. That was so, we later noted, because "Ohio was the corporation's principal, if temporary, place of business." *Keeton*, 465 U.S. at 780 n.11.

* * *

The next case on point, *Helicopteros*, 466 U.S. 408, arose from a helicopter crash in Peru. Four U.S. citizens perished in that accident; their survivors and representatives brought suit in Texas state court against the helicopter's owner and operator, a Colombian corporation. That company's contacts with Texas were confined to "sending its chief executive officer to Houston for a contract-negotiation session; accepting into its New York bank account checks drawn on a Houston bank; purchasing helicopters, equipment, and training services from [a Texas-based helicopter company] for substantial sums; and sending personnel to [Texas] for training." *Id.* at 416. Notably, those contacts bore no apparent relationship to the accident that gave rise to the suit. We held that the company's Texas connections did not resemble the "continuous and systematic general business contacts ... found to exist in *Perkins*." *Id.* "[M]ere purchases, even if occurring at regular intervals," we clarified, "are not enough to warrant a State's assertion of *in personam* jurisdiction over a nonresident corporation in a cause of action not related to those purchase transactions." *Id.* at 418.

Most recently, in *Goodyear*, we answered the question: "Are foreign subsidiaries of a United States parent corporation amenable to suit in state court on claims unrelated to any activity of the subsidiaries in the forum State?" 564 U.S. at ___, 131 S. Ct. at 2850. That case arose from a bus accident outside Paris that killed two boys from North Carolina. The boys' parents brought a wrongful-death suit in North Carolina state court alleging that the bus's tire was defectively manufactured. The complaint named as defendants not only The Goodyear Tire and Rubber Company (Goodyear), an Ohio corporation, but also Goodyear's Turkish, French, and Luxembourgian subsidiaries. Those foreign subsidiaries, which manufactured tires for sale in Europe and Asia, lacked any affiliation with North Carolina. A small percentage of tires manufactured by the foreign subsidiaries were distributed in North Carolina, however, and on that ground, the North Carolina Court of Appeals held the subsidiaries amenable to the general jurisdiction of North Carolina courts.

We reversed, observing that the North Carolina court's analysis "elided the essential difference between case-specific and all-purpose (general) jurisdiction." *Id.* at ___, 131 S. Ct. at 2855. Although the placement of a product into the stream of commerce "may bolster an affiliation germane to *specific* jurisdiction," we explained, such contacts "do not warrant a determination that, based on those ties, the forum has *general* jurisdiction over a defendant." *Id.* at ___, 131 S. Ct. at 2867. As *International Shoe* itself teaches, a corporation's "continuous activity of some sorts within a state is not enough to support the demand that the corporation be amenable to suits unrelated to that activity." 326 U.S. at 318. Because Goodyear's foreign subsidiaries were "in no sense at home in North Carolina," we held, those subsidiaries could not be required to submit to the general jurisdiction of that State's courts. 564 U.S. at ___, 131 S. Ct. at 2857.

As is evident from *Perkins*, *Helicopteros*, and *Goodyear*, general and specific jurisdiction have followed markedly different trajectories post-*International Shoe*. Specific jurisdiction has been cut loose from *Pennoyer*'s sway, but we have declined to stretch general jurisdiction beyond limits traditionally recognized. As this Court has increasingly trained on the "relationship among the defendant, the forum, and the litigation," *Shaffer*, 433 U.S. at 204, *i.e.*, specific jurisdiction, general jurisdiction has come to occupy a less dominant place in the contemporary scheme.

IV

With this background, we turn directly to the question whether Daimler's affiliations with California are sufficient to subject it to the general (all-purpose) personal jurisdiction of that State's courts. In the proceedings below, the parties agreed on, or failed to contest, certain points we now take as given. Plaintiffs have never attempted to fit this case into the *specific* jurisdiction category. Nor did plaintiffs challenge on appeal the District Court's holding that Daimler's own contacts with California were, by themselves, too sporadic to justify the exercise of general jurisdiction. While plaintiffs ultimately persuaded the Ninth Circuit to impute MBUSA's California contacts to Daimler on an agency theory, at no point have they maintained that MBUSA is an alter ego of Daimler.

Daimler, on the other hand, failed to object below to plaintiffs' assertion that the California courts could exercise all-purpose jurisdiction over MBUSA. We will assume then, for purposes of this decision only, that MBUSA qualifies as at home in California.

A

In sustaining the exercise of general jurisdiction over Daimler, the Ninth Circuit relied on an agency theory, determining that MBUSA acted as Daimler's agent for jurisdictional purposes and then attributing MBUSA's California contacts to Daimler. The Ninth Circuit's agency analysis derived from Circuit precedent considering principally whether the subsidiary "performs services that are sufficiently important to the foreign corporation that if it did not have a representative to perform them, the corporation's own officials would undertake to perform substantially similar services."

This Court has not yet addressed whether a foreign corporation may be subjected to a court's general jurisdiction based on the contacts of its in-state subsidiary....

The Ninth Circuit's agency finding rested primarily on its observation that MBUSA's services were "important" to Daimler, as gauged by Daimler's hypothetical readiness to perform those services itself if MBUSA did not exist. Formulated this way, the inquiry into importance stacks the deck, for it will always yield a pro-jurisdiction answer: "Anything a corporation does through an independent contractor, subsidiary, or distributor is presumably something that the corporation would do 'by other means' if the independent contractor, subsidiary, or distributor did not exist." 676 F.3d at 777 (O'Scannlain, J., dissenting from denial of reh'g en banc). The Ninth Circuit's agency theory thus appears to subject foreign corporations to general jurisdiction whenever they have an in-state subsidiary or affiliate, an outcome that would sweep beyond even the "sprawling view of general jurisdiction" we rejected in *Goodyear*, 564 U.S. at ___, 131 S. Ct. at 2856.

B

Even if we were to assume that MBUSA is at home in California, and further to assume MBUSA's contacts are imputable to Daimler, there would still be no basis to subject Daimler to general jurisdiction in California, for Daimler's slim contacts with the State hardly render it at home there.

Goodyear made clear that only a limited set of affiliations with a forum will render a defendant amenable to all-purpose jurisdiction there. "For an individual, the paradigm forum for the exercise of general jurisdiction is the individual's domicile; for a corporation, it is an equivalent place, one in which the corporation is fairly regarded as at home." 564 U.S. at ___, 131 S. Ct. at 2853–54. With respect to a corporation, the place of incorporation and principal place of business are "paradig[m] ... bases for general jurisdiction." *Id.* at 735. Those affiliations have the virtue of being unique—that is, each ordinarily indicates only one place—as well as easily ascertainable. These bases afford plaintiffs recourse to at least one clear and certain forum in which a corporate defendant may be sued on any and all claims.

Goodyear did not hold that a corporation may be subject to general jurisdiction *only* in a forum where it is incorporated or has its principal place of business; it simply typed those places paradigm all-purpose forums. Plaintiffs would have us look beyond the exemplar bases *Goodyear* identified, and approve the exercise of general jurisdiction in every State in which a corporation "engages in a substantial, continuous, and systematic course of business." That formulation, we hold, is unacceptably grasping.

As noted, the words "continuous and systematic" were used in *International Shoe* to describe instances in which the exercise of *specific* jurisdiction would be appropriate. *See* 326 U.S. at 317 (jurisdiction can be asserted where a corporation's in-state activities are not only "continuous and systematic, but also give rise to the liabilities sued on"). Turning to all-purpose jurisdiction, in contrast, *International Shoe* speaks of "instances in which the continuous corporate operations within a state [are] so substantial and of such a nature as to justify suit ... *on causes of action arising from dealings entirely distinct from those activities.*" *Id.* at 318. Accordingly, the inquiry under *Goodyear* is not whether a foreign corporation's in-forum contacts can be said to be in some sense "continuous and systematic," it is whether that corporation's "affiliations with the State are so 'continuous and systematic' as to render [it] essentially at home in the forum State." 564 U.S. ___, 131 S. Ct. at 2851.

Here, neither Daimler nor MBUSA is incorporated in California, nor does either entity have its principal place of business there. If Daimler's California activities sufficed to allow adjudication of this Argentina-rooted case in California, the same global reach would presumably be available in every other State in which MBUSA's sales are sizable. Such exorbitant exercises of all-purpose jurisdiction would scarcely permit out-of-state defendants "to structure their primary conduct with some minimum assurance as to where that conduct will and will not render them liable to suit." *Burger King*, 471 U.S. at 472.

It was therefore error for the Ninth Circuit to conclude that Daimler, even with MBUSA's contacts attributed to it, was at home in California, and hence subject to suit there on claims by foreign plaintiffs having nothing to do with anything that occurred or had its principal impact in California.[20]

C

Finally, the transnational context of this dispute bears attention. The Court of Appeals emphasized, as supportive of the exercise of general jurisdiction, plaintiffs' assertion of claims under the Alien Tort Statute (ATS), and the Torture Victim Protection Act of 1991 (TVPA). Recent decisions

---

20. .... Justice Sotomayor would reach the same result, but for a different reason. Rather than concluding that Daimler is not at home in California, Justice Sotomayor would hold that the exercise of general jurisdiction over Daimler would be unreasonable "in the unique circumstances of this case." In other words, she favors a resolution fit for this day and case only. True, a multipronged reasonableness check was articulated in *Asahi*, but not as a free-floating test. Instead, the check was to be essayed when *specific* jurisdiction is at issue. First, a court is to determine whether the connection between the forum and the episode-in-suit could justify the exercise of specific jurisdiction. Then, in a second step, the court is to consider several additional factors to assess the reasonableness of entertaining the case. When a corporation is genuinely at home in the forum State, however, any second-step inquiry would be superfluous.

Justice Sotomayor fears that our holding will "lead to greater unpredictability by radically expanding the scope of jurisdictional discovery." But it is hard to see why much in the way of discovery would be needed to determine where a corporation is at home. Justice Sotomayor's proposal to import *Asahi*'s "reasonableness" check into the general jurisdiction determination, on the other hand, would indeed compound the jurisdictional inquiry. The reasonableness factors identified in *Asahi* include "the burden on the defendant," "the interests of the forum State," "the plaintiff's interest in obtaining relief," "the interstate judicial system's interest in obtaining the most efficient resolution of controversies," "the shared interest of the several States in furthering fundamental substantive social policies," and, in the international context, "the procedural and substantive policies of other *nations* whose interests are affected by the assertion of jurisdiction." Imposing such a checklist in cases of general jurisdiction would hardly promote the efficient disposition of an issue that should be resolved expeditiously at the outset of litigation.

of this Court, however, have rendered plaintiffs' ATS and TVPA claims infirm.

The Ninth Circuit, moreover, paid little heed to the risks to international comity its expansive view of general jurisdiction posed. Other nations do not share the uninhibited approach to personal jurisdiction advanced by the Court of Appeals in this case. In the European Union, for example, a corporation may generally be sued in the nation in which it is "domiciled," a term defined to refer only to the location of the corporation's "statutory seat," "central administration," or "principal place of business." European Parliament and Council Reg. 1215/2012, Arts. 4(1), and 63(1), 2012 O.J. (L. 351) 7, 18. The Solicitor General informs us, in this regard, that "foreign governments' objections to some domestic courts' expansive views of general jurisdiction have in the past impeded negotiations of international agreements on the reciprocal recognition and enforcement of judgments." U.S. Brief 2 (citing Junger, *The American Law of General Jurisdiction*, 2001 U. CHI. LEGAL FORUM 141, 161–62). Considerations of international rapport thus reinforce our determination that subjecting Daimler to the general jurisdiction of courts in California would not accord with the "fair play and substantial justice" due process demands.

For the reasons stated, the judgment of the United States Court of Appeals for the Ninth Circuit is

Reversed.

Justice Sotomayor, concurring in the judgment.

I agree with the Court's conclusion that the Due Process Clause prohibits the exercise of personal jurisdiction over Daimler in light of the unique circumstances of this case. I concur only in the judgment, however, because I cannot agree with the path the Court takes to arrive at that result.

The Court acknowledges that Mercedes-Benz USA, LLC (MBUSA), Daimler's wholly owned subsidiary, has considerable contacts with California. It has multiple facilities in the State, including a regional headquarters. Each year, it distributes in California tens of thousands of cars, the sale of which generated billions of dollars in the year this suit was brought. And it provides service and sales support to customers throughout the State. Daimler has conceded that California courts may exercise general jurisdiction over MBUSA on the basis of these contacts, and the Court assumes that MBUSA's contacts may be attributed to Daimler for the purpose of deciding whether Daimler is also subject to general jurisdiction.

Are these contacts sufficient to permit the exercise of general jurisdiction over Daimler? The Court holds that they are not, for a reason wholly foreign to our due process jurisprudence. The problem, the Court says, is not that Daimler's contacts with California are too few, but that its contacts with other forums are too many. In other words, the Court does not dispute that the presence of multiple offices, the direct distribution of thousands of products accounting for billions of dollars in sales, and continuous interaction with customers throughout a State would be enough to support the exercise of general jurisdiction over some businesses. Daimler is just not one of those businesses, the Court concludes, because its California contacts must be viewed in the context of its extensive "nationwide and worldwide" operations. In recent years, Americans have grown accustomed to the concept of multinational corporations that are supposedly "too big to fail"; today the Court deems Daimler "too big for general jurisdiction."

The Court's conclusion is wrong as a matter of both process and substance. As to process, the Court decides this case on a ground that was neither argued nor passed on below, and that Daimler raised for the first time in a footnote to its brief. As to substance, the Court's focus on Daimler's operations outside of California ignores the lodestar of our personal jurisdiction jurisprudence: A State may subject a defendant to the burden of suit if the defendant has sufficiently taken advantage of the State's laws and protections through its contacts in the State; whether the defendant has contacts elsewhere is immaterial.

Regrettably, these errors are unforced. The Court can and should decide this case on the far simpler ground that, no matter how extensive Daimler's contacts with California, that State's exercise of jurisdiction would be unreasonable given that the case involves foreign plaintiffs suing a foreign defendant based on foreign conduct, and given that a more appropriate forum is available. Because I would reverse the judgment below on this ground, I concur in the judgment only.

I

I begin with the point on which the majority and I agree: The Ninth Circuit's decision should be reversed.

Our personal jurisdiction precedents call for a two-part analysis. The contacts prong asks whether the defendant has sufficient contacts with the forum State to support personal jurisdiction; the reasonableness prong asks whether the exercise of jurisdiction would be unreasonable under the circumstances. *Burger King.* As the majority points out, all of the cases in which we have applied the reasonableness prong have involved specific as opposed to general jurisdiction. Whether the reasonableness prong should apply in the general jurisdiction context is therefore a question we have never decided, and it is one on which I can appreciate the arguments on both sides. But it would be imprudent to decide that question in this case given that respondents have failed to argue against the application of the reasonableness prong during the entire 8-year history of this litigation. As a result, I would decide this case under the reasonableness prong without foreclosing future consideration of whether that prong should be limited to the specific jurisdiction context.

Exercise 2-12(a): *Daimler* Applied to a U.S.-Based Corporation — *BNSF Railway Co. v. Tyrrell*

The Supreme Court of the United States recently had the opportunity to apply *Daimler* to a United States-based corporation. As you read *BNSF Railway Co. v. Tyrrell*, answer the following questions.

1. What is Montana's long arm statute? Do BNSF's activities in Montana fall within the statute?

2. Why is this not a case of specific jurisdiction?

3. How did the Montana Supreme Court try to distinguish *Daimler*? Why was it not successful in doing so?

4. Where does this case leave corporate consent to jurisdiction? Is this still a viable option for a state wishing to assert jurisdiction over out-of-state corporations that do business in that state?

5. Justice Sotomayor dissents in part in the case. Why does she disagree with the majority?

BNSF Railway Co. v. Tyrrell
581 U.S. ___, 137 S. Ct. 1549 (2017)

Ginsburg, J.

The two cases we decide today arise under the Federal Employers' Liability Act (FELA), 35 Stat. 65, as amended, 45 U.S.C. §51 et seq., which makes railroads liable in money damages to their employees for on-the-job injuries. Both suits were pursued in Montana state courts although the injured workers did not reside in Montana, nor were they injured there. The defendant railroad, BNSF Railway Company (BNSF), although "doing business" in Montana when the litigation commenced, was not incorporated in Montana, nor did it maintain its principal place of business in that State.

* * *

I

In March 2011, respondent Robert Nelson, a North Dakota resident, brought a FELA suit against BNSF in a Montana state court to recover damages for knee injuries Nelson allegedly sustained while working for BNSF as a fuel-truck driver. In May 2014, respondent Kelli Tyrrell, appointed in South Dakota as the administrator of her husband Brent Tyrrell's estate, similarly sued BNSF under FELA in a Montana state court. Brent Tyrrell, his widow alleged, had developed a fatal kidney cancer from his exposure to carcinogenic chemicals while working for BNSF. Neither plaintiff alleged injuries arising from or related to work performed in Montana; indeed, neither Nelson nor Brent Tyrrell appears ever to have worked for BNSF in Montana.

BNSF is incorporated in Delaware and has its principal place of business in Texas. It operates railroad lines in 28 States. BNSF has 2,061 miles of railroad track in Montana (about 6% of its total track mileage of 32,500), employs some 2,100 workers there (less than 5% of its total work force of 43,000), generates less than 10% of its total revenue in the State, and maintains only one of its 24 automotive facilities in Montana (4%). Contending that it is not "at home" in Montana, as required for the exercise of general personal jurisdiction under *Daimler AG v. Bauman*, 571 U.S. ___, ___, 134 S. Ct. 746, 754 (2014) (internal quotation marks omitted), BNSF moved to dismiss both suits for lack of personal jurisdiction. Its motion was granted in Nelson's case and denied in Tyrrell's.

After consolidating the two cases, the Montana Supreme Court held that Montana courts could exercise general personal jurisdiction over BNSF. Section 56 [of the FELA], the court determined, authorizes state courts to exercise personal jurisdiction over railroads "doing business" in the State. In addition, the court observed, Montana law provides for the exercise of general jurisdiction over "[a]ll persons found within" the State. 383 Mont. 417, 427, 373 P.3d, at 8 (2016) (quoting Mont. Rule Civ. Proc. 4(b)(1) (2015)). In view of the railroad's many employees and miles of track in Montana, the court concluded, BNSF is both "doing business" and "found within" the State, such that both FELA and Montana law authorized the exercise of personal jurisdiction. 383 Mont. at 426, 428, 373 P.3d, at 7–8 (internal quotation marks omitted). The due process limits articulated in *Daimler*, the court added, did not control, because Daimler did not involve a FELA claim or a railroad defendant.

* * *

We granted certiorari to resolve whether § 56 [of the FELA] authorizes state courts to exercise personal jurisdiction over railroads doing business in their States but not incorporated or headquartered there, and whether the Montana courts' exercise of personal jurisdiction in these cases comports with due process. [The Court concluded that § 56 of the FELA did not provide authority for the assertion of personal jurisdiction over the railroad, and therefore could not form a basis for the Montana courts' exercise of jurisdiction in these cases.]

* * *

III

Because FELA does not authorize state courts to exercise personal jurisdiction over a railroad solely on the ground that the railroad does some business in their States, the Montana courts' assertion of personal jurisdiction over BNSF here must rest on Mont. Rule Civ. Proc. 4(b)(1), the State's provision for the exercise of personal jurisdiction over "persons found" in Montana. BNSF does not contest that it is "found within" Montana as the State's courts comprehend that rule. We therefore inquire whether the Montana courts' exercise of personal jurisdiction under Montana law comports with the Due Process Clause of the Fourteenth Amendment.

In *International Shoe*, this Court explained that a state court may exercise personal jurisdiction over an out-of-state defendant who has "certain minimum contacts with [the State] such that the maintenance of the suit does not offend 'traditional notions of fair play and substantial justice.'" 326 U.S. at 316. Elaborating on this guide, we have distinguished between specific or case-linked jurisdiction and general or all-purpose jurisdiction. *See, e.g., Daimler*, 571 U.S. at ___, 134 S. Ct. at 754; *Goodyear Dunlop Tires Operations, S.A. v. Brown*, 564 U.S. 915, 919 (2011); *Helicopteros Nacionales de Colombia, S.A. v. Hall*, 466 U.S. 408, 414, nn. 8, 9 (1984). Because neither Nelson nor Tyrrell alleges any injury from work in or related to Montana, only the propriety of general jurisdiction is at issue here.

Goodyear and *Daimler* clarified that "[a] court may assert general jurisdiction over foreign (sister-state or foreign-country) corporations to hear any and all claims against them when their affiliations with the State are so 'continuous and systematic' as to render them essentially at home in the forum State." *Daimler*, 571 U.S. at ___, 134 S. Ct. at 754 (quoting *Goodyear*, 564 U.S. at 919). The "paradigm" forums in which a corporate defendant is "at home," we explained, are the corporation's place of incorporation and its principal place of business. *Daimler*, 571 U.S. at ___, 134 S. Ct. at 760; *Goodyear*, 564 U.S. at 924. The exercise of general jurisdiction is not limited to these forums; in an "exceptional case," a corporate defendant's operations in another forum "may be so substantial and of such a nature as to render the corporation at home in that State." *Daimler*, 571 U.S. at ___, n. 19, 134 S. Ct. at 761, n. 19. We suggested that *Perkins v. Benguet Consol. Mining Co.*, 342 U.S. 437 (1952), exemplified such a case. *Daimler*, 571 U.S. at ___, n. 19, 134 S. Ct. at 761, n. 19. In *Perkins*, war had forced the defendant corporation's owner to temporarily relocate the enterprise from the Philippines to Ohio. 342 U.S. at 447–448. Because Ohio then became "the center of the corporation's wartime activities," *Daimler*, 571 U.S. at ___, n. 8, 134 S. Ct. at 756, n. 8, suit was proper there, *Perkins*, 342 U.S. at 448.

The Montana Supreme Court distinguished Daimler on the ground that we did not there confront "a FELA claim or a railroad defendant." 383 Mont. at 424, 373 P.3d at 6. The Fourteenth Amendment due process constraint described in *Daimler*, however, applies to all state-court assertions of general jurisdiction over nonresident defendants; the constraint does not vary with the type of claim asserted or business enterprise sued.

BNSF, we repeat, is not incorporated in Montana and does not maintain its principal place of business there. Nor is BNSF so heavily engaged in activity in Montana "as to render [it] essentially at home" in that State. *See Daimler*, 571 U.S. at ___, 134 S. Ct. at 761 (internal quotation marks omitted). As earlier noted, BNSF has over 2,000 miles of railroad track and more than 2,000 employees in Montana. But, as we observed in *Daimler*, "the general jurisdiction inquiry does not focus solely on the magnitude of the defendant's in-state contacts." Id. at ___, n. 20, 134 S. Ct. at 762, n. 20 (internal quotation marks and alterations omitted). Rather, the inquiry "calls for an appraisal of a corporation's activities in their entirety"; "[a] corporation that operates in many places can scarcely be deemed at home in all of them." Id. In short, the business BNSF does in Montana is sufficient to subject the railroad to specific personal jurisdiction in that State on claims related to the business it does in Montana. But in-state business, we clarified in *Daimler* and *Goodyear*, does not suffice to permit the assertion of general jurisdiction over claims like Nelson's and Tyrrell's that are unrelated to any activity occurring in Montana.

IV

Nelson and Tyrrell present a further argument—that BNSF has consented to personal jurisdiction in Montana. The Montana Supreme Court did not address this contention, so we do not reach it.

For the reasons stated, the judgment of the Montana Supreme Court is reversed, and the cases are remanded for further proceedings not inconsistent with this opinion.

It is so ordered.

Sotomayor, J., concurring in part and dissenting in part.

... I continue to disagree with the path the Court struck in *Daimler AG v. Bauman*, 571 U.S. ___, 134 S. Ct. 746 (2014), which limits general jurisdiction over a corporate defendant only to those States where it is "'essentially at home,'" id. at ___, 134 S. Ct. at 761. And even if the Court insists on adhering to that standard, I dissent from its decision to apply it here in the first instance rather than remanding to the Montana Supreme Court for it to conduct what should be a fact-intensive analysis under the proper legal framework. Accordingly, I join Parts I and II of the Court's opinion, but dissent from Part III and the judgment.

The Court would do well to adhere more faithfully to the direction from *International Shoe Co. v. Washington*, 326 U.S. 310 (1945), which instructed that general jurisdiction is proper when a corporation's "continuous corporate operations within a state [are] so substantial and of such a nature as to justify suit against it on causes of action arising from dealings entirely distinct from those activities." *Id.* at 318. Under International Shoe, in other words, courts were to ask whether the benefits a defendant attained in the forum State warranted the burdens associated with general personal jurisdiction. *See id.* at 317–318. The majority itself acknowledges that International Shoe should govern, describing the question as whether a defendant's affiliations with a State are sufficiently " 'continuous and systematic' " to warrant the exercise of general jurisdiction there. If only its analysis today reflected that directive. Instead, the majority opinion goes on to reaffirm the restrictive "at home" test set out in *Daimler* — a test that, as I have explained, has no home in our precedents and creates serious inequities. *See* 571 U.S. at ___–___, 134 S. Ct. at 767–773 (Sotomayor, J., concurring in judgment).

The majority's approach grants a jurisdictional windfall to large multistate or multinational corporations that operate across many jurisdictions. Under its reasoning, it is virtually inconceivable that such corporations will ever be subject to general jurisdiction in any location other than their principal places of business or of incorporation. Foreign businesses with principal places of business outside the United States may never be subject to general jurisdiction in this country even though they have continuous and systematic contacts within the United States. *See id.* at ___–___, 134 S. Ct. at 759–760. What was once a holistic, nuanced contacts analysis backed by considerations of fairness and reasonableness has now effectively been replaced by the rote identification of a corporation's principal place of business or place of incorporation. The result? It is individual plaintiffs, harmed by the actions of a farflung foreign corporation, who will bear the brunt of the majority's approach and be forced to sue in distant jurisdictions with which they have no contacts or connection.

* * *

I respectfully concur in part and dissent in part.

Exercise 2-13. *Daimler* and *BNSF* Revisited

1. After *Daimler* and *BNSF*, is the assertion of general jurisdiction limited to a corporate defendant's principal place of business and the state of its incorporation?

2. How do you determine whether to use general jurisdiction or specific jurisdiction in a given case?

3. Apply the rule of the *Daimler* and *BNSF* cases to determine whether the court can assert jurisdiction over the defendants in the following cases.

   a. In the Wal-Mart example given in the Note on General Jurisdiction above, would the Tennessee court have jurisdiction over Wal-Mart with respect to a claim that arose out of a slip and fall accident in a store in North Carolina? What if Wal-Mart has 20 stores and a distribution center in Tennessee?

   b. The plaintiff truck driver sues an oil company after it loaded the wrong chemicals on his truck in Michigan and it exploded in Ohio, causing the truck driver injuries. The truck driver sued the oil company in Louisiana, where he lives, although the oil company has neither its principal place of business nor its place of incorporation in Louisiana. However, 12% of its total refinery tanks are located in Louisiana, and 30% of both its refining capacity and total refinery-related tank storage capacity is in Louisiana. The only other state where the oil company has greater storage capacity is Texas. In the year the accident took place, 5% of the oil company's income was generated from sales in Louisiana and 9% of its workforce was located in Louisiana. Does the Louisian court have jurisdiction? *See Stewart v. Marathon Petroleum Co. LP*, 2018 WL 3220554 (E.D. La. July 2, 2018) (no).

   c. The plaintiff sues a Delaware corporation with its principal place of business in Los Angeles, California, regarding a contract that was supposed to be performed in Texas. Does a Delaware state court have jurisdiction?

   d. Republic, a garbage company, damaged a restaurant in Michigan while retrieving a dumpster. The Tennessee-based holding company that owned the restaurant sued Republic, an Arizona corporation, in Tennessee state court for damages. The restaurant company had five agreements with Republic for waste removal services — one for the Michigan restaurant and four for services in Tennessee. The four Tennessee agreements were negotiated on behalf of the restaurant company by a broker located in Franklin, Tennessee. All the agreements were signed by the restaurant company in Nashville, Tennessee. Republic sent invoices for services provided under the four contracts to Franklin, Tennessee for payment by the restaurant company. Four of the agreements, including the one for the Michigan restaurant, were on a form prepared by and bearing the logo of Allied Waste Services. The billing address listed on all five agreements is the same post office box in Franklin, Tennessee. Republic does business as Allied Waste Company. Does the Tennessee court have general jurisdiction over Republic? *See J. Alexander's Holdings, LLC v. Republic Services, Inc.*, 2017 WL 1969763, (Tenn. Ct. of App. May 12, 2017) (yes).

6. Personal Jurisdiction and the Internet

The Internet has added an interesting wrinkle to personal jurisdiction analysis. Many individuals and businesses conduct transactions online or simply have an informational website that describes the company's products or services. Under what circumstances does a court have jurisdiction over an out-of-state defendant when that person simply clicked send, filled in a form, posted a website, or agreed to a click wrap agreement? This also has implications for tort law, given that it is easy to defame someone online in a variety of ways; for example, a person can commit such a tort by e-mail, by blog post, or by commenting online. *See Shrader v. Biddinger*, 633 F.3d 1235 (10th Cir. 2011) (holding that an allegedly defamatory statement about a forum resident did not create a sufficient connection to the forum state for purposes of jurisdiction); *Bancroft & Masters, Inc. v. Augusta National, Inc.*, 223 F.3d 1082, 1087 (9th Cir. 2000) (explaining that jurisdiction can be established by directing "wrongful conduct [into a state] individually targeting a known forum resident").

Lower court cases have discussed under what circumstances a website can render a defendant subject to jurisdiction. An early case on the subject that is often cited by lower courts, *Zippo Manufacturing Co. v. Zippo Dot Com, Inc.*, 952 F. Supp. 1119 (W.D. Pa. 1997), set up a sliding scale approach:

> At one end of the spectrum are situations where a defendant clearly does business over the internet.... [A]t the opposite end are situations where a defendant has simply posted information on an Internet Web site which is accessible to users in foreign jurisdictions.... The middle ground is occupied by interactive Web sites where a user can exchange information with the host computer. In these cases, the exercise of jurisdiction is determined by examining the level of interactivity and commercial nature of the exchange of information that occurs on the Web site.

952 F. Supp. at 1124. While some courts have followed the *Zippo* court's approach, *see, e.g, Marvrix Photo, Inc. v. Brand Techs., Inc.*, 647 F.3d 1218, 1226–27 (9th Cir. 2011), others have not adopted it. *See, e.g., Shrader v. Biddinger*, 633 F.3d 1235, 1242 n.5 (10th Cir. 2011). The United States Supreme Court has yet to weigh in on these cases.

Exercise 2-14. *Plixer International, Inc. v. Scrutinizer GMBH*

Plixer presents an example of the a federal court applying Federal Rule of Civil Procedure 4(k)(2) and an assessment of a defendant's contacts with the United States as a whole for purposes of the due process clause of the Fifth Amendment. As you read *Plixer*, answer the follow questions:

1. The court uses a de novo standard of review in this case. Look up this term. What does it mean for the ability of the appellate court to overturn the trial court's decision?

2. Why does the court use the Fifth Amendment's Due Process clause rather than the Fourteenth Amendment's Due Process clause?

3. Does the court's analysis change because it is applying the Fifth Amendment's Due Process clause rather than the Fourteenth Amendment Due Process clause, which was used by the courts in other cases you have read?

4. Why doesn't the forum selection clause and choice of law clause play a significant role in the court's analysis in *Plixer*?

5. The defendant, Scrutinizer, concedes that the claim arises out of or relates to the defendant's forum activities. Why do you think it conceded this point?

6. How does the court parse the varying justices' decisions in *Nicastro* to support its holding in this case?

Plixer International, Inc. v. Scrutinizer GMBH
905 F.3d 1 (1st Cir. 2018)

Lynch, Circuit Judge.

Given the particular facts of this case, we affirm the thoughtful holding of the district court that the exercise of specific personal jurisdiction against a German corporation under Federal Rule of Civil Procedure 4(k)(2) does not offend the Due Process Clause of the United States Constitution. We note that this is an area in which the Supreme Court has not yet had the occasion to give clear guidance, and so we deliberately avoid creating any broad rules.

I.

We take the following facts from the undisputed record. Scrutinizer GmbH (Scrutinizer) is a German corporation with its principal place of business in Kassel, Germany. Through its interactive, English-language website, Scrutinizer runs a "self-service platform" that helps customers build better software. Scrutinizer brings its customers' code from a third-party hosting service like GitHub to its "controlled cloud environment," where it runs "software analysis tools" meant to "improve source-code quality, eliminate bugs, and find security vulnerabilities." Scrutinizer offers potential customers a fourteen-day free trial. In the course of its activities, Scrutinizer employs Google Analytics.

Customers who contract to use Scrutinizer's online service can pay only in euros. Scrutinizer's standard contract with those customers contains a forum-selection clause and a choice-of-law clause that provide that all lawsuits relating to the contract be brought in German courts and under German law. Scrutinizer maintains no U.S. office, phone number, or agent for service of process; it directs no advertising at the United States; and its employees do not go to the United States on business.

Scrutinizer provides its service globally. In an affidavit, Scrutinizer's founder said that customers can use the service "anywhere where Internet access is available." Scrutinizer's website states that it is "[t]rusted by over 5000 projects and companies around the world." Over three-and-a-half years, from January 2014 to June 2017, Scrutinizer sold its services to 156 U.S. customers. These sales occurred in thirty states, and the revenue from the contracts remitted to Scrutinizer €165,212.07. This amount was just under $200,000 in June 2017. The record does not reveal what percentage of Scrutinizer's total revenue comes from the United States. It does, however, detail Scrutinizer's customer numbers by state: from fifty-one in California to one in each of eight other states. During the three-and-a-half year period, Scrutinizer had two Maine customers, who collectively paid Scrutinizer €3,100 for its services.

Plixer International, Inc. (Plixer), a Maine corporation, sued Scrutinizer in federal district court in Maine on November 21, 2016, for trademark infringement. Plixer owns the U.S. registered mark "Scrutinizer," for which it filed in July 2015. Plixer's trademark application said that Plixer used the mark as early as November 2005. That application covered "[c]omputer software and hardware for analyzing, reporting and responding to malware infections and application performance problems, used in the field of information technology." In its complaint, Plixer alleged that Scrutinizer's use of the term "Scrutinizer" caused "confusion, mistake or deception as to the source" of Scrutinizer's services; that the use "will infringe and/or dilute Plixer's prior rights" in the mark; that the use "will interfere with Plixer's use" of its mark; and that Scrutinizer's "services are closely related to the services covered by Plixer's" mark, so "the public is likely to be confused about whether Plixer is the source of [Scrutinizer's] services or whether Plixer is affiliated with or the sponsor of [Scrutinizer's] services."

Plixer gave two bases for personal jurisdiction over Scrutinizer, only one of which is at issue in this appeal. It said that Scrutinizer's nationwide contacts with the United States supported specific jurisdiction under Federal Rule of Civil Procedure 4(k)(2). After rejecting an initial motion to dismiss, the district court allowed limited jurisdictional discovery.

In January 2017, after this lawsuit began, Scrutinizer filed a U.S. trademark application for "Scrutinizer." The record is silent on the reasons why Scrutinizer filed this application.

On prima facie review, the district court found that it could constitutionally exercise specific personal jurisdiction over Scrutinizer under Rule 4(k)(2). *Plixer Int'l, Inc. v. Scrutinizer GmbH*, 293 F.Supp.3d 232, 245 (D. Me. 2017). It held that Scrutinizer "operated a highly interactive website that sold its cloud-based services directly through the website, that it was open to business throughout the world, that it accepted recurrent business from the United States in a substantial amount, and that it did so knowingly." *Id.* at 241. The district court concluded that the criteria for purposeful availment in the United States had been met. The district court also found that the exercise of jurisdiction was reasonable and that Scrutinizer had not carried its burden of proving otherwise.

As part of its analysis, the district court considered Scrutinizer's application for U.S. trademark protection. The record gave the district court "no hint" why Scrutinizer had filed the application. *Id.* at 243. The district court did not find that contact conclusive, but said that "it does confirm [Scrutinizer's] desire to deal with the American market." *Id.* at 243.

We granted this interlocutory appeal on the district court's recommendation.

II.

A. Standard of Review

The district court held that Plixer had made a prima facie showing of personal jurisdiction. On prima facie review, we take the plaintiff's evidentiary proffers as true and we consider uncontradicted facts proffered by the defendant. *C.W. Downer & Co. v. Bioriginal Food & Sci. Corp.*, 771 F.3d 59, 65 (1st Cir. 2014). The plaintiff's burden is to proffer evidence "sufficient to support findings of all facts essential to personal jurisdiction" without relying on unsupported allegations. *A Corp. v. All Am. Plumbing, Inc.*, 812 F.3d 54, 58 (1st Cir. 2016). We review de novo the district court's conclusion that Plixer met its burden of proffering sufficient evidence to support findings of all facts essential to personal jurisdiction. *See Foster-Miller, Inc. v. Babcock & Wilcox Can.*, 46 F.3d 138, 147 (1st Cir. 1995).

B. Personal Jurisdiction

Plixer's basis for asserting personal jurisdiction over Scrutinizer is Federal Rule of Civil Procedure 4(k)(2). Rule 4(k)(2) has three requirements: (1) the cause of action must arise under federal law; (2) the defendant must not be subject to the personal jurisdiction of any state court of general jurisdiction; and (3) the federal court's exercise of personal jurisdiction must comport with due process. *United States v. Swiss Am. Bank, Ltd.* (*Swiss I*), 191 F.3d 30, 38 (1st Cir. 1999). All parties agree that the first two requirements are met here. The question is whether personal jurisdiction comports with due process.

This is a federal question case, so constitutional limits on jurisdiction come from the Due Process Clause of the Fifth Amendment. *United States v. Swiss Am. Bank, Ltd.* (*Swiss II*), 274 F.3d 610, 618 (1st Cir. 2001). The Fifth Amendment Due Process Clause requires the plaintiff to "show that the defendant has adequate contacts with the United States as a whole, rather than with a particular state." *Id.* To see if Scrutinizer's nationwide contacts are adequate, we turn to the familiar "minimum contacts" framework.

Due process requires that the defendant "have certain minimum contacts with [the forum] such that the maintenance of the suit does not offend 'traditional notions of fair play and substantial justice.'" *Int'l Shoe Co. v. Washington*, 326 U.S. 310, 316 (1945) (*quoting Milliken v. Meyer*, 311 U.S. 457, 463 (1940)). Plixer has asserted specific personal jurisdiction over Scrutinizer, so the minimum contacts inquiry has three prongs: relatedness, purposeful availment, and reasonableness. That is, Plixer must show that (1) its claim directly arises out of or relates to the defendant's forum activities; (2) the defendant's forum contacts represent a purposeful availment of the privilege of conducting activities in that forum, thus invoking the benefits and protections of the forum's laws and rendering the defendant's involuntary presence in the forum's courts foreseeable; and (3) the exercise of jurisdiction is reasonable. *A Corp.*, 812 F.3d at 59.

Plixer must show that it has met all three requirements to establish personal jurisdiction. *C.W. Downer*, 771 F.3d at 65. Scrutinizer has conceded the first requirement; we hold that Plixer has met the remaining two.

1. Purposeful Availment

Plixer bears the burden of demonstrating that Scrutinizer has purposefully availed "itself of the privilege of conducting activities within the forum [ ], thus invoking the benefits and protections of its laws." *Hanson v. Denckla*, 357 U.S. 235, 253 (1958). The purposeful availment requirement ensures that the exercise of jurisdiction is essentially voluntary and foreseeable, *C.W. Downer*, 771 F.3d at 66, not premised on a defendant's "random, fortuitous, or attenuated contacts," *Carreras v. PMG Collins, LLC*, 660 F.3d 549, 555 (1st Cir. 2011) (*quoting Burger King Corp. v. Rudzewicz*, 471 U.S. 462, 475 (1985)). This requirement applies to foreign defendants. *See C.W. Downer*, 771 F.3d at 66 (*citing J. McIntyre Mach., Ltd. v. Nicastro*, 564 U.S. 873, 885–87 (2011) (plurality opinion)).

The Supreme Court has not definitively answered how a defendant's online activities translate into contacts for purposes of the minimum contacts analysis. Instead, in *Walden v. Fiore*, it "le[ft] questions about virtual contacts for another day." 571 U.S. 277, 290 n.9 (2014). In the absence of Supreme Court guidance, we are extremely reluctant to fashion any general guidelines beyond those that exist in law, so we emphasize that our ruling is specific to the facts of this case.

This Court has twice addressed "virtual contacts," but in cases whose factual scenarios are far-removed from this one. One baseline principle has emerged: a website operator does not necessarily purposefully avail itself of the benefits and protections of every state in which its website is accessible. *See A Corp.*, 812 F.3d at 61 (holding that "the mere availability of a passive website" cannot by itself subject a defendant to personal jurisdiction in the forum); *Cossaboon v. Maine Med. Ctr.*, 600 F.3d 25, 35 (1st Cir. 2010) (noting that the running of a "website that is visible in a forum and that gives information about a company and its products" cannot alone support the exercise of jurisdiction) (*quoting McBee v. Delica Co.*, 417 F.3d 107, 124 (1st Cir. 2005)). The district court held that Scrutinizer had not merely made its website available in the United States; it had used that website to engage "in sizeable and continuing commerce with United States customers." *Plixer*, 293 F.Supp.3d at 242. As a result, Scrutinizer "should not be surprised at United States-based litigation." *Id.* We agree.

Scrutinizer attacks the district court ruling with three arguments. Scrutinizer first says that it did no more than enter its product into the stream of commerce. Second, it argues that its contacts with the United States were not its own but instead the product of its customers' unilateral actions. And third, it says that because it did not specifically target the United States it is not subject to specific personal jurisdiction in a United States forum. We reject each attack.

First, this is not the prototypical stream-of-commerce case. Cases including a standard stream-of-commerce analysis usually involve entities who cannot necessarily predict or control where downstream their products will land; intervening actors like distributors may take the products to unforeseeable markets. But no intervening actor can bring Scrutinizer's product somewhere unexpected. Scrutinizer's service goes only to the customers that Scrutinizer has accepted. This means that we have an objectively clearer picture of Scrutinizer's intent to serve the forum, the crux of the purposeful availment inquiry. *See C.W. Downer*, 771 F.3d at 66.

World-Wide Volkswagen Corp. v. Woodson, 444 U.S. 286 (1980), illustrates a significant difference between this case and the prototypical stream-of-commerce one. There, the Audi-owning plaintiff drove his car into Oklahoma, a market that the defendant did not then serve. *See id.* at 295. A car manufacturer cannot limit where its customers take its product. In contrast, Scrutinizer can take steps to limit access to its website. For instance, Scrutinizer could design its site to not interact with U.S. users, *cf. Yahoo! Inc. v. La Ligue Contre Le Racisme et L'Antisemitisme*, 433 F.3d 1199, 1203 (9th Cir. 2006), but it has not done so. And Scrutinizer could take the low-tech step of posting a disclaimer that its service is not intended for U.S. users. *See Bensusan Restaurant Corp. v. King*, 126 F.3d 25, 27 (2d Cir. 1997); cf. *Illinois v. Hemi Group LLC*, 622 F.3d 754, 755 (7th Cir. 2010). Again, it has not done so. Instead, Scrutinizer's website (https://scrutinizer-ci.com/) is globally accessible. In fact, the website gives no indication that it is not meant for U.S. consumption, or even that it is run by a German company.

Scrutinizer says that we should not consider whether a defendant blocks access to its website — access-blocking software is imperfect, developing technology. If a defendant tries to limit U.S. users' ability to access its website, however, that is surely relevant to its intent not to serve the United States. The converse is true here: Scrutinizer's failure to implement such restrictions, coupled with its substantial U.S. business, provides an objective measure of its intent to serve customers in the U.S. market and thereby profit. And Scrutinizer's warnings about the inefficacy of access-blocking technology are misplaced based on the record before us. Scrutinizer can track where its customers are from — it provided state-by-state customer information in response to Plixer's discovery request.

Second, Scrutinizer voluntarily served U.S. customers. Specific personal jurisdiction must be based on a defendant's voluntary contact with the forum; it "may not rest on the 'unilateral activity of another party or a third person.'" *Ticketmaster-New York, Inc. v. Alioto*, 26 F.3d 201, 208 (1st Cir. 1994) (*quoting Burger King*, 471 U.S. at 475). Here, Scrutinizer made a globally accessible website and U.S. customers used that website to purchase and pay for Scrutinizer's service. Further, Scrutinizer knew that it was serving U.S. customers and took no steps to limit its website's reach or block its use by U.S. customers. After three-and-a-half years of knowingly serving U.S. customers, Scrutinizer cannot now claim that its contact with the United States was involuntary. *Cf. Walden*, 571 U.S. at 286 (noting that the exercise of jurisdiction may be constitutional even though a defendant's forum contacts are "intertwined with his transactions or interactions with the plaintiff or other parties").

Third, Scrutinizer's purposeful U.S. contacts were sufficient to put Scrutinizer on notice that it should expect to be haled into U.S. court. Scrutinizer has "target[ed] the world" by making its website globally accessible. *See Nicastro*, 564 U.S. at 890 (Breyer, J., concurring). But Scrutinizer says that it could not reasonably anticipate specific jurisdiction because it did not specifically target the United States with its business. We disagree.

Supreme Court precedent does not establish specific targeting of a forum as the only means of showing that the purposeful availment test has been met. The Supreme Court last considered personal jurisdiction over a foreign defendant in *Nicastro*. The *Nicastro* plurality would have permitted the exercise of jurisdiction "only where the defendant can be said to have targeted the forum." 564 U.S. at 882. That is the same rule that Scrutinizer urges us to adopt. However, this rule did not command a majority on the Court and so is not binding here. "When a fragmented Court decides a case and no single rationale explaining the result enjoys the assent of five justices, 'the holding of the Court may be viewed as that position taken by those Members who concurred in the judgment on the narrowest grounds.'" *Marks v. United States*, 430 U.S. 188, 193 (1977) (*quoting Gregg v. Georgia*, 428 U.S. 153, 169 n.15 (1976) (opinion of Stewart, Powell, and Stevens, JJ)). In *Nicastro*, Justice Breyer held that "resolving [the] case require[d] no more than adhering to [the Supreme Court's] precedents." 564 U.S. at 890 (Breyer, J., concurring). That holding was the narrowest and so controls here. *Accord Williams v. Romarm*, SA, 756 F.3d 777, 784 (D.C. Cir. 2014) (finding Justice Breyer's concurring opinion controlling under *Marks*); *Ainsworth v. Moffett Eng'g, Ltd.*, 716 F.3d 174, 178 (5th Cir. 2013) (same); *AFTG-TG, LLC v. Nuvoton Tech. Corp.*, 689 F.3d 1358, 1363 (Fed. Cir. 2012) (same).

Justice Breyer found no jurisdiction under any of the Court's precedents. There was "no 'regular ... flow' or 'regular course' of sales," as required by the concurrences in *Asahi Metal Industry Co. v. Superior Court of California*, 480 U.S. 102 (1987), *see id.* at 117 (Brennan, J., concurring in part and concurring in judgment); *id.* at 122 (Stevens, J., concurring in part and concurring in judgment). *Nicastro*, 564 U.S. at 889 (Breyer, J., concurring). And there was "no 'something more'" that the *Asahi* plurality would have required, *see Asahi*, 480 U.S. at 111–12 (opinion of O'Connor, J.). *Nicastro*, 564 U.S. at 889 (Breyer, J., concurring). As such, "the plurality's seemingly strict no-jurisdiction rule" was unnecessary. *Id.* at 890. Justice Breyer also criticized New Jersey's test, which would subject a foreign defendant to jurisdiction so long as it "knows or reasonably should know that its products are distributed through a nationwide distribution system that might lead to those products being sold in any of the fifty states." *Id.* at 891. We need not adopt such a broad rule as the New Jersey court's to uphold the exercise of specific personal jurisdiction over Scrutinizer.

Ultimately, although a close call, we conclude that the German company could have "reasonably anticipated" the exercise of specific personal jurisdiction based on its U.S. contacts. Scrutinizer's "regular flow or regular course of sales" in the United States show that it has purposefully availed itself of the U.S. forum. The record does not reveal what percentage of Scrutinizer's business came from the United States. Nor does the record reveal whether Scrutinizer ever did an online trademark search for the term "Scrutinizer," either before or after it sought U.S. customers. But the record does show that Scrutinizer used its website to obtain U.S. customer contracts. Those contracts yielded nearly $200,000 in business over three-and-a-half years. This is not a situation where a defendant merely made a website accessible in the forum. *See, e.g., Scottsdale Capital Advisors Corp. v. The Deal, LLC*, 887 F.3d 17, 21 (1st Cir. 2018). Instead, Scrutinizer's voluntary service of the U.S. market and its not insubstantial income from that market show that it could have "reasonably anticipated" being haled into U.S. court.

This holding accords with Supreme Court precedent. In *Keeton v. Hustler Magazine*, the Supreme Court upheld the exercise of jurisdiction because the magazine publisher defendant had "continuously and deliberately exploited the [forum] market." 465 U.S. 770, 781 (1984). The magazine publisher had a nationwide market—it had not targeted the forum particularly—but the court held it should reasonably anticipate suit based on its "substantial number of" sales. *Id.*

This conclusion is also consistent with post-Nicastro rulings from around the country. For instance, the en banc Oregon Supreme Court found a regular course of sales where the defendant sold "over 1,100 CTE battery chargers within Oregon over a two-year period," with in-state sales totaling about $30,000. *Willemsen v. Invacare Corp.*, 352 Or. 191, 282 P.3d 867, 874, 871 (2012) (en banc). This "pattern of sales" made the exercise of personal jurisdiction over the defendant constitutional. *Id.* at 877. In contrast, a New Jersey federal district court found no regular course of sales when, over about a year, fewer than ten in-state sales brought the defendant "less than $3,383 in revenue." *Oticon, Inc. v. Sebotek Hearing Sys., LLC*, 865 F.Supp.2d 501, 514–15 (D. N.J. 2011). "Such scant sales activity" did not "justify the exercise of specific jurisdiction" there. *Id.* Scrutinizer's U.S. business more resembles the former example than the latter one.

Further, our holding is in accord with those of our sister circuits. The Ninth Circuit upheld the exercise of jurisdiction over a defendant who "continuously and deliberately exploited" the forum market, and who specifically targeted its website at the forum market. *Mavrix Photo, Inc. v. Brand Techs., Inc.*, 647 F.3d 1218, 1230 (9th Cir. 2011). The Sixth Circuit upheld the exercise of jurisdiction over a defendant who "regularly [chose] to do business with [forum] residents." *Bird v. Parsons*, 289 F.3d 865, 875 (6th Cir. 2002). In contrast, the Seventh Circuit found no jurisdiction when the plaintiff pointed to no litigation-related in-forum sales and to no efforts to specifically target the forum. *See Advanced Tactical Ordnance Sys., LLC v. Real Action Paintball, Inc.*, 751 F.3d 796, 801, 803 (7th Cir. 2014). And the Fourth Circuit found that a Maryland court had no jurisdiction over a nonprofit defendant who limited its services to Illinois and who accepted, over ten years, less than $1,600 in donations from Marylanders. *See Carefirst of Md., Inc. v. Carefirst Pregnancy Ctrs., Inc.*, 334 F.3d 390, 395, 401 (4th Cir. 2003). We think each of these are consistent with our holding that Scrutinizer is subject to personal jurisdiction.

Finally, we consider Scrutinizer's U.S. trademark application, filed after this litigation began. We have stated that "in most cases, contacts coming into existence after the cause of action arose will not be relevant." *Harlow*, 432 F.3d at 62. But we made that statement in a suit where the plaintiff alleged medical malpractice. *See id.* at 53. That discrete-in-time tort is unlike the alleged continuing "tortious" conduct at issue here. Moreover, *Harlow* based its general rule on the concept of "relatedness," *see id.* at 62, which Scrutinizer has conceded. Because Scrutinizer's trademark application lies outside Harlow's rule, we consider the application for whatever impact it has.

The parties have not spoken to why Scrutinizer filed the application, except to suggest that filing may be a precondition for sending a cease and desist letter. We agree with the district court that this contact confirms Scrutinizer's desire to deal with the U.S. market, but does not "tip the scales." *Plixer*, 293 F.Supp.3d at 243.

2. Reasonableness

Though Plixer has satisfied the first two prongs of the analysis, we must still see whether the exercise of jurisdiction here is fair and reasonable. We consider five "gestalt" factors:

> (1) the defendant's burden of appearing [in the forum], (2) the [forum's] interest in adjudicating the dispute, (3) the plaintiff's interest in obtaining convenient and effective relief, (4) the judicial system's interest in obtaining the most effective resolution of the controversy, and (5) the common interests of all sovereigns in promoting substantive social policies.

Ticketmaster, 26 F.3d at 209 (*citing Burger King*, 471 U.S. at 477). These factors typically "play a larger role in cases ... where the minimum contacts question is very close." *C.W. Downer*, 771 F.3d at 69 (*quoting Adelson v. Hananel* (*Adelson I*), 510 F.3d 43, 51 (1st Cir. 2007)). The defendant bears the burden of establishing that the exercise of jurisdiction would be unreasonable, *Burger King*, 471 U.S. at 477, and, although the question is close, Scrutinizer has not shown that it would be unreasonable to assert jurisdiction here.

We consider first the burden on Scrutinizer. That a foreign defendant is involved here is of some weight. Subjecting a defendant to a foreign legal system poses "unique burdens" that carry "significant weight in assessing the reasonableness" of jurisdiction. *Asahi*, 480 U.S. at 114. We acknowledge this significant burden, but do not find it dispositive. Scrutinizer does substantial and recurrent business in the U.S. As such it "cannot wholly expect to escape the reach of United States courts." *Jet Wine & Spirits, Inc. v. Bacardi & Co., Ltd.*, 298 F.3d 1, 12 (1st Cir. 2002). Although this factor points in Scrutinizer's favor, its weight is somewhat diminished by Scrutinizer's substantial U.S. business.

For further support, Scrutinizer points to the burden of cross-Atlantic travel. But "mounting an out-of-state defense most always means added trouble and cost," *BlueTarp Fin., Inc. v. Matrix Constr. Co.*, 709 F.3d 72, 83 (1st Cir. 2013), and modern travel "creates no especially ponderous burden for business travelers," *Pritzker v. Yari*, 42 F.3d 53, 64 (1st Cir. 1994). A defendant hoping to show that travel burdens should make the difference must show that those burdens are "special or unusual." *BlueTarp*, 709 F.3d at 83 (quoting *Hannon v. Beard*, 524 F.3d 275, 285 (1st Cir. 2008)) (internal quotation marks omitted). Scrutinizer has not done so. As we noted in *C.W. Downer*, many of the case's logistical challenges "can be resolved through the use of affidavits and video devices." 771 F.3d at 70.

On the second factor, Scrutinizer does not dispute that the United States has an interest in adjudicating a dispute over the application of U.S. trademark law. *See, e.g., McBee v. Delica Co., Ltd.*, 417 F.3d 107, 121 (1st Cir. 2005) (noting the "core purposes of the Lanham Act, which are both to protect the ability of American consumers to avoid confusion and to help assure a trademark's owner that it will reap the financial and reputational rewards associated with having a desirable name or product"). Further, the United States has an interest in remedying an alleged injury that occurs in the United States. *See Keeton*, 465 U.S. at 777.

As to the final three factors, Scrutinizer presents no arguments tending to show that the exercise of jurisdiction would be unreasonable here. It concedes that Plixer has an interest in obtaining effective relief in a U.S. forum. And it doubts whether the fourth and fifth factors apply. Even if the last two factors "weighed against jurisdiction, this alone would be 'insufficient to tip the constitutional balance' on the facts presented here." *Adelson v. Hananel (Adelson II)*, 652 F.3d 75, 84 (1st Cir. 2011) (*quoting Adelson I*, 510 F.3d at 51).

The gestalt factors do not support Scrutinizer's protests. "When minimum contacts have been established, often the interests of the plaintiff and the forum in the exercise of jurisdiction will justify even the serious burdens placed on the alien defendant." *Asahi*, 480 U.S. at 114. Scrutinizer has not shown that the exercise of jurisdiction here would be unreasonable.

* * *

Our role is limited to adjudicating the precise issue in front of us. This appeal raised only one issue: whether the exercise of specific personal jurisdiction over Scrutinizer would violate the Fifth Amendment's Due Process Clause. We conclude that on the facts here the exercise of jurisdiction would not violate the Due Process Clause.

III.

The judgment of the district court is affirmed.

Exercise 2-15. Synthesis Exercise

You have now read a series of United States Supreme Court cases on personal jurisdiction. Given the cases as they currently stand, how would you approach a personal jurisdiction problem? What would the steps in your decision making process look like? This exercise involves case synthesis—putting together what you know about the cases you have read into a coherent approach to solving the particular legal problem. Your synthesis should include different lines of personal jurisdiction analysis—one for general jurisdiction and one for specific jurisdiction. How do you determine whether to use a general or specific jurisdiction analysis?

Recall the chapter problem. In it, Sherry wishes to arrange for a wrongful death lawsuit in California. Her brother, Kevin, died in a plane crash in Scotland. Both Sherry and Kevin are citizens of Scotland. The plane involved in the crash was manufactured by the Piper Aircraft Company in Pennsylvania. The plane was owned and operated by corporations that were organized under the laws of the United Kingdom. The four other passengers and the pilot, all of whom died in the crash, are from Scotland. In addition, a preliminary investigation into the crash revealed that there might have been a mechanical problem with the plane's propeller.

Hartzell Propeller, Inc., manufactured the plane's propeller in Ohio. Hartzell does not sell any propellers to plane manufacturers in California. Piper incorporated the Hartzell propeller into the plane at issue in this case in its Pennsylvania plant. Piper manufactures planes in Pennsylvania that are used in California and throughout the rest of the United States as well as in foreign countries. Using case synthesis, analyze whether a California state court would have jurisdiction over Piper and Hartzell. Would a Pennsylvania court have jurisdiction over Piper and Hartzell?

7. Professional Development Reflection

In cases like *Daimler v. Bauman*, and the *Piper* case that forms the basis for the chapter problem, the plaintiffs' attorneys fought hard to keep the lawsuit in a United States court. Why did they try to bring these cases in the United States courts when the lawsuits involved alleged wrongdoing that occurred in another country and foreign citizens? Was it ethical for the lawyers in these cases to choose a U.S. forum? Would it have been unethical for the plaintiffs' attorneys not to at least attempt to bring these lawsuits in a United States court?

Chapter 3
Notice and Opportunity to Be Heard

1. Chapter Problem

Service and a Hearing

Pat and Dee are former friends and business partners who are in a dispute involving a $200,000 loan from Pat to Dee. Pat and Dee met in college. They shared a passion for writing code and developing new types of software. After graduation, they became business partners in a tech start up. To grow the business, Pat and Dee needed to invest capital. Pat invested $200,000 of Pat's money in the business. Since Dee did not have cash to invest, Pat loaned Dee $200,000 to invest in the business as well.

Pat and Dee developed innovative apps to facilitate personal fitness. Unfortunately, the apps never really caught on. Eventually, the business burned through the $400,000 investment. As cash became tighter, the relationship between Pat and Dee grew more and more adversarial. Pat began to spend less time on the business and more time on other, more successful ventures. After two years of intense effort, the business failed.

After the failure of their business, Pat and Dee each moved on to other tech ventures. Pat demanded that Dee repay the $200,000 loan, plus 10% interest, under the terms of the promissory note Pat and Dee signed. Dee refused to pay because Dee believed that Pat had forgiven the debt during the time when Dee was spending 100 hours per week on the business while Pat was spending very little time on the business but lots of time on other ventures.

The relationship between Pat and Dee became toxic. Pat threatened to sue Dee for $200,000 plus interest. Dee told Pat, "Go ahead. Sue me. You know that I owe you nothing. You will never get a dime out of me, lawsuit or not. Good luck trying to serve me. Even if you get a judgment, you will never be able to collect."

Pat's lawyer intends to file a lawsuit against Dee in federal court in Wisconsin to collect on the loan. During an extensive pre-suit investigation, Pat's lawyer has learned:

- Dee sometimes lives with a roommate in a gated community in Madison, Wisconsin;

- Dee regularly visits aging parents in Chicago, Illinois;

- Dee has successfully avoided service when other potential plaintiffs have tried to initiate lawsuits;
- Dee has transferred substantial sums to bank accounts outside of the U.S.;
- Dee currently has $100,000 worth of computer equipment at an office in Milwaukee, Wisconsin.

1. Pat's lawyer has drafted a summons and complaint. What options does Pat's lawyer have for serving those documents to successfully initiate the lawsuit?

2. Assume that Pat successfully serves the summons and complaint and then immediately uses Wisconsin's prejudgment attachment statutes to seize Dee's computer equipment in Milwaukee without any prior notice to Dee. Does Dee's lawyer have plausible grounds to attack the constitutionality of that seizure?

2. Introduction

Chapter 2 explored the limits on a court's exercise of personal jurisdiction over defendants imposed by the Due Process Clause of the U.S. Constitution and state long arm statutes. Chapter 3 addresses additional constitutional and statutory constraints on notice to the defendant in a lawsuit and the defendant's opportunity to be heard.

- Section 3 — Due Process Limits on Notice
- Section 4 — Statutory Limits on Notice
- Section 5 — Due Process Limits on the Opportunity to Be Heard
- Section 6 — Professional Development Reflection

3. Due Process Limits on Notice

Exercise 3-1. *Mullane v. Central Hanover Bank & Trust*

As you read *Mullane*, use your case analysis skills to address the following questions:

1. Facts — What is the purpose of the common trust funds authorized under New York Banking Law?

2. Facts — What is the purpose of the judicial settlement of common trust fund accounts required by the New York Banking Law?

3. Issue — What was the issue before the court in *Mullane*?

4. Law — At a minimum, what does the Due Process Clause of the 14th Amendment require before a person is deprived of life, liberty, or property?

5. Law—What test does the court adopt to determine the constitutional validity of notice?

6. Application—What type of notice is constitutional for the beneficiaries whose interests or addresses are unknown? Why?

7. Application—What type of notice is constitutional for the beneficiaries whose interests and addresses are known? Why?

8. Application—Why isn't personal service required for any of the beneficiaries?

Mullane v. Central Hanover Bank & Trust Co.

339 U.S. 306 (1950)

Mr. Justice Jackson delivered the opinion of the Court.

This controversy questions the constitutional sufficiency of notice to beneficiaries on judicial settlement of accounts by the trustee of a common trust fund established under the New York Banking Law. The New York Court of Appeals considered and overruled objections that the statutory notice contravenes requirements of the Fourteenth Amendment and that by allowance of the account beneficiaries were deprived of property without due process of law.

Common trust fund legislation is addressed to a problem appropriate for state action. Mounting overheads have made administration of small trusts undesirable to corporate trustees. In order that donors and testators of moderately sized trusts may not be denied the service of corporate fiduciaries, the District of Columbia and some thirty states other than New York have permitted pooling small trust estates into one fund for investment administration. The income, capital gains, losses and expenses of the collective trust are shared by the constituent trusts in proportion to their contribution. By this plan, diversification of risk and economy of management can be extended to those whose capital standing alone would not obtain such advantage.

* * *

In January, 1946, Central Hanover Bank and Trust Company established a common trust fund in accordance with these provisions [of New York Banking Law], and in March, 1947, it petitioned the Surrogate's Court for settlement of its first account as common trustee. During the accounting period a total of 113 trusts, approximately half *inter vivos* and half testamentary, participated in the common trust fund, the gross capital of which was nearly three million dollars. The record does not show the number or residence of the beneficiaries, but they were many and it is clear that some of them were not residents of the State of New York.

The only notice given beneficiaries of this specific application was by publication in a local newspaper in strict compliance with the minimum requirements of N.Y. Banking Law.... Thus the only notice required, and the only one given, was by newspaper publication setting forth merely the name and address of the trust company, the name and the date of establishment of the common trust fund, and a list of all participating estates, trusts or funds.

At the time the first investment in the common fund was made on behalf of each participating estate, however, the trust company, pursuant to the requirements of [N.Y. Banking Law] had notified by mail each person of full age and sound mind whose name and address was then known to it and who was "entitled to share in the income therefrom * * * (or) * * * who would be entitled to share in the principal if the event upon which such estate, trust or fund will become distributable should have occurred at the time of sending such notice." Included in the notice was a copy of those provisions of the Act relating to the sending of the notice itself and to the judicial settlement of common trust fund accounts.

* * *

Appellant appeared specially, objecting that notice and the statutory provisions for notice to beneficiaries were inadequate to afford due process under the Fourteenth Amendment, and therefore that the court was without jurisdiction to render a final and binding decree. Appellant's objections were entertained and overruled, the Surrogate holding that the notice required and given was sufficient. A final decree accepting the accounts has been entered, affirmed by the Appellate Division of the Supreme Court and by the Court of Appeals of the State of New York.

The effect of this decree, as held below, is to settle all questions respecting the management of the common fund. We understand that every right which beneficiaries would otherwise have against the trust company, either as trustee of the common fund or as trustee of any individual trust, for improper management of the common trust fund during the period covered by the accounting is sealed and wholly terminated by the decree.

* * *

Quite different from the question of a state's power to discharge trustees is that of the opportunity it must give beneficiaries to contest. Many controversies have raged about the cryptic and abstract words of the Due Process Clause but there can be no doubt that at a minimum they require that deprivation of life, liberty or property by adjudication be preceded by notice and opportunity for hearing appropriate to the nature of the case.

In two ways this proceeding does or may deprive beneficiaries of property. It may cut off their rights to have the trustee answer for negligent or illegal impairments of their interests. Also, their interests are presumably subject to diminution in the proceeding by allowance of fees and expenses to one who, in their names but without their knowledge, may conduct a fruitless or uncompensatory contest. Certainly the proceeding is one in which they may be deprived of property rights and hence notice and hearing must measure up to the standards of due process.

Personal service of written notice within the jurisdiction is the classic form of notice always adequate in any type of proceeding. But the vital interest of the State in bringing any issues as to its fiduciaries to a final settlement can be served only if interests or claims of individuals who are outside of the State can somehow be determined. A construction of the Due Process Clause which would place impossible or impractical obstacles in the way could not be justified.

Against this interest of the State we must balance the individual interest sought to be protected by the Fourteenth Amendment.... [T]he fundamental requisite of due process of law is the opportunity to be heard. This right to be heard has little reality or worth unless one is informed that the matter is pending and can choose for himself whether to appear or default, acquiesce or contest.

The Court has not committed itself to any formula achieving a balance between these interests in a particular proceeding or determining when constructive notice may be utilized or what test it must meet. Personal service has not in all circumstances been regarded as indispensable to the process due to residents, and it has more often been held unnecessary as to nonresidents....

An elementary and fundamental requirement of due process in any proceeding which is to be accorded finality is notice reasonably calculated, under all the circumstances, to apprise interested parties of the pendency of the action and afford them an opportunity to present their objections. *Milliken v. Meyer*, 311 U.S. 311 (1940). The notice must be of such nature as reasonably to convey the required information, and it must afford a reasonable time for those interested to make their appearance. But if with due regard for the practicalities and peculiarities of the case these conditions are reasonably met the constitutional requirements are satisfied.

* * *

But when notice is a person's due, process which is a mere gesture is not due process. The means employed must be such as one desirous of actually informing the absentee might reasonably adopt to accomplish it. The reasonableness and hence the constitutional validity of any chosen method may be defended on the ground that it is in itself reasonably certain to inform those affected or, where conditions do not reasonably permit such notice, that the form chosen is not substantially less likely to bring home notice than other of the feasible and customary substitutes.

It would be idle to pretend that publication alone as prescribed here, is a reliable means of acquainting interested parties of the fact that their rights are before the courts. It is not an accident that the greater number of cases reaching this Court on the question of adequacy of notice have been concerned with actions founded on process constructively served through local newspapers. Chance alone brings to the attention of even a local resident an advertisement in small type inserted in the back pages of a newspaper, and if he makes his home outside the area of the newspaper's normal circulation the odds that the information will never reach him are large indeed. The chance of actual notice is further reduced when as here the notice required does not even name those whose attention it is supposed to attract, and does not inform acquaintances who might call it to attention....

Nor is publication here reinforced by steps likely to attract the parties' attention to the proceeding. It is true that publication traditionally has been acceptable as notification supplemental to other action which in itself may reasonably be expected to convey a warning. The ways for an owner with tangible property are such that he usually arranges means to learn of any direct attack upon his possessory or proprietary rights. Hence, libel of a ship, attachment of a chattel or entry upon real estate in the name of law may reasonably be expected to come promptly to the owner's attention. When the state within which the owner has located such property seizes it for some reason, publication or posting affords an additional measure of notification. A state may indulge the assumption that one who has left tangible property in the state either has abandoned it or that he has left some caretaker under a duty to let him know that it is being jeopardized.

* * *

In the case before us there is, of course, no abandonment. On the other hand these beneficiaries do have a resident fiduciary as caretaker of their interest in this property. But it is their caretaker who in the accounting becomes their adversary. Their trustee is released from giving notice of jeopardy, and no one else is expected to do so....

This Court has not hesitated to approve of resort to publication as a customary substitute in another class of cases where it is not reasonably possible or practicable to give more adequate warning. Thus it has been recognized that, in the case of persons missing or unknown, employment of an indirect and even a probably futile means of notification is all that the situation permits and creates no constitutional bar to a final decree foreclosing their rights.

Those beneficiaries represented by appellant whose interests or whereabouts could not with due diligence be ascertained come clearly within this category. As to them the statutory notice is sufficient. However great the odds that publication will never reach the eyes of such unknown parties, it is not in the typical case much more likely to fail than any of the choices open to legislators endeavoring to prescribe the best notice practicable.

Nor do we consider it unreasonable for the State to dispense with more certain notice to those beneficiaries whose interests are either conjectural or future or, although they could be discovered upon investigation, do not in due course of business come to knowledge of the common trustee. Whatever searches might be required in another situation under ordinary standards of diligence, in view of the character of the proceedings and the nature of the interests here involved we think them unnecessary. We recognize the practical difficulties and costs that would be attendant on frequent investigations into the status of great numbers of beneficiaries, many of whose interests in the common fund are so remote as to be ephemeral; and we have no doubt that such impracticable and extended searches are not required in the name of due process. The expense of keeping informed from day to day of substitutions among even current income beneficiaries and presumptive remaindermen, to say nothing of the far greater number of contingent beneficiaries, would impose a severe burden on the plan, and would likely dissipate its advantages....

Accordingly we overrule appellant's constitutional objections to published notice insofar as they are urged on behalf of any beneficiaries whose interests or addresses are unknown to the trustee.

As to known present beneficiaries of known place of residence, however, notice by publication stands on a different footing. Exceptions in the name of necessity do not sweep away the rule that within the limits of practicability notice must be such as is reasonably calculated to reach interested parties. Where the names and post office addresses of those affected by a proceeding are at hand, the reasons disappear for resort to means less likely than the mails to apprise them of its pendency.

The trustee has on its books the names and addresses of the income beneficiaries represented by appellant, and we find no tenable ground for dispensing with a serious effort to inform them personally of the accounting, at least by ordinary mail to the record addresses. Certainly sending them a copy of the statute months and perhaps years in advance does not answer this purpose. The trustee periodically remits their income to them, and we think that they might reasonably expect that with or apart from their remittances word might come to them personally that steps were being taken affecting their interests....

Of course personal service even without the jurisdiction of the issuing authority serves the end of actual and personal notice, whatever power of compulsion it might lack. However, no such service is required under the circumstances. This type of trust presupposes a large number of small interests. The individual interest does not stand alone but is identical with that of a class. The rights of each in the integrity of the fund and the fidelity of the trustee are shared by many other beneficiaries. Therefore notice reasonably certain to reach most of those interested in objecting is likely to safeguard the interests of all, since any objections sustained would inure to the benefit of all. We think that under such circumstances reasonable risks that notice might not actually reach every beneficiary are justifiable.

* * *

The statutory notice to known beneficiaries is inadequate, not because in fact it fails to reach everyone, but because under the circumstances it is not reasonably calculated to reach those who could easily be informed by other means at hand. However it may have been in former times, the mails today are recognized as an efficient and inexpensive means of communication. Moreover, the fact that the trust company has been able to give mailed notice to known beneficiaries at the time the common trust fund was established is persuasive that postal notification at the time of accounting would not seriously burden the plan.

* * *

We hold the notice of judicial settlement of accounts required by the New York Banking Law is incompatible with the requirements of the Fourteenth Amendment as a basis for adjudication depriving known persons whose whereabouts are also known of substantial property rights. Accordingly the judgment is reversed and the cause remanded for further proceedings not inconsistent with this opinion.

Reversed.

Exercise 3-2. *Greene v. Lindsey*

1. Recall *Shaffer v. Heitner* from Chapter 2, addressing *in personam* and *in rem* bases for personal jurisdiction. How is the majority opinion in *Greene* consistent with *Shaffer*?

2. What legal rules and facts does the majority rely on to invalidate service by posting in *Greene*?

3. On what basis does the dissent conclude that posting does not violate due process in *Greene*?

Greene v. Lindsey

456 U.S. 444 (1982)

Justice Brennan delivered the opinion of the Court.

A Kentucky statute provides that in forcible entry or detainer actions, service of process may be made under certain circumstances by posting a summons on the door of a tenant's apartment. The question presented is whether this statute, as applied to tenants in a public housing project, fails to afford those tenants the notice of proceedings initiated against them required by the Due Process Clause of the Fourteenth Amendment.

I

Appellees Linnie Lindsey, Barbara Hodgens, and Pamela Ray are tenants in a Louisville, Ky., housing project. Appellants are the Sheriff of Jefferson County, Ky., and certain unnamed Deputy Sheriffs charged with responsibility for serving process in forcible entry and detainer actions. In 1975, the Housing Authority of Louisville initiated detainer actions against each of appellees, seeking repossession of their apartments. Service of process was made pursuant to [a Kentucky statute], which states: "If the officer directed to serve notice on the defendant in forcible entry or detainer proceedings cannot find the defendant on the premises mentioned in the writ, he may explain and leave a copy of the notice with any member of the defendant's family thereon over sixteen (16) years of age, and if no such person is found he may serve the notice by posting a copy thereof in a conspicuous place on the premises. The notice shall state the time and place of meeting of the court."

In each instance, notice took the form of posting a copy of the writ of forcible entry and detainer on the door of the tenant's apartment. Appellees claim never to have seen these posted summonses; they state that they did not learn of the eviction proceedings until they were served with writs of possession, executed after default judgments had been entered against them, and after their opportunity for appeal had lapsed.

Thus without recourse in the state courts, appellees filed this suit as a class action in the United States District Court for the Western District of Kentucky, seeking declaratory and injunctive relief under 42 U.S.C. § 1983. They claimed that the notice procedure employed as a predicate to these eviction proceedings did not satisfy the minimum standards of constitutionally adequate notice described in *Mullane v. Central Hanover Bank & Trust*, and that the Commonwealth of Kentucky had thus failed to afford them the due process of law guaranteed by the Fourteenth Amendment....

On cross-motions for summary judgment, the District Court granted judgment for appellants. In an unreported opinion, the court noted that some 70 years earlier, in *Weber v. Grand Lodge of Kentucky, F. & A. M.,* 169 F. 522 (1909), the Court of Appeals for the Sixth Circuit had held that constructive notice by posting on the door of a building, provided an adequate constitutional basis upon which to commence an eviction action, on the ground that it was reasonable for the State to presume that a notice posted on the door of the building in dispute would give the tenant actual notice in time to contest the action. Although the District Court recognized that "conditions have changed since the decision in *Weber* ... and ... that there is undisputed testimony in this case that notices posted on the apartment doors of tenants are often removed by other tenants," the court nevertheless concluded that the procedures employed did not deny due process in light of the fact "that posting only comes into play after the officer directed to serve notice cannot find the defendant on the premises.

The Court of Appeals for the Sixth Circuit reversed the grant of summary judgment in favor of appellants. Acknowledging that its decision in *Weber* directed a contrary result, the Court of Appeals examined the doctrinal basis of that decision, and concluded that it rested in part on distinctions between actions *in rem* and actions *in personam* that had been drawn in cases such as *Pennoyer v. Neff,* and that had been substantially undercut by intervening decisions of this Court. In overruling *Weber,* the Court of Appeals cited *International Shoe Co. v. Washington, Mullane,* and *Shaffer v. Heitner* as cases calling for a more realistic appraisal of the adequacy of process provided by the State. Turning to the circumstances of this case, ... the Court of Appeals noted that while there may have been "a time when posting provided a surer means of giving notice than did mailing, [t]hat time has passed. The uncontradicted testimony by process servers themselves that posted summonses are not infrequently removed by persons other than those served constitutes effective confirmation of the conclusion that notice by posting 'is not reasonably calculated to reach those who could easily be informed by other means at hand,'" (quoting *Mullane*). The court held, therefore, that the notice provided pursuant to [the Kentucky statute] was constitutionally deficient. We noted probable jurisdiction and now affirm.

II

A

The fundamental requisite of due process of law is the opportunity to be heard. And the right to be heard has little reality or worth unless one is informed that the matter is pending and can choose for himself whether to appear or default, acquiesce or contest. Personal service guarantees actual notice of the pendency of a legal action; it thus presents the ideal circumstance under which to commence legal proceedings against a person, and has traditionally been deemed necessary in actions styled *in personum.*

Nevertheless, certain less rigorous notice procedures have enjoyed substantial acceptance throughout our legal history; in light of this history and the practical obstacles to providing personal service in every instance, we have allowed judicial proceedings to be prosecuted in some situations on the basis of procedures that do not carry with them the same certainty of actual notice that inheres in personal service. But we have also clearly recognized that the Due Process Clause does prescribe a constitutional minimum: "An elementary and fundamental requirement of due process in any proceeding which is to be accorded finality is *notice reasonably calculated, under all the circumstances, to apprise interested parties of the pendency of the action* and afford them an opportunity to present their objections." *Mullane* (emphasis added). It is against this standard that we evaluate the procedures employed in this case.

B

Appellants argue that because a forcible entry and detainer action is an action *in rem*, notice by posting is *ipso facto* constitutionally adequate. Appellees concede that posting has traditionally been deemed appropriate for *in rem* proceedings, but argue that detainer actions can now encompass more than the simple issue of the tenant's continued right to possession, and that they therefore require the more exacting forms of notice customarily provided for proceedings *in personam*.

As in *Mullane*, we decline to resolve the constitutional question based upon the determination whether the particular action is more properly characterized as one *in rem* or *in personum*. That is not to say that the nature of the action has no bearing on a constitutional assessment of the reasonableness of the procedures employed. The character of the action reflects the extent to which the court purports to extend its power, and thus may roughly describe the scope of potential adverse consequences to the person claiming a right to more effective notice.... In this case, appellees have been deprived of a significant interest in property: indeed, of the right to continued residence in their homes. In light of this deprivation, it will not suffice to recite that because the action is *in rem*, it is only necessary to serve notice upon the thing itself. The sufficiency of notice must be tested with reference to its ability to inform people of the pendency of proceedings that affect their interests. In arriving at the constitutional assessment, we look to the realities of the case before us....

It is, of course, reasonable to assume that a property owner will maintain superintendence of his property, and to presume that actions physically disturbing his holdings will come to his attention. The frequent restatement of this rule impresses upon the property owner the fact that a failure to maintain watch over his property may have significant legal consequences for him, providing a spur to his attentiveness, and a consequent reinforcement to the empirical foundation of the principle. Upon this understanding, a State may in turn conclude that in most cases, the secure posting of a notice on the property of a person is likely to offer that property owner sufficient warning of the pendency of proceedings possibly affecting his interests.

The empirical basis of the presumption that notice posted upon property is adequate to alert the owner or occupant of property of the pendency of legal proceedings would appear to make the presumption particularly well founded where notice is posted at a residence. With respect to claims affecting the continued possession of that residence, the application of this presumption seems particularly apt: If the tenant has a continuing interest in maintaining possession of the property for his use and occupancy, he might reasonably be expected to frequent the premises; if he no longer occupies the premises, then the injury that might result from his not having received actual notice as a consequence of the posted notice is reduced. Short of providing personal service, then, posting notice on the door of a person's home would, in many or perhaps most instances, constitute not only a constitutionally acceptable means of service, but indeed a singularly appropriate and effective way of ensuring that a person who cannot conveniently be served personally is actually apprised of proceedings against him.

But whatever the efficacy of posting in many cases, it is clear that, in the circumstances of this case, merely posting notice on an apartment door does not satisfy minimum standards of due process. In a significant number of instances, reliance on posting results in a failure to provide actual notice to the tenant concerned. Indeed, appellees claim to have suffered precisely such a failure of actual notice. As the process servers were well aware, notices posted on apartment doors in the area where these tenants lived were not infrequently removed by children or other tenants before they could have their intended effect. Under these conditions, notice by posting on the apartment door cannot be considered a reliable means of acquainting interested parties of the fact that their rights are before the courts.

Of course, the reasonableness of the notice provided must be tested with reference to the existence of "feasible and customary" alternatives and supplements to the form of notice chosen.... [T]he statute requires the officer serving notice to make a visit to the tenant's home and to attempt to serve the writ personally on the tenant or some member of his family. But if no one is at home at the time of that visit, as is apparently true in a "good percentage" of cases, posting follows forthwith. Neither the statute, nor the practice of the process servers, makes provision for even a second attempt at personal service, perhaps at some time of day when the tenant is more likely to be at home. The failure to effect personal service on the first visit hardly suggests that the tenant has abandoned his interest in the apartment such that mere *pro forma* notice might be held constitutionally adequate.

[A]s we noted in *Mullane*, the mails provide an efficient and inexpensive means of communication, upon which prudent men will ordinarily rely in the conduct of important affairs. Notice by mail in the circumstances of this case would surely go a long way toward providing the constitutionally required assurance that the State has not allowed its power to be invoked against a person who has had no opportunity to present a defense despite a continuing interest in the resolution of the controversy. Particularly where the subject matter of the action also happens to be the mailing address of the defendant, and where personal service is ineffectual, notice by mail may reasonably be relied upon to provide interested persons with actual notice of judicial proceedings. Where an inexpensive and efficient mechanism such as mail service is available to enhance the reliability of an otherwise unreliable notice procedure, the State's continued exclusive reliance on an ineffective means of service is not notice "reasonably calculated to reach those who could easily be informed by other means at hand." *Mullane.*

III

We conclude that in failing to afford appellees adequate notice of the proceedings against them before issuing final orders of eviction, the State has deprived them of property without the due process of law required by the Fourteenth Amendment. The judgment of the Court of Appeals is therefore

Affirmed.

Justice O'Connor, with whom The Chief Justice and Justice Rehnquist join, dissenting.

Today, the Court holds that the Constitution prefers the use of the Postal Service to posted notice. The Court reaches this conclusion despite the total absence of any evidence in the record regarding the speed and reliability of the mails. The sole ground for the Court's result is the scant and conflicting testimony of a handful of process servers in Kentucky. On this flimsy basis, the Court confidently overturns the work of the Kentucky Legislature and, by implication, that of at least 10 other States.

* * *

The Court rejects these established procedures as unconstitutional, though it does not cite a single case, other than the decision below, supporting its position that notice by posting is constitutionally inadequate in summary eviction proceedings. Instead, the Court relies solely on the deposition testimony of a few Kentucky process servers.

The testimony is hardly compelling. For example, one process server, Mr. S. Carter Bacon, reported having seen children in the Village West housing development pull down posted writs "probably a couple of times." The Court neglects to mention, however, that another process server, cast doubt on Mr. Bacon's testimony by stating: "The six months I was working at it there was no occasion where I saw anyone tear the Writs off of the door." Another process server testified that in order to avoid problems with children, the process servers "always put [the writs] up high. So we never had any problems with that." Corroborating this testimony, moreover, is the testimony of yet another process server, who asserted: "we always try to put the paper up above where, a, say a small child can't reach it." This server, asked whether he had "had complaints about small children ripping them off," answered that he had never had a complaint and had never seen a child try to rip a notice off.

The Court, holds that notice via the mails is so far superior to posted notice that the difference is of constitutional dimension. How the Court reaches this judgment remains a mystery, especially since the Court is unable, on the present record, to evaluate the risks that notice mailed to public housing projects might fail due to loss, misdelivery, lengthy delay, or theft. Furthermore, the advantages of the mails over posting, if any, are far from obvious. It is no secret, after all, that unattended mailboxes are subject to plunder by thieves. Moreover, unlike the use of the mails, posting notice at least gives assurance that the notice has gotten as far as the tenant's door.

* * *

I respectfully dissent.

Exercise 3-3. Due Process Notice Analysis — *Dusenbery v. United States*

In a forfeiture action brought by the government, do service by publication and certified mail to the prison where the defendant is incarcerated comport with due process when the defendant does not receive actual notice of the action?

When executing a search warrant, the FBI seized the defendant's car, gun, knife, drugs, and over $221,000 in cash. After defendant pled guilty to violations of the Controlled Substances Act, the FBI initiated forfeiture proceedings in order to dispose of defendant's property. The FBI followed the applicable service statute, which required the FBI to serve notice of the forfeiture action on the defendant via publication for three consecutive weeks in a newspaper of general circulation and via certified mail. The FBI sent the certified mail to the prison where defendant was incarcerated. The normal process for mail delivery at the prison was to log in the mail and then deliver it to prisoners during mail call. When the government did not receive a reply, the FBI disposed of the defendant's property. After being released from prison, the defendant challenged the forfeiture on the grounds that his due process rights were violated because he did not receive actual notice of the forfeiture and because it would not have been difficult for the government to have provided it. Apply *Mullane* and *Greene*. Did the FBI's manner of service comport with due process?

See Dusenbery v. United States, 534 U.S. 161 (2002).

Exercise 3-4. Due Process Notice Analysis — *Jones v. Flowers*

When notice of a tax sale is mailed to the owner and returned undelivered, must the government take additional reasonable steps to provide notice before taking the owner's property?

In 1967, petitioner Gary Jones purchased a house in Little Rock, Arkansas. He lived in the house with his wife until they separated in 1993. Jones then moved into an apartment in Little Rock, and his wife continued to live in the house. Jones paid his mortgage each month for 30 years, and the mortgage company paid Jones's property taxes. After Jones paid off his mortgage in 1997, the property taxes went unpaid, and the property was certified as delinquent. In April 2000, the Commissioner of State Lands (Commissioner), attempted to notify Jones of his tax delinquency and his right to redeem the property by mailing a certified letter to Jones at the house. Nobody was home to sign for the letter, and nobody appeared at the post office to retrieve the letter, so the post office returned the unopened packet to the Commissioner marked "unclaimed." Two years later, the Commissioner mailed another certified letter to Jones at the North Bryan Street address, attempting to notify him that his house would be sold to Flowers if he did not pay his taxes. Like the first letter, the second was also returned to the Commissioner marked "unclaimed." Flowers purchased the house, which the parties stipulated in the trial court had a fair market value of $80,000, for $21,042.15. Flowers had an unlawful detainer notice delivered to the property. The notice was served on Jones's daughter, who contacted Jones and notified him of the tax sale. Jones filed a lawsuit in Arkansas state court against the Commissioner and Flowers, alleging that the Commissioner's failure to provide notice of the tax sale and of Jones's right to redeem resulted in the taking of his property without due process. Apply *Mullane, Greene,* and *Dusenbery*. Did the government's manner of service comport with due process?

See *Jones v. Flowers,* 547 U.S. 220 (2006).

Exercise 3-5. Due Process Notice Policy

In *Mullane*, the Court sets out the basic requirements of procedural due process: "An elementary and fundamental requirement of due process in any proceeding which is to be accorded finality is notice reasonably calculated, under all the circumstances, to apprise interested parties of the pendency of the action and afford them an opportunity to present their objections." Why then does the court reject the argument that due process requires that the defendant receive *actual* notice of the initiation of civil litigation in *Greene* and *Jones*? What policies support the Court's rejection of an actual notice requirement? What policies would support an actual notice requirement?

4. Statutory Limits on Notice

The Due Process Clauses of the Fifth and Fourteenth Amendments to the U.S. Constitution, as interpreted by the Supreme Court in cases such as *Mullane, Greene, Dusenbery,* and *Jones,* establish the minimum requirements for notice. Those constitutional requirements are designed to protect parties in civil litigation from deprivations of life, liberty, and property without adequate notice of the lawsuit.

Nothing prevents federal and state legislatures from providing *additional* protection for parties via notice requirements set out in federal and state statutes and rules. In fact, every state court system and the federal court system have enacted notice provisions in statutes and rules. In federal court, the fundamental requirements of notice to initiate a lawsuit are provided in Federal Rule of Civil Procedure 4. In state court, the statutes and rules of the forum state set out notice requirements.

When a plaintiff initiates a lawsuit, the method of service on the defendant must comply with both the U.S. Constitution and the notice rules and statutes of the court in which the case is filed. For example, to initiate a suit in Florida state court, service must comply with the U.S. Constitution and Florida rules and statutes. In federal court, service must meet the requirements of the U.S. Constitution and Rule 4.

Exercise 3-6. Statutory Analysis — Rule 4 Service Requirements

Chapter 1 laid out a five-step process for analyzing a statute or rule. The first step is to carefully read the words of the applicable statutory provision. The following questions address the basic notice requirement of Rule 4. Carefully read Rule 4(a), (c), (l), and (m) and answer these questions.

1. Who is allowed to serve process?

2. What must be served?

3. When must service be accomplished?

4. How should a private process server prove service?

The second step in statutory analysis is to identify the purpose of the statute.

5. Rule 4(c)(2) prevents parties to the lawsuit from serving process. Why do you think the rule drafters included this provision?

Practice Pointer

To get a better sense of how the requirements of Rule 4 play out in practice, the following three documents are examples of a summons, complaint, and proof of service in a very simple hypothetical lawsuit in federal court.

UNITED STATES DISTRICT COURT FOR
THE EASTERN DISTRICT OF WASHINGTON

Fran Bell, Plaintiff

CV 2019303

v.   Summons

Jan Ring, Defendant

To:
Jan Ring
311 Sherman Avenue
Coeur d'Alene, ID 83814

A lawsuit has been filed against you.

Within 21 days after service of this summons on you (not counting the day you received it) you must serve on the plaintiff an answer to the attached complaint or a motion under Rule 12 of the Federal Rules of Civil Procedure. The answer or motion must be served on the plaintiff's attorney, whose name and address is:

Pat Munn
Attorney for Plaintiff
111 North Street
Spokane, WA 99220
(509) 555-1212
PMunn@gmail.com

If you fail to respond, judgment by default will be entered against you for the relief demanded in the complaint. You also must file your answer or motion with the court.

August 15, 2019

Fran Alliera

Fran Alliera
Clerk of Court

UNITED STATES DISTRICT COURT FOR
THE EASTERN DISTRICT OF WASHINGTON

Fran Bell, Plaintiff

CV 2019303

v.

Complaint for Negligence

Jan Ring, Defendant

1. Plaintiff is a citizen of Washington. Defendant is a citizen of Idaho. The amount in controversy exceeds $75,000. This court has jurisdiction under 28 U.S.C § 1332.

2. On May 5, 2019, at the corner of Dakota and Sharp in Spokane, Washington, Defendant negligently drove a motor vehicle into Plaintiff's motor vehicle.

3. Defendant was negligent because Defendant failed to stop at a stop sign. The Spokane Police Department issued Defendant a citation for failing to stop at the stop sign. (See attached Police Report # 9914456.)

4. As a result of Defendant's negligence, Plaintiff suffered a broken arm, severe cuts to the face, and multiple bruises. As a result of those injuries, Plaintiff has incurred lost wages, medical expenses, and pain. In addition, plaintiff's 2016 Honda Accord was destroyed.

Plaintiff requests judgment against Defendant for damages in an amount to be proved at trial and for the costs of this action.

Dated: August 15, 2019.

Pat Munn

Pat Munn
Attorney for Plaintiff
111 North Street
Spokane, WA 99220
(509) 555-1212
PMunn@gmail.com

Civil Action No. CV 2019303

Proof of Service

The Summons for _Jan Ring_ was received by me on _August 15, 2019_.

_____ I personally served the Summons on the individual at
(*place*) _____
on (*date*) _____.

_X_ I left the Summons at the individual's residence or usual place of abode
with (*name*) _Fran Ring_, a person of suitable age and discretion who resides
there, on (*date*) _August 16, 2019_.

_____ I served the Summons on (*name of individual*) _____
who is designated by law to accept service of process on behalf of (*name of
organization*) _____ on (*date*) _____.

_____ Other (*specify*) _____
_____ .

_____ I returned the Summons unexecuted because _____
_____ .

My fees are _$45_ (*travel*) and _$35_ (*services*) for a total of _$80_.

I declare under penalty of perjury that this information is true.

(*date*) _August 16, 2019_

C.J. Vale
Vale Legal Process

Exercise 3-7. Rule 4(e) — Service on Individuals

Read FRCP 4(e) regarding service on individuals.

In *Kolker*, how does Judge Pieras apply the facts to each subpart of the rule to assess whether service was proper?

Kolker v. Hurwitz

269 F.R.D. 119 (D. Puerto Rico 2010)

Plaintiff Paul Kolker ("Kolker") and his wife purchased lot 19 in the community Surfside in Palmas del Mar with the idea of building a vacation home. However, Plaintiff and his wife never built the vacation home because Plaintiff's wife became ill and passed away in 1992.

Kolker occasionally visited Palmas del Mar after his wife's death and noticed that Defendant Charles Hurwitz ("Hurwitz") had cemented over a portion of the green area in front of Hurwitz's residence to build a pool and gazebo. Also, Hurwitz installed a generator and a large garbage receptacle in the green area adjacent to Kolker's property. Defendants Surfside Development Corporation and Hurwitz did not seek and/or receive Kolker's consent to the acts committed by Defendants in the covenanted green area.

In January 2007, Hurwitz called Kolker in order to seek his permission to add further structures in the green area adjacent to lot 19. Kolker denied Hurwitz's request because the restrictive covenants preserving the existing green area had been determinative in his decision to purchase lot 19. During the same time period, Kolker met with the Palmas del Mar Architectural Review Board and informed them of his objections to Hurwitz's adverse possession of the covenanted green areas.

* * *

Plaintiff alleges that, in January 2007, Hurwitz, through Palmas Realty Corporation, tried to coerce Kolker to accept the breach of the covenant by offering him lesser properties. The properties offered did not possess the 280-degree view and untouched green area found in lot 19. As such, Kolker declined the offers.

On July 21, 2009, Defendant Palmas del Mar Properties, Inc. sent Kolker a letter stating that Kolker had unreasonably withheld his consent to allow construction of the green area.... The parties continued to exchange correspondence and met with each other in the hopes of resolving their disagreements.

* * *

Kolker then filed the complaint in this case on September 4, 2009. The first cause of action seeks a declaratory judgment that the existing pool, gazebo, generator, and garbage receptacle are in breach of the Palmas Master Plan and Puerto Rico law. The second cause of action seeks to enjoin Defendants from using the existing structures and building additional structures in the covenanted green areas because the existing and proposed structures violate Puerto Rico law and the Palmas Master Plan.... The third cause of action charges that the existing structures constitute a breach of contract. Lastly, the fourth cause of action requests damages pursuant to Puerto Rico's tort action statute....

* * *

Defendants move for the Court to dismiss Plaintiff's complaint. Specifically, Defendants Charles Hurwitz and Barbara Hurwitz argue that Plaintiff has failed to properly serve them....

Plaintiffs attempted to serve Defendants Charles Hurwitz and Barbara Hurwitz by having Joe Barak leave copies of the complaint and summons with a security guard at the entrance of their apartment complex. Defendants argue that this attempt by Plaintiff does not comply with the applicable rules and, as such, the action should be dismissed pursuant to Federal Rule of Civil Procedure ("FRCP") 12(b)(5).

When serving an individual within a judicial district of the United States, process can served by following the laws of the jurisdiction where either the district court sits or where service is made. FRCP 4(e)(1). Also, service could be made by either: (1) delivering a copy of the summons and of the complaint to the individual personally; (2) leaving a copy of the summons and complaint at the individual's dwelling or usual place of abode with someone of suitable age and discretion who resides there; or (3) delivering a copy of the summons and complaint to an agent authorized by appointment or by law to receive service of process. FRCP 4(e)(2).

1. Service Under FRCP 4(e)(1)

Under FRCP 4(e)(1), service would have to be made, in this case, under the laws of either Puerto Rico or Texas because this Court is located in the District of Puerto and because service was attempted on Defendants Charles Hurwitz and Barbara Hurwitz in Texas.

i. Puerto Rico Laws

Puerto Rico Rules of Civil Procedure provide for service of process upon a nonresident by publication of an edict in a newspaper of general circulation in Puerto Rico and by mailing a copy of the summons and complaint to Defendant by certified mail with acknowledgment of receipt within ten days of the edict being published.

In the instant case, Plaintiff sought, and was granted, permission to serve Defendants Charles Hurwitz and Barbara Hurwitz by publication.

However, Plaintiff has failed to present evidence that the edict was in fact published. Moreover, Plaintiff has not submitted evidence that he sent Defendants a copy of the summons and complaint by certified mail with acknowledgment of receipt. As such, Plaintiff has not complied with the Puerto Rico rules on service of process.

ii. Texas Laws

Pursuant to the Texas Rules of Civil Procedure, service is made by either delivering a copy of the summons and complaint to Defendant personally or by mailing a copy of each to Defendant by registered or certified mail return receipt requested. When Plaintiff is unable to personally serve Defendant, the rules provide for service by either leaving a copy of the complaint and summons with anyone over sixteen years of age at Defendant's usual place of business or usual place of abode, or in any other manner that will be reasonably effective to give Defendant notice of the suit. See TexR.Civ.P. 106(b). However, to effect service under Texas Rule 106(b), Plaintiff must file an affidavit showing his unsuccessful attempts to serve process upon Defendant and must receive Court authorization.

In the instant case, Plaintiff has presented no evidence that he has either personally served Defendants Charles Hurwitz and Barbara Hurwitz, or mailed copy of the complaint and summons to Defendants by registered or certified mail return receipt requested. Also, in this case, Plaintiff has not obtained leave from Court to serve Defendants through Texas Rule 106(b). Plaintiff has therefore not complied with the Texas rules for service of process.

2. Service Under FRCP 4(e)(2)

Under FRCP 4(e)(2), service can be made by either: (A) delivering a copy of the summons and the complaint to the individual personally; (B) leaving a copy of the summons and complaint at the individual's dwelling or usual place of abode with someone of suitable age and discretion who resides there; or (C) delivering a copy of the summons and complaint to an agent authorized by appointment or by law to receive service of process.

i. Personal Service

In the instant case, there is no evidence, and Plaintiff does not argue, that Defendants Charles Hurwitz and Barbara Hurwitz were personally served....

ii. Leaving Copy at Individual's Dwelling or Usual Place of Abode with Someone of Suitable Age and Discretion who Resides There

Plaintiff argues that service was appropriate when Plaintiff's process server left a copy of the summons and the complaint with the security guard in Defendants Charles Hurwitz and Barbara Hurwitz's apartment complex because the individual had an obligation to notify Defendants.

Defendants counter that Plaintiff did not comply with FRCP 4(e)(2)(B) when the process server left the complaint and summons with the security guard....

After considering the arguments, the Court agrees with Defendants. The treatise and case cited by Plaintiff does not support his contention that service was performed correctly in this case. The treatise cited by Kolker indicates that under some circumstances leaving a copy of the summons and complaint with a building manager and/or landlord may be sufficient to satisfy the requirements of FRCP 4(e)(2)(B). 4A Charles Allan Wright & Arthur R. Miller, *Federal Practice and Procedure*, 1096 (3d. ed.). However, the key to whether service is sufficient in these cases is whether the person who receives the complaint and summons has an obligation to relay the information to the tenants or guests.... Similarly, other cases have relied on the need of some form of similar authorization, whether express or by customary practice, to receive correspondence on behalf of the building tenants.

In the instant case ... there is no evidence or argumentation supporting a finding that the security guard had any authority to accept and sign for deliveries to the Hurwitz's residence or that the security guard at the Hurwitz's residence had a duty to inform Defendants of any correspondence received. Accordingly, Plaintiff's attempt to serve process on Charles Hurwitz and Barbara Hurwitz is not sufficient to satisfy the requirements of FRCP 4(e)(2)(B).

iii. Authorized Agent

In the instant case, there is also no evidence that Plaintiff has served the summons and complaint to an agent authorized by appointment or by law to receive service of process. The only argument by Plaintiff is that Defendants' attorney refused to accept service on Charles Hurwitz and Barbara Hurwitz behalf. However, no evidence has been presented that Charles Hurwitz and/or Barbara Hurwitz have either appointed or authorized their attorney to receive service on their behalf....

Accordingly, the Court finds that Plaintiff has failed to properly serve Defendants Charles Hurwitz, Barbara Hurwitz, and the conjugal partnership formed between them. Thus, the Court will dismiss the complaint without prejudice against said Defendants.

Exercise 3-8. Rule 4(e)(2)(B) Analysis

In *Kolker*, Judge Pieras concluded that the service on the security guard did not satisfy Rule 4(e)(2)(B) because there was no evidence that the security guard had authority to accept and sign for deliveries or that the security guard had a duty to inform defendants of correspondence received. Read Rule 4(e)(2)(B) carefully.

1. Identify all of the requirements of Rule 4(e)(2)(B).

2. Identify the purpose of Rule 4(e)(2)(B). Why do you think the rule drafters allow this type of service?

3. Make an argument based on the language of Rule 4(e)(2)(B) that the plaintiffs failed to demonstrate compliance with the requirements of the rule.

Exercise 3-9. *National Development Corp. v. Triad*

Like *Kolker*, the following case deals with Rule 4(e)(2)(B). In *Kolker*, the court applied that rule to the facts of the case. In *National Development Corp.*, the court not only applies the rule, it interprets the rule.

1. How does the court's interpretation expand and contract the scope of "usual house of abode?"

2. What role, if any, do you think the defendant's nationality, lifestyle, and wealth played in this decision?

Nat'l Develop. Corp. v. Triad Holding Corp.

930 F.2d 253 (2d Cir. 1991)

For more than a half-century, the Federal Rules of Civil Procedure have permitted service upon an individual by leaving a summons and complaint "at the individual's dwelling house or usual place of abode." ... With approximately 1.16 billion passengers annually engaging in international airline travel, and an estimated five million people with second homes in the United States, determining a person's "dwelling house or usual place of abode" is no longer as easy as in those early days of yesteryear.

We ponder this problem upon review of an order of the United States District Court for the Southern District of New York refusing ... to vacate a default judgment entered against defendant-appellant Adnan Khashoggi ("Khashoggi"). In essence, Khashoggi argues that, although he has numerous residences world-wide, his "dwelling house or usual place of abode" is in Saudi Arabia and, absent personal delivery, service of process pursuant to [FRCP 4(e)(2)(B)] is proper only at his compound there. Therefore, he concludes that a purported service at his apartment at the Olympic Tower in New York was void and conferred no jurisdiction. We disagree and affirm the order of the district court.

Background

Plaintiff-appellee National Development Company ("NDC") is a corporation wholly-owned by the Republic of the Philippines. The dispute between NDC and Khashoggi arose from the dissolution of Triad Asia, Ltd. ("Triad Asia"), a joint venture formed by NDC and Triad Holding Corporation ("Triad Holding"), a company controlled by Khashoggi. NDC claims that Khashoggi converted approximately $3.5 million of Triad Asia's assets....

* * *

It is the service of the summons and complaint on Khashoggi on December 22, 1986 that forms the basis of this appeal. On that day, NDC handed a copy of the summons and complaint to Aurora DaSilva, a housekeeper at Khashoggi's Olympic Tower condominium apartment on Fifth Avenue.... On September 23, 1987, after Khashoggi failed to appear in the district court action, a default judgment was entered.... On October 25, 1989, Khashoggi filed a motion pursuant to FRCP 60(b)(4) to vacate the ... 1987 default judgment....

The district court held an evidentiary hearing on the service of process issue, at which Khashoggi and his housekeeper, Ms. DaSilva, testified. Ms. DaSilva confirmed that Khashoggi was in New York and staying at his Olympic Tower apartment from December 15 through December 23, 1986. The parties stipulated that Ms. DaSilva accepted delivery of a copy of the summons and complaint on December 22, 1986. Ms. DaSilva testified that during 1986, Khashoggi stayed at his Olympic Tower apartment for a total of 34 days.

To call it an apartment is perhaps to denigrate it. Valued at approximately $20–25 million, containing more than 23,000 square feet on at least two floors, the Olympic Tower apartment contains a swimming pool, a sauna, an office and four separate furnished "apartments" to accommodate guests and Khashoggi's brother. The complex requires the attention of two full-time and three part-time staff persons.

Khashoggi testified that he is a citizen of Saudi Arabia and resides in a ten-acre, six-villa compound in its capital city, Riyadh. In 1986, Khashoggi stayed in the Riyadh compound for only three months. During the remaining nine months, Khashoggi travelled throughout the world, staying another two months at a "home" in Marabella, Spain. Khashoggi testified that he purchased the Olympic Tower apartment in 1974. Khashoggi personally hired contractors to complete a remodeling project costing over $1 million. The results of the remodeling project were prominently featured in the June 1984 issue of *House and Garden*.

With regard to the NDC lawsuit, Khashoggi testified that he first learned of it in 1989, when NDC personally served him with its post-judgment discovery requests.

In an opinion dated June 11, 1990, the district court denied Khashoggi's motion to vacate the default judgment.... [T]he district court found that the Olympic Tower apartment was not a "dwelling house or usual place of abode" for purposes of [FRCP 4(e)(2)(B)], but that service was nevertheless proper because Khashoggi had actual notice. We reject the notion that "actual notice" suffices to cure a void service, but we affirm the district court because we conclude that the Olympic Tower apartment is properly characterized as Khashoggi's "dwelling house or usual place of abode," and service at that location was therefore valid.

Discussion

[FRCP 4(e)(2)(B)] permits service by delivering a copy of the summons and of the complaint to the individual personally or by leaving copies at the individual's dwelling house or usual place of abode with some person of suitable age and discretion [who resides there].

There is no dispute that Ms. DaSilva, with whom the papers were left, is a person of suitable age and discretion then residing at the Olympic Tower apartment. We are called upon only to determine whether the Olympic Tower apartment was Khashoggi's "dwelling house or usual place of abode", terms that thus far have eluded "any hard and fast definition." 2 J. Moore, Moore's Federal Practice ¶ 4.11[2] at 4-128 (2d ed. 1990)....

As leading commentators observe, "[i]n a highly mobile and affluent society, it is unrealistic to interpret [FRCP 4(e)(2)(B)] so that the person to be served has only one dwelling house or usual place of abode at which process may be left." *Id.* at 79–80. This case presents a perfect example of how ineffectual so wooden a rule would be.

Khashoggi is a wealthy man and a frequent intercontinental traveller. Although he is a citizen of Saudi Arabia and considers the Riyadh compound his domicile, he spent only three months there in 1986. Khashoggi testified that the Olympic Tower apartment was only one of twelve locations around the world where he spends his time, including a "home" which he owns in Marabella, Spain, and "houses" in Rome, Paris and Monte Carlo. The conclusion that only one of these locations is Khashoggi's "usual place of abode", since he does not "usually" stay at any one of them, commends itself to neither common sense nor sound policy.

There is nothing startling in the conclusion that a person can have two or more "dwelling houses or usual places of abode," provided each contains sufficient indicia of permanence.... Some courts have expressly required that the defendant sought to be served be actually living at the residence at the time service is effected....

Although federal practice under [FRCP 4(e)(2)(B)] has not produced consistent results, *compare Capitol Life Ins. Co. v. Rosen*, 69 F.R.D. 83

(E.D.Pa.1975) (service at defendant's brother's house sufficient where defendant frequently journeyed but kept a room and personal belongings at brother's house and paid rent therefor) *and Blackhawk Heating & Plumbing Co. v. Turner*, 50 F.R.D. 144 (D.Ariz.1970) (service at house in Arizona deemed proper where evidence suggested that defendant was living at the time in California but received actual notice) *with First Nat'l Bank & Trust Co. v. Ingerton*, 207 F.2d 793 (10th Cir.1953) (usual place of abode was hotel in New Mexico notwithstanding defendant's temporary stay in Denver) *and Shore v. Cornell-Dubilier Elec. Corp.*, 33 F.R.D. 5 (D.Mass.1963) (service on defendant who divided his time between residences in New York and New Jersey improper where made at a house he owned in Massachusetts that was used by him only when conducting business there), we believe that application of the rule to uphold service is appropriate under these facts.

It cannot seriously be disputed that the Olympic Tower apartment has sufficient indicia of permanence. Khashoggi owned and furnished the apartment and spent a considerable amount of money remodelling it to fit his lifestyle. Indeed, in July 1989, Khashoggi listed the Olympic Tower apartment as one of his residences in a bail application submitted in connection with the criminal proceedings. Since Khashoggi was actually living in the Olympic Tower apartment on December 22, 1986, service there on that day was, if not the most likely method of ensuring that he received the summons and complaint, reasonably calculated to provide actual notice of the action. Surely, with so itinerant a defendant as Khashoggi, plaintiff should not be expected to do more.

We conclude, therefore, that service of process on Khashoggi should be sustained under [FRCP 4(e)(2)(B)] because the Olympic Tower apartment was a "dwelling house or usual place of abode" in which he was actually living at the time service was effected. We express no opinion upon the validity of service had Khashoggi not been actually living at the Olympic Tower apartment when service was effected.

Exercise 3-10. Service by Publication

Most states allow service by publication in some circumstances. The following statute (Arizona Rule of Civil Procedure 4.1(l)) is typical:

Service by Publication.

(1) Generally. A party may serve by publication only if:

(A) the last-known address of the person to be served is in Arizona but:

(i) the serving party, despite reasonably diligent efforts, has been unable to ascertain the person's current address: or

(ii) the person to be served has intentionally avoided service of process; and

(B) service by publication is the best means practicable in the circumstances for providing the person with notice of the action's commencement.

(2) Procedure

(A) Generally. Service by publication is accomplished by publishing the summons and a statement describing how a copy of the pleading being served may be obtained at least once a week for 4 successive weeks:

(i) in a newspaper published in the county where the action is pending; and

(ii) if the last known address of the person to be served is in a different county, in a newspaper in that county.

***

(D) Effective Date of Service. Service is complete 30 days after the summons and statement is first published in all newspapers where publication is required.

Return to the facts of the Chapter Problem in Section 1. Pat's lawyer had hired a process server who has not succeeded in serving Dee personally because Dee has been hiding out. The process server then tried to serve Dee by leaving the summons and complaint with Dee's roommate, but the guard at Dee's gated community would not allow the process server into the community. Consequently, Pat's lawyer served process by publication, following the requirements of Wisconsin's service by publication rule (assume that the Wisconsin rule is identical to the Arizona rule).

1. Would Pat's manner of service satisfy Federal Rule of Civil Procedure 4? Explain why or why not.

2. Would Pat's manner of service satisfy the Due Process Clause? Explain why or why not.

Exercise 3-11. Serving a Corporation

In *Piper Aircraft Co. v. Reyno*, assume that you are the plaintiffs' lawyer and you decide to bring suit in federal court in California. You are considering how to serve process on defendant Piper Aircraft Co., the manufacturer of the plane. Your factual and legal research reveals the following:

- State statutes in California allow plaintiffs to serve process on corporations in several ways, including via certified mail anywhere in the United States to an officer or director of the corporation;

- Piper's president and vice president work most days at Piper's headquarters in Pittsburgh, Pennsylvania;

- Piper's board of directors will meet next week in Honolulu;

- Piper has appointed an agent for service of process in Delaware; and

- Pennsylvania case law allows plaintiffs to serve process on corporations via email to an officer, if the officer acknowledges receipt of the email.

1. Identify at least four options Pat has for serving the summons and complaint on Piper in compliance with Rule 4(h).

2. Do any of those options fail to satisfy the requirements of the Due Process clause?

Exercise 3-12. Waiver of Service

Return to the facts of the Chapter Problem in Section 1 above. While researching service options for a suit in federal court, Pat's lawyer finds the waiver of service provisions of Rule 4(d). Carefully read the rule and answer these questions. For questions 1–4, assume Pat's lawyer decided to request that Dee waive service:

1. What documents must accompany the request for waiver?

2. Could Pat email the request for waiver and appropriate documents to Dee?

3. Rule 4(d)(3) contains an incentive for Dee to agree to waive service— Dee would have 60 days to answer the complaint, rather than 21 days that Rule 12(a) usually gives a defendant to answer. What penalty does Rule 4(d) impose on Dee if Dee refuses to waive service?

4. If Dee waives service, does Dee waive proper court defenses?

5. Despite the provisions of Rule 4(d), it is highly unlikely that Pat would choose to request that Dee waive service. Why?

6. In what circumstances would you choose to request that the defendant waive service?

5. Opportunity to Be Heard

In *Mullane*, the Supreme Court captured in a sentence the most basic protections of procedural due process: "An elementary and fundamental requirement of due process in any proceeding which is to be accorded finality is notice reasonably calculated, under all the circumstances, to apprise interested parties of the pendency of the action and afford them an opportunity to present their objections." 339 U.S. 306, 314 (1950). When, if ever, can the government impinge on a person's liberty or property interests without prior notice and a hearing? That question is the subject of the next case.

Connecticut v. Doehr

501 U.S. 1 (1991)

Justice White delivered an opinion, Parts I, II, and III of which are the opinion of the Court.

This case requires us to determine whether a state statute that authorizes prejudgment attachment of real estate without prior notice or hearing, without a showing of extraordinary circumstances, and without a requirement that the person seeking the attachment post a bond, satisfies the Due Process Clause of the Fourteenth Amendment. We hold that, as applied to this case, it does not.

I

On March 15, 1988, petitioner John F. DiGiovanni submitted an application to the Connecticut Superior Court for an attachment in the amount of $75,000 on respondent Brian K. Doehr's home in Meriden, Connecticut. DiGiovanni took this step in conjunction with a civil action for assault and battery that he was seeking to institute against Doehr in the same court. The suit did not involve Doehr's real estate, nor did DiGiovanni have any pre-existing interest either in Doehr's home or any of his other property.

Connecticut law authorizes prejudgment attachment of real estate without affording prior notice or the opportunity for a prior hearing to the individual whose property is subject to the attachment. The State's prejudgment remedy statute provides, in relevant part:

> "The court or a judge of the court may allow the prejudgment remedy to be issued by an attorney without hearing as provided in sections 52-278c and 52-278d upon verification by oath of the plaintiff or of some competent affiant, that there is probable cause to sustain the validity of the plaintiff's claims and (1) that the prejudgment remedy requested is for an attachment of real property...."

The statute does not require the plaintiff to post a bond to insure the payment of damages that the defendant may suffer should the attachment prove wrongfully issued or the claim prove unsuccessful.

As required, DiGiovanni submitted an affidavit in support of his application. In five one-sentence paragraphs, DiGiovanni stated that the facts set forth in his previously submitted complaint were true; that "I was willfully, wantonly and maliciously assaulted by the defendant, Brian K. Doehr"; that "[s]aid assault and battery broke my left wrist and further caused an ecchymosis to my right eye, as well as other injuries"; and that "I have further expended sums of money for medical care and treatment." The affidavit concluded with the statement, "In my opinion, the foregoing facts are sufficient to show that there is probable cause that judgment will be rendered for the plaintiff."

On the strength of these submissions the Superior Court Judge, by an order dated March 17, found "probable cause to sustain the validity of the plaintiff's claim" and ordered the attachment on Doehr's home "to the value of $75,000." The sheriff attached the property four days later, on March 21. Only after this did Doehr receive notice of the attachment. He also had yet to be served with the complaint, which is ordinarily necessary for an action to commence in Connecticut. As the statute further required, the attachment notice informed Doehr that he had the right to a hearing: (1) to claim that no probable cause existed to sustain the claim; (2) to request that the attachment be vacated, modified, or dismissed or that a bond be substituted; or (3) to claim that some portion of the property was exempt from execution.

Rather than pursue these options, Doehr filed suit against DiGiovanni in Federal District Court, claiming that [the statute] (a)(1) was unconstitutional under the Due Process Clause of the Fourteenth Amendment. The District Court upheld the statute and granted summary judgment in favor of DiGiovanni. On appeal, a divided panel of the United States Court of Appeals for the Second Circuit reversed. Judge Pratt, who wrote the opinion for the court, concluded that the Connecticut statute violated due process in permitting *ex parte* attachment absent a showing of extraordinary circumstances.

A further reason to invalidate the statute, the court ruled, was the highly factual nature of the issues in this case. In ... *Mathews v. Eldridge*, 424 U.S. 319 (1976), where an evidentiary hearing was not required prior to the termination of disability benefits, the determination of disability was "sharply focused and easily documented." Judge Pratt observed that in contrast the present case involved the fact-specific event of a fist fight and the issue of assault. He doubted that the judge could reliably determine probable cause when presented with only the plaintiff's version of the altercation.

"Because the risk of a wrongful attachment is considerable under these circumstances, we conclude that dispensing with notice and opportunity for a hearing until after the attachment, without a showing of extraordinary circumstances, violates the requirements of due process."

Judge Pratt went on to conclude that in his view, the statute was also constitutionally infirm for its failure to require the plaintiff to post a bond for the protection of the defendant in the event the attachment was ultimately found to have been improvident.

* * *

II

With this case we return to the question of what process must be afforded by a state statute enabling an individual to enlist the aid of the State to deprive another of his or her property by means of the prejudgment attachment or similar procedure. Our cases reflect the numerous variations this type of remedy can entail. In *Snidach v. Family Finance Corp of Bay view*, 395 U.S. 337 (1969), the Court struck down a Wisconsin statute that permitted a creditor to effect prejudgment garnishment of wages without notice and prior hearing to the wage earner. In *Fuentes v. Shevin*, 407 U.S. 67 (1972), the Court likewise found a due process violation in state replevin provisions that permitted vendors to have goods seized through an *ex parte* application to a court clerk and the posting of a bond. Conversely, the Court upheld a Louisiana *ex parte* procedure allowing a lienholder to have disputed goods sequestered in *Mitchell v. W.T. Grant Co.*, 416 U.S. 600 (1974), *Michell* however, carefully noted that *Fuentes* was decided against "a factual and legal background sufficiently different ... that it does not require the invalidation of the Louisiana sequestration statute." Those differences included Louisiana's provision of an immediate postdeprivation hearing along with the option of damages; the requirement that a judge rather than a clerk determine that there is a clear showing of entitlement to the writ; the necessity for a detailed affidavit; and an emphasis on the lienholder's interest in preventing waste or alienation of the encumbered property. In *North Georgia Finishing, Inc. v. Di-Chem, Inc.*, 419 U.S. 601 (1975), the Court again invalidated an *ex parte* garnishment statute that not only failed to provide for notice and prior hearing but also failed to require a bond, a detailed affidavit setting out the claim, the determination of a neutral magistrate, or a prompt postdeprivation hearing.

* * *

In *Mathews*, we drew upon our prejudgment remedy decisions to determine what process is due when the government itself seeks to effect a deprivation on its own initiative. That analysis resulted in the now familiar threefold inquiry requiring consideration of "the private interest that will be affected by the official action"; "the risk of an erroneous deprivation of such interest through the procedures used, and the probable value, if any, of additional or substitute safeguards"; and lastly "the Government's interest, including the function involved and the fiscal and administrative burdens that the additional or substitute procedural requirement would entail."

Here the inquiry is similar, but the focus is different. Prejudgment remedy statutes ordinarily apply to disputes between private parties rather than between an individual and the government. Such enactments are designed to enable one of the parties to "make use of state procedures with the overt, significant assistance of state officials," and they undoubtedly involve state action "substantial enough to implicate the Due Process Clause." Nonetheless, any burden that increasing procedural safeguards entails primarily affects not the government, but the party seeking control of the other's property. For this type of case, therefore, the relevant inquiry requires, as in *Mathews* first, consideration of the private interest that will be affected by the prejudgment measure; second, an examination of the risk of erroneous deprivation through the procedures under attack and the probable value of additional or alternative safeguards; and third, in contrast to *Mathews* principal attention to the interest of the party seeking the prejudgment remedy, with, nonetheless, due regard for any ancillary interest the government may have in providing the procedure or forgoing the added burden of providing greater protections.

We now consider the *Mathews* factors in determining the adequacy of the procedures before us, first with regard to the safeguards of notice and a prior hearing, and then in relation to the protection of a bond.

III

We agree with the Court of Appeals that the property interests that attachment affects are significant. For a property owner like Doehr, attachment ordinarily clouds title; impairs the ability to sell or otherwise alienate the property; taints any credit rating; reduces the chance of obtaining a home equity loan or additional mortgage; and can even place an existing mortgage in technical default where there is an insecurity clause. Nor does Connecticut deny that any of these consequences occurs.

Instead, the State correctly points out that these effects do not amount to a complete, physical, or permanent deprivation of real property; their impact is less than the perhaps temporary total deprivation of household goods or wages. But the Court has never held that only such extreme deprivations trigger due process concern. To the contrary, our cases show that even the temporary or partial impairments to property rights that attachments, liens, and similar encumbrances entail are sufficient to merit due process protection. Without doubt, state procedures for creating and enforcing attachments, as with liens, are subject to the strictures of due process.

We also agree with the Court of Appeals that the risk of erroneous deprivation that the State permits here is substantial. By definition, attachment statutes premise a deprivation of property on one ultimate factual contingency—the award of damages to the plaintiff which the defendant may not be able to satisfy. For attachments before judgment, Connecticut mandates that this determination be made by means of a procedural inquiry that asks whether "there is probable cause to sustain the validity of the plaintiff's claim." The statute elsewhere defines the validity of the claim in terms of the likelihood "that judgment will be rendered in the matter in favor of the plaintiff." What probable cause means in this context, however, remains obscure. The State initially took the position, as did the dissent below, that the statute requires a plaintiff to show the objective likelihood of the suit's success. Doehr, citing ambiguous state cases, reads the provision as requiring no more than that a plaintiff demonstrate a subjective good-faith belief that the suit will succeed. At oral argument, the State shifted its position to argue that the statute requires something akin to the plaintiff stating a claim with sufficient facts to survive a motion to dismiss.

We need not resolve this confusion since the statute presents too great a risk of erroneous deprivation under any of these interpretations. If the statute demands inquiry into the sufficiency of the complaint, or, still less, the plaintiff's good-faith belief that the complaint is sufficient, requirement of a complaint and a factual affidavit would permit a court to make these minimal determinations. But neither inquiry adequately reduces the risk of erroneous deprivation. Permitting a court to authorize attachment merely because the plaintiff believes the defendant is liable, or because the plaintiff can make out a facially valid complaint, would permit the deprivation of the defendant's property when the claim would fail to convince a jury, when it rested on factual allegations that were sufficient to state a cause of action but which the defendant would dispute, or in the case of a mere good-faith standard, even when the complaint failed to state a claim upon which relief could be granted. The potential for unwarranted attachment in these situations is self-evident and too great to satisfy the requirements of due process absent any countervailing consideration.

Even if the provision requires the plaintiff to demonstrate, and the judge to find, probable cause to believe that judgment will be rendered in favor of the plaintiff, the risk of error was substantial in this case. As the record shows, and as the State concedes, only a skeletal affidavit need be, and was, filed. The State urges that the reviewing judge normally reviews the complaint as well, but concedes that the complaint may also be conclusory. It is self-evident that the judge could make no realistic assessment concerning the likelihood of an action's success based upon these one-sided, self-serving, and conclusory submissions. And as the Court of Appeals said, in a case like this involving an alleged assault, even a detailed affidavit would give only the plaintiff's version of the confrontation. Unlike determining the existence of a debt or delinquent payments, the issue does not concern "ordinarily uncomplicated matters that lend themselves to documentary proof." *Mitchell.* The likelihood of error that results illustrates that fairness can rarely be obtained by secret, one-sided determination of facts decisive of rights.... [And n]o better instrument has been devised for arriving at truth than to give a person in jeopardy of serious loss notice of the case against him and opportunity to meet it.

What safeguards the State does afford do not adequately reduce this risk. Connecticut points out that the statute also provides an "expeditiou[s]" postattachment adversary hearing, notice for such a hearing, judicial review of an adverse decision, and a double damages action if the original suit is commenced without probable cause. Similar considerations were present in *Mitchell* where we upheld Louisiana's sequestration statute despite the lack of predeprivation notice and hearing. But in *Mitchell* the plaintiff had a vendor's lien to protect, the risk of error was minimal because the likelihood of recovery involved uncomplicated matters that lent themselves to documentary proof, and the plaintiff was required to put up a bond. None of these factors diminishing the need for a predeprivation hearing is present in this case. It is true that a later hearing might negate the presence of probable cause, but this would not cure the temporary deprivation that an earlier hearing might have prevented.

"The Fourteenth Amendment draws no bright lines around three-day, 10-day or 50-day deprivations of property. Any significant taking of property by the State is within the purview of the Due Process Clause." *Fuentes.*

Finally, we conclude that the interests in favor of an *ex parte* attachment, particularly the interests of the plaintiff, are too minimal to supply such a consideration here. The plaintiff had no existing interest in Doehr's real estate when he sought the attachment. His only interest in attaching the property was to ensure the availability of assets to satisfy his judgment if he prevailed on the merits of his action. Yet there was no allegation that Doehr was about to transfer or encumber his real estate or take any other action during the pendency of the action that would render his real estate unavailable to satisfy a judgment. Our cases have recognized such a properly supported claim would be an exigent circumstance permitting postponing any notice or hearing until after the attachment is effected. Absent such allegations, however, the plaintiff's interest in attaching the property does not justify the burdening of Doehr's ownership rights without a hearing to determine the likelihood of recovery.

No interest the government may have affects the analysis. The State's substantive interest in protecting any rights of the plaintiff cannot be any more weighty than those rights themselves. Here the plaintiff's interest is *de minimis.* Moreover, the State cannot seriously plead additional financial or administrative burdens involving predeprivation hearings when it already claims to provide an immediate post-deprivation hearing.

* * *

Connecticut's statute appears even more suspect in light of current practice. A survey of state attachment provisions reveals that nearly every State requires either a preattachment hearing, a showing of some exigent circumstance, or both, before permitting an attachment to take place. Twenty-seven States, as well as the District of Columbia, permit attachments only when some extraordinary circumstance is present. In such cases, preattachment hearings are not required but postattachment hearings are provided. Ten States permit attachment without the presence of such factors but require prewrit hearings unless one of those factors is shown. Six States limit attachments to extraordinary circumstance cases, but the writ will not issue prior to a hearing unless there is a showing of some even more compelling condition. Three States always require a preattachment hearing. Only Washington, Connecticut, and Rhode Island authorize attachments without a prior hearing in situations that do not involve any purportedly heightened threat to the plaintiff's interests. Even those States permit *ex parte* deprivations only in certain types of cases: Rhode Island does so only when the claim is equitable; Connecticut and Washington do so only when real estate is to be attached, and even Washington requires a bond. Conversely, the States for the most part no longer confine attachments to creditor claims. This development, however, only increases the importance of the other limitations.

We do not mean to imply that any given exigency requirement protects an attachment from constitutional attack. Nor do we suggest that the statutory measures we have surveyed are necessarily free of due process problems or other constitutional infirmities in general. We do believe, however, that the procedures of almost all the States confirm our view that the Connecticut provision before us, by failing to provide a preattachment hearing without at least requiring a showing of some exigent circumstance, clearly falls short of the demands of due process.

IV

Although a majority of the Court does not reach the issue, Justices Marshall, Sevens, O'Connor, and I deem it appropriate to consider whether due process also requires the plaintiff to post a bond or other security in addition to requiring a hearing or showing of some exigency.

As noted, the impairments to property rights that attachments effect merit due process protection. Several consequences can be severe, such as the default of a homeowner's mortgage. In the present context, it need only be added that we have repeatedly recognized the utility of a bond in protecting property rights affected by the mistaken award of prejudgment remedies.

Without a bond, at the time of attachment, the danger that these property rights may be wrongfully deprived remains unacceptably high even with such safeguards as a hearing or exigency requirement. The need for a bond is especially apparent where extraordinary circumstances justify an attachment with no more than the plaintiff's *ex parte* assertion of a claim. We have already discussed how due process tolerates, and the States generally permit, the otherwise impermissible chance of erroneously depriving the defendant in such situations in light of the heightened interest of the plaintiff. Until a postattachment hearing, however, a defendant has no protection against damages sustained where no extraordinary circumstance in fact existed or the plaintiff's likelihood of recovery was nil. Such protection is what a bond can supply. Both the Court and its individual Members have repeatedly found the requirement of a bond to play an essential role in reducing what would have been too great a degree of risk in precisely this type of circumstance.

But the need for a bond does not end here. A defendant's property rights remain at undue risk even when there has been an adversarial hearing to determine the plaintiff's likelihood of recovery. At best, a court's initial assessment of each party's case cannot produce more than an educated prediction as to who will win. This is especially true when, as here, the nature of the claim makes any accurate prediction elusive. In consequence, even a full hearing under a proper probable-cause standard would not prevent many defendants from having title to their homes impaired during the pendency of suits that never result in the contingency that ultimately justifies such impairment, namely, an award to the plaintiff. Attachment measures currently on the books reflect this concern. All but a handful of States require a plaintiff's bond despite also affording a hearing either before, or (for the vast majority, only under extraordinary circumstances) soon after, an attachment takes place. Bonds have been a similarly common feature of other prejudgment remedy procedures that we have considered, whether or not these procedures also included a hearing.

The State stresses its double damages remedy for suits that are commenced without probable cause. This remedy, however, fails to make up for the lack of a bond. As an initial matter, the meaning of "probable cause" in this provision is no more clear here than it was in the attachment provision itself. Should the term mean the plaintiff's good faith or the facial adequacy of the complaint, the remedy is clearly insufficient. A defendant who was deprived where there was little or no likelihood that the plaintiff would obtain a judgment could nonetheless recover only by proving some type of fraud or malice or by showing that the plaintiff had failed to state a claim. Problems persist even if the plaintiff's ultimate failure permits recovery. At best a defendant must await a decision on the merits of the plaintiff's complaint. Settlement, under Connecticut law, precludes seeking the damages remedy, a fact that encourages the use of attachments as a tactical device to pressure an opponent to capitulate. An attorney's advice that there is probable cause to commence an action constitutes a complete defense, even if the advice was unsound or erroneous. Finally, there is no guarantee that the original plaintiff will have adequate assets to satisfy an award that the defendant may win.

Nor is there any appreciable interest against a bond requirement. [The statute] does not require a plaintiff to show exigent circumstances nor any pre-existing interest in the property facing attachment. A party must show more than the mere existence of a claim before subjecting an opponent to prejudgment proceedings that carry a significant risk of erroneous deprivation.

Our foregoing discussion compels the four of us to consider whether a bond excuses the need for a hearing or other safeguards altogether. If a bond is needed to augment the protections afforded by preattachment and postattachment hearings, it arguably follows that a bond renders these safeguards unnecessary. That conclusion is unconvincing, however, for it ignores certain harms that bonds could not undo but that hearings would prevent. The law concerning attachments has rarely, if ever, required defendants to suffer an encumbered title until the case is concluded without any prior opportunity to show that the attachment was unwarranted. Our cases have repeatedly emphasized the importance of providing a prompt postdeprivation hearing at the very least. Every State but one, moreover, expressly requires a preattachment or postattachment hearing to determine the propriety of an attachment.

The necessity for at least a prompt postattachment hearing is self-evident because the right to be compensated at the end of the case, if the plaintiff loses, for all provable injuries caused by the attachment is inadequate to redress the harm inflicted, harm that could have been avoided had an early hearing been held. An individual with an immediate need or opportunity to sell a property can neither do so, nor otherwise satisfy that need or recreate the opportunity. The same applies to a parent in need of a home equity loan for a child's education, an entrepreneur seeking to start a business on the strength of an otherwise strong credit rating, or simply a homeowner who might face the disruption of having a mortgage placed in technical default. The extent of these harms, moreover, grows with the length of the suit. Here, oral argument indicated that civil suits in Connecticut commonly take up to four to seven years for completion. Many state attachment statutes require that the amount of a bond be anywhere from the equivalent to twice the amount the plaintiff seeks. These amounts bear no relation to the harm the defendant might suffer even assuming that money damages can make up for the foregoing disruptions. It should be clear, however, that such an assumption is fundamentally flawed. Reliance on a bond does not sufficiently account for the harms that flow from an erroneous attachment to excuse a State from reducing that risk by means of a timely hearing.

If a bond cannot serve to dispense with a hearing immediately after attachment, neither is it sufficient basis for not providing a preattachment hearing in the absence of exigent circumstances even if in any event a hearing would be provided a few days later. The reasons are the same: a wrongful attachment can inflict injury that will not fully be redressed by recovery on the bond after a prompt postattachment hearing determines that the attachment was invalid.

Once more, history and contemporary practices support our conclusion. Historically, attachments would not issue without a showing of extraordinary circumstances even though a plaintiff bond was almost invariably required in addition. Likewise, all but eight States currently require the posting of a bond. Out of this 42-State majority, all but one requires a preattachment hearing, a showing of some exigency, or both, and all but one expressly require a postattachment hearing when an attachment has been issued *ex parte*. This testimony underscores the point that neither a hearing nor an extraordinary circumstance limitation eliminates the need for a bond, no more than a bond allows waiver of these other protections. To reconcile the interests of the defendant and the plaintiff accurately, due process generally requires all of the above.

Because Connecticut's prejudgment remedy provision, violates the requirements of due process by authorizing prejudgment attachment without prior notice or a hearing, the judgment of the Court of Appeals is affirmed, and the case is remanded to that court for further proceedings consistent with this opinion.

Opportunity to Be Heard — Notes and Exercises

In *Connecticut v. Doehr*, the Court addressed the due process right to be heard in the context of prejudgment attachment. The Court briefly discussed four of its previous cases that arose in the context of prejudgment deprivations of property:

- *Snidach v. Family Finance Corp of Bay View*, 395 U.S. 337 (1969), invalidating a Wisconsin statute that permitted a creditor to effect prejudgment garnishment of wages without providing notice and prior hearing to the wage earner.

- *Fuentes v. Shevin*, 407 U.S. 67 (1972), finding a due process violation in state replevin provisions that permitted vendors to have goods seized through an *ex parte* application to a court clerk and the posting of a bond.

- *Mitchell v. W.T. Grant Co.*, 416 U.S. 600 (1974), upholding a Louisiana *ex parte* procedure allowing a lien-holder to have disputed goods sequestered due to Louisiana's provision of an immediate post-deprivation hearing along with the option of damages; the requirement that a judge rather than a clerk determine that there is a clear showing of entitlement to the writ; and the necessity for a detailed affidavit.

- *North Georgia Finishing, Inc. v. Di-Chem, Inc.*, 419 U.S. 61 (1975), invalidating an *ex parte* garnishment statute that failed to provide for notice and prior hearing and also failed to require a bond, a detailed affidavit setting out the claim, the determination of a neutral magistrate, or a prompt post-deprivation hearing.

The Court in *Doehr* applied the three-part test it first articulated in *Mathews v. Eldridge*, 424 U.S. 319, 335 (1976), requiring consideration of:

1. "the private interest that will be affected by the official action";

2. "the risk of an erroneous deprivation of such interest through the procedures used, and the probable value, if any, of additional or substitute safeguards"; and

3. "the Government's interest, including the function involved and the fiscal and administrative burdens that the additional or substitute procedural requirement would entail."

Mathews involved the termination of disability benefits. Eldridge was receiving disability payments from the Social Security Administration (SSA), which was reevaluating his benefits. The SSA collected medical reports on Eldridge's condition and ultimately determined that he was no longer disabled and that it would terminate his benefits. Eldridge disputed the termination but was again denied after his written appeal was considered. He was not afforded any hearing to present evidence other than the option to apply for reconsideration in six months. The Court held that the termination procedures did not violate Eldridge's due process rights. Although Eldridge was entitled to due process for the taking of his benefits, the Court decided that the procedures employed by the SSA were constitutionally sufficient.

Apply the *Mathews v. Eldridge* test in the following three situations to determine whether the government provided an opportunity to be heard that satisfied the Due Process Clause.

Exercise 3-13. Opportunity to Be Heard — *Mackey v. Montrym*

A Massachusetts statute mandates suspension of a driver's license for refusing to take a breath-analysis test upon arrest for operating a motor vehicle while under the influence of intoxicating liquor. The Registrar of Motor Vehicles must order a 90-day suspension upon receipt of the police report of the licensee's refusal to take such test; the licensee, after surrendering his license, is entitled to an immediate hearing before the Registrar. Appellee, whose license was suspended under the statute, brought a class action in federal district court alleging that the Massachusetts statute was unconstitutional on its face and as applied in that it authorized the suspension of his license without affording him a pre-suspension hearing. Apply the *Mathews* test. How should the court rule?

See *Mackey v. Montrym*, 443 U.S. 1 (1979).

Exercise 3-14. Opportunity to Be Heard — *Cleveland Bd. of Educ. v. Loudermill*

The Board of Education hired Loudermill as a security guard. On his job application, Loudermill stated that he had never been convicted of a felony. Subsequently, upon discovering that he had in fact been convicted of grand larceny, the Board dismissed him for dishonesty in filling out the job application. He was not afforded an opportunity to respond to the dishonesty charge or to challenge the dismissal. Under Ohio law, Loudermill was a "classified civil servant," and by statute, as such an employee, could be terminated only for cause and was entitled to a post-termination administrative review of the dismissal. He filed an appeal with the Civil Service Commission and argued that his conviction was a misdemeanor, not a felony. The Commission upheld the dismissal some nine months after the appeal had been filed. Loudermill filed suit in Federal District Court, alleging that the Ohio statute providing for administrative review was unconstitutional on its face because it provided no opportunity for a discharged employee to respond to charges against him prior to removal, thus depriving him of liberty and property without due process. Apply the *Mathews* test. How should the court rule?

See Cleveland Bd. of Educ. v. Loudermill, 470 U.S. 532 (1985).

Exercise 3-15. Opportunity to Be Heard — *City of Los Angeles v. David*

David paid Los Angeles $134.50 to recover his car, which had been towed from a spot where parking was prohibited, and requested a hearing to recover the money. The hearing was held 27 days after the car was towed. His claim was denied. He then filed a 42 U.S.C. § 1983 suit, claiming that the city violated his due process rights by failing to provide a sufficiently prompt hearing. Apply the *Mathews* test. How should the court rule?

See City of Los Angeles v. David, 538 U.S. 715 (2003).

Exercise 3-16. Constitutionality of Wisconsin Prejudgment Attachment Statutes

Return to Part 2 of the Problem at the beginning of the chapter. Below are the applicable provisions of the Wisconsin prejudgment attachment statutes. Apply the opportunity to be heard analysis from Section 5 above to assess whether Dee has a viable constitutional challenge to the attachment of Dee's computer equipment.

Wisconsin Prejudgment Attachment Statutes

811.01 Attachment. Any creditor may attach the property of his or her debtor, in the cases, upon the conditions, and in the manner prescribed in this chapter.

811.02 Writ. The writ of attachment shall be issued by a judge or other judicial officer on the request of the plaintiff at any time before final judgment and after a summons and a complaint are filed. It shall be directed to the sheriff of some county in which the property of the defendant is supposed to be, and shall require the sheriff to attach all the property of the defendant within the county or so much thereof as may be sufficient to satisfy the plaintiff's demand, together with costs and expenses.

811.03 Basis for attachment.

(1) ON CONTRACT OR JUDGMENT. Before any writ of attachment shall be executed the plaintiff or someone in the plaintiff's behalf shall make and annex thereto an affidavit setting forth specific factual allegations to show that the defendant is indebted, or that property of the defendant is available, to the plaintiff in a sum exceeding $50 specifying the amount above all setoffs, and that the same is due upon contract or upon a judgment and that the affiant knows or has good reason to believe either:

(a) That the defendant is absent from this state, or is concealed therein so that summons cannot be served on the defendant; or

(b) That the defendant has disposed of or concealed or is about to dispose of or conceal the defendant's property or some part thereof with intent to defraud the defendant's creditors; or

(c) That the defendant has removed or is about to remove property out of this state with intent to defraud the defendant's creditors;

811.06 Bond. Before the writ of attachment is executed, a bond on the part of the plaintiff in a sum set by the judge or the judicial officer issuing the writ of attachment in an amount sufficient to provide adequate security to the defendant for any damages the defendant may sustain by reason of the attachment, shall be filed with the court to the effect that if the defendant recovers judgment the plaintiff shall pay all damages which the defendant may sustain by reason of the attachment.

811.18 Vacation or modification of writ. The court or the presiding judge thereof may, at any time vacate or modify the writ of attachment upon motion of the defendant for any sufficient cause.

811.19 Hearing on motion to vacate or modify. A motion to vacate or modify shall be heard forthwith by the court. On the motion, the burden of proof shall be upon the plaintiff.

6. Professional Development Reflection

The initiation of a lawsuit gives rise to many professionalism issues in real life practice. Both plaintiffs and defendants can abuse the service and hearing requirements.

Plaintiffs abuse the service requirement via unscrupulous process servers. The abuse, known as "sewer service," goes like this. The process server makes no effort to actually serve the defendant. Instead, the process server throws the summons and complaint in the trash but files with the court a proof of service affidavit claiming that the process server personally served the defendant. The defendant has no notice of the suit, so the defendant never responds to the complaint. The plaintiff proceeds to get a default judgment. Then the plaintiff attempts to satisfy the judgment through execution or garnishment. The defendant first learns of the suit when the defendant's property is seized or wages garnished. Plaintiffs can also abuse the prejudgment attachment statutes by fudging an affidavit and getting the sheriff to seize the defendant's property without prior notice or a hearing for the defendant.

Defendants abuse the service requirement by frustrating the plaintiff's attempt to use the civil ligation system to adjudicate a legitimate dispute by intentionally avoiding service of process. Defendants can also make fraudulent transfers of their assets so that plaintiffs will be unable to collect a judgment.

Exercise 3-17. Service Professionalism

The manner in which a lawyer chooses to serve process can significantly affect the lawyer's reputation, the public's confidence in the civil litigation system, and the administration of justice. Consider the following problems, both of which arose in real life practice.

1. Lawyers hire process servers, who proceed to attempt to serve the defendant and who submit affidavits of service to the court. The selection of a process server is important because civil litigation cannot begin unless the defendant is served and because the process server's actions and affidavits reflect directly on the lawyer who hired the process server. With this in mind, identify the characteristics of the type of process server you would like to hire.

2. You represent the plaintiff in an acrimonious dispute involving former partners who have come to detest one another. You are about to initiate a lawsuit on behalf of the plaintiff. You believe that the defendant will be quite easy to serve. The defendant is a politician who works in an office that is open to the public and who is often at public appearances outside of the office. You have no reason to believe that the defendant will try to avoid service. The plaintiff tells you the defendant is getting married on Saturday. The plaintiff urges you to have the summons and complaint served on the defendant at the wedding. What would you say to the plaintiff?

Chapter 4

Subject Matter Jurisdiction

1. Chapter Problem

Memorandum

To: Associate
From: Mary Rogers, Partner
Re: Potential Wrongful Death Action

I received your memorandum regarding the California court's assertion of personal jurisdiction over Piper Aircraft and Hartzell Propeller. Another issue has arisen in the case. I am concerned that if we file this case in California state court, the defendants will remove the case from state court to federal court. It's possible that a federal jury might not be as sympathetic to our client's claim as a state court jury.

As I mentioned in my previous memo on this case, Piper manufactured the aircraft at its Pennsylvania facility. Hartzell manufactured the propeller in Ohio. While our client, Sherry, and her deceased brother are from Scotland, I intend to have Jill Reyno, one of my administrative assistants who is a resident of the state of California, appointed the administrator of the estate. Jill will bring the lawsuit on behalf of the estate. The complaint will include state tort claims.

If the parties to the lawsuit encompass this plaintiff and these defendants, will the defendants be able to remove the case to federal court?

---

2. Introduction

Subject matter jurisdiction refers to the power of a court to hear a particular type of case. What is your preliminary answer to the partner's question in the chapter problem? Why do you think this is the correct answer? The cases in this chapter will help you understand how lawyers and courts reason through a problem of subject matter jurisdiction.

Subject matter jurisdiction is a relative of personal jurisdiction. However, while the question answered when personal jurisdiction is at issue is, "does the court have jurisdiction over a particular defendant," the question answered for subject matter

153

jurisdiction is, "does the court have jurisdiction over the particular type of case?" Different court systems have various ways of approaching subject matter jurisdiction. For example, some states have a court system that is set up based on the amount of damages, i.e., claims for less than $1000 go to small claims court, whereas claims for $1000 to $10,000 go to district court, and claims for over $10,000 go to circuit court. Cases also may be assigned to courts based on subject matter, such as specialized probate courts that only hear probate matters. Each individual state sets up its own court system. Thus, for the state court systems, which case goes to which court is a matter of state law.

This chapter focuses on federal law, because it is universal in that it applies in every federal court in the country. Thus, whether you file a claim in federal court in New York or in California (or any state in between), the same subject matter jurisdiction rules apply.

Subject matter jurisdiction, like personal jurisdiction, is fundamental to a court's ability to hear a case. Because subject matter jurisdiction goes to the power of the court to hear the type of case the plaintiff has brought, a decision rendered by a court that does not have subject matter jurisdiction is void. However, unlike personal jurisdiction, subject matter jurisdiction is not based on an individual right. Therefore, the parties may not waive it. You probably can see why subject matter jurisdiction is so important. If the court were to issue a judgment without subject matter jurisdiction, that court would have wasted its time deciding a case it did not have the power to decide. This results in courts' policing their jurisdiction closely. Federal courts have a duty to raise the issue of subject matter jurisdiction and often do so sua sponte (of their own accord). It's important for you as a lawyer to make sure you have filed your case in a court with appropriate subject matter jurisdiction or you run the risk of wasting the court's and your own time (and your client's money). Like personal jurisdiction, subject matter jurisdiction is an issue you must resolve before you file a lawsuit or you will face a challenge to the court's authority to hear your client's case.

Like situations in which a court lacks personal jurisdiction, a court need not give full faith and credit to the judgment of a court that did not have subject matter jurisdiction to render the judgment. The Supreme Court of the United States addressed the full faith credit given to another state's decision in the context of subject matter jurisdiction challenge involving a same-sex couple adoption in *V.L. v. E.L.*, ___ U.S. ___, 136 S. Ct. 1017 (2016) (per curiam). Two women were in a relationship raising three children together. One of the women gave birth to the children. A Georgia state court granted the adoption of the non-birth mother while recognizing the birth mother's continued parental rights. The couple separated while living in Alabama, and the non-birth mother sued in Alabama state court for custody and visitation rights. The Alabama court refused to give full faith and credit to the Georgia court's adoption decision, holding that the Georgia court did not have subject matter jurisdiction to grant an adoption while still recognizing the other parent's parental rights. The Supreme Court disagreed, reasoning that the Georgia code explicitly gave the state's superior court's jurisdiction over adoption matters. Noting that there is a distinction between the subject matter jurisdiction of the courts and the underlying merits of the case, the Court reasoned that if the particular element of Georgia's adoption law that the Alabama court found lacking was considered jurisdictional, all the elements necessary to adopt would become jurisdictional. As the Court explained, "[t]his result would comport neither with Georgia law nor with common sense." 136 S. Ct. at 1021. Thus, it is important to make sure any challenge to subject matter jurisdiction actually is based on the power of the court—not the merits of the underlying cause of action.

There is another reason that subject matter jurisdiction is considered important. It dictates the judicial forum—state or federal—in which you can file a suit. Sometimes a lawyer has a preference for state or federal court, depending on a variety of factors. For example, if you represented an individual plaintiff in a lawsuit against a huge multi-national corporation, in what court would you prefer to bring the lawsuit—in the defendant's local state court, in your client's local state court, or in federal court? Note that state courts usually draw their juries from a much smaller geographic area than the federal courts. Often, the jury members reside in the same county in which you filed the lawsuit. A federal jury is drawn from a much larger geographic area. For smaller states, it can be the entire state. Studies suggest that plaintiffs who initially file in state court choose that forum for good reasons. Professors Kevin Clermont and Theodore Eisenberg compared the difference in plaintiff win rates for cases removed to federal court with those cases that the plaintiff initially filed in federal court. They found that the plaintiff win rate for cases removed to federal court was 36.77%, whereas the plaintiff win rate for cases originally filed in federal court was 57.97%. Differences in plaintiff win rates were even more stark in cases brought in federal court based on diversity jurisdiction, which you will learn more about in this chapter. Plaintiff win rates drop from 71% for cases brought originally in federal court to 34% for cases that are removed to federal court. *See* Kevin M. Clermont & Theodore Eisenberg, *Do Case Outcomes Really Reveal Anything about the Legal System? Win Rates and Removal Jurisdiction*, 83 Cornell L. Rev. 581, 593 (1998). This suggests that plaintiffs who initially filed in state court had good reasons for thinking their chances might be better before those courts. As Professor Clermont explained in a later article:

> The name of the game is forum shopping, as many have observed elsewhere. Lawyers all know this and have lived by it forever. The contribution of recent empirical research, besides confirming the existence of the phenomenon, has been to show that all of those lawyers were not wasting their clients' money on forum fights—because, in fact, forum matters. Forum is worth fighting over because outcome often turns on forum ...

Kevin M. Clermont, *Litigation Realities Redux*, 84 Notre Dame L. Rev. 1919, 1921 (2009). Thus, where you bring a lawsuit matters, and subject matter jurisdiction and venue, which will be covered in Chapter 5, like personal jurisdiction, affect your forum options.

This chapter explores the varying bases for the assertion of federal court subject matter jurisdiction. It proceeds as follows:

- Section 3 describes the statutory and constitutional bases for federal court subject matter jurisdiction.
- Section 4 covers diversity jurisdiction—one of the most controversial bases for federal jurisdiction.
- Section 5 covers cases "arising under" the Constitution, statutes, and treaties of the United States. Sometimes referred to as "federal question" jurisdiction, this text will refer to it as "arising under" jurisdiction to more accurately track the language of the statute and Constitutional provisions that establish this form of jurisdiction.
- Section 6 explores supplemental jurisdiction, the form of jurisdiction that permits parties to join state and federal claims in the same federal lawsuit.
- Section 7 describes the requirements for removal, the process by which a defendant can "remove" a case that the plaintiff filed in state court to a federal court when a basis for federal jurisdiction exists. You will see cases referring to a defendant's removal of a case to federal court in other sections of this chapter as well.
- Section 8 contains the professional development reflection for subject matter jurisdiction.

3. Statutory and Constitutional Bases for Federal Court Subject Matter Jurisdiction

The federal courts are courts of "limited jurisdiction." This means that they are limited in the types of cases that they are permitted to hear. State courts have broader jurisdiction and are often referred to as courts of "general jurisdiction," meaning that they can hear most types of claims. Federal courts' jurisdiction is based on the Constitution and statutes that provide for the assertion of specific types of jurisdiction. Beginning with the Constitution, Article III, Section 2, states:

> The judicial power shall extend to all cases, in law and equity, arising under this Constitution, the laws of the United States, and treaties made, or which shall be made, under their authority;—to all cases affecting ambassadors, other public ministers and consuls;—to all cases of admiralty and maritime jurisdiction;—to controversies to which the United States shall be a party;— to controversies between two or more states;—between a state and citizens of another state;—between citizens of different states;—between citizens of the same state claiming lands under grants of different states, and between a state, or the citizens thereof, and foreign states, citizens or subjects.

Article III extends the federal judicial power to a variety of cases, some of which involve federal interests (such as those that arise under the Constitution, laws, and treaties of the United States) and others that involve lawsuits between citizens of differing states, foreign states, or aliens. The authority granted in the Constitution is not self-executing. Congress has codified the various grants of jurisdiction explicitly in the United States code. In this chapter, we will be most concerned with three most common bases for jurisdiction—diversity jurisdiction, arising under jurisdiction, and supplemental jurisdiction. Congress codified the three most common bases for federal court jurisdiction in 28 U.S.C. §§ 1331,1332, and 1367, which can be found in your course supplement or by searching the statutes online. However, if you browse the 1330's sections of chapter 28 of the U.S. Code, you will see that Congress has codified a variety of bases for federal court jurisdiction. In addition, sometimes a basis for the federal court's jurisdiction appears in the substantive law itself. *See, e.g.,* 42 U.S.C. § 2000e-5(f)(3) (explicit grant of federal court jurisdiction for Title VII cases). The three that are the focus of this chapter are the most general.

4. Diversity Jurisdiction

Read 28 U.S.C. § 1332(a). As you can tell from reading § 1332(a), in order for a federal court to have diversity jurisdiction, a case must meet two basic requirements. First, the parties must be completely diverse. At its most basic level, this means that no plaintiff can be from the same state as any defendant, although there are other combinations worth noting involving alien parties as well. *Strawbridge v. Curtiss,* 7 U.S. (3 Cranch) (1806). Second, the plaintiff must establish the "amount in controversy"—the overall value of the case to whichever party prevails. Section 1332 sets the threshold for this value. While this amount has varied over the years, Congress currently has set it at in excess of $75,000. The chart below shows how the amount in controversy has changed over time.

Amount in Controversy (must exceed)		
Year	28 USC 1331	28 USC 1332
Before 1980	$10,000	$10,000
1980	$0	$10,000
1988	$0	$50,000
1997 to present	$0	$75,000

Claims based on diversity are state law claims. Thus, a plaintiff can bring a run of the mill breach of contract action or state tort claim in federal court if it meets the two requirements for diversity jurisdiction. Why would the federal courts be concerned with such state law claims? Wouldn't it make sense to reserve the federal courts for federal law cases? Why does the Constitution contemplate, and section 1332 permit, plaintiffs to bring these cases in federal court?

One of the main purposes of diversity jurisdiction is to avoid bias directed at out-of-state defendants. This was considered important for business transactions. For example, a business located in New York might be reluctant to enter into a contract with a Mississippi company if it thought the Mississippi company could sue it in Mississippi state court. The perception was that those courts would favor the

Mississippi-based business. That in many states judges are elected exacerbates concerns about bias aimed at out-of-state defendants. Thus, that New York business might be facing a Mississippi business before a Mississippi state court judge who has to worry about reelection and how a decision affects his or her constituents. While not all states elect their judges, federal judges are appointed pursuant to Article III of the Constitution. The Constitution grants them lifetime jobs and salaries that are guaranteed not to be reduced. Thus, federal judges are, at least in theory, insulated from the political pressures under which elected state court judges may operate. While it is not precisely clear that this out-of-state bias exists, many argue that diversity is justified simply because out-of-state bias is thought to exist. The perception of bias itself would stop business from flowing across state lines. Thus, keeping federal courts available to out-of-state litigants is thought to be necessary for commerce.

Diversity jurisdiction is rather controversial. Many argue that these cases are not of great importance to the federal courts and are better handled by state courts, which have more expertise in state law matters. In addition, diversity cases are thought to clog the federal court system. For example, in 2017, diversity cases made up about 31% of federal cases filed. *See* United States Courts, Federal Judicial Caseload Statistics 2017, http://www.uscourts.gov/statistics-reports/federal-judicial-caseload-statistics-2017. Thus, they are a significant portion of the federal courts' dockets. As you read the cases in this section, ask yourself whether diversity jurisdiction still is necessary, given the national and international nature of commerce as well as the transient nature of individuals.

Exercise 4-1. Understanding and Applying the Federal Diversity Statute

Read 28 U.S.C. § 1332(a), (b), and (c). Many important rules governing civil procedure do not appear in the Federal Rules of Civil Procedure, but instead in chapter 28 of the United States Code. Thus, along with reading rules, in order to fully understand civil procedure, you will also need to become adept at reading statutes. After reading 28 U.S.C. § 1332, answer the following questions about diversity jurisdiction to test your ability to read and interpret the statute.

1. What are the two fundamental requirements for diversity jurisdiction?

2. How do you determine the state citizenship of a corporation?

3. How do you determine the state citizenship of an insurance company?

4. Under what circumstances is an alien considered a state citizen for purposes of diversity jurisdiction?

5. What are the potential consequences for a party if the amount of damages awarded does not reach the jurisdictional amount?

6. What are the different combinations of citizens and citizens of foreign states that will provide a basis for diversity jurisdiction? It is helpful to diagram the different sets of plaintiff and defendant combinations. Using this diagram, which of the following sets of parties are completely diverse? If you need more information to formulate your answer, what is that information and what impact does it have on your analysis?

   a. Jennifer, who lives in Missouri, sues Michael, who lives in Arkansas.

   b. Jennifer, who lives in Arkansas, sues Michael, who lives in Arkansas.

   c. Jennifer, who lives in Arkansas, sues Michael's insurance company. Michael lives in Arkansas, but his insurance company is a Delaware corporation with its principal place of business in Chicago, Illinois.

   d. Jennifer, who lives in Arkansas, sues Big-Mart, a Delaware corporation with its principal place of business in Arkansas.

   e. Jennifer, who lives in Missouri, sues Big-Mart, a Delaware corporation with its principal place of business in Arkansas.

   f. Health Breads, Inc., a Delaware corporation with its principal place of business in San Francisco, California, sues Big-Mart, a Delaware corporation with its principal place of business in Arkansas.

   g. Health Breads, Inc., a California corporation with its principal place of business in San Francisco, California, sues Big-Mart, a Delaware corporation with its principal place of business in Los Angeles, California.

   h. Health Breads, Inc., a Delaware corporation with its principal place of business in San Francisco, California, sues Big-Mart, an Arkansas corporation with its principal place of business in Arkansas and distribution facilities in Oakland, California and San Bernadino, California.

   i. A bus accident occurs in Oklahoma. Carrie, a New York resident, John, a New Jersey resident, and Mary, an Oklahoma resident, sue Springer Bus Lines, a Delaware corporation with its principal place of business in Phoenix, Arizona, John King, a New Jersey truck driver whose big rig hit the bus, and Cross-Country Trucking, a Delaware corporation with its principal place of business in Baltimore, Maryland.

   j. Robert, a graduate student in New York who is a citizen of the United Kingdom, sues Mega-Mart, a Delaware corporation with its principal place of business in Rochester, New York.

   k. Edward, a permanent resident of California who is a citizen of Canada, sues Hollywood Studios, a Delaware corporation with its principal place of business in Los Angeles, California.

Exercise 4-2. *Mas v. Perry*

Sometimes it is difficult to determine the state citizenship of a particular person. The following case considers how you determine the state citizenship of an individual for purposes of diversity jurisdiction. As you read the case, answer the following questions.

1. What court decided this case? For what courts is this case precedent? How do you determine whether other jurisdictions follow the *Mas* Court's approach?

2. What happens to a court's jurisdiction if a plaintiff moves to the same state as the defendant after the lawsuit has started? Does the court still have diversity jurisdiction?

3. Who has the burden of showing the court has jurisdiction?

4. What is the difference between a place of residence and domicile?

5. You and your classmates are students who were born and raised in a variety of states. How does the court in *Mas* determine your and your classmates' citizenship? Consider what facts might support a party's citizenship in a particular state.

6. Note that the amount in controversy at the time of the *Mas* case was $10,000. Aside from the change in the amount in controversy, does the current version of 28 U.S.C. § 1332 change the outcome of this case?

7. *Mas* also reveals distinctions between men and women that at the time of the case were part of the law. What problem does the court identify with the legal status of wives?

8. *Mas* also discusses and applies the standard for the amount in controversy. What is the standard?

9. What policy concerns does the *Mas* court discuss in reaching its result?

Mas v. Perry

489 F.2d 1396 (5th Cir. 1974), *cert. denied*, 419 U.S. 842 (1974)

Ainsworth, Circuit Judge:

This case presents questions pertaining to federal diversity jurisdiction under 28 U.S.C. § 1332, which, pursuant to article III, section II of the Constitution, provides for original jurisdiction in federal district courts of all civil actions that are between, inter alia, citizens of different States or citizens of a State and citizens of foreign states and in which the amount in controversy is more than $10,000.

Appellees Jean Paul Mas, a citizen of France, and Judy Mas were married at her home in Jackson, Mississippi. Prior to their marriage, Mr. and Mrs.

Mas were graduate assistants, pursuing coursework as well as performing teaching duties, for approximately nine months and one year, respectively, at Louisiana State University in Baton Rouge, Louisiana. Shortly after their marriage, they returned to Baton Rouge to resume their duties as graduate assistants at LSU. They remained in Baton Rouge for approximately two more years, after which they moved to Park Ridge, Illinois. At the time of the trial in this case, it was their intention to return to Baton Rouge while Mr. Mas finished his studies for the degree of Doctor of Philosophy. Mr. and Mrs. Mas were undecided as to where they would reside after that.

Upon their return to Baton Rouge after their marriage, appellees rented an apartment from appellant Oliver H. Perry, a citizen of Louisiana. This appeal arises from a final judgment entered on a jury verdict awarding $5,000 to Mr. Mas and $15,000 to Mrs. Mas for damages incurred by them as a result of the discovery that their bedroom and bathroom contained "two-way" mirrors and that they had been watched through them by the appellant during three of the first four months of their marriage.

At the close of the appellees' case at trial, appellant made an oral motion to dismiss for lack of jurisdiction. The motion was denied by the district court. Before this Court, appellant challenges the final judgment below solely on jurisdictional grounds, contending that appellees failed to prove diversity of citizenship among the parties and that the requisite jurisdictional amount is lacking with respect to Mr. Mas. Finding no merit to these contentions, we affirm. Under section 1332(a)(2), the federal judicial power extends to the claim of Mr. Mas, a citizen of France, against the appellant, a citizen of Louisiana. Since we conclude that Mrs. Mas is a citizen of Mississippi for diversity purposes, the district court also properly had jurisdiction under section 1332(a)(1) of her claim.

It has long been the general rule that complete diversity of parties is required in order that diversity jurisdiction obtain; that is, no party on one side may be a citizen of the same State as any party on the other side. This determination of one's State Citizenship for diversity purposes is controlled by federal law, not by the law of any State. As is the case in other areas of federal jurisdiction, the diverse citizenship among adverse parties must be present at the time the complaint is filed. Jurisdiction is unaffected by subsequent changes in the citizenship of the parties. The burden of pleading the diverse citizenship is upon the party invoking federal jurisdiction, and if the diversity jurisdiction is properly challenged, that party also bears the burden of proof.

To be a citizen of a State within the meaning of section 1332, a natural person must be both a citizen of the United States, and a domiciliary of that State. For diversity purposes, citizenship means domicile; mere residence in the State is not sufficient.

Court defines domicile. A person's domicile is the place of "his true, fixed, and permanent home and principal establishment, and to which he has the intention of returning whenever he is absent therefrom...." *Stine v. Moore,* [213 F.2d 446, 448 (5th Cir. 1954)]. A change of domicile may be effected only by a combination of two elements: (a) taking up residence in a different domicile with (b) the intention to remain there.

It is clear that at the time of her marriage, Mrs. Mas was a domiciliary of the State of Mississippi. While it is generally the case that the domicile of the wife — and, consequently, her State citizenship for purposes of diversity jurisdiction — is deemed to be that of her husband, and we find no precedent for extending this concept to the situation here, in which the husband is a citizen of a foreign state but resides in the United States. Indeed, such a fiction would work absurd results on the facts before us. If Mr. Mas were considered a domiciliary of France — as he would be since he had lived in Louisiana as a student-teaching assistant prior to filing this suit, — then Mrs. Mas would also be deemed a domiciliary, and thus, fictionally at least, a citizen of France. She would not be a citizen of any State and could not sue in a federal court on that basis; nor could she invoke the alienage jurisdiction to bring her claim in federal court, since she is not an alien. On the other hand, if Mrs. Mas's domicile were Louisiana, she would become a Louisiana citizen for diversity purposes and could not bring suit with her husband against appellant, also a Louisiana citizen, on the basis of diversity jurisdiction. These are curious results under a rule arising from the theoretical identity of person and interest of the married couple.

An American woman is not deemed to have lost her United States citizenship solely by reason of her marriage to an alien. Similarly, we conclude that for diversity purposes a woman does not have her domicile or State Citizenship changed solely by reason of her marriage to an alien.

Mrs. Mas's Mississippi domicile was disturbed neither by her year in Louisiana prior to her marriage nor as a result of the time she and her husband spent at LSU after their marriage, since for both periods she was a graduate assistant at LSU. Though she testified that after her marriage she had no intention of returning to her parents' home in Mississippi, Mrs. Mas did not effect a change of domicile since she and Mr. Mas were in Louisiana only as students and lacked the requisite intention to remain there. Until she acquires a new domicile, she remains a domiciliary, and thus a citizen, of Mississippi.

Appellant also contends that Mr. Mas's claim should have been dismissed for failure to establish the requisite jurisdictional amount for diversity cases of more than $10,000. In their complaint Mr. and Mrs. Mas alleged that they had each been damaged in the amount of $100,000. As we have noted, Mr. Mas ultimately recovered $5,000.

It is well settled that the amount in controversy is determined by the amount claimed by the plaintiff in good faith. Federal jurisdiction is not lost because a judgment of less than the jurisdictional amount is awarded. That Mr. Mas recovered only $5,000 is, therefore, not compelling. As the Supreme Court stated in *St. Paul Mercury Indemnity Co. v. Red Cab Co.*, 303 U.S. 283, 288–290 (1938):

> The sum claimed by the plaintiff controls if the claim is apparently made in good faith.
>
> It must appear to a legal certainty that the claim is really for less than the jurisdictional amount to justify dismissal. The inability of the plaintiff to recover an amount adequate to give the court jurisdiction does not show his bad faith or oust the jurisdiction....
>
> ... His good faith in choosing the federal forum is open to challenge not only by resort to the face of his complaint, but by the facts disclosed at trial, and if from either source it is clear that his claim never could have amounted to the sum necessary to give jurisdiction there is no injustice in dismissing the suit.

Having heard the evidence presented at the trial, the district court concluded that the appellees properly met the requirements of section 1332 with respect to jurisdictional amount. Upon examination of the record in this case, we are also satisfied that the requisite amount was in controversy.

Thus the power of the federal district court to entertain the claims of appellees in this case stands on two separate legs of diversity jurisdiction: a claim by an alien against a State citizen; and an action between citizens of different States. We also note, however, the propriety of having the federal district court entertain a spouse's action against a defendant, where the district court already has jurisdiction over a claim, arising from the same transaction, by the other spouse against the same defendant. In the case before us, such a result is particularly desirable. The claims of Mr. and Mrs. Mas arise from the same operative facts, and there was almost complete interdependence between their claims with respect to the proof required and the issues raised at trial. Thus, since the district court had jurisdiction of Mr. Mas's action, sound judicial administration militates strongly in favor of federal jurisdiction of Mrs. Mas's claim.

Policy

Affirmed.

Exercise 4-3. *Mas v. Perry* Revisited

Given the court's reasoning in *Mas*, what are the domiciles of the following parties for purposes of diversity jurisdiction?

1. Where is Mark Zuckerberg's domicile? Mark Zuckerberg, founder of Facebook, established a company in California. He was born in New York, graduated from high school in New Hampshire, attended college in Massachusetts, and lived in California the summer after his sophomore year in college. He took a leave of absence from his Massachusetts university and returned to California, where the company he founded was incorporated. However, he planned to return to college and continued to use his parents' New York address as his permanent residence. Under *Mas*, what state is his state of domicile for purposes of diversity jurisdiction? *See Connectu LLD v. Zuckerberg*, 482 F. Supp. 2d 3 (D. Mass. 2007), *rev'd on other grounds*, 522 F.3d 82 (1st Cir. 2008) (court held he was domiciled in New York).

2. Tracy attends law school in California. She grew up in Chicago, Illinois, and attended college in North Carolina. During the summers while she was in college, she returned to her family home in Chicago. Tracy now lives in Los Angeles. She has a California driver's license and California car tags on her car, but still lists her home in Chicago as her official address on her law school records. She is registered to vote in Illinois. Where is Tracy's domicile?

   a. Does your analysis change if Tracy has interviewed for jobs only with law firms in Chicago?

   b. Does your analysis change if Tracy has interviewed for jobs only with law firms in California?

   c. Does your analysis change if Tracy has interviewed with law firms in Chicago, New York, Washington, D.C., Los Angeles, and Boston?

Exercise 4-4. *Hertz Corp. v. Friend* and the Problem of Corporations

A corporation, under 28 U.S.C. § 1332(c)(1), is a citizen of two places — its place of incorporation and its principal place of business. A corporation's place of incorporation is generally easy to find and is a matter of public record. Many state secretary of state offices have this information available online for corporations that are registered to do business in the state. While a case like *Mas* dealt with individuals, courts continued to struggle in determining the principal place of business of corporations for purposes of diversity. Lower courts developed a variety of approaches. As you read *Hertz Corp. v. Friend*, answer the following questions.

1. The *Hertz* Court identified three different tests lower courts used to determine a corporation's principal place of business for purposes of diversity. Can you describe them? What test did the *Hertz* Court adopt for determining the principal place of business for a corporation?

2. What factors played a role in the Court's adoption of this test?

3. The plaintiffs brought the *Hertz* case as a class action. Look up "class action" in a legal dictionary. You will learn about class actions in Chapter 8.

Hertz Corp. v. Friend
559 U.S. 77 (2010)

Justice Breyer delivered the opinion of the Court.

The federal diversity jurisdiction statute provides that "a corporation shall be deemed to be a citizen of any State by which it has been incorporated *and of the State where it has its principal place of business.*" 28 U.S.C. § 1332(c)(1) (emphasis added). We seek here to resolve different interpretations that the Circuits have given this phrase. In doing so, we place primary weight upon the need for judicial administration of a jurisdictional statute to remain as simple as possible. And we conclude that the phrase "principal place of business" refers to the place where the corporation's high level officers direct, control, and coordinate the corporation's activities. Lower federal courts have often metaphorically called that place the corporation's "nerve center." We believe that the "nerve center" will typically be found at a corporation's headquarters.

I

In September 2007, respondents Melinda Friend and John Nhieu, two California citizens, sued petitioner, the Hertz Corporation, in a California state court. They sought damages for what they claimed were violations of California's wage and hour laws. And they requested relief on behalf of a potential class composed of California citizens who had allegedly suffered similar harms.

Hertz filed a notice seeking removal to a federal court. Hertz claimed that the plaintiffs and the defendant were citizens of different States. Hence, the federal court possessed diversity-of-citizenship jurisdiction. Friend and Nhieu, however, claimed that the Hertz Corporation was a California citizen, like themselves, and that, hence, diversity jurisdiction was lacking.

To support its position, Hertz submitted a declaration by an employee relations manager that sought to show that Hertz's "principal place of business" was in New Jersey, not in California. The declaration stated, among other things, that Hertz operated facilities in 44 States; and that California—which had about 12% of the Nation's population—accounted for 273 of Hertz's 1,606 car rental locations; about 2,300 of its 11,230 full-time employees; about $811 million of its $4.371 billion in annual revenue; and about 3.8 million of its approximately 21 million annual transactions, *i.e.,* rentals. The declaration also stated that the "leadership of Hertz and its domestic subsidiaries" is located at Hertz's "corporate headquarters" in Park Ridge, New Jersey; that its "core executive and administrative functions ... are carried out" there and "to a lesser extent" in Oklahoma City, Oklahoma; and that its "major administrative operations ... are found" at those two locations.

[The district court held that Hertz's principal place of business was in California for purposes of diversity jurisdiction. Hertz appealed to the Ninth Circuit, which affirmed the district court's decision.]

III

We begin our "principal place of business" discussion with a brief review of relevant history. The Constitution provides that the "judicial Power shall extend" to "Controversies ... between Citizens of different States." Art. III, § 2. This language, however, does not automatically confer diversity jurisdiction upon the federal courts. Rather, it authorizes Congress to do so and, in doing so, to determine the scope of the federal courts' jurisdiction within constitutional limits.

[The Court provided a lengthy description of congressional changes to the statutory rules for diversity jurisdiction.]

* * *

IV

The phrase "principal place of business" has proved more difficult to apply than its originators likely expected....

[C]ourts were ... uncertain as to where to look to determine a corporation's "principal place of business" for diversity purposes. If a corporation's headquarters and executive offices were in the same State in which it did most of its business, the test seemed straightforward. The "principal place of business" was located in that State.

But suppose those corporate headquarters, including executive offices, are in one State, while the corporation's plants or other centers of business activity are located in other States? In 1959 a distinguished federal district judge, Edward Weinfeld, relied on the Second Circuit's interpretation of the Bankruptcy Act to answer this question in part:

> "Where a corporation is engaged in far-flung and varied activities which are carried on in different states, its principal place of business is the nerve center from which it radiates out to its constituent parts and from which its officers direct, control and coordinate all activities without regard to locale, in the furtherance of the corporate objective. The test applied by our Court of Appeals, is that place where the corporation has an 'office from which its business was directed and controlled'—the place where 'all of its

business was under the supreme direction and control of its officers.'" *Scot Typewriter Co. v. Underwood Corp.*, 170 F. Supp. [862], 865 [(SDNY 1959)].

Numerous Circuits have since followed this rule, applying the "nerve center" test for corporations with "far-flung" business activities.

Scot's analysis, however, did not go far enough. For it did not answer what courts should do when the operations of the corporation are not "far-flung" but rather limited to only a few States. When faced with this question, various courts have focused more heavily on where a corporation's actual business activities are located.

Perhaps because corporations come in many different forms, involve many different kinds of business activities, and locate offices and plants for different reasons in different ways in different regions, a general "business activities" approach has proved unusually difficult to apply. Courts must decide which factors are more important than others: for example, plant location, sales or servicing centers; transactions, payrolls, or revenue generation.

The number of factors grew as courts explicitly combined aspects of the "nerve center" and "business activity" tests to look to a corporation's "total activities," sometimes to try to determine what treatises have described as the corporation's "center of gravity."... Not surprisingly, different circuits (and sometimes different courts within a single circuit) have applied these highly general multifactor tests in different ways

This complexity may reflect an unmediated judicial effort to apply the statutory phrase "principal place of business" in light of the general purpose of diversity jurisdiction, *i.e.*, an effort to find the State where a corporation is least likely to suffer out-of-state prejudice when it is sued in a local court. But, if so, that task seems doomed to failure. After all, the relevant purposive concern — prejudice against an out-of-state party — will often depend upon factors that courts cannot easily measure, for example, a corporation's image, its history, and its advertising, while the factors that courts can more easily measure, for example, its office or plant location, its sales, its employment, or the nature of the goods or services it supplies, will sometimes bear no more than a distant relation to the likelihood of prejudice. At the same time, this approach is at war with administrative simplicity. And it has failed to achieve a nationally uniform interpretation of federal law, an unfortunate consequence in a federal legal system.

Policy discussed here.

V

A

In an effort to find a single, more uniform interpretation of the statutory phrase, we have reviewed the Courts of Appeals' divergent and increasingly complex interpretations. Having done so, we now return to, and expand,

Judge Weinfeld's approach, as applied in the Seventh Circuit. We conclude that "principal place of business" is best read as referring to the place where a corporation's officers direct, control, and coordinate the corporation's activities. It is the place that Courts of Appeals have called the corporation's "nerve center." And in practice it should normally be the place where the corporation maintains its headquarters — provided that the headquarters is the actual center of direction, control, and coordination, *i.e.*, the "nerve center," and not simply an office where the corporation holds its board meetings (for example, attended by directors and officers who have traveled there for the occasion).

Three sets of considerations, taken together, convince us that this approach, while imperfect, is superior to other possibilities. First, the statute's language supports the approach. The statute's text deems a corporation a citizen of the "State where it has its principal place of business." The word "place" is in the singular, not the plural. The word "principal" requires us to pick out the "main, prominent" or "leading" place. 12 OXFORD ENGLISH DICTIONARY 495 (2d ed. 1989) (def.(A)(I)(2)). And the fact that the word "place" follows the words "State where" means that the "place" is a place *within* a State. It is not the State itself.

Note the Court's use of the dictionary to define terms.

A corporation's "nerve center," usually its main headquarters, is a single place. The public often (though not always) considers it the corporation's main place of business. And it is a place within a State. By contrast, the application of a more general business activities test has led some courts, as in the present case, to look, not at a particular place within a State, but incorrectly at the State itself, measuring the total amount of business activities that the corporation conducts there and determining whether they are "significantly larger" than in the next-ranking State. *Friend v. Hertz Corp.*, 297 Fed. Appx. 690 (9th Cir. 2008).

This approach invites greater litigation and can lead to strange results, as the Ninth Circuit has since recognized. Namely, if a "corporation may be deemed a citizen of California on th[e] basis" of "activities [that] roughly reflect California's larger population ... nearly every national retailer — no matter how far flung its operations — will be deemed a citizen of California for diversity purposes." But why award or decline diversity jurisdiction on the basis of a State's population, whether measured directly, indirectly (say proportionately), or with modifications?

Second, administrative simplicity is a major virtue in a jurisdictional statute. Complex jurisdictional tests complicate a case, eating up time and money as the parties litigate, not the merits of their claims, but which court is the right court to decide those claims. Complex tests produce appeals and reversals, encourage gamesmanship, and, again, diminish the likelihood that results and settlements will reflect a claim's legal and factual merits. Judicial resources too are at stake. Courts have an independent obligation to determine whether subject-matter jurisdiction exists, even when no party challenges it. So courts benefit from straightforward rules under which they can readily assure themselves of their power to hear a case.

Simple jurisdictional rules also promote greater predictability. Predictability is valuable to corporations making business and investment decisions. Predictability also benefits plaintiffs deciding whether to file suit in a state or federal court.

A "nerve center" approach, which ordinarily equates that "center" with a corporation's headquarters, is simple to apply *comparatively speaking*. The metaphor of a corporate "brain," while not precise, suggests a single location. By contrast, a corporation's general business activities more often lack a single principal place where they take place. That is to say, the corporation may have several plants, many sales locations, and employees located in many different places. If so, it will not be as easy to determine which of these different business locales is the "principal" or most important "place."

Third, the statute's legislative history, for those who accept it, offers a simplicity-related interpretive benchmark. The Judicial Conference provided an initial version of its proposal that suggested a numerical test. A corporation would be deemed a citizen of the State that accounted for more than half of its gross income. The Conference changed its mind in light of criticism that such a test would prove too complex and impractical to apply. That history suggests that the words "principal place of business" should be interpreted to be no more complex than the initial "half of gross income" test. A "nerve center" test offers such a possibility. A general business activities test does not.

B

We recognize that there may be no perfect test that satisfies all administrative and purposive criteria. We recognize as well that, under the "nerve center" test we adopt today, there will be hard cases. For example, in this era of telecommuting, some corporations may divide their command and coordinating functions among officers who work at several different locations, perhaps communicating over the Internet. That said, our test nonetheless points courts in a single direction, towards the center of overall direction, control, and coordination. Courts do not have to try to weigh corporate functions, assets, or revenues different in kind, one from the other. Our approach provides a sensible test that is relatively easier to apply, not a test that will, in all instances, automatically generate a result.

We also recognize that the use of a "nerve center" test may in some cases produce results that seem to cut against the basic rationale for 28 U.S.C. § 1332. For example, if the bulk of a company's business activities visible to the public take place in New Jersey, while its top officers direct those activities just across the river in New York, the "principal place of business" is New York. One could argue that members of the public in New Jersey would be *less* likely to be prejudiced against the corporation than persons in New York—yet the corporation will still be entitled to remove a New Jersey state case to federal court. And note too that the same corporation would be unable to remove a New York state case to federal court, despite the New York public's presumed prejudice against the corporation.

We understand that such seeming anomalies will arise. However, in view of the necessity of having a clearer rule, we must accept them. Accepting occasionally counterintuitive results is the price the legal system must pay to avoid overly complex jurisdictional administration while producing the benefits that accompany a more uniform legal system.

The burden of persuasion for establishing diversity jurisdiction, of course, remains on the party asserting it. When challenged on allegations of jurisdictional facts, the parties must support their allegations by competent proof. And when faced with such a challenge, we reject suggestions such as, for example, the one made by petitioner that the mere filing of a form like the Securities and Exchange Commission's Form 10-K listing a corporation's "principal executive offices" would, without more, be sufficient proof to establish a corporation's "nerve center." Such possibilities would readily permit jurisdictional manipulation, thereby subverting a major reason for the insertion of the "principal place of business" language in the diversity statute. Indeed, if the record reveals attempts at manipulation—for example, that the alleged "nerve center" is nothing more than a mail drop box, a bare office with a computer, or the location of an annual executive retreat—the courts should instead take as the "nerve center" the place of actual direction, control, and coordination, in the absence of such manipulation.

VI

Petitioner's unchallenged declaration suggests that Hertz's center of direction, control, and coordination, its "nerve center," and its corporate headquarters are one and the same, and they are located in New Jersey, not in California. Because respondents should have a fair opportunity to litigate their case in light of our holding, however, we vacate the Ninth Circuit's judgment and remand the case for further proceedings consistent with this opinion.

It is so ordered.

Exercise 4-5. Applying *Hertz*

Given the test the Court adopted in *Hertz*, where is the principal place of business for purposes of diversity jurisdiction for the following corporations?

1. A Delaware corporation with stores in all 50 states, distribution facilities in Texas, California, Ohio, and Maryland, and its CEO, CFO and Vice Presidents located in an office in New Haven, Connecticut.

2. A Delaware corporation with offices in 25 states, with managing vice presidents in each office who report to a president who is located in Raleigh, North Carolina, but a Board of Directors that meets quarterly in Miami, Florida.

3. An Ohio Corporation that purports to have its principal place of business in Columbus, Ohio. The corporation's entire Board of Directors is located in Columbus. Additionally, from its office in Columbus, 22 out of the corporation's 27 officers—including its Chief Executive Officer, Chief Financial Officer, Secretary, and Treasurer—make significant corporate decisions and set corporate policy. Together, they decide the location and construction of power plants and transmission lines, and they negotiate and execute contracts for the procurement of fuel for the corporation's hydroelectric facilities, pump storage facilities, coal-fired power plants, and gas power plants; all of which are decisions at the core of the corporation's business. The Columbus officers handle environmental permitting for work at the corporation's West Virginia facilities and calculate and pay taxes owed on these facilities. Moreover, they collect and disburse revenues, control and direct the filings made with the SEC and the FERC, determine human resource policies and codes of conduct, and oversee the corporation's legal affairs. On the other hand, 5 out of the corporation's 27 officers are based in Charleston, West Virginia. The Charleston officers are responsible for implementing the large-scale directives received from Columbus and for managing the corporation's day-to-day operations in West Virginia, Virginia, and Tennessee. Of the five officers in West Virginia, one oversees all aspects of the corporation's day-to-day operations. Another oversees its distribution operations, including line trucks and service trucks. A third interacts with state and local government and monitors legislation, while a fourth oversees the operation of its power plants. And, finally, the fifth oversees the regulatory operations in West Virginia, Virginia, and Tennessee. *See Hoschar v. Appalachian Power Co.*, 739 F.3d 163 (4th Cir. 2014) (Ohio was principal place of business).

4. A corporation organized under Delaware law that is licensed to do busy in Kentucky and lists a Kentucky address with the Kentucky Secretary of state as the organization's "principal office address." The corporation's parent company is located in Japan. The corporation's human resources manager submits a declaration stating that the corporate officers located at

the corporation's parent-company headquarters in Japan exercise ultimate authority over the corporation's activities in Kentucky, make significant corporate decision pertaining to it, and direct and control its corporate policies. *See Elliott v. Yamamoto FB Engineering, Inc.*, 2018 WL 852375 (W.D. Ky. Feb. 13, 2018) (Japan was principal place of business).

Exercise 4-6. Domicile of Other Business Entities

In addition to traditional corporations, a variety of business entities do not have corporate statuses, but the courts still must determine their places of domicile. In *Americold Realty Trust v. Conagra Foods, Inc.*, ___ U.S. ___, 136 S. Ct. 1012 (2016), the Supreme Court of the United States considered the citizenship of a real estate investment trust formed under Maryland law. The entity involved was not incorporated, but instead was an " 'unincorporated business trust or association' in which property is held and managed 'for the benefit and profit of any person who may become a shareholder' " under Maryland law. *Id.* at 1016 (quoting Md. Corp. & Assn. Code Ann. §§ 8-101(c), 9-102 (2014)). The Court reasoned that the shareholders of such an entity are in the same position as partners in a limited partnership for purposes of diversity. Thus, courts should consider the citizenship of the shareholders for purposes of determining whether the requirements of diversity jurisdiction are met. In doing so, the Court rejected treating the citizenship of the entity, though it is called a "trust" under state law, like it treats the citizenship of a trustee who sues on behalf of a trust. When a trustee sues on behalf of a trust, only the trustee's citizenship is considered for purposes of diversity—not the citizenship of the beneficiaries of the trust or those who contributed to the trust. The Court distinguished situations in which the entity itself sued from those in which the trustee sued on behalf of a trust. Noting that many entities are called "trusts" that are not set up as traditional trusts, the Court reasoned that where the entity itself sues, its shareholder's citizenship is relevant for diversity. The Court also rejected treating the entity like a corporation, because Congress was explicit in the diversity statute with respect to the citizenship of corporations. There is no explicit statutory language for entities such as this. Based on what you know about diversity jurisdiction and the policies behind it, where do you think the following entities are domiciled for purposes of diversity jurisdiction?

1. A partnership with partners located in New York, New Jersey, and Connecticut.

2. A Tennessee corporation that has ceased to do business. *See Midatlantic Nat'l Bank v. E.F. Hansen*, 48 F.3d 693 (3d Cir. 1995) (inactive corporation is domiciled in state of incorporation only); *but see Passalacqua Builders, Inc. v. Resnick Developers South, Inc.*, 933 F.2d 131 (2d Cir. 1991) (inactive corporation also domiciled in its last place of business).

3. An unincorporated association made up of members from the States of Washington, Oregon, Montana, and Idaho. *See C.T. Carden v. Arkoma Associates*, 494 U.S. 185 (1990) (citizenship of limited partners must be considered in determining diversity jurisdiction).

Exercise 4-7. *Harshey v. Advanced Bionics Corp. & Carroll v. Stryker Corp.*

Along with complete diversity between parties, a party seeking diversity jurisdiction also must meet the amount in controversy, which is currently greater than $75,000. Recall that the court in *Mas* set out the basic standard for the amount in controversy. The sum claimed by the plaintiff is accepted if alleged in good faith. It must appear to a legal certainty that damages are less than the jurisdictional amount to justify a court's dismissal of the case based on the inability of the plaintiff to meet the jurisdictional amount. However, it is not always the plaintiff who is seeking the federal court's jurisdiction. Sometimes the defendant is trying to remove the case from state court to federal court, a process that is discussed in more detail in section 7 of this chapter. Does the standard change when the plaintiff challenges the jurisdictional amount? Who has the burden to show that the jurisdictional amount is likely to be met in the case? The *Harshey* and *Carroll* cases address these issues. As you read the cases, answer the following questions.

1. In what court did the plaintiffs originally bring these cases?

2. What court is issuing the judgment in each case? What does that mean for each decision's precedential effect?

3. What is meant by aggregation as the court mentions in the *Harshey* case?

4. What's the standard of proof the party seeking diversity jurisdiction must meet?

5. Who raised the issue of subject matter jurisdiction in each case? At what point in the litigation was it raised?

6. What is the effect of a plaintiff stipulating that his or her damages are less than $75,000?

7. How did the defendants try to show that the jurisdictional amount was met in these cases?

Harshey v. Advanced Bionics Corp.

No. 1:09-cv-905-DFH-TAB, 2009 WL 3617756 (S.D. Ind. Oct. 29, 2009)

David F. Hamilton, Chief Judge.

Plaintiff Kenneth A. Harshey had surgery in 2007 for implantation of a pulse generator manufactured by defendants. Harshey filed this action alleging that the device has malfunctioned and has subjected him to painful and dangerous electrical shocks, causing "severe and permanent injuries." Harshey's wife has joined as a plaintiff with a claim for loss of consortium, and his son has joined with a claim for negligent infliction of emotional distress. Plaintiffs originally filed the action in state court, and defendants removed the case by invoking the court's diversity jurisdiction under 28 U.S.C. § 1332, which requires diversity of citizenship and an amount in controversy exceeding $75,000, exclusive of interest and costs. Plaintiffs have moved to remand the case to state court for failure to show that the jurisdictional amount is in controversy.

Plaintiffs have submitted post-removal stipulations stating that none of them individually seeks, demands, or will accept any recovery in excess of $75,000. To meet their burden of establishing that federal jurisdiction is proper, defendants rely on the statement of their counsel that their "experience with personal injury litigation" and the general descriptions of plaintiffs' alleged injuries in the complaint show that the amount in controversy requirement is satisfied. The court disagrees and grants the motion to remand.

Let's lay out the basic ground rules here. First, the parties seeking federal jurisdiction have the burden of showing that jurisdiction is proper.

Second, the separate claims of the three plaintiffs may not be aggregated to satisfy the jurisdictional amount in controversy requirement. At least one of the claims must satisfy the requirement. If one does, the other related claims of the plaintiffs may be joined in one federal case under the supplemental jurisdiction statute, 28 U.S.C. § 1367. *Exxon Mobil Corp. v. Allapattah Services, Inc.*, 545 U.S. 546, 549 (2005).

Third, plaintiffs' post-removal stipulations to limit their claims are not binding or otherwise effective to defeat a removal that was proper at the time it occurred. The stipulations and the motion to remand are sufficient, however, to put the burden on defendants to show that jurisdiction is proper. Under current Seventh Circuit authority, the burden is on defendants in this situation to support with "competent proof" their assertion that the amount in controversy requirement is satisfied.

The pivotal question here is whether defense counsel's assertion based on "experience with personal injury litigation" is sufficient to meet defendants' burden of providing competent proof. The court finds that it is not. From defendants' response to the motion to remand, it is clear that the comparisons are not to other claims similar to these plaintiffs' claims but to a wide array of catastrophic personal injury cases. Defendants cite the following reported verdicts in Indiana state and federal courts:

$2,730,000 for severe and permanent injuries including broken bones and a wound complication.

$259,375 for medical malpractice injuring the laryngeal nerve.

$550,000 for a lost eye.

$1,210,000 for persistent post-operative pain.

Recognizing that none of these cases involved claims for electrical shocks delivered by an implanted medical device, defendants cite cases from other jurisdictions involving electrical shocks, but those cases involved heavy electrical equipment, not implanted medical devices. The one cited case involving an implanted medical device involved a claim for permanent brain damage.

In short, the cited cases offer no meaningful guidance about the value of Kenneth Harshey's claim, about which the record shows very little. Assuming that comparisons to other cases can be used to satisfy the defendants' burden on the amount in controversy, a much stronger showing of close similarity should be required. Personal injury cases are so individual and varied that the cases cited by defendants provide no valuable guidance on the question before the court — the amount in controversy for these plaintiffs' claims for injuries stemming from the asserted malfunction of the implanted medical device.

If the court were to accept defendants' showing in this case, the result could be very troubling for similarly situated defendants and would tend to require courts to decide similar amount-in-controversy disputes based on speculation and guesswork. Recall that if it is clear from the outset that a case is removable, a defendant must decide whether to remove in no more than 30 days. But if it is not clear, the defendant has up to one year to determine whether to remove, providing an opportunity for informal or formal discovery. If the 30-day clock began to run based on nothing more than defense counsel's experience and information about cases as different as those cited by defendants in this case, the clock would run out quickly with little information to go on.

The better approach is to require more of a removing defendant and to give that defendant a reasonable opportunity to learn more about the scope of the plaintiff's claim. This can be done quickly with a letter or more formal interrogatory or request for admission as to whether plaintiff is willing to state definitively that he seeks no more than $75,000, exclusive of interest and costs. Direct answers, and even evasions and failures to respond, can give both defendants and federal courts a much stronger foundation for exercising federal jurisdiction than the guesswork and speculation that underlie the comparisons relied upon in this case.

Plaintiffs' motion to remand is granted. The case is remanded to the Marion Superior Court from which it was removed.

So ordered.

————————

Carroll v. Stryker Corp.
658 F.3d 675 (7th Cir. 2011)

Sykes, Circuit Judge.

Matthew Carroll was a commissioned sales representative assigned to solicit orders in Wisconsin for Stryker Corporation ("Stryker"), a medical-instrument manufacturer based in Michigan. Stryker terminated Carroll's employment in 2008 because he failed to meet his quarterly sales quota. When Stryker refused to pay him a commission he felt he was rightfully owed, Carroll sued Stryker in state court for unpaid wages under Wisconsin's wage-claim statute and alternatively sought recovery under equitable contract doctrines. Stryker removed the action to federal court and later moved for summary judgment, arguing that Carroll was barred from pursuing a statutory wage claim because he worked on commission, and also that equitable contract relief was unavailable because Carroll's compensation was the subject of an express contract.

Carroll responded by voluntarily dismissing his statutory claim and seeking leave to amend his complaint to add a cause of action for breach of contract. The district court entered summary judgment for Stryker, agreeing that Carroll could not recover under any equitable contract doctrine. The court also denied Carroll's motion for leave to amend because the deadline for amending the pleadings had long since passed and no reasonable cause had been shown for the undue delay. Carroll appealed.

At oral argument we noted a possible jurisdictional issue regarding the amount in controversy. We ordered supplemental briefing and now conclude that the damages Carroll seeks exceed the $75,000 threshold for diversity jurisdiction. *See* 28 U.S.C. § 1332(a).

* * *

II. Discussion
A. Jurisdiction

Although neither the parties nor the district court addressed subject-matter jurisdiction, we have an independent obligation to satisfy ourselves that jurisdiction is secure before proceeding to the merits. At oral argument we asked whether it was clear that the $75,000 amount-in-controversy requirement for diversity jurisdiction was met, and ordered the parties to file supplemental briefs on the matter. Not surprisingly, Carroll argued against federal jurisdiction, while Stryker supported it.

As the party removing the case to federal court, Stryker had the initial burden of establishing by a preponderance of the evidence facts that suggest the jurisdictional amount has been satisfied. Once it has made this showing, jurisdiction will be defeated only if it appears to a legal certainty that the stakes of the lawsuit do not exceed $75,000. The amount in controversy is evaluated as of the time of removal, although events subsequent to removal may clarify what the plaintiff was actually seeking when the case was removed.

If Carroll's damages were measured by reference to the *statutory* claim alone, the "legal certainty" test might kick in to defeat jurisdiction. As the Wisconsin Department of Workforce Development informed both Carroll and Stryker before the suit was filed, Wisconsin's wage-claim statute was amended in 2003 to specifically exclude commissioned salespersons. So Carroll was not a proper claimant under that statute and could not receive its enhanced recovery of a 50% penalty and attorney's fees. The Department told Carroll that he could potentially file suit under section 134.93, which provides a statutory cause of action to recover payment of commissions owed to independent sales representatives and applies to any sales representative "who is compensated, in whole or in part, by commission."

The legal-certainty test sets the bar high for excluding federal subject-matter jurisdiction, and for good reason: District courts should not get bogged down at the time of removal in evaluating claims on the merits to determine if jurisdiction exists. Nonetheless, removal is obviously improper if jurisdiction never existed in the first place. Counting the statutory damages—including the 50% penalty and attorney's fees—toward the jurisdictional amount when the statute by its terms does not apply would rest jurisdiction on a form of recovery that was legally impossible. True, this case does not involve a statutory or contractual cap on damages—common examples of claims that are considered "legally impossible" for jurisdictional purposes. But from the face of the statute and Carroll's complaint, it was clear from the beginning that as a sales representative who worked on commission, he could not recover under section 109.03.

But statutory damages are not the sole measure of the amount in controversy in this case. The complaint also demands "wages and other compensation and benefits" as general compensatory damages under the equitable contract doctrines of quantum meruit and unjust enrichment. In its supplemental brief in this court, Stryker supplied evidence of Carroll's damages demand under these doctrines. First, Stryker pointed to a letter from Carroll's counsel sent before the state-court suit was initiated. In it Carroll demanded $41,122.35 in lost commissions, nine months of draw in the amount of $54,000, and prefiling attorney's fees of $19,105, for a total of $114,227.35 in damages. Minus the attorney's fees, Carroll's damages demand totaled $95,122.35. Moreover, Carroll testified in deposition that he was seeking $50,000 to $60,000 in commissions, $200,000 to $300,000 in lost salary (presumably future salary in the form of commissions), a 10% bonus, a 401K distribution, and $15,000 to $20,000 in attorney's fees.

Finally, during the pendency of the case in federal court, Carroll's counsel sent a settlement offer to Stryker's counsel by email stating that Carroll had reduced his demand from an earlier figure of "$100,000 or more" and would now settle for $60,000 plus certain nonmonetary relief. We also note that the parties agreed in their proposed findings of fact that Carroll was seeking $200,000 to $300,000 in lost wages and that the jurisdictional amount had been met. While litigants cannot create federal jurisdiction where none exists, we take this agreement as further proof that the stakes of the suit exceeded the $75,000 jurisdictional threshold at the time of removal.

This evidence is enough to establish that the jurisdictional amount has been satisfied. In his supplemental brief arguing against jurisdiction, Carroll concentrates solely on the subject of statutory damages, ignoring the abundant evidence that the stakes of the suit exceeded the jurisdictional threshold when just the common-law claims are considered. We conclude that Stryker has shown more than the "theoretical availability of certain categories of damages," it has established that "what the plaintiff hopes to get out of the litigation," was well over $75,000. Subject-matter jurisdiction is secure, removal was proper, and we proceed to the merits.

Exercise 4-8. *Harshey* and *Carroll* Revisited

Based on the *Harshey* and *Carroll* cases, would the plaintiffs in the following cases meet the jurisdictional amount?

1. Three victims of a car accident who claim $50,000, $25,000, and $60,000 in damages, respectively.

2. Three victims of a car accident who claim $80,000, $25,000, and $16,000 in damages.

3. A tort claim brought by a plaintiff who broke his leg. In the state where he brought his case, cases brought for broken limbs received damage awards of $10,000 (arm), $13,000 (wrist), $50,000 (ankle), and $1.2 million (back).

4. A company that sues for an injunction to stop its former sales representative from breaching a one year covenant not to compete where the sales representative brought in, on average, $300,000 in sales at his former company, but has yet to bring in any sales at his new company. *See A.F.A. Tours, Inc. v. Whitchurch*, 937 F.2d 82 (2d Cir. 1991) (potential profits for new employer sufficient to meet the jurisdictional amount).

Note on Minimal Diversity Jurisdiction Statutes

When you read §1332, you probably noticed part (d) of the rule, which covers certain class actions as well as mass actions. This part of the statute is known as the Class Action Fairness Act ("CAFA"). CAFA allows plaintiffs to bring certain state law class actions and mass actions in federal court as well as permits defendants to remove these actions to federal court. The basic class action provision is in 28 U.S.C. §1332 (d)(2), which provides that the federal courts have jurisdiction over a state law class action if: (1) there are more than 100 members in the class; (2) the amount in controversy exceeds $5 million; and (3) there is minimal diversity between the plaintiffs and defendant(s). Minimal diversity means that at least one plaintiff is from a different state from at least one defendant. Thus, complete diversity is not required in these cases.

CAFA also contemplates "mass actions," an action brought by numerous plaintiffs who are not seeking class certification. *See* 28 U.S.C. §1332(d)(11). Cases falling under CAFA's jurisdictional grant are also removable to federal court, which is discussed in Part 7 of this chapter. *See* 28 U.S.C. §1453. CAFA has several exceptions, some of which are quite complex. *See* 28 U.S.C. §1332(d)(3), (4) & (9). A noteworthy difference between CAFA and §1332(a) diversity jurisdiction is that CAFA provides that an unincorporated association is a citizen of the state where it has its principal place of business as well as the state under whose laws it is organized. 28 U.S.C. §1332(d)(10). An unincorporated association is located in all the states of its members under §1332(a) diversity. *See Navarro Sav. Ass'n v. Lee*, 446 U.S. 458, 461 (1980). CAFA is the result of a perceived national problem related to plaintiff-friendly state courts that would certify purportedly meritless class actions. Those opposing CAFA saw it as an effort to bring class actions into the federal courts, which were less likely to certify the class. *See* Scott L. Nelson, *CAFA in the Congress: The Eight-Year Struggle*, in The Class Action Fairness Act: Law and Strategy 23 (Gregory C. Cook, ed., 2013).

A variant on the aggregated actions provisions above is the Multiparty, Multiforum Jurisdiction statute, 28 U.S.C. §1369. Like §1332(d), this statute requires minimal diversity between adverse parties. The other requirement is that the lawsuit arises out of a single incident in which at least 75 people have died in a single location. Like CAFA, there are exceptions to this grant of jurisdiction.

For purposes of this chapter, it is enough that you know there are specific grants of federal court jurisdiction over certain minimal-diversity state law class actions, mass actions, and mass disaster cases. Class actions and other rules for joining parties are covered in more detail in chapter 8.

Note on Exceptions to Diversity Jurisdiction

Two big areas of state law are not subject to diversity jurisdiction even if the parties are completely diverse and the amount in controversy requirement is met. Those areas are domestic relations, *Barber v. Barber*, 62 U.S. (21 How.) 582, 584 (1859), *In re Burrus*, 136 U.S. 586, 593–94 (1890), and probate cases, *In re Broderick's Will*, 88 U.S. 503 (1874). Why are there exceptions for these types of cases? What types of parties do these cases generally involve? Do the policies underlying the reasons for providing diversity jurisdiction apply to these cases?

5. Cases "Arising under the Constitution, Laws, or Treaties of the United States"

Along with diversity jurisdiction, federal trial courts are authorized to hear civil cases "arising under the Constitution, laws, or treaties of the United States." 28 U.S.C. § 1331. The district courts can exercise this type of jurisdiction, known as "arising under" or "federal question" jurisdiction, without regard to the amount in controversy. Like any statute, Section 1331 has "wiggle room"—terms that are not sufficiently definite to provide concrete answers in all cases. Can you identify the "wiggly" terminology in Section 1331? The courts' difficulty with federal question jurisdiction comes from the term "arising under." What does it mean for a claim to arise under federal law for purposes of federal jurisdiction? The answer to this question is easy when federal law creates the cause of action. Certainly such cases arise under federal law. But what happens if a federal issue is introduced by the defendant or is one element of a state law claim with several elements? Do these cases "arise under" federal law for purposes of federal jurisdiction? The cases that follow will help you identify the factors that the courts look to in making this determination.

Before reading the cases, a review of the history of arising under jurisdiction is helpful to understanding its current application. If you read Article III of the United States Constitution, it only establishes the United States Supreme Court. It leaves the creation of federal trial courts and intermediate appellate courts to Congress. At the time of the ratification of the Constitution, state trial courts existed that could handle trying most cases. Except for a brief attempt in 1801, Congress did not enact the precursor to current Section 1331 until 1875, creating a general grant of jurisdiction in the federal trial courts over cases arising under federal law. Paul J. Mishkin, *The Federal "Question" in the District Courts*, 53 Colum. L. Rev. 157, 157–59 (1953). What policies are promoted by this jurisdiction? Why is it useful to have federal trial courts interpreting federal law instead of state courts?

One of the earliest discussions of what "arising under" means comes from a case interpreting that language in Article III. *Osborn v. Bank of the United States*, 22 U.S. (9 Wheat) 738 (1824), involved a lawsuit brought in federal court by the Bank of the United States, an entity created by act of Congress, to enjoin the state auditor of Ohio from collecting a tax from the bank. The bank alleged that the tax was unconstitutional. The trial court enjoined the auditor from collecting the tax, but the auditor collected the tax anyway! The act creating the bank authorized it to sue and be sued in any circuit court of the United States. In a companion case to *Osborn*, *Bank of the United States v. Planters Bank of Georgia*, 22 U.S. (9 Wheat) 904 (1824), the bank sued because it had purchased some notes from a state bank that the state bank refused to honor. This companion case arose under state breach of contract law. In deciding the *Osborn* case, Justice John Marshall explained "when a question to which the judicial power of the union is extended by the constitution, forms an ingredient in the original cause, it is in the power of Congress to give the [federal] Circuit Courts jurisdiction of that cause, although other questions of fact or law may be involved in it." *Osborn*, 22 U.S. at 823. Because the bank was the creation of a federal act, every act of the bank necessarily grew out of the law that created it and endowed it with all the capacities it possessed. Thus, every case involving the bank, even one that amounted to a simple breach of contract, arose under the laws of the United States—an original ingredient—for purposes of federal question jurisdiction.

That federal courts have jurisdiction over a civil claim does not mean that the state courts do not have jurisdiction. Note that, with some exceptions specifically carved out by Congress, the default rule is that state courts can hear federal claims as well. However, the pleading of a federal claim in a state court case can form the basis for a defendant to remove the case to federal court. Thus, if a lawyer wants to keep his or her client's case in the state court system, the choice is often to omit any federal claims.

It is noteworthy that the "arising under" language appears not only in § 1331, but also in a variety of other explicit grants of jurisdiction in the Section 1330s of Title 28. Included, for example, are cases "arising under" patent, trademark, and copyright law (28 U.S.C. § 1338(a)) and postal matters (28 U.S.C. § 1339). In the case of patent, trademark, and copyright law, Congress has made federal court jurisdiction "exclusive," meaning that states cannot hear these claims. Why would Congress carve out an exception to the general rule that state courts also can hear federal claims for these types of cases?

Exercise 4-9. *Louisville & Nashville R. Co. v. Mottley*

The *Mottley* case is an early interpretation of "arising under" jurisdiction. As you read the case, answer the following questions.

1. In what court did the Mottleys first file this case?

2. Why is there no diversity jurisdiction in this case?

3. What's the claim in the *Mottley* case?

4. Who raised the issue of subject matter jurisdiction in *Mottley*?

5. What is the argument that the Mottley's case arises under federal law for purposes of federal jurisdiction even though their claim is a state law claim?

6. What rule does the Court set in this case?

Louisville & Nashville R. Co. v. Mottley
211 U.S. 149 (1908)

Mr. Justice Moody delivered the opinion of the Court:

The appellees (husband and wife), being residents and citizens of Kentucky, brought this suit in equity in the circuit court of the United States for the western district of Kentucky against the appellant, a railroad company and a citizen of the same state.

* * *

The bill alleged that in September, 1871, plaintiffs, while passengers upon the defendant railroad, were injured by the defendant's negligence, and released their respective claims for damages in consideration of the agreement for transportation during their lives, expressed in the contract. It is alleged that the contract was performed by the defendant up to January 1, 1907, when the defendant declined to renew the passes. The bill then alleges that the refusal to comply with the contract was based solely upon that part of the act of Congress of June 29, 1906, which forbids the giving of free passes or free transportation. The bill further alleges: First, that the act of Congress referred to does not prohibit the giving of passes under the circumstances of this case; and, second, that, if the law is to be construed as prohibiting such passes, it is in conflict with the 5th Amendment of the Constitution, because it deprives the plaintiffs of their property without due process of law. The defendant demurred to the bill. The judge of the circuit court overruled the demurrer, entered a decree for the relief prayed for, and the defendant appealed directly to this court.

* * *

... We do not deem it necessary ... to consider [the merits of the claims], because, in our opinion, the court below was without jurisdiction of the cause. Neither party has questioned that jurisdiction, but it is the duty of this court to see to it that the jurisdiction of the circuit court, which is defined and limited by statute, is not exceeded. This duty we have frequently performed of our own motion.

There was no diversity of citizenship, and it is not and cannot be suggested that there was any ground of jurisdiction, except that the case was a "suit … arising under the Constitution or laws of the United States." 25 Stat. at L. 434, ch. 866, U.S. Comp. Stat. 1901, p. 509. It is the settled interpretation of these words, as used in this statute, conferring jurisdiction, that a suit arises under the Constitution and laws of the United States only when the plaintiff's statement of his own cause of action shows that it is based upon those laws or that Constitution. It is not enough that the plaintiff alleges some anticipated defense to his cause of action, and asserts that the defense is invalidated by some provision of the Constitution of the United States. Although such allegations show that very likely, in the course of the litigation, a question under the Constitution would arise, they do not show that the suit, that is, the plaintiff's original cause of action, arises under the Constitution.

* * *

"The only way in which it might be claimed that a Federal question was presented would be in the complainant's statement of what the defense of defendants would be, and complainant's answer to such defense. Under these circumstances the case is brought within the rule laid down in *Tennessee v. Union & Planters' Bank*, [a case brought by the state of Tennessee in federal court to recover taxes owed by the defendant pursuant to state law. The plaintiff alleged that the defendant claimed immunity from the taxation because it was unconstitutional as applied to it. The Court held that the circuit court did not have jurisdiction, because 'A suggestion of one party, that the other will or may set up a claim under the Constitution or laws of the United States, does not make the suit one arising under that Constitution or those laws.' 152 U.S. 454, 464 (1894)]. That case has been cited and approved many times since."

* * *

It is ordered that the judgment be reversed and the case remitted to the circuit court with instructions to dismiss the suit for want of jurisdiction.

Exercise 4-10. *Mottley* Revisited

The rule coming out of the *Mottley* case is often referred to as the "well pleaded complaint" rule. Essentially, it holds that the federal issue must appear in the plaintiff's complaint as a legitimate part of the plaintiff's cause of action. The Mottleys refiled their case in state court. It was ultimately appealed again to the United States Supreme Court on the merits of the constitutional claim. The Supreme Court held for the railroad three years later. *Louisville & Nashville R. Co. v. Mottley*, 219 U.S. 467 (1911). What was gained by making the Mottleys return to state court to pursue a case that ultimately made its way back to the United States Supreme Court on the federal issue anyway? Given the rule in *Mottley*, assess whether the following cases "arise under" federal law for purposes of Section 1331.

1. A defamation case brought by a plaintiff who also addresses in her complaint a First Amendment defense that the defendant likely will raise.

2. A defamation case brought by a plaintiff who addresses in her complaint a First Amendment argument she will make in response to a state law defense that the defendant is likely to raise. *See Bracken v. Matgouranis*, 296 F.3d 160 (3d Cir. 2002) (federal arising under jurisdiction lacking).

3. A case brought by a plaintiff concerning four songs copyrighted under federal copyright laws alleging that the defendant copyright holder improperly assigned his rights to the songs to a third party in violation of its contract with the defendant. *See T.B. Harms Co. v. Eliscu*, 339 F.2d 823 (2d Cir. 1964) (claims arose under state contract law—not federal law).

4. A household fan manufacturer files a declaratory judgment action in federal court requesting a judgment that it has not infringed on a competitor's trade dress (a state law claim). The defendant counterclaims for patent infringement, a claim that is exclusively within the federal court's jurisdiction under 28 U.S.C. § 1338(a). *See Holmes Group, Inc. v. Vornado Air Circulation Systems, Inc.*, 535 U.S. 826 (2002) (federal court does not have arising under jurisdiction over state law claim even though defendant raises federal counterclaim in answer), *superseded in part by statute*, Leahy-Smith America Invents Act § 19(b), Pub. L. No. 112-29, 125 Stat. 284 (2011) (amending 28 U.S.C. § 1295(a)(1) to add compulsory patent counterclaims).

Note on State Law Claims that Incorporate Federal Standards — An Exercise in Reconciling Conflicting Cases

One skill that lawyers must develop is the ability to reconcile cases that appear to come to opposite conclusions when addressing a similar issue. The key to reconciling cases is in recognizing facts or nuances in legal rules that result in the cases being distinguishable from one another. Reconciling cases is important, because lawyers must know how to apply the law to their own client's case. Thus, knowing why a court came to one conclusion under one set of circumstances and the opposite under a slightly different set of circumstances is key to knowing how to apply the cases to a new set of facts. Two cases involving federal arising under jurisdiction provide an opportunity to practice this skill. This exercise asks you to try this yourself, but also provides you with an example of how to do so for these two cases. Exercise 4-13 will provide you with the opportunity to synthesize and reconcile cases on your own.

In addition to situations in which a defendant alleges a defense or counterclaim that arises under federal law, sometimes state law itself incorporates a federal standard. For example, in your torts class you have learned or will learn about negligence per se. Under many states' laws, a negligence per se claim exists if a defendant violates a state or federal law meant to protect the public. Thus, a federal issue can creep into a state tort action if the plaintiff alleges a breach of a federal standard in its state law claim. Is this sufficient for the plaintiff's claim to "arise under" federal law for purposes of federal jurisdiction?

Early case law on this issue was somewhat confused. In 1921, in *Smith v. Kansas Title & Trust Co.*, 255 U.S. 180 (1921), the United States Supreme Court decided that a case in which a shareholder of a corporation sued to enjoin the corporation from investing in federal bonds that the shareholder alleged were issued as a result of an unconstitutional law did arise under federal law for purposes of arising under jurisdiction. The underlying claim in the case was based on a Missouri law that made the investment in unauthorized securities an enjoinable act. Thus, Missouri law provided the basis for the plaintiff's claim. The Court set out this rule in the case: "The general rule is that where it appears from the [complaint] of the plaintiff that the right to relief depends upon the construction or application of the Constitution or laws of the United States, and that such federal claim is not merely colorable, and results upon a reasonable foundation, the District Court has jurisdiction." 255 U.S. at 199.

Justice Holmes dissented in *Smith*, explaining that " 'a suit arises under the law that creates the cause of action.' " 255 U.S. at 215 (quoting *American Well Works Co. v. Layne & Bowler Co.*, 241 U.S. 257, 260 (1916)). Because Missouri law created the plaintiff's cause of action in *Smith*, according to Holmes, it arose under Missouri state law—not federal law—for purposes of arising under jurisdiction. This principle is often referred to as the "Holmes Creation Test." While it is a handy rule to determine whether a claim is within the courts' arising under jurisdiction, the United States Supreme Court has noted that it is not as useful for excluding state law claims that contain a federal issue from the federal court's jurisdiction, because it excludes some state law claims that do arise under federal law for jurisdictional purposes. *See Franchise Tax Bd. of State of California v. Construction Laborers Vacation Trust for Southern California*, 463 U.S. 1, 9 (1983).

Compare and contrast *Smith* with *Moore v. Chesapeake & Ohio Ry. Co.*, 291 U.S. 205 (1934), a case decided thirteen years later that involved a plaintiff's action under a Kentucky law that provided a plaintiff could not be held responsible for contributory negligence or assumption of risk when his or her injury resulted from the violation of any state or federal statute enacted for the safety of employees. The plaintiff alleged that his injury was due to the defendant's failure to comply with the Federal Safety Appliance Act, which set safety precautions on railroad trains and locomotives. In this case, the Court held that the case did not arise under federal law for purpose of federal jurisdiction. The Court explained that where a case is brought under a state statute that creates a breach of duty under state law because of a requirement imposed by a federal statute, a federal question was not implicated.

Exercise 4-11. Reconciling Seemingly Conflicting Case Law

How do you reconcile *Smith* and *Moore*? What factual circumstances and/ or legal issues addressed in each case distinguish one from the other? Here are several ways to distinguish these two cases. First, the federal interest in each case was decidedly different. In *Smith*, the plaintiff alleged that an act of Congress was unconstitutional. This contention always has significant implications for federal interests, which make it an important case for a federal court to decide. In addition, federal courts have more expertise in federal issues of this sort. On the other hand, the *Moore* case simply involved application of a federal standard set out in a federal statute. There was no challenge to the authority of Congress to enact that statute.

Another potential distinguishing characteristic is the nature of the underlying determination required in each case. In *Smith*, the issue was one the courts could determine as a matter of law. It was not heavily fact-based. Either Congress had the authority under the Constitution to issue the bonds or it did not. *Moore*, on the other hand, was very fact-based. The fact finder would have to determine whether, factually, the defendant violated the Federal Safety Appliance Act resulting in the plaintiff's injury as well as any state law issue that might arise from that violation.

The potential for additional cases that might use similar theories might also account for the difference in results. Federal courts are courts of limited jurisdiction—they only hear cases as permitted by Article III and Congress. However, if a case like *Moore* were to create a federal question, a plaintiff could then bring any state negligence per se claim that relies on a federal standard in federal court. The federal courts' caseload would be significantly broadened for cases that involve state law tort claims. On the other hand, whether an Act of Congress is constitutional is decided once and for all for all cases that involve that Act. While the case would have to be appealed to the United States Supreme Court for it to become binding precedent nationwide, the issue would obviously be one of general importance to the federal system of government and would not obviously lead to a plethora of additional cases. Note that some of these reasons are policy-laden in terms of the types of cases that are important to the federal courts as well as the caseload of the federal courts.

Finally, one could argue that one of the cases was incorrect. Indeed, Justice Brennan argued in a subsequent case that *Moore* was incorrectly decided. *See Merrell Dow Pharmaceuticals, Inc. v. Thompson*, 478 U.S. 804, 821 n.1 (1986) (Brennan, J., dissenting). In subsequent cases you will have an opportunity to read how the Court itself distinguishes these two cases.

Exercise 4-12. *Grable & Sons Metal Products, Inc. v. Darue Engineering & Manufacturing* and Its Progeny

In the last ten years, the Court has revisited the issue of when a court has arising under jurisdiction over a state law claim that raises federal issues. As you read the next three cases, see if you can find a pattern in these cases to help identify those that will fall within arising under jurisdiction. Read these cases with an eye toward trying to synthesize them at the end. An exercise following all three will provide you with the opportunity to synthesize and apply your synthesis to new fact patterns. As you read the cases, answer the following questions.

1. How did each case reach a federal court?

2. What is the underlying claim in each case?

3. What are the four factors the *Grable* Court identifies for determining whether a claim arises under federal law when federal law does not create the cause of action?

4. The *Grable* Court discusses *Merrell Dow Pharmaceuticals, Inc. v. Thompson,* 478 U.S. 804 (1986). From the Court's description in *Grable,* what were the facts of *Merrell Dow,* and what did the Court hold in that case? How are *Grable* and *Merrell Dow* distinguishable?

5. How does the *Empire* majority distinguish *Grable*?

6. How does the *Gunn* majority distinguish *Grable*?

Grable & Sons Metal Products, Inc. v. Darue Engineering & Manufacturing

545 U.S. 308 (2005)

Justice Souter delivered the opinion of the Court.

The question is whether want of a federal cause of action to try claims of title to land obtained at a federal tax sale precludes removal to federal court of a state action with nondiverse parties raising a disputed issue of federal title law. We answer no, and hold that the national interest in providing a federal forum for federal tax litigation is sufficiently substantial to support the exercise of federal-question jurisdiction over the disputed issue on removal, which would not distort any division of labor between the state and federal courts, provided or assumed by Congress.

I

In 1994, the Internal Revenue Service seized Michigan real property belonging to petitioner Grable & Sons Metal Products, Inc., to satisfy

Grable's federal tax delinquency. Title 26 U.S.C. § 6335 required the IRS to give notice of the seizure, and there is no dispute that Grable received actual notice by certified mail before the IRS sold the property to respondent Darue Engineering & Manufacturing. Although Grable also received notice of the sale itself, it did not exercise its statutory right to redeem the property within 180 days of the sale, and after that period had passed, the Government gave Darue a quitclaim deed.

Five years later, Grable brought a quiet title action in state court, claiming that Darue's record title was invalid because the IRS had failed to notify Grable of its seizure of the property in the exact manner required by § 6335 (a), which provides that written notice must be "given by the Secretary to the owner of the property [or] left at his usual place of abode or business." Grable said that the statute required personal service, not service by certified mail.

Darue removed the case to Federal District Court as presenting a federal question, because the claim of title depended on the interpretation of the notice statute in the federal tax law. The District Court declined to remand the case at Grable's behest after finding that the "claim does pose a 'significant question of federal law,'" and ruling that Grable's lack of a federal right of action to enforce its claim against Darue did not bar the exercise of federal jurisdiction. On the merits, the court granted summary judgment to Darue, holding that although § 6335 by its terms required personal service, substantial compliance with the statute was enough. [The Court of Appeals for the Sixth Circuit affirmed.]

We granted certiorari on the jurisdictional question ... to resolve a split within the Courts of Appeals on whether [prior case law] always requires a federal cause of action as a condition for exercising federal-question jurisdiction. We now affirm.

II

Darue was entitled to remove the quiet title action if Grable could have brought it in federal district court originally, as a civil action "arising under the Constitution, laws, or treaties of the United States." This provision for federal-question jurisdiction is invoked by and large by plaintiffs pleading a cause of action created by federal law. There is, however, another longstanding, if less frequently encountered, variety of federal "arising under" jurisdiction, this Court having recognized for nearly 100 years that in certain cases federal-question jurisdiction will lie over state-law claims that implicate significant federal issues. The doctrine captures the commonsense notion that a federal court ought to be able to hear claims recognized under state law that nonetheless turn on substantial questions of federal law, and thus justify resort to the experience, solicitude, and hope of uniformity that a federal forum offers on federal issues.

The classic example is *Smith*, a suit by a shareholder claiming that the defendant corporation could not lawfully buy certain bonds of the National Government because their issuance was unconstitutional. Although Missouri law provided the cause of action, the Court recognized federal-question jurisdiction because the principal issue in the case was the federal constitutionality of the bond issue. *Smith* thus held, in a somewhat generous statement of the scope of the doctrine, that a state-law claim could give rise to federal-question jurisdiction so long as it "appears from the [complaint] that the right to relief depends upon the construction or application of [federal law]." *Smith v. Kansas City Title & Trust Co.*, 255 U.S. 180, 199 (1921).

The *Smith* statement has been subject to some trimming to fit earlier and later cases recognizing the vitality of the basic doctrine, but shying away from the expansive view that mere need to apply federal law in a state-law claim will suffice to open the "arising under" door.... It has in fact become a constant refrain in such cases that federal jurisdiction demands not only a contested federal issue, but a substantial one, indicating a serious federal interest in claiming the advantages thought to be inherent in a federal forum.

But even when the state action discloses a contested and substantial federal question, the exercise of federal jurisdiction is subject to a possible veto. For the federal issue will ultimately qualify for a federal forum only if federal jurisdiction is consistent with congressional judgment about the sound division of labor between state and federal courts governing the application of § 1331.... Because arising-under jurisdiction to hear a state-law claim always raises the possibility of upsetting the state-federal line drawn (or at least assumed) by Congress, the presence of a disputed federal issue and the ostensible importance of a federal forum are never necessarily dispositive; there must always be an assessment of any disruptive portent in exercising federal jurisdiction.

These considerations have kept us from stating a "single, precise, all-embracing" test for jurisdiction over federal issues embedded in state-law claims between nondiverse parties. *Christianson v. Colt Industries Operating Corp.*, 486 U.S. 800, 821 (1988). We have not kept them out simply because they appeared in state raiment, as Justice Holmes would have done, see *Smith*, 255 U.S. at 214 (dissenting opinion), but neither have we treated "federal issue" as a password opening federal courts to any state action embracing a point of federal law. Instead, the question is, does a state-law claim necessarily raise a stated federal issue, actually disputed and substantial, which a federal forum may entertain without disturbing any congressionally approved balance of federal and state judicial responsibilities.

III

A

This case warrants federal jurisdiction. Grable's state complaint must specify "the facts establishing the superiority of [its] claim," and Grable has premised its superior title claim on a failure by the IRS to give it adequate notice, as defined by federal law. Whether Grable was given notice within the meaning of the federal statute is thus an essential element of its quiet title claim, and the meaning of the federal statute is actually in dispute; it appears to be the only legal or factual issue contested in the case. The meaning of the federal tax provision is an important issue of federal law that sensibly belongs in a federal court. The Government has a strong interest in the "prompt and certain collection of delinquent taxes," *United States v. Rodgers*, 461 U.S. 677, 709 (1983), and the ability of the IRS to satisfy its claims from the property of delinquents requires clear terms of notice to allow buyers like Darue to satisfy themselves that the Service has touched the bases necessary for good title. The Government thus has a direct interest in the availability of a federal forum to vindicate its own administrative action, and buyers (as well as tax delinquents) may find it valuable to come before judges used to federal tax matters. Finally, because it will be the rare state title case that raises a contested matter of federal law, federal jurisdiction to resolve genuine disagreement over federal tax title provisions will portend only a microscopic effect on the federal-state division of labor.

This conclusion puts us in venerable company, quiet title actions having been the subject of some of the earliest exercises of federal-question jurisdiction over state-law claims. [Court describes and cites cases.] ... Consistent with those cases, the recognition of federal jurisdiction is in order here.

B

Merrell Dow Pharmaceuticals, Inc. v. Thompson, 478 U.S. 804 (1986), on which Grable rests its position, is not to the contrary. *Merrell Dow* considered a state tort claim resting in part on the allegation that the defendant drug company had violated a federal misbranding prohibition, and was thus presumptively negligent under Ohio law. The Court assumed that federal law would have to be applied to resolve the claim, but after closely examining the strength of the federal interest at stake and the implications of opening the federal forum, held federal jurisdiction unavailable. Congress had not provided a private federal cause of action for violation of the federal branding requirement, and the Court found "it would ... flout, or at least undermine, congressional intent to conclude that federal courts might nevertheless exercise federal-question jurisdiction and provide remedies for violations of that federal statute solely because the violation ... is said to be a ...'proximate cause' under state law." *Id.* at 812.

Because federal law provides for no quiet title action that could be brought against Darue, Grable argues that there can be no federal jurisdiction here, stressing some broad language in *Merrell Dow* (including the passage just quoted) that on its face supports Grable's position. But an opinion is to be read as a whole, and *Merrell Dow* cannot be read whole as overturning decades of precedent, as it would have done by effectively adopting the Holmes dissent in *Smith*, and converting a federal cause of action from a sufficient condition for federal-question jurisdiction into a necessary one.

* * *

... *Merrell Dow* should be read in its entirety as treating the absence of a federal private right of action as evidence relevant to, but not dispositive of, the "sensitive judgments about congressional intent" that § 1331 requires. The absence of any federal cause of action affected *Merrell Dow*'s result two ways. The Court saw the fact as worth some consideration in the assessment of substantiality. But its primary importance emerged when the Court treated the combination of no federal cause of action and no preemption of state remedies for misbranding as an important clue to Congress's conception of the scope of jurisdiction to be exercised under § 1331. The Court saw the missing cause of action not as a missing federal door key, always required, but as a missing welcome mat, required in the circumstances, when exercising federal jurisdiction over a state misbranding action would have attracted a horde of original filings and removal cases raising other state claims with embedded federal issues. For if the federal labeling standard without a federal cause of action could get a state claim into federal court, so could any other federal standard without a federal cause of action. And that would have meant a tremendous number of cases.

One only needed to consider the treatment of federal violations generally in garden variety state tort law. "The violation of federal statutes and regulations is commonly given negligence per se effect in state tort proceedings." RESTATEMENT (THIRD) OF TORTS § 14, Reporters' Note, Comment *a*, p. 195 (Tent. Draft No. 1, Mar. 28, 2001). A general rule of exercising federal jurisdiction over state claims resting on federal mislabeling and other statutory violations would thus have heralded a potentially enormous shift of traditionally state cases into federal courts. Expressing concern over the "increased volume of federal litigation," and noting the importance of adhering to "legislative intent," *Merrell Dow* thought it improbable that the Congress, having made no provision for a federal cause of action, would have meant to welcome any state-law tort case implicating federal law "solely because the violation of the federal statute is said to [create] a rebuttable presumption [of negligence] ... under state law." *Merrell Dow*, 478 U.S. at 811–12. In this situation, no welcome mat meant keep out. *Merrell Dow*'s analysis thus fits within the framework of examining the importance of having a federal forum for the issue, and the consistency of such a forum with Congress's intended division of labor between state and federal courts.

As already indicated, however, a comparable analysis yields a different jurisdictional conclusion in this case. Although Congress also indicated ambivalence in this case by providing no private right of action to Grable, it is the rare state quiet title action that involves contested issues of federal law. Consequently, jurisdiction over actions like Grable's would not materially affect, or threaten to affect, the normal currents of litigation. Given the absence of threatening structural consequences and the clear interest the Government, its buyers, and its delinquents have in the availability of a federal forum, there is no good reason to shirk from federal jurisdiction over the dispositive and contested federal issue at the heart of the state-law title claim.

IV

The judgment of the Court of Appeals, upholding federal jurisdiction over Grable's quiet title action, is affirmed.

It is so ordered.

<h2 style="text-align:center">Empire HealthChoice Assurance, Inc. v. McVeigh</h2>
547 U.S. 677 (2006)

Justice Ginsburg delivered the opinion of the Court.

The Federal Employees Health Benefits Act of 1959 (FEHBA), establishes a comprehensive program of health insurance for federal employees. The Act authorizes the Office of Personnel Management (OPM) to contract with private carriers to offer federal employees an array of health-care plans. Largest of the plans for which OPM has contracted ... is the Blue Cross Blue Shield Service Benefit Plan (Plan), administered by local Blue Cross Blue Shield companies. This case concerns the proper forum for reimbursement claims when a Plan beneficiary, injured in an accident, whose medical bills have been paid by the Plan administrator, recovers damages (unaided by the carrier-administrator) in a state-court tort action against a third party alleged to have caused the accident.

* * *

FEHBA itself provides for federal-court jurisdiction only in actions against the United States. Congress could decide and provide that reimbursement claims of the kind here involved warrant the exercise of federal-court jurisdiction. But claims of this genre, seeking recovery from the proceeds of state-court litigation, are the sort ordinarily resolved in state courts. Federal courts should await a clear signal from Congress before treating such auxiliary claims as "arising under" the laws of the United States.

* * *

II

Petitioner Empire HealthChoice Assurance, Inc., doing business as Empire Blue Cross Blue Shield (Empire), is the entity that administers the BCBSA Plan as it applies to federal employees in New York State. Respondent Denise Finn McVeigh (McVeigh) is the administrator of the estate of Joseph E. McVeigh (Decedent), a former enrollee in the Plan. The Decedent was injured in an accident in 1997. Plan payments for the medical care he received between 1997 and his death in 2001 amounted to $157,309. McVeigh, on behalf of herself, the Decedent, and a minor child, commenced tort litigation in state court against parties alleged to have caused Decedent's injuries. On learning that the parties to the state-court litigation had agreed to settle the tort claims, Empire sought to recover the $157,309 it had paid out for the Decedent's medical care. Of the $3,175,000 for which the settlement provided, McVeigh, in response to Empire's asserted reimbursement right, agreed to place $100,000 in escrow.

Empire then filed suit in the United States District Court for the Southern District of New York, alleging that McVeigh was in breach of the reimbursement provision of the Plan. As relief, Empire demanded $157,309, with no offset for attorney's fees or other litigation costs McVeigh incurred in pursuing the state-court settlement. McVeigh moved to dismiss on various grounds, among them, lack of subject-matter jurisdiction. [The district court granted McVeigh's motion, dismissing the case for lack of subject matter jurisdiction. The Second Circuit affirmed.]

III

Title 28 U.S.C. § 1331 vests in federal district courts "original jurisdiction" over "all civil actions arising under the Constitution, laws, or treaties of the United States." A case "aris[es] under" federal law within the meaning of § 1331, this Court has said, if "a well-pleaded complaint establishes either that federal law creates the cause of action or that the plaintiff's right to relief necessarily depends on resolution of a substantial question of federal law." *Franchise Tax Bd. of Cal. v. Construction Laborers Vacation Trust for Southern Cal.*, 463 U.S. 1, 27–28 (1983).

... The United States argues ... that there is federal jurisdiction here, as demonstrated by our recent decision in *Grable*, because "federal law is a necessary element of [Empire's] claim."

* * *

C

We turn ... to the argument that Empire's reimbursement claim, even if it does not qualify as a "cause of action created by federal law," nevertheless arises under federal law for § 1331 purposes, because federal law is "a necessary element of the [carrier's] claim for relief." (quoting *Grable* 545 U.S. 308, 312 and *Jones v. R.R. Donnelley & Sons Co.*, 541 U.S. 369, 376 (2004)). This case, we are satisfied, does not fit within the special and small category in which the United States would place it ...

* * *

This case is poles apart from *Grable*. The dispute there centered on the action of a federal agency (IRS) and its compatibility with a federal statute, the question qualified as "substantial," and its resolution was both dispositive of the case and would be controlling in numerous other cases. Here, the reimbursement claim was triggered, not by the action of any federal department, agency, or service, but by the settlement of a personal-injury action launched in state court, and the bottom-line practical issue is the share of that settlement properly payable to Empire.

Grable presented a nearly "pure issue of law," one "that could be settled once and for all and thereafter would govern numerous tax sale cases." [R. FALLON, D. MELTZER, & D. SHAPIRO, HART AND WECHSLER'S THE FEDERAL COURTS AND THE FEDERAL SYSTEM 65 (2005 Supp.).] In contrast, Empire's reimbursement claim, McVeigh's counsel represented without contradiction, is fact-bound and situation-specific. McVeigh contends that there were overcharges or duplicative charges by care providers, and seeks to determine whether particular services were properly attributed to the injuries caused by the 1997 accident and not rendered for a reason unrelated to the accident.

The United States observes that a claim for reimbursement may also involve as an issue "[the] extent, if any, to which the reimbursement should take account of attorney's fees expended ... to obtain the tort recovery." Indeed it may. But it is hardly apparent why a proper "federal-state balance," would place such a nonstatutory issue under the complete governance of federal law, to be declared in a federal forum. The state court in which the personal-injury suit was lodged is competent to apply federal law, to the extent it is relevant, and would seem best positioned to determine the lawyer's part in obtaining, and his or her fair share in, the tort recovery.

The United States no doubt "has an overwhelming interest in attracting able workers to the federal workforce," and "in the health and welfare of the federal workers upon whom it relies to carry out its functions." But those interests, we are persuaded, do not warrant turning into a discrete and costly "federal case" an insurer's contract-derived claim to be reimbursed from the proceeds of a federal worker's state-court-initiated tort litigation.

In sum, *Grable* emphasized that it takes more than a federal element "to open the 'arising under' door." This case cannot be squeezed into the slim category *Grable* exemplifies.

* * *

For the reasons stated, the judgment of the Court of Appeals for the Second Circuit is

Affirmed.

Justice Breyer, with whom Justice Kennedy, Justice Souter, and Justice Alito join, dissenting.

This case involves a dispute about the meaning of terms in a federal health insurance contract. The contract, between a federal agency and a private carrier, sets forth the details of a federal health insurance program created by federal statute and covering 8 million federal employees. In all this the Court cannot find a basis for federal jurisdiction. I believe I can.

* * *

It is enough here ... to assume that federal common law means federal jurisdiction where Congress so intends. If so, there are strong reasons for the federal courts ... to assume jurisdiction and apply federal common law to resolve this case.

First, although the nominal plaintiff in this case is the carrier, the real party in interest is the United States. Any funds that the petitioner recovers here it must pay directly to the United States, by depositing those funds in the FEHBA United States Treasury account managed by the federal agency. The carrier simply administers the reimbursement proceeding for the United States, just as it administers the rest of the agency/carrier contract. Accordingly, this case ... concerns the "rights of the United States under its contracts." *Boyle v. United Technologies Corp.*, 487 U.S. 500, 504 (1988).

Second, the health insurance system FEHBA establishes is a federal program. The Federal Government pays for the benefits, receives the premiums, and resolves disputes over claims for medical services. Given this role, the Federal Government's need for uniform interpretation of the contract is great. Given the spread of Government employees throughout the Nation and the unfairness of treating similar employees differently, the employees' need for uniform interpretation is equally great. That interest in uniformity calls for application of federal common law to disputes about the meaning of the words in the agency/carrier contract and brochure. And that interest in uniformity also suggests that the doors of the federal courts should be open to decide such disputes.

Third, ... the provisions at issue here are just a few scattered islands in a sea of federal contractual provisions, all of which federal courts will interpret and apply (when reviewing the federal agency's resolution of disputes regarding benefits). Given this context, why would Congress have wanted the courts to treat those islands any differently? I can find no convincing answer.

Gunn v. Minton

568 U.S. 251 (2013)

Chief Justice Roberts delivered the opinion of the Court.

Federal courts have exclusive jurisdiction over cases "arising under any Act of Congress relating to patents." 28 U.S.C. § 1338(a). The question presented is whether a state law claim alleging legal malpractice in the handling of a patent case must be brought in federal court.

I

In the early 1990s, respondent Vernon Minton developed a computer program and telecommunications network designed to facilitate securities trading. In March 1995, he leased the system — known as the Texas Computer Exchange Network, or TEXCEN — to R.M. Stark & Co., a securities brokerage. A little over a year later, he applied for a patent for an interactive securities trading system that was based substantially on TEXCEN. The U.S. Patent and Trademark Office issued the patent in January 2000.

Patent in hand, Minton filed a patent infringement suit in Federal District Court against the National Association of Securities Dealers, Inc. (NASD) and the NASDAQ Stock Market, Inc. He was represented by Jerry Gunn and the other petitioners. NASD and NASDAQ moved for summary judgment.... [T]he District Court granted the summary judgment motion and declared Minton's patent invalid.

Minton then filed a motion for reconsideration in the District Court, arguing for the first time that the lease agreement with Stark was part of ongoing testing of TEXCEN and therefore fell within the "experimental use" exception to the on-sale bar. The District Court denied the motion. [The Federal Circuit affirmed, agreeing that Minton had waived the experimental-use argument.]

Minton, convinced that his attorneys' failure to raise the experimental-use argument earlier had cost him the lawsuit and led to invalidation of his patent, brought this malpractice action in Texas state court. His former lawyers defended on the ground that the lease to Stark was not, in fact, for an experimental use, and that therefore Minton's patent infringement claims would have failed even if the experimental-use argument had been timely raised. The trial court agreed, holding that Minton had put forward "less than a scintilla of proof" that the lease had been for an experimental purpose. It accordingly granted summary judgment to Gunn and the other lawyer defendants. [On appeal, Minton raised the argument that, because his malpractice claim hinged on a patent claim, the state court did not have jurisdiction. The Texas Court of Appeals rejected Minton's argument, but the Texas Supreme Court reversed, holding that

Minton's claim involved a substantial federal issue that warranted federal court jurisdiction.]

* * *

II

"Federal courts are courts of limited jurisdiction," possessing "only that power authorized by Constitution and statute." *Kokken v. Guardian Life Ins. Co. of America*, 511 U.S. 375, 377 (1994). There is no dispute that the Constitution permits Congress to extend federal court jurisdiction to a case such as this one, the question is whether Congress has done so.

As relevant here, Congress has authorized the federal district courts to exercise original jurisdiction in "all civil actions arising under the Constitution, laws, or treaties of the United States," 28 U.S.C. § 1331, and, more particularly, over "any civil action arising under any Act of Congress relating to patents," § 1338(a). Adhering to the demands of "[l]inguistic consistency," we have interpreted the phrase "arising under" in both sections identically, applying our § 1331 and § 1338 precedents interchangeably. *See Christianson v. Colt Industries Operating Corp.*, 486 U.S. 800, 808–09 (1988). For cases falling within the patent-specific arising under jurisdiction of § 1338(a), however, Congress has not only provided for federal jurisdiction but also eliminated state jurisdiction, decreeing that "[n]o State court shall have jurisdiction over any claim for relief arising under any Act of Congress relating to patents." 28 U.S.C. § 1338(a). To determine whether jurisdiction was proper in the Texas courts, therefore, we must determine whether it would have been proper in a federal district court— whether, that is, the case "aris [es] under any Act of Congress relating to patents."

For statutory purposes, a case can "aris[e] under" federal law in two ways. Most directly, a case arises under federal law when federal law creates the cause of action asserted. As a rule of inclusion, this "creation" test admits of only extremely rare exceptions and accounts for the vast bulk of suits that arise under federal law....

But even where a claim finds its origins in state rather than federal law—as Minton's legal malpractice claim indisputably does—we have identified a "special and small category" of cases in which arising under jurisdiction still lies. In outlining the contours of this slim category, we do not paint on a blank canvas. Unfortunately, the canvas looks like one that Jackson Pollock got to first.

In an effort to bring some order to this unruly doctrine several Terms ago, we condensed our prior cases into the following inquiry: Does the "state-law claim necessarily raise a stated federal issue, actually disputed and substantial, which a federal forum may entertain without disturbing any congressionally approved balance of federal and state judicial responsibilities"? *Grable*, 545 U.S. at 314. That is, federal jurisdiction over a state law claim will lie if a federal issue is: (1) necessarily raised, (2) actually disputed, (3) substantial, and (4) capable of resolution in federal court without disrupting the federal-state balance approved by Congress. Where all four of these requirements are met, we held, jurisdiction is proper because there is a "serious federal interest in claiming the advantages thought to be inherent in a federal forum," which can be vindicated without disrupting Congress's intended division of labor between state and federal courts. *Id.*, at 313–314.

III

Applying *Grable*'s inquiry here, it is clear that Minton's legal malpractice claim does not arise under federal patent law. Indeed, for the reasons we discuss, we are comfortable concluding that state legal malpractice claims based on underlying patent matters will rarely, if ever, arise under federal patent law for purposes of § 1338(a). Although such cases may necessarily raise disputed questions of patent law, those cases are by their nature unlikely to have the sort of significance for the federal system necessary to establish jurisdiction.

A

To begin, we acknowledge that resolution of a federal patent question is "necessary" to Minton's case. Under Texas law, a plaintiff alleging legal malpractice must establish four elements: (1) that the defendant attorney owed the plaintiff a duty; (2) that the attorney breached that duty; (3) that the breach was the proximate cause of the plaintiff's injury; and (4) that damages occurred. In cases like this one, in which the attorney's alleged error came in failing to make a particular argument, the causation element requires a "case within a case" analysis of whether, had the argument been made, the outcome of the earlier litigation would have been different. To prevail on his legal malpractice claim, therefore, Minton must show that he would have prevailed in his federal patent infringement case if only petitioners had timely made an experimental-use argument on his behalf. That will necessarily require application of patent law to the facts of Minton's case.

B

The federal issue is also "actually disputed" here—indeed, on the merits, it is the central point of dispute. Minton argues that the experimental-use exception properly applied to his lease to Stark, saving his patent from the on-sale bar; petitioners argue that it did not. This is just the sort of "'dispute ... respecting the ... effect of [federal] law'" that *Grable* envisioned. *Grable*, 545 U.S. at 313 (quoting *Shulthis v. McDougal*, 225 U.S. 561, 569 (1912)).

C

Minton's argument founders on *Grable*'s next requirement, however, for the federal issue in this case is not substantial in the relevant sense. In reaching the opposite conclusion, the Supreme Court of Texas focused on the importance of the issue to the plaintiff's case and to the parties before it. As our past cases show, however, it is not enough that the federal issue be significant to the particular parties in the immediate suit; that will *always* be true when the state claim "necessarily raise[s]" a disputed federal issue, as *Grable* separately requires. The substantiality inquiry under *Grable* looks instead to the importance of the issue to the federal system as a whole.

In *Grable* itself, for example, the Internal Revenue Service had seized property from the plaintiff and sold it to satisfy the plaintiff's federal tax delinquency. Five years later, the plaintiff filed a state law quiet title action against the third party that had purchased the property, alleging that the IRS had failed to comply with certain federally imposed notice requirements, so that the seizure and sale were invalid. In holding that the case arose under federal law, we primarily focused not on the interests of the litigants themselves, but rather on the broader significance of the notice question for the Federal Government. We emphasized the Government's "strong interest" in being able to recover delinquent taxes through seizure and sale of property, which in turn "require [d] clear terms of notice to allow buyers ... to satisfy themselves that the Service has touched the bases necessary for good title." The Government's "direct interest in the availability of a federal forum to vindicate its own administrative action" made the question "an important issue of federal law that sensibly belong[ed] in a federal court." *Grable*, 545 U.S. at 315.

A second illustration of the sort of substantiality we require comes from *Smith*, which *Grable* described as "[t]he classic example" of a state claim arising under federal law. 545 U.S. at 312. In *Smith* the plaintiff argued that the defendant bank could not purchase certain bonds issued by the Federal Government because the Government had acted unconstitutionally in issuing them. We held that the case arose under federal law, because the "decision depends upon the determination" of "the constitutional validity of an act of Congress which is directly drawn in question." *Smiths*, 255 U.S. at 201. Again, the relevant point was not the importance of the question to the parties alone but rather the importance more generally of a determination that the Government "securities were issued under an unconstitutional law, and hence of no validity." *Id*.

Here, the federal issue carries no such significance. Because of the backward-looking nature of a legal malpractice claim, the question is posed in a merely hypothetical sense: *If* Minton's lawyers had raised a timely experimental-use argument, would the result in the patent infringement proceeding have been different? No matter how the state courts resolve that hypothetical "case within a case," it will not change the real-world result of the prior federal patent litigation. Minton's patent will remain invalid.

Nor will allowing state courts to resolve these cases undermine "the development of a uniform body of [patent] law." *Bonito Boats, Inc. v. Thunder Craft Boats, Inc.*, 489 U.S. 141, 162 (1989). Congress ensured such uniformity by vesting exclusive jurisdiction over actual patent cases in the federal district courts and exclusive appellate jurisdiction in the Federal Circuit. In resolving the nonhypothetical patent questions those cases present, the federal courts are of course not bound by state court case-within-a-case patent rulings. In any event, the state court case-within-a-case inquiry asks what would have happened in the prior federal proceeding if a particular argument had been made. In answering that question, state courts can be expected to hew closely to the pertinent federal precedents. It is those precedents, after all, that would have applied had the argument been made.

As for more novel questions of patent law that may arise for the first time in a state court "case within a case," they will at some point be decided by a federal court in the context of an actual patent case, with review in the Federal Circuit. If the question arises frequently, it will soon be resolved within the federal system, laying to rest any contrary state court precedent; if it does not arise frequently, it is unlikely to implicate substantial federal interests. The present case is "poles apart from *Grable*" in which a state court's resolution of the federal question "would be controlling in numerous other cases." *Empire v. Healthchoice Assurance, Inc.*, 547 U.S. 677, 700 (2006).

Minton also suggests that state courts' answers to hypothetical patent questions can sometimes have real-world effect on other patents through issue preclusion. Minton, for example, has filed what is known as a "continuation patent" application related to his original patent. He argues that, in evaluating this separate application, the patent examiner could be bound by the Texas trial court's interpretation of the scope of Minton's original patent. It is unclear whether this is true. The Patent and Trademark Office's Manual of Patent Examining Procedure provides that res judicata is a proper ground for rejecting a patent "only when the earlier decision was a decision of the Board of Appeals" or certain federal reviewing courts, giving no indication that state court decisions would have preclusive effect. In fact, Minton has not identified any case finding such preclusive effect based on a state court decision. But even assuming that a state court's case-within-a-case adjudication may be preclusive under some circumstances, the result would be limited to the parties and patents that had been before the state court. Such "fact-bound and situation-specific" effects are not sufficient to establish federal arising under jurisdiction. *Empire*, 547 U.S. at 701.

Nor can we accept the suggestion that the federal courts' greater familiarity with patent law means that legal malpractice cases like this one belong in federal court. It is true that a similar interest was among those we considered in *Grable*. But the possibility that a state court will incorrectly resolve a state claim is not, by itself, enough to trigger the federal courts' exclusive patent jurisdiction, even if the potential error finds its root in a misunderstanding of patent law.

There is no doubt that resolution of a patent issue in the context of a state legal malpractice action can be vitally important to the particular parties in that case. But something more, demonstrating that the question is significant to the federal system as a whole, is needed. That is missing here.

D

It follows from the foregoing that *Grable*'s fourth requirement is also not met. That requirement is concerned with the appropriate "balance of federal and state judicial responsibilities." *Grable*, 545 U.S. at 314. We have already explained the absence of a substantial federal issue within the meaning of *Grable*. The States, on the other hand, have "a special responsibility for maintaining standards among members of the licensed professions." *Ohralik v. Ohio State Bar Assn.*, 436 U.S. 447, 460 (1978). Their "interest ... in regulating lawyers is especially great since lawyers are essential to the primary governmental function of administering justice, and have historically been officers of the courts." *Goldfarb v. Virginina State Bar*, 421 U.S. 773, 792 (1975) (internal quotation marks omitted). We have no reason to suppose that Congress—in establishing exclusive federal jurisdiction over patent cases—meant to bar from state courts state legal malpractice claims simply because they require resolution of a hypothetical patent issue.

* * *

As we recognized a century ago, "[t]he Federal courts have exclusive jurisdiction of all cases arising under the patent laws, but not of all questions in which a patent may be the subject-matter of the controversy." *New Marshall Engine Co., v. Marshall Engine Co.*, 223 U.S. 473, 478 (1912). In this case, although the state courts must answer a question of patent law to resolve Minton's legal malpractice claim, their answer will have no broader effects. It will not stand as binding precedent for any future patent claim; it will not even affect the validity of Minton's patent. Accordingly, there is no "serious federal interest in claiming the advantages thought to be inherent in a federal forum," *Grable*, 545 U.S. at 313. Section 1338(a) does not deprive the state courts of subject matter jurisdiction.

The judgment of the Supreme Court of Texas is reversed, and the case is remanded for further proceedings not inconsistent with this opinion.

It is so ordered.

Exercise 4-13. Synthesizing *Grable*, *Empire*, and *Gunn*

You have just read the three most recent United States Supreme Court cases addressing whether a federal issue embedded in a state law claim creates arising under jurisdiction. How would you put these cases together to apply to future cases? A good place to start is with the four factors set out in *Grable*. Make a chart with those four factors and use the cases as examples of how the Court applies the factors in differing situations. After you do that, apply your approach to the following fact patterns to determine whether a federal court would have federal question jurisdiction.

1. Plaintiff brought a wrongful death action against a railroad, a train engineer, and conductor after her husband was killed when his car was hit by a train at a railroad crossing. Plaintiff alleged that the railroad failed to properly maintain the crossing and right-of-way, failed to construct properly the cross, and failed to provide adequate warning devices to warn drivers about oncoming trains. In her complaint, the plaintiff cited the Manual on Uniform Traffic Control Devices, a federal publication, and 23 C.F.R. §646.214(b)(3), a federal regulation, to support her theory that the railroad owed a duty to a motorist such as her husband. *See Connolly v. Union Pacific Railroad Co.*, 453 F. Supp. 2d 1104 (E.D. Mo. 2006) (arising under jurisdiction not present).

2. A cable television customer sued his cable television provider for breach of contract for violating the terms of its uniform customer agreement. That agreement provides that the company's rates and any changes to those rates are subject to applicable law. Federal law provides that cable service providers who are the only providers in a geographic area must provide uniform rates to all customers. Plaintiff alleged that some customers were offered discounted winter rates that he was never offered. Plaintiff's complaint also included claims for fraud and unjust enrichment. *See Broder v. Cablevision Systems Corp.*, 418 F.3d 187 (2d Cir. 2005) (action removable on the basis of arising under jurisdiction).

3. The Rhode Island Fishermen's Alliance, a trade organization, and eight individual lobster fisherman sued the Rhode Island Department of Environmental Management ("DEM") under the Rhode Island constitution and various Rhode Island state laws. The DEM adopted a regulation for lobster fishing to bring the state in compliance with a policy adopted by the Atlantic States Marine Fisheries Commission, an interstate body created by federal law to prepare and adopt interstate fishery management plans.

The particular policy at issue was designed to prevent overfishing of lobster. It required Rhode Island and Massachusetts to allocate lobster traps to fishermen based on each fisherman's documented lobster catch during 2001–2003. The lawsuit challenged the DEM regulation implementing this federal policy. The plaintiffs argued, in part, that the federal policy did not require DEM to adopt the particular limit. *See Rhode Island Fishermen's Alliance, Inc. v. Rhode Island Dept. of Environmental Management*, 585 F.3d 42 (1st Cir. 2009) (plaintiff's claim included embedded federal question for purposes of arising jurisdiction).

4. Aircraft passengers and bystanders brought an action against an airline, the aircraft manufacturer, and the city owning the airport involved under state law, including claims of negligence, conscious disregard for safety, and product liability, for injuries resulting when an aircraft overran its runway, broke through a fence, and eventually came to stop on a residential city street. The aviation industry is highly regulated by the federal government. *See Bennett v. Southwest Airlines Co.*, 484 F.3d 907 (7th Cir. 2007) (tort claims did not arise under federal law for purposes of federal jurisdiction).

Note on Other Situations That Implicate (or Do Not Implicate) Arising under Jurisdiction

Several other types of cases implicating arising under jurisdiction are worth noting. First, as noted earlier in the chapter, when a cause of action is created by federal law, under the Holmes Creation Test, the claim falls within arising under jurisdiction. However, it is not always easy to determine whether a federal statute creates a cause of action. In some statutes, such as Title VII of the Civil Rights Act of 1964, the statute itself provides that a person harmed by a violation of the statute may sue. 42 U.S.C. §2000e-5(f)(1). However, sometimes a statute prohibits conduct but does not indicate whether someone harmed by that conduct can sue. Under these circumstances, the Court initially looked to a multi-factored test to determine whether it could imply a cause of action into a federal law.

The Court set out the four factor test in *Cort v. Ash*, 422 U.S. 66, 78 (1975):

In determining whether a private remedy is implicit in a statute not expressly providing one, several factors are relevant. First, is the plaintiff "one of the class for whose especial benefit the statute was enacted," — that is, does the statute create a federal right in favor of the plaintiff? Second, is there any indication of legislative intent, explicit or implicit, either to create such a remedy or to deny one? Third, is it consistent with the underlying purposes of the legislative scheme to imply such a remedy for the plaintiff? And finally, is the cause of action one traditionally relegated to state law, in an area basically the concern of the States, so that it would be inappropriate to infer a cause of action based solely on federal law?

Modernly, the Supreme Court has emphasized the second factor — legislative intent. Thus, the focus is on determining whether Congress, although it did not explicitly provide for a private cause of action in a statute, meant to do so. *Touche Ross & Co. v. Redington*, 442 U.S. 560, 575 (1979) ("[t]he central inquiry remains whether Congress intended to create, either expressly or by implication, a private cause of action."). Courts use the other three *Cort* factors to help determine legislative intent. *See id.* at 575–76.

There are also areas of federal common law that qualify for arising under jurisdiction. As you probably have realized from your torts and contracts courses, much law in the United States is developed by the courts themselves — not just legislatures. Thus, in certain areas where the federal government has distinct interests, the federal courts have arising under jurisdiction. For example, the United States' rights and duties with respect to commercial paper that it issues are governed by federal law. *See Clearfield Trust Co. v. United States*, 318 U.S. 363, 366 (1943). Likewise, the United States' obligations and rights under its own contracts are governed by federal common law. *Boyle v. United Technologies Corp.*, 487 U.S. 500, 504 (1988). Thus, even where a statute does not provide for a cause of action, there are areas of federal common law that provide a basis for arising under jurisdiction.

In addition, if federal law covers the entire area of law, arising under jurisdiction exists based on "field preemption." However, for field preemption to apply, the federal coverage of the field of law in question must be complete, meaning that the federal law leaves no areas for states to regulate within the field. Even though ordinarily preemption is a defense that would not result in federal court jurisdiction under *Mottley*'s well-pleaded complaint rule, if Congress intended to preempt the entire field, the case is one for federal court. Two examples of statutes that create this type of preemption are the Employee Retirement Income Security Act of 1974 (commonly known as "ERISA"), *Metropolitan Life Ins. Co. v. Taylor*, 481 U.S. 58, 67 (1987), and the Labor Management Relations Act (commonly known as the "LMRA"), *Avco Corp v. Machinists*, 390 U.S. 557 (1968). This is often raised by defendants using the "artful pleading" doctrine. Defendants use this doctrine to argue that a case arises under federal law when the plaintiff has no stated federal claim in the case, but the claim is necessarily federal. A claim that is preempted by federal law presents the most compelling case for using this doctrine.

On the other hand, there are areas of federal law that incorporate state law that the Court has held do not provide a basis for arising under jurisdiction. The classic case of this is *Shoshone Mining Co. v. Royal J. Rutter*, 177 U.S. 505 (1900). The *Shoshone* case involved federal legislation providing that persons who had a dispute regarding ownership of land granted by the United States government could sue to determine the right of possession of the property. The determination of who owned the property was made by looking at local customs and statutory provisions at the time that controlled the right of possession of property. This determination usually involved a question of fact based on application of local customs, such as the location of the claim or a determination of the meaning of certain local rules and customs followed by miners in the particular area. Thus, it did not necessarily involve an issue of federal law. Accordingly, the Court in *Shoshone* remanded the case for dismissal for lack of subject matter jurisdiction because, even though federal law allowed potential property owners to resolve these disputes, there was no federal question in the case. Another interesting example the *Shoshone* Court provided comes directly from the Constitution. Article I, §2 of the Constitution provides that electors in each state of members of the House of Representatives "shall have the qualifications requisite for electors of the most numerous branch of the state legislature." The *Shoshone* Court noted that even though this provision appears in the Constitution, the issue is one of state law because it relies on qualifications set by state law. *Shoshone*, 177 U.S. at 508.

6. Supplemental Jurisdiction

a. The History of Supplemental Jurisdiction

What happens when a case between two non-diverse parties includes a federal question, for example an employment discrimination case under Title VII of the Civil Rights Act of 1964, and a claim under a state anti-discrimination law? Can you bring both claims in the same federal lawsuit? Similarly, assume you represent three plaintiffs who are diverse from the defendant who wish to assert state tort claims in federal court, but only one of them has a claim that meets the jurisdictional amount. Can you bring the claims of all three in federal court? Supplemental jurisdiction is a form of "tag along" jurisdiction that permits a plaintiff to bring claims that would not otherwise qualify for federal court jurisdiction because these additional claims are related to claims over which the federal courts have subject matter jurisdiction.

Supplemental jurisdiction is codified at 28 U.S.C. §1367. Prior to its codification by Congress, the courts at common law created a set of rules that permitted parties to bring these "tag along" state law claims. The common law concepts that the courts developed included ancillary and pendent jurisdiction. Pendent jurisdiction permitted a plaintiff to append a claim lacking an independent basis for federal subject matter jurisdiction to a claim that did come within the federal court's jurisdiction. Ancillary jurisdiction permitted a plaintiff or defendant to bring in a claim and sometimes a party lacking an independent basis for federal subject matter jurisdiction by way of counterclaim (when a defendant counter-sues a plaintiff), cross-claim (when a co-party sues another co-party), or a third party complaint (when a defendant brings in a third party and sues them in the same action). The rules governing the addition of claims and parties are covered under the subject of Joinder, which is detailed in Chapter 8. For now, it is enough that you know the basics of these concepts.

While both of these types of jurisdiction are now subsumed under the concept of supplemental jurisdiction, it's important to know what ancillary and pendent jurisdiction are, because courts still use these terms.

A pivotal case that predates the codification of supplemental jurisdiction, but greatly influenced it, is *United Mine Workers v. Gibbs*, 383 U.S. 715 (1966). In *Gibbs*, the Court addressed a case brought in federal court by Gibbs, a superintendent of mining operations, against the United Mine Workers for tortious interference with contract under state law as well as a secondary boycott under Section 303 of the Labor Management Relations Act ("LMRA"), a federal law. The jury held for Gibbs on both claims. However, the trial judge set aside the verdict on the secondary boycott claim, holding that the LMRA claim failed as a matter of law. The court upheld the jury's verdict on the state law claim. Once the federal claim was dismissed, the defendant challenged the court's subject matter jurisdiction to hear the remaining state law claim. The Supreme Court held that the federal trial court had jurisdiction in the case. In doing so, the Court explained that for a federal court to hear a state law claim along with a federal claim, the claims must derive from a "common nucleus of operative fact." In addition, the plaintiff's claims must be "such that he would ordinarily be expected to try them all in one judicial proceeding." Finally, the federal issue must be substantial. State claims satisfying this standard were considered part of the "same case or controversy" as the claim over which the federal court has original jurisdiction for purposes of jurisdiction under Article III of the Constitution. Thus, the court's exercise of such jurisdiction over the state law claims was within the constitutional authority of the federal courts.

Applied in the *Gibbs* case, the two claims clearly arose out of a common nucleus of operative fact—both claims involved interference with Gibbs's ability to complete his duties under his contract with the mines due to the Union's interference. In addition, the federal issue was substantial. The federal claim remained in the case all the way through the jury's verdict; thus, it was sufficient to support the court's jurisdiction.

The *Gibbs* Court was careful to acknowledge that keeping such state law claims in federal court was within the trial judge's discretion. That decision also remains open throughout the litigation. Thus, the court could dismiss the state law claims later if it determined that was appropriate. The Court offered guidance on what the trial court should consider in exercising this discretion:

> Certainly, if the federal claims are dismissed before trial, even though not insubstantial in a jurisdictional sense, the state claims should be dismissed as well. Similarly, if it appears that the state issues substantially predominate, whether in terms of proof, of the scope of the issues raised, or of the comprehensiveness of the remedy sought, the state claims may be dismissed without prejudice and left for resolution to state tribunals. There may, on the other hand, be situations in which the state claim is so closely tied to questions of federal policy that the argument for exercise of pendent jurisdiction is particularly strong.... Finally, there may be reasons independent of jurisdictional considerations, such as the likelihood of jury confusion in treating divergent legal theories of relief, that would justify separating state and federal claims for trial. If so, jurisdiction should ordinarily be refused.

Gibbs, 383 U.S. 736–37. In *Gibbs*, these problems were not implicated. The Court did note that if there was a problem of jury confusion, the court could use a special verdict form to guide the jurors through their decision making process.

In 1989, the Supreme Court began to rein in this type of jurisdiction. In *Finley v. United States*, 490 U.S. 545 (1989), the Court held that a woman suing for the death of her husband and children in a plane crash could not bring both state and federal claims in federal court, even though one of her claims was within the exclusive jurisdiction of the federal courts. In this case, Finley sued the Federal Aviation Administration under the Federal Tort Claims Act. She also sued the City of San Diego and a local utility company under state tort laws. The plaintiff was not diverse from either the City or the utility. The Court held that she could not bring her state law claims against additional parties when there was no independent basis for federal subject jurisdiction over those additional claims. The result for Finley was that she would have to maintain two lawsuits—one in federal court against the FAA and one in state court against the utility and the City. Yet, both cases involved the same facts. In that case, the Court invited Congress to codify a fix to this problem. It did so in 28 U.S.C. § 1367.

b. Modern Supplemental Jurisdiction

Read 28 U.S.C. § 1367. This statute is quite complex, and it helps to diagram it to understand it. The statute is broken into three basic parts. Taking it apart section by section is helpful to understanding how it functions.

First, the court can exercise jurisdiction if the requirements of § 1367(a) are met, subject to exceptions set out for diversity cases in § 1367(b), which are discussed in the next paragraph. Use of Section 1367(a) hinges on the existence of an "anchor claim"—a claim over which the court has original jurisdiction. That original jurisdiction can be based on diversity, arising under jurisdiction, or some other grant of federal court jurisdiction. Section 1367(a) permits the court to exercise supplemental jurisdiction over an additional claim—the "supplemental" claim—as long as that additional claim forms part of the "same case or controversy" for purposes of Article III. Recall the standard set for this determination in *Gibbs*. In order to be part of the "same case or controversy," both claims must derive from a common nucleus of operative fact.

Section 1367(b) provides several exceptions to the exercise of supplemental jurisdiction when the anchor claim is based on diversity jurisdiction. If the court's jurisdiction over the anchor claim is based on arising under jurisdiction, Section 1367(b)'s exceptions do not apply. Even in cases of diversity, the exceptions apply only in certain situations in which parties are joined. Joinder is covered in detail in Chapter 8. For purposes of the discussion here, it is enough for you to know that two of the exceptions apply only to claims made by plaintiffs against joined parties. The other two exceptions bar claims made either by such a joined party or against such a joined party. The best way to apply this section is to first note whether the anchor claim is based on diversity and then determine whether you have one of the joinder situations set out in subsection (b).

Even where the exceptions contained in Section 1367(b) do not apply, the court still has discretion to remand the state law claims if the policies in § 1367(c) are implicated in the case. Thus, the statute retains the discretionary nature of the court's assertion of jurisdiction over these state law claims that the Court set out in *Gibbs*. Note that the discretionary factors set out in § 1367(c) include some, but not all, of the factors set out in the *Gibbs* case. Do you think Congress meant to codify the *Gibbs* discretionary factors in § 1367(c)? Can the court use factors set out in *Gibbs* that don't appear in the statute?

Exercise 4-14. Applying 28 U.S.C. § 1367

Using what you know about federal question and diversity jurisdiction as well as § 1367, would a federal trial court have jurisdiction in the following cases?

1. Plaintiff was fired from her job at Powerco, the local electric company for Little Rock, Arkansas. Plaintiff is an Arkansas resident. She believes she was fired because of her sex, i.e., being female, in violation of Title VII of the Civil Rights Act of 1964, a federal statute that creates a private right of action for employees whose employers violate the Act. Plaintiff also wishes to sue under the Arkansas Civil Rights Act, which also prohibits employment discrimination based on sex.

2. Plaintiff was fired from her job at Powerco, the local electric company for Little Rock, Arkansas. Plaintiff is an Arkansas resident. She believes she was fired because of her sex, i.e., being female, in violation of Title VII of the Civil Rights Act of 1964, a federal statute. Plaintiff also wishes to sue in the same lawsuit for breach of contract, because she was under a three-year contact with Powerco, which would expire in one more year.

3. Plaintiff opened up a garbage company in California and began to solicit business from industrial clients to haul their recyclables. At first, business was booming; the company was picking up all sorts of recyclable waste, and the business looked like it would be very profitable. Suddenly, business fell off entirely. The plaintiff found out that other garbage companies were colluding to stop their clients from using its services because those companies wanted to begin to pick up recyclables. The plaintiff sues several garbage companies under both state and federal antitrust statutes.

4. Plaintiff was working on scaffolding that collapsed. It was manufactured by Shakey Corp. She was severely injured and was out of work for one full year. She also continued to have residual back pain due to the injury. Plaintiff lives in Arkansas. Shakey is a Texas corporation with its principal place of business in Dallas. The plaintiff files suit in federal court based on diversity. Shakey claims that the defective part that caused plaintiff's injury was manufactured by Rice Materials Company. Rice is an Arkansas corporation with its principal place of business in Pine Bluff. If Shakey

brings in Rice as a third party defendant under Rule 14, may the plaintiff amend her complaint to assert a claim against Rice?

A couple of lingering ambiguities persisted even after the codification of §1367. The first was how to apply it to Rule 23 class actions. Prior to enactment of §1367, the Court held in *Zahn v. International Paper Co.*, 414 U.S. 291 (1973), that while only the named plaintiffs and defendants needed to be completely diverse, every member of the class had to meet the jurisdictional amount for class actions brought in federal court based on diversity jurisdiction. In addition, it was not clear whether some, but not all, of the plaintiffs in a non-class action diversity case needed to meet the jurisdictional amount. Prior case law established that when a single plaintiff sued a single defendant, the plaintiff could aggregate the amount of damages it had against that defendant from more than one claim to reach the amount in controversy. Thus, the plaintiff could add up the varying amounts of its claims against the defendant, and if together they exceeded the jurisdictional amount, diversity was proper. However, aggregation of claims by different plaintiffs was permitted only if they had a common, undivided interest, such as a joint tenancy in a piece of real property. *Clark v. Paul Gray, Inc.*, 306 U.S. 583 (1939). Thus, if three plaintiffs sued a driver who was responsible for their injuries in a car accident, under *Clark*, each individual plaintiff's damages would have to meet the jurisdictional amount for the federal court to hear the case. If only one plaintiff's claim did, he or she would have to sue alone. The other plaintiffs could bring their claims in the state court system. Section 1367 called both approaches into question. The *Exxon Mobile* case answers some questions raised by the codification of Section 1367.

Exercise 4-15. *Exxon Mobile Corp. v. Allapattah Services, Inc.*

As you read *Exxon Mobile*, answer the following questions:

1. The Court discusses the indivisibility theory and the contamination theory. What are these theories? Does it reject them or accept them in *Exxon Mobile*? Why does it do so?

2. What is the Court's holding in this case? Is it consistent with your reading of §§ 1367(a) and (b)?

3. Why did the Supreme Court of the United States grant certiorari in this case?

Exxon Mobile Corp. v. Allapattah Services, Inc.

545 U.S. 546 (2005)

Justice Kennedy delivered the opinion of the Court.

These consolidated cases present the question whether a federal court in a diversity action may exercise supplemental jurisdiction over additional plaintiffs whose claims do not satisfy the minimum amount-in-controversy requirement, provided the claims are part of the same case or controversy as the claims of plaintiffs who do allege a sufficient amount in controversy. Our decision turns on the correct interpretation of 28 U.S.C. § 1367. The question has divided the Courts of Appeals, and we granted certiorari to resolve the conflict.

We hold that, where the other elements of jurisdiction are present and at least one named plaintiff in the action satisfies the amount-in-controversy requirement, § 1367 does authorize supplemental jurisdiction over the claims of other plaintiffs in the same Article III case or controversy, even if those claims are for less than the jurisdictional amount specified in the statute setting forth the requirements for diversity jurisdiction. We affirm the judgment of the Court of Appeals for the Eleventh Circuit…, and we reverse the judgment of the Court of Appeals for the First Circuit.

I

In 1991, about 10,000 Exxon dealers filed a class-action suit against the Exxon Corporation in the United States District Court for the Northern District of Florida. The dealers alleged an intentional and systematic scheme by Exxon under which they were overcharged for fuel purchased from Exxon. The plaintiffs invoked the District Court's 1332(a) diversity jurisdiction. After a unanimous jury verdict in favor of the plaintiffs, the District Court certified the case for interlocutory review, asking whether it had properly exercised § 1367 supplemental jurisdiction over the claims of class members who did not meet the jurisdictional minimum amount in controversy. [The 11th Circuit upheld the trial court's use of supplemental jurisdiction.]

* * *

In the other case now before us the Court of Appeals for the First Circuit took a different position on the meaning of § 1367(a). In that case, a 9-year-old girl sued Star-Kist in a diversity action in the United States District Court for the District of Puerto Rico, seeking damages for unusually severe injuries she received when she sliced her finger on a tuna can. Her family joined in the suit, seeking damages for emotional distress and certain medical expenses. The District Court granted summary judgment to Star-Kist, finding that none of the plaintiffs met the minimum amount-in-controversy requirement. The Court of Appeals for the First Circuit, however, ruled that the injured girl, but not her family members, had made allegations of damages in the requisite amount. [The 1st Circuit held that supplemental jurisdiction over the family members' claims that fell below the jurisdictional amount was improper. Thus, the 1st Circuit (as well as other courts that agreed with its holding) and 11th Circuit were in conflict on this issue.]

II

A

The district courts of the United States, as we have said many times, are "courts of limited jurisdiction. They possess only that power authorized by Constitution and statute." *Kokkonen v. Guardian Life Ins. Co. of America*, 511 U.S. 375, 377 (1994). In order to provide a federal forum for plaintiffs who seek to vindicate federal rights, Congress has conferred on the district courts original jurisdiction in federal-question cases — civil actions that arise under the Constitution, laws, or treaties of the United States. 28 U.S.C. § 1331. In order to provide a neutral forum for what have come to be known as diversity cases, Congress also has granted district courts original jurisdiction in civil actions between citizens of different States, between U.S. citizens and foreign citizens, or by foreign states against U.S. citizens. § 1332. To ensure that diversity jurisdiction does not flood the federal courts with minor disputes, § 1332(a) requires that the matter in controversy in a diversity case exceed a specified amount, currently $75,000.

Although the district courts may not exercise jurisdiction absent a statutory basis, it is well established — in certain classes of cases — that, once a court has original jurisdiction over some claims in the action, it may exercise supplemental jurisdiction over additional claims that are part of the same case or controversy. The leading modern case for this principle is *Mine Workers v. Gibbs*.

* * *

We have not, however, applied *Gibbs'* expansive interpretive approach to other aspects of the jurisdictional statutes. For instance, we have consistently interpreted § 1332 as requiring complete diversity: In a case with multiple plaintiffs and multiple defendants, the presence in the action of a single plaintiff from the same State as a single defendant deprives the district court of original diversity jurisdiction over the entire action. The complete diversity requirement is not mandated by the Constitution, or by the plain text of § 1332(a). The Court, nonetheless, has adhered to the complete diversity rule in light of the purpose of the diversity requirement, which is to provide a federal forum for important disputes where state courts might favor, or be perceived as favoring, home-state litigants. The presence of parties from the same State on both sides of a case dispels this concern, eliminating a principal reason for conferring § 1332 jurisdiction over any of the claims in the action.... In order for a federal court to invoke supplemental jurisdiction under *Gibbs*, it must first have original jurisdiction over at least one claim in the action. Incomplete diversity destroys original jurisdiction with respect to all claims, so there is nothing to which supplemental jurisdiction can adhere.

* * *

B

In *Finley* we emphasized that "[w]hatever we say regarding the scope of jurisdiction conferred by a particular statute can of course be changed by Congress." 490 U.S. 545, 556 (1921). In 1990, Congress accepted the invitation. It passed the Judicial Improvements Act, 104 Stat. 5089, which enacted §1367, the provision which controls these cases.

* * *

Section 1367(a) is a broad grant of supplemental jurisdiction over other claims within the same case or controversy, as long as the action is one in which the district courts would have original jurisdiction. The last sentence of §1367(a) makes it clear that the grant of supplemental jurisdiction extends to claims involving joinder or intervention of additional parties. The single question before us, therefore, is whether a diversity case in which the claims of some plaintiffs satisfy the amount-in-controversy requirement, but the claims of other plaintiffs do not, presents a "civil action of which the district courts have original jurisdiction." If the answer is yes, §1367(a) confers supplemental jurisdiction over all claims, including those that do not independently satisfy the amount-in-controversy requirement, if the claims are part of the same Article III case or controversy. If the answer is no, §1367(a) is inapplicable and ... the district court has no statutory basis for exercising supplemental jurisdiction over the additional claims.

We now conclude the answer must be yes. When the well-pleaded complaint contains at least one claim that satisfies the amount-in-controversy requirement, and there are no other relevant jurisdictional defects, the district court, beyond all question, has original jurisdiction over that claim. The presence of other claims in the complaint, over which the district court may lack original jurisdiction, is of no moment. If the court has original jurisdiction over a single claim in the complaint, it has original jurisdiction over a "civil action" within the meaning of §1367(a), even if the civil action over which it has jurisdiction comprises fewer claims than were included in the complaint. Once the court determines it has original jurisdiction over the civil action, it can turn to the question whether it has a constitutional and statutory basis for exercising supplemental jurisdiction over the other claims in the action.

Section 1367(a) commences with the direction that §§1367(b) and (c), or other relevant statutes, may provide specific exceptions, but otherwise §1367(a) is a broad jurisdictional grant, with no distinction drawn between pendent-claim and pendent-party cases. In fact, the last sentence of §1367(a) makes clear that the provision grants supplemental jurisdiction over claims involving joinder or intervention of additional parties. The terms of §1367 do not acknowledge any distinction between pendent jurisdiction and the doctrine of so-called ancillary jurisdiction. Though the doctrines of pendent and ancillary jurisdiction developed separately as a historical matter, the Court has recognized that the doctrines are "two species of the same generic problem," *Owen Equipment and Erection Co. v. Kroger*, 437 U.S. 365, 370 (1978). Nothing in § 1367 indicates a congressional intent to recognize, preserve, or create some meaningful, substantive distinction between the jurisdictional categories we have historically labeled pendent and ancillary.

If § 1367(a) were the sum total of the relevant statutory language, our holding would rest on that language alone. The statute, of course, instructs us to examine § 1367(b) to determine if any of its exceptions apply, so we proceed to that section. While § 1367(b) qualifies the broad rule of § 1367(a), it does not withdraw supplemental jurisdiction over the claims of the additional parties at issue here. The specific exceptions to § 1367(a) contained in § 1367(b), moreover, provide additional support for our conclusion that § 1367(a) confers supplemental jurisdiction over these claims. Section 1367(b), which applies only to diversity cases, withholds supplemental jurisdiction over the claims of plaintiffs proposed to be joined as indispensable parties under Federal Rule of Civil Procedure 19, or who seek to intervene pursuant to Rule 24. Nothing in the text of § 1367(b), however, withholds supplemental jurisdiction over the claims of plaintiffs permissively joined under Rule 20 (like the additional plaintiffs in [the Star-Kist tuna can case]) or certified as class-action members pursuant to Rule 23 (like the additional plaintiffs in [the class action case]). The natural, indeed the necessary, inference is that § 1367 confers supplemental jurisdiction over claims by Rule 20 [covering joinder of plaintiffs] and Rule 23 [covering class actions] plaintiffs. This inference, at least with respect to Rule 20 plaintiffs, is strengthened by the fact that § 1367(b) explicitly excludes supplemental jurisdiction over claims against defendants joined under Rule 20.

We cannot accept the view, urged by some of the parties, commentators, and Courts of Appeals, that a district court lacks original jurisdiction over a civil action unless the court has original jurisdiction over every claim in the complaint. As we understand this position, it requires assuming either that all claims in the complaint must stand or fall as a single, indivisible "civil action" as a matter of definitional necessity—what we will refer to as the "indivisibility theory"—or else that the inclusion of a claim or party falling outside the district court's original jurisdiction somehow contaminates every other claim in the complaint, depriving the court of original jurisdiction over any of these claims—what we will refer to as the "contamination theory."

The indivisibility theory is easily dismissed, as it is inconsistent with the whole notion of supplemental jurisdiction. If a district court must have original jurisdiction over every claim in the complaint in order to have "original jurisdiction" over a "civil action," then in *Gibbs* there was no civil action of which the district court could assume original jurisdiction under § 1331, and so no basis for exercising supplemental jurisdiction over any of the claims. The indivisibility theory is further belied by our practice — in both federal-question and diversity cases — of allowing federal courts to cure jurisdictional defects by dismissing the offending parties rather than dismissing the entire action.... If the presence of jurisdictionally problematic claims in the complaint meant the district court was without original jurisdiction over the single, indivisible civil action before it, then the district court would have to dismiss the whole action rather than particular parties.

We also find it unconvincing to say that the definitional indivisibility theory applies in the context of diversity cases but not in the context of federal-question cases. The broad and general language of the statute does not permit this result. The contention is premised on the notion that the phrase "original jurisdiction of all civil actions" means different things in §§ 1331 and 1332. It is implausible, however, to say that the identical phrase means one thing (original jurisdiction in all actions where at least one claim in the complaint meets the following requirements) in § 1331 and something else (original jurisdiction in all actions where every claim in the complaint meets the following requirements) in § 1332.

The contamination theory, as we have noted, can make some sense in the special context of the complete diversity requirement because the presence of nondiverse parties on both sides of a lawsuit eliminates the justification for providing a federal forum. The theory, however, makes little sense with respect to the amount-in-controversy requirement, which is meant to ensure that a dispute is sufficiently important to warrant federal-court attention. The presence of a single nondiverse party may eliminate the fear of bias with respect to all claims, but the presence of a claim that falls short of the minimum amount in controversy does nothing to reduce the importance of the claims that do meet this requirement.

It is fallacious to suppose, simply from the proposition that § 1332 imposes both the diversity requirement and the amount-in-controversy requirement, that the contamination theory germane to the former is also relevant to the latter. There is no inherent logical connection between the amount-in-controversy requirement and § 1332 diversity jurisdiction. After all, federal-question jurisdiction once had an amount-in-controversy requirement as well. If such a requirement were revived under § 1331, it is clear beyond peradventure that § 1367(a) provides supplemental jurisdiction over federal-question cases where some, but not all, of the federal-law claims involve a sufficient amount in controversy....

* * *

We also reject the argument ... that while the presence of additional claims over which the district court lacks jurisdiction does not mean the civil action is outside the purview of § 1367(a), the presence of additional parties does. The basis for this distinction is not altogether clear, and it is in considerable tension with statutory text. Section 1367(a) applies by its terms to any civil action of which the district courts have original jurisdiction, and the last sentence of § 1367(a) expressly contemplates that the court may have supplemental jurisdiction over additional parties. So it cannot be the case that the presence of those parties destroys the court's original jurisdiction, within the meaning of § 1367(a), over a civil action otherwise properly before it. Also, § 1367(b) expressly withholds supplemental jurisdiction in diversity cases over claims by plaintiffs joined as indispensable parties under Rule 19. If joinder of such parties were sufficient to deprive the district court of original jurisdiction over the civil action within the meaning of § 1367(a), this specific limitation on supplemental jurisdiction in § 1367(b) would be superfluous. The argument that the presence of additional parties removes the civil action from the scope of § 1367(a) also would mean that § 1367 left the *Finley* result undisturbed. *Finley* after all, involved a Federal Tort Claims Act suit against a federal defendant and state-law claims against additional defendants not otherwise subject to federal jurisdiction. Yet all concede that one purpose of § 1367 was to change the result reached in *Finley*.

Finally, it is suggested that our interpretation of § 1367(a) creates an anomaly regarding the exceptions listed in § 1367(b): It is not immediately obvious why Congress would withhold supplemental jurisdiction over plaintiffs joined as parties "needed for just adjudication" under Rule 19 but would allow supplemental jurisdiction over plaintiffs permissively joined under Rule 20. The omission of Rule 20 plaintiffs from the list of exceptions in § 1367(b) may have been an "unintentional drafting gap." *Meritcare Inc. v. St. Paul Mercury Ins. Co.*, 166 F.3d 214, 221 & n.6 (3d Cir. 1999). If that is the case, it is up to Congress rather than the courts to fix it. The omission may seem odd, but it is not absurd. An alternative explanation for the different treatment of Rules 19 and 20 is that Congress was concerned that extending supplemental jurisdiction to Rule 19 plaintiffs would allow circumvention of the complete diversity rule: A nondiverse plaintiff might be omitted intentionally from the original action, but joined later under Rule 19 as a necessary party. The contamination theory described above, if applicable, means this ruse would fail, but Congress may have wanted to make assurance double sure. More generally, Congress may have concluded that federal jurisdiction is only appropriate if the district court would have original jurisdiction over the claims of all those plaintiffs who are so essential to the action that they could be joined under Rule 19.

To the extent that the omission of Rule 20 plaintiffs from the list of § 1367(b) exceptions is anomalous, moreover, it is no more anomalous than the inclusion of Rule 19 plaintiffs in that list would be if the alternative view of § 1367(a) were to prevail. If the district court lacks original jurisdiction over a civil diversity action where any plaintiff's claims fail to comply with all the requirements of § 1332, there is no need for a special § 1367(b) exception for Rule 19 plaintiffs who do not meet these requirements. Though the omission of Rule 20 plaintiffs from § 1367(b) presents something of a puzzle on our view of the statute, the inclusion of Rule 19 plaintiffs in this section is at least as difficult to explain under the alternative view.

And so we circle back to the original question. When the well-pleaded complaint in district court includes multiple claims, all part of the same case or controversy, and some, but not all, of the claims are within the court's original jurisdiction, does the court have before it "any civil action of which the district courts have original jurisdiction"? It does. Under § 1367, the court has original jurisdiction over the civil action comprising the claims for which there is no jurisdictional defect. No other reading of § 1367 is plausible in light of the text and structure of the jurisdictional statute. Though the special nature and purpose of the diversity requirement mean that a single nondiverse party can contaminate every other claim in the lawsuit, the contamination does not occur with respect to jurisdictional defects that go only to the substantive importance of individual claims.

It follows from this conclusion that the threshold requirement of § 1367(a) is satisfied in cases, like those now before us, where some, but not all, of the plaintiffs in a diversity action allege a sufficient amount in controversy. We hold that § 1367 by its plain text ... authorized supplemental jurisdiction over all claims by diverse parties arising out of the same Article III case or controversy, subject only to enumerated exceptions not applicable in the cases now before us.

* * *

The judgment of the Court of Appeals for the Eleventh Circuit is affirmed. The judgment of the Court of Appeals for the First Circuit is reversed, and the case is remanded for proceedings consistent with this opinion.

It is so ordered.

Note on Tolling under 28 U.S.C. § 1367(d)

28 U.S.C. § 1367(d) states:

The period of limitations for any claim asserted under subsection (a), and for any other claim in the same action that is voluntarily dismissed at the same time as or after the dismissal of the claim under subsection (a), shall be tolled while the claim is pending and for a period of 30 days after it is dismissed unless State law provides for a longer tolling period.

This portion of the statute grants a plaintiff a grace period in which to refile in state court should the claims that form the basis for federal court jurisdiction be dismissed. The Supreme Court of the United States recently considered how this section applied in the context of a plaintiff who filed her state action beyond the thirty-day grace period. In *Artis v. District of Columbia*, ___ U.S. ___, 138 S. Ct. 594 (2018), plaintiff Artis filed her state law claims fifty-nine days after the dismissal of the federal action. When the plaintiff first filed her state law claims in federal court, two and a half years remained of the three-year state statute of limitations. By the time the action was dismissed under 28 U.S.C. § 1367(c)(3), the remaining two and half years had passed. The Court considered what "tolled" meant under Section (d) — did the state statute of limitations cease to run while the federal action was pending, or did Artis merely have the thirty-day grace period left in which to file her claims in state court? The Court concluded that the statute meant that the state statute of limitations ceased to run during the pendency of the federal action. In other words, Artis still had two and a half years in which to file her state law claims after they were dismissed. The thirty-day grace period instead functioned for those cases in which the state law claims were filed on or near the last day of the statute of limitations.

7. Removal

Federal statutes permit a defendant to remove a case to federal court that has subject matter jurisdiction under certain circumstances. To "remove" a case means to force a case that the plaintiff initially filed in state court to be litigated in federal court instead — in effect, to veto the plaintiff's forum choice of state court. While the main statute permitting removal is 28 U.S.C. § 1441, there are other statutes that permit removal for specific types of cases. For example, 28 U.S.C. § 1442 permits removal of cases brought against the United States as well as officers of the United States, among others. In addition, Congress has specified that certain actions cannot be removed. An example of this is actions brought under the Federal Employers Liability Act, which a defendant cannot remove even though a plaintiff could bring such action in federal court if it wished to do so in the first instance. 28 U.S.C. § 1445(a). Likewise, a defendant cannot remove a case brought under state worker's compensation laws even if it involves diverse parties. 28 U.S.C. § 1445(c). Other statutes, specifically 28 U.S.C. §§ 1446–1448, discuss the details of the process for removal. If a plaintiff thinks the defendant improperly removed her lawsuit, she can make a motion to remand the case.

Only the defendant can remove a case. Section 1441(a) specifies only defendants, and the Court has held that even if the defendant counterclaims with a claim that falls within the federal court's subject matter jurisdiction, the plaintiff (even though it is a defendant vis à vis the counterclaim) cannot remove. *Shamrock Oil & Gas Corp. v. Sheets*, 313 U.S. 100 (1941). The Court reasoned that the plaintiff, by initially filing the action in state court, had submitted itself to the state court's jurisdiction and elected its forum. The Court construed the statute strictly, permitting only the original defendant to remove. Finally, if there are multiple defendants sued in the lawsuit, all must agree to removal.

Exercise 4-16. Understanding the Removal Statutes

Read and diagram 28 U.S.C. § 1441(a), (b), and (c), the general provisions governing removal. Note that § 1441(b) applies only to diversity cases. Based on your understanding of the statute, answer the following questions.

1. If a plaintiff domiciled in Arkansas files a claim under Title VII of the Civil Rights Act of 1964, a federal claim, against an Arkansas corporation in state court in Arkansas, can the defendant remove the case to federal court? What part of § 1441 did you rely upon to make your decision?

2. If a plaintiff domiciled in Missouri files a claim requesting $100,000 in damages under the Arkansas Civil Rights Act against an Arkansas corporation in state court in Arkansas, can the defendant remove the case to federal court? What part of § 1441 did you rely upon in making your decision?

3. If a plaintiff domiciled in Arkansas files a claim under Title VII of the Civil Rights Act of 1964 and the Arkansas Civil Rights Act against an Arkansas corporation, can the defendant remove the case to federal court? What part of § 1441 did you rely upon in making your decision?

4. If a plaintiff domiciled in Missouri files a claim requesting $100,000 in damages under the Arkansas Civil Rights Act against an Arkansas corporation, and the defendant counterclaims under federal securities laws, can the plaintiff remove the case to federal court? What part of § 1441 did you rely upon in making your decision?

Exercise 4-17. Federal Subject Matter Jurisdiction Revisited: Putting It All Together

You've now had the opportunity to learn about several common bases for federal court jurisdiction. By now, you also should be able to diagram the requirements for each area of federal court jurisdiction. Putting all your diagrams together, explain why or why not the federal trial courts would have subject matter jurisdiction over the following cases.

1. Recall the Chapter Problem at the beginning of this chapter. In it, a plane manufactured by Piper at its Pennsylvania facility crashed in Scotland. Hartzell manufactured the plane's propeller in Ohio. The client, Sherry, and her deceased brother are from Scotland. However, Jill Reyno, one of the plaintiff's attorney's administrative assistants who is a resident of the state of California, was appointed the administrator of the estate and brings the lawsuit in state court in California on behalf of the Estate. The

complaint includes state tort claims. If the parties to the lawsuit encompass this plaintiff and these defendants, will the defendants be able to remove the case to federal court?

2. An Arkansas resident who is in a car accident with a Missouri resident in Arkansas files a tort lawsuit in Arkansas federal court against the Missouri resident.

3. Nora Smith works for Piggy Slaughterhouse. While working in the meat packing branch of Piggy's operations, located in Lonoke, Arkansas, Ms. Smith was hurt by some machinery that was defectively maintained in violation of OSHA guidelines. OSHA is a federal agency that, pursuant to Acts of Congress, promulgates guidelines for employers. Its guidelines appear in the Code of Federal Regulations. Arkansas has a statute that states, "Any violation of an OSHA guideline that results in an injury to a worker in Arkansas gives rise to a cause of action for strict liability." Ms. Smith files her lawsuit in federal court.

4. General Computers, a Delaware corporation with its corporate headquarters in Arkansas and manufacturing facilities in Mexico, entered into a contract with BigTime Advertising, a New York-based advertising agency that is incorporated in Delaware and has an office in New Orleans. BigTime breached its agreement by not acquiring advertising time for General Computers during the Super Bowl. General Computers files its lawsuit in federal court.

5. Plaintiff had a contract with the United States government to provide hot meals to the federal court house in Little Rock, Arkansas. The United States, dissatisfied with plaintiff's service, hired the Applebee corporation to handle its food service needs. Plaintiff files a breach of contract claim against the federal government in federal court.

6. Laura Little, Sigourney Smith, and Joseph Jackson, all of whom are from Little Rock, Arkansas, got into a car wreck with Abe Long on I-40 between Memphis, Tennessee and Little Rock. Long was driving a tractor trailer from Atlanta to its final destination in Oklahoma City. Long works for an Atlanta-based trucking company. He lives in the suburbs of Atlanta. Laura, Sigourney and Joseph sue Long and his trucking company, Atlanta Express, in state court in Arkansas, alleging that Long was negligent in driving the truck. Laura, who was driving, broke her arm as a result of her air bag's deploying. Her bills for the break were $750. Sigourney was in the back seat and experienced severe whiplash as a result of the accident. She had to go through six months or physical therapy at a cost of $1,800. Joseph, however, was severely injured, as he was not wearing his seatbelt. He was ejected from the car, breaking a vertebra in his lower back as well as his left leg. He was in the hospital for six weeks and required surgery for his back injury. He also continues in physical therapy as well as a result of muscle damage to his back. As of now, his injuries have resulted in

$120,000 in medical/physical therapy bills. It's predicted that he will need another year of physical therapy at a cost of $2,000. Can the defendants remove this case to federal court?

7. Loretta Young files a suit for divorce in an Arkansas state court against her husband, John Young, who has left her and their three sons in Little Rock, Arkansas. John is now living in Chicago, Illinois. Can John remove the case to federal court?

8. Professional Development Reflection

At the beginning of this chapter, studies were discussed that suggest that plaintiffs who file in state court and remain there fare better than plaintiffs whose cases are removed to federal court. Do these data suggest that there are problems in the federal, state, or both court systems? As an attorney, do you have an obligation to try to keep your client's case in the court in which you believe you will obtain the most favorable judgment? How can you assure that your client remains in state court if the case is a diversity case involving multiple defendants? What if the case involves a mixture of state and federal claims?

Chapter 5
Venue and Forum Non Conveniens

1. Chapter Problem

Memorandum

To: Associate
From: John Carter, Partner
Re: Wrongful Death Suit Brought Against Hartzell

Our client, Hartzell Propellers, was recently sued by Jill Reyno, the representative of the estate of Kevin Leland, a citizen of Scotland. Apparently, a plane manufactured by Piper Aircraft crashed in Scotland, and Mr. Leland was one of the passengers who died in the accident. Hartzell manufactured the propeller of the plane involved in the accident. The lawsuit was filed in state court in San Diego County, California, where Ms. Reyno resides.

I'd like you to investigate where the proper venue is for this case. Our client is an Ohio corporation, and the purportedly defective propeller was manufactured in Ohio. It was installed in the plane at Piper's facility in Pennsylvania. However, the accident occurred in Scotland, where the wreckage from the plane is now located and any witnesses to the crash are situated. In addition, an investigation into the crash has taken place there. Also, the relatives of those who died in the crash have filed a lawsuit in England against the estate of the pilot (a citizen of the UK who also died in the crash) as well as the company that operated the plane, which is a UK corporation.

Let me know whether there is a basis for challenging venue in California. It would be easier for our client if this case were in Ohio or Pennsylvania. However, it might be best to move the case to England, where the wrongful death and products liability laws are not as beneficial to plaintiffs.

---

2. Introduction

You have finally figured out what court has personal jurisdiction over the defendant, a way to serve the defendant in that jurisdiction, and what court has subject matter jurisdiction over the type of lawsuit you are about to file. Assume all these determinations result in your deciding to file your lawsuit in California state court. How do you determine in which county to file your lawsuit? What if you decide to file your

lawsuit in federal court instead? California has four federal district courts—the Northern, the Central, the Eastern, and the Southern Districts of California. In which
federal district court do you file your lawsuit? Venue rules help you decide where to
file within a particular jurisdiction. Venue transfer rules also permit, under certain
circumstances, a party to transfer a case if there is a better venue or if the initial venue
was improper. Like subject matter jurisdiction and service rules, the state and federal
courts have different rules for laying proper venue.

Let's look at a more exotic example of a venue dilemma. What about the chapter
problem above? Here is a case in which the witnesses and most (but not all) of the
evidence related to the accident are in a different country. What if the most appropriate
place for a lawsuit to go forward is in a foreign venue? A court in the United States
generally has no authority to transfer a case to a foreign jurisdiction. The best the
court can do is dismiss the case with the promise that the plaintiff will refile in the
appropriate foreign jurisdiction. When a court does not have authority to transfer
the case, it uses the rules governing forum non conveniens, which means "a forum
that is not convenient." Forum non conveniens also sometimes is used if a state court
rules that another sovereign's courts are more appropriate. Once again, a state court,
like California in the example above, does not have authority to transfer a case to
another state's court, to a federal court, or to a foreign jurisdiction. In the federal
courts, forum non conveniens is a creation of common law. In the state courts, it is
a creation of either statutory or common law.

Different jurisdictions take a variety of approaches to venue rules. Some are based
on where a particular party is located—such as the defendant, the plaintiff, or the seat
of government for lawsuits in which the plaintiff sues the government. Others are based
on where the property involved in the lawsuit is located. Still others premise venue on
where a particular event related to the lawsuit took place. The policies behind venue
rules include convenience of the parties and witnesses, access to necessary evidence, as
well as other traditional jurisdictional principals, such as where the property is located.

Venue rules involve considerations of convenience and strategy. Plaintiffs will lay
venue in a place that is most beneficial to them—whether it be because the law is
better for them there, the evidence they need is readily available, or it is a very inconvenient and/or inhospitable venue for the defendant. Similarly, defendants want
to avoid venues that are better for plaintiffs and instead would prefer a venue that
works in their favor. Venue, like personal jurisdiction and subject matter jurisdiction,
can lead parties to forum shop for the best place for the case to go forward from that
party's perspective. As you review the venue rules below, ask yourself if there is sufficient protection in the rules to avoid plaintiffs laying venue in a location that is extraordinarily inconvenient for the defendant.

This chapter will focus on federal venue rules, because they apply in every federal
court in the country. This chapter proceeds as follows.

- Section 3 provides an example of a state venue rule and its application.

- Section 4 covers federal venue rules, including cases applying those rules.

- Section 5 explores forum non conveniens—the common law concept that covers situations in which venue may be proper in another country, as in the chapter problem.

- Section 6 discusses rules governing the transfer and dismissal of cases because either there is a problem with the original venue or there is a better place for the case to go forward.

- Section 7 contains the professional development reflection for venue.

3. State Venue

State venue rules vary. It is important to consult state venue rules for state practice. To give you a sense of this variation, one state venue case is provided below.

Exercise 5-1. *Reasor-Hill Corp. v. Harrison*

Reasor-Hill is a rather old case from the Supreme Court of Arkansas. This case discusses majority and minority rules. A majority rule is one that most jurisdictions have adopted. A minority rule is an alternative rule that fewer than a majority of jurisdictions have adopted. As you read the case, answer the following questions.

1. Who sued whom for what in this lawsuit?
2. If Barton cannot bring this lawsuit in Arkansas, what will happen to his claim against Reasor-Hill? Under modern personal jurisdiction rules, would Barton be able to sue Reasor-Hill in Missouri?
3. The Court mentions the statute of limitations in this case. Consult a legal dictionary to determine what a statute of limitations is.
4. What is the difference between a local and transitory action?
5. What is the majority rule? What are the origins of this rule?
6. What minority rule does Arkansas adopt? Why does the Arkansas Supreme Court reject the various justifications for the majority rule?
7. Why does Justice McFaddin disagree with the majority's analysis?

Reasor-Hill Corp. v. Harrison
220 Ark. 521 (1952)

George Rose Smith, Justice.

Petitioner asks us to prohibit the circuit court of Mississippi County from taking jurisdiction of a cross-complaint filed by D. M. Barton. In the court below the petitioner moved to dismiss the cross-complaint for the reason that it stated a cause of action for injury to real property in the state of Missouri. When the motion to dismiss was overruled the present application for prohibition was filed in this court.

The suit below was brought by the Planters Flying Service to collect an account for having sprayed insecticide upon Barton's cotton crop in Missouri. In his answer Barton charged that the flying service had damaged his growing crop by using an adulterated insecticide, and by cross-complaint he sought damages from the petitioner for its negligence in putting on the market a chemical unsuited to spraying cotton. The petitioner is an Arkansas corporation engaged in manufacturing insecticides and is not authorized to do business in Missouri.

The question presented is one of first impression: May the Arkansas courts entertain a suit for injuries to real property situated in another State? For the respondent it is rightly pointed out that if the suit is not maintainable Barton has no remedy whatever. The petitioner cannot be served with summons in Missouri; so unless it is subject to suit in Arkansas it can escape liability entirely by staying out of Missouri until the statute of limitations has run. The petitioner answers this argument by showing that with the exception of the Supreme Court of Minnesota every American court that has passed upon the question (and there have been about twenty) has held that jurisdiction does not exist.

We agree that the weight of authority is almost unanimously against the respondent, although in some States the rule has been changed by statute and in others it has been criticized by the courts and restricted as narrowly as possible. But before mechanically following the majority view we think it worthwhile to examine the origin of the rule and the reasons for its existence.

The distinction between local and transitory actions was recognized at the beginning of the fourteenth century in the common law of England. Before then all actions had to be brought where the cause of action arose, because the members of the jury were required to be neighbors who would know something of the litigants and of the dispute as well. But when cases were presented that involved separate incidents occurring in different communities the reason for localizing the action disappeared, for it was then impossible to obtain a jury who knew all the facts. Consequently the courts developed the distinction between a case that might have arisen anywhere, which was held to be transitory, and one that involved a particular piece of land, which was held to be local. Within a short time this distinction was embodied in English statutes.

As between judicial districts under the same sovereign the rule has many advantages and has been followed in America. As between counties our statutes in Arkansas require that actions for injury to real estate be brought where the land lies. But we permit the defendant to be served anywhere in the State, so the plaintiff is not denied a remedy even though the defendant is a resident of another county.

The English courts, in developing the law of local and transitory actions, applied it also to suits for injuries to real property lying outside England. If, for example, there had been a trespass upon land in France, the courts would not permit the plaintiff to bring suit in England, even though the defendant lived in England and could not be subjected to liability in France. The American courts, treating the separate States as independent sovereigns, have followed the English decisions.

In the United States the leading case is unquestionably *Livingston v. Jefferson.* That suit was a part of the famous litigation between Edward Livingston and Thomas Jefferson. The case was heard by Marshall as circuit justice and Tyler as district judge. Both agreed that the suit, which was for a wrongful entry upon land in Louisiana, could not be maintained in Virginia. In Marshall's concurring opinion he examined the English precedents and concluded that the law was so firmly established that the court was bound to follow it, though Marshall expressed his dissatisfaction with a rule which produced "the inconvenience of a clear right without a remedy." 1 Brock. 203, 4 Hall, Law J. 78 (1811).

Since then the American courts have relied almost uniformly upon the *Livingston* case in applying the rule to interstate litigation in this country. At least three reasons have been offered to justify the rule, but it is easy to show that each reason is more applicable to international controversies than to interstate disputes.

First, the ground most frequently relied upon is that the courts are not in a position to pass upon the title to land outside the jurisdiction. As between nations this reasoning may be sound. The members of this court have neither the training nor the facilities to investigate questions involving the ownership of land in France, in Russia, or in China. But the same difficulties do not exist with respect to land in another State. In our library we have the statutes and decisions of every other State, and it seldom takes more than a few hours to find the answer to a particular question. Furthermore, the American courts do not hesitate to pass upon an out-of-state title when the issue arises in a transitory action. If, for example, Barton had charged that this petitioner converted a mature crop in Missouri and carried it to Arkansas, our courts would decide the case even though it became necessary to pass upon conflicting claims of title to the land in Missouri. Again, a suit for damages for nonperformance of a contract to purchase land is transitory and may be maintained in another State, even though the sole issue is the validity of the seller's title. To put an extreme example, suppose that two companion suits, one local and one transitory, were presented to the same court together. In those States where the courts disclaim the ability to pass upon questions of title in local actions it might be necessary for the court to dismiss the local action for that reason and yet to decide the identical question in the allied transitory case.

Second, it has been argued that since the tort must take place where the land is situated the plaintiff should pursue his remedy before the defendant leaves the jurisdiction. This argument, too, has merit when nations are concerned. A sovereign, by its control of passports and ports of entry, may detain those who wish to cross its borders. But the citizens of the various States have a constitutional right to pass freely from one jurisdiction to another. In the case at bar the poison was spread by airplane, and Barton could hardly be expected to discover the damage and file an attachment suit before the pilot returned to his landing field in Arkansas.

Third, there is an understandable reluctance to subject one's own citizens to suits by aliens, especially if the other jurisdiction would provide no redress if the situation were reversed.... One may have some sympathy for this position in international disputes, but it has no persuasive effect when the States are involved. We do not feel compelled to provide a sanctuary in Arkansas for those who have willfully and wrongfully destroyed property, torn down houses, uprooted crops, polluted streams, and inflicted other injuries upon innocent landowners in our sister States. Yet every jurisdiction which follows the rule of the *Livingston* case affords that refuge to any person — whether one of its citizens or not — who is successful in fleeing from the scene of such misdeeds.

The truth is that the majority rule has no basis in logic or equity and rests solely upon English cases that were decided before America was discovered and in circumstances that are not even comparable to those existing in our Union. Basic principles of justice demand that wrongs should not go unredressed. Our own Bill of Rights puts the matter well enough: "Every person is entitled to a certain remedy in the laws for all injuries or wrongs he may receive in his person, property or character." Ark. Const. Art. 2, § 13. If Barton has been wronged he should have a remedy; to deny it is to encourage skepticism as to the ability of the courts to do their duty. Under the majority rule we should have to tell Barton that he would have been much better off had the petitioner stolen his cotton outright instead of merely damaging it. And the only reason we could give for this unfortunate situation would be that English juries in the thirteenth century were expected to have personal knowledge of the disputes presented to them. We prefer to afford this litigant his day in court.

Writ denied.

McFaddin, J., with Ward, J., dissenting.

The definite question to be considered is clearly stated in the majority opinion in these words: "May the Arkansas courts entertain a suit for injuries to real property situated in another State?" The majority answers the question in the affirmative; and I answer it in the negative.

Insofar as Barton's defense against the Planters Flying Service is concerned, the Arkansas Court has jurisdiction.[2] The difficulty arises on Barton's cross-complaint against Reasor-Hill. In that so-called cross-complaint, Barton claimed that Reasor-Hill sold to the Planters Flying Service — not to Barton, I stress, — an insecticide that damaged Barton's cotton crop growing on his lands in Missouri. This complaint of Barton against Reasor-Hill was an entirely new cause of action and was a claim by Barton against Reasor-Hill for damages to a crop growing on lands in Missouri.

In *Western Union Tel. Co. v. Bush*, 191 Ark. 1085 (1935), we held that damage to a growing crop was a damage to real property, and that an action to recover such damage *must* be brought in the County in which the land is situated. That case clearly holds two points: (1) Damage to growing crops is damage to realty; and (2) an action for damage to realty *must* be brought in the County in which the land is situated. In the present case, the majority concedes the first point, but refuses to follow the second point; and it is in regard to this second point that this dissent is directed.

The majority in the present case candidly admits that every American Jurisdiction — save only the State of Minnesota — has followed the holding in the original case of *Livingston v. Jefferson;* yet the majority, in seeing fit to depart from such time honored holding, advances three reasons, which do not seem to me to be sufficient for such a radical departure.

In the first place, the majority says that we have ample facilities to determine the land laws of other States in the United States.... This statement about the size of the law library seems rather weak, because land actions are tried in lower courts and not in the Supreme Court library. Just because we have a fine law library does not mean that we are prepared to determine the title to lands in Texas,[4] Missouri, Vermont, or any other State. But if we have the jurisdiction which the majority claims, then we could determine ejectment actions involving ownership of lands in other States....

Secondly, the majority says that the rule, requiring that an action be brought in the jurisdiction in which the land is situated, is a good rule

---

2. Ed. Note. The Planters Flying Service brought action against Barton to collect the account for spraying his cotton crop. Barton defended against the action by claiming that the insecticide was not as represented. The Arkansas Court had jurisdiction of this action because it was an action on account and was transitory.

4. The writer knows by experience that only one skilled in Texas Land Law can successfully handle an action of Trespass to Try Title in the State of Texas.

between Nations, but is not good as between States in the American Union. For answer to this, I say: I have always understood that each of the American States is Sovereign; that the Federal Government is a government of delegated powers; and that all powers not delegated to the Federal Government are retained by the States and the People. Surely the majority is not attempting to reduce our American States to the level of mere local administrative units. Yet such, unfortunately, is the natural conclusion to which the majority opinion would carry us, when it concedes one rule for Nations and another for States.

Thirdly, the majority says that it does not desire to afford Arkansas Citizens a sanctuary from damage actions by citizens of other States. This is an argument that should be made—if at all—in the Legislative branch of Government, rather than in a judicial opinion. It is for the Legislative Department to determine when and where actions may be prosecuted. The opinion of the majority in the case at bar is therefore judicial legislation, minus only the enacting clause required of legislative determinations.

* * *

Because of the views herein stated, I respectfully dissent from the majority in the case at bar; and I am authorized to state that Mr. Justice Ward concurs in this dissent.

Exercise 5-2. *Reasor-Hill* Revisited

1. Does it make sense to treat individual states like they are foreign countries for purposes of venue rules? Whose position is more sensible—that of Justice Smith or Justice McFaddin? What policy underlies Justice Smith's position? What policy underlies Justice McFaddin's position?

2. Do you think the *Reasor-Hill* court would have ruled the same if it were possible for Barton to sue Reasor-Hill in Missouri? Why or why not?

3. Review the majority and minority position on this venue rule. Would venue be proper in a court following the majority position in the following cases? Would it be proper for a court following the minority position?

   a. A quiet title action brought in Missouri regarding land in Arkansas.

   b. An action for conversion of crops from land located in Missouri brought in court in Arkansas, because the crops are now in Arkansas.

   c. An action for trespass onto land in Missouri brought in Missouri.

   d. An action for trespass onto land in Arkansas brought in Missouri.

4. Federal Venue Rules

Federal venue rules are set out in several statutes. The general statute that covers venue in most federal court cases is 28 U.S.C. § 1391. Other more specialized statutes cover venue in specific cases. For example, 28 U.S.C. § 1396 is a special provision governing venue in cases involving taxes. Section 1397 governs venue in interpleader cases, a subject that will be covered in Chapter 8. Section 1400 concerns venue in patent and copyright cases. In *TC Heartland LLC v. Kraft Foods Group Brands LLC*, ___ U.S. ___, 137 S. Ct. 1514 (2017), the Supreme Court of the United States made clear that the amendments to 28 U.S.C. § 1391 that extend the residence of corporations for venue purposes to places in which a court can exercise personal jurisdiction over a corporation do not modify the patent venue statute, 28 U.S.C. § 1400(b). The patent venue statute lays venue "in the judicial district where the defendant resides, or where the defendant has committed acts of infringement and has a regular and established place of business." 28 U.S.C. § 1400(b). Unlike Section 1391, a domestic corporation defendant "resides" only in its state of incorporation for purposes of venue in cases involving patent infringement. If you browse through §§ 1391–1413 of Title 28, you will find other specialized venue statutes. In addition, there are venue statutes throughout the U.S. Code that specify venue for particular types of cases. For example, 42 U.S.C. § 2000e-5(f)(3) sets venue for claims brought under Title VII of the Civil Rights Act of 1964.

Section 1391 does not apply to removed cases, because 28 U.S.C. § 1441(a) permits removal to the "the district and division embracing the place where such action is pending." Courts interpreting the removal statute have held that this provision covers venue in removed cases.

Venue operates like personal jurisdiction and proper service in that it is waivable. If a defendant fails to assert a problem with venue relatively early in the lawsuit, any venue defect is waived. You will learn more about waiver of defenses in Chapter 10.

Exercise 5-3. Reading and Applying the Federal Venue Statute

Read 28 U.S.C. § 1391. Note that § 1391(a)(2) does away with the distinction between local and transitory actions described in *Reasor-Hill*. Note also that § 1391(b) sets out the general venue rules applicable to most actions. Diagram § 1391(b). You should also note the specific rules for particular types of defendants and/or cases in §§ 1391(c)–(g). Based on your reading and diagramming of the statute, answer the following questions.

1. What are the three basic places where it is proper for a plaintiff to lay venue?

    Assuming other jurisdictional requirements are met, where would venue be proper under federal law in the following cases? In some instances, more than one venue may be proper.

2. Plaintiff sues three Missouri residents regarding a car accident that occurred in Arkansas.

3. Plaintiff sues two Missouri residents and one Arkansas resident regarding a car accident that occurred in Tennessee.

4. Plaintiff sues a Missouri corporation regarding a slip and fall accident that occurred in a store owned by the defendant that is located in Tennessee.

5. Plaintiff sues a local Missouri car dealership, the American importer of the car, which is incorporated in Delaware and has its principal place of business in Los Angeles, California, and the foreign manufacturer of the car, which is a German corporation, for products liability after the car's anti-lock brakes failed resulting in an accident in California.

6. Plaintiff sues a local Los Angeles, California, car dealership, the American importer of the car, which is incorporated in Delaware and has its principal place of business in Los Angeles, California, and the foreign manufacturer of the car, which is a German corporation, for products liability after the car's anti-lock brakes failed, resulting in an accident in California.

7. Plaintiff sues the foreign manufacturer of her car, a German corporation, for products liability after the car's anti-lock brakes failed resulting in an accident in California.

Exercise 5-4. *Bates v. C & S Adjustors, Inc.* and *Jenkins Brick Co. v. Bremer*

Section 1391(b)(2) has "wiggle" room, meaning that determining where "a substantial part of the events or omission giving rise to the claim occurred" is not precise language. It is open to interpretation. Venue under this section is commonly referred to as "transactional venue" because venue is proper in the district(s) where the actions took place related to the underlying transaction that gives rise to the claim in the lawsuit. Most courts that have examined this section have concluded that more than one venue can be appropriate under this standard. As you read the following cases interpreting this part of the statute, answer the following questions.

1. Do the courts examine the activities of the defendant, plaintiff, or both in determining venue under § 1391(b)(2)? Whose or what activities should they consider?

2. How do both courts distinguish personal jurisdiction questions from venue questions?

3. How does the *Jenkins Brick* court use cases to support its position? What does the *Bates* court use to support its position?

Bates v. C & S Adjustors, Inc.

980 F.2d 865 (2d Cir. 1992)

Jon O. Newman, Circuit Judge:

This appeal concerns venue in an action brought under the Fair Debt Collection Practices Act. Specifically, the issue is whether venue exists in a district in which the debtor resides and to which a bill collector's demand for payment was forwarded. The issue arises on an appeal by Phillip E. Bates from the May 21, 1992, judgment of the District Court for the Western District of New York ... dismissing his complaint because of improper venue. We conclude that venue was proper under 28 U.S.C. § 1391(b)(2), and therefore reverse and remand.

Background

Bates commenced this action in the Western District of New York upon receipt of a collection notice from C & S Adjusters, Inc. ("C & S"). Bates alleged violations of the Fair Debt Collection Practices Act, and demanded statutory damages, costs, and attorney's fees. The facts relevant to venue are not in dispute. Bates incurred the debt in question while he was a resident of the Western District of Pennsylvania. The creditor, a corporation with its principal place of business in that District, referred the account to C & S, a local collection agency which transacts no regular business in New York. Bates had meanwhile moved to the Western District of New York. When C & S mailed a collection notice to Bates at his Pennsylvania address, the Postal Service forwarded the notice to Bates' new address in New York.

In its answer, C & S asserted two affirmative defenses and also counterclaimed for costs, alleging that the action was instituted in bad faith and for purposes of harassment. C & S subsequently filed a motion to dismiss for improper venue, which the District Court granted.

Discussion

1. Venue and the 1990 amendments to 28 U.S.C. § 1391(b)

Bates concedes that the only plausible venue provision for this action is 28 U.S.C. § 1391(b)(2), which allows an action to be brought in "a judicial district in which a substantial part of the events or omissions giving rise to the claim occurred." Prior to 1990, section 1391 allowed for venue in "the judicial district ... in which the claim arose." This case represents our first opportunity to consider the significance of the 1990 amendments.

* * *

2. Fair Debt Collection Practices Act

Under the version of the venue statute in force from 1966 to 1990, at least three District Courts held that venue was proper under the Fair Debt Collection Practices Act in the plaintiff's home district if a collection agency had mailed a collection notice to an address in that district or placed a phone call to a number in that district. None of these cases involved the unusual fact, present in this case, that the defendant did not deliberately direct a communication to the plaintiff's district.

We conclude, however, that this difference is inconsequential, at least under the current venue statute. The statutory standard for venue focuses not on whether a defendant has made a deliberate contact—a factor relevant in the analysis of personal jurisdiction—but on the location where events occurred. Under the new version of section 1391(b)(2), we must determine only whether a "substantial part of the events … giving rise to the claim" occurred in the Western District of New York.

In adopting this statute, Congress was concerned about the harmful effect of abusive debt practices on consumers. This harm does not occur until receipt of the collection notice. Indeed, if the notice were lost in the mail, it is unlikely that a violation of the Act would have occurred. Moreover, a debt collection agency sends its dunning letters so that they will be received. Forwarding such letters to the district to which a debtor has moved is an important step in the collection process. If the bill collector prefers not to be challenged for its collection practices outside the district of a debtor's original residence, the envelope can be marked "do not forward." We conclude that receipt of a collection notice is a substantial part of the events giving rise to a claim under the Fair Debt Collection Practices Act.…

[T]he alleged violations of the Act turn largely not on the collection agency's intent, but on the content of the collection notice. The most relevant evidence—the collection notice—is located in the Western District of New York. Because the collection agency appears not to have marked the notice with instructions not to forward, and has not objected to the assertion of personal jurisdiction, trial in the Western District of New York would not be unfair.

Conclusion

The judgment of the District Court is reversed, and the matter is remanded for further proceedings consistent with this decision.

Jenkins Brick Co. v. Bremer
321 F.3d 1366 (11th Cir. 2003)

Tjoflat, Circuit Judge:

I.

Jenkins Brick Company ("Jenkins Brick") contemplated the idea of expanding its Alabama-based operations into the Savannah, Georgia area. John Bremer, a Savannah native who had spent many years working in the brick business that his family owned since 1914, proved to be an ideal candidate to help Jenkins Brick facilitate this expansion. Bremer and Jenkins Brick united on March 31, 1997, when Jenkins Brick hired Bremer to sell brick and block throughout the sales territory that consisted of a fifty-mile radius around Savannah.

In January 1998, a non-compete agreement was presented to Bremer in Savannah by Leon Hawk, Vice President of Jenkins Brick. Hawk told Bremer that his signature was a necessary condition of his continued employment with the company. The lengthy agreement prohibited a variety of competitive practices, including all competition with Jenkins Brick within a fifty mile radius of any Jenkins Brick office or plant for the two years following the conclusion of Bremer's employment. The agreement also prevented Bremer from soliciting business from any existing or prospective customer with whom Bremer had contact during his tenure as a Jenkins Brick employee. Finally, the agreement contained clauses stating that it was to be governed by Alabama law and that it was executed in Alabama.

Bremer's employment came to an end in February 2001, when Bremer voluntarily tendered his resignation. He immediately began working for a Savannah competitor in violation of the non-compete agreement. Jenkins Brick responded by filing suit in the U.S. District Court for the Middle District of Alabama, seeking injunctive and monetary relief. Bremer moved the court to dismiss the case for lack of venue or, alternatively, to transfer the case to the U.S. District Court for the Southern District of Georgia. After hearing argument of counsel, the district court transferred the case to the Southern District of Georgia pursuant to 28 U.S.C. § 1404(a), implicitly holding that venue was proper in Alabama and explicitly holding that the Georgia court would be a more convenient forum.

* * *

III

A

Both parties agree that the focus of this appeal is how this court should interpret subsection 2 of the statute governing venue in diversity cases. *See* 28 U.S.C. § 1391(a)(2) (allowing for venue in any "judicial district in which a substantial part of the events or omissions giving rise to the claim occurred"). This language was added in 1990, amending the former subsection 2 which provided for venue only in the single district "in which the claim arose." Congress believed that the old phrase was "litigation-breeding," partly because it did not cover the situation "in which substantial parts of the underlying events have occurred in several districts." *See* H.R. Report of the Committee on the Judiciary, Rep. No. 101-734, at 23 (1990). The old language was problematic because it was oftentimes difficult to pinpoint the single district in which a "claim arose." Consider, for example, a breach-of-contract case with these facts: the agreement is executed in

Oregon; the defendant fails to deliver goods to New York and California; and the defendant makes an anticipatory repudiation of the rest of the contract from its home office in Utah. Or consider a toxic tort case in which the defendant's factories in Colorado and Missouri pollute a river, causing injury to Arkansas and Louisiana citizens who ingest the water. If one had to pick a single district in which the tort or contract claim "arose," each scenario would require the district court, after extensive litigation, to pick a district in an arbitrary fashion.

The new language thus contemplates some cases in which venue will be proper in two or more districts. This does not mean, however, that the amended statute no longer emphasizes the importance of the place where the wrong has been committed. Rather, the statute merely allows for additional play in the venue joints, reducing the degree of arbitrariness in close cases. The statute's language is instructive: venue is proper in "a judicial district in which a *substantial* part of the *events or omissions giving rise to the claim occurred.*" 28 U.S.C. § 1391(a)(2) (emphasis added). Only the events that directly give rise to a claim are relevant. And of the places where the events have taken place, only those locations hosting a "substantial part" of the events are to be considered.

In this vein, we approve of cases such as *Woodke v. Dahm*, 70 F.3d 983 (8th Cir. 1995). In that case, the plaintiff, a designer and seller of semi-trailers under a federally registered trademark, asserted that the defendant was passing off trailers under an identical trademark. The plaintiff sued in the state of his residency, Iowa, even though he had no evidence of wrongdoing in that state. The Eighth Circuit found that venue was improper, holding that "[t]he place where the alleged passing off occurred . . . provides an obviously correct venue." *Id.* at 985. Importantly, the court noted that the statute protects defendants, and Congress therefore "meant to require courts to focus on relevant activities of the defendant, not of the plaintiff." *Id.* When the plaintiff pointed to a host of facts tending to show a relationship between the defendant and Iowa, the plaintiff was rebuffed. Although the trailers were manufactured in Iowa and an agreement between the plaintiff and defendant was executed in Iowa, the court found that "[t]hese activities [had] an insubstantial connection with the kinds of events that give rise to a claim." *Id.* The court conceded that "[i]t is true that manufacturing the trailers was a necessary event, in a causal sense, to an attempt to pass them off." *Id.* However, the court did not "think that [manufacturing] is an event giving rise to [the plaintiff's] claim because it was not itself wrongful." *Id.* at 986. We think this analytical framework, which considered as relevant only those acts and omissions that have a close nexus to the wrong, is a good interpretation of a statute.

Contrast this decision with another line of cases cited by Jenkins Brick, epitomized by *U.S. Surgical Corp. v. Imagyn Medical Technologies, Inc.*,

25 F. Supp. 2d 40 (D. Conn. 1998). That case, like the case at bar, involved an employee's breach of a non-compete agreement. The court's venue analysis focused on a host of factors, including: (1) where the contract was to be performed; (2) where the contract was allegedly breached; (3) where the contract was negotiated and executed; (4) where the defendant attended training classes; and (5) where the defendant attended sales meetings. *Id.* at 45. We think this case was incorrect because its flavor was that of a "minimum contacts" personal jurisdiction analysis rather than a proper venue analysis. We do not believe, for example, that a defendant's attendance at sales meetings is an "event giving rise to a claim" for breach of a covenant not to compete. Accordingly, we disapprove of this line of cases.

B

What acts or omissions by Bremer "gave rise" to Jenkins Brick's claim? Of those acts, did a "substantial part" of them take place in Alabama? The events that gave rise to Jenkins Brick's claim occurred exclusively in Georgia. The contract was not negotiated; rather, it was presented to Bremer in Georgia. It was executed in Georgia because that is where Bremer signed the contract. The non-compete agreement was also intended to be performed primarily in Savannah in order to protect the Savannah business and goodwill that Jenkins Brick acquired with the help of Bremer. After all, Bremer's sales territory comprised only Savannah and the surrounding area; there was no goodwill garnered by Bremer in other territories that needed to be "protected" by virtue of the non-compete provision. Perhaps this is why Jenkins Brick seeks to enforce the agreement only in the Savannah territory. Finally, and most importantly, the contract was breached when Bremer failed to perform his post-employment obligation to refrain from competing against Jenkins Brick—conduct that occurred only in Georgia. In sum, none of the acts giving rise to Jenkins Brick's claim occurred in Alabama, much less a "substantial part" of them.

Jenkins Brick, citing to cases such as *U.S. Surgical,* points to other facts: sales and training meetings were held in Alabama, salary and benefits ultimately came from Alabama, and the agreement was allegedly sent by Bremer to Alabama. As we have indicated, these facts do not have a close nexus with the cause of action for breach of contract, and they are therefore irrelevant. Jenkins Brick also argues that the contract was "executed" in Alabama because the contract says so on its face. However, this does not mean that the contract was, in fact, executed in Alabama; indeed, the record undeniably shows that it was executed in Georgia. We do not believe that a "place of execution" clause can, standing alone, make something true. Unlike a forum selection clause, a "place of execution" clause merely recites a fact about the world which can be refuted with empirical evidence to the contrary. This kind of clause is more akin to a contractual "agreement" that the sky is green. If a court later finds that the sky is blue, it would not have to defer to a contractual provision to the contrary.

In sum, we agree with the district court that all of the events "giving rise to" Jenkins Brick's claims occurred in Georgia. All of the relevant factors point in one direction: Georgia is the only proper venue for this litigation.

Exercise 5-5. *Bates v. C & S Adjustors, Inc.* and *Jenkins Brick Co. v. Bremer* **Revisited**

1. What approach(es) do the two courts take in determining where a "substantial part of the events or omission giving rise to the claim occurred?" What facts does the *Bates* court emphasize? What facts does the *Jenkins Brick* court emphasize?

2. The *Jenkins Brick* court disagrees with the district court's decision in *U.S. Surgical*. How would you go about determining whether your jurisdiction followed *Bremer* or *U.S. Surgical*?

3. Given the decisions in these cases, where would venue be proper under § 1391(b)(2) in the following cases:

   a. Plaintiff sues the manufacturer of her car, a Delaware corporation with its principal place of business in Detroit, Michigan, for products liability after the car's anti-lock brakes failed resulting in an accident in California. The brakes were designed in Detroit and manufactured in China. They were installed in plaintiff's car in Alabama.

   b. Plaintiff, an Iowa corporation with its principal place of business in Orange City, Iowa, sues defendant, a Missouri Corporation with its principal place of business in St. Louis, Missouri, for breach of contract in federal court in Iowa. Plaintiff contracted with defendant to install a roof on a grain storage facility in Minnesota. Plaintiff alleges that the defendant breached that contract by failing to install the roof properly. The contract was signed in Orange City, Iowa. The plaintiff and defendant negotiated the contract by telephone and in person in Iowa. Other telephone discussions (including extensive communications before and after execution of the contract), facsimile transmissions, and in-person negotiations (including execution of the contract) occurred in Iowa.

Note on Pendent Venue

In Chapter 4, you learned about supplemental jurisdiction over claims that formed part of the same claim or controversy as the claim over which the federal court has subject matter jurisdiction. A similar concept comes up in the context of venue under § 1391(b)(2). What happens if the court has venue over a claim because a substantial part of the events giving rise to that claim occurred in, let's say, New York, but does not have venue over a related claim, because a substantial part of the events giving rise to that claim occurred in New Jersey? To avoid the inefficiency of a plaintiff pursuing two transactionally related claims in two different venues, some courts use the concept of pendent venue. If a claim qualifies for supplemental jurisdiction under § 1367, it will qualify for pendent venue under court precedent. However, other courts are more cautious about expanding venue without congressional approval where the pendent claim involves a restrictive venue statute. Pendent venue can also become an issue when claims are added through joinder.

5. Forum Non Conveniens

Forum non conveniens was developed by the courts to handle situations in which the plaintiff has laid proper venue, but an alternative court exists that is a better place to hear the lawsuit. Generally, if there is a better federal court to hear a case, the federal court can now transfer the case under 28 U.S.C. § 1404, which is discussed in the next section of this chapter. Likewise, if a lawsuit is filed in one county in a particular state, but there is a better county for the lawsuit, some states permit transfer to the appropriate county's court. In forum non conveniens situations, the court that currently has the case does not have the power to transfer it to that other, better court. Thus, a successful motion based on forum non conveniens results in dismissal of the lawsuit, which the plaintiff must refile in the more appropriate forum.

The Supreme Court provided a list of factors that courts often consider in deciding a motion based on forum non conveniens in *Gulf Oil Corp. v. Gilbert*, 330 U.S. 501, 508–09 (1946), a case that predates 28 U.S.C. § 1404. In that case, the Court identified both "private" interest and "public" interest factors for the courts to consider:

> An interest to be considered, and the one likely to be most pressed, is the private interest of the litigant. Important considerations are the relative ease of access to sources of proof; availability of compulsory process for attendance of unwilling, and the cost of obtaining attendance of willing, witnesses; possibility of view of premises, if view would be appropriate to the action; and all other practical problems that make trial of a case easy, expeditious and inexpensive. There may also be questions as to the enforcibility [sic] of a judgment if one is obtained. The court will weigh relative advantages and obstacles to fair trial. It is often said that the plaintiff may not, by choice of an inconvenient forum, 'vex,' 'harass,' or 'oppress' the defendant by inflicting upon him expense or trouble not necessary to his own right to pursue his remedy. But unless the balance is strongly in favor of the defendant, the plaintiff's choice of forum should rarely be disturbed.

> Factors of public interest also have place in applying the doctrine. Administrative difficulties follow for courts when litigation is piled up in congested

centers instead of being handled at its origin. Jury duty is a burden that ought not to be imposed upon the people of a community which has no relation to the litigation. In cases which touch the affairs of many persons, there is reason for holding the trial in their view and reach rather than in remote parts of the country where they can learn of it by report only. There is a local interest in having localized controversies decided at home. There is an appropriateness, too, in having the trial of a diversity case in a forum that is at home with the state law that must govern the case, rather than having a court in some other forum untangle problems in conflict of laws, and in law foreign to itself.

The Court in the following case applied these factors.

Exercise 5-6. *Piper Aircraft v. Reyno*

As you read the *Piper Aircraft* case, answer the following questions.

1. Procedurally, how does this case make its way from state court in California to the Supreme Court of the United States?

2. What is choice of law? How does it factor into the Court's decision?

3. What is the standard of review for the appellate court when reviewing a district court's decision on a forum non conveniens motion?

4. How does the Court apply and evaluate each of the *Gilbert* factors in this case?

Piper Aircraft Co. v. Reyno

454 U.S. 235 (1981)

Justice Marshall delivered the opinion of the Court.

These cases arise out of an air crash that took place in Scotland. Respondent, acting as representative of the estates of several Scottish citizens killed in the accident, brought wrongful-death actions against petitioners that were ultimately transferred to the United States District Court for the Middle District of Pennsylvania. Petitioners moved to dismiss on the ground of *forum non conveniens*. After noting that an alternative forum existed in Scotland, the District Court granted their motions. The United States Court of Appeals for the Third Circuit reversed. The Court of Appeals based its decision, at least in part, on the ground that dismissal is automatically barred where the law of the alternative forum is less favorable to the plaintiff than the law of the forum chosen by the plaintiff. Because we conclude that the possibility of an unfavorable change in law should not, by itself, bar dismissal, and because we conclude that the District Court did not otherwise abuse its discretion, we reverse.

I

A

In July 1976, a small commercial aircraft crashed in the Scottish high-lands during the course of a charter flight from Blackpool to Perth. The pilot and five passengers were killed instantly. The decedents were all Scottish subjects and residents, as are their heirs and next of kin. There were no eyewitnesses to the accident. At the time of the crash the plane was subject to Scottish air traffic control.

The aircraft, a twin-engine Piper Aztec, was manufactured in Pennsylvania by petitioner Piper Aircraft Co. (Piper). The propellers were manufactured in Ohio by petitioner Hartzell Propeller, Inc. (Hartzell). At the time of the crash the aircraft was registered in Great Britain and was owned and maintained by Air Navigation and Trading Co., Ltd. (Air Navigation). It was operated by McDonald Aviation, Ltd. (McDonald), a Scottish air taxi service. Both Air Navigation and McDonald were organized in the United Kingdom. The wreckage of the plane is now in a hangar in Farnsborough, England.

The British Department of Trade investigated the accident shortly after it occurred. A preliminary report found that the plane crashed after developing a spin, and suggested that mechanical failure in the plane or the propeller was responsible. At Hartzell's request, this report was reviewed by a three-member Review Board, which held a 9-day adversary hearing attended by all interested parties. The Review Board found no evidence of defective equipment and indicated that pilot error may have contributed to the accident. The pilot, who had obtained his commercial pilot's license only three months earlier, was flying over high ground at an altitude considerably lower than the minimum height required by his company's operations manual.

In July 1977, a California probate court appointed respondent Gaynell Reyno administratrix of the estates of the five passengers. Reyno is not related to and does not know any of the decedents or their survivors; she was a legal secretary to the attorney who filed this lawsuit. Several days after her appointment, Reyno commenced separate wrongful-death actions against Piper and Hartzell in the Superior Court of California, claiming negligence and strict liability. Air Navigation, McDonald, and the estate of the pilot are not parties to this litigation. The survivors of the five passengers whose estates are represented by Reyno filed a separate action in the United Kingdom against Air Navigation, McDonald, and the pilot's estate. Reyno candidly admits that the action against Piper and Hartzell was filed in the United States because its laws regarding liability, capacity to sue, and damages are more favorable to her position than are those of Scotland. Scottish law does not recognize strict liability in tort. Moreover, it permits wrongful-death actions only when brought by a decedent's relatives. The relatives may sue only for "loss of support and society."

On petitioners' motion, the suit was removed to the United States District Court for the Central District of California. Piper then moved for transfer to the United States District Court for the Middle District of Pennsylvania, pursuant to 28 U.S.C. § 1404(a). Hartzell moved to dismiss for lack of personal jurisdiction, or in the alternative, to transfer.[5] In December 1977, the District Court quashed service on Hartzell and transferred the case to the Middle District of Pennsylvania. Respondent then properly served process on Hartzell.

B

In May 1978, after the suit had been transferred, both Hartzell and Piper moved to dismiss the action on the ground of *forum non conveniens.* The District Court granted these motions in October 1979. It relied on the balancing test set forth by this Court in *Gulf Oil Corp. v. Gilbert,* and its companion case, *Koster v. Lumbermens Mut. Cas. Co.,* 330 U.S. 518 (1947). In those decisions, the Court stated that a plaintiff's choice of forum should rarely be disturbed. However, when an alternative forum has jurisdiction to hear the case, and when trial in the chosen forum would "establish ... oppressiveness and vexation to a defendant ... out of all proportion to plaintiff's convenience," or when the "chosen forum [is] inappropriate because of considerations affecting the court's own administrative and legal problems," the court may, in the exercise of its sound discretion, dismiss the case. *Koster,* 330 U.S. at 524. To guide trial court discretion, the Court provided a list of "private interest factors" affecting the convenience of the litigants, and a list of "public interest factors" affecting the convenience of the forum. *Gilbert,* 330 U.S. at 508–09.

* * *

[The district court dismissed the case using the *Gilbert* factors, reasoning that the lawsuit should be refiled in Scotland. The Court of Appeals reversed and remanded, reasoning that the district court abused its discretion in applying the *Gilbert* factors and dismissal was never proper where the laws of the foreign jurisdiction were less favorable to the plaintiff.]

II

The Court of Appeals erred in holding that plaintiffs may defeat a motion to dismiss on the ground of *forum non conveniens* merely by showing that the substantive law that would be applied in the alternative forum is less favorable to the plaintiffs than that of the present forum. The possibility of a change in substantive law should ordinarily not be given conclusive or even substantial weight in the *forum non conveniens* inquiry.

---

5. The District Court concluded that it could not assert personal jurisdiction over Hartzell consistent with due process. However, it decided not to dismiss Hartzell because the corporation would be amenable to process in Pennsylvania.

* * *

[B]y holding that the central focus of the *forum non conveniens* inquiry is convenience, *Gilbert* implicitly recognized that dismissal may not be barred solely because of the possibility of an unfavorable change in law. Under *Gilbert*, dismissal will ordinarily be appropriate where trial in the plaintiff's chosen forum imposes a heavy burden on the defendant or the court, and where the plaintiff is unable to offer any specific reasons of convenience supporting his choice.[15] If substantial weight were given to the possibility of an unfavorable change in law, however, dismissal might be barred even where trial in the chosen forum was plainly inconvenient.

The Court of Appeals' decision is inconsistent with this Court's earlier *forum non conveniens* decisions in another respect. Those decisions have repeatedly emphasized the need to retain flexibility. In *Gilbert*, the Court refused to identify specific circumstances "which will justify or require either grant or denial of remedy." 330 U.S. at 508....

In fact, if conclusive or substantial weight were given to the possibility of a change in law, the *forum non conveniens* doctrine would become virtually useless. Jurisdiction and venue requirements are often easily satisfied. As a result, many plaintiffs are able to choose from among several forums. Ordinarily, these plaintiffs will select that forum whose choice-of-law rules are most advantageous. Thus, if the possibility of an unfavorable change in substantive law is given substantial weight in the *forum non conveniens* inquiry, dismissal would rarely be proper.

Except for the court below, every Federal Court of Appeals that has considered this question after *Gilbert* has held that dismissal on grounds of *forum non conveniens* may be granted even though the law applicable in the alternative forum is less favorable to the plaintiff's chance of recovery.

The Court of Appeals' approach is not only inconsistent with the purpose of the *forum non conveniens* doctrine, but also poses substantial practical problems. If the possibility of a change in law were given substantial weight, deciding motions to dismiss on the ground of *forum non conveniens* would become quite difficult. Choice-of-law analysis would become extremely important, and the courts would frequently be required to interpret the law of foreign jurisdictions. First, the trial court would have to determine what law would apply if the case were tried in the chosen forum, and what law would apply if the case were tried in the alternative forum. It would then have to compare the rights, remedies, and procedures available under the law that would be applied in each forum. Dismissal would

---

15. In other words, *Gilbert* held that dismissal may be warranted where a plaintiff chooses a particular forum, not because it is convenient, but solely in order to harass the defendant or take advantage of favorable law. This is precisely the situation in which the Court of Appeals' rule would bar dismissal.

be appropriate only if the court concluded that the law applied by the alternative forum is as favorable to the plaintiff as that of the chosen forum. The doctrine of *forum non conveniens*, however, is designed in part to help courts avoid conducting complex exercises in comparative law. As we stated in *Gilbert*, the public interest factors point towards dismissal where the court would be required to "untangle problems in conflict of laws, and in law foreign to itself." 330 U.S. at 509.

Upholding the decision of the Court of Appeals would result in other practical problems. At least where the foreign plaintiff named an American manufacturer as defendant, a court could not dismiss the case on grounds of *forum non conveniens* where dismissal might lead to an unfavorable change in law. The American courts, which are already extremely attractive to foreign plaintiffs, would become even more attractive. The flow of litigation into the United States would increase and further congest already crowded courts.

* * *

We do not hold that the possibility of an unfavorable change in law should *never* be a relevant consideration in a *forum non conveniens* inquiry. Of course, if the remedy provided by the alternative forum is so clearly inadequate or unsatisfactory that it is no remedy at all, the unfavorable change in law may be given substantial weight; the district court may conclude that dismissal would not be in the interests of justice.[22] In these cases, however, the remedies that would be provided by the Scottish courts do not fall within this category. Although the relatives of the decedents may not be able to rely on a strict liability theory, and although their potential damages award may be smaller, there is no danger that they will be deprived of any remedy or treated unfairly.

III

The Court of Appeals also erred in rejecting the District Court's *Gilbert* analysis. The Court of Appeals stated that more weight should have been given to the plaintiff's choice of forum, and criticized the District Court's analysis of the private and public interests. However, the District Court's decision regarding the deference due plaintiff's choice of forum was appropriate. Furthermore, we do not believe that the District Court abused its discretion in weighing the private and public interests.

---

22. At the outset of any *forum non conveniens* inquiry, the court must determine whether there exists an alternative forum. Ordinarily, this requirement will be satisfied when the defendant is "amenable to process" in the other jurisdiction. *Gilbert*, 330 U.S. at 506–07. In rare circumstances, however, where the remedy offered by the other forum is clearly unsatisfactory, the other forum may not be an adequate alternative, and the initial requirement may not be satisfied. Thus, for example, dismissal would not be appropriate where the alternative forum does not permit litigation of the subject matter of the dispute.

A

The District Court acknowledged that there is ordinarily a strong presumption in favor of the plaintiff's choice of forum, which may be overcome only when the private and public interest factors clearly point towards trial in the alternative forum. It held, however, that the presumption applies with less force when the plaintiff or real parties in interest are foreign.

The District Court's distinction between resident or citizen plaintiffs and foreign plaintiffs is fully justified. In *Koster*, the Court indicated that a plaintiff's choice of forum is entitled to greater deference when the plaintiff has chosen the home forum. When the home forum has been chosen, it is reasonable to assume that this choice is convenient. When the plaintiff is foreign, however, this assumption is much less reasonable. Because the central purpose of any *forum non conveniens* inquiry is to ensure that the trial is convenient, a foreign plaintiff's choice deserves less deference.

Respondent argues that since plaintiffs will ordinarily file suit in the jurisdiction that offers the most favorable law, establishing a strong presumption in favor of both home and foreign plaintiffs will ensure that defendants will always be held to the highest possible standard of accountability for their purported wrongdoing. However, the deference accorded a plaintiff's choice of forum has never been intended to guarantee that the plaintiff will be able to select the law that will govern the case.

B

The *forum non conveniens* determination is committed to the sound discretion of the trial court. It may be reversed only when there has been a clear abuse of discretion; where the court has considered all relevant public and private interest factors, and where its balancing of these factors is reasonable, its decision deserves substantial deference. *Gilbert; Koster....*

(1)

In analyzing the private interest factors, the District Court stated that the connections with Scotland are "overwhelming." This characterization may be somewhat exaggerated. Particularly with respect to the question of relative ease of access to sources of proof, the private interests point in both directions. As respondent emphasizes, records concerning the design, manufacture, and testing of the propeller and plane are located in the United States. She would have greater access to sources of proof relevant to her strict liability and negligence theories if trial were held here. However, the District Court did not act unreasonably in concluding that fewer evidentiary problems would be posed if the trial were held in Scotland. A large proportion of the relevant evidence is located in Great Britain.

The Court of Appeals found that the problems of proof could not be given any weight because Piper and Hartzell failed to describe with specificity the evidence they would not be able to obtain if trial were held in the United States. It suggested that defendants seeking *forum non conveniens* dismissal must submit affidavits identifying the witnesses they would call and the testimony these witnesses would provide if the trial were held in the alternative forum. Such detail is not necessary. Piper and Hartzell have moved for dismissal precisely because many crucial witnesses are located beyond the reach of compulsory process, and thus are difficult to identify or interview. Requiring extensive investigation would defeat the purpose of their motion. Of course, defendants must provide enough information to enable the District Court to balance the parties' interests. Our examination of the record convinces us that sufficient information was provided here. Both Piper and Hartzell submitted affidavits describing the evidentiary problems they would face if the trial were held in the United States.

The District Court correctly concluded that the problems posed by the inability to implead potential third-party defendants clearly supported holding the trial in Scotland. Joinder of the pilot's estate, Air Navigation, and McDonald is crucial to the presentation of petitioners' defense. If Piper and Hartzell can show that the accident was caused not by a design defect, but rather by the negligence of the pilot, the plane's owners, or the charter company, they will be relieved of all liability. It is true, of course, that if Hartzell and Piper were found liable after a trial in the United States, they could institute an action for indemnity or contribution against these parties in Scotland. It would be far more convenient, however, to resolve all claims in one trial. The Court of Appeals rejected this argument. Forcing petitioners to rely on actions for indemnity or contributions would be "burdensome" but not "unfair." Finding that trial in the plaintiff's chosen forum would be burdensome, however, is sufficient to support dismissal on grounds of *forum non conveniens*.

(2)

The District Court's review of the factors relating to the public interest was also reasonable. On the basis of its choice-of-law analysis, it concluded that if the case were tried in the Middle District of Pennsylvania, Pennsylvania law would apply to Piper and Scottish law to Hartzell. It stated that a trial involving two sets of laws would be confusing to the jury. It also noted its own lack of familiarity with Scottish law. Consideration of these problems was clearly appropriate under *Gilbert*; in that case we explicitly held that the need to apply foreign law pointed towards dismissal. The Court of Appeals found that the District Court's choice-of-law analysis was incorrect, and that American law would apply to both Hartzell and Piper. Thus, lack of familiarity with foreign law would not be a problem. Even if the Court of Appeals' conclusion is correct, however, all other public interest factors favored trial in Scotland.

Scotland has a very strong interest in this litigation. The accident occurred in its airspace. All of the decedents were Scottish. Apart from Piper and Hartzell, all potential plaintiffs and defendants are either Scottish or English. As we stated in *Gilbert*, there is "a local interest in having localized controversies decided at home." Respondent argues that American citizens have an interest in ensuring that American manufacturers are deterred from producing defective products, and that additional deterrence might be obtained if Piper and Hartzell were tried in the United States, where they could be sued on the basis of both negligence and strict liability. However, the incremental deterrence that would be gained if this trial were held in an American court is likely to be insignificant. The American interest in this accident is simply not sufficient to justify the enormous commitment of judicial time and resources that would inevitably be required if the case were to be tried here.

IV

The Court of Appeals erred in holding that the possibility of an unfavorable change in law bars dismissal on the ground of *forum non conveniens*. It also erred in rejecting the District Court's *Gilbert* analysis. The District Court properly decided that the presumption in favor of the respondent's forum choice applied with less than maximum force because the real parties in interest are foreign. It did not act unreasonably in deciding that the private interests pointed towards trial in Scotland. Nor did it act unreasonably in deciding that the public interests favored trial in Scotland. Thus, the judgment of the Court of Appeals is

Reversed.

Exercise 5-7. *Piper Aircraft* Revisited

1. What is the Court's ruling in this case? Does it carve out exceptions? If so, what are they?

2. Is there a prerequisite that must be met before a court can dismiss a case based on forum non conveniens? What is it?

3. In the following cases, assess whether the court should grant a forum non conveniens motion.

   a. The plaintiff's ship, the Iolair, was struck by the defendant's ship, the Beaufort, about 44 miles off the coast of Mexico. Companies with an interest in the Iolair are located in the Bahamas, Luxembourg, and Mexico. Companies with an interest in the Beaufort are located in the United States, although they conduct business in Mexico through subsidiaries or related companies. At the time of the accident, both ships were performing services for the Mexico state-owned oil company. The

Beaufort's owner filed two petitions in the Mexican courts to limit its liability. The plaintiffs filed an action in the federal district court for the Southern District of Texas for negligence and the unseaworthiness of the Beaufort. The statute of limitations on the plaintiff's claims, if it decided to file a lawsuit in Mexico, had already lapsed. The Beaufort had been seized by a Louisiana federal court. Should the court in the Southern District of Texas dismiss the lawsuit? *See Cotemar v. Hornbeck Offshore Services*, 569 Fed. Appx. 187 (5th Cir. 2014) (trial court should consider timeliness of action in alternative forum as well as seizure of additional vessel in making forum non conveniens determination).

b. A former Russian national who is now a naturalized American citizen living in New York and her Delaware LLC brought an action in federal court in New York for misappropriation and conversion, fraud, conspiracy to defraud and breach of fiduciary duty against a group of Russian nationals and entities. The plaintiffs allege that defendants, most of whom are Russian citizens living in Russia, conspired to loot a Russian corporation owned and controlled by the plaintiffs. The Delaware LLC owned a controlling interest in a Russian real estate company that held significant real estate and development rights in Moscow. Should the federal court in New York dismiss the lawsuit? *See RiGroup LLC v. Trefonisco Management Ltd.*, 949 F. Supp. 2d 546 (S.D.N.Y. 2013) (case dismissed based on forum non conveniens).

c. Plaintiffs, Guatemalan nationals residing in the United States, sued the defendants in the federal district court for the Southern District of Florida under the Alien Tort Act and Torture Victim Protection Act after defendants allegedly kidnapped and tortured them in Guatemala as the result of a labor dispute in that country. Plaintiffs were granted political asylum in the United States. Should the Southern District of Florida dismiss the lawsuit? *See Villeda Aldana v. Fresh Del Monte Produce, Inc.*, 2007 WL 3054986 (S.D. Fla. Oct. 16, 2007) (case dismissed based on forum non conveniens).

6. Transfer and Dismissal Based on Venue Issues

Federal statutes permit courts to transfer cases under two distinct circumstances. First, a court can transfer a case in which the plaintiff laid venue improperly to a court where venue is proper. Such cases are governed by 28 U.S.C. § 1406. Second, a court can transfer a case in which the plaintiff laid venue properly to a court where it is more convenient for the case to go forward. This type of transfer is governed by 28 U.S.C. § 1404, which codifies forum non conveniens for transfers between federal courts. Read and diagram both statutes. What do they require?

Section 1404(a) specifies that a court can transfer a case to a district or division "where it might have been brought or to any district or division to which all parties have consented." As you might expect, if one party, assume the defendant, wishes to transfer the case to another court in the federal court system, it is likely that the defendant perceives some advantage to itself in having the case go forward there. On the other hand, the plaintiff, who laid venue in the first court, likely believes that this is the best place for her case and thus doesn't want the case transferred. While the rule contemplates that the parties might all consent to a transfer, this is unlikely to happen. Thus, litigants and courts are often faced with deciding "where [the case] might have been brought" in determining to which court the case may be transferred. What do you think this phrase means? Does it mean a court that has personal jurisdiction and venue? The Supreme Court resolved this issue in *Hoffman v. Blaski*, 363 U.S. 335 (1960).

In *Hoffman*, the plaintiffs brought a patent infringement suit in the Northern District of Texas, where the defendants were located. The defendants moved to transfer the case under § 1404(a) to the Northern District of Illinois, which the Texas court granted. That order was upheld by the 5th Circuit. Once the case was transferred to Illinois, the plaintiffs moved to transfer it back to Texas, because they could not have brought the case in Illinois in the first instance due to venue problems. The Illinois court agreed with the plaintiffs, and transferred the case back to Texas. That decision was upheld on appeal by the 7th Circuit. The U.S. Supreme Court sided with the plaintiffs, holding that the language of the statute indicates that the plaintiff must be able to bring the case in the transferee court in the first instance in order for a court to transfer it to that district under § 1404. The Court was unimpressed with the defendants' arguments that venue and personal jurisdiction were waivable and that they could choose to waive them for purposes of transfer. Thus, absent consent by all the parties, a party seeking transfer must ascertain whether the plaintiff could bring the lawsuit in the transferee court in the first instance. Both Sections 1404 and 1406 contain language that requires this determination. While Section 1404 permits a court to transfer venue to a place "where it [the lawsuit] might have been brought," Section 1406 states that the court may transfer venue to a court where the lawsuit "could have been brought." The net effect of the language of both statutes is the same. In what way would it be unfair to plaintiffs if the defendants could simply waive venue and personal jurisdiction problems in order to seek a more favorable venue?

You should also be aware that states often have transfer rules that permit the court to transfer a case if venue is laid improperly. In addition, some states permit transfer if the defendant will experience unfair prejudice in the county in which the plaintiff laid venue or if another venue is more convenient. The rules on transfer vary from state to state.

Exercise 5-8. Applying the Transfer Statutes

Apply § 1404 and § 1406 to the following fact patterns. Bear in mind that you might need to look back at § 1391 to determine if the plaintiff properly laid venue in the first instance. Which statute applies? Should the court transfer the case?

1. Plaintiff, who is now a California resident, brings a breach of contract claim against her former employer in federal court in California. The defendant is a Delaware corporation with its principal place of business in New York. At the time of the alleged breach, plaintiff worked for defendant in Rochester, New York. Assume the defendant is a small corporation that operates two restaurants in New York. Defendant would prefer that the case go forward in New York. If the defendant requests it, will the court transfer, dismiss, or retain venue?

2. Plaintiff sues her former employer for employment discrimination under Title VII of the Civil Rights Act of 1964 in the Central District of California. The defendant is a Delaware corporation with its principal place of business in New York. The corporation runs a national chain of restaurants. Plaintiff worked at a Los Angeles, California, location of the chain, where the alleged discriminatory acts took place. Defendant would prefer that the case go forward in New York. If the defendant requests it, will the court transfer, dismiss, or retain venue?

3. Plaintiff is in an automobile accident with an 18-wheeler outside of Chicago, Illinois. He was driving from San Francisco, California, where he is domiciled, to New York, New York, as part of a vacation. Plaintiff was severely injured, requiring a six-week stay in the hospital as well as six months of rehabilitation. Plaintiff sues the driver as well as the trucking company that owned the truck. The trucking company is a Pennsylvania corporation with its principal place of business in Harrisburg, Pennsylvania. It transports goods throughout the eastern half of the United States. The particular truck involved in the accident was delivering goods to Chicago, Illinois, the farthest point west to which the company delivers. Plaintiff sues three days before the statute of limitations for such claims runs under California law in federal court in the Northern District of California. Defendant would prefer the case go forward in Illinois, where the accident occurred, or Pennsylvania, where it is located. If the defendant requests it, will the court transfer, dismiss, or retain venue?

Exercise 5-9. *Atlantic Marine Construction Co., Inc. v. U.S. District Court for the Western District of Texas*

The *Atlantic Marine* case is the Court's latest discussion of both §§ 1404 and 1406. This case addresses several issues and sets up a general approach to both transfer and forum non conveniens. Take your time reading it. As you read the case, answer the following questions.

1. What is a forum selection clause? Do the federal courts generally enforce them?

2. This case was appealed through a writ of mandamus. Look this term up in a legal dictionary. What does it mean?

3. The Court refers repeatedly to Federal Rule of Civil Procedure 12(b)(3). Read Rule 12(b)(3). Why is it relevant to this case? You will learn more about this rule in Chapter 10.

4. The *Atlantic Marine* Court relies heavily on the *Van Dusen* case. From the *Atlantic Marine* Court's description of *Van Dusen*, what happened in that case?

5. According to the Court, how do §§ 1391(b)(1), (2), and (3) operate? Is this consistent with your earlier diagram of the statute?

6. What is the "plaintiff's venue privilege?" How does the principle work in a case involving a forum selection clause?

7. The Court describes § 1391(b)(3) as a "fallback" position. What does it mean by this?

8. Which party bears the burden of showing that transfer is proper under § 1404(a) when the case involves a forum selection clause? Does it differ when the case does not involve a forum selection clause?

Atlantic Marine Construction Co., Inc. v. U.S. Dist. Ct. for the Western District of Texas

571 U.S. 49 (2013)

Justice Alito delivered the opinion of the Court.

The question in this case concerns the procedure that is available for a defendant in a civil case who seeks to enforce a forum-selection clause. We reject petitioner's argument that such a clause may be enforced by a motion to dismiss under 28 U.S.C. § 1406(a) or Rule 12(b)(3) of the Federal Rules of Civil Procedure. Instead, a forum-selection clause may be enforced by a motion to transfer under § 1404(a), which provides that "[f]or the convenience of parties and witnesses, in the interest of justice, a district court may transfer any civil action to any other district or division where it might have been brought or to any district or division to which all parties have consented." When a defendant files such a motion, we conclude, a district court should transfer the case unless extraordinary circumstances unrelated to the convenience of the parties clearly disfavor a transfer. In the present case, both the District Court and the Court of Appeals misunderstood the standards to be applied in adjudicating a § 1404(a)

motion in a case involving a forum-selection clause, and we therefore reverse the decision below.

I

Petitioner Atlantic Marine Construction Co., a Virginia corporation
with its principal place of business in Virginia, entered into a contract
with the United States Army Corps of Engineers to construct a child-de-
velopment center at Fort Hood in the Western District of Texas. Atlantic
Marine then entered into a subcontract with respondent J-Crew Management, Inc., a Texas corporation, for work on the project. This subcontract
included a forum-selection clause, which stated that all disputes between
the parties " 'shall be litigated in the Circuit Court for the City of Norfolk,
Virginia, or the United States District Court for the Eastern District of
Virginia, Norfolk Division.' "

When a dispute about payment under the subcontract arose, however,
J-Crew sued Atlantic Marine in the Western District of Texas, invoking
that court's diversity jurisdiction. Atlantic Marine moved to dismiss the
suit, arguing that the forum-selection clause rendered venue in the Western
District of Texas "wrong" under § 1406(a) and "improper" under Federal
Rule 12(b)(3). In the alternative, Atlantic Marine moved to transfer the
case to the Eastern District of Virginia under § 1404(a). J-Crew opposed
these motions.

[The district court denied both motions. Atlantic Marine petitioned the
Court of Appeals for a writ of mandamus directing the district court to
dismiss the case under § 1404(a) or to transfer it under § 1406(a). The appellate court denied the petition and upheld the district court's decision
not to transfer the case under § 1404(a).]

II

Atlantic Marine contends that a party may enforce a forum-selection
clause by seeking dismissal of the suit under § 1406(a) and Rule 12(b)(3).
We disagree. Section 1406(a) and Rule 12(b)(3) allow dismissal only when
venue is "wrong" or "improper." Whether venue is "wrong" or "improper"
depends exclusively on whether the court in which the case was brought
satisfies the requirements of federal venue laws, and those provisions say
nothing about a forum-selection clause.

A

Section 1406(a) provides that "[t]he district court of a district in which
is filed a case laying venue in the wrong division or district shall dismiss,
or if it be in the interest of justice, transfer such case to any district or division in which it could have been brought."* Rule 12(b)(3) states that a

---

* Ed. Note. An earlier version of § 1404(a) did not include the language "in to any district or division to which all parties have consented." This language was added in 2011.

party may move to dismiss a case for "improper venue." These provisions therefore authorize dismissal only when venue is "wrong" or "improper" in the forum in which it was brought.

This question—whether venue is "wrong" or "improper"—is generally governed by 28 U.S.C. § 1391. That provision states that "[e]xcept as otherwise provided by *law* ... this section *shall* govern the venue of *all civil actions* brought in district courts of the United States." § 1391(a)(1) (emphasis added). It further provides that "[a] civil action may be brought in—(1) a judicial district in which any defendant resides, if all defendants are residents of the State in which the district is located; (2) a judicial district in which a substantial part of the events or omissions giving rise to the claim occurred, or a substantial part of property that is the subject of the action is situated; or (3) if there is no district in which an action may otherwise be brought as provided in this section, any judicial district in which any defendant is subject to the court's personal jurisdiction with respect to such action." § 1391(b). When venue is challenged, the court must determine whether the case falls within one of the three categories set out in § 1391(b). If it does, venue is proper; if it does not, venue is improper, and the case must be dismissed or transferred under § 1406(a). Whether the parties entered into a contract containing a forum-selection clause has no bearing on whether a case falls into one of the categories of cases listed in § 1391(b). As a result, a case filed in a district that falls within § 1391 may not be dismissed under § 1406(a) or Rule 12(b)(3).

Petitioner's contrary view improperly conflates the special statutory term "venue" and the word "forum." It is certainly true that, in some contexts, the word "venue" is used synonymously with the term "forum," but § 1391 makes clear that venue in "all civil actions" must be determined in accordance with the criteria outlined in that section. That language cannot reasonably be read to allow judicial consideration of other, extrastatutory limitations on the forum in which a case may be brought.

The structure of the federal venue provisions confirms that they alone define whether venue exists in a given forum. In particular, the venue statutes reflect Congress' intent that venue should always lie in *some* federal court whenever federal courts have personal jurisdiction over the defendant. The first two paragraphs of § 1391(b) define the preferred judicial districts for venue in a typical case, but the third paragraph provides a fallback option: If no other venue is proper, then venue will lie in "*any judicial district* in which any defendant is subject to the court's personal jurisdiction" § 1391(b) (emphasis added). The statute thereby ensures that so long as a federal court has personal jurisdiction over the defendant, venue will always lie somewhere.... Yet petitioner's approach would mean that in some number of cases—those in which the forum-selection clause points to a state or foreign court—venue would not lie in any federal district. That would not comport with the statute's design, which contemplates that venue will always exist in some federal court.

The conclusion that venue is proper so long as the requirements of §1391(b) are met, irrespective of any forum-selection clause, also follows from our prior decisions construing the federal venue statutes. In *Van Dusen v. Barrack*, 376 U.S. 612 (1964), we considered the meaning of 1404(a), which authorizes a district court to "transfer any civil action to any other district or division where it might have been brought." 28 U.S.C. §1404(a). The question in *Van Dusen* was whether §1404(a) allows transfer to a district in which venue is proper under §1391 but in which the case could not have been pursued in light of substantive state-law limitations on the suit. In holding that transfer is permissible in that context, we construed the phrase "where it might have been brought," 376 U.S. at 624, to refer to "the federal laws delimiting the districts in which such an action 'may be brought,'" noting that "the phrase 'may be brought' recurs at least 10 times" in §§ 1391–1406. *Id.* at 622. We perceived "no valid reason for reading the words 'where it might have been brought' to narrow the range of permissible federal forums beyond those permitted by federal venue statutes."

As we noted in *Van Dusen*, §1406(a) "shares the same statutory context" as §1404(a) and "contain[s] a similar phrase." It instructs a court to transfer a case from the "wrong" district to a district "in which it could have been brought." *Id.* at 618. The most reasonable interpretation of that provision is that a district cannot be "wrong" if it is one in which the case could have been brought under §1391. Under the construction of the venue laws we adopted in *Van Dusen* a "wrong" district is therefore a district other than "those districts in which Congress has provided *by its venue statutes* that the action 'may be brought.'" (emphasis added). If the federal venue statutes establish that suit may be brought in a particular district, a contractual bar cannot render venue in that district "wrong."

* * *

B

Although a forum-selection clause does not render venue in a court "wrong" or "improper" within the meaning of §1406(a) or Rule 12(b)(3), the clause may be enforced through a motion to transfer under §1404(a). That provision states that "[f]or the convenience of parties and witnesses, in the interest of justice, a district court may transfer any civil action to any other district or division where it might have been brought or to any district or division to which all parties have consented." Unlike §1406(a), §1404(a) does not condition transfer on the initial forum's being "wrong." And it permits transfer to any district where venue is also proper (*i.e.*, "where [the case] might have been brought") or to any other district to which the parties have agreed by contract or stipulation.

Section 1404(a) therefore provides a mechanism for enforcement of forum-selection clauses that point to a particular federal district. And for the reasons we address in Part III, *infra,* a proper application of § 1404(a) requires that a forum-selection clause be "given controlling weight in all but the most exceptional cases." *Stewart v. Ricoh Corp.,* 487 U.S. 22, 33 (1988) (Kennedy, J., concurring).

Atlantic Marine argues that § 1404(a) is not a suitable mechanism to enforce forum-selection clauses because that provision cannot provide for transfer when a forum-selection clause specifies a state or foreign tribunal, and we agree with Atlantic Marine that the Court of Appeals failed to provide a sound answer to this problem. The Court of Appeals opined that a forum-selection clause pointing to a nonfederal forum should be enforced through Rule 12(b)(3), which permits a party to move for dismissal of a case based on "improper venue." As Atlantic Marine persuasively argues, however, that conclusion cannot be reconciled with our construction of the term "improper venue" in § 1406 to refer only to a forum that does not satisfy federal venue laws. If venue is proper under federal venue rules, it does not matter for the purpose of Rule 12(b)(3) whether the forum-selection clause points to a federal or a nonfederal forum.

Instead, the appropriate way to enforce a forum-selection clause pointing to a state or foreign forum is through the doctrine of *forum non conveniens.* Section 1404(a) is merely a codification of the doctrine of *forum non conveniens* for the subset of cases in which the transferee forum is within the federal court system; in such cases, Congress has replaced the traditional remedy of outright dismissal with transfer.... For the remaining set of cases calling for a nonfederal forum, § 1404(a) has no application, but the residual doctrine of *forum non conveniens* "has continuing application in federal courts." *Sinochem Int'l Co. v. Malaysiz Int'l Shipping Corp.,* 549 U.S. 422, 430 (2007) (internal quotation marks and brackets omitted). And because both § 1404(a) and the *forum non conveniens* doctrine from which it derives entail the same balancing-of-interests standard, courts should evaluate a forum-selection clause pointing to a nonfederal forum in the same way that they evaluate a forum-selection clause pointing to a federal forum....

* * *

III

Although the Court of Appeals correctly identified § 1404(a) as the appropriate provision to enforce the forum-selection clause in this case, the Court of Appeals erred in failing to make the adjustments required in a § 1404(a) analysis when the transfer motion is premised on a forum-selection clause. When the parties have agreed to a valid forum-selection clause, a district court should ordinarily transfer the case to the forum specified in that clause.[5] Only under extraordinary circumstances unrelated to the convenience of the parties should a § 1404(a) motion be denied. And no such exceptional factors appear to be present in this case.

A

In the typical case not involving a forum-selection clause, a district court considering a § 1404(a) motion (or a *forum non conveniens* motion) must evaluate both the convenience of the parties and various public-interest considerations. Ordinarily, the district court would weigh the relevant factors and decide whether, on balance, a transfer would serve "the convenience of parties and witnesses" and otherwise promote "the interest of justice." § 1404(a).

The calculus changes, however, when the parties' contract contains a valid forum-selection clause, which "represents the parties' agreement as to the most proper forum." *Stewart*, 487 U.S. at 31. The "enforcement of valid forum-selection clauses, bargained for by the parties, protects their legitimate expectations and furthers vital interests of the justice system." *Id.* at 33 (Kennedy, J., concurring). For that reason, and because the overarching consideration under § 1404(a) is whether a transfer would promote "the interest of justice," "a valid forum-selection clause [should be] given controlling weight in all but the most exceptional cases." *Id.* at 33. The presence of a valid forum-selection clause requires district courts to adjust their usual § 1404(a) analysis in three ways.

First, the plaintiff's choice of forum merits no weight. Rather, as the party defying the forum-selection clause, the plaintiff bears the burden of establishing that transfer to the forum for which the parties bargained is unwarranted. Because plaintiffs are ordinarily allowed to select whatever forum they consider most advantageous (consistent with jurisdictional and venue limitations), we have termed their selection the "plaintiff's venue privilege." *Van Dusen*, 376 U.S. at 635. But when a plaintiff agrees by contract to bring suit only in a specified forum—presumably in exchange for other binding promises by the defendant—the plaintiff has effectively exercised its "venue privilege" before a dispute arises. Only that initial choice deserves deference, and the plaintiff must bear the burden of showing why the court should not transfer the case to the forum to which the parties agreed.

Second, a court evaluating a defendant's § 1404(a) motion to transfer based on a forum-selection clause should not consider arguments about the parties' private interests. When parties agree to a forum-selection

---

5. Our analysis presupposes a contractually valid forum-selection clause.

clause, they waive the right to challenge the preselected forum as inconvenient or less convenient for themselves or their witnesses, or for their pursuit of the litigation. A court accordingly must deem the private-interest factors to weigh entirely in favor of the preselected forum. As we have explained in a different but "'instructive'" context, *Stewart*, "[w]hatever 'inconvenience' [the parties] would suffer by being forced to litigate in the contractual forum as [they] agreed to do was clearly foreseeable at the time of contracting." *The Bremen v. Zapata Off-Shore Co.*, 407 U.S. 1, 17–18 (1972).

As a consequence, a district court may consider arguments about public-interest factors only. Because those factors will rarely defeat a transfer motion, the practical result is that forum-selection clauses should control except in unusual cases. Although it is "conceivable in a particular case" that the district court "would refuse to transfer a case notwithstanding the counterweight of a forum-selection clause," *Stewart*, 476 U.S. at 30–31, such cases will not be common.

* * *

B

The District Court's application of § 1404(a) in this case did not comport with these principles. The District Court improperly placed the burden on Atlantic Marine to prove that transfer to the parties' contractually preselected forum was appropriate. As the party acting in violation of the forum-selection clause, J-Crew must bear the burden of showing that public-interest factors overwhelmingly disfavor a transfer.

The District Court also erred in giving weight to arguments about the parties' private interests, given that all private interests, as expressed in the forum-selection clause, weigh in favor of the transfer. The District Court stated that the private-interest factors "militat[e] against a transfer to Virginia" because "compulsory process will not be available for the majority of J-Crew's witnesses" and there will be "significant expense for those willing witnesses." But when J-Crew entered into a contract to litigate all disputes in Virginia, it knew that a distant forum might hinder its ability to call certain witnesses and might impose other burdens on its litigation efforts. It nevertheless promised to resolve its disputes in Virginia, and the District Court should not have given any weight to J-Crew's current claims of inconvenience.

* * *

We reverse the judgment of the Court of Appeals for the Fifth Circuit. Although no public-interest factors that might support the denial of Atlantic Marine's motion to transfer are apparent on the record before us, we remand the case for the courts below to decide that question.

It is so ordered.

Exercise 5-10. *Atlantic Marine* Revisited

1. What are the advantages to using a forum selection clause? Which party does it benefit most?

2. How do transfer and forum non conveniens interact? Where is it appropriate to use one and not the other in cases involving forum selection clauses?

3. Does the *Atlantic Marine* case change the standard for forum non conveniens from the one set out in *Piper Aircraft*?

4. If your client wants to file a lawsuit in a jurisdiction other than that provided in the forum selection clause, what types of arguments would you make to try to undermine enforcement of the clause?

5. How must a federal trial court adjust its § 1404(a) analysis when a forum selection clause is present?

6. How does the availability of witnesses impact the court's analysis of venue when a forum selection clause is present? Does this seem fair?

Note on Law that Applies to Transferred Cases

One issue that arose in cases that were transferred under Section 1404 was what state law applies if the case includes state law claims. For example, if venue was properly laid in a case involving state law claims in California, but then transferred to Arizona based on Section 1404, should California or Arizona law apply to the state law claims? This question was answered in by the Supreme Court in 1964 in *Van Dusen v. Barrack*, 376 U.S. 612 (1964):

> We conclude ... that in cases such as the present, where the defendants seek to transfer, the transferee district court must be obligated to apply the state law that would have been applied if there had been no change of venue. A change of venue under § 1404(a) generally should be, with respect to state law, but a change of courtrooms.

Id. at 639. What state law should apply if the transfer is pursuant to Section 1406—the law of the transferor court or the law of the transferee court?

Note on Transfer Due to Jurisdictional Defect

In addition to 28 U.S.C. §§ 1404 and 1406, 28 U.S.C. § 1631 permits a court to transfer a case when jurisdiction is improper in the court where the case was initially filed. Read 28 U.S.C. § 1631. What do you think is meant by jurisdiction in this statute? Does it refer to personal jurisdiction, subject matter jurisdiction, or both? What is the legal standard under this statute? Under what circumstances would it be appropriate to transfer a case using this statute?

Exercise 5-11. Transfers in the Interest of Justice for Want of Jurisdiction

The following two case excerpts provide examples of how lower courts apply § 1631. As you read the cases, answer the following questions.

1. What court ruled in each case? What does this mean for each case's precedential value?

2. In the two cases that follow, what type of jurisdictional defect is present — subject matter jurisdiction or personal jurisdiction?

3. The *Hays* decision is "per curiam." Look this term up in a legal dictionary. What does it mean?

4. What is the standard of review that the courts of appeals use in reviewing a trial court's decision under § 1631? Does that make it difficult or easy for the party opposing the trial court's decision to win on appeal?

Hays v. Postmaster General of the United States

868 F.2d 328 (9th Cir. 1989)

Per Curiam:

Arthur Hays petitioned the district court for review of a decision by the Merit Systems Protection Board (MSPB) upholding his removal from his job with the Postal Service. The district court held that it lacked jurisdiction. We review the district court's determination de novo.

FACTS

Hays received a notice of proposed removal from his job on January 28, 1985. On February 3, he appealed this decision to the MSPB, but did not make any discrimination claims; on February 24, he filed a formal Equal Employment Opportunity (EEO) complaint, charging discrimination based on race, sex and physical handicap. Under Equal Employment Opportunity Commission (EEOC) regulations, an aggrieved person may file an EEO complaint based on discrimination and nondiscrimination claims (termed a "mixed" case complaint), or file a mixed case appeal with the MSPB, but may not do both. Moreover, the regulations provide how the election of remedies is made: "[W]hichever is filed first (the EEO complaint or the MSPB appeal) shall be considered an election to proceed in that forum." As the appeal to the MSPB preceded the filing of the EEO complaint, the MSPB's presiding official considering Hays' appeal correctly determined that the MSPB had jurisdiction.

The presiding official upheld Hays' removal on April 25, 1986. Under the regulations then in effect, Hays had 30 days to petition the full MSPB for a review of the decision. On May 3, 1986, the Postal Service notified Hays that his EEO complaint had been rejected pursuant to regulations which require rejection of a mixed case complaint when the case had been appealed to the MSPB. The Postal Service advised him to "bring the allegations of discrimination contained in this rejected complaint to the attention of the Merit Systems Protection Board ... within twenty (20) calendar days...." Hays did not attempt to bring his discrimination claims to the attention of the MSPB. As Hays failed to file a petition for review before the full MSPB, the presiding official's decision became final on May 30, 1986.

On June 13, Hays petitioned the district court for review of the MSPB's decision and for remedies based on his claim that he had suffered discrimination on account of a mental handicap, in violation of section 501 of the Rehabilitation Act of 1973. Defendants moved the court to dismiss the case for lack of subject matter jurisdiction or to transfer it to the United States Court of Appeals for the Federal Circuit pursuant to 28 U.S.C. § 1631. The district court granted the motion to dismiss.

Discussion I

[The court concluded that under federal law, the court of appeals for the federal circuit had subject matter jurisdiction over the plaintiff's appeal. Thus, the Ninth Circuit did not have jurisdiction to hear this case.]

II

Hays contends that once the district court determined it lacked jurisdiction, it should have transferred the petition for review to the Federal Circuit, pursuant to 28 U.S.C. § 1631. Under section 1631, whenever the court finds a lack of jurisdiction, it "shall, if it is in the interest of justice, transfer such action or appeal to any other such court in which the action or appeal could have been brought at the time it was filed or noticed." *Id.* Although Hays did not move the court to transfer the case, we have held that "[a] motion to transfer is unnecessary because of the mandatory cast of section 1631's instructions." *Harris v. McCauley*, 814 F.2d 1350, 1352 (9th Cir. 1987).

We review a district court's failure to transfer a case under section 1631 for an abuse of discretion. Once the district court has determined that it lacks jurisdiction, but that another federal court has authority to hear the case, the district court "must consider whether the action would have been timely if it had been filed in the proper forum on the date filed, and if so, whether a transfer would be 'in the interest of justice.'" *Taylor v. Social Sec. Admin.*, 842 F.2d 232, 233 (9th Cir. 1988).

Here the district court indicated that the Federal Circuit would have jurisdiction over Hays' action, but failed to consider either of the issues required by *Taylor*. We note that Hays' petition for review would have been timely if it had been filed in the Federal Circuit. As the district court failed to exercise its discretion pursuant to section 1631, we remand with directions to consider whether the transfer of Hays' action to the Federal Circuit would be in the interest of justice.

Affirmed in part, reversed in part, and remanded.

———————

Nationwide Contractor Audit Service v. National Compliance Management Services, Inc.

622 F. Supp. 2d 276 (W.D. Pa. 2008)

MEMORANDUM OPINION

William L. Standish, District Judge.

In this tortious interference and unfair competition case, Defendant National Compliance Management Services, Inc. ("NCMS"), has filed a motion to dismiss pursuant to Federal Rule of Civil Procedure 12(b)(2), arguing that Plaintiff Nationwide Contractor Audit Service, Inc. ("Nationwide"), cannot establish the Constitutional prerequisites which would allow this Court to exercise either specific or general jurisdiction over Defendant. For the reasons discussed below, Defendant's Motion is granted. However, the Court will exercise its discretion and transfer this matter to the District of Kansas for further consideration.

[The district court concluded that it did not have personal jurisdiction over the defendant, but that the courts of Kansas would have jurisdiction.]

* * *

V. TRANSFER

"Whenever a civil action is filed in a court ... and that court finds that there is a want of jurisdiction, the court shall, if it is in the interest of justice, transfer such action or appeal to any other such court in which the action or appeal could have been brought at the time it was filed." 28 U.S.C. § 1631 (transfer to cure want of jurisdiction). The Court will therefore not dismiss this case entirely, but will transfer it to the District of Kansas. Neither of the parties has requested such a transfer, but we conclude it is within our discretion to do so even in the absence of such a request....

Alternatively, this Court may transfer an action pursuant to 28 U.S.C. § 1406(a) despite the lack of personal jurisdiction over Defendant. Under 28 U.S.C. § 1406, a district court may transfer a case that was improperly filed in the wrong district to "any district or division in which it could have been brought" to further "the interests of justice."

Jurisdiction and venue are appropriate in Kansas because that State has general jurisdiction over Defendant inasmuch as its principal place of business is in Hutchinson, Kansas, and the events which allegedly led to the tortious interference claim ... occurred there. Similarly, the NCMS website which Plaintiff alleges contains false and misleading assertions about DOT approval allegedly in violation of the Lanham Act is controlled from Kansas. Third, Mr. Rippert, Plaintiff's president, resides in Kansas and presumably has access to the company's files and records, as well as to his own records, at that location.

In addition, we find no policy impediments to transferring this case to Kansas. Should Defendant be found liable to Nationwide for any of the claims brought against it, a money judgment will be easily enforceable in that jurisdiction. None of the claims require interpretation of unique Pennsylvania law and there are no choice of law clauses requiring application of Pennsylvania law which would be potentially burdensome for a Kansas court. Moreover, transferring the case rather than dismissing it without prejudice will further the interests of justice because it will allow Nationwide to avoid the filing and service costs associated with refiling in Kansas.

An appropriate Order follows.

Exercise 5-12. Transfers in the Interest of Justice for Want of Jurisdiction Revisited

1. What do you think are some common reasons that a court will transfer a case under § 1631 rather than dismiss it?

2. Does it seem constitutional to permit a court that does not have subject matter or personal jurisdiction to transfer a case? Why or why not?

3. In the following cases, should the court dismiss the lawsuit or transfer it under § 1631?

   a. A case that the plaintiff mistakenly filed in the federal district court in Florida when the federal court of claims had jurisdiction over the claim, and the claim would be untimely if refiled in the federal court of claims.

   b. A case filed by the plaintiff in the Southern District of New York in which that court determines that it does not have jurisdiction over the defendant, who is domiciled in New Jersey.

Note on Multidistrict Litigation Transfers

In addition to transfers under 28 U.S.C. § 1404 and § 1406, courts can transfer cases under 28 U.S.C. § 1407. This statute addresses situations in which similar lawsuits against the same defendant are filed in several federal courts throughout the country. Section 1407 permits such cases to be transferred to one court for pretrial proceedings, such as discovery. What are the advantages of this? The judicial panel for multidistrict litigation assigns the case to a particular judge for the pretrial proceedings. However, the court must return the cases to the courts where the plaintiffs originally filed them after the pretrial process is completed. *Lexecon v. Milberg Weiss Bershad Hynes & Lerach*, 523 U.S. 26 (1998). Examples of cases that have been transferred for pretrial proceedings include those involving exposure to Agent Orange during the Vietnam war and products liability actions brought against silicone gel breast implant makers.

Exercise 5-13. Multi-District Litigation Transfers

Read 28 U.S.C. § 1407. Based on your reading of the statute, answer the following questions.

1. Who can initiate the process of having a case transferred under § 1407?

2. How does a party challenge a decision by the judicial panel for multidistrict litigation?

3. Can a case be transferred under § 1407 if the parties to the lawsuit object to the transfer?

4. What are the benefits of this type of pretrial consolidation?

5. Are there any exceptions to transfers of this type? If so, what are they?

Exercise 5-14. Chapter Problem Revisited: Putting It All Together and Applying It

You now have learned the basic law of venue, transfer, and forum non conveniens. Put all your diagrams of the rules together and apply to the following problems.

1. Plaintiff Home Health Services ("HHS") brought an action against EBC, a software design company, in the federal district court for the Eastern District of New York for fraud, breach of contract, and breach of professional duty. HHS is a New York corporation with an office in Brooklyn, New York, that provides home health care services in the state of New York. EBC is a software company that contracted with HHS to provide health insurance billing services for HHS. EBC is a New Jersey corporation with an office is Piscataway, New Jersey. HHS alleges that EBC failed to submit the necessary bills on its behalf, resulting in HHS's losing over $7 million in health insurance payments for its services. EBC processed HHS's bills by accessing its computers remotely and processing the insurance

claims at EBC's offices in New Jersey. Ten EBC employees in New Jersey are witnesses who would be necessary for EBC to defend itself in the lawsuit. If EBC makes a motion to transfer venue to New Jersey or, in the alternative, to dismiss the case, will it be successful? Why or why not?

2. Plaintiff Ernest Johnson was injured while working on a construction project in Omaha, Nebraska. At the time of the accident, Johnson was a Nebraska resident. Freedom Mutual Insurance Company is a national insurance company that does business in both Iowa and Nebraska. It provided liability insurance and workers' compensation insurance for Johnson's employer at the time of the accident. Johnson's employer was a subcontractor on the project. Johnson filed a personal injury suit in Nebraska state court against several defendants, including the general contractor. Johnson eventually moved to Iowa and built a home that could accommodate his disabilities due to the accident. Freedom Mutual provided some funding for the home and has paid him weekly disability payments since May 2006. In a telephone conversation with Johnson, a Freedom Mutual representative, he stated that Freedom Mutual did not have a right to any proceeds from the personal injury suit. After Johnson reached a settlement with the general contractor in the personal injury suit, Freedom Mutual told Johnson that it would seek reimbursement for some of its payments to him from the proceeds of the settlement. Johnson filed an action against Freedom Mutual in the United States District Court for the Southern District of Iowa, asserting a claim of fraudulent misrepresentation, including a request for punitive damages, and breach of contract. If Freedom Mutual files a motion to transfer to a federal court in Nebraska or, in the alternative, to dismiss based on forum non conveniens, will the court grant the motion?

7. Professional Development Reflection

Venue and forum non conveniens can involve situations in which plaintiffs are laying venue in a manner that most benefits themselves and/or most inconveniences the defendant. Likewise, defendants can use transfer and forum non conveniens to benefit themselves at the expense of plaintiffs. As a lawyer, what is your role in advising clients about making these choices? For example, should you advise your client to make a motion to transfer a case to a very inconvenient forum for the plaintiff when venue is properly laid in the first instance? As a plaintiff's lawyer, should you lay venue in a place that is most inconvenient for the defendant? What are the downsides to taking such an approach?

Chapter 6

What Law Governs?

1. Chapter Problem

Memorandum

To: Associate
From: Mary Rogers, Partner
Re: Wrongful Death Action

I would like to speak with you later today about our plane crash case from Scotland. Recall that the plane crash happened in Scotland, but the plane was manufactured by Piper Aircraft Company in Pennsylvania (a company that does significant business in California), and we attempted to capture a favorable court by designating a California estate administrator and filing in California state court. As you know, the case was removed to federal court, and then transferred to the Middle District of Pennsylvania. We still have a few procedural fights on our hands, but we know that the issue of what law will apply to the two claims we have will come up.

Since a preliminary investigation into the crash revealed that there might have been a mechanical problem with the plane's propeller, and since Hartzell Propeller, Inc. manufactured the plane's propeller in Ohio, Pennsylvania's state courts would likely apply Ohio law to the claim against Hartzell, were the case initially filed there. But since the plane itself was manufactured by Piper in Pennsylvania, California's courts would likely apply Pennsylvania's law to the claim against Piper, were the case proceeding there. We know that the California federal court did not have personal jurisdiction or proper venue over the claim against Hartzell, but it may have had both over the claim against Piper, notwithstanding the transfer of venue to the Middle District of Pennsylvania.

I believe that both parties are going to file motions to dismiss on a forum non conveniens theory. To help me prepare, I need to know which law the Pennsylvania federal court will likely choose to govern the forum non conveniens motion. The federal courts use a complex, multi-factor approach to decide such motions, while the courts of both Pennsylvania and California privilege the availability of witnesses and co-defendants and the potential for jury confusion due to foreign law as the sole factors. Be ready to discuss this with me later today.

---

2. Introduction

Chapters 2–5 examined the many doctrines that litigants must consider when choosing a court. Chapter 6 addresses one very important additional consideration, one which can come up at any stage of the case, but which must be considered before filing: What law will apply to the dispute? This Chapter will proceed through the following Sections:

- Section 3 — Basic Choice of Law Concepts. This Section introduces the concept of choice of law and distinguishes between its two main varieties in the United States judicial system — horizontal and vertical choice of law.

- Section 4 — The Rules of Decision Act Problem. This Section addresses the vertical choice-of-law problem that exists when a state-law case finds its way into federal court.

- Section 5 — The Rules Enabling Act Problem. This Section addresses the complexity that is introduced to the vertical choice-of-law problem by virtue of the existence of a set of uniform federal rules of procedure.

- Section 6 — Reconciling Vertical and Horizontal Choice of Law. This Section outlines some special problems that exist in choice-of-law due to the interaction of vertical and horizontal choice of law in the same case.

Chapter 6 ends with a discussion of professional and ethical standards and the choice-of-law problems surrounding them.

3. Basic Choice of Law Concepts

The law of "choice of law," or "conflict of laws," as it is often called, is one of the most complex and frustrating areas of procedural law. It is so complex in its full scope that most, if not all, law schools offer an entire three-credit course (or its quarter-hour equivalent) in Conflict of Laws. Thankfully, in the first-year Civil Procedure course, we need only be concerned with one portion of this material — the choice between federal and state law in a state-law case that has found its way to federal court. But, to understand this portion of the conflict of laws world, we need a basic introduction to that world.

The need for a body of legal doctrine relating to choice or law or conflict of laws arises from the presence of sovereign or quasi-sovereign borders. Each state in the United States, and the United States itself, has the power to designate laws that will operate on those who are subject to their jurisdiction, and to exercise that jurisdiction to apply and enforce those laws. Much of what you have studied thus far in this course relates to that notion of sovereignty.

But what happens where the parties to a lawsuit are plausibly subject to the jurisdiction of more than one state, either because the parties live in different states, the events giving rise to the suit occurred in different states, or some combination of the two? In such cases, whatever court in which the lawsuit is filed must make a "choice of law" to apply to the suit, or to different claims or issues within the suit.

One possibility is that the court where the suit is filed can just apply the law of that state to the suit, and this would seem to make sense. After all, it would be very easy. But consider what that might mean for fairness to the litigants. What if the events giving rise to the suit, say, a car accident, occurred in a completely different state, and the suit is only in the court it is in because the defendant lives in that state, where none of the events giving rise to the suit occurred? Would it be fair to apply the law of that forum state, when nothing of consequence happened there?

No state court in the United States has gone with this easy-but-unfair approach to determining what law to apply. Instead, state courts apply a variety of tests to determine which state's law the courts *must* apply. The two most popular tests ask, on the one hand, which state has the "most significant relationship" with the facts giving rise to the case; and on the other, which state has the greatest public policy-based "interest" in resolving the case. Other tests apply different categorical rules to each area of law—for example, the tendency of some state courts to choose the law of the "place of the injury" to govern a tort claim. These determinations of state courts of whether to apply their own law or the law of other states is generally referred to as "horizontal" choice of law because it involves co-equal quasi-sovereigns in our federalist system of law and government deciding which law to apply among themselves.

You may notice that the factor-based metrics described above are quite similar to the factor-based analysis of some personal jurisdiction questions as promulgated in the *Burger King* case, but there are two very, very important differences. First, whereas the factors considered in a personal jurisdiction analysis are overwhelmingly directed at the activities of the defendant (because it is the defendant who is claiming a lack of contacts with, or purposeful availment of, the forum state), in a choice-of-law analysis, the activities of *all* parties (and sometimes non-parties) are considered. The reason for this is the second major difference. In personal jurisdiction law, the court merely must determine whether the forum state in which the lawsuit was filed is *an* appropriate forum for the dispute (i.e., is the forum state one where the lawsuit can proceed, acknowledging that there *may* be other places where it can also proceed). In contrast, in choice-of-law analysis, the court's task is to determine which state's law provides *the* law for the dispute, claim, or issue (i.e., which state's law is the law that *must* decide the dispute, claim, or issue).

You may have also noticed that we used the words, "dispute, claim, or issue" above. You can infer from this usage that one case may involve several different choice-of-law determinations, and the choice of law for one claim, issue, or party in the dispute may end up pointing toward the law of a state different from the state that provides the law for other claims, issues, or parties to the dispute. Or, one state may provide the law for the entire substantive dispute between all of the parties. As you can see, choice-of-law determinations can become very complex very quickly, and anyone who hopes to litigate claims that may involve more than one state would be very well-advised to take the course in Conflict of Laws.

So, hopefully, by now you have a basic sense of what state courts do when they adjudicate cases that involve more than one state—they engage a detailed, factor-based analysis and determine whether they can apply their own law, or whether another state's (or other states') laws must be applied. So, what should a federal court do when it adjudicates a state-law claim (as in a diversity action), and that case arose from transactions or occurrences that happened in more than one state (as in our Chapter Problem)?

The first part of this question is answered by what we generally refer to as the "*Erie* Doctrine." What we generally call the *Erie* Doctrine, however, now encompasses more than just the seminal case of *Erie Railroad Co. v. Tompkins*. The modern analysis now proceeds along two "tracks," each of which addresses one of two choice-of-law problems in the federal courts. We term the first problem the Rules of Decision Act Problem, and we term the second problem the Rules Enabling Act Problem. Each of these problems requires the federal court where the lawsuit is proceeding to determine whether to apply federal or state law to a dispute, claim, or issue. We call this "vertical" choice of law because it involves a choice between the "supreme" sovereign entity in our federalist system (the United States) and one or more of the subordinate, quasi-sovereign entities in that system (the several states).

The remainder of the question above is answered by a branch of the *Erie* Doctrine involving one case you have not seen yet—*Klaxon Company v. Stentor Electric Manufacturing Company*—and another two that you have already seen in the venue context—*Van Dusen v. Barrack* and *Atlantic Marine Construction Co. v. U.S. District Court*, three cases that help the federal courts reconcile the often competing considerations of horizontal choice of law (the choice between the laws of two or more states) and vertical choice of law (the choice between federal and state law). We begin with the Rules of Decision Act Problem.

4. The Rules of Decision Act Problem

In 1789, Congress passed the Judiciary Act, Section 34 of which has since come to be known as the Rules of Decision Act (the "RDA"). The RDA, codified in its current form at 28 U.S.C. § 1652, provides:

> The laws of the several states, except where the Constitution or treaties of the United States or Acts of Congress otherwise require or provide, shall be regarded as rules of decision in civil actions in the courts of the United States, in cases where they apply.

As with most statutes, rules, and other codified sources of law, this statute contains a number of words and phrases that require interpretation. For example, just what are "the laws of the several states"? What are "rules of decision"? And which cases are the "cases where they [i.e., 'the laws of the several states'] apply"?

The following case is a seminal case in the law of civil procedure (it has an entire "doctrine" named after it). The case attempts to address the uncertainty wrought by

Congress's use of one of the phrases identified above: "the laws of the several states." As you will see, the ultimate resolution of this uncertainty was not without its detractors, but it had a profound effect on federal civil litigation practice. As you will also see, the other two phrases identified above present some of the more persistent problems in federal-state choice of law — problems we are still trying to work out to this very day.

Exercise 6-1: *Swift v. Tyson & Erie R. Co. v. Tompkins*

The case below, *Erie Railroad Co. v. Tompkins*, reconsiders what was then a 100-year-old precedent, *Swift v. Tyson*. As you read *Erie*, use your case analysis skills to address the following questions:

1. Issue — What was the issue before the court in *Erie*?

2. Law — Based on your reading of *Erie*, what was the old "rule" of *Swift*? What is the new "rule" of *Erie*?

3. Law — Does *Erie* overrule *Swift*?

Erie R. Co. v. Tompkins
304 U.S. 64 (1938)

Justice Brandeis delivered the opinion of the Court.

The question for decision is whether the oft-challenged doctrine of *Swift v. Tyson* shall now be disapproved.

Tompkins, a citizen of Pennsylvania, was injured on a dark night by a passing freight train of the Erie Railroad Company while walking along its right of way at Hughestown in that State. He claimed that the accident occurred through negligence in the operation, or maintenance, of the train; that he was rightfully on the premises as licensee because on a commonly used beaten footpath which ran for a short distance alongside the tracks, and that he was struck by something which looked like a door projecting from one of the moving cars. To enforce that claim, he brought an action in the federal court for southern New York, which had jurisdiction because the company is a corporation of that State. It denied liability, and the case was tried by a jury.

The Erie insisted that its duty to Tompkins was no greater than that owed to a trespasser. It contended, among other things, that its duty to Tompkins, and hence its liability, should be determined in accordance with the Pennsylvania law; that, under the law of Pennsylvania, as declared by its highest court, persons who use pathways along the railroad right of way — that is, a longitudinal pathway, as distinguished from a crossing —

are to be deemed trespassers, and that the railroad is not liable for injuries to undiscovered trespassers resulting from its negligence unless it be wanton or willful. Tompkins denied that any such rule had been established by the decisions of the Pennsylvania courts, and contended that, since there was no statute of the State on the subject, the railroad's duty and liability is to be determined in federal courts as a matter of general law.

The trial judge refused to rule that the applicable law precluded recovery. The jury brought in a verdict of $30,000, and the judgment entered thereon was affirmed by the Circuit Court of Appeals, which held, 90 F.2d 603, 604, that it was unnecessary to consider whether the law of Pennsylvania was as contended, because the question was one not of local, but of general, law, and that,

> upon questions of general law, the federal courts are free, in the absence of a local statute, to exercise their independent judgment as to what the law is, and it is well settled that the question of the responsibility of a railroad for injuries caused by its servants is one of general law.... Where the public has made open and notorious use of a railroad right of way for a long period of time and without objection, the company owes to persons on such permissive pathway a duty of care in the operation of its trains.... It is likewise generally recognized law that a jury may find that negligence exists toward a pedestrian using a permissive path on the railroad right of way if he is hit by some object projecting from the side of the train.

The Erie had contended that application of the Pennsylvania rule was required, among other things, by §34 of the Federal Judiciary Act of September 24, 1789, c. 20, 28 U.S.C. §725* which provides:

> The laws of the several States, except where the Constitution, treaties, or statutes of the United States otherwise require or provide, shall be regarded as rules of decision in trials at common law, in the courts of the United States, in cases where they apply.

Because of the importance of the question whether the federal court was free to disregard the alleged rule of the Pennsylvania common law, we granted certiorari.

First. *Swift v. Tyson*, 16 Pet. 1, 18, held that federal courts exercising jurisdiction on the ground of diversity of citizenship need not, in matters of general jurisprudence, apply the unwritten law of the State as declared by its highest court; that they are free to exercise an independent judgment as to what the common law of the State is—or should be, and that, as there stated by Mr. Justice Story:

---

* Ed. Note. This is also a reference to the Rules of Decision Act, which is now codified at 28 U.S.C. §1652.

the true interpretation of the thirty-fourth section limited its application to state laws strictly local, that is to say, to the positive statutes of the state, and the construction thereof adopted by the local tribunals, and to rights and titles to things having a permanent locality, such as the rights and titles to real estate, and other matters immovable and intraterritorial in their nature and character. It never has been supposed by us that the section did apply, or was intended to apply, to questions of a more general nature, not at all dependent upon local statutes or local usages of a fixed and permanent operation, as, for example, to the construction of ordinary contracts or other written instruments, and especially to questions of general commercial law, where the state tribunals are called upon to perform the like functions as ourselves, that is, to ascertain upon general reasoning and legal analogies what is the true exposition of the contract or instrument, or what is the just rule furnished by the principles of commercial law to govern the case.

The Court, in applying the rule of § 34 to equity cases, in *Mason v. United States*, 260 U.S. 545, 559, said: "The statute, however, is merely declarative of the rule which would exist in the absence of the statute." The federal courts assumed, in the broad field of "general law," the power to declare rules of decision which Congress was confessedly without power to enact as statutes. Doubt was repeatedly expressed as to the correctness of the construction given § 34, and as to the soundness of the rule which it introduced. But it was the more recent research of a competent scholar, who examined the original document, which established that the construction given to it by the Court was erroneous, and that the purpose of the section was merely to make certain that, in all matters except those in which some federal law is controlling, the federal courts exercising jurisdiction in diversity of citizenship cases would apply as their rules of decision the law of the State, unwritten as well as written.[5]

Criticism of the doctrine became widespread after the decision of *Black & White Taxicab Co. v. Brown & Yellow Taxicab Co.*, 276 U.S. 518. There, Brown and Yellow, a Kentucky corporation owned by Kentuckians, and the Louisville and Nashville Railroad, also a Kentucky corporation, wished that the former should have the exclusive privilege of soliciting passenger and baggage transportation at the Bowling Green, Kentucky, railroad station, and that the Black and White, a competing Kentucky corporation, should be prevented from interfering with that privilege. Knowing that such a contract would be void under the com-

---

5. Charles Warren, *New Light on the History of the Federal Judiciary Act of 1789* (1923) 37 Harv. L. Rev. 49, 51–52, 81–88, 108.

mon law of Kentucky, it was arranged that the Brown and Yellow reincorporate under the law of Tennessee, and that the contract with the railroad should be executed there. The suit was then brought by the Tennessee corporation in the federal court for western Kentucky to enjoin competition by the Black and White; an injunction issued by the District Court was sustained by the Court of Appeals, and this Court, citing many decisions in which the doctrine of *Swift v. Tyson* had been applied, affirmed the decree.

Second. Experience in applying the doctrine of *Swift v. Tyson* had revealed its defects, political and social, and the benefits expected to flow from the rule did not accrue. Persistence of state courts in their own opinions on questions of common law prevented uniformity; and the impossibility of discovering a satisfactory line of demarcation between the province of general law and that of local law developed a new well of uncertainties.

On the other hand, the mischievous results of the doctrine had become apparent. Diversity of citizenship jurisdiction was conferred in order to prevent apprehended discrimination in state courts against those not citizens of the State. *Swift v. Tyson* introduced grave discrimination by noncitizens against citizens. It made rights enjoyed under the unwritten "general law" vary according to whether enforcement was sought in the state or in the federal court, and the privilege of selecting the court in which the right should be determined was conferred upon the noncitizen.[9] Thus, the doctrine rendered impossible equal protection of the law. In attempting to promote uniformity of law throughout the United States, the doctrine had prevented uniformity in the administration of the law of the State.

The discrimination resulting became, in practice, far-reaching. This resulted in part from the broad province accorded to the so-called "general law" as to which federal courts exercised an independent judgment. In addition to questions of purely commercial law, "general law" was held to include the obligations under contracts entered into and to be performed within the State, the extent to which a carrier operating within a State may stipulate for exemption from liability for his own negligence or that of his employee; the liability for torts committed within the State upon person resident or property located there, even where the question of liability depended upon the scope of a property right conferred by the State and the right to exemplary or punitive damages. Furthermore, state decisions construing local deeds, mineral conveyances, and even devises of real estate were disregarded.

---

9. It was even possible for a nonresident plaintiff defeated on a point of law in the highest court of a State nevertheless to win out by taking a nonsuit and renewing the controversy in the federal court. *Compare Gardner v. Michigan Cent. R. Co.*, 150 U.S. 349; *Harrison v. Foley*, 206 Fed. 57 (C.C.A. 8); *Interstate Realty & Inv. Co. v. Bibb County*, 293 Fed. 721 (C.C.A. 5); *see Mills, supra*, note 4, at 52.

In part, the discrimination resulted from the wide range of persons held entitled to avail themselves of the federal rule by resort to the diversity of citizenship jurisdiction. Through this jurisdiction, individual citizens willing to remove from their own State and become citizen of another might avail themselves of the federal rule.* And, without even change of residence, a corporate citizen of the State could avail itself of the federal rule by reincorporating under the laws of another State, as was done in the *Taxicab* case.**

The injustice and confusion incident to the doctrine of *Swift v. Tyson* have been repeatedly urged as reasons for abolishing or limiting diversity of citizenship jurisdiction. Other legislative relief has been proposed. If only a question of statutory construction were involved, we should not be prepared to abandon a doctrine so widely applied throughout nearly a century. But the unconstitutionality of the course pursued has now been made clear, and compels us to do so.

Third. Except in matters governed by the Federal Constitution or by Acts of Congress, the law to be applied in any case is the law of the State. And whether the law of the State shall be declared by its Legislature in a statute or by its highest court in a decision is not a matter of federal concern. There is no federal general common law. Congress has no power to declare substantive rules of common law applicable in a State, whether they be local in their nature or "general," be they commercial law or a part of the law of torts. And no clause in the Constitution purports to confer such a power upon the federal courts. As stated by Mr. Justice Field when protesting in *Baltimore & Ohio R. Co. v. Baugh*, 149 U.S. 368, 401, against ignoring the Ohio common law of fellow servant liability:

> I am aware that what has been termed the general law of the country — which is often little less than what the judge advancing the doctrine thinks at the time should be the general law on a particular subject — has been often advanced in judicial opinions of this court to control a conflicting law of a State. I admit that learned judges have fallen into the habit of repeating this doctrine as a convenient mode of brushing aside the law of a State in conflict with their views. And I confess that, moved and governed by the authority of the great names of those judges, I have, myself, in many instances, unhesitatingly and confidently,

---

* Ed. Note. Recall from your study of subject matter jurisdiction that an in-state defendant does not have the power to remove a diversity case to federal court. 28 U.S.C. § 1441(b)(2).

** Ed. Note. For most of its existence, including much of the time between *Swift* and *Erie*, the diversity jurisdiction statute, 28 U.S.C. § 1332, provided that the citizenship of a corporation was its place of incorporation only. Today, a corporation is also a citizen of the state that is its "principal place of business."

but I think now erroneously, repeated the same doctrine. But, notwithstanding the great names which may be cited in favor of the doctrine, and notwithstanding the frequency with which the doctrine has been reiterated, there stands, as a perpetual protest against its repetition, the Constitution of the United States, which recognizes and preserves the autonomy and independence of the States — independence in their legislative and independence in their judicial departments. Supervision over either the legislative or the judicial action of the States is in no case permissible except as to matters by the Constitution specifically authorized or delegated to the United States. Any interference with either, except as thus permitted, is an invasion of the authority of the State and, to that extent, a denial of its independence.

The fallacy underlying the rule declared in *Swift v. Tyson* is made clear by Mr. Justice Holmes. The doctrine rests upon the assumption that there is "a transcendental body of law outside of any particular State but obligatory within it unless and until changed by statute," that federal courts have the power to use their judgment as to what the rules of common law are, and that, in the federal courts, "the parties are entitled to an independent judgment on matters of general law":

> but law in the sense in which courts speak of it today does not exist without some definite authority behind it. The common law so far as it is enforced in a State, whether called common law or not, is not the common law generally, but the law of that State existing by the authority of that State without regard to what it may have been in England or anywhere else....

> the authority and only authority is the State, and, if that be so, the voice adopted by the State as its own [whether it be of its Legislature or of its Supreme Court] should utter the last word.

Thus, the doctrine of *Swift v. Tyson* is, as Mr. Justice Holmes said,

> an unconstitutional assumption of powers by courts of the United States which no lapse of time or respectable array of opinion should make us hesitate to correct.

In disapproving that doctrine, we do not hold unconstitutional § 34 of the Federal Judiciary Act of 1789 or any other Act of Congress. We merely declare that, in applying the doctrine, this Court and the lower courts have invaded rights which, in our opinion, are reserved by the Constitution to the several States.

Fourth. The defendant contended that, by the common law of Pennsylvania as declared by its highest court in *Falchetti v. Pennsylvania R. Co.*, 307 Pa. 203; 160 A. 859, the only duty owed to the plaintiff was to refrain from willful or wanton injury. The plaintiff denied that such is the Pennsylvania law.[24] In support of their respective contentions the parties discussed and cited many decisions of the Supreme Court of the State. The Circuit Court of Appeals ruled that the question of liability is one of general law, and on that ground declined to decide the issue of state law. As we hold this was error, the judgment is reversed and the case remanded to it for further proceedings in conformity with our opinion.

Reversed.

Justice Cardozo took no part in the consideration or decision of this case.

Justice Butler dissented (opinion omitted)

Reed, J. concurred separately (opinion omitted)

Exercise 6-2. Understanding the *Erie* Doctrine

1. What justifies the decision in *Erie*? Is it a case of statutory or constitutional interpretation?

2. What role does the Rules of Decision Act play in the Court's decision?

3. The *Erie* Court holds that the "course pursued" in the federal courts since *Swift* is unconstitutional. Which provision(s) of the Constitution does this "course pursued" violate? In a small study group, read the Constitution (it's quite short, but feel free to divide it up), and try to identify all of the provisions that the "course pursued" as a result of *Swift* could have plausibly violated. Try to articulate why each provision you identify is violated by the *Swift* doctrine.

Exercise 6-3. Application

Imagine that you are litigating a contract case in federal court, and the law of the state where the federal court sits says that only written contracts can be enforced, while the more general understanding among courts, both in the United States and in England, has always been that both written and oral contracts can be enforced. If the underlying contract is oral, will the contract be enforced? Why or why not?

Exercise 6-4. Application

What if the contract is written, but unlike the courts of every other state, the courts of the state where the court sits require a plaintiff to attach a copy

24. Tompkins also contended that the alleged rule of the *Falchetti* case is not, in any event, applicable here because he was struck at the intersection of the longitudinal pathway and a transverse crossing. The court below found it unnecessary to consider this contention, and we leave the question open.

of the contract to the complaint or suffer dismissal—should the claim be dismissed in federal court if this plaintiff forgot to attach the contract?

Note: Cases Applying *Erie*

Most of the discussion in *Erie* deals with the problem of interpreting what "the laws of the several states" means (or, in Justice Brandeis's terms, what the phrase can and cannot constitutionally mean) in the Rules of Decision Act. As you saw there, the answer to this question is not obvious, and the analysis of the Court in *Erie* is subject to legitimate criticism for being unduly vague and somewhat forced, as the Justices who wrote separately in that case pointed out.

But the "rule" of *Erie* is simple to express. For state-law claims that end up in federal court, the court is required to apply state law (regardless of its source) as the "rules of decision." In essence, Congress has directed the federal courts to choose state law when conducting their choice of law determinations in cases presenting state-law claims. Simple!

But what is a "rule of decision"? Traditionally in choice-of-law analysis, the court where an action proceeds has always had the prerogative to apply its own "procedural" law, even though it is duty-bound to apply the "substantive" law of the state to which its choice-of-law analysis points as the law that determines who wins or loses on the merits. This is also true in federal-state choice-of-law analysis, so even the *Erie* doctrine is understood to require only the application of state *substantive* law, not state *procedural* law. In other words, the federal courts are entitled to have their own procedural rules and statutes that apply to *all* cases, whether such cases arise out of state or federal law, even though the federal courts are mandated to apply state substantive law as the rules of decision in the cases that arise out of state law. Another way of saying this is that only *substantive* rules of law can be considered "rules of decision." But what makes a law "procedural" or "substantive"?

Surprisingly (or maybe not), this is a very, very difficult question. You can probably imagine what sorts of rules and statutes would clearly constitute "procedural" law. A court rule on paper or font size or proper courtroom attire would come to mind, for example. You also can probably imagine laws that all reasonable people would consider completely "substantive." The tort duty of care at issue in *Erie* would come to mind, for example. In between these two extremes, however, the distinction becomes much more difficult to draw.

Several cases decided by the Supreme Court after *Erie* presented conflicts between state and federal law containing both procedural and substantive elements. The first of these, *Guaranty Trust Co. v. York*, 326 U.S. 99 (1945), involved a class action for breach of fiduciary duty against a bond trustee for allegedly fraudulently inducing bondholders to enter into an unfavorable deal in satisfaction of their claims against the debtor. New York's applicable statute of limitations would have barred the suit because the plaintiff class did not file it on or before the statutorily imposed deadline. But under the equitable doctrine of "laches" (which federal courts generally apply to "equity" claims,* such as a claim for breach of fiduciary duty), the court generally asks whether the plaintiff filed the claim soon enough under the totality of the circumstances, rather than simply applying a date cutoff, so the suit could have been allowed to proceed.

The Supreme Court considered whether the *Erie* doctrine required the federal court in which the action was proceeding to apply the New York statute, or whether it could instead apply the equitable doctrine of laches. Understanding that merely labeling the statute of limitations a "substantive" or "procedural" statute would just beg the question, Justice Frankfurter had to devise a test of substantivity. The test that Justice Frankfurter devised has come to be known as the "outcome determinative test."

Under this test, Justice Frankfurter asked whether the application of either state or federal law to the case would alter the outcome of the case on the merits. In other words, would the selection of either state or federal law determine who would win the case? If so, then the law of time limits on actions would be 'substantive enough' to require the application of state law under *Erie*. If not, then the law would be adjudged more procedural than substantive, and the federal courts would be free to apply (or even to craft) their own approach to time limits. Since state law in New York would decide the case in favor of the defendants on the merits on the statute of limitations ground, while the federal approach to laches would potentially result in a full trial and a plaintiff victory, the outcome would be meaningfully different depending on which law the court chose to apply. Accordingly, since it was 'substantive enough' to alter the outcome of the case, the New York statute of limitations was substantive enough to form a "rule of decision" in the case, and the *Erie* doctrine therefore mandated the application of the New York statute.

More than a decade after *York*, the Court addressed a similar question in *Byrd v. Blue Ridge Rural Electric Cooperative, Inc.*, 356 U.S. 525 (1958). Although the Court addressed other federal-state choice-of-law cases during this time, *York* and *Byrd* are often discussed together, so we discuss *Byrd* before moving on to the intervening cases.

Byrd involved a personal injury suit brought by the employee of an independent contractor that had been engaged by Blue Ridge to install power lines in South Carolina. The suit ended up in federal court due to diversity jurisdiction, and the pertinent dispute involved Blue Ridge's defense to Byrd's tort claim. The defense contended that the South Carolina worker's compensation statute barred the suit because under the statute, Byrd was Blue Ridge's "statutory employee,"** and all employees injured

---

 * Ed. Note. The distinction between "law" claims and "equity" claims is an ancient one, and while the Federal Rules do not distinguish between them, many doctrines, such as laches, depend on a determination of whether the claim is an "equity" claim or a "law" claim. We cover the distinction in detail in the Chapter on Trials, where it has the most salience.

 ** Ed. Note. Because Byrd was actually the employee of the independent contractor that Blue Ridge engaged to install the lines, Blue Ridge had to argue that, under the statute, and for the purposes of his suit and the exclusivity defense, Byrd should nevertheless be treated as Blue Ridge's employee because his work was of the nature of the work that Blue Ridge's employees normally performed. Such a status is termed, "statutory employee."

in the line of duty must seek their recovery through the provisions of the worker's compensation statute, rather than through tort suits. The wrinkle that made the case an *Erie* case was this: under South Carolina judicial practice, the determination of whether a plaintiff was a statutory employee was one for the court alone. Under established federal practices (and arguably the Seventh Amendment), the question was required to be decided by a jury.

In his majority opinion, Justice Brennan conceded, mostly for the sake of argument, that the outcome-determinative test developed in *York* would require the Court to apply state law and allow the judge to decide the statutory employer question. But Justice Brennan added a wrinkle to this test. Brennen explained that, notwithstanding the outcome-determinativeness of the choice of law, in some cases, "countervailing federal interests" will nevertheless require the federal courts to apply federal law to a state-law claim. In *Byrd*, the state judicial practice of allowing the judge to decide the statutory employee question could not be squared with what Brennan referred to as "the influence, if not the command, of the Seventh Amendment." As Justice Brennan explained, since the state judicial practice was not "bound up" with the rights of the parties, and was merely a matter of administrative convenience in resolving cases, the important, constitutionally significant federal interest in preserving the right to trial by jury outweighed any state administrative interest in allowing judges to decide the issue.

So, following *Byrd*, one seeking to apply the outcome determinative test would have to first ask the outcome determinativeness question, then inquire as to whether any countervailing federal interest existed that should be weighed against the state's interest in seeing its law applied, and then, finally, conduct a weighing of these competing interests and determine whether to override the choice of state law. The *York/Byrd* approach remained the approach the federal courts used to decide *Erie* questions until *Hanna v. Plumer* was decided in 1965.

In between its decisions in *York* and *Byrd*, in 1949, and relevant as precursors to *Hanna*, the Supreme Court decided three other cases presenting *Erie* questions. In *Ragan v. Merchants Transfer & Warehouse Co.*, 337 U.S. 530 (1949), a traffic accident case arising out of Kansas wound up in federal court due to diversity. The conflict between state and federal law was similar to that in *York*. Kansas law provided a statute of limitations of two years, and the plaintiff did indeed file the complaint within two years of the accident, which, under the general federal court approach to Rule 3,* would have stopped the statute from running ("tolled" it, in statute of limitations parlance). However, under Kansas law, the statute of limitations did not stop running until the defendant was validly served with the complaint. Filing alone was not enough. Although the plaintiff had filed the case within the statute's deadline, the defendant was not served until the deadline was past. This made the distinction be-

---

* Ed. Note. Federal Rule of Civil Procedure 3 provides, "A civil action is commenced by filing a complaint with the court." Typically a statute of limitation states that an action must be "commenced" by a certain deadline to be timely.

tween the federal "tolled at filing" approach and the state "tolled at service" approach "outcome determinative" in the sense developed in *York*, so the Court held that state law must be applied.

In *Cohen v. Beneficial Industrial Loan Corp.*, 337 U.S. 541 (1949), a New Jersey shareholder's derivative suit filed in federal court under what is now Federal Rule of Civil Procedure 23.1, the Court again was faced with a conflict between federal and state law. New Jersey law at the time required any minor shareholder* wishing to sue the board of directors of the corporation on behalf of the shareholders to pay the legal fees of the corporation if the board of directors were to prevail. The plaintiff also was required to post a bond to secure these expenses. Federal law, embodied in Rule 23.1, did not contain any bond requirement, but the defendant board contended that the New Jersey requirement must be applied. Reasoning that a plaintiff meeting the statute's requirements (as this plaintiff did) would be completely denied a cause of action absent the bond in New Jersey, and would be allowed to proceed on the merits under Rule 23.1, the Court concluded that the New Jersey provision was "outcome determinative," and ordered that state law be applied.

Finally, in *Woods v. Interstate Realty Co.*, 337 U.S. 535 (1949), the Court addressed a suit seeking a real estate commission, brought by a Tennessee corporation which had not registered to do business in Mississippi, the state where the commission was allegedly earned. Mississippi law provided that corporations could not sue in the state's courts unless they first registered to do business in the state and appointed an in-state agent for service of process, while Federal Rule of Civil Procedure 17 states that a corporation may sue under the laws of its state of organization, regardless of whether it is registered in the state where the suit is filed. The defendant urged the federal court to apply the Mississippi statute, and the court agreed, awarding summary judgment to the defendant based on the Mississippi statutory exclusion. The Supreme Court agreed, once again on the reasoning that, under state law, the plaintiff would have no claim, while under federal law (which contained no requirement for a corporation to register in order to sue), the plaintiff would have a cause of action. Accordingly, the Court held, the difference in law was outcome-determinative, and state law must be applied.

---

5. The Rules Enabling Act Problem

The preceding three cases represent three straightforward, pre-*Byrd* applications of *York* to federal-state conflicts of law, as in each case, the choice of either federal or state law would have determined the outcome of the case. But these three cases differed from both *York* and *Byrd* in an important way. In each of these three cases,

---

* Ed. Note. This provision applied to shareholders holding less than 5% of the corporation's stock, or less than $50,000 of its value. Consider why this rule might be adopted. Can you see the policy goal the New Jersey Legislature was attempting to serve?

the federal approach plausibly could have been described as being mandated by a Federal Rule of Civil Procedure (Rule 3, on filing an action, in *Ragan*; Rule 23.1, on shareholder's derivative suits, in *Cohen*; and Rule 17, on the capacity of corporations to sue, in *Woods*). If these provisions of the Federal Rules indeed mandated the federal approach in these three cases, it would seem odd to privilege state law over them.

The main reason for this is the Supremacy Clause of the United States Constitution, article VI, clause 2, which provides:

> This Constitution, and the Laws of the United States which shall be made in pursuance thereof; and all treaties made, or which shall be made, under the authority of the United States, shall be the supreme law of the land; and the judges in every state shall be bound thereby, anything in the constitution or laws of any state to the contrary notwithstanding.

It would seem that, if the Federal Rules of Civil Procedure are "Laws of the United States made in pursuance" of the Constitution, then they should be "supreme" over any conflicting state laws in all cases. As it turns out, whether the Federal Rules of Civil Procedure are in fact "Laws" made "in pursuance of" the Constitution depends on — you guessed it — whether the Rules are "procedural," as opposed to "substantive."

The case below, *Hanna v. Plumer*, 380 U.S. 460 (1965), addresses this difficult aspect of drawing the substance-procedure distinction, and develops a test that courts can use to resolve the question in some cases.

Exercise 6-5. *Hanna v. Plumer*

1. Why does the *Hanna* Court reject the application of *Erie*, *York*, and *Byrd* to the case? What is different about the issue presented in *Hanna*?

2. What is the "test" of *Hanna*? How do we know whether a federal rule of civil procedure must be applied over a contrary state procedure, like the state service rule here?

3. What if the state legislature here had stated, as part of the service law's Preamble, its legislative finding that in-hand service is vital to protecting the substantive rights of estate executors? Would or should that change the result?

Hanna v. Plumer

380 U.S. 460 (1965)

Chief Justice Warren delivered the opinion of the Court.

The question to be decided is whether, in a civil action where the jurisdiction of the United States district court is based upon diversity of citizenship between the parties, service of process shall be made in the manner prescribed by state law or that set forth in Rule 4(d)(1) of the Federal Rules of Civil Procedure.

On February 6, 1963, petitioner, a citizen of Ohio, filed her complaint in the District Court for the District of Massachusetts, claiming damages in excess of $10,000 for personal injuries resulting from an automobile accident in South Carolina, allegedly caused by the negligence of one Louise Plumer Osgood, a Massachusetts citizen deceased at the time of the filing of the complaint. Respondent, Mrs. Osgood's executor and also a Massachusetts citizen, was named as defendant. On February 8, service was made by leaving copies of the summons and the complaint with respondent's wife at his residence, concededly in compliance with Rule 4(d)(1),* which provides:

> The summons and complaint shall be served together. The plaintiff shall furnish the person making service with such copies as are necessary. Service shall be made as follows:

> (1) Upon an individual other than an infant or an incompetent person, by delivering a copy of the summons and of the complaint to him personally or by leaving copies thereof at his dwelling house or usual place of abode with some person of suitable age and discretion then residing therein....

Respondent filed his answer on February 26, alleging, inter alia, that the action could not be maintained because it had been brought "contrary to and in violation of the provisions of Massachusetts General Laws (Ter. Ed.) Chapter 197, Section 9." That section provides:

> Except as provided in this chapter, an executor or administrator shall not be held to answer to an action by a creditor of the deceased which is not commenced within one year from the time of his giving bond for the performance of his trust, or to such an action which is commenced within said year unless before the expiration thereof the writ in such action has been served by delivery in hand upon such executor or administrator or service thereof accepted by him or a notice stating the name of the estate, the name and address of the creditor, the amount of the claim and the court in which the action has been brought has been filed in the proper registry of probate.... Mass. Gen. Laws Ann., c. 197, §9 (1958).[1]

---

*   Ed. Note. Former Rule 4(d)(1) is now codified as Rule 4(e)(2).

1. Section 9 is in part a statute of limitations, providing that an executor need not "answer to an action ... which is not commenced within one year from the time of his giving bond...." This part of the statute, the purpose of which is to speed the settlement of estates, *Spaulding v. McConnell*, 307 Mass. 144, 146, 29 N. E. 2d 713, 715 (1940); *Doyle v. Moylan*, 141 F. Supp. 95 (D. C. D. Mass. 1956), is not involved in this case, since the action clearly was timely commenced. (Respondent filed bond on March 1, 1962; the complaint was filed February 6, 1963, and the service — the propriety of which

On October 17, 1963, the District Court granted respondent's motion for summary judgment, citing *Ragan v. Merchants Transfer Co.*, 337 U.S. 530, and *Guaranty Trust Co. v. York*, 326 U.S. 99, in support of its conclusion that the adequacy of the service was to be measured by §9, with which, the court held, petitioner had not complied. On appeal, petitioner admitted noncompliance with §9, but argued that Rule 4(d)(1) defines the method by which service of process is to be effected in diversity actions. The Court of Appeals for the First Circuit, finding that "[r]elatively recent amendments [to §9] evince a clear legislative purpose to require personal notification within the year," concluded that the conflict of state and federal rules was over "a substantive rather than a procedural matter," and unanimously affirmed. 331 F. 2d 157. Because of the threat to the goal of uniformity of federal procedure posed by the decision below, we granted certiorari, 379 U.S. 813.

We conclude that the adoption of Rule 4(d)(1), designed to control service of process in diversity actions, neither exceeded the congressional mandate embodied in the Rules Enabling Act nor transgressed constitutional bounds, and that the Rule is therefore the standard against which the District Court should have measured the adequacy of the service. Accordingly, we reverse the decision of the Court of Appeals.

The Rules Enabling Act, 28 U.S.C. §2072 (1958 ed.), provides, in pertinent part:

> The Supreme Court shall have the power to prescribe, by general rules, the forms of process, writs, pleadings, and motions, and the practice and procedure of the district courts of the United States in civil actions.

> Such rules shall not abridge, enlarge or modify any substantive right and shall preserve the right of trial by jury....

Under the cases construing the scope of the Enabling Act, Rule 4(d)(1) clearly passes muster. Prescribing the manner in which a defendant is to be notified that a suit has been instituted against him, it relates to the practice and procedure of the district courts.

---

is in dispute—was made on February 8, 1963.) 331 F. 2d, at 159. *Cf. Guaranty Trust Co. v. York*, *supra*; *Ragan v. Merchants Transfer Co.*, *supra*.

Section 9 also provides for the manner of service. Generally, service of process must be made by "delivery in hand," although there are two alternatives: acceptance of service by the executor, or filing of a notice of claim, the components of which are set out in the statute, in the appropriate probate court. The purpose of this part of the statute, which is involved here, is, as the court below noted, to insure that executors will receive actual notice of claims. Actual notice is of course also the goal of Rule 4(d)(1); however, the Federal Rule reflects a determination that this goal can be achieved by a method less cumbersome than that prescribed in §9. In this case the goal seems to have been achieved; although the affidavit filed by respondent in the District Court asserts that he had not been served in hand nor had he accepted service, it does not allege lack of actual notice.

"The test must be whether a rule really regulates procedure,—the judicial process for enforcing rights and duties recognized by substantive law and for justly administering remedy and redress for disregard or infraction of them." *Sibbach v. Wilson & Co.*, 312 U.S. 1, 14.

In *Mississippi Pub. Corp. v. Murphree*, 326 U.S. 438, this Court upheld Rule 4 (f), which permits service of a summons anywhere within the State (and not merely the district) in which a district court sits:

> We think that Rule 4(f) is in harmony with the Enabling Act.... Undoubtedly most alterations of the rules of practice and procedure may and often do affect the rights of litigants. Congress' prohibition of any alteration of substantive rights of litigants was obviously not addressed to such incidental effects as necessarily attend the adoption of the prescribed new rules of procedure upon the rights of litigants who, agreeably to rules of practice and procedure, have been brought before a court authorized to determine their rights. *Sibbach v. Wilson & Co.*, 312 U.S. 1, 11–14. The fact that the application of Rule 4(f) will operate to subject petitioner's rights to adjudication by the district court for northern Mississippi will undoubtedly affect those rights. But it does not operate to abridge, enlarge or modify the rules of decision by which that court will adjudicate its rights. *Id.*, at 445–446.

Thus were there no conflicting state procedure, Rule 4(d)(1) would clearly control. However, respondent, focusing on the contrary Massachusetts rule, calls to the Court's attention another line of cases, a line which—like the Federal Rules—had its birth in 1938. *Erie R. Co. v. Tompkins*, 304 U.S. 64, overruling *Swift v. Tyson*, 16 Pet. 1, held that federal courts sitting in diversity cases, when deciding questions of "substantive" law, are bound by state court decisions as well as state statutes. The broad command of *Erie* was therefore identical to that of the Enabling Act: federal courts are to apply state substantive law and federal procedural law. However, as subsequent cases sharpened the distinction between substance and procedure, the line of cases following *Erie* diverged markedly from the line construing the Enabling Act. *Guaranty Trust Co. v. York*, 326 U.S. 99, made it clear that *Erie*-type problems were not to be solved by reference to any traditional or common-sense substance-procedure distinction:

> "And so the question is not whether a statute of limitations is deemed a matter of 'procedure' in some sense. The question is ... does it significantly affect the result of a litigation for a federal court to disregard a law of a State that would be controlling in an action upon the same claim by the same parties in a State court?" 326 U.S., at 109.

Respondent, by placing primary reliance on *York* and *Ragan*, suggests that the *Erie* doctrine acts as a check on the Federal Rules of Civil Procedure, that despite the clear command of Rule 4(d)(1), *Erie* and its progeny demand the application of the Massachusetts rule. Reduced to essentials, the argument is: (1) *Erie*, as refined in *York*, demands that federal courts apply state law whenever application of federal law in its stead will alter the outcome of the case. (2) In this case, a determination that the Massachusetts service requirements obtain will result in immediate victory for respondent. If, on the other hand, it should be held that Rule 4(d)(1) is applicable, the litigation will continue, with possible victory for petitioner. (3) Therefore, *Erie* demands application of the Massachusetts rule. The syllogism possesses an appealing simplicity, but is for several reasons invalid.

In the first place, it is doubtful that, even if there were no Federal Rule making it clear that in-hand service is not required in diversity actions, the *Erie* rule would have obligated the District Court to follow the Massachusetts procedure. "Outcome-determination" analysis was never intended to serve as a talisman. *Byrd v. Blue Ridge Cooperative*, 356 U.S. 525, 537. Indeed, the message of *York* itself is that choices between state and federal law are to be made not by application of any automatic, "litmus paper" criterion, but rather by reference to the policies underlying the *Erie* rule.

The *Erie* rule is rooted in part in a realization that it would be unfair for the character or result of a litigation materially to differ because the suit had been brought in a federal court.

> Diversity of citizenship jurisdiction was conferred in order to prevent apprehended discrimination in state courts against those not citizens of the State. *Swift v. Tyson* introduced grave discrimination by non-citizens against citizens. It made rights enjoyed under the unwritten 'general law' vary according to whether enforcement was sought in the state or in the federal court; and the privilege of selecting the court in which the right should be determined was conferred upon the non-citizen. Thus, the doctrine rendered impossible equal protection of the law.

The decision was also in part a reaction to the practice of "forum-shopping" which had grown up in response to the rule of *Swift v. Tyson*. That the *York* test was an attempt to effectuate these policies is demonstrated by the fact that the opinion framed the inquiry in terms of "substantial" variations between state and federal litigation. Not only are nonsubstantial, or trivial, variations not likely to raise the sort of equal protection problems which troubled the Court in *Erie*; they are also unlikely to influence the choice of a forum. The "outcome-determination" test therefore cannot be read without reference to the twin aims of the

Erie rule: discouragement of forum-shopping and avoidance of inequitable administration of the laws.[9]

The difference between the conclusion that the Massachusetts rule is applicable, and the conclusion that it is not, is of course at this point "outcome-determinative" in the sense that if we hold the state rule to apply, respondent prevails, whereas if we hold that Rule 4(d)(1) governs, the litigation will continue. But in this sense every procedural variation is "outcome-determinative." For example, having brought suit in a federal court, a plaintiff cannot then insist on the right to file subsequent pleadings in accord with the time limits applicable in the state courts, even though enforcement of the federal timetable will, if he continues to insist that he must meet only the state time limit, result in determination of the controversy against him.[10] So it is here. Though choice of the federal or state rule will at this point have a marked effect upon the outcome of the litigation, the difference between the two rules would be of scant, if any, relevance to the choice of a forum. Petitioner, in choosing her forum, was not presented with a situation where application of the state rule would wholly bar recovery; rather, adherence to the state rule would have resulted only in altering the way in which process was served.[11] Moreover, it is difficult to argue that permitting service of defendant's wife to take the place of in-hand service of defendant himself alters the

---

9. The Court of Appeals seemed to frame the inquiry in terms of how "important" §9 is to the State. In support of its suggestion that §9 serves some interest the State regards as vital to its citizens, the court noted that something like §9 has been on the books in Massachusetts a long time, that §9 has been amended a number of times, and that §9 is designed to make sure that executors receive actual notice. *See* note 1, supra. The apparent lack of relation among these three observations is not surprising, because it is not clear to what sort of question the Court of Appeals was addressing itself. One cannot meaningfully ask how important something is without first asking "important for what purpose?" *Erie* and its progeny make clear that when a federal court sitting in a diversity case is faced with a question of whether or not to apply state law, the importance of a state rule is indeed relevant, but only in the context of asking whether application of the rule would make so important a difference to the character or result of the litigation that failure to enforce it would unfairly discriminate against citizens of the forum State, or whether application of the rule would have so important an effect upon the fortunes of one or both of the litigants that failure to enforce it would be likely to cause a plaintiff to choose the federal court.

10. *See Guaranty Trust Co. v. York, supra*, at 108–109; *Ragan v. Merchants Transfer Co., supra*, at 532; *Woods v. Interstate Realty Co., supra*, note 5, at 538.

Similarly, a federal court's refusal to enforce the New Jersey rule involved in *Cohen v. Beneficial Loan Corp.*, 337 U.S. 541, requiring the posting of security by plaintiffs in stockholders' derivative actions, might well impel a stockholder to choose to bring suit in the federal, rather than the state, court.

11. *Cf. Monarch Insurance Co. of Ohio v. Spach*, 281 F. 2d 401, 412 (C. A. 5th Cir. 1960). We cannot seriously entertain the thought that one suing an estate would be led to choose the federal court because of a belief that adherence to Rule 4(d)(1) is less likely to give the executor actual notice than §9, and therefore more likely to produce a default judgment. Rule 4(d)(1) is well designed to give actual notice, as it did in this case. *See* note 1, *supra*.

mode of enforcement of state-created rights in a fashion sufficiently "substantial" to raise the sort of equal protection problems to which the *Erie* opinion alluded.

There is, however, a more fundamental flaw in respondent's syllogism: the incorrect assumption that the rule of *Erie R. Co. v. Tompkins* constitutes the appropriate test of the validity and therefore the applicability of a Federal Rule of Civil Procedure. The *Erie* rule has never been invoked to void a Federal Rule. It is true that there have been cases where this Court has held applicable a state rule in the face of an argument that the situation was governed by one of the Federal Rules. But the holding of each such case was not that *Erie* commanded displacement of a Federal Rule by an inconsistent state rule, but rather that the scope of the Federal Rule was not as broad as the losing party urged, and therefore, there being no Federal Rule which covered the point in dispute, *Erie* commanded the enforcement of state law.

> Respondent contends, in the first place, that the charge was correct because of the fact that Rule 8(c) of the Rules of Civil Procedure makes contributory negligence an affirmative defense. We do not agree. Rule 8(c) covers only the manner of pleading. The question of the burden of establishing contributory negligence is a question of local law which federal courts in diversity of citizenship cases [*Erie R. Co. v. Tompkins*, 304 U.S. 64] must apply. *Palmer v. Hoffman*, 318 U.S. 109, 117.

(Here, of course, the clash is unavoidable; Rule 4(d)(1) says—implicitly, but with unmistakable clarity—that in-hand service is not required in federal courts.) At the same time, in cases adjudicating the validity of Federal Rules, we have not applied the *York* rule or other refinements of *Erie*, but have to this day continued to decide questions concerning the scope of the Enabling Act and the constitutionality of specific Federal Rules in light of the distinction set forth in *Sibbach*.

Nor has the development of two separate lines of cases been inadvertent. The line between "substance" and "procedure" shifts as the legal context changes. Each implies different variables depending upon the particular problem for which it is used. It is true that both the Enabling Act and the *Erie* rule say, roughly, that federal courts are to apply state "substantive" law and federal "procedural" law, but from that it need not follow that the tests are identical. For they were designed to control very different sorts of decisions. When a situation is covered by one of the Federal Rules, the question facing the court is a far cry from the typical, relatively unguided *Erie* choice: the court has been instructed to apply the Federal Rule, and can refuse to do so only if the Advisory Committee, this Court, and Congress erred in their prima facie judgment that the Rule in question transgresses neither the terms of the Enabling Act nor constitutional restrictions.

We are reminded by the *Erie* opinion that neither Congress nor the federal courts can, under the guise of formulating rules of decision for federal courts, fashion rules which are not supported by a grant of federal authority contained in Article I or some other section of the Constitution; in such areas state law must govern because there can be no other law. But the opinion in *Erie*, which involved no Federal Rule and dealt with a question which was "substantive" in every traditional sense (whether the railroad owed a duty of care to Tompkins as a trespasser or a licensee), surely neither said nor implied that measures like Rule 4(d)(1) are unconstitutional. For the constitutional provision for a federal court system (augmented by the Necessary and Proper Clause) carries with it congressional power to make rules governing the practice and pleading in those courts, which in turn includes a power to regulate matters which, though falling within the uncertain area between substance and procedure, are rationally capable of classification as either. Neither *York* nor the cases following it ever suggested that the rule there laid down for coping with situations where no Federal Rule applies is coextensive with the limitation on Congress to which *Erie* had adverted. Although this Court has never before been confronted with a case where the applicable Federal Rule is in direct collision with the law of the relevant State,[15] courts of appeals faced with such clashes have rightly discerned the implications of our decisions.

* * *

Erie and its offspring cast no doubt on the long-recognized power of Congress to prescribe housekeeping rules for federal courts even though some of those rules will inevitably differ from comparable state rules. "When, because the plaintiff happens to be a non-resident, such a right is enforceable in a federal as well as in a State court, the forms and mode of enforcing the right may at times, naturally enough, vary because the two judicial systems are not identic." *Guaranty Trust Co. v. York, supra,* at 108. Thus, though a court, in measuring a Federal Rule against the standards contained in the Enabling Act and the Constitution, need not wholly blind itself to the degree to which the Rule makes the character and result of the federal litigation stray from the course it would follow in state courts, it cannot be forgotten that the *Erie* rule, and the guidelines suggested in *York*, were created to serve another purpose altogether. To hold that a Federal Rule of Civil Procedure must cease to function whenever it alters the mode of enforcing state-created rights would be to disembowel either the Constitution's grant of power over federal procedure or Congress'

---

15. In *Sibbach v. Wilson & Co., supra,* the law of the forum State (Illinois) forbade the sort of order authorized by Rule 35. However, *Sibbach* was decided before *Klaxon Co. v. Stentor Co., supra,* note 7, and the *Sibbach* opinion makes clear that the Court was proceeding on the assumption that if the law of any State was relevant, it was the law of the State where the tort occurred (Indiana), which, like Rule 35, made provision for such orders. 312 U.S., at 6–7, 10–11.

attempt to exercise that power in the Enabling Act. Rule 4(d)(1) is valid and controls the instant case.

Reversed.

Justice Black concurs in the result.

Justice Harlan, concurring.

It is unquestionably true that up to now *Erie* and the cases following it have not succeeded in articulating a workable doctrine governing choice of law in diversity actions. I respect the Court's effort to clarify the situation in today's opinion. However, in doing so I think it has misconceived the constitutional premises of *Erie* and has failed to deal adequately with those past decisions upon which the courts below relied.

Erie was something more than an opinion which worried about "forum-shopping and avoidance of inequitable administration of the laws," *ante*, p. 468, although to be sure these were important elements of the decision. I have always regarded that decision as one of the modern cornerstones of our federalism, expressing policies that profoundly touch the allocation of judicial power between the state and federal systems. *Erie* recognized that there should not be two conflicting systems of law controlling the primary activity of citizens, for such alternative governing authority must necessarily give rise to a debilitating uncertainty in the planning of everyday affairs. And it recognized that the scheme of our Constitution envisions an allocation of law-making functions between state and federal legislative processes which is undercut if the federal judiciary can make substantive law affecting state affairs beyond the bounds of congressional legislative powers in this regard. Thus, in diversity cases *Erie* commands that it be the state law governing primary private activity which prevails.

The shorthand formulations which have appeared in some past decisions are prone to carry untoward results that frequently arise from over-simplification. The Court is quite right in stating that the "outcome-determinative" test of *Guaranty Trust Co. v. York*, 326 U.S. 99, if taken literally, proves too much, for any rule, no matter how clearly "procedural," can affect the outcome of litigation if it is not obeyed. In turning from the "outcome" test of *York* back to the unadorned forum-shopping rationale of *Erie*, however, the Court falls prey to like over-simplification, for a simple forum-shopping rule also proves too much; litigants often choose a federal forum merely to obtain what they consider the advantages of the Federal Rules of Civil Procedure or to try their cases before a supposedly more favorable judge. To my mind the proper line of approach in determining whether to apply a state or a federal rule, whether "substantive" or "procedural," is to stay close to basic principles by inquiring if the choice of rule would substantially affect those primary decisions respecting human conduct which our constitutional system leaves to state regulation. If so, *Erie* and the Constitution require that the state rule prevail, even in the face of a conflicting federal rule.

* * *

So long as a reasonable man could characterize any duly adopted federal rule as "procedural," the Court, unless I misapprehend what is said, would have it apply no matter how seriously it frustrated a State's substantive regulation of the primary conduct and affairs of its citizens. Since the members of the Advisory Committee, the Judicial Conference, and this Court who formulated the Federal Rules are presumably reasonable men, it follows that the integrity of the Federal Rules is absolute. Whereas the unadulterated outcome and forum-shopping tests may err too far toward honoring state rules, I submit that the Court's "arguably procedural, ergo constitutional" test moves too fast and far in the other direction.

* * *

As [the application of Rule 4(d)(1)] does not seem enough to give rise to any real impingement on the vitality of the state policy which the Massachusetts rule is intended to serve, I concur in the judgment of the Court.

Note: Understanding *Hanna* and Its Progeny

As you can see, *Hanna* takes the *Erie* analysis and divides it into two "tracks." Track One, which we will call the RDA Track (because it applies the Rules of Decision Act), is the basic *Erie* analysis. It requires that, where a state law is 'substantive enough' to determine the outcome of the case, that law must be applied over contrary federal law. What *Hanna* adds to this is the vantage point from which the court asks the outcome determinativeness question. Unlike *York*, *Ragan*, *Cohen*, and *Woods*, which simply asked the question from the vantage point of the cases before the Court in their then-current procedural posture, *Hanna* shifts the vantage point to the point at which a litigant makes the choice of forum between state and federal court.

And this makes very good sense, in light of what the *Hanna* Court identifies as the "twin aims" of *Erie*—to eliminate forum shopping to avoid inequitable administration of the law. Simply put, if the difference in law would cause a litigant with the ability to make a forum choice to choose federal over state court (ostensibly because the forum chosen would be less fair to the litigant's opponent), then the difference in law is outcome determinative, and is therefore 'substantive enough' to require application under the *Erie* doctrine. So, to apply the RDA Track *Erie* analysis, put yourself in the shoes of the litigant who chooses the federal forum—either the plaintiff deciding where to file or the defendant deciding whether to remove the case from state to federal court—and decide whether a litigant in one of those positions would choose federal court simply to capture the difference in law. If so, then the difference in law is outcome-determinative, and state law must be applied. Remember, this is a hypothetical inquiry—don't fall victim to the fallacy of asking whether *this plaintiff* or *this defendant* in fact chose federal court to capture a difference in law—that's not relevant.

But *Hanna*'s real importance lies in specifying that there is another analytical track. Track Two, which we will call the REA Track (because it applies the Rules Enabling Act), is the analysis set forth in *Hanna* beginning with the words, "There is, however, a more fundamental flaw in respondent's syllogism ..."* Under the REA Track, the analysis is much simpler. The Supremacy Clause of the Constitution, article VI, clause 2, specifies that the Constitution, along with all laws made in conformity with it, are "supreme" over any state laws that conflict with them. By virtue of the "Courts Clause" (art. I, § 8, cl. 9), read in conjunction with the "Necessary and Proper Clause" (art. I, § 8, cl. 18), Congress has the power under the Constitution to make laws relating to practice and procedure in the federal courts.

Through the Rules Enabling Act, Congress delegated part of this power to the federal courts, which are empowered to make rules of practice, procedure, and evidence (through the Judicial Conference of the United States, pursuant to a lengthy notice and comment procedure), and these rules will have the force of federal statutes unless objected to or amended by Congress before their effective date. *See* 28 U.S.C. §§ 2071 *et seq.* Accordingly, where the courts comply with the procedures set forth in the REA, and they promulgate rules to which Congress does not object or pass amendments, these rules constitute "laws made in pursuance" of the Constitution, and are therefore "supreme" over any state laws that conflict with them. This means that, in a conflict between a Federal Rule of Civil Procedure and any provision of state law (the state constitution, a state statute, a state judicial decision, a state rule of procedure, etc.), the federal rule should prevail.

But remember that Congress did not delegate *all* of its lawmaking power to the courts, even where they follow the procedures for rulemaking under the REA. Rather, in the most pertinent portion of the REA, 28 U.S.C. § 2072, Congress specified limits on the courts' rulemaking power:

> (a) The Supreme Court shall have the power to prescribe general rules of practice and procedure and rules of evidence for cases in the United States district courts (including proceedings before magistrate judges thereof) and courts of appeals.
>
> (b) Such rules shall not abridge, enlarge or modify any substantive right....

So, the courts are limited to promulgating "general rules of practice and procedure and rules of evidence" (subsection (a)). These rules also must not "abridge, enlarge

---

* Ed. Note. Many civil procedure professors refer to this part of the opinion as "*Hanna* Part II," while terming the *Erie* analysis portion of the opinion (which is mostly *dicta*), "*Hanna* Part I." *See, e.g.,* Joseph W. Glannon, Civil Procedure: Examples & Explanations (7th ed. 2013, Aspen). This can be a useful shorthand, and you should use it if it works for you, but we prefer to name the tracks based on the federal statutes that they apply, to help you keep straight just how and why the two analyses set forth in *Hanna* are different.

or modify any substantive right" (subsection (b)). Since *Hanna* was decided, the courts have had a very difficult time in deciding exactly what limitations these two provisions place on judicial rulemaking. Three efforts to do so are worth noting before moving on to the most recent case, *Shady Grove Orthopedics v. Allstate Insurance Co.*, which sets forth the best approximation of the state of the law today.

First, in *Walker v. Armco Steel Corp.*, 446 U.S. 740 (1980), an action arising out of Oklahoma was filed in federal court within the statute of limitations. But the defendant, a foreign corporation, was not served until nearly four months after the complaint was filed. Like the Kansas statute of limitations at issue in *Ragan*, the Oklahoma statute provided that the statute would not be tolled until the defendant was served with process. The defendant contended that the Oklahoma statute must be applied, on the authority of *Ragan* (meaning that the statute would only be tolled at service, and the complaint would be dismissed as untimely), while the plaintiff contended that Federal Rule of Civil Procedure 3's language regarding "commenc[ing]" a cause of action should set the date for the tolling of the statute (meaning that it would have been tolled at filing, and the complaint would have been timely). Thus, *Walker* provided a perfect, post-*Hanna* opportunity for the Court to overrule *Ragan* and solidify the *Hanna* approach to conflicts between state law and the Federal Rules of Civil Procedure. But the Court chose another path — one that has made a significant difference in recent cases. Reading Rule 3, the Court determined that the Rule was not drafted as a way of tolling any statute of limitations, but instead was written as a baseline to which all of the other time limits in the Federal Rules could relate. In fact, a number of federal statutes places requirements other than filing on the tolling of statutes of limitation, and Rule 3 does not conflict with those provisions, so it should not conflict with the Oklahoma statute at issue in the case. This case established that federal rules could be read narrowly to avoid conflicts with state law.

Next, in *Burlington Northern Railroad Co. v. Woods*, 480 U.S. 1 (1987), a plaintiff won a judgment in a case arising from a motorcycle accident. The defendant appealed, but the judgment was affirmed. Under Alabama law at the time, an unsuccessful appellant was automatically assessed a 10% penalty. Under Federal Rule of Appellate Procedure 38,* in contrast, the court, in its discretion, may award single or double costs to the successful appellee if the court determines that an appeal was "frivolous." Applying the REA Track analysis in *Hanna*, the Supreme Court held that, since the availability of a penalty for an unsuccessful appeal was not part of the underlying substantive rights of the parties in the action, but was merely part of the forms and modes of enforcing those rights, the penalty under FRAP 38 was procedural, and was therefore "supreme" over the conflicting Alabama law.

Stewart Organization, Inc. v. Ricoh Corp., 487 U.S. 22 (1988), presented the REA Track problem in the federal statutory context. Also arising out of Alabama law, this case involved a breach of contract claim. The defendant sought a convenience-based

---

* Ed. Note. The Federal Rules of Appellate Procedure are treated the same as the Federal Rules of Civil Procedure for the purposes of choice-of-law analysis.

transfer of venue to the Southern District of New York, in part based on a "forum-selection clause" in the contract between the parties, stating that all suits concerning the contract must be litigated in the courts embracing the borough of Manhattan in New York City. The federal District Court in Alabama denied the motion to transfer venue, in pertinent part because the court determined that Alabama law treats forum-selection clauses with disfavor. Essentially, the court held that the forum-selection clause could not be considered among the convenience factors in the 28 U.S.C. § 1404 analysis. As you know from your study of venue, forum-selection clauses are considered relevant, albeit not dispositive, to a § 1404 transfer motion, so the Alabama approach was in conflict with the federal approach.

Applying *Hanna*'s reasoning to the statutory conflict context, the Court held that, since the federal courts generally consider forum-selection clauses for the procedural purpose of deciding which venue is most convenient for the parties, the consideration of such clauses is part and parcel of the clearly procedural transfer-of-venue statute, and therefore is "supreme" over state law when used in this way. Important to note here is that, while the analysis is similar where a federal statute conflicts with state law and where a federal rule does, the analysis is not identical. For a federal rule, one must examine whether the congressional delegation of rulemaking authority to the courts in the Rules Enabling Act is satisfied. That is, one must determine whether the rule is question is a 'rule of practice, procedure, or evidence,' and if so, one must then determine whether the rule in question 'abridges, enlarges or modifies any substantive right.' For a statutory conflict, since there is no delegation of authority at issue (statutes are directly passed as laws by Congress and signed by the President), one must simply ask whether Congress had the constitutional authority to enact the statute. For a procedural statute, that typically amounts to asking whether the Courts Clause, read in light of the Necessary and Proper Clause, justifies the enactment. If so, then the statute is "supreme" over state law.

Exercise 6-6. Testing Your Understanding

Based on your understanding of federal-state choice of law from the cases above, attempt to resolve the following problems:

1. Plaintiff, a New Hampshire resident, brings an action in federal court against a Maine hospital based on negligence. Maine law requires a pre-litigation hearing before a panel of medical experts before a purported victim of medical malpractice can file suit. The state law also provides that the findings of a unanimous panel may be admitted into evidence in court without explanation. The federal rules of evidence permit both parties to inquire into the credibility of the other side's evidence. Which standard should the court apply?

2. Plaintiff, an Arkansas resident, sues a Missouri hospital for malpractice in federal court. The hospital moves for summary judgment. Plaintiff ar-

gues for application of the Missouri standard for summary judgment, which provides that a defendant must disprove each element of plaintiff's case in order to prevail. Defendant argues that the court should apply the federal standard for summary judgment, which only requires the defendant to establish that the plaintiff does not have sufficient evidence to support one element of the claim at trial. Which standard should apply?

3. Plaintiffs, California residents, are injured in a car wreck in Pennsylvania, when they are rear-ended by a truck driven by an Ohio truck driver working for an Ohio company. The plaintiffs sue in federal court in Pennsylvania and win. Pursuant to Rule 238 of the Pennsylvania Rules of Civil Procedure, Plaintiffs request prejudgment interest as part of their recovery. The Pennsylvania rule applies only if a defendant makes no offer of settlement. No federal statutes or procedural rules make provision for prejudgment interest. Defendants never offer to settle the case prior to the verdict, which goes in favor of Plaintiffs. Should the court award prejudgment interest?

4. Plaintiff, a sixteen-year-old high school girl, receives counseling at her public high school. The high school counselor makes inappropriate sexual remarks to the plaintiff and eventually sexually abuses her. The school principal earlier received complaints from another student regarding inappropriate behavior by the same counselor. Plaintiff sues the school and counselor under various federal and state theories. The plaintiff specifically sues the counselor under state tort law for professional negligence. An Oklahoma statute requires a plaintiff in a professional negligence action to attach an affidavit to his or her complaint attesting that the plaintiff has consulted a qualified expert and obtained the expert's written opinion regarding the merits of the plaintiff's claim. The affidavit must be attached to the complaint, or the claim will be dismissed with prejudice. The plaintiff does not attach any affidavit to her complaint. If the counselor makes a motion to dismiss under Rule 12(b)(6), should the court dismiss the professional negligence claim?

The modern choice-of-law cases have become quite complex, and they have led to disputes among the Justices that reveal three potential approaches to federal-state conflicts of law. In *Gasperini v. Center for Humanities*, 518 U.S. 415 (1996), a freelance photographer sued an arts center for losing 300 valuable photographic slides that he had produced while studying the Central American hostilities in the 1980s and loaned to the Center for use in an educational film. Gasperini, the photographer, prevailed at trial, and based on the testimony of his expert witness (which was uncontroverted) the jury awarded him $450,000 in compensatory damages, or $1,500 per slide. The Center moved for a new trial based on the alleged excessiveness of the damages, but the District Court denied the motion. The Second Circuit applied New York's Civil Practice Laws and Rules, Section 5501(c), which provided both (1) that any jury award appealed after the denial of a new trial motion should be reviewed independently by the appellate court; and (2) that the appellate court should order a new trial or impose a conditional remittitur* if the jury's award "deviates materially from reasonable compensation." The Second Circuit held that the award did indeed "deviate materially," and ordered a new trial conditioned on the plaintiff's failure to accept a remittitur to $100,000.

In the Supreme Court, the case presented several potential federal-state conflicts of law. One involved the Seventh Amendment's Reexamination Clause, which provides that "no fact tried by a jury, shall be otherwise reexamined in any court of the United States, than according to the rules of the common law." Under the rules of the common law at the time of the ratification of the Seventh Amendment, motions for new trial were permitted, but the federal courts have interpreted the state of the common law at that time to require that the trial judge order a new trial only where a jury verdict is so excessive as to "shock the conscience of the court." Obviously, this standard is more difficult to meet than a mere requirement that the jury's award "deviates materially from reasonable compensation," as the New York rule provided.

In addition, unlike the New York rule, which required both the trial court and the appellate court to ask the "deviates materially" question independent of each other, only the trial court in the federal system may decide whether a verdict is so excessive as to "shock the conscience of the court." The role of the federal Courts of Appeal is limited to determining whether the District Court abused its discretion in making this determination—a very deferential standard.

Along with these conflicts with the Constitution, the New York rule also plausibly conflicted with Federal Rule of Civil Procedure 38, which essentially "rulifies" the Seventh Amendment's right to trial by jury, as well as Federal Rule of Civil Procedure 59, which governs both the procedure and standards for seeking a new trial, essentially "rulifying" the Seventh Amendment's Reexamination Clause. Faced with all of these sources of federal law in conflict with New York's civil procedure code, and in light of the REA Track analysis set forth in *Hanna*, one might think that *Gasperini* should have been an easy, unanimous decision requiring state law to yield. But in fact, the Court's splintered resolution of *Gasperini* was much more complex.

Justice Ginsburg, writing the majority, noted the "substantive" nature of the right against excessive damages, and sought to give effect to the New York policy of limiting damages awards to those which are reasonable. Since the New York rule clashed with both the Seventh Amendment and potentially two Federal Rules of Civil Procedure, she could not simply ignore the Supremacy Clause and apply state law. So, she devised

---

* Ed. Note. In many cases involving excessive jury awards, the court can condition the grant of a motion for new trial on the plaintiff's failure to accept a court-imposed reduction of the damage award, which is termed a "remittitur." The most famous of these cases involved an elderly woman who suffered third-degree burns from extremely hot McDonald's coffee, and was initially awarded $2,860,000 in both compensatory and punitive damages. The court ultimately granted the defendant's motion for new trial, but conditioned this grant on the plaintiff's failure to accept a remittitur of the damages to a total of $640,000. Both parties appealed, and the case ultimately settled. *See Liebeck v. McDonald's Restaurants*, No. D-202 CV-93-02419, 1995 WL 360309 (D.N.M. August 18, 1994).

an accommodative approach. Under Justice Ginsburg's approach, on remand, the federal *trial court* would apply the New York "deviates materially" standard, rather than the federal "shocks the conscience" standard, and the federal appellate court would have no independent power to review that determination, other than for abuse of discretion.

Justice Stevens dissented not to the decision to give effect to the New York rule, but to the identification of the alleged conflict with the Reexamination Clause. Stevens contended that the Reexamination Clause would not bar an appellate court from ordering a new trial because a jury's damage award exceeded a statutory cap, so it should not bar such review where a less mathematical "cap" is the reason for the new trial grant. He would have simply affirmed the Second Circuit, including the conditional remittitur it imposed, rather than reversing and remanding for a trial court redetermination, as Justice Ginsburg's plurality did.

Justice Scalia dissented to the Court's failure to order the application of federal law to the motion for new trial, as well as to the appellate review of that motion. Scalia saw the New York rule as being squarely in conflict with the Reexamination Clause, as well as with the Federal Rules of Civil Procedure. Accordingly, he would have reversed the Second Circuit and remanded to the trial court to apply the federal "shocks the conscience" standard, subject to appellate review for abuse of discretion. Two other Justices joined this opinion, making the Court's split 5–1–3.

A few principles emerge from *Gasperini*, (read along with *Walker*, *Ricoh*, and *Burlington Northern*) that help one to read *Shady Grove*. The first is that most of the current sitting Justices view the judicial interpretation of a Federal Rule (or statute) as being part of the Rule (or statute). This makes sense if one considers that this is how we also view constitutional provisions (e.g., the Fifth Amendment does not say anything about *Miranda* warnings, but we all understand the *Miranda* requirement to be part of the Fifth Amendment right against self-incrimination). This means that a federal rule or statute will be found to be in "conflict" with state law even if the reason for the conflict arises from judicial interpretation of the rule or statute. Moreover, the definition of "conflict" can include the failure of a federal rule to provide for or require something that a similar state law does provide for or require, as with the corporate registration requirement at issue in *Woods*, or the bond requirement at issue in *Cohen*.

Second, the Court is very splintered in how it views the Supremacy Clause in federal-state conflicts of law where the federal source of law is a rule, statute, or provision of the Constitution. On one extreme, some Justices are willing to seek accommodations between federal and state laws, even where Federal Rules and the Constitution are at issue, to attempt to give effect to both federal procedural and state substantive policies, and to foster both comity and federalism. On the other, the REA Track of *Hanna* is seen as an inexorable command: if a Federal Rule is on point, and state law conflicts with it, then state law must yield. Period. (This approach is the same for statutes and constitutional provisions.) In the middle, some Justices are willing to read federal law narrowly to avoid identifying conflicts with state law in the first place.

Exercise 6-7. Three Current Approaches —
Shady Grove v. Allstate

1. Recall Question (3) of Exercise 6-2, which asked whether a state legislature's inclusion of a legislative finding that its procedural requirement is necessary to protect a substantive right should change the outcome of the case. How do you think each the Justices who authored opinions in the *Shady Grove* case (Scalia, Stevens, and Ginsburg) would answer that question?

2. Research the difference between "facial" and "as-applied" challenges to statutes. If the Plaintiffs' side of the *Shady Grove* dispute can be considered a "challenge" to the application of Federal Rule of Civil Procedure 23, then is this challenge "facial" or "as-applied"? How would each of the Justices who authored opinions in the case answer that question?

Shady Grove Orthopedic Associates v. Allstate Ins. Co.
559 U.S. 393 (2010)

Justice Scalia announced the judgment of the Court and delivered the opinion of the Court with respect to Parts I and II-A, an opinion with respect to Parts II-B and II-D, in which the Chief Justice, Justice Thomas, and Justice Sotomayor join, and an opinion with respect to Part II-C, in which the Chief Justice and Justice Thomas join.

New York law prohibits class actions in suits seeking penalties or statutory minimum damages.[1] We consider whether this precludes a federal

---

1. N.Y. Civ. Prac. Law Ann. §901 (West 2006) provides:

(a) One or more members of a class may sue or be sued as representative parties on behalf of all if:

    1. the class is so numerous that joinder of all members, whether otherwise required or permitted, is impracticable;

    2. there are questions of law or fact common to the class which predominate over any questions affecting only individual members;

    3. the claims or defenses of the representative parties are typical of the claims or defenses of the class;

    4. the representative parties will fairly and adequately protect the interests of the class; and

    5. a class action is superior to other available methods for the fair and efficient adjudication of the controversy.

(b) Unless a statute creating or imposing a penalty, or a minimum measure of recovery specifically authorizes the recovery thereof in a class action, an action to recover a penalty, or minimum measure of recovery created or imposed by statute may not be maintained as a class action.

district court sitting in diversity from entertaining a class action under Federal Rule of Civil Procedure 23.[2]

I

The petitioner's complaint alleged the following: Shady Grove Orthopedic Associates, P. A., provided medical care to Sonia E. Galvez for injuries she suffered in an automobile accident. As partial payment for that care, Galvez assigned to Shady Grove her rights to insurance benefits under a policy issued in New York by Allstate Insurance Co. Shady Grove tendered a claim for the assigned benefits to Allstate, which under New York law had 30 days to pay the claim or deny it. *See* N.Y. Ins. Law Ann. § 5106(a) (West 2009). Allstate apparently paid, but not on time, and it refused to pay the statutory interest that accrued on the overdue benefits (at two percent per month).

Shady Grove filed this diversity suit in the Eastern District of New York to recover the unpaid statutory interest. Alleging that Allstate routinely refuses to pay interest on overdue benefits, Shady Grove sought relief on behalf of itself and a class of all others to whom Allstate owes interest. The District Court dismissed the suit for lack of jurisdiction. It reasoned that N.Y. Civ. Prac. Law Ann. § 901(b), which precludes a suit to recover a "penalty" from proceeding as a class action, applies in diversity suits in federal court, despite Federal Rule of Civil Procedure 23. Concluding that statutory interest is a "penalty" under New York law, it held that § 901(b) prohibited the proposed class action. And, since Shady Grove conceded that its individual claim (worth roughly $500) fell far short of the amount-in-controversy requirement for individual suits under 28 U.S.C. § 1332(a), the suit did not belong in federal court.[3]

The Second Circuit affirmed. The court did not dispute that a federal rule adopted in compliance with the Rules Enabling Act, 28 U.S.C. § 2072, would control if it conflicted with § 901(b). But there was no conflict because (as we will describe in more detail below) the Second Circuit con-

---

2. Rule 23(a) provides:
  (a) Prerequisites. One or more members of a class may sue or be sued as representative parties on behalf of all members only if:
    (1) the class is so numerous that joinder of all members is impracticable;
    (2) there are questions of law or fact common to the class;
    (3) the claims or defenses of the representative parties are typical of the claims or defenses of the class; and
    (4) the representative parties will fairly and adequately protect the interests of the class.
  Subsection (b) says that "[a] class action may be maintained if Rule 23(a) is satisfied and if" the suit falls into one of three described categories (irrelevant for present purposes).
3. Shady Grove had asserted jurisdiction under 28 U.S.C. § 1332(d)(2), which relaxes, for class actions seeking at least $5 million, the rule against aggregating separate claims for calculation of the amount in controversy. *See Exxon Mobil Corp. v. Allapattah Services, Inc.,* 545 U.S. 546, 571, 125 S.Ct. 2611, 162 L.Ed.2d 502 (2005).

cluded that Rule 23 and § 901(b) address different issues. Finding no federal rule on point, the Court of Appeals held that § 901(b) is "substantive" within the meaning of *Erie R. Co. v. Tompkins*, 304 U.S. 64 (1938), and thus must be applied by federal courts sitting in diversity.

We granted certiorari.

II

The framework for our decision is familiar. We must first determine whether Rule 23 answers the question in dispute. If it does, it governs — New York's law notwithstanding — unless it exceeds statutory authorization or Congress's rulemaking power. *See Hanna v. Plumer*, 380 U.S. 460, 463–464 (1965). We do not wade into *Erie*'s murky waters unless the federal rule is inapplicable or invalid.

A

The question in dispute is whether Shady Grove's suit may proceed as a class action. Rule 23 provides an answer. It states that "[a] class action may be maintained" if two conditions are met: The suit must satisfy the criteria set forth in subdivision (a) (i.e., numerosity, commonality, typicality, and adequacy of representation), and it also must fit into one of the three categories described in subdivision (b). Fed. Rule Civ. Proc. 23(b). By its terms this creates a categorical rule entitling a plaintiff whose suit meets the specified criteria to pursue his claim as a class action. (The Federal Rules regularly use "may" to confer categorical permission, as do federal statutes that establish procedural entitlements.) Thus, Rule 23 provides a one-size-fits-all formula for deciding the class-action question. Because § 901(b) attempts to answer the same question — i.e., it states that Shady Grove's suit "may *not* be maintained as a class action" (emphasis added) because of the relief it seeks — it cannot apply in diversity suits unless Rule 23 is *ultra vires*.

The Second Circuit believed that § 901(b) and Rule 23 do not conflict because they address different issues. Rule 23, it said, concerns only the criteria for determining whether a given class can and should be certified; section 901(b), on the other hand, addresses an antecedent question: whether the particular type of claim is eligible for class treatment in the first place — a question on which Rule 23 is silent. Allstate embraces this analysis.

We disagree. To begin with, the line between eligibility and certifiability is entirely artificial. Both are preconditions for maintaining a class action. Allstate suggests that eligibility must depend on the "particular cause of action" asserted, instead of some other attribute of the suit. But that is not so. Congress could, for example, provide that only claims involving more than a certain number of plaintiffs are "eligible" for class treatment in federal court. In other words, relabeling Rule 23(a)'s prerequisites "eligibility criteria" would obviate Allstate's objection — a sure sign that its eligibility-certifiability distinction is made-to-order.

There is no reason, in any event, to read Rule 23 as addressing only whether claims made eligible for class treatment by some other law should be certified as class actions. Allstate asserts that Rule 23 neither explicitly nor implicitly empowers a federal court "to certify a class in each and every case" where the Rule's criteria are met. But that is exactly what Rule 23 does: It says that if the prescribed preconditions are satisfied "[a] class action may be *maintained*" (emphasis added)—not "a class action may be *permitted*." Courts do not maintain actions; litigants do. The discretion suggested by Rule 23's "may" is discretion residing in the plaintiff: He may bring his claim in a class action if he wishes. And like the rest of the Federal Rules of Civil Procedure, Rule 23 automatically applies "in all civil actions and proceedings in the United States district courts," Fed. Rule Civ. Proc. 1.

Allstate points out that Congress has carved out some federal claims from Rule 23's reach—which shows, Allstate contends, that Rule 23 does not authorize class actions for all claims, but rather leaves room for laws like § 901(b). But Congress, unlike New York, has ultimate authority over the Federal Rules of Civil Procedure; it can create exceptions to an individual rule as it sees fit—either by directly amending the rule or by enacting a separate statute overriding it in certain instances. The fact that Congress has created specific exceptions to Rule 23 hardly proves that the Rule does not apply generally. In fact, it proves the opposite. If Rule 23 did not authorize class actions across the board, the statutory exceptions would be unnecessary.

Allstate next suggests that the structure of § 901 shows that Rule 23 addresses only certifiability. Section 901(a), it notes, establishes class-certification criteria roughly analogous to those in Rule 23 (wherefore it agrees that subsection is preempted). But § 901(b)'s rule barring class actions for certain claims is set off as its own subsection, and where it applies § 901(a) does not. This shows, according to Allstate, that § 901(b) concerns a separate subject. Perhaps it does concern a subject separate from the subject of § 901(a). But the question before us is whether it concerns a subject separate from the subject of Rule 23—and for purposes of answering that question the way New York has structured its statute is immaterial. Rule 23 permits all class actions that meet its requirements, and a State cannot limit that permission by structuring one part of its statute to track Rule 23 and enacting another part that imposes additional requirements. Both of § 901's subsections undeniably answer the same question as Rule 23: whether a class action may proceed for a given suit.

The dissent argues that § 901(b) has nothing to do with whether Shady Grove may maintain its suit as a class action, but affects only the remedy it may obtain if it wins. Whereas "Rule 23 governs procedural aspects of class litigation" by "prescrib[ing] the considerations relevant to class certification and postcertification proceedings," §901(b) addresses only "the size of a monetary award a class plaintiff may pursue." Accordingly, the dissent says, Rule 23 and New York's law may coexist in peace.

We need not decide whether a state law that limits the remedies available in an existing class action would conflict with Rule 23; that is not what §901(b) does. By its terms, the provision precludes a plaintiff from "maintain[ing]" a class action seeking statutory penalties. Unlike a law that sets a ceiling on damages (or puts other remedies out of reach) in properly filed class actions, §901(b) says nothing about what remedies a court may award; it prevents the class actions it covers from coming into existence at all. Consequently, a court bound by §901(b) could not certify a class action seeking both statutory penalties and other remedies even if it announces in advance that it will refuse to award the penalties in the event the plaintiffs prevail; to do so would violate the statute's clear prohibition on "maintain[ing]" such suits as class actions.

The dissent asserts that a plaintiff can avoid §901(b)'s barrier by omitting from his complaint (or removing) a request for statutory penalties. Even assuming all statutory penalties are waivable, the fact that a complaint omitting them could be brought as a class action would not at all prove that §901(b) is addressed only to remedies. If the state law instead banned class actions for fraud claims, a would-be class-action plaintiff could drop the fraud counts from his complaint and proceed with the remainder in a class action. Yet that would not mean the law provides no remedy for fraud; the ban would affect only the procedural means by which the remedy may be pursued. In short, although the dissent correctly abandons Allstate's eligibility-certifiability distinction, the alternative it offers fares no better.

The dissent all but admits that the literal terms of §901(b) address the same subject as Rule 23—i.e., whether a class action may be maintained—but insists the provision's purpose is to restrict only remedies. ("[W]hile phrased as responsive to the question whether certain class actions may begin, §901(b) is unmistakably aimed at controlling how those actions must end"). Unlike Rule 23, designed to further procedural fairness and efficiency, §901(b) (we are told) "responds to an entirely different concern": the fear that allowing statutory damages to be awarded on a class-wide basis would "produce overkill." (internal quotation marks omitted). The dissent reaches this conclusion on the basis of (1) constituent concern recorded in the law's bill jacket; (2) a commentary suggesting that the Legislature "apparently fear[ed]" that combining class actions and statutory penalties "could result in annihilating punishment of the defendant"; (3) a remark by the Governor in his signing statement that §901(b) "provides a controlled remedy"; and (4) a state court's statement that the final text of §901(b) "was the result of a compromise among competing interests."

This evidence of the New York Legislature's purpose is pretty sparse. But even accepting the dissent's account of the Legislature's objective at face value, it cannot override the statute's clear text. Even if its aim is to restrict the remedy a plaintiff can obtain, § 901(b) achieves that end by limiting a plaintiff's power to maintain a class action. The manner in which the law could have been written has no bearing; what matters is the law the Legislature did enact. We cannot rewrite that to reflect our perception of legislative purpose.[6] The dissent's concern for state prerogatives is frustrated rather than furthered by revising state laws when a potential conflict with a Federal Rule arises; the state-friendly approach would be to accept the law as written and test the validity of the Federal Rule.

The dissent's approach of determining whether state and federal rules conflict based on the subjective intentions of the state legislature is an enterprise destined to produce "confusion worse confounded," *Sibbach v. Wilson & Co.*, 312 U.S. 1, 14 (1941). It would mean, to begin with, that one State's statute could survive pre-emption (and accordingly affect the procedures in federal court) while another State's identical law would not, merely because its authors had different aspirations. It would also mean that district courts would have to discern, in every diversity case, the purpose behind any putatively pre-empted state procedural rule, even if its text squarely conflicts with federal law. That task will often prove arduous. Many laws further more than one aim, and the aim of others may be impossible to discern. Moreover, to the extent the dissent's purpose-driven approach depends on its characterization of § 901(b)'s aims as substantive, it would apply to many state rules ostensibly addressed to procedure. Pleading standards, for example, often embody policy preferences about the types of claims that should succeed—as do rules governing summary judgment, pretrial discovery, and the admissibility of certain evidence. Hard cases will abound. It is not even clear that a state supreme court's pronouncement of the law's purpose would settle the issue, since existence of the factual predicate for avoiding federal pre-emption is ultimately a federal question. Predictably, federal judges would be condemned to poring

---

6. Our decision in *Walker v. Armco Steel Corp.*, 446 U.S. 740 (1980), discussed by the dissent, is not to the contrary. There we held that Rule 3 (which provides that a federal civil action is "'commenced'" by filing a complaint in federal court) did not displace a state law providing that "'[a]n action shall be deemed commenced, within the meaning of this article [the statute of limitations], as to each defendant, at the date of the summons which is served on him....'" 446 U.S. at 743, n. 4. Rule 3, we explained, "governs the date from which various timing requirements of the Federal Rules begin to run, but does not affect state statutes of limitations" or tolling rules, which it did not "purpor[t] to displace." 446 U.S. at 751, 750. The texts were therefore not in conflict. While our opinion observed that the State's actual-service rule was (in the State's judgment) an "integral part of the several policies served by the statute of limitations," *id.* at 751, nothing in our decision suggested that a federal court may resolve an obvious conflict between the texts of state and federal rules by resorting to the state law's ostensible objectives.

through state legislative history—which may be less easily obtained, less thorough, and less familiar than its federal counterpart.

But while the dissent does indeed artificially narrow the scope of §901(b) by finding that it pursues only substantive policies, that is not the central difficulty of the dissent's position. The central difficulty is that even artificial narrowing cannot render §901(b) compatible with Rule 23. Whatever the policies they pursue, they flatly contradict each other. Allstate asserts (and the dissent implies) that we can (and must) interpret Rule 23 in a manner that avoids overstepping its authorizing statute. If the Rule were susceptible of two meanings—one that would violate §2072(b) and another that would not—we would agree. But it is not. Rule 23 unambiguously authorizes any plaintiff, in any federal civil proceeding, to maintain a class action if the Rule's prerequisites are met. We cannot contort its text, even to avert a collision with state law that might render it invalid. What the dissent's approach achieves is not the avoiding of a conflict between Rule 23 and §901(b), but rather the invalidation of Rule 23 (pursuant to §2072(b) of the Rules Enabling Act) to the extent that it conflicts with the substantive policies of §901. There is no other way to reach the dissent's destination. We must therefore confront head-on whether Rule 23 falls within the statutory authorization.

B

Erie involved the constitutional power of federal courts to supplant state law with judge-made rules. In that context, it made no difference whether the rule was technically one of substance or procedure; the touchstone was whether it "significantly affect[s] the result of a litigation." *Guaranty Trust Co. v. York*, 326 U.S. 99, 109 (1945). That is not the test for either the constitutionality or the statutory validity of a Federal Rule of Procedure. Congress has undoubted power to supplant state law, and undoubted power to prescribe rules for the courts it has created, so long as those rules regulate matters "rationally capable of classification" as procedure. *Hanna*, 380 U.S. at 472. In the Rules Enabling Act, Congress authorized this Court to promulgate rules of procedure subject to its review, 28 U.S.C. §2072(a), but with the limitation that those rules "shall not abridge, enlarge or modify any substantive right," §2072(b).

We have long held that this limitation means that the Rule must "really regulat[e] procedure,—the judicial process for enforcing rights and duties recognized by substantive law and for justly administering remedy and redress for disregard or infraction of them," *Sibbach*, 312 U.S. at 14. The test is not whether the rule affects a litigant's substantive rights; most procedural rules do. What matters is what the rule itself regulates: If it governs only "the manner and the means" by which the litigants' rights are "enforced," it is valid; if it alters "the rules of decision by which [the] court will adjudicate [those] rights," it is not. *Id.* at 446 (internal quotation marks omitted).

Applying that test, we have rejected every statutory challenge to a Federal Rule that has come before us. We have found to be in compliance with § 2072(b) rules prescribing methods for serving process, and requiring litigants whose mental or physical condition is in dispute to submit to examinations. Likewise, we have upheld rules authorizing imposition of sanctions upon those who file frivolous appeals, or who sign court papers without a reasonable inquiry into the facts asserted. Each of these rules had some practical effect on the parties' rights, but each undeniably regulated only the process for enforcing those rights; none altered the rights themselves, the available remedies, or the rules of decision by which the court adjudicated either.

Applying that criterion, we think it obvious that rules allowing multiple claims (and claims by or against multiple parties) to be litigated together are also valid. *See, e.g.,* Fed. Rules Civ. Proc. 18 (joinder of claims), 20 (joinder of parties), 42(a) (consolidation of actions). Such rules neither change plaintiffs' separate entitlements to relief nor abridge defendants' rights; they alter only how the claims are processed. For the same reason, Rule 23 — at least insofar as it allows willing plaintiffs to join their separate claims against the same defendants in a class action — falls within § 2072(b)'s authorization. A class action, no less than traditional joinder (of which it is a species), merely enables a federal court to adjudicate claims of multiple parties at once, instead of in separate suits. And like traditional joinder, it leaves the parties' legal rights and duties intact and the rules of decision unchanged.

Allstate contends that the authorization of class actions is not substantively neutral: Allowing Shady Grove to sue on behalf of a class "transform[s][the] dispute over a five hundred dollar penalty into a dispute over a five million dollar penalty." Allstate's aggregate liability, however, does not depend on whether the suit proceeds as a class action. Each of the 1,000-plus members of the putative class could (as Allstate acknowledges) bring a freestanding suit asserting his individual claim. It is undoubtedly true that some plaintiffs who would not bring individual suits for the relatively small sums involved will choose to join a class action. That has no bearing, however, on Allstate's or the plaintiffs' legal rights. The likelihood that some (even many) plaintiffs will be induced to sue by the availability of a class action is just the sort of incidental effect we have long held does not violate § 2072(b).

Allstate argues that Rule 23 violates § 2072(b) because the state law it displaces, § 901(b), creates a right that the Federal Rule abridges — namely, a "substantive right ... not to be subjected to aggregated class-action liability" in a single suit. To begin with, we doubt that that is so. Nothing in the text of § 901(b) (which is to be found in New York's procedural code) confines it to claims under New York law; and of course New York has no power to alter substantive rights and duties created by other sovereigns. As we have said, the consequence of excluding certain class actions may be to cap the damages a defendant can face in a single suit, but the law itself alters only procedure. In that respect, §901(b) is no different from a state law forbidding simple joinder. As a fallback argument, Allstate argues that even if §901(b) is a procedural provision, it was enacted "for substantive *reasons*." Its end was not to improve "the conduct of the litigation process itself" but to alter "the outcome of that process."

The fundamental difficulty with both these arguments is that the substantive nature of New York's law, or its substantive purpose, makes no difference. A Federal Rule of Procedure is not valid in some jurisdictions and invalid in others—or valid in some cases and invalid in others—depending upon whether its effect is to frustrate a state substantive law (or a state procedural law enacted for substantive purposes). That could not be clearer in *Sibbach*:

> The petitioner says the phrase ['substantive rights' in the Rules Enabling Act] connotes more; that by its use Congress intended that in regulating procedure this Court should not deal with important and substantial rights theretofore recognized. Recognized where and by whom? The state courts are divided as to the power in the absence of statute to order a physical examination. In a number such an order is authorized by statute or rule....

> The asserted right, moreover, is no more important than many others enjoyed by litigants in District Courts sitting in the several states before the Federal Rules of Civil Procedure altered and abolished old rights or privileges and created new ones in connection with the conduct of litigation.... If we were to adopt the suggested criterion of the importance of the alleged right we should invite endless litigation and confusion worse confounded. The test must be whether a rule really regulates procedure.... 312 U.S. at 13–14 (footnotes omitted).

Hanna unmistakably expressed the same understanding that compliance of a Federal Rule with the Enabling Act is to be assessed by consulting the Rule itself, and not its effects in individual applications:

> [T]he court has been instructed to apply the Federal Rule, and can refuse to do so only if the Advisory Committee, this Court, and Congress erred in their prima facie judgment that the Rule in question transgresses neither the terms of the Enabling Act nor constitutional restrictions. 380 U.S. at 471.

In sum, it is not the substantive or procedural nature or purpose of the affected state law that matters, but the substantive or procedural nature of the Federal Rule. We have held since *Sibbach*, and reaffirmed repeatedly, that the validity of a Federal Rule depends entirely upon whether it regulates procedure. If it does, it is authorized by § 2072 and is valid in all jurisdictions, with respect to all claims, regardless of its incidental effect upon state-created rights.

C

A few words in response to the concurrence. We understand it to accept the framework we apply—which requires first, determining whether the federal and state rules can be reconciled (because they answer different questions), and second, if they cannot, determining whether the Federal Rule runs afoul of § 2072(b). The concurrence agrees with us that Rule 23 and § 901(b) conflict, and departs from us only with respect to the second part of the test, i.e., whether application of the Federal Rule violates § 2072(b). Like us, it answers no, but for a reason different from ours.

The concurrence would decide this case on the basis, not that Rule 23 is procedural, but that the state law it displaces is procedural, in the sense that it does not "function as a part of the State's definition of substantive rights and remedies." A state procedural rule is not preempted, according to the concurrence, so long as it is "so bound up with," or "sufficiently intertwined with," a substantive state-law right or remedy "that it defines the scope of that substantive right or remedy."

This analysis squarely conflicts with *Sibbach*, which established the rule we apply. The concurrence contends that *Sibbach* did not rule out its approach, but that is not so. Recognizing the impracticability of a test that turns on the idiosyncrasies of state law, *Sibbach* adopted and applied a rule with a single criterion: whether the Federal Rule "really regulates procedure." That the concurrence's approach would have yielded the same result in *Sibbach* proves nothing; what matters is the rule we did apply, and that rule leaves no room for special exemptions based on the function or purpose of a particular state rule.[10] We have rejected an attempt to read into *Sibbach* an exception with no basis in the opinion, and we see no reason to find such an implied limitation today.

In reality, the concurrence seeks not to apply *Sibbach*, but to overrule it (or, what is the same, to rewrite it). Its approach, the concurrence insists, gives short shrift to the statutory text forbidding the Federal Rules from "abridg[ing], enlarg[ing], or modify[ing] any substantive right,"

---

10. The concurrence insists that we have misread *Sibbach*, since surely a Federal Rule that "in most cases" regulates procedure does not do so when it displaces one of those "rare" state substantive laws that are disguised as rules of procedure. *Post* at 1455 n. 13. This mistakes what the Federal Rule regulates for its incidental effects. As we have explained, *supra*, at 1442–1443, most Rules have some effect on litigants' substantive rights or their ability to obtain a remedy, but that does not mean the Rule itself regulates those rights or remedies.

§ 2072(b). There is something to that. It is possible to understand how it
can be determined whether a Federal Rule "enlarges" substantive rights
without consulting State law: If the Rule creates a substantive right, even
one that duplicates some state-created rights, it establishes a new federal
right. But it is hard to understand how it can be determined whether a
Federal Rule "abridges" or "modifies" substantive rights without knowing
what state-created rights would obtain if the Federal Rule did not exist.
Sibbach's exclusive focus on the challenged Federal Rule — driven by the
very real concern that Federal Rules which vary from State to State would
be chaos — is hard to square with § 2072(b)'s terms.

   Sibbach has been settled law, however, for nearly seven decades. Setting
aside any precedent requires a "special justification" beyond a bare belief
that it was wrong. *Patterson v. McLean Credit Union*, 491 U.S. 164, 172
(1989) (internal quotation marks omitted). And a party seeking to overturn
a statutory precedent bears an even greater burden, since Congress remains
free to correct us, and adhering to our precedent enables it do so. We do
Congress no service by presenting it a moving target. In all events, Allstate
has not even asked us to overrule *Sibbach*, let alone carried its burden of
persuading us to do so. Why we should cast aside our decades-old decision
escapes us, especially since (as the concurrence explains) that would not
affect the result.[13]

   The concurrence also contends that applying *Sibbach* and assessing
whether a Federal Rule regulates substance or procedure is not always
easy. Undoubtedly some hard cases will arise (though we have managed
to muddle through well enough in the 69 years since *Sibbach* was decided).
But as the concurrence acknowledges, the basic difficulty is unavoidable:
The statute itself refers to "substantive right[s]," § 2072(b), so there is no

---

13. The concurrence is correct, *post* at 1453, n. 9, that under our disposition any rule that "really
regulates procedure," *Sibbach, supra* at 14, 61 S.Ct. 422, will pre-empt a conflicting state rule, however
"bound up" the latter is with substantive law. The concurrence is wrong, however, that that result
proves our interpretation of § 2072(b) implausible, *post* at 1453, n. 9. The result is troubling only if
one stretches the term "substantive rights" in § 2072(b) to mean not only state-law rights themselves,
but also any state-law procedures closely connected to them. Neither the text nor our precedent supports that expansive interpretation. The examples the concurrence offers — statutes of limitations,
burdens of proof, and standards for appellate review of damages awards — do not make its broad
definition of substantive rights more persuasive. They merely illustrate that in rare cases it may be
difficult to determine whether a rule "really regulates" procedure or substance. If one concludes the
latter, there is no pre-emption of the state rule; the Federal Rule itself is invalid.
   The concurrence's concern would make more sense if many Federal Rules that effectively alter
state-law rights "bound up with procedures" would survive under *Sibbach*. But as the concurrence
concedes, *post* at 1454, n. 10, very few would do so. The possible existence of a few outlier instances
does not prove *Sibbach*'s interpretation is absurd. Congress may well have accepted such anomalies
as the price of a uniform system of federal procedure.

escaping the substance-procedure distinction. What is more, the concurrence's approach does nothing to diminish the difficulty, but rather magnifies it many times over. Instead of a single hard question of whether a Federal Rule regulates substance or procedure, that approach will present hundreds of hard questions, forcing federal courts to assess the substantive or procedural character of countless state rules that may conflict with a single Federal Rule. And it still does not sidestep the problem it seeks to avoid. At the end of the day, one must come face to face with the decision whether or not the state policy (with which a putatively procedural state rule may be "bound up") pertains to a "substantive right or remedy" — that is, whether it is substance or procedure. The more one explores the alternatives to *Sibbach*'s rule, the more its wisdom becomes apparent.

D

We must acknowledge the reality that keeping the federal-court door open to class actions that cannot proceed in state court will produce forum shopping. That is unacceptable when it comes as the consequence of judge-made rules created to fill supposed "gaps" in positive federal law. For where neither the Constitution, a treaty, nor a statute provides the rule of decision or authorizes a federal court to supply one, "state law must govern because there can be no other law." [*Hanna*, 380 U.S. at 471–472.] But divergence from state law, with the attendant consequence of forum shopping, is the inevitable (indeed, one might say the intended) result of a uniform system of federal procedure. Congress itself has created the possibility that the same case may follow a different course if filed in federal instead of state court. The short of the matter is that a Federal Rule governing procedure is valid whether or not it alters the outcome of the case in a way that induces forum shopping. To hold otherwise would be to disembowel either the Constitution's grant of power over federal procedure or Congress's exercise of it.

* * *

The judgment of the Court of Appeals is reversed, and the case is remanded for further proceedings.

It is so ordered.

Justice Stevens, concurring in part and concurring in the judgment.

The New York law at issue, N.Y. Civ. Prac. Law Ann. (CPLR) § 901(b) (West 2006), is a procedural rule that is not part of New York's substantive law. Accordingly, I agree with Justice Scalia that Federal Rule of Civil Procedure 23 must apply in this case and join Parts I and II-A of the Court's opinion. But I also agree with Justice Ginsburg that there are some state procedural rules that federal courts must apply in diversity cases because they function as a part of the State's definition of substantive rights and remedies.

I

* * *

It is important to observe that the balance Congress has struck turns, in part, on the nature of the state law that is being displaced by a federal rule. And in my view, the application of that balance does not necessarily turn on whether the state law at issue takes the form of what is traditionally described as substantive or procedural. Rather, it turns on whether the state law actually is part of a State's framework of substantive rights or remedies.

Applying this balance, therefore, requires careful interpretation of the state and federal provisions at issue....

In our federalist system, Congress has not mandated that federal courts dictate to state legislatures the form that their substantive law must take. And were federal courts to ignore those portions of substantive state law that operate as procedural devices, it could in many instances limit the ways that sovereign States may define their rights and remedies. When a State chooses to use a traditionally procedural vehicle as a means of defining the scope of substantive rights or remedies, federal courts must recognize and respect that choice.

II

When both a federal rule and a state law appear to govern a question before a federal court sitting in diversity, our precedents have set out a two-step framework for federal courts to negotiate this thorny area. At both steps of the inquiry, there is a critical question about what the state law and the federal rule mean.

The court must first determine whether the scope of the federal rule is sufficiently broad to control the issue before the court, thereby leaving no room for the operation of seemingly conflicting state law. If the federal rule does not apply or can operate alongside the state rule, then there is no "Ac[t] of Congress" governing that particular question, 28 U.S.C. § 1652, and the court must engage in the traditional Rules of Decision Act inquiry under *Erie* and its progeny. In some instances, the plain meaning of a federal rule will not come into direct collision with the state law, and both can operate. In other instances, the rule when fairly construed, with sensitivity to important state interests and regulatory policies, will not collide with the state law.[5]

---

5. I thus agree with Justice Ginsburg that a federal rule, like any federal law, must be interpreted in light of many different considerations, including "sensitivity to important state interests" and "regulatory policies." *See Stewart Organization, Inc. v. Ricoh Corp.*, 487 U.S. 22, 37–38 (1988) (Scalia, J., dissenting) ("We should assume ... when it is fair to do so, that Congress is just as concerned as we have been to avoid significant differences between state and federal courts in adjudicating claims.... Thus, in deciding whether a federal ... Rule of Procedure encompasses a particular issue, a broad

If, on the other hand, the federal rule is sufficiently broad to control the issue before the Court, such that there is a direct collision, the court must decide whether application of the federal rule represents a valid exercise of the rulemaking authority bestowed on this Court by the Rules Enabling Act. That Act requires, *inter alia*, that federal rules "not abridge, enlarge or modify any substantive right." 28 U.S.C. §2072(b) (emphasis added). Unlike Justice Scalia, I believe that an application of a federal rule that effectively abridges, enlarges, or modifies a state-created right or remedy violates this command. Congress may have the constitutional power to "supplant state law" with rules that are "rationally capable of classification as procedure," but we should generally presume that it has not done so. Indeed, the mandate that federal rules "shall not abridge, enlarge or modify any substantive right" evinces the opposite intent, as does Congress' decision to delegate the creation of rules to this Court rather than to a political branch.

Thus, the second step of the inquiry may well bleed back into the first. When a federal rule appears to abridge, enlarge, or modify a substantive right, federal courts must consider whether the rule can reasonably be interpreted to avoid that impermissible result. And when such a "saving" construction is not possible and the rule would violate the Enabling Act, federal courts cannot apply the rule. A federal rule, therefore, cannot govern a particular case in which the rule would displace a state law that is procedural in the ordinary use of the term but is so intertwined with a state right or remedy that it functions to define the scope of the state-created right. And absent a governing federal rule, a federal court must engage in the traditional Rules of Decision Act inquiry, under the *Erie* line of cases. This application of the Enabling Act shows "sensitivity to important state interests" and "regulatory policies," but it does so as Congress authorized, by ensuring that federal rules that ordinarily "prescribe general rules of practice and procedure," §2072(a), do "not abridge, enlarge or modify any substantive right," §2072(b).

* * *

III

* * *

Rule 23 Controls Class Certification

When the District Court in the case before us was asked to certify a class action, Federal Rule of Civil Procedure 23 squarely governed the de-

---

reading that would create significant disuniformity between state and federal courts should be avoided if the text permits"). I disagree with Justice Ginsburg, however, about the degree to which the meaning of federal rules may be contorted, absent congressional authorization to do so, to accommodate state policy goals.

termination whether the court should do so. That is the explicit function of Rule 23. Rule 23, therefore, must apply unless its application would abridge, enlarge, or modify New York rights or remedies.

Notwithstanding the plain language of Rule 23, I understand the dissent to find that Rule 23 does not govern the question of class certification in this matter because New York has made a substantive judgment that such a class should not be certified, as a means of proscribing damages. Although I do not accept the dissent's view of § 901(b), I also do not see how the dissent's interpretation of Rule 23 follows from that view.[15] I agree with Justice Ginsburg that courts should "avoi[d] immoderate interpretations of the Federal Rules that would trench on state prerogatives," and should in some instances "interpre[t] the federal rules to avoid conflict with important state regulatory policies." But that is not what the dissent has done. Simply because a rule should be read in light of federalism concerns, it does not follow that courts may rewrite the rule.

At bottom, the dissent's interpretation of Rule 23 seems to be that Rule 23 covers only those cases in which its application would create no *Erie* problem. The dissent would apply the Rules of Decision Act inquiry under *Erie* even to cases in which there is a governing federal rule, and thus the Act, by its own terms, does not apply. But "[w]hen a situation is covered by one of the Federal Rules, the question facing the court is a far cry from the typical, relatively unguided *Erie* choice." *Hanna*, 380 U.S. at 471. The question is only whether the Enabling Act is satisfied. Although it reflects a laudable concern to protect "state regulatory policies," Justice Ginsburg's approach would, in my view, work an end run around Congress' system of uniform federal rules and our decision in

---

15. Nor do I see how it follows from the dissent's premises that a class cannot be certified. The dissent contends that § 901(b) is a damages "limitation," *post* at 1463, n. 2, 1464, 1464–1465, 1466, 1473, or "proscription," *post* at 1466, n. 6, 1471, whereas Rule 23 "does not command that a particular remedy be available when a party sues in a representative capacity," *post* at 1465, and that consequently both provisions can apply. Yet even if the dissent's premises were correct, Rule 23 would still control the question whether petitioner may certify a class, and § 901(b) would be relevant only to determine whether petitioner, at the conclusion of a class-action lawsuit, may collect statutory damages.

It may be that if the dissent's interpretation of § 901(b) were correct, this class could not (or has not) alleged sufficient damages for the federal court to have jurisdiction, see 28 U.S.C. § 1332(d)(6). But that issue was not raised in respondent's motion to dismiss (from which the case comes to this Court), and it was not squarely presented to the Court. In any event, although the lead plaintiff has "acknowledged that its individual claim" is for less than the required amount in controversy, see 549 F.3d 137, 140 (C.A.2 2008), we do not know what actual damages the entire class can allege. Thus, even if the Court were to adopt all of the dissent's premises, I believe the correct disposition would be to vacate and remand for further consideration of whether the required amount in controversy has or can be met.

Hanna. Federal courts can and should interpret federal rules with sensitivity to "state prerogatives," but even when "state interests ... warrant our respectful consideration," federal courts cannot rewrite the rules. If my dissenting colleagues feel strongly that § 901(b) is substantive and that class certification should be denied, then they should argue within the Enabling Act's framework. Otherwise, the Federal Rule applies regardless of contrary state law.

Applying Rule 23 Does Not Violate the Enabling Act

As I have explained, in considering whether to certify a class action such as this one, a federal court must inquire whether doing so would abridge, enlarge, or modify New York's rights or remedies, and thereby violate the Enabling Act. This inquiry is not always a simple one because "[i]t is difficult to conceive of any rule of procedure that cannot have a significant effect on the outcome of a case," [Wright, Miller & Cooper, Federal Practice and Procedure, § 4508, at 232–233 (2d ed. 1996)], and almost "any rule can be said to have ...'substantive effects,' affecting society's distribution of risks and rewards," [Ely, *The Irrepressible Myth of Erie*, 87 Harv. L. Rev. 693, 724, n. 170 (1974)]. Faced with a federal rule that dictates an answer to a traditionally procedural question and that displaces a state rule, one can often argue that the state rule was really some part of the State's definition of its rights or remedies.

In my view, however, the bar for finding an Enabling Act problem is a high one. The mere fact that a state law is designed as a procedural rule suggests it reflects a judgment about how state courts ought to operate and not a judgment about the scope of state-created rights and remedies. And for the purposes of operating a federal court system, there are costs involved in attempting to discover the true nature of a state procedural rule and allowing such a rule to operate alongside a federal rule that appears to govern the same question. The mere possibility that a federal rule would alter a state-created right is not sufficient. There must be little doubt.

The text of CPLR § 901(b) expressly and unambiguously applies not only to claims based on New York law but also to claims based on federal law or the law of any other State. And there is no interpretation from New York courts to the contrary. It is therefore hard to see how § 901(b) could be understood as a rule that, though procedural in form, serves the function of defining New York's rights or remedies. This is all the more apparent because lawsuits under New York law could be joined in federal class actions well before New York passed § 901(b) in 1975, and New York had done nothing to prevent that. It is true, as the dissent points out, that there is a limited amount of legislative history that can be read to suggest that the New York officials who supported § 901(b) wished to create a "limitation" on New York's "statutory damages." *Post* at 1464. But, as Justice SCALIA notes, that is not the law that New York adopted.

* * *

Because Rule 23 governs class certification, the only decision is whether certifying a class in this diversity case would "abridge, enlarge or modify" New York's substantive rights or remedies. § 2072(b). Although one can argue that class certification would enlarge New York's "limited" damages remedy, see post at 1463, n. 2, 1464, 1464–1465, 1466, 1473, such arguments rest on extensive speculation about what the New York Legislature had in mind when it created § 901(b). But given that there are two plausible competing narratives, it seems obvious to me that we should respect the plain textual reading of § 901(b), a rule in New York's procedural code about when to certify class actions brought under any source of law, and respect Congress' decision that Rule 23 governs class certification in federal courts. In order to displace a federal rule, there must be more than just a possibility that the state rule is different than it appears.

Accordingly, I concur in part and concur in the judgment.

Justice Ginsburg, with whom Justice Kennedy, Justice Breyer, and Justice Alito join, dissenting.

The Court today approves Shady Grove's attempt to transform a $500 case into a $5,000,000 award, although the State creating the right to recover has proscribed this alchemy. If Shady Grove had filed suit in New York state court, the 2% interest payment authorized by New York Ins. Law Ann. § 5106(a) (West 2009) as a penalty for overdue benefits would, by Shady Grove's own measure, amount to no more than $500. By instead filing in federal court based on the parties' diverse citizenship and requesting class certification, Shady Grove hopes to recover, for the class, statutory damages of more than $5,000,000. The New York Legislature has barred this remedy, instructing that, unless specifically permitted, "an action to recover a penalty, or minimum measure of recovery created or imposed by statute may not be maintained as a class action." N.Y. Civ. Prac. Law Ann. (CPLR) § 901(b) (West 2006). The Court nevertheless holds that Federal Rule of Civil Procedure 23, which prescribes procedures for the conduct of class actions in federal courts, preempts the application of § 901(b) in diversity suits.

The Court reads Rule 23 relentlessly to override New York's restriction on the availability of statutory damages. Our decisions, however, caution us to ask, before undermining state legislation: Is this conflict really necessary? Had the Court engaged in that inquiry, it would not have read Rule 23 to collide with New York's legitimate interest in keeping certain monetary awards reasonably bounded. I would continue to interpret Federal Rules with awareness of, and sensitivity to, important state regulatory policies. Because today's judgment radically departs from that course, I dissent.

* * *

Exercise 6-8. Visualizing Vertical Choice of Law

Shady Grove is a long and complex case, as the edited case excerpt above illustrates. Two main disputes animate the Court's three separate opinions. One, between Justices Scalia and Ginsburg, involves the proper way to calibrate the scope of a federal rule of civil procedure, as a means to identify a "collision" with state law. The other, between Justices Scalia and Stevens, involves the independent significance that should be afforded the "abridge, enlarge, or modify" portion of the Rules Enabling Act. This latter dispute is, at bottom, a dispute over whether a challenge to a federal rule is a "facial" or "as-applied" challenge.

These disputes are unresolved today, and will remain unresolved at least until the Court grants certiorari on another choice-of-law case. For now, as a law student, the best approach is to attempt to understand how the three approaches interact, and where in the analysis the disputes identified above fit. One very useful way in which to do this is through flowcharting. Attempt to flowchart the analyses set forth in the competing opinions in *Shady Grove* as follows:

1. Flowchart each of the opinions' analyses, step by step, by itself. (You'll have to read the opinions of Justices Scalia and Stevens to infer Justice Ginsburg's precise approach, but it draws heavily from *Gasperini*, which is summarized in the notes prior to *Shady Grove*.)

2. Attempt to create one flowchart that includes all three competing analyses, signifying where the approaches diverge from each other. Experiment with different colors for the boxes that apply to the different Justices, etc., in an attempt to arrive at creating a useful visual aid for your studying.

6. Reconciling Vertical and Horizontal Choice of Law

Exercise 6-9. What Law Applies if the "Law" Is Not Clear?

Resolving the *Erie/Hanna* question in favor of state law is often not the end of the matter for the federal court. If a vertical choice-of-law determination points toward state law, then the court must determine what state law provides or requires. In many cases, this is clear, and it is known to the court at the time of the choice-of-law determination (usually because a statute or a decision of the state's highest court clearly states what that law is on the point in question). But in many others, the content of state law is vague, ambiguous, or even non-existent (e.g., if no statute exists, and no state court has ever considered the question, or the intermediate state appellate courts disagree with each other). In such cases, federal courts have one or two options, depending on what state law provides. If state law provides for it, the federal court can "certify a question," usually to the state's highest court, which then provides an advisory opinion to the federal court, which that court can then use to adjudicate the issue in question. If not, or even if so (in the discretion of the federal court), the court can make what is generally called an "*Erie* guess," or a prediction of what the state's highest court would decide on the question of law at issue. Below is one case considering each of these paths and ultimately choosing to certify two questions of law to the state court.

As you read *Craig* below, articulate exactly why the Court refused (1) to apply the precedent urged on it, and (2) to make an "*Erie* guess."

Craig v. FedEx Ground Package System, Inc.
686 F. 3d 423 (7th Cir. 2012)

Before Easterbrook, Chief Judge, and Rovner and Tinder, Circuit Judges.

Per Curiam.

FedEx Ground ("FedEx") provides small package pick-up and delivery services through a network of pick-up and delivery drivers. The plaintiffs are current and former drivers for FedEx who allege that they were employees rather than independent contractors under the laws of the states in which they worked and under federal law. The Judicial Panel on Multidistrict Litigation consolidated these actions and transferred them to the District Court for the Northern District of Indiana. That court used the *Carlene M. Craig, et al.* case, which was based on the Employee Retirement Income Security Act ("ERISA") and Kansas law, as its "lead" case. The court certified a nationwide class seeking relief under ERISA and certified statewide classes under Federal Rule of Civil Procedure Rule 23(b)(3).[1] The Kansas class has 479 members. They allege that they were improperly classified as independent contractors rather than employees under the Kansas Wage Payment Act ("KWPA" or "Act"), Kan. Stat. Ann. §§ 44-313 *et seq.*, and that as employees, they are entitled to repayment of all costs and expenses they paid during their time as FedEx employees. They also seek payment of overtime wages.

---

1. The Kansas class is defined as "All persons who: 1) entered or will enter into a FXG Ground or FXG Home Delivery form Operating Agreement ...; 2) drove or will drive a vehicle on a full-time basis (meaning exclusive of time off for commonly excused employment absences) from February 11, 1998, through October 15, 2007, to provide package pick-up and delivery services pursuant to the Operating Agreement; and 3) were dispatched out of a terminal in the state of Kansas." See In re Fedex Ground Package Sys., Inc., Emp't Practices Litig., No. 3:05-md-527 RM (MDL-1700), 2007 WL 3027405, at *14 (N.D.Ind. Oct. 15, 2007), & Dist. Ct. Op. & Ord. entered Apr. 4, 2008.

Cross summary judgment motions presented the question of whether the FedEx drivers are employees or independent contractors under the KWPA. The evidence presented through the competing motions essentially comprised a stipulated record revolving around a form Operating Agreement FedEx entered with each of the class members and certain FedEx work practices. FedEx asserted that the undisputed facts before the district court must result in a determination that the drivers are not employees under the KWPA. The drivers contended that the same record required the court to find that they are employees under that Act or, in the alternative, that the undisputed evidence, along with reasonable inferences that could be drawn from it, entitled them to a trial on that question. In a thorough opinion and order, the district court granted FedEx summary judgment and denied the plaintiffs summary judgment, effectively deciding that they could not prevail on their claims. The court then drew on its decision in *Craig* and ruled in FedEx's favor on summary judgment on the question of the plaintiffs' employment status in the other cases. Judgments and amended judgments were entered.

Twenty-one cases are on appeal. They present substantially the same issue: whether the district court erred by deciding as a matter of law that the certified classes of plaintiffs were independent contractors and thus could not prevail on their claims. Each case, however, arises under a different state's substantive law. The parties proposed that we begin with the *Craig* appeal and stay the remaining appeals, proceeding as the district court did. We suspended briefing in the other appeals pending further order and now address the *Craig* appeal....

I.

When sitting in diversity, "our task is to ascertain the substantive content of state law as it either has been determined by the highest court of the state or as it would be by that court if the present case were before it now." *Thomas v. H & R Block E. Enters.*, 630 F.3d 659, 663 (7th Cir. 2011).

The KWPA requires employers to pay their employees "all wages due." Kan. Stat. Ann. § 44-314(a). The Act provides an expansive definition of "employee": "any person allowed or permitted to work by an employer." Kan. Stat. Ann. § 44-313(b). The Act also defines "employer" broadly as well to include any corporation "employing any person." Kan. Stat. Ann. § 44-313(a). The Kansas Supreme Court has stated that the statute's definition of "employee" is "virtually identical" to the definition of "employee" in the workers' compensation statute. *Coma Corp. v. Kansas Dep't of Labor*, 283 Kan. 625, 154 P.3d 1080, 1092 (2007) (comparing definition of "employee" in Kan. Stat. Ann. § 44-313 with definition of "workman," "employee," and "worker" in Kan. Stat. Ann. § 44-508(b)).... Importantly, the [KWPA] regulations provide that "[a]llowed or permitted to work" within § 44-313(b) "shall not include an independent contractor, as defined by rules, regulations, and interpretations of the United States secretary of labor for the purposes of the fair labor standards act." Kan. Admin. Regs. §49-20-1(e).

Kansas courts look to the workers' compensation statute when construing the KWPA. Kansas courts have defined an independent contractor as "one who, in exercising an independent employment, contracts to do certain work according to his own methods, without being subject to the control of his employer, except as to the results or product of his work." *Falls v. Scott*, 249 Kan. 54, 815 P.2d 1104, 1112 (1991). No absolute rule exists for determining whether a worker is an independent contractor or an employee. Each case must be decided based on its own facts and circumstances. The primary consideration is the "right of control" test: "whether the employer has the right of control and supervision over the work of the alleged employee, and the right to direct the manner in which the work is to be performed, as well as the result which is to be accomplished." *Falls*, 815 P.2d at 1112. The Kansas Supreme Court has said: "It is not the actual interference or exercise of the control by the employer, but the existence of the right or authority to interfere or control, which renders one a servant rather than an independent contractor." *Id.*

The "right of control" test is the most important consideration in determining whether an employment relationship exists, but it is not the only one. Courts may consider other factors, including the ones enumerated in the Restatement (Second) of Agency §220(2) (1958):

(a) the extent of control which, by the agreement, the master may exercise over the details of the work;

(b) whether or not the one employed is engaged in a distinct occupation or business;

(c) the kind of occupation, with reference to whether, in the locality, the work is usually done under the direction of the employer or by a specialist without supervision;

(d) the skill required in the particular occupation;

(e) whether the employer or the workman supplies the instrumentalities, tools, and the place of work for the person doing the work;

(f) the length of time for which the person is employed;

(g) the method of payment, whether by the time or by the job;

(h) whether or not the work is a part of the regular business of the employer;

(i) whether or not the parties believe they are creating the relation of master and servant; and

(j) whether the principal is or is not in business.

Olds-Carter v. Lakeshore Farms, Inc., 45 Kan.App.2d 390, 250 P.3d 825, 834 (2011).[2]

In looking for guidance on the meaning of the KWPA, we are directed to Kansas cases addressing the employee/independent contractor status of truck drivers. The Kansas Supreme Court has found the existence of the right of control so as to support a finding of employee status in a number of such cases. *See Knoble v. Nat'l Carriers, Inc.*, 212 Kan. 331, 510 P.2d 1274, 1280 (1973) (concluding the company "exercised or had the right to exercise as much control over the drivers ... as it desired"); *Anderson v. Kinsley Sand & Gravel, Inc.*, 221 Kan. 191, 558 P.2d 146, 152 (1976) (concluding there was evidence of an employment relationship where truck driver engaged in "an inherent part of [the company's] business operation," and the company determined the kind and quantity of material to be loaded into the truck and where each load was to be delivered); *Watson v. W.S. Dickey Clay Mfg. Co.*, 202 Kan. 366, 450 P.2d 10 (1969) (stating that when a trucker reports to the company to deliver its products, he "agrees to submit to the controls that are imposed by [the company]; otherwise he hauls none of [its] products"); *Wilbeck v. Grain Belt Transp. Co.*, 181 Kan. 512, 313 P.2d 725, 726–27 (1957) (holding employment relationship existed where driver hauled freight for company whose business was exclusively the transportation of shipments of freight); *Shay v. Hill*, 133 Kan. 157, 299 P. 263 (1931) (individual who furnished his own truck, equipped and operated it at his expense, and hauled animal carcasses for another at a piece rate was an employee under the Workmen's Compensation Act). On the other hand, the court has found the right of control absent in other truck-driver cases. *See Christensen v. Builders Sand Co.*, 180 Kan. 761, 308 P.2d 69, 70 (1957) (drivers "could come and go as they chose," were not compelled to accept any loads, and could haul "as many or as few loads as [they] wished"); *Brownrigg v. Allvine Dairy Co.*, 137 Kan. 209, 19 P.2d 474, 475 (1933) (driver had no route or district and sold milk wherever he wanted).

Knoble, Anderson, Wilbeck, and *Shay* were decided under the Kansas Workers' Compensation Act and Watson involved an interpretation of that Act, the provisions of which "are to be liberally construed to bring workers under the Act...." *Hollingsworth v. Fehrs Equip. Co.*, 240 Kan. 398,

---

2. Section 220 of Restatement (Second) of Agency is now part of section 7.07 of Restatement (Third) of Agency, which identifies essentially the same factors. Because the Kansas courts have relied on section 220, we believe they would similarly look to section 7.07. See Kansas City Brigade, Inc. v. DTG Operations, Inc., No. 103,769, 251 P.3d 112 (Kan.Ct.App. Apr. 29, 2011) (unpublished). However, there may be some tension between the Kansas decisions, see, e.g., Hartford Underwriters, 32 P.3d at 1151; Falls, 815 P.2d at 1112 (distinguishing between the exercise of the control and the right to control) and section 7.07 (making relevant "the extent of control that the principal has exercised in practice over the details of the agent's work"). And the plaintiff class "was certified on the basis of right to control, not actual exercise of control." FedEx Ground, 734 F.Supp.2d at 560.

729 P.2d 1214, 1217 (1986). And all but Watson involved limited judicial review of a compensation appeal. *See, e.g., Knoble*, 510 P.2d at 1277. Perhaps this explains the different outcomes in the cases discussed above. Nonetheless, the cases are difficult to reconcile and reflect that the determination of whether an employer-employee relationship exists is based on the facts in each case. Where some of the factors weigh in favor of finding employee status, some weigh in favor of independent contractor status, and some "cut both ways," a court must weigh the factors according to some legal principle or principles. But other than the point that the right of control is the primary factor, what is the underlying principle (or principles) that guides that weighing process in close cases such as this seeking to establish an employment relationship under the KWPA? We are unsure.

Moreover, there is tension between *Knoble* and *Crawford v. State, Dep't of Human Resources*, 17 Kan.App.2d 707, 845 P.2d 703 (1989), that further complicates our ability to predict how the Kansas Supreme Court would decide the issues before us. In *Knoble*, the court noted that the company had offered explanations for the control it exercised over the drivers by pointing to governmental regulatory requirements, but the reasons behind the control didn't matter: "While such regulations may indeed furnish reasons for at least part of the control exercised, they do not alter the fact of its existence." 510 P.2d at 1280. In the more recent *Crawford* case, however, the court of appeals seems to have taken the view that the reasons for the right to control do matter. 845 P.2d at 706–08 (concluding that evidence did not support a finding of an employment relationship where "the restrictions came not from [the business owner who provided the demonstrators] but from the manufacturers or the individual stores" and that "any control [the owner] had would have had to arise from her being able to enforce the requirements ... of the manufacturers or stores").

Thus, the impact, if any, of the reasons behind FedEx's control over the drivers is unclear. The district court thought that the reasons FedEx retained control mattered. *See, e.g., In re FedEx Ground*, 734 F.Supp.2d at 568 (noting the testimony that "contractors must use a scanner so that customers can track their packages" and "[t]he scanners are connected to FedEx's computer system and transmit package tracking information to FedEx's website for customers to view"), 569 (noting that driver's [*sic*] were required to pick up and deliver at specific times when FedEx negotiated a pick-up or delivery window with a customer). The court found that "[m]any general instructions set forth by FedEx are based on customer demands" and FedEx required "that drivers meet these customer demands," *id.* at 588, which the court concluded involved "the results of the drivers' work," *id.* Of course, it is FedEx that decides what services are provided to its customers, and when. *See id.* at 591. The district court later recognized that "[d]rawing the line between means and results is a challenging, highly contextual and fact-specific task," 758 F.Supp.2d at 658, and "what constitutes control of results in one case ... may constitute control of means in another case," *id.* at 693, albeit in ruling in the other pending cases following its decision in *Craig*.

In addition to our considerable doubt as to how the Kansas Supreme Court would apply its law to the facts and circumstances of this case, we are aware that other courts have reached different conclusions regarding FedEx drivers' employment status. The District of Columbia Circuit held that FedEx single route drivers were independent contractors under the National Labor Relations Act, see *FedEx Home Delivery v. NLRB*, 563 F.3d 492 (D.C.Cir.2009) (reviewing the same or substantially same Operating Agreement), but the Eighth Circuit reversed the grant of summary judgment in favor of FedEx, concluding that there was a genuine issue of material fact as to whether under Missouri law the driver of a tractor trailer bearing FedEx insignia was a FedEx employee or independent contractor, see *Huggins v. FedEx Ground Package Sys., Inc.*, 592 F.3d 853 (8th Cir.2010). Other reported decisions only add to the uncertainty as to the FedEx drivers' status. *Compare Johnson v. FedEx Home Delivery*, No. 04-CV-4935 (JG) (VVP), 2011 WL 6153425 (E.D.N.Y. Dec. 12, 2011) (holding plaintiffs who contracted to provide delivery services to FedEx under the Operating Agreement were independent contractors under New York law), *with Estrada v. FedEx Ground Package Sys.*, Inc., 154 Cal.App.4th 1, 64 Cal.Rptr.3d 327 (2007) (holding single work area drivers were employees rather than independent contractors under California law).

As noted, the KWPA was intended to protect wages and wage earners. *Campbell*, 255 P.3d at 6–7. "It is an expansive and comprehensive legislative scheme that is broad in its scope and the rights created for Kansas workers to secure unpaid wages earned from their labors." *Id.* at 6. The Act "embeds within its provisions a public policy of protecting wage earners' rights to their unpaid wages and benefits." *Id.* at 7; *see also Coma*, 154 P.3d at 1092 (stating that protection of wages and wage earners had been a principal objective of numerous Kansas state laws including the KWPA). Perhaps the Kansas public policy tips the scales in favor of finding employee status for purposes of the KWPA in close cases such as this. We cannot be sure, and the Kansas Supreme Court is in a far better position to provide a definitive answer on this controlling question of state law than are we.

In deciding whether certification is appropriate, see Circuit Rule 52(a); Kan. Stat. Ann. §60-3201, "the most important consideration guiding the exercise of [our] discretion ... is whether [we] find[] [ourselves] genuinely uncertain about a question of state law that is vital to a correct disposition of the case." *Cedar Farm, Harrison Cnty., Inc. v. Louisville Gas & Elec. Co.*, 658 F.3d 807, 812–13 (7th Cir.2011) (quotation and citation omitted). "[C]ertification is appropriate when the case concerns a matter of vital public concern, where the issue will likely recur in other cases, where resolution of the question to be certified is outcome determinative of the case, and where the state supreme court has yet to have an opportunity to illuminate a clear path on the issue." *Id.* at 813. When considering certification, we are mindful of the state courts' already busy dockets. We "consider several factors when deciding whether to certify a question," *State Farm Mut. Auto. Ins. Co. v. Pate*, 275 F.3d 666, 671 (7th Cir.2001), including whether the issue "is of interest to the state supreme court in its development of state law," *id.* at 672. However, "'questions that are tied to the specific facts of a case are typically not ideal candidates for certification. Thus, if certification would produce a fact bound, particularized decision'" without broad precedential significance, certification is generally inappropriate. *Thomas v. H & R Block E. Enters., Inc.*, 630 F.3d 659, 667 (7th Cir.2011).

* * *

The question of the plaintiffs' employment status under Kansas law is outcome determinative and we are unguided by any controlling Kansas Supreme Court precedent. The question appears to be a close one. And the issue is of great importance not just to this case but to the structure of the American workplace. The number of independent contractors in this country is growing. There are several economic incentives for employers to use independent contractors and there is a potential for abuse in misclassifying employees as independent contractors. Employees misclassified as independent contractors are denied access to certain benefits and protections. Misclassification results in significant costs to government: "[B]etween 1996 and 2004, $34.7 billion of Federal tax revenues went uncollected due to the misclassification of workers and the tax loopholes that allow it." 156 Cong. Rec. S7135-01, S7136 (daily ed. Sept. 15, 2010). And misclassification "puts employers who properly classify their workers at a disadvantage in the marketplace[.]" Vice President Joe Biden, quoted in Press Release, John Kerry, White House Endorses Legislation to Close Tax Loophole That Hurts Workers and Businesses (Sept. 15, 2010). FedEx has approximately 15,000 delivery drivers in the U.S. This case will have far-reaching effects on how FedEx runs its business, not only in Kansas but also throughout the United States. And it seems likely that employers in other industries may have similar arrangements with workers, whether delivery drivers or other types of workers. Thus, the decision in this case will have ramifications beyond this particular case and FedEx's business practices, affecting FedEx's competitors and employers in other industries as well.

Although we are presented with a particular contract and specific facts and circumstances, this appeal requires an interpretation of the meaning of "employee" under the KWPA in light of the Kansas public policy of protecting workers' rights to their wages and benefits. Under these circumstances, we believe that the Kansas Supreme Court is in a better position than we to say what Kansas law is and should have the first opportunity to address the issues before us. Certification would further the interests of cooperative federalism.

II.

We respectfully request the Kansas Supreme Court, in an exercise of its sound discretion, to answer the following certified questions:

1. Given the undisputed facts presented to the district court in this case, are the plaintiff drivers employees of FedEx as a matter of law under the KWPA?

2. Drivers can acquire more than one service area from FedEx. *See* 734 F.Supp.2d at 574. Is the answer to the preceding question different for plaintiff drivers who have more than one service area?

We invite reformulation of the questions presented, if necessary, and nothing in this certification should be read to limit the scope of the inquiry to be undertaken by the Kansas Supreme Court. Further proceedings in this court are stayed while this matter is under consideration by that court.

The clerk of this court shall transmit the briefs and appendices in this case as well as a copy of this opinion under official seal to the Kansas Supreme Court, and at that court's request, will transmit the full record.

QUESTIONS CERTIFIED.

Exercise 6-10. What Law Applies If the "Law" Is Choice-of-Law Rules?

1. As you read *Klaxon* below, consider whether the Court's resolution is the best one for the general run of the cases. Would it be better to develop a federal common law of choice of law for diversity and other state-law cases? Or is it better to deem choice-of-law rules "substantive" and apply the basic *Erie* rule to them? What are the advantages and disadvantages of each approach?

2. If the *Klaxon* case were to arise as a case of first impression today, how do you think each of the Justices who wrote opinions in the *Shady Grove* case would decide it?

Klaxon Co. v. Stentor Elec. Mfg. Co.

313 U.S. 487 (1941)

Justice Reed delivered the opinion of the Court.

The principal question in this case is whether in diversity cases the federal courts must follow conflict of laws rules prevailing in the states in which they sit. We left this open in *Ruhlin v. New York Life Insurance Co.*, 304 U.S. 202, 208, n. 2. The frequent recurrence of the problem, as well as the conflict of approach to the problem between the Third Circuit's opinion here and that of the First Circuit in *Sampson v. Channell*, 110 F.2d 754, 759–62, led us to grant certiorari.

In 1918, respondent, a New York corporation, transferred its entire business to petitioner, a Delaware corporation. Petitioner contracted to use its best efforts to further the manufacture and sale of certain patented devices covered by the agreement, and respondent was to have a share of petitioner's profits. The agreement was executed in New York, the assets were transferred there, and petitioner began performance there although later it moved its operations to other states. Respondent was voluntarily dissolved under New York law in 1919. Ten years later it instituted this action in the United States District Court for the District of Delaware, alleging that petitioner had failed to perform its agreement to use its best efforts. Jurisdiction rested on diversity of citizenship. In 1939 respondent recovered a jury verdict of $100,000, upon which judgment was entered. Respondent then moved to correct the judgment by adding interest at the rate of six percent from June 1, 1929, the date the action had been brought. The basis of the motion was the provision in §480 of the New York Civil Practice Act directing that in contract actions interest be added to the principal sum "whether theretofore liquidated or unliquidated."[1] The District Court granted the motion, taking the view that the rights of the parties were governed by New York law and that under New York law the addition of such interest was mandatory. 30 F. Supp. 425, 431. The Circuit Court of Appeals affirmed, 115 F.2d 268, and we granted certiorari, limited

---

1. Section 480, New York Civil Practice Act:

"Interest to be included in recovery. Where in any action, except as provided in section four hundred eighty—a, final judgment is rendered for a sum of money awarded by a verdict, report or decision, interest upon the total amount awarded, from the time when the verdict was rendered or the report or decision was made to the time of entering judgment, must be computed by the clerk, added to the total amount awarded, and included in the amount of the judgment. In every action wherein any sum of money shall be awarded by verdict, report or decision upon a cause of action for the enforcement of or based upon breach of performance of a contract, express or implied, interest shall be recovered upon the principal sum whether theretofore liquidated or unliquidated and shall be added to and be a part of the total sum awarded."

to the question whether § 480 of the New York Civil Practice Act is applicable to an action in the federal court in Delaware. 312 U.S. 674.

The Circuit Court of Appeals was of the view that under New York law the right to interest before verdict under § 480 went to the substance of the obligation, and that proper construction of the contract in suit fixed New York as the place of performance. It then concluded that § 480 was applicable to the case because "it is clear by what we think is undoubtedly the better view of the law that the rules for ascertaining the measure of damages are not a matter of procedure at all, but are matters of substance which should be settled by reference to the law of the appropriate state according to the type of case being tried in the forum. The measure of damages for breach of a contract is determined by the law of the place of performance; Restatement, Conflict of Laws § 413." The court referred also to § 418 of the Restatement, which makes interest part of the damages to be determined by the law of the place of performance. Application of the New York statute apparently followed from the court's independent determination of the "better view" without regard to Delaware law, for no Delaware decision or statute was cited or discussed.

We are of opinion that the prohibition declared in *Erie R. Co. v. Tompkins*, 304 U.S. 64, against such independent determinations by the federal courts, extends to the field of conflict of laws. The conflict of laws rules to be applied by the federal court in Delaware must conform to those prevailing in Delaware's state courts.[2] Otherwise, the accident of diversity of citizenship would constantly disturb equal administration of justice in coordinate state and federal courts sitting side by side. *See Erie R. Co. v. Tompkins, supra*, at 74–77. Any other ruling would do violence to the principle of uniformity within a state, upon which the *Tompkins* decision is based. Whatever lack of uniformity this may produce between federal courts in different states is attributable to our federal system, which leaves to a state, within the limits permitted by the Constitution, the right to pursue local policies diverging from those of its neighbors. It is not for the federal courts to thwart such local policies by enforcing an independent "general law" of conflict of laws. Subject only to review by this Court on any federal question that may arise, Delaware is free to determine whether a given matter is to be governed by the law of the forum or some other law. This Court's views are not the decisive factor in determining the applicable conflicts rule. And the proper function of the Delaware federal court is to ascertain what the state law is, not what it ought to be.

* * *

---

2. An opinion in *Sampson v. Channell*, 110 F.2d 754, 759–62, reaches the same conclusion, as does an opinion of the Third Circuit handed down subsequent to the case at bar, *Waggaman v. General Finance Co.*, 116 F.2d 254, 257. *See also* Goodrich, Conflict of Laws, § 12.

Respondent makes the further argument that the judgment must be affirmed because, under the full faith and credit clause of the Constitution, the state courts of Delaware would be obliged to give effect to the New York statute. The argument rests mainly on the decision of this Court in *John Hancock Mutual Life Ins. Co. v. Yates*, 299 U.S. 178, where a New York statute was held such an integral part of a contract of insurance, that Georgia was compelled to sustain the contract under the full faith and credit clause. Here, however, § 480 of the New York Civil Practice Act is in no way related to the validity of the contract in suit, but merely to an incidental item of damages, interest, with respect to which courts at the forum have commonly been free to apply their own or some other law as they see fit. Nothing in the Constitution ensures unlimited extraterritorial recognition of all statutes or of any statute under all circumstances. The full faith and credit clause does not go so far as to compel Delaware to apply § 480 if such application would interfere with its local policy.

Accordingly, the judgment is reversed and the case remanded to the Circuit Court of Appeals for decision in conformity with the law of Delaware.

Reversed.

––––––––––

Under *Klaxon*, what should a court do if a case is initially filed in one federal District Court, but is then transferred under 28 U.S.C. § 1404 to another District Court situated in another state? Which state's choice of law principles should apply to the case? It is clear that, if the transfer were one for improper venue, then the law of the state in which the transferee court sits would supply the appropriate choice-of-law rules, since the initial court in such a case would not have been a proper court. But what if both the transferor court and the transferee court have proper jurisdiction and venue, as is the case with the typical § 1404 transfer. Can a party secure a change in law through a change in venue, thereby frustrating the plaintiff's forum shopping though its own venue shopping? The Supreme Court answered this question in *Van Dusen v. Barrack*, 376 U.S. 612 (1964), holding that, in the case of a § 1404 transfer, the choice-of-law rules of the transferor District follow the case to the transferee District. Colloquially, lawyers refer to this rule as the "suitcase rule," in that the parties essentially "pack up the law in a suitcase" and take it with them to the new District when the case is transferred.

In Chapter 5, you studied venue and transfer of venue, and you learned from the *Atlantic Marine* case that venue transfer motions are evaluated using a set of non-dispositive factors, one of which may be the existence and content of a contractual clause termed a "forum selection clause." Omitted from the *Atlantic Marine* case as presented there was a portion of the opinion addressing the question above. That omitted portion is below.

Atlantic Marine Construction Co., Inc. v.
U.S. Dist. Ct. for the Western District of Texas

134 S. Ct. 568 (2013)

Justice Alito delivered the opinion of the Court.

* * *

Third, when a party bound by a forum-selection clause flouts its contractual obligation and files suit in a different forum, a § 1404(a) transfer of venue will not carry with it the original venue's choice-of-law rules — a factor that in some circumstances may affect public-interest considerations. A federal court sitting in diversity ordinarily must follow the choice-of-law rules of the State in which it sits. *See Klaxon Co. v. Stentor Elec. Mfg. Co.*, 313 U.S. 487, 494–96 (1941). However, we previously identified an exception to that principle for § 1404(a) transfers, requiring that the state law applicable in the original court also apply in the transferee court. We deemed that exception necessary to prevent "defendants, properly subjected to suit in the transferor State," from "invok[ing] § 1404(a) to gain the benefits of the laws of another jurisdiction. . . ." *Van Dusen.*

The policies motivating our exception to the *Klaxon* rule for § 1404(a) transfers, however, do not support an extension to cases where a defendant's motion is premised on enforcement of a valid forum-selection clause. To the contrary, those considerations lead us to reject the rule that the law of the court in which the plaintiff inappropriately filed suit should follow the case to the forum contractually selected by the parties. In *Van Dusen* we were concerned that, through a § 1404(a) transfer, a defendant could "defeat the state-law advantages that might accrue from the exercise of [the plaintiff's] venue privilege." But as discussed above, a plaintiff who files suit in violation of a forum-selection clause enjoys no such "privilege" with respect to its choice of forum, and therefore it is entitled to no concomitant "state-law advantages." Not only would it be inequitable to allow the plaintiff to fasten its choice of substantive law to the venue transfer, but it would also encourage gamesmanship. Because "§ 1404(a) should not create or multiply opportunities for forum shopping," *Ferens v. John Deere Co.*, 494 U.S. 516, 523 (1990), we will not apply the *Van Dusen* rule when a transfer stems from enforcement of a forum-selection clause: The court in the contractually selected venue should not apply the law of the transferor venue to which the parties waived their right.[8]

When parties have contracted in advance to litigate disputes in a particular forum, courts should not unnecessarily disrupt the parties' settled

---

8. For the reasons detailed above, see Part II-B, *supra*, the same standards should apply to motions to dismiss for *forum non conveniens* in cases involving valid forum-selection clauses pointing to state or foreign forums. . . .

expectations. A forum-selection clause, after all, may have figured centrally in the parties' negotiations and may have affected how they set monetary and other contractual terms; it may, in fact, have been a critical factor in their agreement to do business together in the first place. In all but the most unusual cases, therefore, "the interest of justice" is served by holding parties to their bargain.

* * *

The District Court also held that the public-interest factors weighed in favor of keeping the case in Texas because Texas contract law is more familiar to federal judges in Texas than to their federal colleagues in Virginia. That ruling, however, rested in part on the District Court's belief that the federal court sitting in Virginia would have been required to apply Texas' choice-of-law rules, which in this case pointed to Texas contract law. But for the reasons we have explained, the transferee court would apply Virginia choice-of-law rules. It is true that even these Virginia rules may point to the contract law of Texas, as the State in which the contract was formed. But at minimum, the fact that the Virginia court will not be required to apply Texas choice-of-law rules reduces whatever weight the District Court might have given to the public-interest factor that looks to the familiarity of the transferee court with the applicable law. And, in any event, federal judges routinely apply the law of a State other than the State in which they sit. We are not aware of any exceptionally arcane features of Texas contract law that are likely to defy comprehension by a federal judge sitting in Virginia.

Exercise 6-11. Choice of Law and Contracts

Imagine that you represent a client, incorporated in Delaware and with its principal place of business in Georgia, that manufactures tax preparation software and sells it nationwide to customers, mostly over the Internet. Because of the prevalence of mistakes in tax preparation, the company is sued fairly often. The company's lawyers have noticed that the law of Wyoming is particularly favorable to it on these claims, and the general counsel would like to find a way to ensure that, as often as possible, its claims are evaluated under Wyoming law. In addition, the company's president, who likes to be personally involved in all litigation against the company, would prefer that any such lawsuits occur in federal court in Georgia, where he lives.

You have been hired to draft the company's new "Terms and Conditions" agreement, a contract to which all purchasers must "agree" before using the software. After reading *Klaxon*, *Van Dusen*, and the above excerpt from *At-*

lantic Marine, what sections would you draft as part of the contract to ensure that your client's wishes are followed and upheld in court?

1. Attempt to draft the language you would use to secure that result.

2. Read another student's draft. Can you think of ways in which you might argue against its enforcement in court?

7. Professional Development Reflection: Horizontal Choice of Law

Every state in the United States licenses attorneys, and each state promulgates, maintains, and enforces its own Code of Ethics or Rules of Professional Responsibility that applies to all attorneys licensed in the state. This means that attorneys licensed in more than one state might be subject to conflicting rules of ethics and professional conduct. In addition, merely serving a client or performing legal services within the borders of a state can make an attorney (even one not licensed in that state) subject to the state's ethics and professional responsibility rules.

Thankfully, there is no "national" or "federal" professional responsibility code (the ABA's Model Rules of Professional Conduct are just that — "model" rules), so vertical choice of law does not present any problems — professional sanctions and discipline are handled entirely at the state level. But even at that state level, where an attorney's conduct has crossed state lines in some way, it may be necessary for the state in which that attorney is licensed to make a horizontal choice-of-law determination to decide whether professional sanctions are appropriate. Fortunately, most state professional responsibility codes are similar to each other, and in the cases where they differ, the codes of most states contain specific provisions governing choice of law.

The following exercise takes you into this difficult terrain. Use the professional responsibility code of the state in which your school sits, or if you prefer, the state in which you plan to become licensed, to complete the exercise.

Exercise 6-12. Choice of Professionalism Law

Imagine that you are the general counsel of a large supermarket corporation with locations in four states: Indiana, Ohio, Kentucky, and Tennessee. The CEO has decided to expand the company's locations into Illinois, and as part of the due diligence phase of decision making, she sends you to Illinois to discuss with the State Comptroller the possibility of obtaining tax incentives for the opening of several locations in the state. While you are there, you discover that the state attorney ethics code requires any corporate counsel to register with the state bar and affiliate with a local attorney before providing legal services of any kind inside the state borders (ignore any outside knowledge you may have of Illinois's actual requirements on this point). Your home state's attorney ethics code contains no such requirement, and indeed, like most state's codes, allows an out-of-state attorney to represent the interests of a single corporate client in non-litigation matters without obtaining any special permissions or registering.

Understanding that, by first traveling to Illinois to gather data to inform your advice to your client without registering or affiliating with a local attorney, you are technically violating the Illinois Code, you travel home to research whether you can be disciplined for it. Using the actual attorney ethics code of your home state, determine whether you are subject to discipline.

Exercise 6-13. Chapter Problem and Discussion

Refer back to the Chapter Problem set forth at the beginning of this Chapter. The problem is based on the actual facts of *Piper Aircraft v. Reyno*, which you studied in detail in the Section on *forum non conveniens*. After studying the material in this Chapter, how would you answer your partner's questions? Draft an informal memo that you can submit to the partner by email before discussing the matter with her.

Chapter 7

Pleading

1. Chapter Problem

Memorandum

To: Associate
From: Jermaine Sutherland, Partner
Re: Martin v. Coalrock, Inc. & Unnamed Employee

Our client, Thomas Martin, is a resident of Pikeville, KY, and the surviving spouse of the woman you may have read about in the paper a couple of years back, who was run off a mountain road and killed in Eastern Kentucky by a truck fully loaded with coal. The truck was driven by a person whose name Mr. Martin does not remember, but who was hauling coal in a truck painted with the logo for Coalrock, Inc., a large coal company incorporated and headquartered in North Carolina.

I would like to get a complaint together for a wrongful death suit as soon as possible, as I believe the statute of limitations is about to run out [*Kentucky's statute of limitations for ve-hicle-related personal injuries and wrongful death is 2 years. KRS 304.39-230(6).*]. Please put to-gether a list of information we need to put together a complaint against both this company and its unnamed employee that will allow us to get to discovery, along with a plan for how best to obtain that information. Send it to me in a memo, with a copy to the file.

---

2. Introduction

Chapters 2–6 outlined the many factors that litigants have to consider when deciding where to file their actions, from personal and subject matter jurisdiction, to the convenience of the venue, to the service of process on the defendant, to the law that will apply to the action based on where it is filed. Chapter 7 moves from these very important, place-bound considerations to the actual litigation of the suit, beginning with the plaintiff's filing of the Complaint—the first pleading that begins any lawsuit in federal court—and moving through the responsive pleadings that each party must or may file. The remainder of Chapter 7 is divided into the following Sections:

- Section 3—The Complaint. This Section addresses the document that begins a litigation by stating the Plaintiff's claims.

- Section 4—Responsive Pleadings. This Section addresses the pleadings that are required or permitted in response to pleadings in which claims are stated.

- Section 5—Amending Pleadings. This Section addresses the standards that courts apply when parties want to make changes to pleadings they have already filed, as well as the consequences of such changes.

- Section 6—Truthfulness, Good Faith, and Professionalism in Pleading. This Section addresses the duties that lawyers have to be candid and truthful in their communications with the court.

Before moving into these sections, a brief introduction to the subject of pleading will help to set the stage. Title III of the Federal Rules of Civil Procedure, "Pleadings and Motions," sets forth rules of pleading that greatly simplified the prior practices that we had adopted and adapted from English pleading.* The Federal Rules recognize three main forms of documents that litigants can file with the court. The first, only referred to sparingly, is typically termed a "notice." *See, e.g.*, Rule 41(a) (permitting a plaintiff to voluntarily dismiss his own case by providing notice to the court and the opposing party(ies)); Rule 7.1 (requiring notice to the court of the corporations with a potential interest in the litigation—terming the notice a "statement"). A notice filed with the court simply tells the court something. No other party need respond to a filed notice, and the typical filed notice does not ask anything of the court.**

Next is a filed document form called a "motion." A motion is a specific request to the court for something—judgment, dismissal of a claim, an extension of time, the scheduling of a conference, sanctions against an opposing party, etc. The point is that a motion is a *request*—one that may be granted or denied (or stayed, or taken under advisement, or deferred until a later stage of the case, etc.). For example, Rule 56 sets forth detailed requirements for moving (not "motioning") the court for summary judgment (judgment without having to go through a trial, covered in Chapter 10). If a party files a motion for summary judgment, the opposing party must respond to that motion, and the court must issue a ruling, usually either granting or denying it. Unlike a notice, then, the court needs to act on a motion in some way, and in

---

* Ed. Note. A detailed comparison of pleading under the Federal Rules and the pleading systems that came before the Rules would be far beyond the scope of this introductory casebook, but knowledge of what came before can be quite illuminating. It can also help with one's state-court litigation practice because many states retain elements of the old pleading systems. For a leading article discussing both English common law pleading and "code" pleading—the first effort to break away from English common law pleading prior to the adoption of the Federal Rules in 1938—see Charles E. Clark, *The Complaint in Code Pleading*, 35 Yale L.J. 259 (1926). We recommend reading Clark's article *after* studying the material in this Chapter.

** Ed. Note. In some cases, the Rules provide that one party should provide "notice" to the other party(ies) in the case—e.g., notice of intent to seek sanctions under Rule 11—and in these cases, the party(ies) receiving notice, which is not "filed" with the court but simply "served" on the other party(ies), often must do something in response (e.g., in the case of Rule 11 sanctions, the party in receipt of the notice has 21 days from such receipt to cure whatever is the ground for sanctions).

most cases, the other party(ies) to the litigation have the right to respond before the court acts. Also, because a motion's purpose is to convince the court to grant some sort of relief to the movant (the person who files the motion), a motion is usually accompanied by a persuasive memorandum of law (sometimes called a "memorandum in support" or a "memorandum of points and authorities").

The third main form of document that a litigant may file is called a "pleading." Whereas a *notice* informs the court of something, and a *motion* directly requests some sort of relief from the court, a pleading carries some of each of these functions, while having as its main function a narrow, foundational role. Mainly, the pleadings *delineate the scope of the entire dispute* and provide the foundation for everything that will occur in the case from the close of the pleadings forward to judgment. A pleading simply constitutes the statement of a party's claims and/or defenses. It provides notice of these claims and/or defenses to the court and the other parties in the cases, and in some cases it "demands" or "prays for" relief from the court (a trial by jury, damages, an injunction, etc.). Nevertheless, even though some pleadings directly request relief from the judge, unlike a motion, a judge need not do anything to "grant" or "deny" a pleading. Pleadings are allowed as a matter of course, and if one party thinks that the pleading of another is insufficient or should be disallowed in whole or in part, that party must file a motion stating a request to have the pleading stricken or dismissed.*

As Rule 7 states, the federal courts recognize only seven types of pleadings, four of which are derivative of the other three:

(a) Pleadings. Only these pleadings are allowed:

(1) a complaint;

(2) an answer to a complaint;

(3) an answer to a counterclaim designated as a counterclaim;

(4) an answer to a crossclaim;

(5) a third-party complaint;

(6) an answer to a third-party complaint; and

(7) if the court orders one, a reply to an answer.

You will understand better what each of these pleadings is once you have studied the material on aggregating claims and parties ("joinder"), but as you can see, stripping out the modifiers, a pleading always takes the form of either a complaint, an answer, or a reply.

A complaint is the initial statement of the claim(s) that a party has against the other party or parties to the case, along with the factual foundation for these claim(s). Fed. R. Civ. P. 8(a). An answer is the response to another party's complaint. It gen-

---

* Ed. Note. While it is true that courts can always move *sua sponte* to dismiss pleadings or portions of them on their own, such action is rare, and is typically employed only to police extreme or foundational defects, such as lack of subject matter jurisdiction.

erally must admit or deny the allegations in the complaint. Fed. R. Civ. P. 8(b). It must also state any affirmative or other defenses that the respondent has, and lay a factual foundation for these defenses, if any. Fed. R. Civ. P. 8(c); Fed. R. Civ. P. 12(f). A reply, which is allowed only with the court's permission, usually presents the response to some affirmative defense or other defense(s) contained in the answer. Replies are generally disfavored, but they are nevertheless filed in many federal cases each year.

Along with a basis for the court's jurisdiction and a demand for judgment (both of which are usually, but not always, *pro forma* elements), Fed. R. Civ. P. 8(a) states that a complaint must contain a "a short and plain statement of the claim showing that the pleader is entitled to relief." Fed. R. Civ. P. 8(a)(2). This brief provision in the Federal Rules has generated some very important case law, particularly recently. In the following Section, we outline the approach that the Supreme Court has instructed the lower courts to take in evaluating whether a complaint contains "a short and plain statement of the claim showing that the pleader is entitled to relief."

In reading the cases and other materials in Section 3, it is helpful to know that, to challenge a complaint as being out of compliance with Rule 8(a), the defendant must file a Motion to Dismiss for Failure to State a Claim upon which Relief May Be Granted, a motion authorized by Rule 12(b)(6), and often referred to by lawyers as a "12(b)(6) Motion." This arrangement helps to illustrate the difference between pleadings and motions. The relevant *pleading* in each of these cases is the Complaint, while the relevant *motion* is the document asking the court to dismiss the Complaint.

3. The Complaint

Exercise 7-1. *Swierkiewicz v. Sorema*

In 1957, the Supreme Court decided *Conley v. Gibson*, 355 U.S. 41 (1957), famously proclaiming that "a complaint should not be dismissed for failure to state a claim unless it appears beyond doubt that the plaintiff can prove no set of facts in support of his claim which would entitle him to relief." *Id.* at 46. This very deferential standard governed motions to dismiss for failure to state a claim until very recently, but the defense bar was never in support of it, and it was beset by both legislative and judicial detractors almost as soon as it was penned.

The basis for these objections was that, while the *Conley* standard was protective of the general orientation of the federal rules away from the traditional English and Colonial practices of form-based pleading (which often rewarded litigants and their counsel for their craftiness and artfulness in pleading, rather than for the merits of their claims), and code-based pleading (which required pleaders and courts to distinguish between "ultimate facts," which had to be pleaded, and "evidentiary facts," which were not permitted in a pleading), the *Conley* standard nevertheless traveled too far in the opposite direction, allowing even patently frivolous claims with no express factual foundation to proceed based on the ability of the court to conceive of a *hypothetical* "set of facts" that would prove the claim. As the costs of discovery began to rise during the latter half of the Twentieth Century, these challenges to the *Conley* standard began to find more adherents.

Some of these adherents had some early success in the employment discrimination realm. Employment discrimination is the intentional mistreatment of an employee due to the employee's physical or personal characteristics, such as race, color, gender, pregnancy, genetics, national origin, religion, disability, or age. But most employment discrimination cases do not involve defendants who admit their intent to discriminate against the plaintiff, and it is difficult, in the absence of such an admission, to prove directly that the defendant had this evil intent. Thus, rather than using this sort of "direct evidence," employment discrimination plaintiffs usually prove their claims through a circumstantial evidence-based framework, first laid out in a case called *McDonnell Douglas Corp. v. Green*, 411 U.S. 792 (1973).

Simplified, this framework requires, first, that the plaintiff establish a "prima facie case" of discrimination. This means that the plaintiff must show a set of circumstances from which a jury can infer that intentional discrimination occurred. In the typical case, this requires the plaintiff to show that (1) she was a member of a "protected class" under the employment discrimination statutes; (2) she was "qualified" for her position (or the position sought); (3) she suffered an "adverse employment action" (such as dismissal or failure to promote); and (4) other circumstances existed at the time that would allow a jury to infer discrimination (such as that other, similarly situated employees or applicants outside the protected class were treated more favorably). If the plaintiff is able to establish this prima facie case (usually at the summary judgment stage), then the parties engage in a burden-shifting proof battle, at the conclusion of which the judge decides whether enough evidence exists to allow the jury to rule for either party.

1. As you read *Swierkiewicz v. Sorema* below, try to discern exactly what is wrong with requiring the plaintiff to *plead* the prima facie case in the Complaint. Wouldn't such a requirement improve the "notice" that Justice Thomas correctly says is the purpose of Rule 8(a)'s standards, and isn't more notice better than less? What distinction is Justice Thomas (who was the head of the EEOC himself for several years, and thus was very familiar with this area of the law) trying to draw, and why does this distinction mean that a plaintiff cannot be required to plead the prima facie case?

2. What does "expressio unius est exlusio alterius" mean? How does Justice Thomas use this "canon of statutory construction" to resolve an issue

in the *Sorema* case? How do Rules 8(a) and 9(b) differ, based on this construction?

Swierkiewicz v. Sorema N.A.

534 U.S. 506 (2002)

Thomas, J., delivered the opinion for a unanimous Court.

This case presents the question whether a complaint in an employment discrimination lawsuit must contain specific facts establishing a *prima facie* case of discrimination under the framework set forth by this Court in *McDonnell Douglas Corp. v. Green*, 411 U.S. 792 (1973). We hold that an employment discrimination complaint need not include such facts and instead must contain only "a short and plain statement of the claim showing that the pleader is entitled to relief." Fed. Rule Civ. Proc. 8(a)(2).

I

Petitioner Akos Swierkiewicz is a native of Hungary, who at the time of his complaint was 53 years old.[1] In April 1989, petitioner began working for respondent Sorema N. A., a reinsurance company headquartered in New York and principally owned and controlled by a French parent corporation. Petitioner was initially employed in the position of senior vice president and chief underwriting officer (CUO). Nearly six years later, François M. Chavel, respondent's Chief Executive Officer, demoted petitioner to a marketing and services position and transferred the bulk of his underwriting responsibilities to Nicholas Papadopoulo, a 32-year-old who, like Mr. Chavel, is a French national. About a year later, Mr. Chavel stated that he wanted to "energize" the underwriting department and appointed Mr. Papadopoulo as CUO. Petitioner claims that Mr. Papadopoulo had only one year of underwriting experience at the time he was promoted, and therefore was less experienced and less qualified to be CUO than he, since at that point he had 26 years of experience in the insurance industry.

Following his demotion, petitioner contends that he "was isolated by Mr. Chavel ... excluded from business decisions and meetings and denied the opportunity to reach his true potential at SOREMA." Petitioner unsuccessfully attempted to meet with Mr. Chavel to discuss his discontent.

---

1. Because we review here a decision granting respondent's motion to dismiss, we must accept as true all of the factual allegations contained in the complaint. *See, e. g., Leatherman v. Tarrant County Narcotics Intelligence and Coordination Unit*, 507 U.S. 163, 164 (1993).

Finally, in April 1997, petitioner sent a memo to Mr. Chavel outlining his grievances and requesting a severance package. Two weeks later, respondent's general counsel presented petitioner with two options: He could either resign without a severance package or be dismissed. Mr. Chavel fired petitioner after he refused to resign.

Petitioner filed a lawsuit alleging that he had been terminated on account of his national origin in violation of Title VII of the Civil Rights Act of 1964, and on account of his age in violation of the Age Discrimination in Employment Act of 1967 (ADEA). The United States District Court for the Southern District of New York dismissed petitioner's complaint because it found that he "ha[d] not adequately alleged a *prima facie* case, in that he ha[d] not adequately alleged circumstances that support an inference of discrimination." The United States Court of Appeals for the Second Circuit affirmed the dismissal, relying on its settled precedent, which requires a plaintiff in an employment discrimination complaint to allege facts constituting a *prima facie* case of discrimination under the framework set forth by this Court in *McDonnell Douglas*. The Court of Appeals held that petitioner had failed to meet his burden because his allegations were "insufficient as a matter of law to raise an inference of discrimination." 5 Fed. App'x. 63, 65 (CA2 2001). We granted certiorari to resolve a split among the Courts of Appeals concerning the proper pleading standard for employment discrimination cases,[2] and now reverse.

II

Applying Circuit precedent, the Court of Appeals required petitioner to plead a *prima facie* case of discrimination in order to survive respondent's motion to dismiss. In the Court of Appeals' view, petitioner was thus required to allege in his complaint: (1) membership in a protected group; (2) qualification for the job in question; (3) an adverse employment action; and (4) circumstances that support an inference of discrimination.

The *prima facie* case under *McDonnell Douglas*, however, is an evidentiary standard, not a pleading requirement. In *McDonnell Douglas*, this Court made clear that "[t]he critical issue before us concern[ed] the *order and allocation of proof* in a private, non-class action challenging employment discrimination." 411 U. S., at 800 (emphasis added). In subsequent cases,

---

2. The majority of Courts of Appeals have held that a plaintiff need not plead a *prima facie* case of discrimination under *McDonnell Douglas Corp. v. Green*, 411 U. S. 792 (1973), in order to survive a motion to dismiss. *See, e. g., Sparrow v. United Air Lines, Inc.*, 216 F. 3d 1111, 1114 (CADC 2000); *Bennett v. Schmidt*, 153 F. 3d 516, 518 (CA7 1998); *Ring v. First Interstate Mortgage, Inc.*, 984 F. 2d 924 (CA8 1993). Others, however, maintain that a complaint must contain factual allegations that support each element of a *prima facie* case. In addition to the case below, see *Jackson v. Columbus*, 194 F. 3d 737, 751 (CA6 1999).

this Court has reiterated that the *prima facie* case relates to the employee's burden of presenting evidence that raises an inference of discrimination.

This Court has never indicated that the requirements for establishing a *prima facie* case under *McDonnell Douglas* also apply to the pleading standard that plaintiffs must satisfy in order to survive a motion to dismiss. For instance, we have rejected the argument that a Title VII complaint requires greater "particularity," because this would "too narrowly constric[t] the role of the pleadings." *McDonald v. Santa Fe Trail Transp. Co.*, 427 U. S. 273, 283, n. 11 (1976). Consequently, the ordinary rules for assessing the sufficiency of a complaint apply. *See, e. g., Scheuer v. Rhodes*, 416 U. S. 232, 236 (1974) ("When a federal court reviews the sufficiency of a complaint, before the reception of any evidence either by affidavit or admissions, its task is necessarily a limited one. The issue is not whether a plaintiff will ultimately prevail but whether the claimant is entitled to offer evidence to support the claims").

In addition, under a notice pleading system, it is not appropriate to require a plaintiff to plead facts establishing a *prima facie* case because the *McDonnell Douglas* framework does not apply in every employment discrimination case. For instance, if a plaintiff is able to produce direct evidence of discrimination, he may prevail without proving all the elements of a *prima facie* case.... Under the Second Circuit's heightened pleading standard, a plaintiff without direct evidence of discrimination at the time of his complaint must plead a *prima facie* case of discrimination, even though discovery might uncover such direct evidence. It thus seems incongruous to require a plaintiff, in order to survive a motion to dismiss, to plead more facts than he may ultimately need to prove to succeed on the merits if direct evidence of discrimination is discovered.

Moreover, the precise requirements of a *prima facie* case can vary depending on the context and were never intended to be rigid, mechanized, or ritualistic.... Before discovery has unearthed relevant facts and evidence, it may be difficult to define the precise formulation of the required *prima facie* case in a particular case. Given that the *prima facie* case operates as a flexible evidentiary standard, it should not be transposed into a rigid pleading standard for discrimination cases.

Furthermore, imposing the Court of Appeals' heightened pleading standard in employment discrimination cases conflicts with Federal Rule of Civil Procedure 8(a)(2), which provides that a complaint must include only "a short and plain statement of the claim showing that the pleader is entitled to relief." Such a statement must simply "give the defendant fair notice of what the plaintiff's claim is and the grounds upon which it rests." *Conley v. Gibson*, 355 U. S. 41, 47 (1957). This simplified notice pleading standard relies on liberal discovery rules and summary judgment motions to define disputed facts and issues and to dispose of unmeritorious claims.

Leatherman v. Tarrant County Narcotics Intelligence and Coordination Unit, 507 U. S. 163, 168–169 (1993). "The provisions for discovery are so flexible and the provisions for pretrial procedure and summary judgment so effective, that attempted surprise in federal practice is aborted very easily, synthetic issues detected, and the gravamen of the dispute brought frankly into the open for the inspection of the court." 5 C. WRIGHT & A. MILLER, FEDERAL PRACTICE AND PROCEDURE § 1202, p. 76 (2d ed. 1990).

Rule 8(a)'s simplified pleading standard applies to all civil actions, with limited exceptions. Rule 9(b), for example, provides for greater particularity in all averments of fraud or mistake.[3] This Court, however, has declined to extend such exceptions to other contexts. In *Leatherman* we stated: "[T]he Federal Rules do address in Rule 9(b) the question of the need for greater particularity in pleading certain actions, but do not include among the enumerated actions any reference to complaints alleging municipal liability under § 1983. *Expressio unius est exclusio alterius.*" 507 U. S., at 168. Just as Rule 9(b) makes no mention of municipal liability under 42 U. S. C. § 1983, neither does it refer to employment discrimination. Thus, complaints in these cases, as in most others, must satisfy only the simple requirements of Rule 8(a).[4]

Other provisions of the Federal Rules of Civil Procedure are inextricably linked to Rule 8(a)'s simplified notice pleading standard. Rule 8(e)(1) states that "[n]o technical forms of pleading or motions are required," and Rule 8(f) provides that "[a]ll pleadings shall be so construed as to do substantial justice." Given the Federal Rules' simplified standard for pleading, "[a] court may dismiss a complaint only if it is clear that no relief could be granted under any set of facts that could be proved consistent with the allegations." *Hishon v. King & Spalding,* 467 U. S. 69, 73 (1984). If a pleading fails to specify the allegations in a manner that provides sufficient notice, a defendant can move for a more definite statement under Rule 12(e) before responding. Moreover, claims lacking merit may be dealt with through summary judgment under Rule 56. The liberal notice pleading of Rule 8(a) is the starting point of a simplified pleading system, which was adopted to focus litigation on the merits of a claim. *See Conley, supra,*

---

3. "In all averments of fraud or mistake, the circumstances constituting fraud or mistake shall be stated with particularity. Malice, intent, knowledge, and other condition of mind of a person may be averred generally." [Fed. R. Civ. P. 9(b).]

4. These requirements are exemplified by the Federal Rules of Civil Procedure Forms, which "are sufficient under the rules and are intended to indicate the simplicity and brevity of statement which the rules contemplate." Fed. Rule Civ. Proc. 84. For example, Form 9 [Note: Now, Form 11, to be deleted from the Federal Rules absent congressional action as of December 2015] sets forth a complaint for negligence in which plaintiff simply states in relevant part: "On June 1, 1936, in a public highway called Boylston Street in Boston, Massachusetts, defendant negligently drove a motor vehicle against plaintiff who was then crossing said highway."

at 48 ("The Federal Rules reject the approach that pleading is a game of skill in which one misstep by counsel may be decisive to the outcome and accept the principle that the purpose of pleading is to facilitate a proper decision on the merits").

Applying the relevant standard, petitioner's complaint easily satisfies the requirements of Rule 8(a) because it gives respondent fair notice of the basis for petitioner's claims. Petitioner alleged that he had been terminated on account of his national origin in violation of Title VII and on account of his age in violation of the ADEA. His complaint detailed the events leading to his termination, provided relevant dates, and included the ages and nationalities of at least some of the relevant persons involved with his termination. These allegations give respondent fair notice of what petitioner's claims are and the grounds upon which they rest. In addition, they state claims upon which relief could be granted under Title VII and the ADEA.

Respondent argues that allowing lawsuits based on conclusory allegations of discrimination to go forward will burden the courts and encourage disgruntled employees to bring unsubstantiated suits. Whatever the practical merits of this argument, the Federal Rules do not contain a heightened pleading standard for employment discrimination suits. A requirement of greater specificity for particular claims is a result that "must be obtained by the process of amending the Federal Rules, and not by judicial interpretation." *Leatherman, supra*, at 168. Furthermore, Rule 8(a) establishes a pleading standard without regard to whether a claim will succeed on the merits. "Indeed it may appear on the face of the pleadings that a recovery is very remote and unlikely but that is not the test." *Scheuer*, 416 U. S., at 236.

For the foregoing reasons, we hold that an employment discrimination plaintiff need not plead a *prima facie* case of discrimination and that petitioner's complaint is sufficient to survive respondent's motion to dismiss. Accordingly, the judgment of the Court of Appeals is reversed, and the case is remanded for further proceedings consistent with this opinion.

It is so ordered.

Notice Pleading and Heightened Pleading

In *Sweirkiewicz*, the Court reaffirmed that no "heightened pleading standard" applies to claims for employment discrimination. In support, Justice Thomas quoted the *Leatherman* case, which employed a canon of statutory construction, "*Expressio unius est exclusio alterius*," or "the expression of one thing implies the exclusion of others." The *Leatherman* Court pointed out that the Federal Rules of Civil Procedure do, in fact establish a heightened pleading standard in Rule 9(b), which requires a party to plead "all averments of fraud or mistake with particularity." Since Rule 9(b) specifically mentions only "fraud or mistake," the proper interpretation is that anything other than fraud or mistake does not require pleading with particularity.*

Heightened pleading standards do appear in other areas of federal law. For example, Rule 23.1 applies a particularity standard to some aspects of a shareholder's derivative complaint. In the statutory context, the Private Securities Litigation Reform Act requires that a complaint "state with particularity facts giving rise to a strong inference that the defendant acted with the required state of mind." 15 U.S.C. §78u-4(b)(2); *see also Tellabs Inc. v. Makor Issues & Rights, Ltd.*, 551 U.S. 308 (2007) (interpreting "strong inference" to require an inference that the required state of mind existed to be "at least as likely as any plausible opposing inference"). But the general requirement for pleading in the federal courts is best described by the term "notice pleading." The plaintiff is only required to "give the defendant fair notice of what the plaintiff's claim is and the grounds upon which it rests." *Conley v. Gibson*, 355 U.S. 41, 47 (1957).

Exercise 7-2. Situating *Swierkiewicz*

Justice Thomas's opinion for the unanimous Court in *Swierkiewicz* appeared to be the death knell for the many challenges to the *Conley* standard that had found success in employment discrimination cases and other contexts. As you see in the opinion, the Court reaffirms the *Conley* "no set of facts" standard, rejects a proposed carve-out from that standard for employment discrimination cases, and says, in no uncertain terms, that tightening up the pleading standard under Rule 8(a)(2) is a matter for rulemaking or congressional legislation.

However, just three years later, the Court issued its decision in *Bell Atlantic v. Twombly*, the next principal case in this Section. As you will see soon, in *Twombly*, which was decided by a 7–2 majority, the Court purported to "retire" the *Conley* "no set of facts" standard. As you read, try to discern what factors may have caused such a stark change. Also, consider whether the Court had the duty to explicitly overrule *Swierkiewicz* in order to establish the *Twombly* rule, and if not, why not?

Bell Atlantic Corp. v. Twombly
550 U.S. 544 (2007)

Justice Souter delivered the opinion of the Court.

Liability under §1 of the Sherman Act, 15 U.S.C. §1, requires a "contract, combination..., or conspiracy, in restraint of trade or com-

---

* Ed. Note. Averments that a condition precedent has not been established must also be pleaded with particularity, but usually, that is done in an answer, rather than in a complaint. *See* Rule 9(c).

merce." The question in this putative class action is whether a § 1 complaint can survive a motion to dismiss when it alleges that major telecommunications providers engaged in certain parallel conduct unfavorable to competition, absent some factual context suggesting agreement, as distinct from identical, independent action. We hold that such a complaint should be dismissed.

I

The upshot of the 1984 divestiture of the American Telephone & Telegraph Company's (AT & T) local telephone business was a system of regional service monopolies (variously called "Regional Bell Operating Companies," "Baby Bells," or "Incumbent Local Exchange Carriers" (ILECs)), and a separate, competitive market for long-distance service from which the ILECs were excluded. More than a decade later, Congress withdrew approval of the ILECs' monopolies by enacting the Telecommunications Act of 1996 (1996 Act), which fundamentally restructured local telephone markets and "subjected ILECs to a host of duties intended to facilitate market entry. In recompense, the 1996 Act set conditions for authorizing ILECs to enter the long-distance market. *See* 47 U.S.C. § 271.

Central to the [new] scheme was each ILEC's obligation to share its network with competitors, which came to be known as "competitive local exchange carriers" (CLECs). A CLEC could make use of an ILEC's network in any of three ways: by (1) purchasing local telephone services at wholesale rates for resale to end users, (2) leasing elements of the ILEC's network on an unbundled basis, or (3) interconnecting its own facilities with the ILEC's network. Owing to the considerable expense and effort required to make unbundled network elements available to rivals at wholesale prices. the ILECs vigorously litigated the scope of the sharing obligation imposed by the 1996 Act, with the result that the Federal Communications Commission (FCC) three times revised its regulations to narrow the range of network elements to be shared with the CLECs. *See Covad Communications Co. v. FCC*, 450 F.3d 528, 533–534 (C.A.D.C. 2006) (summarizing the 10-year-long regulatory struggle between the ILECs and CLECs).

Respondents William Twombly and Lawrence Marcus (hereinafter plaintiffs) represent a putative class consisting of all "subscribers of local telephone and/or high speed internet services ... from February 8, 1996 to present." In this action against petitioners, a group of ILECs, plaintiffs seek treble damages and declaratory and injunctive relief for claimed violations of § 1 of the Sherman Act, 15 U.S.C. § 1, which prohibits "[e]very contract, combination in the form of trust or otherwise, or conspiracy, in restraint of trade or commerce among the several States, or with foreign nations."

The complaint alleges that the ILECs conspired to restrain trade in two ways, each supposedly inflating charges for local telephone and high-speed Internet services. Plaintiffs say, first, that the ILECs "engaged in parallel conduct" in their respective service areas to inhibit the growth of upstart CLECs. Their actions allegedly included making unfair agreements with the CLECs for access to ILEC networks, providing inferior connections to the networks, overcharging, and billing in ways designed to sabotage the CLECs' relations with their own customers. According to the complaint, the ILECs' "compelling common motivatio[n]" to thwart the CLECs' competitive efforts naturally led them to form a conspiracy; "[h]ad any one [ILEC] not sought to prevent CLECs … from competing effectively…, the resulting greater competitive inroads into that [ILEC's] territory would have revealed the degree to which competitive entry by CLECs would have been successful in the other territories in the absence of such conduct."

Second, the complaint charges agreements by the ILECs to refrain from competing against one another. These are to be inferred from the ILECs' common failure "meaningfully [to] pursu[e]" "attractive business opportunit[ies]" in contiguous markets where they possessed "substantial competitive advantages," and from a statement of Richard Notebaert, chief executive officer (CEO) of the ILEC Qwest, that competing in the territory of another ILEC " 'might be a good way to turn a quick dollar but that doesn't make it right.' "

The complaint couches its ultimate allegations this way:

> "In the absence of any meaningful competition between the [ILECs] in one another's markets, and in light of the parallel course of conduct that each engaged in to prevent competition from CLECs within their respective local telephone and/or high speed internet services markets and the other facts and market circumstances alleged above, Plaintiffs allege upon information and belief that [the ILECs] have entered into a contract, combination or conspiracy to prevent competitive entry in their respective local telephone and/or high speed internet services markets and have agreed not to compete with one another and otherwise allocated customers and markets to one another."

The United States District Court for the Southern District of New York dismissed the complaint for failure to state a claim upon which relief can be granted. The District Court acknowledged that "plaintiffs may allege a conspiracy by citing instances of parallel business behavior that suggest an agreement," but emphasized that "while '[c]ircumstantial evidence of consciously parallel behavior may have made heavy inroads into the traditional judicial attitude toward conspiracy[, …] 'conscious parallelism' has not yet read conspiracy out of the Sherman Act entirely.' " 313 F.Supp.2d 174,

179 (2003). Thus, the District Court understood that allegations of parallel business conduct, taken alone, do not state a claim under § 1; plaintiffs must allege additional facts that "ten[d] to exclude independent self-interested conduct as an explanation for defendants' parallel behavior." 313 F.Supp.2d, at 179. The District Court found plaintiffs' allegations of parallel ILEC actions to discourage competition inadequate because "the behavior of each ILEC in resisting the incursion of CLECs is fully explained by the ILEC's own interests in defending its individual territory." As to the ILECs' supposed agreement against competing with each other, the District Court found that the complaint does not "alleg[e] facts ... suggesting that refraining from competing in other territories as CLECs was contrary to [the ILECs'] apparent economic interests, and consequently [does] not rais[e] an inference that [the ILECs'] actions were the result of a conspiracy."

The Court of Appeals for the Second Circuit reversed, holding that the District Court tested the complaint by the wrong standard. It held that "plus factors are not required to be pleaded to permit an antitrust claim based on parallel conduct to survive dismissal." 425 F.3d 99, 114 (2005) (emphasis in original). Although the Court of Appeals took the view that plaintiffs must plead facts that "include conspiracy among the realm of 'plausible' possibilities in order to survive a motion to dismiss," it then said that "to rule that allegations of parallel anticompetitive conduct fail to support a plausible conspiracy claim, a court would have to conclude that there is no set of facts that would permit a plaintiff to demonstrate that the particular parallelism asserted was the product of collusion rather than coincidence." *Ibid.*

We granted certiorari to address the proper standard for pleading an antitrust conspiracy through allegations of parallel conduct, 548 U.S. 93 (2006), and now reverse.

II
A

Because § 1 of the Sherman Act does not prohibit all unreasonable restraints of trade, but only restraints effected by a contract, combination, or conspiracy, the crucial question is whether the challenged anticompetitive conduct stems from independent decision or from an agreement, tacit or express. While a showing of parallel business behavior is admissible circumstantial evidence from which the fact finder may infer agreement, it falls short of conclusively establishing agreement or itself constituting a Sherman Act offense. Even "conscious parallelism," a common reaction of "firms in a concentrated market [that] recogniz[e] their shared economic interests and their interdependence with respect to price and output decisions" is "not in itself unlawful." *Brooke Group Ltd. v. Brown & Williamson Tobacco Corp.*, 509 U.S. 209, 227 (1993).

The inadequacy of showing parallel conduct or interdependence, without more, mirrors the ambiguity of the behavior: consistent with conspiracy, but just as much in line with a wide swath of rational and competitive business strategy unilaterally prompted by common perceptions of the market.... Accordingly, we have previously hedged against false inferences from identical behavior at a number of points in the trial sequence. An antitrust conspiracy plaintiff with evidence showing nothing beyond parallel conduct is not entitled to a directed verdict; proof of a § 1 conspiracy must include evidence tending to exclude the possibility of independent action; and at the summary judgment stage a § 1 plaintiff's offer of conspiracy evidence must tend to rule out the possibility that the defendants were acting independently.

B

This case presents the antecedent question of what a plaintiff must plead in order to state a claim under § 1 of the Sherman Act. Federal Rule of Civil Procedure 8(a)(2) requires only "a short and plain statement of the claim showing that the pleader is entitled to relief," in order to "give the defendant fair notice of what the ... claim is and the grounds upon which it rests," *Conley v. Gibson*, 355 U.S. 41, 47 (1957). While a complaint attacked by a Rule 12(b)(6) motion to dismiss does not need detailed factual allegations, a plaintiffs obligation to provide the "grounds" of his "entitle[ment] to relief" requires more than labels and conclusions, and a formulaic recitation of the elements of a cause of action will not do, see *Papasan v. Allain*, 478 U.S. 265, 286 (1986) (on a motion to dismiss, courts "are not bound to accept as true a legal conclusion couched as a factual allegation"). Factual allegations must be enough to raise a right to relief above the speculative level, on the assumption that all the allegations in the complaint are true (even if doubtful in fact).

In applying these general standards to a § 1 claim, we hold that stating such a claim requires a complaint with enough factual matter (taken as true) to suggest that an agreement was made. Asking for plausible grounds to infer an agreement does not impose a probability requirement at the pleading stage; it simply calls for enough facts to raise a reasonable expectation that discovery will reveal evidence of illegal agreement. And, of course, a well-pleaded complaint may proceed even if it strikes a savvy judge that actual proof of those facts is improbable, and that a recovery is very remote and unlikely. In identifying facts that are suggestive enough to render a § 1 conspiracy plausible, we have the benefit of the prior rulings and considered views of leading commentators, already quoted, that lawful parallel conduct fails to be-speak unlawful agreement. It makes sense to say, therefore, that an allegation of parallel conduct and a bare assertion of conspiracy will not suffice. Without more, parallel conduct does not suggest conspiracy, and a conclusory allegation of agreement at some unidentified point does not supply facts adequate to show illegality. Hence, when allegations of parallel conduct are set out in order to make a § 1 claim, they must be placed in a context that raises a suggestion of a preceding agreement, not merely parallel conduct that could just as well be independent action.

The need at the pleading stage for allegations plausibly suggesting (not merely consistent with) agreement reflects the threshold requirement of Rule 8(a)(2) that the "plain statement" possess enough heft to "show that the pleader is entitled to relief." A statement of parallel conduct, even conduct consciously undertaken, needs some setting suggesting the agreement necessary to make out a § 1 claim; without that further circumstance pointing toward a meeting of the minds, an account of a defendant's commercial efforts stays in neutral territory. An allegation of parallel conduct is thus much like a naked assertion of conspiracy in a § 1 complaint: it gets the complaint close to stating a claim, but without some further factual enhancement it stops short of the line between possibility and plausibility of entitlement to relief. *Cf. DM Research, Inc. v. College of Am. Pathologists*, 170 F.3d 53, 56 (C.A.1 1999) ("[T]erms like 'conspiracy,' or even 'agreement,' are border-line: they might well be sufficient in conjunction with a more specific allegation—for example, identifying a written agreement or even a basis for inferring a tacit agreement, ... but a court is not required to accept such terms as a sufficient basis for a complaint").

We alluded to the practical significance of the Rule 8 entitlement requirement in *Dura Pharmaceuticals, Inc. v. Broudo*, 544 U.S. 336 (2005), when we explained that something beyond the mere possibility of loss causation must be alleged, lest a plaintiff with "'a largely groundless claim'" be allowed to "'take up the time of a number of other people, with the right to do so representing an *in terrorem* increment of the settlement value.'" *Id.*, at 347. So, when the allegations in a complaint, however true, could not raise a claim of entitlement to relief, this basic deficiency should ... be exposed at the point of minimum expenditure of time and money by the parties and the court.

Thus, it is one thing to be cautious before dismissing an antitrust complaint in advance of discovery, but quite another to forget that proceeding to antitrust discovery can be expensive. As we indicated over 20 years ago in *Associated Gen. Contractors of Cal., Inc. v. Carpenters*, 459 U.S. 519, 528, n. 17 (1983), "a district court must retain the power to insist upon some specificity in pleading before allowing a potentially massive factual controversy to proceed." *See also Car Carriers, Inc. v. Ford Motor Co.*, 745 F.2d 1101, 1106 (C.A.7 1984) ("[T]he costs of modern federal antitrust litigation and the increasing caseload of the federal courts counsel against sending the parties into discovery when there is no reasonable likelihood that the plaintiffs can construct a claim from the events related in the complaint") ... That potential expense is obvious enough in the present

case: plaintiffs represent a putative class of at least 90 percent of all subscribers to local telephone or high-speed Internet service in the continental
United States, in an action against America's largest telecommunications
firms (with many thousands of employees generating reams and gigabytes
of business records) for unspecified (if any) instances of antitrust violations
that allegedly occurred over a period of seven years.

It is no answer to say that a claim just shy of a plausible entitlement to
relief can, if groundless, be weeded out early in the discovery process
through "careful case management," given the common lament that the
success of judicial supervision in checking discovery abuse has been on
the modest side. *See, e.g.,* Easterbrook, *Discovery as Abuse,* 69 B.U. L. Rev.
635, 638 (1989) ("Judges can do little about impositional discovery when
parties control the legal claims to be presented and conduct the discovery
themselves"). And it is self-evident that the problem of discovery abuse
cannot be solved by "careful scrutiny of evidence at the summary judgment
stage," much less "lucid instructions to juries"; the threat of discovery expense will push cost-conscious defendants to settle even anemic cases before reaching those proceedings. Probably, then, it is only by taking care
to require allegations that reach the level suggesting conspiracy that we
can hope to avoid the potentially enormous expense of discovery in cases
with no reasonably founded hope that the [discovery] process will reveal
relevant evidence to support a § 1 claim.

Plaintiffs do not, of course, dispute the requirement of plausibility and
the need for something more than merely parallel behavior..., and their
main argument against the plausibility standard at the pleading stage is
its ostensible conflict with an early statement of ours construing Rule 8.
Justice Black's opinion for the Court in *Conley v. Gibson* spoke not only
of the need for fair notice of the grounds for entitlement to relief but of
"the accepted rule that a complaint should not be dismissed for failure to
state a claim unless it appears beyond doubt that the plaintiff can prove
no set of facts in support of his claim which would entitle him to relief."
355 U.S., at 45–46. This "no set of facts" language can be read in isolation
as saying that any statement revealing the theory of the claim will suffice
unless its factual impossibility may be shown from the face of the pleadings;
and the Court of Appeals appears to have read *Conley* in some such way
when formulating its understanding of the proper pleading standard.

On such a focused and literal reading of *Conley*'s "no set of facts," a
wholly conclusory statement of claim would survive a motion to dismiss
whenever the pleadings left open the possibility that a plaintiff might later
establish some "set of [undisclosed] facts" to support recovery. So here,
the Court of Appeals specifically found the prospect of unearthing direct
evidence of conspiracy sufficient to preclude dismissal, even though the
complaint does not set forth a single fact in a context that suggests an

agreement. It seems fair to say that this approach to pleading would dispense with any showing of a "'reasonably founded hope'" that a plaintiff would be able to make a case; Mr. Micawber's optimism would be enough.

Seeing this, a good many judges and commentators have balked at taking the literal terms of the *Conley* passage as a pleading standard. *See, e.g., Car Carriers*, 745 F.2d, at 1106 ("*Conley* has never been interpreted literally") and, "[i]n practice, a complaint ... must contain either direct or inferential allegations respecting all the material elements necessary to sustain recovery under some viable legal theory" (internal quotation marks omitted; emphasis and omission in original); *Ascon Properties, Inc. v. Mobil Oil Co.*, 866 F.2d 1149, 1155 (C.A.9 1989) (tension between *Conley*'s "no set of facts" language and its acknowledgment that a plaintiff must provide the "grounds" on which his claim rests); *O'Brien v. DiGrazia*, 544 F.2d 543, 546, n. 3 (C.A.1 1976) ("[W]hen a plaintiff ... supplies facts to support his claim, we do not think that *Conley* imposes a duty on the courts to conjure up unpleaded facts that might turn a frivolous claim of unconstitutional ... action into a substantial one"); *McGregor v. Industrial Excess Landfill, Inc.*, 856 F.2d 39, 42–43 (C.A.6 1988) (quoting *O'Brien*'s analysis); Hazard, *From Whom No Secrets Are Hid*, 76 Tex. L. Rev. 1665, 1685 (1998) (describing *Conley* as having "turned Rule 8 on its head"); Marcus, *The Revival of Fact Pleading Under the Federal Rules of Civil Procedure*, 86 Colum. L. Rev. 433, 463–465 (1986) (noting tension between *Conley* and subsequent understandings of Rule 8).

We could go on, but there is no need to pile up further citations to show that *Conley*'s "no set of facts" language has been questioned, criticized, and explained away long enough. To be fair to the *Conley* Court, the passage should be understood in light of the opinion's preceding summary of the complaint's concrete allegations, which the Court quite reasonably understood as amply stating a claim for relief. But the passage so often quoted fails to mention this understanding on the part of the Court, and after puzzling the profession for 50 years, this famous observation has earned its retirement. The phrase is best forgotten as an incomplete, negative gloss on an accepted pleading standard: once a claim has been stated adequately, it may be supported by showing any set of facts consistent with the allegations in the complaint. *Conley*, then, described the breadth of opportunity to prove what an adequate complaint claims, not the minimum standard of adequate pleading to govern a complaint's survival.

III

When we look for plausibility in this complaint, we agree with the District Court that plaintiffs' claim of conspiracy in restraint of trade comes up short. To begin with, the complaint leaves no doubt that plaintiffs rest their § 1 claim on descriptions of parallel conduct and not on any independent allegation of actual agreement among the ILECs. Although in form a few stray statements speak directly of agreement, on fair reading these are merely legal conclusions resting on the prior allegations. Thus, the complaint first takes account of the alleged "absence of any meaningful competition between [the ILECs] in one another's markets," "the parallel course of conduct that each [ILEC] engaged in to prevent competition from CLECs," "and the other facts and market circumstances alleged [earlier]"; "in light of" these, the complaint concludes "that [the ILECs] have entered into a contract, combination or conspiracy to prevent competitive entry into their ... markets and have agreed not to compete with one another." The nub of the complaint, then, is the ILECs' parallel behavior, consisting of steps to keep the CLECs out and manifest disinterest in becoming CLECs themselves, and its sufficiency turns on the suggestions raised by this conduct when viewed in light of common economic experience.

We think that nothing contained in the complaint invests either the action or inaction alleged with a plausible suggestion of conspiracy. As to the ILECs' supposed agreement to disobey the 1996 Act and thwart the CLECs' attempts to compete, we agree with the District Court that nothing in the complaint intimates that the resistance to the upstarts was anything more than the natural, unilateral reaction of each ILEC intent on keeping its regional dominance. The 1996 Act did more than just subject the ILECs to competition; it obliged them to subsidize their competitors with their own equipment at wholesale rates. The economic incentive to resist was powerful, but resisting competition is routine market conduct, and even if the ILECs flouted the 1996 Act in all the ways the plaintiffs allege, there is no reason to infer that the companies had agreed among themselves to do what was only natural anyway; so natural, in fact, that if alleging parallel decisions to resist competition were enough to imply an antitrust conspiracy, pleading a § 1 violation against almost any group of competing businesses would be a sure thing.

The complaint makes its closest pass at a predicate for conspiracy with the claim that collusion was necessary because success by even one CLEC in an ILEC's territory "would have revealed the degree to which competitive entry by CLECs would have been successful in the other territories." But, its logic aside, this general premise still fails to answer the point that there was just no need for joint encouragement to resist the 1996 Act; as the District Court said, "each ILEC has reason to want to avoid dealing with CLECs" and "each ILEC would attempt to keep CLECs out, regardless of the actions of the other ILECs." 313 F.Supp.2d, at 184; *cf. Kramer v. Pollock-Krasner Foundation*, 890 F. Supp. 250, 256 (S.D.N.Y.1995) (while the plaintiff "may believe the defendants conspired..., the defendants' allegedly conspiratorial actions could equally have been prompted by lawful, independent goals which do not constitute a conspiracy").

Plaintiffs' second conspiracy theory rests on the competitive reticence among the ILECs themselves in the wake of the 1996 Act, which was supposedly passed in the "'hop[e] that the large incumbent local monopoly companies ... might attack their neighbors' service areas, as they are the best situated to do so.'" Contrary to hope, the ILECs declined "'to enter each other's service territories in any significant way,'" and the local telephone and high speed Internet market remains highly compartmentalized geographically, with minimal competition. Based on this state of affairs, and perceiving the ILECs to be blessed with "especially attractive business opportunities" in surrounding markets dominated by other ILECs, the plaintiffs assert that the ILECs' parallel conduct was "strongly suggestive of conspiracy."

But it was not suggestive of conspiracy, not if history teaches anything. In a traditionally unregulated industry with low barriers to entry, sparse competition among large firms dominating separate geographical segments of the market could very well signify illegal agreement, but here we have an obvious alternative explanation. In the decade preceding the 1996 Act and well before that, monopoly was the norm in telecommunications, not the exception. The ILECs were born in that world, doubtless liked the world the way it was, and surely knew the adage about him who lives by the sword. Hence, a natural explanation for the noncompetition alleged is that the former Government-sanctioned monopolists were sitting tight, expecting their neighbors to do the same thing.

In fact, the complaint itself gives reasons to believe that the ILECs would see their best interests in keeping to their old turf. Although the complaint says generally that the ILECs passed up "especially attractive business opportunit[ies]" by declining to compete as CLECs against other ILECs, it does not allege that competition as CLECs was potentially any more lucrative than other opportunities being pursued by the ILECs during the same period, and the complaint is replete with indications that any CLEC faced nearly insurmountable barriers to profitability owing to the ILECs' flagrant resistance to the network sharing requirements of the 1996 Act. Not only that, but even without a monopolistic tradition and the peculiar difficulty of mandating shared networks, "[f]irms do not expand without limit and none of them enters every market that an outside observer might regard as profitable, or even a small portion of such markets." AREEDA & HOVENKAMP ¶ 307d, at 155 (Supp.2006) (commenting on the case at bar). The upshot is that Congress may have expected some ILECs to become CLECs in the legacy territories of other ILECs, but the disappointment does not make conspiracy plausible. We agree with the District Court's assessment that antitrust conspiracy was not suggested by the facts adduced under either theory of the complaint, which thus fails to state a valid § 1 claim.

Plaintiffs say that our analysis runs counter to *Swierkiewicz v. Sorema N. A.*, 534 U.S. 506, 508 (2002), which held that "a complaint in an employment discrimination lawsuit [need] not contain specific facts establishing a *prima facie* case of discrimination under the framework set forth in *McDonnell Douglas Corp. v. Green*, 411 U.S. 792 (1973)." They argue that just as the *prima facie* case is a "flexible evidentiary standard" that "should not be transposed into a rigid pleading standard for discrimination cases," "transpos[ing] 'plus factor' summary judgment analysis woodenly into a rigid Rule 12(b)(6) pleading standard ... would be unwise." As the District Court correctly understood, however, "*Swierkiewicz* did not change the law of pleading, but simply re-emphasized ... that the Second Circuit's use of a heightened pleading standard for Title VII cases was contrary to the Federal Rules' structure of liberal pleading requirements." 313 F.Supp.2d, at 181 (citation and footnote omitted). Even though Swierkiewicz's pleadings "detailed the events leading to his termination, provided relevant dates, and included the ages and nationalities of at least some of the relevant persons involved with his termination," the Court of Appeals dismissed his complaint for failing to allege certain additional facts that Swierkiewicz would need at the trial stage to support his claim in the absence of direct evidence of discrimination. We reversed on the ground that the Court of Appeals had impermissibly applied what amounted to a heightened pleading requirement by insisting that Swierkiewicz allege "specific facts" beyond those necessary to state his claim and the grounds showing entitlement to relief.

Here, in contrast, we do not require heightened fact pleading of specifics, but only enough facts to state a claim to relief that is plausible on its face. Because the plaintiffs here have not nudged their claims across the line from conceivable to plausible, their complaint must be dismissed.

* * *

The judgment of the Court of Appeals for the Second Circuit is reversed, and the cause is remanded for further proceedings consistent with this opinion.

It is so ordered.

Justice Stevens dissented (opinion omitted).

Exercise 7-3. Understanding *Twombly*

1. After reading and discussing the excerpts from *Twombly*, how would you instruct a new attorney in your office to conduct an analysis of whether a complaint is sufficient to meet the requirements of Rule 8(a)? In other words, what is the "test" for the validity of a complaint? It may help to flowchart the analysis.

2. In applying *Twombly*, how is a court supposed to determine whether a certain set of non-conclusory allegations make out a "plausible claim for relief"? What makes a set of allegations "plausible"?

Exercise 7-4. From *Twombly* to *Iqbal*

After the Court decided *Twombly*, observers of federal practice were understandably confused. Many practitioners and academic commentators attempted to reconcile the decision with the half-century of jurisprudence regarding federal pleading that had preceded it, and some (perhaps most) were inclined to believe (or at least to hope) that the decision was limited to highly complex cases, such as the nationwide antitrust class action in *Twombly* itself. This position seemed quite sensible at the time, since the discovery costs of such complex cases (one of the main concerns stated in Justice Souter's majority opinion as a basis for rejecting *Conley*) tend to be much higher, and especially since, just two weeks after *Twombly* was decided, the Court decided *Erickson v. Pardus*, 551 U.S. 89 (2007), reversing a trial court's dismissal of a *pro se* prisoner's complaint against his jailers for failing to provide him with proper medication. Importantly, the alleged flaw in the prisoner's complaint in *Erickson* was similar to that in *Twombly*—the complaint did not state non-conclusory factual allegations connecting the jailers' conduct to the plaintiff's injury. But the Court rejected this reading, even going so far as to chastise the lower courts for requiring more than simple "notice" of the claim, especially from a *pro se* plaintiff.

Reading *Erickson*, and seeing that *Twombly* did not purport to overrule *Swierkiewicz*, many civil procedure observers therefore concluded that *Twombly* was a one-off decision, which might be relied on in other highly complex cases, but which did not undo the established, lenient rules of federal pleading. And then along came *Iqbal*. As you read *Iqbal*, note that it is a 5–4 decision, and that the author of *Twombly* is the author of a dissent to *Iqbal*. Are the cases meaningfully different, such that they should have come out differently on the pleading question?

Exercise 7-5. Understanding *Iqbal*

After reading and discussing the excerpt from *Iqbal*, would you alter your instructions to the new attorney in your office? In other words, does the "test" for sufficiency of a complaint change at all? If not, then why the full opinion in the Supreme Court?

Ashcroft v. Iqbal

556 U.S. 662 (2009)

Justice Kennedy delivered the opinion of the Court.

Respondent Javaid Iqbal is a citizen of Pakistan and a Muslim. In the wake of the September 11, 2001, terrorist attacks he was arrested in the United States on criminal charges and detained by federal officials. Respondent claims he was deprived of various constitutional protections while in federal custody. To redress the alleged deprivations, respondent filed a complaint against numerous federal officials, including John Ashcroft, the former Attorney General of the United States, and Robert Mueller, the Director of the Federal Bureau of Investigation (FBI). Ashcroft and Mueller are the petitioners in the case now before us. As to these two petitioners, the complaint alleges that they adopted an unconstitutional policy that subjected respondent to harsh conditions of confinement on account of his race, religion, or national origin.

In the District Court petitioners raised the defense of qualified immunity* and moved to dismiss the suit, contending the complaint was not sufficient to state a claim against them. The District Court denied the motion to dismiss, concluding the complaint was sufficient to state a claim despite petitioners' official status at the times in question. Petitioners brought an interlocutory appeal in the Court of Appeals for the Second Circuit. The court ... affirmed the District Court's decision.

Respondent's account of his prison ordeal could, if proved, demonstrate unconstitutional misconduct by some governmental actors. But the allegations and pleadings with respect to these actors are not before us here. This case instead turns on a narrower question: Did respondent, as the plaintiff in the District Court, plead factual matter that, if taken as true, states a claim that petitioners deprived him of his clearly established constitutional rights. We hold respondent's pleadings are insufficient.

I

Following the 2001 attacks, the FBI and other entities within the Department of Justice began an investigation of vast reach to identify the assailants and prevent them from attacking anew. The FBI dedicated more than 4,000 special agents and 3,000 support personnel to the endeavor. By September 18 "the FBI had received more than 96,000 tips or potential leads from the public." Dept. of Justice, Office of Inspector General, The

---

* Ed. Note. The doctrine of qualified immunity protects federal and state officials when they are sued in their individual capacities (as opposed to their official capacities) for damages resulting from their own constitutional violations. It is a presumptive immunity from suit for damages, which a plaintiff can overcome by showing that the defendant violated a clearly established rule of constitutional law of which a reasonable official in the defendant's position would have been aware.

September 11 Detainees: A Review of the Treatment of Aliens Held on Immigration Charges in Connection with the Investigation of the September 11 Attacks 1, 11–12 (Apr. 2003) (hereinafter OIG Report).

In the ensuing months the FBI questioned more than 1,000 people with suspected links to the attacks in particular or to terrorism in general. Of those individuals, some 762 were held on immigration charges; and a 184-member subset of that group was deemed to be "of 'high interest'" to the investigation. The high-interest detainees were held under restrictive conditions designed to prevent them from communicating with the general prison population or the outside world.

Respondent was one of the detainees. According to his complaint, in November 2001 agents of the FBI and Immigration and Naturalization Service arrested him on charges of fraud in relation to identification documents and conspiracy to defraud the United States. Pending trial for those crimes, respondent was housed at the Metropolitan Detention Center (MDC) in Brooklyn, New York. Respondent was designated a person "of high interest" to the September 11 investigation and in January 2002 was placed in a section of the MDC known as the Administrative Maximum Special Housing Unit (ADMAX SHU). As the facility's name indicates, the ADMAX SHU incorporates the maximum security conditions allowable under Federal Bureau of Prison regulations. ADMAX SHU detainees were kept in lockdown 23 hours a day, spending the remaining hour outside their cells in handcuffs and leg irons accompanied by a four-officer escort.

Respondent pleaded guilty to the criminal charges, served a term of imprisonment, and was removed to his native Pakistan. He then filed a *Bivens* action* in the United States District Court for the Eastern District of New York against 34 current and former federal officials and 19 "John Doe" federal corrections officers. *See Bivens v. Six Unknown Fed. Narcotics Agents*, 403 U.S. 388 (1971). The defendants range from the correctional officers who had day-to-day contact with respondent during the term of his confinement, to the wardens of the MDC facility, all the way to petitioners — officials who were at the highest level of the federal law enforcement hierarchy.

The 21-cause-of-action complaint does not challenge respondent's arrest or his confinement in the MDC's general prison population. Rather, it concentrates on his treatment while confined to the ADMAX SHU. The

---

* Ed. Note. A *Bivens* action is a suit under an implied right of action recognized in that case to enforce one's federal constitutional rights against a federal official or officials, whether acting in their official or individual capacity. The analogous action one would bring to enforce federal constitutional rights against *state* officials would be the express cause of action under 42 U.S.C. §1983. Qualified immunity doctrine applies identically to both causes of action.

complaint sets forth various claims against defendants who are not before us. For instance, the complaint alleges that respondent's jailors "kicked him in the stomach, punched him in the face, and dragged him across" his cell without justification; subjected him to serial strip and body-cavity searches when he posed no safety risk to himself or others; and refused to let him and other Muslims pray because there would be "[n]o prayers for terrorists."

The allegations against petitioners are the only ones relevant here. The complaint contends that petitioners designated respondent a person of high interest on account of his race, religion, or national origin, in contravention of the First and Fifth Amendments to the Constitution. The complaint alleges that "the [FBI], under the direction of Defendant Mueller, arrested and detained thousands of Arab Muslim men ... as part of its investigation of the events of September 11." It further alleges that "[t]he policy of holding post-September-11th detainees in highly restrictive conditions of confinement until they were 'cleared' by the FBI was approved by Defendants Ashcroft and Mueller in discussions in the weeks after September 11, 2001." Lastly, the complaint posits that petitioners "each knew of, condoned, and willfully and maliciously agreed to subject" respondent to harsh conditions of confinement "as a matter of policy, solely on account of [his] religion, race, and/or national origin and for no legitimate penological interest." The pleading names Ashcroft as the "principal architect" of the policy, and identifies Mueller as "instrumental in [its] adoption, promulgation, and implementation."

Petitioners moved to dismiss the complaint for failure to state sufficient allegations to show their own involvement in clearly established unconstitutional conduct. The District Court denied their motion. Accepting all of the allegations in respondent's complaint as true, the court held that "it cannot be said that there [is] no set of facts on which [respondent] would be entitled to relief as against" petitioners. *Id.*, at 136a–137a (relying on *Conley v. Gibson*, 355 U.S. 41 (1957)). Invoking the collateral-order doctrine,* petitioners filed an interlocutory appeal in the United States Court of Appeals for the Second Circuit. While that appeal was pending, this Court decided *Bell Atlantic Corp. v. Twombly*, 550 U.S. 544 (2007), which discussed the standard for evaluating whether a complaint is sufficient to survive a motion to dismiss.

The Court of Appeals considered *Twombly*'s applicability to this case. Acknowledging that *Twombly* retired the *Conley* no-set-of-facts test relied upon by the District Court, the Court of Appeals' opinion discussed at

---

* Ed. Note. The collateral order doctrine is a judicially crafted exception to the "final judgment rule," 28 U.S.C. § 1291, which typically must be satisfied before an appeal can be taken. Chapter 12 discusses these rules in detail.

length how to apply this Court's "standard for assessing the adequacy of pleadings." 490 F.3d, at 155. It concluded that *Twombly* called for a "flexible 'plausibility standard,' which obliges a pleader to amplify a claim with some factual allegations in those contexts where such amplification is needed to render the claim plausible." The court found that petitioners' appeal did not present one of "those contexts" requiring amplification. As a consequence, it held respondent's pleading adequate to allege petitioners' personal involvement in discriminatory decisions which, if true, violated clearly established constitutional law.

Judge Cabranes concurred. He agreed that the majority's "discussion of the relevant pleading standards reflect[ed] the uneasy compromise ... between a qualified immunity privilege rooted in the need to preserve the effectiveness of government as contemplated by our constitutional structure and the pleading requirements of Rule 8(a) of the Federal Rules of Civil Procedure." Judge Cabranes nonetheless expressed concern at the prospect of subjecting high-ranking Government officials — entitled to assert the defense of qualified immunity and charged with responding to "a national and international security emergency unprecedented in the history of the American Republic" — to the burdens of discovery on the basis of a complaint as nonspecific as respondent's. Reluctant to vindicate that concern as a member of the Court of Appeals, Judge Cabranes urged this Court to address the appropriate pleading standard "at the earliest opportunity." We granted certiorari, 554 U.S. ___ (2008), and now reverse.

II

* * *

We proceed to consider the merits of petitioners' appeal.

III

In *Twombly*, the Court found it necessary first to discuss the antitrust principles implicated by the complaint. Here too we begin by taking note of the elements a plaintiff must plead to state a claim of unconstitutional discrimination against officials entitled to assert the defense of qualified immunity.

In *Bivens* — proceeding on the theory that a right suggests a remedy — this Court "recognized for the first time an implied private action for damages against federal officers alleged to have violated a citizen's constitutional rights." *Correctional Services Corp. v. Malesko*, 534 U.S. 61, 66 (2001). Because implied causes of action are disfavored, the Court has been reluctant to extend *Bivens* liability to any new context or new category of defendants. That reluctance might well have disposed of respondent's First Amendment claim of religious discrimination. For while we have allowed a *Bivens* action to redress a violation of the equal protection component of the Due Process Clause of the Fifth Amendment, we have not found an implied damages remedy under the Free Exercise Clause. Indeed, we have declined to extend *Bivens* to a claim sounding in the First Amendment. *Bush v. Lucas*, 462 U.S. 367 (1983). Petitioners do not press this argument, however, so we assume, without deciding, that respondent's First Amendment claim is actionable under *Bivens*.

In the limited settings where *Bivens* does apply, the implied cause of action is the federal analog to suits brought against state officials under Rev. Stat. § 1979, 42 U.S.C. § 1983. Based on the rules our precedents establish, respondent correctly concedes that Government officials may not be held liable for the unconstitutional conduct of their subordinates under a theory of respondeat superior. *See Monell v. New York City Dept. of Social Servs.*, 436 U.S. 658, 691 (1978) (finding no vicarious liability for a municipal "person" under 42 U.S.C. § 1983). Because vicarious liability is inapplicable to *Bivens* and § 1983 suits, a plaintiff must plead that each Government official defendant, through the official's own individual actions, has violated the Constitution.

The factors necessary to establish a *Bivens* violation will vary with the constitutional provision at issue. Where the claim is invidious discrimination in contravention of the First and Fifth Amendments, our decisions make clear that the plaintiff must plead and prove that the defendant acted with discriminatory purpose. *Washington v. Davis*, 426 U.S. 229, 240 (1976) (Fifth Amendment). Under extant precedent purposeful discrimination requires more than "intent as volition or intent as awareness of consequences." *Personnel Administrator of Mass. v. Feeney*, 442 U.S. 256, 279 (1979). It instead involves a decisionmaker's undertaking a course of action " 'because of,' not merely 'in spite of,' [the action's] adverse effects upon an identifiable group." *Ibid.* It follows that, to state a claim based on a violation of a clearly established right, respondent must plead sufficient factual matter to show that petitioners adopted and implemented the detention policies at issue not for a neutral, investigative reason but for the purpose of discriminating on account of race, religion, or national origin.

Respondent disagrees. He argues that, under a theory of "supervisory liability," petitioners can be liable for "knowledge and acquiescence in their subordinates' use of discriminatory criteria to make classification decisions among detainees." That is to say, respondent believes a supervisor's mere knowledge of his subordinate's discriminatory purpose amounts to the supervisor's violating the Constitution. We reject this argument. Respondent's conception of "supervisory liability" is inconsistent with his accurate stipulation that petitioners may not be held accountable for the misdeeds of their agents. In a § 1983 suit or a *Bivens* action — where masters do not answer for the torts of their servants — the term "supervisory liability" is a misnomer. Absent vicarious liability, each Gov-

ernment official, his or her title notwithstanding, is only liable for his or
her own misconduct. In the context of determining whether there is a
violation of clearly established right to overcome qualified immunity,
purpose rather than knowledge is required to impose *Bivens* liability on
the subordinate for unconstitutional discrimination; the same holds true
for an official charged with violations arising from his or her superintendent responsibilities.

IV

A

We turn to respondent's complaint. Under Federal Rule of Civil Procedure 8(a)(2), a pleading must contain a "short and plain statement of
the claim showing that the pleader is entitled to relief." As the Court held
in *Twombly*, 550 U.S. 544, the pleading standard Rule 8 announces does
not require "detailed factual allegations," but it demands more than an
unadorned, the-defendant-unlawfully-harmed-me accusation. A pleading
that offers labels and conclusions or a formulaic recitation of the elements
of a cause of action will not do. Nor does a complaint suffice if it tenders
naked assertions devoid of further factual enhancement.

To survive a motion to dismiss, a complaint must contain sufficient
factual matter, accepted as true, to "state a claim to relief that is plausible
on its face." *Id.*, at 570. A claim has facial plausibility when the plaintiff
pleads factual content that allows the court to draw the reasonable inference
that the defendant is liable for the misconduct alleged. The plausibility
standard is not akin to a "probability requirement," but it asks for more
than a sheer possibility that a defendant has acted unlawfully. Where a
complaint pleads facts that are "merely consistent with" a defendant's liability, it "stops short of the line between possibility and plausibility of
'entitlement to relief.'"

Two working principles underlie our decision in *Twombly*. First, the
tenet that a court must accept as true all of the allegations contained in a
complaint is inapplicable to legal conclusions. Threadbare recitals of the
elements of a cause of action, supported by mere conclusory statements,
do not suffice. Rule 8 marks a notable and generous departure from the
hyper-technical, code-pleading regime of a prior era, but it does not
unlock the doors of discovery for a plaintiff armed with nothing more
than conclusions. Second, only a complaint that states a plausible claim
for relief survives a motion to dismiss. Determining whether a complaint
states a plausible claim for relief will, as the Court of Appeals observed,
be a context-specific task that requires the reviewing court to draw on its
judicial experience and common sense. But where the well-pleaded facts
do not permit the court to infer more than the mere possibility of misconduct, the complaint has alleged—but it has not "show[n]"—"that
the pleader is entitled to relief." Fed. Rule Civ. Proc. 8(a)(2).

In keeping with these principles, a court considering a motion to dismiss can choose to begin by identifying pleadings that, because they are no more than conclusions, are not entitled to the assumption of truth. While legal conclusions can provide the framework of a complaint, they must be supported by factual allegations. When there are well-pleaded factual allegations, a court should assume their veracity and then determine whether they plausibly give rise to an entitlement to relief.

Our decision in *Twombly* illustrates the two-pronged approach. There, we considered the sufficiency of a complaint alleging that incumbent telecommunications providers had entered an agreement not to compete and to forestall competitive entry, in violation of the Sherman Act, 15 U.S.C. § 1. Recognizing that § 1 enjoins only anticompetitive conduct "effected by a contract, combination, or conspiracy," the plaintiffs in *Twombly* flatly pleaded that the defendants "ha[d] entered into a contract, combination or conspiracy to prevent competitive entry ... and ha[d] agreed not to compete with one another." The complaint also alleged that the defendants' "parallel course of conduct ... to prevent competition" and inflate prices was indicative of the unlawful agreement alleged.

The Court held the plaintiffs' complaint deficient under Rule 8. In doing so it first noted that the plaintiffs' assertion of an unlawful agreement was a " 'legal conclusion' " and, as such, was not entitled to the assumption of truth. Had the Court simply credited the allegation of a conspiracy, the plaintiffs would have stated a claim for relief and been entitled to proceed perforce. The Court next addressed the "nub" of the plaintiffs' complaint—the well-pleaded, nonconclusory factual allegation of parallel behavior—to determine whether it gave rise to a "plausible suggestion of conspiracy." Acknowledging that parallel conduct was consistent with an unlawful agreement, the Court nevertheless concluded that it did not plausibly suggest an illicit accord because it was not only compatible with, but indeed was more likely explained by, lawful, unchoreographed free-market behavior. Because the well-pleaded fact of parallel conduct, accepted as true, did not plausibly suggest an unlawful agreement, the Court held the plaintiffs' complaint must be dismissed.

B

Under *Twombly*'s construction of Rule 8, we conclude that respondent's complaint has not "nudged [his] claims" of invidious discrimination "across the line from conceivable to plausible."

We begin our analysis by identifying the allegations in the complaint that are not entitled to the assumption of truth. Respondent pleads that petitioners "knew of, condoned, and willfully and maliciously agreed to subject [him]" to harsh conditions of confinement "as a matter of policy, solely on account of [his] religion, race, and/or national origin and for no legitimate penological interest." The complaint alleges that Ashcroft was the "principal architect" of this invidious policy, and that Mueller was "instrumental" in adopting and executing it. These bare assertions, much like the pleading of conspiracy in *Twombly*, amount to nothing more than a "formulaic recitation of the elements" of a constitutional discrimination claim, namely, that petitioners adopted a policy "'because of,' not merely 'in spite of,' its adverse effects upon an identifiable group." As such, the allegations are conclusory and not entitled to be assumed true. To be clear, we do not reject these bald allegations on the ground that they are unrealistic or nonsensical. We do not so characterize them any more than the Court in *Twombly* rejected the plaintiffs' express allegation of a "'contract, combination or conspiracy to prevent competitive entry,'" because it thought that claim too chimerical to be maintained. It is the conclusory nature of respondent's allegations, rather than their extravagantly fanciful nature, that disentitles them to the presumption of truth.

We next consider the factual allegations in respondent's complaint to determine if they plausibly suggest an entitlement to relief. The complaint alleges that "the [FBI], under the direction of Defendant Mueller, arrested and detained thousands of Arab Muslim men ... as part of its investigation of the events of September 11." It further claims that "[t]he policy of holding post-September-11th detainees in highly restrictive conditions of confinement until they were 'cleared' by the FBI was approved by Defendants Ashcroft and Mueller in discussions in the weeks after September 11, 2001." Taken as true, these allegations are consistent with petitioners' purposefully designating detainees "of high interest" because of their race, religion, or national origin. But given more likely explanations, they do not plausibly establish this purpose.

The September 11 attacks were perpetrated by 19 Arab Muslim hijackers who counted themselves members in good standing of al Qaeda, an Islamic fundamentalist group. Al Qaeda was headed by another Arab Muslim— Osama bin Laden—and composed in large part of his Arab Muslim disciples. It should come as no surprise that a legitimate policy directing law enforcement to arrest and detain individuals because of their suspected link to the attacks would produce a disparate, incidental impact on Arab Muslims, even though the purpose of the policy was to target neither Arabs nor Muslims. On the facts respondent alleges the arrests Mueller oversaw were likely lawful and justified by his nondiscriminatory intent to detain aliens who were illegally present in the United States and who had potential connections to those who committed terrorist acts. As between that "obvious alternative explanation" for the arrests, and the purposeful, invidious discrimination respondent asks us to infer, discrimination is not a plausible conclusion.

But even if the complaint's well-pleaded facts give rise to a plausible inference that respondent's arrest was the result of unconstitutional discrimination, that inference alone would not entitle respondent to relief. It is important to recall that respondent's complaint challenges neither the constitutionality of his arrest nor his initial detention in the MDC. Respondent's constitutional claims against petitioners rest solely on their ostensible "policy of holding post-September-11th detainees" in the ADMAX SHU once they were categorized as "of high interest." To prevail on that theory, the complaint must contain facts plausibly showing that petitioners purposefully adopted a policy of classifying post-September-11 detainees as "of high interest" because of their race, religion, or national origin.

This the complaint fails to do. Though respondent alleges that various other defendants, who are not before us, may have labeled him a person of "of high interest" for impermissible reasons, his only factual allegation against petitioners accuses them of adopting a policy approving "restrictive conditions of confinement" for post-September-11 detainees until they were "'cleared' by the FBI." Accepting the truth of that allegation, the complaint does not show, or even intimate, that petitioners purposefully housed detainees in the ADMAX SHU due to their race, religion, or national origin. All it plausibly suggests is that the Nation's top law enforcement officers, in the aftermath of a devastating terrorist attack, sought to keep suspected terrorists in the most secure conditions available until the suspects could be cleared of terrorist activity. Respondent does not argue, nor can he, that such a motive would violate petitioners' constitutional obligations. He would need to allege more by way of factual content to "nudg[e]" his claim of purposeful discrimination "across the line from conceivable to plausible."

To be sure, respondent can attempt to draw certain contrasts between the pleadings the Court considered in *Twombly* and the pleadings at issue here. In *Twombly*, the complaint alleged general wrongdoing that extended over a period of years, whereas here the complaint alleges discrete wrongs — for instance, beatings — by lower level Government actors. The allegations here, if true, and if condoned by petitioners, could be the basis for some inference of wrongful intent on petitioners' part. Despite these distinctions, respondent's pleadings do not suffice to state a claim. Unlike in *Twombly*, where the doctrine of respondeat superior could bind the corporate defendant, here, as we have noted, petitioners cannot be held liable unless they themselves acted on account of a constitutionally protected characteristic. Yet respondent's complaint does not contain any factual allegation sufficient to plausibly suggest petitioners' discriminatory state of mind. His pleadings thus do not meet the standard necessary to comply with Rule 8.

It is important to note, however, that we express no opinion concerning the sufficiency of respondent's complaint against the defendants who are not before us. Respondent's account of his prison ordeal alleges serious official misconduct that we need not address here. Our decision is limited to the determination that respondent's complaint does not entitle him to relief from petitioners.

C

Respondent offers three arguments that bear on our disposition of his case, but none is persuasive.

1

Respondent first says that our decision in *Twombly* should be limited to pleadings made in the context of an antitrust dispute. This argument is not supported by *Twombly* and is incompatible with the Federal Rules of Civil Procedure. Though *Twombly* determined the sufficiency of a complaint sounding in antitrust, the decision was based on our interpretation and application of Rule 8. That Rule in turn governs the pleading standard "in all civil actions and proceedings in the United States district courts." Fed. Rule Civ. Proc. 1. Our decision in *Twombly* expounded the pleading standard for "all civil actions," and it applies to antitrust and discrimination suits alike.

2

Respondent next implies that our construction of Rule 8 should be tempered where, as here, the Court of Appeals has "instructed the district court to cabin discovery in such a way as to preserve" petitioners' defense of qualified immunity "as much as possible in anticipation of a summary judgment motion." We have held, however, that the question presented by a motion to dismiss a complaint for insufficient pleadings does not turn on the controls placed upon the discovery process. *Twombly, supra,* at 559 ("It is no answer to say that a claim just shy of a plausible entitlement to relief can, if groundless, be weeded out early in the discovery process through careful case management given the common lament that the success of judicial supervision in checking discovery abuse has been on the modest side" (internal quotation marks and citation omitted)).

Our rejection of the careful-case-management approach is especially important in suits where Government-official defendants are entitled to assert the defense of qualified immunity. The basic thrust of the qualified-immunity doctrine is to free officials from the concerns of litigation, including "avoidance of disruptive discovery." *Siegert v. Gilley,* 500 U.S. 226, 236 (1991) (Kennedy, J., concurring in judgment). There are serious and legitimate reasons for this. If a Government official is to devote time to his or her duties, and to the formulation of sound and responsible policies, it is counterproductive to require the substantial diversion that is attendant to participating in litigation and making informed decisions as to how it should proceed. Litigation, though necessary to ensure that officials comply with the law, exacts heavy costs in terms of efficiency and expenditure of valuable time and resources that might otherwise be directed to the proper execution of the work of the Government. The costs of diversion are only magnified when Government officials are charged with responding to, as Judge Cabranes aptly put it, "a national and international security emergency unprecedented in the history of the American Republic."

It is no answer to these concerns to say that discovery for petitioners can be deferred while pretrial proceedings continue for other defendants. It is quite likely that, when discovery as to the other parties proceeds, it would prove necessary for petitioners and their counsel to participate in the process to ensure the case does not develop in a misleading or slanted way that causes prejudice to their position. Even if petitioners are not yet themselves subject to discovery orders, then, they would not be free from the burdens of discovery.

We decline respondent's invitation to relax the pleading requirements on the ground that the Court of Appeals promises petitioners minimally intrusive discovery. That promise provides especially cold comfort in this pleading context, where we are impelled to give real content to the concept of qualified immunity for high-level officials who must be neither deterred nor detracted from the vigorous performance of their duties. Because respondent's complaint is deficient under Rule 8, he is not entitled to discovery, cabined or otherwise.

3

Respondent finally maintains that the Federal Rules expressly allow him to allege petitioners' discriminatory intent "generally," which he equates with a conclusory allegation. (citing Fed. Rule Civ. Proc. 9). It follows, respondent says, that his complaint is sufficiently well pleaded because it claims that petitioners discriminated against him "on account of [his] religion, race, and/or national origin and for no legitimate penological interest." Were we required to accept this allegation as true, respondent's complaint would survive petitioners' motion to dismiss. But the Federal Rules do not require courts to credit a complaint's conclusory statements without reference to its factual context.

It is true that Rule 9(b) requires particularity when pleading "fraud or mistake," while allowing "[m]alice, intent, knowledge, and other conditions of a person's mind [to] be alleged generally." But "generally" is a relative term. In the context of Rule 9, it is to be compared to the particularity requirement applicable to fraud or mistake. Rule 9 merely excuses a party from pleading discriminatory intent under an elevated pleading standard. It does not give him license to evade the less rigid—though still operative—strictures of Rule 8. And Rule 8 does not empower respondent to plead the bare elements of his cause of action, affix the label "general allegation," and expect his complaint to survive a motion to dismiss.

V

We hold that respondent's complaint fails to plead sufficient facts to state a claim for purposeful and unlawful discrimination against petitioners. The Court of Appeals should decide in the first instance whether to remand to the District Court so that respondent can seek leave to amend his deficient complaint.

The judgment of the Court of Appeals is reversed, and the case is remanded for further proceedings consistent with this opinion.

It is so ordered.

[Justices Souter dissented, and this dissent was joined by Justices Stevens, Ginsburg, and Breyer (opinion omitted)].

Exercise 7-6. Understanding Rule 8(a) and Rule 12(b)(6)

In *Twombly* and *Iqbal*, two Supreme Court majorities found the allegations of two very lengthy complaints to be insufficient under Rule 8(a)(2) and ordered the dismissal of the complaints pursuant to motions under Rule 12(b)(6). How, exactly, were these complaints "insufficient," though?

As it turns out, there are two kinds of "insufficiency" that will cause a complaint to run afoul of Rule 8(a)(2) (and will accordingly require the court to grant a motion to dismiss under Rule 12(b)(6)). The first, and easiest to see, can be termed "legal insufficiency." This type of insufficiency is the type you are most familiar with from your "common law" courses, such as Torts and Contracts. In these courses, the cases you read often arise from motions to dismiss testing the sufficiency of tort or contract claims, and you learn the content of tort or contract law by seeing what courts do with these claims—whether they allow the claims to go forward or not. The clearest examples are the tort "duty" cases. If the law does not recognize a "duty" to protect against a certain risk (e.g., injuries to unknown trespassers due to the ordinary negligence of the property owner), then no matter what the complaint says, a claim seeking recovery on that risk will fail—legally, not factually.

A more extreme example will illustrate. Imagine that John files a complaint against Mary, stating (in addition to the basis for the court's jurisdiction):

On December 12, 2012, at 4:30, PM, in the northwest corner of Room 271 of Willet Hall on the campus of Academica University, Defendant Mary, without cause, privilege, or justification, by inhaling deeply in proximity to Plaintiff John, and within no more than one meter of Plaintiff John's mouth and nasal passages, did breathe Plaintiff John's rightful air. As a result, Plaintiff John was denied his rightful air to breathe and was damaged in an amount to be determined justly by the court.

In such a case, it does not matter that the complaint appears to supply more than adequate factual detail. No matter how much detail that John adds to the complaint, he will never be able to state a claim against Mary for "breathing John's rightful air" because the law does not recognize such a silly claim. Another way of thinking about this is that Mary could admit every factual allegation in the complaint, and she would still win because the complaint is legally insufficient.

The second kind of insufficiency can be termed, "factual insufficiency." This kind of insufficiency is much trickier to identify, but its basic meaning is that the complaint at issue is attempting to state a claim that the law does in fact recognize (such as a negligence claim based on a slip-and-fall in a supermarket), but the plaintiff has not provided enough factual detail to give the defendant adequate notice of the claim against him (for instance, the complaint does not say where the plaintiff was when he fell).

The easiest way to see it is through another extreme example. Imagine that John and Mary get into a car accident in the parking lot outside of Willet Hall after their air-breathing confrontation. Assume that John is distracted by a text message, and he taps the bumper of Mary's car as they are leaving the parking lot. Can Mary state a claim against John by stating in her complaint (in addition to the jurisdictional allegations and prayer for relief), "*Defendant John injured Plaintiff Mary*"? Of course not. It is obvious that there is so little factual detail in Mary's complaint that John would have no idea what is being claimed against him. As we add more and more detail to the complaint, at some point it will *become* factually sufficient, and it will survive a motion to dismiss unless it is *legally* insufficient. In granting motions to dismiss on factual insufficiency grounds, courts often permit plaintiffs to re-plead their complaints, on the theory that the failure to include sufficient factual detail could have been careless, but a dismissal for legal insufficiency usually will not come with permission to re-plead because there usually is no point to re-pleading a claim the law does not recognize.

So, now that you know the two kinds of insufficiency, how would you describe the problems with the claims at issue in *Twombly* and *Iqbal*? Are they legally insufficient? Factually insufficient? A little of both? Why? What does the Court say to lead you to your conclusion?

Pleading Your Legal Theory

Do *Twombly* and *Iqbal* require a plaintiff to plead the precise legal theories that allow his claim to prevail? The Supreme Court addressed this issue by summary ruling, and the answer it gave was "No." *Johnson v. City of Shelby*, 574 U. S. ___, 135

S. Ct. 346 (2014). In *Johnson*, several police officers claimed that their due process rights were violated when they were fired in retaliation for exposing official corruption, a cause of action that would be asserted under the general federal civil rights statute, 42 U.S.C. § 1983, which provides a cause of action for a person who has been deprived of her federal rights by another person operating "under color of state law." The *Johnson* plaintiffs stated a factually sufficient complaint, but they failed to cite 42 U.S.C. § 1983, and the District Court dismissed the complaint for lack of notice to the defendant employer as to the legal theory grounding their claims. The Court rejected this ruling summarily (meaning without oral argument and unanimously), stating:

> Our decisions in *Bell Atlantic Corp. v. Twombly*, 550 U. S. 544 (2007), and *Ashcroft v. Iqbal*, 556 U. S. 662 (2009), are not in point, for they concern the factual allegations a complaint must contain to survive a motion to dismiss. A plaintiff, they instruct, must plead facts sufficient to show that her claim has substantive plausibility. Petitioners' complaint was not deficient in that regard. Petitioners stated simply, concisely, and directly events that, they alleged, entitled them to damages from the city. Having informed the city of the factual basis for their complaint, they were required to do no more to stave off threshold dismissal for want of an adequate statement of their claim. [*citations omitted*].

Thus, the most recent Supreme Court case on this topic draws a nice distinction between factual insufficiency and legal insufficiency, and makes clear that the failure to specify the precise legal theory under which one proceeds does not make the complaint legally insufficient.

Exercise 7-7. Applying *"Twiqbal"*

In applying *Twombly* and *Iqbal* (together referred to by many as *"Twiqbal"*), how would you state a claim for negligence in connection with the following facts, as reflected in the following email from a prospective client?

Sent October 29, 2014
From: Prospective Client
To: Lawyer
Subject: I Need Your Help!!!!!!

I was at a four-way stop the other day, and this jerk T-Boned my car while I was in the intersection. I got his license and insurance information, and I want you to sue him. His name is Tommy Tortfeasor, and he works at the Quicky Lube down the street from the intersection where he hit me. Let me know when you have filed the suit. Thanks.

Signed, Prospective Client.

1. Is this enough information for you? If you need to know more, what more do you need to know? Draft the portion of the complaint stating a claim for your client. Determine where you might have to improve the allegations to meet the *Twiqbal* standard.

2. Assuming that you need to know more from your prospective client, how would you choose to communicate that need? Think about how you might craft a responsive email to this prospective client, and draft the email.

4. The Answer, Defenses, and Affirmative Defenses

Once the plaintiff files a complaint, and it survives a motion to dismiss (or the defendant chooses not to ask the court to dismiss it), the defendant must then file an **answer** with the court. Rules 8(b) and (c) impose several requirements on parties filing answers.

First and foremost, a party filing an answer has the duty to "admit or deny the allegations asserted against it by an opposing party." Rule 8(b)(1)(B). This seems simple enough, until one considers that complaints do not always state verifiably true or false allegations, and that some knowledge that would be required for a party to, in good faith, admit or deny an allegation may not be in the possession of that party. For example, consider an assault complaint that alleges that the plaintiff "feared bodily harm." Can the defendant really admit or deny this allegation? Only by guessing or by just denying the statement regardless of her knowledge. But neither of these responses would be offered based on the defending party's own knowledge.

So, the Rule gives the defending party another option. Rule 8(b)(5) provides that "A party that lacks knowledge or information sufficient to form a belief about the truth of an allegation must so state, and the statement has the effect of a denial." This solves the problem of speculating, guessing, or just summarily denying statements when one truly does not know whether they are true or false.

Beyond this simple set of choices of "admit," "deny," and "claim lack of sufficient knowledge," though, lies a more demanding set of requirements. Lack of care in pleading, as much as outright bad faith, can cause a party (or that party's attorney) to run afoul of these requirements. One is that "A denial must fairly respond to the substance of the allegation." Rule 8(b)(2). Within this small sentence are a number of potential landmines, including what we will discuss below as "improper forms of denial." Another is that one must deny only that which one actually intends to deny, and admit only that which one actually intends to admit. Rule 8(b)(3) & (4). This requirement short-circuits any attempt to avoid parsing through the allegations in the complaint and just deny everything. Finally, under Rule 8(b), "An allegation — other than one relating to the amount of damages — is admitted if a responsive pleading is required and the allegation is not denied." Thus, the defending party must take care to respond to every allegation, and every part thereof, to avoid risking an admission by default.

Important to note here is that, where an allegation is admitted (either explicitly or by default) that allegation is "true" for the purposes of the trial and the jury's deliberations, *regardless of whether it can be shown to be false in the real world.* Thus, there is great danger in being careless in one's response to a complaint—one may end up making something "true" for the purposes of the case that the plaintiff would have had no hope of proving.

Beyond the duty to admit, deny, or claim lack of sufficient knowledge as to every part of every allegation in the complaint, the defending party must also provide notice to the court and the opposing party(ies) of any defenses that the defending party has to the complaint and its claims. Defenses are not denials. Rather, a defense is a kind of excuse of the wrongdoing alleged in the complaint. Some of these excuses take the form of a procedural challenge to the suit as filed, such as a challenge to the court's jurisdiction, while others have developed as substantive defenses (traditionally called "avoidances") that absolve the defending party of responsibility on the merits, even if the facts as stated in the complaint are completely true. Today, these latter defenses are generally referred to as "affirmative defenses" because the defending party must not only plead them, but also bears an affirmative burden of proving them.

Reflecting this distinction, Rule 8 recognizes both "defenses," Rule 8(b)(1)(A), and "affirmative defenses," Rule 8(c). Rule 8(b)(1)(A) requires that a defending party plead a "short and plain statement" of each defense that that party has against each claim asserted against it. Rule 8(c) requires that a defending party "affirmatively state any avoidance or affirmative defense." This language—particularly the "short and plain" language of Rule 8(b)(1)(A), has caused commentators and courts to wonder whether the *Twiqbal* standards of pleading also apply to defenses. Thus far, the Supreme Court has not weighed in on the question. When read in light of Rule 12(f)'s authorization of a motion to "strike from a pleading an insufficient defense," however, it appears that the Rule's drafters intended for defenses to meet some standard of sufficiency.

Below, we provide an example of a party's answer that ran afoul of some of the requirements set forth above.

ELK LIGHTING, INC.'S ANSWER AND DEFENSES TO INFINITI GROUP INTERNATIONAL, INC.'S COMPLAINT FOR TRADEMARK INFRINGEMENT, FALSE ADVERTISING AND UNFAIR COMPETITION

[selected provisions]

1. Plaintiff, Infiniti Group International, Inc, ("IGI") is an Illinois corporation, with its principal place of business located at 14047 Petronella Dr #107, Libertyville, IL 60048.

   ANSWER: Defendant lacks knowledge or information sufficient to form a belief about the truth of the allegations of Paragraph 1 and therefore denies them.

2. IGI is engaged in the business of selling clocks.

   ANSWER: Defendant lacks knowledge or information sufficient to form a belief about the truth of the allegations of Paragraph 2 and therefore denies them.

* * *

7. IGI began adopting and using the trademark Sterling & Noble ("the Mark"), in connection with clocks, at least as early as June of 1994, and in commerce at least as early as December of 1994.

ANSWER: Defendant lacks knowledge or information sufficient to form a belief about the truth of the allegations of Paragraph 7 and therefore denies them.

8. Sample uses of the Sterling & Noble Mark by IGI are attached hereto as Group Exhibit A and made a part hereof.

ANSWER: Defendant lacks knowledge or information sufficient to form a belief about the truth of the allegations of Paragraph 8 and therefore denies them.

9. IGI's clocks have been widely advertised, extensively offered for sale, and sold under the Sterling & Noble Mark throughout the United States and worldwide and the Mark has become, through widespread use and favorable public acceptance and recognition, a famous Mark and asset of substantial value as a symbol of IGI, its quality clocks and its goodwill.

ANSWER: Defendant lacks knowledge or information sufficient to form a belief about the truth of the allegations of Paragraph 9 and therefore denies them.

* * *

11. In recognition of the inherent distinctiveness and exclusive rights of use, on April 22, 1997, the United States Patent and Trademark Office granted IGI Registration No. 2,055,787 for the Sterling & Noble trademark in connection with "clocks." A copy of the Certificate of Registration is attached hereto as Exhibit B and made a part hereof.

ANSWER: Defendant admits that IGI obtained U.S. Registration No. 2,055,787 for the Sterling & Noble trademark in connection with "clocks" on April 22, 1997, and Defendant admits that a copy of that Certificate of Registration is attached to the Complaint as Exhibit B. Defendant lacks knowledge or information sufficient to form a belief about the truth of the remaining allegations of Paragraph 11 and therefore denies them.

12. Registration No. 2,499,880 remains in full force and effect and has become incontestable.
ANSWER: Defendant lacks knowledge or information sufficient to form a belief about the truth of the allegations of Paragraph 12 and therefore denies them. Defendant avers that Registration No. 2,499,880 is for a mark that is not at issue in this action.

13. The certificate of registration constitutes "conclusive evidence" of "the validity of the registered Mark, of the registrant's ownership of the Mark and of the registrant's exclusive right to use the Mark in connection with the goods or services specified in the registration" 15 U.S.C. § 1115.

ANSWER: Defendant lacks knowledge or information sufficient to form a belief about the truth of the allegations of Paragraph 13 and therefore denies them.

* * *

16. Without authorization from IGI, Defendant has improperly begun advertising, offering for sale, and selling clocks bearing the Sterling & Noble Mark.

ANSWER: Defendant denies the allegations of Paragraph 16.

17. Sample uses of the Sterling & Noble Mark by Defendant are attached hereto as Group Exhibit C and made a part hereof.

ANSWER: Defendant denies the allegations of Paragraph 17.

* * *

24. Despite the notice and demand by IGI's counsel, Defendant continued and continues to improperly use the Sterling & Noble Mark.

ANSWER: Defendant denies the allegations of Paragraph 24.

AFFIRMATIVE AND OTHER DEFENSES

1. This Court lacks jurisdiction over the person of Defendant, which is not a resident of the State of Illinois, does not do business in the State of Illinois, and is not otherwise subject to jurisdiction in Illinois pursuant to 735 Ill. Comp. Stat. 5/2-209 (2011).

2. This Court is not the proper venue for the trial of the claims alleged. The Defendant does not reside in the judicial district of this Court, a substantial part of the events giving rise to this claim did not occur in the judicial district of this Court, and the Defendant may not be found in the judicial district of this Court.

Exercise 7-8. Improper Denials

The excerpt of a filed answer that you see above comes from the intellectual property case of *Infiniti Group International, Inc. v. Elk Lighting, Inc.*, Case No. 1:11-cv-07735, Doc. 15 (N.D. Ill. 2012). In reading the responses above, do any problems jump out at you? What if you were informed that the case did not involve any dispute over whether the Defendant was in fact selling Sterling & Noble clocks in its stores, but instead whether these sales constituted a violation of the Lanham Act, a trademark statute (all of which the court was apprised of during a hearing on a motion for default judgment, after the deadline for the Defendant to file its answer initially passed).

In the actual case, the court took up the issue of the sufficiency of the answer on its own motion (*sua sponte*), which is permitted under Rule 12(f). The court's short opinion (which we will revisit when we discuss Rule 12 motions) appears below.

Infiniti Group International, Inc. v.
Elk Lighting, Inc., d/b/a Sterling Industries, Inc.

No. 11 C 7735 (N.D. Ill. 2012)

MEMORANDUM ORDER

Milton I. Shadur, Senior District Judge.

Elk Lighting, Inc. ("Elk") has filed its Answer and Defenses ("ADs") to the intellectual property action brought against it by Infiniti Group International, Inc. ("Infiniti"). This *sua sponte* memorandum order is triggered by both (1) some problematic aspects of the Answer[1] and (2) the two ADs advanced by Elk.

To begin with the Answer, a number of its paragraphs (Answer ¶¶ 1, 2, 7–9, 11–13 and 15) follow a meticulous invocation of the disclaimer permitted by Fed. R. Civ. P. ("Rule") 8(b)(5) with the language "and therefore denies them." That is of course oxymoronic — how can a party that asserts (presumably in good faith) that it lacks even enough information to form a belief as to the truth of an allegation then proceed to deny it in accordance with Rule 11(b)? Accordingly the quoted phrase is stricken wherever it appears in the Answer.

Next, though this Court has made no effort to analyze the propriety of the host of flat-out denials contained in the Answer, a couple of them have figuratively jumped off the page and caught this reader's eye. Thus Answer ¶¶ 16 and 24 would appear to call for denial only of the "improperly" characterization contained in Infiniti's allegations, while going on to admit the allegations except for that term.[2] Even more directly problematic, this Court is mystified by the unequivocal denial set out in Answer ¶ 17.

Given those examples, this Court will leave it to Elk's counsel to take a fresh look at all of the denials in the Answer to make certain that they past [*sic*] muster under objective good faith standard prescribed by Rule 11(b). In the meantime, however, two more substantive issues call for current handling.

First, AD 1 (like Answer ¶ 4) asserts the absence of in personam jurisdiction over Elk. If Elk's counsel are serious in that contention, they should promptly bring the issue on by an appropriately supported motion so that the case can be dispatched at the outset if that is called for. Failing such a prompt submission, this Court will treat that defense as having been waived — no litigant can properly keep such an issue in reserve, to be

---

1. At the risk of being charged with applying a double standard, this Court views errors of the type hereafter set out in the text as particularly disturbing when they are committed by a member of a major law firm.

2. Elk's total-denial usage seems to carry overtones somewhat similar to the form of common-law pleading that carried the label "negative pregnant."

368 PLEADING 7 ·

brought to the forefront if the case is lost (or appears to be lost) on the merits.

What has just been said is equally true of AD 2, which echos [*sic*] Answer ¶¶ 5 and 6. Once again, Elk must "use it or lose it" — it must bring the venue issue on forthwith or forgo it.

Exercise 7-9. "Negative Pregnants" and Other Improper Denial Forms

Several types of what might be called "artful pleading" concern the judge enough to cause him to call up and grant his own motion to strike. As to the denials, Judge Shadur identifies nine paragraphs with one type of problem, two more with another, and one with still another, while also referencing yet another, more ancient, form of improper denial in footnote 2. Let's go through them.

1. As to the nine flagged paragraphs, Judge Shadur's concern is that the defendant is attempting to "have it both ways" under Rule 8(b). As you can see from reading the Rule's text, a pleader has only three options at the answer stage: (1) admit; (2) deny; or (3) claim lack of knowledge sufficient to form a belief in the truth or falsity of the allegation. The pleader can even use each of these choices as to *part* of an allegation, while using another choice as to another part. For example, in response to the allegation, "At 3:00 PM on December 5, 2012, Defendant was driving through the intersection at Main St. and Elm St. and negligently struck the Plaintiff, causing her significant physical injury," the pleader can say, "Defendant admits that he was present at the intersection at the time alleged, but denies that his car struck Plaintiff. Defendant lacks sufficient knowledge of Plaintiff's injuries, if any, to form a belief as to the truth or falsity of Plaintiff's claim of injury." The point is that if you use more than one form of response, it must be clear why you are doing so. Why was the use of the denial and the claim of lack of knowledge together in the nine paragraphs improper, then?

2. Paragraphs 16 and 24 deny the entirety of the allegations in each of those paragraphs wholesale. This is not necessarily improper, but when it is used, the pleader must actually intend, in good faith, to deny everything being alleged. What does Judge Shadur see as the problem with these paragraphs?

3. In footnote 2, dropped in reference to Judge Shadur's discussion of the two paragraphs above, the judge mentions the improper form of denial termed a "negative pregnant." He sees the improper denial that the defendants filed as being similar to this improper denial form.

So, what is a "negative pregnant"? Well, it is a *denial* that is "pregnant" with an unspoken and concealed *admission*. For example, imagine that the response to the allegations in Paragraph 16 was instead, "Defendant denies that it has improperly begun advertising, offering for sale, and sell-ing clocks bearing the Sterling & Noble Mark." Such a denial, tracking the literal statements in the allegation, is bound to make some judges wonder whether it masks an admission.

This example might mask at least three possible admissions. The first two are masked by the overly literal repetition of a verb and an adverb (choose these wisely when you are pleading, and avoid adverbs as much as you can, to prevent this sort of gamesmanship). Perhaps the defendant has not "begun" selling these clocks, but has been doing so for some time. Or perhaps the allegation is true in its entirety, and all that the defendant means to deny is the word "improperly." The literal repetition of the exact words of the allegation masks both of these possible admissions.

The third possible admission in this example results from the repetition of the list, "advertising, offering for sale, and selling" from the allegation. What if the defendant is in fact "offering for sale" and "selling" the clocks, but is not "advertising" them? By using what is referred to as a "conjunctive" denial and denying the list of items, joined by the conjunction "and," the defendant would be misleadingly masking what it should admit — that it is "offering for sale" and "selling" the clocks. Many judges — perhaps most — will not pick up on negative pregnant denials, but using them is bad practice and is unprofessional. Judges who do catch litigants using negative pregnants generally react harshly.

That said, as a plaintiff, you also should not use sloppy allegations con-taining more modifiers than necessary, or containing lists of infractions that could be stated separately as their own allegations. This sort of plead-ing invites unprofessional denials.

4. Finally, what is the problem with Paragraph 17 of the answer? Obviously, it "denies" the existence of a paper that it could clearly see was attached to the complaint. Your denials must reflect what you can observe through a reasonable investigation or inquiry, and you are bound to conduct that inquiry before pleading. More on that when we discuss Rule 11.

Exercise 7-10. Defenses

1. The defendants in the Infiniti Group case assert two defenses. Are either or both of these defenses "affirmative defenses" or "avoidances"? Ask your-self whether either of these defenses go to the merits of the cause of action asserted.

2. Why does Judge Shadur move *sua sponte* to strike both of these defenses? Does this action seem correct or incorrect to you? Why?

3. What if, in addition to asserting the two defenses above, the defendants had asserted the doctrine of *in pari delicto*, or "unclean hands" (a common

defense to trademark claims that asserts that the plaintiff cannot recover because the plaintiff is also a wrongdoer, who therefore comes to the court with "unclean hands"), as a third defense to the claims asserted against them? Assuming that it is a sound disposition of the jurisdiction and venue defenses, should Judge Shadur's "use it or lose it" rule apply to the "unclean hands" defense, as well? Why or why not?

5. Amending and Supplementing Pleadings

Everyone, including every great lawyer, makes mistakes from time to time. As we mention above, the pleadings to a lawsuit define the scope of the entire action and form the foundation of everything that comes after them. The overall goal of the Federal Rules of seeking to "secure the just, speedy, and inexpensive determination of every action and proceeding," (Fed. R. Civ. P. 1), would therefore be frustrated if there were no way to correct mistakes a party or that party's counsel makes in framing a pleading. However, it would be just as contrary to the purpose of the Rules to allow parties unlimited changes to their filings, or unlimited time to make such changes.

Do you see why? Not allowing correction of mistakes at all would work against the requirement of "just[ness]," or fairness. Allowing unlimited corrections, or unlimited time to make corrections, would work against the requirements of "speed[iness]" and "inexpensive[ness]." Accordingly, in the area of pleading (as in many other areas of procedural law) a court must balance these values and goals to allow a reasonable, but limited, opportunity for a party to amend that party's pleadings. Rule 15 governs this opportunity and its limits. Read Rule 15.

Exercise 7-11. *Beeck v. Aquaslide*

A leading case on the amendment of pleadings is *Beeck v. Aquaslide*, excerpted below. The case presents a gut-wrenching scenario, where a plaintiff is clearly and very seriously harmed, but sues the wrong defendant due to the slide on which he was injured being a counterfeit. The sloppy pleading practice of the defendant causes the plaintiff to lose his cause of action when the defendant is allowed to correct its mistake after the statute of limitations has already run.

Which of the standards found in Rule 15 are applied here? Was this case decided correctly? Can you see (and defend, based on the terms of the rule) another way that the case could have come out? What would be the weakness of your alternative outcome?

Beeck v. Aquaslide 'n' Dive Corp.

562 F.2d 537 (1977)

Before Bright and Henley, Circuit Judges, and Benson, District Judge.*

Benson, District Judge.

This case is an appeal from the trial court's exercise of discretion on procedural matters in a diversity personal injury action.

Jerry A. Beeck was severely injured on July 15, 1972, while using a water slide. He and his wife, Judy A. Beeck, sued Aquaslide 'N' Dive Corporation (Aquaslide), a Texas corporation, alleging it manufactured the slide involved in the accident, and sought to recover substantial damages on theories of negligence, strict liability and breach of implied warranty.

Aquaslide initially admitted manufacture of the slide, but later moved to amend its answer to deny manufacture; the motion was resisted. The district court granted leave to amend. On motion of the defendant, a separate trial was held on the issue of "whether the defendant designed, manufactured or sold the slide in question."** This motion was also resisted by the plaintiffs. The issue was tried to a jury, which returned a verdict for the defendant, after which the trial court entered summary judgment of dismissal of the case. Plaintiffs took this appeal, and stated the issues presented for review to be:

1. Where the manufacturer of the product, a water slide, admitted in its Answer and later in its Answer to Interrogatories both filed prior to the running of the statute of limitations that it designed, manufactured and sold the water slide in question, was it an abuse of the trial court's discretion to grant leave to amend to the manufacturer in order to deny these admissions after the running of the statute of limitations?

2. After granting the manufacturer's Motion for Leave to Amend in order to deny the prior admissions of design, manufacture and sale of the water slide in question, was it an abuse of the trial court's discretion to further grant the manufacturer's Motion for a Separate Trial on the issue of manufacture?

I. Facts.

A brief review of the facts found by the trial court in its order granting leave to amend, and which do not appear to have been in dispute, is essential to a full understanding of appellants' claims.

---

* The Honorable Paul Benson, Chief Judge, United States District Court for the District of North Dakota, sitting by designation.

** Ed. Note. Rule 42(b) allows a judge to sever or bifurcate a trial for "convenience, to avoid prejudice, or to expedite and economize." Which of these reasons do you think justified bifurcation here?

In 1971 Kimberly Village Home Association of Davenport, Iowa, ordered an Aquaslide product from one George Boldt, who was a local distributor handling defendant's products. The order was forwarded by Boldt to Sentry Pool and Chemical Supply Co. in Rock Island, Illinois, and Sentry forwarded the order to Purity Swimming Pool Supply in Hammond, Indiana. A slide was delivered from a Purity warehouse to Kimberly Village, and was installed by Kimberly employees. On July 15, 1972, Jerry A. Beeck was injured while using the slide at a social gathering sponsored at Kimberly Village by his employer, Harker Wholesale Meats, Inc. Soon after the accident investigations were undertaken by representatives of the separate insurers of Harker and Kimberly Village. On October 31, 1972, Aquaslide first learned of the accident through a letter sent by a representative of Kimberly's insurer to Aquaslide, advising that "one of your Queen Model # Q-3D slides" was involved in the accident. Aquaslide forwarded this notification to its insurer. Aquaslide's insurance adjuster made an on-site investigation of the slide in May, 1973, and also interviewed persons connected with the ordering and assembly of the slide. An inter-office letter dated September 23, 1973, indicates that Aquaslide's insurer was of the opinion the "Aquaslide in question was definitely manufactured by our insured." The complaint was filed October 15, 1973. Investigators for three different insurance companies, representing Harker, Kimberly and the defendant, had concluded that the slide had been manufactured by Aquaslide, and the defendant, with no information to the contrary, answered the complaint on December 12, 1973, and admitted that it "designed, manufactured, assembled and sold" the slide in question.[4]

The statute of limitations on plaintiff's personal injury claim expired on July 15, 1974. About six and one-half months later Carl Meyer, president and owner of Aquaslide, visited the site of the accident prior to the taking of his deposition by the plaintiff.[5] From his on-site inspection of the slide, he determined it was not a product of the defendant. Thereafter, Aquaslide moved the court for leave to amend its answer to deny manufacture of the slide.

II. Leave to Amend.

Amendment of pleadings in civil actions is governed by Rule 15(a), F.R.Civ.P., which provides in part that once issue is joined in a lawsuit, a party may amend his pleading "only by leave of court or by written consent of the adverse party; and leave shall be freely given when justice so requires."

---

4. In answers to interrogatories filed on June 3, 1974, Aquaslide again admitted manufacture of the slide in question.

5. Plaintiffs apparently requested Meyer to inspect the slide prior to the taking of his deposition to determine whether it was defectively installed or assembled.

In *Foman v. Davis*, 371 U.S. 178 (1962), the Supreme Court had occasion to construe that portion of Rule 15(a) set out above:

> Rule 15(a) declares that leave to amend "shall be freely given when justice so requires," this mandate is to be heeded.... If the underlying facts or circumstances relied upon by a plaintiff may be a proper subject of relief, he ought to be afforded an opportunity to test his claim on the merits. In the absence of any apparent or declared reason—such as undue delay, bad faith or dilatory motive on the part of the movant, repeated failure to cure deficiencies by amendments previously allowed, undue prejudice to the opposing party by virtue of allowance of the amendment, futility of amendment, etc.—the leave sought should, as the rules require, be "freely given." Of course, the grant or denial of an opportunity to amend is within the discretion of the District Court, ...

371 U.S. at 182.

This Court in *Hanson v. Hunt Oil Co.*, 398 F.2d 578, 582 (8th Cir. 1968), held that "[p]rejudice must be shown." The burden is on the party opposing the amendment to show such prejudice. In ruling on a motion for leave to amend, the trial court must inquire into the issue of prejudice to the opposing party, in light of the particular facts of the case. *Standard Title Ins. Co. v. Roberts*, 349 F.2d at 622.

Certain principles apply to appellate review of a trial court's grant or denial of a motion to amend pleadings. First, as noted in *Foman v. Davis*, allowance or denial of leave to amend lies within the sound discretion of the trial court, and is reviewable only for an abuse of discretion. The appellate court must view the case in the posture in which the trial court acted in ruling on the motion to amend. *Izaak Walton League of America v. St. Clair*, 497 F.2d 849, 854 (8th Cir.), *cert. denied*, 419 U.S. 1009 (1974).

It is evident from the order of the district court that in the exercise of its discretion in ruling on defendant's motion for leave to amend, it searched the record for evidence of bad faith, prejudice and undue delay which might be sufficient to overbalance the mandate of Rule 15(a), F.R.Civ.P., and *Foman v. Davis*, that leave to amend should be "freely given." Plaintiffs had not at any time conceded that the slide in question had not been manufactured by the defendant, and at the time the motion for leave to amend was at issue, the court had to decide whether the defendant should be permitted to litigate a material factual issue on its merits.

In inquiring into the issue of bad faith, the court noted the fact that the defendant, in initially concluding that it had manufactured the slide, relied upon the conclusions of three different insurance companies,[6] each

---

6. The insurer of Beeck's employer, the insurer of Kimberly Village, as well as the defendant's insurer had each concluded the slide in question was an Aquaslide.

of which had conducted an investigation into the circumstances surrounding the accident. This reliance upon investigations of three insurance companies, and the fact that "no contention has been made by anyone that the defendant influenced this possibly erroneous conclusion," persuaded the court that "defendant has not acted in such bad faith as to be precluded from contesting the issue of manufacture at trial." The court further found "[t]o the extent that 'blame' is to be spread regarding the original identification, the record indicates that it should be shared equally."

In considering the issue of prejudice that might result to the plaintiffs from the granting of the motion for leave to amend, the trial court held that the facts presented to it did not support plaintiffs' assertion that, because of the running of the two year Iowa statute of limitations on personal injury claims, the allowance of the amendment would sound the "death knell" of the litigation. In order to accept plaintiffs' argument, the court would have had to assume that the defendant would prevail at trial on the factual issue of manufacture of the slide, and further that plaintiffs would be foreclosed, should the amendment be allowed, from proceeding against other parties if they were unsuccessful in pressing their claim against Aquaslide. On the state of the record before it, the trial court was unwilling to make such assumptions,[7] and concluded "[u]nder these circumstances, the Court deems that the possible prejudice to the plaintiffs is an insufficient basis on which to deny the proposed amendment." The court reasoned that the amendment would merely allow the defendant to contest a disputed factual issue at trial, and further that it would be prejudicial to the defendant to deny the amendment.

The court also held that defendant and its insurance carrier, in investigating the circumstances surrounding the accident, had not been so lacking in diligence as to dictate a denial of the right to litigate the factual issue of manufacture of the slide.

On this record we hold that the trial court did not abuse its discretion in allowing the defendant to amend its answer.

---

7. The district court noted in its order granting leave to amend that plaintiffs may be able to sue other parties as a result of the substituting of a "counterfeit" slide for the Aquaslide, if indeed this occurred. The court added:

> [a]gain, the Court is handicapped by an unclear record on this issue. If, in fact, the slide in question is not an Aquaslide, the replacement entered the picture somewhere along the Boldt to Sentry, Sentry to Purity, Purity to Kimberly Village chain of distribution. Depending upon the circumstances of its entry, a cause of action sounding in fraud or contract might lie. If so, the applicable statute of limitations period would not have run. Further, as defendant points out, the doctrine of equitable estoppel might possibly preclude another defendant from asserting the two-year statute as a defense.

67 F.R.D. at 415.

III. Separate Trials.

* * *

We hold the Rule 42(b) separation was not an abuse of discretion.

The judgment of the district court is affirmed.

Exercise 7-12. *Beeck v. Aquaslide*: An Appeal

Assume that the plaintiff in the *Beeck* case appeals to the United States Supreme Court. The plaintiff argues that the Court of Appeals erred in affirming the trial court's decision to grant defendant's motion to amend the answer. You will be assigned to represent the plaintiff or defendant. Prepare a legal argument addressing whether the court of appeals erred. The material available for your argument is limited to Rules 1 and 15, and the text of the *Beeck* opinion above. Your argument should (1) identify the issue, (2) set out the applicable law and the applicable policies, and (3) apply the relevant facts to the law and policy.

Exercise 7-13. Beeck's Options

Of course, the result of the *Beeck* case—that a severely disabled plaintiff with what appears to be a good cause of action cannot recover against the party that harmed him through its negligent manufacture of a counterfeit slide—does not please anyone who reads this case for the first time. But did this *have* to be the end for Beeck? Rule 15(c) allows a party to amend that party's pleadings and to treat the amended pleading as "relating back" to the date of the initial pleading (thus potentially eliminating Beeck's statute of limitations problem if he were to sue the actual counterfeit manufacturer). Could/should Beeck's lawyers have responded to the motion to amend the answer by tendering an amended complaint swapping Aquaslide for the proper defendant(s)? What would have been the challenges presented by this plan?

Krupski v. Costa Crociere S. p. A.

130 S. Ct. 2485 (2010)

Justice SOTOMAYOR delivered the opinion of the Court.

Rule 15(c) of the Federal Rules of Civil Procedure governs when an amended pleading "relates back" to the date of a timely filed original pleading and is thus itself timely even though it was filed outside an applicable statute of limitations. Where an amended pleading changes a party or a party's name, the Rule requires, among other things, that "the party to be brought in by amendment . . . knew or should have known that the action would have been brought against it, but for a mistake concerning the proper party's identity." Rule 15(c)(1)(C). In this case, the Court of Appeals held that Rule 15(c) was not satisfied because the plaintiff knew or should have known of the proper defendant before filing her original complaint. The court also held that relation back was not appropriate because the plaintiff had unduly delayed in seeking to amend. We hold that relation back under Rule 15(c)(1)(C) depends on what the party to be added knew or should have known, not on the amending party's knowledge or its timeliness in seeking to amend the pleading. Accordingly, we reverse the judgment of the Court of Appeals.

I

On February 21, 2007, petitioner, Wanda Krupski, tripped over a cable and fractured her femur while she was on board the cruise ship Costa Magica. Upon her return home, she acquired counsel and began the process of seeking compensation for her injuries. Krupski's passenger ticket—which explained that it was the sole contract between each passenger and the carrier, included a variety of requirements for obtaining damages for an injury suffered on board one of the carrier's ships. The ticket identified the carrier as "Costa Crociere S. p. A., an Italian corporation, and all Vessels and other ships owned, chartered, operated, marketed or provided by Costa Crociere, S. p. A., and all officers, staff members, crew members, independent contractors, medical providers, concessionaires, pilots, suppliers, agents and assigns onboard said Vessels, and the manufacturers of said Vessels and all their component parts."

The ticket required an injured party to submit "written notice of the claim with full particulars ... to the carrier or its duly authorized agent within 185 days after the date of injury." The ticket further required any lawsuit to be "filed within one year after the date of injury" and to be "served upon the carrier within 120 days after filing." Ibid. For cases arising from voyages departing from or returning to a United States port in which the amount in controversy exceeded $75,000, the ticket designated the United States District Court for the Southern District of Florida in Broward County, Florida, as the exclusive forum for a lawsuit. *Id.*, at 36a. The ticket extended the "defenses, limitations and exceptions ... that may be invoked by the CARRIER" to "all persons who may act on behalf of the CARRIER or on whose behalf the CARRIER may act," including "the CARRIER's parents, subsidiaries, affiliates, successors, assigns, representatives, agents, employees, servants, concessionaires and contractors" as well as "Costa Cruise Lines N. V.," identified as the "sales and marketing agent for the CARRIER and the issuer of this Passage Ticket Contract." *Id.*, at 29a. The front of the ticket listed Costa Cruise Lines' address in Florida and stated that an entity called "Costa Cruises" was "the first cruise company in the world" to obtain a certain certification of quality. *Id.*, at 25a.

On July 2, 2007, Krupski's counsel notified Costa Cruise Lines of Krupski's claims. On July 9, 2007, the claims administrator for Costa Cruise requested additional information from Krupski "[i]n order to facilitate our future attempts to achieve a pre-litigation settlement." The parties were unable to reach a settlement, however, and on February 1, 2008—three weeks before the 1-year limitations period expired—Krupski filed a negligence action against Costa Cruise, invoking the diversity jurisdiction of the Federal District Court for the Southern District of Florida. The complaint alleged that Costa Cruise "owned, operated, managed, supervised and controlled" the ship on which Krupski had injured herself; that Costa Cruise had extended to its passengers an invitation to enter onto the ship; and that Costa Cruise owed Krupski a duty of care, which it breached by failing to take steps that would have prevented her accident. The complaint further stated that venue was proper under the passenger ticket's forum selection clause and averred that, by the July 2007 notice of her claims, Krupski had complied with the ticket's presuit requirements. Krupski served Costa Cruise on February 4, 2008.

Over the next several months—after the limitations period had expired—Costa Cruise brought Costa Crociere's existence to Krupski's attention three times. First, on February 25, 2008, Costa Cruise filed its answer, asserting that it was not the proper defendant, as it was merely the North American sales and marketing agent for Costa Crociere, which was the actual carrier and vessel operator. Second, on March 20, 2008, Costa Cruise listed Costa Crociere as an interested party in its corporate disclosure statement. Finally, on May 6, 2008, Costa Cruise moved for summary judgment, again stating that Costa Crociere was the proper defendant.

On June 13, 2008, Krupski responded to Costa Cruise's motion for summary judgment, arguing for limited discovery to determine whether Costa Cruise should be dismissed. According to Krupski, the following sources of information led her to believe Costa Cruise was the responsible party: The travel documents prominently identified Costa Cruise and gave its Florida address; Costa Cruise's Web site listed Costa Cruise in Florida as the United States office for the Italian company Costa Crociere; and the Web site of the Florida Department of State listed Costa Cruise as the only "Costa" company registered to do business in that State. Krupski also observed that Costa Cruise's claims administrator had responded to her claims notification without indicating that Costa Cruise was not a responsible party. With her response, Krupski simultaneously moved to amend her complaint to add Costa Crociere as a defendant.

On July 2, 2008, after oral argument, the District Court denied Costa Cruise's motion for summary judgment without prejudice and granted Krupski leave to amend, ordering that Krupski effect proper service on Costa Crociere by September 16, 2008. Complying with the court's deadline, Krupski filed an amended complaint on July 11, 2008, and served

Costa Crociere on August 21, 2008. On that same date, the District Court issued an order dismissing Costa Cruise from the case pursuant to the parties' joint stipulation, Krupski apparently having concluded that Costa Cruise was correct that it bore no responsibility for her injuries.

Shortly thereafter, Costa Crociere—represented by the same counsel who had represented Costa Cruise, moved to dismiss, contending that the amended complaint did not relate back under Rule 15(c) and was therefore untimely. The District Court agreed. Rule 15(c), the court explained, imposes three requirements before an amended complaint against a newly named defendant can relate back to the original complaint. First, the claim against the newly named defendant must have arisen "out of the conduct, transaction, or occurrence set out—or attempted to be set out—in the original pleading." Fed. Rules Civ. Proc. 15(c)(1)(B), (C). Second, "within the period provided by Rule 4(m) for serving the summons and complaint" (which is ordinarily 120 days from when the complaint is filed, see Rule 4(m)), the newly named defendant must have "received such notice of the action that it will not be prejudiced in defending on the merits." Rule 15(c)(1)(C)(i). Finally, the plaintiff must show that, within the Rule 4(m) period, the newly named defendant "knew or should have known that the action would have been brought against it, but for a mistake concerning the proper party's identity." Rule 15(c)(1)(C)(ii).

The first two conditions posed no problem, the court explained: The claim against Costa Crociere clearly involved the same occurrence as the original claim against Costa Cruise, and Costa Crociere had constructive notice of the action and had not shown that any unfair prejudice would result from relation back. But the court found the third condition fatal to Krupski's attempt to relate back, concluding that Krupski had not made a mistake concerning the identity of the proper party. Relying on Eleventh Circuit precedent, the court explained that the word "mistake" should not be construed to encompass a deliberate decision not to sue a party whose identity the plaintiff knew before the statute of limitations had run. Because Costa Cruise informed Krupski that Costa Crociere was the proper defendant in its answer, corporate disclosure statement, and motion for summary judgment, and yet Krupski delayed for months in moving to amend and then in filing an amended complaint, the court concluded that Krupski knew of the proper defendant and made no mistake.

The Eleventh Circuit affirmed in an unpublished per curiam opinion. *Krupski v. Costa Cruise Lines, N. V., LLC*, 330 Fed. Appx. 892 (2009). Rather than relying on the information contained in Costa Cruise's filings, all of which were made after the statute of limitations had expired, as evidence that Krupski did not make a mistake, the Court of Appeals noted that the relevant information was located within Krupski's passenger ticket, which she had furnished to her counsel well before the end of the limitations period. Because the ticket clearly identified Costa Crociere as the carrier, the court stated, Krupski either knew or should have known of Costa Crociere's identity as a potential party. It was therefore appropriate to treat Krupski as having chosen to sue one potential party over another. Alternatively, even assuming that she first learned of Costa Crociere's identity as the correct party from Costa Cruise's answer, the Court of Appeals observed that Krupski waited 133 days from the time she filed her original complaint to seek leave to amend and did not file an amended complaint for another month after that. In light of this delay, the Court of Appeals concluded that the District Court did not abuse its discretion in denying relation back.

We granted certiorari to resolve tension among the Circuits over the breadth of Rule 15(c)(1)(C)(ii), and we now reverse.

II

. . . .

In our view, neither of the Court of Appeals' reasons for denying relation back under Rule 15(c)(1)(C)(ii) finds support in the text of the Rule. We consider each reason in turn.

A

The Court of Appeals first decided that Krupski either knew or should have known of the proper party's identity and thus determined that she had made a deliberate choice instead of a mistake in not naming Costa Crociere as a party in her original pleading. By focusing on Krupski's knowledge, the Court of Appeals chose the wrong starting point. The question under Rule 15(c)(1)(C)(ii) is not whether Krupski knew or should have known the identity of Costa Crociere as the proper defendant, but whether Costa Crociere knew or should have known that it would have been named as a defendant but for an error. Rule 15(c)(1)(C)(ii) asks what the prospective defendant knew or should have known during the Rule 4(m) period, not what the plaintiff knew or should have known at the time of filing her original complaint.

Information in the plaintiff's possession is relevant only if it bears on the defendant's understanding of whether the plaintiff made a mistake regarding the proper party's identity. For purposes of that inquiry, it would be error to conflate knowledge of a party's existence with the absence of mistake. A mistake is "[a]n error, misconception, or misunderstanding; an erroneous belief." Black's Law Dictionary 1092 (9th ed.2009); *see also* Webster's Third New International Dictionary 1446 (2002) (defining "mistake" as "a misunderstanding of the meaning or implication of something"; "a wrong action or statement proceeding from faulty judgment, inadequate knowledge, or inattention"; "an erroneous belief"; or "a state of mind not in accordance with the facts"). That a plaintiff knows of a party's existence does not preclude her from making a mistake with respect to that party's identity. A plaintiff may know that a prospective defendant — call him party A — exists, while erroneously believing him to have the status of party B. Similarly, a plaintiff may know generally what party A does while misunderstanding the roles that party A and party B played in the "conduct, transaction, or occurrence" giving rise to her claim. If the plaintiff sues party B instead of party A under these circumstances, she has made a "mistake concerning the proper party's identity" notwithstanding her knowledge of the existence of both parties. The only question under Rule 15(c)(1)(C)(ii), then, is whether party A knew or should have known that, absent some mistake, the action would have been brought against him.

Respondent urges that the key issue under Rule 15(c)(1)(C)(ii) is whether the plaintiff made a deliberate choice to sue one party over another. We agree that making a deliberate choice to sue one party instead of another while fully understanding the factual and legal differences between the two parties is the antithesis of making a mistake concerning the proper party's identity. We disagree, however, with respondent's position that any time a plaintiff is aware of the existence of two parties and chooses to sue the wrong one, the proper defendant could reasonably believe that the plaintiff made no mistake. The reasonableness of the mistake is not itself at issue. As noted, a plaintiff might know that the prospective defendant exists but nonetheless harbor a misunderstanding about his status or role in the events giving rise to the claim at issue, and she may mistakenly choose to sue a different defendant based on that misimpression. That kind of deliberate but mistaken choice does not foreclose a finding that Rule 15(c)(1)(C)(ii) has been satisfied.

This reading is consistent with the purpose of relation back: to balance the interests of the defendant protected by the statute of limitations with the preference expressed in the Federal Rules of Civil Procedure in general, and Rule 15 in particular, for resolving disputes on their merits. A prospective defendant who legitimately believed that the limitations period had passed without any attempt to sue him has a strong interest in repose. But repose would be a windfall for a prospective defendant who understood, or who should have understood, that he escaped suit during the limitations period only because the plaintiff misunderstood a crucial fact about his identity. Because a plaintiff's knowledge of the existence of a party does not foreclose the possibility that she has made a mistake of identity about which that party should have been aware, such knowledge does not support that party's interest in repose.

Our reading is also consistent with the history of Rule 15(c)(1)(C). That provision was added in 1966 to respond to a recurring problem in suits against the Federal Government, particularly in the Social Security context.

Individuals who had filed timely lawsuits challenging the administrative denial of benefits often failed to name the party identified in the statute as the
proper defendant—the current Secretary of what was then the Department
of Health, Education, and Welfare—and named instead the United States;
the Department of Health, Education, and Welfare itself; the nonexistent
"Federal Security Administration"; or a Secretary who had recently retired
from office. By the time the plaintiffs discovered their mistakes, the statute
of limitations in many cases had expired, and the district courts denied the
plaintiffs leave to amend on the ground that the amended complaints would
not relate back. Rule 15(c) was therefore "amplified to provide a general
solution" to this problem. It is conceivable that the Social Security litigants
knew or reasonably should have known the identity of the proper defendant
either because of documents in their administrative cases or by dint of the
statute setting forth the filing requirements. Nonetheless, the Advisory Committee clearly meant their filings to qualify as mistakes under the Rule.

Respondent suggests that our decision in *Nelson v. Adams USA, Inc.*,
529 U.S. 460, 120 S.Ct. 1579 (2000), forecloses the reading of Rule
15(c)(1)(C)(ii) we adopt today. We disagree. In that case, Adams USA,
Inc. (Adams), had obtained an award of attorney's fees against the corporation of which Donald Nelson was the president and sole shareholder.
After Adams became concerned that the corporation did not have sufficient funds to pay the award, Adams sought to amend its pleading to add
Nelson as a party and simultaneously moved to amend the judgment to
hold Nelson responsible. The District Court granted both motions, and
the Court of Appeals affirmed. We reversed, holding that the requirements
of due process, as codified in Rules 12 and 15 of the Federal Rules of
Civil Procedure, demand that an added party have the opportunity to
respond before judgment is entered against him. *Id.*, at 465–467, 120
S.Ct. 1579. In a footnote explaining that relation back does not deny the
added party an opportunity to respond to the amended pleading, we
noted that the case did not arise under the "mistake clause" of Rule 15(c):
"Respondent Adams made no such mistake. It knew of Nelson's role and
existence and, until it moved to amend its pleading, chose to assert its
claim for costs and fees only against [Nelson's company]." *Id.*, at 467, n.
1, 120 S.Ct. 1579.

Contrary to respondent's claim, *Nelson* does not suggest that Rule
15(c)(1)(C)(ii) cannot be satisfied if a plaintiff knew of the prospective
defendant's existence at the time she filed her original complaint. In that
case, there was nothing in the initial pleading suggesting that Nelson was
an intended party, while there was evidence in the record (of which Nelson
was aware) that Adams sought to add him only after learning that the
company would not be able to satisfy the judgment. *Id.*, at 463–464, 120
S.Ct. 1579. This evidence countered any implication that Adams had orig-

inally failed to name Nelson because of any "mistake concerning the proper party's identity," and instead suggested that Adams decided to name Nelson only after the fact in an attempt to ensure that the fee award would be paid. The footnote merely observes that Adams had originally been under no misimpression about the function Nelson played in the underlying dispute. We said, after all, that Adams knew of Nelson's "role" as well as his existence. *Id.*, at 467, n. 1, 120 S.Ct. 1579. Read in context, the footnote in *Nelson* is entirely consistent with our understanding of the Rule: When the original complaint and the plaintiff's conduct compel the conclusion that the failure to name the prospective defendant in the original complaint was the result of a fully informed decision as opposed to a mistake concerning the proper defendant's identity, the requirements of Rule 15(c)(1)(C)(ii) are not met. This conclusion is in keeping with our rejection today of the Court of Appeals' reliance on the plaintiff's knowledge to deny relation back.

B

The Court of Appeals offered a second reason why Krupski's amended complaint did not relate back: Krupski had unduly delayed in seeking to file, and in eventually filing, an amended complaint. The Court of Appeals offered no support for its view that a plaintiff's dilatory conduct can justify the denial of relation back under Rule 15(c)(1)(C), and we find none. The Rule plainly sets forth an exclusive list of requirements for relation back, and the amending party's diligence is not among them. Moreover, the Rule mandates relation back once the Rule's requirements are satisfied; it does not leave the decision whether to grant relation back to the district court's equitable discretion. See Rule 15(c)(1) ("An amendment ... *relates back* ... when" the three listed requirements are met (emphasis added)).

The mandatory nature of the inquiry for relation back under Rule 15(c) is particularly striking in contrast to the inquiry under Rule 15(a), which sets forth the circumstances in which a party may amend its pleading before trial. By its terms, Rule 15(a) gives discretion to the district court in deciding whether to grant a motion to amend a pleading to add a party or a claim. Following an initial period after filing a pleading during which a party may amend once "as a matter of course," "a party may amend its pleading only with the opposing party's written consent or the court's leave," which the court "should freely give ... when justice so requires." Rule 15(a)(1)-(2). We have previously explained that a court may consider a movant's "undue delay" or "dilatory motive" in deciding whether to grant leave to amend under Rule 15(a). *Foman v. Davis*, 371 U.S. 178, 182, 83 S.Ct. 227 (1962). As the contrast between Rule 15(a) and Rule 15(c) makes clear, however, the speed with which a plaintiff moves to amend her complaint or files an amended complaint after obtaining leave to do so has no bearing on whether the amended complaint relates back.

Rule 15(c)(1)(C) does permit a court to examine a plaintiff's conduct during the Rule 4(m) period, but not in the way or for the purpose respondent or the Court of Appeals suggests. As we have explained, the question under Rule 15(c)(1)(C)(ii) is what the prospective defendant reasonably should have understood about the plaintiff's intent in filing the original complaint against the first defendant. To the extent the plaintiff's postfiling conduct informs the prospective defendant's understanding of whether the plaintiff initially made a "mistake concerning the proper party's identity," a court may consider the conduct. *Cf. Leonard v. Parry*, 219 F.3d 25, 29 (C.A.1 2000) ("[P]ost-filing events occasionally can shed light on the plaintiff's state of mind at an earlier time" and "can inform a defendant's reasonable beliefs concerning whether her omission from the original complaint represented a mistake (as opposed to a conscious choice)"). The plaintiff's postfiling conduct is otherwise immaterial to the question whether an amended complaint relates back.

C

Applying these principles to the facts of this case, we think it clear that the courts below erred in denying relation back under Rule 15(c)(1)(C)(ii). The District Court held that Costa Crociere had "constructive notice" of Krupski's complaint within the Rule 4(m) period. Costa Crociere has not challenged this finding. Because the complaint made clear that Krupski meant to sue the company that "owned, operated, managed, supervised and controlled" the ship on which she was injured, and also indicated (mistakenly) that Costa Cruise performed those roles, Costa Crociere should have known, within the Rule 4(m) period, that it was not named as a defendant in that complaint only because of Krupski's misunderstanding about which "Costa" entity was in charge of the ship—clearly a "mistake concerning the proper party's identity."

Respondent contends that because the original complaint referred to the ticket's forum requirement and presuit claims notification procedure, Krupski was clearly aware of the contents of the ticket, and because the ticket identified Costa Crociere as the carrier and proper party for a lawsuit, respondent was entitled to think that she made a deliberate choice to sue Costa Cruise instead of Costa Crociere. Brief for Respondent 13. As we have explained, however, that Krupski may have known the contents of the ticket does not foreclose the possibility that she nonetheless misunderstood crucial facts regarding the two companies' identities. Especially because the face of the complaint plainly indicated such a misunderstanding, respondent's contention is not persuasive. Moreover, respondent has articulated no strategy that it could reasonably have thought Krupski was pursuing in suing a defendant that was legally unable to provide relief.

. . . .

It is also worth noting that Costa Cruise and Costa Crociere are related corporate entities with very similar names; "crociera" even means "cruise" in Italian. Cassell's Italian Dictionary 137, 670 (1967). This interrelationship and similarity heighten the expectation that Costa Crociere should suspect a mistake has been made when Costa Cruise is named in a complaint that actually describes Costa Crociere's activities. *Cf. Morel v. DaimlerChrysler AG*, 565 F.3d 20, 27 (C.A.1 2009) (where complaint conveyed plaintiffs' attempt to sue automobile manufacturer and erroneously named the manufacturer as Daimler-Chrysler Corporation instead of the actual manufacturer, a legally distinct but related entity named Daimler-Chrysler AG, the latter should have realized it had not been named because of plaintiffs' mistake); *Goodman v. Praxair, Inc.*, 494 F.3d 458, 473–475 (C.A.4 2007) (*en banc*) (where complaint named parent company Praxair, Inc., but described status of subsidiary company Praxair Services, Inc., subsidiary company knew or should have known it had not been named because of plaintiff's mistake). In addition, Costa Crociere's own actions contributed to passenger confusion over "the proper party" for a lawsuit. The front of the ticket advertises that "Costa Cruises" has achieved a certification of quality, without clarifying whether "Costa Cruises" is Costa Cruise Lines, Costa Crociere, or some other related "Costa" company. Indeed, Costa Crociere is evidently aware that the difference between Costa Cruise and Costa Crociere can be confusing for cruise ship passengers. *See, e.g., Suppa v. Costa Crociere, S.p.A.*, No. 07-60526-CIV, 2007 WL 4287508, *1, (S.D.Fla., Dec.4, 2007) (denying Costa Crociere's motion to dismiss the amended complaint where the original complaint had named Costa Cruise as a defendant after "find[ing] it simply inconceivable that Defendant Costa Crociere was not on notice ... that ... but for the mistake in the original Complaint, Costa Crociere was the appropriate party to be named in the action").

In light of these facts, Costa Crociere should have known that Krupski's failure to name it as a defendant in her original complaint was due to a mistake concerning the proper party's identity. We therefore reverse the judgment of the Court of Appeals for the Eleventh Circuit and remand the case for further proceedings consistent with this opinion.

It is so ordered.

SCALIA, J., concurred in part and concurred in the judgment (opinion omitted).

Exercise 7-14. Applying Rule 15 and Relation-Back

1. Under *Krupski*, what is the definition of "mistake," and why was Costa Crociere not successful in convincing the Court that the failure to name the Italian carrier was not a "mistake"?

2. Although it is not really an issue in *Krupski*, many first-year students have problems properly applying the time-knowledge requirement of Rule 15(c), as well as keeping straight which portions of Rule 15 apply to which questions when a party seeks to amend its pleading. Justice Sotomayor does a good job of cutting through some of the confusion, but a brief example will help illustrate further:

   Imagine that Mary Swanson is injured in a car accident with John Smith, and that the statute of limitations for negligence claims in the relevant state is one year. Plaintiff files suit against Defendant on the 300th day after her accident, but unbeknownst to her, the driver of the car, John Smith, is the cousin of the man to whom the car is registered, also named John Smith, and the John Smith who owns the car was not driving it on the date of the accident. Mary realizes this a year after filing suit (and therefore 300 days after the statute of limitations has lapsed). Once she realizes her error, she files a motion for leave to amend her complaint. Her opponent, John Smith the owner, opposes this motion, knowing that she cannot prove that he was in the car at the time of the accident, and knowing that denial of leave to amend will keep his cousin, John Smith the driver, from being sued. Assume that Defendant Smith's argument in opposition to the motion is that leave to amend would be "futile" (one of the possible reasons that "justice may [not] require" leave to be given, as listed in the Foman *case discussed in* Beeck*) because the new defendant, once subbed in, would just move successfully to dismiss the case due to the lapse in the statute of limitations. Will Mary be able to make this amendment successfully?*

   Now, the first thing you have to understand is that a fight over leave to amend requires, first and foremost, the application of Rule 15(a), not necessarily 15(c). The standard for whether leave to amend is given is "freely when justice so requires." Only when one party makes the argument that justice *does not* "so require" (in this hypothetical, due to the futility of the amendment because the statute of limitations has lapsed)* does the court have to consider Rule 15(c) and relation-back. Otherwise, judges consider

---

   * Ed. Note. There are reasons other than the statute of limitations lapsing that can render an amendment "futile." For example, the claim sought to be asserted is legally insufficient, and no amount of additional fact development will rescue it; the intended plaintiff is beyond the personal jurisdiction of the court, or will destroy venue or subject matter jurisdiction; etc. Only when the alleged defect is a lapse of the statute of limitations is relation-back under Rule 15(c) relevant. Otherwise, only Rule 15(a) or (b) will be relevant, depending on the procedural posture of the case.

Rule 15(c) only if the opposing party moves to dismiss or moves for summary judgment *based on the statute of limitations lapsing* (i.e., the plaintiff sets up the amendment and relation-back as a defense to the motion, as in *Krupski*).

In this case, though, the defendant has presented the argument for futility, premised on the lapsing of the statute of limitations, in opposition to Mary's motion for leave to amend, so the court's consideration of whether "justice so requires" inevitably requires the judge to determine whether the amended complaint will relate back to the initial filing date, thus eliminating the statute of limitations problem.

Second, is "mistake" an issue in this case? In a word, no. Here, we have a genuine mistake, and even better, it is a mistake "as to the party's identity." The mistake is even less tenuous than that in *Krupski*, so the mistake portion of Rule 15(c) appears to be satisfied.

Is the remainder of the Rule satisfied, then? Did the driver John Smith know, within 120 days of the filing of the complaint, that the wrong John Smith had been sued, and that, but for a mistake in identity, he would have been the one sued? As to this question, we can only speculate based on the facts provided above. If the two live together, for example, it is more likely that the driver John Smith has known about the suit since the beginning (he might have even accepted service of process on behalf of the owner John Smith under Rule 4(e)(2)(b)). If they are together only infrequently (e.g., for holiday dinners), then the driver John Smith might not have known about the suit. If their contacts are really infrequent, then it may not even be the case that the driver John Smith "should have known" about the mistake in identity. The point is that the three standards: (1) the "freely when justice so requires" standard of Rule 15(a); (2) the "mistake in the identity of the party" standard of Rule 15(c); and the "knew or should have known" within 120 days of the initial filing of the pleading to be amended standard of Rule 15(c), all serve different functions, and some or all of these standards might be at issue where a party seeks to amend a pleading to assert a time-barred claim.

6. Truthfulness, Good Faith, and Professionalism in Pleading

In *Worthington v. Wilson*, 8 F.3d 1253 (7th Cir. 1993), a police brutality case, the Seventh Circuit held that an amendment made after the statute of limitations lapsed, substituting named officers for "John Doe" defendants named in the original complaint did not relate back because the complete lack of knowledge of the officers' identities could not constitute a "mistake as to [their] identity." *Krupski* may abrogate *Worthington*, but assuming it does not, could the plaintiff in *Worthington* have simply chosen three officers of the Police Department at random and named them as defendants to get the discovery process rolling, and then substituted the three correct police officers for the randomly selected defendants? For three important reasons, his lawyer would not have been well-advised to do that, and that is probably why he chose to file a complaint against "three unknown named officers."

The first is that it would be unprofessional to do so. ABA Model Rule of Professional Conduct 3.1 provides, in pertinent part,

> A lawyer shall not bring or defend a proceeding, or assert or controvert an issue therein, unless there is a basis in law and fact for doing so that is not frivolous, which includes a good faith argument for an extension, modification or reversal of existing law.

Naming defendants whom you suspect are not the correct defendants likely fails this requirement for good-faith advocacy.

The second is that such a strategy likely would not succeed because the purported "mistake" under this strategy would be much more like the purported "mistake" in *Worthington* than the actual mistake in *Krupski*. As we have framed it, unlike the plaintiff in *Krupski*, the plaintiff here is not confused about the identity of his assailants — he just doesn't know who they were. That he chooses three names at random, even if these names come from the roster of the Police Department employees, does not change this fact.

The third, which is the subject of the materials below, is that naming three random employees of the Department, absent a good-faith factual basis for naming them personally as defendants, would likely violate the main provision of the Federal Rules that policies the truthfulness of parties in their pleading: Fed. R. Civ. P. 11. It also might justify an attorney's fee award under 28 U.S.C. § 1927 for "unreasonably and vexatiously" multiplying the proceedings. The case below shows how these provisions interact to police untruthful and bad-faith pleading.

Rule 11 contains a number of requirements, and it must be read as a whole to get a sense of how these requirements interact. First, it requires that "Every pleading, written motion, and other paper must be signed by at least one attorney of record in the attorney's name — or by a party personally if the party is unrepresented." Fed. R. Civ. P. 11(a). This signature requirement forces the person who files the pleading to certify four representations to the court. The first is that the paper "is not being presented for any improper purpose, such as to harass, cause unnecessary delay, or needlessly increase the cost of litigation." Fed. R. Civ. P. 11(b)(1). This certification polices attorneys who would make filings that are technically justified, but that the attorneys do not need to make, and that they are just making to delay the proceedings or cause the opposing party(ies) to incur expenses.

The second is that "the claims, defenses, and other legal contentions are warranted by existing law or by a nonfrivolous argument for extending, modifying, or reversing existing law or for establishing new law." Fed. R. Civ. P. 11(b)(2). This certification ensures that whoever files the pleading has conducted thorough research of the underlying law and knows either that the pleading complies with that law, or that a credible argument exists that the law is wrong.

The third is that "the factual contentions have evidentiary support or, if specifically so identified, will likely have evidentiary support after a reasonable opportunity for further investigation or discovery." Fed. R. Civ. P. 11(b)(3). After *Twiqbal*, this requirement may *seem* superfluous, as all pleadings that rely on factual allegations must contain enough of these factual allegations to convince the court that the claim or affirmative defense they underlie is plausible. But what if a complaint contains the required amount of factual material, but this material is just made up? Can *Twiqbal* police that? In a word, no. The *Twiqbal* rule still requires courts to accept factual allegations as true for the purposes of evaluating a pleading, so absent this requirement for a good-faith certification that an allegation does or will have evidentiary support, a pleader could just make things up to get the complaint from filing to discovery, hoping to obtain a settlement (although he would likely run afoul of his state's professional responsibility code in doing so).

The fourth, which only applies to denials of factual allegations and is thus the mirror image of the third, is that "the denials of factual contentions are warranted on the evidence or, if specifically so identified, are reasonably based on belief or a lack of information." Fed. R. Civ. P. 11(b)(4). This certification serves the same function as Rule 11(b)(3), just for denials rather than for the allegations themselves. Importantly, though, just as the others do, it applies to both pleadings and motions, so denying a factual contention made in a motion for summary judgment, for example, would also fall under the Rule's strictures. Also important to note is that Rule 11 explicitly does *not* apply to discovery, which has its own rules for sanctions. Fed. R. Civ. P. 11(d).

What is the consequence of making these certifications? Well, if one makes these certifications, and it later becomes clear that one or more of them was not made truthfully or in good faith, then the court is empowered to order "an appropriate sanction on any attorney, law firm, or party that violated the rule or is responsible for the violation." Rule 11(c)(1). And a law firm will usually be held responsible for the conduct of its attorneys, as well. *Id.* However, since the Rule bases its provisions on papers filed with the court (whether the target of the sanctions is the person who "sign[ed], fil[ed], submit[ted], or later advocate[ed] it," Fed. R. Civ. P. 11(b)), it also contains what is generally referred to as a "safe harbor" provision. Fed. R. Civ. P. 11(c)(2). The case below fleshes out how this "safe harbor" provision works and when it applies.

Ridder v. City of Springfield
109 F. 3d 288 (6th Cir. 1997)

Before: Suhrheinrish and Moore, Circuit Judges; McKinley, District Judge.*

Moore, Circuit Judge.

In this appeal we are asked to determine the propriety of sanctions under Fed. R. Civ. P. 11, as amended in 1993, when a motion for sanctions

---

* The Honorable Joseph H. McKinley, Jr., United States District Judge for the Western District of Kentucky, sitting by designation.

is filed without satisfying the requisite "safe harbor" period and after a court has entered summary judgment. Following a protracted civil rights litigation resulting in summary judgment for defendants on all claims, Defendant City of Springfield moved for sanctions against Plaintiff Stephen M. Ridder's counsel, Dwight D. Brannon, pursuant to Rule 11 and 28 U.S.C. § 1927, without first serving the motion on plaintiff's counsel for a "safe harbor" period as instructed by the 1993 Amendments to Rule 11. Agreeing with Springfield's contention that over the five-year litigation period Ridder had failed to put forth any evidence of a proper basis for municipal liability, the magistrate judge imposed sanctions in the form of a $32,546.02 fine against Ridder's counsel. As explained below, we disallow the Rule 11 sanctions because Springfield failed to comply with the rule's explicit procedural prerequisite. Springfield is entitled to $32,546.02 in attorney fees, however, under § 1927 insofar as Ridder's counsel unreasonably and vexatiously multiplied the proceedings. Therefore, we affirm the magistrate judge's order awarding fees.

I. Background

In January 1990, Stephen M. Ridder commenced an action under 42 U.S.C. § 1983 against the City of Springfield, Ohio, and other defendants as a result of his arrest and pre-trial incarceration for a number of rape and related charges. Ridder essentially alleged that the actions of Springfield police officers in withholding from a search warrant affidavit inconsistent information given by various rape victims and in failing to investigate fully Ridder's alibis deprived Ridder of his constitutional right to due process of law.

The events that formed the basis of Ridder's suit stemmed from a series of rapes that occurred in and around Springfield between January 1986 and July 1988. In July 1988, Ridder's hand was nearly severed in an industrial accident. While physicians reattached his hand, a hospital employee identified Ridder's voice as that of her attacker. Police began investigating Ridder. He could be placed in the general location at the time of several of the rapes, and five of eight victims identified him in a lineup. Pursuant to a fourteen-count indictment, Springfield police officers arrested Ridder on September 8, 1988. He was detained in the Clark County Jail from then until January 4, 1989, when DNA tests exonerated him. Ridder was released from jail on January 4, 1989, and all charges against him were later dropped.

On January 4, 1990, Ridder filed a complaint against the City of Springfield, Clark County, Prosecutor Stephen A. Schumaker, Clark County Sheriff Gene A. Kelly, Springfield Chief of Police Roger Evans, Sergeant Robert Marcum, Detectives Ronald Mendah and Robert Kerr, and Dr. Walter Lawrence alleging several causes of action pursuant to 42 U.S.C. § 1983, 42 U.S.C. § 1985, and state law. The assigned magistrate judge, Michael R. Merz, noted several pleading deficiencies as to who was being sued for what and gave Ridder an opportunity to amend the complaint. On October 1, 1990, Ridder filed an amended complaint. The magistrate judge subsequently dismissed most claims in the amended complaint as failing to state a claim upon which relief could be granted or as barred by qualified immunity.

Ridder then obtained leave to file a second amended complaint, which he filed on May 11, 1992. With respect to this complaint, the magistrate judge granted a defense motion for a more definite statement, noting that "still the Court is faced with a pleading that is not explicit about who is being sued for what." The magistrate judge also decided *sua sponte* that the filing of the second amended complaint constituted a violation of 28 U.S.C. § 1927 in that it multiplied proceedings vexatiously and unreasonably. This § 1927 ruling, however, never became final as the magistrate judge granted Ridder leave to file a third amended complaint.

Ridder filed his third amended complaint on August 17, 1993. In the intervening period, the Supreme Court in *Leatherman v. Tarrant County Narcotics Intelligence and Coordination Unit*, 507 U.S. 163 (1993), held that a civil rights complaint alleging municipal liability cannot be subject to a heightened pleading standard. Recognizing *Leatherman*'s effect on Ridder's municipal liability claims, the magistrate judge deemed the third amended complaint sufficient for Ridder's case to progress beyond the pleading stage.

Proceeding on the basis of the third amended complaint, the parties undertook discovery throughout 1994. Near the end of that year, Springfield moved for summary judgment. Even assuming that the Springfield police officers deprived Ridder of a constitutional right, the magistrate judge found that Ridder offered no evidence that the officers acted pursuant to any policy, custom, or usage of the City of Springfield, as required by *Monell v. Department of Social Servs.*, 436 U.S. 658, 690 (1978).* Ridder admitted in interrogatories that he was not relying on any written policy, and the magistrate judge found no evidence that the officers' conduct toward Ridder was pursuant to a pattern, much less amounted to a policy, custom, or usage. *Id.* Accordingly, the magistrate judge dismissed the § 1983 claims against Springfield, as well as all other claims against the City and other defendants.

On March 28, 1995, one month after the magistrate judge entered judgment in favor of the City, Springfield moved for attorney fees and/or sanc-

---

* Ed. Note. In a Section 1983 suit, when the municipal employer is the defendant, rather than (or in addition to) the officials who actually carried out the constitutional violation, the plaintiff must prove that the violation stemmed from a pattern, practice, policy, or custom of the municipality. Unlike qualified immunity, which protects the officials themselves when they are sued in their individual capacities, this "pattern, practice, policy, or custom" rule is a standard of fault, not an affirmative defense.

tions pursuant to 42 U.S.C. § 1988, 28 U.S.C. § 1927, and Rule 11. Early in the case Springfield had determined that separate counsel would be retained to defend the individual police officers, thereby avoiding conflict inherent in having one attorney represent both the officers and the City. Accordingly, Springfield sought reimbursement for the fees earned by the retained counsel and not for the time and effort of the Law Director for the City of Springfield, who represented the City's interests throughout Ridder's suit.

Springfield urged that Ridder's counsel should be sanctioned under Rule 11 for "failing to reasonably investigate, pre-filing, claims made against Defendant City, and for continuing in their claims long after it became, or should have become, clear that there was no factual or legal basis for municipal liability." Springfield acknowledged the "safe harbor" provision of amended Rule 11 which instructs that a motion should be served on offending counsel twenty-one days prior to any filing with the court, yet the City admitted that it did not serve such a motion on Ridder's counsel. Finally, Springfield insisted that by pursuing the case over five years, Ridder's counsel unreasonably and vexatiously multiplied the litigation within the meaning of 28 U.S.C. § 1927. Ridder unsuccessfully moved the magistrate judge to stay decision on Springfield's motion for sanctions pending appeal to this court of the underlying civil rights action.

On October 11, 1995, the magistrate judge ordered Ridder's counsel, Dwight D. Brannon, to pay the City of Springfield $32,546.02 pursuant to Rule 11 and 28 U.S.C. § 1927. According to the magistrate judge, Ridder's counsel asserted frivolous claims against Springfield at the outset of the case, and continued to maintain the claims without ever developing evidentiary support. As to Rule 11's "safe harbor" provision, the magistrate judge reasoned:

> The purpose of this requirement in the Rule is to allow a party threatened with sanctions to withdraw an offending paper, thereby avoiding the need to litigate the Rule 11 questions. Here the Motion is directed to Plaintiff's counsel's conduct in maintaining the case at all and keeping the City of Springfield in the case from the beginning through summary judgment. Plaintiff has vigorously defended against motions to dismiss and certainly did not withdraw his claims against the City of Springfield when confronted with their motion for summary judgment. Serving Plaintiff's counsel with the Rule 11 Motion 21 days before filing it would have been in this case an empty formality. In any event, the requirement does not appear to be jurisdictional; amended Rule 11 does not forbid the award of sanctions when this particular requirement is not met.

Thus, according to the magistrate judge, the failure of Springfield to comport with Rule 11's "safe harbor" provision was essentially harmless.

II. Rule 11 Sanctions
A. Standard of Review

In this circuit the test for imposition of Rule 11 sanctions is whether the attorney's conduct was reasonable under the circumstances. We review all aspects of a court's Rule 11 determination for abuse of discretion. A court necessarily abuses its discretion if it bases its ruling on an erroneous view of the law or a clearly erroneous assessment of the evidence.

B. The 1993 Amendments to Rule 11

Originally enacted in 1937 but rarely utilized for over four decades, Rule 11 became a popular tool for regulating attorney behavior following the rule's major overhaul in 1983. The 1983 version of Rule 11 mandated sanctions when an attorney failed to satisfy an objective standard of reasonable pre-filing inquiry into the facts or law underlying a claim. The 1983 amendment was designed to reduce a perceived reluctance of courts to impose sanctions, thereby discouraging dilatory and abusive litigation tactics and streamlining the litigation process. Fed. R. Civ. P. 11 Advisory Committee Notes (1983 Amendment). The application of the 1983 version of Rule 11 provoked considerable commentary and was criticized for spawning satellite litigation, abusing the rule's potential as a fee-shifting device, exacerbating incivility among lawyers and between bench and bar, chilling creative advocacy, and disproportionately impacting plaintiffs over defendants, particularly in the civil rights arena.

Responding to these concerns, Rule 11 was substantially revised in 1993. The new language broadens the scope of attorney obligations but places greater constraints on the imposition of sanctions. Under the amended rule:

> By presenting to the court (whether by signing, filing, submitting, or later advocating) a pleading, written motion, or other paper, an attorney or unrepresented party is certifying that to the best of the person's knowledge, information, and belief, formed after an inquiry reasonable under the circumstances,—
>
> (1) it is not being presented for any improper purpose, such as to harass or to cause unnecessary delay or needless increase in the cost of litigation;
>
> (2) the claims, defenses, and other legal contentions therein are warranted by existing law or by a nonfrivolous argument for the extension, modification, or reversal of existing law or the establishment of new law;
>
> (3) the allegations and other factual contentions have evidentiary support or, if specifically so identified, are likely to have evidentiary support after a reasonable opportunity for further investigation or discovery; and

(4) the denials of factual contentions are warranted on the evidence or, if specifically so identified, are reasonably based on a lack of information or belief.

Fed. R. Civ. P. 11(b). Insofar as the amended rule liberalizes certification standards for factual allegations by validating a potential need for discovery, it reciprocates by embracing a continuing duty of candor: "[I]f evidentiary support is not obtained after a reasonable opportunity for further investigation or discovery, the party has a duty under the rule not to persist with that contention." Fed. R. Civ. P. 11 Advisory Committee Notes (1993 Amendments). Thus, litigants may be sanctioned under the amended rule for continuing to insist upon a position that is no longer tenable.

In a significant turnabout, the amended rule now makes the imposition of sanctions for violations discretionary, rather than mandatory. *See* Fed. R. Civ. P. 11(c). In line with Rule 11's ultimate goal of deterrence, rather than compensation, the amended rule also de-emphasizes monetary sanctions and discourages direct payouts to the opposing party. Fed. R. Civ. P. 11 Advisory Committee Notes (1993 Amendments).

C. "Safe Harbor" Provision

The 1993 amendments prescribe specific procedural requirements for the imposition of Rule 11 sanctions, a conspicuous change from the former version. "A motion for sanctions under this rule shall be made separately from other motions or requests and shall describe the specific conduct alleged to violate [Rule 11(b)]." Fed. R. Civ. P. 11(c)(1)(A). In accord with the amended rule, a party seeking sanctions must follow a two-step process: first, serve the Rule 11 motion on the opposing party for a designated period (at least twenty-one days); and then file the motion with the court. Critical new language directs that the motion for sanctions:

> [S]hall not be filed with or presented to the court unless, within 21 days after service of the motion (or such other period as the court may prescribe), the challenged paper, claim, defense, contention, allegation, or denial is not withdrawn or appropriately corrected.

Id. In the Advisory Committee Notes, the drafters correspondingly state:

> These provisions are intended to provide a type of "safe harbor" against motions under Rule 11 in that a party will not be subject to sanctions on the basis of another party's motion unless, after receiving the motion, it refuses to withdraw that position or to acknowledge candidly that it does not currently have evidence to support a specified allegation.... [T]he timely withdrawal of a contention will protect a party against a motion for sanctions.

Fed. R. Civ. P. 11 Advisory Committee Notes (1993 Amendments). Thus, the 1993 amendments allow for a twenty-one day period of "safe harbor," whereby the offending party can avoid sanctions altogether by withdrawing or correcting the challenged document or position after receiving notice of the allegedly violative conduct. In that way, the "safe harbor" provision works in conjunction with the duty of candor, giving the proponent of a questionable claim an opportunity to assess the claim's validity without immediate repercussion.

The inclusion of a "safe harbor" provision is expected to reduce Rule 11's volume, formalize appropriate due process considerations of sanctions litigation, and diminish the rule's chilling effect. By providing immunity from sanctions through self-regulation, the "safe harbor" period also serves the streamlining purpose that the 1983 architects of Rule 11 originally envisioned. Undoubtedly, the drafters also anticipated that civility among attorneys and between bench and bar would be furthered by having attorneys communicate with each other with an eye toward potentially resolving their differences prior to court involvement.

On the other hand, the creation of a "safe harbor" period minimizes the risks of engaging in inappropriate litigation tactics. Justice Scalia, dissenting from the Supreme Court's adoption of the 1993 amendments to Rule 11, noted as much, believing the revisions render Rule 11 "toothless," in part because the "safe harbor" provision allows for an offending attorney to "escape with no sanction at all.... Under the revised Rule, parties will be able to file thoughtless, reckless, and harassing pleadings, secure in the knowledge that they have nothing to lose." Amendments to the Federal Rules of Civil Procedure, Dissenting Statement of Justice Scalia, 146 F.R.D. 507–08 (1993). The "safe harbor" provision has also been criticized as increasing litigation costs by forcing litigants to review, research, and reconsider any pleading that the other party believes may be sanctionable. However, the burden imposed by the new procedure does not appear to be significantly more onerous than that imposed by the prior rule or "the dictates of good professional practice." *See* 5A CHARLES A. WRIGHT & ARTHUR MILLER, FEDERAL PRACTICE & PROCEDURE, CIVIL 2A. § 1332 (Supp. 1996).

D. Timing of Rule 11 Motion

The now-discarded 1983 version of Rule 11 designated no particular time for filing a Rule 11 motion. Rather, the Advisory Committee Notes under the 1983 amendment contemplated that, although the court had discretion with respect to when sanctions could be imposed, Rule 11 issues stemming from the pleadings "normally [would] be determined at the end of the litigation." Fed. R. Civ. P. 11 Advisory Committee Notes (1983 Amendment). It became settled law, before the 1993 amendments took effect, that a Rule 11 motion could be made after final judgment, subject to local rules establishing timeliness standards. This is no longer the case.

Although the text of the amended rule fails to specify when a Rule 11 motion should be brought, the drafters advise early action:

> The revision leaves for resolution on a case-by-case basis, considering the particular circumstances involved, the question as to when a motion for violation of Rule 11 should be served and when, if filed, it should be decided. Ordinarily the motion should be served promptly after the inappropriate paper is filed, and, if delayed too long, may be viewed as untimely. In other circumstances, it should not be served until the other party has had a reasonable opportunity for discovery. Given the "safe harbor" provisions … a party cannot delay serving its Rule 11 motion until conclusion of the case (or judicial rejection of the offending contention).

Fed. R. Civ. P. 11 Advisory Committee Notes (1993 Amendments). Thus, the 1993 amendments work a significant change in the timing of a Rule 11 motion. By virtue of the fact that under the 1993 amendments, a Rule 11 motion cannot be made unless there is some paper, claim, or contention that can be withdrawn, it follows that a party cannot wait to seek sanctions until after the contention has been judicially disposed. A party must now serve a Rule 11 motion on the allegedly offending party at least twenty-one days prior to conclusion of the case or judicial rejection of the offending contention. If the court disposes of the offending contention before the twenty-one day "safe harbor" period expires, a motion for sanctions cannot be filed with or presented to the court. Any other interpretation would defeat the rule's explicit requirements. Once a motion is properly filed with the court, the drafters prudently permit the court to defer ruling on the sanctions motion until after the final resolution of the case. *See* Fed. R. Civ. P. 11 Advisory Committee Notes (1993 Amendments).

E.

* * *

F. Springfield's Motion for Rule 11 Sanctions

There is no question that Springfield failed to comply with the "safe harbor" procedural prerequisite of the amended rule. Springfield admits that it did not serve the motion for sanctions on Ridder's counsel prior to filing the motion with the court:

> Finally, counsel for Defendant City is not unaware of the amendment of Rule 11 effective December 1, 1993, particularly insofar as paragraph (c)(1)(A) now sets forth a procedure for service of a motion upon the offending counsel prior to filing with the Court, and the twenty-one (21) day "safe harbor" provision that is also now in Rule 11. Further, the Defendant City has not served such a motion upon Plaintiff's counsel in this case.

Motion at 10 (emphasis added). Notwithstanding this admission, Springfield insists that complying with the "safe harbor" provision would have been a "vain act," for Ridder's counsel "clearly evidenced a willingness to persist in meritless claims." Motion at 11.

Rule 11 cases emerging in the wake of the 1993 amendments have found the "safe harbor" provision to be an absolute requirement. We agree that the rule is unquestionably explicit with respect to this issue. The plain language of Rule 11 specifies that unless a movant has complied with the twenty-one day "safe harbor" service, the motion for sanctions "shall not be filed with or presented to the court." Fed. R. Civ. P. 11(c)(1)(A). Springfield did not comply with the "safe harbor" procedural prerequisite; therefore, the City's Rule 11 motion should not have been presented to the court.

Nonetheless, the magistrate judge found and Springfield argues that the "safe harbor" provision is rendered a mere "empty formality" when a motion for sanctions comes after summary judgment has been granted. We fully agree with that observation. By virtue of its nature, the "safe harbor" provision cannot have any effect if the court has already rendered its judgment in the case; it is too late for the offending party to withdraw the challenged claim. Given the futility of the "safe harbor" provision in this context, Springfield deduces that compliance is unnecessary. This is where we depart from Springfield's logic. Rather than excusing Springfield's non-compliance, we instead hold that Springfield has given up the opportunity to receive an award of Rule 11 sanctions in this case by waiting to file the motion until after the entry of summary judgment. As stated above, a motion for sanctions under Rule 11 must be served on the offending party for a period of "safe harbor" at least twenty-one days prior to the entry of final judgment or judicial rejection of the offending contention. A party seeking sanctions must leave sufficient opportunity for the opposing party to choose whether to withdraw or cure the offense voluntarily before the court disposes of the challenged contention.

Pragmatic realities require such strict adherence to the rule's outlined procedure. By delaying the motion until after summary judgment was granted, Springfield deprived Ridder's counsel of the "safe harbor" to which the rule says he is entitled. Had Ridder's counsel been allotted his "safe harbor" service, he could have avoided sanction by withdrawing the claims against Springfield. That is the very essence of a "safe harbor." Instead, Ridder's counsel was unable to choose for himself whether to continue asserting claims against the City when faced with a potential payout from his own pocket. Neither the opposing party nor the magistrate judge should, with hindsight, step into the attorney's shoes to speculate as to whether the prospect of a fine or other sanctions would have sufficiently motivated the attorney to withdraw the offense. Moreover, had the twenty-one day "safe harbor" period been provided, and Ridder withdrawn his claims, the magistrate judge would have been spared the need to rule on the City's summary judgment motion.

In sum, adhering to the rule's explicit language and overall structure, we hold that sanctions under Rule 11 are unavailable unless the motion for sanctions is served on the opposing party for the full twenty-one day "safe harbor" period before it is filed with or presented to the court; this service and filing must occur prior to final judgment or judicial rejection of the offending contention. Quite clearly then, a party cannot wait until after summary judgment to move for sanctions under Rule 11.[8]

By filing a motion for sanctions without previously having served the motion on the opposing party for the designated period and by waiting until summary judgment had been entered, Springfield failed to afford Ridder's counsel the twenty-one day "safe harbor" period mandated by the 1993 revised rule. We conclude that the magistrate judge's decision to impose Rule 11 sanctions in this case was based upon an erroneous view of the rule and thus amounted to an abuse of the magistrate judge's discretion. For this reason, we vacate the imposition of sanctions under Rule 11.

III. Counsel's Liability Under 28 U.S.C. § 1927

The unavailability of Rule 11 sanctions in the present case does not rule out the possibility that attorney fees were properly assessed against Ridder's counsel pursuant to 28 U.S.C. § 1927. Unlike Rule 11 sanctions, a motion for excess costs and attorney fees under § 1927 is not predicated upon a "safe harbor" period, nor is the motion untimely if made after the final judgment in a case. Therefore, this avenue for upholding the fee award against Ridder remains viable.

Having found sanctions appropriate under Rule 11, the magistrate judge concluded that he:

> [N]eed not analyze the 28 U.S.C. § 1927 authority as well except to state that it also supports the same award since the conduct of counsel being sanctioned is pleading the policy claim against Springfield in the beginning and then failing to develop any evidence in support of it. The excess costs incurred by Springfield and recoverable under § 1927 against Mr. Brannon are the same amount to be awarded under Rule 11.

Decision, Oct. 11, 1995 at 7. Thus, the magistrate judge did enter a finding that the $32,546.02 fee award was also justified under § 1927, although his explanation leaves little for us to review. In the interest of preventing

---

8. Our construction of Rule 11's "safe harbor" provision does not in any way preclude the ability of a district or magistrate judge, on his or her own initiative, to enter an order describing the offending conduct and directing the offending attorney to show cause why Rule 11 has not been violated. See Fed. R. Civ. P. 11(c)(1)(B). There is no corresponding "safe harbor" period for court-initiated sanctions.

further delay in this already protracted litigation, we will determine whether a § 1927 fine against Ridder's counsel was warranted. As with Rule 11 sanctions, we review an order awarding attorney fees under § 1927 for abuse of discretion.

Section 1927 provides that any attorney "who so multiplies the proceedings in any case unreasonably and vexatiously may be required by the court to satisfy personally the excess costs, expenses, and attorneys' fees reasonably incurred because of such conduct." 28 U.S.C. § 1927.

Initially, this circuit understood the statute as punishing "an intentional departure from proper conduct, or, at a minimum, ... a reckless disregard of the duty owed by counsel to the court." *United States v. Ross*, 535 F.2d 346, 349 (6th Cir.1976). After Congress amended the statutory language in 1980, we dispensed with the subjective standard, holding that § 1927 "authorizes a court to assess fees against an attorney for 'unreasonable and vexatious' multiplication of litigation despite the absence of any conscious impropriety." *Jones v. Continental Corp.*, 789 F.2d 1225, 1230 (6th Cir.1986). Fees may be assessed without a finding of bad faith, "at least when an attorney knows or reasonably should know that a claim pursued is frivolous, or that his or her litigation tactics will needlessly obstruct the litigation of nonfrivolous claims." *Id.*

The objective standard enunciated in *Jones* remains sound in this circuit, but we have since reinforced that:

> [S]imple inadvertence or negligence that frustrates the trial judge will not support a sanction under section 1927. There must be some conduct on the part of the subject attorney that trial judges, applying the collective wisdom of their experience on the bench, could agree falls short of the obligations owed by a member of the bar to the court and which, as a result, causes additional expense to the opposing party.

In re Ruben, 825 F.2d 977, 984 (6th Cir. 1987). Under this formulation, the mere finding that an attorney failed to undertake a reasonable inquiry into the basis for a claim does not automatically imply that the proceedings were intentionally or unreasonably multiplied.

We believe that Ridder's counsel, Mr. Brannon, should be liable for excess costs resulting from his initial filing and persistent assertion of meritless claims, conduct that amounted to unreasonable and vexatious multiplication of the proceedings. Mr. Brannon brought suit against the City of Springfield and individual Springfield police officers without any evidence to support a basis for municipal liability, and he persisted in pressing the allegations for over five years, despite unearthing no evidentiary support for the claims even after full discovery. Thus, Mr. Brannon pursued the case against Springfield long after it should have become clear that the claims lacked any plausible factual basis. Under the circumstances, Mr. Brannon's conduct fell short of the obligations owed by a member of the bar and caused considerable expense to the City of Springfield.

An attorney is liable under § 1927 solely for excessive costs resulting from the violative conduct. Mr. Brannon's failure to withdraw the claims against Springfield and the individual police officers forced the City to defend this action for a period in excess of five years. Since we agree with the magistrate judge that Mr. Brannon's unreasonable and vexatious behavior began with the filing of the complaint and persisted throughout the pendency of the case, the magistrate judge did not abuse his discretion by awarding the full amount of attorney fees incurred by counsel separately retained by Springfield to defend the case against the individual officers. Of the many obstacles encountered during the "procedural odyssey" that became this case, we believe many, if not most, are directly attributable to inadequate advocacy by plaintiff's counsel.

We remain sensitive that an award of attorney's fees against a losing plaintiff in a civil rights action is an extreme sanction, and must be limited to truly egregious cases of misconduct. It is a function of the intrinsic nature of civil rights actions that on occasion plaintiffs may not possess full evidentiary support at the onset. However, a civil rights plaintiff does not have free rein to bring and pursue frivolous claims. Here, Mr. Brannon should have diligently withdrawn the claims against the City upon realizing that he was unable to amass any evidentiary support after five years and full discovery. Moreover, the magistrate judge delivered a poignant warning to Mr. Brannon that he had crossed the line into "unreasonable and vexatious multiplication of proceedings" by imposing § 1927 liability for the filing of the second amended complaint, only to rescind that award in response to Mr. Brannon's request for leave yet again to amend the complaint. Surely, at that point, Mr. Brannon should have proceeded cautiously when asserting the same claims in the third amended complaint. Thereafter, however, Mr. Brannon continued asserting the same frivolous claims up to and including plaintiff's motion in opposition to summary judgment, all the while revealing no plausible factual basis for municipal liability.

IV. Conclusion

Pursuant to the "safe harbor" provision of the 1993 amendments to Rule 11, a motion for Rule 11 sanctions must be served on the opposing party at least twenty-one days before it is filed with or presented to the court; this "safe harbor" service and delayed filing must be completed prior to final judgment or judicial rejection of the offending contention. Because Springfield did not comply with the twenty-one day "safe harbor" procedural prerequisite before filing its motion for Rule 11 sanctions, the award of sanctions under Rule 11 was improper. Therefore, of the two alternate bases for imposing a fee award against Ridder's counsel in this case, the order of the magistrate judge is Vacated to the extent that it imposed Rule 11 sanctions, but Affirmed insofar as it awarded attorney fees to Springfield pursuant to 28 U.S.C. § 1927.

Exercise 7-15. Rule 11 versus § 1927

The *Ridder* case illustrates several important principles, among these that the current version of Rule 11 is markedly different from the immediate prior one, which was itself far more rigorous than the original version. Clearly, the Rules drafters have wrestled with the difficulty of establishing a standard of fault justifying sanctions. You will see this issue come up again when we discuss discovery sanctions under Rule 37 (recall that Rule 11 does not apply to discovery).

Another important principle established in *Ridder* is the mandatory nature of the "safe harbor." Note, though, that judges may bring up Rule 11 sanctions on their own motions, and that the only procedural step required there is an order to show cause why sanctions should not be ordered, so Justice Scalia was wrong to say that plaintiffs can plead under the current Rule with reckless abandon, trusting on the "safe harbor" to protect them in all cases.

Finally, we see the overlap between Rule 11 and § 1927. This court approves sanctions under § 1927 for the same conduct that, absent the "safe harbor," would seem to have justified sanctions under Rule 11. Are the two provisions coterminous as to what, and whom, they punish? On your own, try to come up with a list of differences, based both on the *Ridder* case and the text of both the Rule and the Statute. Once you have, share your list with another student from your class and discuss any differences.

Exercise 7-16. Professionalism Exercise

You represent the plaintiff in a breach of contract case. Assume that opposing counsel files and serves an answer that contains a dozen affirmative defenses, many of which obviously lack a legal or factual basis (e.g., "contributory negligence").

1. Would you serve on opposing counsel a Rule 11 motion for sanctions?

2. Would you contact opposing counsel before serving a Rule 11 motion to discuss your concerns about the answer?

3. What factors would guide your ultimate decision on whether to serve a Rule 11 motion?

Exercise 7-17. Putting the Standards Together

Given the facts set forth in the Chapter Problem, what steps would you take to make sure that you could plead your client's case, while (1) meeting the strictures of *Twiqbal*, and also (2) not running afoul of Rule 11 or § 1927, not to mention your professional ethical obligations?

Form a group of two or four, with half of the group as representatives of the plaintiff and the other half as representatives of the defendant. Based on the correspondence file that your professor provides each half of the group [*this file is part of the teacher materials*], draft the complaint and answer it.

Chapter 8

Aggregating Claims and Parties

1. Chapter Problem

The "Shoretown Effect"

Harry and Joe are business partners who own a controlling interest in the Love Island News, Inc. (LINI), which publishes and distributes a newspaper by the same name throughout the four counties making up Love Island, Old York. As the controlling shareholders, they have elected Joe to be the sole Director of LINI, and Joe has, in turn, hired Harry to be the CEO and chief publications director. LINI is located in Selden, a small town on eastern Love Island about three hours' drive from Old York City. Selden is also located about 10 miles (as the crow flies) from the town of Shoretown on the North Shore of Love Island, where Old York's oldest nuclear power plant is situated.

Both Harry and Joe are lifelong Selden residents, and both remember the day the nuclear reactor was first publicly proposed in 1973, when they were both ten years old, and when eastern Love Island was mostly farmland. Both also remember that, when the plant was finished in 1984, Old York Power Company (OYPCO), the owner of the plant, engaged in some testing of the reactor, turning it on at lower levels than would be required for commercial electricity generation. OYPCO is a Delaware Corporation with power-generation facilities throughout the U.S., but its corporate officers reside and meet in Old York. Ultimately, based on the 1979 nuclear disaster at Three Mile Island in Pennsylvania, anti-nuclear protestors compelled Old York State to deny permits to OYPCO to completely fire up the reactor, and the plant never generated any power beyond that generated by the initial testing on one day in 1984. Since 1984, eastern Love Island has become far more populated, and the area can no longer be considered rural in any sense of the word. Housing costs are astronomical.

In late 2006, Dr. Brown, an oncologist (cancer specialist) at the Love Island Medical Center (the "LIMC"), sees a patient named Molly, who is from Port Jackson, a town in eastern Love Island near Selden and just up the coast from Shoretown. Molly complains of lesions on the skin of her arms that look like liver spots. The only problem is that liver spots generally appear when one is elderly (over 60), and Molly is only thirty years old. Dr. Brown decides to conduct

---

a biopsy, which reveals that Molly's skin lesions are actually melanoma (the most deadly kind of skin cancer) in its early stages.

Dr. Brown calls Molly and instructs her to make an appointment with his office to have the lesions removed as soon as possible. Molly asks what could have caused her to contract skin cancer. Molly explains that she never, ever goes out in the sun. In fact, for the past twenty years, she has been seeing a psychologist for treatment of her irrational fear of sun exposure. In Port Jackson, people know her as the "wrapped lady" because she never goes outside without being covered from head to toe (including gloves and a hood in the summer) to prevent any possible exposure to sunlight. Dr. Brown assures her that he has indeed found melanoma, and that it can be caused by numerous factors other than the sun, including genetics and exposure to radiation. Molly makes an appointment to have the lesions removed the next week.

Later that day, Molly runs into Joe, with whom she has been friends since childhood, and she tells him about her diagnosis. Joe sees a potential human interest story there, and after getting Molly's permission, he shares the tale with Harry for potential follow-up by the newspaper they own. Before her operation, Molly is interviewed by a reporter, and a story is published the next day under the title, "Growing Up in the Shadow of Shoretown." The theme of the story is that the only possible explanation for Molly's melanoma is her exposure to dangerous radiation during the limited testing of the Shoretown nuclear reactor in 1984. The story quotes Molly, purportedly quoting Dr. Brown's statement that exposure to radiation "most likely caused" her skin cancer. The story is published both in print and in the online version of the Love Island News, which is accessible nationwide without fee or registration.

The story is a runaway success, in newspaper terms. Both in print and online, it has the highest readership — by far — of any story ever published by an Old York newspaper, outstripping even the Old York Times's coverage of the end of World War II. Within weeks, thousands of people descend upon Love Island and the LIMC from numerous other states, seeking help for skin cancers that they claim to have developed due to proximity to Shoretown in the early 1980s.

Most of these people seek treatment from Dr. Brown, who enlists several colleagues to help with the volume of new cases. Many cases are in their early stages, like Molly's, but many others are at varying stages of seriousness, requiring treatments ranging from simple surgery (like Molly's); to surgery with radiation; to surgery, radiation, and chemotherapy. Some cases are even so advanced that they are not treatable at all, and Dr. Brown must inform these patients that they cannot be helped by medical science. About 500 of these patients die shortly thereafter before even leaving Love Island. Overall, Dr. Brown and his colleagues see 4,700 new patients over the course of the six months following publication of Molly's story.

Some of these new patients have stories similar to Molly's — fear of the sun or very limited sun exposure. Most, however, have experienced normal sun exposure, and some have spent huge amounts of time in the sun, due to holding outside jobs or living most of their lives in very sunny states. Also, although Molly has no history of cancer in her family, many of Dr. Brown's new patients do have such history, and these family histories vary greatly among the new patients.

Fascinated by this explosion of new cancer cases among people with connections to eastern Love Island, Harry and Joe cause another story to be published as a follow up to their first one. This one carries the title, "The Shoretown Effect Spreads." Dr. Brown declines to comment for the story. Once again, the story sets readership records both online and in print. Real estate values in eastern Love Island promptly plummet.

Consider how the following claims might be structured so that the total number of separately filed lawsuits is as small as possible.

1. A claim by Sally, a local real estate agent in Selden, against the Love Island News for tortious interference with her business relationships.

2. A claim by Sally against Harry for tortious interference with her business relationships.

3. A claim by Sally against Joe for tortious interference with her business relationships.

4. A claim by Harry against Sally for malicious prosecution (wrongful litigation).

5. A claim by Sally against Harry for an unpaid real estate commission from one year ago.

6. A claim by Dr. Brown against the Love Island News for defamation, based on what he considers to be a misleading misquoting of him in the paper.

7. A claim by the heirs of Gladys, a former patient of Dr. Brown's who died of melanoma after treatment, for medical malpractice.

8. A claim by Dr. Brown against Joe for an unpaid medical bill from three months ago.

9. A claim by Joe against Insco, Inc., his insurance company, for indemnity and bad faith denial of insurance proceeds, in connection with his treatment from Dr. Brown.

10. A claim by Molly against the Love Island News for invasion of privacy.

11. A claim by Molly against the LIMC for malpractice related to a flawed prescription that caused her to have an allergic reaction.

12. A claim by the LIMC against Dr. Brown for indemnity and contribution on Molly's malpractice claim.

2. Introduction

Chapter 7 fleshed out the requirements for stating claims and defenses in federal court. But the choice of *what* to plead is only one third of the decision to file a complaint. Another third of that decision is *where* to file the complaint, matter addressed partially in each of chapters 2–5. The final third of the decision is *against whom* to file the complaint. Part of this third involves questions of personal jurisdiction, subject matter jurisdiction, and venue. But assuming that each of these is satisfied, the filer of a claim for relief (usually, but not always, the plaintiff) must also decide against whom to assert that claim, along with whether it is the only claim that the plaintiff has. Chapter 8 addresses these questions.

Since these questions are really questions of how many claims and parties will be *joined together* as part of the same action, the Rules group them under the label, "joinder." Also known as "aggregation," joinder describes the combination of more than one claim or party into the same legal action. The Rules authorize two main types of joinder: Claim Joinder and Party Joinder. There are several kinds of each, ranging from the simple joinder of two claims by the same plaintiff against the same defendant, to the highly complex, numerous-party, multiple-claim class action. This Chapter touches on all of these topics, with more treatment of the simpler types of joinder, understanding that the more complex types of joinder often merit their own course, usually called something like "Complex Litigation."

Joinder doctrine is, perhaps more than any other topic in Civil Procedure, a highly "textual" doctrine, requiring close reading of the rules and strict application of their terms. This is not to say that joinder rules don't require interpretation. However, more than most Civil Procedure topics, the answer to a joinder problem usually lies right in the explicit text of the rule. It's learning to read the rules carefully and completely, including paying close attention to cross-references, that matters most of all. The Chapter is organized as follows:

- Section 3 — Basic Claim Joinder, the aggregation of two or more claims between the same two opponents.

- Section 4 — Basic Party Joinder, the aggregation of claims between more than two opponents.

- Section 5 — Complex Joinder, aggregation of claims and parties to prevent unfairness or injustice.

- Section 6 — Class Actions, aggregation of large numbers of claims and parties, with the litigation of the claims through a representative party or party group.

- Section 7 — Professionalism and Joinder. This Section considers the ethical and professional issues raised by the approaches to joinder that prevail in the federal system.

To begin with, it is important to understand some things about joinder that confuse many 1Ls. First, *each individual claim* against *each individual party* in a lawsuit requires *its own basis for joinder*. You must be able to point to a Rule that justifies the presence of each party and each claim in the action. Inability to properly establish the basis for joinder will usually not lead to dismissal, but it can lead to severance of a misjoined claim or party, thus frustrating one reason for joinder in the first place (efficiency). *See* Fed. R. Civ. P. 21. This means that, while you can never ignore the overall structure of the action, you must also be able to focus in and view each claim against each party as its own unit in order to analyze the propriety of its joinder.

Second, no claim is just a claim. All claims are asserted against some person or entity (in our terms, a party). Thus, even if a Rule authorizes the *claim* joinder considered in isolation, such joinder may upset the requirements of another Rule that justifies the presence of the *party* against whom that claim is asserted in the action. And in the same way, joinder of a claim may depend on the Rule of party joinder that placed the party in the case initially.

Third, joinder of both claims and parties can sometimes impact such threshold considerations as personal jurisdiction and subject matter jurisdiction. For example, joinder of additional defendants into an action can affect where that action can proceed, as an action can only be filed where personal jurisdiction exists over all of the defendants. Also, all of the exceptions to supplemental subject matter jurisdiction found in 28 U.S.C. § 1367(b) are based on the Rule under which the defending party was joined.

What this second and third consideration mean for you is that, though you must be able to focus in and consider each claim against each party in isolation to figure out whether it is properly joined, you must also be able to step back and consider each claim within the overall landscape of the dispute to make sure that its joinder does not upset the other claims. In short, both the forest and the trees are important to analyzing joinder. One of us jokes in class that joinder is the sole reason you had to complete that horrible "games" section on the LSAT, and once you work your way through the materials, you'll see what we mean.

With all of this in mind, some terminology will be useful to us as we work through the material in this Chapter. First, remember that a "party" is a person (or entity) who is part of the action as filed or amended. Every party will be connected to at least one claim, either as the party asserting the claim or as the party against whom the claim is asserted. A "non-party" is a person (or entity) who is not part of the action as filed or amended. When a party proposes to join a non-party, that non-party becomes a party once joined, usually through the filing of an amended or supplemental pleading, as discussed in Chapter 7. A "third party" is usually a party who is not the subject of the main dispute in the case, but who might be liable to one of the other parties if *that* party loses the case.*

You will see very quickly that plaintiffs are not the only parties who file claims — far from it. Accordingly, the Rules provide names for parties who are not plaintiffs, but who nevertheless assert claims — names such as "counterclaimant" and "third-party plaintiff." You will get used to these names the more you use them. Sometimes, however, it is difficult to keep these roles straight in a complex case, especially if joinder has only been proposed, but not yet accomplished. To help out with this

---

* Ed. Note. In discovery, the term "third party" is usually meant to denote a non-party who has in its possession or control materials or information that will be useful to the parties in the case. This dual meaning can be confusing, but the term "third party" has a formal meaning in the joinder context. Its meaning in discovery is more informal.

problem, we will occasionally use the word "claimant" to describe the party who asserts (or seeks to assert) a claim for relief against another party (or prospective party) and "defending party" to describe the claimant's (actual or proposed) adversary. Where it is possible, however, we will use the terms that the Rules provide, and you should too.

Finally, it is important to understand that, once a claim is joined against a party (whether an existing party or one newly added to the case), the party against whom the claim is asserted has all the same rights as the initial defendant to challenge the new claim based on its foundation, jurisdiction, etc. The new claim also requires an answer, just as the initial complaint required one. As a result, joinder after the initial filing of the complaint can greatly lengthen the time it takes to dispose of an action, so courts tend to pay close attention to the propriety of joinder.

Exercise 8-1. Interrogating the Purpose of Joinder

The Federal Rules do not authorize joinder simply as a lark. Very good, policy-based reasons, some of which are explicitly stated within the Rules and the committee notes accompanying them, exist to justify joining claims and parties together in the same action, but other good reasons exist that would counsel against completely unfettered joinder.

As you prepare to engage the material in this Chapter, put yourself in the shoes of one seeking to join multiple claims or parties to an action. From a policy perspective, what are some general reasons that a court should let you do so?

Switching sides, now think of yourself as a party who has not yet been joined into an ongoing action, and who would like to remain that way. From a policy perspective, what reasons would you use to attempt to convince a court that there should be limits on joinder?

---

3. Basic Claim Joinder

Read Rule 18. This is the most basic of all the joinder rules. It authorizes any "party" (a person or entity that has already been joined in the case) to assert as many claims as he has, regardless of whether those claims are related to one another, against "an opposing party" (another party to the case who is already the prospective claimant's adversary as to an existing claim). Under Rule 18, all that is necessary is that the claimant has at least one other claim in the action that is proper both jurisdictionally and under the joinder rules. If so, then that claimant can assert any other claim he has against the same defending party, regardless of any relationship between the initial, or "anchor," claim and the claim(s) joined to that anchor claim under Rule 18.

A diagram of Rule 18 joinder appears below, where claim "A" functions as the "anchor claim," or the claim to which others will be joined, and claim "B" is the claim joined by virtue of Rule 18:

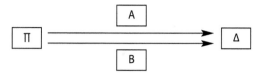

Not all claim joinders are so simple, though, and not all are voluntary.

Rule 13 introduces two more complex forms of basic claim joinder, one of which is sometimes "compulsory," or non-voluntary. Read Rule 13. You will notice that Rule 13 has a few more permutations than Rule 18, but the claims it authorizes are not very difficult to comprehend.

The first two subsections ((a) and (b)) describe a claim asserted by an existing defending party against an existing claimant who has already asserted a claim against that defending party (usually, this means a claim asserted back against the plaintiff by the defendant, but this is not always so in a case with multiple claims filed by multiple parties). That is why the Rule terms such a claim a "counterclaim" — it "counters" a claim already asserted by asserting a claim against the original claimant. The only difference between subsections (a) and (b) is that, if a claim meets the requirements of subsection (a), it *must* be asserted (unless one of the exceptions applies), whereas if it does not, it only *may* be asserted (meaning that the claimant can choose not to assert it in this action and instead file a separate action on that claim). In either case, the claimant does not need to seek leave of court to assert the counterclaim — the difference in the subsections only determines whether the claimant *must* assert the counterclaim, or *may* wait and assert it in another lawsuit. A diagram of a counterclaim appears below, where the initial claim is represented by "A," and the counterclaim is represented by "B.":

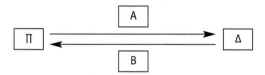

Subsection (g) governs crossclaims, which are claims between two existing parties who are already adversaries of the same opposing party. The Rule describes the person against whom one may assert a crossclaim as a coparty, basically meaning a party on the same side of the "v" as the crossclaimant. This part of the Rule thus only applies where the case involves either more than one plaintiff or more than one defendant. If the case only involves one plaintiff and one defendant, then no "crossclaims" are possible because crossclaims can be asserted only against "coparties." Here is a diagram of a crossclaim, where the original claims by the plaintiff against the two defendants (the coparties) are represented by "A" and "B," and the crossclaim is represented by "C."

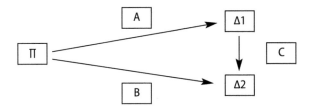

Exercise 8-2. Compulsory and Permissive Joinder of Claims

Consider the following hypothetical. Decide whether each claim can be joined against the party it is asserted against, and note the subsection of the rule that authorizes joinder if so.

While visiting his vacation home in Tennessee, Bart Johnson, a domiciliary of Kentucky, takes his car, a rare Bentley worth over $300,000, to AAA Auto, the local luxury car garage, for a tune-up. After leaving the garage, he notices a persistent rattling that was not there before he brought the car to the garage. Thinking that the mechanics must have inadvertently left a tool in the engine compartment, he drives the two blocks back to the garage, but while pulling into the garage's parking lot, he is broad-sided by another customer pulling into the parking lot from the opposite direction. When the other customer, Bill Parker, gets out of the car, he claims that he could not see Bart's car due to a reflection of the sun's light coming off the front window of the garage, which temporarily blinded him. He apologizes to Bart, and they exchange insurance information.

Bart pulls his Bentley (which is banged up, but still driveable) over to the garage bay where his tune-up was performed. The mechanic opens the hood and finds a large crescent wrench that was left on top of the engine before the hood was closed and is now tightly wedged into the engine. Unfortunately, the mechanic also finds that the car's state-of-the-art engine computer, which calibrates the engine's performance down to a microscopic level of efficiency rivaled only by the Space Shuttle, has been smashed beyond repair. He says that this computer will have to be replaced right away, or Bart will risk losing control of the car on the way home. The mechanic says he can install a new engine computer in the Bentley for the bargain price of $80,000. Bart is furious. He shouts, "You mean that I have to *pay* you to fix what you just broke by carelessly leaving a wrench in my engine?!" The mechanic says, "Looks to me like the wreck you were just in broke the computer, not my wrench."

Bart storms out and drives (slowly) to another garage, where he pays $80,000 to have a new computer installed. Later, Bart resolves to sue both Bill and AAA Auto, both of whom are domiciled in Tennessee, for the damage to his car.

Bart files a complaint in Tennessee federal court against both Bill and AAA for property damage in the amount of $80,000. Bill decides to "sue Bart back," in his words, so he files a claim for damage to his own vehicle against

Bart. AAA, for its part, believes that both Bart and Bill damaged part of its front entrance when their cars crashed into each other, so AAA files claims against both Bart and Bill for that damage. As it happens, AAA also has an unpaid invoice from Bill dating back a few months, so AAA decides to sue Bill for that payment, as well. Finally, Bill also has a preexisting dispute with AAA, but that dispute stems from service that AAA provided him (and for which he paid in full) three months prior to the service for which he has not yet paid. He sues AAA for a refund of that prior payment, contending that AAA failed to repair his vehicle competently.

Which Rule(s) (and which precise subsection(s) of such Rule(s)) justify joining each of these claims? Are any of the claims compulsory? Is each claim joined properly under its respective Rule? Diagram the claims and parties.

Related Claims and Joinder

You will note that joinder under Rule 13 depends in part on whether the claims involved arose under the same "transaction or occurrence." This determination makes the difference in determining whether a counterclaim is compulsory or not, and whether two existing parties may file cross claims against each other. But what does it mean for two claims to be related in this way? The following cases consider the question. They also consider a matter that has generated a split of authority among the federal Circuits: whether the "same transaction or occurrence" requirement of Rule 13(a) (and several other joinder rules) differs meaningfully from the "same case or controversy" requirement of the supplemental jurisdiction statute, 28 U.S.C. § 1367(a).

Jones v. Ford Motor Credit Co.
358 F.3d 205 (2004)

Before: NEWMAN, SOTOMAYOR, and WESLEY, Circuit Judges.

Opinion

JON O. NEWMAN, Circuit Judge.

This appeal concerns the availability of subject matter jurisdiction for permissive counterclaims. It also demonstrates the normal utility of early decision of a motion for class certification. Defendant-Appellant Ford Motor Credit Company ("Ford Credit") appeals from the June 14, 2002, judgment of the United States District Court for the Southern District of New York dismissing for lack of jurisdiction its permissive counterclaims against three of the four Plaintiffs-Appellees and its conditional counterclaims against members of the putative class that the Plaintiffs-Appellees seek to certify. We conclude that supplemental jurisdiction authorized by 28 U.S.C. § 1367 may be available for the permissive counterclaims, but that the District Court's discretion under subsection 1367(c) should not be exercised in this case until a ruling on the Plaintiffs' motion for class certification. We therefore vacate and remand.

Background

Plaintiffs-Appellees Joyce Jones, Martha L. Edwards, Lou Cooper, and Vincent E. Jackson ("Plaintiffs"), individually and as class representatives, sued Ford Credit alleging racial discrimination under the Equal Credit Opportunity Act ("ECOA"), 15 U.S.C. § 1691 *et seq.* (2003). They had purchased Ford vehicles under Ford Credit's financing plan. They alleged that the financing plan discriminated against African-Americans. Although the financing rate was primarily based on objective criteria, Ford Credit permitted its dealers to mark up the rate, using subjective criteria to assess non-risk charges. The Plaintiffs alleged that the mark-up policy penalized African-American customers with higher rates than those imposed on similarly situated Caucasian customers.

In its Answer, Ford Credit denied the charges of racial discrimination and also asserted state-law counterclaims against Jones, Edwards, and Cooper for the amounts of their unpaid car loans. Ford Credit alleged that Jones was in default on her obligations under her contract for the purchase of a 1995 Ford Windstar, and that Edwards and Cooper were in default on payments for their joint purchase of a 1995 Mercury Cougar. Additionally, in the event that a class was certified, Ford Credit asserted conditional counterclaims against any member of that class who was in default on a car loan from Ford Credit. The Plaintiffs moved to dismiss Ford Credit's counterclaims for lack of subject matter jurisdiction, lack of personal jurisdiction, improper venue, and failure to state a claim upon which relief could be granted.

The District Court granted the Plaintiffs' motion and dismissed Ford Credit's counterclaims, summarizing its reasons for doing so as follows: "[D]efendant's counterclaims do not meet the standard for compulsory counterclaims[, and] … pursuant to § 1367(c)(4), … there are compelling reasons to decline to exercise jurisdiction over the counterclaims."

In reaching these conclusions, Judge McKenna acknowledged some uncertainty. After determining that the counterclaims were permissive, he expressed doubt as to the jurisdictional consequence of that determination. On the one hand, he believed, as the Plaintiffs maintain, that permissive counterclaims must be dismissed if they lack an independent basis of federal jurisdiction. On the other hand, he acknowledged that "there [was] some authority to suggest that … the court should determine, based on the particular circumstances of the case, whether it ha[d] authority to exercise supplemental jurisdiction under § 1367(a)" over a counterclaim, regardless of whether it was compulsory or permissive.

To resolve his uncertainty, Judge McKenna initially ruled that the counterclaims, being permissive, "must be dismissed for lack of an independent basis of federal jurisdiction." He then ruled that, if he was wrong and if supplemental jurisdiction under section 1367 was available, he would still dismiss the counterclaims in the exercise of the discretion subsection 1367(c) gives district courts. Without explicitly stating on which of the four subdivisions of subsection 1367(c) he relied, Judge McKenna gave the following reasons for declining to exercise supplemental jurisdiction:

> [1] The claims and counterclaims arise out of the same occurrence only in the loosest terms.... There does not exist a logical relationship between the essential facts [to be proven] in the claim and those of the counterclaims.

> [2] [A]llowing defendant's counterclaims to proceed in this forum might undermine the ECOA enforcement scheme by discouraging plaintiffs from bringing ECOA claims due to the fear of counterclaims.

> [3] [T]he interests of judicial economy will not be served by joining the claim and counterclaims in one suit [because of] what would most likely be a tremendous number of separate collection actions, each based on facts specific to the individual plaintiffs involved.

Judge McKenna stated his belief that it would be "unfair and inexpedient" to require absent class members who resided outside of New York to litigate their debt collection actions in the Southern District of New York and that there was no good reason to litigate the debt collection actions in a federal court.

On March 27, 2003, the District Court entered judgment pursuant to Fed.R.Civ.P. 54(b) in favor of the Plaintiffs, dismissing Ford Credit's counterclaims without prejudice. Ford Credit appeals from this decision.

Discussion

I. Are Ford Credit's Counterclaims Permissive?

Fed.R.Civ.P. 13(a) defines a compulsory counterclaim as

any claim which at the time of serving the pleading the pleader has against any opposing party, if it arises out of the transaction or occurrence that is the subject matter of the opposing party's claim and does not require for its adjudication the presence of third parties of whom the court cannot obtain jurisdiction.

Such counterclaims are compulsory in the sense that if they are not raised, they are forfeited. Fed.R.Civ.P. 13(b) defines a permissive counterclaim as "any claim against an opposing party not arising out of the transaction or occurrence that is the subject matter of the opposing party's claim."

Whether a counterclaim is compulsory or permissive turns on whether the counterclaim "arises out of the transaction or occurrence that is the subject matter of the opposing party's claim," and this Circuit has long considered this standard met when there is a "logical relationship" between the counterclaim and the main claim. Although the "logical relationship" test does not require "an absolute identity of factual backgrounds," the " 'essential facts of the claims [must be] so logically connected that considerations of judicial economy and fairness dictate that all the issues be resolved in one lawsuit.' " Critical-Vac, 233 F.3d at 699 (emphasis omitted) (quoting Adam v. Jacobs, 950 F.2d 89, 92 (2d Cir.1991)); see also Harris v. Steinem, 571 F.2d 119, 123 (2d Cir.1978); United Artists Corp. v. Masterpiece Productions, Inc., 221 F.2d 213, 216 (2d Cir.1955).

We agree with the District Court that the debt collection counterclaims were permissive rather than compulsory. The Plaintiffs' ECOA claim centers on Ford Credit's mark-up policy, based on subjective factors, which allegedly resulted in higher finance charges on their purchase contracts than on those of similarly situated White customers. Ford Credit's debt collection counterclaims are related to those purchase contracts, but not to any particular clause or rate. Rather, the debt collection counterclaims concern the individual Plaintiffs' non-payment after the contract price was set. Thus, the relationship between the counterclaims and the ECOA claim is "logical" only in the sense that the sale, allegedly on discriminatory credit terms, was the "but for" cause of the non-payment. That is not the sort of relationship contemplated by our case law on compulsory counterclaims. The essential facts for proving the counterclaims and the ECOA claim are not so closely related that resolving both sets of issues in one lawsuit would yield judicial efficiency. Indeed, Ford Credit does not even challenge the ruling that its counterclaims are permissive.

II. Is There Jurisdiction over the Permissive Counterclaims?

For several decades federal courts have asserted that permissive counterclaims require an independent basis of jurisdiction, i.e., that the counterclaim must be maintainable in a federal district court on some jurisdictional basis that would have sufficed had it been brought in a separate action. The origin of this proposition, the questioning of it before the statutory authorization of supplemental jurisdiction in section 1367, and the impact of that provision upon the proposition all merit careful consideration.

. . . .

(C) The impact of section 1367. The judge-made doctrine of ancillary jurisdiction, which had been invoked to provide a jurisdictional basis for compulsory counterclaims, was given statutory undergirding when Congress added section 1367 to Title 28 in 1990. See Judicial Improvements Act of 1990, Pub.L. No. 101-650, Title III, §310(c), 104 Stat. 5114 (1990). The newly labeled "supplemental" jurisdiction explicitly extended federal courts' authority to "all other claims" in a civil action "so related to claims in the action within [the district court's] original jurisdiction that they form part of the same case or controversy under Article III of the United States Constitution." 28 U.S.C. §1367(a) (2000).

The explicit extension to the limit of Article III of a federal court's jurisdiction over "all other claims" sought to be litigated with an underlying claim within federal jurisdiction recast the jurisdictional basis of permissive counterclaims into constitutional terms. After section 1367, it is no longer sufficient for courts to assert, without any reason other than *dicta* or even holdings from the era of judge-created ancillary jurisdiction, that permissive counterclaims require independent jurisdiction. Rising to the challenge, after enactment of section 1367, in a case strikingly similar to our pending case, the Seventh Circuit vacated the dismissal of a permissive counterclaim and remanded for exercise of the discretion contemplated by section 1367. *Channell v. Citicorp National Services, Inc.*, 89 F.3d 379 (7th Cir.1996). *Channell* involved a creditor's counterclaims to collect debts in a class action alleging violations of the Consumer Leasing Act, 15 U.S.C. §§1667–1667e (2000). As Judge Easterbrook stated, "Now that Congress has codified the supplemental jurisdiction in §1367(a), courts should use the language of the statute to define the extent of their powers." *Id.* at 385. He viewed section 1367's reach to the constitutional limits of Article III as requiring only "[a] loose factual connection between the claims," *id.* (internal quotation marks omitted), a standard that appears to be broader than the *Gibbs* test of "a common nucleus of operative facts," appropriate for permitting joinder of a plaintiff's non-federal claim. In *Channell*, he readily found the requisite "loose connection" to exist between the Consumer Leasing Act claim and the debt collection counterclaim. *Id.* at 385–86.

We share the view that section 1367 has displaced, rather than codified, whatever validity inhered in the earlier view that a permissive counterclaim requires independent jurisdiction (in the sense of federal question or diversity jurisdiction). The issue in this case therefore becomes whether supplemental jurisdiction is available for Ford Credit's counterclaims.

III. Application of Section 1367's Standards for Supplemental Jurisdiction

Whether or not the *Gibbs* "common nucleus" standard provides the outer limit of an Article III "case," and is therefore a requirement for entertaining a permissive counterclaim that otherwise lacks a jurisdictional basis, the facts of Ford Credit's counterclaims and those of the Plaintiffs' ECOA claims satisfy that standard, even though the relationship is not such as would make the counterclaims compulsory. The counterclaims and the underlying claim bear a sufficient factual relationship (if one is necessary) to constitute the same "case" within the meaning of Article III and hence of section 1367. Both the ECOA claim and the debt collection claims originate from the Plaintiffs' decisions to purchase Ford cars.

Satisfying the constitutional "case" standard of subsection 1367(a), however, does not end the inquiry a district court is obliged to make with respect to permissive counterclaims. A trial court must consider whether any of the four grounds set out in subsection 1367(c) are present to an extent that would warrant the exercise of discretion to decline assertion of supplemental jurisdiction.

[The court discussed the application of the factors in 28 U.S.C. § 1367(c), concluding that the case should be remanded for further consideration in light of 2d Circuit precedent].

Conclusion

The judgment dismissing Ford Credit's counterclaims is vacated, and the case is remanded for further proceedings consistent with this opinion. No costs.

Ginwright v. Exeter Finance Corp.

2016 WL 5867443 (D. Md. 2016)

MEMORANDUM OPINION

THEODORE D. CHUANG, United States District Judge

On February 26, 2016, Plaintiff Billy Ginwright filed this action against Defendant Exeter Finance Corporation ("Exeter") for violations of the Telephone Consumer Protection Act ("TCPA"), 47 U.S.C. § 227 (2012), and the Maryland Telephone Consumer Protection Act ("MTCPA"), Md. Code Ann., Com. Law §§ 14-3201 to -3202 (West 2013). On May 11, 2016, Exeter filed its Amended Answer and Counterclaim, alleging that Ginwright breached the contract that led Exeter to seek to collect a debt by telephone. Pending before the Court is Ginwright's Motion to Dismiss Exeter's Counterclaim. For the following reasons, the Motion is granted.

BACKGROUND

In May 2013, Ginwright entered into a contract with BW Auto Outlet of Hanover, Maryland to finance the purchase of a vehicle. Within the contract, BW Auto Outlet assigned all of its rights under the contract to Exeter. In his Complaint, Ginwright alleges that in seeking to collect a debt under the contract, Exeter called Ginwright's cellular phone "hundreds of times" by means of an automatic dialing system. Compl. ¶¶ 22–23. Ginwright maintains that Exeter made the calls for non-emergency purposes and without his prior express consent. He also asserts that he repeatedly told Exeter to cease calling him, to no avail. Rather, Exeter representatives told him that they would not stop calling his cellular phone, and that the calls would continue through the automatic dialing system. As a result, with rare exceptions, Ginwright received three to seven calls from Exeter every day between December 4 and December 17, 2014; March 5 and April 29, 2015; and May 10 and June 5, 2015.

In its Counterclaim, Exeter alleges that Ginwright breached the original contract when he failed to make car payments, requiring Exeter to repossess the vehicle. Exeter contends that, following the sale of the vehicle and the application of the sale proceeds to the full amount owed, Ginwright owed a remainder of $23,782.17 under the contract as of May 3, 2016.

DISCUSSION

Ginwright is seeking dismissal of the counterclaim pursuant to Federal Rule of Civil Procedure 12(b)(1) for lack of subject matter jurisdiction. Ginwright asserts that Exeter has failed to assert any independent basis for jurisdiction over the counterclaim and that this Court may not exercise supplemental jurisdiction over the counterclaim because it is a permissive counterclaim. Exeter counters that, since the enactment of 28 U.S.C. § 1367, a court may exercise supplemental jurisdiction over a permissive counterclaim, and that, in any event, its counterclaim is compulsory.

I. Legal Standard

It is the burden of the party asserting jurisdiction to show that subject matter jurisdiction exists. Rule 12(b)(1) allows a party to move for dismissal when it believes that the claimant has failed to make that showing. When a plaintiff asserts that the facts alleged in a counterclaim are not sufficient to establish subject matter jurisdiction, the allegations in the counterclaim are assumed to be true under the same standard as in a Rule 12(b)(6) motion, and "the motion must be denied if the [counterclaim] alleges sufficient facts to invoke subject matter jurisdiction." Kerns v. United States, 585 F.3d 187, 192 (4th Cir. 2009).

II. Supplemental Jurisdiction

In asserting its counterclaim, Exeter does not allege that the Court has federal question jurisdiction or diversity jurisdiction. Rather, Exeter asserts that jurisdiction is proper under the supplemental jurisdiction statute, 28 U.S.C. § 1367. In determining whether a court has supplemental jurisdiction over a counterclaim, the United States Court of Appeals for the Fourth Circuit has traditionally distinguished between compulsory counterclaims, which must be stated by a defendant in its answer, and permissive counterclaims, which need not be. Fed. R. Civ. P. 13. The Fourth Circuit has held that, absent an independent basis of jurisdiction, a federal court has supplemental jurisdiction over a compulsory counterclaim but not a permissive counterclaim. *Painter v. Harvey*, 863 F.2d 329, 331 (4th Cir. 1988);

Whigham v. Beneficial Finance Co., 599 F.2d 1322 (4th Cir. 1979) ("A federal court has ancillary jurisdiction over compulsory counterclaims, but it cannot entertain permissive counterclaims unless they independently satisfy federal jurisdictional requirements.").

Exeter argues that the Fourth Circuit rule has been superseded by the 1990 enactment of the supplemental jurisdiction statute, which provides that "in any civil action of which the district courts have original jurisdiction, the district courts shall have supplemental jurisdiction over all other claims that are so related to" claims already within the court's jurisdiction "that they form part of the same case or controversy under Article III of the United States Constitution." 28 U.S.C. § 1367(a). Exeter contends that the "all other claims" language encompasses counterclaims and that the "same case or controversy" language encompasses at least certain types of permissive counterclaims.

Several courts of appeals have agreed with this view and have interpreted § 1367 to permit the exercise of supplemental jurisdiction over "at least some permissive counterclaims." Within the Fourth Circuit, however, district courts have continued to follow the binding precedent of *Painter* and limit supplemental jurisdiction to compulsory counterclaims. *See, e.g.,* *Williams v. Long*, 558 F. Supp. 2d 601, 603 & n.1 (D. Md. 2008) [string citation omitted].

In *Williams*, the court offered a rationale for the continuing applicability of the Fourth Circuit rule based on the premise that § 1367 did not materially alter the jurisdictional landscape applicable to this issue. The United States Supreme Court has stated that § 1367 "codified" existing common law doctrines of pendent and ancillary jurisdiction "under a common heading" of supplemental jurisdiction. *City of Chicago v. Int'l Coll of Surgeons*, 522 U.S. 156, 165 (1997). The pre-§ 1367 doctrine of pendent jurisdiction provided federal jurisdiction over claims that "derive from a common nucleus of operative fact" such that "the entire action before the court comprises but one constitutional 'case.'" *Id.* at 164–65 (quoting *United Mine Workers v. Gibbs*, 383 U.S. 715, 725 (1966)). In *International College of Surgeons*, when the Court applied the "common nucleus of operative fact" test to conclude that there was supplemental jurisdiction under the "same case or controversy" requirement of § 1367, it effectively equated the two tests. In *Williams*, the court concluded that because the "common nucleus of operative fact" standard remains applicable after § 1367, the Fourth Circuit rule of providing supplemental jurisdiction over compulsory counterclaims only, which was premised on that pre-§ 1367 standard, remains intact. Where the Fourth Circuit has not addressed whether § 1367 altered the rule articulated in *Whigham* and *Painter*, the district courts within this circuit continue to adhere to that rule, and a principled basis exists for doing so, the Court declines to deviate from

Fourth Circuit precedent and will continue to apply the rule that a federal court has supplemental jurisdiction over compulsory counterclaims only.

III. Permissive Counterclaim

In assessing whether a counterclaim is compulsory or permissive, courts consider four inquiries:

(1) Are the issues of fact and law raised in the claim and counterclaim largely the same?

(2) Would res judicata bar a subsequent suit on the party's counterclaim, absent * the compulsory counterclaim rule?

(3) Will substantially the same evidence support or refute the claim as well as the counterclaim? and

(4) Is there any logical relationship between the claim and counterclaim?

Painter, 863 F.2d at 331. These inquiries are more akin to a set of guidelines than a rigid test, such that a "court need not answer all these questions in the affirmative for the counterclaim to be compulsory." *Id.*

Applying the four inquiries here, the Court concludes that Exeter's counterclaim is permissive. First, the issues of fact and law raised in the TCPA claim and breach of contract counterclaim are largely dissimilar. The TCPA bars "any call (other than a call made for emergency purposes or made with the prior express consent of the called party) using any automatic telephone dialing system or an artificial or prerecorded voice" to any telephone number assigned to a cellular telephone service. 47 U.S.C. § 227(b)(1)(A)(iii). Thus, to prevail on this claim, Ginwright must establish that Exeter made calls to the plaintiff's cellular phone, by means of an automatic dialing system, without Ginwright's express consent or an emergency purpose. There is no requirement to show any underlying contractual dispute or debt that led to such phone calls. Meanwhile, the breach of contract counterclaim requires proof of an agreement between the parties and a failure by Ginwright to honor the terms of that agreement to make timely car payments. According to Ginwright, his defense may be based on the assertion that Exeter did not comply with the statutorily required repossession and resale procedures contained in the Creditor Grantor Closed End Credit ("CLEC") provisions of the Maryland Commercial Law Article, which must be satisfied in order for a lender to collect a deficiency judgment for an unpaid car loan. There is no requirement to show any use or lack of use of telephone calls to the borrower. Thus, there is little overlap between the two sets of legal and factual issues.

Second, because the legal and factual issues are different, the evidence would not be "substantially the same." While the alleged contract underlying the counterclaim might be admissible on the TCPA claim to the extent that it is relevant to establishing prior express consent for phone calls or the lack thereof, the evidence on the TCPA claim will primarily consist of records and testimony about the number of calls received and the use of the automatic dialing system, which would be of no relevance to the breach of contract counterclaim. Likewise, Exeter's counterclaim, which contains no allegations relating to phone calls or an automatic dialing system, will rely primarily on evidence that does not pertain to the TCPA claim, such as proof of Ginwright's failure to make car payments and evidence that Exeter did or did not repossess the car and resell it in accordance with Maryland's CLEC requirements.

Third, *res judicata* would not bar a subsequent suit on the breach of contract counterclaim. "The preclusive effect of a federal-court judgment is determined by federal common law." An action is precluded when:

> 1) the prior judgment was final and on the merits, and rendered by a court of competent jurisdiction in accordance with the requirements of due process; 2) the parties are identical, or in privity, in the two actions; and, 3) the claim[ ] in the second matter [is] based upon the same cause of action involved in the earlier proceeding.

Claims "based upon the same cause of action" are those which "arise out of the same transaction or series of transactions, or the same core of operative facts." As discussed above, Exeter's counterclaim, which is associated with the sales agreement for a vehicle, derives from a different core set of facts than Ginwright's TCPA claim, which is based on numerous phone calls placed to his cellular phone from December 2014 to July 2015. Thus, *res judicata* would not bar a subsequent breach of contract claim by Exeter.

Fourth, any logical relationship between the TCPA claim and the breach of contract counterclaim is a loose one. Although the TCPA claim would likely not have arisen in the absence of the original contract at issue on the counterclaim, there is little or no connection between a claim concerning the misuse of an automatic dialing system and a counterclaim alleging the failure to pay back a loan. *Cf. Peterson v. United Accounts, Inc.*, 638 F.2d 1134, 1137 (8th Cir. 1981) (holding that a Fair Debt Collection Practices Act claim relating to the practices followed in collecting a debt and a counterclaim for collection of the debt itself "bear no logical relationship to one another").

Considering all of the factors, the Court concludes that Exeter's counterclaim is permissive. Although the Fourth Circuit has not addressed this precise issue, it has held that where a plaintiff alleged a violation of the disclosure requirements of the Truth-in-Lending Act ("TILA"), a counterclaim seeking payment of the underlying debt was permissive. *Whigham*, 599 F.2d at 1323. In *Whigham*, the court concluded that the counterclaim raised "significantly different" issues of law and fact than those presented by the TILA claim and that evidence on the two claims differed because only the counterclaim depended on verification of the debt and proof of default. It also concluded that the claims were "not logically related" because although the federal claim involved the same loan, it did not "arise from the obligations created by the contractual transaction." These same conclusions apply here, where Ginwright's TCPA claim involves different issues of fact and law, relies on different evidence, and is no more logically related to the counterclaim than the TILA claim in *Whigham* was to its counterclaim.

The Court's conclusion is consistent with those of several district courts that have held that, in the case of a TCPA claim, a counterclaim alleging a failure to pay the debt that was the subject of the telephone calls was permissive. [String citation omitted].

Exeter's citation to a single district court case reaching the contrary conclusion, *Horton v. Calvary Portfolio Servs.*, 301 F.R.D. 547, 551 (S.D. Cal. July 23, 2014), is unpersuasive. In *Horton*, the court applied the "logical relationship" test, followed by the United States Court of Appeals for the Ninth Circuit in determining whether a counterclaim is compulsory or permissive, which differs from the Fourth Circuit's four-part inquiry. Moreover, other courts applying a logical relationship test have concluded that a breach of contract counterclaim to a TCPA claim is permissive.

Having concluded that Exeter's counterclaim is permissive, the Court concludes that it must be dismissed for lack of jurisdiction.

IV. 28 U.S.C. § 1367(c)

Even if the Court could exercise supplemental jurisdiction over a permissive counterclaim, the Court may decline to do so under certain circumstances. 28 U.S.C. § 1367(c).

> [*The court concluded that, even if the counterclaim were related enough to be subject to the court's supplemental jurisdiction, Section 1367(c) would justify declining jurisdiction.*]

CONCLUSION

For the foregoing reasons, Ginwright's Motion to Dismiss Counterclaim is GRANTED. A separate Order shall issue.

Exercise 8-3. "Same Transaction or Occurrence"

In the case immediately above, the court sets forth the main tests for whether a claim arises out of the "same transaction or occurrence" as another claim in the action. This determination is very important to several areas of joinder law, as well as to the law of claim preclusion, so you will need it again.

Here is the test, as the court frames it:

"A counterclaim is compulsory if: (1) the issues of fact and law raised by the principal claim and the counterclaim are largely the same; (2) *res judicata* [i.e., claim preclusion] would bar a subsequent suit on defendant's claim; (3) the same evidence supports or refutes the principal claim and the counterclaim; and, (4) there is a logical relationship between the claim and counterclaim."

Is this test useful? Based on the analysis in the case above, which of the factors stated here are really doing the analytical "work," and why?

Important to note is that some courts, such as the District of Maryland in *Ginwright*, view this "test" as a set of factors, all of which must be satisfied, while others view each of these four enumerations as alternative ways of making the "same transaction or occurrence" determination. Still other courts, such as the Second Circuit in *Jones*, hold that only one of these ways of making the determination — the "logical relationship" test — is the correct one, rejecting all of the others. Which of these three groups of courts seems most likely to be correct?

4. Basic Party Joinder

Rule 20 provides for the most basic form of party joinder. Read Rule 20. As you can see, this provision differs from the two already discussed because it focuses on joining additional *parties* to the action, rather than on simply adding more *claims* to the action between existing parties. Of course, each new party joined to an action must either become the claiming party or the defending party on at least one claim, but the focus with party joinder is on the addition of parties to the case.

Note the subtle difference in terminology between the two subsections above: a plaintiff "may join," but a defendant "may be joined." We can infer an important point from this difference. In most cases, plaintiffs may decide for themselves whether to become part of an action — whether proposed or existing. Defendants (or prospective defendants) do not have that choice, other than in very limited, more complex circumstances. This is the main reason that the threshold defenses that make up much of the content of the first half of this book (personal jurisdiction, service, venue, *forum non conveniens*), and the due process rights that ground those provisions, focus mostly on the interests of defending parties — they are the ones who usually do not have the choice whether to become parties to a lawsuit.

So, Rule 20(a) authorizes more than one plaintiff to decide to litigate together in the same action, and Rule 20(b) authorizes a plaintiff to assert claims against more than one defendant. This is as simple as party joinder gets. A diagram of each of these scenarios appears below, with claim "A" representing an anchor claim between two parties, and claim "B" representing a claim that would be joined under either subsection (a) or (b) of Rule 20.

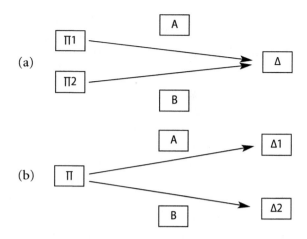

The party seeking to accomplish joinder under Rule 20 must establish two predicate elements: (1) that the claim asserted by or against the party proposed to be joined arise from the "same transaction or occurrence, or series of transactions or occurrences" as another claim in the action, and (2) that the claim asserted by or against the party proposed to be joined share at least one "common question of law or fact" with that existing claim. Both predicate elements must be met, and each is evaluated independently.

In comparison with the only other joinder rules you have seen thus far that contain predicate elements, Rules 13(a) and (g), Rule 20 differs in important ways. First, neither Rule 13(a) nor Rule 13(g) contains a "common question of law or fact" requirement. In addition, the "same transaction or occurrence" language that you saw in Rule 13 is modified and arguably broadened to, "same transaction, occurrence, or series of transactions or occurrences." Under conventional views of statutory interpretation, this textual distinction should make a difference in how Rules 13 and 20 are applied, but in practical application, this does not appear to be so, at least as to the "same transaction or occurrence" requirement. The "logical relationship" test (whether considered part of a four-factor analysis or whether used on its own as "the" test) seems to bring a related series of transactions or occurrences within the basic meaning of "same transaction or occurrence." The case below illustrates this point.

King v. Pepsi Cola Metropolitan Bottling Co.

86 F.R.D. 4 (E.D. Pa. 1979)

Memorandum of Decision

McGlynn, District Judge.

This is an action brought originally by plaintiffs on behalf of themselves and the class they purport to represent, alleging both specific and general practices of racial discrimination against their employer, Pepsi Cola Metropolitan Bottling Company ("Pepsi"). In an order of March 23, 1979, this court dismissed plaintiffs' claims for relief under the Thirteenth and Fourteenth Amendments, as well as the claims of each plaintiff as individually named plaintiffs under Title VII of the 1964 Civil Rights Act, 42 U.S.C. Section 2000e *et seq.* The remaining claims allege a right to relief under Section 2 of the Civil Rights Act of 1866, 42 U.S.C. Section 1981.

Defendant has filed a motion in the alternative seeking a severance of the plaintiffs or separate trials before a separate jury for each plaintiff, which, of course, is the same as a severance. Defendant asserts that since the plaintiffs did not move for a class action determination within the ninety (90) day period after the filing of the complaint, as prescribed by Rule 45 of the Local Rules of the United States District Court for the Eastern District of Pennsylvania, plaintiffs are left with only their individual claims for relief under 42 U.S.C. Section 1981.

Rule 20(a) of the Federal Rules of Civil Procedure permits the joinder of plaintiffs in an action "if they assert any right to relief ... arising out of the same transaction, occurrence, or series of transactions or occurrences" and presenting any question of law or fact common to all the persons to be joined. This requirement is cumulative in nature, that is, both the common question and the same transaction portions must be satisfied. Rule 21 of the Federal Rules of Civil Procedure gives the court the power to remedy the misjoinder of parties, either on motion of any party or on its own initiative, by order that a party be dropped or added or that the claim against any party should be severed and proceeded with separately.

The question of what constitutes the same transaction or occurrence or series thereof arises here. This court recognizes the policy favoring the broadest possible scope of action consistent with fairness to the parties, strongly encouraging joinder of parties, claims and remedies, which was defined by the United States Supreme Court in *United Mine Workers of America v. Gibbs*, 383 U.S. 715, 724 (1966). In *Mosley v. General Motors Corporation*, 497 F.2d 1330 (8th Cir. 1974), the court upheld the joinder of ten plaintiffs who had alleged a general policy of discrimination against Negroes by General Motors and two of its divisions, Chevrolet and Fisher Body. The Court looked to the construction given to "transaction or occurrence" under Federal Rule of Civil Procedure 13(a), finding that the connection of events depended not on their immediateness in time but rather on their logical relationship to each other. Under Rule 13, all "logically related" events entitling a person to institute legal action against another constitutes a transaction or occurrence. Applying this interpretation by analogy to Rule 20(a), the *Mosley* court reasoned that the Rule would permit all "reasonably related" claims for relief by or against different parties to be tried in a single proceeding. Absolute identity of all events is unnecessary. *Mosley, supra* at 1333.

Here, plaintiffs' complaint alleges that specific instances of discrimination occurred against each of named plaintiffs as well as a general and pervasive corporate policy of discrimination by Pepsi against blacks. Thus, the allegations of a pervasive policy of discrimination by Pepsi would bring the complaints of the individual plaintiffs under the rubric of the "same series of transactions." The failure of the plaintiffs to seek a class designation does not preclude them from proving that Pepsi discriminates as a matter of policy. Each plaintiff alleges that he is the victim of a pervasive corporate policy of discrimination and raises the common factual question of whether such a policy does indeed exist.

The complaint alleges that plaintiffs, King, Carter, Wilson and Taylor all were assigned to the production unit at Pepsi's Northeast Philadelphia plant and were all either directly or indirectly under the supervision of Cliff Rissell, a Pepsi employee. Plaintiff Minot, although assigned to the engineering unit, was assigned to set up production equipment at the Northeast plant, and it was here that Minot allegedly encountered harassment from the same Cliff Rissell. Even though proof of the discrimination will involve the various work records of each plaintiff, there will also be a substantial overlap in the evidence presented. Since these five plaintiffs worked in the same unit, many of the witnesses who will testify as to conditions within the unit and also to the individual instances alleged by each will be the same. Further, each plaintiff alleges that Cliff Rissell played an integral role in carrying out the alleged discriminatory company policy. It follows, then, that each of the five will present evidence concerning Rissell's activities. The court can economically and expeditiously hear this evidence in one trial. The dangers of jury confusion are no greater here than in any other case. The claims here are not so diverse and multiple, centered as they are around a central theme of a company discriminatory policy, that a reasonable jury cannot segregate the evidence and decide the separate claims.

Plaintiff Bobby Coatney presents a different situation, since he was assigned to a separate department within the company with different supervisors. It is conceded that his case will involve evidence different from the others in some respects. However, his claim is united with the others by the allegations of a company policy of discrimination. For the convenience of the parties and in the interests of judicial economy, Coatney's claim should also be tried with the other five named plaintiffs.

For these reasons, then, defendant's motion to sever parties or for separate trials will be denied.

Exercise 8-4. Misjoinder and Rule 21

In *King*, the court considers the propriety of basic party joinder in the same way that most courts consider it — through the mechanism of a motion to sever or drop parties under Rule 21, titled "Misjoinder and Nonjoinder of Parties," which provides:

> "Misjoinder of parties is not a ground for dismissing an action. On motion or on its own, the court may at any time, on just terms, add or drop a party. The court may also sever any claim against a party."

Note that the Rule does not appear to limit severance or the dropping or adding of a party to instances of *misjoinder* (joining parties improperly under the Rules) or the related problem of *nonjoinder* (the failure to join a party who should have been joined, which you will learn about soon). But given its presence in the joinder section of the Federal Rules, as well as its title and the mention of "misjoinder" obliquely in the text, courts have generally concluded that Rule 21 severance, addition, or dropping of parties must be justified both by "just terms" and by a plausible argument that joinder is somehow improper. Note, also, that although "misjoinder" is not a ground for dismissal, "nonjoinder" certainly is. Just look at Rule 12(b)(7).

Why might a party want to sever the claim of another party, or convince the court to drop that party altogether? Why do you think the *King* defendant wanted to sever the claims of the different plaintiffs for trial, even though it had already established that their class action claims could not go forward due to their failure to comply with a Local Rule?*

The next case illustrates a particularly inventive use of Rule 21 (one that ultimately failed), as well as another approach to applying Rule 20.

John S. Clark Co., Inc. v. Travelers Indemnity Co. of Ill.

359 F. Supp. 2d 429 (M.D.N.C. 2004).

Memorandum Opinion

Bullock, District Judge.

Before the court are two motions to remand this civil action to the General Court of Justice, Superior Court Division, Guilford County, North Carolina, separately filed by John S. Clark Company, Inc. ("Plaintiff"), and by Ignacio Herrera, Marina Herrera, and Herrera Masonry, Inc. (collectively "the Herrera Defendants"). Plaintiff's motion to remand includes Plaintiff's request for an award of costs and attorney fees upon remand

---

* Ed. Note. Every Federal District Court in the country has its own Local Rules and bar admissions procedures. To practice in the courts of a specific Federal District, you must be admitted and remain in good standing in that District's bar, and you must maintain familiarity with that District's Local Rules of practice and procedure. These Local Rules have the same importance as the Federal Rules of Civil Procedure in the courts that promulgate them. Many federal practitioners have run afoul of the courts by paying insignificant attention to the Local Rules.

pursuant to 28 U.S.C. § 1447(c). Also before the court is Travelers Indemnity Company of Illinois' ("Travelers") motion to dismiss the Herrera Defendants pursuant to Federal Rules of Civil Procedure 19 and 21. For the following reasons, Plaintiff's motion to remand will be granted, the Herrera Defendants' motion to remand will be granted, and Plaintiff's request for an award of costs and attorney fees upon remand will be granted. As a result, Travelers' motion to dismiss the Herrera Defendants will be denied as moot.

Facts

Plaintiff is a building contractor incorporated under the laws of a state other than North Carolina and registered to do business in North Carolina. Plaintiff maintains an office in Guilford County, North Carolina, and qualifies as a citizen of North Carolina for jurisdictional purposes. Ignacio Herrera and Marina Herrera are individuals whose domiciles and primary residences are located in North Carolina. Herrera Masonry, Inc., is a North Carolina corporation with its principal place of business in Forsyth County, North Carolina. Travelers is an insurance company incorporated under the laws of a state other than North Carolina with its principal place of business in Hartford, Connecticut.

This civil action arises from several construction problems that Plaintiff encountered during the construction of a Parish Life Center and other associated renovations of the Saint Therese Catholic Church in Mooresville, North Carolina ("the construction project"). Before Plaintiff began the construction project, Plaintiff obtained multiple layers of insurance to cover the construction project itself and Plaintiff's liabilities while working on the construction project, including a series of commercial general liability insurance policies that Travelers issued to Plaintiff with effective dates of January 1, 2000, through May 1, 2002 (collectively "the CGL Policies"). According to Plaintiff's complaint, the CGL Policies provided Plaintiff with coverage for property damage arising from work performed by subcontractors on Plaintiff's behalf as well as coverage for costs that Plaintiff might incur to repair or replace defective work during the construction project.

On August 11, 2000, Plaintiff hired the Herrera Defendants as masonry subcontractors to perform work on the construction project pursuant to the terms and conditions of a written agreement between Plaintiff and the Herrera Defendants ("the Herrera Contract"). The Herrera Contract allegedly contained an agreement between Plaintiff and the Herrera Defendants in which the Herrera Defendants assumed responsibility "for assuring that [their] workmanship and material [were] in compliance with all local, state and/or federal codes." According to Plaintiff's complaint, the Herrera Contract also contained the Herrera Defendants' warranty "against all deficiencies and defects in materials and/or workmanship" as well as the Herrera Defendants' promise to indemnify Plaintiff "from and against all claims, damages, loss and expenses ... arising out of or resulting from the performance of [their] work."

On January 19, 2001, a portion of the construction project collapsed for a number of alleged reasons, including errors, omissions, and deficiencies in the Herrera Defendants' masonry. Following the collapse on January 19, 2001, Plaintiff repaired and rebuilt the collapsed portion of the construction project. Plaintiff also corrected and repaired other portions of the construction project in which Plaintiff discovered structural defects "of a similar character to [the defects] contained in [the] walls which disintegrated on January 19, 2001." According to Plaintiff's complaint, "[a]ll of the damages, errors, omissions and deficiencies, including, but not limited to those associated with the January 19, 2001 incident, have been rebuilt, repaired, corrected, or otherwise remedied."

On January 19, 2004, Plaintiff filed this civil action in the General Court of Justice, Superior Court Division, Guilford County, North Carolina, demanding payment and indemnity from both Travelers and the Herrera Defendants for "losses and damages, including, but not limited to, property damage, loss of use, delay and acceleration damages, other charges assessed by the Owner and other actual, consequential, and special damages." Plaintiff's complaint stated two claims against the Herrera Defendants for breach of contract and negligence based on the Herrera Defendants' alleged improper installation of rebar in certain sections of masonry, failure to install rebar in certain sections of masonry, failure to install grout in certain sections of masonry, and faulty workmanship, which Plaintiff apparently discovered throughout the construction project. Plaintiff's complaint also stated three separate claims against Travelers for breach of contract, bad faith, and unfair and deceptive trade practices, in violation of North Carolina General Statute § 75-1.1 et seq., based on Travelers' alleged failure to investigate and pay Plaintiff's claims for costs that Plaintiff incurred to repair and rebuild the collapsed portion of the construction project and costs that Plaintiff incurred to repair portions of the construction project which contained structural defects but did not collapse.

On February 26, 2004, Travelers responded to Plaintiff's complaint by filing a notice of removal to this court pursuant to 28 U.S.C. §§ 1441 and 1446, which cited 28 U.S.C. § 1332 as the only basis for federal jurisdiction of the subject matter of this civil action. On March 22, 2004, the Herrera Defendants filed an answer to Plaintiff's complaint and a motion to remand this civil action to the General Court of Justice, Superior Court Division, Guilford County, North Carolina, for lack of subject matter jurisdiction. In their answer to Plaintiff's complaint, the Herrera Defendants denied the material allegations contained in Plaintiff's complaint and asserted several affirmative defenses to the allegations contained in

Plaintiff's complaint, including the affirmative defense of contributory negligence. In support of their motion to remand, the Herrera Defendants contend that the court lacks jurisdiction of the subject matter of this civil action because "Plaintiff and the Herrera Defendants are all citizens of the State of North Carolina, [and] there is not complete diversity between the parties."

On March 29, 2004, Plaintiff filed its own motion to remand this civil action to the General Court of Justice, Superior Court Division, Guilford County, North Carolina, pursuant to 28 U.S.C. § 1447(c). In support of its motion to remand, Plaintiff contends that the court lacks jurisdiction of the subject matter of this civil action because there is not complete diversity between Plaintiff and the Herrera Defendants. Plaintiff also contends that remand is appropriate because Travelers' notice of removal is "defective on its face" as a result of the Herrera Defendants' failure to join in or otherwise consent to Travelers' removal of this civil action.

On April 5, 2004, Travelers filed an answer to Plaintiff's complaint and a motion to dismiss the Herrera Defendants. In its answer to Plaintiff's complaint, Travelers denied the material allegations contained in Plaintiff's complaint and asserted several affirmative defenses to the allegations contained in Plaintiff's complaint. In support of its motion to dismiss and in opposition to Plaintiff's and the Herrera Defendants' motions to remand, Travelers contends that the court should disregard the Herrera Defendants for jurisdictional purposes and dismiss the Herrera Defendants because the Herrera Defendants do not qualify as necessary parties or proper parties to the controversy between Plaintiff and Travelers. According to Travelers, the court should retain jurisdiction of Plaintiff's claims against Travelers and Plaintiff should pursue its separate claims against the Herrera Defendants in North Carolina state court.

Discussion

* * *

In the instant case, Travelers does not dispute that a lack of complete diversity exists between Plaintiff and the Herrera Defendants because Plaintiff and the Herrera Defendants qualify as citizens of North Carolina for jurisdictional purposes. *See* 28 U.S.C. § 1332(c). Instead, Travelers contends that the court should dismiss the Herrera Defendants and disregard the Herrera Defendants' citizenship for jurisdictional purposes because they are neither necessary nor indispensable parties under Federal Rule of Civil Procedure 19* and because they are not proper parties who may be joined under Federal Rule of Civil Procedure 20. According to Travelers, Federal Rule of Civil Procedure 21 permits the court to drop

---

* Ed. Note. Rule 19 is a rule that requires joinder of a non-party in certain circumstances. We discuss Rule 19 in great detail in the next Section, which covers complex joinder.

any party from a civil action because of misjoinder, and the court has discretion to drop nondiverse parties in order to maintain or achieve diversity jurisdiction as long as they do not qualify as indispensable parties under Federal Rule of Civil Procedure 19.

The doctrine of fraudulent joinder is a judicially created exception to the statutory requirement of complete diversity under Section 1332 of Title 28 and permits removal when a non-diverse party is (or has been) a defendant in the case. The fraudulent joinder doctrine permits a district court to assume jurisdiction of a case, even if there is a lack of complete diversity between the parties, in order to dismiss nondiverse defendants and thereby retain diversity jurisdiction of the case. To establish fraudulent joinder in the Fourth Circuit, the removing party must demonstrate either outright fraud in the plaintiff's pleading of jurisdictional facts or that there is no possibility that the plaintiff can establish a cause of action against the in-state defendant in state court. In order to determine whether an attempted joinder is fraudulent, the court is not bound by the allegations of the pleadings, but may instead consider the entire record, and determine the basis of joinder by any means available. There is nothing in the record to establish that the Herrera Defendants were fraudulently joined in this action.

Procedural misjoinder of parties is a relatively new concept that has emerged from the Eleventh Circuit and appears to be part of the doctrine of fraudulent joinder at least in that circuit. *See Tapscott v. MS Dealer Serv. Corp.*, 77 F.3d 1353, 1359–60 (11th Cir. 1996) (concluding that misjoinder may be just as fraudulent as joinder of a resident defendant against whom a plaintiff has no cause of action if the plaintiff's attempted joinder of the resident defendant pursuant to Federal Rule of Civil Procedure 20 is so egregious that it amounts to fraudulent joinder). While the Fourth Circuit has not recognized procedural misjoinder as a form of fraudulent joinder, other courts have determined that procedural misjoinder may rise to the level of fraudulent joinder in certain cases. Even assuming that the Fourth Circuit would recognize procedural misjoinder as a form of fraudulent joinder, the record shows that Plaintiff has properly joined the Herrera Defendants in this civil action according to the conditions for permissive joinder set forth in Federal Rule of Civil Procedure 20(a).

Federal Rule of Civil Procedure 20(a) permits joinder of multiple defendants in a single action when "there is asserted against them jointly, severally, or in the alternative, any right to relief in respect of or arising out of the same transaction, occurrence, or series of transactions or occurrences and if any question of law or fact common to all defendants will arise in the action." Fed.R.Civ.P. 20(a). Federal Rule of Civil Procedure 20(a) thus allows a plaintiff to "join multiple defendants in a single action only if [the] plaintiff asserts at least one claim to relief against each of them that arises out of the same transaction or occurrence and presents questions of law or fact common to all." 7 CHARLES A. WRIGHT, ARTHUR R. MILLER, AND MARY KAY KANE, FEDERAL PRACTICE AND PROCEDURE § 1655, at 420–21 (3d ed.2001). Once a plaintiff has satisfied the requirements for permissive joinder under Federal Rule of Civil Procedure 20(a), Federal Rule of Civil Procedure 18 permits the "plaintiff to join as many other claims as [the] plaintiff has against the multiple defendants or any combination of them, even though the additional claims do not involve common questions of law or fact and arise from unrelated transactions." *Id.* at 421.

Federal Rule of Civil Procedure 21 provides a mechanism to correct misjoinder or non-joinder of parties and states that "[p]arties may be dropped or added by order of the court on motion of any party or of its own initiative at any stage of the action and on such terms as are just." Fed.R.Civ.P. 21. "Dismissal of a misjoined party under Rule 21 is without prejudice; a claim by or against such a party may be refiled as a separate suit." 4 MOORE'S FEDERAL PRACTICE § 21.03 (Matthew Bender 3d ed.2003). Although Federal Rule of Civil Procedure 21 does not contain a clear definition of misjoinder, federal courts have uniformly held that misjoinder occurs when a single party or multiple parties fail to satisfy the conditions for permissive joinder set forth in Federal Rule of Civil Procedure 20(a). Federal Rule of Civil Procedure 21 thus "applies when the claims asserted by or against the joined parties do not arise out of the same transaction or occurrence or do not present some common question of law or fact." WRIGHT, MILLER, AND KANE, *supra* (emphasis added).

In construing the Federal Rules of Civil Procedure, the impulse is toward entertaining the broadest possible scope of action consistent with fairness to the parties; joinder of claims, parties and remedies is strongly encouraged. Federal Rule of Civil Procedure 20(a)'s requirement that claims asserted against joined parties arise out of the same transaction or occurrence permits all reasonably related claims for relief by or against different parties to be tried in a single proceeding. *See Moore v. N.Y. Cotton Exch.*, 270 U.S. 593, 610 (1926) ("'Transaction' is a word of flexible meaning. It may comprehend a series of many occurrences, depending not so much upon the immediateness of their connection as upon their logical relationship."). An absolute identity of all events is not necessary for permissive joinder and courts must construe Federal Rule of Civil Procedure 20(a) in light of its purpose, which is to promote trial convenience and expedite the final determination of disputes, thereby preventing multiple lawsuits.

Whether claims against joined parties arise out of the same transaction or occurrence, or the same series of transactions or occurrences, is ordinarily determined on a case-by-case basis. Plaintiff's claims against the Herrera Defendants for breach of contract and negligence as well as Plaintiff's claim against Travelers for breach of contract arise out of problems with the construction project allegedly caused by the Herrera Defendants' improper or defective work on the construction project, and Plaintiff has demanded payment and indemnity from both Travelers and the Herrera Defendants for costs that Plaintiff allegedly incurred because of the Herrera Defendants' improper or defective work on the construction project. Although Plaintiff has stated separate claims against Travelers based on Travelers' alleged breach of the terms and conditions of coverage listed in the CGL Policies and Travelers' alleged failure to investigate and pay Plaintiff's claims under the CGL Policies, Plaintiff's claim against Travelers for breach of contract appears to be logically related to Plaintiff's claims against the Herrera Defendants because Plaintiff seeks coverage under the CGL Policies for the losses that Plaintiff allegedly incurred because of the Herrera Defendants' improper or defective work on the construction project. Therefore, the court finds that Plaintiff's claim against Travelers for breach of contract and Plaintiff's claims against the Herrera Defendants arise out of the same series of transactions or occurrences for purposes of Federal Rule of Civil Procedure 20(a).

The second requirement for permissive joinder under Federal Rule of Civil Procedure 20(a) is that separate claims asserted by or against the joined parties must raise at least one question of law or fact common to all the parties. *See* Fed.R.Civ.P. 20(a); *see also* WRIGHT, MILLER, AND KANE, *supra* § 1653, at 413 ("Rule 20(a) does not require that every question of law or fact in the action be common among the parties; rather, the rule permits party joinder whenever there will be at least one common question of law or fact."). To support its claims against the Herrera Defendants, Plaintiff must prove that the Herrera Defendants performed improper or defective work on the construction project and that Plaintiff actually incurred a loss or damages as a result of the Herrera Defendants' alleged improper or defective work on the construction project. Plaintiff also must prove these same facts related to causation and damages to support its claim against Travelers for breach of contract because Travelers has denied material allegations related to causation and damages contained in Plaintiff's complaint, including Plaintiff's allegation that the Herrera Defendants performed "[s]ome of the damaged work and the work out of which the damage constituting [Plaintiff]'s Claims arises."

According to Plaintiff's complaint, the CGL Policies provided Plaintiff with coverage for property damage arising from work performed by subcontractors on Plaintiff's behalf and coverage for costs that Plaintiff might incur to repair or replace defective work. Although Plaintiff must support its claim against Travelers for breach of contract with proof that the CGL Policies actually contained these terms and conditions of coverage, Travelers' obligations and liabilities as well as the Herrera Defendants' obligations and liabilities depend upon facts showing what caused the partial collapse of the construction project on January 19, 2001, and facts showing what caused structural defects in other portions of the construction project which did not collapse. The obligations and liabilities of all defendants also depend upon the amount of loss or damages that Plaintiff incurred as a result of the partial collapse of the construction project and the structural defects in other portions of the construction project which did not collapse. *See Gravett*, 262 F.Supp.2d at 647 (concluding that an injured motorist's negligence claim against another driver and breach of contract claim against her automobile insurer for underinsured motorist benefits shared common issues of fact and were properly joined because "[t]he legal obligations of both defendants [were] based upon a factual showing of [the other driver]'s negligence" and because "the extent of [the injured motorist]'s damages will have a bearing on the extent of each defendant's liability"); *see also Eichinger v. Fireman's Fund Ins. Co.*, 20 F.R.D. 204, 208 (D.Neb.1957) (explaining that claims by the owner of a grain elevator destroyed in an explosion and claims by the owner of destroyed grain against the contractor who constructed the elevator and against insurers of the elevator should not be severed for separate trials under Rule 20(b) because evidence in both trials would concern the character and extent of the plaintiffs' damages, as well as the cause of the plaintiffs' damages, "for, though with a notably different thrust, the cause of the damage, that is to say the collapse of the elevator, [was] at the heart of each claim, the one against the insurance companies [for coverage] and the one against [the contractor for negligence]").

Plaintiff's claim against Travelers for breach of contract and Plaintiff's claims against the Herrera Defendants share at least one common issue of fact for purposes of Federal Rule of Civil Procedure 20(a). Therefore, the court concludes that Plaintiff has properly joined the Herrera Defendants in this civil action according to the conditions for permissive joinder set forth in Federal Rule of Civil Procedure 20(a).

Travelers contends that even if the Herrera Defendants do qualify as proper parties who may be joined in this civil action under Federal Rule of Civil Procedure 20(a), Federal Rule of Civil Procedure 21 permits the court to drop the Herrera Defendants in order to create complete diversity and to establish proper jurisdiction of the subject matter of this civil action. "[I]t is well settled that Rule 21 invests district courts with authority to allow a dispensable nondiverse party to be dropped at any time...." *Newman-Green, Inc. v. Alfonzo-Larrain*, 490 U.S. 826, 832 (1989). *See also Caperton v. Beatrice Pocahontas Coal Co.*, 585 F.2d 683, 691 (4th Cir. 1978) ("There is, of course, sound authority for the view that non-diverse parties whose presence is not essential under Rule 19 may be dropped to achieve diversity between the plaintiffs and the defendants...."). However, the decision of whether to drop parties from a case in order to create or maintain diversity between the remaining parties is a decision that rests within the discretion of the trial court.

Neither Plaintiff nor the Herrera Defendants contend that the Herrera Defendants qualify as necessary or indispensable parties under Federal Rule of Civil Procedure 19. Therefore, the court must decide whether to drop the Herrera Defendants from the instant case in order to create complete diversity between Plaintiff and Travelers and to establish proper jurisdiction of the subject matter of this civil action. As stated above, Federal Rule of Civil Procedure 21 permits courts to drop parties or add parties "on motion of any party or of its own initiative at any stage of the action and on such terms as are just." Fed.R.Civ.P. 21. In deciding whether to drop parties, add parties, or retain parties under Federal Rule of Civil Procedure 21, courts ordinarily consider basic principles such as fundamental fairness and judicial economy, whether an order under Federal Rule of Civil Procedure 21 would prejudice any party or would result in undue delay, and the threats of duplicitous litigation and inconsistent jury verdicts.

Based on considerations of fundamental fairness, judicial economy, prejudice, and undue delay, as well as the dual threat of duplicitous litigation and inconsistent verdicts, the court concludes that the Herrera Defendants should remain in this civil action as defendants properly joined under Federal Rule of Civil Procedure 20(a). Claims like Plaintiff's claims against Travelers and Plaintiff's claims against the Herrera Defendants are routinely adjudicated in North Carolina state courts and traditionally present substantive legal issues exclusive to North Carolina law. Although Travelers might prefer to defend against Plaintiff's claims in federal court, Plaintiff would likely incur significant costs and additional expenses by pursuing its claims against Travelers and its claims against the Herrera Defendants in separate forums because discovery and separate trials in separate forums would likely be more expensive than discovery and a single trial in one forum. Furthermore, if the court decided to drop the Herrera Defendants from this civil action, Plaintiff would have to re-file its claims against the Herrera Defendants in North Carolina state court, which would likely cause a substantial delay in the resolution of Plaintiff's claims against the Herrera Defendants.

As stated above, Plaintiff's claim against Travelers for breach of contract and Plaintiff's claims against the Herrera Defendants depend upon proof of common issues of fact related to causation and damages. If the court decided to drop the Herrera Defendants from this civil action, Plaintiff would likely present the same evidence of causation and damages in its state court action against the Herrera Defendants and in its federal court action against Travelers because Plaintiff would have to prove the same facts relevant to causation and damages in each case. In addition to the threat of duplicitous litigation posed by dropping the Herrera Defendants, separate trials could result in inconsistent verdicts even if Plaintiff presented the same evidence of causation and damages during each trial.

Travelers contends that the court should drop the Herrera Defendants because "a suit by [Plaintiff] against the Herrera Defendants and Travelers, would inform a jury of insurance potentially paying a claim against the Herrera [D]efendants, [which is] a fact that prejudices Travelers' ability to obtain a fair trial." Assuming that Travelers might suffer prejudice by having issues of insurance coverage heard by the same jury deciding the Herrera Defendants' liability for Plaintiff's losses, the North Carolina Rules of Civil Procedure provide safeguards to counter prejudice and many other potentially harsh effects of broad joinder rules. These include severability of the issues or bifurcation of the trial. Each is available to a party upon proper motion and subject to a discretionary ruling of the [state] trial court.

For these reasons, the court in its discretion will decline to drop the Herrera Defendants from the case in order to create complete diversity between Plaintiff and Travelers. Because complete diversity does not exist between the parties, the court lacks jurisdiction of this case under Section 1332(a)(1) of Title 28, as a basis for removal under Section 1441(a) of Title 28, and all defendants properly joined in this civil action have failed to join in or otherwise consent to Travelers' notice of removal as required by Section 1446(a) of Title 28. Therefore, the court will grant Plaintiff's and the Herrera Defendants' motions to remand this civil action to the General Court of Justice, Superior Court Division, Guilford County, North Carolina.

* * *

Conclusion

Plaintiff elected to file this action in North Carolina state court and properly joined Travelers and the Herrera Defendants in a single action by asserting claims against them that arise out of the same series of transactions or occurrences and raise common issues of fact. Travelers has sought to defeat Plaintiff's choice of forum by asking the court to drop the Herrera Defendants pursuant to Federal Rule of Civil Procedure 21 in order to create complete diversity between the parties so that Travelers may defend against Plaintiff's claims in federal court. An exercise of the court's discretion under Federal Rule of Civil Procedure 21 in these circumstances would be fundamentally unfair. Therefore, Plaintiff's motion to remand will be granted, the Herrera Defendants' motion to remand will be granted, and Plaintiff's request for an award of costs and attorney fees will be granted. Travelers' motion to dismiss the Herrera Defendants will be denied as moot.

Exercise 8-5. Using Rules 20 and 21

1. Should Travelers have been subject to Rule 11 sanctions for moving to have the Herrera Defendants dropped as parties under Rule 21 solely to manufacture diversity jurisdiction?

2. Aside from Rule 11, this case is a good example of a court that interprets Rule 20 on its own terms, without reference to Rule 13. Is the outcome meaningfully different from that in *King* as to that interpretation? If so, how? If not, should it be?

Rule 14 governs what the Rules term "Third Party Practice," and what is generally referred to as "Impleader" (not to be confused with "Interpleader," which is discussed in the Complex Joinder Section). Read Rule 14.

As you can see, this rule allows any party who is a defending party to a claim in an existing action to force a non-party into the action (to "implead" that non-party, thereby making him/her/it into a party). The rule refers to the party who forces the non-party into the action as the "Third-Party Plaintiff," and to the non-party who is forced in as the "Third-Party Defendant." A diagram of an impleader appears below, where claim "A" represents the "anchor" claim (the existing claim to which the third-party claim must be joined), and claim "B" represents the impleader/third-party claim.

Note, however, that this Rule contains a predicate element that differs from the others' predicate elements, which focus on the relatedness of the claims. For a defending party to force another person or entity into a lawsuit, the rules require more than mere transactional relatedness or identity of issues. Rather, the nonparty sought to be joined must be a nonparty "who is or may be liable to [the proposed third-party plaintiff] for all or part of the claim against it."

We call this sort of liability "derivative liability" because the liability of the third-party defendant does not arise at all to the third party plaintiff unless that third-party plaintiff ends up liable to some *other* party. A liability insurance contract is the best example of this form of liability. When you purchase liability insurance, you are purchasing a contract of "indemnity," which is type of derivative liability. If you purchase automobile liability insurance, for example, and you rear-end another driver on a public street, your insurance company will be liable to you, but only if *you* are found to be liable to the other driver. The insurance company's liability is therefore "derivative" of your own liability. Only such derivative liability can justify an impleader under Rule 14.

Although derivative liability by contract is a fairly simple concept, and a number of federal and state statutes establish derivative liability by law, the case below illustrates some ways in which derivative liability might arise without a contract or statute, based instead on the conduct of the parties.

Santana Products, Inc., Plaintiff, v. Bobrick Washroom Equipment, Inc., Defendants and Third-Party Plaintiffs, v. Formica Corp., Third-Party Defendant

69 F. Supp. 2d 678 (M.D. Pa. 1999)

Memorandum

Vanaskie, District Judge.

I. Background

On October 1, 1996, plaintiff Santana Products, Inc. (Santana) instituted this action against defendants Bobrick Washroom Equipment, Bobrick Corporation, The Hornyak Group, Inc., Vogel Sales Company, Sylvester & Associates, Ltd., and Fred Sylvester. Santana alleges that Bobrick and other toilet compartment manufacturers conspired to enforce a product standard that had the effect of excluding Santana's high density polyethylene ("HDPE") compartments from the relevant market. Specifically, Santana contends that Bobrick and others falsely represented that toilet compartments were subject to flame and smoke standards applicable to a "wall finish," rather than the standard for furniture and fixtures. According to Santana, Bobrick (and its alleged co-conspirators) then informed prospective purchasers that Santana's HDPE product did not meet the wall finish standard to dissuade the prospective purchasers from selecting Santana's product. Santana seeks to recover under §§ 1 and 2 of the Sherman Act, 15 U.S.C. §§ 1 and 2, § 43(a) of the Lanham Act, 15 U.S.C. § 1125(a), and the common law of tortious interference with prospective contractual relationships.

Santana's lawsuit against Bobrick was preceded by a lawsuit filed in this Court by Santana against eleven other toilet compartment manufacturers and the Formica Corporation, referred to collectively by Santana as the Toilet Partition Manufacturer's Council ("TPMC"). As in this case, Santana's claims in the TPMC action included alleged violations of §§ 1 and 2 of the Sherman Act, and § 43(a) of the Lanham Act, as well as tortious interference with prospective contractual relations. As does this case, the TPMC action focused on an alleged conspiracy "to use scare tactics to discourage specification and acceptance of Santana's HDPE partitions in lieu of or as a replacement material for conventional [toilet partition] materials by falsely alleging that Santana's partitions posed a dangerous fire hazard." Santana alleges in both actions that Formica, a manufacturer of phenolic sheets used by toilet partition manufacturers other than Santana, induced its customers to use a Formica videotape that falsely depicted the flammability of Santana's HDPE partitions.

In early 1995, Formica and other TPMC members sued in the TPMC action settled with Santana and that lawsuit was dismissed. The "Release and Covenant Not to Sue" executed in connection with the settlement specified that it was governed by New York law.

On June 1, 1998, Bobrick filed a Third-Party Complaint against Formica, asserting counts for (1) contribution, (2) indemnification, (3) fraud, and (4) negligent misrepresentation. Bobrick's Third-Party Complaint focuses on the Formica videotape purporting to depict the flammability of Santana's product. The Formica videotape showed one of Santana's HDPE toilet partitions actually being set on fire with a lighter. Bobrick alleges that Formica encouraged Bobrick to use the videotape in its marketing efforts. Bobrick alleges that Formica failed to inform it that the videotape contained false representations and information. Bobrick contends that it reasonably relied upon the Formica videotape and that, as a result of that reliance, Bobrick has been sued by Santana.

Formica has moved to dismiss the Third-Party Complaint. Formica asserts that Bobrick may not maintain an action for contribution for alleged violations of the Sherman Act and the Lanham Act. Formica also contends that any claim for contribution is barred by the release it executed to settle its liability in the TPMC action. Formica further argues that Bobrick has failed to allege a proper claim for indemnification in that (1) Bobrick was not a passive tortfeasor, and (2) any indemnification claim is premature. Finally, Formica contends that the state law claims of fraud and negligent misrepresentation are not proper third-party claims.

II. Discussion
A. Contribution

[The court declined to recognize an implied right of action for contribution under the Sherman Act or the Lanham Act.]

* * *

Accordingly, Bobrick's claim for contribution will be dismissed.

B. Indemnification

While § 15-108 bars a claim for contribution, it does not foreclose a claim for indemnification. As with the contribution claim, however, there is no federal common law right to indemnification and Congress has not explicitly or implicitly provided such a right to indemnification under the

Sherman Act or the Lanham Act. Thus, indemnification with respect to violations of federal law is foreclosed. Bobrick, however, also seeks indemnification as to Santana's common law claims. Therefore, the viability of Bobrick's indemnification claim will be considered.

In a third-party action for indemnity, the third-party plaintiff must demonstrate that its liability is secondary or passive. *See Twin City Fire Ins. Co. v. Pierce Leahy Co.*, No. 92-6370, 1993 WL 131333, at *2 (E.D.Pa. Apr. 23, 1993) ("If the party seeking indemnity had 'any part in causing the injury,' indemnity is not available."); *Schiele v. Simpson Safety Equip., Inc.*, No. 91-1872, 1992 WL 73588, at *2 (E.D.Pa. Apr.7, 1992) ("Under Pennsylvania law, indemnity is limited to those situations in which the defendant's liability is secondary or passive."). As noted by the Pennsylvania Supreme Court, indemnification arises "only when a defendant who has been held liable to a plaintiff solely by operation of law, seeks to recover his loss from a defendant who was actually responsible for the accident which occasioned the loss." *Sirianni v. Nugent Bros., Inc.*, 506 A.2d 868, 871 (1986).

Santana's complaint against Bobrick contains no allegations of negligence. Instead, the complaint alleges repeatedly that Bobrick knowingly and intentionally attempted to exclude Santana from the toilet partition market, knowingly made false and disparaging statements about Santana's products, and intentionally and maliciously interfered with Santana's prospective business relations. The allegations in Santana's complaint clearly encompass intentional acts by Bobrick, not passive actions that would entitle Bobrick to indemnification.

The claims asserted by Santana require proof that Bobrick acted intentionally. To succeed on its claim under § 1 of the Sherman Antitrust Act, Santana must show: (1) concerted action by Bobrick; (2) that was designed to achieve an unlawful objective; (3) that produced anti-competitive effects within the relevant product and geographic markets; and (4) that the concerted action injured Santana. Critical to any § 1 determination is the necessity of collusive conduct that was competitively unreasonable, and that produced an "antitrust injury." The cornerstone of a § 1 claim is an allegation that two or more distinct entities entered into an understanding or agreement to take joint action against a plaintiff to achieve an unlawful objective. In terms of the § 1 claim, Santana will be required to prove that Bobrick knowingly entered into an agreement with Formica and/or others to take joint action against Santana to achieve an unlawful objective. Thus, the viability of Santana's § 1 claim rests upon Bobrick's active conduct in knowingly joining an antitrust conspiracy.

Section 2 of the Sherman Act provides that "[e]very person who shall monopolize, or attempt to monopolize, or combine or conspire to monopolize, any part of the trade or commerce among the several states ...

shall be deemed guilty of a felony." 15 U.S.C. § 2. In order to support its § 2 claim, Santana must demonstrate: (1) that the defendant has engaged in predatory or anticompetitive conduct with (2) a specific intent to monopolize and (3) a dangerous probability of achieving monopoly power. Thus, in order to succeed under its § 2 claim, Santana must prove that Bobrick acted with the specific intent to monopolize trade. Thus, any judgment against Bobrick in relation to the § 2 claim must be based upon a finding that Bobrick did not act passively.

With respect to the Lanham Act claim, Santana alleges that Bobrick knowingly made false misrepresentations regarding Santana's HDPE partitions. In addition to Bobrick's use of the Formica videotape, Santana has also alleged that Bobrick created its own videotape which compared the differences between HDPE partitions and other available partitions. Santana contends that Bobrick knowingly made numerous false statements in its videotape concerning HDPE partitions. Moreover, Santana alleges that Bobrick used its false videotape to persuade potential customers to reject Santana's HDPE toilet partitions. Santana's complaint also contains allegations that Bobrick created a bulletin that contained false allegations concerning Santana's HDPE product. Santana contends that Bobrick circulated a memorandum to its architectural representatives in which it again falsely represented Santana's HDPE partitions. In another instance, Santana alleges that Bobrick created and circulated a bulletin that falsely stated that HDPE partitions posed a fire and smoke hazard. Thus, the allegations in Santana's complaint make clear that Bobrick's action was not limited to passively distributing Formica's videotape without regard to its accuracy. Instead, the complaint contains numerous allegations of Bobrick actively creating and knowingly distributing false advertising material. It is thus clear that even if there was a right to indemnification under the Lanham Act, the allegations of the pleadings preclude an indemnification claim here.

Finally, in terms of Santana's claim that Bobrick interfered with Santana's prospective business advantage, such a claim requires Santana to prove: (1) a prospective contractual relation; (2) Bobrick's intent to harm Santana by preventing the relation from occurring; (3) the absence of privilege or justification on the part of Bobrick; and (4) damage arising from Bobrick's conduct. Therefore, Santana must prove that Bobrick purposefully interfered with its business relations — clearly active, not passive, conduct.

In short, a review of the Bobrick's third-party complaint and Santana's original complaint warrants a finding that Bobrick may not assert a claim for indemnification on these facts. Any liability that Bobrick suffers will result from Santana's proof of its claims that Bobrick acted knowingly and intentionally in falsely representing Santana's products to potential customers. As noted by Formica: "Thus, Bobrick will be found liable to Santana only if it engaged in knowing and intentional misconduct, which would bar Bobrick's claim for indemnity against Formica. If, on the other hand, Bobrick proves that it did not engage in knowing or intentional misconduct, Santana's claims will fail, and thus, Bobrick will not require indemnity from Formica." The pleadings make clear that Santana seeks to hold Bobrick liable as an active, not passive, party. Therefore, Formica's motion to dismiss Bobrick's third-party indemnification claim will be granted.

C. Fraud and Negligent Misrepresentation Claims

Bobrick's claims for fraud and negligent misrepresentation do not present a theory of secondary or derivative liability as required under Federal Rule of Civil Procedure 14(a). As noted by this Court:

> [A third-party complaint] must set forth a claim of secondary liability such that, if the third-party plaintiff is found liable, the third-party defendant will be liable to him/her under a theory of indemnification, contribution or some other theory of derivative liability recognized by the relevant substantive law. Any third-party complaint which does not facially meet this test is not proper under Rule 14 and thus falls outside of this Court's ancillary jurisdiction.*

Toberman v. Copas, 800 F. Supp. 1239, 1242 (M.D.Pa.1992) (citations omitted); *see also FDIC v. Bathgate*, 27 F.3d 850, 873 (3d Cir. 1994) ("A third party claim may be asserted under Rule 14(a) only when the third party's liability is in some way dependent on the outcome of the main claim or when the third party is secondarily liable to defendant."); *Ronson v. Talesnick*, 33 F.Supp.2d 347, 356 (D.N.J.1999) ("A third-party complaint that does not make a facial showing of secondary liability will not be entertained by the court."); *Damar, Inc. v. Advanced Global Design, Inc.*, No. 98-3435, 1998 WL 967549, at *1 (E.D.Pa. Nov.19, 1998) (finding that third-party complaint that alleged torts committed by third-party defendant, but no allegations of secondary liability, could not be maintained under Rule 14); *Lawyer's Title Ins. Co. v. Suburban Abstract Assoc., L.P.*, No. 94-6127, 1995 WL 321885, at *1 (E.D.Pa. May 25, 1995) ("First and foremost, a third-party complaint must seek relief under a theory of secondary or derivative liability.").

While Bobrick properly alleged claims for contribution and indemnification in its third-party complaint, those claims have been dismissed. Bobrick's independent claims for fraud and negligent misrepresentation against Formica cannot form the basis of a third-party complaint as they

---

* Ed. Note. Some courts (such as the one cited here) used to employ what was then termed "ancillary jurisdiction" to take jurisdiction over state-law claims that did not have their own bases for subject matter jurisdiction, but were joined with claims that did. Today, 28 U.S.C. § 1367, which governs Supplemental Jurisdiction (described in Chapter 4), governs these claims.

do not assert derivative or secondary liability. In its third-party complaint, Bobrick alleges it

> has been damaged by the alleged [fraudulent misrepresentation and/or negligent misrepresentations] of Formica by being subject to a lawsuit and having to expend substantial sums in defending itself against allegations based directly upon Bobrick or its independent architectural representatives showing the Videotape to specifiers, building code officials, architects and builders.

Clearly, the fraud and negligent misrepresentation claims relate to damages that Bobrick suffered defending against Santana's claims relating to the Formica videotape. The fraud and negligent misrepresentation claims are not dependent upon the outcome of the underlying action. Rather, these claims exist without regard to the ultimate success or failure of Santana's action. Nor do the fraud and negligent misrepresentation claims shift responsibility for Santana's damages; rather, Bobrick seeks to recover its own damages independent of the success of Santana's action. Therefore, because the fraud and negligent misrepresentation claims do not present secondary liability claims and cannot be maintained under Rule 14, Formica's motion to dismiss the fraud and negligent misrepresentation claims will be granted.

III. Conclusion

There is no right to contribution or indemnification under the Sherman Act or the Lanham Act. Moreover, the release between Formica and Santana bars Bobrick's contribution claim against Formica. Because Santana's underlying action depends upon Bobrick's knowing and intentional acts, a third-party claim for indemnification is unavailable. Finally, the claims for fraud and negligent misrepresentation are not derivative claims for secondary liability, but rather independent tort claims which may not be maintained independently through a third-party complaint under Rule 14(a). For all of these reasons, Formica's motion to dismiss the third-party complaint will be granted.

Exercise 8-6. Indemnity or Indemnity?

You will recall that, when we introduced the concept of indemnity by contract above, we used the example of automobile liability insurance to illustrate the point. That sort of relationship always requires that the person covered by the insurance (the indemnified person) has committed some sort of wrong that the insurance policy covers, meaning that the insurance company (the indemnitor) will only be liable where the covered insured has done something wrong.

How does the common law form of indemnity discussed in the case above differ from this sort of indemnity? What are the consequences for this proposed third-party plaintiff?

Exercise 8-7. Contribution and Impleader

Note that one of Bobrick's theories of derivative liability in the case above is contribution under the Lanham Act, the main federal Trademark statute. Although the analysis is omitted from the above edited version of the case because it is more an evaluation of whether the right to contribution exists or not under the Lanham Act (and thus is better placed under the heading of Rule 8 and Rule 12(b)(6)), the question of whether Rule 14 joinder was proper would essentially be the same question because a claim for contribution is a quintessential claim for derivative liability. Simply put, a party may not recover from co-wrongdoer for contribution if the claiming party has not otherwise been held liable to some other party.

However, it is important to understand that merely being a joint tortfeasor (or a joint violator of a statute) is not enough to justify a derivative claim against one's co-tortfeasor (or co-violator). Under which of the following scenarios would a derivative claim be possible if only one of several co-tortfeasors or co-statutory violators were sued?

1. The statute creating liability states that co-violators may seek contribution from other co-violators.

2. A state's tort doctrine recognizes apportionment of fault among joint tortfeasors when one or more are not made defendants to a lawsuit, but holds that liability among them is "several."

3. A state's tort doctrine recognizes apportionment of fault among joint tortfeasors when one or more are not made defendants to a lawsuit, but holds that liability among them is "joint and several."

Exercise 8-8. Review of Basic Joinder Practice

Review the problems below and determine, for each claim, the appropriate response choice(s). Be sure to consult the Rules in making your choices. Also, it will be very helpful to you if you diagram the party alignments as we have diagrammed them for you in this Chapter.

1. Abbott sues Brady for negligence. Brady impleads Costello for indemnity. Abbott then amends his complaint and adds Drogba as a party-defendant. Assume that the claims against Costello and Drogba are properly joined. May Drogba now cross-claim against Costello?

   a. Yes, if the claim arises out of the same transaction or occurrence as the claim by Abbott against Brady.

   b. Yes, if the claim arises out of the same transaction or occurrence as the claim by Brady against Costello.

    c. Yes, if the claim arises out of the same transaction or occurrence as the claim by Abbott against Drogba.

    d. No.

2. Assume the facts from the previous question, and assume that all claims stated there are properly joined. May Abbott file a claim against Costello?

    a. Yes, if the claim arises out of the same transaction or occurrence as the claim by Abbott against Brady.

    b. No, unless Costello first files a claim against Abbott.

    c. Yes, if the claim arises out of the same transaction or occurrence as any other claim asserted in the action.

    d. No.

3. Assume the facts from the previous question, and assume that all claims are properly joined. May Costello file a permissive counterclaim against Abbott?

    a. Yes, if the claim arises out of the same transaction or occurrence as the claim by Abbott against Brady.

    b. No, unless Costello joins it to a compulsory counterclaim against Abbott using Rules 13 and 18 together.

    c. Yes, regardless of whether the counterclaim arises out of the same transaction or occurrence as any other claim asserted in the action.

    d. No.

4. Assume the facts from the previous question, and assume that all claims are properly joined. May Costello now implead Falco and assert an indemnity claim against Falco?

    a. Yes, if the claim is derived from the claim by Abbott against Costello.

    b. Yes, if the claim arises out of the same transaction as the claim by Abbott against Brady.

    c. Yes, if the claim is derived from the claim by Brady against Costello.

    d. Either (a) or (c).

    e. No. Third-party defendants cannot act as third-party plaintiffs.

5. Assume the facts from the previous question, and assume that Costello impleads Falco successfully. May Costello now assert claims against Falco other than for indemnity?

    a. Yes, if each such claim arises out of the same transaction or occurrence as the claim by Abbott against Brady.

    b. Yes, if each such claim arises out of the same transaction or occurrence as the claim by Costello against Falco.

c. Yes, regardless of whether the claim arises out of the same transaction or occurrence as any other claim asserted in the action.

d. No.

6. Assume the facts from the previous question, and assume that all claims have been properly joined. Which of the claims would require a summons?

a. Abbott's initial claim against Brady.

b. Costello's counterclaim against Abbott.

c. Costello's indemnity claim against Falco.

d. Costello's cross-claim against Drogba.

5. Complex Joinder

The preceding Sections introduced the concept of joinder and explained the basic forms of claim and party joinder. This Section, along with Section 6, which is devoted to introducing the unique joinder device called the class action, introduce and explain the more complex forms of joinder available under the Federal Rules. Even more so than the simpler forms of joinder, these more complex forms of joinder are highly textual, so we include substantial portions of each of the relevant joinder rules here in the text to assist you with your learning.

Other than the class action, there are three complex forms of joinder — compulsory joinder of a party needed for just adjudication (Rule 19 and Rule 12(b)(7)); interpleader (Rule 22 and 28 U.S.C. § 1335); and intervention (Rule 24 and several federal statutes). The bad news is that the rules and statutes governing these doctrines are among the more difficult ones you will encounter. The good news is that the standards each of the rules impose are quite similar, so if you master one rule, you will be a long way down the path toward mastering the others.

a. Required Joinder of Parties

The most sensible place to begin is with Rule 19, titled, "Required Joinder of Parties."[*] Read Rule 19 very carefully on your own. As you can see, this Rule contains more stringent requirements than the others you have studied thus far. To break them out:

IF joining an absent party would not destroy the court's subject matter jurisdiction; and

IF that absent party can be validly served with process;

The court MUST order the joinder of the absent party if ANY of the following are true:

---

[*] Ed. Note. Older sources will refer to this sort of joinder as "compulsory" joinder.

1. *Failing to join the absent party will prevent the court from providing "complete relief" to the "existing parties."* This potential basis for required joinder concerns the interests of the parties already in the case. For example, if litigation concerns ownership of a piece of real property, and that property is owned jointly by the defendant and the absent party, and state law is such that both joint owners must surrender their ownership interests for the property to be validly transferred to another, then "complete relief" is impossible among the "existing parties" unless the absent joint owner is joined.

2. *The absent party claims an interest in the "subject matter of the litigation," and adjudicating the case in his or her absence may, "as a practical matter impair or impede the person's ability to protect the interest."* In contrast with the first basis, this basis for required joinder concerns the interest of the absent party. If the absent party has an interest in the property or other subject matter over which the existing litigants are litigating, and if allowing that litigation to come to a conclusion without the absent party would prevent the absent party from protecting his or her interest "as a practical matter" (which is something broader than "as a legal matter"), then the court must join the absent party. For example, imagine that twin sons each separately received the same promise from their father—that on their 18th birthday, he would give them his pickup truck, as long as they refrained from dating before then. Perhaps their father thought that it was unlikely that both would forego dating before turning 18, but as it turns out, they both do. Now that they are both 18, and there remains only one pickup truck for their father to give away, he refuses to give it to either of them. One of the brothers sues the father, seeking specific performance, and the father moves to include the other. The absent brother should be joined because he has an interest in the pickup truck, and, if the existing case results in his brother obtaining the truck, his interest will be impaired.

3. *The absent party claims an interest in the "subject matter of the litigation," and adjudicating the case in his or her absence may "leave an existing party subject to a substantial risk of incurring double, multiple, or otherwise inconsistent obligations because of the interest."* For example, imagine an insurance policy that is payable on death to a named beneficiary. Assume that the beneficiary is one of two daughters of the deceased. The non-named daughter brings suit to challenge the validity of the insurance policy, claiming that she was originally the named beneficiary, and the change that replaced her name with her sister's was not in compliance with the policy's terms. The absent sister here has a very strong interest in seeing that the amendment that made her the beneficiary is upheld, but she is not part of the suit. If the insurance company is required to pay the proceeds over to her sister, then the absent sister is likely to sue herself, and will not be precluded from doing so. This would present the insurance company with the prospect of having to pay the same proceeds twice. To prevent that, the absent sister should be joined.

So, although the language of the provisions is not the clearest, each of the possible scenarios that would justify compulsory joinder is a familiar one. However, each of these scenarios is subject to a very important "unless." That is, if one (or more) of the above qualifications is met, joinder must occur UNLESS it is not "feasible." Two clues as to when joinder is not feasible appear in the text of the Rule—if joinder would destroy the court's subject matter jurisdiction or if the party sought to be joined cannot be validly served (including if the party is not subject to the personal jurisdiction of the court—see Rule 4(k)). It is possible to imagine others, but the real question is, if joinder is not "feasible," then what should the court do?

Under the terms of the Rule, if joinder is not "feasible," then the court must decide between two options: (1) continue with the litigation even without the absent party, despite the risk to that party's and/or the existing parties' interests; or (2) dismiss the case in its entirety. This latter option is the reason that most Rule 19 arguments come up as part of a motion to dismiss under Rule 12(b)(7), which provides a defending party with a way to seek dismissal of the case due to the "failure to join a party needed for just adjudication." Simply put, most parties making Rule 19-based arguments are attempting to get the case dismissed, first, and to make it more fair only if it cannot be dismissed. This is one of the weaknesses of Rule 19 joinder—it depends in part on the interests of an absent party, but leaves the raising of that interest to the existing parties.

You will see, however, that the other complex joinder rules account for this weakness. For now, it will be useful to see how a court decides both the joinder question and the question of whether the case should be dismissed when joinder is not feasible. The case below does both.

Equal Employment Opportunity Commission v. Peabody Western Coal Company; Navajo Nation

610 F.3d 1070 (9th Cir. 2010)

Opinion

William A. Fletcher, Circuit Judge:

The Equal Employment Opportunity Commission ("EEOC") appeals various rulings of the district court in its suit against Peabody Western Coal Company ("Peabody"). Peabody leases mines from the Navajo Nation ("the Nation"), and maintains a preference for employing Navajo workers at these mines. EEOC alleges that in maintaining its employment preference Peabody discriminates against non-Navajo Indians, including two members of the Hopi Nation and one member of the Otoe tribe, in violation of Title VII, 42 U.S.C. § 2000e-2(a)(1). The district court first dismissed EEOC's suit in 2002. We heard EEOC's appeal from that dismissal in *EEOC v. Peabody Western Coal Co.* ("Peabody II"), 400 F.3d 774 (9th Cir. 2005). We reversed, holding that it was feasible to join the Nation under Federal Rule of Civil Procedure 19 and that the suit did not present a nonjusticiable political question.* On remand, the district court granted summary judgment to Peabody. EEOC appeals.

In this appeal, we address questions arising out of the joinder of two different parties. We first address the joinder of the Nation. We hold that the amended complaint filed by EEOC after our remand does not render it infeasible to join the Nation. We next address the joinder of the Secretary of the Interior ("the Secretary"). We hold that the Secretary is a required party under Rule 19(a), and that joining him is not feasible. We hold further that Peabody and the Nation may not bring a third-party damages claim against the Secretary under Federal Rule of Civil Procedure 14(a), and that EEOC's claim against Peabody for damages must therefore be dismissed under Rule 19(b). However, we hold that Peabody and the Nation may bring a third-party claim against the Secretary for prospective relief under Rule 14(a), and that EEOC's injunctive claim against Peabody should therefore be allowed to proceed.

We vacate the remainder of the district court's rulings and remand for further proceedings consistent with this opinion.

I. Background
A. Factual Background

Peabody mines coal at the Black Mesa Complex and Kayenta Mine on the Navajo and Hopi reservations in northeastern Arizona. Peabody does so pursuant to leases with the Navajo and Hopi tribes inherited from its predecessor-in-interest, Sentry Royalty Company ("Sentry"). This case involves two leases Sentry entered into with the Nation: a 1964 lease permitting it to mine on the Navajo reservation (lease no. 8580) and a 1966 lease permitting it to mine on the Navajo portion of land jointly used by the Navajo and Hopi nations (lease no. 9910).

Both leases require that Peabody provide an employment preference to Navajo job applicants. The 1964 lease provides that Peabody "agrees to employ Navajo Indians when available in all positions for which, in the

---

* Ed. Note. A nonjusticiable political question describes a case that a federal court must dismiss on prudential grounds, even though it has formal subject matter jurisdiction, because the issues presented by the case impair the separation of powers for one or more reasons. *See Baker v. Carr*, 369 U.S. 186 (1962), which provides a list of the reasons that have justified dismissal on political question grounds in the past.

judgment of [Peabody], they are qualified," and that Peabody "shall make a special effort to work Navajo Indians into skilled, technical and other higher jobs in connection with [Peabody's] operations under this Lease." The 1966 lease provides similarly, but also states that Peabody may "at its option extend the benefits of this Article [containing the Navajo employment preference] to Hopi Indians." We will refer to these provisions as "Navajo employment preference provisions." Many business leases on the Navajo reservation contain similar employment preferences for Navajo job applicants.

As we noted in *Peabody II*, the Department of the Interior ("DOI") approved both mining leases, as well as subsequent amendments and extensions, under the Indian Mineral Leasing Act of 1938 ("IMLA"). Former Secretary of the Interior Stewart Udall, who served as Secretary during the period the leases were drafted and approved, stated in a declaration submitted to the district court that DOI drafted the leases and required the inclusion of the Navajo employment preferences. This statement is undisputed. The leases provide that, if their terms are violated, both the Nation and the Secretary retain the power to cancel them after a notice and cure period. Amendments to the leases must be approved by the Secretary.

B. Procedural Background

This is the latest in a series of cases involving Navajo employment preferences. We discussed the history of Navajo employment preferences in detail in the first appeal in this case. *See Peabody II*, 400 F.3d at 777.

EEOC filed this suit against Peabody in June 2001, alleging that Peabody was unlawfully discriminating on the basis of national origin by implementing the Navajo employment preferences contained in the leases. EEOC's complaint charged that Peabody had refused to hire non-Navajo Indians including two members of the Hopi and one now-deceased member of the Otoe tribe, as well as unspecified other non-Navajo Indians, for positions for which they were otherwise qualified. EEOC alleged that such conduct violated Title VII, 42 U.S.C. § 2000e-2(a)(1), which prohibits employers from refusing to hire applicants because of their national origin. EEOC's position throughout this litigation has been that the Indian preference exception of Title VII, § 2000e-2(i), permits discrimination in favor of Indians living on or near a particular tribe's reservation, but does not permit discrimination against Indians who live on or near that reservation but are members of another tribe. EEOC alleged further that Peabody had violated the recordkeeping requirements of § 2000e-8(c). EEOC requested three forms of relief: (1) an injunction prohibiting Peabody from continuing to discriminate on the basis of national origin and requiring Peabody to provide equal employment opportunities for non-Navajo Indians living on or near the Navajo reservation; (2) damages, including back pay with interest, compensatory damages, and punitive damages; and (3) an order requiring Peabody to make and preserve records in compliance with Title VII.

Peabody moved for summary judgment and for dismissal of the action. Peabody argued, first, that Rule 19 required dismissal because the Nation was a necessary and indispensable party to the action and, second, that the action presented a nonjusticiable political question between EEOC and DOI because DOI had approved the mining leases. The district court agreed and granted Peabody's motion to dismiss on both grounds. The district court also dismissed EEOC's recordkeeping claim, even though Peabody had not sought dismissal of this claim.

We reversed in *Peabody II*. First, we held that the Nation was a necessary party under Rule 19, but that EEOC's suit need not be dismissed because joinder of the Nation was feasible. Because EEOC is an agency of the United States, the Nation could not assert sovereign immunity as a defense to joinder. Although EEOC lacked statutory authority to state a cause of action against the Nation, joinder of the Nation for the purposes of *res judicata* was still possible and would be effective in providing "complete relief between the parties." Second, we held that EEOC's claim did not present a nonjusticiable political question. Third, we held that the district court erred in dismissing EEOC's recordkeeping claim. We remanded for further proceedings with the Nation joined under Rule 19.

On remand, EEOC filed an amended complaint that included the same claims and prayer for relief as its initial complaint. The newly joined Nation moved to dismiss under Rule 19, arguing, *inter alia*, that EEOC's amended complaint impermissibly seeks affirmative relief against the Nation, and that the Secretary of the Interior is a necessary and indispensable party. Peabody filed its own motion to dismiss. *Inter alia*, it agreed with the Nation's argument that the Secretary was a necessary and indispensable party. This was the first time in this litigation that anyone had argued that the Secretary was a necessary and indispensable party.

The district court converted the motions to dismiss into motions for summary judgment. The district court granted summary judgment against EEOC, holding, in the alternative, that (1) EEOC was seeking affirmative relief against the Nation in its amended complaint, and that the Nation therefore could not be joined under Rule 19; (2) the Secretary was a necessary and indispensable party for whom joinder was not feasible; and (3) the Rehabilitation Act of 1950, 25 U.S.C. §631–638, authorized the tribe-specific preferences challenged by EEOC. The district court also granted the Nation's motions to strike two EEOC exhibits and to strike an EEOC footnote reference. Finally, the court denied EEOC's motion to strike two forms upon which Peabody relied. EEOC timely appealed all of the district court's rulings.

We reach only holdings (1) and (2), as to which we reverse the district court. We vacate the rest of the court's decision and remand for further proceedings.

II. Standard of Review

We review a district court's decision on joinder for abuse of discretion, and we review the legal conclusions underlying that decision de novo.

III. Discussion

This case continues to present somewhat complex compulsory party joinder issues.

* * *

Although the wording of Rule 19 has changed since the district court dismissed this case, its meaning remains the same. When dealing with the amended rule in this opinion, we will use the new language.

A Rule 19 motion poses three successive inquiries. First, the court must determine whether a nonparty should be joined under Rule 19(a). That nonparty (or "absentee") is now referred to as a "person required to be joined if feasible." If an absentee meets the requirements of Rule 19(a), "the second stage is for the court to determine whether it is feasible to order that the absentee be joined. Finally, if joinder is not feasible, the court must determine at the third stage whether the case can proceed without the absentee" or whether the action must be dismissed. A non-party in whose absence an action must be dismissed is one who "not only has an interest in the controversy, but has an interest of such a nature that a final decree cannot be made without either affecting that interest, or leaving the controversy in such a condition that its final termination may be wholly inconsistent with equity and good conscience." *Shields v. Barrow*, 58 U.S. 130, 139 (1855). With these principles in mind, we consider the Rule 19 joinder of both the Navajo Nation and the Secretary of the Interior.

A. Joinder of the Navajo Nation under Rule 19

In *Peabody II*, we held that the Navajo Nation was a necessary party for whom joinder was feasible. It is undisputed that the Nation was a necessary party, and is now, under the amended rule, a person required to be joined if feasible. As we explained in *Peabody II*, the Nation is a party to the leases whose employment preference is challenged in this lawsuit.

If the EEOC is victorious in this suit but the Nation has not been joined, the Nation could possibly initiate further action to enforce the employment preference against Peabody, even though that preference would have been held illegal in this litigation. Peabody would then be between the proverbial rock and a hard place—comply with the injunction prohibiting the hiring preference policy or comply with the lease requiring it. By similar logic, we have elsewhere found that tribes are necessary parties to actions that might have the result of directly undermining authority they would otherwise exercise. We held that it was feasible to join the Nation even though under Title VII no affirmative relief was available to EEOC against the Nation.

After our remand, EEOC amended its complaint to add the Nation as a defendant. The district court held that EEOC sought affirmative relief against the Nation in its amended complaint even though we had specifically held in *Peabody II* that such relief was not available. Under its reading of EEOC's amended complaint, the district court dismissed EEOC's suit on the ground that the Nation could not, after all, be joined. For the reasons that follow, we hold that the district court should not have dismissed EEOC's amended complaint on this ground.

In *Peabody II*, Peabody made two arguments why joinder of the Nation was not feasible. We disagreed with both of them. First, Peabody argued that the Nation could not be joined because of sovereign immunity. We held that the Nation's sovereign immunity did not shield it from a suit brought by EEOC and therefore did not bar its joinder. We explained, "Tribal sovereign immunity does not act as a shield against the United States, even when Congress has not specifically abrogated tribal immunity." *Id.*, [400 F.3d at 780.]

Second, Peabody argued that because Title VII exempts the Nation from the definition of employer, 42 U.S.C. § 2000e(b), EEOC could not state a claim against the Nation. Therefore, Peabody argued, the Nation could not be joined in a suit brought by EEOC. But a plaintiff's inability to state a direct cause of action against an absentee does not prevent the absentee's joinder under Rule 19. An absentee can be joined under Rule 19 in order to subject it, under principles of *res judicata*, to the minor and ancillary effects of a judgment. We wrote that

> EEOC has no claim against the party it seeks to join and is not seeking any affirmative relief directly from that party. Joinder is necessary for the "sole purpose" of effecting complete relief between the parties ... by ensuring that both Peabody and the Nation are bound to any judgment upholding or striking down the challenged lease provision.

Peabody II, 400 F.3d at 783.

On remand, the district court concluded that EEOC's amended complaint sought affirmative relief against the Nation. The district court found that "with the benefit of the filing of the Amended Complaint and limited discovery, it is apparent to this Court that the EEOC is not merely seeking relief against Peabody Coal, but all parties acting in concert with it, which includes the Navajo Nation." In so holding, the district court relied on the language in the amended complaint seeking "a permanent injunction enjoining Peabody ... and all persons in active concert or participation with it, from engaging in discrimination on the basis of national origin." The court found that

> there can be no doubt that the Navajo Nation falls within the scope of affirmative relief sought by the EEOC.... Should the EEOC prevail in this suit and obtain the broad relief sought, the Navajo Nation would then be enjoined from implementing and requiring such lease provisions in the future as it would already be subject to injunctive relief from this Court based upon the determination that such provisions are contrary to Title VII. As such, there can be little doubt that the EEOC seeks affirmative relief not only against Peabody Coal but the Navajo Nation as well.

The language added to the amended complaint provides, in its entirety:

> Defendant Navajo Nation is a party to a lease agreement with the Defendant employer, Peabody Coal Company, and is therefore named as a party pursuant to Rule 19(a) of the Federal Rules of Civil Procedure, in that, in its absence, complete relief cannot be accorded among those already parties, and it has an interest in the subject of this action.

This added language says nothing about any kind of relief against the Nation.

The original complaint was before us when we decided *Peabody II*. The language in the amended complaint upon which the district court relied to conclude that EEOC was seeking affirmative relief is word-for-word the same as in the original complaint. It is, in its entirety:

> Wherefore, the Commission respectfully requests that this Court:
>
> A. Grant a permanent injunction enjoining Peabody, its officers, successors, assigns, and all persons in active concert or participation with it, from engaging in discrimination on the basis of national origin.

Some of this added language is standard boilerplate drawn from Rule 65(d)(2)(C), describing the "persons bound" by "every injunction" as including "other persons who are in active concert or participation" with the party or parties served with an injunction.

There are two possible readings of the amended complaint. Under one reading, EEOC is not seeking any injunctive relief against the Nation. The Nation is "bound" by the injunction only in the sense that it is *res judicata* as to the Nation, not in the sense that the injunction affirmatively requires the Nation to do something. In our view, this is the better reading of the boilerplate language in the complaint, given that the explicit premise of our holding in *Peabody II* was that EEOC has no cause of action against the Nation under Title VII and that, as a necessary corollary, EEOC can obtain no injunctive relief against the Nation. However, the district court did not adopt this reading.

Under the reading adopted by the district court, EEOC sought injunctive relief against the Nation in its amended complaint. Even if this is the correct reading, the district court nonetheless erred in dismissing EEOC's suit. Because we had held in *Peabody II* that joinder of the Nation was feasible despite the unavailability of injunctive relief against it, the proper response of the district court would have been simply to deny EEOC's request for injunctive relief. As we held in *Peabody II*, joinder of the Nation is feasible, and dismissal under Rule 19 is not required even though injunctive relief is unavailable.

The district court therefore erred in dismissing EEOC's complaint on the ground that it sought injunctive relief against the Nation.

B. Joinder of the Secretary of the Interior under Rule 19

On remand from *Peabody II*, Peabody and the newly joined Nation argued under Rule 19 that the suit could not proceed without joinder of the Secretary. Even though Peabody had been a defendant in the suit from the outset, this was the first time it made this argument. Because the Nation had just been joined, this was its first opportunity to make the argument. We agree with Peabody and the Nation that the Secretary is a person to be joined if feasible under Rule 19. But we do not agree that the entirety of EEOC's suit must be dismissed.

The central problem is that Peabody is caught in the middle of a dispute not of its own making. EEOC contends that the Navajo employment preference provision contained in the leases violates Title VII. The Secretary required that this provision be included in the leases. EEOC seeks damages and an injunction against Peabody, which has complied with the lease terms upon which the Secretary insisted.

If the district court were to hold that the Navajo employment preference provision violates Title VII and to award damages against Peabody, it would be profoundly unfair if Peabody could not seek indemnification from the Secretary. It would be similarly unfair if the district court were to grant an injunction requiring Peabody to disregard the preference provision, but leaving the Secretary free, despite the court's holding, to insist that Peabody comply with it.

The same is true, though to a lesser extent, for the Nation. As we held in *Peabody II*, EEOC can obtain neither damages nor injunctive relief against the Nation. But if the district court holds that the employment preference provision violates Title VII, the Nation will be bound to that result by *res judicata*. If the Secretary is not made a party to the suit, he may ignore the court's judgment and place conflicting demands upon the Nation who will be required by *res judicata* to honor the judgment.

1. The Secretary as a Required Party under Rule 19(a)

A person is required to be joined if feasible under Rule 19(a)(1)(A) if, "in that person's absence, the court cannot accord complete relief among the existing parties" or under Rule 19(a)(1)(B) if "that person claims an interest relating to the subject of the action and is so situated that disposing of the action in the person's absence may: (i) as a practical matter impair or impede the person's ability to protect the interest; or (ii) leave an existing party subject to a substantial risk of incurring double, multiple, or otherwise inconsistent obligations because of the interest." There is no precise formula for determining whether a particular nonparty should be joined under Rule 19(a). The determination is heavily influenced by the facts and circumstances of each case. The Secretary meets the standards of both Rule 19(a)(1)(A) and Rule 19(a)(1)(B).

First, under Rule 19(a)(1)(A), in the absence of the Secretary, the district court cannot accord complete relief among the existing parties. The record makes clear that the Secretary insisted that the disputed employment preference provision be included in the leases between Peabody and the Nation, and that the Secretary is ultimately responsible for its continued inclusion in the leases. If EEOC prevails in its interpretation of Title VII, it may recover damages from Peabody based on Peabody's compliance with the employment preference provision. In that event, Peabody will be obliged to pay damages for having engaged in conduct that was mandated by the Secretary. If the Secretary is not made a party, Peabody will not be able to seek indemnification from the Secretary.

Further, if EEOC prevails it may obtain an injunction ordering Peabody to disregard the employment preference provision. The Secretary has the power, if the lease terms are violated, to cancel the leases after a notice and cure period, and Peabody is unable to modify the terms of the leases without the approval of the Secretary. If the Secretary is not made a party, Peabody may be obliged by the court to disregard the preference provision, while the Secretary would remain free to insist that Peabody honor it, upon pain of losing the leases. *See, e.g., Associated Dry Goods Corp. v. Towers Fin. Corp.*, 920 F.2d 1121, 1124 (2d Cir. 1990) (holding that landlord was required party in suit brought by tenant against subtenant, as subtenant would not be able to obtain complete relief in counterclaims against tenant for increased electrical capacity without approval of landlord); *Wymbs v. Republican State Executive Comm.*, 719 F.2d 1072, 1080 (11th Cir. 1983) (holding that national political party committee was required party in suit on the constitutionality of a local political party's delegate selection rule when the local rule was derived from the national rule and the national party still had the ability to determine which delegates would be seated).

Second, under Rule 19(a)(1)(B), the Secretary has an interest in the subject matter of this action. Resolving this action in the Secretary's absence may both impair the Secretary's ability to protect that interest and leave Peabody and the Nation subject to a substantial risk of incurring inconsistent obligations. If the Secretary is not joined, he will be unable to defend his interest in the legality of the lease provisions. We have repeatedly held that no procedural principle is more deeply imbedded in the common law than that, in an action to set aside a lease or a contract, all parties who may be affected by the determination of the action are indispensable.

Although [our prior precedent] involved parties who were signatories to a contract, which the Secretary is not, the underlying principle applies here. The Secretary mandated the provisions and continues to exercise oversight over the leases. A public entity has an interest in a lawsuit that could result in the invalidation or modification of one of its ordinances, rules, regulations, or practices. *See, e.g., Davis v. United States*, 192 F.3d 951, 959 (10th Cir. 1999) (holding that Seminole Nation of Oklahoma was necessary party as a ruling on the merits would modify the Nation's ordinances); *Ricci v. State Bd. of Law Exam'rs*, 569 F.2d 782, 784 (3d Cir. 1978) (holding that Pennsylvania Supreme Court was indispensable party to an action that would, if it succeeded, invalidate one of the Court's rules of admission). The Secretary thus has an interest in an action that would require him to modify the terms of leases he approves for entities conducting business on the Navajo reservation. The Secretary therefore qualifies as a person to be joined under Rule 19(a)(1)(B)(i).

If the Secretary is not made a party and if EEOC prevails, the Secretary may choose to cancel the leases or to modify them to eliminate the Navajo employment preference. Alternatively, the Secretary may choose to continue the leases in their current form, ignoring the judgment in the case to which he has not been made a party. If the Secretary chooses to do this, he will put both Peabody and the Nation "between the proverbial rock and a hard place," forcing them to choose between complying with the injunction or risking cancellation of the leases for violating terms mandated by the Secretary. The Secretary therefore qualifies as a person to be joined under Rule 19(a)(1)(B)(ii).

EEOC argues that the Secretary is not a person required to be joined under Rule 19(a), citing to the Navajo Nation line of cases decided by the Supreme Court. In these cases, the Court held that the DOI did not owe a fiduciary duty to the Navajo Nation in managing, negotiating, or approving leases under the statutes at issue in this litigation, and that the Nation therefore could not state a cause of action against DOI for breach of fiduciary duty. *United States v. Navajo Nation* ("Navajo Nation II"), 556 U.S. 287, ___, 129 S. Ct. 1547, 1558 (2009) (holding that the Navajo-Hopi Rehabilitation Act of 1950 and Surface Mining Control and Reclamation Act of 1977 do not provide a cause of action to the Navajo Nation against the United States for breach of trust in its approval of coal mining leases); *Navajo Nation I*, 537 U.S. at 506, 123 S. Ct. 1079 (holding the same for the IMLA). These cases indicate the limits of DOI's fiduciary duty to the Nation with respect to the leases, but they say nothing about whether DOI possesses a cognizable interest in the outcome of litigation challenging lease terms mandated by the Secretary.

We therefore hold that the Secretary is a person required to be joined if feasible under Rule 19(a)(1)(A) and Rule 19(a)(1)(B).

2. Feasibility of Joining the Secretary

Rule 19(a) contemplates that a required party be joined as either a plaintiff or defendant. In the posture of this suit, the Secretary would be joined as a defendant rather than a plaintiff. However, we conclude that EEOC cannot join the Secretary as a defendant.

EEOC is prevented by 42 U.S.C. § 2000e-5(f)(1) from filing suit against the Secretary on its own authority. Section 2000e-5(f)(1) provides that if EEOC is not able to obtain a conciliation agreement with a governmental agency, it cannot itself bring suit against that agency. Instead, § 2000e-5(f)(1) provides that if EEOC is unable to obtain an agreement, it "shall take no further action and shall refer the case to the Attorney General who may bring a civil action against such respondent in the appropriate United States district court." We were told at oral argument by EEOC's attorney that EEOC has no expectation that the Attorney General will file suit against the Secretary. While there is no evidence in the record of a formal referral to and refusal by the Attorney General, we assume for purposes of our decision that the Attorney General either has refused or will refuse to file suit against the Secretary.

3. Dismissal "In Equity and Good Conscience"

If a required party under Rule 19(a) cannot be joined as a plaintiff or defendant, we look to the factors provided in Rule 19(b) to determine whether, "in equity and good conscience, the action should proceed among the existing parties or should be dismissed." Fed.R.Civ.P. 19(b). Rule 19(b) provides four factors that we must consider in making this determination: (1) the extent to which a judgment rendered in the person's absence might prejudice that person or the existing parties; (2) the extent to which any prejudice could be lessened or avoided by shaping the judgment or the relief; (3) whether a judgment rendered in the person's absence would be adequate; and (4) whether the plaintiff would have an adequate remedy if the action were dismissed. *Id.* The heart of this inquiry is the question of "equity and good conscience." The inquiry is a practical one and fact specific ... and is designed to avoid the harsh results of rigid application.

For the reasons that follow, we conclude that EEOC's claim for damages against Peabody must be dismissed under Rule 19(b), but that its claim for an injunction against Peabody should be permitted to proceed.

a. EEOC's Claim for Damages

If EEOC's suit against Peabody were allowed to proceed, the district court would almost certainly award damages against Peabody if it concludes that the Navajo employment preference provision violates Title VII. In that event, Peabody would quite reasonably look to the Secretary for indemnification, given that the preference provision was included in the leases at the insistence of the Secretary. Rule 14(a) would permit Peabody to file a third-party complaint against the Secretary for indemnification. But because Peabody's indemnification suit would seek damages, it would be barred by the government's sovereign immunity unless that immunity is waived by statute. We can find no waiver of sovereign immunity to such a suit.

The Tucker Act, 28 U.S.C. § 1346(a)(2), waives the government's sovereign immunity in damage suits based on contract, as well as for some claims arising under the Constitution and statutes of the United States. Under the Tucker Act, a party's claims must either rest upon a contract, seek the return of money paid by them to the Government, or establish an entitlement to money damages under a federal statute that can fairly be interpreted as mandating compensation by the Federal Government for the damage sustained. The Federal Tort Claims Act, 28 U.S.C. § 1346(b), waives the sovereign immunity of the United States for suits in tort. However, neither the Tucker Act nor the Federal Tort Claims Act waives the government's sovereign immunity in the circumstances of this case.

Title VII also waives the government's sovereign immunity to some extent. Based on that waiver, a federal employee may sue the government for damages under Title VII, provided that administrative remedies with EEOC have been exhausted. 42 U.S.C. § 2000e-16(c). But we can find nothing in Title VII that waives the government's sovereign immunity to a damages suit brought by a private employer that has itself violated Title VII.

Peabody's only sin, if indeed it was a sin, was to comply with an employment preference provision inserted in its lease at the insistence of the Secretary. It would be profoundly unfair for a court to award damages against Peabody while allowing Peabody no redress against the government. We are unable to see any way to mitigate this unfairness by, for example, "protective provisions in the judgment; ... shaping relief; or ... other measures." Fed.R.Civ.P. 19(b)(2)(A–C). We therefore conclude that "in equity and good conscience" EEOC's damages claim against Peabody must be dismissed under Rule 19(b).

b. EEOC's Claim for an Injunction

If EEOC's suit is allowed to proceed and if the district court were to hold that the Navajo employment preference provision violates Title VII, the district court would almost certainly grant an injunction requiring Peabody to ignore the provision in making its employment decisions. This injunction would not only require Peabody to take certain actions; it would also operate as *res judicata* against the Nation. In the event such an injunction were issued, Peabody and the Nation would quite reasonably want to seek prospective relief preventing the Secretary from enforcing the provision. Rule 14(a) would permit Peabody and the Nation to file a third-party complaint seeking such relief against the Secretary. Sovereign immunity does not bar prospective injunctive relief against the Secretary. We conclude that the availability of prospective relief through a third-party complaint under Rule 14(a) means that "in equity and good conscience" EEOC's suit against Peabody should be permitted to proceed.

i. Sovereign Immunity

A claim to which sovereign immunity is not a defense may be entertained even if another claim in the suit is dismissed because of sovereign immunity. Therefore, the district court may entertain Peabody and the Nation's third-party claim for prospective relief if it is not barred by the United States' sovereign immunity, even if a Peabody claim for damages would have to be dismissed.

Prospective relief requiring, or having the effect of requiring, governmental officials to obey the law has long been available. Sovereign immunity does not bar such relief. The case often cited for this proposition is *Ex parte Young*, 209 U.S. 123 (1908), which permitted an injunction against the Attorney General of Minnesota despite the Eleventh Amendment.

* * *

However, since 1976 federal courts have looked to §702 of the Administrative Procedure Act ("APA"), 5 U.S.C. §702, to serve the purposes of the *Ex parte Young* fiction in suits against federal officers. In *Presbyterian Church (U.S.A.) v. United States*, 870 F.2d 518 (9th Cir. 1989), we explained that after §702 was amended in 1976, it replaced the *Ex parte Young* fiction as the doctrinal basis for a claim for prospective relief.

* * *

"Agency action" under the APA is defined as "the whole or a part of an agency rule, order, license, sanction, relief, or the equivalent or denial thereof, or failure to act." 5 U.S.C. §551(13). "Persons" entitled to judicial review under the APA include "an individual, partnership, corporation, association, or public or private organization other than an agency." 5 U.S.C. §701(b)(2) (providing that, for purposes of provisions on judicial review, definition of "person" in 5 U.S.C. §551 applies); *id.* §551(providing definition of "person"). Both Peabody and the Navajo Nation come within this definition of "person." Peabody is a corporation, and the Nation is a "public organization." *Id.* Therefore, under § 702 of the APA, as would be the case under the *Ex parte Young* fiction, either Peabody or the Nation may assert a claim against the Secretary requesting injunctive or declaratory relief. We therefore conclude that neither Peabody nor the Nation is barred by sovereign immunity from bringing a third-party complaint seeking prospective relief against the Secretary under Rule 14(a).

ii. Third-party Complaints under Rule 14(a)

If a required party under Rule 19(a) cannot be joined as a plaintiff or defendant, the court must determine whether under Rule 19(b) the action must be dismissed "in equity and good conscience." Among the factors to be considered in making that determination is whether, under Rule 19(b)(2)(C), "measures" may be taken that would lessen or avoid any prejudice. To the degree that Peabody and the Nation may be prejudiced by the absence of the Secretary as a plaintiff or defendant, that prejudice may be eliminated by a third-party complaint against the Secretary under Rule 14(a).

The courts of appeals that have addressed the question are unanimous in holding that if an absentee can be brought into an action by impleader under Rule 14(a), a dismissal under Rule 19(b) is inappropriate. In *Pasco International (London) Ltd. v. Stenograph Corp.*, 637 F.2d 496 (2d Cir. 1980), the Second Circuit repeatedly indicated that prejudice to existing parties could be eliminated by impleader under Rule 14(a). The court wrote, "Stenograph can always protect itself from the possibility of inconsistent verdicts by impleading Croxford under Rule 14 [.] ... [T]he existence of the Rule 14 provisions demonstrates that parties such as Croxford who may be impleaded under Rule 14 are not indispensable parties within Rule 19(b)." *Id.* at 503. It summarized, "[A]ll persons subject to impleader by the defendant are not indispensable parties. This is ... merely an extension of the settled doctrine that Rule 19(b) was not intended to require the joinder of persons subject to impleader under Rule 14 such as potential indemnitors." *Id.* at 505 n. 20. The other circuits that have addressed the question have come to the same conclusion.

c. Summary

We conclude that prospective relief in the form of an injunction or declaratory judgment is available in a Rule 14(a) impleader against the Secretary. Such prospective relief against the Secretary is enough to protect Peabody and the Nation, both with respect to EEOC's request for injunctive relief against Peabody and with respect to any *res judicata* effect against the Nation. Such relief would also protect the Secretary because, once brought in as a third-party defendant, he will be able to defend his position on the legality of the leases. We therefore conclude, "in equity and good conscience," that EEOC's claim against Peabody for injunctive relief should be allowed to proceed.

C. Remaining Issues

EEOC has appealed the district court's various other rulings, including its holding that the Navajo employment preference does not violate Title VII. We vacate all of these rulings to allow reconsideration once the Secretary has been brought into the suit as a third-party defendant. This will allow the court to consider the arguments of the Secretary on the legality of the employment preferences before issuing a final ruling. We note, further, that the presentation of the Secretary's views in the district court, and the district court's considered ruling taking those views into account, will be useful to us in the event of a further appeal.

Conclusion

We again hold that joinder of the Navajo Nation under Rule 19 is feasible. We hold that the Secretary of the Interior is a party required to be joined if feasible under Rule 19(a), but that joinder of the Secretary as a defendant is not feasible. We hold that EEOC's damages claim against Peabody must be dismissed under Rule 19(b). Finally, we hold that EEOC's injunctive claim against Peabody should be allowed to proceed. We vacate the other rulings of the district court and remand for further proceedings consistent with this opinion.

Reversed in part and vacated in part. Each party to bear its own costs.

Exercise 8-9. The Complexity of Required Joinder

As you can see, complex joinder issues often arise in complex litigation. In the case above, the decision whether the absent parties had to be joined, as well as the decision whether some claims had to be dismissed, involved considerations of sovereign immunity, claim preclusion (res judicata), and the effects of judicial injunctions, not to mention the powers of the EEOC and the rights to the employees affected by the conduct giving rise to the litigation.

Can you articulate exactly why the EEOC was required to join the Nation to its action? Can you do so for the Secretary? What are the particular harms that would result if either of these non-parties were left out of the action, and which subsections of Rule 19 require joinder where these harms are likely?

Now, can you articulate why the joinder of the Nation was deemed "feasible," while the joinder of the Secretary was deemed "not feasible"?

Finally, can you articulate why it was not necessary to dismiss the case even though it was not feasible to join the Secretary?

Exercise 8-10. Alternatives to Required Joinder

Rule 19 is but one avenue for ensuring that a litigation does not proceed to an unfair resolution when it can be made more fair by bringing a non-party into the action. For a Rule 19(a)(1)(A) situation, where those who would be harmed by virtue of the non-party's absence are the existing parties to the litigation, we can feel secure that those parties would act in their own best interests to make sure that the non-party is made a party to the action.

But what about the other two scenarios under Rule 19? If, as is true under Rule 19(a)(1)(B)(i), the non-party's interests are the only ones that will be harmed by virtue of that non-party's absence, can we really expect the existing parties to look out for that interest? In some cases, yes, but in many cases, no. To account for this reality, we have Rule 24, which allows an absent non-party to move to "intervene" in an existing action.

And what about the other interest protected by Rule 19(a)(1)(B)(ii) — the interest of an existing party in avoiding "double, multiple, or otherwise inconsistent obligations" because one or more parties who have legitimate claims against it is absent from the case? The existing party might be able to prevail on a Rule 19 motion to force the joinder of the absent party, but he/she/it might also fail at that attempt. Since one of the consequences of a successful Rule 19 motion is dismissal of the entire case, courts are understandably strict in applying its terms. To account for this practicality, the rules drafters have provided another alternative path, termed "interpleader." Interpleader, governed by Rule 22 and 28 U.S.C. § 1335, allows a party in possession of a piece of property over which it has no interest to force two or more parties who each claim to have interests in that same property to litigate the issue in the same action.

Read Rules 22 and 24, and review Rule 19. Try to imagine a hypothetical fact situation where Rule 19 joinder would be rejected, but where a party might nevertheless be successful at accomplishing joinder under either Rule 22 or 24.

---

b. Interpleader

Both Rules 22 and 24 contain a number of challenges for the courts and for parties. To begin with, Rule 22 must be read along with 28 U.S.C. § 1335 and 1397, but the provisions are not necessarily consistent with each other. Section 1335 purports to be a subject matter jurisdiction statute (and is augmented by 28 U.S.C. § 2361, a nationwide service of process statute, and § 1397 a venue provision specific to statutory interpleader actions), while Rule 22 simply defines and authorizes interpleader as a form of joinder. Courts often have to wrestle with whether a given interpleader is merely a "rule" interpleader, to which the normal rules of subject matter jurisdiction, personal jurisdiction, and venue apply; or instead a "statutory" interpleader, for which Section 1335 governs subject matter jurisdiction, Section 2361 governs service of process (and therefore personal jurisdiction — see Rule 4(k)), and Section 1397 governs venue. The following case illustrates the consequences that can result from proceeding under the Rule, rather than the statute.

Metropolitan Life Ins. Co. v. Price
501 F.3d 271 (3d Cir. 2007)

Before: Scirica, Chief Judge, Fuentes and Chagares, Circuit Judges.

Opinion of the Court

Chagares, Circuit Judge.

Appellant Metropolitan Life Insurance Company ("MetLife") is the claims fiduciary of an "employee welfare benefit plan." *See* Employee Retirement Income Security Act of 1974 ("ERISA") § 3(1), 29 U.S.C. § 1002(1). After one of the plan's participants died, MetLife received competing claims to the decedent's life-insurance benefits. It responded by filing this interpleader action against the competing claimants. The District Court raised the issue of subject matter jurisdiction *sua sponte* and dismissed. In our view, however, the District Court had federal question jurisdiction. Accordingly, we will vacate and remand.

I

The New Jersey Transit Corporation sponsors a Basic Life Plan for the benefit of its employees. The plan is funded through a group life insurance policy issued by MetLife to New Jersey Transit. MetLife is the plan's "claims fiduciary."

Paul Price was a participant in the plan. He was a bus driver with New Jersey Transit and had enrolled for $20,000 in life insurance benefits. In May 2002, Paul passed away. He was survived by his widow, Sandra Price, and his children from a previous marriage, Shannon and Andre Price.

After Paul's death, his widow and his children submitted competing claims for the life insurance benefits. MetLife investigated the matter and discovered that, in or around February 2000, Paul designated his widow as the primary beneficiary. MetLife then informed the children's attorney that it was denying their claims. MetLife explained that it had a fiduciary duty "to administer claims in accordance with ERISA and the terms of the plan." As such, it had to "pay the proceeds to the named beneficiary only."

The children's attorney requested a review of the claim. Paul's first marriage had ended in 1995 with a final judgment of divorce in New Jersey Superior Court. Paragraph 11 of that judgment specifically referenced Paul's life insurance:

> The Husband currently has life insurance upon his life. The Husband shall amend these policies in order to name the children of the marriage as irrevocable beneficiaries until such time as Andre Price, the son of the marriage[,] is emancipated. The Husband shall name the Wife as trustee.

Since Andre remained unemancipated at the time of Paul's death, the children claimed they were the rightful beneficiaries under the divorce judgment's plain terms.

This left MetLife in a quandary. Under ERISA, it had a duty to administer claims "in accordance with the documents and instruments governing the plan." 29 U.S.C. § 1104(a)(1)(D). These documents instructed MetLife to pay the benefits to Paul's designated beneficiary—his widow. Under the New Jersey divorce judgment, however, the children were to be designated "irrevocable beneficiaries."

Normally, ERISA preempts any state law that "relate[s] to" an employee benefit plan. 29 U.S.C. § 1144(a); *Egelhoff v. Egelhoff*, 532 U.S. 141, 147–48 (2001). However, ERISA (as amended by the Retirement Equity Act of 1984) contains an exception from this general rule for "qualified domestic relations orders" ("QDROs"). 29 U.S.C. §§ 1144(b)(7), 1056(d)(3)(B)–(E). A QDRO "assigns to an alternate payee the right to ... receive all or a portion of the benefits payable with respect to a participant under a plan." 29 U.S.C. § 1056(d)(3)(B)(i).

MetLife informed the competing claimants that it could not tell "whether a court would find that th[e] divorce decree is a QDRO." It noted that if the New Jersey judgment is a QDRO, then in all likelihood the children should get the $20,000. It further noted that if the judgment is not a QDRO, then Price's widow is entitled to the money. MetLife stated that if the claimants did not resolve the matter amicably, it would bring suit. Price's widow and the children negotiated, but they failed to reach an agreement. The children's attorney then asked MetLife to "[k]indly initiate an interpleader action."

MetLife obliged, bringing this suit in the United States District Court for the District of New Jersey. On its own motion, the District Court raised the issue of subject matter jurisdiction and dismissed. This appeal followed. We review *de novo* the District Court's dismissal for lack of subject matter jurisdiction.

MetLife
negotiate or forced
to sue

II

The equitable remedy of interpleader allows a person holding property to join in a single suit two or more persons asserting claims to that property. The plaintiff in an interpleader action is a stakeholder that admits it is liable to one of the claimants, but fears the prospect of multiple liability. Interpleader allows the stakeholder to file suit, deposit the property with the court, and withdraw from the proceedings. The competing claimants are left to litigate between themselves. The result is a win-win situation. The stakeholder avoids multiple liability. The claimants settle their dispute in a single proceeding, without having to sue the stakeholder first and then face the difficulties of finding assets and levying execution.

helps stakeholder avoid liability

There are two methods for bringing an interpleader in federal court. The first is the interpleader statute, 28 U.S.C. § 1335. District Courts have subject matter jurisdiction under this provision if there is "minimal diversity" between two or more adverse claimants, and if the amount in controversy is $500 or more. The second is Federal Rule of Civil Procedure 22. Unlike its statutory counterpart, rule interpleader is no more than a procedural device; the plaintiff must plead and prove an independent basis for subject matter jurisdiction.

Two methods
1) Statute
2) FRCP 22

In this case, MetLife does not rely on the interpleader statute, nor could it, as the adverse claimants are all New Jerseyans. Rather, it has styled its lawsuit as a rule interpleader action. MetLife argues that jurisdiction exists under the federal question statute, 28 U.S.C. § 1331, and ERISA's jurisdictional provision, 29 U.S.C. § 1132(e).

A federal question interpleader is a rarity. Statutory "arising under" jurisdiction requires that a federal question appear on the face of the plaintiff's well-pleaded complaint. *See Louisville & Nashville R.R. v. Mottley*, 211 U.S. 149, 152 (1908). This requirement poses a problem for an interpleader plaintiff, as all the complaint seeks is an order releasing and discharging the plaintiff from liability. It is difficult to characterize such a request as asserting either federal or state rights. Thus, at least at first blush, it is hard to see how a request for interpleader could raise a federal question.

But only at first blush. Some interpleader actions do raise federal questions. Indeed, our sister courts of appeals have recognized that an interpleader "arises under" federal law when brought by an ERISA fiduciary against competing claimants to plan benefits.

We agree with these courts. Federal question jurisdiction exists when the plaintiff's well-pleaded complaint establishes that "federal law creates the cause of action." *Franchise Tax Bd. v. Constr. Laborers Vacation Trust*, 463 U.S. 1, 27–28 (1983). MetLife brings this suit under section 502(a)(3) of ERISA, 29 U.S.C. § 1132(a)(3). That provision creates a cause of action for fiduciaries "to obtain … appropriate equitable relief … to enforce any provisions of this subchapter or the terms of the plan." 29 U.S.C. § 1132(a)(3)(B)(ii). As courts have noted, "[t]he interconnection between the basis of the District Court's jurisdiction — ERISA — and the elements of [an] ERISA claim[ ] makes it easy to confuse the question of the court's subject matter jurisdiction with the question of the plaintiff's ability to state a claim." *Carlson v. Principal Fin. Group*, 320 F.3d 301, 307 (2d Cir. 2003). The test we must apply is a familiar one. For jurisdictional purposes, the issue is not whether MetLife will ultimately be successful in sustaining its cause of action under section 502(a)(3). Rather, dismissal for lack of subject-matter jurisdiction because of the inadequacy of the federal claim is proper only when the claim is so insubstantial, implausible, foreclosed by prior decisions of the Supreme Court, or otherwise completely devoid of merit as not to involve a federal controversy.

Here, MetLife brings suit as a fiduciary, and it adequately invokes the District Court's subject matter jurisdiction by seeking "appropriate equitable relief … to enforce any provisions of this subchapter or the terms of the plan." ERISA § 502(a)(3), 29 U.S.C. § 1132(a)(3). Specifically, MetLife seeks interpleader, which is a form of "equitable relief." *See U.S. Fire Ins. Co. v. Asbestospray, Inc.*, 182 F.3d 201, 208 (3d Cir. 1999). Through its interpleader action, MetLife seeks to enforce the provisions of ERISA and the plan by ensuring that funds are disbursed to the proper beneficiary. MetLife thus presents a substantial, non-frivolous claim for relief under section 502(a)(3). This is enough to confer subject matter jurisdiction under ERISA.[4]

---

4. Even apart from MetLife's cause of action as a fiduciary, there may be an additional basis for subject matter jurisdiction in this case. A rule interpleader is quite similar to a declaratory judgment action. Both the declaratory judgment statute and Rule 22 are purely procedural. *See NYLife*, 72 F.3d at 372 n. 1; *Aetna Life Ins. Co. v. Haworth*, 300 U.S. 227, 240 (1937). Neither provision enlarges the subject-matter jurisdiction of the federal courts. Compare Fed.R.Civ.P. 82 ("These rules shall not be construed to extend … the jurisdiction of the United States district courts.…"), with 28 U.S.C. § 2201 (authorizing a federal court to issue a declaratory judgment "[i]n a case of actual controversy within its jurisdiction") (emphasis added). Rather, both simply provide plaintiffs with a means to "anticipate and accelerate … coercive action[s] by … defendant[s]." *Bell & Beckwith v. United States*, 766 F.2d 910, 914 (6th Cir. 1985). Based on these similarities, some courts have held that the jurisdictional test applicable in declaratory judgment cases applies equally to a rule interpleader. *See, e.g., Commercial Nat'l Bank of Chicago v. Demos*, 18 F.3d 485, 488 (7th Cir. 1994); *Commercial Union Ins. Co. v. United States*, 999 F.2d 581, 585 (D.C. Cir. 1993); *Morongo Band of Mission Indians v. Cal. State Bd. of Equalization*, 858 F.2d 1376, 1384 (9th Cir. 1988); *Bell & Beckwith*, 766 F.2d at 913–14.

In the declaratory judgment context, "[f]ederal courts have regularly taken original jurisdiction over … suits in which, if the declaratory judgment defendant brought a coercive action to enforce its rights, that suit would necessarily present a federal question." *Franchise Tax*, 463 U.S. at 19, 103 S.Ct. 2841; *see also* Richard H. Fallon, Jr., et. al, Hart & Wechsler's Federal Courts 900 (5th ed. 2003) (stating that *Franchise Tax* "appears to endorse" an approach that "would uphold jurisdiction over a declaratory action if jurisdiction would exist in a hypothetical nondeclaratory action brought by either party against the other."); *but see Textron Lycoming Reciprocating Engine Div., Avco Corp. v. UAW*, 523

III

∗ ∗ ∗

IV

In sum, the District Court erred when it dismissed MetLife's complaint for want of subject matter jurisdiction. MetLife's well-pleaded complaint establishes that its cause of action arises under ERISA. The exhaustion requirement is a nonjurisdictional affirmative defense, and that affirmative defense did not require MetLife to make a decision on the QDRO issue before seeking interpleader in federal court. We will vacate the District Court's judgment and remand for further proceedings consistent with this opinion.

---

c. Intervention

Rule 24 provides two varieties—intervention "of right" (Rule 24(a)) and "permissive" intervention (Rule 24(b)). The consequence of intervention under both provisions is the same—the party allowed to intervene is then permitted to participate in the action the same as the other parties. The main difference is judicial discretion. In the case of intervention "of right," the court has little to no discretion in allowing intervention if the standards of the Rule are met. The standard in the intervention "of right" case is almost identical to the standard for requiring joinder under Rule 19(a)(1)(B)(i): whether the prospective intervenor possesses an interest in the subject matter of the action that the prospective intervenor will be unable to protect, as a practical matter, if the ligation proceeds as filed. The only difference is that, even if this standard is met under Rule 24, the prospective intervenor may still be denied intervention if "existing parties adequately represent that interest." Fed. R. Civ. P. 24(a)(2).

In the case of "permissive" intervention, the court's discretion is far greater. The only standard, unless the prospective intervenor is given a conditional right to intervene by the text of a statute or is a government official or agency, is that the prospec-

---

U.S. 653, 659–60 (1998) (expressing doubt about whether a "declaratory-judgment complaint raising a nonfederal defense to an anticipated federal claim ... would confer § 1331 jurisdiction") (emphasis in original). If the practice described by *Franchise Tax* is correct, and if the principle extends to rule interpleader, then jurisdiction exists whenever one of "the coercive actions anticipated by the [interpleader] complaint would arise under federal law." *Morongo*, 858 F.2d at 1385.

MetLife's interpleader complaint anticipates coercive actions by both Price's widow and his children. Both hypothetical claims would seek to recover "benefits due ... under the terms of [a] plan," 29 U.S.C. § 1132(a)(1)(B), and would necessarily present federal questions. *See Taylor*, 481 U.S. at 66–67, 107 S.Ct. 1542. Thus, the approach adopted by our sister courts of appeals in cases like *Bell & Beckwith* and *Morongo* might provide an alternative basis for subject matter jurisdiction. Nonetheless, in light of our determination that federal law creates MetLife's cause of action, we need not take a position on the propriety of those decisions.

tive intervenor's claim or defense share "a common question of law or fact" with a claim or defense in the existing action. If that standard is met, the judge may decide (subject to appellate review for abuse of discretion only) whether to allow intervention. Obviously, then, if one seeks to intervene in an ongoing action, one would prefer to be able to meet the standards for intervention "of right." The following case illustrates how difficult establishing a right to intervene can be.

Arakaki v. Cayetano

324 F.3d 1078 (9th Cir. 2003)

Before: Hug, Alarcon, and Graber, Circuit Judges.

Hug, Circuit Judge:

Josiah Hoohuli and other native Hawaiians (collectively "Hoohuli") seek to intervene in a lawsuit challenging the provision of benefits by the Office of Hawaiian Affairs ("OHA"), the Department of Hawaiian Home Lands ("DHHL"), and the Hawaiian Homes Commission ("HHC") to native Hawaiians[1] and Hawaiians.[2] Hoohuli, lessees of Hawaiian homestead lands or applicants for such leases, seek intervention on the grounds that they have an interest in continuing to receive benefits as native Hawaiians, and an interest to stop the provision of benefits to Hawaiians by limiting the eligibility to only native Hawaiians.

We address whether the district court erred in denying Hoohuli's motion to intervene as a matter of right.

I

On March 4, 2002, Plaintiffs Arakaki et al. (collectively "Plaintiffs") filed a civil action against the State of Hawaii and various state agencies, challenging the constitutionality of race-based privileges. This suit follows closely on the heels of the Supreme Court's recent *Rice v. Cayetano* decision, which held that limiting voter eligibility to elect the trustees to the OHA to members of the racial classifications Hawaiian and native Hawaiian violated the Fifteenth Amendment. 528 U.S. at 499.

Plaintiffs challenge the exclusive benefits given to Hawaiians and native Hawaiians by the OHA, the HHC, and the DHHL. Plaintiffs allege the provision of such benefits is racially discriminatory and violates the Equal

---

1. "Native Hawaiians" are those who are descendants of the races inhabiting the Hawaiian Islands prior to 1778 with at least 50% Hawaiian blood quantum. Haw.Rev.Stat. § 10-2.

2. "Hawaiians" are those who are descendants of the races inhabiting the Hawaiian Islands prior to 1778 without reference to blood quantum. Id. This broader class includes the narrower class "native Hawaiians." Rice v. Cayetano, 528 U.S. 495, 499 (2000).

Protection clauses of the Fifth and Fourteenth Amendments. They also allege that, as beneficiaries of § 5(f) of the Hawaii Admission Act's public land trust, the State and HHC/DHHL discriminate against them, which constitutes a breach of trust. Pub. L. 86-3, 73 Stat. 4, § 5(f) (1959) ("Admission Act"). Plaintiffs asserted standing as taxpayers, and as beneficiaries of the public land trust established by Congress in § 5(f).

On March 18, 2002, the district court granted proposed defendants-intervenors State Council of Hawaiian Homestead Association ("SCHHA"), and Anthony Sang, Sr.'s ("Sang") Motion to Intervene. The SCHHA is an organization of native Hawaiian HHC homestead lessee associations; Sang is a lessee.

On March 25, 2002, Hoohuli filed its motion to intervene. Hoohuli alleged two interests justifying intervention: (1) to ensure continued receipt of benefits for native Hawaiians; and (2) to limit the class of eligible beneficiaries to only native Hawaiians, at the exclusion of the broader Hawaiian class. Additionally, Hoohuli sought to raise as a defense to its receipt of benefits that, absent discrimination by the United States, it should be entitled to tribal status, and its benefits scrutinized under rational basis review pursuant to *Morton v. Mancari*, 417 U.S. 535 (1974). A magistrate judge denied this motion on May 2, 2002. Hoohuli timely appealed to the district court.

On May 8, 2002, the district court dismissed for lack of standing Plaintiffs' breach of the public land trust claims. It ruled that Plaintiffs' claim for relief, invalidating the stated purpose of § 5(f), rather than alleging an actual breach of the trust created by § 5(f), amounted to a generalized grievance. Since Plaintiffs were not proceeding on the basis of any direct injury, they lacked standing to complain. The district court held that the only claims remaining were Plaintiffs' equal protection challenges asserted as taxpayers against the direct expenditures of tax revenues by the legislature. Plaintiffs' motion for reconsideration of this order was denied on June 18, 2002. Plaintiffs have not appealed this order to the Ninth Circuit.

On June 13, 2002, the district court denied Hoohuli's motion to intervene, both as a matter of right and permissively. The district court first held that since Plaintiffs' public land trust claims were dismissed, Hoohuli had no significantly protectable interest in those claims at this time. The district court ruled that Hoohuli's intervention to assert additional claims of breaches of public land trusts, specifically that benefits should be limited to only native Hawaiians, was not raised by existing parties and clearly separable from Plaintiffs' remaining equal protection challenge. The district court also noted that nothing prevented Hoohuli from filing its own breach of trust suit against the State to claim benefits should be allocated to only native Hawaiians.

Next, the district court addressed Hoohuli's motion to intervene in Plaintiffs' equal protection claims. The district court observed that Hoohuli had a significantly protectable interest in the manner in which its tax dollars are used. A ruling in Plaintiffs' favor would impair Hoohuli's interest in the continued receipt of homestead leases. Hoohuli's interest in limiting benefits to native Hawaiians, however, was not encompassed by the issues before the court. Additionally, Hoohuli failed to demonstrate that the State defendants would not adequately represent their interests. The court ruled that Defendants and Hoohuli have the same ultimate objective, and that to date, Defendants have demonstrated that they will vigorously oppose Plaintiffs' challenges to the provision of benefits to native Hawaiians. The court rejected Hoohuli's proffered justification that Defendants are inadequate because they will not argue as a defense that the Department of the Interior is engaging in unconstitutional race discrimination by excluding native Hawaiians in the definition of "Indian tribe."

The district court denied Hoohuli's request for permissive intervention because it sought to interject new issues into this action beyond the scope of Plaintiffs' claims. Hoohuli's participation would unnecessarily complicate the litigation, and existing Defendants, including native Hawaiian lessees, would vigorously seek to uphold the provision of these benefits.[3]

Jurisdiction is proper before this Court pursuant to 28 U.S.C. § 1291.

II

The district court's decision regarding intervention as a matter of right pursuant to Federal Rule of Civil Procedure 24(a)(2) is reviewed *de novo*.

III

Rule 24 traditionally receives liberal construction in favor of applicants for intervention. Courts are guided primarily by practical and equitable considerations.

Rule 24(a)(2) gives a person the right to intervene:

> [u]pon timely application ... (2) when the applicant claims an interest relating to the property or transaction which is the subject of the action and the applicant is so situated that the disposition of the action may as a practical matter impair or impede the applicant's ability to protect that interest, unless the applicant's interest is adequately represented by existing parties.

Fed.R.Civ.P. 24(a)(2).

A party seeking to intervene as of right must meet four requirements: (1) the applicant must timely move to intervene; (2) the applicant must

---

3. On appeal, Hoohuli does not challenge the denial of this request for permissive intervention. Therefore our review is limited to whether intervention as of right was appropriate pursuant to Rule 24(a)(2).

have a significantly protectable interest relating to the property or transaction that is the subject of the action; (3) the applicant must be situated such that the disposition of the action may impair or impede the party's ability to protect that interest; and (4) the applicant's interest must not be adequately represented by existing parties. Each of these four requirements must be satisfied to support a right to intervene.

When a plaintiff's action is narrowed by court order, the court may consider the case as restructured in ruling on a motion to intervene.

A. Public Land Trust Beneficiary Claim

Hoohuli seeks to intervene to support in part and to challenge in part Plaintiffs' public land trust beneficiary claim created by § 5(f) of the Admission Act. Hoohuli joins in the view that provision of leasehold benefits to Hawaiians is illegal, but believes that providing benefits to native Hawaiians does not breach § 5(f) of the Act.

Assuming Hoohuli timely filed its motion to intervene, intervention is nevertheless inappropriate for the public land trust beneficiary claim. Rule 24(a) requires an applicant to demonstrate a significantly protectable interest relating to the property or transaction that is the subject of the action. *Donnelly*, 159 F.3d at 409. Here, Plaintiffs' § 5(f) public trust claim has been dismissed by the district court and not subsequently appealed before this Court. Because this trust claim is no longer the subject of Plaintiffs' action, intervention is inappropriate as a matter of right.

We offer no comment on Hoohuli's option of filing its own § 5(f) breach of trust suit against the State to raise the claim that benefits should be restricted to native Hawaiians. We only hold that intervention is not necessary when the litigation will not impair or impede the applicant's ability to protect its interests because the claim is no longer a subject of the plaintiff's action.

B. Equal Protection Claim

Hoohuli seeks to intervene as of right to address Plaintiffs' equal protection claims challenging the expenditure of tax revenues for programs that benefit only Hawaiians and native Hawaiians.

1. Timeliness

All parties concede that Hoohuli timely filed its motion to intervene. The district court did not abuse its discretion by finding Hoohuli's motion, filed three weeks after the filing of Plaintiffs' complaint, timely.

2. Significantly Protectable Interest

The requirement of a significantly protectable interest is generally satisfied when "the interest is protectable under some law, and that there is a relationship between the legally protected interest and the claims at issue." *Sierra Club v. EPA*, 995 F.2d 1478, 1484 (9th Cir. 1993). The applicant must satisfy each element. "An applicant generally satisfies the 're-lationship' requirement only if the resolution of the plaintiff's claims actually will affect the applicant." Id.

The Supreme Court has yet to provide any clear definition of the nature of the "interest relating to the property or transaction which is the subject of the action." 7C Charles Alan Wright, Arthur R. Miller & Mary Kay Kane, Federal Practice and Procedure: Civil 2d § 1908, at 21 (Supp.2002). Wright suggests the term "significantly protectable interest" has not been a term of art in the law, and sufficient room for disagreement exists over the meaning of the term. *Id.*

Hoohuli claims that the district court found, as it was compelled to do under *Price v. Akaka*, 928 F.2d 824, 826–27 (9th Cir. 1990), that it had a protectable interest in the subject of the action. In *Price*, plaintiffs filed a § 1983 claim against the State of Hawaii, alleging that OHA managed income derived from § 5(b) lands for purposes not provided in § 5(f) on the Admission Act. Section 5(f) lists various purposes for the trust lands and the income derived therefrom. The district court dismissed plaintiffs' suit for lack of subject matter jurisdiction and failure to state a claim. This Court reversed, holding that plaintiffs, as beneficiaries of the § 5(f) trust, had standing to enforce the spending provisions of § 5(f). Plaintiffs demonstrated an injury in fact through the trustees' expenditure of income on purposes not specified by § 5(f). Allowing plaintiffs to enforce § 5(f) was also consistent with common law trusts. This Court additionally held that subject matter jurisdiction was appropriate and the Eleventh Amendment did not bar the suit.

Hoohuli's reference to *Price* does not advance its motion to intervene. *Price* does not justify intervention, but rather provides authority for standing to a beneficiary seeking to enforce the § 5(f) provisions of the Admission Act. In other words, Hoohuli may rely upon *Price* to support an independent suit as a beneficiary challenging the provision of benefits to Hawaiians under § 5(f). Hoohuli's standing for a collateral suit under *Price*, however, does not alone justify a Rule 24(a) right to intervene in any § 5(f) breach of trust or equal protection litigation. Instead, to successfully intervene as of right in a pending case, Hoohuli must satisfy the four *Donnelly* requirements.

We agree with the district court that Hoohuli has a significantly protectable interest in the manner in which its tax dollars are used, specifically a continued receipt of benefits. Hoohuli, as lessees of Hawaiian homestead lands or applicants for such leases, have a stake in the outcome of Plaintiffs' equal protection challenge. Consequently, Hoohuli's protectable interest in the continued receipt of benefits supports intervention.

Hoohuli also asserts an interest in limiting the class of beneficiaries to native Hawaiians. In order to intervene on this basis, Hoohuli must demonstrate a relationship between its interests and the claims raised by Plaintiffs. *Sierra Club*, 995 F.2d at 1484.

Here, Hoohuli does not adequately demonstrate a relationship between its dilution interest and the claims raised by Plaintiffs. Plaintiffs claim the provision of benefits from the OHA, HHC, and DHHL is racially-based and violates equal protection, and make no distinction between the grant of benefits to Hawaiians and native Hawaiians. Hoohuli's interests, on the other hand, are twofold: continuing to receive benefits, and preventing the dilution of benefits by limiting eligibility to only native Hawaiians. The district court held that Hoohuli's interest in preventing dilution of benefits went beyond the claims at issue. We agree.

Hoohuli asserts that the district court misinterpreted *Portland Audubon Society v. Hodel*, 866 F.2d 302 (9th Cir. 1989), to reject Hoohuli's interest in the litigation as unrelated to the interests presented by either party. Hoohuli correctly observes this Circuit clarified the holding of *Portland Audubon* in *Sierra Club*. In *Sierra Club*, this Court distinguished *Portland Audubon* by broadening the scope of a "protectable interest" to include rights that are generally protected by law, and not only those interests protected by the statute under which the litigation is brought. *Sierra Club*, 995 F.2d at 1484.

Hoohuli's analysis is misplaced. First, a small technical matter: nowhere in the district court's order does it cite *Portland Audubon*. Rather, the district court cites *Sierra Club*, 995 F.2d at 1484, as authority for the proposition that a significantly protectable interest be both protectable under law and related to the claims at issue. Without directly citing any case, the district court concludes that Hoohuli's interest in limiting the receipt of land trust benefits to only native Hawaiians was separable from the interests asserted by Plaintiffs because it was not raised by any existing party.

The magistrate judge cites *Portland Audubon* as authority for requiring an interest that the laws at issue were intended to protect. The magistrate judge also cites *Sierra Club* for requiring a relationship between the interest and the claim at issue. Neither the district judge nor the magistrate judge discuss either case beyond the general rule. This citation by the magistrate judge to *Portland Audubon* is harmless, though, because the district court does not cite this rule or rely upon the magistrate judge's analysis.

Second, despite *Sierra Club* distinguishing *Portland Audubon* on the scope of a "protectable interest," it reaffirmed the requirement that some relationship exist between the legally protected interest and the claims at issue. The integrity of *Sierra Club* is not questioned. This Court recently discussed this two-step standard for a significantly protectable interest in *Donnelly*, 159 F.3d at 409. This relationship requirement is dispositive of Hoohuli's dilution interest.

Hoohuli also relies on a First Circuit case granting intervention to black police officers to defend their promotions, as interests related to the action, against white officers alleging an impermissible promotion practice based on racial grounds. *Cotter v. Mass. Ass'n of Minority Law Enforcement Officers*, 219 F.3d 31 (1st Cir. 2000). While *Cotter* supports Hoohuli's claim that it has an interest in defending the continued receipt of benefits, it does nothing to support its interest in preventing dilution of its benefits due to unrelatedness.

We agree with the district court that Hoohuli has a significantly protectable interest against Plaintiffs' equal protection challenge in the continued receipt of benefits as native Hawaiians. We also agree that Hoohuli does not have a significantly protectable interest in its dilution claim to limit benefits to native Hawaiians. This claim is unrelated to Plaintiffs' equal protection challenge seeking to invalidate all benefits to Hawaiians and native Hawaiians. Hoohuli is not permitted to inject new, unrelated issues into the pending litigation.

3. Impairment of Interest

We agree with the district court's conclusion that a ruling in favor of Plaintiffs' equal protection challenge would impair Hoohuli's ability to protect its interest in the continued receipt of benefits as native Hawaiians. Hoohuli's interest in limiting the class of beneficiaries to native Hawaiians is not impaired by Plaintiffs' equal protection claim. We offer no comment on the merits of Hoohuli's own equal protection lawsuit challenging the provision of benefits to Hawaiians.

4. Adequacy of Representation

This Court follows the guidance of Rule 24 advisory committee notes that state that "if an absentee would be substantially affected in a practical sense by the determination made in an action, he should, as a general rule, be entitled to intervene." As noted above, Hoohuli's continued receipt of benefits will cease altogether should Plaintiffs prevail. Hoohuli would be justified in intervention to protect the continued receipt of benefits if it demonstrates that existing parties do not adequately protect its interest. The burden on proposed intervenors in showing inadequate representation is minimal, and would be satisfied if they could demonstrate that representation of their interests "may be" inadequate.

This Court considers three factors in determining the adequacy of representation: (1) whether the interest of a present party is such that it will undoubtedly make all of a proposed intervenor's arguments; (2) whether the present party is capable and willing to make such arguments; and (3) whether a proposed intervenor would offer any necessary elements to the proceeding that other parties would neglect.

The most important factor in determining the adequacy of representation is how the interest compares with the interests of existing parties. When an applicant for intervention and an existing party have the same ultimate objective, a presumption of adequacy of representation arises. If the applicant's interest is identical to that of one of the present parties, a compelling showing should be required to demonstrate inadequate representation.

There is also an assumption of adequacy when the government is acting on behalf of a constituency that it represents. In the absence of a "very compelling showing to the contrary," it will be presumed that a state adequately represents its citizens when the applicant shares the same interest. 7C WRIGHT, MILLER & KANE, § 1909, at 332. Where parties share the same ultimate objective, differences in litigation strategy do not normally justify intervention.

Hoohuli has not overcome the presumption that existing parties will adequately represent its interests. First, based on the record before this Court, present parties have demonstrated they are capable and willing to make all of Hoohuli's arguments. Hoohuli's chief objection is that existing parties will not raise as a defense that, absent discrimination by the United States, native Hawaiians should be entitled to tribal status. It claims the federal government racially discriminates against native Hawaiians through the Indian Reorganization Act, 25 U.S.C. § 479, and the Indian Self Determination Act, 25 U.S.C. § 450. These Acts allow native persons from Alaska and the continental United States to seek tribal status. Hawaii is excluded. Consequently, native Hawaiians are not presently granted tribal recognition by Congress.

Tribal recognition is significant because it allows a more deferential rational basis review of government benefit programs to persons of tribal ancestry under *Morton v. Mancari*. Due to the Supreme Court's recent ruling in *Rice v. Cayetano*, holding the classification "native Hawaiian" to be racial, the provision of benefits pursuant to this classification may be subject to the more demanding strict scrutiny review. We observe that in *Rice*, the Supreme Court did not address the merits of native Hawaiians' equal protection claim against the United States for the denial of tribal status, staying, in the words of the Court, "far off that difficult terrain." 528 U.S. at 519. The Supreme Court likewise avoided addressing the constitutionality of the benefits and trust structure at issue today, limiting its opinion only to the voting restriction. The district court and eventually this Court may in the course of this litigation be required to venture onto this challenging terrain to resolve this difficult issue. The only question we must resolve, however, is whether existing defendants are capable and willing to make this argument should it be necessary.

We conclude that the State defendants will adequately represent Hoohuli's interest at trial. Counsel for the State and HHC/DHHL, and

OHA have stated before this Court that it will make all arguments necessary to defend the benefits to native Hawaiians. Additionally, we are aware of no conflict that prevents the State and its agency defendants from raising this argument.

Second, Hoohuli fails to demonstrate it would offer any necessary elements to the proceeding that other parties would neglect. Hoohuli shares the same ultimate objective as the State and its agencies. The State and HHC/DHHL defendants are directed by section 4 of the Admission Act, and Article XII of the Hawaii Constitution to provide benefits to native Hawaiians. In such circumstances a presumption of adequacy of representation arises.

Finally, native Hawaiian homestead lessees, the SCHHA, have already successfully intervened as parties to the litigation. Counsel for SCHHA have stated that they are willing to speak with Hoohuli and raise some of its arguments. Not every native Hawaiian group could or should be entitled to intervene.

The presence of SCHHA as a similarly situated intervenor, combined with the State defendants' specific statutory and constitutional obligations to protect native Hawaiians' interests, distinguishes this case from those in which we have permitted intervention on the government's side in recognition that the intervenors' interests are narrower than that of the government and therefore may not be adequately represented. *See, e.g.,* *Southwest Ctr.*, 268 F.3d at 823 ("the City's range of considerations in development is broader than the profit-motives animating [intervening] developers"); *Californians for Safe Dump Truck Transp. v. Mendonca*, 152 F.3d 1184, 1190 (9th Cir. 1998) (the intervenor's interest "were potentially more narrow and parochial than the interests of the public at large"); *cf. Forest Conservation Council v. U.S. Forest Serv.*, 66 F.3d 1489, 1499 (9th Cir. 1995) ("The Forest Service is required to represent a broader view than the more narrow, parochial interests of the [state and local government intervenors]."). For these reasons, we hold that Hoohuli does not overcome its compelling burden to demonstrate that the State and its agencies do not adequately represent its interests.

IV

The district court did not err in denying Hoohuli's Rule 24 motion to intervene as a matter of right. Hoohuli cannot intervene in Plaintiffs' breach of trust challenge to § 5(f) because this claim has been dismissed due to lack of standing. Hoohuli does have a significantly protectable interest at stake in Plaintiffs' equal protection challenge. Intervention is improper, however, because its interests are adequately represented by existing parties. The district court is Affirmed.

Exercise 8-11. Framing a Motion to Intervene

Motions to intervene are fairly common in environmental law, natural resources law, and other areas of the law involving public goods. More and more common in recent years have been motions to intervene filed by parties seeking to preserve ameliorative laws benefiting them and those similarly situated to them against challenges of what is sometimes called "reverse discrimination." The case above presents one such intervention attempt (and note that another Native Hawaiian group was actually successful before the Hoohuli group made its attempt), and cites a few others. Another high-profile attempt was made in the famous law school affirmative action case of *Grutter v. Bollinger* by groups seeking to defend affirmative action policies. That attempt succeeded, primarily because the Sixth Circuit decided that the District Courts had applied too strict a standard as to whether the existing parties would "adequately protect" the prospective intervenors' interests. According to the Sixth Circuit, only a showing that their interests "might" not be adequately protected was required. *See Grutter v. Bollinger*, 188 F.3d 394, 397 (6th Cir. 1999).

In framing the Motion to Intervene and the related memorandum in support in the *Hoohuli* case, how might you proceed differently to obtain the result that the intervenors in *Grutter* were able to obtain? If you had to change one aspect of the *Hoohuli* prospective intervenors' approach to framing their arguments, what would it be? Would that be enough? Under this court's decision, what do you see as necessary to rebut the presumption that a state defendant will protect the interests of its citizens?

6. Class Actions

The final form of aggregation that we will discuss is the class action. A class action is typically a large-scale aggregation of many claims against one or more defendants, litigated through an individual or small group that acts as the representative of the entire class. So, a class action differs markedly from the forms of joinder reviewed above in several ways: (1) the plaintiff (or defendant, in some cases) class is much larger than a typical group of plaintiffs (or defendants) whose claims or defenses have been joined; (2) an individual or small group stands as the representative of the entire class, which might number into the millions, and the non-representative members have little to no input as to how these representatives pursue the case; (3) one attorney, or at most a few attorneys, litigates the case on behalf of both the named representatives and the entire membership of the class, and these lawyers generally only interact personally with the named representatives; and (4) in order to proceed as a class, a group of plaintiffs must specifically ask the court for its permission to do so—this is called a motion to certify a class.

As a policy matter, the class action form promotes efficiency, economy, ease of presentation and proof, and for the defendant(s), repose (due to the knowledge that all claims have been resolved once the class action has come to completion).* In thinking about class actions, you must keep in mind that these values are all at stake because the requirements for certifying a class action are built in part on these concerns. But you must also remember what you learned in Chapter 3 of this casebook—the foundational organizing principle of all civil procedure is the concept of due process. The values outlined above for recognizing the class action form therefore must be weighed against the equally important value in affording every person or entity bound by a judicial action the due process of law. And the primary rule governing class certification—Rule 23—embeds a strong notion of due process within its standards.

Exercise 8-12. Statutory Analysis — Rule 23 Certification Requirements

Chapter 1 laid out a five-step process for analyzing a statute or rule. Recalling this process, carefully read FRCP 23(a), (b), (c), (e) and (g) and answer these questions.

1. What are the four prerequisites for certifying any class action under Rule 23?

2. Once those prerequisites are established, how does one know what kind of class action one should pursue for certification?

3. What is the purpose of the notice provisions? What interest(s) is/are being protected through them? Why does it treat one kind of class action differently from the other two?

4. How do your answers to the above differ in considering the settlement provisions? Are additional interests at stake? If so, what are they?

5. Why do you think the rules drafters made it so difficult to be appointed as class counsel?

Class actions are highly controversial. Several motion pictures have focused on high-profile class actions, news stories seem to report about them daily, and interest groups work very hard to move the law of class certification in the directions they prefer. Occasionally, a high-profile case makes it to the Supreme Court on the issue of class certification, and the result is often surprising, or even disappointing. The following case is the Supreme Court's most recent high-profile foray into this area of law, a case that made headlines for months—both positive and negative, and one which continues to exert influence over the behavior of legal actors. For your purposes

---

* Ed. Note. As you will see, many aspects of class certification can frustrate this interest in repose, but it is an important defense-side interest in class litigation that is often overlooked in cases and commentary.

as students, it also illustrates the ambiguity that exists in some of the seemingly-clear terms of Rule 23.

Wal-Mart Stores, Inc. v. Dukes
131 S. Ct. 2541 (2011)

Justice Scalia delivered the opinion of the Court.

We are presented with one of the most expansive class actions ever. The District Court and the Court of Appeals approved the certification of a class comprising about one and a half million plaintiffs, current and former female employees of petitioner Wal-Mart who allege that the discretion exercised by their local supervisors over pay and promotion matters violates Title VII by discriminating against women. In addition to injunctive and declaratory relief, the plaintiffs seek an award of backpay. We consider whether the certification of the plaintiff class was consistent with Federal Rules of Civil Procedure 23(a) and (b)(2).

I

A

Petitioner Wal-Mart is the Nation's largest private employer. It operates four types of retail stores throughout the country: Discount Stores, Supercenters, Neighborhood Markets, and Sam's Clubs. Those stores are divided into seven nationwide divisions, which in turn comprise 41 regions of 80 to 85 stores apiece. Each store has between 40 and 53 separate departments and 80 to 500 staff positions. In all, Wal-Mart operates approximately 3,400 stores and employs more than one million people.

Pay and promotion decisions at Wal-Mart are generally committed to local managers' broad discretion, which is exercised "in a largely subjective manner." Local store managers may increase the wages of hourly employees (within limits) with only limited corporate oversight. As for salaried employees, such as store managers and their deputies, higher corporate authorities have discretion to set their pay within preestablished ranges.

Promotions work in a similar fashion. Wal-Mart permits store managers to apply their own subjective criteria when selecting candidates as "support managers," which is the first step on the path to management. Admission to Wal-Mart's management training program, however, does require that a candidate meet certain objective criteria, including an above-average performance rating, at least one year's tenure in the applicant's current position, and a willingness to relocate. But except for those requirements, regional and district managers have discretion to use their own judgment when selecting candidates for management training. Promotion to higher office—e.g., assistant manager, co-manager, or store manager—is similarly at the discretion of the employee's superiors after prescribed objective factors are satisfied.

B

The named plaintiffs in this lawsuit, representing the 1.5 million members of the certified class, are three current or former Wal-Mart employees who allege that the company discriminated against them on the basis of their sex by denying them equal pay or promotions, in violation of Title VII of the Civil Rights Act of 1964, 42 U.S.C. § 2000e-1 *et seq.*

Betty Dukes began working at a Pittsburgh, California, Wal-Mart in 1994. She started as a cashier, but later sought and received a promotion to customer service manager. After a series of disciplinary violations, however, Dukes was demoted back to cashier and then to greeter. Dukes concedes she violated company policy, but contends that the disciplinary actions were in fact retaliation for invoking internal complaint procedures and that male employees have not been disciplined for similar infractions. Dukes also claims two male greeters in the Pittsburgh store are paid more than she is.

Christine Kwapnoski has worked at Sam's Club stores in Missouri and California for most of her adult life. She has held a number of positions, including a supervisory position. She claims that a male manager yelled at her frequently and screamed at female employees, but not at men. The manager in question "told her to 'doll up,' to wear some makeup, and to dress a little better."

The final named plaintiff, Edith Arana, worked at a Wal-Mart store in Duarte, California, from 1995 to 2001. In 2000, she approached the store manager on more than one occasion about management training, but was brushed off. Arana concluded she was being denied opportunity for advancement because of her sex. She initiated internal complaint procedures, whereupon she was told to apply directly to the district manager if she thought her store manager was being unfair. Arana, however, decided against that and never applied for management training again. In 2001, she was fired for failure to comply with Wal-Mart's timekeeping policy.

These plaintiffs, respondents here, do not allege that Wal-Mart has any express corporate policy against the advancement of women. Rather, they claim that their local managers' discretion over pay and promotions is exercised disproportionately in favor of men, leading to an unlawful disparate impact on female employees, see 42 U.S.C. § 2000e-2(k). And, respondents say, because Wal-Mart is aware of this effect, its refusal to cabin its managers' authority amounts to disparate treatment, see § 2000e-2(a). Their complaint seeks injunctive and declaratory relief, punitive damages, and backpay. It does not ask for compensatory damages.

Importantly for our purposes, respondents claim that the discrimination to which they have been subjected is common to all Wal-Mart's female employees. The basic theory of their case is that a strong and uniform "corporate culture" permits bias against women to infect, perhaps subconsciously, the discretionary decisionmaking of each one of Wal-Mart's thousands of managers—thereby making every woman at the company the victim of one common discriminatory practice. Respondents therefore wish to litigate the Title VII claims of all female employees at Wal-Mart's stores in a nationwide class action.

C

Class certification is governed by Federal Rule of Civil Procedure 23. Under Rule 23(a), the party seeking certification must demonstrate, first, that:

"(1) the class is so numerous that joinder of all members is impracticable,

"(2) there are questions of law or fact common to the class,

"(3) the claims or defenses of the representative parties are typical of the claims or defenses of the class, and

"(4) the representative parties will fairly and adequately protect the interests of the class" (paragraph breaks added).

Second, the proposed class must satisfy at least one of the three requirements listed in Rule 23(b). Respondents rely on Rule 23(b)(2), which applies when "the party opposing the class has acted or refused to act on grounds that apply generally to the class, so that final injunctive relief or corresponding declaratory relief is appropriate respecting the class as a whole."[2]

Invoking these provisions, respondents moved the District Court to certify a plaintiff class consisting of "[a]ll women employed at any Wal-Mart

---

2. Rule 23(b)(1) allows a class to be maintained where "prosecuting separate actions by or against individual class members would create a risk of" either "(A) inconsistent or varying adjudications," or "(B) adjudications ... that, as a practical matter, would be dispositive of the interests of the other members not parties to the individual adjudications or would substantially impair or impeded their ability to protect their interests." Rule 23(b)(3) states that a class may be maintained where "questions of law or fact common to class members predominate over any questions affecting only individual members," and a class action would be "superior to other available methods for fairly and efficiently adjudicating the controversy." The applicability of these provisions to the plaintiff class is not before us.

domestic retail store at any time since December 26, 1998, who have been or may be subjected to Wal-Mart's challenged pay and management track promotions policies and practices." As evidence that there were indeed "questions of law or fact common to" all the women of Wal-Mart, as Rule 23(a)(2) requires, respondents relied chiefly on three forms of proof: statistical evidence about pay and promotion disparities between men and women at the company, anecdotal reports of discrimination from about 120 of Wal-Mart's female employees, and the testimony of a sociologist, Dr. William Bielby, who conducted a "social framework analysis" of Wal-Mart's "culture" and personnel practices, and concluded that the company was "vulnerable" to gender discrimination. 603 F.3d 571, 601 (C.A.9 2010) (*en banc*).

Wal-Mart unsuccessfully moved to strike much of this evidence. It also offered its own countervailing statistical and other proof in an effort to defeat Rule 23(a)'s requirements of commonality, typicality, and adequate representation. Wal-Mart further contended that respondents' monetary claims for backpay could not be certified under Rule 23(b)(2), first because that Rule refers only to injunctive and declaratory relief, and second because the backpay claims could not be manageably tried as a class without depriving Wal-Mart of its right to present certain statutory defenses. With one limitation not relevant here, the District Court granted respondents' motion and certified their proposed class.

D

A divided en banc Court of Appeals substantially affirmed the District Court's certification order. 603 F.3d 571. The majority concluded that respondents' evidence of commonality was sufficient to "raise the common question whether Wal-Mart's female employees nationwide were subjected to a single set of corporate policies (not merely a number of independent discriminatory acts) that may have worked to unlawfully discriminate against them in violation of Title VII." *Id.*, at 612 (emphasis deleted). It also agreed with the District Court that the named plaintiffs' claims were sufficiently typical of the class as a whole to satisfy Rule 23(a)(3), and that they could serve as adequate class representatives, see Rule 23(a)(4). *Id.*, at 614–615. With respect to the Rule 23(b)(2) question, the Ninth Circuit held that respondents' backpay claims could be certified as part of a (b)(2) class because they did not "predominat[e]" over the requests for declaratory and injunctive relief, meaning they were not "superior in strength, influence, or authority" to the nonmonetary claims. *Id.*, at 616 (internal quotation marks omitted).

Finally, the Court of Appeals determined that the action could be manageably tried as a class action because the District Court could adopt the approach the Ninth Circuit approved in *Hilao v. Estate of Marcos*, 103 F.3d 767, 782–787 (1996). There compensatory damages for some 9,541 class members were calculated by selecting 137 claims at random, referring those claims to a special master for valuation, and then extrapolating the validity and value of the untested claims from the sample set. The Court of Appeals "s[aw] no reason why a similar procedure to that used in *Hilao* could not be employed in this case." *Id.*, at 627. It would allow Wal-Mart "to present individual defenses in the randomly selected 'sample cases,' thus revealing the approximate percentage of class members whose unequal pay or non-promotion was due to something other than gender discrimination."

We granted certiorari.

II

The class action is an exception to the usual rule that litigation is conducted by and on behalf of the individual named parties only. In order to justify a departure from that rule, a class representative must be part of the class and possess the same interest and suffer the same injury as the class members. Rule 23(a) ensures that the named plaintiffs are appropriate representatives of the class whose claims they wish to litigate. The Rule's four requirements — numerosity, commonality, typicality, and adequate representation — effectively limit the class claims to those fairly encompassed by the named plaintiff's claims.

A

The crux of this case is commonality — the rule requiring a plaintiff to show that "there are questions of law or fact common to the class." Rule 23(a)(2).[5] That language is easy to misread, since "[a]ny competently crafted class complaint literally raises common 'questions.'" Nagareda, *Class Certification in the Age of Aggregate Proof,* 84 N.Y.U. L. REV. 97, 131–132 (2009). For example: Do all of us plaintiffs indeed work for Wal-Mart? Do our managers have discretion over pay? Is that an unlawful employment practice? What remedies should we get? Reciting these questions is not sufficient to obtain class certification. Commonality requires the plaintiff to demonstrate that the class members "have suffered the same injury," *Falcon, supra,* at 157. This does not mean merely that they have all suffered a violation of the same provision of law. Title VII, for example, can be violated in many ways — by intentional discrimination, or by hiring and promotion criteria that result in disparate impact, and by the use of these practices on the part of many different superiors in a

---

5. We have previously stated in this context that "[t]he commonality and typicality requirements of Rule 23(a) tend to merge. Both serve as guideposts for determining whether under the particular circumstances maintenance of a class action is economical and whether the named plaintiff's claim and the class claims are so interrelated that the interests of the class members will be fairly and adequately protected in their absence. Those requirements therefore also tend to merge with the adequacy-of-representation requirement, although the latter requirement also raises concerns about the competency of class counsel and conflicts of interest." *General Telephone Co. of Southwest v. Falcon,* 457 U.S. 147, 157–158, n. 13 (1982). In light of our disposition of the commonality question, however, it is unnecessary to resolve whether respondents have satisfied the typicality and adequate-representation requirements of Rule 23(a).

single company. Quite obviously, the mere claim by employees of the same company that they have suffered a Title VII injury, or even a disparate-impact Title VII injury, gives no cause to believe that all their claims can productively be litigated at once. Their claims must depend upon a common contention—for example, the assertion of discriminatory bias on the part of the same supervisor. That common contention, moreover, must be of such a nature that it is capable of classwide resolution—which means that determination of its truth or falsity will resolve an issue that is central to the validity of each one of the claims in one stroke.

> "What matters to class certification ... is not the raising of common 'questions'—even in droves—but, rather the capacity of a classwide proceeding to generate common answers apt to drive the resolution of the litigation. Dissimilarities within the proposed class are what have the potential to impede the generation of common answers." *Nagareda, supra,* at 132.

Rule 23 does not set forth a mere pleading standard. A party seeking class certification must affirmatively demonstrate his compliance with the Rule—that is, he must be prepared to prove that there are in fact sufficiently numerous parties, common questions of law or fact, etc. We recognized in *Falcon* that "sometimes it may be necessary for the court to probe behind the pleadings before coming to rest on the certification question," 457 U.S., at 160, and that certification is proper only if "the trial court is satisfied, after a rigorous analysis, that the prerequisites of Rule 23(a) have been satisfied." Frequently that "rigorous analysis" will entail some overlap with the merits of the plaintiff's underlying claim. That cannot be helped. The class determination generally involves considerations that are enmeshed in the factual and legal issues comprising the plaintiff's cause of action. Nor is there anything unusual about that consequence: The necessity of touching aspects of the merits in order to resolve preliminary matters, e.g., jurisdiction and venue, is a familiar feature of litigation.

In this case, proof of commonality necessarily overlaps with respondents' merits contention that Wal-Mart engages in a pattern or practice of discrimination.[7] That is so because, in resolving an individual's Title VII claim, the crux of the inquiry is the reason for a particular employment decision. Here respondents wish to sue about literally millions of employment decisions at once. Without some glue holding the alleged reasons

---

7. In a pattern-or-practice case, the plaintiff tries to "establish by a preponderance of the evidence that ... discrimination was the company's standard operating procedure[,] the regular rather than the unusual practice." *Teamsters v. United States,* 431 U.S. 324, 358 (1977); *see also Franks v. Bowman Transp. Co.,* 424 U.S. 747, 772 (1976). If he succeeds, that showing will support a rebuttable inference that all class members were victims of the discriminatory practice, and will justify "an award of prospective relief," such as "an injunctive order against the continuation of the discriminatory practice." *Teamsters, supra,* at 361.

for all those decisions together, it will be impossible to say that examination of all the class members' claims for relief will produce a common answer to the crucial question why was I disfavored.

B

This Court's opinion in *Falcon* describes how the commonality issue must be approached. There an employee who claimed that he was deliberately denied a promotion on account of race obtained certification of a class comprising all employees wrongfully denied promotions and all applicants wrongfully denied jobs. We rejected that composite class for lack of commonality and typicality, explaining:

> "Conceptually, there is a wide gap between (a) an individual's claim that he has been denied a promotion [or higher pay] on discriminatory grounds, and his otherwise unsupported allegation that the company has a policy of discrimination, and (b) the existence of a class of persons who have suffered the same injury as that individual, such that the individual's claim and the class claim will share common questions of law or fact and that the individual's claim will be typical of the class claims." *Id.*, at 157–158.

Falcon suggested two ways in which that conceptual gap might be bridged. First, if the employer "used a biased testing procedure to evaluate both applicants for employment and incumbent employees, a class action on behalf of every applicant or employee who might have been prejudiced by the test clearly would satisfy the commonality and typicality requirements of Rule 23(a)." *Id.*, at 159, n. 15. Second, "[s]ignificant proof that an employer operated under a general policy of discrimination conceivably could justify a class of both applicants and employees if the discrimination manifested itself in hiring and promotion practices in the same general fashion, such as through entirely subjective decisionmaking processes." *Ibid.* We think that statement precisely describes respondents' burden in this case. The first manner of bridging the gap obviously has no application here; Wal-Mart has no testing procedure or other companywide evaluation method that can be charged with bias. The whole point of permitting discretionary decisionmaking is to avoid evaluating employees under a common standard.

The second manner of bridging the gap requires "significant proof" that Wal-Mart "operated under a general policy of discrimination." That is entirely absent here. Wal-Mart's announced policy forbids sex discrimination, and as the District Court recognized the company imposes penalties for denials of equal employment opportunity. The only evidence of a "general policy of discrimination" respondents produced was the testimony of Dr. William Bielby, their sociological expert. Relying on "social framework" analysis, Bielby testified that Wal-Mart has a "strong corporate culture," that makes it " 'vulnerable' " to "gender bias." He could not, however, "determine with any specificity how regularly stereotypes play a meaningful role in employment decisions at Wal-Mart. At his deposition ... Dr. Bielby conceded that he could not calculate whether 0.5 percent or 95 percent of the employment decisions at Wal-Mart might be determined by stereotyped thinking." The parties dispute whether Bielby's testimony even met the standards for the admission of expert testimony under Federal Rule of Civil Procedure 702 and our *Daubert* case, see *Daubert v. Merrell Dow Pharmaceuticals, Inc.*, 509 U.S. 579 (1993)....

We doubt that is so, but even if properly considered, Bielby's testimony does nothing to advance respondents' case. "[W]hether 0.5 percent or 95 percent of the employment decisions at Wal-Mart might be determined by stereotyped thinking" is the essential question on which respondents' theory of commonality depends. If Bielby admittedly has no answer to that question, we can safely disregard what he has to say. It is worlds away from "significant proof" that Wal-Mart "operated under a general policy of discrimination."

C

The only corporate policy that the plaintiffs' evidence convincingly establishes is Wal-Mart's "policy" of allowing discretion by local supervisors over employment matters. On its face, of course, that is just the opposite of a uniform employment practice that would provide the commonality needed for a class action; it is a policy against having uniform employment practices. It is also a very common and presumptively reasonable way of doing business—one that we have said "should itself raise no inference of discriminatory conduct," *Watson v. Fort Worth Bank & Trust*, 487 U.S. 977, 990 (1988).

To be sure, we have recognized that, "in appropriate cases," giving discretion to lower-level supervisors can be the basis of Title VII liability under a disparate-impact theory—since an employer's undisciplined system of subjective decisionmaking [can have] precisely the same effects as a system pervaded by impermissible intentional discrimination. But the recognition that this type of Title VII claim "can" exist does not lead to the conclusion that every employee in a company using a system of discretion has such a claim in common. To the contrary, left to their own devices most managers in any corporation—and surely most managers in a corporation that forbids sex discrimination—would select sex-neutral, performance-based criteria for hiring and promotion that produce no actionable disparity at all. Others may choose to reward various attributes that produce disparate impact—such as scores on general aptitude tests or educational achievements. And still other managers may be guilty of intentional discrimination that produces a sex-based disparity. In such a company, demonstrating the invalidity of one manager's use of discretion will do nothing to demonstrate the invalidity of another's.

A party seeking to certify a nationwide class will be unable to show that all the employees' Title VII claims will in fact depend on the answers to common questions.

Respondents have not identified a common mode of exercising discretion that pervades the entire company—aside from their reliance on Dr. Bielby's social frameworks analysis that we have rejected. In a company of Wal-Mart's size and geographical scope, it is quite unbelievable that all managers would exercise their discretion in a common way without some common direction. Respondents attempt to make that showing by means of statistical and anecdotal evidence, but their evidence falls well short.

The statistical evidence consists primarily of regression analyses performed by Dr. Richard Drogin, a statistician, and Dr. Marc Bendick, a labor economist. Drogin conducted his analysis region-by-region, comparing the number of women promoted into management positions with the percentage of women in the available pool of hourly workers. After considering regional and national data, Drogin concluded that "there are statistically significant disparities between men and women at Wal-Mart ... [and] these disparities ... can be explained only by gender discrimination." Bendick compared work-force data from Wal-Mart and competitive retailers and concluded that Wal-Mart "promotes a lower percentage of women than its competitors."

Even if they are taken at face value, these studies are insufficient to establish that respondents' theory can be proved on a classwide basis. In *Falcon*, we held that one named plaintiff's experience of discrimination was insufficient to infer that "discriminatory treatment is typical of [the employer's employment] practices." 457 U.S., at 158. A similar failure of inference arises here. As Judge Ikuta observed in her dissent, "[i]nformation about disparities at the regional and national level does not establish the existence of disparities at individual stores, let alone raise the inference that a company-wide policy of discrimination is implemented by discretionary decisions at the store and district level." 603 F.3d, at 637. A regional pay disparity, for example, may be attributable to only a small set of Wal-Mart stores, and cannot by itself establish the uniform, store-by-store disparity upon which the plaintiffs' theory of commonality depends.

There is another, more fundamental, respect in which respondents' statistical proof fails. Even if it established (as it does not) a pay or promotion pattern that differs from the nationwide figures or the regional figures in all of Wal-Mart's 3,400 stores, that would still not demonstrate that commonality of issue exists. Some managers will claim that the availability of women, or qualified women, or interested women, in their stores' area does not mirror the national or regional statistics. And almost all of them will claim to have been applying some sex-neutral, performance-based criteria—whose nature and effects will differ from store to store.

In the landmark case of ours which held that giving discretion to lower-level supervisors can be the basis of Title VII liability under a disparate-impact theory, the plurality opinion conditioned that holding on the corollary that merely proving that the discretionary system has produced a racial or sexual disparity is not enough. "[T]he plaintiff must begin by identifying the specific employment practice that is challenged." *Watson*, 487 U.S., at 994. That is all the more necessary when a class of plaintiffs is sought to be certified. Other than the bare existence of delegated discretion, respondents have identified no "specific employment practice" — much less one that ties all their 1.5 million claims together. Merely showing that Wal-Mart's policy of discretion has produced an overall sex-based disparity does not suffice.

Respondents' anecdotal evidence suffers from the same defects, and in addition is too weak to raise any inference that all the individual, discretionary personnel decisions are discriminatory. In *Teamsters v. United States*, 431 U.S. 324 (1977), in addition to substantial statistical evidence of company-wide discrimination, the Government (as plaintiff) produced about 40 specific accounts of racial discrimination from particular individuals. *See id.*, at 338. That number was significant because the company involved had only 6,472 employees, of whom 571 were minorities, and the class itself consisted of around 334 persons. The 40 anecdotes thus represented roughly one account for every eight members of the class. Moreover, the Court of Appeals noted that the anecdotes came from individuals "spread throughout" the company who "for the most part" worked at the company's operational centers that employed the largest numbers of the class members. Here, by contrast, respondents filed some 120 affidavits reporting experiences of discrimination — about 1 for every 12,500 class members — relating to only some 235 out of Wal-Mart's 3,400 stores. More than half of these reports are concentrated in only six States (Alabama, California, Florida, Missouri, Texas, and Wisconsin); half of all States have only one or two anecdotes; and 14 States have no anecdotes about Wal-Mart's operations at all. Even if every single one of these accounts is true, that would not demonstrate that the entire company "operate[s] under a general policy of discrimination," *Falcon, supra*, at 159, n. 15, which is what respondents must show to certify a companywide class.

The dissent misunderstands the nature of the foregoing analysis. It criticizes our focus on the dissimilarities between the putative class members on the ground that we have "blend[ed]" Rule 23(a)(2)'s commonality requirement with Rule 23(b)(3)'s inquiry into whether common questions "predominate" over individual ones. That is not so. We quite agree that for purposes of Rule 23(a)(2) " '[e]ven a single [common] question' " will do, *post*, at 2566, n. 9 (quoting Nagareda, *The Preexistence Principle and the Structure of the Class Action*, 103 COLUM. L. REV. 149, 176, n. 110

(2003)). We consider dissimilarities not in order to determine (as Rule 23(b)(3) requires) whether common questions predominate, but in order to determine (as Rule 23(a)(2) requires) whether there is "[e]ven a single [common] question." And there is not here. Because respondents provide no convincing proof of a companywide discriminatory pay and promotion policy, we have concluded that they have not established the existence of any common question.

In sum, we agree with Chief Judge Kozinski that the members of the class:

> "held a multitude of different jobs, at different levels of Wal-Mart's hierarchy, for variable lengths of time, in 3,400 stores, sprinkled across 50 states, with a kaleidoscope of supervisors (male and female), subject to a variety of regional policies that all differed.... Some thrived while others did poorly. They have little in common but their sex and this lawsuit." 603 F.3d, at 652 (dissenting opinion).

III

We also conclude that respondents' claims for backpay were improperly certified under Federal Rule of Civil Procedure 23(b)(2). Our opinion in *Ticor Title Ins. Co. v. Brown*, 511 U.S. 117, 121 (1994) (*per curiam*) expressed serious doubt about whether claims for monetary relief may be certified under that provision. We now hold that they may not, at least where (as here) the monetary relief is not incidental to the injunctive or declaratory relief.

A

Rule 23(b)(2) allows class treatment when "the party opposing the class has acted or refused to act on grounds that apply generally to the class, so that final injunctive relief or corresponding declaratory relief is appropriate respecting the class as a whole." One possible reading of this provision is that it applies only to requests for such injunctive or declaratory relief and does not authorize the class certification of monetary claims at all. We need not reach that broader question in this case, because we think that, at a minimum, claims for individualized relief (like the backpay at issue here) do not satisfy the Rule. The key to the (b)(2) class is "the indivisible nature of the injunctive or declaratory remedy warranted—the notion that the conduct is such that it can be enjoined or declared unlawful only as to all of the class members or as to none of them." Nagareda, 84 N.Y.U.L.Rev., at 132. In other words, Rule 23(b)(2) applies only when a single injunction or declaratory judgment would provide relief to each member of the class. It does not authorize class certification when each individual class member would be entitled to a different injunction or declaratory judgment against the defendant. Similarly, it does not authorize class certification when each class member would be entitled to an individualized award of monetary damages.

That interpretation accords with the history of the Rule. Because Rule 23 "stems from equity practice" that predated its codification, *Amchem Products, Inc. v. Windsor*, 521 U.S. 591, 613 (1997), in determining its meaning we have previously looked to the historical models on which the Rule was based. As we observed in *Amchem*, "[c]ivil rights cases against parties charged with unlawful, class-based discrimination are prime examples" of what (b)(2) is meant to capture. 521 U.S., at 614. In particular, the Rule reflects a series of decisions involving challenges to racial segregation — conduct that was remedied by a single classwide order. In none of the cases cited by the Advisory Committee as examples of (b)(2)'s antecedents did the plaintiffs combine any claim for individualized relief with their classwide injunction. See Advisory Committee's Note, 39 F.R.D. 69, 102 (1966) (citing cases).

Permitting the combination of individualized and classwide relief in a (b)(2) class is also inconsistent with the structure of Rule 23(b). Classes certified under (b)(1) and (b)(2) share the most traditional justifications for class treatment — that individual adjudications would be impossible or unworkable, as in a(b)(1) class,[11] or that the relief sought must perforce affect the entire class at once, as in a (b)(2) class. For that reason these are also mandatory classes: The Rule provides no opportunity for (b)(1) or (b)(2) class members to opt out, and does not even oblige the District Court to afford them notice of the action. Rule 23(b)(3), by contrast, is an "adventuresome innovation" of the 1966 amendments, *Amchem*, 521 U.S., at 614 (internal quotation marks omitted), framed for situations "in which 'class-action treatment is not as clearly called for'" *id.*, at 615 (quoting Advisory Committee's Notes, 28 U.S.C.App., p. 697 (1994 ed.)). It allows class certification in a much wider set of circumstances but with greater procedural protections. Its only prerequisites are that "the questions of law or fact common to class members predominate over any questions affecting only individual members, and that a class action is superior to other available methods for fairly and efficiently adjudicating the controversy." Rule 23(b)(3). And unlike (b)(1) and (b)(2) classes, the (b)(3) class is not mandatory; class members are entitled to receive "the best notice

---

11. Rule 23(b)(1) applies where separate actions by or against individual class members would create a risk of "establish[ing] incompatible standards of conduct for the party opposing the class," Rule 23(b)(1)(A), such as "where the party is obliged by law to treat the members of the class alike," *Amchem Products, Inc. v. Windsor*, 521 U.S. 591, 614 (1997), or where individual adjudications "as a practical matter, would be dispositive of the interests of the other members not parties to the individual adjudications or would substantially impair or impede their ability to protect their interests," Rule 23(b)(1)(B), such as in "'limited fund' cases, ... in which numerous persons make claims against a fund insufficient to satisfy all claims," *Amchem, supra*, at 614.

that is practicable under the circumstances" and to withdraw from the class at their option. *See* Rule 23(c)(2)(B).

Given that structure, we think it clear that individualized monetary claims belong in Rule 23(b)(3). The procedural protections attending the (b)(3) class—predominance, superiority, mandatory notice, and the right to opt out—are missing from (b)(2) not because the Rule considers them unnecessary, but because it considers them unnecessary to a (b)(2) class. When a class seeks an indivisible injunction benefitting all its members at once, there is no reason to undertake a case-specific inquiry into whether class issues predominate or whether class action is a superior method of adjudicating the dispute. Predominance and superiority are self-evident. But with respect to each class member's individualized claim for money, that is not so—which is precisely why (b)(3) requires the judge to make findings about predominance and superiority before allowing the class. Similarly, (b)(2) does not require that class members be given notice and opt-out rights, presumably because it is thought (rightly or wrongly) that notice has no purpose when the class is mandatory, and that depriving people of their right to sue in this manner complies with the Due Process Clause. In the context of a class action predominantly for money damages we have held that absence of notice and opt-out violates due process. *See Phillips Petroleum Co. v. Shutts,* 472 U.S. 797, 812 (1985). While we have never held that to be so where the monetary claims do not predominate, the serious possibility that it may be so provides an additional reason not to read Rule 23(b)(2) to include the monetary claims here.

B

Against that conclusion, respondents argue that their claims for backpay were appropriately certified as part of a class under Rule 23(b)(2) because those claims do not "predominate" over their requests for injunctive and declaratory relief. They rely upon the Advisory Committee's statement that Rule 23(b)(2) "does not extend to cases in which the appropriate final relief relates exclusively or predominantly to money damages." The negative implication, they argue, is that it does extend to cases in which the appropriate final relief relates only partially and nonpredominantly to money damages. Of course it is the Rule itself, not the Advisory Committee's description of it, that governs. And a mere negative inference does not in our view suffice to establish a disposition that has no basis in the Rule's text, and that does obvious violence to the Rule's structural features. The mere "predominance" of a proper (b)(2) injunctive claim does nothing to justify elimination of Rule 23(b)(3)'s procedural protections: It neither establishes the superiority of class adjudication over individual adjudication nor cures the notice and opt-out problems. We fail to see why the Rule should be read to nullify these protections whenever a plaintiff class, at its option, combines its monetary claims with a request — even a "predominating request" — for an injunction.

Respondents' predominance test, moreover, creates perverse incentives for class representatives to place at risk potentially valid claims for monetary relief. In this case, for example, the named plaintiffs declined to include employees' claims for compensatory damages in their complaint. That strategy of including only backpay claims made it more likely that monetary relief would not "predominate." But it also created the possibility (if the predominance test were correct) that individual class members' compensatory-damages claims would be precluded by litigation they had no power to hold themselves apart from. If it were determined, for example, that a particular class member is not entitled to backpay because her denial of increased pay or a promotion was not the product of discrimination, that employee might be collaterally estopped from independently seeking compensatory damages based on that same denial. That possibility underscores the need for plaintiffs with individual monetary claims to decide for themselves whether to tie their fates to the class representatives' or go it alone — a choice Rule 23(b)(2) does not ensure that they have.

The predominance test would also require the District Court to reevaluate the roster of class members continually. The Ninth Circuit recognized the necessity for this when it concluded that those plaintiffs no longer employed by Wal-Mart lack standing to seek injunctive or declaratory relief against its employment practices. The Court of Appeals' response to that difficulty, however, was not to eliminate all former employees from the certified class, but to eliminate only those who had left the company's employ by the date the complaint was filed. That solution has no logical connection to the problem, since those who have left their Wal-Mart jobs since the complaint was filed have no more need for prospective relief than those who left beforehand. As a consequence, even though the validity of a (b)(2) class depends on whether "final injunctive relief or corresponding declaratory relief is appropriate respecting the class as a whole," Rule 23(b)(2) (emphasis added), about half the members of the class approved by the Ninth Circuit have no claim for injunctive or declaratory relief at all. Of course, the alternative (and logical) solution of excising plaintiffs from the class as they leave their employment may have struck the Court of Appeals as wasteful of the District Court's time. Which indeed it is, since if a backpay action were properly certified for class treatment under (b)(3), the ability to litigate a plaintiff's backpay claim as part of the class would not turn on the irrelevant question whether she is still employed at Wal-Mart. What follows from this, however, is not that some arbitrary limitation on class membership should be imposed but that the backpay claims should not be certified under Rule 23(b)(2) at all.

Finally, respondents argue that their backpay claims are appropriate for a (b)(2) class action because a backpay award is equitable in nature. The latter may be true, but it is irrelevant. The Rule does not speak of "equitable" remedies generally but of injunctions and declaratory judgments. As Title VII itself makes pellucidly clear, backpay is neither. *See* 42 U.S.C. § 2000e-5(g)(2)(B)(i) and (ii) (distinguishing between declaratory and injunctive relief and the payment of "backpay," see § 2000e-5(g)(2)(A)).

C

In *Allison v. Citgo Petroleum Corp.*, 151 F.3d 402, 415 (C.A.5 1998), the Fifth Circuit held that a (b)(2) class would permit the certification of monetary relief that is "incidental to requested injunctive or declaratory relief," which it defined as "damages that flow directly from liability to the class as a whole on the claims forming the basis of the injunctive or declaratory relief." In that court's view, such "incidental damage should not require additional hearings to resolve the disparate merits of each individual's case; it should neither introduce new substantial legal or factual issues, nor entail complex individualized determinations." *Ibid.* We need not decide in this case whether there are any forms of "incidental" monetary relief that are consistent with the interpretation of Rule 23(b)(2) we have announced and that comply with the Due Process Clause. Respondents do not argue that they can satisfy this standard, and in any event they cannot.

Contrary to the Ninth Circuit's view, Wal-Mart is entitled to individualized determinations of each employee's eligibility for backpay. Title VII includes a detailed remedial scheme. If a plaintiff prevails in showing that an employer has discriminated against him in violation of the statute, the court "may enjoin the respondent from engaging in such unlawful employment practice, and order such affirmative action as may be appropriate, [including] reinstatement or hiring of employees, with or without backpay … or any other equitable relief as the court deems appropriate." § 2000e-5(g)(1). But if the employer can show that it took an adverse employment action against an employee for any reason other than discrimination, the court cannot order the "hiring, reinstatement, or promotion of an individual as an employee, or the payment to him of any backpay." § 2000e-5(g)(2)(A).

We have established a procedure for trying pattern-or-practice cases that gives effect to these statutory requirements. When the plaintiff seeks individual relief such as reinstatement or backpay after establishing a pattern or practice of discrimination, a district court must usually conduct additional proceedings to determine the scope of individual relief. At this phase, the burden of proof will shift to the company, but it will have the right to raise any individual affirmative defenses it may have, and to demonstrate that the individual applicant was denied an employment opportunity for lawful reasons.

The Court of Appeals believed that it was possible to replace such proceedings with Trial by Formula. A sample set of the class members would be selected, as to whom liability for sex discrimination and the backpay owing as a result would be determined in depositions supervised by a master. The percentage of claims determined to be valid would then be applied to the entire remaining class, and the number of (presumptively) valid claims thus derived would be multiplied by the average backpay award in the sample set to arrive at the entire class recovery—without further individualized proceedings. We disapprove that novel project. Because the Rules Enabling Act forbids interpreting Rule 23 to "abridge, enlarge or modify any substantive right," 28 U.S.C. § 2072(b), a class cannot be certified on the premise that Wal-Mart will not be entitled to litigate its statutory defenses to individual claims. And because the necessity of that litigation will prevent backpay from being "incidental" to the classwide injunction, respondents' class could not be certified even assuming, arguendo, that "incidental" monetary relief can be awarded to a 23(b)(2) class.

* * *

The judgment of the Court of Appeals is

Reversed.

Justice Ginsburg, with whom Justice Breyer, Justice Sotomayor, and Justice Kagan join, concurred in part and dissented in part (opinion omitted).

Exercise 8-13. Applying *Wal-Mart v. Dukes*

Imagine that you are contacted by the *Dukes* plaintiffs and their counsel on remand. Based on the Court's decision above, what would you advise them to do differently in pursuing their claims further, if the goal is to put together some kind of class action? Reading Justice Ginsburg's dissent (omitted from this casebook due to space limitations) may help to generate some ideas.

Exercise 8-14. Chapter Problem Revisited

Assume the facts of the Chapter Problem. Now, imagine that you are a solo practitioner in the state of Old York, with offices in Selden, and that you are interested in trying your hand for the first time at litigating a class action. One day, two potential clients come to see you. One is Molly, from the Chapter Problem. The other is Richard, who is the executive of his brother Tom's estate. Tom died recently from melanoma that Dr. Brown could not treat.

They ask you to file and secure certification of a class action that would include their claims and all similar ones. The best estimate they have of the size of the class is "around 50,000 people."

1. In addition to the facts related in the Chapter Problem and here, what do you need to know before proceeding? What questions might you ask Molly and Richard?

2. What legal concerns do you have, if any, regarding the possibility of certifying the class action that Molly and Richard would like you to file?

3. Assume that you do file a putative class action suit against OYPCO. Prior to certification, OYPCO makes motions to join others to the suit, and some non-parties also seek to join. Evaluate each of the following potential joinder motions:

   a. A motion by OYPCO for leave to file a third-party complaint against its insurer, Insco, Inc., for indemnity on the claims.

   b. A motion by OYPCO to dismiss, or in the alternative to force the joinder of Nukem, Inc., the outside contractor that OYPCO hired to do the testing that purportedly made everyone sick, under Rule 12(b)(7).

   c. A motion by the Old York Committee on Tort Reform to intervene, either as of right or permissively, to "defend Old York's business-friendly tort doctrines."

4. Assume that, after Tom's death, both his sister and his brother filed benefit claims with Tom's life insurance company, Insco, Inc., for payment of Tom's death benefit. As it happens, the current policy documents reflect that Tom's sister is the 100% beneficiary, while the old documents, which are still on record, reflect that Tom's brother is the beneficiary. The amount to the paid is over $1 million. What can Insco do to resolve this?

7. Professionalism and Joinder

Joinder decisions do not obviously implicate the ethical duties of lawyers, but ethical considerations nevertheless permeate joinder decisions. For example, consider whether it is ethical for a plaintiff's counsel to advise that an action be filed excluding a person that Rule 19 would consider to be a "party required for just adjudication." Considering that Rule 19, in part, exists to protect the absent party's interests, it stands to reason that an opportunistic attorney might act to prevent that absent party's participation, hoping to deprive the absent party of the interest in a way that will preclude the absent party from protecting it. Rule 19 recognizes this danger, and accordingly places upon any pleader the duty to disclose whether a required party exists who has not been joined, and the reasons for not joining that party. Rule 19(c).

Consider also whether the attorney for a "putative" class (one that is proposed, but not yet certified) bears any duties toward the many members of the class outside the named representatives. Difficult issues arise during the time after filing of the action and before certification because only at the certification stage does the court formally appoint class counsel. Should the putative counsel engage in communication with the members of the putative class? If so, does the attorney-client privilege attach to these communications? These issues, among many others, are so thorny that courts have taken to issuing communications orders prior to class certification in some cases, specifying what sorts of limited communications are permitted between putative counsel and the members of a putative class.

Of course, more serious ethical (sometimes reaching the level of criminal) actions can also result from a lawyer's foray into the class action field. The most serious of these issues is likely fees. Excessive fee arrangements are quite possible — and quite unethical — in the class context because the aggregation of claims allows for a significant multiplier on the average contingency fee of 40%. In addition, because most of the members of a class participate in the action only passively, it is relatively easy for class counsel to convince the class that an exorbitant fee is fair to the class, when in fact it is not. Rule 23 contains a number of safeguards against this sort of conduct, but the discretion of a lawyer over what his fee will be continues to generate problems — and sometimes even prosecutions.

Exercise 8-15. Fraudulent Joinder and Professionalism

In the *John S. Clark Co., Inc. v. Travelers Indemnity Co. of Ill.* case above, you learned about fraudulent joinder and how a court can dismiss a party who has been joined solely to destroy subject matter jurisdiction, with the determination of whether joinder was fraudulent entirely in the hands of the court. If a court makes such a determination, should there be an ethical sanction against the attorney who accomplished the joinder?

Model Rule of Professional Conduct 3.3, which has been adopted in most jurisdictions, requires "candor to the tribunal," meaning that lawyers cannot participate in, conceal, or fail to disclose fraudulent conduct in connection with a judicial proceeding. Does/should fraudulent joinder violate this provision? Why or why not?

Chapter 9

Discovery

The rules of discovery provide a variety of tools lawyers and parties can use to discover facts and evidence that the other party or third parties to the litigation possess. They also govern the general scope of what parties to a lawsuit may discover. As you read the following problem, consider what kind of information you want to discover and who would be a likely source for such information. The Federal Rules of Civil Procedure and cases covered in this chapter will help you develop the type of discovery plan requested in the problem as well as anticipate any problems that might arise in trying to obtain that information.

1. Chapter Problem

Memorandum

To: Associate
From: Mary Rogers, Partner
Re: Discovery in Wrongful Death Action

Now that the Piper case is finally situated in the federal court in Pennsylvania, it's time to begin discovery regarding the plaintiff's claims. Our client, the plaintiff in this case, represents the estate of one of the decedents, who was a resident of Scotland. The plane on which he was a passenger was manufactured by the Piper Aircraft Company in Pennsylvania. The plane was owned and operated by corporations that were organized under the laws of the United Kingdom. The four other passengers and the pilot, all of whom died in the crash, are from Scotland. In addition, a preliminary investigation into the crash revealed that there might have been a mechanical problem with the plane's propeller. Defendant Hartzell Propeller, Inc., manufactured the plane's propeller in Ohio. Our complaint alleges wrongful death and products liability causes of action. We are also making claims for loss of consortium on behalf of the decedent's wife as well as compensation for emotional distress.

Please draft a discovery plan covering all aspects of discovery, including the various tools we should use to develop facts that support our client's claims and that will help us counter any defenses that the defendants may make.

---

2. Introduction

The discovery process is the main way a party finds information that is relevant to a lawsuit. It performs a variety of functions. It can help parties preserve evidence for trial. It can isolate issues that are actually in controversy, so that a trial need not involve issues upon which the parties agree. It also helps avoid surprise at trial. Unlike what you might see in an old Perry Mason episode, if the civil discovery process has worked properly, each party to a lawsuit should know before trial what evidence the other side possesses to support its position. However, this depends on the parties asking the correct questions and being forthcoming about the information they possess. What is found out in discovery can also lead the parties to settle a case early.

Discovery is one aspect of the litigation process in which parties are often accused of abuse. Defendants argue that plaintiffs engage in "fishing expeditions" by using the discovery process to bolster claims that are flimsy or frivolous at the time the plaintiff filed the case. Parties argue that opposing counsels "stiff" them in discovery, increasing costs by requiring attorneys to file motions to compel to obtain information that is clearly relevant to the case. All of these purported abuses increase the costs of litigation, in some instances making plaintiffs settle for less and defendants settle cases that they would otherwise defend if the costs were not so high. These complaints have spurred several reforms to the discovery process. However, there is evidence that claims of abuse may be folklore.

Studies of the discovery process suggest that the costs of discovery are not out of control in relation to the amount at stake in most lawsuits. In a study of federal cases closed in the 2008 calendar year, the Federal Judicial Center found the median cost of litigation (including attorneys' fees) was not as high as expected—the median for defendants was $20,000 and for plaintiffs was $15,000. Furthermore, discovery costs did not appear disproportionate. The median percentage of litigation costs attributable to discovery was 20% for plaintiffs and 27% for defendants. Perhaps more significant was that discovery costs (including attorneys' fees attributable thereto) were 1.6% of the stake in the case for plaintiffs and 3.3% of the stake for defendants. In addition, 2008 apparently was not an anomalous year; these statistics are consistent with other studies of parties' costs in the civil justice system. *See* Danya Shocair Reda, *The Cost-and-Delay Narrative in Civil Justice Reform: Its Fallacies and Functions*, 90 Or. L. Rev. 1085, 1088–89 (2012) (describing studies). In earlier studies by RAND and the Federal Judicial Center, in 38% (RAND) to around 50% (Federal Judicial Center) of civil cases there was no discovery at all. *See* Linda S. Mullenix, *The Pervasive Myth of Pervasive Discovery Abuse: The Sequel*, 39 B.C. L. Rev. 683, 684 (1998) (citing and describing studies). Instead, discovery problems are limited to a minority of cases. James S. Kakalik et al., Rand Inst. for Civil Justice, *Discovery Management: Further Analysis of the Civil Justice Reform Act Evaluation Data* § II(A) (1998), *reprinted in* 39 B.C. L. Rev. 613 (1998). Of course, this does not mean that parties (through their lawyers) do not occasionally abuse the discovery process.

Before looking at the rules covering discovery, consider how you might go about finding information relevant to a case prior to filing a lawsuit. There are other ways to discover information that is helpful in a lawsuit. For example, information in the possession of governmental entities is sometimes publicly available through Freedom of Information laws. Also, it is sometimes possible simply to track down a witness and ask them if they are willing to talk to you. Components of investigation not requiring formal discovery might include:

- Client interviews

- Witness interviews

- Legal research

- Document research

- Clients' documents, such as contracts, insurance, medical records

- Public documents available through governmental agencies

- Internet research

- Viewing the scene.

However, without using an official discovery tool, any answers you receive will not be provided under penalty of perjury and thus may not be as reliable or usable in court. Thus, it is sometimes helpful to depose even a friendly witness to make certain his or her story doesn't change by the time of trial.

There are six basic discovery tools: required disclosures; depositions; interrogatories to parties; requests for documents, things, and entry onto property; requests for physical and mental examinations; and requests for admission (also referred to as requests to admit). Some of these tools, such as depositions, can be quite costly. Others, such as propounding interrogatories, are relatively inexpensive for the party propounding them, but can be quite expensive for the party answering such a request.

This chapter is organized as follows.

- Section 3 explores the general scope of discovery. What kinds of information can a party request and from whom? It takes up special limitations in the context of discovery, including the attorney-client privilege and related doctrines.

- Section 4, entitled "the tools," walks you through each discovery device, discussing how an attorney might use each to find useful information.

- Section 5 describes what happens when attorneys and parties fail to comply with discovery requests. This section includes motions to compel and sanctions based on discovery abuse.

- Section 6 finishes the chapter with a professional development question related to discovery.

3. General Scope of Discovery and Its Limits

a. General Scope

The general scope of discovery in the federal court system is broad. As you learned in Chapter 7, the federal rules, at least in theory, only require notice pleading. As the Supreme Court of the United States has explained, the "simplified notice pleading standard relies on liberal discovery rules and summary judgment motions to define disputed facts and issues and to dispose of unmeritorious claims." *Swierkiewicz v. Sorema, N.A.*, 534 U.S. 506, 512 (2002). Thus, "[b]road discovery is a cornerstone of the litigation process contemplated by the Federal Rules of Civil Procedure." *Jones v. Goord*, No. 95 Civ. 8026, 2002 WL 1007614, at *1 (S.D.N.Y. May 16, 2002).

Rule 26(b)(1) sets out the general scope of discovery in civil cases. Read Rule 26(b)(1). The rule provides for the discovery of nonprivileged information "that is relevant to any party's claim or defense." This rule was revised in 2015 to include language indicating that the discovery be "proportional to the needs of the case." It then provides a list of considerations in making this determination, including "the importance of the issues at stake in the action, the amount in controversy, the parties' relative access to relevant information, the parties' resources, the importance of the discovery in resolving the issues, and whether the burden or expense of the proposed discovery outweighs its likely benefit." The advisory committee notes to the amendments explain that the proportionality addition to Rule 26(b)(1) was intended to "restore" these factors "to their original place in defining the scope of discovery." Advisory Committee notes to 2015 amendments. The notes also indicate that the proportionality additions were in part a response to e-discovery, which has increased the cost of discovery. The advisory committee contemplates the dynamic nature of e-discovery, explaining that "[c]ourts and parties should be willing to consider the opportunities for reducing the burden or expense of discovery as reliable means of searching electronically stored information become available." The advisory committee explained that the proportionality change is not intended to allow a party opposing discovery to refuse requests by making blanket objections that the discovery requested is not "proportional."

The amended rule eliminates any reference to the phrase that information is discoverable if it is "reasonably calculated to lead to the discovery of admissible evidence," which appeared in prior versions of the rule. The advisory committee notes indicate that this phrase had been incorrectly used to define the scope of discovery and could swallow other limitations. The new rule leaves intact the provision that the information sought need not be admissible in evidence in court. Issues of admissibility are covered by the Federal Rules of Evidence, which are the subject of evidence courses. Federal Rule of Evidence 401 states that evidence is relevant if "(a) it has any tendency to make a fact more or less probable than it would be without the evidence; and (b) the fact is of consequence in determining the action." Fed. R. Evid. 401.

The scope of discovery can be understood as a two-step process. First, what is within the scope of discovery? The box below illustrates the general scope.

Relevance Box — Broad Scope of Discovery — Rule 26(b)(1)

Any unprivileged matter, relevant to any party's claim or defense

Second, additional limits apply to the scope of discovery. Read Rules 26(b)(1), (2), (3), (4) and 26(c). The limits contained in these rules can be summed up by the following limits box.

Limits on Scope of Discovery

26(b)(1)	privilege, proportionality
26(b)(2)	burden, expense
26(b)(3)	work product
26(b)(4)	experts
26(c)	protective orders

In addition to requesting discovery within the parameters of this rule, Federal Rule of Civil Procedure 26(a) provides for required initial disclosures. The initial disclosures are discussed among the tools of discovery, although they differ from other tools in that a party need not ask for this information. Aside from information provided based on initial disclosures, a party must ask for information in order to receive it. Such requests are governed by the general scope of discovery. The notes of the advisory committee, which developed the current rule, provide insight into the broad nature of this rule.

> A variety of types of information not directly pertinent to the incident in suit could be relevant to the claims or defenses raised in a given action. For example, other incidents of the same type, or involving the same product, could be properly discoverable under the revised standard. Information about organizational arrangements or filing systems of a party could be discoverable if likely to yield or lead to the discovery of admissible information. Similarly, information that could be used to impeach a likely witness, although not otherwise relevant to the claims or defenses, might be properly discoverable. In each instance, the determination whether such information is discoverable because it is relevant to the claims or defenses depends on the circumstances of the pending action.

Amendments to the Federal Rules of Civil Procedure, Federal Rules of Evidence, Federal Rules of Criminal Procedure and Federal Rules of Bankruptcy Procedure, 192 F.R.D. 389 (2000). As noted in Chapter 1, the notes of the advisory committee that developed a particular rule can be helpful in interpreting that rule. With respect to Rule 26(b), the drafters of the rule admitted, "[t]he dividing line between information relevant to the claims and defenses and that relevant only to the subject matter of the action cannot be defined with precision."

Exercise 9-1. *Giacchetto v. Patchogue-Medford Union Free School Dist.*

As you read *Giacchetto v. Patchogue-Medford Union Free School Dist.*, answer the following questions.

1. What varying approaches to the discoverability of social networking information does the *Giacchetto* court identify?

2. The court mentions "in camera" review. Using a legal dictionary, find out what this means.

3. The court also mentions an "ad damnum clause." Using a legal dictionary, find out what this means.

4. The *Giacchetto* court distinguishes between producing information for purposes of discovery related to physical damages as opposed to emotional distress damages. Why does the court make this distinction?

Giacchetto v. Patchogue-Medford Union Free School Dist.

293 F.R.D. 112 (E.D.N.Y. 2013)

A. Kathleen Tomlinson, United States Magistrate Judge:

Plaintiff Theresa Giacchetto ("Plaintiff") asserts claims against Defendant Patchogue-Medford Union Free School District (the "School District" or "Defendant") for violations of the Americans with Disabilities Act ("ADA"), and the New York State Human Rights Law ("NYSHRL"). Pending before the Court is Defendant's motion to compel Plaintiff to provide authorizations for the release of all records from Plaintiff's social networking accounts, including but not limited to her Facebook, Twitter, and MySpace accounts. For the reasons that follow, the motion is granted in part and denied in part.

According to the Amended Complaint, Plaintiff began working as an elementary education teacher for Defendant in 1996. On December 21, 2010, Plaintiff asserts she was diagnosed with adult Attention Deficit Hyperactivity Disorder ("ADHD"). Plaintiff claims that when she informed Defendant of her ADHD diagnosis, Dr. Tania M. Dalley repeatedly mocked Plaintiff within earshot of others. On January 5, 2011, Plaintiff filed a complaint with the New York State Division of Human Rights ("DHR") alleging disability discrimination. Thereafter, Plaintiff alleges that she was treated differently from other employees who did not have a disability and who did not file DHR complaints. For example, Plaintiff asserts that the School District issued her numerous counseling letters and transferred her to a different classroom and grade level against her will. Plaintiff further alleges that the School District refused to accommodate her disability. Based on these allegations, Plaintiff is seeking "compensatory, pension, medical benefits, emotional, physical, and punitive damages (where applicable), lost pay, front pay, interest, injunctive relief, and any other damages permitted by law."

Defendant argues that information from Plaintiff's social networking accounts is relevant to Plaintiff's claims of physical and emotional damages because it reflects her "levels of social interaction and daily functioning" and her "emotional and psychological state." Defendant also argues that any accounts of the events alleged in the Amended Complaint are discoverable. Plaintiff argues that Defendant's request is based on pure speculation and a fishing expedition "designed to harass Plaintiff and unnecessarily impinge on her privacy in the hopes that it will produce something that can be used against Plaintiff."

A. Legal Standard

Federal Rule of Civil Procedure 26(b)(1) provides that parties "may obtain discovery regarding any nonprivileged matter that is relevant to any party's claim or defense." The definition of relevancy under Rule 26 is to be "construed broadly to encompass any matter that bears on, or that reasonably could lead to other matter that could bear on, any issue that is or may be in th[e] case." *Oppenheimer Fund, Inc. v. Sanders*, 437 U.S. 340, 351 (1978).

The fact that Defendant is seeking social networking information as opposed to traditional discovery materials does not change the Court's analysis. The Court also notes that the "fact that the information [Defendant] seeks is in an electronic file as opposed to a file cabinet does not give [it] the right to rummage through the entire file." *Howell v. Buckeye Ranch, Inc.*, No. 11-CV-1014, 2012 WL 5265170, at *1 (S.D. Ohio Oct. 1, 2012).[1]

---

1. Some courts have held that the private section of a Facebook account is only discoverable if the party seeking the information can make a threshold evidentiary showing that the plaintiff's public Facebook profile contains information that undermines the plaintiff's claims. *See Potts v. Dollar Tree Stores, Inc.*, No. 11-CV-1180, 2013 WL 1176504, at *3 (M.D. Tenn. March 20, 2013); *Keller v. Nat'l Farmers Union Property & Casualty Co.*, No. 12-CV-72, 2013 WL 27731, at *4 (D. Mont. Jan. 2, 2013); *Tompkins v. Detroit Metro Airport*, 278 F.R.D. 387, 388 (E.D. Mich. 2012); *Romano v. Steelcase Inc.*, 30 Misc. 3d 426, 432, 907 N.Y.S. 2d 650 (Sup. Ct. 2010). This approach can lead to results that are both too broad and too narrow. On the one hand, a plaintiff should not be required to turn over the private section of his or her Facebook profile (which may or may not contain relevant information) merely because the public section undermines the plaintiff's claims. On the other hand, a plaintiff should be required to review the private section and produce any relevant information, regardless of what is reflected in the public section. The Federal Rules of Civil Procedure do not require a party

B. Discussion

Although Defendant apparently initially sought unlimited access to Plaintiff's entire social networking accounts, Defendant's motion to compel is limited to three categories of information: (1) postings about Plaintiff's emotional and psychological well-being; (2) postings about Plaintiff's physical damages; and (3) any accounts of the events alleged in Plaintiff's Amended Complaint. The Court will address each of these categories, as well as the proper method of producing the information which the Court deems relevant.

1. Emotional Damages

Courts have reached varying conclusions regarding the relevance of social networking postings in cases involving claims for emotional distress damages. Some courts have held that such information is relevant. Other courts have questioned the probative value of the material. This Court agrees with the latter approach. The fact that an individual may express some degree of joy, happiness, or sociability on certain occasions sheds little light on the issue of whether he or she is actually suffering emotional distress. If the Court were to allow broad discovery of Plaintiff's social networking postings as part of the emotional distress inquiry, then there would be no principled reason to prevent discovery into every other personal communication the Plaintiff had or sent since [the] alleged incident. As explained by Magistrate Judge Francis in *Rozell v. Ross-Holst*:

> To be sure, anything that a person says or does might in some theoretical sense be reflective of her emotional state. But that is hardly justification for requiring the production of every thought she may have reduced to writing or, indeed, the deposition of everyone she might have talked to.

No. 05-CV-2936, 2006 WL 163143, at *3 (S.D.N.Y. Jan. 20, 2006) (ruling on motion to compel emails that defendants claimed provided a contemporaneous record of plaintiff's emotional state). Thus, a plaintiff's entire social networking account is not necessarily relevant simply because he or she is seeking emotional distress damages.

In *Offenback v. L.M. Bowman, Inc.*, the defendants argued that the plaintiff's Facebook and MySpace accounts were relevant to his claim that he suffered physical and psychological injuries as a result of a vehicular accident. No. 10-CV-1789, 2011 WL 2491371, at *1 (M.D. Pa. June 22, 2011). Specifically, the defendants argued that the plaintiff's "social activities, transportation related activities, and expressions of emotion [were] relevant." *Id.* The court conducted an *in camera* review and ruled that while

---

to prove the existence of relevant material before requesting it. Furthermore, this approach improperly shields from discovery the information of Facebook users who do not share any information publicly. For all of the foregoing reasons, the Court will conduct a traditional relevance analysis.

certain posts reflecting that the plaintiff rode a motorcycle, possibly rode a mule, and hunted after the alleged accident were relevant, the remainder of the postings were not. *Id.* at *2–3. Notably, the Court did not order the production of any expressions of emotion or information about the plaintiff's social activities despite the fact that the plaintiff engaged in "routine communications with family and friends." *Id.* at *3. Although the court did not directly address the issue, *Offenback* underscores an important distinction between the relevance of social networking information to claims for physical damages and claims for emotional damages. While the relevance of a posting reflecting engagement in a physical activity that would not be feasible given the plaintiff's claimed physical injury is obvious, the relationship of routine expressions of mood to a claim for emotional distress damages is much more tenuous. For example, a severely depressed person may have a good day or several good days and choose to post about those days and avoid posting about moods more reflective of his or her actual emotional state. *See* Kathryn R. [Brown], *The Risks of Taking Facebook at Face Value: Why the Psychology of Social Networking Should Influence the Evidentiary Relevance of Facebook Photographs*, 14 VAND. J. ENT. & TECH. L. 357, 365 (2012) ("Because social networking websites enable users to craft a desired image to display to others, social scientists have posited that outside observers can misinterpret that impression.").

Based on the foregoing information, the Court concludes that Plaintiff's routine status updates and/or communications on social networking websites are not, as a general matter, relevant to her claim for emotional distress damages, nor are such communications likely to lead to the discovery of admissible evidence regarding the same. The Court does find, however, ... that certain limited social networking postings should be produced. First, Plaintiff must produce any specific references to the emotional distress she claims she suffered or treatment she received in connection with the incidents underlying her Amended Complaint (e.g., references to a diagnosable condition or visits to medical professionals). Moreover, in seeking emotional distress damages, Plaintiff has opened the door to discovery into other potential sources/causes of that distress. Thus, any postings on social networking websites that refer to an alternative potential stressor must also be produced. These materials are to be served upon Defendant's counsel as directed in Section B.4. below. However, unfettered access to Plaintiff's social networking history will not be permitted simply because Plaintiff has a claim for emotional distress damages.

b. Physical Damages

Defendant also seeks information bearing on Plaintiff's claim for physical damages. Postings or photographs on social networking websites that reflect physical capabilities inconsistent with a plaintiff's claimed injury are relevant. In this case, however, other than a brief reference to physical damages in the *ad damnum* clause, Plaintiff does not describe any physical damages and the Court is unaware of what type of physical harm she suffered. As such, the Court is directing Plaintiff to confirm in writing that she is pursuing relief for physical damages and, if so, specify the claimed harm. This statement is to be served on Defendant's counsel, with five (5) days of the Court's Order. The Court will address the scope of social networking discovery as it pertains to physical damages upon receipt of Plaintiff's statement.

3. Allegations in the Amended Complaint

Defendant also seeks "any accounts of the events alleged in plaintiff's Amended Complaint—contradictory or otherwise...." Such information is relevant and to the extent that such information exists on any social networking account maintained by the Plaintiff, Plaintiff must produce that information. Plaintiff is therefore required to produce, as directed in Section 4.B. below, any social networking postings that refer or relate to any of the events alleged in the Amended Complaint.

4. Method of Production

Having determined the scope of relevant information, the Court turns to the final issue raised in the parties' submissions—the method of producing information from Plaintiff's social networking accounts. Defendant seeks authorizations for the release of records from these accounts and presumably intends to subpoena the companies which host Plaintiff's accounts. Defendant also requests that Plaintiff's counsel conduct an independent review of the accounts for relevant material, instead of relying on the Plaintiff's conclusion that there is no relevant information in the account as counsel has previously done. Plaintiff takes no position on these issues.

First, the Court sees no basis at this time why Defendant should go through a third-party provider to access Plaintiff's social networking postings when Plaintiff has access to this information herself. This Court finds the approach utilized in *Howell* to be persuasive and reasonable. Therefore, the Court directs that Plaintiffs postings be reviewed for relevance by Plaintiff's counsel and that Plaintiff's counsel—*not Plaintiff*—make a determination regarding the relevance of the postings, keeping in mind the broad scope of discovery contemplated under Rule 26. The review and production of any relevant material is to be completed within 21 days.

———————

This case is decided by a federal magistrate judge. Magistrate judges hear motions and can try cases, with the consent of the parties, to help ease the caseload of federal district court judges. They are not protected by life tenure and guaranteed salaries; however, they are appointed by the federal judges for the particular district in which they sit and have eight year terms of appointment. Aside from a magistrate's job being eliminated by Congress due to a downturn in cases, a magistrate can only be removed during his or her term for "incompetency, misconduct, neglect of duty, or physical or mental disability," 28 U.S.C. §631(i). Thus, they are somewhat protected from political influences. Magistrates are permitted to hear certain pretrial matters in civil cases, subject to review by the federal judge appointing the magistrate to the matter. *See* 28 U.S.C. §636(b).

Before people posted much of their daily life on social media sites, it was much more expensive and difficult to discover information about individuals. For example, if a defendant wanted to find evidence that a plaintiff was faking his or her injuries, the defendant might hire a private investigator to follow the plaintiff to take video or photographs that suggested the plaintiff was not as harmed as alleged in the complaint. Such a method costs money and takes time. Now, through social media, one can find similar photographs and even video of a plaintiff suggesting that he or she does not have the extensive physically injuries he or she claims by simply making a discovery request. This costs relatively little for the requesting party compared to old-school methods of gathering information.

Exercise 9-2. *Giacchetto v. Patchogue-Medford Union Free School Dist.* Revisited

1. The court identifies a variety of approaches courts take to the production of social networking information. Can you determine which approach your jurisdiction takes to the production of such information? What is it?

2. Some courts permit very broad access to social media information. *See Sourdiff v. Texas Roadhouse Holdings, LLC*, No. 10-CV-0408, 2011 WL 7560647, at *1 (N.D.N.Y. Oct. 24, 2011) ("[P]laintiffs' counsel shall provide to defendant any photographs, profile information, postings, messages, comments and status updates and/or other posts, including deleted content, that are in any way related to plaintiff's emotional or mental state, her physical condition, activity level, employment, this litigation, and the injuries and damages claimed by plaintiffs in their complaint in this action."). Why might this information be less reliable? What are some policy arguments for limiting access through discovery?

3. Other courts, as indicated in footnote 1 of the decision, only permit discovery if the party's public information suggests that there may be information relevant to the underlying claims or defenses available in the non-public area of the site. What are the advantages and disadvantages of this approach?

4. Should the courts limit access to social media information that might be relevant to emotional distress damages using the discovery process? If this information is less reliable, might the better approach be to permit discovery but limit its admissibility into evidence?

5. The *Giacchetto* court ordered the plaintiff's lawyer to review the postings for relevance under the standards it set. Does this raise concerns about bias? Who else might review the postings?

6. Consider whether the following would be discoverable:

   a. In the chapter problem, the defendant Piper requests "any and all postings, photographs, or video on plaintiff's Facebook, Twitter, or other social media accounts that reflect decedent's wife's current emotional state as well as her emotional state immediately after the accident."

   b. In a breach of employment contract case in which the defendant employer alleges that the plaintiff was terminated for breaching the contract by disclosing trade secrets, the defendant requests "any and all postings, photographs, or video on plaintiff's Facebook, Twitter, or other social media accounts that mention the defendant or any of the defendant's products."

   c. In a personal injury case, the defendant requests "any and all postings, photographs, or video on plaintiff's Facebook, Twitter, or other social media accounts from one year prior to the accident alleged in the complaint to the present that reflect the plaintiff's physical or mental condition."

b. Proportionality and Limits on Discovery

Several provisions in the discovery rules permit or require the court to limit discovery under certain circumstances. The following exercise walks you through the limits set out in these rules.

Exercise 9-3. Reading Rules that Limit Discovery

1. Read Rule 26(b)(2)(C). What are the three general situations in which the rule requires a court to limit discovery?

2. Rule 26(b)(2)(B) limits discovery of electronically stored information. What standard does it set?

3. Rule 26(c) permits a court to issue a protective order. Read Rule 26(c). Based on the language of the rule,

   a. Who moves for a protective order?

   b. What must be shown in order for a court to issue a protective order?

c. What are the limits a court can place on discovery in a protective order?

4. Read Rule 26(d)(2). How might a court use this rule to fashion a protective order?

If a party finds a discovery request objectionable, it can object and refuse to respond. The party requesting the discovery must then meet and confer with the other party's attorney or the party (if the responding party is pro se) to determine whether they can agree on what will be produced. If that negotiation fails, the party requesting the information may make a motion to compel in order to receive the information. Motions to compel are covered in more detail later in this chapter.

Exercise 9-4. *Marrese v. American Academy of Orthopaedic Surgeons*

Marrese v. American Academy of Orthopaedic Surgeons is a case that eventually made its way to the Supreme Court of the United States on a claim preclusion issue, a subject covered in Chapter 13 of this book. This case was reversed on other grounds. In a portion of the case that the Supreme Court did not reverse, the en banc Seventh Circuit considered an interesting discovery problem that makes this case worthwhile reading. As you read *Marrese*, answer the following questions.

1. The Seventh Circuit heard this case "en banc." Look in a legal dictionary to determine what this means.

2. The *Marrese* court identifies a variety of tools at the trial court's disposal to protect a party from invasive discovery. What are they?

3. What is the standard of review for a trial court's decision regarding a discovery dispute of the type discussed in *Marrese*?

4. What legal standard does the *Marrese* court set under Rule 26(c)?

5. What is the "First Amendment interest" acknowledged by the court in *Marrese*?

Marrese v. American Academy of Orthopaedic Surgeons

726 F.2d 1150 (7th Cir. 1984) (en banc)

Posner, Circuit Judge.

These consolidated appeals present important questions relating to ... the responsibilities of federal district judges in controlling pretrial discovery.

In 1976 the American Academy of Orthopaedic Surgeons, a private association, rejected the plaintiffs' applications for membership, without a hearing or a statement of reasons. [The plaintiffs initially sued the Academy on state law grounds in the Illinois state courts. They lost that case. They subsequently brought a case in federal court for damages and injunctive relief under the Sherman Antitrust Act, a federal claim. The plaintiffs asked the Academy to produce its files relating to all denials of membership applications between 1970 and 1980. The Academy refused. When the Academy persisted in its refusal after the district judge issued an order to produce, the judge held the Academy in criminal contempt and fined it $10,000.]

* * *

We turn to … the Academy's appeal from the $10,000 fine for contempt of Judge Shadur's discovery order.

* * *

… Rule 37(a)(2), authorizing discovery orders, must be read in light of Rule 26(c), which empowers the district court to "make any order which justice requires to protect a party or person from annoyance, embarrassment, oppression, or undue burden or expense, including … that discovery not be had …," and Rule 26(d), which empowers the court, "upon motion, for the convenience of parties and witnesses and in the interests of justice," to control the sequence and timing of discovery. Of course the effective management of complex litigation requires that the district judge be allowed a broad discretion in guiding the discovery process, and hence in deciding whether to limit discovery in accordance with Rules 26(c) or (d). But his discretion is not unlimited; if we have a firm conviction that he has made a mistake, we must reverse. …

A motion under Rule 26(c) to limit discovery requires the district judge to compare the hardship to the party against whom discovery is sought, if discovery is allowed, with the hardship to the party seeking discovery if discovery is denied. He must consider the nature of the hardship as well as its magnitude and thus give more weight to interests that have a distinctively social value than to purely private interests; and he must consider the possibility of reconciling the competing interests through a carefully crafted protective order. He must go through the same analysis under Rule 26(d) except that an order merely postponing a particular discovery request obviously should be granted more freely than one denying the request altogether.

In an effort to show that more than purely private interests are at stake the Academy argues that its membership files are protected by the First Amendment. If meant to establish a complete immunity from pretrial discovery of these materials[,] the argument is untenable in light of *Memorial Hospital for McHenry Cty. v. Shadur*, 664 F.2d 1058, 1063 (7th Cir. 1981) (per curiam), which rejected a claim of privilege for a hospital's records of disciplinary proceedings against staff physicians. Even if the Academy were engaged in advocating controversial views and the publication of its internal files would expose members to retaliation for those views, it would not have an absolute privilege against discovery, though the plaintiffs would then have the burden of showing that the information sought was essential to their case and unobtainable by other means that would be less likely to discourage such advocacy.

Yet there is in this case, if not a First Amendment right, at least a First Amendment interest, which the discovery sought by the plaintiffs would impair and which differentiates this case from the usual antitrust case, where discovery is sought of invoices or salesmen's reports or the minutes of a board of directors' meeting. In *NAACP v. Alabama*, 357 U.S. 449 (1958), a case involving resistance to pretrial discovery of membership lists, the Supreme Court recognized a First Amendment right of association for the purpose of expressing ideas. The American Academy of Orthopaedic Surgeons is not the NAACP, but neither is it a country club or a trade association; it is a professional association and a forum for exchanges of information about surgical techniques and related matters of substantial public interest.... If the Academy has to reveal its membership files, members may be reluctant to offer candid evaluations of applicants, and the atmosphere of mutual confidence that encourages a free exchange of ideas will be eroded.

The Constitution to one side, one does not have to be a student of Aristotle and de Tocqueville to know that voluntary associations are important to many people, Americans in particular, and that voluntary professional associations are important to American professionals (the premise of the plaintiffs' antitrust suit, as it was of their Illinois suits). Since an association would not be genuinely voluntary if the members were not allowed to consider applications for new members in confidence, the involuntary disclosure of deliberations on membership applications cannot but undermine the voluntary character of an association and therefore harm worthy interests, whether or not those interests derive any additional dignity from the First Amendment. The threat to such interests is more than speculative in this case. Dr. Marrese's counsel said at the rehearing en banc that he wants to use the membership files as a source of names of Academy members to depose in an effort to find out the motives behind their opposition to his client's application. It is hard to believe that after members of the Academy find themselves deposed for this purpose they will still be willing to offer candid evaluations of prospective members.

The other side of the coin is that barring the plaintiffs or their counsel from all access to the membership files would probably make it impossible for them to prove their antitrust case. But there were various devices that the district judge could have used to reconcile the parties' competing needs. For example, he could have examined the membership files himself *in camera,* a procedure described by the Supreme Court in a related context as "a relatively costless and eminently worthwhile method to insure that the balance between petitioners' claims of irrelevance and privilege and plaintiffs' asserted need for the documents is correctly struck." *Kerr v. United States Dist. Ct.,* 426 U.S. 394 (1976). We are told the membership files may be voluminous. No doubt the files in *all* cases between 1970 and 1980 where applications for membership in the Academy were refused are voluminous, but the place to start an *in camera* examination would be with the files on Drs. Marrese and Treister. If the judge found no evidence in those files of any anticompetitive purpose attributable to the Academy, he would not have to look at any other files....

Better yet, the judge might have followed the procedure discussed in this court's recent decision in *EEOC v. University of Notre Dame Du Lac,* 715 F.2d 331, 338–39 (7th Cir. 1983). There we ordered the files of faculty tenure deliberations edited ("redacted") to remove the names of the deliberating faculty members and any other information that might enable them to be identified, and we directed that on remand the redaction be reviewed *in camera* by the district judge, who would have the originals before him to compare with (and thereby assure the accuracy of) the redactions. Had the same procedure been followed here, the plaintiffs' counsel would have been able to read the files personally. If the files had turned out to contain evidence or leads to evidence of anticompetitive conduct, the plaintiffs' counsel could then have requested the judge to order names revealed to counsel so that the relevant individuals could be deposed. We do not think that only universities should be entitled to such consideration.

The protective order that the judge did enter ... was not well designed to protect the privacy of the Academy's members. It not only allowed the plaintiffs themselves—two disappointed applicants for membership—to read the files on their own applications; it allowed the plaintiffs' counsel "to discuss with plaintiffs the general contents" of all of the other files and to depose anyone whose name they found in the files. The order was not calculated to allay the Academy's justifiable anxiety for the confidentiality of its membership deliberations.

Rule 26(d) (control of the sequence and timing of discovery) provided another method of accommodating the competing interests here with minimal damage to either. If there is other discovery that a plaintiff must complete in order to be able to resist a motion by the defendant for summary judgment, and thus a significant probability that his case will fail regardless of what the internal files he is seeking may show, the district judge has the power under Rule 26(d) to require the plaintiff to complete the other, nonsensitive discovery first. And in an appropriate case he has the duty. "As a threshold matter, the court should be satisfied that a claim is not frivolous, a pretense for using discovery powers in a fishing expedition. In this case, plaintiff should show that it can establish jury issues on the essential elements of its case not the subject of the contested discovery." *Bruno & Stillman, Inc. v. Globe Newspaper Co.*, 633 F.2d 583, 597 (1st Cir. 1980).

Of course, if the plaintiffs do not need anything beyond the contents of the Academy's membership files to prove their case, they cannot be asked to do any other discovery before getting access to the files. At oral argument we asked Dr. Marrese's counsel whether his discovery would be complete after he saw the membership files and followed up any leads the files contained. He answered that at that point he would file a motion for summary judgment arguing that the Academy had committed a per se violation of the Sherman Act, but that if the motion was denied he would conduct additional discovery, which he admitted would be necessary to prove a Rule of Reason violation. It is unlikely that the district judge would allow him to proceed in so piecemeal a fashion. The judge probably would tell him to complete discovery before moving for summary judgment. Assuming discovery would not be at an end when the files were turned over and any leads contained in them were tracked down, Rule 26(d) could have been used to schedule the sensitive discovery last.

We do not hold that all files of all voluntary associations are sacrosanct; we do not even hold that the membership files of an association of medical professionals are sacrosanct. They are discoverable in appropriate circumstances, subject to appropriate safeguards. But we may not ignore as judges what we know as lawyers — that discovery of sensitive documents is sometimes sought not to gather evidence that will help the party seeking discovery to prevail on the merits of his case but to coerce his opponent to settle regardless of the merits rather than have to produce the documents....

Many other judges and commentators have voiced concern over the use of discovery to force settlement in groundless cases. There is at least a hint of predatory discovery in this case in the fact that the plaintiffs did not seek access to the federal court system with its liberal discovery rules till after they had lost their state-court suit, and in the determination expressed by Dr. Marrese's counsel to use the Academy's membership files as the basis for deposing the individuals who voted against his client's membership application.

There are so many ways in which Judge Shadur could have prevented the plaintiffs from abusing the discovery process, without denying them any information essential to developing their case, that we are left with the firm conviction that the discovery order he issued, when he issued it, was erroneous. Our conclusion is consistent with the evolving concept of the district judge's managerial responsibility in complex litigation....

This case illustrates the pathological delays that are all too frequent in modern litigation. After nearly eight years of state and federal litigation, the case remains stalled in the earliest stages of discovery. It has gone on long enough.... [T]he contempt judgment is reversed with directions to dismiss the contempt proceeding....

Harlington Wood, Jr., Circuit Judge, with whom Cummings, Chief Judge, and Cudahy, Circuit Judge, join, dissenting.

* * *

Judge Posner's opinion now finds fault in the district court's failure to incorporate other protective devices for resolving the discovery dispute, such as an in camera inspection of the Academy's files or production of a redacted version of the files. I, too, believe that the trial judge could have improved on his discovery order. First, he could have been well-served by taking a look in camera at the Academy files on plaintiffs to see whether the files contained what plaintiffs claimed to need so badly, and whether the Academy had good reason to fight so desperately to keep the files out of sight.

The Supreme Court has commended an in camera view of documents in a discovery dispute to insure the striking of a proper balance between the interests in confidentiality and disclosure. Failure to make an in camera inspection, however, is not in itself an abuse of discretion. While the district court did not view the Academy's files, it apparently was aware that the state trial court had conducted an in camera inspection of the files in the earlier state court litigation between the same parties. After viewing the files, the state court ordered production over the Academy's objections. Thus, one judge had viewed these materials and determined that the contents were relevant and disclosure was appropriate. We should not ignore the state court's first-hand determination. Further, the Academy has maintained that an in camera inspection would not improve the discovery order. In the Academy's view, as I understand it, an in camera inspection could lead to a discovery order which, even if including redaction of the files, would be an abuse of discretion at this stage of the litigation.

The propriety of the district court's order to produce the unredacted files also must be considered in light of the surrounding circumstances. In the early stages of this litigation, plaintiffs expressed their willingness to accept a redacted version of the Academy's files, at least as the first phase of discovery. The Academy refused plaintiffs' early offer to enter a redaction agreement, and plaintiffs later rescinded the offer. Both sides submitted proposed protective orders to the district court; apparently neither provided for redaction.

* * *

Judge Posner's opinion discusses the misuse of discovery tools to coerce settlement, and apparently concludes that the district court's discovery order failed to prevent plaintiffs from abusing the discovery process. The opinion finds two "hints" of predatory discovery here: first, that plaintiffs sought access to federal court—and its liberal discovery rules—only after losing in the state court; and further, that plaintiffs planned to use information from the Academy's files as the basis for further discovery. The first hint merely returns us to the res judicata issue in the context of a dual court system. The second hint, plaintiffs' plan to follow up leads found in the files, is one of the conventional purposes of discovery.

Upon questioning at oral argument, counsel for the Academy labeled plaintiffs' suit a "fishing expedition," an attempt to gain access to otherwise unavailable information. Under the circumstances, however, plaintiffs' pursuit of the files and plan to seek further discovery using leads from the files were within the bounds of appropriate discovery. The discovery record in this case evidences not the slightest abuse, harassment, or coercion to pressure a settlement. Judicial concern about discovery abuse is always legitimate, but such arguments are gratuitous in the context of this case. The abuse of discovery here instead is the Academy's obstinate defiance of the trial court, which now is sanctioned by this court.

Although not condemning any one omission as an abuse of discretion, the discovery majority is left with the "firm conviction" that the district court's discovery order was erroneous. I am not. The district court sought and received proposed protective orders from the parties, and mediated negotiations on this issue. Bifurcation of discovery was not mandatory in this case, and the court reasonably provided for the Academy's confidentiality concerns through the protective order. The Academy should not now reap a windfall from reversal of the discovery order because the order did not incorporate certain provisions that the Academy still would refuse to accept. The Academy treated the trial judge's reasonable discovery order with contempt and its contempt should be recognized by this court.

* * *

Although the discovery order could have been improved, the district court's fashioning of the terms was not an abuse of discretion under the circumstances of this case. What the merits of this case would have turned out to be, we now will never know; but we must not let a prejudgment on the merits cloud our review of the discovery order. Plaintiffs ... deserve the opportunity within reasonable limits to develop their case, and then the opportunity to try it before a judge and jury. I would affirm the district court's contempt holding, but on remand I would direct the court to view the Academy's files in camera and to consider possible redaction before actually enforcing the discovery order.

Exercise 9-5. *Marrese* Revisited

1. What role does the First Amendment play in Judge Posner's analysis of this case?

2. What role does Judge Posner envision for trial judges during the discovery process?

3. Judge Wood, dissenting and applying an abuse of discretion standard of review, argues that the trial judge did not violate this standard. How does he reach this conclusion? Who has the better argument — Judge Posner or Judge Wood?

4. Given the standard for protective orders set by the *Marrese* court, would a court issue a protective order in the following cases?

a. A defendant in a sexual harassment case seeks discovery of information related to plaintiff's sexual activities outside the workplace. If the plaintiff makes a motion for a protective order, will the court grant it?

b. In a products liability action against a tire manufacturer based on an automobile accident, the plaintiff requests information about accidents involving tires similar to the tire involved in the accident. If the defendant makes a motion for a protective order, will the court grant it?

c. In a patent infringement action, the plaintiff requests information regarding the defendant's product that it alleged infringes on the plaintiff's patent. If the defendant makes a motion for a protective order, will the court grant it?

d. A retail company brings an action against the issuer of credit cards and asserts state law claims based on the credit card issuer's imposition of noncompliance fines and reimbursement assessments after a cyberattack involving credit card purchases at the retailer's stores. The credit card issuer requests evidence of the retailer's voluntary changes to its credit card system designed to avoid a future cyberattack. If the retail company makes a motion for a protective order, will the court grant it? *See Genesco, Inc. v. VISA U.S.A., Inc.*, 302 F.R.D. 168 (M.D. Tenn. 2014) (court refused discovery of subsequent remedial measures).

c. Special Limits on Discovery

(1) Work Product Doctrine

Rule 26(b)(3) limits discovery of material created by attorneys in preparation for trial. Read Rule 26(b)(3). Known as the work product doctrine, this protects the work of lawyers, including private notes, from disclosure to the opposing side. Rule 26(b)(3) sets a two-tiered discovery process for attorney work product. First, the material is discoverable under very limited circumstances. While the first prong of this rule—the material may be discovered if it is relevant to a claim or defense of a party (Rule 26(b)(1))—is more easily satisfied, the second prong makes it unlikely that an opposing party will be permitted to discover attorney work product. Showing that there is a substantial need for information to prepare a case and that the party cannot obtain the substantial equivalent by other means without undue hardship is difficult. However, even if a party does satisfy Rule 26(b)(3)(A), part B of the rule protects against disclosure "mental impressions, opinions, or legal theories of a party's attorney." This part of the Rule suggests that these materials are never discoverable. How might you produce, for example, a memorandum created by you as an attorney that contained some material covered by Rule 26(b)(3)(B)?

Before the work product doctrine was codified in the Federal Rules of Civil Procedure, the United States Supreme Court sought to lay out the parameters of the protection in a case involving discovery—*Hickman v. Taylor*.

Exercise 9-6. *Hickman v. Taylor*

Hickman v. Taylor is the classic United States Supreme Court case that discusses the work product doctrine. As you read the case, answer the following questions.

1. The *Hickman* case is a rare Supreme Court case dealing with a discovery issue. Discovery matters are rarely appealed, because parties generally need to wait to the end of the entire lawsuit to bring an appeal. How did this case get to the Supreme Court of the United States?

2. What standard does the Court use for discovery of work product in this case? Does the plaintiff meet this standard?

3. What policies underlying the work product doctrine does the Court identify in *Hickman*?

4. According to the court, why doesn't the attorney-client privilege apply in this case?

Hickman v. Taylor
329 U.S. 495 (1947)

Mr. Justice Murphy delivered the opinion of the Court.

This case presents an important problem under the Federal Rules of Civil Procedure ... as to the extent to which a party may inquire into oral and written statements of witnesses, or other information, secured by an adverse party's counsel in the course of preparation for possible litigation after a claim has arisen....

On February 7, 1943, the tug "J. M. Taylor" sank while engaged in helping to tow a car float of the Baltimore & Ohio Railroad across the Delaware River at Philadelphia. The accident was apparently unusual in nature, the cause of it still being unknown. Five of the nine crew members were drowned. Three days later the tug owners and the underwriters employed a law firm, of which respondent Fortenbaugh is a member, to defend them against potential suits by representatives of the deceased crew members and to sue the railroad for damages to the tug.

A public hearing was held on March 4, 1943, before the United States Steamboat Inspectors, at which the four survivors were examined. This testimony was recorded and made available to all interested parties. Shortly thereafter, Fortenbaugh privately interviewed the survivors and took statements from them with an eye toward the anticipated litigation; the survivors signed these statements on March 29. Fortenbaugh also interviewed other persons believed to have some information relating to the accident and in some cases he made memoranda of what they told him. At the time when Fortenbaugh secured the statements of the survivors, representatives of two of the deceased crew members had been in communication with him. Ultimately claims were presented by representatives of all five of the deceased; four of the claims, however, were settled without litigation. The fifth claimant, petitioner herein, brought suit in a federal court under the Jones Act on November 26, 1943, naming as defendants the two tug owners, individually and as partners, and the railroad.

One year later, petitioner filed 39 interrogatories directed to the tug owners. The 38th interrogatory read: "State whether any statements of the members of the crews of the Tugs 'J. M. Taylor' and 'Philadelphia' or of any other vessel were taken in connection with the towing of the car float and the sinking of the Tug 'John M. Taylor.' Attach hereto exact copies of all such statements if in writing, and if oral, set forth in detail the exact provisions of any such oral statements or reports." Supplemental interrogatories asked whether any oral or written statements, records, reports or other memoranda had been made concerning any matter relative to the towing operation, the sinking of the tug, the salvaging and repair of the tug, and the death of the deceased. If the answer was in the affirmative, the tug owners were then requested to set forth the nature of all such records, reports, statements or other memoranda.

The tug owners, through Fortenbaugh, answered all of the interrogatories except No. 38 and the supplemental ones just described. While admitting that statements of the survivors had been taken, they declined to summarize or set forth the contents. They did so on the ground that such requests called "for privileged matter obtained in preparation for litigation" and constituted "an attempt to obtain indirectly counsel's private files." It was claimed that answering these requests "would involve practically turning over not only the complete files, but also the telephone records and, almost, the thoughts of counsel."

[The district court held that the information was not privileged and ordered it produced. When Fortenbaugh and the tug owners refused, they were held in contempt of court and imprisoned. The Third Circuit reversed the district court.]

* * *

[The court began by addressing a procedural irregularity in the case that will make more sense once you have reviewed the various discovery tools later in this chapter. The plaintiff used Rule 33, governing interrogatories to parties, to attempt to obtain this information. However, Rule 33 does not permit a party to request information from a non-party (such as Fortenbaugh) or to obtain documents. In addition, to the extent the request can be reframed as a Rule 34 request for documents, such a request cannot be aimed at a non-party such as Fortenbaugh. The plaintiff should have used Rule 45 to subpoena documents from a non-party.]

… But in the present circumstances, for the purposes of this decision, the procedural irregularity is not material. Having noted the proper procedure, we may accordingly turn our attention to the substance of the underlying problem.

In urging that he has a right to inquire into the materials secured and prepared by Fortenbaugh, petitioner emphasizes that the deposition-discovery portions of the Federal Rules of Civil Procedure are designed to enable the parties to discover the true facts and to compel their disclosure wherever they may be found. It is said that inquiry may be made under these rules, epitomized by Rule 26, as to any relevant matter which is not privileged; and since the discovery provisions are to be applied as broadly and liberally as possible, the privilege limitation must be restricted to its narrowest bounds. On the premise that the attorney-client privilege is the one involved in this case, petitioner argues that it must be strictly confined to confidential communications made by a client to his attorney. And since the materials here in issue were secured by Fortenbaugh from third persons rather than from his clients, the tug owners, the conclusion is reached that these materials are proper subjects for discovery under Rule 26.

As additional support for this result, petitioner claims that to prohibit discovery under these circumstances would give a corporate defendant a tremendous advantage in a suit by an individual plaintiff. Thus in a suit by an injured employee against a railroad or in a suit by an insured person against an insurance company the corporate defendant could pull a dark veil of secrecy over all the pertinent facts it can collect after the claim arises merely on the assertion that such facts were gathered by its large staff of attorneys and claim agents. At the same time, the individual plaintiff, who often has direct knowledge of the matter in issue and has no counsel until some time after his claim arises could be compelled to disclose all the intimate details of his case. By endowing with immunity from disclosure all that a lawyer discovers in the course of his duties, it is said, the rights of individual litigants in such cases are drained of vitality and the lawsuit becomes more of a battle of deception than a search for truth.

But framing the problem in terms of assisting individual plaintiffs in their suits against corporate defendants is unsatisfactory. Discovery concededly may work to the disadvantage as well as to the advantage of individual plaintiffs. Discovery, in other words, is not a one-way proposition. It is available in all types of cases at the behest of any party, individual or corporate, plaintiff or defendant. The problem thus far transcends the situation confronting this petitioner. And we must view that problem in light of the limitless situations where the particular kind of discovery sought by petitioner might be used.

We agree, of course, that the deposition-discovery rules are to be accorded a broad and liberal treatment. No longer can the time-honored cry of "fishing expedition" serve to preclude a party from inquiring into the facts underlying his opponent's case. Mutual knowledge of all the relevant facts gathered by both parties is essential to proper litigation. To that end, either party may compel the other to disgorge whatever facts he has in his possession. The deposition-discovery procedure simply advances the stage at which the disclosure can be compelled from the time of trial to the period preceding it, thus reducing the possibility of surprise. But discovery, like all matters of procedure, has ultimate and necessary boundaries. As indicated by Rules 30(b) and (d) and 31(d), limitations inevitably arise when it can be shown that the examination is being conducted in bad faith or in such a manner as to annoy, embarrass or oppress the person subject to the inquiry. And as Rule 26(b) provides, further limitations come into existence when the inquiry touches upon the irrelevant or encroaches upon the recognized domains of privilege.

We also agree that the memoranda, statements and mental impressions in issue in this case fall outside the scope of the attorney-client privilege and hence are not protected from discovery on that basis. It is unnecessary here to delineate the content and scope of that privilege as recognized in the federal courts. For present purposes, it suffices to note that the protective cloak of this privilege does not extend to information which an attorney secures from a witness while acting for his client in anticipation of litigation. Nor does this privilege concern the memoranda, briefs, communications and other writings prepared by counsel for his own use in prosecuting his client's case; and it is equally unrelated to writings which reflect an attorney's mental impressions, conclusions, opinions or legal theories.

But the impropriety of invoking that privilege does not provide an answer to the problem before us. Petitioner has made more than an ordinary request for relevant, non-privileged facts in the possession of his adversaries or their counsel. He has sought discovery as of right of oral and written statements of witnesses whose identity is well known and whose availability to petitioner appears unimpaired. He has sought production of these matters after making the most searching inquiries of his opponents as to the circumstances surrounding the fatal accident, which inquiries were sworn to have been answered to the best of their information and belief. Interrogatories were directed toward all the events prior to, during and subsequent to the sinking of the tug. Full and honest answers to such broad inquiries would necessarily have included all pertinent information gleaned by Fortenbaugh through his interviews with the witnesses. Petitioner makes no suggestion, and we cannot assume, that the tug owners or Fortenbaugh were incomplete or dishonest in the framing of their answers. In addition, petitioner was free to examine the public testimony of the witnesses taken before the United States Steamboat Inspectors. We are thus dealing with an attempt to secure the production of written statements and mental impressions contained in the files and the mind of the attorney Fortenbaugh without any showing of necessity or any indication or claim that denial of such production would unduly prejudice the preparation of petitioner's case or cause him any hardship or injustice. For aught that appears, the essence of what petitioner seeks either has been revealed to him already through the interrogatories or is readily available to him direct from the witnesses for the asking.

The District Court, after hearing objections to petitioner's request, commanded Fortenbaugh to produce all written statements of witnesses and to state in substance any facts learned through oral statements of witnesses to him. Fortenbaugh was to submit any memoranda he had made of the oral statements so that the court might determine what portions should be revealed to petitioner. All of this was ordered without any showing by petitioner, or any requirement that he make a proper showing, of the necessity for the production of any of this material or any demonstration that denial of production would cause hardship or injustice. The court simply ordered production on the theory that the facts sought were material and were not privileged as constituting attorney-client communications.

In our opinion, neither Rule 26 nor any other rule dealing with discovery contemplates production under such circumstances. That is not because the subject matter is privileged or irrelevant, as those concepts are used in these rules. Here is simply an attempt, without purported necessity or justification, to secure written statements, private memoranda and personal recollections prepared or formed by an adverse party's counsel in the course of his legal duties. As such, it falls outside the arena of discovery and contravenes the public policy underlying the orderly prosecution and defense of legal claims. Not even the most liberal of discovery theories can justify unwarranted inquiries into the files and the mental impressions of an attorney.

Historically, a lawyer is an officer of the court and is bound to work for the advancement of justice while faithfully protecting the rightful interests of his clients. In performing his various duties, however, it is essential that a lawyer work with a certain degree of privacy, free from unnecessary intrusion by opposing parties and their counsel. Proper preparation of a client's case demands that he assemble information, sift what he considers to be the relevant from the irrelevant facts, prepare his legal theories and plan his strategy without undue and needless interference. That is the historical and the necessary way in which lawyers act within the framework of our system of jurisprudence to promote justice and to protect their clients' interests. This work is reflected, of course, in interviews, statements, memoranda, correspondence, briefs, mental impressions, personal beliefs, and countless other tangible and intangible ways—aptly though roughly termed by the Circuit Court of Appeals in this case as the "Work product of the lawyer." Were such materials open to opposing counsel on mere demand, much of what is now put down in writing would remain unwritten. An attorney's thoughts, heretofore inviolate, would not be his own. Inefficiency, unfairness and sharp practices would inevitably develop in the giving of legal advice and in the preparation of cases for trial. The effect on the legal profession would be demoralizing. And the interests of the clients and the cause of justice would be poorly served.

We do not mean to say that all written materials obtained or prepared by an adversary's counsel with an eye toward litigation are necessarily free from discovery in all cases. Where relevant and non-privileged facts remain hidden in an attorney's file and where production of those facts is essential to the preparation of one's case, discovery may properly be had. Such written statements and documents might, under certain circumstances, be admissible in evidence or give clues as to the existence or location of relevant facts. Or they might be useful for purposes of impeachment or corroboration. And production might be justified where the witnesses are no longer available or can be reached only with difficulty. Were production of written statements and documents to be precluded under such circumstances, the liberal ideals of the deposition-discovery portions of the Federal Rules of Civil Procedure would be stripped of much of their meaning. But the general policy against invading the privacy of an attorney's course of preparation is so well recognized and so essential to an orderly working of our system of legal procedure that a burden rests on the one who would invade that privacy to establish adequate reasons to justify production through a subpoena or court order. That burden, we believe, is necessarily implicit in the rules as now constituted.

Rule 30(b), as presently written, gives the trial judge the requisite discretion to make a judgment as to whether discovery should be allowed as to written statements secured from witnesses. But in the instant case there was no room for that discretion to operate in favor of the petitioner. No attempt was made to establish any reason why Fortenbaugh should be forced to produce the written statements. There was only a naked, general demand for these materials as of right and a finding by the District Court that no recognizable privilege was involved. That was insufficient to justify discovery under these circumstances and the court should have sustained the refusal of the tug owners and Fortenbaugh to produce.

But as to oral statements made by witnesses to Fortenbaugh, whether presently in the form of his mental impressions or memoranda, we do not believe that any showing of necessity can be made under the circumstances of this case so as to justify production. Under ordinary conditions, forcing an attorney to repeat or write out all that witnesses have told him and to deliver the account to his adversary gives rise to grave dangers of inaccuracy and untrustworthiness. No legitimate purpose is served by such production. The practice forces the attorney to testify as to what he remembers or what he saw fit to write down regarding witnesses' remarks. Such testimony could not qualify as evidence; and to use it for impeachment or corroborative purposes would make the attorney much less an officer of the court and much more an ordinary witness. The standards of the profession would thereby suffer.

Denial of production of this nature does not mean that any material, non-privileged facts can be hidden from the petitioner in this case. He need not be unduly hindered in the preparation of his case, in the discovery of facts or in his anticipation of his opponents' position. Searching interrogatories directed to Fortenbaugh and the tug owners, production of written documents and statements upon a proper showing and direct interviews with the witnesses themselves all serve to reveal the facts in Fortenbaugh's possession to the fullest possible extent consistent with public policy. Petitioner's counsel frankly admits that he wants the oral statements only to help prepare himself to examine witnesses and to make sure that he has overlooked nothing. That is insufficient under the circumstances to permit him an exception to the policy underlying the privacy of Fortenbaugh's professional activities. If there should be a rare situation justifying production of these matters, petitioner's case is not of that type.
Mr. Justice Jackson, concurring.

* * *

The primary effect of the practice advocated here would be on the legal profession itself. But it too often is overlooked that the lawyer and the law office are indispensable parts of our administration of justice. Law-abiding people can go nowhere else to learn the ever changing and constantly multiplying rules by which they must behave and to obtain redress for their wrongs. The welfare and tone of the legal profession is therefore of prime consequence to society, which would feel the consequences of such a practice as petitioner urges secondarily but certainly. "Discovery" is one of the working tools of the legal profession....

To consider first the most extreme aspect of the requirement in litigation here, we find it calls upon counsel, if he has had any conversations with any of the crews of the vessels in question or of any other, to "set forth in detail the exact provision of any such oral statements or reports." Thus the demand is not for the production of a transcript in existence but calls for the creation of a written statement not in being. But the statement by counsel of what a witness told him is not evidence when written. Plaintiff could not introduce it to prove his case. What, then, is the purpose sought to be served by demanding this of adverse counsel?

Counsel for the petitioner candidly said on argument that he wanted this information to help prepare himself to examine witnesses, to make sure he overlooked nothing. He bases his claim to it in his brief on the view that the Rules were to do away with the old situation where a law suit developed into "a battle of wits between counsel." But a common law trial is and always should be an adversary proceeding. Discovery was hardly intended to enable a learned profession to perform its functions either without wits or on wits borrowed from the adversary.

The real purpose and the probable effect of the practice ordered by the district court would be to put trials on a level even lower than a "battle of wits." I can conceive of no practice more demoralizing to the Bar than to require a lawyer to write out and deliver to his adversary an account of what witnesses have told him. Even if his recollection were perfect, the statement would be his language permeated with his inferences. Every one who has tried it knows that it is almost impossible so fairly to record the expressions and emphasis of a witness that when he testifies in the environment of the court and under the influence of the leading question there will not be departures in some respects. Whenever the testimony of the witness would differ from the "exact" statement the lawyer had delivered, the lawyer's statement would be whipped out to impeach the witness. Counsel producing his adversary's "inexact" statement could lose nothing by saying, "Here is a contradiction, gentlemen of the jury. I do not know whether it is my adversary or his witness who is not telling the truth, but one is not." Of course, if this practice were adopted, that scene would be repeated over and over again. The lawyer who delivers such statements often would find himself branded a deceiver afraid to take the stand to support his own version of the witness's conversation with him, or else he will have to go on the stand to defend his own credibility—perhaps against that of his chief witness, or possibly even his client.

Every lawyer dislikes to take the witness stand and will do so only for grave reasons. This is partly because it is not his role; he is almost invariably a poor witness. But he steps out of professional character to do it. He regrets it; the profession discourages it. But the practice advocated here is one which would force him to be a witness, not as to what he has seen or done but as to other witnesses' stories, and not because he wants to do so but in self-defense.

And what is the lawyer to do who has interviewed one whom he believes to be a biased, lying or hostile witness to get his unfavorable statements and know what to meet? He must record and deliver such statements even though he would not vouch for the credibility of the witness by calling him. Perhaps the other side would not want to call him either, but the attorney is open to the charge of suppressing evidence at the trial if he fails to call such a hostile witness even though he never regarded him as reliable or truthful.

The question remains as to signed statements or those written by witnesses. Such statements are not evidence for the defendant. Nor should I think they ordinarily could be evidence for the plaintiff. But such a statement might be useful for impeachment of the witness who signed it, if he is called and if he departs from the statement. There might be circumstances, too, where impossibility or difficulty of access to the witness or his refusal to respond to requests for information or other facts would show that the interests of justice require that such statements be made available. Production of such statements are governed by Rule 34 and on "showing good cause therefor" the court may order their inspection, copying or photographing. No such application has here been made; the demand is made on the basis of right, not on showing of cause.

I agree to the affirmance of the judgment of the Circuit Court of Appeals which reversed the district court.

Exercise 9-7. *Hickman v. Taylor* Revisited

1. *Hickman* predates the current codification of the work product doctrine in Rule 26(b)(3). Is the code section consistent with the *Hickman* Court's approach to work product?

2. As noted earlier, the *Hickman* case is a rather rare United States Supreme Court case on discovery. It is rare because, in the federal court system,

for the most part, an appellate court can only review "final judgments." By the time the case reaches final judgment, often there is little to be gained by appealing a discovery matter. An exception to this rule is when a party is held in contempt. *See United States v. Ryan*, 402 U.S. 530 (1971). Why was an appeal permitted here?

3. The Court notes that a fact is not protected from discovery simply because a party's lawyer knows it or discovers it. Here, the plaintiff gathered information using other discovery tools, such as interrogatories. Fortenbaugh disclosed information he discovered during this process. What exactly is the Court protecting here?

4. Note that the Court is concerned that, if attorney notes are routinely discoverable, attorneys will be witnesses in cases they are pursuing or defending on behalf of clients. Why is this problematic?

5. Given the rules governing work product, would the court permit discovery of the following information?

   a. In a breach of contract action involving the purported negligent drilling of oil and gas wells resulting in an employee's being injured, the defendant requests "all communications between the plaintiff's legal counsel and its insurers arising out of or related to the investigation of the accident." *See Sundance Energy Oklahoma, LLC v. Dan D. Drilling Corp.*, No. CV-13-991-R, 2014 WL 6306742 (W.D. Okla. Nov. 13, 2014) (forensic investigator's records and communications were protected).

   b. Plaintiff insured brought an action against its insurer for insurance bad faith in the handling of a claim plaintiff made against its policy. The claim involved property damage resulting from a hurricane. Plaintiff requested that the defendant insurer produce the entire file underlying its claim. The file includes notes from an attorney who reviewed the claim. *See Fox Haven of Foxfire Condominium IV Assoc., Inc., v. Nationwide Mut. Fire Ins. Co.*, No. 2:13-CV-399-FtM-29Cm, 2014 WL 6389668 (M.D. Fla. Nov. 14, 2014) (communications with counsel about plaintiff's case privileged, but communications regarding business advice were not).

   c. Plaintiff brings a civil rights action against a city and police officer based on a police shooting. The local prosecutor had conducted an investigation into the shooting to determine whether criminal charges should be filed. No charges were filed against the officer. Plaintiff requests the prosecutor's files from the criminal investigation, which include notes about witness statements. *See Vazquez v. City of New York*, No. 10-CCV-6277, 2014 WL 6356941 (S.D.N.Y. Nov. 14, 2014) (some documents discoverable with "core work product" redacted).

(2) Attorney-Client Privilege

Rule 26(b) permits a party to obtain discovery of "nonprivileged" matter. A variety of statutory and common law privileges are available in the state and federal court systems. A privilege permits a party or non-party to refuse to respond to a discovery request. One of most commonly invoked privileges is the attorney-client privilege. However, there are additional privileges, such as the spousal privilege and the doctor-patient privilege. Because the attorney-client privilege is most relevant for attorneys, it will be the main focus of this section.

A frequently cited case that sets out the elements of the attorney-client privilege is *United States v. United Shoe Machinery Corp.*, 89 F. Supp. 357, 358–59 D. Mass. 1950). In that case, Judge Wyzanski stated the conditions under which the attorney-client privilege applies:

> The privilege applies only if (1) the asserted holder of the privilege is or sought to become a client; (2) the person to whom the communication was made (a) is a member of the bar of a court, or his subordinate and (b) in connection with this communication is acting as a lawyer; (3) the communication relates to a fact of which the attorney was informed (a) by his client (b) without the presence of strangers (c) for the purpose of securing primarily either (i) an opinion on law or (ii) legal services or (iii) assistance in some legal proceeding, and not (d) for the purpose of committing a crime or tort; and (4) the privilege has been (a) claimed and (b) not waived by the client.

Exercise 9-8. When Does the Attorney-Client Privilege Apply?

Lawyers need to know when the attorney-client privilege applies. While the privilege usually is covered in legal ethics classes, it also has implications for discovery, because it is one of the primary objections a lawyer can raise to a discovery request. Based on the definition supplied by Judge Wyzanski in the *United Shoe Machinery Corp.* case, does the privilege apply in the following circumstances?

1. If someone comes to you for consultation regarding a potential lawsuit, and you ultimately do not represent them in the case, is that person a client for purposes of attorney-client privilege?

2. The client comes in and provides information relevant to her case to your paralegal. Is this privileged?

3. Your client asks whether he can start a fire at his annoying neighbor's home. Is this privileged?

4. A translator is present during your consultations with a client because your client does not speak English. Does the translator's presence break the privilege?

5. Your client brings her best friend with her during her consultation with you. Is the ensuing conversation privileged?

6. You and another lawyer at your firm are discussing what a client told you about a pending lawsuit in a crowded elevator on your way to lunch. Is this conversation privileged?

When you represent an individual, it's simple to determine who your client is for purposes of the attorney-client privilege. However, when your client is a corporation, who exactly is the client? The person who is in charge? The person who did something that might make the corporation liable? All employees of the corporation?

Exercise 9-9. Who Is the Client for Purposes of the Privilege? *Upjohn Co. v. United States*

As you read *Upjohn Co. v. United States*, answer the following questions.

1. The Court considers using two different tests to determine who is the client when a corporation is a client. What test does the Court choose and why?

2. What is the purpose of the attorney-client privilege?

3. This case involves the work product doctrine as well. What is the issue concerning the work product doctrine? How does the Court resolve it?

Upjohn Co. v. United States
449 U.S. 383 (1981)

Justice Rehnquist delivered the opinion of the Court.

We granted certiorari in this case to address important questions concerning the scope of the attorney-client privilege in the corporate context and the applicability of the work-product doctrine in proceedings to enforce tax summonses. With respect to the privilege question the parties and various *amici* have described our task as one of choosing between two "tests" which have gained adherents in the courts of appeals. We are acutely aware, however, that we sit to decide concrete cases and not abstract propositions of law. We decline to lay down a broad rule or series of rules to govern all conceivable future questions in this area, even were we able to do so. We can and do, however, conclude that the attorney-client privilege protects the communications involved in this case from compelled disclosure and that the work-product doctrine does apply in tax summons enforcement proceedings.

I

Petitioner Upjohn Co. manufactures and sells pharmaceuticals here and abroad. In January 1976 independent accountants conducting an audit of one of Upjohn's foreign subsidiaries discovered that the subsidiary made payments to or for the benefit of foreign government officials in order to secure government business. The accountants, so informed petitioner, Mr. Gerard Thomas, Upjohn's Vice President, Secretary, and General Counsel. Thomas is a member of the Michigan and New York Bars, and has been Upjohn's General Counsel for 20 years. He consulted with outside counsel and ... Upjohn's Chairman of the Board. It was decided that the company would conduct an internal investigation of what were termed "questionable payments." As part of this investigation the attorneys prepared a letter containing a questionnaire which was sent to "All Foreign General and Area Managers" over the Chairman's signature. The letter began by noting recent disclosures that several American companies made "possibly illegal" payments to foreign government officials and emphasized that the management needed full information concerning any such payments made by Upjohn. The letter indicated that the Chairman had asked Thomas, identified as "the company's General Counsel," "to conduct an investigation for the purpose of determining the nature and magnitude of any payments made by the Upjohn Company or any of its subsidiaries to any employee or official of a foreign government." The questionnaire sought detailed information concerning such payments. Managers were instructed to treat the investigation as "highly confidential" and not to discuss it with anyone other than Upjohn employees who might be helpful in providing the requested information. Responses were to be sent directly to Thomas. Thomas and outside counsel also interviewed the recipients of the questionnaire and some 33 other Upjohn officers or employees as part of the investigation.

On March 26, 1976, the company voluntarily submitted a preliminary report to the Securities and Exchange Commission on Form 8-K disclosing certain questionable payments. A copy of the report was simultaneously submitted to the Internal Revenue Service, which immediately began an investigation to determine the tax consequences of the payments. Special agents conducting the investigation were given lists by Upjohn of all those interviewed and all who had responded to the questionnaire. On November 23, 1976, the Service issued a summons ... demanding production of:

> All files relative to the investigation conducted under the supervision of Gerard Thomas to identify payments to employees of foreign governments and any political contributions made by the Upjohn Company or any of its affiliates since January 1, 1971 and to determine whether any funds of the Upjohn Company had been improperly accounted for on the corporate books during the same period.

> The records should include but not be limited to written questionnaires sent to managers of the Upjohn Company's foreign af-

filiates, and memorandums or notes of the interviews conducted in the United States and abroad with officers and employees of the Upjohn Company and its subsidiaries.

The company declined to produce the documents specified in the second paragraph on the grounds that they were protected from disclosure by the attorney-client privilege and constituted the work product of attorneys prepared in anticipation of litigation. On August 31, 1977, the United States filed a petition seeking enforcement of the summons ... in the United States District Court for the Western District of Michigan. That court adopted the recommendation of a Magistrate who concluded that the summons should be enforced. Petitioners appealed to the Court of Appeals for the Sixth Circuit which rejected the Magistrate's finding of a waiver of the attorney-client privilege, but agreed that the privilege did not apply "[t]o the extent that the communications were made by officers and agents not responsible for directing Upjohn's actions in response to legal advice ... for the simple reason that the communications were not the 'client's.'" The court reasoned that accepting petitioners' claim for a broader application of the privilege would encourage upper-echelon management to ignore unpleasant facts and create too broad a "zone of silence." Noting that Upjohn's counsel had interviewed officials such as the Chairman and President, the Court of Appeals remanded to the District Court so that a determination of who was within the "control group" could be made. In a concluding footnote the court stated that the work-product doctrine "is not applicable to administrative summonses...."

II

... The attorney-client privilege is the oldest of the privileges for confidential communications known to the common law. Its purpose is to encourage full and frank communication between attorneys and their clients and thereby promote broader public interests in the observance of law and administration of justice. The privilege recognizes that sound legal advice or advocacy serves public ends and that such advice or advocacy depends upon the lawyer's being fully informed by the client.... Admittedly complications in the application of the privilege arise when the client is a corporation, which in theory is an artificial creature of the law, and not an individual; but this Court has assumed that the privilege applies when the client is a corporation, and the Government does not contest the general proposition.

The Court of Appeals, however, considered the application of the privilege in the corporate context to present a "different problem," since the client was an inanimate entity and "only the senior management, guiding and integrating the several operations, ... can be said to possess an identity analogous to the corporation as a whole." [This is known as the "control group" test.] ...

[W]e think [the control group test] overlooks the fact that the privilege exists to protect not only the giving of professional advice to those who can act on it but also the giving of information to the lawyer to enable him to give sound and informed advice. The first step in the resolution of any legal problem is ascertaining the factual background and sifting through the facts with an eye to the legally relevant....

In the case of the individual client the provider of information and the person who acts on the lawyer's advice are one and the same. In the corporate context, however, it will frequently be employees beyond the control group as defined by the court below — "officers and agents ... responsible for directing [the company's] actions in response to legal advice" — who will possess the information needed by the corporation's lawyers. Middle-level — and indeed lower-level — employees can, by actions within the scope of their employment, embroil the corporation in serious legal difficulties, and it is only natural that these employees would have the relevant information needed by corporate counsel if he is adequately to advise the client with respect to such actual or potential difficulties....

The control group test adopted by the court below thus frustrates the very purpose of the privilege by discouraging the communication of relevant information by employees of the client to attorneys seeking to render legal advice to the client corporation. The attorney's advice will also frequently be more significant to noncontrol group members than to those who officially sanction the advice, and the control group test makes it more difficult to convey full and frank legal advice to the employees who will put into effect the client corporation's policy.

The narrow scope given the attorney-client privilege by the court below not only makes it difficult for corporate attorneys to formulate sound advice when their client is faced with a specific legal problem but also threatens to limit the valuable efforts of corporate counsel to ensure their client's compliance with the law. In light of the vast and complicated array of regulatory legislation confronting the modern corporation, corporations, unlike most individuals, "constantly go to lawyers to find out how to obey the law," Burnham, *The Attorney-Client Privilege in the Corporate Arena*, 24 Bus. Law. 901, 913 (1969), particularly since compliance with the law in this area is hardly an instinctive matter. The test adopted by the court below is difficult to apply in practice, though no abstractly formulated and unvarying "test" will necessarily enable courts to decide questions such as this with mathematical precision. But if the purpose of the attorney-client privilege is to be served, the attorney and client must be able to predict with some degree of certainty whether particular discussions will be protected. An uncertain privilege, or one which purports to be certain but results in widely varying applications by the courts, is little better than no privilege at all. The very terms of the test adopted by the

court below suggest the unpredictability of its application. The test restricts
the availability of the privilege to those officers who play a "substantial
role" in deciding and directing a corporation's legal response. Disparate
decisions in cases applying this test illustrate its unpredictability.

The communications at issue were made by Upjohn employees to counsel
for Upjohn acting as such, at the direction of corporate superiors in order
to secure legal advice from counsel. As the Magistrate found, "Mr. Thomas
consulted with the Chairman of the Board and outside counsel and thereafter conducted a factual investigation to determine the nature and extent
of the questionable payments *and to be in a position to give legal advice to
the company with respect to the payments.*" (Emphasis supplied.) Information,
not available from upper-echelon management, was needed to supply a
basis for legal advice concerning compliance with securities and tax laws,
foreign laws, currency regulations, duties to shareholders, and potential
litigation in each of these areas. The communications concerned matters
within the scope of the employees' corporate duties, and the employees
themselves were sufficiently aware that they were being questioned in order
that the corporation could obtain legal advice. The questionnaire identified
Thomas as "the company's General Counsel" and referred in its opening
sentence to the possible illegality of payments such as the ones on which
information was sought. A statement of policy accompanying the questionnaire clearly indicated the legal implications of the investigation. The
policy statement was issued "in order that there be no uncertainty in the
future as to the policy with respect to the practices which are the subject
of this investigation." It began "Upjohn will comply with all laws and regulations," and stated that commissions or payments "will not be used as a
subterfuge for bribes or illegal payments" and that all payments must be
"proper and legal." Any future agreements with foreign distributors or agents
were to be approved "by a company attorney" and any questions concerning
the policy were to be referred "to the company's General Counsel." This
statement was issued to Upjohn employees worldwide, so that even those
interviewees not receiving a questionnaire were aware of the legal implications of the interviews. Pursuant to explicit instructions from the Chairman
of the Board, the communications were considered "highly confidential"
when made, and have been kept confidential by the company. Consistent
with the underlying purposes of the attorney-client privilege, these communications must be protected against compelled disclosure.

The Court of Appeals declined to extend the attorney-client privilege
beyond the limits of the control group test for fear that doing so would
entail severe burdens on discovery and create a broad "zone of silence"
over corporate affairs. Application of the attorney-client privilege to communications such as those involved here, however, puts the adversary in
no worse position than if the communications had never taken place. The

privilege only protects disclosure of communications; it does not protect disclosure of the underlying facts by those who communicated with the attorney.... Here the Government was free to question the employees who communicated with Thomas and outside counsel. Upjohn has provided the IRS with a list of such employees, and the IRS has already interviewed some 25 of them. While it would probably be more convenient for the Government to secure the results of petitioner's internal investigation by simply subpoenaing the questionnaires and notes taken by petitioner's attorneys, such considerations of convenience do not overcome the policies served by the attorney-client privilege. As Justice Jackson noted in his concurring opinion in *Hickman v. Taylor*, 329 U.S. at 516, "Discovery was hardly intended to enable a learned profession to perform its functions ... on wits borrowed from the adversary."

Needless to say, we decide only the case before us, and do not undertake to draft a set of rules which should govern challenges to investigatory subpoenas.... While such a "case-by-case" basis may to some slight extent undermine desirable certainty in the boundaries of the attorney-client privilege, it obeys the spirit of the Rules. At the same time we conclude that the narrow "control group test" sanctioned by the Court of Appeals, in this case cannot, consistent with "the principles of the common law as ... interpreted ... in the light of reason and experience," Fed. Rule Evid. 501, govern the development of the law in this area.

III

Our decision that the communications by Upjohn employees to counsel are covered by the attorney-client privilege disposes of the case so far as the responses to the questionnaires and any notes reflecting responses to interview questions are concerned. The summons reaches further, however, and Thomas has testified that his notes and memoranda of interviews go beyond recording responses to his questions. To the extent that the material subject to the summons is not protected by the attorney-client privilege as disclosing communications between an employee and counsel, we must reach the ruling by the Court of Appeals that the work-product doctrine does not apply to summonses....

* * *

The Government stresses that interviewees are scattered across the globe and that Upjohn has forbidden its employees to answer questions it considers irrelevant. The [exception to the work product doctrine discussed in] *Hickman*, however, did not apply to "oral statements made by witnesses ... whether presently in the form of [the attorney's] mental impressions or memoranda."[329 U.S.] at 512. As to such material the Court did "not believe that any showing of necessity can be made under the circumstances of this case so as to justify production.... If there should be a rare situation justifying production of these matters petitioner's case is not of that type." *Id.* at 512–13. Forcing an attorney to disclose notes and memoranda of witnesses' oral statements is particularly disfavored because it tends to reveal the attorney's mental processes.

* * *

... It is clear that the Magistrate applied the wrong standard when he concluded that the Government had made a sufficient showing of necessity to overcome the protections of the work-product doctrine. The Magistrate applied the "substantial need" and "without undue hardship" standard articulated in the first part of Rule 26(b)(3). The notes and memoranda sought by the Government here, however, are work product based on oral statements. If they reveal communications, they are, in this case, protected by the attorney-client privilege. To the extent they do not reveal communications, they reveal the attorneys' mental processes in evaluating the communications. As Rule 26 and *Hickman* make clear, such work product cannot be disclosed simply on a showing of substantial need and inability to obtain the equivalent without undue hardship.

While we are not prepared at this juncture to say that such material is always protected by the work-product rule, we think a far stronger showing of necessity and unavailability by other means than was made by the Government or applied by the Magistrate in this case would be necessary to compel disclosure. Since the Court of Appeals thought that the work-product protection was never applicable in an enforcement proceeding such as this, and since the Magistrate whose recommendations the District Court adopted applied too lenient a standard of protection, we think the best procedure with respect to this aspect of the case would be to reverse the judgment of the Court of Appeals for the Sixth Circuit and remand the case to it for such further proceedings in connection with the work-product claim as are consistent with this opinion.

Accordingly, the judgment of the Court of Appeals is reversed, and the case remanded for further proceedings.

It is so ordered.

Exercise 9-10. *Upjohn* Revisited

1. After the *Upjohn* case, is it still difficult to determine who is covered by the attorney-client privilege? Does the *Upjohn* court set a specific standard?

2. The client's identity in the corporate context can create ethical dilemmas for counsel. Model Rule of Professional Conduct 1.13 makes clear that when an attorney represents an organization, his or her duty is to the organization. Sometimes corporations argue that the employee who engaged

in wrongdoing was not acting on behalf of the corporation at the time he or she did so. Yet, as an attorney representing the corporation, you would like to ask that employee for his or her version of the facts. As an attorney talking to an employee/witness, you must be clear about who you represent. The employee may reasonably believe, given that she works for the corporation, that you are her counsel as well. Thus, the employee may say something she reasonably believes is privileged only to find out that the corporation will use it against her to avoid its own liability. Yet, once a lawyer reveals that she really represents the corporation, do you think the employee will be very forthcoming?

4. The Tools of Discovery

Now that you know the scope of and some common exceptions to discovery, it's time to explore the various tools that are available to parties in the discovery process. Go back to the chapter problem and begin to think about what information you need for your client's case against Piper and Hartzell. Recall that your client is claiming wrongful death. It's also useful to look at this fact pattern from Piper's and Hartzell's perspectives. Thus, throughout this section, you'll be asked to consider how you might use these tools to gather information for both the plaintiff and the defendants in that litigation.

a. Initial Disclosures

Initial disclosures are distinguishable from other available discovery tools in that a party is simply entitled to this information from an opposing party. Thus, a party need not ask for the types of information covered by the initial disclosures. While the initial disclosures are required in all federal civil cases except those exempted by Rule 26(a)(1)(B), most state court systems do not have an initial disclosure requirement. In states without initial disclosures, a party only receives information from the opposing side by requesting it.

Exercise 9-11. Initial Disclosures

Read the required disclosures listed in Rule 26(a)(1)(A). Based on your reading of the Rule, answer the following questions:

1. Who must disclose?

2. To whom?

3. What must be disclosed?

   a. Names and contact information for which individuals?

   b. Copies of which documents and electronic information?

> c. What information related to damages?
>
> d. Copies of what type of insurance?
>
> 4. When are they due?
>
> 5. Would a defendant in a tort case involving a car accident have to disclose pursuant to Rule 26(a)(1)(A) a witness that supported the plaintiff's position?

b. Depositions

Depositions are one of the most valuable, and the most expensive, tools in an attorney's discovery arsenal. Depositions allow an attorney to ask a witness or party questions under penalty of perjury that the witness or party must answer, subject to any claims of privilege or protective orders. Depositions are valuable in a variety of contexts. From a defendant's point of view, they permit a defendant to nail down the plaintiff's version of the facts. From a plaintiff's point of view, they allow a plaintiff to question the defendant about facts within its particular knowledge. Depositions also provide attorneys with an opportunity to see how a witness or party handles live questions. But depositions go well beyond parties. Depositions are one of the few discovery tools that parties can use on non-parties. Subject to the subpoena power of the courts for non-parties, an attorney can depose anyone with information relevant to a claim or defense in the action.

Let's go back to the *Piper* case. Who would you want to depose if you represented the plaintiff? If you represented Piper or Hartzell, who would you want to depose?

One of the main downsides to depositions is the cost. The party taking the deposition pays for the costs, including hiring a court reporter. Court reporters charge a fee for depositions, including a per page price for creating a transcript. In addition, if the deposition is videotaped, there are costs associated with creating the video as well. You also have attorney time in preparation for the deposition as well as in taking the deposition. Consider the depositions in the *Piper* case in light of their cost. Attorneys often limit depositions to the most important potential witnesses because of these costs.

As noted above, an attorney can request that a deposition be taken by videotape under the Rules. There are several advantages to videotaped depositions. First, if a witness will be unavailable at trial, this provides you with a means of presenting his or her testimony that is more compelling than simply reading a dry transcript. In addition, videotape is particularly useful in cross-examinations. It is very powerful for the fact finder to see a witness or party taking a position in court that is subsequently contradicted by the witness's own videotaped testimony during a deposition. Finally, videotape is a way to control a difficult witness or opposing counsel. Some people will behave better if they know they are being filmed. Thus, if you believe a witness or party will be uncooperative, videotaping the deponent may be helpful. In addition, if the deponent is still evasive in spite of the videotape, videotape footage is very useful if you must move to compel answers from that deponent. To get a sense of how evasive a deponent can be, search out Justin Bieber's deposition testimony on YouTube. Do you think it is helpful to a party's position in a lawsuit if he or she is evasive in responding to deposition questions? As an attorney, would you advise your client to do so?

Parties must attend depositions. Non-party witnesses, because they are not parties to the lawsuit, are not under an obligation to submit themselves to a deposition. Thus, in order to guarantee the attendance of a non-party, the witness must be subpoenaed under Rule 45. The witness must then attend or risk being held in contempt of court. A non-party who believes he or she has been improperly subpoenaed for a deposition may make a motion to quash the subpoena. If the court agrees with the witness that the deposition is outside the scope of discovery, it will grant the motion, and the deposition will not occur.

Sometimes the non-party witness an attorney wishes to depose is a friendly witness. Can you imagine how someone might feel receiving a subpoena? Do you think they still will be as friendly to your client's case? One way to offset the fear generated by a subpoena is to let the witness know that subpoenas are standard practice for non-party depositions in civil cases. This will also offer you the opportunity to schedule the deposition at a time that is convenient for the witness. While the rule states that a party must provide "reasonable notice" of a deposition, it is common to consult with opposing counsel and/or the witness (for those not represented by counsel) to make certain that the deponent will be available on the date set for the deposition. Note that when it comes to parties, attorneys must make arrangements for the time and place of a deposition through a party's counsel when that party is represented by counsel in the litigation.

Federal Rules of Civil Procedure 28 through 32 govern deposition practice. Rule 28 sets out before whom a deposition can be taken. Rule 29(a) provides that parties may stipulate about the time, place, and manner in which a deposition will be taken as well as stipulate to other discovery matters. Rule 30 is the main rule covering oral depositions. Rule 31 sets out a process for taking depositions by written questions, an alternative to asking questions live for the first time during the deposition. Rule 32 governs how parties can use depositions in court proceedings. Finally, the not-often-used Rule 27 permits a would-be party to take a deposition before a lawsuit is filed, but the rule applies in very limited circumstances, as the next exercise shows.

Exercise 9-12. Reading and Applying Rule 27

Read Rule 27. Based on your reading of the rule, what does it require? Rule 27 only permits a pre-lawsuit deposition to perpetuate testimony when a potential plaintiff cannot file the lawsuit prior to taking that deposition. Given this, can the plaintiff in the following fact patterns take a deposition pursuant to Rule 27?

1. A woman is interested in suing local police officers and the local police department, because a police officer shot and killed her father during a traffic stop. However, she does not know what happened during the stop or which officer actually shot her father. Can she depose the chief of police to determine this information prior to filing her lawsuit? See *In re Petition of Sheila Roberts Ford*, 170 F.R.D. 504 (M.D. Ala. 1997) (pre-lawsuit deposition not permitted).

2. A trucking company is considering suing a truck driver who acted as its subcontractor for losses the company incurred due to an accident involving the driver. The driver is dying of cancer and is not expected to live for more than one more month. Can the trucking company depose the driver prior to filing its lawsuit?

3. An investor wishes to sue her securities brokerage firm for securities fraud. The investor's main investment advisor at the company is being transferred to the company's Berlin, Germany office. Can the investor take the deposition of the advisor prior to filing the lawsuit?

Exercise 9-13. Reading Rule 30

The following exercises are designed to walk you through Rule 30 and pick out the important points in that rule.

1. Read Rule 30(a). Based on your reading of that rule:
   a. Who may a party depose?
   b. What must a party do to guarantee the attendance of a non-party at a deposition?
   c. What is the default limit on the number of depositions a party may take?
   d. How does a party obtain more depositions than the limit?
   e. Under what other circumstances must a party obtain leave of court to take a deposition?

2. Read Rule 30(b). Based on your reading of that rule:
   a. What must be in the notice of deposition?
   b. Can a party or witness be asked to produce documents at the deposition? If so, how?
   c. What means can a party use to record the deposition?
   d. How do you notice a deposition when you need information from an organization, such as a corporation, and are unsure who has that information within that organization?

3. Read Rule 30(c). Based on your reading of that rule:
   a. Can you object at a deposition?
   b. If an attorney objects to a question, must the witness answer it?

c. Under what circumstances can an attorney instruct a witness or party being deposed not to answer a question?

4. Read Rule 30(d). Based on your reading of that rule:

a. How long is a deposition?

b. Under what circumstances will a court permit a deposition for a longer period of time?

c. Under what circumstances may a deponent terminate a deposition?

d. What forms of a relief can a deponent who terminates a deposition seek?

5. Read Rule 30(e). Based on your reading of that rule:

a. Can a deponent or party review the transcript or recording of a deposition?

b. Can a deponent or party make changes to the transcript or recording?

6. Read Rule 30(g). Based on your reading of that rule:

a. What may happen if a party noticing a deposition fails to inform opposing counsel that the deposition is not going forward?

b. What may happen if a party fails to subpoena a non-party witness who fails to attend his or her deposition?

You now know the basic rule regarding taking depositions. Whose deposition will you notice on behalf of the estate of the decedent in the *Piper* case? If you represent Piper or Hartzell, whose deposition will you notice? What types of questions will you ask?

Rule 30(b)(6) covers noticing depositions of organizations when you are not certain who in the organization has the relevant knowledge. In addition, sometimes a party knows precisely whom they wish to depose in an organization. For example, the plaintiffs in the *Piper* chapter problem likely will want to depose people who have knowledge about the propeller's design. However, as the plaintiff's attorney, you probably will not know whose deposition to notice to obtain this information. Noticing a deposition under Rule 30(b)(6) asking for the person who has knowledge of the propeller design requires that Hartzell produce that person.

Exercise 9-14. Depositions by Remote Means

The internet has provided remote access to potential deponents. Under what circumstances should the court permit a deposition by Skype or some other internet conferencing provider? *Delgado v. Magical Cruise Co.* discusses this issue in the context of a plaintiff who resides outside the United States.

1. The defendant uses both a motion to quash and a motion for a protective order. Look up these two terms. What's the difference between these two procedures?

2. Why does the court permit a video deposition of the plaintiff in this case?

3. Why might the defendant prefer to have the plaintiff present for his or her deposition?

4. Why was the plaintiff not permitted to depose a representative of the defendant? Does this seem fair to you?

Delgado v. Magical Cruise Co.

Case No. 6:15-cv-2130-Orl-4aTBS (M.D. Fla. May 30, 2017)

Thomas B. Smith, Magistrate Judge

ORDER

Pending before the Court are Defendant's Motion for Protective Order, Motion to Quash, and Motion to Compel Plaintiff to apply for a Visa, and Defendant's Motion for Protective Order and Motion to Quash Plaintiff's Unilateral Notice of Defendant's 30(b)(6) Corporate Representative Deposition. The Court has reviewed Plaintiff Jorge Delgado's responses to the motions and heard oral argument.

Background

Delgado served as a crewmember aboard Defendant's ships. In April 2014, during the course of his shipboard employment, Delgado suffered a herniated disk injury as a result of the alleged negligence of Defendant. Delgado was medically disembarked and repatriated to his native country of Peru. In Lima, he received medical care and treatment provided by Defendant's network of doctors. Delgado represents that on February 23, 2015, Dr. Gomez declared that he had reached maximum medical improvement for his injury. This lawsuit was filed in December 2015.

Although the parties' initial case management meeting was held on May 11, 2016 (thus starting the period allowed for discovery) and the discovery deadline is set to expire June 5, 2017, neither party has taken the deposition of the other. On May 15, 2017, Delgado noticed his own deposition to occur on May 25, 2017 "via Skype." On May 18, 2017, Delgado served a Notice of Taking Deposition of Defendant's corporate representative, to occur May 30, 2017. Defendant objects to both depositions on various grounds. When asked at hearing why Defendant did not notice Delgado's deposition, its counsel said Defendant made a "business decision" to wait until after the April 24, 2017 mediation to determine whether it was necessary to depose Delgado. When Delgado was asked about his own delay in seeking to depose Defendant's corporate representative, his lawyer claimed that defense counsel have "refused to produce their calendars," thus forcing him to unilaterally schedule the deposition to occur before the discovery cut-off.

Motion regarding the taking of Delgado's deposition

Rule 26(c) allows the Court to enter a protective order, for good cause, to protect a party from annoyance, embarrassment, oppression, or undue burden or expense. Fed. R. Civ. P. 26(c)(1). Defendant relies on the rule here, and objects to the unilateral scheduling of Delgado's deposition via Skype, arguing that Delgado should be compelled to apply for a visa in order to appear in Florida for his deposition and "possible" Rule 35 examination. Defendant also seeks an extension of time to complete Delgado's deposition and "if necessary" Rule 35 examination, and also requests an extension until July 1 for Defendant's expert physician disclosures. Defendant requests attorney's fees and costs associated with bringing its motion. The Court finds that for the most part, the motion is without merit.

The last minute and unilateral scheduling of Delgado's deposition by Delgado would normally be enough to warrant quashing the notice. But at hearing, Delgado's attorney represented that visa difficulties will most likely preclude his client's presence at trial, making testimony by remote means essential to preserve Delgado's testimony for trial. As Defendant did not timely attempt to take Plaintiff's deposition for reasons of its own, Delgado cannot be faulted for setting it himself.

Depositions by remote means are not unusual, given the strides of technology, and it is undisputed that Delgado needs but does not have the visa necessary to enter the United States for this purpose. In addition, Delgado represents that he is an unemployed seaman with scarce financial means and travel for this purpose is a great economic hardship. While the Court acknowledges that deposing Delgado from Peru via Skype is not as desirable as a face to face deposition in Florida, to the extent this is a burden on Defendant, such burden is not "undue" under the circumstances. *See* Rule 30(b)(4) (allowing deposition "by remote means"); Balu v. Costa Crociere S.P.A., No. 11-60031-CIV, 2011 U.S. Dist. LEXIS 85299, 2011 WL 3359681, at *2 (S.D. Fla. Aug. 3, 2011) (noting "depositions are now readily taken inexpensively by internet video (e.g., Skype) or through somewhat more expensive, but still efficient, video conferencing facilities."); Hernandez v. Hendrix Produce, Inc., 297 F.R.D. 538, 541 (S.D. Ga. 2014) ("Skype depositions have been used where travel is cost prohibitive" — collecting cases); In re Willingham, No. 3:11-AP-00269-JAF, 2014 Bankr. LEXIS 3180, 2014 WL 3697556, at *4 (Bankr. M.D. Fla. July 18, 2014) ("ample case law recognizes that a videoconference deposition can be an adequate substitute for an in-person deposition, particularly when significant expenses are at issue" — collecting cases). As noted in a case cited by Defendant: "[I]f a plaintiff demonstrates hardship or burden that outweighs any prejudice to the defendant, the general rule requiring a plaintiff to appear for deposition in the forum 'may yield to the exigencies of the particular case.'" Arval Serv. Lease S.A. v. Clifton, No. 3:14-CV-1047-J-

39MCR, 2015 U.S. Dist. LEXIS 183645, 2015 WL 12818837, at *3 (M.D. Fla. June 23, 2015), quoting Palma v. Safe Hurricane Shutters, Inc., 2009 U.S. Dist. LEXIS 22704, 2009 WL 653305, *4 (S.D. Fla. Mar. 12, 2009). Here, I find no reason to compel Delgado to apply for a visa or incur the expense of traveling to Florida for his deposition.

* * *

Now, Defendant's motion is denied to the extent it seeks to quash the deposition of Delgado, compel Delgado to obtain a visa in order to come to Florida, for an award of costs, and for an extension of time to make expert witness disclosures. Defendant's motion is granted to the extent it seeks an extension of time to complete Delgado's deposition, as follows: Delgado may be deposed in Peru by remote means (Skype, videoconferencing or similar) at a time mutually convenient to the parties, but no later than July 31, 2017. If taking the deposition by videographic means proves to be demonstrably insufficient and Defendant can show good cause, Defendant may move to tax the costs of defense counsel taking the deposition in person in Peru. Consistent with the requirements of the Case Management and Scheduling Order, any discovery conducted after the dispositive motions date will not be available for summary judgment purposes and the delay in taking this deposition is not grounds for extension of the summary judgment deadline.

Motion regarding the taking of Defendant's deposition

Defendant moves for a protective order and to quash Delgado's unilateral Notice of Deposition of Defendant's 30(b)(6) Corporate Representative, contending that it was not timely served, was not coordinated with defense counsel, and Defendant's chosen counsel is not available on the date selected, or any other date prior to the expiration of discovery.

Rule 30(b)(1) provides that "[a] party who wants to depose a person by oral questions must give reasonable written notice to every other party." Fed. R. Civ. P. 30(b)(1). Pursuant to our local rule: "Unless otherwise stipulated by all interested parties…, a party desiring to take the deposition of any person upon oral examination shall give at least fourteen (14) days' notice in writing to every other party to the action and to the deponent (if the deponent if not a party)." L. R. 3.02. As the Notice of Taking a May 30, 2017 Deposition of Defendant's corporate representative was served on May 18 (Doc. 32-1), it is untimely.

Delgado does not dispute the untimeliness of the Notice, contending only that as defense counsel "refused to produce their calendars to facilitate scheduling," Delgado's counsel "had no choice but to notice the deposition to occur before the discovery cutoff." Delgado suggests a discovery extension would remedy the objection, noting that, although Defendant is at fault for not producing calendars or providing sworn affidavits as to counsel's stated unavailability, Delgado's counsel is "nevertheless … willing to confer in good faith to coordinate mutually agreeable times and dates for the depositions." I am not persuaded. Although Delgado's counsel claims that he "had no choice but to notice the deposition" for this time, I disagree. Delgado had a year in which to depose Defendant. He chose to wait until the waning days of discovery to serve his Notice. There are consequences to such a choice. I find no showing of good cause for the unreasonable delay evident here. Therefore, I see no reason to extend the discovery deadline to accommodate Delgado's failure to timely secure Defendant's deposition. Defendant's motion is GRANTED to the extent it seeks to preclude the taking of the corporate deposition.

Defendant seeks an award of reasonable fees and costs associated with bringing the motion, under Fed. R. Civ. P. 26(c)(3) (incorporating Rule 37(a)(5)'s award of expenses for motions for protective order). I am not persuaded. The course of conduct evidenced in the papers and at hearing make it clear that counsel on both sides share responsibility for the situation giving rise to these motions. Accordingly, the motion is DENIED as to fees and costs. *See* Rule 37(a)(5)(A)(iii) (no costs "if other circumstances make an award of expenses unjust").

DONE and ORDERED in Orlando, Florida on May 30, 2017.

Note on Objections During Depositions

Rule 32 governs the use of depositions during court proceedings. As Rule 32(a)(2) suggests, one of the main uses of a deposition during trial is for impeachment. Rule 32(a)(4) permits its use when a witness is unavailable at the time of trial. In addition, a party can use deposition testimony during trial for any other purpose permitted by the Rules of Evidence. Because an attorney can use deposition testimony at trial, one issue that comes up during depositions is objections—when to make them, what types of objections an attorney can make, and what the implications are of not making an objection during a deposition.

Rule 32(d) governs when a party's attorney waives objections by not making them during a deposition. Objections to the notice of depositions and to the officer's qualifications are easily waived under Rule 32(d)(1) and (2). However, objections of this sort are rare. Rule 32(d)(3) explains which objections are waived and which are not if they are not made during the deposition. It's important to know this so that you make appropriate objections during a deposition and don't waive any valid objections.

Read Rule 32(d) again. Beginning with Rule 32(d)(3)(A), the rule explains that objections related to a deponent's competence, the relevance of testimony, or the materiality of testimony are not waived by an attorney's failure to object on this basis during the deposition. However, this rule has a caveat. If the grounds for objection could have been corrected during the deposition and the attorney did not make an objection, it is waived. Given that possibility, would you make an objection during a deposition based on competence, relevance, or materiality?

Rule 32(d)(2)(B) states that objections as to any error or irregularity during the deposition are waived if related to the manner in which the deposition is taken, such as the form of a question or answer, the oath, a party's conduct, or any other matter that could have been corrected at the time of the deposition. This is important to know because attorneys sometimes ask questions that are not properly phrased during a deposition. If you do not object to the manner in which the question is posed, you will waive that objection. For example, one common objection of this sort is based on compound questions. These are questions that actually consist of two or more questions. The problem with such questions is that it can be difficult to know which question the deponent actually is answering. An objection can result in the deposing attorney breaking the question up into its component parts and thereby curing the defect and clarifying the deponent's answer.

Note that Rule 32(b) makes clear that, subject to Rule 32(d)(3), an attorney can still make an objection to deposition testimony at trial as if the deponent were testifying live. So, many objections are preserved for trial. However, that does not mean that attorneys do not object during depositions even though the particular objection is preserved. Why might an attorney still object even though she may raise the objection at trial without fear of waiver? Some attorneys representing deponents tell the deponent to listen carefully to any objections. Attorneys sometimes use objections to "coach" witnesses. *See, e.g., Community Assoc. Underwrites of America, Inc. v. Queensboro Flooring Corp.*, No. 3:10-CV-1559, 2014 WL 3055358 (M.D. Pa. July 3, 2014) (party moved for sanctions in part because attorney "coached" witness using objections). For example, if an attorney objects that a question has already been asked and answered by the deponent, this clues the deponent in that he or she should answer consistently with a prior answer. Does this sound ethically questionable to you?

Finally, an objection raised during a deposition does not generally result in a witness's not answering the question. Aside from privileged matter or matter protected by a protective order under Rule 26(c), the party must answer the question even though an attorney raised an objection. *See* Fed. R. Civ. P. 30(c)(2). An attorney may only instruct a deponent not to answer if the matter is privileged, covered by a protective order, or if the attorney intends to seek a protective order to prohibit disclosure.

c. Interrogatories to Parties

Interrogatories are written questions that one party propounds on another party to which the receiving party must respond. They cannot be used on non-parties. Like other forms of discovery, the receiving party may object if it believes that a particular interrogatory is objectionable. Interrogatories are governed by Rule 33. They have the advantage of being very inexpensive to propound, but they can be costly to answer.

Think about the *Piper* case again. What questions would you ask Piper and Hartzell? If you represented Piper, what questions would you ask the plaintiff?

Exercise 9-15. Rule 33 and Interrogatories

Read Rule 33. Based on your reading of the rule, answer the following questions.

1. How many interrogatories is a party permitted to serve in a federal civil case? Many states have no limit on the number of interrogatories a party may propound on another party. Find out if the state in which you intend to practice has a limit.

2. If a party wishes to serve more interrogatories than permitted, how does it go about increasing this amount?

3. Is an interrogatory to a plaintiff proper if it requests the facts supporting a particular contention in the complaint?

4. How long does a party have to respond to interrogatories?

5. What does a party do if she needs more time to respond to a set of interrogatories?

6. What happens if a party fails to object to an interrogatory that it subsequently finds objectionable?

7. Who signs the response to interrogatories?

8. How are interrogatories used at trial?

9. How may a party respond to an interrogatory if the information requested must be culled out of business records?

10. Draft three interrogatories on behalf of the plaintiff in *Piper* directed at Piper. What are some objections Piper might raise to your interrogatories?

11. Draft three interrogatories on Piper's behalf directed at the plaintiff. What are some of the objections the plaintiff might raise to your interrogatories?

---

d. Requests for Documents, Tangible Things, and Entering Land

Rule 34 permits a party to request documents, including data compilations, tangible things, as well as entry onto land or property. Like depositions, an attorney may make these requests to non-parties as well, but must do so by subpoena under Rule 45. Unlike interrogatories and depositions, there are no limits on the number of requests a party can make, although if such requests become too burdensome, they are subject to the limitations set out in Rule 26(b).

Exercise 9-16. *Zubulake v. UBS Warburg LLC*

As you read the *Zubulake* decision, answer the following questions.

1. When UBS refused to provide additional e-mails that were responsive to Zubulake's document request, what action did Zubulake's attorney take?

2. Who generally pays for the costs of document requests?

3. Judge Scheindlin creates a seven-factor test to determine whether the costs of discovery should be shifted to another party. What is her test? Determine whether the jurisdiction in which you intend to practice follows it.

Zubulake v. UBS Warburg LLC

217 F.R.D. 309 (S.D.N.Y. 2003)

Scheindlin, District Judge.

The world was a far different place in 1849, when Henry David Thoreau opined (in an admittedly broader context) that "[t]he process of discovery is very simple." [HENRY DAVID THOREAU, A WEEK ON THE CONCORD AND MERRIMACK RIVERS (1849)]. That hopeful maxim has given way to rapid technological advances, requiring new solutions to old problems. The issue presented here is one such problem, recast in light of current technology: To what extent is inaccessible electronic data discoverable, and who should pay for its production?

I. Introduction

... [T]he reliance on broad discovery has hit a roadblock. As individuals and corporations increasingly do business electronically—using computers to create and store documents, make deals, and exchange e-mails—the universe of discoverable material has expanded exponentially. The more information there is to discover, the more expensive it is to discover all the relevant information until, in the end, "discovery is not just about uncovering the truth, but also about how much of the truth the parties can afford to disinter." [*Rowe Entm't, Inc. v. William Morris Agency, Inc.*, 205 F.R.D. 421, 423 (S.D.N.Y. 2002).]

This case provides a textbook example of the difficulty of balancing the competing needs of broad discovery and manageable costs. Laura Zubulake is suing UBS Warburg LLC, UBS Warburg, and UBS AG (collectively, "UBS" or the "Firm") under Federal, State and City law for gender discrimination and illegal retaliation. Zubulake's case is certainly not frivolous[8] and if she prevails, her damages may be substantial.[9] She contends that key evidence is located in various e-mails exchanged among UBS employees that now exist only on backup tapes and perhaps other archived media. According to UBS, restoring those e-mails would cost approximately $175,000.00, exclusive of attorney time in reviewing the e-mails. Zubulake now moves for an order compelling UBS to produce those e-mails at its expense.

II. Background A. Zubulake's Lawsuit

UBS hired Zubulake on August 23, 1999, as a director and senior salesperson on its U.S. Asian Equities Sales Desk (the "Desk"), where she reported to Dominic Vail, the Desk's manager. At the time she was hired, Zubulake was told that she would be considered for Vail's position if and when it became vacant.

In December 2000, Vail indeed left his position to move to the Firm's London office. But Zubulake was not considered for his position, and the Firm instead hired Matthew Chapin as director of the Desk. Zubulake alleges that from the outset Chapin treated her differently than the other members of the Desk, all of whom were male. In particular, Chapin "undermined Ms. Zubulake's ability to perform her job by, *inter alia:* (a) ridiculing and belittling her in front of co-workers; (b) excluding her from work-related outings with male co-workers and clients; (c) making sexist remarks in her presence; and (d) isolating her from the other senior salespersons on the Desk by seating her apart from them." No such actions were taken against any of Zubulake's male co-workers.

... On February 15, 2002, Zubulake filed the instant action, suing [UBS] for sex discrimination and retaliation under Title VII, the New York State Human Rights Law, and the Administrative Code of the City of New York. UBS timely answered on March 12, 2002, denying the allegations....

B. The Discovery Dispute

Discovery in this action commenced on or about June 3, 2002, when Zubulake served UBS with her first document request. At issue here is request number twenty-eight, for "[a]ll documents concerning any communication by or between UBS employees concerning Plaintiff." The term document in Zubulake's request "includ[es], without limitation, electronic or computerized data compilations." On July 8, 2002, UBS responded by

---

8. Indeed, Zubulake has already produced a sort of "smoking gun": an e-mail suggesting that she be fired "ASAP" after her EEOC charge was filed, in part so that she would not be eligible for year-end bonuses.

9. At the time she was terminated, Zubulake's salary was approximately $500,000. Were she to receive full back pay and front pay, Zubulake estimates that she may be entitled to as much as $13,000,000 in damages, not including punitive damages or attorney's fees.

producing approximately 350 pages of documents, including approximately 100 pages of e-mails. UBS also objected to a substantial portion of Zubulake's requests.

* * *

UBS ... produced no additional e-mails and insisted that its initial production (the 100 pages of e-mails) was complete. As UBS's opposition to the instant motion makes clear—although it remains unsaid—UBS never searched for responsive e-mails on any of its backup tapes. To the contrary, UBS informed Zubulake that the cost of producing e-mails on backup tapes would be prohibitive (estimated at the time at approximately $300,000.00).

Zubulake, believing that [an earlier agreement concerning discovery] included production of e-mails from backup tapes, objected to UBS's non-production. In fact, Zubulake *knew* that there were additional responsive e-mails that UBS had failed to produce because she herself had produced approximately 450 pages of e-mail correspondence. Clearly, numerous responsive e-mails had been created and deleted at UBS, and Zubulake wanted them.

On December 2, 2002, the parties ... appeared before Judge Gorenstein, who ordered UBS to produce for deposition a person with knowledge of UBS's e-mail retention policies in an effort to determine whether the backup tapes contained the deleted e-mails and the burden of producing them. In response, UBS produced Christopher Behny, Manager of Global Messaging, who was deposed on January 14, 2003. Mr. Behny testified to UBS's e-mail backup protocol, and also to the cost of restoring the relevant data.

C. UBS's E-Mail Backup System

In the first instance, the parties agree that e-mail was an important means of communication at UBS during the relevant time period. Each salesperson, including the salespeople on the Desk, received approximately 200 e-mails each day. Given this volume, and because Securities and Exchange Commission regulations require it, UBS implemented extensive e-mail backup and preservation protocols. In particular, e-mails were backed up in two distinct ways: on backup tapes and on optical disks.

1. Backup Tape Storage

... With limited exceptions, *all* e-mails sent or received by *any* UBS employee are stored onto backup tapes.... Once e-mails have been stored onto backup tapes, the restoration process is lengthy. Each backup tape routinely takes approximately five days to restore, although resort to an outside vendor would speed up the process (at greatly enhanced costs, of course). Because each tape represents a snapshot of one server's hard drive in a given month, each server/month must be restored separately onto a hard drive. Then, a program called Double Mail is used to extract a particular individual's e-mail file. That mail file is then exported into a Microsoft Outlook data file, which in turn can be opened in Microsoft Outlook, a common e-mail application. A user could then browse through the mail file and sort the mail by recipient, date or subject, or search for key words in the body of the e-mail.

Fortunately, NetBackup also created indexes of each backup tape. Thus, Behny was able to search through the tapes from the relevant time period and determine that the e-mail files responsive to Zubulake's requests are contained on a total of ninety-four backup tapes.

2. Optical Disk Storage

In addition to the e-mail backup tapes, UBS also stored certain e-mails on optical disks. For certain "registered traders," probably including the members of the Desk, a copy of *all* e-mails sent to or received from outside sources (*i.e.,* e-mails from a "registered trader" at UBS to someone at another entity, or vice versa) was simultaneously written onto a series of optical disks. Internal e-mails, however, were not stored on this system.

UBS has retained each optical disk used since the system was put into place in mid-1998. Moreover, the optical disks are neither erasable nor rewritable. Thus, UBS has *every* e-mail sent or received by registered traders (except internal e-mails) during the period of Zubulake's employment, even if the e-mail was deleted instantaneously on that trader's system.

The optical disks are easily searchable ...

III. Legal Standard

* * *

The application of these various discovery rules is particularly complicated where electronic data is sought because otherwise discoverable evidence is often only available from expensive-to-restore backup media. That being so, courts have devised creative solutions for balancing the broad scope of discovery prescribed in Rule 26(b)(1) with the cost-consciousness of Rule 26(b)(2). By and large, the solution has been to consider cost-shifting: forcing the requesting party, rather than the answering party, to bear the cost of discovery.

* * *

IV. Discussion A. Should Discovery of UBS's Electronic Data Be Permitted?

Under Rule 34, a party may request discovery of any document, "including writings, drawings, graphs, charts, photographs, phonorecords, and other data compilations...." The "inclusive description" of the term document "accord[s] with changing technology." "It makes clear that Rule 34 applies to *electronics* [sic] data compilations." Thus, "[e]lectronic documents are no less subject to disclosure than paper records." [*Rowe*, 205 F.R.D. at 205.] This is true not only of electronic documents that are currently in use, but also of documents that may have been deleted and now reside only on backup disks.

That being so, Zubulake is entitled to discovery of the requested e-mails so long as they are relevant to her claims, which they clearly are. As noted, e-mail constituted a substantial means of communication among UBS employees. To that end, UBS has already produced approximately 100 pages of e-mails, the contents of which are unquestionably relevant.

Nonetheless, UBS argues that Zubulake is not entitled to any further discovery because it already produced all responsive documents, to wit, the 100 pages of e-mails. This argument is unpersuasive for two reasons. *First,* because of the way that UBS backs up its e-mail files, it clearly could not have searched all of its e-mails without restoring the ninety-four backup tapes (which UBS admits that it has not done). UBS therefore cannot represent that it has produced all responsive e-mails. *Second,* Zubulake herself has produced over 450 pages of relevant e-mails, including e-mails that would have been responsive to her discovery requests but were never produced by UBS. These two facts strongly suggest that there are e-mails that Zubulake has not received that reside on UBS's backup media.

B. Should Cost-Shifting Be Considered?

Because it apparently recognizes that Zubulake is entitled to the requested discovery, UBS expends most of its efforts urging the court to shift the cost of production to "protect [it] ... from undue burden or expense." Faced with similar applications, courts generally engage in some sort of cost-shifting analysis ...

The first question, however, is whether cost-shifting must be considered in every case involving the discovery of electronic data, which — in today's world — includes virtually all cases. In light of the accepted principle, stated above, that electronic evidence is no less discoverable than paper evidence, the answer is, "No." The Supreme Court has instructed that "the presumption is that the responding party must bear the expense of complying with discovery requests...." [*Oppenheimer Fund*, 437 U.S. at 358.] Any principled approach to electronic evidence must respect this presumption.

Courts must remember that cost-shifting may effectively end discovery, especially when private parties are engaged in litigation with large corporations. As large companies increasingly move to entirely paper-free environments, the frequent use of cost-shifting will have the effect of crippling discovery in discrimination and retaliation cases. This will both undermine the "strong public policy favor[ing] resolving disputes on their merits," [Pecarsky v. Galaxiworld.com, Inc., 249 F.3d 167, 172 (2d Cir. 2001)] and may ultimately deter the filing of potentially meritorious claims.

Thus, cost-shifting should be considered *only* when electronic discovery imposes an "undue burden or expense" on the responding party. The burden or expense of discovery is, in turn, "undue" when it "outweighs its likely benefit, taking into account the needs of the case, the amount in controversy, the parties' resources, the importance of the issues at stake in the litigation, and the importance of the proposed discovery in resolving the issues." [Fed. R. Civ. P. 26(b)(2)(iii)].

Many courts have automatically assumed that an undue burden or expense may arise simply because electronic evidence is involved. This makes no sense. Electronic evidence is frequently cheaper and easier to produce than paper evidence because it can be searched automatically, key words can be run for privilege checks, and the production can be made in electronic form obviating the need for mass photocopying.

In fact, whether production of documents is unduly burdensome or expensive turns primarily on whether it is kept in an *accessible or inaccessible* format ... But in the world of electronic data, thanks to search engines, any data that is retained in a machine readable format is typically accessible.

Whether electronic data is accessible or inaccessible turns largely on the media on which it is stored....

... Information deemed "accessible" is stored in a readily usable format. Although the time it takes to actually access the data ranges from milliseconds to days, the data does not need to be restored or otherwise manipulated to be usable. "Inaccessible" data, on the other hand, is not readily usable. Backup tapes must be restored using a process similar to that previously described, fragmented data must be de-fragmented, and erased data must be reconstructed, all before the data is usable. That makes such data inaccessible.

The case at bar is a perfect illustration of the range of accessibility of electronic data. As explained above, UBS maintains e-mail files in three forms: (1) active user e-mail files; (2) archived e-mails on optical disks; and (3) backup data stored on tapes. The active ... data is obviously the most accessible: it is online data that resides on an active server, and can be accessed immediately. The optical disk ... data is only slightly less accessible.... The e-mails are on optical disks that need to be located and read with the correct hardware, but the system is configured to make searching the optical disks simple and automated once they are located. For these sources of e-mails—active mail files and e-mails stored on optical disks—it would be wholly inappropriate to even consider cost-shifting. UBS maintains the data in an accessible and usable format, and can respond to Zubulake's request cheaply and quickly. Like most typical discovery requests, therefore, the producing party should bear the cost of production.

E-mails stored on backup tapes..., however, are an entirely different matter. Although UBS has already identified the ninety-four potentially responsive backup tapes, those tapes are not currently accessible. In order to search the tapes for responsive e-mails, UBS would have to engage in the costly and time-consuming process.... It is therefore appropriate to *consider* cost shifting.

C. What Is the Proper Cost-Shifting Analysis?

* * *

c. A New Seven-Factor Test

Set forth below is a new seven-factor test [to determine whether costs should be shifted to the requesting party] ...

1. The extent to which the request is specifically tailored to discover relevant information;

2. The availability of such information from other sources;

3. The total cost of production, compared to the amount in controversy;

4. The total cost of production, compared to the resources available to each party;

5. The relative ability of each party to control costs and its incentive to do so;

6. The importance of the issues at stake in the litigation; and

7. The relative benefits to the parties of obtaining the information.

2. The Seven Factors Should Not Be Weighted Equally

Whenever a court applies a multi-factor test, there is a temptation to treat the factors as a check-list, resolving the issue in favor of whichever column has the most checks. But "we do not just add up the factors." When evaluating cost-shifting, the central question must be, does the request impose an "undue burden or expense" on the responding party? Put another way, "how important is the sought-after evidence in comparison to the cost of production?" The seven-factor test articulated above provide [sic] some guidance in answering this question, but the test cannot be mechanically applied at the risk of losing sight of its purpose.

Weighting the factors in descending order of importance may solve the problem and avoid a mechanistic application of the test. The first two factors—comprising the marginal utility test—are the most important. These factors include: (1) The extent to which the request is specifically tailored to discover relevant information and (2) the availability of such information from other sources. The substance of the marginal utility test was well described in *McPeek v. Ashcroft:*

> The more likely it is that the backup tape contains information that is relevant to a claim or defense, the fairer it is that the [responding party] search at its own expense. The less likely it is, the more unjust it would be to make the [responding party] search at its own expense. The difference is "at the margin." [*McPeek v. Ashcroft,* 202 F.R.D. 31, 34 (S.D.N.Y, 2002)]

The second group of factors addresses cost issues: "How expensive will this production be?" and, "Who can handle that expense?" These factors include: (3) the total cost of production compared to the amount in controversy, (4) the total cost of production compared to the resources available to each party and (5) the relative ability of each party to control costs and its incentive to do so. The third "group" — (6) the importance of the litigation itself — stands alone, and as noted earlier will only rarely come into play. But where it does, this factor has the potential to predominate over the others. Collectively, the first three groups correspond to the three explicit considerations of Rule 26(b)(2)(iii). Finally, the last factor — (7) the relative benefits of production as between the requesting and producing parties — is the least important because it is fair to presume that the response to a discovery request generally benefits the requesting party. But in the unusual case where production will also provide a tangible or strategic benefit to the responding party, that fact may weigh *against* shifting costs.

D. A Factual Basis Is Required to Support the Analysis

* * *

Requiring the responding party to restore and produce responsive documents from a small sample of backup tapes will inform the cost-shifting analysis laid out above. When based on an actual sample, the marginal utility test will not be an exercise in speculation — there will be tangible evidence of what the backup tapes may have to offer. There will also be tangible evidence of the time and cost required to restore the backup tapes, which in turn will inform the second group of cost-shifting factors. Thus, by requiring a sample restoration of backup tapes, the entire cost-shifting analysis can be grounded in fact rather than guesswork.

Exercise 9-17. *Zubulake* Revisited

1. The *Zubulake* court divided electronic data into categories of accessible and inaccessible data. As an attorney representing a party seeking discovery of electronic data, how would you determine in which category the data you requested fell?

2. The court contemplates that cost shifting should be considered for inaccessible data. Review the factors set out by the *Zubulake* court. Do you think these are appropriate factors? Is anything missing? Should any of these factors be excluded?

Note on Implications of 2015 Amendments and e-Discovery

The 2015 amendments to the discovery rules contemplate that e-discovery has added increased cost and complexity to the discovery process. In addition to the added proportionality language of Rule 26(b)(1) noted earlier in this chapter, Rule 26(c)(1)(B), governing protective orders, states that the court may issue a protective order "specifying ... the allocation of expenses." This contemplates that the court may shift the costs of discovery to the requesting party. However, the advisory committee notes state that this change does not "imply that cost-shifting should become a common practice." Instead, the default is still that the responding party bears the costs. In addition to this change, Rule 34 was also amended in several respects that partly respond to problems with e-discovery. The Rule allows the requesting parties to specify the form in which they wish to receive electronically stored information, but permits the responding parties to object to the requested form of producing electronically stored information and provide another form instead. Fed. R. Civ. Pro. 34(b)(2)(D).

The case law on e-discovery is evolving. However, a group of attorneys, academics, judges, and consultants formed the Sedona Conference in an effort to create best practices for e-discovery. Federal courts have cited the Sedona Principles favorably. *See, e.g., John B. v. Goetz*, 531 F.3d 448, 459–60 (6th Cir. 2008); *Regan-Touhy v. Walgreen Co.*, 526 F.3d 641, 649 n.5 (10th Cir. 2008). The Conference is now on its third edition of suggested principles governing e-discovery. These principles include:

1. Electronically stored information is generally subject to the same preservation and discovery requirements as other relevant information.

2. When balancing the cost, burden, and need for electronically stored information, courts and parties should apply the proportionality standard embodied in Fed. R. Civ. P. 26(b)(1) and its state equivalents, which requires consideration of the importance of the issues at stake in the action, the amount in controversy, the parties' relative access to relevant information, the parties' resources, the importance of the discovery in resolving the issues, and whether the burden or expense of the proposed discovery outweighs its likely benefit.

3. As soon as practicable, parties should confer and seek to reach agreement regarding the preservation and production of electronically stored information.

4. Discovery requests for electronically stored information should be as specific as possible; responses and objections to discovery should disclose the scope and limits of the production.

5. The obligation to preserve electronically stored information requires reasonable and good faith efforts to retain information that is expected to be relevant to claims or defenses in reasonably anticipated or pending litigation. However, it is unreasonable to expect parties to take every conceivable step or disproportionate steps to preserve each instance of relevant electronically stored information.

6. Responding parties are best situated to evaluate the procedures, methodologies, and technologies appropriate for preserving and producing their own electronically stored information.

7. The requesting party has the burden on a motion to compel to show that the responding party's steps to preserve and produce relevant electronically stored information were inadequate.

8. The primary sources of electronically stored information to be preserved and produced should be those readily accessible in the ordinary course. Only when electronically stored information is not available through such primary sources should parties move down a continuum of less accessible sources until the information requested to be preserved or produced is no longer proportional.

9. Absent a showing of special need and relevance, a responding party should not be required to preserve, review, or produce deleted, shadowed, fragmented, or residual electronically stored information.

10. Parties should take reasonable steps to safeguard electronically stored information, the disclosure or dissemination of which is subject to privileges, work product protections, privacy obligations, or other legally enforceable restrictions.

11. A responding party may satisfy its good faith obligations to preserve and produce relevant electronically stored information by using technology and processes, such as sampling, searching, or the use of selection criteria.

12. The production of electronically stored information should be made in the form or forms in which it is ordinarily maintained or that is reasonably usable given the nature of the electronically stored information and the proportional needs of the case.

13. The costs of preserving and producing relevant and proportionate electronically stored information ordinarily should be borne by the responding party.

14. The breach of a duty to preserve electronically stored information may be addressed by remedial measures, sanctions, or both: remedial measures are appropriate to cure prejudice; sanctions are appropriate only if a party acted with intent to deprive another party of the use of relevant electronically stored information.

The Sedona Principles 51–53 (3d ed. 2018).

Rule 34 also was amended to eliminate boilerplate objections to document requests, adding language that objections must "state with specificity the grounds for objecting" as well as "whether any responsive materials are being withheld." Fed. R. Civ. Pro. 34(b)(2)(B) & (C). The advisory committee notes explain that the amendments were "aimed at reducing the potential to impose unreasonable burdens by objections to requests to produce." In addition, the rule now states that "production must then be completed no later than the time for inspection specified in the request or another reasonable time specified in the response." Fed. R. Civ. Pro. 26(b)(2)(B). Rule 26 and 34 were amended to permit the serving of Rule 34 requests prior to the Rule 26(f) discovery conference, although responses to such an early request must be provided within thirty days after the first Rule 26(f) conference. Fed. R. Civ. Pro. 26(d)(2), 34(b)(2)(A).

e. Physical and Mental Examinations

Physical and mental examinations are governed by Rule 35. Read Rule 35. From your reading, what would you have to show to obtain a mental or physical exam? If you represented Piper or Hartzell instead of the plaintiff in the chapter problem, would you request any physical or mental examinations?

Exercise 9-18. *Schlagenhauf v. Holder*

As you read *Schlagenhauf v. Holder*, answer the following questions.

1. Begin by diagramming this case. Procedurally, who is suing whom and for what?

2. What procedural tool did the defendants' lawyer use to get this case to the Supreme Court of the United States?

3. What is Schlagenhauf's argument that Rule 35 does not apply to defendants? How does the Court address this argument?

Schlagenhauf v. Holder
379 U.S. 104 (1964)

Mr. Justice Goldberg, delivered the opinion of the Court.

This case involves the validity and construction of Rule 35(a) of the Federal Rules of Civil Procedure as applied to the examination of a defendant in a negligence action....

I.

An action based on diversity of citizenship was brought in the District Court seeking damages arising from personal injuries suffered by passengers of a bus which collided with the rear of a tractor-trailer. The named defendants were The Greyhound Corporation, owner of the bus; petitioner, Robert L. Schlagenhauf, the bus driver; Contract Carriers, Inc., owner of the tractor; Joseph L. McCorkhill, driver of the tractor; and National Lead Company, owner of the trailer. Answers were filed by each of the defendants denying negligence.

Greyhound then cross-claimed against Contract Carriers and National Lead for damage to Greyhound's bus, alleging that the collision was due solely to their negligence in that the tractor-trailer was driven at an unreasonably low speed, had not remained in its lane, and was not equipped with proper rear lights. Contract Carriers filed an answer to this cross-claim denying its negligence and asserting "(t)hat the negligence of the driver of the ... bus (petitioner Schlagenhauf) proximately caused and contributed to ... Greyhound's damages."

Pursuant to a pretrial order, Contract Carriers filed a letter—which the trial court treated as, and we consider to be, part of the answer—alleging that Schlagenhauf was "not mentally or physically capable" of driving a bus at the time of the accident.

Contract Carriers and National Lead then petitioned the District Court for an order directing petitioner Schlagenhauf to submit to both mental and physical examinations by one specialist in each of the following fields:

(1) Internal medicine;

(2) Ophthalmology;

(3) Neurology; and

(4) Psychiatry.

For the purpose of offering a choice to the District Court of one specialist in each field, the petition recommended two specialists in internal medicine, ophthalmology, and psychiatry, respectively, and three specialists in neurology—a total of nine physicians. The petition alleged that the mental and physical condition of Schlagenhauf was "in controversy" as it had been raised by Contract Carriers' answer to Greyhound's cross-claim. This was supported by a brief of legal authorities and an affidavit of Contract Carriers' attorney stating that Schlagenhauf had seen red lights 10 to 15 seconds before the accident, that another witness had seen the rear lights of the trailer from a distance of three-quarters to one-half mile, and that Schlagenhauf had been involved in a prior accident.

* * *

While disposition of this petition was pending, National Lead filed its answer to Greyhound's cross-claim and itself "cross-claimed" against Greyhound and Schlagenhauf for damage to its trailer. The answer asserted generally that Schlagenhauf's negligence proximately caused the accident. The cross-claim additionally alleged that Greyhound and Schlagenhauf were negligent "(b)y permitting said bus to be operated over and upon said public highway by the said defendant, Robert L. Schlagenhauf, when both the said Greyhound Corporation and said Robert L. Schlagenhauf knew that the eyes and vision of the said Robert L. Schlagenhauf was (sic) impaired and deficient."

The District Court, on the basis of the petition filed by Contract Carriers, and without any hearing, ordered Schlagenhauf to submit to nine examinations — one by each of the recommended specialists — despite the fact that the petition clearly requested a total of only four examinations.

Petitioner applied for a writ of mandamus in the Court of Appeals against the respondent, the District Court Judge, seeking to have set aside the order requiring his mental and physical examinations. The Court of Appeals denied mandamus ...

We granted certiorari to review undecided questions concerning the validity and construction of Rule 35.

* * *

III.

Rule 35 on its face applies to all "parties," which under any normal reading would include a defendant. Petitioner contends, however, that the application of the Rule to a defendant would be an unconstitutional invasion of his privacy, or, at the least, be a modification of substantive rights existing prior to the adoption of the Federal Rules of Civil Procedure and thus beyond the congressional mandate of the Rules Enabling Act.

These same contentions were raised in *Sibbach v. Wilson & Co.*, 312 U.S. 1 [(1941)], by a plaintiff in a negligence action who asserted a physical injury as a basis for recovery. The Court, by a closely divided vote, sustained the Rule as there applied.... Petitioner does not challenge the holding in *Sibbach* as applied to plaintiffs. He contends, however, that it should not be extended to defendants. We can see no basis under the *Sibbach* holding for such a distinction. Discovery "is not a one-way proposition. *Hickman v. Taylor*, 329 U.S. 495, 507 [(1947)]. Issues cannot be resolved by a doctrine of favoring one class of litigants over another.

We recognize that, insofar as reported cases show, this type of discovery in federal courts has been applied solely to plaintiffs, and that some early state cases seem to have proceeded on a theory that a plaintiff who seeks redress for injuries in a court of law thereby "waives" his right to claim the inviolability of his person.

However, it is clear that *Sibbach* was not decided on any "waiver" theory....

... We therefore agree with the Court of Appeals that the District Court had power to apply Rule 35 to a party defendant in an appropriate case.

IV.

There remains the issue of the construction of Rule 35....

Petitioner contends that even if Rule 35 is to be applied to defendants, which we have determined it must, nevertheless it should not be applied to him as he was not a party in relation to Contract Carriers and National Lead—the movants for the mental and physical examinations—at the time the examinations were sought. The Court of Appeals agreed with petitioner's general legal proposition, holding that the person sought to be examined must be an opposing party vis-a-vis the movant (or at least one of them). While it is clear that the person to be examined must be a party to the case, we are of the view that the Court of Appeals gave an unduly restrictive interpretation to that term. Rule 35 only requires that the person to be examined be a party to the "action," not that he be an opposing party vis-a-vis the movant. There is no doubt that Schlagenhauf was a "party" to this "action" by virtue of the original complaint. Therefore, Rule 35 permitted examination of him (a party defendant) upon petition of Contract Carriers and National Lead (codefendants), provided, of course, that the other requirements of the Rule were met. Insistence that the movant have filed a pleading against the person to be examined would have the undesirable result of an unnecessary proliferation of cross-claims and counterclaims and would not be in keeping with the aims of a liberal, nontechnical application of the Federal Rules.

* * *

Petitioner next contends that his mental or physical condition was not "in controversy" and "good cause" was not shown for the examinations, both as required by the express terms of Rule 35.

* * *

Rule 35 ... requires discriminating application by the trial judge, who must decide, as an initial matter in every case, whether the party requesting a mental or physical examination or examinations has adequately demonstrated the existence of the Rule's requirements of "in controversy" and "good cause," which requirements, as the Court of Appeals in this case itself recognized, are necessarily related. This does not, of course, mean that the movant must prove his case on the merits in order to meet the requirements for a mental or physical examination. Nor does it mean that an evidentiary hearing is required in all cases. This may be necessary in some cases, but in other cases the showing could be made by affidavits or other usual methods short of a hearing. It does mean, though, that the movant must produce sufficient information, by whatever means, so that the district judge can fulfill his function mandated by the Rule.

Of course, there are situations where the pleadings alone are sufficient to meet these requirements. A plaintiff in a negligence action who asserts mental or physical injury, *cf. Sibbach v. Wilson & Co.*, places that mental or physical injury clearly in controversy and provides the defendant with good cause for an examination to determine the existence and extent of such asserted injury. This is not only true as to a plaintiff, but applies equally to a defendant who asserts his mental or physical condition as a defense to a claim, such as, for example, where insanity is asserted as a defense to a divorce action.

Here, however, Schlagenhauf did not assert his mental or physical condition either in support of or in defense of a claim. His condition was sought to be placed in issue by other parties. Thus, under the principles discussed above, Rule 35 required that these parties make an affirmative showing that petitioner's mental or physical condition was in controversy and that there was good cause for the examinations requested. This, the record plainly shows, they failed to do.

The only allegations in the pleadings relating to this subject were the general conclusory statement in Contract Carriers' answer to the cross-claim that "Schlagenhauf was not mentally or physically capable of operating" the bus at the time of the accident and the limited allegation in National Lead's cross-claim that, at the time of the accident, "the eyes and vision of ... Schlagenhauf was (sic) impaired and deficient."

The attorney's affidavit attached to the petition for the examinations provided:

> "That ... Schlagenhauf, in his deposition ... admitted that he saw red lights for 10 to 15 seconds prior to a collision with a semi-tractor trailer unit and yet drove his vehicle on without reducing speed and without altering the course thereof.

> "The only eye-witness to this accident known to this affiant * * * testified that immediately prior to the impact between the bus and truck that he had also been approaching the truck from the rear and that he had clearly seen the lights of the truck for a distance of three-quarters to one-half mile to the rear thereof.

> "... Schlagenhauf has admitted in his deposition ... that he was involved in a (prior) similar type rear end collision...."

This record cannot support even the corrected order which required one examination in each of the four specialties of internal medicine, ophthalmology, neurology, and psychiatry. Nothing in the pleadings or affidavit would afford a basis for a belief that Schlagenhauf was suffering from a mental or neurological illness warranting wide-ranging psychiatric or neurological examinations. Nor is there anything stated justifying the broad internal medicine examination.

The only specific allegation made in support of the four examinations ordered was that the "eyes and vision" of Schlagenhauf were impaired.

Considering this in conjunction with the affidavit, we would be hesitant to set aside a visual examination if it had been the only one ordered. However, as the case must be remanded to the District Court because of the other examinations ordered, it would be appropriate for the District Judge to reconsider also this order in light of the guidelines set forth in this opinion.

The Federal Rules of Civil Procedure should be liberally construed, but they should not be expanded by disregarding plainly expressed limitations. The "good cause" and "in controversy" requirements of Rule 35 make it very apparent that sweeping examinations of a party who has not affirmatively put into issue his own mental or physical condition are not to be automatically ordered merely because the person has been involved in an accident — or, as in this case, two accidents — and a general charge of negligence is lodged. Mental and physical examinations are only to be ordered upon a discriminating application by the district judge of the limitations prescribed by the Rule. To hold otherwise would mean that such examinations could be ordered routinely in automobile accident cases. The plain language of Rule 35 precludes such an untoward result.

Accordingly, the judgment of the Court of Appeals is vacated and the case remanded to the District Court to reconsider the examination order in light of the guidelines herein formulated and for further proceedings in conformity with this opinion.

Vacated and remanded.

Mr. Justice Black, with whom Mr. Justice Clark joins, concurring in part and dissenting in part.

* * *

In a collision case like this one, evidence concerning very bad eyesight or impaired mental or physical health which may affect the ability to drive is obviously of the highest relevance. It is equally obvious, I think, that when a vehicle continues down an open road and smashes into a truck in front of it although the truck is in plain sight and there is ample time and room to avoid collision, the chances are good that the driver has some physical, mental or moral defect. When such a thing happens twice, one is even more likely to ask, "What is the matter with that driver? Is he blind or crazy?" Plainly the allegations of the other parties were relevant and put the question of Schlagenhauf's health and vision "in controversy." The Court nevertheless holds that these charges were not a sufficient basis on which to rest a court-ordered examination of Schlagenhauf. It says with reference to the charges of impaired physical or mental health that the charges are "conclusory." I had not thought there was anything strange about pleadings being "conclusory" — that is their function, at least since modern rules of procedure have attempted to substitute simple pleadings for the complicated and redundant ones which long kept the common-law courts in disrepute. I therefore cannot agree that the charges about Schlagenhauf's health and vision were not sufficient upon which to base an order under Rule 35(a), particularly since he was a party who raised every technical objection to being required to subject himself to an examination but never once denied that his health and vision were bad. In these circumstances the allegations here should be more than enough to show probable cause to justify a court order requiring some kind of physical and mental examination....

Exercise 9-19. *Schlagenhauf v. Holder* Revisited

When is the physical and mental condition of a party "in controversy"? Based on the Court's analysis in this case, is the party's physical or mental condition "in controversy" in the following cases?

1. Plaintiff files a civil rights action against certain police officers and the police department alleging false arrest, excessive force, and violation of the equal protection clause. His damages include injuries suffered to his right elbow and arm as well as emotional distress. Will the defendant be able to obtain a physical and mental examination? *See Said v. County of San Diego*, Civ. No. 12 CV 2437, 2014 WL 5800218 (S.D. Cal. Nov. 7, 2014) (exams permitted).

2. Plaintiff files an action under the Americans with Disabilities Act against a city due to problems he has gaining access to a public pool run by the city. In his complaint, he states that he must be carried up and down a flight of stairs to gain access to the pool area and that this is frustrating and embarrassing to him. If the city requests a mental exam, will the court grant it? *See Robertson v. City of San Diego*, No. 13 CV 1460 W, 2014 WL 6810726 (S.D. Cal. Dec. 2, 2014) (exam denied).

3. An insurance company brings an action to determine who should receive the proceeds from an insurance policy. The insurance policy states that the proceeds will go to a living child of the decedent, if one exists. The decedent signed an order of parentage acknowledging a son as his biological child. The sister of the decedent, also a defendant in the case, contests that the son is the biological child of her brother and requests a DNA test under Rule 35. State law creates a presumption that a man is the natural father of a child if he and the child's biological mother have signed an acknowledgement of parentage. Will the court grant the request for the DNA test? *See Minnesota Life Ins. Co. v. Jones*, 771 F.3d 387 (7th Cir. 2014) (district court did not abuse discretion in denying request for DNA test).

f. Requests for Admission

Requests for admission are much like the name suggests—a series of written statements that an opposing party is asked to admit or deny. A party may propound requests for admission only on parties. A party cannot use them on non-parties. Lawyers find requests for admissions useful at two points in the litigation process. Sometimes they are useful early in a lawsuit to identify issues upon which both sides agree. Most lawyers use them at the end of the discovery process to limit the issues that are in dispute for trial. Requests for admission are particularly useful for admissions related to the genuineness of documents that an attorney plans to use at trial. Rule 36 governs requests for admission.

Exercise 9-20. Reading Rule 36

Read Rule 36. Based on your reading of Rule 36, answer the following questions.

1. What types of admissions may a party request?

2. How does one make a request to admit the genuineness of a document?

3. How long does a party have to respond to a request to admit?

4. How does a party obtain more time to respond to a request to admit?

5. What happens when a party fails to respond to a request to admit?

6. Why would an attorney want to pay particularly close attention to the response deadline for a request for admission?

7. What are the ways in which a party can respond to a particular request to admit? (Hint: look at Rule 36(a)(4)).

8. If a party propounding requests for admission believes some of the answers are insufficient, how can it obtain a sufficient response?

9. What can happen to a party who responds to a request to admit improperly?

10. What is the effect of an admission?

11. What can a party do if it has admitted something erroneously?

Note on Failure to Admit Something That the Requesting Party Later Proves

Rule 37(c)(2) provides a remedy for a party who propounds a request to admit that a party denies that the propounding party later proves. The propounding party can make a motion that the party who failed to admit the matter pay the reasonable expenses, including attorney's fees, that the propounding party incurred in proving the matter. For example, assume you represent a landowner who brings a toxic contamination tort case against an adjoining landowner. The defendant is cleaning up the plaintiff's property by order of state and federal officials under state and federal environmental laws. As the attorney representing the plaintiff, you realize it would be much less costly for your client if you did not need to hire an expert to prove that the defendant contaminated your client's property. You propound a request to admit that asks the defendant to admit that toxic substances contained in its underground storage tank leaked onto your client's adjacent property. The defendant denies this. If you prove at trial that the defendant did contaminate your client's property (which is quite likely, given that the defendant is going to the expense of cleaning up your client's property), you can make a motion that the defendant pay not only for the costs of your expert, but also any attorney's fees you incurred in developing the evidence to support this fact. That could result in the defendant's paying quite a bit of money.

The rule does provide some caveats. For example, if the request was held objectionable, the request was not of "substantial importance," the party who failed to admit thought it had reasonable ground to believe it might prevail on the matter at trial, or there was other good reasons for failing to admit, then the court is not required to order that the party pay the propounding party's costs. Rule 37(c)(2)(A)–(D). Consider the toxic contamination example posed above. Can the party who failed to admit that it contaminated the propounding party's property wiggle out of liability for costs under the grounds specified in Rule 37(c)(2)(A)–(D)?

An attorney can find this aspect of the rule useful in the meet and confer process prior to making a motion to compel. As you will learn in the next section of this chapter, in order to make a motion to compel answers to a request for admission, the propounding party must meet and confer with the party failing to fully respond before moving to compel an answer. Thus, if a party denies something in a request for admission that the facts show is obviously true, an attorney during the meet and confer process can remind the attorney of the party that submitted the denial that, under Rule 37(c)(2), the court may award costs against her client if the matter is proven true at trial. This can be an effective way to convince the answering party to respond fully to the request and simply admit what is obviously true.

5. Motions to Compel, Sanctions, and the Duty to Supplement Responses

a. Motions to Compel and Sanctions for Discovery Non-Compliance

Rule 37 governs the process an attorney must follow to compel answers to discovery requests when the answering party does not respond or does not respond fully. In order to compel a party to respond, the requesting party must make a motion to compel discovery. As mentioned earlier in this chapter, any such motion must include "certification that the movant has in good faith conferred or attempted to confer with the person or party failing to make disclosure or discovery in an effort to obtain it without court action." Fed. R. Civ. P. 37(a)(1).

If such a motion is granted, the court "must" order that the party or deponent (in the case of deposition) whose behavior necessitated the motion pay the reasonable expenses incurred in making the motion. This explicitly includes attorney's fees. Fed. R. Civ. P. 37(a)(5)(A). However, like the Rule about failure to admit an item that the opposing party later proves, this rule is subject to several caveats. These include that the moving party did not meet and confer before making the motion, the failure to respond was "substantially justified," and other circumstances suggesting that award of expenses would be "unjust." Fed. R. Civ. P. 37(a)(5)(A)(i)–(iii).

The purported abuses of the discovery process have led to amendments to discovery rules designed to curb such abuse. Thus, there are other provisions of Rule 37 that apply to specific failures on the part of a responding party, including failing to disclose under Rule 26(a) (Rule 37(c)(1)), failing to appear for a deposition (Rule 37(d)(1)(A)(i)), or failing to respond to a discovery request (Rule 37(d)(1)(A)(ii)), to name a few. Reading Rule 37 carefully reveals others.

Failure to comply with a court's order compelling discovery can have significant consequences for a party. For example, the court can order issues sanctions. An issue sanction occurs when a court finds against a party on an issue because that party was uncooperative in discovery pertaining to that issue. This is a very significant penalty. It means that party cannot contest the issue in court. *See* Rule 37(b)(2)(A)(i)–(ii). The next case provides a compelling example.

Insurance Corp. of Ireland, Ltd. v. Compagnie des Bauxites de Guinee

456 U.S. 962 (1982)

Justice White delivered the opinion of the Court.

Rule 37(b), Federal Rules of Civil Procedure, provides that a district court may impose sanctions for failure to comply with discovery orders. Included among the available sanctions is:

> "An order that the matters regarding which the order was made or any other designated facts shall be taken to be established for the purposes of the action in accordance with the claim of the party obtaining the order." Rule 37(b)(2)(A).

The question presented by this case is whether this Rule is applicable to facts that form the basis for personal jurisdiction over a defendant. May a district court, as a sanction for failure to comply with a discovery order directed at establishing jurisdictional facts, proceed on the basis that personal jurisdiction over the recalcitrant party has been established?

Petitioners urge that such an application of the Rule would violate due process: If a court does not have jurisdiction over a party, then it may not create that jurisdiction by judicial fiat. They contend also that until a court has jurisdiction over a party, that party need not comply with orders of the court; failure to comply, therefore, cannot provide the ground for a sanction. In our view, petitioners are attempting to create a logical conundrum out of a fairly straightforward matter.

I

Respondent Compagnie des Bauxites de Guinee (CBG) is a Delaware corporation, 49% of which is owned by the Republic of Guinea and 51% is owned by Halco (Mining) Inc. CBG's principal place of business is in the Republic of Guinea, where it operates bauxite mines and processing facilities. Halco, which operates in Pennsylvania, has contracted to perform certain administrative services for CBG. These include the procurement of insurance.

In 1973, Halco instructed an insurance broker, Marsh & McLennan, to obtain $20 million worth of business interruption insurance to cover CBG's operations in Guinea. The first half of this coverage was provided by the Insurance Company of North America (INA). The second half, or what is referred to as the "excess" insurance, was provided by a group of 21 foreign insurance companies, 14 of which are petitioners in this action (the excess insurers).

* * *

Sometime after February 12, CBG allegedly experienced mechanical problems in its Guinea operation, resulting in a business interruption loss in excess of $10 million. Contending that the loss was covered under its policies, CBG brought suit when the insurers refused to indemnify CBG for the loss. Whatever the mechanical problems experienced by CBG, they were perhaps minor compared to the legal difficulties encountered in the courts.

In December 1975, CBG filed a two-count suit in the Western District of Pennsylvania, asserting jurisdiction based on diversity of citizenship. The first count was against INA; the second against the excess insurers. INA did not challenge personal or subject-matter jurisdiction of the District Court. The answer of the excess insurers, however, raised a number of defenses, including lack of *in personam* jurisdiction. Subsequently, this alleged lack of personal jurisdiction became the basis of a motion for summary judgment filed by the excess insurers. The issue in this case requires an account of respondent's attempt to use discovery in order to demonstrate the court's personal jurisdiction over the excess insurers.

Respondent's first discovery request—asking for "[c]opies of all business interruption insurance policies issued by Defendant during the period from January 1, 1972 to December 31, 1975"—was served on each defendant in August 1976. In January 1977, the excess insurers objected, on grounds of burdensomeness, to producing such policies. Several months later, respondent filed a motion to compel petitioners to produce the requested documents. In June 1978, the court orally overruled petitioners' objections. This was followed by a second discovery request in which respondent narrowed the files it was seeking to policies which "were delivered in ... Pennsylvania ... or covered a risk located in ... Pennsylvania." Petitioners now objected that these documents were not in their custody or control; rather, they were kept by the brokers in London. The court ordered petitioners to request the information from the brokers, limiting the request to policies covering the period from 1971 to date. That was in July 1978; petitioners were given 90 days to produce the information. On November 8, petitioners were given an additional 30 days to complete discovery. On November 24, petitioners filed an affidavit offering to make their records, allegedly some 4 million files, available at their offices in London for inspection by respondent. Respondent countered with a motion to compel production of the previously requested documents. On December 21, 1978, the court, noting that no conscientious effort had yet been made to produce the requested information and that no objection had been entered to the discovery order in July, gave petitioners 60 more days to produce the requested information. The District Judge also issued the following warning:

> "[I]f you don't get it to him in 60 days, I am going to enter an order saying that because you failed to give the information as requested, that I am going to assume, under Rule of Civil Procedure 37(b), subsection 2(A), that there is jurisdiction."

A few moments later he restated the warning as follows: "I will assume that jurisdiction is here with this court unless you produce statistics and other information in that regard that would indicate otherwise."

On April 19, 1979, the court, after concluding that the requested material had not been produced, imposed the threatened sanction, finding that "for the purpose of this litigation the Excess Insurers are subject to the in personam jurisdiction of this Court due to their business contacts with Pennsylvania." Independently of the sanction, the District Court found two other grounds for holding that it had personal jurisdiction over petitioners....

Except with respect to three excess insurers, the Court of Appeals for the Third Circuit affirmed the jurisdictional holding, relying entirely upon the validity of the sanction. That court specifically found that the discovery orders of the District Court did not constitute an abuse of discretion and that imposition of the sanction fell within the limits of trial court discretion under Rule 37(b)....

Because the decision below directly conflicts with the decision of the Court of Appeals for the Fifth Circuit..., we granted certiorari.

II

In *McDonald v. Mabee*, 243 U.S. 90 (1917), another case involving an alleged lack of personal jurisdiction, Justice Holmes wrote for the Court, "great caution should be used not to let fiction deny the fair play that can be secured only by a pretty close adhesion to fact." *Id.* at 91. Petitioners' basic submission is that to apply Rule 37(b)(2) to jurisdictional facts is to allow fiction to get the better of fact and that it is impermissible to use a fiction to establish judicial power, where, as a matter of fact, it does not exist. In our view, this represents a fundamental misunderstanding of the nature of personal jurisdiction.

The validity of an order of a federal court depends upon that court's having jurisdiction over both the subject matter and the parties. The concepts of subject-matter and personal jurisdiction, however, serve different purposes, and these different purposes affect the legal character of the two requirements. Petitioners fail to recognize the distinction between the two concepts—speaking instead in general terms of "jurisdiction"—although their argument's strength comes from conceiving of jurisdiction only as subject-matter jurisdiction.

* * *

... The requirement that a court have personal jurisdiction flows not from Art. III, but from the Due Process Clause. The personal jurisdiction requirement recognizes and protects an individual liberty interest. It represents a restriction on judicial power not as a matter of sovereignty, but as a matter of individual liberty. Thus, the test for personal jurisdiction requires that "the maintenance of the suit ... not offend 'traditional notions of fair play and substantial justice.'" *International Shoe Co. v. Washington*, 326 U.S. 310, 316 (1945), quoting *Milliken v. Meyer*, 311 U.S. 457, 463 (1940).

Because the requirement of personal jurisdiction represents first of all an individual right, it can, like other such rights, be waived. [Court detailed various ways in which a defendant can waive personal jurisdiction.]

In sum, the requirement of personal jurisdiction may be intentionally waived, or for various reasons a defendant may be estopped from raising the issue. These characteristics portray it for what it is—a legal right protecting the individual. The plaintiff's demonstration of certain historical facts may make clear to the court that it has personal jurisdiction over the defendant as a matter of law—*i.e.*, certain factual showings will have legal consequences—but this is not the only way in which the personal jurisdiction of the court may arise. The actions of the defendant may amount to a legal submission to the jurisdiction of the court, whether voluntary or not.

The expression of legal rights is often subject to certain procedural rules: The failure to follow those rules may well result in a curtailment of the rights. Thus, the failure to enter a timely objection to personal jurisdiction constitutes, under Rule 12(h)(1), a waiver of the objection. A sanction under Rule 37(b)(2)(A) consisting of a finding of personal jurisdiction has precisely the same effect. As a general proposition, the Rule 37 sanction applied to a finding of personal jurisdiction creates no more of a due process problem than the Rule 12 waiver. Although "a court cannot conclude all persons interested by its mere assertion of its own power," *Chicago Life Ins. Co. v. Cherry*, 244 U.S. 25, 29 (1917), not all rules that establish legal consequences to a party's own behavior are "mere assertions" of power.

Rule 37(b)(2)(A) itself embodies the standard established in *Hammond Packing Co. v. Arkansas*, 212 U.S. 322 (1909), for the due process limits on such rules. There the Court held that it did not violate due process for a state court to strike the answer and render a default judgment against a defendant who failed to comply with a pretrial discovery order. Such a rule was permissible as an expression of "the undoubted right of the lawmaking power to create a presumption of fact as to the bad faith and untruth of an answer begotten from the suppression or failure to produce the proof ordered ... [T]he preservation of due process was secured by the presumption that the refusal to produce evidence material to the administration of due process was but an admission of the want of merit in the asserted defense." *Id.* at 350–351.

The situation in *Hammond* was specifically distinguished from that in *Hovey v. Elliott*, 167 U.S. 409 (1897), in which the Court held that it did violate due process for a court to take similar action as "punishment" for failure to obey an order to pay into the registry of the court a certain sum of money. Due process is violated only if the behavior of the defendant will not support the *Hammond Packing* presumption. A proper application of Rule 37(b)(2) will, as a matter of law, support such a presumption. If there is no abuse of discretion in the application of the Rule 37 sanction, as we find to be the case here (see Part III), then the sanction is nothing more than the invocation of a legal presumption, or what is the same thing, the finding of a constructive waiver.

Petitioners argue that a sanction consisting of a finding of personal jurisdiction differs from all other instances in which a sanction is imposed, including the default judgment in *Hammond Packing*, because a party need not obey the orders of a court until it is established that the court has personal jurisdiction over that party. If there is no obligation to obey a judicial order, a sanction cannot be applied for the failure to comply. Until the court has established personal jurisdiction, moreover, any assertion of judicial power over the party violates due process.

This argument again assumes that there is something unique about the requirement of personal jurisdiction, which prevents it from being established or waived like other rights. A defendant is always free to ignore the judicial proceedings, risk a default judgment, and then challenge that judgment on jurisdictional grounds in a collateral proceeding. By submitting to the jurisdiction of the court for the limited purpose of challenging jurisdiction, the defendant agrees to abide by that court's determination on the issue of jurisdiction: That decision will be res judicata on that issue in any further proceedings. As demonstrated above, the manner in which the court determines whether it has personal jurisdiction may include a variety of legal rules and presumptions, as well as straightforward factfinding. A particular rule may offend the due process standard of *Hammond Packing*, but the mere use of procedural rules does not in itself violate the defendant's due process rights.

III

Even if Rule 37(b)(2) may be applied to support a finding of personal jurisdiction, the question remains as to whether it was properly applied under the circumstances of this case. Because the District Court's decision to invoke the sanction was accompanied by a detailed explanation of the reasons for that order and because that decision was upheld as a proper exercise of the District Court's discretion by the Court of Appeals, this issue need not detain us for long. What was said in *National Hockey League v. Metropolitan Hockey Club, Inc.*, 427 U.S. 639, 642 (1976), is fully applicable here: "The question, of course, is not whether this Court, or whether the Court of Appeals, would as an original matter have [applied the sanction]; it is whether the District Court abused its discretion in so doing" (citations omitted). For the reasons that follow, we hold that it did not.

Rule 37(b)(2) contains two standards — one general and one specific — that limit a district court's discretion. First, any sanction must be "just"; second, the sanction must be specifically related to the particular "claim" which was at issue in the order to provide discovery. While the latter requirement reflects the rule of *Hammond Packing, supra*, the former represents the general due process restrictions on the court's discretion.

In holding that the sanction in this case was "just," we rely specifically on the following. First, the initial discovery request was made in July 1977. Despite repeated orders from the court to provide the requested material, on December 21, 1978, the District Court was able to state that the petitioners "haven't even made any effort to get this information up to this point." The court then warned petitioners of a possible sanction. Confronted with continued delay and an obvious disregard of its orders, the trial court's invoking of its powers under Rule 37 was clearly appropriate. Second, petitioners repeatedly agreed to comply with the discovery orders within specified time periods. In each instance, petitioners failed to comply with their agreements. Third, respondent's allegation that the court had personal jurisdiction over petitioners was not a frivolous claim, and its attempt to use discovery to substantiate this claim was not, therefore, itself a misuse of judicial process. The substantiality of the jurisdictional allegation is demonstrated by the fact that the District Court found, as an alternative ground for its jurisdiction, that petitioners had sufficient contacts with Pennsylvania to fall within the State's long-arm statute. Fourth, petitioners had ample warning that a continued failure to comply with the discovery orders would lead to the imposition of this sanction. Furthermore, the proposed sanction made it clear that, even if there was not compliance with the discovery order, this sanction would not be applied if petitioners were to "produce statistics and other information" that would indicate an absence of personal jurisdiction. In effect, the District Court simply placed the burden of proof upon petitioners on the issue of personal jurisdiction. Petitioners failed to comply with the discovery order; they also failed to make any attempt to meet this burden of proof. This course of behavior, coupled with the ample warnings, demonstrates the "justice" of the trial court's order.

Neither can there be any doubt that this sanction satisfies the second requirement. CBG was seeking through discovery to respond to petitioners' contention that the District Court did not have personal jurisdiction. Having put the issue in question, petitioners did not have the option of blocking the reasonable attempt of CBG to meet its burden of proof. It surely did not have this option once the court had overruled petitioners' objections. Because of petitioners' failure to comply with the discovery orders, CBG was unable to establish the full extent of the contacts between petitioners and Pennsylvania, the critical issue in proving personal jurisdiction. Petitioners' failure to supply the requested information as to its contacts with Pennsylvania supports "the presumption that the refusal to produce evidence ... was but an admission of the want of merit in the asserted defense." *Hammond Packing*, 212 U.S. at 351. The sanction took as established the facts — contacts with Pennsylvania — that CBG was seeking to establish through discovery. That a particular legal consequence — personal jurisdiction of the court over the defendants — follows from this, does not in any way affect the appropriateness of the sanction.

IV

Because the application of a legal presumption to the issue of personal jurisdiction does not in itself violate the Due Process Clause and because there was no abuse of the discretion granted a district court under Rule 37(b)(2), we affirm the judgment of the Court of Appeals.

So ordered.

———————

b. Duty to Supplement Discovery Responses

The federal rules provide that a party has a duty to supplement its responses to discovery requests. Rule 26(e) requires parties supplement or correct any disclosures pursuant to Rule 26(a) as well as any interrogatory, request for production, or request for admission in a timely manner. If a party fails to do so, the party will not be permitted to use that information or witness (in the case of a disclosure under 26(a)) at a hearing or trial unless the failure is "substantially justified or is harmless." Fed. R. Civ. P. 37(c)(1). Thus, it's good practice to continually update discovery responses and disclosures as new information or witnesses become known. In addition, it's smart to review discovery responses before the close of discovery to make sure no additions or modifications are necessary. Although Rule 26(e) contemplates that a party need not supplement if the change or additional witness was made known to the other parties in the lawsuit, given that the court can potentially stop an attorney from using this information or calling the witness, it's better to be safe and supplement.

Exercise 9-21. The Chapter Problem Revisited

You now have reviewed the general scope of discovery, some limits on that scope, and the tools themselves. Recall the Piper lawsuit from the chapter problem. Draft a discovery plan on behalf of the plaintiff that includes what tools you would use to find facts and depose witnesses that would be helpful to or hurt your client's case as well as what you would ask using those tools. Include information you expect to get from the Rule 26(a) initial disclosures. What problems do you anticipate in obtaining some of the information?

---

6. Professional Development Question

As noted earlier, many attorneys and judges believe that attorneys and parties abuse the discovery process, increasing the costs of litigation. Although studies do not suggest that this is commonly the case, what is to be gained by an attorney or party in doing so? As an attorney, how does propounding 350 interrogatories in a simple debt collection case make you appear to opposing counsel and the court? Are there advantages to your client in propounding such a large request? What are they? Are there disadvantages to your professional reputation and to your client's interests in the lawsuit from doing so? What would you do if an opposing counsel propounded 350 interrogatories on your client?

Chapter 10

Disposition without Trial

1. Chapter Problem

"Icelandic-Nordic"

Imagine that you are a defense attorney who represents a Delaware corporation. One day, you are called to the front of your office to accept service on behalf of your client for a suit brought by one of its employees claiming race discrimination in promotions. The complaint in the suit states that the plaintiff was denied a promotion due to her race, which she describes as "Icelandic-Nordic."

The statute she sues under, Title VII of the Civil Rights Act of 1964, indeed prohibits race discrimination in promotion decisions, but it contains a set of exhaustion requirements, along with deadlines for each stage if the exhaustion process that must be observed for a claim to be deemed timely. A quick glance at the complaint reveals that the date on which the plaintiff claims to have been denied a promotion due to her race falls well outside the time limits specified in Title VII, so the claim is barred by the statute of limitations. As an experienced employment discrimination lawyer, you are also pretty sure you can win the case at trial because "Icelandic-Nordic" has never been recognized in any case as being its own unique racial group, as distinguished from "White non-Hispanic." Finally, you have also noticed that the complaint omits the required jurisdictional statement (*See* Rule 8(b)(1)).

What should you do?

---

2. Introduction

The preceding chapters mostly treated the many aspects of filing or framing a cause of action. From threshold considerations, such as jurisdiction, service, and venue, to more technical matters such as whom to sue, what law will govern the suit, and how to plead a claim under that law, most of the doctrines you have studied thus far get you to the point of filing and framing your side of the action. The exception is discovery—that process taught you how to marshal the evidence falling within the scope of the pleading that you have filed, against whom you have decided to sue, on the claims you have decided to assert, under the law you have determined will apply to those claims, and to organize that evidence to prepare to win your case, whether you are trying to prove a claim or defend against it.

This chapter focuses instead on how you can use that information to win the case in various ways without having to proceed to a full jury trial (which can be very expensive, as well as uncertain). Estimates vary, and the numbers change slightly from year to year, but generally, over 90% of the cases filed in the federal district courts do not proceed to a full trial on the merits.* These cases may be disposed of through a motion for default judgment, a motion for judgment on the pleadings, a motion to dismiss, a summary judgment motion, or through various litigation alternatives, which will be discussed in Chapter 14. This Chapter focuses on the various motions that each party may file to attempt to "take the case away from the jury." The rest of the chapter is organized as follows:

- Section 3 — Default and Default Judgment
- Section 4 — Dismissal and Judgment on the Pleadings
- Section 5 — Summary Judgment

Chapter 10 ends with Section 6, which addresses professionalism issues that arise by virtue of the availability of summary adjudication.

3. Default and Default Judgment

Look back at the Chapter Problem. At the end of the narrative, it asks, "What should you do?" How about doing nothing? If the case is a loser (and you have already determined it is a loser, on pleading grounds, on statute of limitations grounds, and on more traditional merits grounds), why go through the hassle of litigating it?

Generally, a civil defendant has three options upon the receipt of a plaintiff's complaint: (1) Do nothing, and wait for it to "go away"; (2) Move to dismiss the complaint, or one or more of the claims within it, under Rule 12; or (3) Answer the complaint under Rule 8. In addition to options (2) and (3), the defendant might also move for a more definite statement — to clarify a pleading that is so vague or unreadable as to make it impossible to answer (Rule 12(e)); or to strike portions of the complaint that are "redundant, immaterial, impertinent, or scandalous" (Rule 12(f)). But ultimately, the defendant will have to choose one of the three options above, and will have to make the election within the time limit for responding to a complaint: "within 21 days after being served with the summons and complaint." Rule 12(a).

The first of these options is to do nothing, and just let the deadline pass. At times, this can even be the *best* option. But what are the consequences of doing nothing?

---

* Ed. Note. *See, e.g.,* United States Courts, Judicial Business of the United States Courts: District Courts, at Tables 3 & T-4 (2013), *available at*: http://www.uscourts.gov/Statistics/Judicial Business/2013/us-district-courts.aspx (last visited Jan. 28, 2015) (read together, showing a trial rate of 6.6% for 2013).

This section discusses the main consequence—default and default judgment. *Default* denotes a change in the status of the defendant in a pending case. Entered on the docket by the Clerk of Court, default signifies that the defendant has failed to respond to the complaint, and that the plaintiff may now move for a default judgment. A *default judgment* is a judgment that is rendered against the defendant on the merits, due to the defendant's failure to defend. That is, a default judgment is a final judgment on the merits—equivalent to a judgment entered after a full trial and a jury verdict. The assumption underlying a default judgment is that, if the defendant had any viable defenses, the defendant would show up an assert those defenses. Since the defendant has failed to respond, the court can safely assume that the plaintiff's statement of the claim is correct.

If that is the case, though, should the court leave it *entirely* up to the plaintiff how a claim is stated? And what if the complaint seeks damages? Should it be entirely up to the plaintiff what amount of damages is awarded? Obviously, the potential for injustice would be too great if either of the above were the correct rule. Accordingly, even in the case of a default judgment, courts often take it upon themselves to conduct a *sua sponte Twombly/Iqbal* review of the complaint, and in every case involving damages (other than in cases where damages are for a "sum certain," such as for an unpaid bill reflected in an invoice), the court must hold an evidentiary hearing (basically, a mini-trial) to determine the proper damages award. Fed. R. Civ. P. 55(b)(2).

Exercise 10-1. Reading Rule 55

Read Rule 55, and answer the questions below:

1. What steps must you take to secure a default judgment if you are the plaintiff and the defendant has not answered your complaint by the deadline?

2. What if you are suing a minor?

3. What if your case is one for negligence in connection with a car accident? Must you do anything to recover the damages you claim in the complaint?

4. Assume that you secure a default judgment for $100,000, and you attempt to enforce the judgment by forcing the sale of some of the defendant's property. If the forced sale proceedings are the first time that the defendant has ever heard of the case, what can/must the defendant do?

Still, we should not be entirely comfortable that a court (and in many cases the Clerk) is permitted to enter a judgment on the merits, awarding damages and potentially other relief, against a party who has not been heard on any matter in the case. Indeed, *ex parte* proceedings (proceedings between the court and only one side of a controversy) for matters such as preliminary injunctions and discovery disputes, and in most other areas of procedural law, are highly disfavored, as you learned in reading *Connecticut v. Doehr* in Chapter 3. So, how can we be comfortable with the idea of a default judgment, which is an *ex parte* proceeding on the merits and results in awarding final judgment against the defendant?

The answer is twofold. First, both the policy of fairness to the defendant and compensation or other relief for the plaintiff must be balanced. You can probably imagine what defendants would do if there were no possibility of a default judgment—they would just never show up to defend their cases. Plaintiffs' rights to relief would be broadly frustrated.

Second, however, acknowledging that the possibility of mistake and injustice is much greater in an *ex parte* proceeding, the Rules provide for a safety valve—the motion to set aside default or a default judgment. The motion to set aside default aims to reverse the simple docket status change that the Clerk is supposed to make when a defendant fails to respond to the complaint on time. The motion to set aside a default judgment seeks relief from the final judgment that the Clerk or the court enters, closing the case and often awarding damages against the defendant. Under Rule 55, setting aside a default requires "good cause," while a default judgment may only be set aside for the reasons that any other final judgment might be set aside under Rule 60(b), reasons elaborated in Chapter 11, which focuses on Trial and Post-Trial.

Focusing on setting aside "default," then, what does "good cause" mean, and how does a court weigh damages evidence when only one party is before it? The next case illustrates how courts approach these questions.

Stephenson v. El-Batrawi
524 F.3d 907 (8th Cir. 2008)

Before Wollman and Smith, Circuit Judges, and Gritzner, District Judge.

Gritzner, District Judge.

Ramy El-Batrawi (El-Batrawi) appeals the decisions of the district court denying El-Batrawi's motion to set aside default, granting a motion for default judgment in favor of the Trustee for the Estate of MJK Clearing, Inc. (MJK Trustee) and against El-Batrawi, and entering a money judgment against El-Batrawi in the amount of $67.5 million. We affirm in part, and remand for further proceedings regarding the determination of the damages.

I. Background

The financial transactions underlying the claims herein are many, intricate and complex. For purposes of this appeal from the entry of default and a default judgment, the matter may be addressed in summary fashion from the allegations below.

MJK Clearing, Inc. (MJK) was a Minneapolis-based securities clearing company that entered into stock-loan transactions involving Genesis Intermedia, Inc. (GENI) stock. Stock lending involves a lending broker, who lends shares of stock to a borrowing broker, who in turn provides the lending broker cash collateral equal to the market value of the borrowed stock. If the price of the stock goes up while the stock is on loan to the borrowing broker, the borrowing broker must provide the lending broker with more cash collateral to cover the increase in price. Conversely, if the value of the stock goes down, the lending broker must return some of the cash collateral to the borrowing broker. This transfer of cash collateral based on the price of the stock is called "marking to the market."

GENI's primary focus was making infomercials and installing internet kiosks in shopping centers. El-Batrawi was the CEO, chairman of the board, and a major stockholder in GENI. The GENI stock-loan scheme commenced in the summer of 1999; GENI stock passed through several securities lending companies and ultimately landed at Deutsche Bank SL. In a typical GENI stock loan, El-Batrawi and Ultimate Holdings, another major GENI shareholder, would lend GENI stock to Native Nations, which in turn loaned GENI stock to MJK; MJK in turn loaned GENI stock to other brokers/dealers, such as Maple Partners, which then loaned GENI stock to Deutsche Bank SL, where the GENI stock would remain. Deutsche Bank SL would give the brokers/dealers, such as Maple Partners, the cash collateral for the stock. The cash collateral would then pass down the chain through the other brokers/dealers, until it reached the hands of El-Batrawi and Ultimate Holdings.

As the GENI stock sat at Deutsche Bank SL, and thus out of public circulation, the perpetrators of the scheme would manipulate the price of the stock by offering the few remaining public shares. As the price of the stock increased, the brokers/dealers in the chain marked to market, sending more cash collateral down the chain to El-Batrawi and Ultimate Holdings.

In the market atmosphere following the September 11, 2001, terrorist attacks, the market rigging could no longer be sustained, forcing Native Nations out of business and causing the GENI stock-loan scheme to collapse. Native Nations did not return over $200 million in cash collateral it owed to MJK for the stock loans. Irrespective of Native Nations' failure to return the funds to MJK, MJK had an independent obligation to return the funds to the broker/dealer behind it in the chain. Unable to absorb this over $200 million loss, MJK contacted officials at the Federal Reserve Bank and almost immediately ceased operations. A SIPA liquidation of MJK was commenced in the United States District Court for the District of Minnesota, and the entire liquidation proceeding was removed to the United States Bankruptcy Court for the District of Minnesota.

The MJK Trustee originally brought an adversary proceeding in the United States Bankruptcy Court for the District of Minnesota against various defendants, including El-Batrawi and Deutsche Bank SL, alleging the defendants were jointly and severally liable in committing various violations of the Securities Exchange Act of 1934, 15 U.S.C. §§ 78a–78nn; the Minnesota Securities Act, Minn. Stat. § 80A.40–.50; and Rackateer [*sic*] Influenced and Corrupt Organizations (RICO) Act, 18 U.S.C. §§ 1961–1968; in addition to allegations of common law fraud, conspiracy to defraud, and violations of the Minnesota Consumer Protection Act, Minn. Stat. §§ 324–338. Thereafter, the MJK Trustee's action was transferred to the United States District Court for the District of Minnesota.

On November 5, 2002, the MJK Trustee served the complaint on El-Batrawi by first-class mail at 3040 Beckman Drive, Los Angeles, California (Beckman address). Proof of service was filed with the Bankruptcy Court on November 18, 2002. The amended complaint was served on El-Batrawi at the Beckman address by first-class mail on November 22, 2002, and proof of service was filed on December 2, 2002. The mailings sent to the Beckman address were never returned to the MJK Trustee. Copies of the summons and amended complaint were also mailed by first-class mail to El-Batrawi at three additional addresses; each of these attempts were returned to the MJK Trustee indicating El-Batrawi no longer resided at those addresses, and no forwarding contact information was provided.

El-Batrawi did not appear to defend in the action after this service on the Beckman address. On April 30, 2003, the MJK Trustee filed for leave to serve El-Batrawi by publication, and on May 27, 2003, the district court granted the MJK Trustee's motion to serve El-Batrawi by publication in the Los Angeles Times once a week for four consecutive weeks. Service by publication was completed on July 27, 2003. El-Batrawi did not file or serve any pleading in response to the service by publication. On August 22, 2003, the MJK Trustee filed for entry of default against El-Batrawi, and the Clerk of Court entered default against El-Batrawi that same day.

In 2005, the MJK Trustee reached a settlement with the Deutsche Bank SL for $147.5 million in cash, waivers, and the withdrawal of certain claims valuing approximately $120 million, for a total settlement value of $267.5 million. According to the MJK Trustee, after reaching the Deutsche Bank SL settlement, approximately $67.5 million in uncompensated damages remained.

On April 7, 2006, and again on June 7, 2006, the MJK Trustee filed a motion for default judgment for the remaining $67.5 million in damages yet to be recovered by the MJK Trustee against El-Batrawi and other defendants who did not participate in the Deutsche Bank SL settlement agreement. Less than a week after the filing of the second motion for default judgment, but three and one-half years after service of the complaint and summons at the Beckman address, El-Batrawi made his first appearance in the case, filing a motion to set aside the default that had been entered against him in 2003. Without explanation of how he became aware of the MJK Trustee's action, El-Batrawi denied that he ever obtained actual notice and urged the district court to set aside the default against him, arguing he had meritorious defenses.

On January 26, 2007, the United States Magistrate Judge issued a Report and Recommendation, recommending El-Batrawi's motion to set aside be denied and the MJK Trustee's motion for default judgment be granted. After entertaining objections and responses to the Report and Recommendation, on March 8, 2007, the district court adopted the Report and Recommendation in its entirety. Judgment was entered on April 20, 2007, in the amount of $67.5 million against El-Batrawi and the remaining co-defendants, jointly and severally. El-Batrawi timely appealed.

El-Batrawi argues the district court abused its discretion in denying his motion to set aside default so he could make an appearance and defend the litigation pending in the district court, and that the district court erred in granting the MJK Trustee's motion for default judgment as against him and in entering a money judgment against him, jointly and severally with other defendants, in the amount of $67.5 million, plus post-judgment interest.

II. Discussion
A. Entry of Default

We review the denial of a motion to set aside default for an abuse of discretion. "The court may set aside an entry of default for good cause, and it may set aside a default judgment under Rule 60(b)." Fed.R.Civ.P. 55(c). When examining whether good cause exists, the district court should weigh "whether the conduct of the defaulting party was blameworthy or culpable, whether the defaulting party has a meritorious defense, and whether the other party would be prejudiced if the default were excused." *Johnson v. Dayton Elec. Mfg. Co.*, 140 F.3d 781, 784 (8th Cir.1998).

1. Blameworthy or Culpable Conduct

In an effort to show he was not blameworthy or culpable, El-Batrawi claims he did not receive "actual" notice of the lawsuit, although counsel for El-Batrawi conceded at oral argument that service was legally effective. The district court, in adopting the Report and Recommendation of the Magistrate Judge in its entirety, concluded the MJK Trustee properly served El-Batrawi. The MJK Trustee mailed copies of the initial summons and complaint, and the amended complaint, to El-Batrawi at the Beckman address, pursuant to Federal Rule of Bankruptcy Procedure 7004. Because those documents were never returned to the MJK Trustee by the United States Postal Service, the law presumes El-Batrawi was effectively served. "The fact that the summons and complaint were mailed to the correct street address, city and state, combined with the evidence that they were not returned to the trustee ... constitute *prima facie* evidence of the validity of the service." *In re Foos*, 204 B.R. 545, 547–48 (Bankr.N.D.Ill.1997); *see also In re Ms. Interpret,* 222 B.R. 409, 413 (Bankr.S.D.N.Y.1998) ("Courts uniformly presume that an addressee receives a properly mailed item when the sender presents proof that it properly addressed, stamped, and deposited the item in the mail."); *In re Thole,* 31 B.R. 548, 550 (Bankr.D.Minn.1983) (recognizing the strong presumption that letters duly mailed are duly received). In addition to the efforts of the MJK Trustee, the sworn affidavit of Elizabeth Fox (Fox), authorized process server for CIBC World Markets, Inc., a plaintiff in an action consolidated with the MJK Trustee case, states that on October 4, 2004, she served an individual she recognized as El-Batrawi at the Beckman address.

The MJK Trustee contacted El-Batrawi's business associates in an attempt to locate El-Batrawi's whereabouts. El-Batrawi's business associates provided no assistance. Counsel for the MJK Trustee asked attorney David C. Scheper, El-Batrawi's counsel in a related California class action, if Scheper would accept service of process on behalf of El-Batrawi. Mr. Scheper declined. Like the district court, we find it implausible that Mr. Scheper, El-Batrawi's attorney, upon being informed of the Minnesota action, would not inform his client of that lawsuit. Even more compelling toward this conclusion is the transfer of the California class action lawsuit pending against El-Batrawi to the District of Minnesota for consolidated pretrial proceedings.

After service on the Beckman address did not generate an appearance by El-Batrawi, the MJK Trustee also took the additional step of serving El-Batrawi by publication in the Los Angeles Times once a week for four successive weeks as permitted by the court. The MJK Trustee made a thorough investigation and inquiry into the whereabouts of El-Batrawi before resorting to service by publication.

The law presumes the documents mailed to the Beckman address were received by El-Batrawi, and his mere denial is insufficient to overcome this presumption. *See In re Outboard Marine Corp.,* 359 B.R. 893, 898 (Bankr.N.D.Ill.2007) ("[M]ere denial of receipt of the summons and complaint falls short of what is required to overcome the *prima facie* evidence of service."). El-Batrawi was also served by publication. Service by publication allows a case to move forward when other attempts at service fail to produce an appearance by a necessary party. El-Batrawi's attorney was fully aware of the existence of the pending action in Minnesota. And, the district court had a reasonable basis upon which to conclude El-Batrawi had actual notice through personal service of another of the consolidated cases.

The district court had more than enough information to conclude El-Batrawi had notice of the litigation through one or more of the foregoing means, and that El-Batrawi's assertions to the contrary lacked credibility. We conclude the district court did not abuse its discretion in concluding El-Batrawi was properly served, was evading service of process, and therefore was not blameless in his failure to timely appear.

2. Meritorious Defense

El-Batrawi argues the district court should have granted his motion to set aside default because he had potentially meritorious defenses, namely that he did not engage in market manipulation, he gave full disclosure, he did not participate in the alleged misconduct, he had no scienter, and the plaintiffs would not be able to prove any of the claimed damages. The district court, citing *Fink v. Swisshelm*, 182 F.R.D. 630 (D. Kan. 1998), for support, concluded El-Batrawi did not provide any factual support for his allegation that he was merely a bystander to the alleged stock-loan fraud that occurred, and accordingly, El-Batrawi had failed to establish the existence of a meritorious defense. El-Batrawi argues on appeal that the district court applied the incorrect legal standard in determining whether he had any meritorious defenses and misapplied the holding of *Fink*.

In *Fink*, the court concluded the defendant's motion to set aside default failed to make any effort to demonstrate a meritorious defense to the action. *Fink*, 182 F.R.D. at 632. The *Fink* court observed that while the defendant's answer listed two affirmative defenses, "bald allegation[s] ... without the support of facts underlying the defense, will not sustain the burden of the defaulting party to show cause why the entry of default should be set aside; the trial court must have before it more than mere allegations that a defense exists." *Id.* at 633. We agree.

Whether a meritorious defense exists is determined by examining whether the proffered evidence would permit a finding for the defaulting party. "The underlying concern is ... whether there is some possibility that the outcome ... after a full trial will be contrary to the result achieved by the default." *Augusta Fiberglass*, 843 F.2d at 812.

The record shows that while El-Batrawi offered up defenses, he did not provide a sufficient elaboration of facts or evidence to permit the district court to determine whether, if believed, the defenses were meritorious. Instead, the proffered defenses were nothing more than simple assertions unsupported by specific facts or evidence. The district court correctly concluded El-Batrawi did not provide minimally adequate factual support to illustrate the potential viability of his asserted defenses, and thus failed to establish the existence of a meritorious defense.

3. No Prejudice

Finally, El-Batrawi argues vacating the default would not prejudice the MJK Trustee, because any burden to the MJK Trustee in having to actually prove his claims against El-Batrawi and obtain the $67.5 million judgment on the merits is clearly outweighed by El-Batrawi's own due process entitlement to defend himself against the claims.

The district court found between the entry of default against El-Batrawi in 2003 and his eventual appearance in June 2006, the MJK Trustee had conducted extensive discovery, engaged in exhaustive motion practice, and made comprehensive trial preparations. The district court, in observing the case had been litigated for many years, concluded that to allow El-Batrawi to appear at this advanced stage in the litigation would result in the MJK Trustee having to re-litigate the case against El-Batrawi, which would cause substantial prejudice to the MJK Trustee. The district court found El-Batrawi had every opportunity to defend himself in the action but declined to do so in a timely manner.

Of course delay alone, or the fact the defaulting party would be permitted to defend on the merits, are insufficient grounds to establish the requisite prejudice to the plaintiff. Setting aside a default must prejudice plaintiff in a more concrete way, such as loss of evidence, increased difficulties in discovery, or greater opportunities for fraud and collusion. Applying this analysis to a case of this nature and magnitude demonstrates concrete prejudice.

This litigation involves complex stock loan transactions and necessarily involves numerous witnesses and voluminous documentary evidence. The MJK Trustee did not have the benefit of any discovery from El-Batrawi. The MJK Trustee's trial preparation was premised on the fact that a default had already been entered against El-Batrawi, and thus the MJK Trustee had no need to prepare for trial as against El-Batrawi. Given the length of delay between the commencement of this action and El-Batrawi's appearance, and the amount of litigation that occurred in the case during the intervening years, the district court correctly determined setting aside the default would clearly result in increased difficulties in discovery given the amount of time that has elapsed; and the MJK Trustee would be substantially prejudiced in having to re-litigate its claims against El-Batrawi at this late stage of the proceedings.

El-Batrawi waited almost three years from the time default was entered to file his motion to set aside, and that motion appears to have only been prompted by the MJK Trustee's motion for default judgment. We find no abuse of discretion by the district court in denying El-Batrawi's motion to set aside the entry of default.

B. Entry of Default Judgment

El-Batrawi argues it was a violation of his due process rights for the district court to enter a default judgment against him in the amount of $67.5 million for damages that El-Batrawi describes as unproven, uncertain, and unliquidated. El-Batrawi claims the record does not support the district court's findings that a sum of money even approximating $67.5 million is attributable to El-Batrawi's conduct in the alleged complaint.

It is a familiar practice and an exercise of judicial power for a court upon default, by taking evidence when necessary or by computation from facts of record, to fix the amount which the plaintiff is lawfully entitled to recover and to give judgment accordingly. "The court may conduct hearings or make referrals ... when, to enter or effectuate judgment, it needs to ... determine the amount of damages." Fed.R.Civ.P. 55(b)(2)(B). Once the amount of damages has been established, the court may enter judgment pursuant to the rule. The district court recognized it could hold an evidentiary hearing to determine the amount of damages, as requested by El-Batrawi, but deemed an evidentiary hearing unnecessary, finding each category of damages was supported by extensive documentary evidence.

A district court's findings regarding damages are reviewed for clear error. We reject El-Batrawi's argument that a *de novo* review should be employed where, as here, the district court held no hearing on the issue of damages. The need for a hearing is within the sound discretion of the district court under Fed.R.Civ.P. 55(b)(2)(B). As the authorities posited by El-Batrawi for a different standard are inapposite as they relate to fundamentally different procedural circumstances, we follow our established standard of review to determine if the damages findings by the district court are clearly erroneous.

The district court found there were three categories of damages at issue for which El-Batrawi and the other defaulting defendants were jointly and severally liable: (1) losses associated with the stock-loan chains at issue (i.e. the cash collateral not returned to MJK through the GENI loan chain); (2) the costs of liquidating the Estate of MJK Clearing, Inc.; and (3) the lost value of the MJK and Miller Johnson Steichen Kinnard, Inc. (MJSK) businesses.

The MJK Trustee claimed: (1) the expert reports of Mary D. Jepperson and Dr. Robert Comment established losses associated with the stock-loan chains of $200 million; (2) losses associated with the value of MJK and MJSK, as set forth in the report of James R. Hitchner, established losses in the amount of $85 million; and (3) liquidation costs for the MJK estate, as substantiated in the proceedings and documents filed with the bankruptcy court in connection with the liquidation of the MJK estate, established losses in the amount of $50 million. The MJK Trustee asserted the total of these losses amounted to $335 million, and after accounting for the $267.5 million settlement, $67.5 in uncompensated damages remained.

The district court, in concluding these three categories of losses amounted to a total of $335 million, as requested by the MJK Trustee, found: (1) the expert reports of Jepperson and Dr. Comment established the losses associated with the stock-loan chains were $200 million; (2) the losses associated with the value of MJK and MJSK were set forth in the report of James Hitchner and amounted to $85 million; and (3) the cost of liquidating the MJK estate amounted to $50 million in damages. The district court concluded the Deutsche Bank SL defendants had recompensated the MJK Trustee for $267.5 million of these damages through the settlement agreement, and therefore only $67.5 million in uncompensated damages remained.

The district court, however, never referenced a specific portion of Jepperson's 64-page report in concluding the report established $200 million in stock-loan chain losses. The district court concluded the cost of liquidating the MJK estate amounted to $50 million; again, however, neither the MJK Trustee nor the district court referenced any specific document in the bankruptcy proceedings to support $50 million in liquidation costs.

Other than general reference to the experts' reports, the district court did not identify with any specificity how it reached a loss amount of $200 million due to the stock-loan losses. Hitchner's report found a maximum loss value of $84 million. Without articulating any basis for deviating from the maximum amount of damages found in Hitchner's report, the district court concluded the lost value of businesses was $85 million. Without identifying upon which bankruptcy filing it relied in assessing the proper amount of liquidation costs, the district court concluded liquidation costs were $50 million, the exact amount requested by the MJK Trustee. It is not clear on this record what the basis is for the discrepancy between the value of the damages as set forth in the reports and the bankruptcy pleadings and the amount of damages sought by the MJK Trustee, and ultimately awarded by the district court.

The MJK Trustee has not extensively documented the mathematical calculation used to reach the final amount in each category of damages requested from the district court. The district court did not state the basis upon which each category of damages was calculated, nor did it refer to any specific portions of the experts' reports, or the bankruptcy proceedings, in support of the amount of each category of damages.

The district court's generic reference to evidentiary support for the damages determination leaves this court unable to discern the basis for that court's conclusions, and our own review of the record reveals inconsistencies between the supporting documents and the damages award. Because we have no adequate record for the evaluation of the district court's damages determinations, we conclude remand is necessary. *See Ackra Direct Mktg. Corp. v. Fingerhut Corp.*, 86 F.3d 852, 857 (8th Cir.1996) ("[W]e may remand when the lack of findings by the district court would substantially hinder our review.").

III. Conclusion

For the reasons stated, we affirm the denial of El-Batrawi's motion to set aside default. We vacate the default judgment and remand this case with instructions for the district court to make findings regarding the evidentiary support and any necessary calculations for any damage award it may enter. In this posture, and recognizing the discretion inherent in

Federal Rule of Civil Procedure 55(b)(2), we state no opinion at this time as to the need for or nature of any evidentiary hearing.

Exercise 10-2. Reading *Stephenson v. El-Batrawi*

1. Why is El-Batrawi unable to convince the court to reverse the denial of its motion to set aside the default? What factors are important to the appellate court in determining whether "good cause" exists, and why are those factors not satisfied?

2. Why does the court remand for a re-determination of damages? If the entry of default was proper, then why was the damages award improper?

3. Will the lower court have to conduct a full evidentiary hearing or mini-trial on remand? If the court does so, what sort of evidence should be admitted to prove the quantum of damages?

Exercise 10-3. "Efficient" Default

In some cases defaulting on purpose may be the most efficient way of responding to the complaint. For example, if you are sued in a federal court sitting in a state far from your home on a state-law cause of action for damages resulting from a car accident that amounted to no more than a fender-bender (i.e., minimal damage to the cars and no injuries to the drivers), would it make sense to appear and defend the case? Any decision the court renders will be invalid, due to lack of subject matter jurisdiction (the amount in controversy likely does not exceed $75,000), and if the plaintiff comes to your state to enforce the judgment, you will likely be able to defeat that action through a collateral attack on the lack of subject matter jurisdiction in the first suit.

Recall the *Pennoyer v. Neff* case from the personal jurisdiction portion of these materials. If you were Mr. Neff's attorney, and you did, in fact, know of the *Mitchell v. Neff* lawsuit (which, you may recall, resulted in Mitchell's attachment and auction purchase of Neff's land and the resulting assignment of it to the unfortunate Mr. Pennoyer), would you have advised Mr. Neff to default on purpose? What would be the pros and cons of such a strategy? What would have been the danger in showing up to defend the suit (which, you may recall, was a suit for unpaid legal bills)?

---

4. Dismissal and Judgment on the Pleadings

Of the three options set forth above that defendants have upon receiving a complaint, the second is to file a motion to dismiss. Rule 12(b) provides the grounds for moving to dismiss a claim based on the pleadings. By now, you are quite familiar with most, if not all, of these bases for dismissal, which include (1) lack of subject matter jurisdiction; (2) lack of personal jurisdiction; (3) lack of venue; (4) insufficient process; (5) insufficient service of process; (6) failure to state a claim upon which relief may be granted; and (7) failure to join a party required for just adjudication.

After studying jurisdiction, venue, service, joinder, and pleading, you know the standards that courts apply in deciding each of these motions, but how do you put these grounds for dismissal into operation?

a. Motion Practice in General

The most sensible place to begin is with what we call "motion practice" in general. When lawyers refer to *motion practice*, they mean the various motions that each side files in an attempt to secure victories—large and small—and to set its case up for those victories. During the course of a litigation, a party might file a motion to dismiss, to file a paper out of time, for preliminary injunctive relief, for expedited discovery, to compel discovery or to protect evidence from it, for sanctions against an opposing party, to exclude evidence, for judgment without trial, for a new trial, for stay of a judgment following a trial, and many, many other matters.

Many of these motions will require that the filer, or *movant*, has first consulted with all those who might oppose the motion to see whether they consent to the relief it requests. Can you see why? The reason is that most matters of procedure—even disputed ones—can be worked out if the parties just attempt to communicate with each other. People (even lawyers) are generally reasonable, and you will find that, if you just ask your opposing counsel to agree to something procedural, chances are that he or she will.

Of course, this is not the case with motions to dismiss, motions for summary judgment, motions for default judgment, or motions for sanctions, but in many cases, a motion simply asks for some minor procedural benefit or privilege, and it does not do the other parties to the case any good to spend money fighting it. If the motion is the kind that does not require prior consultation, or if the parties consulted do not give their consent for the relief requested, however, then they must oppose it through a response brief, which must be filed with the court. This process will typically also include a hearing, and while the Federal Rules do not generally specify any deadlines for response briefs, often the Local Rules of each District Court do. *E.g.*, U.S. Dist. Ct., N. Dist. Fla., Local Rule 7.1(c) (specifying a 14-day deadline for a response brief). One approach more common in state courts than in federal court today requires the non-movant to count backwards a number of days from the date of the scheduled hearing, if any, and file the response at that time.

In some cases, the Rules do establish a deadline for the filing of a *motion*, though. And that is where Rules 5 and 6 come in. Rules 5 and 6 govern the computation of time in the federal courts, and they can be the source of a great deal of angst for new lawyers. The following exercise will help you work through them in the context of a Rule 12(b)(6) motion.

Exercise 10-4. Responding to a Motion (or a Pleading)

This exercise will help you move through Rules 5 and 6. Although this example is tied to motion practice, the same rules apply when you are responding to a pleading, a discovery request, or any other paper that must be responded to by a deadline.

Imagine that you are plaintiff's counsel in a tort case filed in the United States District Court for the District of Academica. You have filed the complaint, and the defendant has answered and stated a counterclaim against your client for damages. Defendant's counsel filed the counterclaim on December 31, 2012 and served it on you by email that same day, pursuant to a written agreement between you two that you will accept service in this way. You would like to move to dismiss the counterclaim under Rule 12(b)(6).

1. What method(s) may/must you use to *serve* the motion to dismiss on your opponent?

2. What method(s) may/must you use to *file* the motion?

3. Assuming that you would like to file the motion electronically through the District of Academica's e-filing system, what is the latest **date** and **time** at which you can file your motion?

b. The Motion to Dismiss and the Motion for Judgment on the Pleadings

Having studied pleading, you have already had significant exposure to the motion to dismiss for failure to state a claim, and in the prior chapters, you saw most of the other Rule 12 defenses (those based on jurisdiction, venue, and service) in action. In the joinder chapter, you were introduced to dismissal based on the failure to join a party required for just adjudication. That leaves us with the Motion for Judgment on the Pleadings (the Rule 12(c) motion). This motion greatly resembles a motion to dismiss for failure to state a claim, in that the court is limited to consideration of the pleadings — no evidence. But it differs as to the *state of the pleadings* at the time of the motion. The Rule 12(c) motion may be filed by either party (or both, as "cross-motions"), but it may be filed and decided only once each party has filed all of the pleadings that it intends to file (complaint(s), answer(s), and reply(ies), if the latter are permitted). Similar to the case with the motion to dismiss, the court's review is limited to the pleadings themselves, along with any documents that have been attached to the pleadings and incorporated by reference (e.g., a contract or a bill).

Since the two motions are so similar, should the motion for judgment on the pleadings be evaluated using the *Twombly/Iqbal* standard? Or should a different standard apply, given that the court is able to review the answer, in addition to the complaint, and determine whether the parties dispute any factual issues between them? For example, what if the complaint states the date of a car accident that gave rise to the suit, and the answer states the affirmative defense of statute of limitations? Even if the plaintiff's complaint states a "plausible" claim for relief on its own terms, surely the additional defense allegation that the statute of limitations has run (along with the judge taking judicial notice of the date of filing) ought to justify judgment on behalf of defendant, right? The following case illustrates the general approach courts take to evaluating motions for judgment on the pleadings. Does it help us resolve the statute of limitations question?

Wee Care Child Center, Inc. v. Lumpkin

680 F.3d 841 (6th Cir. 2012)

Before: Cole and McKeague, Circuit Judges; Zatkoff, District Judge.

Cole, Circuit Judge.

Plaintiffs-Appellants Wee Care Child Center, Inc. and Tonya Brown appeal the district court's grants of the Defendants' motion to dismiss under Federal Rule of Civil Procedure Rule 12(b)(6) and cross-motion for judgment on the pleadings under Rule 12(c). This case comes to us as the latest in a long history of litigation between the Plaintiffs and various state and local government agencies and officials over the licensing of Wee Care Child Center. After reviewing this lengthy procedural history, we find many of the Plaintiffs' current claims waived. Because we also find the remaining unwaived claims barred by the Local Government Antitrust Act of 1984, we affirm.

I.

A. Factual Background

Plaintiff Brown is the owner and operator of Wee Care Child Center, Inc., ("Wee Care"), a now-defunct Columbus, Ohio, day care center that provided child care services for children of low-income parents. The Ohio Department of Job and Family Services ("ODJFS") originally granted Wee Care an operating license under Ohio Revised Code § 5104.02 *et seq.*, and when this license expired in December 2005, Wee Care timely applied for a renewal. This renewal application remained pending without any official decision for fifteen months, from December 2005 to March 2007. During this time period, ODJFS issued three expired licenses, in July 2006, August 2006, and January 2007, gradually reducing Wee Care's capacity from eighty-eight to thirty-eight children. These expired licenses remained valid operating licenses throughout the pendency of the renewal process. *See* Ohio Rev. Code § 119.06.

To provide its service, Wee Care primarily relied on funding contracts under Title XX, which provides government assistance for child care. *See* 42 U.S.C. § 1397 *et seq.* In May or June 2006, the Franklin County Department of Job and Family Services ("FCDJFS") — the agency responsible for distributing and negotiating Title XX funding contracts — decided to discontinue providing public assistance for Wee Care's child care services. FCDJFS based this decision on a proposed adjudication order from ODJFS, which would reject Wee Care's renewal application based on its failure to provide a safe environment for children. Among ODJFS's justifications for rejecting the renewal application were Wee Care's alleged improper use of physical discipline and failure to adequately ensure that its employees did not have disqualifying criminal convictions.

In July 2006, Wee Care requested an evidentiary hearing from ODJFS on the proposed adjudication order. This hearing was originally scheduled for October 2006, but was later delayed until November 2006. Prior to the scheduled hearing, ODJFS withdrew the proposed adjudication order, purportedly with the intent to re-file it at a later date with an additional charge. Wee Care, however, contends that ODJFS withdrew the order because it had insufficient evidence to prove its allegations against Wee Care.

Although ODJFS permitted Wee Care to continue operating its day care center under the expired licenses, Wee Care experienced difficulty negotiating and renewing third-party contracts, including its liability insurance contract and renewal certification from the Ohio Bureau of Workers' Compensation, as well as its Title XX contract. These losses eventually forced Wee Care to go out of business on March 3, 2007.

B. Procedural Background

Wee Care's long-fought battle with Ohio state and local government over its renewal application and Title XX funding contract began in November 2007 when Wee Care filed suit in the United States District Court for the Southern District of Ohio ("Wee Care I"). Wee Care raised a claim under 42 U.S.C. § 1983, as well as state law tort claims of tortious interference with contracts and business relationships. Wee Care requested eighty-eight million dollars in damages against ODJFS and three individuals, Helen Jones-Kelley, Barbara Riley, and Peggy Blevins. ODJFS filed a motion to dismiss and Wee Care voluntarily dismissed the suit without prejudice.

In February 2008, Wee Care again filed suit in the United States District Court for the Southern District of Ohio, asserting the same § 1983 and state tort law causes of action. This suit ("Wee Care II") also named Tonya Brown as a plaintiff and added an allegation that the defendants' actions were motivated by racial animus. The suit again requested eighty-eight million dollars in damages and was filed against ODJFS and the three original individual defendants as well as ODJFS employees, Lemuel Harrison and Michelle Vent. In December 2008, while *Wee Care II* was pending, Wee Care and Brown filed suit in the Ohio Court of Claims against ODJFS and the State of Ohio ("Wee Care III"), requesting the same monetary damages and alleging similar legal issues as the prior lawsuits.

After *Wee Care III* was filed in the Ohio Court of Claims, the *Wee Care II* defendants filed a motion to dismiss, arguing that the plaintiffs' claims against the individual defendants had been waived under § 2743.02(A)(1) of the Ohio Revised Code. The *Wee Care II* court "found that, by electing to sue ODJFS in the Court of Claims, Plaintiffs had waived their claims against the individual State Defendants" and granted the motion to dismiss as to the individual defendants. *Wee Care Child Center, Inc. v. Lumpkin*, No. 2:09-cv-1059, 2010 WL 3463369, at *2 (S.D. Ohio Aug. 30, 2010). The state also argued that Eleventh Amendment sovereign immunity barred the plaintiffs' claims against the state, and the court dismissed the claims against ODJFS on that basis.

Following the dismissal of *Wee Care II*, the *Wee Care III* plaintiffs requested a hearing to determine whether the individual defendants were entitled to immunity as government defendants. The *Wee Care III* court decided, over the plaintiffs' objection, to hold the immunity hearing at the same time as the trial on the merits. Thereafter, the plaintiffs voluntarily dismissed *Wee Care III*.

Three days after voluntarily dismissing *Wee Care III*, Wee Care again filed suit in the United States District Court for the Southern District of Ohio ("*Wee Care IV*"). In *Wee Care IV*, Wee Care and Brown named sixteen employees of ODJFS and FCDJFS as defendants. An amended complaint named eleven ODJFS employees ("State Defendants") and five FCDJFS employees ("County Defendants"). Wee Care raised four causes of action, alleging that the State and County Defendants violated Section 1 of the Sherman Antitrust Act, and that the County Defendants tortiously interfered with Wee Care's contracts and business relationships, and engaged in a civil conspiracy. The State Defendants filed a motion to dismiss under Rule 12(b)(6) on the basis of Ohio Revised Code § 2743.02(A)(1) waiver, qualified immunity, the state action doctrine, and a failure to satisfy pleading standards. The district court granted this motion, concluding that Wee Care's claims were waived because *Wee Care IV* involves the same act or omission alleged in *Wee Care III*. The court further concluded that § 2743.02(A)(1) waiver applied irrespective of Wee Care's attempt to couch *Wee Care IV* in a new antitrust cause of action.

The County Defendants and Wee Care also both filed motions for judgment on the pleadings under Rule 12(c). The County Defendants alleged immunity from money damages under the Local Government Antitrust Act of 1984 ("LGAA"), 15 U.S.C. §§ 34–36, as well as asserted qualified immunity, the state action doctrine, and failure to satisfy pleading standards as additional bases for judgment in their favor. The district court granted the County Defendants' motion, finding the LGAA to bar Wee Care's request for relief on the antitrust claim and then declined to exercise supplemental jurisdiction over the remaining state law claims. Wee Care timely appeals the district court's orders and it is *Wee Care IV* that is currently before this Court.

In November 2010, following the district court's decision in *Wee Care IV*, Wee Care again filed suit in the Ohio Court of Claims ("*Wee Care V*"), against ODJFS and five individual defendants, raising allegations nearly identical to *Wee Care III*. The Ohio Court of Claims has stayed proceedings in *Wee Care V* in response to the appeal of *Wee Care IV* currently before this Court.

II.

A. Standard of Review

We review a district court's grant of a motion to dismiss under Federal Rule of Civil Procedure 12(b)(6) *de novo*. "To survive a motion to dismiss, [the plaintiff] must allege 'enough facts to state a claim to relief that is plausible on its face.'" *Traverse Bay Area Intermediate Sch. Dist. v. Mich. Dep't of Educ.*, 615 F.3d 622, 627 (6th Cir. 2010) (quoting *Bell Atlantic Corp. v. Twombly*, 550 U.S. 544, 570 (2007)). The Court must construe the complaint in light most favorable to the plaintiff, accept all the factual allegations as true, and determine whether the plaintiff can prove any set of facts in support of her claim that would entitle her to relief. We also review the district court's decision regarding a motion for judgment on the pleadings pursuant to Federal Rule of Civil Procedure 12(c) using the same *de novo* standard of review as a motion to dismiss under Rule 12(b)(6).

B. Wee Care's Claims Against the State Defendants

The *Wee Care IV* complaint raises one claim against the State Defendants, a *per se* violation of Section 1 of the Sherman Antitrust Act. Wee Care bases its antitrust action on ODJFS's allegedly improper process of responding to license renewal applications, which involves a procedure Wee Care characterizes as a "zero out scheme." Under this alleged zero out scheme, Wee Care contends that ODJFS would not respond timely to renewal applications and, with the cooperation of FCDJFS, would deny Title XX funding to day care centers awaiting a renewal decision. As the day care centers were left to operate under expired licenses that often reduced the number of children the center could serve, the day care centers would have trouble negotiating necessary third-party contracts. With fewer clients and no Title XX funding, the businesses eventually would be forced to close.

Wee Care alleges that ODJFS implemented this zero out procedure as a means to control the day care market and drive disfavored businesses out of the market without providing the due process hearing required by Ohio law. Section 119.06(C) of the Ohio Revised Code requires any licensing agency to "afford a hearing upon the request of a person whose application for a license has been rejected...." Ohio Rev. Code § 119.06(C). Wee Care alleges that when ODJFS wanted to deny an application, rather than affording the day care operator a hearing, the State Defendants would delay the hearing for such lengthy periods of time that the day care center eventually went out of business, mooting the request for a hearing.

Wee Care's attempt to establish an antitrust claim against the State Defendants based on this alleged zero out scheme fails both as a matter of state and federal law. As a threshold matter, as the district court correctly concluded, § 2743.02(A)(1) expressly prohibits Wee Care from raising any claims regarding any such zero out procedure against individual government employees. In this section, Ohio law provides a limited waiver of sovereign immunity and consent to suit in the Court of Claims. However, it also provides that a plaintiff who elects to sue the state in that court waives the right to raise claims against individual employees of the state. Section 2743.02(A)(1) states that "filing a civil action in the court of claims results in a complete waiver of any cause of action, based on the same act or omission, which the filing party has against any officer or employee...." This waiver is void if "the court determines that the act or omission was manifestly outside the scope of the officer's or employee's office or employment or that the officer or employee acted with malicious purpose, in bad faith, or in a wanton or reckless manner." *Id.*

When Wee Care filed *Wee Care III* in the Court of Claims against ODJFS and the State of Ohio, it waived any claims against the individual officers and employees that arose from the same act or omission. Wee Care contends that *Wee Care III* does not involve the same acts or omissions as *Wee Care IV*, because its current complaint couches its causes of action in terms of antitrust and conspiracy violations, whereas prior iterations of the complaint were presented as due process violations. Although the parties dispute whether Wee Care even raised this new claim of conspiracy against the State Defendants, even assuming that the conspiracy claim was properly raised, we have previously rejected the argument that a plaintiff may evade the reach of § 2743.02(A)(1) by employing a new cause of action. In *Thomson v. Harmony*, we held that because § 2743.02(A)(1) "specifically refers to an 'act' rather than an 'allegation' or 'claim,'" waiver applies if the two cases involve the same acts or omissions regardless of whether they "share the same legal or theoretical foundation...." 65 F.3d 1314, 1319 (6th Cir.1995) (emphasis omitted). Because the case before this Court involves the same issue previously raised in the Court of Claims in *Wee Care III*—the impropriety of ODJFS and FCDJFS's purported zero out scheme—under §2743.02(A)(1), Wee Care is barred from suing individual government employees and the district court properly dismissed the case.

Regardless of the waiver issue, the State Defendants are further entitled to dismissal under Rule 12(b)(6) because Wee Care has failed to state a claim to relief that is plausible on its face. Viewing Wee Care's complaint in the light most favorable to it and accepting all its well-pleaded allegations as true, Wee Care has not alleged facts that would plausibly allow it to show that the State Defendants violated antitrust laws. To prove antitrust injury, the key inquiry is whether competition—not necessarily a competitor—suffered as a result of the challenged business practice. Because protecting competition is the *sine qua non* of the antitrust laws, a complaint alleging only adverse effects suffered by an individual competitor cannot establish an antitrust injury.

A review of Wee Care's complaint reveals that it has not set forth "sufficient factual matter ... to state a claim to relief that is plausible on its face," *Ashcroft v. Iqbal*, 556 U.S. 662, 678 (2009), because it lacks any factual basis for concluding a harm to competition beyond adverse effects suffered by an individual competitor. Wee Care provides no facts, beyond mere conclusory statements, to support the allegation that ODJFS's procedures harmed competition. "While legal conclusions can provide the framework of a complaint, they must be supported by factual allegations." *Iqbal*, 556 U.S. at 679. A complaint, such as that in *Wee Care IV*, that solely "tenders naked assertion[s] devoid of further factual enhancement," cannot survive a motion to dismiss under Rule 12(b)(6). *Id.* at 678 (internal quotation marks omitted) (alteration in original). As such, the district court properly granted the State Defendants' motion to dismiss and we need not address the State Defendants' defenses under qualified immunity and the state action doctrine.

C. Wee Care's Claims Against the County Defendants

The *Wee Care IV* complaint raises four claims against the County Defendants: a *per se* violation of Section 1 of the Sherman Antitrust Act, tortious interference with contract, tortious interference with business relationships, and civil conspiracy. The district court dismissed all four causes of action, finding the LGAA to bar the antitrust claim and declining to exercise supplemental jurisdiction under 28 U.S.C. §1367(c)(3) on the remaining state law claims. The LGAA, enacted in response to the voluminous antitrust litigation against local governments, provides that "[n]o damages, interest on damages, costs, or attorney's fees may be recovered [for antitrust violations] ... from any local government, or official or employee thereof acting in an official capacity." 15 U.S.C. §35(a). Wee Care contends that the County Defendants' actions underlying the antitrust claim were not made in their official capacity because they participated in the allegedly improper zero out scheme and, therefore, asks this Court to deny LGAA immunity.

As the question of whether the County Defendants were "acting in an official capacity" is dispositive to Wee Care's argument, we must first explore the meaning of this requirement. We have not previously defined, for purposes of the LGAA, the phrase "acting in an official capacity." However, the Fourth Circuit has reasoned that:

> Our position [is] that an affirmative grant of explicit authority is not required for an employee or government official to be acting in an official capacity under the LGAA.... [T]he phrase 'acting in an official capacity' includes those lawful actions, undertaken in the course of a defendant's performance of his duties, that reasonably can be construed to be within the scope of his duties and consistent with the general responsibilities and objectives of his position.

Sandcrest Outpatient Servs., P.A. v. Cumberland Cnty. Hosp. Sys., Inc., 853 F.2d 1139, 1145 (4th Cir.1988). We agree with the Fourth Circuit that "acting in an official capacity" should be read broadly for purposes of the LGAA.

Applying this broad reading, Wee Care's argument that the County Defendants were acting outside the scope of their official capacity when negotiating Title XX funding contracts is untenable. Municipal employees act within their official capacity when conducting duties that are "consistent with the general responsibilities and objectives" of their positions. *Sandcrest Outpatient Servs., P.A.*, 853 F.2d at 1145. There is no question that the negotiation of Title XX funding contracts falls within the "general responsibilities and objectives" of the County Defendants' positions. And, to the extent that Wee Care seeks to argue that the County Defendants undertook this general responsibility with an improper motive, that argument fails because "[t]he LGAA makes no provision for consideration of a defendant's motives...." *Id.* at 1146. Therefore, the LGAA shields the County Defendants from antitrust liability and the district court properly granted their cross-motion for judgment on the pleadings under Rule 12(c).

As Wee Care's one federal claim was properly dismissed, it was likewise proper for the district court to decline to exercise supplemental jurisdiction over the remaining state law claims.

* * *

III.

The district court's grants of the State Defendants' motion to dismiss under Rule 12(b)(6) and the County Defendants' cross-motion for judgment on the pleadings under Rule 12(c) are affirmed.

> ## Exercise 10-5. Motion to Dismiss vs. Motion for Judgment on the Pleadings
>
> You know from the introductory material above that a big difference between a motion to dismiss and a motion for judgment on the pleadings is the state of the pleadings at the time of the motion. For a motion to dismiss, only the complaint is before the court. For a motion for judgment on the pleadings, all of the pleadings are before the court (but nothing else—note that, in either case, introducing evidentiary matter going beyond the pleadings and any attached documents automatically converts the motion to a motion for summary judgment—see Rule 12(d)).
>
> 1. As you can see from the above case, the nature of the defense offered can influence which type of motion is filed. In *Wee Care IV* (the case above), the state defendants filed a motion to dismiss, while the county defendants filed a motion for judgment on the pleadings. What is it about the defenses that each offered that justified these differences in strategy?
>
> 2. Why do you think that Wee Care also filed a motion for judgment on the pleadings (thus making the motions "cross-motions")? Why didn't Wee Care file a "cross-motion" to dismiss against the state defendants?
>
> 3. What are the differences in the standards that apply to review of each motion (if any)?

c. Waiver of Defenses under Rule 12

One of the more difficult aspects of Rule 12 and its defenses is determining whether any of the defenses are waived. The doctrine of waiver exists in many areas of the law—both procedural (e.g., the procedural waiver in *Wee Care IV* above) and substantive (e.g., a waiver of breach in a contract dispute). Waiver of one's threshold defenses depends on the application of Rule 12(g) and (h), which must be read together (and very, very carefully). Read Rules 12(g) and (h).

As you can see from such a reading, Rule 12(g) provides two governing principles: (1) that a movant may join together any combination of the Rule 12(b) grounds in one motion; and (2) that, once a party makes any motion under Rule 12, that same party may not make any other motion under Rule 12 if that second motion raises a defense that was "available" to the party, but omitted from the first motion.

This latter part means that, for example, if you know you have a defense based on personal jurisdiction at the time you move for dismissal based on subject matter jurisdiction, you cannot omit the personal jurisdiction ground from your initial Rule 12 motion. If you do, you cannot assert the personal jurisdiction ground through a later Rule 12 motion if you lose on the subject matter jurisdiction ground. Now, if at the time of your initial motion, you are not (or should not be) aware of the personal jurisdiction defense (for example, if the case arose out of communications, and it is not clear where those communications originated or were directed until later), then you are still able to move to dismiss under your personal jurisdiction ground when the ground becomes "available" (i.e., you find out about it). Otherwise, you *waive* your personal jurisdiction ground by failing to assert it in your first motion (or in your answer, if you choose *not* to move to dismiss *at all*).

Rule 12(h) specifies exactly which defenses can be waived in this way, and which defenses are not so easily waived. The defenses stated in Rule 12(b)(2)–(5) (personal jurisdiction, venue, insufficient process, and insufficient service of process) are all waived due to failure to assert them in the initial motion (or pleading, if no motion is filed), but the other Rule 12 defenses are not so easily waived.

Why are the Rule 12(b)(2)–(5) defenses treated so harshly? Think about the nature of these defenses. They are personal to the defendant (i.e., they protect the defendant's right to due process of law, along with the defendant's reasonable expectation of a convenient forum and venue). They do not involve the merits, as a Rule 12(b)(6) motion does. They do not involve including or excluding other parties, as a Rule 12(b)(7) motion does. And most importantly, they all present matters that should be knowable before a defending party chooses whether to answer or move to dismiss. A defendant is very likely to know, at the earliest stages of the case, his connections with the forum state (personal jurisdiction), his own residence state (venue), the contents of the process served on him (insufficient process), and whether he was served properly, or at all (insufficient service). It does no good to leave these matters unaddressed and allow money and time to be spent on later stages of the case if they are all known or knowable at the outset.

In contrast, whether a complaint states a plausible claim for relief can depend on later factual development that allows a defendant to better understand the allegations in the complaint. If a complaint is truly incomprehensible, or something close to that, the defendant can always move for a more definite statement under Rule 12(e), but the standard for such motions is high,* and a complaint can be unclear or ambiguous without requiring a more definite statement. If we have one of these complaints — not a model of clarity, but also not a complete mess — then the later stages of the case may clarify what the plaintiff meant by some of the more opaque allegations in the complaint, and it may be that, once clarified, they allow for the complaint to be dismissed on legal grounds (recall that both legal and factual insufficiency are grounds for granting a Rule 12(b)(6) motion). For this reason, Rule 12(h) allows a party to move to dismiss based on Rule 12(b)(6) at any time before the jury is asked to deliberate.

Rule 12(b)(7) motions are treated similarly under Rule 12(h). Here again, it may not be clear at the outset that a party needed for just adjudication has been left out of the action (either deliberately or negligently). But later stages of the case may make

---

* Ed. Note. A Rule 12(e) motion may be granted only if the complaint "is so vague or ambiguous that the party cannot reasonably prepare a response." Fed. R. Civ. P. 12(e).

it clear that either an absent party's interests are likely to be impaired, or the fairness of the case between the existing parties is likely to be impaired, without joining the absent party. In such cases, it is possible to accomplish required joinder (or dismissal, if joinder is not feasible and the factors weigh in favor of it) at any time before the jury is asked to deliberate. Fed. R. Civ. P. 12(h)(2).

What about subject matter jurisdiction (Rule 12(b)(1))? Subject matter jurisdiction has most of the features of the other "threshold" defenses subject to waiver if they are not asserted in a timely way, but subject matter jurisdiction qualifies for special treatment under Rule 12(h)(3)—it is never waived. As you know from studying subject matter jurisdiction, even if the parties fail to bring it up, the court can make *its own motion* to consider subject matter jurisdiction. The reason we treat the subject matter jurisdiction defense in this way is that it goes to the basic power of the court over the action. This is an issue that is personal to the *court*, not the *parties*, because it involves the legitimacy of the decision. A court with no constitutional and statutory power over an action cannot issue legitimate orders in that action affecting the rights of the parties. So, we are very careful about subject matter jurisdiction, and we allow it to be raised at any stage of the case, by any party, or even by the court, even if the first time it is raised is in an appeal to the Supreme Court.* The next Exercise helps you to work your way back through these difficult provisions.

Exercise 10-6. Applying Rule 12(g) & (h)

For each of the questions below, choose the best response based on your careful reading of Rule 12(g) and (h).

1. Can a defendant make a motion to dismiss under Rule 12(b)(2) after having an earlier motion under Rule 12(b)(6) denied?

   a. Yes, because you can make a Rule 12(b)(2) motion at any time.

   b. No, because the 12(b)(2) defense is waived.

2. Can a defendant make a motion to dismiss under Rule 12(b)(2) after it files its answer?

   a. Yes, because a Rule 12(b)(2) defense is never waivable.

---

* Ed. Note. The only way to really lose the subject matter jurisdiction defense is to allow a case to proceed through all the stages of litigation, reach a judgment, and exhaust all appeals without anyone raising the issue. At that time, because the parties and the court all had the opportunity at every stage, we deem the issue waived. But this doctrine is a matter of federal common law, not a matter specified in the rules. *See Insurance Corp. of Ireland v. Compagnie des Bauxites de Guinee*, 456 U.S. 694, 702 n.9 (1982) ("A party that has had an opportunity to litigate the question of subject-matter jurisdiction may not, however, reopen that question in a collateral attack upon an adverse judgment. It has long been the rule that principles of *res judicata* apply to jurisdictional determinations—both subject matter and personal.") (citing *Chicot County Drainage Dist. v. Baxter State Bank*, 308 U.S. 371 (1940); *Stoll v. Gottlieb*, 305 U.S. 165 (1938)).

    b. Yes, because the defendant did not raise the defense in an initial Rule 12 motion.

    c. No, because the defendant must raise the defense in its answer.

    d. No, because the defendant waived the defense by not raising it in a Rule 12 motion prior to answering.

3. Defendant makes no pre-trial Rule 12 motion and includes no Rule 12 defenses in its answer. He loses at trial. On appeal, can he raise the defense set out in Rule 12(b)(1)?

    a. No, because he failed to raise the defense in a Rule 12 motion or an answer.

    b. Yes, because he can raise the defense anytime.

    c. No, because he must raise the defense at some point before the jury is charged.

    d. Yes, if he has preserved the defense for appeal.

4. If a defendant makes a pre-answer Rule 12(b)(1) motion and loses, can she move once again to dismiss the case pursuant to Rule 12(b)(1) after she loses at trial?

    a. Yes, because she can raise the defense at any time.

    b. No, because once the court has decided the issue, she must wait to raise it on appeal.

    c. Yes, as long as she objects during the trial.

    d. No, because the court has no authority to reconsider its own motions.

5. Defendant loses a motion to dismiss based on Rule 12(b)(3). Can she now make a motion under Rule 12(f)?

    a. Yes, because this is not a Rule 12(b) motion and therefore is not waived.

    b. No, because a defendant must make this Rule 12 motion with her initial Rule 12(b)(3) motion.

    c. Yes, because this ground is never waived.

    d. No, because only a plaintiff can challenge scandalous matter in a complaint.

Recall that Rule 12(g)(2) provides that, once a party makes any motion "under this rule" (Rule 12), that same party cannot make another motion "under this rule" raising "defenses" that were available at the time of the first motion. Note that this prohibition is subject to the exceptions stated in Rule 12(h). That is, even if the 12(b)(1), (6), and/or (7) defenses are "available" to a party when that party makes its first motion (or files its answer, if no motion is filed), they may still be raised later. But what about Rule 12 motions that are *not* motions to dismiss? Does this prohibition on later motions apply to those? The next case addresses the issue.

Marrero-Gutierrez v. Molina

491 F.3d 1 (1st Cir. 2007)

Young, District Judge.

Enid Marrero-Gutierrez ("Marrero") and Alejandro Bou Santiago ("Bou") (collectively "the Plaintiffs") sued Esperanza Molina ("Molina"), Ivan Velez ("Velez"), Luis Coss ("Coss") a/k/a Tito, Gabriel Alonso ("Alonso"), Ileana Echegoyen, Nilsa Enid Negron, Ramonita Garcia, and Wanda Roman in their personal capacities; Myrna Crespo-Saavedra in her official capacity; and the Housing Department of the Commonwealth of Puerto Rico ("Housing Department") (collectively "the Defendants") for political discrimination and violations of the Plaintiffs' rights under the First, Fifth, and Fourteenth Amendments to the United States Constitution. The Plaintiffs also asserted various state-law claims. Acting on a motion for judgment on the pleadings, the district court granted judgment to the Defendants on all claims. The Plaintiffs now appeal. After careful consideration, we affirm.

I. Factual and Procedural History

The Plaintiffs are former employees of the Housing Department and active members of the New Progressive Party ("NPP") — a political party that campaigns for Puerto Rican statehood. In 2000, Puerto Rico held its general elections, and the Popular Democratic Party ("PDP") won control of the government. The PDP is a political adversary of the NPP.

Bou worked in the Housing Department for ten years. In May 2000, he received a promotion to the position of Administrative Director II and was appointed as the Director of the Office of Security and Emergency Management of the Housing Department. As a result of PDP's winning the elections that year, Coss — a member of the PDP — was appointed Special Assistant to the Secretary of the Housing Department. Bou alleges that Coss gave instructions to the Human Resources personnel of the Housing Department to find a way to replace him with a PDP adherent. Specifically, Bou alleges that Coss made this request to Angel Semidey ("Semidey") who, despite being a PDP adherent, refused to help Coss and subsequently resigned. On March 7, 2001, Bou was demoted. On July 27, 2002, Bou encountered Semidey at a celebration and, for the first time, learned that his demotion resulted from his affiliation with NPP.

Marrero held a career position as Director of the Section 8 Program starting in 1994. Marrero alleges that her job performance garnered only praise from her supervisors. Marrero managed to receive such positive performance feedback despite serving under different party administrations during her career at the Housing Department.

Marrero alleges that after Molina retired in June 2002, the Housing Department was reorganized without following federal guidelines. As part of the reorganization, Alonso was brought in to supervise the Section 8 Program. The reorganization amounted to a constructive demotion of Marrero by reducing her responsibilities and subjecting her to an abusive work environment. Specifically, her new responsibilities failed to include functions that she was entitled to perform under the Housing Department's prior reclassification program. Marrero also alleges that her subordinates often circumvented her, that her supervisors treated her in a discourteous manner by harassing and intimidating her, and that Molina openly disparaged the NPP in front of Marrero and her personnel. Finally, Marrero suffered several humiliating events arising out of her health status. Marrero was surgically treated for cancer in her reproductive system. The Defendants allegedly mocked her as a result of this condition, claiming that she was not really sick and simply attempting to avoid returning to work by faking her illness.

On or about May 3, 2002, while still on medical leave, Marrero received a letter dated April 18, 2002, stating the intention to remove her from office. This letter, and a subsequent one, accused her of failing to perform job duties and of committing illegal acts. These accusations mirrored ones levied against Velez—a member of the PDP—who directly supervised Marrero during this time. The Housing Department also notified Velez that it intended to terminate him. Velez was initially demoted and later terminated. In both letters, Marrero was summoned to an informal hearing, which she alleges was a sham designed to tarnish her reputation. Despite her characterization of the hearing, Marrero was able to proffer evidence rebutting the accusations against her. Marrero was allowed to continue working at the Housing Department pending the final disposition. The hearing officer submitted a negative report. On March 10, 2002, the Housing Department notified Marrero of her separation from employment and salary, which constituted the last alleged act of discrimination by the Defendants.

This action commenced in the district court on March 10, 2003. The Housing Department successfully moved to dismiss, on Eleventh Amendment grounds, the claims against it for monetary relief. Marrero does not appeal this ruling. Thereafter, upon motions duly briefed by both sides, the district court granted the Defendants judgment on the pleadings pursuant to Federal Rule of Civil Procedure 12(c). The appeal of this order is before this Court.

II. Analysis

* * *

B. Marrero's Threshold Arguments

Marrero advances three threshold, procedural challenges to the dismissal of her section 1983 claims. She argues that the district court erred in allowing the Defendants' motion for a judgment on the pleadings because the Defendants had waived the grounds upon which the district judge relied by failing to consolidate their defenses and raise them in the first motion to dismiss. Second, Marrero contends that the district judge improperly converted the Defendants' motion for judgment on the pleadings into a motion for summary judgment. Finally, Marrero raises the argument that the district court ought not have dismissed the ancillary state law claims after finding no cognizable section 1983 claim. These threshold issues are easily dispensed with before addressing the arguments on the merits.

1. Failure to Consolidate Defenses

The district court dismissed the Plaintiffs' claims by allowing a narrow motion to dismiss and then subsequently allowing a broader motion for judgment on the pleadings. Marrero attacks the district court's allowance of the second motion by parroting the general rule for consolidation of defenses found in Federal Rule of Civil Procedure 12(g). According to Marrero, the Defendants waived the grounds upon which the district court relied in the second motion by failing to raise them when the Housing Department moved to dismiss on Eleventh Amendment grounds.

Federal Rule of Civil Procedure 12(g) provides that:

> A party who makes a motion under this rule may join with it any other motions herein provided for and then available to the party. If a party makes a motion under this rule but omits therefrom any defense or objection then available to the party which this rule permits to be raised by motion, the party shall not thereafter make a motion based on the defense or objection so omitted, except a motion as provided in subdivision (h)(2) hereof on any of the grounds there stated.*

Fed.R.Civ.P. 12(g) (emphasis added).

Marrero ignores the rule's express exception that cross-references subdivision (h)(2) and permits a "defense of failure to state a claim upon which relief can be granted" to be raised "by motion for judgment on the pleadings." Fed. R. Civ. P. 12(h)(2).

Here, the district court entertained and allowed a motion for judgment on the pleadings that raised a defense of failure to state a claim. The district court's action thus squarely meets the exception to the general rule expressed in Rule 12(g) and undermines Marrero's argument.

---

* Ed. Note. This is an older version of Rule 12(g), which was amended for stylistic purposes on December 1, 2007.

2. Improper Conversion

Marrero also argues that the district court improperly converted the motion for judgment on the pleadings into a motion for summary judgment. This argument marries with Marrero's contention that factual issues existed on the merits of her section 1983 claim. Marrero, consumed by her belief that such factual issues existed, concludes that the district judge must have converted the motion for judgment on the pleadings into a motion for summary judgment in order to dismiss the case. There is, however, no support that such a conversion occurred.

The record shows that the district court properly considered the matter as a motion for judgment on the pleadings. The Defendants did not attach any documents or exhibits outside their pleadings, and the district court never allowed the parties to supplement the record.

Of course, the implication of this holding is that we will review, as we do below, Marrero's arguments as to why factual issues remained as to her section 1983 claims under the standard for a motion for judgment on the pleadings, which requires the plaintiff to meet only a deferential, notice-pleading requirement to survive dismissal.

3. Supplemental Jurisdiction

* * *

C. Marrero's Merits Arguments

After dispensing with the threshold, procedural arguments, we must carefully review the district court's dismissal on a motion for judgment on the pleadings of Marrero's section 1983 claim. Such a review must be conducted by considering the adequacy of *Marrero*'s complaint in light of the Supreme Court's admonition that there can be no "heightened pleading standard" or a "more demanding rule for pleading a complaint under § 1983 than for pleading other kinds of claims for relief." *Leatherman v. Tarrant County Narcotics Intelligence and Coordination Unit*, 507 U.S. 163, 167–68 (1993). We consider each of Marrero's theories in turn.

1. Procedural Due Process Claim

In order to establish a procedural due process claim under section 1983, a plaintiff "must allege first that it has a property interest as defined by state law and, second, that the defendants, acting under color of state law, deprived it of that property interest without constitutionally adequate process." *PFZ Props., Inc. v. Rodriguez*, 928 F.2d 28, 30 (1st Cir.1991).

To establish a constitutionally protected property interest in employment, a plaintiff must demonstrate that she has a legally-recognized expectation that she will retain her position. A legitimate expectation of continued employment may derive from a statute, a contract, or an officially sanctioned rule of the workplace. Here, it is undisputed that under the laws of Puerto Rico, career or tenured employees have property rights in their continued employment.

This inquiry, therefore, narrows to whether Marrero received constitutionally adequate process. Such a standard naturally requires us to consider what process was provided to Marrero and whether it was constitutionally adequate. In this case, we must decide whether the pre-termination hearing provided to Marrero satisfies this standard.

Due process requires only that the pre-termination hearing fulfill the purpose of "an initial check against mistaken decisions — essentially, a determination of whether there are reasonable grounds to believe that the charges against the employee are true and support the proposed action." *Cepero-Rivera v. Fagundo*, 414 F.3d 124, 135 (1st Cir.2005). This initial check requires the employee to receive notice of the charges, an explanation of the evidence that supports those charges, and the ability to refute that evidence. *See id.* at 134. Any standard that would require more process than this would unduly impede the government in removing poorly performing employees. *See id.*

Marrero concedes in her amended complaint that on May 3, 2002, she received a letter informing her of the Housing Department's intention to remove her from office. This letter, along with a second letter, required her to appear at an informal meeting to discuss the removal proceedings. She attended the meeting and was given a full opportunity to respond to each of the allegations. Even drawing all inferences in Marrero's favor, the process provided her in this pre-termination hearing comported with due process guarantees by providing her notice and an opportunity to be heard. As a result, the pre-termination hearing provided constitutionally adequate process without necessitating a post-termination hearing.

2. Equal Protection Claim

Under the Equal Protection Clause, persons similarly situated must be accorded similar governmental treatment. In order to establish this claim, Marrero needs to allege facts indicating that, "compared with others similarly situated, [she] was selectively treated ... based on impermissible considerations such as race, religion, intent to inhibit or punish the exercise of constitutional rights, or malicious or bad faith intent to injure a person." *Rubinovitz v. Rogato*, 60 F.3d 906, 910 (1st Cir.1995).

The formula for determining whether individuals or entities are "similarly situated" for equal protection purposes is not always susceptible to precise demarcation. Instead, the test is whether an objective person would see two people similarly situated based upon the incident and context in question.

Here, Marrero fails even to implicate this test by failing to make any allegation that persons similarly situated were treated more favorably. In fact, the complaint includes allegations to the contrary by admitting that Velez, despite his PDP membership, was accused of similar charges, accorded similar process, and eventually received a similar reprimand. Accordingly, Marrero's equal protection claim was correctly dismissed.

3. Political Discrimination

Finally, we address Marrero's claim of political discrimination. The First Amendment protects non-policymaking public employees from adverse employment actions based on their political opinions. To establish a *prima facie* case, a plaintiff must show that party affiliation was a substantial or motivating factor behind a challenged employment action. "While plaintiffs are not held to higher pleading standards in § 1983 actions, they must plead enough for a necessary inference to be reasonably drawn." *Torres-Viera v. Laboy-Alvarado*, 311 F.3d 105, 108 (1st Cir. 2002).

Here, Marrero's allegations are limited to stating that she was badly treated at work and that her political party was mocked. Thus, Marrero has failed to set forth any sort of causal connection between her demotion and the political animus that she alleges prompted it. Merely juxtaposing that she is an active member of the NPP and that the defendants are affiliated with the PDP is insufficient, standing alone, to create a causal link. *See Bell Atlantic Corp.*, 127 S. Ct. at 1966. True, such a connection is one among a myriad of possible inferences. Yet even drawing all reasonable inferences in Marrero's favor, it would be speculative to draw the forbidden inference from the range of possibilities. *See Bell Atlantic Corp. v. Twombly*, 127 S. Ct. 1955, 1966 (2007) (stating that a naked assertion of conspiracy gets the complaint close to stating a claim, but "without some further factual enhancement it stops short of the line between possibility and plausibility of entitlement to relief"). Accordingly, the district court correctly concluded that her complaint failed to state a cause of action upon which relief could be granted.

III. Conclusion

Each of the Plaintiff's arguments fails to state a claim upon which relief could be granted. Therefore, the district court's ruling ought be, and hereby is, affirmed.

Exercise 10-7. Waiver, Exceptions, and Litigation Strategy

As you can see from the case above, courts may entertain motions founded on the less-easily-waived grounds listed in Rule 12(h)(2) and (3), even where those grounds would have been available at the time of an earlier Rule 12(b) motion. In *Marerro*, one of the defendants initially moved to dismiss for failure to state a claim, based on sovereign immunity, and then that defendant, along with the remaining defendants, were able to move later for judgment on the pleadings, also on the theory that the complaint failed to state a claim on which relief could be granted (you will also note that the standards for both motions are identical — this opinion even cites *Twombly*).

What do you think the strategy was behind the non-immune defendants' waiting to move for judgment on the pleadings? Was the failure to move to dismiss earlier simply an oversight? Consider the nature of the defense initially asserted by the Housing Department and the nature of the later defense asserted in the motion for judgment on the pleadings? Are they meaningfully different? Would it make sense to have the court consider them separately?

d. Voluntary Dismissal

The dismissal motions you have encountered thus far were all seeking "involuntary" dismissals. For such dismissals, the movant files a motion to dismiss the complaint, and the court orders its dismissal, against the wishes of the claiming party. Rule 41(a) provides for another process — "voluntary dismissal," and sets forth the effects of obtaining a voluntary dismissal. Read Rule 41.

Why would a party "volunteer" to dismiss her own case? Settlement is one very common reason. A settlement itself is just a contract between the litigants. It does nothing to end the litigation between them. To do that, the plaintiff must inform the court in some way that there is no longer a dispute between the parties, so the court can close the docket. Most of the time, this is done through a notice of voluntary dismissal (Fed. R. Civ. P. 41(a)(1)(A)(i)), or a notice to the court that the parties have stipulated dismissal of the case between them (Fed. R. Civ. P. 41(a)(1)(A)(ii)).

However, there are times when a dismissal by notice is not possible — the notice must be filed "before the opposing party serves either an answer or a motion for summary judgment." And the opposing party may not be willing to stipulate to a dismissal if the dismissal is not pursuant to a settlement. For example, if the defendant has served the plaintiff with a notice of intent to seek Rule 11 sanctions, the defendant is not likely to assist the plaintiff in dismissing the offending claim(s). Also, if the defendant has stated a counterclaim, the defendant is not likely to agree to the dismissal of the entire action, including her counterclaim.

In such cases, a party may seek leave from the court — by motion, of course — to voluntarily dismiss her case. The court has nearly complete discretion as to whether to grant or deny the motion, but cannot do so if a counterclaim is present, and the counterclaim cannot be severed from the main claim to proceed on its own (e.g., it does not have its own basis for subject matter jurisdiction).

Some causes of action require that, even in the case of an agreed settlement, the court must approve a voluntary dismissal, even though Rule 41(a) does not contain any such requirement in the event of a stipulated dismissal or a timely dismissal by notice. One example is the Fair Labor Standards Act (the "FLSA"), which protects the rights of employees to a minimum hourly wage and overtime pay. Because employees in such cases are relatively powerless, and because the amounts owed to plaintiffs tend to be very small, courts police settlements to make sure that they are both fair and not intended to hide the settled claim from other potential plaintiffs with meritorious claims. Class actions under Rule 23 also may be settled only with court approval (along with many other procedural requirements) (Fed. R. Civ. P. 23(e)), and derivative suits against the principals of business entities come in for similar treatment (Fed. R. Civ. P. 23.1; 23.2).

Exercise 10-8. Voluntary Dismissal

Assume that you represent the plaintiff in a serious automobile accident case, and that you initially filed your action in state court in a state that requires the plaintiff to plead punitive damages "with particularity" in the complaint, and that does not allow any amendments to pleadings. You plead punitive damages only generally, and the defense counsel files a motion for summary judgment on any claims seeking punitive damages, citing the insufficiency of your pleading. You move for leave to dismiss your claim voluntarily, hoping to re-plead in federal court where you will have more flexibility, both in terms of amending your pleadings and in terms of pleading your client's entitlement to punitive damages less particularly.

1. Why can't you just dismiss by notice?

2. Why might your opponent be unlikely to stipulate to a dismissal in this case?

3. What are the dangers of following this strategy of seeking leave to dismiss? If you want to dismiss the claim again, will you be able to do so? Any other potential consequences?

Exercise 10-9. The Effects of Dismissal

Rule 41 distinguishes between dismissal "without prejudice" and dismissals that "operate[] as an adjudication on the merits." A dismissal "without prejudice" is a purely procedural dismissal. If your complaint is dismissed in this way, you can turn around and re-file it the next day, even in the exact same court (though it would be smart to fix the flaws that led to dismissal in the first place), because the court has not considered or addressed the merits of your claims in any way.

A dismissal "with prejudice" is one that "operates as an adjudication on the merits." This means that the complaint's dismissal is the equivalent of a full trial to a verdict on the merits, and the judgment that results from it is equivalent to a judgment entered on a jury's verdict (other than as to the standards of review applicable on appeal — see Chapter 12). Obviously, then, if your client's complaint is dismissed, you hope that it will be dismissed "without prejudice" unless, of course, you achieved a settlement.

Rule 41 specifies which kinds of dismissals are with and without prejudice. Consider the following dismissal hypotheticals and, assuming that the relevant orders do not specify either, determine which would constitute dismissals with prejudice, and which would constitute dismissals without prejudice:

1. You file an action in federal court, and on the day after your initial filing, you realize that the district court in which you filed does not have personal jurisdiction over the defendant. You file a notice of voluntary dismissal with the court's electronic filing system that day.

2. In Exercise 10-6 above, before answering your complaint in federal court, your opposing counsel serves you with a notice of intent to seek Rule 11 sanctions, and you realize from reading his draft motion that he has a point. You immediately file with the court's electronic filing system a notice of voluntary dismissal.

3. You file an action in federal district court. Your opposing counsel moves to dismiss the action for failure to join a party needed for just adjudication. The court grants the motion.

4. You file an action in federal district court. Your opposing counsel files a motion to dismiss for lack of subject matter jurisdiction, lack of personal jurisdiction, and failure to state a claim upon which relief may be granted. The court denies the motion on the first two grounds, but grants it on the third.

5. You file an action in federal district court on behalf of your client, a large business entity, seeking damages for tortious interference with your customer relationships against another large business entity. The case proceeds to the discovery phase, where you and your opposing counsel do battle over the discovery of electronically stored information. Sadly, your client is found to have "spoliated" (lost, defaced, or destroyed) several gigabytes of relevant emails, and the court finds that agents of the company did so intentionally to avoid having to produce them in discovery. As a sanction for this behavior, the court orders dismissal of your complaint.

Exercise 10-10. Researching Dismissal Without Prejudice

Imagine that you file an action on behalf of your client, an employee seeking to sue a former employer for breach of contract based on what the employee believes was a wrongful termination without cause. Because the client comes to you after debating seeking a lawyer for several months, you file the action two days before the one-year statute of limitations lapses. Your opposing counsel files a motion to dismiss for insufficient service of process, and the court grants the motion, dismissing the case without prejudice. Since the date of your filing, three months have elapsed. Upon receiving the order entering judgment against your client dismissing the case without prejudice, you gather your materials together and re-file the complaint, paying a new filing fee. You properly serve the defendant, and your opposing counsel promptly moves for summary judgment on the theory that the statute of limitations has lapsed.

Will this motion succeed? Research the law relating to dismissals without prejudice of claims that have become time-barred during the pendency of ongoing litigation, and attempt to answer this question.

Exercise 10-11. Researching Failure to Prosecute

Note that Rule 41(b) provides that, "If the plaintiff fails to prosecute," the defendant may move to dismiss on that basis. What does it mean to "fail to prosecute"?

Putting aside what you know about "prosecution" in the criminal law context, the word has a particular meaning in the civil litigation context. To "prosecute" means to move the case forward diligently and expeditiously. We have an adversarial (as opposed to inquisitorial) system of adjudication in the United States, and under this system, which is party-focused (as opposed to judge-focused), the plaintiff in any case has the duty to move the case forward—neither the judge nor the defendant has any duty to do so. However, just as there are faster and slower workers in any workplace, different plaintiffs and their counsel will move more and less quickly to move a case forward by filing pleadings and motions, seeking discovery, and moving for pretrial conferences, hearing dates, and trial dates.

Occasionally, for whatever reason, a plaintiff's counsel does not do any of these things for a long time—years in some cases. In such situations, should the court and defendant have to wait in limbo for the plaintiff to finally do something?

The answer is no. The failure to do anything material to move a case forward for an extended period of time constitutes a failure to prosecute, and it is a ground for dismissal of the complaint with prejudice. How long should a case have to lie dormant for a dismissal on this basis to be warranted? Should there be a rule that the court has to give the plaintiff a "last chance" before ordering dismissal?

What is the approach to these questions favored by the federal district courts of the district where your law school sits? What about the state courts of the state in which your law school sits? If they have not adopted an approach, what approach do you think they would adopt? Research the law of your law school's district, and compose a brief memorandum to your law firm's research file resolving these questions as best you can. Don't forget to check your relevant state statutes and procedural rules, as well.

5. Summary Judgment

Federal Rule of Civil Procedure 56 governs the process of "summary judgment." During much of its existence, Rule 56 has been the subject of contentious judicial rulings and massive amounts of commentary. This should not be surprising, since Rule 56 provides litigants with their principal avenue for prevailing on their claims on the merits without going through a trial. A motion for summary judgment asks the court to assess the evidence that has been produced through the discovery process, in light of the legal arguments made by the parties in their briefs, and determine whether (1) there exists no "genuine dispute as to any material fact" for the jury to decide; and (2) the legal standards, in light of the undisputed facts, entitle the movant to "judgment as a matter of law." *See* Fed. R. Civ. P. 56(a).

Summary judgment is in tension with many bedrock aspects of our judicial system. It is in tension with the Seventh Amendment right to trial by jury, for example, because without a trial, one cannot have a jury. For this reason, the courts interpret the requirement of Rule 56(a) that the movant be "entitled to judgment as a matter of law" to require the court to determine that *no rational jury presented with the evidence contained in the record could render a verdict for the non-movant.* Simply put: if a reasonable jury *could* legitimately rule for the non-movant, then the case must be presented to the jury. In the case of a bench trial, the standard is the same (though "jury" becomes "fact-finder" in those cases), but it of course makes less sense, because the judge decides the summary judgment motion and is the fact-finder who will decide the case if it is tried.

Summary judgment is also in tension with the general notion of due process of law, since summary adjudication, by definition, constitutes less "process" than full trial adjudication. The case law interpreting Rule 56 has accordingly vacillated from an approach to summary judgment that made it very hard to obtain, to an approach that seemed to many to make it too easy to obtain.

In recent years, the Rules drafters have attempted to codify many of the disputed elements of this case law, and their work product remains the subject of much dispute. Nevertheless, it is fair to say that the current version of Rule 56 — substantially amended in December 2010 — codifies something closer to the approach favored by more recent courts, making it relatively easier to obtain summary judgment. The drafters have also codified several augmentations to the summary judgment process that previously appeared mostly in the local rules of some federal districts. (*See* Rule 56(c), outlining procedures for supporting and opposing a summary judgment motion).* The result is a more stylized process, but one where the duties of each party —

---

* Ed. Note. The Local Rules of some District Courts continue to go beyond these strictures. For example, one of us practiced a good bit in the Western District of Tennessee, where Memphis sits, the movant and the non-movant, are more clear than they were under the original version of Rule 56.

That said, much of the current content of Rule 56 codifies a famous—or infamous, depending on your point of view—trio of cases decided by the Supreme Court in 1986 that greatly liberalized the summary judgment standard then prevailing.* Below, we excerpt two of these three cases.

Celotex Corp. v. Catrett
477 U.S. 317 (1986)

Justice Rehnquist delivered the opinion of the Court.

The United States District Court for the District of Columbia granted the motion of petitioner Celotex Corporation for summary judgment against respondent Catrett because the latter was unable to produce evidence in support of her allegation in her wrongful-death complaint that the decedent had been exposed to petitioner's asbestos products. A divided panel of the Court of Appeals for the District of Columbia Circuit reversed, however, holding that petitioner's failure to support its motion with evidence tending to negate such exposure precluded the entry of summary judgment in its favor. *Catrett v. Johns-Manville Sales Corp.*, 756 F.2d 181 (D.C. Cir. 1985). This view conflicted with that of the Third Circuit in *In re Japanese Electronic Products*, 723 F.2d 238 (1983). We granted certiorari to resolve the conflict, 474 U.S. 944 (1985), and now reverse the decision of the District of Columbia Circuit.

Respondent commenced this lawsuit in September 1980, alleging that the death in 1979 of her husband, Louis H. Catrett, resulted from his exposure to products containing asbestos manufactured or distributed by 15 named corporations. Respondent's complaint sounded in negligence, breach of warranty, and strict liability. Two of the defendants filed motions challenging the District Court's *in personam* jurisdiction, and the remaining 13, including petitioner, filed motions for summary judgment. Petitioner's motion, which was first filed in September 1981, argued that summary

---

and to seek summary judgment there, one must not only identify each material fact that is not in genuine dispute and cite to the portions of the record that show that it is not disputed, but also, if the argument for summary judgment is that the opponent cannot produce evidence in support of his claims, must digitally scan and attach all pages of the record supporting that argument. *See* W.D. Tenn. Loc. R. 56.1(a) ("If the movant contends that the opponent of the motion cannot produce evidence to create a genuine issue of material fact, the proponent shall affix to the memorandum copies of the precise portions of the record relied upon as evidence of this assertion.").

* Ed. Note. The standard that prevailed at the time of the Court's decisions in the summary judgment trio of cases is best reflected by the then-seminal case of *Adickes v. S.H. Kress & Co.*, 398 U.S. 144 (1970). It is worth reviewing that case, and those cited within its text, because a number of state courts continue to adhere to the pre-1986 approach to summary judgment, rejecting the more recent federal cases and the 2010 amendments to the Rule.

judgment was proper because respondent had "failed to produce evidence that any [Celotex] product ... was the proximate cause of the injuries alleged within the jurisdictional limits of [the District] Court." In particular, petitioner noted that respondent had failed to identify, in answering interrogatories specifically requesting such information, any witnesses who could testify about the decedent's exposure to petitioner's asbestos products. In response to petitioner's summary judgment motion, respondent then produced three documents which she claimed "demonstrate that there is a genuine material factual dispute" as to whether the decedent had ever been exposed to petitioner's asbestos products. The three documents included a transcript of a deposition of the decedent, a letter from an official of one of the decedent's former employers whom petitioner planned to call as a trial witness, and a letter from an insurance company to respondent's attorney, all tending to establish that the decedent had been exposed to petitioner's asbestos products in Chicago during 1970–1971. Petitioner, in turn, argued that the three documents were inadmissible hearsay* and thus could not be considered in opposition to the summary judgment motion.

In July 1982, almost two years after the commencement of the lawsuit, the District Court granted all of the motions filed by the various defendants. The court explained that it was granting petitioner's summary judgment motion because "there [was] no showing that the plaintiff was exposed to the defendant Celotex's product in the District of Columbia or elsewhere within the statutory period." Respondent appealed only the grant of summary judgment in favor of petitioner, and a divided panel of the District of Columbia Circuit reversed. The majority of the Court of Appeals held that petitioner's summary judgment motion was rendered "fatally defective" by the fact that petitioner "made no effort to adduce any evidence, in the form of affidavits or otherwise, to support its motion." 756 F.2d, at 184. According to the majority, Rule 56(e) of the Federal Rules of Civil Procedure, and this Court's decision in *Adickes v. S.H. Kress & Co.*, 398 U.S. 144, 159 (1970), establish that "the party opposing the motion for summary judgment bears the burden of responding only after the moving party has met its burden of coming forward with proof of the absence of any genuine issues of material fact." 756 F.2d, at 184 (footnote omitted). The majority therefore declined to consider petitioner's argument

---

* Ed. Note. "Hearsay" is defined in the Federal Rules of Evidence as "a statement that: (1) the declarant does not make while testifying at the current trial or hearing; and (2) a party offers in evidence to prove the truth of the matter asserted in the statement." Fed. R. Evid. 801(c). So hearsay essentially describes evidence taking the form of, "My friend told me that ..." Hearsay is generally inadmissible due to the lack of opportunity to cross-examine the person who originally made the statement being offered in court, but there are many exceptions to that rule. You will learn all about those in your course on Evidence. The consideration of hearsay at the summary judgment stage is controversial, as you will see.

that none of the evidence produced by respondent in opposition to the motion for summary judgment would have been admissible at trial. The dissenting judge argued that "[t]he majority errs in supposing that a party seeking summary judgment must always make an affirmative evidentiary showing, even in cases where there is not a triable, factual dispute." 756 F.2d, at 188 (Bork, J., dissenting). According to the dissenting judge, the majority's decision "undermines the traditional authority of trial judges to grant summary judgment in meritless cases." 756 F.2d, at 187.

We think that the position taken by the majority of the Court of Appeals is inconsistent with the standard for summary judgment set forth in Rule 56(c) of the Federal Rules of Civil Procedure. Under Rule 56(c), summary judgment is proper "if the pleadings, depositions, answers to interrogatories, and admissions on file, together with the affidavits, if any, show that there is no genuine issue as to any material fact and that the moving party is entitled to a judgment as a matter of law." In our view, the plain language of Rule 56(c) mandates the entry of summary judgment, after adequate time for discovery and upon motion, against a party who fails to make a showing sufficient to establish the existence of an element essential to that party's case, and on which that party will bear the burden of proof at trial. In such a situation, there can be "no genuine issue as to any material fact," since a complete failure of proof concerning an essential element of the nonmoving party's case necessarily renders all other facts immaterial. The moving party is "entitled to a judgment as a matter of law" because the nonmoving party has failed to make a sufficient showing on an essential element of her case with respect to which she has the burden of proof. "[T]h[e] standard [for granting summary judgment] mirrors the standard for a directed verdict under Federal Rule of Civil Procedure 50(a)...." *Anderson v. Liberty Lobby, Inc.*, 477 U.S. 242, 250 (1986).

Of course, a party seeking summary judgment always bears the initial responsibility of informing the district court of the basis for its motion, and identifying those portions of "the pleadings, depositions, answers to interrogatories, and admissions on file, together with the affidavits, if any," which it believes demonstrate the absence of a genuine issue of material fact. But unlike the Court of Appeals, we find no express or implied requirement in Rule 56 that the moving party support its motion with affidavits or other similar materials negating the opponent's claim. On the contrary, Rule 56(c), which refers to "the affidavits, if any," suggests the absence of such a requirement. And if there were any doubt about the meaning of Rule 56(c) in this regard, such doubt is clearly removed by Rules 56(a) and (b), which provide that claimants and defendants, respectively, may move for summary judgment "with or without supporting affidavits" (emphasis added). The import of these subsections is that, regardless of whether the moving party accompanies its summary judgment motion with affidavits, the motion may, and should, be granted so long as whatever is before the district court demonstrates that the standard for the entry of summary judgment, as set forth in Rule 56(c), is satisfied. One of the principal purposes of the summary judgment rule is to isolate and dispose of factually unsupported claims or defenses, and we think it should be interpreted in a way that allows it to accomplish this purpose.

* * *

We do not mean that the nonmoving party must produce evidence in a form that would be admissible at trial in order to avoid summary judgment. Obviously, Rule 56 does not require the nonmoving party to depose her own witnesses. Rule 56(e) permits a proper summary judgment motion to be opposed by any of the kinds of evidentiary materials listed in Rule 56(c), except the mere pleadings themselves, and it is from this list that one would normally expect the nonmoving party to make the showing to which we have referred.

The Court of Appeals in this case felt itself constrained, however, by language in our decision in *Adickes v. S.H. Kress & Co.*, 398 U.S. 144 (1970). There we held that summary judgment had been improperly entered in favor of the defendant restaurant in an action brought under 42 U.S.C. § 1983. In the course of its opinion, the *Adickes* Court said that "both the commentary on and the background of the 1963 amendment conclusively show that it was not intended to modify the burden of the moving party ... to show initially the absence of a genuine issue concerning any material fact." *Id.*, at 159. We think that this statement is accurate in a literal sense, since we fully agree with the *Adickes* Court that the 1963 amendment to Rule 56(e) was not designed to modify the burden of making the showing generally required by Rule 56(c). It also appears to us that, on the basis of the showing before the Court in *Adickes*, the motion for summary judgment in that case should have been denied. But we do not think the *Adickes* language quoted above should be construed to mean that the burden is on the party moving for summary judgment to produce evidence showing the absence of a genuine issue of material fact, even with respect to an issue on which the nonmoving party bears the burden of proof. Instead, as we have explained, the burden on the moving party may be discharged by "showing" — that is, pointing out to the district court — that there is an absence of evidence to support the nonmoving party's case.

* * *

Our conclusion is bolstered by the fact that district courts are widely acknowledged to possess the power to enter summary judgments *sua sponte*, so long as the losing party was on notice that she had to come forward with all of her evidence. *See* 756 F.2d, at 189 (Bork, J., dissenting);

10A C. Wright, A. Miller, & M. Kane, Federal Practice and Procedure § 2720, pp. 28–29 (1983). It would surely defy common sense to hold that the District Court could have entered summary judgment *sua sponte* in favor of petitioner in the instant case, but that petitioner's filing of a motion requesting such a disposition precluded the District Court from ordering it.

* * *

In this Court, respondent's brief and oral argument have been devoted as much to the proposition that an adequate showing of exposure to petitioner's asbestos products was made as to the proposition that no such showing should have been required. But the Court of Appeals declined to address either the adequacy of the showing made by respondent in opposition to petitioner's motion for summary judgment, or the question whether such a showing, if reduced to admissible evidence, would be sufficient to carry respondent's burden of proof at trial. We think the Court of Appeals with its superior knowledge of local law is better suited than we are to make these determinations in the first instance.

* * *

The judgment of the Court of Appeals is accordingly reversed, and the case is remanded for further proceedings consistent with this opinion.

It is so ordered.

Justice White concurred (opinion omitted).

Anderson v. Liberty Lobby, Inc.

477 U.S. 242 (1986)

Justice White delivered the opinion of the Court.

In *New York Times Co. v. Sullivan*, 376 U.S. 254, 279–280 (1964), we held that, in a libel suit brought by a public official, the First Amendment requires the plaintiff to show that in publishing the defamatory statement the defendant acted with actual malice— "with knowledge that it was false or with reckless disregard of whether it was false or not." We held further that such actual malice must be shown with "convincing clarity." *Id.*, at 285–286. These *New York Times* requirements we have since extended to libel suits brought by public figures as well. *See, e.g., Curtis Publishing Co. v. Butts*, 388 U.S. 130 (1967).

This case presents the question whether the clear-and-convincing-evidence requirement must be considered by a court ruling on a motion for summary judgment under Rule 56 of the Federal Rules of Civil Procedure in a case to which *New York Times* applies. The United States Court of

Appeals for the District of Columbia Circuit held that that requirement need not be considered at the summary judgment stage. We granted *certiorari* because that holding was in conflict with decisions of several other Courts of Appeals, which had held that the *New York Times* requirement of clear and convincing evidence must be considered on a motion for summary judgment. We now reverse.

I

Respondent Liberty Lobby, Inc., is a not-for-profit corporation and self-described "citizens' lobby." Respondent Willis Carto is its founder and treasurer. In October 1981, The Investigator magazine published two articles: "The Private World of Willis Carto" and "Yockey: Profile of an American Hitler." These articles were introduced by a third, shorter article entitled "America's Neo-Nazi Underground: Did Mein Kampf Spawn Yockey's *Imperium*, a Book Revived by Carto's Liberty Lobby?" These articles portrayed respondents as neo-Nazi, anti-Semitic, racist, and Fascist.

Respondents filed this diversity libel action in the United States District Court for the District of Columbia, alleging that some 28 statements and 2 illustrations in the 3 articles were false and derogatory. Named as defendants in the action were petitioner Jack Anderson, the publisher of The Investigator, petitioner Bill Adkins, president and chief executive officer of the Investigator Publishing Co., and petitioner Investigator Publishing Co. itself.

Following discovery, petitioners moved for summary judgment pursuant to Rule 56. In their motion, petitioners asserted that because respondents are public figures they were required to prove their case under the standards set forth in *New York Times*. Petitioners also asserted that summary judgment was proper because actual malice was absent as a matter of law. In support of this latter assertion, petitioners submitted the affidavit of Charles Bermant, an employee of petitioners and the author of the two longer articles. In this affidavit, Bermant stated that he had spent a substantial amount of time researching and writing the articles and that his facts were obtained from a wide variety of sources. He also stated that he had at all times believed and still believed that the facts contained in the articles were truthful and accurate. Attached to this affidavit was an appendix in which Bermant detailed the sources for each of the statements alleged by respondents to be libelous.

Respondents opposed the motion for summary judgment, asserting that there were numerous inaccuracies in the articles and claiming that an issue of actual malice was presented by virtue of the fact that in preparing the articles Bermant had relied on several sources that respondents asserted were patently unreliable. Generally, respondents charged that petitioners had failed adequately to verify their information before publishing.

Respondents also presented evidence that William McGaw, an editor of The Investigator, had told petitioner Adkins before publication that the articles were "terrible" and "ridiculous."

In ruling on the motion for summary judgment, the District Court first held that respondents were limited-purpose public figures and that *New York Times* therefore applied. The District Court then held that Bermant's thorough investigation and research and his reliance on numerous sources precluded a finding of actual malice. Thus, the District Court granted the motion and entered judgment in favor of petitioners.

On appeal, the Court of Appeals affirmed as to 21 and reversed as to 9 of the allegedly defamatory statements. Although it noted that respondents did not challenge the District Court's ruling that they were limited-purpose public figures and that they were thus required to prove their case under *New York Times*, the Court of Appeals nevertheless held that for the purposes of summary judgment the requirement that actual malice be proved by clear and convincing evidence, rather than by a preponderance of the evidence, was irrelevant: To defeat summary judgment respondents did not have to show that a jury could find actual malice with "convincing clarity." The court based this conclusion on a perception that to impose the greater evidentiary burden at summary judgment "would change the threshold summary judgment inquiry from a search for a minimum of facts supporting the plaintiff's case to an evaluation of the weight of those facts and (it would seem) of the weight of at least the defendant's uncontroverted facts as well." 746 F.2d, at 1570. The court then held, with respect to nine of the statements, that summary judgment had been improperly granted because "a jury could reasonably conclude that the ... allegations were defamatory, false, and made with actual malice." 746 F.2d at 1577.

II

A

Our inquiry is whether the Court of Appeals erred in holding that the heightened evidentiary requirements that apply to proof of actual malice in this *New York Times* case need not be considered for the purposes of a motion for summary judgment. Rule 56(c) of the Federal Rules of Civil Procedure provides that summary judgment "shall be rendered forthwith if the pleadings, depositions, answers to interrogatories, and admissions on file, together with the affidavits, if any, show that there is no genuine issue as to any material fact and that the moving party is entitled to a judgment as a matter of law." By its very terms, this standard provides that the mere existence of some alleged factual dispute between the parties will not defeat an otherwise properly supported motion for summary judgment; the requirement is that there be no genuine issue of material fact.

As to materiality, the substantive law will identify which facts are material. Only disputes over facts that might affect the outcome of the suit under the governing law will properly preclude the entry of summary judgment. Factual disputes that are irrelevant or unnecessary will not be counted. This materiality inquiry is independent of and separate from the question of the incorporation of the evidentiary standard into the summary judgment determination. That is, while the materiality determination rests on the substantive law, it is the substantive law's identification of which facts are critical and which facts are irrelevant that governs. Any proof or evidentiary requirements imposed by the substantive law are not germane to this inquiry, since materiality is only a criterion for categorizing factual disputes in their relation to the legal elements of the claim and not a criterion for evaluating the evidentiary underpinnings of those disputes.

More important for present purposes, summary judgment will not lie if the dispute about a material fact is "genuine," that is, if the evidence is such that a reasonable jury could return a verdict for the nonmoving party. In *First National Bank of Arizona v. Cities Service Co.*, 391 U.S. 253 (1968), we affirmed a grant of summary judgment for an antitrust defendant where the issue was whether there was a genuine factual dispute as to the existence of a conspiracy. We noted Rule 56(e)'s provision that a party opposing a properly supported motion for summary judgment " 'may not rest upon the mere allegations or denials of his pleading, but ... must set forth specific facts showing that there is a genuine issue for trial.' " We observed further that

> [i]t is true that the issue of material fact required by Rule 56(c) to be present to entitle a party to proceed to trial is not required to be resolved conclusively in favor of the party asserting its existence; rather, all that is required is that sufficient evidence supporting the claimed factual dispute be shown to require a jury or judge to resolve the parties' differing versions of the truth at trial. 391 U.S., at 288–289.

We went on to hold that, in the face of the defendant's properly supported motion for summary judgment, the plaintiff could not rest on his allegations of a conspiracy to get to a jury without "any significant probative evidence tending to support the complaint." *Id.*, at 290.

Again, in *Adickes v. S.H. Kress & Co.*, 398 U.S. 144 (1970), the Court emphasized that the availability of summary judgment turned on whether a proper jury question was presented. There, one of the issues was whether there was a conspiracy between private persons and law enforcement officers. The District Court granted summary judgment for the defendants, stating that there was no evidence from which reasonably minded jurors might draw an inference of conspiracy. We reversed, pointing out that the moving parties' submissions had not foreclosed the possibility of the existence of certain facts from which "it would be open to a jury ... to infer from the circumstances" that there had been a meeting of the minds. *Id.*, at 158–159.

Our prior decisions may not have uniformly recited the same language in describing genuine factual issues under Rule 56, but it is clear enough from our recent cases that at the summary judgment stage the judge's function is not himself to weigh the evidence and determine the truth of the matter but to determine whether there is a genuine issue for trial. As *Adickes*, *supra*, and *Cities Service*, *supra*, indicate, there is no issue for trial unless there is sufficient evidence favoring the nonmoving party for a jury to return a verdict for that party. If the evidence is merely colorable, or is not significantly probative, summary judgment may be granted.

That this is the proper focus of the inquiry is strongly suggested by the Rule itself. Rule 56(e) provides that, when a properly supported motion for summary judgment is made, the adverse party "must set forth specific facts showing that there is a genuine issue for trial." And, as we noted above, Rule 56(c) provides that the trial judge shall then grant summary judgment if there is no genuine issue as to any material fact and if the moving party is entitled to judgment as a matter of law. There is no requirement that the trial judge make findings of fact. The inquiry performed is the threshold inquiry of determining whether there is the need for a trial—whether, in other words, there are any genuine factual issues that properly can be resolved only by a finder of fact because they may reasonably be resolved in favor of either party.

Petitioners suggest, and we agree, that this standard mirrors the standard for a directed verdict under Federal Rule of Civil Procedure 50(a), which is that the trial judge must direct a verdict if, under the governing law, there can be but one reasonable conclusion as to the verdict. If reasonable minds could differ as to the import of the evidence, however, a verdict should not be directed. As the Court long ago said in *Improvement Co. v. Munson*, 14 Wall. 442, 448 (1872), and has several times repeated:

> Nor are judges any longer required to submit a question to a jury merely because some evidence has been introduced by the party having the burden of proof, unless the evidence be of such a character that it would warrant the jury in finding a verdict in favor of that party. Formerly it was held that if there was what is called a *scintilla* of evidence in support of a case the judge was bound to leave it to the jury, but recent decisions of high authority have established a more reasonable rule, that in every case, before the evidence is left to the jury, there is a preliminary question for the judge, not whether there is literally no evidence, but whether

there is any upon which a jury could properly proceed to find a verdict for the party producing it, upon whom the onus of proof is imposed. (Footnotes omitted.)

The Court has said that summary judgment should be granted where the evidence is such that it "would require a directed verdict for the moving party." *Sartor v. Arkansas Gas Corp.*, 321 U.S. 620, 624 (1944). And we have noted that the "genuine issue" summary judgment standard is "very close" to the "reasonable jury" directed verdict standard: "The primary difference between the two motions is procedural; summary judgment motions are usually made before trial and decided on documentary evidence, while directed verdict motions are made at trial and decided on the evidence that has been admitted." *Bill Johnson's Restaurants, Inc. v. NLRB*, 461 U.S. 731, 745, n. 11 (1983). In essence, though, the inquiry under each is the same: whether the evidence presents a sufficient disagreement to require submission to a jury or whether it is so one-sided that one party must prevail as a matter of law.

B

Progressing to the specific issue in this case, we are convinced that the inquiry involved in a ruling on a motion for summary judgment or for a directed verdict necessarily implicates the substantive evidentiary standard of proof that would apply at the trial on the merits. If the defendant in a run-of-the-mill civil case moves for summary judgment or for a directed verdict based on the lack of proof of a material fact, the judge must ask himself not whether he thinks the evidence unmistakably favors one side or the other but whether a fair-minded jury could return a verdict for the plaintiff on the evidence presented. The mere existence of a *scintilla* of evidence in support of the plaintiff's position will be insufficient; there must be evidence on which the jury could reasonably find for the plaintiff. The judge's inquiry, therefore, unavoidably asks whether reasonable jurors could find by a preponderance of the evidence that the plaintiff is entitled to a verdict—whether there is evidence upon which a jury can properly proceed to find a verdict for the party producing it, upon whom the onus of proof is imposed.

In terms of the nature of the inquiry, this is no different from the consideration of a motion for acquittal in a criminal case, where the beyond-a-reasonable-doubt standard applies and where the trial judge asks whether a reasonable jury could find guilt beyond a reasonable doubt. Similarly, where the First Amendment mandates a "clear and convincing" standard, the trial judge in disposing of a directed verdict motion should consider whether a reasonable factfinder could conclude, for example, that the plaintiff had shown actual malice with convincing clarity.

The case for the proposition that a higher burden of proof should have a corresponding effect on the judge when deciding whether to send the case to the jury was well made by the Court of Appeals for the Second Circuit in *United States v. Taylor*, 464 F.2d 240 (2d Cir.1972), which overruled *United States v. Feinberg*, 140 F.2d 592 (2d Cir.1944), a case holding that the standard of evidence necessary for a judge to send a case to the jury is the same in both civil and criminal cases even though the standard that the jury must apply in a criminal case is more demanding than in civil proceedings. Speaking through Judge Friendly, the Second Circuit said: "It would seem at first blush—and we think also at second—that more 'facts in evidence' are needed for the judge to allow [reasonable jurors to pass on a claim] when the proponent is required to establish [the claim] not merely by a preponderance of the evidence but ... beyond a reasonable doubt." 464 F.2d, at 242. The court could not find a "satisfying explanation in the *Feinberg* opinion why the judge should not place this higher burden on the prosecution in criminal proceedings before sending the case to the jury." *Ibid.* The *Taylor* court also pointed out that almost all the Circuits had adopted something like Judge Prettyman's formulation in *Curley v. United States*, 160 F.2d 229, 232–233 (D.C.Cir.1947):

> The true rule, therefore, is that a trial judge, in passing upon a motion for directed verdict of acquittal, must determine whether upon the evidence, giving full play to the right of the jury to determine credibility, weigh the evidence, and draw justifiable inferences of fact, a reasonable mind might fairly conclude guilt beyond a reasonable doubt. If he concludes that upon the evidence there must be such a doubt in a reasonable mind, he must grant the motion; or, to state it another way, if there is no evidence upon which a reasonable mind might fairly conclude guilt beyond reasonable doubt, the motion must be granted. If he concludes that either of the two results, a reasonable doubt or no reasonable doubt, is fairly possible, he must let the jury decide the matter.

This view is equally applicable to a civil case to which the "clear and convincing" standard applies. Indeed, the *Taylor* court thought that it was implicit in this Court's adoption of the clear-and-convincing-evidence standard for certain kinds of cases that there was a "concomitant duty on the judge to consider the applicable burden when deciding whether to send a case to the jury." 464 F.2d, at 243. Although the court thought that this higher standard would not produce different results in many cases, it could not say that it would never do so.

Just as the "convincing clarity" requirement is relevant in ruling on a motion for directed verdict, it is relevant in ruling on a motion for summary judgment. When determining if a genuine factual issue as to actual malice exists in a libel suit brought by a public figure, a trial judge must bear in mind the actual quantum and quality of proof necessary to support liability under *New York Times*. For example, there is no genuine issue if the evidence presented in the opposing affidavits is of insufficient caliber or quantity to allow a rational finder of fact to find actual malice by clear and convincing evidence.

Thus, in ruling on a motion for summary judgment, the judge must view the evidence presented through the prism of the substantive evidentiary burden. This conclusion is mandated by the nature of this determination. The question here is whether a jury could reasonably find either that the plaintiff proved his case by the quality and quantity of evidence required by the governing law or that he did not. Whether a jury could reasonably find for either party, however, cannot be defined except by the criteria governing what evidence would enable the jury to find for either the plaintiff or the defendant: It makes no sense to say that a jury could reasonably find for either party without some benchmark as to what standards govern its deliberations and within what boundaries its ultimate decision must fall, and these standards and boundaries are in fact provided by the applicable evidentiary standards.

Our holding that the clear-and-convincing standard of proof should be taken into account in ruling on summary judgment motions does not denigrate the role of the jury. It by no means authorizes trial on affidavits. Credibility determinations, the weighing of the evidence, and the drawing of legitimate inferences from the facts are jury functions, not those of a judge, whether he is ruling on a motion for summary judgment or for a directed verdict. The evidence of the non-movant is to be believed, and all justifiable inferences are to be drawn in his favor. Neither do we suggest that the trial courts should act other than with caution in granting summary judgment or that the trial court may not deny summary judgment in a case where there is reason to believe that the better course would be to proceed to a full trial.

In sum, we conclude that the determination of whether a given factual dispute requires submission to a jury must be guided by the substantive evidentiary standards that apply to the case. This is true at both the directed verdict and summary judgment stages. Consequently, where the *New York Times* "clear and convincing" evidence requirement applies, the trial judge's summary judgment inquiry as to whether a genuine issue exists will be whether the evidence presented is such that a jury applying that evidentiary standard could reasonably find for either the plaintiff or the defendant. Thus, where the factual dispute concerns actual malice, clearly a material issue in a *New York Times* case, the appropriate summary judgment question will be whether the evidence in the record could support a reasonable jury finding either that the plaintiff has shown actual malice by clear and convincing evidence or that the plaintiff has not.

III

Respondents argue, however, that whatever may be true of the applicability of the "clear and convincing" standard at the summary judgment or directed verdict stage, the defendant should seldom if ever be granted summary judgment where his state of mind is at issue and the jury might disbelieve him or his witnesses as to this issue. They rely on *Poller v. Columbia Broadcasting System, Inc.*, 368 U.S. 464 (1962), for this proposition. We do not understand *Poller*, however, to hold that a plaintiff may defeat a defendant's properly supported motion for summary judgment in a conspiracy or libel case, for example, without offering any concrete evidence from which a reasonable juror could return a verdict in his favor and by merely asserting that the jury might, and legally could, disbelieve the defendant's denial of a conspiracy or of legal malice. The movant has the burden of showing that there is no genuine issue of fact, but the plaintiff is not thereby relieved of his own burden of producing in turn evidence that would support a jury verdict. Rule 56(e) itself provides that a party opposing a properly supported motion for summary judgment may not rest upon mere allegation or denials of his pleading, but must set forth specific facts showing that there is a genuine issue for trial. Based on that Rule, *Cities Service*, 391 U.S., at 290, held that the plaintiff could not defeat the properly supported summary judgment motion of a defendant charged with a conspiracy without offering "any significant probative evidence tending to support the complaint." As we have recently said, "discredited testimony is not [normally] considered a sufficient basis for drawing a contrary conclusion." *Bose Corp. v. Consumers Union of United States, Inc.*, 466 U.S. 485, 512 (1984). Instead, the plaintiff must present affirmative evidence in order to defeat a properly supported motion for summary judgment. This is true even where the evidence is likely to be within the possession of the defendant, as long as the plaintiff has had a full opportunity to conduct discovery. We repeat, however, that the plaintiff, to survive the defendant's motion, need only present evidence from which a jury might return a verdict in his favor. If he does so, there is a genuine issue of fact that requires a trial.

IV

In sum, a court ruling on a motion for summary judgment must be guided by the *New York Times* "clear and convincing" evidentiary standard in determining whether a genuine issue of actual malice exists — that is, whether the evidence presented is such that a reasonable jury might find that actual malice had been shown with convincing clarity. Because the Court of Appeals did not apply the correct standard in reviewing the District Court's grant of summary judgment, we vacate its decision and remand the case for further proceedings consistent with this opinion.

It is so ordered.

Justice Brennen dissented (opinion omitted).

Justice Rehnquist dissented (opinion omitted).

Exercise 10-12. Codifying the Summary Judgment Trio and Other Decisions

Here are the Committee Notes to the amendment of Rule 56 in 2010:

Committee Notes on Rules — 2010 Amendment

Rule 56 is revised to improve the procedures for presenting and deciding summary-judgment motions and to make the procedures more consistent with those already used in many courts. The standard for granting summary judgment remains unchanged. The language of subdivision (a) continues to require that there be no genuine dispute as to any material fact and that the movant be entitled to judgment as a matter of law. The amendments will not affect continuing development of the decisional law construing and applying these phrases.

Subdivision (a). Subdivision (a) carries forward the summary-judgment standard expressed in former subdivision (c), changing only one word — genuine "issue" becomes genuine "dispute." "Dispute" better reflects the focus of a summary-judgment determination. As explained below, "shall" also is restored to the place it held from 1938 to 2007.

The first sentence is added to make clear at the beginning that summary judgment may be requested not only as to an entire case but also as to a claim, defense, or part of a claim or defense. The subdivision caption adopts the common phrase "partial summary judgment" to describe disposition of less than the whole action, whether or not the order grants all the relief requested by the motion.

"Shall" is restored to express the direction to grant summary judgment. The word "shall" in Rule 56 acquired significance over many decades of use. Rule 56 was amended in 2007 to replace "shall" with "should" as part of the Style Project, acting under a convention that prohibited any use of "shall." Comments on proposals to amend Rule 56, as published in 2008, have shown that neither of the choices available under the Style Project conventions — "must" or "should" — is suitable in light of the case law on whether a district court has discretion to deny summary judgment when there appears to be no genuine dispute as to any material fact. *Compare Anderson v. Liberty Lobby, Inc.*, 477 U.S. 242, 255 (1986) ("Neither do we suggest that the trial courts should act other than with caution in granting summary judgment or that the trial court may not deny summary judgment in a case in which there is reason to believe that the better course would be to proceed to a full trial. *Kennedy v. Silas Mason Co.*, 334 U.S. 249 * * * (1948))," *with Celotex Corp. v. Catrett*, 477 U.S. 317, 322 (1986) ("In our view, the plain language of Rule 56(c) mandates the entry of summary judgment, after adequate time for discovery and upon motion, against a party who fails to make a showing sufficient to establish the existence of an element essential to that party's case, and on which that party will bear the burden of proof at trial."). Eliminating "shall" created an unacceptable risk of changing the summary-judgment standard. Restoring "shall" avoids the unintended consequences of any other word.

Subdivision (a) also adds a new direction that the court should state on the record the reasons for granting or denying the motion. Most courts recognize this practice. Among other advantages, a statement of reasons can facilitate an appeal or subsequent trial-court proceedings. It is particularly important to state the reasons for granting summary judgment. The form and detail of the statement of reasons are left to the court's discretion.

The statement on denying summary judgment need not address every available reason. But identification of central issues may help the parties to focus further proceedings.

Subdivision (b). The timing provisions in former subdivisions (a) and (c) are superseded. Although the rule allows a motion for summary judgment to be filed at the commencement of an action, in many cases the motion will be premature until the nonmovant has had time to file a responsive pleading or other pretrial proceedings have been had. Scheduling orders or other pretrial orders can regulate timing to fit the needs of the case.

Subdivision (c). Subdivision (c) is new. It establishes a common procedure for several aspects of summary-judgment motions synthesized from similar elements developed in the cases or found in many local rules.

Subdivision (c)(1) addresses the ways to support an assertion that a fact can or cannot be genuinely disputed. It does not address the form for providing the required support. Different courts and judges have adopted different forms including, for example, directions that the support be included in the motion, made part of a separate statement of facts, interpolated in the body of a brief or memorandum, or provided in a separate statement of facts included in a brief or memorandum.

Subdivision (c)(1)(A) describes the familiar record materials commonly relied upon and requires that the movant cite the particular parts of the materials that support its fact positions. Materials that are not yet in the record — including materials referred to in an affidavit or declaration — must be placed in the record. Once materials are in the record, the court may, by order in the case, direct that the materials be gathered in an appendix, a party may voluntarily submit an appendix, or the parties may submit a joint appendix. The appendix procedure also may be established by local rule. Pointing to a specific location in an appendix satisfies the citation requirement. So too it may be convenient to direct that a party assist the court in locating materials buried in a voluminous record.

Subdivision (c)(1)(B) recognizes that a party need not always point to specific record materials. One party, without citing any other materials, may respond or reply that materials cited to dispute or support a fact do not establish the absence or presence of a genuine dispute. And a party who does not have the trial burden of production may rely on a showing that a party who does have the trial burden cannot produce admissible evidence to carry its burden as to the fact.

Subdivision (c)(2) provides that a party may object that material cited to support or dispute a fact cannot be presented in a form that would be admissible in evidence. The objection functions much as an objection at trial, adjusted for the pretrial setting. The burden is on the proponent to show that the material is admissible as presented or to explain the admissible form that is anticipated. There is no need to make a separate motion to strike. If the case goes to trial, failure to challenge admissibility at the summary-judgment stage does not forfeit the right to challenge admissibility at trial.

Subdivision (c)(3) reflects judicial opinions and local rules provisions stating that the court may decide a motion for summary judgment without undertaking an independent search of the record. Nonetheless, the rule also recognizes that a court may consider record materials not called to its attention by the parties.

Subdivision (c)(4) carries forward some of the provisions of former subdivision (e)(1). Other provisions are relocated or omitted. The requirement that a sworn or certified copy of a paper referred to in an affidavit or declaration be attached to the affidavit or declaration is omitted as unnecessary given the requirement in subdivision (c)(1)(A) that a statement or dispute of fact be supported by materials in the record.

A formal affidavit is no longer required. 28 U.S.C. § 1746 allows a written unsworn declaration, certificate, verification, or statement subscribed in proper form as true under penalty of perjury to substitute for an affidavit.

Subdivision (d). Subdivision (d) carries forward without substantial change the provisions of former subdivision (f).

A party who seeks relief under subdivision (d) may seek an order deferring the time to respond to the summary-judgment motion.

Subdivision (e). Subdivision (e) addresses questions that arise when a party fails to support an assertion of fact or fails to properly address another party's assertion of fact as required by Rule 56(c). As explained below, summary judgment cannot be granted by default even if there is a complete failure to respond to the motion, much less when an attempted response fails to comply with Rule 56(c) requirements. Nor should it be denied by default even if the movant completely fails to reply to a nonmovant's response. Before deciding on other possible action, subdivision (e)(1) recognizes that the court may afford an opportunity to properly support or address the fact. In many circumstances this opportunity will be the court's preferred first step.

Subdivision (e)(2) authorizes the court to consider a fact as undisputed for purposes of the motion when response or reply requirements are not satisfied. This approach reflects the "deemed admitted" provisions in many local rules. The fact is considered undisputed only for purposes of the motion; if summary judgment is denied, a party who failed to make a proper Rule 56 response or reply remains free to contest the fact in further proceedings. And the court may choose not to consider the fact as undisputed, particularly if the court knows of record materials that show grounds for genuine dispute.

Subdivision (e)(3) recognizes that the court may grant summary judgment only if the motion and supporting materials — including the facts considered undisputed under subdivision (e)(2) — show that the movant is entitled to it. Considering some facts undisputed does not of itself allow summary judgment. If there is a proper response or reply as to some facts, the court cannot grant summary judgment without determining whether those facts can be genuinely disputed. Once the court has determined the set of facts — both those it has chosen to consider undisputed for want of a proper response or reply and any that cannot be genuinely disputed despite a procedurally proper response or reply — it must determine the legal consequences of these facts and permissible inferences from them.

Subdivision (e)(4) recognizes that still other orders may be appropriate. The choice among possible orders should be designed to encourage proper presentation of the record. Many courts take extra care with *pro se* litigants, advising them of the need to respond and the risk of losing by summary judgment if an adequate response is not filed. And the court may seek to reassure itself by some examination of the record before granting summary judgment against a *pro se* litigant.

Subdivision (f). Subdivision (f) brings into Rule 56 text a number of related procedures that have grown up in practice. After giving notice and a reasonable time to respond the court may grant summary judgment for the nonmoving party; grant a motion on legal or factual grounds not raised by the parties; or consider summary judgment on its own. In many cases it may prove useful first to invite a motion; the invited motion will automatically trigger the regular procedure of subdivision (c).

Subdivision (g). Subdivision (g) applies when the court does not grant all the relief requested by a motion for summary judgment. It becomes relevant only after the court has applied the summary-judgment standard carried forward in subdivision (a) to each claim, defense, or part of a claim or defense, identified by the motion. Once that duty is discharged, the court may decide whether to apply the summary-judgment standard to dispose of a material fact that is not genuinely in dispute. The court must take care that this determination does not interfere with a party's ability to accept a fact for purposes of the motion only. A nonmovant, for example, may feel confident that a genuine dispute as to one or a few facts will defeat the motion, and prefer to avoid the cost of detailed response to all facts stated by the movant. This position should be available without running the risk that the fact will be taken as established under subdivision (g) or otherwise found to have been accepted for other purposes.

If it is readily apparent that the court cannot grant all the relief requested by the motion, it may properly decide that the cost of determining whether some potential fact disputes may be eliminated by summary disposition is greater than the cost of resolving those disputes by other means, including trial. Even if the court believes that a fact is not genuinely in dispute it may refrain from ordering that the fact be treated as established. The court may conclude that it is better to leave open for trial facts and issues that may be better illuminated by the trial of related facts that must be tried in any event.

Subdivision (h). Subdivision (h) carries forward former subdivision (g) with three changes. Sanctions are made discretionary, not mandatory, reflecting the experience that courts seldom invoke the independent Rule 56 authority to impose sanctions. *See* Cecil & Cort, Federal Judicial Center Memorandum on Federal Rule of Civil Procedure 56 (g) Motions for Sanctions (April 2, 2007). In addition, the rule text is expanded to recognize the need to provide notice and a reasonable time to respond. Finally, authority to impose other appropriate sanctions also is recognized.

Imagine that you represent a business entity that is suing one of its former employees for misappropriation of trade secrets. Because the relevant jurisdiction requires that a misappropriation of trade secrets be intentional to be actionable, the main dispute appears to be over whether the defendant knew that what he took from the company on his own personal thumb drive on the day he resigned was the company's proprietary trade secret information. Your evidence on this point is largely circumstantial, but an inference can be drawn from this circumstantial evidence that the defendant in fact knew that he was stealing trade secrets. The defendant's only evidence in response to this evidence of yours is his own word, reflected in an affidavit his counsel has filed on his behalf, which is cited in his response to your motion.

Carefully read through the provisions of Rule 56 and the comments above. Assuming that intent is the only issue in the case, should (or rather "shall") the court grant the motion? What arguments do you expect each side to make?

Below are two cases reflecting the post-amendment approach to a summary judgment motion. One aspect of this post-amendment practice is that movants have not been afraid to use the authorization of Rule 56(b) to file a summary judgment motion "at any time until 30 days after the close of all discovery." This provision superseded timing provisions in former Rule 56(a) and (c). Thus, it is now possible for a defendant to file its answer along with a motion for summary judgment. It is even possible for a plaintiff to file the *complaint* along with a motion for summary judgment! One might question whether the availability of such early opportunities for summary judgment (which is always on the merits and with prejudice) will render the motion to dismiss and the motion for judgment on the pleadings superfluous, especially considering the demanding standard for sufficiency of the complaint that *Twombly* and *Iqbal* establish.

One response to this concern is the existence of Rule 56(d), which was renumbered, but not substantially changed, from prior Rule 56(f). That provision permits a party faced with a motion for summary judgment to move the court for leave to conduct additional discovery. In support of this motion, the party opposing summary judgment need only file an affidavit or declaration specifying the reasons that additional discovery is needed — usually to reveal evidence that would dispute the material facts that form the basis of the motion that has been filed against it. If the court views additional discovery as warranted, Rule 56(d) allows the judge to defer ruling on the motion until such discovery can be completed.

Now, when faced with early motions for summary judgment, parties often make Rule 56(d) arguments for additional discovery. Often, if the summary judgment motion has been filed very early, and the case is likely to be fact-intensive, the courts are willing to grant these motions for additional discovery. But in many cases, they are not willing to grant what is requested, sometimes because the legal foundation of a summary judgment motion will not be implicated by additional factual material, and other times because the opponent of summary judgment has not convinced the court through its declaration. The cases below illustrate each of these situations.

Garner v. City of Ozark

587 Fed. App'x 515 (11th Cir. 2014)

Before Tjoflat, Wilson and Cox, Circuit Judges.

Per Curiam:

In this case, the Plaintiff Spring Garner sues Officer Phil Dodson in his individual and official capacity and the City of Ozark (the "Defendants") for injuries her son, Wynter Stokes, suffered while Dodson was attempting to apprehend him. The Defendants bring this interlocutory appeal contending that the district court erred by ignoring a claim of immunity in their motion to dismiss and incorrectly granting Garner discovery and denying their immunity-based summary judgment motion.

I. Facts and Procedural History

According to the allegations of the complaint, Stokes (who is autistic) left his residence, wandered down the street, and entered the yard of a private residence. The owner of the residence called police. Officer Dodson responded to the call. According to the complaint, Dodson arrived on the scene and, without provocation or cause, repeatedly instructed his police canine to attack Stokes.

As a result of these events, Garner (as parent of Stokes) filed this suit alleging multiple claims: excessive force in violation of the Fourth Amendment (Count I); unreasonable seizure in violation of the Fourth Amendment (Count II); unlawful arrest in violation of the Fourth Amendment (Count III); violation of the Americans with Disability Act ("ADA") (Count IV); negligent hiring (Count V); negligence (Count VII); assault (Count VIII); and battery (IX). Although the complaint is hardly a model of clarity, it appears to assert each claim against every Defendant—regardless of whether such assertion is rational. The Defendants moved to dismiss all claims except those of excessive force, assault, and battery against Dodson in his individual capacity. The district court granted the motion to dismiss on all the counts it considered with the exception of the ADA claim. However, the district court did not address the motion to dismiss regarding the assault or battery claims against the city.

The Defendants also moved for summary judgment on all claims. In response to the summary judgment motion, Garner's counsel filed an affidavit stating that she would need to present several expert witnesses in order to respond to the motion. The district court granted Garner discovery under Fed.R.Civ.P. 56(d) and denied the Defendants' summary judgment motion, but with leave to refile at an appropriate time. The Defendants appeal.

II. Issues on Appeal

The Defendants present two issues on appeal. First, Ozark contends that the district court erred by not considering its immunity-based motion to dismiss the state law assault and battery claims. Second, the Defendants contend that the district court abused its discretion by granting Garner's Rule 56(d) motion for discovery and—in doing so—denying the Defendants' summary judgment motion.

III. Standards of Review

… We review a district court's ruling on a Rule 56(d) motion for abuse of discretion.

IV. Discussion

A. The district court erred by denying Ozark immunity on the Alabama state law tort claims.

* * *

B. The district court erred by denying the Defendants' summary judgment motion.

The Defendants contend that the district court erred by granting Garner's Rule 56(d) motion and—in doing so—denying their immunity-based summary judgment motion.

Fed.R.Civ.P. 56(d) allows a district court to deny a summary judgment motion when "a nonmovant shows by affidavit or declaration that, for specified reasons, it cannot present facts essential to justify its opposition." A Rule 56(d) motion must be supported by an affidavit which sets forth with particularity the facts the moving party expects to discover and how those facts would create a genuine issue of material fact precluding summary judgment. Whether to grant or deny a Rule 56(d) motion for discovery requires the court to balance the movant's demonstrated need for discovery against the burden such discovery will place on the opposing party. In qualified immunity cases, the Rule 56(d) balancing is done with a thumb on the side of the scale weighing against discovery. "The basic thrust of the qualified-immunity doctrine is to free officials from the concerns of litigation, including avoidance of disruptive discovery." *Ashcroft v. Iqbal*, 556 U.S. 662, 685 (2009) (quotation omitted). And, the city's immunity claim in this case warrants a ruling on the city's motion for summary judgment without further discovery.

In this case, Garner has not shown that she meets the requirements of Rule 56(d). Garner has not articulated what particular facts she expects to discover. Neither has she provided any explanation of how those facts would be relevant to the issue of immunity. Garner's counsel submitted an affidavit stating that she would like to present expert witnesses on recognition of individuals with autism, proper handling of police dogs, and the nature of Stokes's capacity and propensity for physical violence. Garner does not explain what facts these expert witnesses would provide. Instead, Garner seems to desire the experts for their opinions on the case. Rule 56(d) provides a remedy "when facts are unavailable to the nonmovant." Fed.R.Civ.P. 56(d) (emphasis added). Even assuming Garner's request for expert opinions was proper under Rule 56(d), she does not explain how these experts' opinions would be relevant to the issue of immunity. Accordingly, Garner has not particularly identified any relevant facts she needs to oppose the summary judgment motion.

The district court's order provides no analysis demonstrating that Garner met the requirements of Rule 56(d). Neither does Garner provide any analysis on appeal. Accordingly, we hold that Garner did not meet the requirements of Rule 56(d) and that the district court abused its discretion in granting Garner discovery. It follows then, that the district court also erred by denying the Defendants' summary judgment motion on the basis that Garner needed additional discovery.

V. Conclusion

The district court erred by not addressing Ozark's immunity-based motion to dismiss. Accordingly, we remand and instruct the district court to consider this issue. The district court also abused its discretion by granting Garner's 56(d) motion. Accordingly, we reverse the district court's order on the Rule 56(d) motion, vacate the district court's denial of the Defendants' summary judgment motion, and remand and instruct the court to consider the merits of the Defendants' summary judgment motion.

Reversed in part and remanded with instructions.

Sterk v. Redbox Automated Retail, LLC

770 F.3d 618 (7th Cir. 2014)

Before Flaum, Manion, and Kanne, Circuit Judges.

Opinion

Flaum, Circuit Judge.

Redbox Automated Retail, LLC out-sources its customer service operations to Stream Global Services, which fields Redbox customer inquiries through a customer service call center. To enable Stream to perform this function, Redbox provides Stream with access to its customer database, the disclosure of which Kevin Sterk and Jiah Chung allege violates the Video Privacy Protection Act, 18 U.S.C. §2710. The district court granted summary judgment in Redbox's favor, concluding that Redbox's actions fall within the statutory exception for disclosures in the ordinary course of business—more precisely, disclosures incident to "request processing." We agree, and therefore affirm the district court's decision.

I. Background

Redbox operates automated self-service kiosks—typically located at grocery stores, convenience stores, or drug stores—at which customers rent DVDs and Blu-ray discs with a debit or credit card for a daily rental fee. Although Redbox owns and operates the machines, the company out-sources certain "back office" functions to various service providers, including Stream. Stream provides customer service to Redbox users when, for example, a customer encounters technical problems at a kiosk and requires help from a live person. In such an event, the Redbox customer can call the phone number listed on the machine to speak to a customer service representative to troubleshoot the issue. If resolution of the customer's issue requires accessing that customer's video rental history—for instance, if a Redbox kiosk charges the customer's credit card, but fails to dispense the selected movie—that call center representative (a Stream employee) will do so.

So that Stream can perform Redbox's customer service functions, Redbox has granted Stream access to the database in which Redbox stores relevant customer information. To enable customer service representatives to perform their jobs capably, Stream trains its employees on how to use the database to access the information necessary to respond to customer inquiries. Plaintiffs object both to Stream's ability to access customer rental histories when prompted by a customer call and Stream's use of customer records during the course of employee training exercises. In plaintiffs' view, Redbox's disclosure of customer information to Stream for these purposes violates the Video Privacy Protection Act ("VPPA").

Enacted in 1988 in response to the Washington City Paper's publication of then-Supreme Court nominee Robert Bork's video rental history (a DC-area video store provided it to a reporter), S. Rep. No. 100-599, at 5 (1988), reprinted in 1988 U.S.C.C.A.N. 4342, the VPPA prohibits "video tape service provider[s]" like Redbox from "disclos[ing], to any person, personally identifiable information concerning any consumer of such provider." 18 U.S.C. § 2710(b)(1). Personally identifiable information ("PII") "includes information which identifies a person as having requested or obtained specific video materials or services from a video tape service provider." *Id.* § 2710(a)(3). But the VPPA provides several exceptions to the disclosure prohibition, allowing disclosure of a consumer's video rental history when the consumer has provided written consent, when the party seeking disclosure has obtained a warrant or court order, or (relevant to this case) when the disclosure is incident to the video tape service provider's ordinary course of business. *Id.* § 2710(b)(2). The statute instructs that "'ordinary course of business' means only debt collection activities, order fulfillment, request processing, and the transfer of ownership." *Id.* § 2710(a)(2).

Plaintiffs Kevin Sterk and Jiah Chung are Redbox users who contend that Redbox's disclosure of their PII to Stream is not incident to Redbox's ordinary course of business. Initially, Sterk filed this lawsuit without Chung, alleging in his original complaint only that Redbox violated the VPPA's "destruction of old records" provision, which requires video tape service providers to destroy PII "as soon as practicable, but no later than one year from the date the information is no longer necessary for the purpose for which it was collected and there are no pending requests or orders for access to such information." 18 U.S.C. § 2710(e). After Sterk's case was consolidated with a similar suit, Redbox moved to dismiss Sterk's complaint, arguing that the VPPA does not provide a private right of action for mere "information retention." Sterk then filed an amended complaint, which Chung joined, adding the unlawful disclosure claim at issue here. Redbox again moved to dismiss. The district court denied the motion but certified for interlocutory appeal the issue of whether the VPPA's private right of action extended to improper retention claims. We took up the issue and reversed the district court, holding that the VPPA does not provide a damages remedy for a retention claim, and so plaintiffs could only seek injunctive relief from Redbox for its alleged failure to timely destroy their information. *See Sterk v. Redbox Automated Retail, LLC*, 672 F.3d 535, 538–39 (7th Cir.2012).

While the interlocutory appeal on the retention issue was pending, discovery regarding the disclosure claims proceeded. Fact discovery commenced on December 21, 2011, and originally was set to close on April 6, 2012.

Over Redbox's opposition, plaintiffs moved to extend discovery by a month, and the district court obliged. During this discovery period, we issued our opinion on the retention issue, and the district court granted plaintiffs leave to file another amended complaint. After denying in part and granting in part Redbox's renewed motion to dismiss the retention claims, the district court reopened discovery as to both the disclosure and retention claims for an additional period of time. During discovery, Redbox produced over a thousand pages of documents in response to forty-eight document requests; responded to forty-two interrogatories; and produced witnesses for three depositions, including two Rule 30(b)(6) witnesses. In the end, Redbox produced information concerning every vendor to which Redbox discloses customer information—including the precise information shared to each—and plaintiffs successfully obtained third-party discovery from Stream. Against that backdrop, Redbox moved for summary judgment.

Plaintiffs objected to Redbox's summary judgment motion as premature, arguing (pursuant to Federal Rule of Civil Procedure 56(d)) that they needed more discovery in order to adequately respond to Redbox's arguments. Despite their contention, plaintiffs pointed to just two issues concerning which they desired more discovery: (1) information regarding the "technical" method by which "Stream queries Redbox's database," and (2) information relating to whether Stream accesses all, or just a portion, of Redbox's customer records. The district court denied plaintiffs' request for additional discovery and granted summary judgment as to all counts in Redbox's favor. As to plaintiffs' improper disclosure claim (the only claim at issue in this appeal), the district court concluded that Redbox's disclosure of its customers' PII to Stream constitutes "request processing" and thus falls within the VPPA's "ordinary course of business" exception. Plaintiffs appeal the summary judgment decision, as well as the district court's refusal to permit additional discovery before ruling. Plaintiffs also complain that the district court overlooked a footnote in their opposition brief concerning Iron Mountain, a vendor with which Redbox stores backup tapes of its data. Though victorious below, Redbox takes issue with the district court's standing analysis.

II. Discussion

* * *

D. Plaintiffs' Motion for Additional Discovery

For similar reasons, the district court did not abuse its discretion by denying plaintiffs' motion for more discovery pursuant to Federal Rule of Civil Procedure 56(d). Rule 56 permits a district court to delay consideration of a summary judgment motion and order additional discovery before ruling if the non-movant demonstrates that "it cannot present facts essential to justify its opposition." Fed. R. Civ. P. 56(d). The Rule places the burden on the non-movant that believes additional discovery is required to "state the reasons why the party cannot adequately respond to the summary judgment motion without further discovery." *Deere & Co. v. Ohio Gear*, 462 F.3d 701, 706 (7th Cir.2006).

Plaintiffs identified two discrete areas of discovery that they allegedly needed to further explore in order to respond to Redbox's summary judgment motion as it pertained to Stream: (1) information regarding the "technical" method by which Stream "queries Redbox's database," and (2) information that would shed more light on whether Stream had accessed all, or just some, of Redbox's customer records. Neither of these topics were material to the district court's summary judgment ruling. How Stream accesses Redbox's information is irrelevant to whether disclosures to Stream fall within the VPPA's "ordinary course of business" exception, and the district court made clear in its opinion that it would reach the same conclusion (one which we endorse on appeal) regardless of whether Stream had access to all customer records or just some of them. Plaintiffs therefore fell far short of meeting their burden to identify material facts needed to oppose summary judgment. Accordingly, the district court did not abuse its discretion in denying plaintiffs additional discovery before ruling on Redbox's motion.

III. Conclusion

For the foregoing reasons, we AFFIRM the judgment of the district court.

Exercise 10-13. Denying Additional Discovery

1. Articulate the reasons that additional discovery was denied in the above cases. What would have been the harm that would have resulted from allowing additional discovery in each case?

2. Imagine how you might have framed the need for additional discovery in each case differently to achieve a more favorable outcome. Is it possible in either? Both?

Exercise 10-14. The Summary Judgment Burden Shift

In the summary judgment trio of cases from 1986, as well as in the *Redbox* case above, the courts make clear that the summary judgment process involves a set of shifting burdens of *production*. No party can carry a burden of *proof* at the summary judgment stage because courts cannot weigh evidence or credibility at that stage. Rather, the party that would bear the burden of proof at trial bears the burden of demonstrating at the summary judgment stage that this burden either *could* be satisfied based on the record evidence, or *certainly will* be satisfied, depending on whether that party is the movant or the non-movant.

If the party seeking summary judgment is also the party who will bear the burden of proof at trial, then the movant must come forward with enough evidence to convince the court (1) that there are no genuine disputes of material fact between the parties; and (2) that based on the evidence in the record and the governing legal standards, no rational fact finder could fail to find in the movant's favor. The non-movant then must come forward with its own evidence and/or argument showing either (1) that there exist one or more genuine disputes of material fact; or (2) that the evidence in the record, and the governing legal standards, could rationally justify a verdict for either party.

If the party moving for summary judgment is not the party who will bear the burden of proof at trial, then the movant must come forward with evidence or argument showing (1) that there are no genuine disputes of material fact; and (2) that the evidence in the record, and the governing legal standards, make it so that no rational fact finder could render a verdict in favor of the non-movant. This burden of production may consist entirely of a showing that evidence of one or more elements of the non-movant's cause of action does not exist. The non-movant must then come forward with evidence showing either (1) the existence of a genuine dispute of material fact; or (2) that the evidence in the record, and the governing legal standards, could justify a verdict for either party.

In *Celotex* and *Liberty Lobby*, which party is the party moving for summary judgment—the party that would bear the burden of proof at trial, or the party that would not bear the burden of proof? Why does the evidence going to the burden of production that the non-movants proffer not satisfy the lower courts?

6. Professionalism and Summary Adjudication

The process of summary adjudication—whether by default judgment, dismissal, or summary judgment—is fraught with ethical and professional concerns. Of these three main types of summary adjudication, the most ethically problematic is the default judgment, mostly because of the concerns we discuss above relating to *ex parte* proceedings. Because the United States system of justice is designed on the assumption that each adverse party will be represented by a diligent and competent adversary, *ex parte* proceedings present a significant danger of injustice. Of course, you should always be on the lookout for opposing counsel who might be likely to abuse the default judgment process to "snap up a judgment," as many courts term it—to secure a quick default based on questionable service (incomplete process, insufficient notice, or even proper service of an unrepresented defendant), and then mature that default into a default judgment as quickly as possible without so much as a hint of warning to the defendant.

Exercise 10-15. Default and Professionalism

You represent the plaintiff in a suit against a former business partner—now estranged from your client—for recovery of what your client claims are proceeds of the sale of the business that should have been shared equally between the two. You properly serve the defendant, who at the time is not represented by an attorney. The defendant does not secure counsel until one month later. In the meantime, the Clerk enters a default on the docket on the 21st day after service, due to the defendant's failure to respond to the complaint. Your client urges you to seek a default judgment right away. You say that you are happy to do that, but that you would like to contact the defendant's newly hired attorney to see whether they plan to appear in the case. Your client urges you not to "help out the enemy." Something in your gut tells you that rushing to the courthouse to obtain a default judgment might not be the most professional thing to do, but how do you make your understandably aggrieved client understand this?

How would you explain your preference to him and attempt to get him to agree with your plan to contact the defendant's lawyer as a courtesy before moving for default judgment? Should you do so, or is that a failure to "diligently represent" your client, as every state's professional responsibility code requires a lawyer to do? If you decide to persuade your client, is there any way that you can couch your plan as being in his best interests?

It may help to know that a few state courts, and some federal districts, have recognized a professional duty to inform the defendant in default before seeking a default judgment. Also, in deciding motions to set aside defaults and default judgments, courts often consider it relevant, though not dispositive, that the defendant's counsel was not contacted before a default judgment was sought.

Chapter 11

Trial and Post-Trial

1. Chapter Problem

Jury Trial and Post-Trial Motion

For each problem below, answer the question, state the law and policy that support your answer, and explain your reasoning.

Pam and Dan are each driving cars that collide at an intersection controlled by a traffic light. Pam sues Dan in federal court. In the Complaint, Pam asserts a claim for negligence and requests compensatory damages. In the Answer, Dan (1) denies that he was negligent, (2) asserts an affirmative defense of contributory negligence, alleging that Pam's negligence caused the accident, and (3) demands a "jury trial on all issues triable by a jury in this case."

1. Does Dan have the right to a jury to decide whether he was negligent? Whether Pam was negligent? The amount of damages if Dan was negligent and Pam was not?

The following evidence is presented at trial:

Pam testified that she was traveling at the speed limit of 30 mph as she approached the intersection. She saw the light turn green 100 yards before she got to the intersection and the light remained green as she entered the intersection. Dan ran the red light in front of Pam and the front of her car crashed into the driver's side of Dan's car. Pam's driving record is perfect — no previous accidents or traffic tickets.

Police Officer testified that she responded to the accident. She confirmed Pam's description of the location of the cars in the intersection. Police Officer also testified that she smelled alcohol on Dan's breath and gave him a blood alcohol test. His blood alcohol registered at .07%, just under the legal limit of .08%. Police Officer ticketed Dan for driving while his license was suspended for prior traffic infractions.

Pam's son testified that Pam had a green light when she entered the intersection and that immediately after the accident Dan apologized to him for the accident.

Dan testified that his light turned from green to yellow at the moment he entered the intersection. He stated that he had consumed three beers in the two hours before the accident but that his driving was not impaired by alcohol at the

---

time. He explained that he did not "apologize" to Pam's son, but had simply expressed his concern for Pam and her son after the accident.

Pam testified that her new car was seriously damaged in the accident and that she suffered a broken leg. Pam introduced documents that established the repair cost of her car ($7,000), her medical bills for her leg ($8,000), and her lost wages due to the accident ($5,000). Pam's doctor testified that Pam's compound fracture required six weeks of painful rehabilitation.

Pam moved for a Judgment as a Matter of Law (JMOL) at the close of all evidence. The trial court did not rule on the motion. The jury returned a verdict for Dan. Pam made timely motions for JMOL and New Trial. Assume that the trial court found Pam and her son to be very credible and Dan to be of questionable credibility.

2. How should the trial court rule on the JMOL motion?

3. How should the trial court rule on the New Trial motion?

4. Assume that the trial court granted Pam's JMOL motion and that Dan appealed. How should the appellate court rule?

5. Assume that Pam's only motion was for a New Trial, that the trial court denied the motion, and that Pam appealed. How should the appellate court rule?

6. Assume the jury decided that Dan was negligent and that Pam was not negligent. The jury awarded a verdict of $200,000. Dan made a motion for a new trial on the grounds that the damages were not supported by the evidence. What options does the trial court have when ruling on Dan's motion? What should the trial court decide?

2. Overview

The law, practice skills, and professionalism involved in civil trials are, perhaps surprisingly, not topics covered in detail in most Civil Procedure courses. There are two primary reasons for this. First, few civil cases reach trial. For example, in 2017, less than 1% of the 290,000 civil cases terminated in federal court reached trial. Second, courses in Evidence and Trial Advocacy directly address the substance, skills, and professionalism of trial practice. Those courses typically address a wide range of trial issues, such the admissibility of evidence, objections to evidence, direct and cross examination of witnesses, documentary evidence, opening statements, and closing statements.

This chapter addresses the following aspects of civil trial and post-trial proceedings:

• Section 3—Right to a Jury. Rule 38 recognizes the right to a jury from two sources: (1) the Seventh Amendment to the United States Constitution, and (2) federal statutes. In addition, Rule 39 gives the court discretion to order a jury trial in circumstances where the parties do not have the right to a jury. The focus of this section is on Supreme Court opinions interpreting the Seventh Amendment.

• Section 4—Jury Selection. Rule 47 and Rule 48 deal with the process of jury selection and the number of jurors. Federal statutes govern the selection of people to become part of the pool of potential jurors and the parties' challenges to individuals to become one of the jurors who decides the case. Finally, the Equal Protection Clause of the United States Constitution proscribes limits on the parties' reasons for challenging jurors on the basis of race and gender.

- Section 5 — Jury Instructions. Rule 51 addresses the process the court and parties employ to propose instructions to give the jury regarding the law it is to apply during its deliberations. In addition, Rule 51 deals with objections to proposed instructions and limits on appeals based on allegedly erroneous jury instructions.

- Section 6 — Jury Verdicts. Rule 48 addresses the requirement that the jury verdict be unanimous unless the parties agree to a non-unanimous verdict. Rule 49 covers alternative verdict forms, which determine the types of questions jurors must answer in reaching a verdict.

- Section 7 — Findings of Fact and Conclusions of Law. Rule 52 requires the judge to make findings of fact and conclusions of law in cases tried to the court (without a jury).

- Section 8 — Motions During and After Trial. Rule 50 governs motions for judgment as a matter of law, which parties can raise both during and after trial, asserting that the evidence does not support the opposing party's case. Rule 59 and Rule 61 deal with motions for a new trial, which can be based on a variety of grounds established in case law, including jury misconduct and erroneous evidentiary rulings. Rule 60 provides grounds for parties to request that the court vacate a judgment, such as newly discovered evidence and fraud.

- Section 9 — Professional Development Reflection. Chapter 11 ends with news stories that illustrate issues of professionalism and professional identity that arise in the trial and post-trial process.

3. Right to a Jury

Rule 38(a) preserves the right to a jury trial provided in the Seventh Amendment to the United States Constitution. Read Rule 38(a), the Seventh Amendment, and the Sixth Amendment. As you see, the Seventh Amendment provides, in part: "In suits at common law ... the right of trial by jury shall be preserved...." Contrast that language with the Sixth Amendment, which provides, in part: "In all criminal prosecutions, the accused shall enjoy the right to a speedy and public trial, by an impartial jury...." The Seventh Amendment contains two limits on the right to a jury in civil cases not found in the Sixth Amendment. First, the Sixth Amendment applies to "all criminal prosecutions," while the Seventh Amendment applies to "suits at common law" rather than to all civil cases. Second, while the Sixth Amendment *creates* the right to a jury in criminal cases, the Seventh Amendment *preserves* the right to a jury in civil cases. The Supreme Court cases interpreting the reach of the Seventh Amendment are addressed below.

Rule 38(a) also preserves the right to a jury provided in federal statutes. Congress has created hundreds of statutory schemes that include civil claims that can be brought in federal courts. For example, private plaintiffs can assert civil claims under the Clean Air Act, the Americans with Disabilities Act, and the Copyright Act. Most federal statutory schemes are silent about the right to a jury, but occasionally Congress not only creates a civil claim but also provides the right to a jury. For example, in 28 U.S.C. § 1346(a)(1) Congress provides that federal district courts have jurisdiction over civil actions against the United States to recover tax erroneously collected and in 28 U.S.C. § 2402 Congress provides either party the right to a jury to decide § 1346(a)(1) claims.

Read Rule 38(b), which makes two important points about the process for demanding a jury. First, the unit of analysis for the right to a jury is whether the *issue* is triable by a jury, not whether the entire *case* is triable by a jury. Second, a party must demand a jury trial within 14 days of the last pleading directed to the issue triable by a jury. Thus, in a simple case in which the pleadings consist of a complaint and an answer, either party may serve a jury demand within 14 days of service of the answer. In more complicated cases, with multiple parties and amended pleadings, the 14 day limit is a bit trickier. For a detailed discussion of the 14 day limit, see WRIGHT & MILLER, FEDERAL PRACTICE & PROCEDURE § 2320.

Practice Pointer

To ensure that they comply with the time limit in Rule 38(b), parties often include the jury demand in their first pleading—the complaint for the plaintiff or the answer for the defendant. Typical language for the demand for jury either in a pleading or in a separate document (Demand for Jury Trial) is: "Plaintiff [or Defendant] demands a jury trial for all issues in this lawsuit."

If a party fails to comply with the requirements of Rule 38(b) for demanding a jury, the party waives the right to a jury under Rule 38(d) and Rule 39(b). Read those subsections. Note that Rule 39(b) softens the harshness of the waiver rule somewhat—upon a motion by a party, the court can order a trial by jury on any issue for which a party had the right to a jury but failed to comply with Rule 38(b).

For civil actions in which neither the Seventh Amendment nor a federal statute provides the right to a jury, Rule 39 gives the court discretion to try issues to a jury in two circumstances. First, Rule 39(c)(1) allows the court to use an advisory jury to assist the judge in deciding the case. Federal judges frequently use this provision even though the judge is not bound by the jury's findings. WRIGHT & MILLER, FEDERAL PRACTICE & PROCEDURE § 2335. Second, Rule 39(c)(2) allows the court to try any issue by jury with the parties' consent, in which case the jury verdict has the same effect as if the jury trial had been a matter of right.

Exercise 11-1. Jury Trial Policy and Strategy

1. Trial by jury has been an integral part of civil litigation in the United States since the Bill of Rights became effective in 1791. Yet trial by jury remains controversial, with strong supporters and detractors. Think broadly about trial by jury, rather than trial by a judge. Consider the effects of trial by jury on the jurors, the parties, and society. Articulate advantages and disadvantages of trial by jury.

2. As an attorney representing clients in civil litigation, you will need to decide whether to demand a jury. What considerations would lead you to demand a jury? When would you prefer to have a judge decide the case?

The Supreme Court cases that follow each contribute to the analytical framework the Court has established when deciding whether a right to a jury trial exists in a civil case. Assuming that a party has made a timely demand for a jury, the Court first looks to see if a federal statute grants the right to a jury for the issues involved in the case. If the Court finds a statutory right to a jury, it need not analyze the Seventh Amendment, because Congress has the power to extend the jury trial right beyond the right preserved in the Seventh Amendment. However, in each of the cases below, Congress did not expressly provide the right to a jury, so the Court analyzed the reach of the Seventh Amendment.

Exercise 11-2. *Chauffeurs Local 391 v. Terry*

Recall the brief discussion of the English bifurcated court system in Chapter 1. Common law courts had jurisdiction over a variety of civil claims called "forms of action." Cases were decided by juries and the most common type of relief was compensatory damages. Equity courts had jurisdiction over suits in which the plaintiff had no adequate remedy at law, such as when compensatory damages did not provide a sufficient remedy. Suits in equity were decided by judges, not juries, and a typical remedy was an injunction ordering the defendant to do something or refrain from doing something. As you will see in *Terry*, the distinction between law and equity is critical in Seventh Amendment analysis. As you read *Terry*, answer the following questions.

1. What two factors does the Court analyze when deciding whether a party has the right to a jury under the Seventh Amendment? Which factor is more important?

2. What policy does the Court articulate to guide its analysis and application of the Seventh Amendment?

3. According to the Court, on what issues does the plaintiff have the right to a jury?

4. What alternative analysis does Justice Brennan urge the court to adopt? Why?

5. On what basis does the dissent conclude that the majority opinion is incorrect?

6. How does the dissent respond to Justice Brennan's proposed analysis?

Chauffeurs Local 391 v. Terry

494 U.S. 558 (1990)

Justice Marshall delivered the opinion of the Court, except as to Part III-A.

I

This case presents the question whether an employee who seeks relief in the form of backpay for a union's alleged breach of its duty of fair representation has a right to trial by jury. We hold that the Seventh Amendment entitles such a plaintiff to a jury trial.

McLean Trucking Company and the Chauffeurs, Teamsters, and Helpers Local No. 391 (Union) were parties to a collective-bargaining agreement that governed the terms and conditions of employment at McLean's terminals. The 27 respondents were employed by McLean as truckdrivers in bargaining units covered by the agreement, and all were members of the Union. In 1982 McLean implemented a change in operations that resulted in the elimination of some of its terminals and the reorganization of others. As part of that change, McLean transferred respondents to the terminal located in Winston-Salem and agreed to give them special seniority rights in relation to "inactive" employees in Winston-Salem who had been laid off temporarily.

After working in Winston-Salem for approximately six weeks, respondents were alternately laid off and recalled several times. Respondents filed a grievance with the Union, contesting the order of the layoffs and recalls. Respondents also challenged McLean's policy of stripping any driver who was laid off of his special seniority rights. Respondents claimed that McLean breached the collective-bargaining agreement by giving inactive drivers preference over respondents....

McLean recalled the inactive employees, thereby allowing them to regain seniority rights over respondents. In the next round of layoffs, then, respondents had lower priority than inactive drivers and were laid off first.

Accordingly, respondents filed another grievance, alleging that McLean's actions were designed to circumvent the initial decision of the grievance committee. The Union representative appeared before the grievance committee and presented the contentions of respondents and those of the inactive truck drivers. At the conclusion of the hearing, the committee held that McLean had not violated the committee's first decision.

McLean continued to engage in periodic layoffs and recalls of the workers at the Winston-Salem terminal. Respondents filed a third grievance with the Union, but the Union declined to refer the charges to a grievance committee on the ground that the relevant issues had been determined in the prior proceedings.

In July 1983, respondents filed an action in District Court, alleging that McLean had breached the collective-bargaining agreement in violation of § 301 of the Labor Management Relations Act, and that the Union had violated its duty of fair representation. Respondents requested a permanent injunction requiring the defendants to cease their illegal acts and to reinstate them to their proper seniority status; in addition, they sought, *inter alia,* compensatory damages for lost wages and health benefits. In 1986 McLean filed for bankruptcy; subsequently, the action against it was voluntarily dismissed, along with all claims for injunctive relief.

Respondents had requested a jury trial in their pleadings. The Union moved to strike the jury demand on the ground that no right to a jury trial exists in a duty of fair representation suit. The District Court denied the motion to strike. After an interlocutory appeal, the Fourth Circuit affirmed the trial court, holding that the Seventh Amendment entitled respondents to a jury trial of their claim for monetary relief. We granted the petition for certiorari to resolve a Circuit conflict on this issue, and now affirm the judgment of the Fourth Circuit.

II

The duty of fair representation is inferred from unions' exclusive authority under the National Labor Relations Act (NLRA), to represent all employees in a bargaining unit. The duty requires a union to serve the interests of all members without hostility or discrimination toward any, to exercise its discretion with complete good faith and honesty, and to avoid arbitrary conduct. A union must discharge its duty both in bargaining with the employer and in its enforcement of the resulting collective-bargaining agreement. Thus, the Union here was required to pursue respondents' grievances in a manner consistent with the principles of fair representation.

Because most collective-bargaining agreements accord finality to grievance or arbitration procedures established by the collective-bargaining agreement, an employee normally cannot bring a § 301 action against an employer unless he can show that the union breached its duty of fair representation in its handling of his grievance. Whether the employee sues both the labor union and the employer or only one of those entities, he must prove the same two facts to recover money damages: that the employer's action violated the terms of the collective-bargaining agreement and that the union breached its duty of fair representation.

III

[The Court examined the NLRA and found the Congress did not expressly grant the right to a jury in the Act.]

We turn now to the constitutional issue presented in this case—whether respondents are entitled to a jury trial. The Seventh Amendment provides that "[i]n Suits at common law, where the value in controversy shall exceed twenty dollars, the right of trial by jury shall be preserved." The right to a jury trial includes more than the common-law forms of action recognized in 1791; the phrase "Suits at common law" refers to "suits in which *legal* rights [are] to be ascertained and determined, in contradistinction to those where equitable rights alone [are] recognized, and equitable remedies [are] administered." *Parsons v. Bedford,* 3 Pet. 433, 447 (1830). The right extends to causes of action created by Congress. *Tull v. United States,* 481 U.S. 412 (1987). Since the merger of the systems of law and equity, see FRCP 2, this Court has carefully preserved the right to trial by jury where legal rights are at stake. As the Court noted in *Beacon Theatres, Inc. v. Westover,* 359 U.S. 500, 501 (1959), "Maintenance of the jury as a fact-finding body is of such importance and occupies so firm a place in our history and jurisprudence that any seeming curtailment of the right to a jury trial should be scrutinized with the utmost care."

To determine whether a particular action will resolve legal rights, we examine both the nature of the issues involved and the remedy sought. "First, we compare the statutory action to 18th-century actions brought in the courts of England prior to the merger of the courts of law and equity. Second, we examine the remedy sought and determine whether it is legal or equitable in nature." *Tull, supra,* 481 U.S., at 417–418. The second inquiry is the more important in our analysis. *Granfinanciera, S.A. v. Nordberg,* 492 U.S. 33 (1989).

A

An action for breach of a union's duty of fair representation was unknown in 18th-century England; in fact, collective bargaining was unlawful. We must therefore look for an analogous cause of action that existed in the 18th century to determine whether the nature of this duty of fair representation suit is legal or equitable.

The Union contends that this duty of fair representation action resembles a suit brought to vacate an arbitration award because respondents seek to set aside the result of the grievance process. In the 18th century, an action to set aside an arbitration award was considered equitable....

The arbitration analogy is inapposite, however, to the Seventh Amendment question posed in this case. No grievance committee has considered respondents' claim that the Union violated its duty of fair representation; the grievance process was concerned only with the employer's alleged breach of the collective-bargaining agreement. Thus, respondents' claim against the Union cannot be characterized as an action to vacate an arbitration award because "[t]he arbitration proceeding did not, and indeed, could not, resolve the employee's claim against the union.... Because no arbitrator has decided the primary issue presented by this claim, no arbitration award need be undone, even if the employee ultimately prevails." *DelCostello v. Teamsters,* 462 U.S. 151, 163–164 (1983).

The Union next argues that respondents' duty of fair representation action is comparable to an action by a trust beneficiary against a trustee for breach of fiduciary duty. Such actions were within the exclusive jurisdiction of courts of equity. This analogy is far more persuasive than the arbitration analogy. Just as a trustee must act in the best interests of the beneficiaries, a union, as the exclusive representative of the workers, must exercise its power to act on behalf of the employees in good faith. Moreover, just as a beneficiary does not directly control the actions of a trustee, an individual employee lacks direct control over a union's actions taken on his behalf.

The trust analogy extends to a union's handling of grievances. In most cases, a trustee has the exclusive authority to sue third parties who injure the beneficiaries' interest in the trust, including any legal claim the trustee holds in trust for the beneficiaries. The trustee then has the sole responsibility for determining whether to settle, arbitrate, or otherwise dispose of the claim. Similarly, the union typically has broad discretion in its decision whether and how to pursue an employee's grievance against an employer. Just as a trust beneficiary can sue to enforce a contract entered into on his behalf by the trustee only if the trustee "improperly refuses or neglects to bring an action against the third person," Restatement (Second) of Trusts, §282(2), so an employee can sue his employer for a breach of the collective-bargaining agreement only if he shows that the union breached its duty of fair representation in its handling of the grievance.

Respondents contend that their duty of fair representation suit is less like a trust action than an attorney malpractice action, which was historically an action at law, see, *e.g., Russell v. Palmer,* 2 Wils. K.B. 325, 95 Eng. Rep. 837 (1767). In determining the appropriate statute of limitations for a hybrid §301/duty of fair representation action, this Court in *DelCostello* noted in dictum that an attorney malpractice action is "the closest state-law analogy for the claim against the union." 462 U.S., at 167. The Court in *DelCostello* did not consider the trust analogy, however. Presented with a more complete range of alternatives, we find that, in the context of the

Seventh Amendment inquiry, the attorney malpractice analogy does not capture the relationship between the union and the represented employees as fully as the trust analogy does.

The attorney malpractice analogy is inadequate in several respects. Although an attorney malpractice suit is in some ways similar to a suit alleging a union's breach of its fiduciary duty, the two actions are fundamentally different. The nature of an action is in large part controlled by the nature of the underlying relationship between the parties. Unlike employees represented by a union, a client controls the significant decisions concerning his representation. Moreover, a client can fire his attorney if he is dissatisfied with his attorney's performance. This option is not available to an individual employee who is unhappy with a union's representation, unless a majority of the members of the bargaining unit share his dissatisfaction. Thus, we find the malpractice analogy less convincing than the trust analogy.

Nevertheless, the trust analogy does not persuade us to characterize respondents' claim as wholly equitable. The Union's argument mischaracterizes the nature of our comparison of the action before us to 18th-century forms of action. As we observed in *Ross v. Bernhard*, 396 U.S. 531 (1970), "The Seventh Amendment question depends on the nature of the *issue* to be tried rather than the character of the overall action." *Id.*, at 538 (emphasis added) (finding a right to jury trial in a shareholder's derivative suit, a type of suit traditionally brought in courts of equity, because plaintiffs' case presented legal issues of breach of contract and negligence). As discussed above, to recover from the Union here, respondents must prove both that McLean violated §301 by breaching the collective-bargaining agreement and that the Union breached its duty of fair representation. When viewed in isolation, the duty of fair representation issue is analogous to a claim against a trustee for breach of fiduciary duty. The §301 issue, however, is comparable to a breach of contract claim—a legal issue.

Respondents' action against the Union thus encompasses both equitable and legal issues. The first part of our Seventh Amendment inquiry, then, leaves us in equipoise as to whether respondents are entitled to a jury trial.

B

Our determination under the first part of the Seventh Amendment analysis is only preliminary. *Granfinanciera, S.A. v. Nordberg*, 492 U.S., at 47. In this case, the only remedy sought is a request for compensatory damages representing backpay and benefits. Generally, an action for money damages was "the traditional form of relief offered in the courts of law." *Curtis v. Loether*, 415 U.S. 189, 196 (1974). This Court has not, however, held that "any award of monetary relief must *necessarily* be 'legal' relief." *Id*. Nonetheless, because we conclude that the remedy respondents seek has none of the attributes that must be present before we will find an exception to the general rule and characterize damages as equitable, we find that the remedy sought by respondents is legal.

First, we have characterized damages as equitable where they are restitutionary, such as in "action[s] for disgorgement of improper profits," The backpay sought by respondents is not money wrongfully held by the Union, but wages and benefits they would have received from McLean had the Union processed the employees' grievances properly. Such relief is not restitutionary.

Second, a monetary award "incidental to or intertwined with injunctive relief" may be equitable. *Tull, supra,* 481 U.S., at 424. See, *e.g., Mitchell v. Robert DeMario Jewelry, Inc.,* 361 U.S. 288, 291–292 (1960) (District Court had power, incident to its injunctive powers, to award backpay under the Fair Labor Standards Act; also backpay in that case was restitutionary). Because respondents seek only money damages, this characteristic is clearly absent from the case.

The Union argues that the backpay relief sought here must nonetheless be considered equitable because this Court has labeled backpay awarded under Title VII, of the Civil Rights Act of 1964 as equitable. See *Albemarle Paper Co. v. Moody,* 422 U.S. 405, 415–418 (1975) (characterizing backpay awarded against employer under Title VII as equitable in context of assessing whether judge erred in refusing to award such relief). It contends that the Title VII analogy is compelling in the context of the duty of fair representation because the Title VII backpay provision was based on the NLRA provision governing backpay awards for unfair labor practices, 29 U.S.C. § 160(c) (1982 ed.) ("[W]here an order directs reinstatement of an employee, back pay may be required of the employer or labor organization"). We are not convinced.

The Court has never held that a plaintiff seeking backpay under Title VII has a right to a jury trial. Assuming, without deciding, that such a Title VII plaintiff has no right to a jury trial, the Union's argument does not persuade us that respondents are not entitled to a jury trial here. Congress specifically characterized backpay under Title VII as a form of "equitable relief." 42 U.S.C. § 2000e-5(g) (1982 ed.) ("[T]he court may … order such affirmative action as may be appropriate, which may include, but is not limited to, reinstatement or hiring of employees, with or without back pay…, or any other equitable relief as the court deems appropriate"). See also *Curtis v. Loether, supra,* 415 U.S., at 196–197, (distinguishing backpay under Title VII from damages under Title VIII, the fair housing provision of the Civil Rights Act, 42 U.S.C. §§ 3601–3619 (1982 ed.), which the Court characterized as "legal" for Seventh Amendment purposes). Congress made no similar pronouncement regarding the duty of fair representation. Furthermore, the Court has noted that backpay sought from an employer under Title VII would generally be restitutionary in nature, see *Curtis v. Loether, supra,* at 197, in contrast to the damages sought here from the Union. Thus, the remedy sought in this duty of fair representation case is clearly different from backpay sought for violations of Title VII.

Moreover, the fact that Title VII's backpay provision may have been modeled on a provision in the NLRA concerning remedies for unfair labor practices does not require that the backpay remedy available here be considered equitable. The Union apparently reasons that if Title VII is comparable to one labor law remedy it is comparable to all remedies available in the NLRA context. Although both the duty of fair representation and the unfair labor practice provisions of the NLRA are components of national labor policy, their purposes are not identical. Unlike the unfair labor practice provisions of the NLRA, which are concerned primarily with the public interest in effecting federal labor policy, the duty of fair representation targets the wrong done the individual employee. Thus, the remedies appropriate for unfair labor practices may differ from the remedies for a breach of the duty of fair representation, given the need to vindicate different goals. Certainly, the connection between backpay under Title VII and damages under the unfair labor practice provision of the NLRA does not require us to find a parallel connection between Title VII backpay and money damages for breach of the duty of fair representation.

We hold, then, that the remedy of backpay sought in this duty of fair representation action is legal in nature. Considering both parts of the Seventh Amendment inquiry, we find that respondents are entitled to a jury trial on all issues presented in their suit.

IV

On balance, our analysis of the nature of respondents' duty of fair representation action and the remedy they seek convinces us that this action is a legal one. Although the search for an adequate 18th-century analog revealed that the claim includes both legal and equitable issues, the money damages respondents seek are the type of relief traditionally awarded by courts of law. Thus, the Seventh Amendment entitles respondents to a jury trial, and we therefore affirm the judgment of the Court of Appeals.

Justice Brennan, concurring in part and concurring in the judgment.

I agree with the Court that respondents seek a remedy that is legal in nature and that the Seventh Amendment entitles respondents to a jury trial on their duty of fair representation claims. I therefore join Parts I, II, III-B, and IV of the Court's opinion. I do not join that part of the opinion which reprises the particular historical analysis this Court has employed to determine whether a claim is a "Sui[t] at common law" under the Seventh Amendment because I believe the historical test can and should be simplified.

The current test, first expounded in *Curtis v. Loether*, 415 U.S. 189, 194 (1974), requires a court to compare the right at issue to 18th-century English forms of action to determine whether the historically analogous right was vindicated in an action at law or in equity, and to examine whether the remedy sought is legal or equitable in nature. However, this Court, in expounding the test, has repeatedly discounted the significance of the analogous form of action for deciding where the Seventh Amendment applies. I think it is time we dispense with it altogether. I would decide Seventh Amendment questions on the basis of the relief sought. If the relief is legal in nature, i. e., if it is the kind of relief that historically was available from courts of law, I would hold that the parties have a constitutional right to a trial by jury—unless Congress has permissibly delegated the particular dispute to a non-Article III decisionmaker and jury trials would frustrate Congress' purposes in enacting a particular statutory scheme.

I believe that our insistence that the jury trial right hinges in part on a comparison of the substantive right at issue to forms of action used in English courts 200 years ago needlessly convolutes our Seventh Amendment jurisprudence. For the past decade and a half, this Court has explained that the two parts of the historical test are not equal in weight, that the nature of the remedy is more important than the nature of the right. Since the existence of a right to jury trial therefore turns on the nature of the remedy, absent congressional delegation to a specialized decisionmaker, there remains little purpose to our rattling through dusty attics of ancient writs. The time has come to borrow William of Occam's razor and sever this portion of our analysis.

* * *

Justice Kennedy, with whom Justice O'Connor and Justice Scalia join, dissenting.

* * *

The Seventh Amendment requires us to determine whether the duty of fair representation action "is more similar to cases that were tried in courts of law than to suits tried in courts of equity." *Tull v. United States*, 481 U.S. 412, 417 (1987). Having made this decision in favor of an equitable action, our inquiry should end. Because the Court disagrees with this proposition, I dissent.

* * *

Justice Marshall, speaking for four Members of the Court, states an important and correct reason for finding the trust model better than the malpractice analogy. He observes that the client of an attorney, unlike a union member or beneficiary, controls the significant decisions concerning his litigation and can fire the attorney if not satisfied. Put another way, although a lawyer acts as an agent of his client, unions and trustees do not serve as agents of their members and beneficiaries in the conventional sense of being subject to their direction and control in pursuing claims. An individual union member cannot require his union to pursue a claim, and cannot choose a different representative....

Further considerations fortify the conclusion that the trust analogy is the controlling one here. A union's duty of fair representation accords with a trustee's duty of impartiality. This standard may require a union to act for the benefit of employees who, as in this case, have antithetical interests. Trust law, in a similar manner, long has required trustees to serve the interests of all beneficiaries with impartiality.

A lawyer's duty of loyalty is cast in different terms. Although the union is charged with the responsibility of reconciling the positions of its members, the lawyer's duty of loyalty long has precluded the representation of conflicting interests....

The relief available in a duty of fair representation action also makes the trust action the better model. To remedy a breach of the duty of fair representation, a court must issue an award fashioned to make the injured employee whole. The court may order an injunction compelling the union, if it is still able, to pursue the employee's claim, and may require monetary compensation, but it cannot award exemplary or punitive damages. This relief parallels the remedies prevailing in the courts of equity in actions against trustees for failing to pursue claims.

* * *

For all these reasons, the suit here resembles a trust action, not a legal malpractice action. By this I do not imply that a union acts as a trustee in all instances or that trust law, as a general matter, should inform any particular aspects of federal labor law. Obvious differences between a union and a trustee will exist in other contexts. I would conclude only that, under the analysis directed by our precedents, the respondents may not insist on a jury trial. When all rights and remedies are considered, their action resembles a suit heard by the courts of equity more than a case heard by the courts of law. From this alone it follows that the respondents have no jury trial right on their duty of fair representation claims against the Union.

* * *

The Court must adhere to the historical test in determining the right to a jury because the language of the Constitution requires it. The Seventh Amendment "preserves" the right to jury trial in civil cases. We cannot preserve a right existing in 1791 unless we look to history to identify it. Our precedents are in full agreement with this reasoning and insist on adherence to the historical test. No alternatives short of rewriting the Constitution exist. If we abandon the plain language of the Constitution to expand the jury right, we may expect Courts with opposing views to curtail it in the future.

Exercise 11-3. *Beacon Theatres, Inc. v. Westover*

In *Beacon* the Court addresses a situation that is common in modern litigation—multiple claims asserted and different types of relief requested in the same suit.

1. In the antitrust suit, who are the parties? What claims and counterclaims do they make? What relief do they seek? What issues are common to the claims and counterclaims?

2. Which party requested a jury trial? Why do you think they did so?

3. What is the trial court's decision regarding the jury trial? How does the trial court use Rule 42(b)?

4. According to the Court, which portions of the case should be heard by a jury and which parts should be decided by the judge? In what order? Why?

5. What policies support the trial court's decision? What policies support the Supreme Court's decision?

Beacon Theaters, Inc. v. Westover

359 U.S. 500 (1959)

Petitioner, Beacon Theatres, Inc., sought by mandamus to require a district judge in the Southern District of California to vacate certain orders alleged to deprive it of a jury trial of issues arising in a suit brought against it by Fox West Coast Theatres, Inc. The Court of Appeals for the Ninth Circuit refused the writ, holding that the trial judge had acted within his proper discretion in denying petitioner's request for a jury. We granted certiorari because "Maintenance of the jury as a fact-finding body is of such importance and occupies so firm a place in our history and jurisprudence that any seeming curtailment of the right to a jury trial should be scrutinized with the utmost care." Dimick v. Schiedt, 293 U.S. 474, 486 (1935).

Fox had asked for declaratory relief against Beacon alleging a controversy arising under the Sherman Antitrust Act and under the Clayton Act, which authorizes suits for treble damages against Sherman Act violators. According to the complaint Fox operates a movie theatre in San Bernardino, California, and has long been exhibiting films under contracts with movie distributors. These contracts grant if the exclusive right to show "first run" pictures in the "San Bernardino competitive area" and provide for "clearance"—a period of time during which no other theatre can exhibit the same pictures. After building a drive-in theatre about 11 miles from San Bernardino, Beacon notified Fox that it considered contracts barring simultaneous exhibitions of first-run films in the two theatres to be overt acts in violation of the antitrust laws. Fox's complaint alleged that this notification, together with threats of treble damage suits against Fox and its distributors, gave rise to "duress and coercion" which deprived Fox of a valuable property right, the right to negotiate for exclusive first-run contracts. Unless Beacon was restrained, the complaint continued, irreparable harm would result.

Accordingly, while its pleading was styled a "Complaint for Declaratory Relief," Fox prayed both for a declaration that a grant of clearance between the Fox and Beacon theatres is reasonable and not in violation of the antitrust laws, and for an injunction, pending final resolution of the litigation, to prevent Beacon from instituting any action under the antitrust laws against Fox and its distributors arising out of the controversy alleged in the complaint.

Beacon filed an answer, a counterclaim against Fox, and a cross-claim against an exhibitor who had intervened. These denied the threats and asserted that there was no substantial competition between the two theatres, that the clearances granted were therefore unreasonable, and that a conspiracy existed between Fox and its distributors to manipulate contracts and clearances so as to restrain trade and monopolize first-run pictures in violation of the antitrust laws. Treble damages were asked.

Beacon demanded a jury trial of the factual issues in the case as provided by Federal Rule of Civil Procedure 38(b). The District Court, however, viewed the issues raised by the "Complaint for Declaratory Relief," including the question of competition between the two theatres, as essentially equitable. Acting under the purported authority of Rules 42(b) and 57, it directed that these issues be tried to the court before jury determination of the validity of the charges of antitrust violations made in the counterclaim and cross-claim. A common issue of the "Complaint for Declaratory Relief," the counterclaim, and the cross-claim was the reasonableness of the clearances granted to Fox, which depended, in part, on the existence of competition between the two theatres. Thus the effect of the action of the District Court could be, as the Court of Appeals believed, "to limit the petitioner's opportunity fully to try to a jury every issue which has a bearing upon its treble damage suit, for determination of the issue of clearances by the judge might operate either by way of res judicata or collateral estoppel so as to conclude both parties with respect thereto at the subsequent trial of the treble damage claim."

The District Court's finding that the Complaint for Declaratory Relief presented basically equitable issues draws no support from the Declaratory

Judgment Act, 28 U.S.C. §§ 2201, 2202; Fed. R. Civ. P. 57. That statute, while allowing prospective defendants to sue to establish their nonliability, specifically preserves the right to jury trial for both parties. It follows that if Beacon would have been entitled to a jury trial in a treble damage suit against Fox it cannot be deprived of that right merely because Fox took advantage of the availability of declaratory relief to sue Beacon first. Since the right to trial by jury applies to treble damage suits under the antitrust laws, and is, in fact, an essential part of the congressional plan for making competition rather than monopoly the rule of trade, the Sherman and Clayton Act issues on which Fox sought a declaration were essentially jury questions.

* * *

Assuming that the pleadings can be construed to support such a request and assuming additionally that the complaint can be read as alleging the kind of harassment by a multiplicity of lawsuits which would traditionally have justified equity to take jurisdiction and settle the case in one suit, we are nevertheless of the opinion that, under the Declaratory Judgment Act and the Federal Rules of Civil Procedure, neither claim can justify denying Beacon a trial by jury of all the issues in the antitrust controversy.

The basis of injunctive relief in the federal courts has always been irreparable harm and inadequacy of legal remedies. At least as much is required to justify a trial court in using its discretion under the Federal Rules to allow claims of equitable origins to be tried ahead of legal ones, since this has the same effect as an equitable injunction of the legal claims. And it is immaterial, in judging if that discretion is properly employed, that before the Federal Rules and the Declaratory Judgment Act were passed, courts of equity, exercising a jurisdiction separate from courts of law, were, in some cases, allowed to enjoin subsequent legal actions between the same parties involving the same controversy.... Inadequacy of remedy and irreparable harm are practical terms, however. As such their existence today must be determined, not by precedents decided under discarded procedures, but in the light of the remedies now made available by the Declaratory Judgment Act and the Federal Rules.

Viewed in this manner, the use of discretion by the trial court under Rule 42(b) to deprive Beacon of a full jury trial on its counterclaim and cross-claim, as well as on Fox's plea for declaratory relief, cannot be justified. Under the Federal Rules the same court may try both legal and equitable causes in the same action. Fed. Rules Civ. Proc. 1, 2, 18. Thus any defenses, equitable or legal, Fox may have to charges of antitrust violations can be raised either in its suit for declaratory relief or in answer to Beacon's counterclaim.... Whatever permanent injunctive relief Fox might be entitled to on the basis of the decision in this case could, of course, be given by the court after the jury renders its verdict. In this way the issues between these parties could be settled in one suit giving Beacon a full jury trial of every antitrust issue....

* * *

If there should be cases where the availability of declaratory judgment or joinder in one suit of legal and equitable causes would not in all respects protect the plaintiff seeking equitable relief from irreparable harm while affording a jury trial in the legal cause, the trial court will necessarily have to use its discretion in deciding whether the legal or equitable cause should be tried first. Since the right to jury trial is a constitutional one, however, while no similar requirement protects trials by the court, that discretion is very narrowly limited and must, wherever possible, be exercised to preserve jury trial.... [O]nly under the most imperative circumstances, circumstances which in view of the flexible procedures of the Federal Rules we cannot now anticipate, can the right to a jury trial of legal issues be lost through prior determination of equitable claims. As we have shown, this is far from being such a case.

Exercise 11-4. *Atlas Roofing Co. v. Occupational Health and Safety Review Comm'n*

In *Atlas*, the Court analyzes the Seventh Amendment in the context of federal regulatory statutes. Congress has enacted numerous statutes designed to regulate many aspects of modern life, including public health, safety, the environment, the tax system, and the economy. In many of these statutory schemes, Congress creates new obligations, rights, and remedies along with a federal agency to administer the statute.

1. In what circumstances can Congress require that fact finding be done by an administrative agency or special court, rather than a jury?

2. What examples does the Court give of public rights?

3. What examples does the court give of private rights?

4. What policies support use of an administrative fact finder in *Atlas*?

Atlas Roofing Co. v. Occupational Health and Safety Review Comm'n

430 U.S. 442 (1977)

The issue in these cases is whether, consistent with the Seventh Amendment, Congress may create a new cause of action in the Government for civil penalties enforceable in an administrative agency where there is no jury trial.

After extensive investigation, Congress concluded, in 1970, that work-related deaths and injuries had become a "drastic" national problem. Finding the existing state statutory remedies as well as state common-law actions for negligence and wrongful death to be inadequate to protect the employee population from death and injury due to unsafe working conditions, Congress enacted the Occupational Safety and Health Act of 1970 (OSHA or Act). The Act created a new statutory duty to avoid maintaining unsafe or unhealthy working conditions, and empowers the Secretary of Labor to promulgate health and safety standards. Two new remedies were provided permitting the Federal Government, proceeding before an administrative agency, (1) to obtain abatement orders requiring employers to correct unsafe working conditions and (2) to impose civil penalties on any employer maintaining any unsafe working condition.…

Under the Act, inspectors, representing the Secretary of Labor, are authorized to conduct reasonable safety and health inspections. If a violation is discovered, the inspector, on behalf of the Secretary, issues a citation to the employer fixing a reasonable time for its abatement and, in his discretion, proposing a civil penalty. Such proposed penalties may range from nothing for de minimis and nonserious violations, to not more than $1,000 for serious violations, to a maximum of $10,000 for willful or repeated violations.

If the employer wishes to contest the penalty or the abatement order, he may do so by notifying the Secretary of Labor within 15 days, in which event the abatement order is automatically stayed. An evidentiary hearing is then held before an administrative law judge of the Occupational Safety and Health Review Commission. The Commission consists of three members, appointed for six-year terms, each of whom is qualified "by reason of training, education or experience" to adjudicate contested citations and assess penalties. At this hearing the burden is on the Secretary to establish the elements of the alleged violation and the propriety of his proposed abatement order and proposed penalty; and the judge is empowered to affirm, modify, or vacate any or all of these items, giving due consideration in his penalty assessment to "the size of the business of the employer…, the gravity of the violation, the good faith of the employer, and the history of previous violations." The judge's decision becomes the Commission's final and appealable order unless within 30 days a Commissioner directs that it be reviewed by the full Commission.

If review is granted, the Commission's subsequent order directing abatement and the payment of any assessed penalty becomes final unless the employer timely petitions for judicial review in the appropriate court of appeals. The Secretary similarly may seek review of Commission orders, but, in either case, "(t)he findings of the Commission with respect to questions of fact, if supported by substantial evidence on the record considered as a whole, shall be conclusive." If the employer fails to pay the assessed penalty, the Secretary may commence a collection action in a federal district court in which neither the fact of the violation nor the propriety of the penalty assessed may be retried. Thus, the penalty may be collected without the employer's ever being entitled to a jury determination of the facts constituting the violation.

Petitioners were separately cited by the Secretary and ordered immediately to abate pertinent hazards after inspections of their respective worksites conducted in 1972 revealed conditions that assertedly violated a mandatory occupational safety standard. In each case an employee's death had resulted. Petitioner Ivey was cited for a willful violation of a safety standard promulgated by the Secretary under the Act requiring the sides of trenches in "unstable or soft material" to be "shored, ... sloped, or otherwise supported by means of sufficient strength to protect the employees working within them." The Secretary proposed a penalty of $7,500 for this violation and ordered the hazard abated immediately.

Petitioner Atlas was cited for a serious violation of [standards] which require that roof opening covers be "so installed as to prevent accidental displacement." The Secretary proposed a penalty of $600 for this violation and ordered the hazard abated immediately.

Petitioners timely contested these citations and were afforded hearings before Administrative Law Judges of the Commission. The judges, and later the Commission, affirmed the findings of violations and accompanying abatement requirements and assessed petitioner Irey a reduced civil penalty of $5,000 and petitioner Atlas the civil penalty of $600 which the Secretary had proposed. Petitioners respectively thereupon sought judicial review in the Courts of Appeals for the Third and Fifth Circuits, challenging both the Commission's factual findings that violations had occurred and the constitutionality of the Act's enforcement procedures.

A panel of the Court of Appeals for the Third Circuit affirmed the Commission's orders....

We granted the petitions for writs of certiorari limited to the important question whether the Seventh Amendment prevents Congress from assigning to an administrative agency, under these circumstances, the task of adjudicating violations of OSHA.

The Seventh Amendment provides that "(i)n Suits at common law, where the value in controversy shall exceed twenty dollars, the right of trial by jury shall be preserved...." The phrase "Suits at common law" has been construed to refer to cases tried prior to the adoption of the Seventh Amendment in courts of law in which jury trial was customary as distinguished from courts of equity or admiralty in which jury trial was not....

Petitioners then claim that to permit Congress to assign the function of adjudicating the Government's rights to civil penalties for violation of the statute to a different forum—an administrative agency in which no jury is available—would be to permit Congress to deprive a defendant of his Seventh Amendment jury right. We disagree. At least in cases in which "public rights" are being litigated—e. g., cases in which the Government sues in its sovereign capacity to enforce public rights created by statutes within the power of Congress to enact—the Seventh Amendment does not prohibit Congress from assigning the factfinding function and initial adjudication to an administrative forum with which the jury would be incompatible.

Congress has often created new statutory obligations, provided for civil penalties for their violation, and committed exclusively to an administrative agency the function of deciding whether a violation has in fact occurred. These statutory schemes have been sustained by this Court, albeit often without express reference to the Seventh Amendment. Thus, taxes may constitutionally be assessed and collected together with penalties, with the relevant facts in some instances being adjudicated only by an administrative agency.... Similarly, Congress has entrusted to an administrative agency the task of adjudicating violations of the customs and immigration laws and assessing penalties based thereon.

* * *

[T]he distinction is at once apparent between cases of private right and those which arise between the Government and persons subject to its authority in connection with the performance of the constitutional functions of the executive or legislative departments. The Congress, in exercising the powers confided to it may establish legislative courts to serve as special tribunals to examine and determine various matters, arising between the government and others, which from their nature do not require judicial determination and yet are susceptible of it. But the mode of determining matters of this class is completely within congressional control. Congress may reserve to itself the power to decide, may delegate that power to executive officers, or may commit it to judicial tribunals. Familiar illustrations of administrative of such

matters are found in connection with the exercise of the congressional power as to interstate and foreign commerce, taxation, immigration, the public lands, public health, the facilities of the
post office, pensions, and payments to veterans. [*Cromwell v.
Benson*, 285 U.S. 22, 50–51 (1932).]

In *NLRB v. Jones & Laughlin Steel Corp.*, 301 U.S. 1 (1937), the Court
squarely addressed the Seventh Amendment issue involved when Congress
commits the factfinding function under a new statute to an administrative
tribunal. Under the National Labor Relations Act, Congress had committed to the National Labor Relations Board, in a proceeding brought
by its litigating arm, the task of deciding whether an unfair labor practice
had been committed and of ordering backpay where appropriate. The
Court stated: "The instant case is not a suit at common law or in the nature of such a suit.... It is a statutory proceeding. Reinstatement of the
employee and payment for time lost are requirements (administratively)
imposed for violation of the statute and are remedies appropriate to its
enforcement. The contention under the Seventh Amendment is without
merit." *Id.*, at 48–49.

* * *

In sum, the cases discussed above stand clearly for the proposition that
when Congress creates new statutory "public rights," it may assign their
adjudication to an administrative agency with which a jury trial would be
incompatible, without violating the Seventh Amendment's injunction that
jury trial is to be "preserved" in "suits at common law." Congress is not
required by the Seventh Amendment to choke the already crowded federal
courts with new types of litigation or prevented from committing some
new types of litigation to administrative agencies with special competence
in the relevant field. This is the case even if the Seventh Amendment would
have required a jury where the adjudication of those rights is assigned instead to a federal court of law instead of an administrative agency.

* * *

[Petitioners assert] that the right to jury trial was never intended to depend on the identity of the forum to which Congress has chosen to submit
a dispute; otherwise, it is said, Congress could utterly destroy the right to
a jury trial by always providing for administrative rather than judicial resolution of the vast range of cases that now arise in the courts. The argument
is well put, but it overstates the holdings of our prior cases and is in any
event unpersuasive. Our prior cases support administrative factfinding in
only those situations involving "public rights," e. g., where the Government
is involved in its sovereign capacity under an otherwise valid statute creating
enforceable public rights. Wholly private tort, contract, and property cases,
as well as a vast range of other cases as well are not at all implicated.

More to the point, it is apparent from the history of jury trial in civil matters that factfinding, which is the essential function of the jury in civil cases, was never the exclusive province of the jury under either the English or American legal systems at the time of the adoption of the Seventh Amendment; and the question whether a fact would be found by a jury turned to a considerable degree on the nature of the forum in which a litigant found himself. Critical factfinding was performed without juries in suits in equity, and there were no juries in admiralty, nor were there juries in the military justice system....

The point is that the Seventh Amendment was never intended to establish the jury as the exclusive mechanism for factfinding in civil cases. It took the existing legal order as it found it, and there is little or no basis for concluding that the Amendment should now be interpreted to provide an impenetrable barrier to administrative factfinding under otherwise valid federal regulatory statutes....

Thus, history and our cases support the proposition that the right to a jury trial turns not solely on the nature of the issue to be resolved but also on the forum in which it is to be resolved. Congress found the common-law and other existing remedies for work injuries resulting from unsafe working conditions to be inadequate to protect the Nation's working men and women. It created a new cause of action, and remedies therefor, unknown to the common law, and placed their enforcement in a tribunal supplying speedy and expert resolutions of the issues involved. The Seventh Amendment is no bar to the creation of new rights or to their enforcement outside the regular courts of law.

The judgments below are affirmed.

Exercise 11-5. *Tull v. United States*

In *Tull*, the Court returns to the right to a jury in a federal statutory regulatory scheme — the Clean Water Act (CWA). Like many federal regulatory schemes, the CWA authorizes suits in federal district court to enforce the Act and provides civil penalties for each day the defendant violated the Act. Civil penalties are payable to the federal government.

1. How is the Seventh Amendment issue in *Tull* different from the issue in *Atlas*?

2. What analysis does the Court employ to decide whether the defendant has the right to a jury to decide whether the defendant violated the CWA?

3. On what basis does the Court decide that the judge, rather than the jury, will decide the amount of the civil penalties?

Tull v. United States

481 U.S. 412 (1987)

The question for decision is whether the Seventh Amendment guaranteed petitioner a right to a jury trial on both liability and amount of penalty in an action instituted by the Federal Government seeking civil penalties and injunctive relief under the Clean Water Act.

I

The Clean Water Act prohibits discharging, without a permit, dredged or fill material into "navigable waters," including the wetlands adjacent to the waters. The Government sued petitioner, a real estate developer, for dumping fill on wetlands on the island of Chincoteague, Virginia....

Section 1319 enumerates the remedies available under the Clean Water Act. Subsection (b) authorizes relief in the form of temporary or permanent injunctions. Subsection (d) provides that violators of certain sections of the Act "shall be subject to a civil penalty not to exceed $10,000 per day" during the period of the violation. The Government sought in this case both injunctive relief and civil penalties. When the complaint was filed, however, almost all of the property at issue had been sold by petitioner to third parties. Injunctive relief was therefore impractical except with regard to a small portion of the land. The Government's complaint demanded the imposition of the maximum civil penalty of $22,890,000....

Petitioner's timely demand for a trial by jury was denied by the District Court. During the 15-day bench trial, petitioner did not dispute that he had placed fill at the locations alleged and did not deny his failure to obtain a permit. Petitioner contended, however, that the property in question did not constitute "wetlands." The Government concedes that triable issues of fact were presented by disputes between experts involving the composition and nature of the fillings.

The District Court concluded that petitioner had illegally filled in wetland areas on all properties in question, but drastically reduced the amount of civil penalties sought by the Government, [awarding $325,000 in civil penalties].

* * *

II

The Seventh Amendment provides that, "[i]n Suits at common law, where the value in controversy shall exceed twenty dollars, the right of trial by jury shall be preserved...." The Court has construed this language to require a jury trial on the merits in those actions that are analogous to "Suits at common law." Prior to the Amendment's adoption, a jury trial was customary in suits brought in the English law courts. In contrast, those actions that are analogous to 18th-century cases tried in courts of equity or admiralty do not require a jury trial. This analysis applies not only to common-law forms of action, but also to causes of action created by congressional enactment.

To determine whether a statutory action is more similar to cases that were tried in courts of law than to suits tried in courts of equity or admiralty, the Court must examine both the nature of the action and of the remedy sought. First, we compare the statutory action to 18th-century actions brought in the courts of England prior to the merger of the courts of law and equity. Second, we examine the remedy sought and determine whether it is legal or equitable in nature.

Petitioner analogizes this Government suit under § 1319(d) to an action in debt within the jurisdiction of English courts of law. Prior to the enactment of the Seventh Amendment, English courts had held that a civil penalty suit was a particular species of an action in debt that was within the jurisdiction of the courts of law.

After the adoption of the Seventh Amendment, federal courts followed this English common law in treating the civil penalty suit as a particular type of an action in debt, requiring a jury trial. Actions by the Government to recover civil penalties under statutory provisions therefore historically have been viewed as one type of action in debt requiring trial by jury.

* * *

The Government argues, however, that—rather than an action in debt—the closer historical analog is an action to abate a public nuisance. In 18th-century English law, a public nuisance was an act or omission which obstructs or causes inconvenience or damage to the public in the exercise of rights common to all Her Majesty's subjects." ...

It is true that the subject matter of this Clean Water Act suit—the placement of fill into navigable waters—resembles these two species of public nuisance. Whether, as the Government argues, a public nuisance action is a better analogy than an action in debt is debatable. But we need not decide the question.... It suffices that we conclude that both the public nuisance action and the action in debt are appropriate analogies to the instant statutory action.

* * *

We reiterate our previously expressed view that characterizing the relief sought is "[m]ore important" than finding a precisely analogous common-law cause of action in determining whether the Seventh Amendment guarantees a jury trial. *Curtis v. Loether.*

A civil penalty was a type of remedy at common law that could only be enforced in courts of law. Remedies intended to punish culpable individuals, as opposed to those intended simply to extract compensation or restore the status quo, were issued by courts of law, not courts of equity.

[Punitive damages remedy is legal, not equitable, relief; treble-damages remedy for securities violation is a penalty, which constitutes legal relief.] The action authorized by § 1319(d) is of this character. Subsection (d) does not direct that the "civil penalty" imposed be calculated solely on the basis of equitable determinations, such as the profits gained from violations of the statute, but simply imposes a maximum penalty of $10,000 per day of violation. The legislative history of the Act reveals that Congress wanted the district court to consider the need for retribution and deterrence, in addition to restitution, when it imposed civil penalties. A court can require retribution for wrongful conduct based on the seriousness of the violations, the number of prior violations, and the lack of good-faith efforts to comply with the relevant requirements. It may also seek to deter future violations by basing the penalty on its economic impact. Subsection 1319(d)'s authorization of punishment to further retribution and deterrence clearly evidences that this subsection reflects more than a concern to provide equitable relief.... Because the nature of the relief authorized by § 1319(d) was traditionally available only in a court of law, petitioner in this present action is entitled to a jury trial on demand.

* * *

III

The remaining issue is whether petitioner additionally has a Seventh Amendment right to a jury assessment of the civil penalties. At the time this case was tried, § 1319(d) did not explicitly state whether juries or trial judges were to fix the civil penalties. The legislative history of the 1977 Amendments to the Clean Water Act shows, however, that Congress intended that trial judges perform the highly discretionary calculations necessary to award civil penalties after liability is found. We must decide therefore whether Congress can, consistent with the Seventh Amendment, authorize judges to assess civil penalties.

The Seventh Amendment is silent on the question whether a jury must determine the remedy in a trial in which it must determine liability. The answer must depend on whether the jury must shoulder this responsibility as necessary to preserve the "substance of the common-law right of trial by jury." Colgrove v. Battin, 413 U.S. 149, 157 (1973). Is a jury role necessary for that purpose? We do not think so. Only those incidents which are regarded as fundamental, as inherent in and of the essence of the system of trial by jury, are placed beyond the reach of the legislature. The Amendment was designed to preserve the basic institution of jury trial in only its most fundamental elements. The assessment of a civil penalty is not one of the "most fundamental elements." ...

Congress' assignment of the determination of the amount of civil penalties to trial judges therefore does not infringe on the constitutional right to a jury trial. Since Congress itself may fix the civil penalties, it may delegate that determination to trial judges. In this case, highly discretionary calculations that take into account multiple factors are necessary in order to set civil penalties under the Clean Water Act. These are the kinds of calculations traditionally performed by judges. We therefore hold that a determination of a civil penalty is not an essential function of a jury trial, and that the Seventh Amendment does not require a jury trial for that purpose in a civil action.

IV

We conclude that the Seventh Amendment required that petitioner's demand for a jury trial be granted to determine his liability, but that the trial court and not the jury should determine the amount of penalty, if any.

Justice Scalia, with whom Justice Stevens joins, concurring in part and dissenting in part.

I join the Court's disposition, and Parts I and II of its opinion. I do not join Part III because in my view the right to trial by jury on whether a civil penalty of unspecified amount is assessable also involves a right to trial by jury on what the amount should be. The fact that the Legislature could elect to fix the amount of penalty has nothing to do with whether, if it chooses not to do so, that element comes within the jury-trial guarantee....

While purporting to base its determination (quite correctly) upon historical practice, the Court creates a form of civil adjudication I have never encountered. I can recall no precedent for judgment of civil liability by jury but assessment of amount by the court. Even punitive damages are assessed by the jury when liability is determined in that fashion....

I would reverse and remand for jury determination of both issues.

Exercise 11-6. Right to a Jury Quiz

Answer the following questions. Briefly explain your rationale and the authorities that support your analysis—*Beacon, Terry, Atlas, Tull,* and Rule 38.

1. P sues for negligence and requests compensatory damages only.

    Who decides negligence?

    Who decides damages?

2. P sues for fraud and requests an injunction only.

    Who decides fraud?

    Who decides the injunction?

3. P sues for breach of contract and requests specific performance and compensatory damages.

    Who decides breach of contract?

Who decides damages?

Who decides specific performance?

4. Without violating the Seventh Amendment, could Congress amend the Clean Water Act to provide that a jury will decide whether the defendant violated the Act and if so the amount of the civil penalty?

5. Without violating the Seventh Amendment, could Congress amend the Federal Labor Management Relations Act to provide that a judge will decide whether the employer violated the Act and what amount of back pay, if any, the employee should receive?

6. Without violating the Seventh Amendment, could Congress amend the Clean Air Act to regulate greenhouse gas emissions from coal fired power plants and provide that the EPA will decide whether the defendant violated that portion of the Act and if so the amount of the civil penalty?

7. Without violating the Seventh Amendment, could Congress enact the Medical Malpractice Reform Act, requiring that medical malpractice claims must be presented to the Medical Malpractice Agency, which will decide without a jury whether the defendant is guilty of medical malpractice and, if so, the appropriate remedy, which could include an injunction and compensatory damages?

4. Jury Selection

The starting point in jury selection is to identify a pool of potential jurors for jury duty. This pool of jurors is known as the venire. In *Theil v. Southern Pacific Co.*, 328 U.S. 317 (1946), the Court articulated the legal standard governing the selection of the jury pool.

> The American tradition of trial by jury, considered in connection with either criminal or civil proceedings, necessarily contemplates an impartial jury drawn from a cross-section of the community. This does not mean, of course, that every jury must contain representatives of all the economic, social, religious, racial, political and geographical groups of the community; frequently such complete representation would be impossible. But it does mean that prospective jurors shall be selected by court officials without systematic and intentional exclusion of any of these groups.

In federal court, selection of the venire is governed by the Jury Selection and Service Act of 1968, 28 U.S.C §§ 1861–1869. That statute provides that:

- Jurors will be selected at random from a fair cross section of the community;

- No citizen will be excluded based on race, color, religion, sex, national origin, or economic status;

- Jurors will be selected from voter registration lists or the lists of actual voters; and

- Qualifications to be a juror include that the person is at least 18 years old, a citizen of the United States, able to speak English, and has not been convicted of a felony.

The jury that will actually hear the case is called the petit jury. In many state courts, twelve jurors comprise the petit jury. In federal court, Rule 48 (a) authorizes juries of "at least 6 and no more than 12."

The petit jury is selected through the voir dire process. The purpose of voir dire is to find a qualified and impartial jury. Read Rule 47, which deals with jury selection. Rule 47(a) provides that the court may allow the parties or their attorneys to examine prospective jurors, or the court may do so itself. If the court conducts the examination, it must allow the parties to conduct additional examination or to suggest questions they would like the judge to ask. Judges have broad discretion regarding the voir dire process, including what questions will be put to prospective jurors.

Parties may challenge individual jurors for cause. There are two basic grounds for challenges for cause. First, parties can challenge a juror's qualifications; for example, a party can move to strike a juror on the basis of a felony conviction. Second, parties can challenge a juror's impartiality. The constitutional standard of impartiality is whether jurors "have such fixed opinions that they could not judge impartially" the case. *Patton v. Yount*, 467 U.S. 1025, 1035 (1984). Trial court decisions regarding impartiality of potential jurors often turn on the judge's assessment of the juror's credibility and demeanor; therefore, appellate courts give great deference to trial judge's decisions on these challenges for cause. Trial courts must decide "[a]ll challenges for cause." *See* 28 U.S.C. § 1870. There is no fixed limit on the number of challenges for cause a party can raise.

Parties are also entitled to peremptory challenges of potential jurors. Rule 47(b) requires the court to allow parties the number of peremptory challenges provided by 28 U.S.C. § 1870, which is, in general, three per party in a civil case. Traditionally, parties could use their peremptory challenges to strike potential jurors for any reason and did not have to explain why they struck a juror. As the following case illustrates, the Supreme Court has concluded that the Equal Protection Clause of the United States Constitution imposes some limits on the use of peremptory challenges.

Exercise 11-7. *J.E.B. v. Alabama*

1. Majority opinion.

   What limits does the Equal Protection Clause put on the exercise of peremptory challenges in criminal and civil cases?

   Describe the process trial courts must employ if a party raises Equal Protection objections to another party's exercise of peremptory challenges.

2. Concurring opinion. What are the purposes served by peremptory challenges?

3. Dissenting opinion. Evaluate the effectiveness of the dissent, both in substance and style.

4. Prepare to debate the *J.E.B.* case. Should parties in civil litigation be allowed to use peremptory challenges to strike jurors for any reason? Should parties in civil litigation be prohibited from striking jurors on the basis of race or gender?

J.E.B. v. Alabama

511 U.S. 127 (1994)

Justice Blackmun delivered the opinion of the Court.

In *Batson v. Kentucky,* 476 U.S. 79 (1986), this Court held that the Equal Protection Clause of the Fourteenth Amendment governs the exercise of peremptory challenges by a prosecutor in a criminal trial. The Court explained that although a defendant has no right to a petit jury composed in whole or in part of persons of his own race, the defendant does have the right to be tried by a jury whose members are selected pursuant to nondiscriminatory criteria. Since *Batson,* we have reaffirmed repeatedly our commitment to jury selection procedures that are fair and nondiscriminatory. We have recognized that whether the trial is criminal or civil, potential jurors, as well as litigants, have an equal protection right to jury selection procedures that are free from state-sponsored group stereotypes rooted in, and reflective of, historical prejudice. See *Powers v. Ohio,* 499 U.S. 400 (1991); *Edmonson v. Leesville Concrete Co.,* 500 U.S. 614 (1991); *Georgia v. McCollum,* 505 U.S. 42 (1992).

Although premised on equal protection principles that apply equally to gender discrimination, all our recent cases defining the scope of *Batson* involved alleged racial discrimination in the exercise of peremptory challenges. Today we are faced with the question whether the Equal Protection Clause forbids intentional discrimination on the basis of gender, just as it prohibits discrimination on the basis of race. We hold that gender, like race, is an unconstitutional proxy for juror competence and impartiality.

I

On behalf of relator T.B., the mother of a minor child, respondent State of Alabama filed a complaint for paternity and child support against petitioner J.E.B. in the District Court of Jackson County, Alabama. On October 21, 1991, the matter was called for trial and jury selection began. The trial court assembled a panel of 36 potential jurors, 12 males and 24 females. After the court excused three jurors for cause, only 10 of the remaining 33 jurors were male. The State then used 9 of its 10 peremptory strikes to remove male jurors; petitioner used all but one of his strikes to remove female jurors. As a result, all the selected jurors were female.

Before the jury was empaneled, petitioner objected to the State's peremptory challenges on the ground that they were exercised against male jurors solely on the basis of gender, in violation of the Equal Protection Clause of the Fourteenth Amendment. Petitioner argued that the logic and reasoning of *Batson v. Kentucky,* which prohibits peremptory strikes solely on the basis of race, similarly forbids intentional discrimination on the basis of gender. The court rejected petitioner's claim and empaneled the all-female jury. The jury found petitioner to be the father of the child, and the court entered an order directing him to pay child support. On post judgment motion, the court reaffirmed its ruling that *Batson* does not extend to gender-based peremptory challenges. The Alabama Court of Civil Appeals affirmed.... The Supreme Court of Alabama denied certiorari.

We granted certiorari to resolve a question that has created a conflict of authority—whether the Equal Protection Clause forbids peremptory challenges on the basis of gender as well as on the basis of race. Today we reaffirm what, by now, should be axiomatic: Intentional discrimination on the basis of gender by state actors violates the Equal Protection Clause, particularly where, as here, the discrimination serves to ratify and perpetuate invidious, archaic, and overbroad stereotypes about the relative abilities of men and women.

II

Discrimination on the basis of gender in the exercise of peremptory challenges is a relatively recent phenomenon. Gender-based peremptory strikes were hardly practicable during most of our country's existence, since, until the 20th century, women were completely excluded from jury service. So well entrenched was this exclusion of women that in 1880 this Court, while finding that the exclusion of African-American men from juries violated the Fourteenth Amendment, expressed "no doubt that a State may confine the selection [of jurors] to males." *Strauder v. West Virginia,* 100 U.S. 303, 310 (1880).

* * *

Many States continued to exclude women from jury service well into the present century, despite the fact that women attained suffrage upon ratification of the Nineteenth Amendment in 1920. States that did permit women to serve on juries often erected other barriers, such as registration requirements and automatic exemptions, designed to deter women from exercising their right to jury service.

The prohibition of women on juries was derived from the English common law which, according to Blackstone, rightfully excluded women from juries under "the doctrine of *propter defectum sexus,* literally, the 'defect of sex.'" *United States v. De Gross,* 960 F.2d 1433, 1438 (CA9 1992) (en banc), quoting 2 W. Blackstone, Commentaries. In this country, supporters of the exclusion of women from juries tended to couch their objections in terms of the ostensible need to protect women from the ugliness and depravity of trials. Women were thought to be too fragile and virginal to withstand the polluted courtroom atmosphere.

* * *

This Court in *Ballard v. United States*, 329 U.S. 187 (1946), first questioned the fundamental fairness of denying women the right to serve on juries. Relying on its supervisory powers over the federal courts, it held that women may not be excluded from the venire in federal trials in States where women were eligible for jury service under local law. In response to the argument that women have no superior or unique perspective, such that defendants are denied a fair trial by virtue of their exclusion from jury panels, the Court explained:

> "It is said ... that an all male panel drawn from the various groups within a community will be as truly representative as if women were included. The thought is that the factors which tend to influence the action of women are the same as those which influence the action of men — personality, background, economic status — and not sex. Yet it is not enough to say that women when sitting as jurors neither act nor tend to act as a class. Men likewise do not act like a class.... The truth is that the two sexes are not fungible; a community made up exclusively of one is different from a community composed of both; the subtle interplay of influence one on the other is among the imponderables. To insulate the courtroom from either may not in a given case make an iota of difference. Yet a flavor, a distinct quality is lost if either sex is excluded." *Id.,* at 193–194.

Fifteen years later, however, the Court still was unwilling to translate its appreciation for the value of women's contribution to civic life into an enforceable right to equal treatment under state laws governing jury service. In *Hoyt v. Florida*, 368 U.S. [57, 61 (1961)], the Court found it reasonable, "[d]espite the enlightened emancipation of women," to exempt women from mandatory jury service by statute, allowing women to serve on juries only if they volunteered to serve. The Court justified the differential exemption policy on the ground that women, unlike men, occupied a unique position "as the center of home and family life." *Id.,* at 62.

In 1975, the Court finally repudiated the reasoning of *Hoyt* and struck down, under the Sixth Amendment, an affirmative registration statute nearly identical to the one at issue in *Hoyt.* See *Taylor v. Louisiana*, 419 U.S. 522 (1975). We explained: "Restricting jury service to only special groups or excluding identifiable segments playing major roles in the community cannot be squared with the constitutional concept of jury trial." *Id.*, at 530. The diverse and representative character of the jury must be maintained "partly as assurance of a diffused impartiality and partly because sharing in the administration of justice is a phase of civic responsibility." *Id.*, at 530–531.

* * *

III

Taylor relied on Sixth Amendment principles, but the opinion's approach is consistent with the heightened equal protection scrutiny afforded gender-based classifications. Since *Reed v. Reed*, 404 U.S. 71 (1971), this Court consistently has subjected gender-based classifications to heightened scrutiny in recognition of the real danger that government policies that professedly are based on reasonable considerations in fact may be reflective of archaic and overbroad generalizations about gender or based on outdated misconceptions concerning the role of females in the home rather than in the marketplace and world of ideas.

Despite the heightened scrutiny afforded distinctions based on gender, respondent argues that gender discrimination in the selection of the petit jury should be permitted, though discrimination on the basis of race is not. Respondent suggests that "gender discrimination in this country ... has never reached the level of discrimination" against African-Americans, and therefore gender discrimination, unlike racial discrimination, is tolerable in the courtroom. While the prejudicial attitudes toward women in this country have not been identical to those held toward racial minorities, the similarities between the experiences of racial minorities and women, in some contexts, overpower those differences.

* * *

Certainly, with respect to jury service, African-Americans and women share a history of total exclusion, a history which came to an end for women many years after the embarrassing chapter in our history came to an end for African-Americans.

We need not determine, however, whether women or racial minorities have suffered more at the hands of discriminatory state actors during the decades of our Nation's history. It is necessary only to acknowledge that our Nation has had a long and unfortunate history of sex discrimination, which warrants the heightened scrutiny we afford all gender-based classifications today. Under our equal protection jurisprudence, gender-based classifications require an exceedingly persuasive justification in order to survive constitutional scrutiny. Thus, the only question is whether discrimination on the basis of gender in jury selection substantially furthers the State's legitimate interest in achieving a fair and impartial trial. In making this assessment, we do not weigh the value of peremptory challenges as an institution against our asserted commitment to eradicate invidious discrimination from the courtroom. Instead, we consider whether peremptory challenges based on gender stereotypes provide substantial aid to a litigant's effort to secure a fair and impartial jury.

Far from proffering an exceptionally persuasive justification for its gender-based peremptory challenges, respondent maintains that its decision to strike virtually all the males from the jury in this case "may reasonably have been based upon the perception, supported by history, that men otherwise totally qualified to serve upon a jury in any case might be more sympathetic and receptive to the arguments of a man alleged in a paternity action to be the father of an out-of-wedlock child, while women equally qualified to serve upon a jury might be more sympathetic and receptive to the arguments of the complaining witness who bore the child."

We shall not accept as a defense to gender-based peremptory challenges "the very stereotype the law condemns." *Powers v. Ohio*, 499 U.S., at 410. Respondent's rationale, not unlike those regularly expressed for gender-based strikes, is reminiscent of the arguments advanced to justify the total exclusion of women from juries. Respondent offers virtually no support for the conclusion that gender alone is an accurate predictor of juror's attitudes; yet it urges this Court to condone the same stereotypes that justified the wholesale exclusion of women from juries and the ballot box. Respondent seems to assume that gross generalizations that would be deemed impermissible if made on the basis of race are somehow permissible when made on the basis of gender.

Discrimination in jury selection, whether based on race or on gender, causes harm to the litigants, the community, and the individual jurors who are wrongfully excluded from participation in the judicial process. The litigants are harmed by the risk that the prejudice that motivated the discriminatory selection of the jury will infect the entire proceedings. The community is harmed by the State's participation in the perpetuation of invidious group stereotypes and the inevitable loss of confidence in our judicial system that state-sanctioned discrimination in the courtroom engenders.

When state actors exercise peremptory challenges in reliance on gender stereotypes, they ratify and reinforce prejudicial views of the relative abilities of men and women. Because these stereotypes have wreaked injustice in so many other spheres of our country's public life, active discrimination by litigants on the basis of gender during jury selection "invites cynicism respecting the jury's neutrality and its obligation to adhere to the law." *Powers v. Ohio*, 499 U.S., at 412. The potential for cynicism is particularly acute in cases where gender-related issues are prominent, such as cases involving rape, sexual harassment, or paternity. Discriminatory use of peremptory challenges may create the impression that the judicial system has acquiesced in suppressing full participation by one gender or that the "deck has been stacked" in favor of one side.

In recent cases we have emphasized that individual jurors themselves have a right to nondiscriminatory jury selection procedures. Contrary to respondent's suggestion, this right extends to both men and women. Brief for Respondent 9 (arguing that men deserve no protection from gender discrimination in jury selection because they are not victims of historical discrimination). All persons, when granted the opportunity to serve on a jury, have the right not to be excluded summarily because of discriminatory and stereotypical presumptions that reflect and reinforce patterns of historical discrimination.

* * *

IV

Our conclusion that litigants may not strike potential jurors solely on the basis of gender does not imply the elimination of all peremptory challenges. Neither does it conflict with a State's legitimate interest in using such challenges in its effort to secure a fair and impartial jury. Parties still may remove jurors who they feel might be less acceptable than others on the panel; gender simply may not serve as a proxy for bias. Parties may also exercise their peremptory challenges to remove from the venire any group or class of individuals normally subject to "rational basis" review. Even strikes based on characteristics that are disproportionately associated with one gender could be appropriate, absent a showing of pretext.

If conducted properly, *voir dire* can inform litigants about potential jurors, making reliance upon stereotypical and pejorative notions about a particular gender or race both unnecessary and unwise. *Voir dire* provides a means of discovering actual or implied bias and a firmer basis upon which the parties may exercise their peremptory challenges intelligently.

The experience in the many jurisdictions that have barred gender-based challenges belies the claim that litigants and trial courts are incapable of complying with a rule barring strikes based on gender. As with race-based *Batson* claims, a party alleging gender discrimination must make a prima facie showing of intentional discrimination before the party exercising the challenge is required to explain the basis for the strike. When an explanation is required, it need not rise to the level of a "for cause" challenge; rather, it merely must be based on a juror characteristic other than gender, and the proffered explanation may not be pretextual.

* * *

V

Equal opportunity to participate in the fair administration of justice is fundamental to our democratic system. It not only furthers the goals of the jury system. It reaffirms the promise of equality under the law—

that all citizens, regardless of race, ethnicity, or gender, have the chance to take part directly in our democracy. Indeed, with the exception of voting, for most citizens the honor and privilege of jury duty is their most significant opportunity to participate in the democratic process. When persons are excluded from participation in our democratic processes solely because of race or gender, this promise of equality dims, and the integrity of our judicial system is jeopardized.

* * *

The judgment of the Court of Civil Appeals of Alabama is reversed, and the case is remanded to that court for further proceedings not inconsistent with this opinion.

Justice O'Connor, concurring.

I agree with the Court that the Equal Protection Clause prohibits the government from excluding a person from jury service on account of that person's gender. The State's proffered justifications for its gender-based peremptory challenges are far from the "exceedingly persuasive" showing required to sustain a gender-based classification.... I therefore join the Court's opinion in this case. But today's important blow against gender discrimination is not costless. I write separately to discuss some of these costs....

Batson v. Kentucky itself was a significant intrusion into the jury selection process. *Batson* mini hearings are now routine in state and federal trial courts, and *Batson* appeals have proliferated as well. Demographics indicate that today's holding may have an even greater impact than did *Batson* itself. In further constitutionalizing jury selection procedures, the Court increases the number of cases in which jury selection — once a sideshow — will become part of the main event.

For this same reason, today's decision further erodes the role of the peremptory challenge. The peremptory challenge is a practice of ancient origin and is part of our common law heritage. The principal value of the peremptory is that it helps produce fair and impartial juries. Peremptory challenges, by enabling each side to exclude those jurors it believes will be most partial toward the other side, are a means of eliminat[ing] extremes of partiality on both sides, thereby assuring the selection of a qualified and unbiased jury....

Moreover, the essential nature of the peremptory challenge is that it is one exercised without a reason stated, without inquiry and without being subject to the court's control. Indeed, often a reason for it cannot be stated, for a trial lawyer's judgments about a juror's sympathies are sometimes based on experienced hunches and educated guesses, derived from a juror's responses at voir dire or a juror's bare looks and gestures. That a trial lawyer's instinctive assessment of a juror's predisposition cannot meet the high standards of a challenge for cause does not mean that the lawyer's instinct is erroneous. Our belief that experienced lawyers will often correctly intuit which jurors are likely to be the least sympathetic, and our understanding that the lawyer will often be unable to explain the intuition, are the very reason we cherish the peremptory challenge. But, as we add, layer by layer, additional constitutional restraints on the use of the peremptory, we force lawyers to articulate what we know is often inarticulable.

In so doing we make the peremptory challenge less discretionary and more like a challenge for cause. We also increase the possibility that biased jurors will be allowed onto the jury, because sometimes a lawyer will be unable to provide an acceptable gender-neutral explanation even though the lawyer is in fact correct that the juror is unsympathetic. Similarly, in jurisdictions where lawyers exercise their strikes in open court, lawyers may be deterred from using their peremptories, out of the fear that if they are unable to justify the strike the court will seat a juror who knows that the striking party thought him unfit. Because I believe the peremptory remains an important litigator's tool and a fundamental part of the process of selecting impartial juries, our increasing limitation of it gives me pause.

Nor is the value of the peremptory challenge to the litigant diminished when the peremptory is exercised in a gender-based manner. We know that like race, gender matters. A plethora of studies make clear that in rape cases, for example, female jurors are somewhat more likely to vote to convict than male jurors. Moreover, though there have been no similarly definitive studies regarding, for example, sexual harassment, child custody, or spousal or child abuse, one need not be a sexist to share the intuition that in certain cases a person's gender and resulting life experience will be relevant to his or her view of the case. "Jurors are not expected to come into the jury box and leave behind all that their human experience has taught them." *Beck v. Alabama*, 447 U.S. 625, 642 (1980). Individuals are not expected to ignore as jurors what they know as men — or women.

Today's decision severely limits a litigant's ability to act on this intuition, for the import of our holding is that any correlation between a juror's gender and attitudes is irrelevant as a matter of constitutional law. But to say that gender makes no difference as a matter of law is not to say that gender makes no difference as a matter of fact. I previously have said with regard to *Batson:* "That the Court will not tolerate prosecutors' racially discriminatory use of the peremptory challenge, in effect, is a special rule of relevance, a statement about what this Nation stands for, rather than a statement of fact." *Brown v. North Carolina*, 479 U.S. 940, 941–942, (1986) (opinion concurring in denial of certiorari). Today's decision is a statement that, in an effort to eliminate the potential discriminatory use of the peremptory, gender is now governed by the special rule of relevance formerly reserved for race. Though we gain much from this statement, we cannot ignore what we lose. In extending *Batson* to gender we have added an additional burden to the state and federal trial process, taken a step closer to eliminating the peremptory challenge, and diminished the ability of litigants to act on sometimes accurate gender-based assumptions about juror attitudes.

* * *

Justice Scalia, with whom the Chief Justice and Justice Thomas join, dissenting.

Today's opinion is an inspiring demonstration of how thoroughly up-to-date and right-thinking we Justices are in matters pertaining to the sexes (or as the Court would have it, the genders), and how sternly we disapprove the male chauvinist attitudes of our predecessors. The price to be paid for this display—a modest price, surely—is that most of the opinion is quite irrelevant to the case at hand. The hasty reader will be surprised to learn, for example, that this lawsuit involves a complaint about the use of peremptory challenges to exclude *men* from a petit jury. To be sure, petitioner, a man, used all but one of *his* peremptory strikes to remove *women* from the jury (he used his last challenge to strike the sole remaining male from the pool), but the validity of *his* strikes is not before us. Nonetheless, the Court treats itself to an extended discussion of the historic exclusion of women not only from jury service, but also from service at the bar (which is rather like jury service, in that it involves going to the courthouse a lot). All this, as I say, is irrelevant, since the case involves state action that allegedly discriminates against men....

The Court also spends time establishing that the use of sex as a proxy for particular views or sympathies is unwise and perhaps irrational. The opinion stresses the lack of statistical evidence to support the widely held belief that, at least in certain types of cases, a juror's sex has some statistically significant predictive value as to how the juror will behave. This assertion seems to place the Court in opposition to its earlier Sixth Amendment "fair cross-section" cases. See, *e.g., Taylor v. Louisiana,* 419 U.S. 522, 532, n. 12 (1975) ("Controlled studies ... have concluded that women bring to juries their own perspectives and values that influence both jury deliberation and result"). But times and trends do change, and unisex is unquestionably in fashion. Personally, I am less inclined to demand statistics, and more inclined to credit the perceptions of experienced litigators who have had money on the line....

Of course the relationship of sex to partiality *would have been* relevant if the Court had demanded in this case what it ordinarily demands: that the complaining party have suffered some injury. Leaving aside for the moment the reality that the defendant himself had the opportunity to strike women from the jury, the defendant would have some cause to complain about the prosecutor's striking male jurors if male jurors tend to be more favorable toward defendants in paternity suits. But if men and women jurors are (as the Court thinks) fungible, then the only arguable injury from the prosecutor's "impermissible" use of male sex as the basis for his peremptories is injury to the stricken juror, not to the defendant. Indeed, far from having suffered harm, petitioner, a state actor under our precedents, has himself actually *inflicted* harm on female jurors.... [T]he scientific evidence presented at trial established petitioner's paternity with 99.92% accuracy. Insofar as petitioner is concerned, this is a case of harmless error if there ever was one....

* * *

Although the Court's legal reasoning in this case is largely obscured by anti-male-chauvinist oratory, to the extent such reasoning is discernible it invalidates much more than sex-based strikes. After identifying unequal treatment (by separating individual exercises of peremptory challenge from the process as a whole), the Court applies the "heightened scrutiny" mode of equal protection analysis used for sex-based discrimination, and concludes that the strikes fail heightened scrutiny because they do not substantially further an important government interest. The Court says that the only important government interest that could be served by peremptory strikes is "securing a fair and impartial jury." It refuses to accept respondent's argument that these strikes further that interest by eliminating a group (men) which may be partial to male defendants, because it will not accept any argument based on "the very stereotype the law condemns." This analysis, entirely eliminating the only allowable argument, implies that sex-based strikes do not even rationally further a legitimate government interest, let alone pass heightened scrutiny. That places *all* peremptory strikes based on *any* group characteristic at risk, since they can all be denominated "stereotypes."

Even if the line of our later cases guaranteed by today's decision limits the theoretically boundless *Batson* principle to race, sex, and perhaps other classifications subject to heightened scrutiny (which presumably would include religious belief) much damage has been done. It has been done, first and foremost, to the peremptory challenge system, which loses its whole character when (in order to defend against "impermissible stereotyping" claims) "reasons" for strikes must be given. The right of peremptory challenge is, as Blackstone says, an arbitrary and capricious right; and it must be exercised with full freedom, or it fails of its full purpose. The loss of the real peremptory will be felt most keenly by the criminal defendant, whom we have until recently thought "should not be held to accept a juror, apparently indifferent, whom he distrusted for any reason or for no reason."

And damage has been done, secondarily, to the entire justice system, which will bear the burden of the expanded quest for "reasoned peremptories" that the Court demands. The extension of *Batson* to sex, and almost certainly beyond, will provide the basis for extensive collateral litigation, which especially the criminal defendant (who litigates full time and cost free) can be expected to pursue. While demographic reality places some limit on the number of cases in which race-based challenges will be an issue, every case contains a potential sex-based claim. Another consequence is a lengthening of the *voir dire* process that already burdens trial courts.

In order, it seems to me, not to eliminate any real denial of equal protection, but simply to pay conspicuous obeisance to the equality of the sexes, the Court imperils a practice that has been considered an essential part of fair jury trial since the dawn of the common law. The Constitution of the United States neither requires nor permits this vandalizing of our people's traditions.

For these reasons, I dissent.

Note on *Baston* Challenges

In *Foster v Chatman*, 136 S.Ct. 1737 (2016), the Court applied *Batson* in a *habeas* petition in a capital murder case. Foster was convicted of capital murder and sentenced to death in a Georgia court. During jury selection, the State used peremptory challenges to strike all four black prospective jurors. Foster argued at trial and at a post-conviction state *habeas* proceeding that the State's peremptory challenges were racially motivated, in violation of *Batson v. Kentucky*. The trial court rejected Foster's argument and the Georgia Supreme Court affirmed.

The U.S. Supreme Court reiterated the three step *Batson* process: (1) the defendant must make a prima facie showing that a peremptory challenge has been exercised on the basis of race; (2) if that showing has been made, the prosecution must offer a race-neutral basis for striking the juror; and (3) the trial court must determine whether the defendant has shown purposeful discrimination. The parties agreed that the first two steps were met. After closely examining the extensive racially-neutral justifications the State articulated for striking two of the jurors, the Court held that the evidence showed the State was motivated in substantial part by race when exercising its peremptory challenges.

5. Jury Instructions

The purpose of jury instructions is to allow the trial judge to inform the jury of the law it must apply during its deliberations. The content of the jury instructions is determined primarily by the rules of evidence and the applicable substantive law. The procedure for jury instructions in federal court is governed by Rule 51.

The content of jury instructions is generally beyond the scope of a Civil Procedure course. However, the following example illustrates the typical scope and content of jury instructions. This example comes from a case in federal court in which a Native American nurse alleges that she was fired due to race discrimination and in retaliation for her complaints about sexual harassment. The box below contains some of the instructions the court gave the jury.

Jury Instruction Example

Members of the Jury: Now that you have heard all of the evidence and the arguments of the attorneys, it is my duty to instruct you as to the law of the case.

Each of you has received a copy of these instructions that you may take with you to the jury room to consult during your deliberations.

It is your duty to find the facts from all the evidence in the case. To those facts you will apply the law as I give it to you. You must follow the law as I give it to you whether you agree with it or not.

When a party has the burden of proof on any claim or affirmative defense by a preponderance of the evidence, it means you must be persuaded by the evidence that the claim or affirmative defense is more probably true than not true. You should base your decision on all of the evidence, regardless of which party presented it.

The evidence you are to consider in deciding what the facts are consists of:

1. the sworn testimony of any witness;

2. the exhibits which are received into evidence; and

3. any facts to which all the lawyers have agreed.

Evidence may be direct or circumstantial. Direct evidence is direct proof of a fact, such as testimony by a witness about what that witness personally saw or heard or did. Circumstantial evidence is proof of one or more facts from which you could find another fact. You should consider both kinds of evidence. The law makes no distinction between the weight to be given to either direct or circumstantial evidence. It is for you to decide how much weight to give to any evidence.

In deciding the facts in this case, you may have to decide which testimony to believe and which testimony not to believe. You may believe everything a witness says, or part of it, or none of it. Proof of a fact does not necessarily depend on the number of witnesses who testify about it.

In considering the testimony of any witness, you may take into account:

1. the opportunity and ability of the witness to see or hear or know the things testified to;

2. the witness's memory;

3. the witness's manner while testifying;

4. the witness's interest in the outcome of the case and any bias or prejudice;

5. whether other evidence contradicted the witness's testimony;

6. the reasonableness of the witness's testimony in light of all the evidence; and

7. any other factors that bear on believability.

The weight of the evidence as to a fact does not necessarily depend on the number of witnesses who testify about it.

Plaintiff has brought a claim of employment discrimination against Defendant. Plaintiff claims that her race was a motivating factor for the Defendant's decision to discharge Plaintiff. Defendant denies that Plaintiff's race was a motivating factor for the Defendant's decision to discharge Plaintiff and further claims the decision to discharge Plaintiff was based upon a lawful reason.

As to Plaintiff's claim that her race was a motivating factor for the Defendant's decision to discharge her, Plaintiff has the burden of proving both of the following elements by a preponderance of the evidence:

1. Plaintiff was discharged by Defendant; and

2. Plaintiff's race was a motivating factor in the Defendant's decision to discharge Plaintiff.

If you find that Plaintiff has failed to prove either of these elements, your verdict should be for Defendant. If Plaintiff has proved both of these elements, Plaintiff is entitled to your verdict, even if you find that the Defendant's conduct was also motivated by a lawful reason. If, however, Defendant proves by a preponderance of the evidence that Defendant would have made the same decision even if Plaintiff's race had played no role in the employment decision, your verdict should be for Defendant.

It is the duty of the Court to instruct you about the measure of damages. By instructing you on damages, the Court does not mean to suggest for which party your verdict should be rendered. If you find for Plaintiff on her claim of race discrimination, then you must determine Plaintiff's damages. Plaintiff has the burden of proving damages by a preponderance of the evidence. Damages means the amount of money that will reasonably and fairly compensate Plaintiff for any injury you find was caused by Defendant. You should consider: the nature and extent of the emotional pain, suffering, inconvenience, mental anguish and loss of enjoyment of life experienced.

If you find for Plaintiff, you may, but are not required to, award punitive damages. The purposes of punitive damages are to punish Defendant and to deter similar acts in the future. Punitive damages may not be awarded to compensate Plaintiff.

Plaintiff has the burden of proving by the preponderance of the evidence that punitive damages should be awarded, and, if so, the amount of any such damages.

You may award punitive damages only if you find that Defendant engaged in a discriminatory practice or discriminatory practices with malice or with reckless indifference to the federally protected rights of Plaintiff. Conduct is malicious if it is accompanied by ill will, or spite, or if it is for the purpose of injuring Plaintiff. Conduct is in reckless disregard of Plaintiff's rights if, under the circumstances, it reflects complete indifference to Plaintiff's safety or rights, or if Defendant acts in the face of a perceived risk that its actions will violate Plaintiff's rights under federal law.

If you find that punitive damages are appropriate, you must use reason in setting the amount. Punitive damages, if any, should be in an amount sufficient to fulfill their purposes but should not reflect bias, prejudice or sympathy toward any party. In considering the amount of any punitive damages, consider the degree of reprehensibility of Defendant's conduct. You may not, however, set the amount of any punitive damages in order to punish Defendant for harm to anyone other than Plaintiff in this case. In addition, you may consider the relationship of any award of punitive damages to any actual harm inflicted on Plaintiff.

You will then discuss the case with your fellow jurors to reach agreement if you can do so. Your verdict must be unanimous.

A verdict form has been prepared for you. After you have reached unanimous agreement on a verdict, your presiding juror will fill in the form that has been given to you, sign and date it, and advise the Court that you are ready to return to the courtroom.

Read Rule 51, which governs the jury instruction process in federal court. The purpose of the rule is to provide a clear, fair process for the parties and the court.

Subsection (a) gives parties the right to request jury instructions, allowing the parties the opportunity to participate in the process of generating instructions. Subsection (b) requires the judge to inform the parties of the jury instructions that the judge intends to give to the jury and to give the parties an opportunity to object on the record to the proposed instructions. Subsection (c) details how and when parties can object to an instruction or the judge's failure to give the party's proposed instruction. Subsection (d) deals with appeals of jury instructions, providing that generally the party must make a timely objection to the instruction under Rule 51(c) in order to appeal based on an erroneous instruction. Subsection (d)(2) contains an exception to the objection requirement, allowing appeals of jury instructions containing "plain error."

In *Taita Chemical Co, Ltd v. Westlake Styrene, LP*, 351 F.3d 663, 667–68 (5th Cir. 2003), the court summarized the substantive and procedural standards for a successful appeal based on erroneous jury instructions.

> There are three requirements to successfully challenge jury instructions. First, the appellant must show that viewing the charge as a whole, the charge creates substantial and ineradicable doubt whether the jury has been properly guided in its deliberations. Second, even if erroneous, the appellate court will not reverse if the error could not have affected the outcome of the case. Third, the appellant must show that the proposed instruction offered to the district court correctly stated the law. Perfection is not required as long as the instructions were generally correct and any error was harmless. This standard provides the district court with great latitude concerning the charge.

> A litigant also must have preserved the error in the charge to complain on appeal. Rule 51 of the Federal Rules of Civil Procedure outlines the requirements that one must satisfy in order to assign error for failing to give, or erroneously giving, jury instructions. One may not complain of a jury instruction unless that party objects thereto, stating distinctly the matter objected to and the grounds of the objection. General objections to jury instructions are insufficient to meet Rule 51's requirements. Furthermore, submission of an alternative instruction does not necessarily preserve error for appeal. The proposed instruction must make one's position sufficiently clear to the court to satisfy Rule 51's objection requirement.

> A party may be excused from Rule 51's strict requirements if the party's position has previously been clearly made to the court and it is plain that a further objection would be unavailing. To find reversible error in this instance, the appellate court must be certain that the district court was adequately informed of the objection. Examples of this exception involve clear cases where the exception is justified: a litigant who fails to object when invited to do so but who had previously filed sufficient objections; a litigant

who fails to object after the court intimated that no more objections would be heard; and a previous emphatic ruling by a judge made later objections futile.

If error is not preserved, we review for plain error. To meet this standard, a party must show: (1) that an error occurred; (2) that the error was plain, which means clear or obvious; (3) the plain error must affect substantial rights; and (4) not correcting the error would seriously affect the fairness, integrity, or public reputation of judicial proceedings. The plain error exception is designed to prevent a miscarriage of justice where the error is clear under current law. (Footnotes omitted.)

Exercise 11-8. Jury Instruction Policy

The last sentence from *Taita Chemical* above, articulates the policy behind the plain error exception in Rule 51(d)(2). Articulate policies that support each of the following provisions of Rule 51:

51(a)(1) requirement that parties can propose jury instructions to the court;

51(b) requirement that the court inform the parties of its proposed instructions and proposed action on their requests for instructions before the parties give their final arguments to the jury;

51(c)(1) requirement that parties object to a proposed instruction or failure to give an instruction on the record stating the specific grounds for the objection; and

51(d)(1) requirement that a party make a timely objection to jury instructions to the trial court in order to appeal an erroneous instruction.

---

6. Jury Verdicts

In most civil cases, after closing arguments and jury instructions, the court asks the jury to deliberate and render a general verdict. The typical general verdict is quite simple, asking the jury to find for the plaintiff or defendant and, if it finds for the plaintiff, to award appropriate damages.

Rule 49 gives the court discretion to choose from two alternatives to the general verdict. Read Rule 49. Rule 49(a) authorizes a special verdict, in which the court submits individual fact questions to the jury. Based on the jury's answers to the questions, the judge determines which party prevails. Below is an example of a special verdict from the race discrimination case described in the Jury Instruction section above. Rule 49(b) allows the court to ask the jury for a general verdict along with responses to fact questions.

Special Verdict Example

1. RACE DISCRIMINATION

A. Has Plaintiff proved by a preponderance of the evidence that her race was a motivating factor for Defendant's decision to discharge her?

Yes   No

If the answer to Question A is "No," do not answer any further questions. If the answer to Question A is "Yes," proceed to Question B.

B. Has Defendant proved by a preponderance of the evidence that its decision to discharge Plaintiff was also motivated by a lawful reason?

Yes   No

If the answer to Question B is "No," proceed to Question 2. If the answer to Question B is "Yes," proceed to Question C.

C. Has Defendant proved by a preponderance of the evidence that it would have made the same decision to discharge Plaintiff even if her race had played no role in its decision to discharge her?

Yes   No

If the answer to Question C is "Yes," do not answer any further questions. If your answer to Question C is "No," proceed to Question 2.

2. DAMAGES

A. If instructed to answer this question by Question 1, what amount of compensatory damages, if any, do you award Plaintiff?

$

B. Has Plaintiff proved by a preponderance of the evidence that Defendant is liable for punitive damages?

Yes   No

If the answer to Question B is "Yes," proceed to Question C. If the answer to Question B is "No," please sign and date below. Do not answer any further questions.

C. What amount of punitive damages, if any, do you award Plaintiff?

$

You have now completed your deliberations. The foreperson should sign and date the verdict form on the lines below and then inform the bailiff that you have completed your deliberations and reached a verdict.

The simplicity of general verdict forms provides great flexibility to the jury to reach consensus on what it deems a just result, with the guidance the court provides in jury instructions. Alternatives to the general verdict aim to focus the jury's deliberations on critical factual issues in the case. On the other hand, the complexity of special verdicts and general verdicts with interrogatories can cause problems. For example, special verdicts may neglect to ask questions on every essential element in the case, and both alternative verdict forms can result in the jury making findings that are inconsistent. Rule 49 provides means for the court to deal with omissions and inconsistencies.

7. Findings of Fact and Conclusions of Law

In cases tried to the court without a jury or with an advisory jury, the judge is responsible for finding the facts, applying the law, and deciding the case. In these cases, Rule 52(a) requires the judge to make findings of fact and conclusions of law and to state them on the record or to include them in a written opinion. Read Rule 52.

Courts have articulated several important purposes underlying Rule 52. First, the requirement of findings of fact and conclusions of law is intended to promote careful decision making by the trial court. Second, the findings and conclusions make clear to the parties and public the factual and legal bases for the judge's decision, which can further public confidence in the civil litigation system. Third, the findings and conclusions allow appellate courts to more fully understand the trial court's reasoning, which helps the appellate court decide appeals. Fourth, findings and conclusions allow courts in subsequent litigation to understand precisely what the trial court decided when courts apply claim and issue preclusion doctrines in future cases. *See* Wright & Miller, 9C Fed. Prac. & Proc.§ 35.15 (5th. ed). Former adjudication doctrines are the subject of Chapter 13.

Below is an example of findings of fact and conclusions of law in a simple automobile collision case, based on 4 West's Fed. Forms, District Courts-Civil § 4315 (3d ed.).

Findings of Fact

1. Plaintiff, Raj Deepah, a passenger in an automobile owned and operated by defendant Hemu Achar, was injured as the result of a collision between the car and a mail truck owned by the Defendant U.S. Government, and operated by Shana Jones, one of its employees.

2. The collision occurred between noon and 12:30 p.m. on May 12, 2019 at the intersection of D Street and Oregon Avenue in Washington, D.C.

3. There were stop signs on D Street at the intersection.

4. Immediately before the collision, Achar was proceeding in a southerly direction along D Street and Jones was proceeding in an easterly direction along Oregon Avenue.

5. When Jones first observed Achar's automobile it was 100 feet north of the intersection, moving at the rate of about 40 miles per hour, at which time the mail truck was about 50 feet south of the intersection and moving at about 25 miles per hour.

6. Approaching the intersection, Achar continued to operate Achar's automobile at an excessive rate of speed and failed to heed the "stop" sign facing Achar's vehicle.

7. Immediately before the collision, Jones, to reduce the force of the impact, turned the government vehicle to the right.

8. Achar operated the automobile in a careless and reckless manner and the collision between the Achar's automobile and the Government truck was caused solely through Achar's negligence, James being free from negligence, and Deepah being free from contributory negligence.

9. As a result of the accident, Plaintiff was confined to the hospital for four days and suffered the following injuries, some of which are crippling or serious: compound fracture of the right arm, lacerations to the face.

10. Some of the injuries and scars Plaintiff sustained will be permanent.

11. Plaintiff suffered considerable pain as a result of the accident and will continue to suffer pain as a result.

12. Plaintiff, employed at a salary of $4000 per month, sustained a loss of pay for 60 days as a result of the accident.

13. Plaintiff incurred medical expenses aggregating $102,334.

14. By reason of the collision, Plaintiff has been damaged to the extent of $475,000.

Conclusions of Law

1. Defendant Achar was guilty of negligence, causing the collision between Achar's automobile and the truck operated by Jones, an employee of the Defendant U.S. Government.

2. Defendant U.S. Government, through its employee, was free from negligence.

3. Plaintiff was free from contributory negligence.

4. Plaintiff is entitled to judgment against Defendant Achar in the sum of $475,000, together with the costs and disbursements of this action.

5. Plaintiff's complaint against the Defendant U.S. Government is dismissed.

Rule 52(a) provides a standard of review for appeals of findings of fact. That portion of Rule 52 is discussed in Chapter 12.

8. Motions During and After Trial

After a jury has reached a verdict or after the judge has made findings of fact and conclusions of law in a case tried without a jury, the judge must enter judgment under Rule 58. Here is a basic form for a judgment.

Form for a Judgment in a Case Tried to a Jury

[Caption — see Rule 10(a)]

Judgment for Plaintiff Levon James

This action was tried by a jury with Judge Kim Martin presiding. And the jury has rendered a verdict in favor of Plaintiff Levon James.

It is ordered that: Plaintiff Levon James recover from Defendant Lee Song the amount of $456,000 along with costs.

Dated: February 22, 2020.

James Larsen

_____

James Larsen, Clerk

A party that loses at trial has four basic methods to challenge the jury's verdict or the judgment entered by the trial court. Three of those methods involve motions the party makes to the trial court: (1) judgment as a matter of law, (2) new trial, and (3) relief from judgment. The fourth method, an appeal to an appellate court, is the topic of Chapter 12.

a. Judgment as a Matter of Law

Rule 50 governs motions for judgment as a matter of law in federal court. Read Rule 50(a) and (b). A party may move for judgment as a matter of law ("JMOL") under Rule 50(a), at any time that a party has been fully heard on an issue and before the case is submitted to the jury. For example, the defendant could move for JMOL at the close of the plaintiff's case and either party could move for JMOL at the close of all evidence. Under Rule 50(b), a party may "renew" its previously submitted motion for JMOL after the jury has returned a verdict and the court has entered judgment.

A 1991 amendment to Rule 50 changed its vocabulary. Formerly, a JMOL motion before the case is submitted to a jury was called a motion for a "directed verdict"; a JMOL motion after judgment was called a motion for judgment notwithstanding the verdict ("JNOV"). The Advisory Committee Note makes clear that the change in vocabulary was not intended to change the substantive standards that apply to Rule 50 motions.

Exercise 11-9. *Reeves v. Sanderson Plumbing Products, Inc.*

1. To decide a JMOL motion, the court must apply the proper substantive law. In *Reeves*, the substantive law is the Age Discrimination in Employment Act (ADEA).

   What must the plaintiff prove to establish a prima facie case?

   What can the defendant prove to avoid liability?

   Ultimately, what must the plaintiff prove to prevail?

2. What is the JMOL evidentiary standard in Rule 50(a)?

3. According to the Court, when a trial court decides a JMOL motion:

   What evidence must the court consider?

   How must the court view the evidence?

   What are jury functions and, therefore, not judge functions?

4. Application of JMOL standards to *Reeves*:

   List the evidence that supports the plaintiff.

   List the evidence that supports the defendant.

   Why does the Court affirm the trial court's denial of the defendant's JMOL motion?

Reeves v. Sanderson Plumbing Products, Inc.
530 U.S. 133 (2000)

Justice O'Connor delivered the opinion of the Court.

This case concerns the kind and amount of evidence necessary to sustain a jury's verdict that an employer unlawfully discriminated on the basis of age. Specifically, we must resolve whether a defendant is entitled to judgment as a matter of law when the plaintiff's case consists exclusively of a prima facie case of discrimination and sufficient evidence for the trier of fact to disbelieve the defendant's legitimate, nondiscriminatory explanation for its action. We must also decide whether the employer was entitled to judgment as a matter of law under the particular circumstances presented here.

I

In October 1995, petitioner Roger Reeves was 57 years old and had spent 40 years in the employ of respondent, Sanderson Plumbing Products.

Petitioner worked in a department known as the "Hinge Room," where he supervised the "regular line." Joe Oswalt, in his mid-thirties, supervised the Hinge Room's "special line," and Russell Caldwell, the manager of the Hinge Room and age 45, supervised both petitioner and Oswalt. Petitioner's responsibilities included recording the attendance and hours of those under his supervision, and reviewing a weekly report that listed the hours worked by each employee.

In the summer of 1995, Caldwell informed Powe Chesnut, the director of manufacturing and the husband of company president Sandra Sanderson, that "production was down" in the Hinge Room because employees were often absent and were "coming in late and leaving early." Because the monthly attendance reports did not indicate a problem, Chesnut ordered an audit of the Hinge Room's timesheets for July, August, and September of that year. According to Chesnut's testimony, that investigation revealed "numerous timekeeping errors and misrepresentations on the part of Caldwell, Reeves, and Oswalt." Following the audit, Chesnut, along with Dana Jester, vice president of human resources, and Tom Whitaker, vice president of operations, recommended to company president Sanderson that petitioner and Caldwell be fired. In October 1995, Sanderson followed the recommendation and discharged both petitioner and Caldwell.

In June 1996, petitioner filed suit in the United States District Court for the Northern District of Mississippi, contending that he had been fired because of his age in violation of the Age Discrimination in Employment Act of 1967 (ADEA). At trial, respondent contended that it had fired petitioner due to his failure to maintain accurate attendance records, while petitioner attempted to demonstrate that respondent's explanation was pretext for age discrimination....

During the trial, the District Court twice denied oral motions by respondent for judgment as a matter of law under Rule 50 of the Federal Rules of Civil Procedure, and the case went to the jury. The court instructed the jury that "[i]f the plaintiff fails to prove age was a determinative or motivating factor in the decision to terminate him, then your verdict shall be for the defendant." So charged, the jury returned a verdict in favor of petitioner, awarding him $35,000 in compensatory damages, and found that respondent's age discrimination had been "willfu[l]." The District Court accordingly entered judgment for petitioner in the amount of $70,000, which included $35,000 in liquidated damages based on the jury's finding of willfulness. Respondent then renewed its motion for judgment as a matter of law and alternatively moved for a new trial. The District Court denied respondent's motions....

The Court of Appeals for the Fifth Circuit reversed, holding that petitioner had not introduced sufficient evidence to sustain the jury's finding of unlawful discrimination. After noting respondent's proffered justification for petitioner's discharge, the court acknowledged that petitioner "very well may" have offered sufficient evidence for "a reasonable jury [to] have found that [respondent's] explanation for its employment decision was pretextual." The court explained, however, that this was "not dispositive" of the ultimate issue—namely, "whether Reeves presented sufficient evidence that his age motivated [respondent's] employment decision." ... [T]he court concluded that petitioner had not introduced sufficient evidence for a rational jury to conclude that he had been discharged because of his age.

We granted certiorari, to resolve a conflict among the Courts of Appeals as to whether a plaintiff's prima facie case of discrimination (as defined in *McDonnell Douglas Corp. v. Green,* 411 U.S. 792, 802 (1973)), combined with sufficient evidence for a reasonable factfinder to reject the employer's nondiscriminatory explanation for its decision, is adequate to sustain a finding of liability for intentional discrimination.

II

Under the ADEA, it is "unlawful for an employer ... to fail or refuse to hire or to discharge any individual or otherwise discriminate against any individual with respect to his compensation, terms, conditions, or privileges of employment, because of such individual's age." 29 U.S.C. § 623(a)(1). When a plaintiff alleges disparate treatment, liability depends on whether the protected trait (under the ADEA, age) actually motivated the employer's decision. That is, the plaintiff's age must have "actually played a role in the employer's decisionmaking process and had a determinative influence on the outcome....

McDonnell Douglas and subsequent decisions have established an allocation of the burden of production and an order for the presentation of proof in discriminatory-treatment cases. First, the plaintiff must establish a prima facie case of discrimination. It is undisputed that petitioner satisfied this burden here: (i) at the time he was fired, he was a member of the class protected by the ADEA ("individuals who are at least 40 years of age," (ii) he was otherwise qualified for the position of Hinge Room supervisor, (iii) he was discharged by respondent, and (iv) respondent successively hired three persons in their thirties to fill petitioner's position. The burden therefore shifted to respondent to produce evidence that the plaintiff was rejected, or someone else was preferred, for a legitimate, nondiscriminatory reason. Respondent met this burden by offering admissible evidence sufficient for the trier of fact to conclude that petitioner was fired because of his failure to maintain accurate attendance records. Accordingly, ... the sole remaining issue was discrimination *vel non.*

Although intermediate evidentiary burdens shift back and forth under this framework, the ultimate burden of persuading the trier of fact that the defendant intentionally discriminated against the plaintiff remains at all times with the plaintiff. And in attempting to satisfy this burden, the plaintiff—once the employer produces sufficient evidence to support a nondiscriminatory explanation for its decision—must be afforded the opportunity to prove by a preponderance of the evidence that the legitimate reasons offered by the defendant were not its true reasons, but were a pretext for discrimination. That is, the plaintiff may attempt to establish that he was the victim of intentional discrimination by showing that the employer's proffered explanation is unworthy of credence. Moreover, although the presumption of discrimination drops out of the picture once the defendant meets its burden of production, the trier of fact may still consider the evidence establishing the plaintiff's prima facie case and inferences properly drawn therefrom on the issue of whether the defendant's explanation is pretextual.

In this case, the evidence supporting respondent's explanation for petitioner's discharge consisted primarily of testimony by Chesnut and Sanderson and documentation of petitioner's alleged "shoddy record keeping." Chesnut testified that a 1993 audit of Hinge Room operations revealed "a very lax assembly line" where employees were not adhering to general work rules. As a result of that audit, petitioner was placed on 90 days' probation for unsatisfactory performance. In 1995, Chesnut ordered another investigation of the Hinge Room, which, according to his testimony, revealed that petitioner was not correctly recording the absences and hours of employees. Respondent introduced summaries of that investigation documenting several attendance violations by 12 employees under petitioner's supervision, and noting that each should have been disciplined in some manner. Chesnut testified that this failure to discipline absent and late employees is "extremely important when you are dealing with a union" because uneven enforcement across departments would keep the company "in grievance and arbitration cases, which are costly, all the time." He and Sanderson also stated that petitioner's errors, by failing to adjust for hours not worked, cost the company overpaid wages. Sanderson testified that she accepted the recommendation to discharge petitioner because he had "intentionally falsif[ied] company pay records."

Petitioner, however, made a substantial showing that respondent's explanation was false. First, petitioner offered evidence that he had properly maintained the attendance records. Most of the timekeeping errors cited by respondent involved employees who were not marked late but who were recorded as having arrived at the plant at 7 a.m. for the 7 a.m. shift. Respondent contended that employees arriving at 7 a.m. could not have been at their workstations by 7 a.m., and therefore must have been late. But both petitioner and Oswalt testified that the company's automated timeclock often failed to scan employees' timecards, so that the timesheets would not record any time of arrival. On these occasions, petitioner and Oswalt would visually check the workstations and record whether the employees were present at the start of the shift. They stated that if an employee arrived promptly but the timesheet contained no time of arrival, they would reconcile the two by marking "7 a.m." as the employee's arrival time, even if the employee actually arrived at the plant earlier. On cross-examination, Chesnut acknowledged that the timeclock sometimes malfunctioned, and that if "people were there at their work station[s]" at the start of the shift, the supervisor "would write in seven o'clock." Petitioner also testified that when employees arrived before or stayed after their shifts, he would assign them additional work so they would not be overpaid.

Petitioner similarly cast doubt on whether he was responsible for any failure to discipline late and absent employees. Petitioner testified that his job only included reviewing the daily and weekly attendance reports, and that disciplinary writeups were based on the monthly reports, which were reviewed by Caldwell. Sanderson admitted that Caldwell, and not petitioner, was responsible for citing employees for violations of the company's attendance policy. Further, Chesnut conceded that there had never been a union grievance or employee complaint arising from petitioner's record-keeping, and that the company had never calculated the amount of overpayments allegedly attributable to petitioner's errors. Petitioner also testified that, on the day he was fired, Chesnut said that his discharge was due to his failure to report as absent one employee, Gina Mae Coley, on two days in September 1995. But petitioner explained that he had spent those days in the hospital, and that Caldwell was therefore responsible for any overpayment of Coley. Finally, petitioner stated that on previous occasions that employees were paid for hours they had not worked, the company had simply adjusted those employees' next paychecks to correct the errors.

Based on this evidence, the Court of Appeals concluded that petitioner "very well may be correct" that "a reasonable jury could have found that [respondent's] explanation for its employment decision was pretextual." Nonetheless, the court held that this showing, standing alone, was insufficient to sustain the jury's finding of liability: "We must, as an essential final step, determine whether Reeves presented sufficient evidence that his age motivated [respondent's] employment decision." And in making this determination, the Court of Appeals ignored the evidence supporting petitioner's prima facie case and challenging respondent's explanation for its decision. The court confined its review of evidence favoring petitioner to that evidence showing that Chesnut had directed derogatory, age-based comments at petitioner, and that Chesnut had singled out petitioner for harsher treatment than younger employees....

In so reasoning, the Court of Appeals misconceived the evidentiary burden borne by plaintiffs who attempt to prove intentional discrimination through indirect evidence. This much is evident from our decision in *St. Mary's Honor Center.* There we held that the factfinder's rejection of the employer's legitimate, nondiscriminatory reason for its action does not *compel* judgment for the plaintiff. The ultimate question is whether the employer intentionally discriminated, and proof that the employer's proffered reason is unpersuasive, or even obviously contrived, does not necessarily establish that the plaintiff's proffered reason is correct. In other words, it is not enough to *dis*believe the employer; the factfinder must *believe* the plaintiff's explanation of intentional discrimination.

In reaching this conclusion, however, we reasoned that it is *permissible* for the trier of fact to infer the ultimate fact of discrimination from the falsity of the employer's explanation. Specifically, we stated:

> The factfinder's disbelief of the reasons put forward by the defendant (particularly if disbelief is accompanied by a suspicion of mendacity) may, together with the elements of the prima facie case, suffice to show intentional discrimination. Thus, rejection of the defendant's proffered reasons will *permit* the trier of fact to infer the ultimate fact of intentional discrimination. *St. Mary's Honor Center v. Hicks*, 509 U.S. 502, 511 (1993).

* * *

This is not to say that such a showing by the plaintiff will *always* be adequate to sustain a jury's finding of liability. Certainly there will be instances where, although the plaintiff has established a prima facie case and set forth sufficient evidence to reject the defendant's explanation, no rational factfinder could conclude that the action was discriminatory. For instance, an employer would be entitled to judgment as a matter of law if the record conclusively revealed some other, nondiscriminatory reason for the employer's decision, or if the plaintiff created only a weak issue of fact as to whether the employer's reason was untrue and there was abundant and uncontroverted independent evidence that no discrimination had occurred....

III

The remaining question is whether, despite the Court of Appeals' misconception of petitioner's evidentiary burden, respondent was nonetheless entitled to judgment as a matter of law. Under Rule 50, a court should render judgment as a matter of law when "a party has been fully heard on an issue and there is no legally sufficient evidentiary basis for a reasonable jury to find for that party on that issue." Fed. Rule Civ. Proc. 50(a). The Courts of Appeals have articulated differing formulations as to what evidence a court is to consider in ruling on a Rule 50 motion. Some decisions have stated that review is limited to that evidence favorable to the nonmoving party, while most have held that review extends to the entire record, drawing all reasonable inferences in favor of the nonmovant....

In the analogous context of summary judgment under Rule 56, we have stated that the court must review the record "taken as a whole." *Matsushita Elec. Industrial Co. v. Zenith Radio Corp.*, 475 U.S. 574, 587 (1986). And the standard for granting summary judgment "mirrors" the standard for judgment as a matter of law, such that "the inquiry under each is the same." *Anderson v. Liberty Lobby, Inc.*, 477 U.S. 242, 250–251 (1986). It therefore follows that, in entertaining a motion for judgment as a matter of law, the court should review all of the evidence in the record.

In doing so, however, the court must draw all reasonable inferences in favor of the nonmoving party, and it may not make credibility determinations or weigh the evidence. "Credibility determinations, the weighing of the evidence, and the drawing of legitimate inferences from the facts are jury functions, not those of a judge." *Liberty Lobby, supra,* at 255. Thus, although the court should review the record as a whole, it must disregard all evidence favorable to the moving party that the jury is not required to believe. That is, the court should give credence to the evidence favoring the nonmovant as well as that evidence supporting the moving party that is uncontradicted and unimpeached, at least to the extent that that evidence comes from disinterested witnesses.

Applying this standard here, it is apparent that respondent was not entitled to judgment as a matter of law. In this case, in addition to establishing a prima facie case of discrimination and creating a jury issue as to the falsity of the employer's explanation, petitioner introduced additional evidence that Chesnut was motivated by age-based animus and was principally responsible for petitioner's firing. Petitioner testified that Chesnut had told him that he "was so old [he] must have come over on the Mayflower" and, on one occasion when petitioner was having difficulty starting a machine, that he "was too damn old to do [his] job." According to petitioner, Chesnut would regularly "cuss at me and shake his finger in my face." Oswalt, roughly 24 years younger than petitioner, corroborated that there was an "obvious difference" in how Chesnut treated them. Oswalt explained that Chesnut "tolerated quite a bit" from him even though he "defied" Chesnut "quite often," but that Chesnut treated petitioner "[i]n a manner, as you would … treat … a child when … you're angry with [him]." Petitioner also demonstrated that, according to company records, he and Oswalt had nearly identical rates of productivity in 1993. Yet respondent conducted an efficiency study of only the regular line, supervised by petitioner, and placed only petitioner on probation. Chesnut conducted that efficiency study and, after having testified to the contrary on direct examination, acknowledged on cross-examination that he had recommended that petitioner be placed on probation following the study.

Further, petitioner introduced evidence that Chesnut was the actual decisionmaker behind his firing. Chesnut was married to Sanderson, who made the formal decision to discharge petitioner. Although Sanderson testified that she fired petitioner because he had "intentionally falsif[ied] company pay records," respondent only introduced evidence concerning the inaccuracy of the records, not their falsification. Moreover, Oswalt testified that all of respondent's employees feared Chesnut, and that Chesnut had exercised "absolute power" within the company for "[a]s long as [he] can remember."

In holding that the record contained insufficient evidence to sustain the jury's verdict, the Court of Appeals misapplied the standard of review dictated by Rule 50. Again, the court disregarded critical evidence favorable to petitioner—namely, the evidence supporting petitioner's prima facie case and undermining respondent's nondiscriminatory explanation. The court also failed to draw all reasonable inferences in favor of petitioner. For instance, while acknowledging "the potentially damning nature" of Chesnut's age-related comments, the court discounted them on the ground that they "were not made in the direct context of Reeves's termination." And the court discredited petitioner's evidence that Chesnut was the actual decisionmaker by giving weight to the fact that there was "no evidence to suggest that any of the other decision makers were motivated by age." Moreover, the other evidence on which the court relied—that Caldwell and Oswalt were also cited for poor recordkeeping, and that respondent employed many managers over age 50—although relevant, is certainly not dispositive. In concluding that these circumstances so overwhelmed the evidence favoring petitioner that no rational trier of fact could have found that petitioner was fired because of his age, the Court of Appeals impermissibly substituted its judgment concerning the weight of the evidence for the jury's....

Given that petitioner established a prima facie case of discrimination, introduced enough evidence for the jury to reject respondent's explanation, and produced additional evidence of age-based animus, there was sufficient evidence for the jury to find that respondent had intentionally discriminated. The District Court was therefore correct to submit the case to the jury, and the Court of Appeals erred in overturning its verdict.

For these reasons, the judgment of the Court of Appeals is reversed.

JMOL Notes and Questions

1. Does JMOL violate the Seventh Amendment?

The Seventh Amendment provides that "no fact tried by a jury, shall be otherwise re-examined in any Court of the United States, than according to the rules of the common law." In *Galloway v. United States*, 319 U.S. 372, 389–92 (1943), the Court upheld the constitutionality of the directed verdict process. The Court stated:

If the intention is to claim generally that the Amendment deprives the federal courts of power to direct a verdict for insufficiency of evidence, the short answer is the contention has been foreclosed by repeated decisions made here consistently for nearly a century.

Furthermore, the argument from history is not convincing. It is not that "the rules of the common law" in 1791 deprived trial courts of power to withdraw cases from the jury, because not made out, or appellate courts of power to review such determinations. The jury was not absolute master of fact in 1791. Then as now courts excluded evidence for irrelevancy and relevant proof for other reasons.... [I]n 1791, a litigant could challenge his opponent's evidence, either by the demurrer, which when determined ended the litigation, or by motion for a new trial which if successful, gave the adversary another chance to prove his case....

The Amendment did not bind the federal courts to the exact procedural incidents or details of jury trial according to the common law in 1791, any more than it tied them to the common-law system of pleading or the specific rules of evidence then prevailing....

[T]he Amendment was designed to preserve the basic institution of jury trial in only its most fundamental elements, not the great mass of procedural forms and details, varying even then so widely among common-law jurisdictions.

2. Identify the two requirements that a party must satisfy in order to bring a JMOL motion to the trial court after the judge enters judgment on the jury's verdict.

3. JMOL Standards.

In some states, the JMOL standard is that the trial court should deny the motion unless there is no evidence in support of the non-moving party. It is sometimes called the "scintilla" test—JMOL is inappropriate if there is a scintilla of evidence supporting the non-moving party. Federal courts do not apply the scintilla test, but instead apply the test from Rule 50—whether a reasonable jury would have sufficient evidence to find for the non-moving party.

The JMOL standard is the same at trial and on appeal in federal court. That is, when deciding a JMOL motion, the trial court applies the reasonable jury standard, as defined by the Court in *Reeves*. When an appellate court decides whether a trial court properly granted or denied a JMOL motion, the appellate court also applies the reasonable jury standard.

4. Why might a trial court deny a JMOL motion made at the close of evidence before the case goes to the jury but grant the JMOL motion after the jury returns its verdict?

In *Unitherm Food Sys. Inc. v. Swift-Eckrich, Inc.*, 546 U.S. 394, 405–06 (2006), Justice Thomas answered this question:

The Rule provides that "the court *may* determine" that "there is no legally sufficient evidentiary basis for a reasonable jury to find for [a] party on [a given] issue," and "*may* grant a motion for judgment as a matter of law against that party...." (Emphasis added.) Thus, while a district court is permitted to enter judgment as a matter of law when it concludes that the evidence is legally insufficient, it is not required to do so. To the contrary, the district courts are, if anything, encouraged to submit the case to the jury, rather than granting such motions. As Wright and Miller explain:

Even at the close of all the evidence it may be desirable to refrain from granting a motion for judgment as a matter of law despite the fact that it would be possible for the district court to do so. If judgment as a matter of law is granted and the appellate court holds that the evidence in fact was sufficient to go to the jury, an entire new trial must be had. If, on the other hand, the trial court submits the case to the jury, though it thinks the evidence insufficient, final determination of the case is expedited greatly. If the jury agrees with the court's appraisal of the evidence, and returns a verdict for the party who moved for judgment as a matter of law, the case is at an end. If the jury brings in a different verdict, the trial court can grant a renewed motion for judgment as a matter of law. Then if the appellate court holds that the trial court was in error in its appraisal of the evidence, it can reverse and order judgment on the verdict of the jury, without any need for a new trial. For this reason the appellate courts repeatedly have said that it usually is desirable to take a verdict, and then pass on the sufficiency of the evidence on a post-verdict motion. 9A Federal Practice § 2533, at 319 (footnote omitted).

Exercise 11-10. *Lavender v. Kurn*

In *Lavender v. Kurn*, 327 U.S. 645 (1946), the Estate of L.E. Haney sued the trustees of the St. Louis-San Francisco Railway (RR), alleging that Haney, while employed as a switchtender by the RR in the switchyard of the Grand Central Station in Memphis, Tennessee, was killed as a result of the RR's negligence. Following a trial in the Circuit Court of the City of St. Louis, Missouri, the jury returned a verdict in favor of the Estate and awarded damages in the amount of $30,000. Judgment was entered accordingly. On appeal, however, the Supreme Court of Missouri reversed the judgment, holding that there was no substantial evidence of negligence to support the submission of the case to the jury. The U.S. Supreme Court reversed.

Based on the following evidence, Rule 50, Reeves, and JMOL policy, make an argument that the trial court should have denied the RR's JMOL motion. Then make an argument that the trial court should have granted the RR's JMOL motion.

It was very dark on the evening of December 21, 1939. At about 7:30 p.m. a westbound interstate Frisco passenger train stopped on the Frisco main line, its rear some 20 or 30 feet west of the switch. Haney, in the performance of his duties, threw or opened the switch to permit the train to back into the station. The respondents claimed that Haney was then required to cross to the south side of the track before the train passed the switch; and the conductor of the train testified that he saw Haney so cross. But there was also evidence that Haney's duties required him to wait at the switch north of the track until the train had cleared, close the switch, return to his shanty near the crossing and change the signals from red to green to permit trains on the Illinois Central tracks to use the crossing. The Frisco train cleared the switch, backing at the rate of 8 or 10 miles per hour. But the switch remained open and the signals still were red. Upon investigation Haney was found north of the track near the switch lying face down on the ground, unconscious. An ambulance was called, but he was dead upon arrival at the hospital.

Haney had been struck in the back of the head, causing a fractured skull from which he died. There were no known eye-witnesses to the fatal blow. Although it is not clear there is evidence that his body was extended north and south, the head to the south. Apparently he had fallen forward to the south; his face was bruised on the left side from hitting the ground and there were marks indicating that his toes had dragged a few inches southward as he fell. His head was about 5½ feet north of the Frisco tracks. Estimates ranged from 2 feet to 14 feet as to how far west of the switch he lay.

The injury to Haney's head was evidenced by a gash about two inches long from which blood flowed. The back of Haney's white cap had a corresponding black mark about an inch and a half long and an inch wide, running at an angle downward to the right of the center of the back of the head. A spot of blood was later found at a point 3 or 4 feet north of the tracks. The conclusion following an autopsy was that Haney's skull was fractured by "some fast moving small round object." One of the examining doctors testified that such an object might have been attached to a train backing at the rate of 8 or 10 miles per hour. But he also admitted that the fracture might have resulted from a blow from a pipe or club or some similar round object in the hands of an individual.

The Estate's theory is that Haney was struck by the curled end or tip of a mail hook hanging down loosely on the outside of the mail car of the backing train. This curled end was 73 inches above the top of the rail, which was 7 inches high. The overhang of the mail car in relation to the rails was about 2 to 2½ feet. The evidence indicated that when the mail car swayed or moved around a curve the mail hook might pivot, its curled end swinging out as much as 12 to 14 inches. The curled end could thus be swung out to a point 3 to 3½ feet from the rail and about 73 inches above the top of the rail. Both east and west of the switch, however, was an uneven mound of cinders and dirt rising at its highest points 18 to 24 inches above the top of the rails. Witnesses differed as to how close the mound approached the rails, the estimates varying from 3 to 15 feet. But taking the figures most favorable to the Estate, the mound extended to a point 6 to 12 inches north of the overhanging side of the mail car. If the mail hook end swung out 12 to 14 inches it would be 49 to 55 inches above the highest parts of the mound. Haney was 67 inches tall. If he had been standing on the mound about a foot from the side of the mail car he could have been hit by the end of the mail hook, the exact point of contact depending upon the height of the mound at the particular point. His wound was about 4 inches below the top of his head, or 63½ inches above the point where he stood on the mound-well within the possible range of the mail hook end.

The RR's theory is that Haney was murdered. They point to the estimates that the mound was 10 to 15 feet north of the rail, making it impossible for the mail hook end to reach a point of contact with Haney's head. Photographs were placed in the record to support the claim that the ground was level north of the rail for at least 10 feet. Moreover, it appears that the area immediately surrounding the switch was quite dark. Witnesses stated that it was so dark that it was impossible to see a 3-inch pipe 25 feet away. It also appears that many hoboes and tramps frequented the area at night in order to get rides on freight trains. Haney carried a pistol to protect himself. This pistol was found loose under his body by those who came to his rescue. It was testified, however, that the pistol had apparently slipped out of his pocket or scabbard as he fell. Haney's clothes were not disarranged and there was no evidence of a struggle or fight. No rods, pipes or weapons of any kind, except Haney's own pistol, were found near the scene. Moreover, his gold watch and diamond ring were still on him after he was struck. Six days later his unsoiled billfold was found on a high board fence about a block from the place where Haney was struck and near the point where he had been placed in an ambulance. It contained his social security card and other effects, but no money. His wife testified that he 'never carried much money, not very much more than $10.' Such were the facts in relation to the RR's theory of murder.

b. New Trial

In federal court, Rule 59 and Rule 61 govern motions for a new trial. Read those rules. Rule 59(a) and (b) allow any party to move for a new trial within 28 days of the entry of judgment. Note that this time limit is the same as the time limit for a post-verdict JMOL motion under Rule 50(b), which makes sense because a party making a post-trial motion often joins a JMOL motion with a motion for a new trial. Rule 59(c) allows the trial judge to grant a new trial even without a motion from a party.

The grounds for a new trial are not specified in Rule 59(a). Instead that rule requires parties to rely on federal case law to identify the grounds for a new trial. Rule 61, however, sets out a "harmless error" rule governing new trial motions. Many state courts specify the grounds for new trials in court rules or statutes. See the example from Washington below. The grounds listed in the Washington Civil Rule 59(a) are typical of the grounds that apply in other state and federal courts.

Washington Civil Rule 59(a) Grounds for a New Trial

(1) Irregularity in the proceedings of the court, jury or adverse party, or any order of the court, or abuse of discretion, by which such party was prevented from having a fair trial;

(2) Misconduct of prevailing party or jury . . . ;

(3) Accident or surprise which ordinary prudence could not have guarded against;

(4) Newly discovered evidence, material for the party making the application, which he could not with reasonable diligence have discovered and produced at the trial;

(5) Damages so excessive or inadequate as unmistakably to indicate that the verdict must have been the result of passion or prejudice;

(6) Error in the assessment of the amount of recovery whether too large or too small, when the action is upon a contract, or for the injury or detention of property;

(7) That there is no evidence or reasonable inference from the evidence to justify the verdict or the decision, or that it is contrary to law;

(8) Error in law occurring at the trial and objected to at the time by the party making the application; or

(9) That substantial justice has not been done.

Exercise 11-11. *Dadurian v. Underwriters at Lloyd's of London*

In *Dadurian*, the jury returned a verdict for the plaintiff and the defendant made motions for JMOL and for a new trial. The version of the opinion below omits the JMOL discussion (the trial court denied the JMOL motion and the court of appeals affirmed). Instead, our focus is on the new trial motion, the trial court and appellate court standards on new trial motions, the policy behind those standards, and the application of that law and policy to the evidence in *Dadurian*.

1. Trial Court Standard. One ground for a new trial in federal and state court is that the jury verdict is not supported by sufficient evidence. The verbal formulation that many courts use in describing the standard that the trial court should apply is whether the verdict is against the "clear" weight of

the evidence or against the "great" weight of the evidence. The trial court is not to view the evidence in the light most favorable to the verdict winner; instead the court is to weigh the evidence.

How is the new trial standard different from the JMOL standard?

What policies support this difference?

What policies support allowing the trial court to order a new trial despite the jury's verdict?

2. Appellate Court Standard. When reviewing a trial court's grant or denial of a new trial motion, the appellate court is to reverse the trial court's decision only if the appellate court finds that the trial court "abused its discretion." This standard is very deferential to the trial court. It is rare for an appellate court to find that a trial court abused its discretion in deciding a new trial motion.

What policies explain why the appellate court standard is so deferential to the trial court on new trial motions?

3. Assume that you are the trial judge in *Dadurian*. Based on the applicable law and evidence, explain why you would grant or deny defendant's new trial motion.

4. Assume that you are a judge on the court of appeals. Based on the applicable law and evidence, explain why you would affirm or reverse the trial court's decision to deny defendant's new trial motion.

Dadurian v. Underwriters at Lloyd's of London

787 F.2d 756 (1st Cir. 1986)

This diversity case arose out of the refusal of defendant-appellant Lloyd's, London ("Lloyd's") to indemnify plaintiff-appellee Paul Dadurian after he claimed the loss of certain jewelry that he allegedly owned and that had been insured under a Lloyd's insurance policy. As affirmative defenses to the suit for nonpayment, Lloyd's asserted that Dadurian's claim was fraudulent and that Dadurian had knowingly made false statements about facts material to his claim. The jury entered special verdicts favorable to Dadurian, resulting in his recovering $267,000 plus interest. Lloyd's moved for judgment notwithstanding the verdict, or alternatively, for a new trial. The United States District Court for the District of Rhode Island denied the motion, and Lloyd's now appeals. As we find the jury's verdict was against the great weight of the evidence, we vacate and remand for a new trial.

I

Dadurian claimed that he purchased 12 pieces of "specialty" jewelry for investment purposes over a period of 30 months, from August 1977 to January 1980. The pieces allegedly ranged in price from $12,000 to $35,000, costing him $233,000 in total. Dadurian testified that he purchased all the jewelry from James Howe, a jeweler in Providence, Rhode Island, and paid for each item in cash. Dadurian did not present any sales slips, receipts or other documents of transfer reflecting any of his alleged purchases; and Howe not only presented no records of his sale of the jewelry to Dadurian, but he could not remember from whom he had originally obtained the jewelry and had no records showing that the jewelry had ever actually been in his possession.

On or about March 2, 1980, Dadurian purchased a "Jewelry Floater" policy from Lloyd's, which insured him against loss of the 12 items of jewelry. The jewelry pieces were described on an attached schedule, which also set forth the maximum amount recoverable for each piece. The maximum recoverable under the policy was $267,000. Dadurian obtained the insurance coverage on the strength of eight appraisal certificates for the jewelry, which were prepared by Howe at Dadurian's request. Some certificates were dated on the same day as certain of the alleged purchases, while the others were dated months later.

Dadurian claimed that on or about April 12, 1980, armed robbers entered his home and forced him to open his safe, where the jewelry was kept. He was shot in the right shoulder, allegedly by one of the robbers, and was taken to the hospital. It is Dadurian's contention that the insured pieces of jewelry were stolen during the robbery. After preliminary investigation by an adjuster representing Lloyd's, Dadurian was asked to appear for a formal examination under oath by counsel for Lloyd's. The examination took place on September 10, 1980, and again on May 28, 1981. Because of alleged false and fraudulent statements made under oath by Dadurian at this examination, Lloyd's refused to indemnify Dadurian for the claimed losses.

On March 31, 1982, Dadurian brought this action in the district court seeking compensation for his losses under the jewelry insurance policy issued by Lloyd's. The action was tried before a jury from October 29 through November 5, 1984. The jury rendered four special verdicts, all favorable to Dadurian: that Dadurian had been robbed on April 12, 1980; that he had not given false answers or information on any material subject when he was examined under oath before the commencement of this suit; that he had not made any false statement or fraudulent claims as to any of the 12 jewelry items for which he claimed a loss; and that the total fair market value of all the jewelry on April 12, 1980, was $267,000. Judgment was entered for plaintiff in the amount of $267,000 with interest.

Pursuant to Fed.R.Civ.P. 50, Lloyd's moved for judgment n.o.v. or, in the alternative, for a new trial. The district court denied defendant's motion, and this appeal followed.

II

Lloyd's argues on appeal that Dadurian swore falsely, and necessarily knowingly, with respect to at least two key issues, and that either instance of false swearing was sufficient to void the insurance policy. First, Dadurian is said to have clearly lied in asserting that he purchased and owned the 12 pieces of jewelry for which he later obtained the insurance; and second, he is said to have knowingly lied in telling Lloyd's, at the formal examination under oath conducted before this action was begun, that the cash he used to purchase the jewelry came from certain bank loans. Lloyd's contends that evidence presented at trial was so overwhelmingly against Dadurian on both these issues that no reasonable jury could have rendered a verdict in his favor.

A. The Purchase of the Jewelry

Pointing to the suspicious absence of documentation for any of the jewelry purchases, Lloyd's asserts that the record shows that Dadurian had sworn falsely when he testified to having purchased the jewelry at all. Dadurian procured the Lloyd's insurance on the basis of written appraisals executed by Howe, the man from whom he allegedly purchased all 12 pieces. But he obtained no receipts nor did Howe have any records of the alleged sales to Dadurian. Moreover, although Dadurian testified to specific dates and prices paid for each of his jewelry purchases, in support of his story of ownership, his testimony that he had obtained that information from Howe's records was contradicted by testimony that Howe kept no such records.

But whatever may be thought of Dadurian's story, we cannot say ... the verdict on this issue was so far contrary to the clear weight of the evidence as, by itself, to provide grounds for our ordering the district court to grant a new trial. Not only did Howe testify at trial that he sold each one of the jewelry pieces to Dadurian at the prices Dadurian claimed, but Howe's employees, Cheryl Cousineau and Edward Proulx, gave testimony which, in material respects, tended to support the story that Dadurian purchased at least some jewelry items from Howe with cash. And Howe and Cousineau testified that they did not usually give receipts for cash purchases of "investment jewelry" or of jewelry sold "on consignment," thus tending to explain why Dadurian had no receipts. Despite extensive cross-examination by counsel for Lloyd's, the jury apparently chose to credit the testimony of Dadurian and his witnesses, and the jury was entitled to overlook the lack of any documentation for the purchases.

B. The Source of the Funds

Lloyd's also argues that Dadurian knowingly lied under oath at the formal examination when he swore that certain specific bank loans were the source of the cash he used to buy the jewelry. If Dadurian swore falsely and knowingly on this issue, he is not entitled to recover under the insurance contract. This is so because under the Lloyd's policy Dadurian was required to give "such information and evidence as to the property lost and the circumstances of the Loss as the Underwriters may reasonably require and as may be in the Assured's power"—and it is undisputed that under the policy, as well as under established case law, knowingly false testimony by Dadurian as to any fact considered "material" to his claim voids the policy.

The district court instructed the jury, and Dadurian does not dispute, that the issue of where he obtained the cash used for his jewelry purchases was "material" to his claim. We agree that where Dadurian got the cash was material to his insurance claim, since Dadurian insisted that he paid Howe a total of $233,000 in cash over a 30-month period for the jewelry, and the credibility of this story, and hence of Dadurian's ownership of the insured items, turned in part on his ability to explain plausibly where he obtained such large sums of cash.

The details of Dadurian's testimony about the bank loans are as follows: Soon after the alleged robbery of the jewelry items in April 1980, Dadurian was interviewed by an adjuster for Lloyd's. At this initial interview Dadurian, to explain the sources of his cash, stated that he "may have borrowed from the bank for the purchase of certain of the personal items of jewelry and [would] check [his] records in this regard." He later submitted to Lloyd's certain promissory notes which he contended represented the bank loans used to finance many of his purchases. Apparently still dissatisfied with the information provided by Dadurian, Lloyd's notified Dadurian in a letter dated August 18, 1980, that he would be required to appear at a formal examination under oath for further questioning at which time he "should be prepared to produce ... all documents in any way relating to the occurrence of the loss...."

At the first examination session on September 10, 1980, and again at the second session on May 28, 1981, when he was examined under oath by counsel for Lloyd's, Dadurian testified to the effect that most of his cash had come from loans from the Rhode Island Hospital Trust National Bank ("Hospital Trust"). During the two sessions, Dadurian was specifically questioned in turn about the sources of the cash used to purchase each one of the jewelry pieces. For 11 of the 12 items, Dadurian identified the individual promissory notes of his—by date and by loan amount—that purportedly represented the bank loans he said was used to finance his purchases. In total, he identified 13 specific bank loans as the source of $166,000 of the $233,000 which he claimed to have paid to Howe.

At trial, however, Richard Niedzwiadek, an employee of the bank, testified that the loans associated with four of the jewelry pieces, totalling $49,500, were simply renewals of earlier loans which could not have generated any cash for Dadurian. He also produced bank statements for Dadurian's accounts at Hospital Trust showing that the proceeds from several other loans which Dadurian had identified as having financed a number of the jewelry pieces had been deposited in those accounts and then withdrawn in too small amounts over a period of time to have been used for purchasing the jewelry as Dadurian claimed. Niedzwiadek further testified that the proceeds of yet another loan supposedly associated with a jewelry item had been deposited in the corporate account of a company named U.S. Enterprises, Inc., and that Dadurian had stated the purpose of the loan as "real estate investment." Confronted with this cumulative evidence, Dadurian essentially conceded that some, if not most, of the promissory notes he had selected had been the wrong ones, and that his testimony as to the sources of the funds was therefore in part false. He insisted, however, that he had selected the notes "to the best of [his] recollection" and that he had been honestly mistaken.

Since it is thus uncontroverted that a substantial number of Dadurian's representations under oath about the sources of his cash were untrue, the only remaining question is whether Dadurian made these false statements *knowingly* or whether he was simply mistaken in good faith as he claims. False swearing is "swearing knowingly and intentionally false and not through mere mistake." *Black's Law Dictionary* 725 (rev. 5th ed. 1979). Lloyd's forcefully contends that where Dadurian testified with such certainty, yet incorrectly, about so many of his own promissory notes and bank loans, the inference of intentional falsehood is so compelling as to render the jury's finding contrary, at very least, to the great weight of the evidence.

After carefully considering the entire record, we find that the great weight of the evidence indicates overwhelmingly that Dadurian knew he was giving false testimony. At the formal examination under oath Dadurian specifically identified 13 promissory notes, apparently from those he had given Lloyd's sometime before the examination, and explicitly linked each note to a particular jewelry purchase. He did not qualify his identifications, but rather couched his testimony in terms of misleading certainty. Only when confronted at trial with the patent falsity of his earlier testimony did Dadurian testify, by way of explanation, that he had made his selections only to the "best of his recollection" in order to satisfy the insurance company's inquiries. It was only then that he explained that because he had "files and files" of such notes in his possession, he must have simply selected the wrong ones under pressure of time and circumstances.

This explanation strains credulity. This was not a case where Dadurian was confronted for the first time at the examination with "files and files" of his promissory notes and asked to come up with correct ones "on the spot." Rather it was Dadurian himself who originated and put forward the story that most of his cash had come from bank loans, and it was

Dadurian who apparently first tendered the supposedly relevant promissory notes to Lloyd's at some time before the formal examination. Dadurian admitted at trial that he had known before the first examination session that he would be questioned further about the bank loans. He apparently marked each of the notes before the examination sessions with the number of the jewelry piece with which it was supposedly associated. By the first session in September 1980, and certainly by the May 1981 session, Dadurian had had ample notice as well as opportunity to discover the correct promissory notes or, if he found he was wrong or in doubt, to say so. The uncontested facts simply belie Dadurian's excuse that he was pressured into making identifications prematurely.

Dadurian had much to gain by providing a plausible explanation for the sources of his cash. By piecing together notes executed on dates close to the times of the alleged purchases, he could hope to create an impression of credibility. That he linked the notes to the jewelry purchases so positively—without bothering to ascertain readily available information showing that they were not so related—indicates, at the least, a wilful misrepresentation as to the state of his own knowledge concerning the matters to which he was testifying. We think the only fair inference from this kind of total indifference to the truth or falsity of his assertions was that Dadurian knew that he was not telling the truth.

It follows, we believe, that the jury's verdict was against the clear weight of the evidence insofar as it found that Dadurian did not knowingly give false answers or information on any material subject when he was examined under oath before commencement of this suit. We emphasize that Dadurian himself conceded that some of his answers were incorrect, and it is clear the district court properly found them "material." This leaves open only the question of their possible innocence, which, to be sure, Dadurian attested to—but with implausible explanations as to why he put forward these patently unfounded and incorrect assertions. We conclude that the jury's finding that Dadurian did not give knowingly false answers was contrary to the great weight of the evidence. For that aspect of the verdict to stand would, in our view, amount to a manifest miscarriage of justice. We hold, therefore, that the district court abused its discretion in denying defendant's motion for a new trial, and remand the case for retrial by a new jury.

New Trial Notes and Questions

1. Unfair Surprise.

In *Conway v. Chemical Leaman Tank Lines, Inc.,* 687 F. 2d 108, 111–12 (5th Cir. 1982), the appellate court affirmed the trial court's decision to grant a new trial motion based on unfair surprise. The suit arose out of a collision between two trucks. A factual issue in the case was which truck crossed the center line and caused the collision.

It is well settled that Rule 59 provides a means of relief in cases in which a party has been unfairly made the victim of surprise. The surprise, however, must be "inconsistent with substantial justice" in order to justify a grant of a new trial. FRCP 61. The district court is therefore entitled to grant a new trial only if the admission of the surprise testimony actually prejudiced the plaintiffs' case. This Court has limited reversible error from unfair surprise to situations where a completely new issue is suddenly raised or a previously unidentified expert witness is suddenly called to testify.

The determination of a trial judge to either grant or deny a motion for a new trial is reviewable under an abuse of discretion standard.

In the instant case, Hay was a previously unidentified witness who was called without any forewarning to testify as an expert at trial. Hay's testimony was not cumulative; rather, it introduced the theory that the questioned eastbound tire marks were asphalt marks from another vehicle. No other party— plaintiff or defendant—had presented this theory. Under the circumstances, plaintiffs had no time or opportunity to prepare a response to this unexpected turn of events. The interrogatories answered by the jury in the second trial leave no doubt that the jury was influenced by Hay's testimony.

2. Amount of the Verdict.

A trial court can set aside a jury verdict if the size of the verdict is not supported by the evidence. The judge should not set aside a jury verdict simply because the judge would have awarded a different amount. Instead, the judge should uphold the jury verdict unless the verdict shows that the proceedings have been tainted by prejudice, the amount is unconscionable, or the size of the verdict shocks the conscience.

If the trial court decides that the verdict is not supported by the evidence, the judge has several options. First, Rule 59(a) gives the court the authority to order a new trial "on all or some of the issues...." Consequently, the trial court can order a new trial on damages only, or on liability and damages. "[I]f the issues are sufficiently interwoven, a partial new trial is inappropriate. For example, a new trial on damages only is not proper if there is reason to think that the verdict may represent a compromise among jurors with different views on whether defendant was liable or if for some other reason it appears that the error on the damage issue may have affected the determination of liability." WRIGHT & MILLER, 11 FED. PRAC. & PROC. CIV.§ 2814 (3d ed.).

If the court decides that the verdict is excessive, the court has the option of remittitur. This option gives the plaintiff a choice. The plaintiff can accept a lower amount of damages, determined by the court. If the plaintiff does not accept the amount set by the court, the judge grants defendant's motion for a new trial. Remittitur applies in state and federal court.

If the court decides that the amount of the verdict is insufficient, the court may have the option of additur. In the additur process, defendant has a choice. Defendant can accept a higher damage award, determined by the court. If defendant does not agree to the increased award, the court will grant plaintiff's motion for a new trial.

Additur is available is some states. Additur is not available in federal court. In federal court, if the trial court finds the verdict to be inadequate, the judge can order a new trial on damages alone or a new trial on damages and liability, but the judge cannot use additur. In *Dimick v. Schiedt*, 293 U.S. 474, 486–87 (1935), the Supreme Court held that additur violated the Seventh Amendment:

> Where the verdict is excessive, the practice of substituting a remission of the excess for a new trial is not without plausible support in the view that what remains is included in the verdict along with the unlawful excess — in the sense that it has been found by the jury — and that the remittitur has the effect of merely lopping off an excrescence. But where the verdict is too small, an increase by the court is a bald addition of something which in no sense can be said to be included in the verdict. When, therefore, the trial court here found that the damages awarded by the jury were so inadequate as to entitle plaintiff to a new trial, how can it be held, with any semblance of reason, that that court, with the consent of the defendant only, may, by assessing an additional amount of damages, bring the constitutional right of the plaintiff to a jury trial to an end in respect of a matter of fact which no jury has ever passed upon either explicitly or by implication? To so hold is obviously to compel the plaintiff to forego his constitutional right to the verdict of a jury and accept "an assessment partly made by a jury which has acted improperly, and partly by a tribunal which has no power to assess.

Does this make any sense?

3. Juror Misconduct.

Juror misconduct is a ground for a new trial. Two primary issues arise in juror misconduct cases. The first issue is how to prove juror misconduct, which is governed by Federal Rule of Evidence 606(b):

> (b) During an Inquiry into the Validity of a Verdict or Indictment.
>
> (1) *Prohibited Testimony or Other Evidence.* During an inquiry into the validity of a verdict or indictment, a juror may not testify about any statement made or incident that occurred during the jury's deliberations; the effect of anything on that juror's or another juror's vote; or any juror's mental processes concerning the verdict or indictment. The court may not receive a juror's affidavit or evidence of a juror's statement on these matters.
>
> (2) *Exceptions.* A juror may testify about whether:
>
>> (A) extraneous prejudicial information was improperly brought to the jury's attention;

(B) an outside influence was improperly brought to bear on any juror; or

(C) a mistake was made in entering the verdict on the verdict form.

The Advisory Committee Note to Rule 606(b) discusses the policy and application of the rule.

> Whether testimony, affidavits, or statements of jurors should be received for the purpose of invalidating or supporting a verdict or indictment, and if so, under what circumstances, has given rise to substantial differences of opinion. The values sought to be promoted by excluding the evidence include freedom of deliberation, stability and finality of verdicts, and protection of jurors against annoyance and embarrassment. On the other hand, simply putting verdicts beyond effective reach can only promote irregularity and injustice. The rule offers an accommodation between these competing considerations.
>
> The mental operations and emotional reactions of jurors in arriving at a given result would, if allowed as a subject of inquiry, place every verdict at the mercy of jurors and invite tampering and harassment. The authorities are in virtually complete accord in excluding the evidence.
>
> Under the federal decisions the central focus has been upon insulation of the manner in which the jury reached its verdict, and this protection extends to each of the components of deliberation, including arguments, statements, discussions, mental and emotional reactions, votes, and any other feature of the process. Thus testimony or affidavits of jurors have been held incompetent to show a compromise verdict, a quotient verdict, misinterpretations of instructions, mistake in returning verdict, and interpretation of guilty plea by one defendant as implicating others. The policy does not, however, foreclose testimony by jurors as to prejudicial extraneous information or influences injected into or brought to bear upon the deliberative process. Thus a juror is recognized as competent to testify to statements by the bailiff or the introduction of a prejudicial newspaper account into the jury room.

The Court recently decided two cases involving Federal Rule of Evidence 606 and juror misconduct.

In *Warger v Shauers*, ___ U.S. ___, 135 S. Ct. 521 (2014), Warger sued Shauers in federal court for negligence arising out of a motor vehicle accident. After the jury returned a verdict for Shauers, one of the jurors contacted Warger's counsel, claiming that the jury foreperson had revealed during jury deliberations that the foreperson's daughter had been at fault in a fatal motor vehicle accident, and that a lawsuit would have ruined her daughter's life. Based on an affidavit from the juror, Warger moved for a new trial, arguing that the juror had deliberately lied during *voir dire*. The district court denied Warger's motion, holding that Rule 606(b) barred the affidavit.

The Eighth Circuit affirmed. The Supreme Court affirmed, holding that Rule 606(b)(1), which bars evidence "about any statement made during the jury's deliberations" barred the affidavit and that the exception for "extraneous prejudicial information" did not apply.

In *Pena-Rodriguez v Colorado*, ___ U.S. ___, 137 S. Ct. 855 (2017), the Court found a constitutional exception to Federal Rule of Evidence 606. After a Colorado jury convicted Peña-Rodriguez of harassment and unlawful sexual contact, two jurors told defense counsel that, during deliberations, a juror had expressed anti-Hispanic bias toward the defendant and the defendant's alibi witness. Defense counsel obtained affidavits from the two jurors describing a number of biased statements made by the other juror. The trial court acknowledged the juror's bias but denied the defendant's motion for a new trial on the ground that Colorado Rule of Evidence 606(b) barred the affidavits as to statements made during jury deliberations. The Court reversed, holding that when a juror makes a clear statement indicating that the juror relied on racial stereotypes or animus to convict a criminal defendant, the Sixth Amendment permits the trial court to consider the evidence of the juror's statement and any resulting denial of the jury trial guarantee.

The second issue is what jury misconduct will justify a new trial. The Supreme Court addresses that issue in the following case.

McDonough Power Equipment, Inc. v. Greenwood
464 U.S. 548 (1984)

Justice Rehnquist delivered the opinion of the Court.

Respondents, Billy Greenwood and his parents, sued petitioner McDonough Power Equipment, Incorporated to recover damages sustained by Billy when his feet came in contact with the blades of a riding lawn mower manufactured by petitioner. The United States District Court for the District of Kansas entered judgment for petitioner upon a jury verdict and denied respondents' motion for new trial. On appeal, however, the Court of Appeals for the Tenth Circuit reversed the judgment of the District Court and ordered a new trial. It held that the failure of a juror to respond affirmatively to a question on voir dire seeking to elicit information about previous injuries to members of the juror's immediate family had prejudiced the Greenwoods' right of peremptory challenge. We granted certiorari and now hold that respondents are not entitled to a new trial unless the juror's failure to disclose denied respondents their right to an impartial jury.

During the voir dire prior to the empaneling of the six-member jury, respondents' attorney asked prospective jurors the following question:

"Now, how many of you have yourself or any members of your immediate family sustained any severe injury, not necessarily as severe as Billy, but sustained any injuries whether it was an accident at home, or on the farm or at work that resulted in any disability or prolonged pain and suffering, that is you or any members of your immediate family?"

Ronald Payton, who eventually became a juror, did not respond to this question, which was addressed to the panel as a whole. After a trial which extended over a three-week period, the jury found for petitioner McDonough. Four days after judgment was entered for petitioner, respondents ... asserted that they were "of information and belief" that juror Payton's son may have been injured at one time, a fact which had not been revealed during voir dire....

Respondents moved for a new trial, asserting 18 grounds in justification. Shortly after the parties placed a telephone conference call to juror Payton, the District Court denied respondents' motion for a new trial, finding that the "matter was fairly and thoroughly tried and that the jury's verdict was a just one, well-supported by the evidence." The District Court was never informed of the results of the examination of juror Payton, nor did respondents ever directly assert before the District Court that juror Payton's non-disclosure warranted a new trial.

* * *

This Court has long held that a litigant " 'is entitled to a fair trial but not a perfect one,' for there are no perfect trials." *Brown v. United States*, 411 U.S. 223, 231–232 (1973), quoting *Bruton v. United States*, 391 U.S. 123, 135 (1968).... Trials are costly, not only for the parties, but also for the jurors performing their civic duty and for society which pays the judges and support personnel who manage the trials.... We have also come a long way from the time when all trial error was presumed prejudicial and reviewing courts were considered "citadels of technicality." The harmless error rules adopted by this Court and Congress embody the principle that courts should exercise judgment in preference to the automatic reversal for "error" and ignore errors that do not affect the essential fairness of the trial.

* * *

The ruling of the Court of Appeals in this case must be assessed against this background. One touchstone of a fair trial is an impartial trier of fact—a jury capable and willing to decide the case solely on the evidence before it. Voir dire examination serves to protect that right by exposing possible biases, both known and unknown, on the part of potential jurors. Demonstrated bias in the responses to questions on voir dire may result in a juror being excused for cause; hints of bias not sufficient to warrant challenge for cause may assist parties in exercising their peremptory challenges. The necessity of truthful answers by prospective jurors if this process is to serve its purpose is obvious.

The critical question posed to juror Payton in this case asked about injuries that resulted in any disability or prolonged pain or suffering. Juror Payton apparently believed that his son's broken leg sustained as a result of an exploding tire was not such an injury. In response to a similar question from petitioner's counsel, however, another juror related such a minor incident as the fact that his six-year-old son once caught his finger in a bike chain. Yet another juror failed to respond to the question posed to juror Payton, and only the subsequent questioning of petitioner's counsel brought out that her husband had been injured in a machinery accident.

* * *

To invalidate the result of a three-week trial because of a juror's mistaken, though honest response to a question, is to insist on something closer to perfection than our judicial system can be expected to give. A trial represents an important investment of private and social resources, and it ill serves the important end of finality to wipe the slate clean simply to recreate the peremptory challenge process because counsel lacked an item of information which objectively he should have obtained from a juror on voir dire examination.... We hold that to obtain a new trial in such a situation, a party must first demonstrate that a juror failed to answer honestly a material question on voir dire, and then further show that a correct response would have provided a valid basis for a challenge for cause. The motives for concealing information may vary, but only those reasons that affect a juror's impartiality can truly be said to affect the fairness of a trial.

Generally, motions for a new trial are committed to the discretion of the district court. The Court of Appeals was mistaken in deciding as it did that respondents were entitled to a new trial. In the event that the issue remains relevant after the Court of Appeals has disposed of respondents' other contentions on appeal, the District Court may hold a hearing to determine whether respondents are entitled to a new trial under the principles we state here.

_____

c. Relief from Judgment

Rule 60 governs relief from judgment. Read Rule 60. Rule 60(a) allows the trial court to correct mistakes due to clerical errors, oversights, and omissions in judgments and orders. For example, Rule 60(a) allows the trial court to correct the failure to enter judgment, a missing date, errors in the names of parties, and the failure to include costs in the judgment.

Rule 60(b) provides six enumerated grounds upon which a party may move for relief from a final judgment or order. Decisions on Rule 60(b) motions are within the discretion of the trial court and appellate review is governed by an abuse of discretion standard. Rule 60(b) implicates two core policies — it balances the desire to do substantial justice with the goal of achieving finality in civil litigation. WRIGHT & MILLER, 11 FED. PRAC. & PROC. CIV.§ 2857 (3d ed.).

(1) Mistake, Inadvertence, Surprise, or Excusable Neglect

A common use of Rule 60(b)(1) is a defendant asking the court for relief from a default judgment, thus allowing the defendant to answer the complaint on the merits. The factual and procedural background in *Brandt v. American Bankers Ins. Co. of Florida*, 653 F.3d 1108 (9th Cir. 2011), is typical.

American Bankers issued a flood insurance policy to the Brandts. After the Brandts' home flooded in December of 2007, the Brandts submitted a claim to American Bankers. Although American Bankers paid a portion of the claim, the Brandts believed the payment was too low.

The Brandts brought suit against American Bankers in the U.S. District Court for the Western District of Washington, alleging breach of contract and bad faith under Washington law. The Brandts served process on American Bankers through the Office of the Insurance Commissioner for the State of Washington ("OIC") as permitted by Washington law. The OIC accepted service of the complaint and sent it, via certified mail, to American Bankers' registered agent, Corporations Service Company ("CSC").

Thereafter, CSC forwarded the complaint, via email, to two individuals at Assurant Group, American Bankers' parent company, according to instructions for service on record with CSC. Although personnel at Assurant should have forwarded the complaint to the appropriate personnel at American Bankers, they failed to do so. The Brandts' counsel also mailed a copy of the complaint to the American Bankers claims adjuster handling the matter; however, the claims adjuster stated he did not receive the complaint.

American Bankers did not answer or otherwise respond to the Brandts' complaint, and the Clerk entered default. Upon motion by the Brandts, and following an evidentiary hearing, the district court entered default judgment against American Bankers in the amount of $655,489.42, representing both contractual and extra-contractual state law damages. The following day, counsel for the Brandts sent a letter to American Bankers via fax, demanding payment of the default judgment.

Upon receipt of the Brandts' letter, American Bankers retained counsel, who filed a notice of appearance in the district court. Shortly thereafter, American Bankers filed a motion to set aside default for good cause pursuant to

Fed.R.Civ.P. 55(c), and to set aside the default judgment for excusable neglect pursuant to Fed.R.Civ.P. 60(b)(1).

Id. at 1108–1101.

The Ninth Circuit concluded that the trial court did not abuse its discretion in granting defendant's motion for relief from judgment. The Ninth Circuit summarized the standard trial courts should apply in deciding Rule 60(b)(1) motions:

> Where a defendant seeks relief under Rule 60(b)(1) based upon "excusable neglect," the court applies ... three factors: ... (1) whether the plaintiff will be prejudiced, (2) whether the defendant has a meritorious defense, and (3) whether culpable conduct of the defendant led to the default. The determination of what conduct constitutes "excusable neglect" under Rule 60(b)(1) and similar rules is at bottom an equitable one, taking account of all relevant circumstances surrounding the party's omission.

Id. at 1111.

(2) Newly Discovered Evidence

In *Jones v. Lincoln Elec. Co.,* 188 F.3d 709, 732 (7th Cir. 1999), the Seventh Circuit set out the standard applicable to Rule 60(b)(2) motions.

> Pursuant to Federal Rule of Civil Procedure 60(b)(2), a party may be entitled to relief from the entry of final judgment if that party presents "newly discovered evidence which by due diligence could not have been discovered in time to move for a new trial under Rule 59(b)." Fed. R. Civ. P. 60(b)(2). Relief under Rule 60(b)(2) is an extraordinary remedy that is to be granted only in exceptional circumstances. We have held that the grant of a new trial on the ground of newly discovered evidence requires proof of the following five prerequisites:
>
> 1. The evidence was discovered following trial;
>
> 2. Due diligence on the part of the movant to discover the new evidence is shown or may be inferred;
>
> 3. The evidence is not merely cumulative or impeaching;
>
> 4. The evidence is material; and
>
> 5. The evidence is such that a new trial would probably produce a new result.
>
> If any one of these prerequisites is not satisfied, the movant's Rule 60(b)(2) motion for a new trial must fail.

(3) Fraud, Misrepresentation, or Misconduct by an Opposing Party

In *Rozier v. Ford Motor Co.,* 573 F.2d 1332 (5th Cir. 1978), the Fifth Circuit addressed both fraud or misconduct of an opposing party under Rule 60(b) and fraud on the court under Rule 60(d)(3). Rozier died in an auto accident when his Ford

Galaxie 500 was struck from behind, causing the fuel tank to explode, severely burning Rozier. During discovery, Ford failed to produce documents Plaintiffs requested concerning Ford's cost/benefit analysis of fuel tank designs. After a week-long trial, the jury returned a verdict for Ford. When plaintiff's lawyer learned that Ford had a document that analyzed costs of various fuel tank locations in Ford passenger vehicles, plaintiff moved for relief from judgment and a new trial under Rule 60(b)(3). The trial court denied the motion. The Fifth Circuit reversed, concluding that the trial court abused its discretion in denying the motion. The appellate court addressed the standards, timing, and policy applicable to Rule 60(b)(3) and 60(d)(3).

> The pivotal question in this case is whether the trial judge abused his discretion in denying Mrs. Rozier's motion for a new trial pursuant to Rule 60(b)(3), Fed.R.Civ.P. We hold that he did and reverse on that basis.

* * *

> Under the express terms of the rule, 60(b)(3) motions must be made within a reasonable time, not more than one year, after the challenged judgment was entered. In this case, Mrs. Rozier moved for a new trial, relying on Rule 60, less than a year after entry of the district court's judgment for Ford, and only five days after her counsel received the information upon which the motion was based.

> Because Mrs. Rozier's 60(b)(3) motion was filed timely, we have no occasion to review Ford's conduct in light of the more exacting "fraud upon the court" standard also provided for by Rule 60(b), but not subject to any time limitation....

> Cases in other Circuits make clear that "fraud upon the court" under the saving clause is distinguishable from "fraud ... misrepresentation, or other misconduct" under subsection (3).

> Generally speaking, only the most egregious misconduct, such as bribery of a judge or members of a jury, or the fabrication of evidence by a party in which an attorney is implicated, will constitute a fraud on the court. Less egregious misconduct, such as nondisclosure to the court of facts allegedly pertinent to the matter before it, will not ordinarily rise to the level of fraud on the court.

> Alternately stated, in order to set aside a judgment or order because of fraud upon the court under Rule 60(b) ... it is necessary to show an unconscionable plan or scheme which is designed to improperly influence the court in its decision.

* * *

> One who asserts that an adverse party has obtained a verdict through fraud, misrepresentation or other misconduct has the burden of proving the assertion by clear and convincing evidence. The conduct complained of must be such as prevented the losing party from fully and fairly presenting his case

or defense. Although Rule 60(b)(3) applies to misconduct in withholding information called for by discovery, it does not require that the information withheld be of such nature as to alter the result in the case. This subsection of the Rule is aimed at judgments which were unfairly obtained, not at those which are factually incorrect.

Id. at 1337–39.

(4) Judgment Is Void

A judgment is void if the trial court lacked jurisdiction over the subject matter or the parties.

(5) Judgment Is Based on an Earlier Judgment That Has Been Reversed, or Applying Judgment Prospectively Is No Longer Equitable

The "earlier judgment has been reversed" grounds is limited. It does not apply to cases where the current judgment used a prior case as precedent and the prior case has been reversed. Instead, this ground applies to cases in which the current judgment is based on claim preclusion or issue preclusion where a court has reversed or vacated the prior judgment. WRIGHT & MILLER, 11 FED. PRAC. & PROC. CIV. § 2863 (3d ed.).

In *Horne v. Flores* 557 U.S. 433 (2009), the Supreme Court addressed Rule 60(b)(5) in the context of a school funding case. A group of English Language Learner (ELL) students sued Arizona, alleging inadequate funding in the Nogales school district in violation of the Equal Educational Opportunities Act. In 2000, the trial court entered judgment for the plaintiffs. In subsequent years, the trial court issued injunctions dealing with ELL funding. In 2006, Arizona increased ELL funding and moved for relief under Rule 60(b)(5).

> Federal Rule of Civil Procedure 60(b)(5) permits a party to obtain relief from a judgment or order if, among other things, "applying [the judgment or order] prospectively is no longer equitable." Rule 60(b)(5) may not be used to challenge the legal conclusions on which a prior judgment or order rests, but the Rule provides a means by which a party can ask a court to modify or vacate a judgment or order if a significant change either in factual conditions or in law renders continued enforcement detrimental to the public interest. The party seeking relief bears the burden of establishing that changed circumstances warrant relief, but once a party carries this burden, a court abuses its discretion when it refuses to modify an injunction or consent decree in light of such changes.

> Rule 60(b)(5) serves a particularly important function in what we have termed "institutional reform litigation." For one thing, injunctions issued in such cases often remain in force for many years, and the passage of time frequently brings about changed circumstances — changes in the nature of the underlying problem, changes in governing law or its interpretation by the courts, and new policy insights — that warrant reexamination of the original judgment.

Second, institutional reform injunctions often raise sensitive federalism concerns. Such litigation commonly involves areas of core state responsibility, such as public education.

Id. at 447–48.

(6) Any Other Reason That Justifies Relief

In *Pioneer Inv. Services Co., v. Brunswick Associates Ltd. P'ship*, 507 U.S. 380, 393 (1993), the Supreme Court addressed the distinctions between Rule 60(b)(1) and 60(b)(6).

> Rule 60(b)(1) ... permits courts to reopen judgments for reasons of "mistake, inadvertence, surprise, or excusable neglect," but only on motion made within one year of the judgment. Rule 60(b)(6) goes further, however, and empowers the court to reopen a judgment even after one year has passed for "any other reason justifying relief from the operation of the judgment." These provisions are mutually exclusive, and thus a party who failed to take timely action due to "excusable neglect" may not seek relief more than a year after the judgment by resorting to subsection (6). To justify relief under subsection (6), a party must show "extraordinary circumstances" suggesting that the party is faultless in the delay. If a party is partly to blame for the delay, relief must be sought within one year under subsection (1) and the party's neglect must be excusable. In *Klapprott*, for example, the petitioner had been effectively prevented from taking a timely appeal of a judgment by incarceration, ill health, and other factors beyond his reasonable control. Four years after a default judgment had been entered against him, he sought to reopen the matter under Rule 60(b) and was permitted to do so. As explained by Justice Black:
>
> > It is contended that the one year limitation [of subsection (1)] bars petitioner on the premise that the petition to set aside the judgment showed, at most, nothing but 'excusable neglect.' And of course, the one year limitation would control if no more than 'neglect' was disclosed by the petition. In that event the petitioner could not avail himself of the broad 'any other reason' clause of 60(b). But petitioner's allegations set up an extraordinary situation which cannot fairly or logically be classified as mere 'neglect' on his part. The undenied facts set out in the petition reveal far more than a failure to defend ... due to inadvertence, indifference, or careless disregard of consequences. *Klapprott v. United States*, 335 U.S. 601, 613 (1949).

The Court applied Rule 60(b)(6) in *Buck v. Davis*, 137 S.Ct. 759 (2017). Buck was convicted of capital murder in a Texas court. Under Texas law, the jury was permitted to impose a death sentence only if it found that Buck was likely to commit acts of violence in the future. Buck's attorney called a psychologist whose report stated that Buck was statistically more likely to act violently because he is black. Buck contended that his attorney's introduction of this evidence violated his Sixth Amendment right to the effective assistance of counsel.

Buck sought federal *habeas* relief, which was denied. Following two Supreme Court cases involving ineffective assistance of counsel, Buck sought to reopen his *habeas* case under Federal Rule of Civil Procedure 60(b)(6) in part based on the introduction of expert testimony linking Buck's race to violence. The District Court denied Buck's 60(b) motion on the grounds that any mention of race during sentencing was *de minimis*, and, therefore, Buck had failed to demonstrate extraordinary circumstances.

The Court held that the district court's denial of Buck's Rule 60(b)(6) motion was an abuse of discretion. To determine whether "extraordinary circumstances" were present, the trial court can consider "the risk of injustice to the parties" and "the risk of undermining the public's confidence in the judicial process." The Court found that there was a reasonable probability that Buck was sentenced to death in part because of his race, which supports 60(b)(6) relief.

9. Professional Development Reflection

Motion practice in civil litigation gives rise to numerous professionalism issues. Consider the following news story.

Karen Dorn Steele, *Lawyer says Japanese heritage affected verdict*

Spokesman Review, January 15, 2008

The medical malpractice verdict in Spokane County Superior Court was read on Dec. 7, 2007 — Pearl Harbor Day.

Spokane attorney Mark D. Kamitomo was unhappy with the jury verdict, which went against his clients and cleared a doctor accused of negligence in a cancer diagnosis.

But Kamitomo was more disturbed by what he heard next.

Juror Jack Marchant, a Washington State University professor, sought out the malpractice attorney after the trial was over and told him five jurors — three women and two men — had disparaged Kamitomo in closed-door jury proceedings, calling him "Mr. Kamikaze," "Mr. Miyashi" and "Mr. Miyagi," a character in the movie "The Karate Kid."

"I was surprised," Kamitomo said. "People who are friends often kid around and insult each other. My first inclination was to ask, is this just harmless? But as (Marchant) told his story, that wasn't how it came across.

"It was shocking to him," Kamitomo said.

Marchant also said he believes the jurors' bias impaired their ability to be objective in the malpractice case.

A second juror, Spokane Transit Authority shipping clerk Mark Costigan, also told the same tale of racial bias in the jury deliberations.

"Costigan approached me the same day. He didn't know the other juror had come forward," Kamitomo said. Costigan also has provided an affidavit on what he observed in the jury room.

One juror remarked on the coincidence that their verdict would be read on Pearl Harbor Day — saying that given the date, another juror's racially insulting remark about Kamitomo was "almost appropriate," Costigan's affidavit says.

Kamitomo — whose father, Doug Kamitomo, was 8 years old when his family was seized in Vancouver, B.C., and relocated to an internment camp at Lemon Creek, B.C., after the Japanese attacks on Pearl Harbor — is asking Superior Court Judge Robert D. Austin for a new trial, based in part on the jurors' comments.

"Plaintiffs are entitled to a new trial because the evidence did not support the verdict and, further, the verdict was not decided by an unbiased and unprejudiced jury," his motion says.

Assume that you represent the defendant.

1. If the case had been tried in federal court, what argument could you make that the jurors' statements are not admissible evidence?

2. Would you make that argument in response to plaintiffs' motion for a new trial?

3. Assuming that the jurors' statements are admissible, what argument could you make that the jurors' statements are not sufficient to warrant a new trial?

4. Would you make that argument?

5. If Mr. Kamitomo contacted you and asked your client to stipulate to a new trial, what advice would you give your client?

Here is the rest of the news story.

Brian T. Rekofke, an attorney for Dr. Nathan P. Stime, the Spokane general practitioner who is the defendant in the medical malpractice case, opposes Kamitomo's motion for a new trial for plaintiffs Darlene and Bill Turner.

"The verdict was 10–2," Rekofke said Monday. "The affidavits filed were by the two dissenting jurors. Mark is a hell of a good lawyer, but I'm disappointed that he's playing the race card here."

Rekofke has obtained affidavits from seven other jurors that contradict the claims of racial bias.

"I had trouble pronouncing Mr. Kamitomo's name, as well as Rekofke's," said Melody Weaver, a registered nurse who served on the jury, in her affidavit. "My vote finding that Dr. Stime was not negligent was based on the evidence and not in any manner, shape or form affected by the race or ethnicity of any of the parties or their attorneys," Weaver said.

6. What effect, if any, do these additional facts have on your response to question 5 above?

After a hearing, Judge Austin granted plaintiffs' motion for a new trial.

Karen Dorn Steele, *Racial Remarks Prompt New Trial*

Spokesman Review, January 15, 2008

A Spokane County Superior Court judge has ordered a new trial in a medical malpractice case where a Spokane attorney of Japanese descent was repeatedly referred to as "Mr. Kamikaze" and other racially charged names during jury deliberations.

Judge Robert D. Austin said he was surprised when he received attorney Mark D. Kamitomo's motion for a new trial in mid-December, based in part on the racial comments.

"We'd hoped we'd moved beyond this, and we apparently have not. It's upsetting," a visibly emotional Austin said during a court hearing Friday.

Austin said he could not be confident that the jury verdict that went against Kamitomo's client and cleared a local doctor of negligence was not a result of juror misconduct.

"We have uncontested affidavits that these remarks were made. It's an expression of prejudice to Mr. Kamitomo's ethnicity," Austin said.

Chapter 12

Appeal

1. Chapter Problem

Right to Appeal and Standards of Review

In *Piper Aircraft Co. v. Reyno*, recall that Plaintiffs filed suit in California state court against Piper Aircraft, which manufactured the airplane in Ohio, and Hartzell Propellers, which manufactured the propeller in Pennsylvania. Defendants removed the case to federal court in California.

1. Defendants moved to transfer venue under 28 U.S.C. § 1404(a). After hearing oral argument, the court issued a written opinion granting Defendants' motion. Assume that you are a lawyer for Piper. Plaintiffs' lawyer notifies you that Plaintiffs are planning to seek appellate review from the Ninth Circuit of the California federal court's order granting transfer of venue to a federal court in Pennsylvania. Argue that the Ninth Circuit should not hear the merits of the appeal. If the Ninth Circuit were to hear the merits of the appeal, what standard of review would it apply?

2. After the case was transferred to a federal court in Pennsylvania, Defendants moved to dismiss on the ground of forum non conveniens. After oral argument, the trial court issued a written opinion, weighing a number of public and private factors and granting the motion to dismiss. The trial court entered the order dismissing the suit on October 1, 1979. Plaintiffs filed a notice of appeal of the order dismissing the lawsuit on October 28, 1979. Assume that you are a lawyer for Plaintiffs. Argue that the court of appeals must hear the appeal. What standard of review should the court of appeals apply?

---

2. Introduction and Overview

As demonstrated in Chapter 3, the Due Process clauses in the United States Constitution require that a person receive reasonable notice and an opportunity for a hearing when the person's life, liberty, or property may be deprived. However, the Due Process clauses do not give a person the right to appeal the decision after the hearing. *Dohany v.* Rodgers, 281 U.S. 362 (1930). Nevertheless, in the federal civil litigation system and in most states, the losing party in the trial court has the statutory right to appeal to an appellate court. And in the federal system and most states, the losing party in the appellate court can petition a supreme court for review, but supreme courts have discretion whether to hear the appeal.

Review by appellate courts serves several purposes in the civil litigation system. First, appellate courts can correct errors made by trial courts that have a significant effect on justice for the parties. Second, appellate courts can ensure that law is applied and interpreted somewhat uniformly. Third, appellate courts play a central role in the ongoing development and refinement of the common law. All of the foregoing reinforce public confidence in the rule of law in civil litigation.

Although parties have the right to appeal adverse judgments in the civil litigation system, and although appellate review serves important functions, most civil judgments are not appealed. Although the statistics vary over time, court system, and type of case, typically 10%–20% of civil cases result in appeals. Of the civil cases that are appealed, only about 20% result in reversal of the trial court's judgment.

There are several preconditions to the right to appeal. First, who can appeal? In general, a party that is adversely affected by the trial court's decision may appeal. For example, defendants found liable are adversely affected, as is a plaintiff that does not get the relief to which it claims to be entitled, whether in the amount or quality of the judgment. *Aetna Casualty & Surety Co. v. Cunningham*, 224 F.2d 478 (5th Cir. 1955).

Second, a party generally must preserve an error for appeal by making a specific, timely objection to the trial court. The purpose of the objection requirement is to give the trial court an opportunity to correct an error before it affects the final decision in the case. Rule 46 provides in relevant part: "A formal objection to a ruling or order is unnecessary. When the ruling or order is requested or made, a party need only state the action that it wants the court to take or objects to, along with the grounds for the request or objection." The preservation requirement has exceptions. For example, under Rule 51(d)(1), a party must properly object to a jury instruction to preserve the right to appeal based on an erroneous instruction. However, Rule 51(d)(2) allows a court to consider an error in jury instructions that was not properly preserved if there is a "plain error in the instruction ... and] the error affects substantial rights."

Third, the party that wishes to initiate an appeal must file a timely notice of appeal with the district court. In general, Federal Rule of Appellate Procedure 4(a) requires that a party file the notice of appeal in a civil case "within 30 days after entry of the judgment or order appealed from." The Supreme Court has held that failure to comply with the time limits for filing notice of appeal deprives the court of appeals of subject matter jurisdiction. *Bowles v. Russell*, 551 U.S. 205 (2007).

The remainder of this chapter explores two issues in more depth.

- Section 3 addresses the question of when an aggrieved party may appeal. In general, a party must wait to appeal until the trial court has entered its final decision in the lawsuit—called the "final judgment rule." However, several exceptions to the final judgment rule allow parties to appeal certain decisions during the suit.

- Section 4 concerns various standards of review that appellate courts employ when reviewing trial court decisions. Section 4 addresses the notion of harmless error as well.

Chapter 12 ends with a professional development reflection exercise in Section 5.

3. The Final Judgment Rule and Its Exceptions

The final judgment rule is codified at 28 U.S.C. § 1291: "The courts of appeals ... shall have jurisdiction of appeals from all final decisions of the district courts of the United States...." Note that Congress created a right to appeal in Section 1291 — "shall have jurisdiction of appeals." But the right to appeal is limited to "final decisions" of district courts. In *Caitlin v. United States,* 324 U.S. 229, 233–34 (1945), the Supreme Court defined "final decisions" in the context of a condemnation proceeding and set out some of the basic policies behind the final judgment rule:

> [Section 1291] limits review to "final decisions" in the District Court. A "final decision" generally is one which ends the litigation on the merits and leaves nothing for the court to do but execute the judgment. Hence, ordinarily in condemnation proceedings, appellate review may be had only upon an order or judgment disposing of the whole case, and adjudicating all rights, including ownership and just compensation, as well as the right to take the property.... The foundation of this policy is not in merely technical conceptions of "finality." It is one against piecemeal litigation. The case is not to be sent up in fragments. Reasons other than conservation of judicial energy sustain the limitation. One is elimination of delays caused by inter-locutory appeals.

Exercise 12-1. Final Judgment Rule Policy

1. In the excerpt above from *Caitlin,* the Court articulates policies in favor of the final judgment rule, which allows parties to appeal any error that they preserved during the course of the case if they wait until the trial court has completed the lawsuit. Articulate additional policies in support of the final judgment rule.

2. What are the costs of the final judgment rule? In other words, what policies support interlocutory appeals, which allow parties to appeal from adverse rulings at the time they occur during the lawsuit, rather than waiting for the final decision in the case?

Trial courts make many decisions throughout the life of a civil case. Most of those decisions do not qualify as "final decisions" and therefore, are not appealable under Section 1291. Examples include denial of a motion to dismiss, denial of a motion for summary judgment, granting a motion to compel discovery, and granting a motion for a new trial. Some trial court decisions and orders do not meet the *Caitlin* definition of "final decision" but are final in some sense. The Supreme Court has addressed these decisions via the "collateral order" doctrine, which is the subject of the next case.

Exercise 12-2. *Mohawk Industries, Inc. v. Carpenter*

1. Identify the three elements of the collateral order doctrine.

2. Identify three procedural mechanisms the Court describes, other than the collateral order doctrine, that could facilitate effective appellate review of trial court decisions concerning the applicability or waiver of the attorney-client privilege.

3. What policies does the Court articulate in support of limiting the scope of the collateral order doctrine?

Mohawk Industries, Inc. v. Carpenter

558 U.S. 100 (2009)

Justice Sotomayor delivered the opinion of the Court.

Section 1291 of the Judicial Code confers on federal courts of appeals jurisdiction to review "final decisions of the district courts." Although "final decisions" typically are ones that trigger the entry of judgment, they also include a small set of prejudgment orders that are "collateral to" the merits of an action and "too important" to be denied immediate review. *Cohen v. Beneficial Industrial Loan Corp.*, 337 U.S. 541, 546 (1949). In this case, petitioner Mohawk Industries, Inc., attempted to bring a collateral order appeal after the District Court ordered it to disclose certain confidential materials on the ground that Mohawk had waived the attorney-client privilege. The Court of Appeals dismissed the appeal for want of jurisdiction.

The question before us is whether disclosure orders adverse to the attorney-client privilege qualify for immediate appeal under the collateral order doctrine. Agreeing with the Court of Appeals, we hold that they do not. Postjudgment appeals, together with other review mechanisms, suffice to protect the rights of litigants and preserve the vitality of the attorney-client privilege.

I

In 2007, respondent Carpenter, a former shift supervisor at a Mohawk manufacturing facility, filed suit in the United States District Court for the Northern District of Georgia, alleging that Mohawk had terminated him in violation of 42 U.S.C. § 1985(2) and various Georgia laws. According to Carpenter's complaint, his termination came after he informed a member of Mohawk's human resources department in an e-mail that the company was employing undocumented immigrants. At the time, unbeknownst to Carpenter, Mohawk stood accused in a pending class-action lawsuit of conspiring to drive down the wages of its legal employees by knowingly hiring undocumented workers in violation of federal and state racketeering laws. *See Williams v. Mohawk Indus., Inc.* Company officials directed Carpenter to meet with the company's retained counsel in the Williams case, and counsel allegedly pressured Carpenter to recant his statements. When he refused, Carpenter alleges, Mohawk fired him under false pretenses.

After learning of Carpenter's complaint, the plaintiffs in the Williams case sought an evidentiary hearing to explore Carpenter's allegations. In its response to their motion, Mohawk described Carpenter's accusations as "pure fantasy" and recounted the "true facts" of Carpenter's dismissal. According to Mohawk, Carpenter himself had "engaged in blatant and illegal misconduct" by attempting to have Mohawk hire an undocumented worker. The company "commenced an immediate investigation," during which retained counsel interviewed Carpenter. Because Carpenter's "efforts to cause Mohawk to circumvent federal immigration law" "blatantly violated Mohawk policy," the company terminated him.

As these events were unfolding in the Williams case, discovery was underway in Carpenter's case. Carpenter filed a motion to compel Mohawk to produce information concerning his meeting with retained counsel and the company's termination decision. Mohawk maintained that the requested information was protected by the attorney-client privilege.

The District Court agreed that the privilege applied to the requested information, but it granted Carpenter's motion to compel disclosure after concluding that Mohawk had implicitly waived the privilege through its representations in the Williams case. The court declined to certify its order for interlocutory appeal under 28 U.S.C. § 1292(b). But, recognizing "the seriousness of its [waiver] finding," it stayed its ruling to allow Mohawk to explore other potential "avenues to appeal, such as a petition for mandamus or appealing this Order under the collateral order doctrine."

Mohawk filed a notice of appeal and a petition for a writ of mandamus to the Eleventh Circuit. The Court of Appeals dismissed the appeal for lack of jurisdiction under 28 U.S.C. § 1291, holding that the District Court's ruling did not qualify as an immediately appealable collateral order within the meaning of *Cohen*. "Under *Cohen*," the Court of Appeals explained, "an order is appealable if it (1) conclusively determines the disputed question; (2) resolves an important issue completely separate from the merits of the action; and (3) is effectively unreviewable on appeal from a final judgment." According to the court, the District Court's waiver ruling satisfied the first two of these requirements but not the third, because "a discovery order that implicates the attorney-client privilege" can be adequately reviewed "on appeal from a final judgment." The Court of Appeals also rejected Mohawk's mandamus petition, finding no "clear usurpation of power or abuse of discretion" by the District Court. We granted certiorari to resolve a conflict among the Circuits concerning the availability of collateral appeals in the attorney-client privilege context.

II

A

By statute, Courts of Appeals "have jurisdiction of appeals from all final decisions of the district courts of the United States ... except where a direct review may be had in the Supreme Court." 28 U.S.C. § 1291. A "final decisio[n]" is typically one "by which a district court disassociates itself from a case." *Swint v. Chambers County Comm'n*, 514 U.S. 35, 42 (1995). This Court, however, "has long given" § 1291 a "practical rather than a technical construction." *Cohen*. As we held in *Cohen*, the statute encompasses not only judgments that "terminate an action," but also a "small class" of collateral rulings that, although they do not end the litigation, are appropriately deemed "final." *Id.*, at 545–46. "That small category includes only decisions that are conclusive, that resolve important questions separate from the merits, and that are effectively unreviewable on appeal from the final judgment in the underlying action." *Swint*, 514 U.S. at 42.

In applying *Cohen*'s collateral order doctrine, we have stressed that it must never be allowed to swallow the general rule that a party is entitled to a single appeal, to be deferred until final judgment has been entered. Our admonition reflects a healthy respect for the virtues of the final-judgment rule. Permitting piecemeal, prejudgment appeals, we have recognized, undermines efficient judicial administration and encroaches upon the prerogatives of district court judges, who play a "special role" in managing ongoing litigation. *Richardson-Merrell Inc. v. Koller*, 472 U.S. 424, 436 (1985) ("[T]he district judge can better exercise [his or her] responsibility [to police the prejudgment tactics of litigants] if the appellate courts do not repeatedly intervene to second-guess prejudgment rulings").

The justification for immediate appeal must therefore be sufficiently strong to overcome the usual benefits of deferring appeal until litigation concludes. This requirement finds expression in two of the three traditional *Cohen* conditions. The second condition insists upon important questions separate from the merits. More significantly, the third *Cohen* question, whether a right is adequately vindicable or effectively reviewable, simply cannot be answered without a judgment about the value of the interests that would be lost through rigorous application of a final judgment requirement. That a ruling may burden litigants in ways that are only imperfectly reparable by appellate reversal of a final district court judgment has never sufficed. Instead, the decisive consideration is whether delaying review until the entry of final judgment would imperil a substantial public interest or "some particular value of a high order." *Will v. Hallock*, 546 U.S. 345, 352–53 (2006).

In making this determination, we do not engage in an "individualized jurisdictional inquiry." *Coopers & Lybrand v. Livesay*, 437 U.S. 463, 473 (1978). Rather, our focus is on the entire category to which a claim belongs. As long as the class of claims, taken as a whole, can be adequately vindicated by other means, the chance that the litigation at hand might be speeded, or a particular injustice averted, does not provide a basis for jurisdiction under § 1291.

B

In the present case, the Court of Appeals concluded that the District Court's privilege-waiver order satisfied the first two conditions of the collateral order doctrine — conclusiveness and separateness — but not the third — effective unreviewability. Because we agree with the Court of Appeals that collateral order appeals are not necessary to ensure effective review of orders adverse to the attorney-client privilege, we do not decide whether the other Cohen requirements are met.

Mohawk does not dispute that we have generally denied review of pretrial discovery orders. Mohawk contends, however, that rulings implicating the attorney-client privilege differ in kind from run-of-the-mill discovery orders because of the important institutional interests at stake. According to Mohawk, the right to maintain attorney-client confidences — the sine qua non of a meaningful attorney-client relationship — is "irreparably destroyed absent immediate appeal" of adverse privilege rulings.

We readily acknowledge the importance of the attorney-client privilege....

The crucial question, however, is not whether an interest is important in the abstract; it is whether deferring review until final judgment so imperils the interest as to justify the cost of allowing immediate appeal of the entire class of relevant orders. We routinely require litigants to wait until after final judgment to vindicate valuable rights, including rights central to our adversarial system. See, e.g., *Richardson-Merrell*, 472 U.S., at 426 (holding an order disqualifying counsel in a civil case did not qualify for immediate appeal under the collateral order doctrine....).

We reach a similar conclusion here. In our estimation, postjudgment appeals generally suffice to protect the rights of litigants and assure the vitality of the attorney-client privilege. Appellate courts can remedy the improper disclosure of privileged material in the same way they remedy a host of other erroneous evidentiary rulings: by vacating an adverse judgment and remanding for a new trial in which the protected material and its fruits are excluded from evidence.

* * *

In deciding how freely to speak, clients and counsel are unlikely to focus on the remote prospect of an erroneous disclosure order, let alone on the timing of a possible appeal.... Most district court rulings on these matters involve the routine application of settled legal principles. They are unlikely to be reversed on appeal, particularly when they rest on factual determinations for which appellate deference is the norm. *Reise v. Board of Regents*, 957 F. 2d 293, 295 (CA7 1992) (noting that "almost all interlocutory appeals from discovery orders would end in affirmance" because "the district court possesses discretion, and review is deferential")....

Moreover, were attorneys and clients to reflect upon their appellate options, they would find that litigants confronted with a particularly injurious or novel privilege ruling have several potential avenues of review apart from collateral order appeal. First, a party may ask the district court to certify, and the court of appeals to accept, an interlocutory appeal pursuant to 28 U.S.C. § 1292(b). The preconditions for § 1292(b) review—"a controlling question of law," the prompt resolution of which "may materially advance the ultimate termination of the litigation"—are most likely to be satisfied when a privilege ruling involves a new legal question or is of special consequence, and district courts should not hesitate to certify an interlocutory appeal in such cases. Second, in extraordinary circumstances—i.e., when a disclosure order amounts to a judicial usurpation of power or a clear abuse of discretion, or otherwise works a manifest injustice—a party may petition the court of appeals for a writ of mandamus. While these discretionary review mechanisms do not provide relief in every case, they serve as useful safety valves for promptly correcting serious errors.

Another long-recognized option is for a party to defy a disclosure order and incur court-imposed sanctions. District courts have a range of sanctions from which to choose, including "directing that the matters embraced in the order or other designated facts be taken as established for purposes of the action," "prohibiting the disobedient party from supporting or opposing designated claims or defenses," or "striking pleadings in whole or in part." Fed. Rule Civ. Proc. 37(b)(2)(i)–(iii). Such sanctions allow a party to obtain postjudgment review without having to reveal its privileged information. Alternatively, when the circumstances warrant it, a district court may hold a noncomplying party in contempt. The party can then appeal directly from that ruling, at least when the contempt citation can be characterized as a criminal punishment.

* * *

In short, the limited benefits of applying "the blunt, categorical instrument of § 1291 collateral order appeal" to privilege-related disclosure orders simply cannot justify the likely institutional costs. *Digital Equipment Corp. v. Desktop Direct, Inc.*, 571 U.S. 863, 883 (1994). Permitting parties to undertake successive, piecemeal appeals of all adverse attorney-client rulings would unduly delay the resolution of district court litigation and needlessly burden the Courts of Appeals....

C

In concluding that sufficiently effective review of adverse attorney-client privilege rulings can be had without resort to the *Cohen* doctrine, we reiterate that the class of collaterally appealable orders must remain narrow and selective in its membership. This admonition has acquired special force in recent years with the enactment of legislation designating rulemaking, not expansion by court decision, as the preferred means for determining whether and when prejudgment orders should be immediately appealable. Specifically, Congress in 1990 amended the Rules Enabling Act, 28 U.S.C. § 2071 et seq., to authorize this Court to adopt rules "defin[ing] when a ruling of a district court is final for the purposes of appeal under section 1291." § 2072(c). Shortly thereafter, and along similar lines, Congress empowered this Court to "prescribe rules, in accordance with [§ 2072], to provide for an appeal of an interlocutory decision to the courts of appeals that is not otherwise provided for under [§ 1292]." § 1292(e)....

Indeed, the rulemaking process has important virtues. It draws on the collective experience of bench and bar, and it facilitates the adoption of measured, practical solutions. We expect that the combination of standard post-judgment appeals, § 1292(b) appeals, mandamus, and contempt appeals will continue to provide adequate protection to litigants ordered to disclose materials purportedly subject to the attorney-client privilege. Any further avenue for immediate appeal of such rulings should be furnished, if at all, through rulemaking, with the opportunity for full airing it provides.

In sum, we conclude that the collateral order doctrine does not extend to disclosure orders adverse to the attorney-client privilege. Effective appellate review can be had by other means. Accordingly, we affirm the judgment of the Court of Appeals for the Eleventh Circuit.

Notes on Collateral Order Doctrine and the Final Judgment Rule

1. Collateral Order Doctrine.

The Supreme Court created the collateral order doctrine in *Cohen v. Beneficial Industrial Loan Co.*, 337 U.S. 451 (1949). In *Cohen*, a small stockholder in a corporation brought a shareholder's derivative suit against the board of directors, alleging fraud and mismanagement that enriched the directors at the expense of the corporation. Defendants moved for an order to require plaintiffs to post security for costs and attorneys' fees under a New Jersey state law that entitled defendants to security for costs and fees when the suit was brought by a small percentage of the shareholders. The district court held that the New Jersey law did not apply to this case and did not require security. Before the case was decided on the merits, the defendants appealed the ruling to not require security. The Supreme Court held that the court of appeals had jurisdiction over the appeal under 28 U.S.C. § 1291 of the trial court's final, collateral order regarding security for costs and fees. "This decision appears to fall in that small class of cases which finally determine claims of right separable from, and collateral to, rights asserted in the action, too important to be denied review and too independent of the cause itself to require that appellate consideration be deferred until the whole case is adjudicated." *Cohen*, 377 U.S. at 546.

After *Cohen*, the Court decided a number of collateral order cases: *Moses H. Cone Memorial Hosp. v. Mercury Construction Corp.*, 460 U.S. 1 (1983) (order staying a federal court action pending resolution of a parallel state case was immediately appealable as a collateral order); *Richardson-Merrel, Inc. v. Koller*, 472 U.S. 424 (1985) (orders granting or denying motions to disqualify counsel are not immediately appealable as collateral orders); *Lauro Lines s.r.l. v. Chasser*, 490 U.S. 495 (1989) (order denying motion to dismiss based on forum selection clause is not appealable under the collateral order doctrine); *Puerto Rico Aqueduct & Sewer Auth. v. Metcalf & Eddy, Inc.*, 506 U.S. 139 (1993) (denial of motion to dismiss based on state sovereign immunity is immediately appealable as a collateral order); *Swint v. Chambers Cnty Comm'n*, 514 U.S. 35 (1995) (denial of summary judgment motion not appealable under the collateral order doctrine); *Cunningham v. Hamilton Cnty.*, 527 U.S. 198 (1999) (order imposing costs and attorneys fees due to discovery violations is not appealable under the collateral order doctrine); *Sell v. United States*, 539 U.S. 166 (2003) (order requiring defendant involuntarily to receive medication in order to render defendant competent to stand trial was immediately appealable as a collateral order).

2. Final Judgment Rule.

Hall v. Hall, 138 S. Ct. 1118 (2018). The trial court consolidated two cases (the "individual" case and the "trust" case) under Fed. R. Civ. Proc. 42(a) and held a single trial of the consolidated cases. After trial, the court entered judgment on the individual case and granted a new trial on the trust case. The losing party appealed the individual case but the court of appeals dismissed the appeal on the grounds that the judgment was not final because the trust case was still pending. The Court reversed, holding that the judgment on the individual cases was final under 28 U.S.C. 1291.

Exceptions to the Final Judgment Rule

There are several codified exceptions to the final judgment rule. Five exceptions are addressed below:

- 28 U.S.C. § 1292(a)(1) — injunctions
- 28 U.S.C. § 1292(b) — certified interlocutory orders
- Rule 23(f) — class action certification
- Rule 54(b) — multi-claim, multi-party cases
- 28 U.S.C. § 1651 — writs of mandamus and prohibition.

a. 28 U.S.C. § 1292(a)(1) — Injunctions

Injunctive relief, in which the court orders a party to do or not do something, can be part of the final relief in the lawsuit. For example, the court could order a party to go through with the sale of real property, to rehire an employee who was fired, to refrain from logging a tract of timber, or to not destroy a historic building. An aggrieved party has the right to appeal the grant or denial of the injunction under 28 U.S.C. § 1291, the final judgment rule.

Rule 65 sets out procedures for trial courts to follow when deciding whether to issue temporary restraining orders and preliminary injunctions during the lawsuit. A trial court can issue a temporary restraining order ("TRO") without prior notice or a hearing for the party to be restrained, but TROs normally cannot exceed 14 days. Preliminary injunctions, which require notice and an opportunity for a hearing, can extend from the time of the hearing through the final disposition of the lawsuit.

Aggrieved parties have the right to appeal interlocutory orders granting, continuing, modifying, refusing or dissolving injunctions under 28 U.S.C. § 1292(a)(1). Consequently, parties can immediately appeal preliminary injunction orders. The primary policy supporting Section 1292(a)(1) is that the grant or denial of a preliminary injunction can cause significant, immediate harm to a party. On the other hand, temporary restraining orders generally are not appealable due to their short duration. *See Levesque v. State of Maine*, 587 F.2d 78 (1st Cir. 1978) (although TROs are generally not appealable, the trial court's order, denying a former employee's reinstatement pending a final hearing more than 30 days later, was appealable as of right under Section 1292(a)(1)).

b. 28 U.S.C. § 1292(b) — Certified Interlocutory Orders

Section 1292(b) permits a district court to certify interlocutory orders for immediate appeal if a four-part test is met. Read Section 1292(b). The test requires that the district court certify in writing that the order (1) "involves a controlling question," (2) "of law," (3) "as to which there is substantial ground for difference of opinion," and (4) "that an immediate appeal from the order may materially advance the termination of the litigation." The application for an immediate appeal must be made within 10 days of the entry of the order. If all of these prerequisites are met, the court of appeals has discretion to permit or deny the appeal. The following case applies Section 1292(b).

In re City of Memphis

293 F.3d 345 (6th Cir. 2002)

Plaintiffs brought this action ... challenging the use of minority preferences by the City in awarding construction contracts under the City's Minority & Women Business Enterprise Procurement Program (MWBE program). Plaintiffs alleged that the MWBE program violated the Fourteenth Amendment.

The City adopted the MWBE program in 1996 as a remedy for past discrimination and to prevent future discrimination. At the time of enactment, the City relied on a disparity study covering the period from 1988 to 1992. Based on that study, the City concluded that it was an active and passive participant in discrimination.

In response to this litigation, the City proposed to commission a new study that would cover the period from 1993 to 1998. The City wishes to use this postenactment study as evidence to demonstrate a compelling governmental interest. The district court ruled that the City could not introduce the postenactment study as evidence of a compelling governmental interest.

[The district court certified for appeal under section 1292(b) the question of whether the postenactment study should be allowed as evidence. Assuming that City made an application for appeal within 10 days of the entry of the trial court's order, should the court of appeals hear the merits of the appeal?]

* * *

This court in its discretion may permit an appeal to be taken from an order certified for interlocutory appeal if (1) the order involves a controlling question of law, (2) a substantial ground for difference of opinion exists regarding the correctness of the decision, and (3) an immediate appeal may materially advance the ultimate termination of the litigation. Review under § 1292(b) is granted sparingly and only in exceptional cases.

The City argues that a substantial ground for difference of opinion exists. Some circuits permit postenactment evidence to supplement preenactment evidence. *See Eng'g Contractors Ass'n v. Metro. Dade County,* 122 F.3d 895, 911–12 (11th Cir.1997). The district court relied on these cases to find that there is substantial disagreement as to the proper role played by postenactment evidence. This issue, however, appears to have been resolved in this circuit.

In *Associated General Contractors v. Drabik,* 214 F.3d 730 (6th Cir.2000) ... [the court] held that a governmental entity must have preenactment evidence sufficient to justify a racially conscious statute. It also indicates that this circuit would not favor using postenactment evidence to make that showing.

Even if we concluded that there is a substantial difference of opinion, the issue presented in this case is not a controlling legal issue. A legal issue is controlling if it could materially affect the outcome of the case. A legal question of the type envisioned in § 1292(b), however, generally does not include matters within the discretion of the trial court. A ruling on the admissibility of evidence is reviewed for abuse of discretion....

Finally, resolution of the City's challenge to the district court's evidentiary ruling may not materially advance the ultimate termination of the litigation. When litigation will be conducted in substantially the same manner regardless of [the court's] decision, the appeal cannot be said to materially advance the ultimate termination of the litigation. Under *Drabik,* the City must present preenactment evidence to show a compelling state interest. The City has preenactment evidence. Thus, the City will pursue its defense in substantially the same manner. If the City prevails with its preenactment evidence, the exclusion of postenactment evidence will be moot. If it does not prevail, the City can then appeal on the evidentiary ruling and any other issues that may arise below. The application for permission to appeal, therefore, is DENIED.

---

c. Rule 23(f) — Class Action Certification

In *Coopers & Lybrand v. Livesay,* 437 U.S. 463 (1978), the trial court decertified a class action under Rule 23. Plaintiffs appealed under 28 U.S.C. § 1291, arguing that the decertification order was likely the "death knell" of the litigation because the potential recovery for individual plaintiffs was too small to provide a sufficient incentive for individual litigation. The Court held that the trial court's decertification decision was not immediately appealable as a final judgment under Section 1291.

Recognizing the critical importance of the trial court's orders granting or denying class certification, in 1998 Rule 23(f) was added, effectively overruling the holding in *Coopers & Lybrand*. Rule 23(f) states, in part: "A court of appeals may permit an appeal from an order granting or denying class-action certification under this rule if a petition for permission to appeal is filed with the circuit clerk within 14 days after the order is entered."

The Supreme Court has not yet decided a Rule 23(f) case. Circuit courts have concluded that courts of appeals have broad discretion when deciding whether to permit an appeal under Rule 23(f) and have identified three categories of certification decisions for which immediate appeal would be appropriate.

> First, an appeal ordinarily should be permitted when a denial of class status effectively ends the case (because, say, the named plaintiff's claim is not of a sufficient magnitude to warrant the costs of stand-alone litigation). Second, an appeal ordinarily should be permitted when the grant of class status raises the stakes of the litigation so substantially that the defendant likely will feel irresistible pressure to settle. Third, an appeal ordinarily should be permitted when it will lead to clarification of a fundamental issue of law.

Waste Management Holdings, Inc. v. Mowbray, 208 F. 3d 288, 293 (1st Cir. 2000).

Exercise 12-3. Compare and Contrast Rule 23(f) and 28 U.S.C. § 1292(b)

1. Identify two similarities between Rule 23(f) and 28 U.S.C. § 1292(b).

2. Identify two significant differences between Rule 23(f) and 28 U.S.C. § 1292(b).

Note on Class Action Certification and the Final Judgment Rule

In *Microsoft Corporation v. Backer*, 137 S. Ct. 1702 (2017), the Court addressed an appeal of a district court's order denying class certification. Plaintiffs, Owners of Xbox 360 video game consoles, sued Microsoft, alleging that the consoles were defective. Plaintiffs sought certification of the suit as a class action. The district court denied class certification. Plaintiffs sought to appeal the order denying class certification under Rule 23(f), but the 9th Circuit declined to hear the appeal. Plaintiff's then stipulated to voluntary dismissal of their claims with prejudice and filed an appeal of the order denying class certification under the final judgment rule, 28 U.S,C. § 1291. The 9th Circuit concluded that it had jurisdiction to hear the appeal under 28 U.S,C. § 1291 and remanded the case to the district court for further consideration of the class certification question. The Court reversed, holding that the 9th Circuit lacked jurisdiction under 28 U.S,C. § 1291. The Court reasoned that to allow Plaintiffs to appeal the denial of class certification under 28 U.S,C. § 1291 would undermine the policies that underlie the final judgment rule and undercut the discretionary nature of appeals under Rule 23(f).

d. Rule 54(b) — Multiple-Claim, Multiple-Party Cases

As shown in Chapter 8, the Federal Rules of Civil Procedure allow and often encourage plaintiffs to bring in one lawsuit multiple claims against a party or claims against multiple parties. Pre-trial motions to dismiss and motions for summary judgment can decide some of the claims. For example, if the plaintiff brings discrimination claims against three defendants, the court may grant a motion to dismiss as to one of the defendants, but not as to the other two defendants. Likewise, if the plaintiff brings claims for breach of contract and negligence against a defendant, the court may grant summary judgment for the plaintiff on the breach of contract claim but not on the negligence claim. In both situations, some claims have been decided and others are going forward through the civil litigation process. The court has not entered the final judgment in either lawsuit, so the parties who lost the motions do not have a right to appeal under 28 U.S.C. § 1291. Rule 54(b) provides a means to appeal when at least one, but not all, claims in the case have been finally decided. Read Rule 54(b).

Exercise 12-4. *Curtiss-Wright Corp. v. General Electric Co.*

Rule 54(b) applies to multiple claim or multiple party cases.

1. If the trial court wants to certify some of the claims for immediate appeal, what are the elements of that certification?

2. Describe the two considerations that go into the "no just reason to delay" element?

3. On what basis does the Supreme Court conclude that the court of appeals erred in dismissing the appeal in *Curtiss-Wright*?

4. What policies support immediate appeals of some claims under Rule 54(b)?

Curtiss-Wright Corp. v. General Electric Co.
446 U.S. 1 (1980)

Federal Rule of Civil Procedure 54(b) allows a district court dealing with multiple claims or multiple parties to direct the entry of final judgment as to fewer than all of the claims or parties; to do so, the court must make an express determination that there is no just reason for delay....

I

From 1968 to 1972, respondent General Electric Co. entered into a series of 21 contracts with petitioner Curtiss-Wright Corp. for the manufacture of components designed for use in nuclear powered naval vessels. These contracts had a total value of $215 million.

In 1976, Curtiss-Wright brought a diversity action in the United States District Court for the District of New Jersey, seeking damages and reformation with regard to the 21 contracts. The complaint asserted claims based on alleged fraud, misrepresentation, and breach of contract by General Electric. It also sought $19 million from General Electric on the outstanding balance due on the contracts already performed.

General Electric counterclaimed for $1.9 million in costs allegedly incurred as the result of "extraordinary efforts" provided to Curtiss-Wright during performance of the contracts which enabled Curtiss-Wright to avoid a contract default. General Electric also sought, by way of counterclaim, to recover $52 million by which Curtiss-Wright was allegedly unjustly enriched as a result of these "extraordinary efforts."

The facts underlying most of these claims and counterclaims are in dispute. As to Curtiss-Wright's claims for the $19 million balance due, however, the sole dispute concerns the application of a release clause contained in each of the 21 agreements, which states that "Seller ... agree[s] as a condition precedent to final payment, that the Buyer and the Government ... are released from all liabilities, obligations and claims arising under or by virtue of this order."

When Curtiss-Wright moved for summary judgment on the balance due, General Electric contended that, so long as Curtiss-Wright's other claims remained pending, this provision constituted a bar to recovery of the undisputed balance.

The District Court rejected this contention and granted summary judgment for Curtiss-Wright on this otherwise undisputed claim. The court also ruled that Curtiss-Wright was entitled to prejudgment interest at the New York statutory rate of 6 per annum.

* * *

The court expressly directed entry of final judgment for Curtiss-Wright, and made the determination that there was "no just reason for delay" pursuant to Rule 54(b). The District Court also provided a written statement of reasons supporting its decision to certify the judgment as final. The essential inquiry was stated to be "whether, after balancing the competing factors, finality of judgment should be ordered to advance the interests of sound judicial administration and justice to the litigants."

The District Court then went on to identify the relevant factors in the case before it. It found that certification would not result in unnecessary appellate review; that the claims finally adjudicated were separate, distinct, and independent of any of the other claims or counterclaims involved; that review of these adjudicated claims would not be mooted by any future developments in the case; and that the nature of the claims was such that no appellate court would have to decide the same issues more than once, even if there were subsequent appeals.

Turning to considerations of justice to the litigants, the District Court found that Curtiss-Wright would suffer severe daily financial loss from nonpayment of the $19 million judgment, because current interest rates were higher than the statutory prejudgment rate, a situation compounded by the large amount of money involved. The court observed that the complex nature of the remaining claims could, without certification, mean a delay that "would span many months, if not years."

* * *

A divided panel of the United States Court of Appeals for the Third Circuit held that the case was controlled by its decision in *Allis-Chalmers Corp. v. Philadelphia Electric Co.,* 521 F.2d 360 (1975), where the court had stated: "In the absence of unusual or harsh circumstances, we believe that the presence of a counterclaim, which could result in a set-off against any amounts due and owing to the plaintiff, weighs heavily against the grant of 54(b) certification." In *Allis-Chalmers,* the court defined unusual or harsh circumstances as those factors involving considerations of solvency, economic duress, etc.

The Court of Appeals concluded that the District Court had abused its discretion by granting Rule 54(b) certification in this situation, and dismissed the case for want of an appealable order....

II

Nearly a quarter of a century ago, in *Sears, Roebuck & Co. v. Mackey,* 351 U. S. 427 (1956), this Court outlined the steps to be followed in making determinations under Rule 54(b). A district court must first determine that it is dealing with a "final judgment." It must be a "judgment" in the sense that it is a decision upon a cognizable claim for relief, and it must be "final" in the sense that it is an ultimate disposition of an individual claim entered in the course of a multiple claims action.

Once having found finality, the district court must go on to determine whether there is any just reason for delay. Not all final judgments on individual claims should be immediately appealable, even if they are in some sense separate from the remaining unresolved claims. The function of the district court under the Rule is to act as a dispatcher. It is left to the sound judicial discretion of the district court to determine the "appropriate time" when each final decision in a multiple claims action is ready for appeal. This discretion is to be exercised in the interest of sound judicial administration.

Thus, in deciding whether there are no just reasons to delay the appeal of individual final judgments in a setting such as this, a district court must take into account judicial administrative interests, as well as the equities involved. Consideration of the former is necessary to assure that application of the Rule effectively preserves the historic federal policy against piecemeal appeals....

*   *   *

What the Court of Appeals found objectionable about the District Judge's exercise of discretion was the assessment of the equities involved. The Court of Appeals concluded that the possibility of a setoff required that the *status quo* be maintained unless petitioner could show harsh or unusual circumstances; it held that such a showing had not been made in the District Court.

This holding reflects a misinterpretation of the standard of review for Rule 54(b) certifications and a misperception of the appellate function in such cases.

*   *   *

In *Sears,* the Court stated that the decision to certify was, with good reason, left to the sound judicial discretion of the district court. The Court indicated that the standard against which a district court's exercise of discretion is to be judged is the interest of sound judicial administration. Admittedly this presents issues not always easily resolved, but the proper role of the court of appeals is not to reweigh the equities or reassess the facts, but to make sure that the conclusions derived from those weighings and assessments are juridically sound and supported by the record.

There are thus two aspects to the proper function of a reviewing court in Rule 54(b) cases. The court of appeals must, of course, scrutinize the district court's evaluation of such factors as the interrelationship of the claims so as to prevent piecemeal appeals in cases which should be reviewed only as single units. But once such juridical concerns have been met, the discretionary judgment of the district court should be given substantial deference, for that court is "the one most likely to be familiar with the case and with any justifiable reasons for delay." The reviewing court should disturb the trial court's assessment of the equities only if it can say that the judge's conclusion was clearly unreasonable.

We are satisfied, however, that, on the record here, the District Court's assessment of the equities was reasonable.

One of the equities which the District Judge considered was the difference between the statutory and market rates of interest....

The difference between the prejudgment and market interest rates was not the only factor considered by the District Court. The court also noted that the debts in issue were liquidated and large, and that absent Rule 54(b) certification they would not be paid for "many months, if not years," because the rest of the litigation could be expected to continue for that period of time. The District Judge had noted earlier in his opinion on the merits of the release clause issue that respondent General Electric contested neither the amount of the debt nor the fact that it must eventually be paid. The only contest was over the effect of the release clause on the timing of the payment, an isolated and strictly legal issue on which summary judgment had been entered against respondent.

The question before the District Court thus came down to which of the parties should get the benefit of the difference between the prejudgment and market rates of interest on debts admittedly owing and adjudged to be due while unrelated claims were litigated. The central factor weighing in favor of General Electric was that its pending counterclaims created the possibility of a setoff against the amount it owed petitioner. This possibility was surely not an insignificant factor, especially since the counterclaims had survived a motion to dismiss for failure to state a claim. But the District Court took this into account when it determined that both litigants appeared to be in financially sound condition, and that Curtiss-Wright would be able to satisfy a judgment on the counterclaims should any be entered.

* * *

The District Court having found no other reason justifying delay, we conclude that it did not abuse its discretion in granting petitioner's motion for certification under Rule 54(b). Accordingly, the judgment of the Court of Appeals is vacated, and the case is remanded for proceedings consistent with this opinion.

---

e. 28 U.S.C. § 1651 — Writs of Mandamus and Prohibition

The All Writs Act, 28 U.S.C. § 1651(a), states, "The Supreme Court and all courts established by Act of Congress may issue all writs necessary or appropriate in aid of their respective jurisdictions and agreeable to the usages and principles of law." This law grants appellate courts power to issue writs of mandamus or writs of prohibition. A writ of mandamus is an order to a governmental officer, including a district court judge, to take certain action. A writ of prohibition is an order not to take certain action.

For example, In *World-Wide Volkswagen v. Woodson*, 444 U.S. (1980), plaintiffs brought a product liability suit in state court in Oklahoma and two of the defendants contested personal jurisdiction, asserting that Oklahoma's exercise of jurisdiction would violate the Due Process Clause of the Fourteenth Amendment. After the Oklahoma trial court denied defendants' jurisdictional challenge, defendants sought a writ of prohibition from the Oklahoma Supreme Court to restrain the trial court from exercising jurisdiction. The Oklahoma Supreme Court denied the writ but the United States Supreme Court granted certiorari and determined that Oklahoma courts lacked personal jurisdiction over two of the defendants.

In *Schlagenhauf v. Holder*, 379 U.S. 104 (1964), which appeared in Chapter 9, the trial court ordered, under Rule 35, defendant bus driver to undergo nine physical and mental examinations. The defendant sought a writ of mandamus against the trial judge, but the court of appeals denied mandamus. The Supreme Court held that mandamus was proper to allow interlocutory review when there is "usurpation of judicial power" or a clear abuse of discretion.

Exercise 12-5. *Kerr v. United States District Court*

1. What test does the Court articulate to guide appellate courts in deciding whether to review trial court orders via a writ of mandamus?

2. What policies support a limited use of mandamus to review trial court orders during the litigation?

Kerr v. United States District Court
426 U.S. 394 (1976)

Seven prisoners in the custody of the Department of Corrections of the State of California filed a class action in the United States District Court for the Northern District of California.... Plaintiffs' complaint alleges substantial constitutional violations in the manner in which the California Adult Authority carries out its function of determining the length and conditions of punishment for convicted criminal offenders.

In the course of discovery, plaintiffs submitted requests for the production of a number of documents pursuant to Fed.Rule Civ.Proc. 34, including the personnel files of all members and employees of the Adult Authority, all Adult Authority documents relating to its past, present, or future operation, and all memoranda written by the Chairman of the Adult Authority within the preceding five years....

Plaintiffs requested the opportunity to examine the files of every twentieth inmate at each California Department of Corrections institution....

When presented with the request for the Adult Authority files, petitioners objected, claiming that the files were irrelevant, confidential, and privileged, and suggesting that they should not be required to turn over the file to plaintiffs without prior *in camera* review by the District Court to evaluate the claims of privilege. Plaintiffs moved, pursuant to Fed.Rule Civ.Proc. 37, for an order compelling discovery. The District Court ... ordered the production of the documents. Seeking to limit distribution of the personnel files of the Adult Authority members and their employees, however, the District Court issued a protective order limiting the number of people associated with the plaintiffs who could examine those documents....

Dissatisfied with the District Court's ruling, petitioners filed a petition for a writ of mandamus under 28 U.S.C. § 1651(a), requesting the Court of Appeals for the Ninth Circuit to vacate the District Court's order granting plaintiffs' motion to compel discovery. The Court of Appeals denied the petition....

* * *

The remedy of mandamus is a drastic one, to be invoked only in extraordinary situations.... [T]he writ has traditionally been used in the federal courts only to confine an inferior court to a lawful exercise of its prescribed jurisdiction or to compel it to exercise its authority when it is its duty to do so. And, while we have not limited the use of mandamus by an unduly narrow and technical understanding of what constitutes a matter of "jurisdiction," the fact still remains that only exceptional circumstances amounting to a judicial usurpation of power will justify the invocation of this extraordinary remedy.

Our treatment of mandamus within the federal court system as an extraordinary remedy is not without good reason. As we have recognized before, mandamus actions such as the one involved in the instant case "have the unfortunate consequence of making the [district court] judge a litigant, obliged to obtain personal counsel or to leave his defense to one of the litigants appearing before him" in the underlying case. *Bankers Life and Cas. Co. v. Holland*, 346 U.S. 379, 384–85 (1953). More importantly, particularly in an era of excessively crowded lower court dockets, it is in the interest of the fair and prompt administration of justice to discourage piecemeal litigation. It has been Congress' determination since the Judiciary Act of 1789 that, as a general rule, appellate review should be postponed until after final judgment has been rendered by the trial court. A judicial readiness to issue the writ of mandamus in anything less than an extraordinary situation would run the real risk of defeating the very policies sought to be furthered by that judgment of Congress.

As a means of implementing the rule that the writ will issue only in extraordinary circumstances, we have set forth various conditions for its issuance. Among these are that the party seeking issuance of the writ have no other adequate means to attain the relief he desires, and that he satisfy the burden of showing that his right to issuance of the writ is clear and indisputable....

When looked at in the framework of these factors, it would appear that the actions of the Court of Appeals in this case should be affirmed. What petitioners are seeking here is not a declaration that the documents in question are absolutely privileged and that plaintiffs can never have access to any of them. On the contrary, petitioners request only that "production of the confidential documents not be compelled without a prior informed determination by the district court that plaintiffs' need for them in the action below outweighs their confidentiality." Petitioners ask in essence only that the District Court review the challenged documents *in camera* before passing on whether each one individually should or should not be disclosed. But the Court of Appeals' opinion dealing with the Adult Authority files did not foreclose the possible necessity of such *in camera* review.

Exercise 12-6. *Liberty Mutual Insurance Co. v. Wetzel*

In *Liberty Mutual*, the Court concludes that the court of appeals lacked jurisdiction over the trial court's summary judgment order. *Liberty Mutual* provides a good review of the final judgment rule and its exceptions.

1. Explain why the trial court's order was not appealable under each of the following:

   28 U.S.C. § 1291;

   28 U.S.C. § 1292(a)(1);

   28 U.S.C. § 1292(b); and

   Rule 54(b).

2. Would a writ of mandamus have been appropriate to facilitate review of the trial court's partial summary judgment order?

Liberty Mutual Insurance Co. v. Wetzel
424 U.S. 737 (1976)

Mr. Justice Rehnquist delivered the opinion of the Court.

Respondents filed a complaint in the United States District Court for the Western District of Pennsylvania in which they asserted that petitioner's employee insurance benefits and maternity leave regulations discriminated against women in violation of Title VII of the Civil Rights Act of 1964. The District Court ruled in favor of respondents on the issue of petitioner's liability under that Act, and petitioner appealed to the Court of Appeals for the Third Circuit. That court held that it had jurisdiction of petitioner's appeal under 28 U.S.C. § 1291, and proceeded to affirm on the merits the judgment of the District Court. We granted certiorari and heard argument

on the merits. Though neither party has questioned the jurisdiction of
the Court of Appeals to entertain the appeal, we are obligated to do so
on our own motion if a question thereto exists. Because we conclude that
the District Court's order was not appealable to the Court of Appeals, we
vacate the judgment of the Court of Appeals with instructions to dismiss
petitioner's appeal from the order of the District Court.

Respondents' complaint, after alleging jurisdiction and facts deemed
pertinent to their claim, prayed for a judgment against petitioner embodying the following relief:

> (a) requiring that defendant establish non-discriminatory hiring,
> payment, opportunity, and promotional plans and programs;
>
> (b) enjoining the continuance by defendant of the illegal acts and
> practices alleged herein;
>
> (c) requiring that defendant pay over to plaintiffs and to the mem-
> bers of the class the damages sustained by plaintiffs and the mem-
> bers of the class by reason of defendant's illegal acts and practices,
> including adjusted backpay, with interest, and an additional equal
> amount as liquidated damages, and exemplary damages;
>
> (d) requiring that defendant pay to plaintiffs and to the members
> of the class the costs of this suit and a reasonable attorneys' fee,
> with interest; and
>
> (e) such other and further relief as the Court deems appropriate.

After extensive discovery, respondents moved for partial summary judgment only as to the issue of liability. The District Court finding no issues
of material fact in dispute, entered an order to the effect that petitioner's
pregnancy-related policies violated Title VII of the Civil Rights Act of
1964. It also ruled that Liberty Mutual's hiring and promotion policies
violated Title VII. Petitioner thereafter filed a motion for reconsideration
which was denied by the District Court. Its order denying the motion for
reconsideration, contains the following concluding language:

> In its Order the court stated it would enjoin the continuance of
> practices which the court found to be in violation of Title VII.
> The Plaintiffs were invited to submit the form of the injunction
> order and the Defendant has filed Notice of Appeal and asked for
> stay of any injunctive order. Under these circumstances the court
> will withhold the issuance of the injunctive order and amend the
> Order previously issued under the provisions of Fed.R.Civ.P.
> 54(b), as follows:
>
> And now this 20th day of February, 1974, it is directed that final
> judgment be entered in favor of Plaintiffs that Defendant's policy
> of requiring female employees to return to work within three

months of delivery of a child or be terminated is in violation of the provisions of Title VII of the Civil Rights Act of 1964; that Defendant's policy of denying disability income protection plan benefits to female employees for disabilities related to pregnancies or childbirth are (Sic) in violation of Title VII of the Civil Rights Act of 1964 and that it is expressly directed that Judgment be entered for the Plaintiffs upon these claims of Plaintiffs' Complaint; there being no just reason for delay.

It is obvious from the District Court's order that respondents, although having received a favorable ruling on the issue of petitioner's liability to them, received none of the relief which they expressly prayed for in the portion of their complaint set forth above. They requested an injunction, but did not get one; they requested damages, but were not awarded any; they requested attorneys' fees, but received none.

Counsel for respondents when questioned during oral argument in this Court suggested that at least the District Court's order amounted to a declaratory judgment on the issue of liability. Had respondents sought only a declaratory judgment, and no other form of relief, we would of course have a different case. But even if we accept respondents' contention that the District Court's order was a declaratory judgment on the issue of liability, it nonetheless left unresolved respondents' requests for an injunction, for compensatory and exemplary damages, and for attorneys' fees. It finally disposed of none of respondents' prayers for relief.

The District Court and the Court of Appeals apparently took the view that because the District Court made the recital required by Fed.Rule Civ.Proc. 54(b) that final judgment be entered on the issue of liability, and that there was no just reason for delay, the orders thereby became appealable as a final decision pursuant to 28 U.S.C. § 1291. We cannot agree with this application of the Rule and statute in question.

Rule 54(b) "does not apply to a single claim action. It is limited expressly to multiple claims actions in which 'one or more but less than all' of the multiple claims have been finally decided and are found otherwise to be ready for appeal." *Sears, Roebuck & Co. v. Mackey*, 351 U.S. 427, 435 (1956). Here, however, respondents set forth but a single claim: that petitioner's employee insurance benefits and maternity leave regulations discriminated against its women employees in violation of Title VII of the Civil Rights Act of 1964. They prayed for several different types of relief in the event that they sustained the allegations of their complaint, see Fed.Rule Civ.Proc. 8(a)(3), but their complaint advanced a single legal theory which was applied to only one set of facts. Thus, despite the fact that the District Court undoubtedly made the findings required under the Rule had it been applicable, those findings do not in a case such as this make the order appealable pursuant to 28 U.S.C. § 1291.

We turn to consider whether the District Court's order might have been appealed by petitioner to the Court of Appeals under any other theory. The order, viewed apart from its discussion of Rule 54(b), constitutes a grant of partial summary judgment limited to the issue of petitioner's liability. Such judgments are by their terms interlocutory and where assessment of damages or awarding of other relief remains to be resolved have never been considered to be "final" within the meaning of 28 U.S.C. § 1291. Thus the only possible authorization for an appeal from the District Court's order would be pursuant to the provisions of 28 U.S.C. § 1292.

If the District Court had granted injunctive relief but had not ruled on respondents' other requests for relief, this interlocutory order would have been appealable under § 1292(a)(1). But, as noted above, the court did not issue an injunction....

Nor was this order appealable pursuant to 28 U.S.C. § 1292(b). Although the District Court's findings made with a view to satisfying Rule 54(b) might be viewed as substantial compliance with the certification requirement of that section, there is no showing in this record that petitioner made application to the Court of Appeals within the 10 days therein specified. And that court's holding that its jurisdiction was pursuant to § 1291 makes it clear that it thought itself obliged to consider on the merits petitioner's appeal. There can be no assurance that had the other requirements of § 1292(b) been complied with, the Court of Appeals would have exercised its discretion to entertain the interlocutory appeal.

Were we to sustain the procedure followed here, we would condone a practice whereby a district court in virtually any case before it might render an interlocutory decision on the question of liability of the defendant and the defendant would thereupon be permitted to appeal to the court of appeals without satisfying any of the requirements that Congress carefully set forth....

The judgment of the Court of Appeals is therefore vacated, and the case is remanded with instructions to dismiss the petitioner's appeal.

Note on Appellate Jurisdiction of the United States Supreme Court

Appellate jurisdiction of the United States Supreme Court is governed by 28. U.S.C. § 1254. Virtually all of the cases heard by the Supreme Court come to the court via a petition for a writ of certiorari. The Court exercises its discretion to decide which petitions it will grant. The Court receives thousands of petitions for a writ of certiorari each year but typically grants only 80 or so.

Exercise 12-7. Appellate Jurisdiction of the Supreme Court

Rule 10 of the United States Supreme Court sets out the matters the Court considers when deciding whether to grant a writ and hear a case. Based on Rule 10, what are the primary functions of the Supreme Court's appellate jurisdiction?

Rule 10. Considerations Governing Review on Writ of Certiorari

Review on a writ of certiorari is not a matter of right, but of judicial discretion. A petition for a writ of certiorari will be granted only for compelling reasons. The following, although neither controlling nor fully measuring the Court's discretion, indicate the character of the reasons the Court considers:

(a) a United States court of appeals has entered a decision in conflict with the decision of another United States court of appeals on the same important matter; has decided an important federal question in a way that conflicts with a decision by a state court of last resort; or has so far departed from the accepted and usual course of judicial proceedings, or sanctioned such a departure by a lower court, as to call for an exercise of this Court's supervisory power;

(b) a state court of last resort has decided an important federal question in a way that conflicts with the decision of another state court of last resort or of a United States court of appeals;

(c) a state court or a United States court of appeals has decided an important question of federal law that has not been, but should be, settled by this Court, or has decided an important federal question in a way that conflicts with relevant decisions of this Court.

A petition for a writ of certiorari is rarely granted when the asserted error consists of erroneous factual findings or the misapplication of a properly stated rule of law.

---

4. Standards of Review and Harmless Error

The previous section, dealing with the final judgment rule and its exceptions, is about the subject matter jurisdiction of appellate courts. This section instead focuses on the merits of appellate review, which addresses two questions. First, how much deference will the appellate court give to trial court decisions when the appellate court is determining whether the trial court committed error? Appellate courts apply different standards of review depending on the nature of the issue before the court — questions of law, findings of fact, or exercises of discretion. Second, if the appellate court concludes that the trial court erred, is the error so serious that the court of appeals will reverse the trial court's order or judgment?

Exercise 12-8. *Pierce v. Underwood*

1. Identify the three traditional standards of review and the types of issues to which each applies.

2. As is clear from the opinions of Justice Scalia and Justice White, the question of which standard of review applies to a particular issue can be quite challenging.

   What standard does Justice Scalia apply? Based on what policies?

   What standard does Justice White apply? Based on what policies?

Pierce v. Underwood
487 U.S. 552 (1986)

Justice Scalia delivered the opinion of the Court.

Respondents settled their lawsuit against one of petitioner's predecessors as the Secretary of Housing and Urban Development, and were awarded attorney's fees after the court found that the position taken by the Secretary was not "substantially justified" within the meaning of the Equal Access to Justice Act (EAJA), 28 U.S.C. § 2412(d). The court also determined that "special factors" justified calculating the attorney's fees at a rate in excess of the $75-per-hour cap imposed by the statute. We granted certiorari to resolve a conflict in the Courts of Appeals over important questions concerning the interpretation of the EAJA.

* * *

We first consider whether the Court of Appeals applied the correct standard when reviewing the District Court's determination that the Secretary's position was not substantially justified. For purposes of standard of review, decisions by judges are traditionally divided into three categories, denominated questions of law (reviewable *de novo*), questions of fact (reviewable for clear error), and matters of discretion (reviewable for "abuse of discretion"). The Ninth Circuit treated the issue of substantial justification as involving the last of these; other Courts of Appeals have treated it as involving the first.

For some few trial court determinations, the question of what is the standard of appellate review is answered by relatively explicit statutory command. See, *e.g.*, 42 U.S.C. § 1988 ("[T]he court, in its discretion, may allow the prevailing party … a reasonable attorney's fee"). For most others, the answer is provided by a long history of appellate practice. But when, as here, the trial court determination is one for which neither a clear statutory prescription nor a historical tradition exists, it is uncommonly difficult to derive from the pattern of appellate review of other questions an analytical framework that will yield the correct answer.... [B]ut we are persuaded that significant relevant factors call for an "abuse of discretion" standard in the present case.

We turn first to the language and structure of the governing statute. It provides that attorney's fees shall be awarded "unless *the court finds* that the position of the United States was substantially justified." This formulation, as opposed to simply "unless the position of the United States was substantially justified," emphasizes the fact that the determination is for the district court to make, and thus suggests some deference to the district court upon appeal....

We recently observed, with regard to the problem of determining whether mixed questions of law and fact are to be treated as questions of law or of fact for purposes of appellate review, that sometimes the decision "has turned on a determination that, as a matter of the sound administration of justice, one judicial actor is better positioned than another to decide the issue in question." *Miller v. Fenton*, 474 U.S. 104, 114 (1985). We think that consideration relevant in the present context as well, and it argues in favor of deferential, abuse-of-discretion review. To begin with, some of the elements that bear upon whether the Government's position "*was* substantially justified" may be known only to the district court. Not infrequently, the question will turn upon not merely what was the law, but what was the evidence regarding the facts. By reason of settlement conferences and other pretrial activities, the district court may have insights not conveyed by the record, into such matters as whether particular evidence was worthy of being relied upon, or whether critical facts could easily have been verified by the Government....

* * *

Another factor that we find significant has been described as follows by Professor Rosenberg:

> One of the 'good' reasons for conferring discretion on the trial judge is the sheer impracticability of formulating a rule of decision for the matter in issue. Many questions that arise in litigation are not amenable to regulation by rule because they involve multifarious, fleeting, special, narrow facts that utterly resist generalization—at least, for the time being.

* * *

Rosenberg, *Judicial Discretion of the Trial Court, Viewed from Above*, 22 SYRACUSE L. REV. 635, 662–63 (1971).

We think that the question whether the Government's litigating position has been "substantially justified" is precisely such a multifarious and novel question, little susceptible, for the time being at least, of useful generalization, and likely to profit from the experience that an abuse-of-discretion rule will permit to develop.... Application of an abuse-of-discretion standard to the present question will permit that needed flexibility.

* * *

We reach, at last, the merits of whether the District Court abused its discretion in finding that the Government's position was not "substantially justified." [The Court set out reasonable arguments for and against the finding that the Government's position was not substantially justified.]

* * *

We cannot say that this description commands the conclusion that the Government's position was substantially justified. Accordingly, we affirm the Ninth Circuit's holding that the District Judge did not abuse his discretion when he found it was not.

Justice White, with whom Justice O'Connor joins, concurring in part and dissenting in part.

I agree with the majority's interpretation of the term "substantially justified" as used in the Equal Access to Justice Act (EAJA), 28 U.S.C. §2412(d). However, because I believe that a district court's assessment of whether the Government's legal position was substantially justified should be reviewed *de novo* and that the attorney's fees award in this case could not be sustained under that standard of review, I dissent from Parts II and IV of the majority's opinion.

The majority acknowledges that neither the language nor the structure of the EAJA compels deferential review of a district court's determination of whether the Government's position was substantially justified. In fact, the statute is wholly silent as to the standard under which such determinations are to be reviewed. This congressional silence in the face of both the general rule of *de novo* review of legal issues and the EAJA's special purpose of encouraging meritorious suits against the Government suggests a different result than that reached by the majority.

... Congress would have known that whether or not a particular legal position was substantially justified is a question of law rather than of fact. The historical facts having been established, the question is to be resolved by the legal analysis of the relevant statutory and decisional authorities that appellate courts are expected to perform. As the District of Columbia Circuit has observed, "the special expertise and experience of appellate courts in assessing the relative force of competing interpretations and applications of legal norms makes the case for *de novo* review of judgments [of whether the Government's legal position was substantially justified] even stronger than the case for such review of paradigmatic conclusions of law." *Spencer v. NLRB*, 712 F.2d 539, 563 (1983)....

De novo appellate review of whether the Government's legal position was substantially justified would also foster consistency and predictability in EAJA litigation. A court of appeals may be required under the majority's "abuse of discretion" standard to affirm one district court's holding that the Government's legal position was substantially justified and another district court's holding that the same position was not substantially justified. As long as the district court's opinion about the substantiality of the Government case rests on some defensible construction and application of the statute, the Court's view would command the court of appeals to defer even though that court's own view on the legal issue is quite different. The availability of attorney's fees would not only be difficult to predict but would vary from circuit to circuit or even within a particular circuit....

* * *

Because I would conclude upon *de novo* review that the Secretary's refusal to implement the operating-subsidy program was substantially justified, I would reverse the award of attorney's fees under the EAJA.

Note — Abuse of Discretion Applied to Rule 11 Sanctions Decisions

In *Cooter & Gell v. Hartmarx Corp.*, 496 U.S. 384, 399–402 (1990), the Supreme Court addressed the standard of review for Rule 11 sanctions.

Determining whether an attorney has violated Rule 11 involves a consideration of three types of issues. The court must consider factual questions regarding the nature of the attorney's prefiling inquiry and the factual basis of the pleading or other paper. Legal issues are raised in considering whether a pleading is "warranted by existing law or a good faith argument" for changing the law and whether the attorney's conduct violated Rule 11. Finally, the district court must exercise its discretion to tailor an appropriate sanction.

* * *

Although the Courts of Appeal use different verbal formulas to characterize their standards of review, the scope of actual disagreement is narrow. No dispute exists that the appellate courts should review the district court's selection of a sanction under a deferential standard. In directing the district court to impose an "appropriate" sanction, Rule 11 itself indicates that the district court is empowered to exercise its discretion.

The Circuits also agree that, in the absence of any language to the contrary in Rule 11, courts should adhere to their usual practice of reviewing the district court's finding of facts under a deferential standard. *See* Fed.Rule Civ.Proc. 52(a) ("Findings of fact ... shall not be set aside unless clearly erroneous, and due regard shall be given to the opportunity of the trial court to judge of the credibility of the witnesses"). In practice, the "clearly erroneous" standard requires the appellate court to uphold any district court determination that falls within a broad range of permissible conclusions. When an appellate court reviews a district court's factual findings, the abuse of discretion and clearly erroneous standards are indistinguishable: A court of appeals would be justified in concluding that a district court had abused its discretion in making a factual finding only if the finding were clearly erroneous.

The scope of disagreement over the appropriate standard of review can thus be confined to a narrow issue: whether the court of appeals must defer to the district court's legal conclusions in Rule 11 proceedings. A number of factors have led the majority of Circuits to conclude that appellate courts should review all aspects of a district court's imposition of Rule 11 sanctions under a deferential standard.

The Court has long noted the difficulty of distinguishing between legal and factual issues. Making such distinctions is particularly difficult in the Rule 11 context.... Of course, this standard would not preclude the appellate court's correction of a district court's legal errors. "[I]f a district court's findings rest on an erroneous view of the law, they may be set aside on that basis." *Pullman-Standard v. Swint*, 456 U.S. at 287.

Pierce v. Underwood, 487 U.S. 552 (1988), strongly supports applying a unitary abuse of discretion standard to all aspects of a Rule 11 proceeding. In *Pierce*, the Court held a District Court's determination under the Equal Access to Justice Act (EAJA), that "the position of the United States was substantially justified" should be reviewed for an abuse of discretion. As a position is "substantially justified" if it "has a reasonable basis in law and fact," EAJA requires an inquiry similar to the Rule 11 inquiry as to whether a pleading is "well grounded in fact" and legally tenable....

* * *

Rule 11's policy goals also support adopting an abuse-of-discretion standard. The district court is best acquainted with the local bar's litigation practices, and thus best situated to determine when a sanction is warranted to serve Rule 11's goal of specific and general deterrence. Deference to the determination of courts on the front lines of litigation will enhance these courts' ability to control the litigants before them. Such deference will streamline the litigation process by freeing appellate courts from the duty of reweighing evidence and reconsidering facts already weighed and considered by the district court; it will also discourage litigants from pursuing marginal appeals, thus reducing the amount of satellite litigation.

* * *

In light of our consideration of the purposes and policies of Rule 11 and in accordance with our analysis of analogous EAJA provisions, we reject petitioner's contention that the Court of Appeals should have applied a three-tiered standard of review. Rather, an appellate court should apply an abuse-of-discretion standard in reviewing all aspects of a district court's Rule 11 determination. A district court would necessarily abuse its discretion if it based its ruling on an erroneous view of the law or on a clearly erroneous assessment of the evidence.

Exercise 12-9. *Anderson v. City of Bessemer City, N.C.*

In *Anderson* the Court interprets and applies the "clearly erroneous" standard from Rule 52.

1. Articulate the detailed definition the Court gives the clearly erroneous standard.

2. What policies support the clearly erroneous standard of review for trial courts' findings of fact?

3. How exactly did the court of appeals err in its application of the clearly erroneous standard?

4. How, if at all, is the clearly erroneous standard in *Anderson* different from the abuse of discretion standard in *Pierce*?

Anderson v. City of Bessemer City, N.C.
470 U.S. 564 (1985)

Justice White delivered the opinion of the Court.

In *Pullman-Standard v. Swint*, 456 U.S. 273 (1982), we held that a District Court's finding of discriminatory intent in an action brought under Title VII of the Civil Rights Act of 1964, is a factual finding that may be overturned on appeal only if it is clearly erroneous. In this case, the Court of Appeals for the Fourth Circuit concluded that there was clear error in a District Court's finding of discrimination and reversed. Because our reading of the record convinces us that the Court of Appeals misapprehended and misapplied the clearly-erroneous standard, we reverse.

I

Early in 1975, officials of respondent Bessemer City, North Carolina, set about to hire a new Recreation Director for the city. Although the duties that went with the position were not precisely delineated, the new Recreation Director was to be responsible for managing all of the city's recreational facilities and for developing recreational programs—athletic and otherwise—to serve the needs of the city's residents. A five-member committee selected by the Mayor was responsible for choosing the Recreation Director. Of the five members, four were men; the one woman on the committee, Mrs. Auddie Boone, served as the chairperson.

Eight persons applied for the position of Recreation Director. Petitioner, at the time a 39-year-old schoolteacher with college degrees in social studies and education, was the only woman among the eight. The selection committee reviewed the resumés submitted by the applicants and briefly interviewed each of the jobseekers. Following the interviews, the committee offered the position to Mr. Donald Kincaid, a 24-year-old who had recently graduated from college with a degree in physical education. All four men on the committee voted to offer the job to Mr. Kincaid; Mrs. Boone voted for petitioner.

Believing that the committee had passed over her in favor of a less qualified candidate solely because she was a woman ... petitioner filed this Title VII action.... After a 2-day trial during which the court heard testimony from petitioner, Mr. Kincaid, and the five members of the selection committee, the court issued a brief memorandum of decision setting forth its finding that petitioner was entitled to judgment because she had been denied the position of Recreation Director on account of her sex. In addition to laying out the rationale for this finding, the memorandum requested that petitioner's counsel submit proposed findings of fact and conclusions of law expanding upon those set forth in the memorandum. Petitioner's counsel complied with this request by submitting a lengthy set of proposed findings; the court then requested and received a response setting forth in detail respondent's objections to the proposed findings — objections that were, in turn, answered by petitioner's counsel in a somewhat less lengthy reply. After receiving these submissions, the court issued its own findings of fact and conclusions of law.

As set forth in the formal findings of fact and conclusions of law, the court's finding that petitioner had been denied employment by respondent because of her sex rested on a number of subsidiary findings. First, the court found that at the time the selection committee made its choice, petitioner had been better qualified than Mr. Kincaid to perform the range of duties demanded by the position. The court based this finding on petitioner's experience as a classroom teacher responsible for supervising schoolchildren in recreational and athletic activities, her employment as a hospital recreation director in the late 1950s, her extensive involvement in a variety of civic organizations, her knowledge of sports acquired both as a high school athlete and as a mother of children involved in organized athletics, her skills as a public speaker, her experience in handling money (gained in the course of her community activities and in her work as a bookkeeper for a group of physicians), and her knowledge of music, dance, and crafts. The court found that Mr. Kincaid's principal qualifications were his experience as a student teacher and as a coach in a local youth basketball league, his extensive knowledge of team and individual sports, acquired as a result of his lifelong involvement in athletics, and his formal training as a physical education major in college. Noting that the position of Recreation Director involved more than the management of athletic programs, the court concluded that petitioner's greater breadth of experience made her better qualified for the position.

Second, the court found that the male committee members had in fact been biased against petitioner because she was a woman. The court based this finding in part on the testimony of one of the committee members that he believed it would have been "real hard" for a woman to handle the job and that he would not want his wife to have to perform the duties of the Recreation Director....

Also critical to the court's inference of bias was its finding that petitioner, alone among the applicants for the job, had been asked whether she realized the job would involve night work and travel and whether her husband approved of her applying for the job. The court's finding that the committee had pursued this line of inquiry only with petitioner was based on the testimony of petitioner that these questions had been asked of her and the testimony of Mrs. Boone that similar questions had not been asked of the other applicants....

Finally, the court found that the reasons offered by the male committee members for their choice of Mr. Kincaid were pretextual. The court rejected the proposition that Mr. Kincaid's degree in physical education justified his choice, as the evidence suggested that where male candidates were concerned, the committee valued experience more highly than formal training in physical education....

On the basis of its findings that petitioner was the most qualified candidate, that the committee had been biased against hiring a woman, and that the committee's explanations for its choice of Mr. Kincaid were pretextual, the court concluded that petitioner had met her burden of establishing that she had been denied the position of Recreation Director because of her sex. Petitioner having conceded that ordering the city to hire her would be an inappropriate remedy under the circumstances, the court awarded petitioner backpay in the amount of $30,397 and attorney's fees of $16,971.59.

The Fourth Circuit reversed the District Court's finding of discrimination. In the view of the Court of Appeals, three of the District Court's crucial findings were clearly erroneous: the finding that petitioner was the most qualified candidate, the finding that petitioner had been asked questions that other applicants were spared, and the finding that the male committee members were biased against hiring a woman. Having rejected these findings, the Court of Appeals concluded that the District Court had erred in finding that petitioner had been discriminated against on account of her sex.

II

We must deal at the outset with the Fourth Circuit's suggestion that "close scrutiny of the record in this case [was] justified by the manner in which the opinion was prepared,"—that is, by the District Court's adoption of petitioner's proposed findings of fact and conclusions of law....

We, too, have criticized courts for their verbatim adoption of findings of fact prepared by prevailing parties, particularly when those findings have taken the form of conclusory statements unsupported by citation to the record. We are also aware of the potential for overreaching and exaggeration on the part of attorneys preparing findings of fact when they have already been informed that the judge has decided in their favor. Nonetheless, our previous discussions of the subject suggest that even when the trial judge adopts proposed findings verbatim, the findings are those of the court and may be reversed only if clearly erroneous.

In any event, the District Court in this case does not appear to have uncritically accepted findings prepared without judicial guidance by the prevailing party. The court itself provided the framework for the proposed findings when it issued its preliminary memorandum, which set forth its essential findings and directed petitioner's counsel to submit a more detailed set of findings consistent with them. Further, respondent was provided and availed itself of the opportunity to respond at length to the proposed findings. Nor did the District Court simply adopt petitioner's proposed findings: the findings it ultimately issued—and particularly the crucial findings regarding petitioner's qualifications, the questioning to which petitioner was subjected, and bias on the part of the committeemen—vary considerably in organization and content from those submitted by petitioner's counsel. Under these circumstances, we see no reason to doubt that the findings issued by the District Court represent the judge's own considered conclusions. There is no reason to subject those findings to a more stringent appellate review than is called for by the applicable rules.

III

Because a finding of intentional discrimination is a finding of fact, the standard governing appellate review of a district court's finding of discrimination is that set forth in Federal Rule of Civil Procedure 52(a): "Findings of fact shall not be set aside unless clearly erroneous, and due regard shall be given to the opportunity of the trial court to judge of the credibility of the witnesses."...

Although the meaning of the phrase "clearly erroneous" is not immediately apparent, certain general principles governing the exercise of the appellate court's power to overturn findings of a district court may be derived from our cases. The foremost of these principles is that "[a] finding is 'clearly erroneous' when although there is evidence to support it, the reviewing court on the entire evidence is left with the definite and firm conviction that a mistake has been committed." *United States v. United States Gypsum Co.*, 333 U.S. 364, 395 (1948). This standard plainly does not entitle a reviewing court to reverse the finding of the trier of fact simply because it is convinced that it would have decided the case differently. The reviewing court oversteps the bounds of its duty under Rule 52(a) if it undertakes to duplicate the role of the lower court. "In applying the clearly erroneous standard to the findings of a district court sitting without a jury, appellate courts must constantly have in mind that their function is not to decide factual issues *de novo*." *Zenith Radio Corp. v. Hazeltine Research, Inc.*, 395 U.S. 100, 123 (1969). If the district court's account of the evidence is plausible in light of the record viewed in its entirety, the court of appeals may not reverse it even though convinced that had it been sitting as the trier of fact, it would have weighed the evidence differently. Where there are two permissible views of the evidence, the factfinder's choice between them cannot be clearly erroneous.

This is so even when the district court's findings do not rest on credibility determinations, but are based instead on physical or documentary evidence or inferences from other facts. To be sure, various Courts of Appeals have on occasion asserted the theory that an appellate court may exercise *de novo* review over findings not based on credibility determinations. But it is impossible to trace the theory's lineage back to the text of Rule 52(a), which states straightforwardly that "findings of fact shall not be set aside unless clearly erroneous." That the Rule goes on to emphasize the special deference to be paid credibility determinations does not alter its clear command: Rule 52(a) "does not make exceptions or purport to exclude certain categories of factual findings from the obligation of a court of appeals to accept a district court's findings unless clearly erroneous." *Pullman-Standard v. Swint*, 456 U.S. at 287.

The rationale for deference to the original finder of fact is not limited to the superiority of the trial judge's position to make determinations of credibility. The trial judge's major role is the determination of fact, and with experience in fulfilling that role comes expertise. Duplication of the trial judge's efforts in the court of appeals would very likely contribute only negligibly to the accuracy of fact determination at a huge cost in diversion of judicial resources. In addition, the parties to a case on appeal have already been forced to concentrate their energies and resources on persuading the trial judge that their account of the facts is the correct one; requiring them to persuade three more judges at the appellate level is requiring too much. As the Court has stated in a different context, the trial on the merits should be "the 'main event'... rather than a 'tryout on the road.'" *Wainwright v. Sykes,* 433 U.S. 72, 90 (1977). For these reasons, review of factual findings under the clearly-erroneous standard—with its deference to the trier of fact—is the rule, not the exception.

When findings are based on determinations regarding the credibility of witnesses, Rule 52(a) demands even greater deference to the trial court's findings; for only the trial judge can be aware of the variations in demeanor and tone of voice that bear so heavily on the listener's understanding of and belief in what is said. Documents or objective evidence may contradict the witness' story; or the story itself may be so internally inconsistent or implausible on its face that a reasonable factfinder would not credit it. Where such factors are present, the court of appeals may well find clear error even in a finding purportedly based on a credibility determination. But when a trial judge's finding is based on his decision to credit the testimony of one of two or more witnesses, each of whom has told a coherent and facially plausible story that is not contradicted by extrinsic evidence, that finding, if not internally inconsistent, can virtually never be clear error.

IV

Application of the foregoing principles to the facts of the case lays bare the errors committed by the Fourth Circuit in its employment of the clearly-erroneous standard. In detecting clear error in the District Court's finding that petitioner was better qualified than Mr. Kincaid, the Fourth Circuit improperly conducted what amounted to a *de novo* weighing of the evidence in the record. The District Court's finding was based on essentially undisputed evidence regarding the respective backgrounds of petitioner and Mr. Kincaid and the duties that went with the position of Recreation Director. The District Court, after considering the evidence, concluded that the position of Recreation Director in Bessemer City carried with it broad responsibilities for creating and managing a recreation program involving not only athletics, but also other activities for citizens of all ages and interests....

The Fourth Circuit, reading the same record, concluded that the basic duty of the Recreation Director was to implement an athletic program, and that the essential qualification for a successful applicant would be either education or experience specifically related to athletics....

Based on our own reading of the record, we cannot say that either interpretation of the facts is illogical or implausible. Each has support in inferences that may be drawn from the facts in the record; and if either interpretation had been drawn by a district court on the record before us, we would not be inclined to find it clearly erroneous. The question we must answer, however, is not whether the Fourth Circuit's interpretation of the facts was clearly erroneous, but whether the District Court's finding was clearly erroneous. The District Court determined that petitioner was better qualified, and, as we have stated above, such a finding is entitled to deference notwithstanding that it is not based on credibility determinations. When the record is examined in light of the appropriately deferential standard, it is apparent that it contains nothing that mandates a finding that the District Court's conclusion was clearly erroneous.

Somewhat different concerns are raised by the Fourth Circuit's treatment of the District Court's finding that petitioner, alone among the applicants for the position of Recreation Director, was asked questions regarding her spouse's feelings about her application for the position. Here the error of the Court of Appeals was its failure to give due regard to the ability of the District Court to interpret and discern the credibility of oral testimony. Once the trial court's characterization of Mrs. Boone's remark is accepted, it is apparent that the finding that the male candidates were not seriously questioned about the feelings of their wives cannot be deemed clearly erroneous. The trial judge was faced with the testimony of three witnesses, one of whom (Mrs. Boone) stated that none of the other candidates had been so questioned, one of whom (a male committee member) testified that Mr. Kincaid had been asked such a question "in a way," and one of whom (another committeeman) testified that all the candidates had been subjected to similar questioning. None of these accounts is implausible on its face, and none is contradicted by any reliable extrinsic evidence. Under these circumstances, the trial court's decision to credit Mrs. Boone was not clearly erroneous.

* * *

The Fourth Circuit's refusal to accept the District Court's finding that the committee members were biased against hiring a woman was based to a large extent on its rejection of the finding that petitioner had been subjected to questioning that the other applicants were spared. Given that that finding was not clearly erroneous, the finding of bias cannot be termed erroneous: it finds support not only in the treatment of petitioner in her interview, but also in the testimony of one committee member that he believed it would have been difficult for a woman to perform the job and in the evidence that another member solicited applications for the position only from men.

... The District Court's findings regarding petitioner's superior qualifications and the bias of the selection committee are sufficient to support the inference that petitioner was denied the position of Recreation Director on account of her sex. Accordingly, we hold that the Fourth Circuit erred in denying petitioner relief under Title VII.

In so holding, we do not assert that our knowledge of what happened 10 years ago in Bessemer City is superior to that of the Court of Appeals; nor do we claim to have greater insight than the Court of Appeals into the state of mind of the men on the selection committee who rejected petitioner for the position of Recreation Director. Even the trial judge, who has heard the witnesses directly and who is more closely in touch than the appeals court with the milieu out of which the controversy before him arises, cannot always be confident that he "knows" what happened. Often, he can only determine whether the plaintiff has succeeded in presenting an account of the facts that is more likely to be true than not. Our task — and the task of appellate tribunals generally — is more limited still: we must determine whether the trial judge's conclusions are clearly erroneous. On the record before us, we cannot say that they are. Accordingly, the judgment of the Court of Appeals is reversed.

Note on the *de novo* Standard of Review

In *Salve Regina College v. Russell*, 499 U.S. 225 (1991), the court addressed the standard of review that applies when a federal court of appeals reviews a district court's determination of state law. *Salve Regina* involved a contract dispute between a college and one of its students. The student was 5'6" tall, weighed in excess of 300 pounds when she was accepted in the nursing program. The contract purported to "condition the student's continuation in the nursing program upon weekly attendance at a weight-loss seminar and an average loss of two pounds per week. When the student failed to meet these commitments, she was asked to withdraw from the program. The student sued the college in federal district court, asserting tort and contract claims. One issue in the case required the district court to interpret and apply Rhode Island contract law. The Court articulated its reasoning for adopting the *de novo* standard of review.

> We conclude that a court of appeals should review *de novo* a district court's determination of state law....
>
> Independent appellate review of legal issues best serves the dual goals of doctrinal coherence and economy of judicial administration. District judges preside alone over fast-paced trials: Of necessity they devote much of their energy and resources to hearing witnesses and reviewing evidence. Similarly, the logistical burdens of trial advocacy limit the extent to which trial counsel is able to supplement the district judge's legal research with memoranda and briefs. Thus, trial judges often must resolve complicated legal questions without benefit of "extended reflection [or] extensive information."
>
> Courts of appeals, on the other hand, are structurally suited to the collaborative juridical process that promotes decisional accuracy. With the record having been constructed below and settled for purposes of the appeal, appellate judges are able to devote their primary attention to legal issues. As questions of law become the focus of appellate review, it can be expected that the parties' briefs will be refined to bring to bear on the legal issues more information and more comprehensive analysis than was provided for the

district judge. Perhaps most important, courts of appeals employ multijudge panels that permit reflective dialogue and collective judgment.

Id. at 231–32.

Exercise 12-10. Harmless Error

Rule 61 sets out the harmless error rule applicable to district courts, which was part of the analysis for new trials, discussed in Chapter 11. The harmless error rule applicable to appellate courts is in 28 U.S.C. §2111, which provides in part: "On the hearing of any appeal ... the court shall give judgment after an examination of the record without regard to errors or defects which do not affect the substantial rights of the parties."

1. In *Cochenour v. Cameron Savings and Loan*:

   a. What harmless error test does the court apply to the trial court's evidentiary rulings?

   b. What harmless error test does the court apply to the trial court's decisions concerning final argument?

2. What policies support the harmless error rule?

Cochenour v. Cameron Savings & Loan, F.A.
160 F.3d 1187 (8th Cir. 1998)

Debera Cochenour sued the Cameron Savings and Loan Association, contending that she was fired from her job in violation of the Americans with Disabilities Act, the Age Discrimination in Employment Act, and the Missouri Human Rights Act. Cameron contends that it fired Ms. Cochenour after two customers complained to Cameron's president that Ms. Cochenour and another employee were spreading rumors in the bank about the customers' sexual orientation. Ms. Cochenour maintains that Cameron's stated reason for firing her was pretextual, and that Cameron in fact terminated her employment because of her age and her health problems.

A jury returned a verdict in favor of Cameron, and the trial court denied Ms. Cochenour's motion for a new trial. Ms. Cochenour appealed from certain evidentiary rulings, and we affirm the judgment of the trial court.

Shortly after Ms. Cochenour and the other employee, Beth McDonald, were fired from Cameron, Ms. McDonald received a job offer from Cameron's attorney, who had given legal advice to the bank regarding its decision to terminate the two employees. Ms. Cochenour maintains that the trial court erred in excluding evidence of the job offer. She argues that the jury could have inferred from this job offer that Cameron never had any real intention of depriving Ms. McDonald of employment, and that its stated reason for firing Ms. Cochenour was therefore pretextual.

If a trial court wrongly excludes evidence, we will not set aside the judgment unless we are left with " 'no reasonable assurance that the jury would have reached the same conclusion had the evidence been admitted.' " *Stolzenburg v. Ford Motor Co.,* 143 F.3d 402, 406 (8th Cir. 1998). In this case, the probative value of the proffered testimony regarding the job offer seems to us extremely small, and we believe that any inference of pretext that a reasonable person could draw from that evidence would have to be correspondingly weak. Other than the tenuous circumstantial evidence of the job offer itself, Ms. Cochenour presented no evidence of an agreement or collusion between Cameron and its attorney regarding the offer to Ms. McDonald. Ms. Cochenour admitted, moreover, that she had participated in discussions regarding the customers' sexual orientation, and Cameron presented a strong case to the jury that Ms. Cochenour was fired for that reason alone. We do not believe that evidence regarding the job offer would have had any appreciable effect on the jury's verdict, and we therefore conclude that any error in excluding it was harmless.

Ms. Cochenour also maintains that the trial court erred in excluding testimony regarding a conversation in which Cameron's president allegedly told an employee that she could not continue to work for Cameron because she had become pregnant. The alleged conversation occurred more than 10 years before Ms. Cochenour's termination, however, and we believe in any case that it was sufficiently dissimilar from Ms. Cochenour's claim that any inference that could be drawn from it regarding Cameron's motive for firing Ms. Cochenour would be extraordinarily weak at best. We therefore conclude that any error in excluding this testimony was also harmless.

* * *

We believe that the trial court erred in refusing to allow Ms. Cochenour's attorney to argue that Cameron had a mandatory retirement policy for all employees. It was the province of the jury, not the trial court, to decide whether or not the evidence presented at trial supported such a conclusion. We do not believe, however, that the trial court's restrictions on Ms. Cochenour's closing argument could possibly have altered the jury's verdict. We note that the trial court did allow Ms. Cochenour's attorney to comment at length during closing argument on the statement of Cameron's president to the 72-year-old employee that she should retire....

We think it probable that it was also error for the trial court to permit Cameron's attorney to say during closing argument that Cameron's mandatory retirement policy for officers was permissible under the law, since that comment was a statement about a legal matter on which the jury was not instructed....

[W]e have held that "to constitute reversible error, statements made in closing argument must be plainly unwarranted and clearly injurious." *Griffin v. Hilke*, 804 F.2d 1052, 1057 (8th Cir.1986). Reversal is inappropriate "when the error is harmless and did not affect the substantial rights of the parties." *Williams v. Fermenta Animal Health Co.*, 984 F.2d 261, 266 (8th Cir.1993). Because we do not believe that this isolated remark affected the jury's verdict, we conclude that it, too, was harmless error.

---

5. Professional Development Reflection

Federal Rule of Appellate Procedure 38 provides: "If a court of appeals determines that an appeal is frivolous, it may, after a separately filed motion or notice from the court and reasonable opportunity to respond, award just damages and single or double costs to the appellee."

Exercise 12-11. Frivolous Appeals

What makes an appeal "frivolous"? Find a case in which a federal appeals court determines that an appeal is "frivolous." In a paragraph or two, summarize the appellate court's reasoning.

Chapter 13

Preclusion

You now have a final judgment in a case involving your client. What does this mean for future lawsuits involving the same parties and issues? Preclusion is a concept that prevents a party to a lawsuit from relitigating a claim or issue that arose in a prior case that has come to a final judgment. Essentially, this means that the parties to a lawsuit get one bite at the apple on a particular claim or issue. The following chapter problem is designed to help you focus on the issues that arise in this context.

1. Chapter Problem

To:	Associate
From:	Mary Rogers, Partner
Re:	Piper Aircraft Matter

Ms. Reyno, the executor of the Estate of Kevin Doe, has once again sued our client, Piper Aircraft, as the executor of the estate of another decedent, Jane Roe, who died in the same airplane crash in Scotland. The Estate of Kevin Doe lawsuit that our firm handled for Piper resulted in summary judgment for Piper. The federal trial judge in Pennsylvania granted summary judgment on the issue of liability, holding that Piper could not be held liable for any design flaws in the propellers manufactured by Hartzell Propeller, Inc.

Please research whether we could use preclusion on Piper Aircraft's behalf in an effort to resolve the second lawsuit expeditiously.

2. Introduction

The rules governing preclusion vary depending on whether a party is using it to preclude a claim, referred to as claim preclusion, or an issue, referred to as issue preclusion. Courts also commonly refer to these concepts as res judicata (claim preclusion) and collateral estoppel (issue preclusion), although you will occasionally see a court referring to both claim and issue preclusion under the general topic of res judicata. The more modern terminology is claim preclusion and issue preclusion. This chapter will refer to these concepts using this terminology. However, you will still encounter courts referring to res judicata and collateral estoppel, so it is important that you recognize these terms as well.

Both concepts are specifically listed as affirmative defenses in Federal Rule of Civil Procedure 8(c). This means that the party seeking to stop the opposing party from relitigating the particular claim or issue generally must raise preclusion in the answer as a specific affirmative defense. Like most affirmative defenses, a party can waive preclusion by not asserting it. However, some federal courts have raised preclusion on their own, arguing that public policy favors using preclusion rather than running the risk that two courts will reach differing conclusions on the same claim or issue. *See, e.g, Harris v. Kado*, 391 Fed. Appx. 560, 564 (7th Cir. 2010); *but see Concerned Residents of Santa Fe Estates, Inc. v. Santa Fe Estates, Inc.*, 143 N.M. 811, 818–19 (N.M. Ct. App. 2008); Restatement (Second) of Judgments §§ 24, 26(1) & 26(1) cmt. a) (noting that claim preclusion does not apply where "the defendant has acquiesced" in a second lawsuit and providing as an example a scenario where the defendant fails to object based on preclusion). In certain instances, parties also can raise preclusion offensively, meaning the plaintiff can raise it, for example, to preclude certain affirmative defenses. The chapter problem is an example of defensive use.

The policies supporting both types of preclusion are based on judicial economy and fairness to the parties. It is a waste of court time for parties to relitigate the same claim or issue after another court has already decided it. In addition, the possibility of an inconsistent judgment from the second court would undermine the efficacy and legitimacy of the civil justice system. Likewise, the parties to a lawsuit should be able to rely on that court's judgment as final (aside from appeals), and not be placed in a situation in which they are relitigating a claim or issue that an earlier court judgment already resolved. This is consistent with policies behind the finality of judgments—that once a court resolves a dispute, it is decided once and for all. *See generally Allen v. McCurry*, 449 U.S. 90 (1980). Thus, preclusion serves both public and private values.

The Full Faith and Credit Clause of the United States Constitution, U.S. Const. Art. IV, § 1, generally requires that a state court give a judgment from another state court the same preclusive effect that the original court would give that judgment. So, for example, an Arizona court would be required to give a New York court's judgment the same preclusive effect that the New York court would give it. Likewise, in the federal court system, the Full Faith and Credit Act, 28 U.S.C. § 1738, requires a federal court to give a state court judgment the preclusive effect that the state that issued the judgment would give that judgment. *See Marrese v. Am. Acad. of Orthopaedic Surgeons*, 470 U.S. 373, 380 (1985). The preclusive effect of a federal court judgment in another federal court is determined by the federal common law of preclusion. *See Semtek Int'l Inc. v. Lockheed Martin Corp.*, 531 U.S. 497, 507–08 (2001). However, the federal courts use state preclusion rules in diversity cases and cases that otherwise involve state law issues.

Claim and issue preclusion involve "recognition" of judgments as opposed to "enforcement" of judgments. Enforcement is the process of actually obtaining the relief that a judgment provides. So, for example, if a court awards a tort victim $50,000 in damages, the plaintiff's attorney must use rules related to enforcing judgments in order to obtain that $50,000. However, if that plaintiff tries to sue that defendant again for the same tort involving the same incident, preclusion rules provide a defense for that defendant in the second action. Preclusion is easy to spot in this regard. You need to have two lawsuits or proceedings, with one of those lawsuits or proceedings coming to a final judgment. Without that first judgment, preclusion cannot apply.

There are other doctrines related to preclusion that will not be covered in detail in this chapter. For example, the concept of law of the case generally prevents a party from relitigating an issue that has already been resolved in that same lawsuit, unless the court has stated that it will leave the issue open for potential modification later. *See Pepper v. United States*, 562 U.S. 476, 506 (2011) (quoting *Arizona v. California*, 460 U.S. 605, 618 (1983) (law of the case " 'doctrine posits that when a court decides upon a rule of law, that decision should continue to govern the same issues in subsequent stages in the same case' "). The purpose of this doctrine is "to 'maintain consistency and avoid reconsideration of matters once decided during the course of a single continuing lawsuit.' " *Devilla v. Schriver*, 245 F.3d 192, 197 (2d Cir. 2001) (quoting WRIGHT, MILLER & COOPER, FEDERAL PRACTICE AND PROCEDURE§ 4478 at 788 (3d ed. 1998)). Thus, once a defendant makes a motion to dismiss based on improper venue and loses that motion, it generally cannot make that motion again in the same case. It can wait until the end of the case and appeal the decision, but the doctrine of the law of the case usually means that a court will not reconsider a decision it has already made in the same case. However, that does not stop lawyers from making motions to reconsider when they believe the court has resolved a motion incorrectly or there has been some change in the law or facts since the court made its initial decision.

Another related concept is stare decisis. As you have learned, stare decisis refers to the idea that courts will rule consistently with precedent, especially when that precedent comes from a court with higher authority. So, for example, a decision by the Supreme Court of the United States on the meaning of "supervisor" for purposes of Title VII of the Civil Rights Act of 1964 sets the meaning of that term for all the courts in the country when applying that statute. These concepts are related to preclusion because they bind subsequent court decision making. However, they both operate differently from preclusion, as you will see below.

This chapter addresses preclusion as follows.

- Section 3 begins by exploring the fundamentals of claim preclusion, including cases and problems that will help you understand and apply the elements of claim preclusion.

- Section 4 describes issue preclusion, the legal principle that prevents a party from relitigating an issue that a court has already finally determined.

- Section 5 presents a professional development reflection concerning ethical issues raised by the use of preclusion.

3. Claim Preclusion

Claim preclusion stops a party from relitigating a claim (sometimes referred to as a cause of action) that it has already litigated in an earlier lawsuit that has come to a final judgment. To use claim preclusion, a party must prove the following elements:

- Nature of the First Judgment—the claim must be the subject of
  - a valid
  - final judgment
  - on the merits.
- Same Claim—It must involve the "same claim."
- Same Parties—It must involve the same parties or those in privity with the parties to the first lawsuit.

Claim preclusion includes the concepts of merger and bar. The idea of "merger" is that, as to a transaction or occurrence, all of the potential claims and theories of liability available at the time of the litigation of that transaction or occurrence between two parties are "merged" into the judgment in the case, regardless of which theories or claims were raised, or which ones formed the basis of the judgment. The concept of "bar" is simply the general principle that, once decided, a judgment between those same two parties (or their privies) cannot be relitigated. Together, they mean that the judgment, along with the theories and claims that formed its bases, as well as any other theories or claims that would have been available at the time of the prior litigation, are now "barred" from relitigation, and that is because they are "merged" into the first judgment.

One way to look at this is that a plaintiff cannot "split" a claim by litigating it twice using different theories of liability. For example, a plaintiff who is fired from her job at a public employer brings a lawsuit asserting that her termination was based on sex in violation of Title VII of the Civil Rights Act of 1964's prohibition of sex discrimination in employment. Assume the plaintiff loses this case. If she refiles a new case based on her termination alleging that her public employer violated the Equal Protection Clause of the United States Constitution by firing her based on her sex, the earlier judgment will have preclusive effect even though she is using a different theory of liability—the Equal Protection Clause—in the second lawsuit. In claim preclusion terminology, her Equal Protection cause of action is barred by the earlier judgment against her in the Title VII lawsuit because it was merged into that earlier judgment even though it was not specifically asserted there.

What happens if the plaintiff has filed the same suit in multiple jurisdictions, hedging its bets about where it might obtain a more favorable ruling or judgment? In prior chapters, it was noted that forum shopping by plaintiffs and defendants is a significant issue in the civil justice system. Sometimes a plaintiff or a defendant will file the same lawsuit in two different courts. In addition, a plaintiff may start a case in state court, and, after some initial motions do not go so well for the plaintiff, decide to file the identical case in federal court (or vice versa). Which judgment has claim preclusive effect—the judgment from the first lawsuit filed or the first to come to final judgment? The first lawsuit that comes to final judgment will have preclusive effect on other pending actions, even if it was not the first lawsuit filed. When multiple lawsuits are filed involving the same claim, it is a race to judgment to determine which case will have preclusive effect.

Claim preclusion is generally a common law concept, although occasionally a state will codify it. *See, e.g.,* La. Rev. Stat. Ann. § 13:4231 (West 1990). It can vary from jurisdiction to jurisdiction. For example, in the Arkansas state court system, a party asserting claim preclusion must also show that the first suit was "fully contested in good faith." *See Arkansas Louisiana Gas Co. v. Taylor,* 314 Ark. 62, 66 (1993). While there are some jurisdiction to jurisdiction differences, most require at least the elements set out above.

Defense preclusion also exists, although it is less frequently used. Under this concept, if a plaintiff wins the first lawsuit and files a second lawsuit on the same claim, the defendant cannot raise any additional defenses in the second lawsuit that it had but left out of the first lawsuit. The defendant must raise every available defense in the first action. However, this is an unlikely scenario because the plaintiff's second claim likely would be precluded as well. As you learned in Chapter 8, the defendant also must assert any compulsory counterclaims it possesses in the first action pursuant to Federal Rule of Civil Procedure 13(a). Once the defendant asserts a counterclaim, either the rules of claim preclusion or Rule 13(a) work to bar a defendant from raising in a subsequent lawsuit any causes of action that arise out of the same claim as the counterclaim.

Taking claim preclusion apart element by element is helpful for understanding how it operates.

a. Valid Judgment

Beginning with the first element related to the nature of the judgment, in order for an earlier judgment to have claim preclusive effect, it must be a valid judgment. What makes a judgment invalid? One of the most obvious problems with a judgment is that the court that issued the judgment did not have jurisdiction. Indeed, some courts refine this element to require a court of competent jurisdiction to have rendered the first judgment. We know from Chapter 4 that a court that lacks subject matter jurisdiction cannot render a valid judgment. However, courts still consider a judgment valid for preclusion purposes if the parties to the first action had the opportunity to raise subject matter jurisdiction in the first action and lost on that issue. The United States Supreme Court in *Travelers Indemnity Co. v. Bailey,* 557 U.S. 137, 153 (2009), explained that "So long as [the parties to the second action] or those in privity with them were parties to the [first action], and were given a fair chance to challenge the ... Court's subject-matter jurisdiction, they cannot challenge it now [in the second action] by resisting enforcement [of the judgment in the first action]."

A state or federal court need not render the decision in order for that judgment to have preclusive effect. Sometimes judgments coming from "quasi-judicial" proceedings qualify for claim preclusion. For example, judgments from arbitrators and administrative agencies can have preclusive effect under the right circumstances. *See* Restatement (Second) of Judgments §§ 83 & 84 (1982). Generally, courts have recognized the preclusive effect of judgments by administrative agencies when the "agency is acting in a judicial capacity." *See United States v. Utah Constr. & Mining Co.*, 384 U.S. 394, 422 (1966), *superceded on other grounds* (stating that "[w]hen an administrative agency is acting in a judicial capacity and resolved disputed issues of fact properly before it which the parties have had an adequate opportunity to litigate, the courts have not hesitated to apply res judicata to enforce repose.").

However, some courts have recognized an exception to claim preclusion if the first court that decided the claim did not have jurisdiction over a particular theory of liability involved in the second lawsuit. *See* Restatement (Second) of Judgments § 26(c). This situation sometimes occurs when the judicial body rendering the first judgment is an administrative agency.

b. Final Judgment

The second requirement is that the judgment a party is using for claim preclusion must be a final judgment. From the chapter on appeals, you have some idea about what makes a judgment final. For purposes of claim preclusion, a judgment is final when the court has entered a judgment for the plaintiff or defendant. This judgment can result from a jury verdict or an order resolving a motion, such as the court granting a motion for summary judgment. All that is left to do is execute on the judgment or, if a party wishes to do so, appeal. You should be aware that most courts, including the federal courts, consider a judgment final for preclusion purposes even though there is an appeal pending. *See Tripati v. G.L. Henman*, 857 F.2d 1366, 1367 (9th Cir. 1988); WRIGHT, MILLER & COOPER, 18A FED. PRAC. & PROC.: JURIS. 2D § 4427 (2002).

c. On the Merits

The first judgment also must be on the merits. A case that comes to a final judgment based on the verdict of a judge or jury clearly is on the merits. If a case is dismissed on a preliminary matter, such as improper venue, that dismissal does not have claim preclusive effect on a second lawsuit that is filed in a proper venue. Similarly, preliminary issues such as dismissals for lack of personal jurisdiction, subject matter jurisdiction, and the like do not have claim preclusive effect on a second lawsuit that subsequently is filed in the appropriate jurisdiction. Is a judgment entered based on failure to state a claim under Federal Rule of Civil Procedure 12(b)(6) on the merits for purposes of claim preclusion?

d. Same Claim

The claims in the first and second lawsuits must also be the same. What constitutes the same claim for claim preclusion purposes has caused a bit of confusion for the courts and litigants. For example, some courts have used the "same evidence test" familiar in the compulsory counterclaim context as described in chapter 8. Under this test, the court looks to whether the two lawsuits involve the same evidence. Others adopted a "same primary rights" test, which is described in more detail below. Still others have used a "same transaction or occurrence" test, along with the "logical relationship" way of satisfying that test, both of which also should be familiar to you after studying compulsory counterclaims. Much of the controversy involved whether a single transaction or occurrence could give rise to two or more separate claims for claim preclusion purposes. You already know that a single transaction or occurrence (or series thereof) can give rise to several different causes of action or theories of liability. Is each of these different theories of liability a different claim for claim preclusion purposes even though they all involve the same transaction or occurrence?

The answer in the federal court system is no. The federal courts follow a same transaction or occurrence test for determining whether a subsequent lawsuit is precluded by an earlier final judgment on the same claim. *See Kremer v. Chemical Constr. Corp.*, 456 U.S. 461, 482 n.22 (1982) (acknowledging that "[r]es judicata has recently been taken to ban claims arising from the same transaction even if brought under different statutes"). The federal courts follow the same transaction or occurrence test in part due to the liberal joinder rules available in the federal court system that you learned about in Chapter 8. Because joinder is available, a plaintiff may join many different theories of liability in the same lawsuit. Thus, a plaintiff's failure to raise a theory of liability involving the same transaction or occurrence as the earlier lawsuit against the same defendant bars that plaintiff from raising it in a subsequent lawsuit involving that defendant.

An example helps show how the same transaction or occurrence standard works. Assume a plaintiff brings a federal antitrust case against a competitor. The plaintiff loses that lawsuit. The plaintiff now refiles the identical factual lawsuit in state court, except this time it asserts a state unfair competition theory of liability, which includes different elements from the federal claim. The defendant likely can successfully argue that the plaintiff is precluded from bringing the second lawsuit because it was part of the same transaction or occurrence as the first lawsuit. On the other hand, if a plaintiff sues a defendant for breach of a contract that occurred six weeks ago, a judgment in an earlier lawsuit by the plaintiff against the same defendant involving another contract between the same parties breached five years ago will not bar the second lawsuit. The two suits do not arise from the same transaction or occurrence.

The Restatement (Second) of Judgments likewise uses a same transaction test. Comment a to Section 24 states:

> The present trend is to see claim in factual terms and to make it coterminous with the transaction regardless of the number of substantive theories, or variant forms of relief flowing from those theories, that may be available to the plaintiff; regardless of the number of primary rights that may have been invaded; and regardless of the variations in the evidence needed to support

the theories or rights. The transaction is the basis of the litigative unit or entity which may not be split.

Practice Pointer

The Restatement (Second) of Judgments is a very useful resource for the general rules of preclusion as well as for citations to cases that apply these rules. It is a good place to start research on a preclusion issue. You will see courts refer to it in deciding cases involving claim and issue preclusion.

While the same transaction or occurrence test may be the majority rule, there are some jurisdictions that use different tests for determining what is the same claim for claim preclusion purposes. For example, California uses what it terms a primary rights and wrongs approach. In California, a single transaction can give rise to claims based on multiple primary rights. *See Mycogen Corp v. Monsanto Co.*, 28 Cal. 4th 888, 904 (2002). Take, for example, a car accident in which the plaintiff incurred both personal injuries (a broken leg and a concussion, for example) and injuries to her car (her new Acura was totaled). In California, this fact pattern involves two differing primary rights—the right to be free from bodily injury and the right to be free from property damage. Thus, if the plaintiff wants to do so, she can bring two different tort lawsuits seeking damages for violation of two different primary rights. If she wins the first lawsuit based on her bodily injuries, she can still pursue the second lawsuit for the property damage. It will not be merged into the first judgment. In a jurisdiction that follows the same transaction or occurrence standard, both types of injuries would be part of the same claim, because they both arose out of the same car accident (the "same occurrence"). Therefore, once the court issued a final judgment in the plaintiff's favor on the personal injury claim, any claim for property damage by the plaintiff would be merged into the first judgment. How would you determine what definition your jurisdiction uses for the "same claim"?

Exercise 13-1. *Lisboa v. City of Cleveland Heights*

As you read *Lisboa v. City of Cleveland Heights*, answer the following questions:

1. What court is deciding this case? What does this mean for its precedential effect? The court did not authorize this decision for publication in the Federal Reporter. Does this have any effect on its precedential value?

2. This case involves multiple lawsuits. Diagram the various lawsuits. Who sued whom for what, and what was the outcome?

3. What Rule of Civil Procedure does the defendant use to raise claim preclusion in this case?

4. The court cites 28 U.S.C. § 1738. How is it relevant to preclusion?

5. Why does the federal court follow Ohio preclusion law?

6. This case involves the preclusive effect of a consent decree. Look up this term in a legal dictionary. According to the court, is this a final judgment on the merits for purposes of claim preclusion?

7. What test(s) does the *Lisboa* court use to evaluate whether the two lawsuits involve the same transaction or occurrence?

8. The *Lisboa* court aligns claim preclusion with the compulsory counterclaim rule. Why does it do so? In what ways do these two concepts appear alike?

Lisboa v. City of Cleveland Heights

___ Fed. Appx. ___, 2014 WL 3891290 (6th Cir. Aug. 6, 2014)

Sutton, Circuit Judge.

Kimberly Lisboa and others owned a nightclub in Cleveland Heights, Ohio. When the club generated noise, fights, and other disturbances in the community, the City sued the owners in state court to stop the nuisance, and the owners sued to defend their actions and to charge the City with acting improperly. The parties eventually entered a consent decree that resolved the two lawsuits, that allowed the club to stay open for a while, and that eventually required the owners to close the club. Not long after signing the consent decree, the club owners filed this § 1983 action alleging due process and equal protection violations surrounding the City's public-nuisance action. The district court granted the City judgment on the pleadings based on claim preclusion. We affirm.

I.

In 2011, Lisboa and others opened a nightclub. MYXX, as they named the club, was popular, perhaps too popular. About a year after the club opened, fights, noise problems, and underage drinking prompted the City of Cleveland Heights to declare the place a public nuisance. The City Council authorized the City Manager and Director of Law to take all appropriate legal action to abate the nuisance. Three weeks later, in the early morning hours, a crowd of drunken partiers poured out of the club onto the street. Calls to the police from unhappy neighbors followed, and many officers were dispatched in response. The City was not happy.

Fed up, the City sued the plaintiffs in Ohio state court, seeking an injunction to end the nuisance once and for all. Lisboa beat the City to the punch, filing for an injunction of her own earlier the same day in a separate action in state court. Among other things, Lisboa claimed that the City enforced its ordinances in a racially discriminatory way and that the nuisance charge was baseless. The parties settled the consolidated actions. They memorialized the settlement in a court-approved consent decree, which allowed Lisboa to keep the club open for a little while longer but eventually required her to close it for good. That, it seemed, was the end of that.

Less than two months later, however, Lisboa filed this § 1983 action in federal court. She raised due process and equal protection claims that largely tracked the factual predicates of her state court claims: insufficient evidence to brand MYXX a nuisance, procedural violations of city law, and discriminatory enforcement targeting the club's predominantly black patrons. Invoking the consent decree, the City moved for judgment on the pleadings based on claim preclusion. The district court agreed. It held that Lisboa's constitutional claims were precluded because she could have, and should have, pursued them in the state litigation.

II.

We give fresh review to a district court's grant of judgment on the pleadings under Civil Rule 12(c). As with review of a Civil Rule 12(b)(6) motion, the question is whether the plaintiff's complaint alleges sufficient facts that state a plausible claim for relief.

In federal court, state court judgments receive the same preclusive effect they would receive in the issuing State's courts. 28 U.S.C. § 1738; *Marrese v. Am. Acad. of Orthopaedic Surgeon*, 470 U.S. 373, 380 (1985). That means we look to Ohio's law of claim preclusion (otherwise known as res judicata), which has four elements: "(1) a prior final, valid decision on the merits by a court of competent jurisdiction; (2) a second action involving the same parties, or their privies, as the first; (3) a second action raising claims that were or could have been litigated in the first action; and (4) a second action arising out of the transaction or occurrence that was the subject matter of the previous action." *Hapgood v. City of Warren*, 127 F.3d 490, 493 (6th Cir. 1997); *see also Grava v. Parkman Twp.*, 653 N.E.2d 226, 229 (Ohio 1995). If all four elements are met, claim preclusion bars the later lawsuit.

Lisboa does not dispute that consent judgments satisfy the first element, as well they do. She does not deny that the parties in both actions overlap. And she does not claim that any obstacle prevented her from raising her federal claims when she filed the first lawsuit.

What separates the parties is the fourth inquiry: Did the second action arise out of the same "transaction or occurrence" as the first? Like the district court, we think it did. Two sets of claims meet this test if, in the language of the case law, they arise from a "common nucleus of operative facts," *Grava*, 653 N.E.2d at 229 (quotation omitted), or if, in the language of everyday people, they are "logically related," *Rettig Enterprises, Inc. v.*

Koehler, 626 N.E.2d 99, 103 (Ohio 1994) (quotation omitted). However phrased, the test is met here. Compare the two actions. In the first one, the parties sued each other over the City's effort to abate the nuisance caused by the fighting, underage drinking, and loud noise—the general disorderly conduct—surrounding MYXX and over the allegedly discriminatory manner in which the City enforced its laws. After the consent decree, Lisboa sued the City under § 1983 for its response to those same disturbances: declaring the club a nuisance in violation of the City's own procedures and racially discriminatory enforcement of its laws. The pattern of disruptive activity behind both suits is the same, and the alleged problem with the City's response is the same. On this record, both sets of claims arise from a shared "occurrence" or "common nucleus of operative facts."

Lisboa persists that the facts relevant to her constitutional claims are sufficiently different from those at issue in the City's case to avoid preclusion. In the prior litigation, she submits, her § 1983 claims would have been permissive, rather than compulsory, counterclaims, and thus she would have had no obligation to bring them then. Her argument, as an initial matter, overlooks the reality that she filed her *own* lawsuit against the City in state court, making the premise of this argument a distinction between compulsory and permissive counterclaims—beside the point.

Even if we ignore this reality, her argument still falls short. One premise of this argument, to be sure, is correct; yet the other is not. Lisboa is right that permissive counterclaims are not later precluded. But she is wrong to give the § 1983 claims this label. What makes a counterclaim compulsory is *also* what triggers preclusion: that the claim arises from the same "transaction or occurrence." Just so here, as we noted. Nor, contrary to her suggestion, is a perfect overlap of the claims required to meet the test. "That they are not precisely identical, or that the counterclaim embraces additional allegations does not matter." [*Rettig Enterprises, Inc. v. Koehler*, 68 Ohio St. 3d. 274, 626 N.E.2d 99, 103 (1994)] (internal quotation marks and ellipsis omitted). Lisboa identifies no material differences between the two actions. As a result, the claims Lisboa asserts now were compulsory counterclaims that should have been brought earlier. Having opted to settle the first actions (hers and the City's) through a consent judgment and having presumably benefited from the give and take of settlement discussions (including being able to keep the club open for a while longer), Lisboa had no right under Ohio law to sue the City again over the same disputes.

For these reasons, we affirm.

Note on *Whole Woman's Health v. Hellerstedt*

In *Whole Woman's Health v. Hellerstedt*, ___ U.S. ___, 136 S. Ct. 2292 (2016) (Breyer, J.), the Supreme Court of the United States addressed what constitutes the same claim for purposes of preclusion in the context of repeated challenges to restrictions on abortion providers imposed by the State of Texas. The providers challenged two aspects of the law—a requirement that abortion providers have admitting privileges at a hospital located no more than thirty miles from the facility and a requirement that the facility satisfy the minimum requirements for an ambulatory surgical center. The first lawsuit only involved the admitting privileges requirement. The Court permitted abortion providers to bring a second lawsuit seeking declaratory and injunctive relief from the Texas statutes and their implementing rules even though many of the same providers had lost in the Fifth Circuit in an earlier lawsuit that involved a facial challenge to the admitting privileges law before it was implemented. In the second lawsuit, the plaintiffs brought as-applied challenges to the admitting privileges and surgical center requirements.

In examining the admitting privileges requirement, the Court explained that claim preclusion only applies to the "very same claim." Relying on the Restatement (Second) of Judgments, which "notes that development of new material facts can mean that a new case and an otherwise similar previous case do not present the same claim," the Court permitted a second suit on this aspect of the law. *Id.* at 2305. The Court also highlighted Restatement language stating that in cases in which "'important human values—such as the lawfulness of continuing personal disability or restraint—are at stake, even a slight change of circumstances may afford a sufficient basis for concluding that a second action may be brought.'" *Id.* (quoting Restatement (Second) of Judgments § 24, comment f (1980)). The Court further explained, "[h]ere, petitioners bring an as-applied challenge to the requirement after its enforcement—and after a large number of clinics have in fact closed. The postenforcement consequences of [the Texas law] were unknowable before it went into effect.... And the Court of Appeals in this case properly decided that new evidence presented by petitioner had given rise to a new claim and that petitioners' as-applied challenges are not precluded." *Id.* at 2306 (emphasis in the original). The Court also held that the challenge to the surgical center requirement that was not challenged in the first lawsuit was likewise not precluded, reasoning that challenges to different portions of a statute can give rise to differing claims for preclusion purposes and that there were good reasons for the plaintiffs to wait to challenge the surgical center requirement.

Exercise 13-2. *Lisboa v. City of Cleveland Heights* Revisited

Based on your reading of *Lisboa v. City of Cleveland Heights* as well as the general rules above regarding what constitutes the "same claim," determine whether the following lawsuits involve the "same claim" for claim preclusion purposes.

1. An employee is fired from her job and files a lawsuit under Title VII of the Civil Rights Act of 1964, alleging that she was terminated based on her sex. After a trial on the merits, the jury finds for her and awards her $300,000 in damages. The plaintiff also had a contract of employment with this employer. The term of employment in the contract was three years. Plaintiff had only completed two years of her employment at the time she was fired. If she brings a second lawsuit for breach of contract, will the defendant be successful using a claim preclusion defense? Does your answer change if this is a primary rights jurisdiction? *See Yapp v. Excel Corp.*, 186 F.3d 1222 (10th Cir. 1999) (claim preclusion barred later lawsuit).

2. A plaintiff sues a police officer in state court for battery after the police officer allegedly beat the plaintiff during a traffic stop. This first lawsuit comes to a final judgment in favor of the plaintiff. The plaintiff brings a second lawsuit in federal court against the defendant police officer based on the same traffic stop, alleging violation of 28 U.S.C. §1983, a federal civil rights statute that prohibits violations of the Constitution under color of law. Will the defendant be successful on a claim preclusion defense in the second lawsuit?

3. A plaintiff is injured in an accident while riding a motorcycle. She brings an action for damages to her motorcycle against the driver who caused the accident. The jury awards her $15,000 in damages. Plaintiff brings a second action against the defendant in another court alleging personal injuries due to the accident. Will the defendant be successful in arguing claim preclusion in the second action? *See Rush v. City of Maple Heights*, 167 Ohio St. 221 (1958) (claim preclusion barred subsequent suit).

4. In an effort to help the struggling racehorse industry in Illinois, the state enacted a law that placed a tax on casinos. The proceeds of that tax were paid to the horse racing tracks in the state to help the industry continue. The governor's office purportedly played a role in getting the bill passed. After the law was passed, members of the horseracing industry made a $100,000 contribution to the governor's campaign. Immediately after the Illinois legislature passed the tax, several casinos filed a lawsuit in state court against the state challenging the constitutionality of the tax under both the state and federal constitutions. The horseracing track owners intervened in the lawsuit. The state court granted summary judgment for the defendants, and that decision was upheld by the Illinois Supreme Court. The same race tracks filed a second lawsuit in federal court against the governor and the casinos, alleging a conspiracy to exchange campaign contributions for state action in violation of the Racketeer Influenced and Corrupt Organizations Act ("RICO"). Will the defendants be successful in arguing claim preclusion in the second action? *See Empress Casino Joliet*

> *Corp. v. Johnston*, 763 F.3d 723 (7th Cir. 2014) (claim preclusion did not bar lawsuit).

e. Same Parties

Claim preclusion also requires that the two lawsuits involve the same parties or those in privity with the original parties. Application of this element is simple when the parties in the first lawsuit are identical to the parties in the second lawsuit. However, when a new party is introduced in the second lawsuit that has some relationship with a party to the first lawsuit, the courts apply the rules of privity. Who is in privity with a party can be difficult to determine. Case law in this area is often inconsistent. Some courts have even acknowledged that there is no set definition of privity in this context. *See, e.g., Satsky v. Paramount Communications, Inc.*, 7 F.3d 1464, 1469 (10th Cir. 1993). Thus, it is important to examine case law involving similar parties in the particular jurisdiction in which you are raising privity to determine how a court would address a particular fact pattern.

Privity has due process implications. Due process dictates that a party is entitled to his or her day in court. Privity functions as an exception to this in situations in which the interests of the party in the first lawsuit are so aligned with the interests of the new party in the second lawsuit that it is fair to bind the new party to the earlier judgment. Examples of parties who courts have acknowledged are sometimes in privity include a city and a public library it supported (*see Adefumi v. City of Philadelphia*, 445 Fed. Appx. 610, 610–611 (3d Cir. 2011)), employers and employees (*see Krepps v. Reiner*, 377 Fed. Appx. 65, 68 (2d Cir. 2010)), a guardian and a ward, and a trustee and a beneficiary of the trust. *Richards v. Jefferson County*, 517 U.S. 793, 798 (1996) (noting these as examples of parties who may be in privity).

Note on "Virtual Representation"

Some courts have noted that parties can be in privity "where a party in the prior suit is so closely aligned to her interests as to be her virtual representative." *Eubanks v. FCIC*, 977 F.2d 166, 170 (5th Cir. 1996). Despite the Fifth Circuit's reference to "virtual representation" as a basis for privity, based on the due process implications of binding non-parties to a previous judgment, the United States Supreme Court has rejected the concept of "virtual representation" in *Taylor v. Sturgell*, 553 U.S. 880 (2008).

Taylor involved successive lawsuits brought by different plaintiffs against the same defendant based on Freedom of Information Act requests that the Federal Aviation Administration denied. The plaintiff in the first lawsuit, Herrick, lost. The plaintiff in the second lawsuit, Taylor, was a friend of the plaintiff in the first lawsuit. However, the relationship between the two plaintiffs and their lawsuits was thin. As the Court described,

Taylor is the president of the Antique Aircraft Association, an organization to which Herrick belongs; the two men are "close associate[s]"; Herrick asked Taylor to help restore Herrick's F-45 [airplane], though they had no contract or agreement for Taylor's participation in the restoration; Taylor was represented by the lawyer who represented Herrick in the earlier litigation; and Herrick apparently gave Taylor documents that Herrick had obtained from the FAA during discovery in his suit.

553 U.S. at 889.

Rejecting a "virtual representation" theory, the Court set out six instances in which a prior judgment could bind a non-party.

Though hardly in doubt, the rule against nonparty preclusion is subject to exceptions. For present purposes, the recognized exceptions can be grouped into six categories.

First, "[a] person who agrees to be bound by the determination of issues in an action between others is bound in accordance with the terms of his agreement." 1 Restatement (Second) of Judgments § 40, p. 390 (1980) (hereinafter Restatement). For example, "if separate actions involving the same transaction are brought by different plaintiffs against the same defendant, all the parties to all the actions may agree that the question of the defendant's liability will be definitely determined, one way or the other, in a 'test case.'" D. SHAPIRO, CIVIL PROCEDURE: PRECLUSION IN CIVIL ACTIONS 77–78 (2001) (hereinafter SHAPIRO)....

Second, nonparty preclusion may be justified based on a variety of pre-existing "substantive legal relationship[s]" between the person to be bound and a party to the judgment. SHAPIRO, [supra, at] 78. Qualifying relationships include, but are not limited to, preceding and succeeding owners of property, bailee and bailor, and assignee and assignor. See 2 Restatement §§ 43–44, 52, 55. These exceptions originated "as much from the needs of property law as from the values of preclusion by judgment." 18A C. WRIGHT, A. MILLER, & E. COOPER, FEDERAL PRACTICE AND PROCEDURE § 4448, p. 329 (2d ed. 2002) (hereinafter WRIGHT & MILLER).

Third, we have confirmed that, "in certain limited circumstances," a nonparty may be bound by a judgment because she was "adequately represented by someone with the same interests who [wa]s a party" to the suit. Richards v. Jefferson County, Alabama, 517 U.S. 793, 798 (1996), (internal quotation marks omitted). Representative suits with preclusive effect on nonparties include properly conducted class actions, and suits brought by trustees, guardians, and other fiduciaries.

Fourth, a nonparty is bound by a judgment if she "assume[d] control" over the litigation in which that judgment was rendered. Montana, 440 U.S. at 154. Because such a person has had "the opportunity to present proofs and argument," he has already "had his day in court" even though he was not a formal party to the litigation. [1 Restatement § 39], Comment *a*, p. 382.

Fifth, a party bound by a judgment may not avoid its preclusive force by re-litigating through a proxy. Preclusion is thus in order when a person who did not participate in a litigation later brings suit as the designated representative of a person who was a party to the prior adjudication. And although our decisions have not addressed the issue directly, it also seems clear that preclusion is appropriate when a nonparty later brings suit as an agent for a party who is bound by a judgment.

Sixth, in certain circumstances a special statutory scheme may "expressly foreclos[e] successive litigation by nonlitigants ... if the scheme is otherwise consistent with due process." *Martin*, 490 U.S. at 762 n.2. Examples of such schemes include bankruptcy and probate proceedings, and *quo warranto* actions or other suits that, "under [the governing] law, [may] be brought only on behalf of the public at large," *Richards*, 517 U.S. at 804.

Taylor v. Sturgell, 553 U.S. 880, 893–95 (2008). The Court did note that its decision likely would not affect the many circuits that had adopted varying theories of virtual representation, because many of those cases would fit within the categories described above. Perhaps based on this fact, the lower courts continue to use the term "virtual representation" in spite of the Supreme Court's rejection of it. *See, e.g., White v. Fox*, 576 Fed. Appx. 327, 331 (5th Cir. 2014) (per curiam).

Note on Potential Exceptions to Claim Preclusion

Sometimes a court comes across such a particularly sympathetic case that it strains to find a way around claim preclusion even though the elements of the defense are met. The following case provides an example of such a situation.

Exercise 13-3. *Federated Department Stores, Inc. v. Moitie*

As you read the *Moitie* case, answer the following questions.

1. Were the elements of claim preclusion met in this case? Go through each element to determine whether it was met.

2. What were the court of appeals' arguments that claim preclusion should not be applied to this case? Why did the Supreme Court reject them?

3. What does the result of this case mean for future litigants who lose at the trial court level? As their lawyer, what would you advise them to do? Does this make sense ethically and economically?

Federated Department Stores, Inc. v. Moitie
452 U.S. 394 (1981)

Justice Rehnquist delivered the opinion of the Court.

The only question presented in this case is whether the Court of Appeals for the Ninth Circuit validly created an exception to the doctrine of res judicata. The court held that res judicata does not bar relitigation of an unappealed adverse judgment where, as here, other plaintiffs in similar actions against common defendants successfully appealed the judgments against them. We disagree with the view taken by the Court of Appeals for the Ninth Circuit and reverse.

I

In 1976 the United States brought an antitrust action against petitioners, owners of various department stores, alleging that they had violated § 1 of the Sherman Act, 15 U.S.C. § 1, by agreeing to fix the retail price of women's clothing sold in northern California. Seven parallel civil actions were subsequently filed by private plaintiffs seeking treble damages on behalf of proposed classes of retail purchasers, including that of respondent Moitie in state court (*Moitie I*) and respondent Brown (*Brown I*) in the United States District Court for the Northern District of California. Each of these complaints tracked almost verbatim the allegations of the Government's complaint, though the *Moitie I* complaint referred solely to state law. All of the actions originally filed in the District Court were assigned to a single federal judge, and the *Moitie I* case was removed there on the basis of diversity of citizenship and federal-question jurisdiction. The District Court dismissed all of the actions "in their entirety" on the ground that plaintiffs had not alleged an "injury" to their "business or property" within the meaning of § 4 of the Clayton Act, 15 U.S.C. § 15.

Plaintiffs in five of the suits appealed that judgment to the Court of Appeals for the Ninth Circuit. The single counsel representing Moitie and Brown, however, chose not to appeal and instead refiled the two actions in state court, *Moitie II* and *Brown II.* Although the complaints purported to raise only state-law claims, they made allegations similar to those made in the prior complaints, including that of the Government. Petitioners removed these new actions to the District Court for the Northern District of California and moved to have them dismissed on the ground of res judicata. In a decision rendered July 8, 1977, the District Court first denied respondents' motion to remand. It held that the complaints, though artfully couched in terms of state law, were "in many respects identical" with the prior complaints, and were thus properly removed to federal court because they raised "essentially federal law" claims. The court then concluded that because *Moitie II* and *Brown II* involved the "same parties, the same alleged offenses, and the same time periods" as *Moitie I* and *Brown I*, the doctrine of res judicata required that they be dismissed this time, Moitie and Brown appealed.

Pending that appeal, this Court on June 11, 1979, decided *Reiter v. Sonotone Corp.*, 442 U.S. 330, holding that retail purchasers can suffer an "injury" to their "business or property" as those terms are used in § 4 of the Clayton Act. On June 25, 1979, the Court of Appeals for the Ninth Circuit reversed and remanded the five cases which had been decided with *Moitie I* and *Brown I*, the cases that had been appealed, for further proceedings in light of Reiter.

When *Moitie II* and *Brown II* finally came before the Court of Appeals for the Ninth Circuit, the court reversed the decision of the District Court dismissing the cases. Though the court recognized that a "strict application of the doctrine of res judicata would preclude our review of the instant decision," 611 F.2d 1267, 1269 (9th Cir. 1980), it refused to apply the doctrine to the facts of this case. It observed that the other five litigants in the Weinberg cases had successfully appealed the decision against them. It then asserted that "non-appealing parties may benefit from a reversal when their position is closely interwoven with that of appealing parties," *id.*, and concluded that "[b]ecause the instant dismissal rested on a case that has been effectively overruled," the doctrine of res judicata must give way to "public policy" and "simple justice." *Id.* at 1269–1270. We granted certiorari to consider the validity of the Court of Appeals' novel exception to the doctrine of res judicata.

II

There is little to be added to the doctrine of res judicata as developed in the case law of this Court. A final judgment on the merits of an action precludes the parties or their privies from relitigating issues that were or could have been raised in that action. Nor are the res judicata consequences of a final, unappealed judgment on the merits altered by the fact that the judgment may have been wrong or rested on a legal principle subsequently overruled in another case. As this Court explained in *Baltimore S.S. Co. v. Phillips*, 274 U.S. 316, 325 (1927), an "erroneous conclusion" reached by the court in the first suit does not deprive the defendants in the second action "of their right to rely upon the plea of res judicata.... A judgment merely voidable because based upon an erroneous view of the law is not open to collateral attack, but can be corrected only by a direct review and not by bringing another action upon the same cause [of action]." We have observed that "[t]he indulgence of a contrary view would result in creating elements of uncertainty and confusion and in undermining the conclusive character of judgments, consequences which it was the very purpose of the doctrine of res judicata to avert." *Reed v. Allen*, 286 U.S. 191, 201 (1932).

In this case, the Court of Appeals conceded that the "strict application of the doctrine of res judicata" required that *Brown II* be dismissed. By that, the court presumably meant that the "technical elements" of res judicata had been satisfied, namely, that the decision in *Brown I* was a final judgment on the merits and involved the same claims and the same parties as *Brown II*. The court, however, declined to dismiss *Brown II* because, in its view, it would be unfair to bar respondents from relitigating a claim so "closely interwoven" with that of the successfully appealing parties. We believe that such an unprecedented departure from accepted principles of res judicata is unwarranted. Indeed, the decision below is all but foreclosed by our prior case law.

In *Reed v. Allen*, this Court addressed the issue presented here. The case involved a dispute over the rights to property left in a will. A won an interpleader action for rents derived from the property and, while an appeal was pending, brought an ejectment action against the rival claimant B. On the basis of the decree in the interpleader suit A won the ejectment action. B did not appeal this judgment, but prevailed on his earlier appeal from the interpleader decree and was awarded the rents which had been collected. When B sought to bring an ejectment action against A, the latter pleaded res judicata, based on his previous successful ejectment action. This Court held that res judicata was available as a defense and that the property belonged to A:

> "The judgment in the ejectment action was final and not open to assault collaterally, but subject to impeachment only through some form of direct attack. The appellate court was limited to a review of the interpleader decree; and it is hardly necessary to say that jurisdiction to review one judgment gives an appellate court no power to reverse or modify another and independent judgment. If respondent, in addition to appealing from the [interpleader] decree, had appealed from the [ejectment] judgment, the appellate court, having both cases before it, might have afforded a remedy.... But this course respondent neglected to follow." *Id.* at 198.

This Court's rigorous application of res judicata in *Reed*, to the point of leaving one party in possession and the other party entitled to the rents, makes clear that this Court recognizes no general equitable doctrine, such as that suggested by the Court of Appeals, which countenances an exception to the finality of a party's failure to appeal merely because his rights are "closely interwoven" with those of another party. Indeed, this case presents even more compelling reasons to apply the doctrine of res judicata than did *Reed*. Respondents here seek to be the windfall beneficiaries of an appellate reversal procured by other independent parties, who have no interest in respondents' case, not a reversal in interrelated cases procured, as in *Reed*, by the same affected party. Moreover, in contrast to *Reed*, where it was unclear why no appeal was taken, it is apparent that respondents here made a calculated choice to forgo their appeals.

The Court of Appeals also rested its opinion in part on what it viewed as "simple justice." But we do not see the grave injustice which would be done by the application of accepted principles of res judicata. "Simple justice" is achieved when a complex body of law developed over a period of years is evenhandedly applied. The doctrine of res judicata serves vital public interests beyond any individual judge's ad hoc determination of the equities in a particular case. There is simply "no principle of law or equity which sanctions the rejection by a federal court of the salutary principle of res judicata." *Heiser v. Woodruff*, 327 U.S. 726, 733 (1946).

The Court of Appeals' reliance on "public policy" is similarly misplaced. This Court has long recognized that "[p]ublic policy dictates that there be an end of litigation; that those who have contested an issue shall be bound by the result of the contest, and that matters once tried shall be considered forever settled as between the parties." *Baldwin v. Traveling Men's Assn.*, 283 U.S. 522, 525 (1931). We have stressed that "[the] doctrine of res judicata is not a mere matter of practice or procedure inherited from a more technical time than ours. It is a rule of fundamental and substantial justice, 'of public policy and of private peace,' which should be cordially regarded and enforced by the courts...." *Hart Steel Co. v. Railroad Supply Co.*, 244 U.S. 294, 299 (1917). The language used by this Court half a century ago is even more compelling in view of today's crowded dockets:

> "The predicament in which respondent finds himself is of his own making.... [W]e cannot be expected, for his sole relief, to upset the general and well-established doctrine of res judicata, conceived in the light of the maxim that the interest of the state requires that there be an end to litigation—a maxim which comports with common sense as well as public policy. And the mischief which would follow the establishment of precedent for so disregarding this salutary doctrine against prolonging strife would be greater than the benefit which would result from relieving some case of individual hardship." *Reed v. Allen*, 286 U.S. at 198–199.

Respondents make no serious effort to defend the decision of the Court of Appeals. They do not ask that the decision below be affirmed. Instead, they conclude that "the writ of certiorari should be dismissed as improvidently granted." In the alternative, they argue that "the district court's dismissal on grounds of res judicata should be reversed, and the district court directed to grant respondent's motion to remand to the California state court." In their view, *Brown I* cannot be considered res judicata as to their state-law claims, since *Brown I* raised only federal-law claims and *Brown II* raised additional state-law claims not decided in *Brown I*, such as unfair competition, fraud, and restitution.

It is unnecessary for this Court to reach that issue. It is enough for our decision here that *Brown I* is res judicata as to respondents' federal-law claims. Accordingly, the judgment of the Court of Appeals is reversed, and the cause is remanded for proceedings consistent with this opinion.

It is so ordered.

Exercise 13-4. Applying the Basic Concepts of Claim Preclusion

Recall that claim preclusion has three basic requirements: (1) a valid final judgment on the merits; (2) the same claim; and (3) the same parties or those in privity with the parties. Using the same transaction or occurrence test for "same claim," determine whether the judgment in the first lawsuit would preclude the second lawsuit. As you assess each problem, make sure you consider each element of claim preclusion.

1. Plaintiff brings a lawsuit in the federal district court for the Southern District of New York. Defendant moves to dismiss based on improper service. The court grants the motion under Federal Rule of Civil Procedure 12(b)(5). Plaintiff refiles the lawsuit and serves the defendant properly. Will the defendant be successful using a claim preclusion defense in the second lawsuit?

2. Plaintiff files a lawsuit against the defendant, who fails to answer. Plaintiff makes a motion for a default judgment, which is granted, and judgment is entered in favor of the plaintiff. Plaintiff files a second action in state court against the defendant in the first action, making the same allegations under a parallel state law. Will the defendant be successful in state court using a claim preclusion defense?

3. Plaintiff taxpayers file a lawsuit against a state, challenging a state tax as violating the federal Constitution. The federal court grants summary judgment, holding that the tax is constitutional as a matter of law. The court enters judgment against the taxpayers. A second group of taxpayers files a lawsuit in federal court against the same state challenging the same tax under both the state and federal constitutions. Will the state be successful using a claim preclusion defense?

4. A plaintiff and defendant settle a breach of contract case, and the court enters an order dismissing the case without prejudice. The plaintiff files a second lawsuit for breach of contract based on the same facts. Will the defendant be successful using a claim preclusion defense?

5. Plaintiff mover files an action against a homeowner to whom it provided moving services for failure to pay all moving fees pursuant to a contract between the moving company and the homeowner. While the company

moved items owned by the homeowner and his wife, only the husband signed the contract. The trial court entered summary judgment in favor of the plaintiff mover. The homeowner and his wife file a tort action in federal court based on diversity against the moving company and its local agent who had negotiated the contract, alleging that some of their belongings were broken and that others were simply stolen during the moving process. Will the defendants in the second lawsuit be successful arguing claim preclusion in the tort action? *See Cleckner v. Republic Van and Storage Co., Inc.*, 556 F.2d 766 (5th Cir. 1977) (subsequent action barred by Florida compulsory counterclaim rule).

6. Plaintiffs brought a class action on behalf of homeowners who were provided mortgages by Mortgage Company. The class action alleged that the Mortgage Company set mortgage pricing policies in a manner that discriminated based on race in violation of the federal Fair Housing Act and Equal Credit Opportunity Act. The class was certified, and the parties entered into a settlement agreement, whereby the plaintiff class was awarded money damages. The trial court approved the settlement pursuant to Federal Rule of Civil Procedure 23. Amanda Vargas, a member of the class in the first action, brought a subsequent action on her own behalf alleging that Mortgage Company set terms on her mortgage that violated the Fair Housing Act and Equal Credit Opportunity Act. Will the Mortgage Company be successful in arguing claim preclusion in Ms. Vargas's lawsuit? *See Vargas v. Capital One Financial Advisors*, 559 Fed. Appx. 22 (2d Cir. 2014) (case barred by prior action and release).

4. Issue Preclusion

Issue preclusion prevents a party from relitigating an issue that was already litigated and adjudicated in a prior lawsuit. In an early case involving this concept, *Southern Pacific Railroad Co. v. United States*, 168 U.S. 1, 48–49 (1897), the first Justice Harlan described it:

> The general principle announced in numerous cases is that a right, question, or fact distinctly put in issue and directly determined by a court of competent jurisdiction, as a ground of recovery, cannot be disputed in a subsequent suit between the same parties or their privies; and, even if the second suit is for a different cause of action, the right, question, or fact once so determined must, as between the same parties or their privies, be taken as conclusively established, so long as the judgment in the first suit remains unmodified.

As this quote suggests, issue preclusion has some of the same elements as claim preclusion. It requires a valid final judgment and generally applies to parties and those in privity with parties. There are also some significant differences. The issue that has preclusive effect must have been actually litigated and determined between the parties. This differs from claim preclusion, under which an earlier judgment can preclude theories of liability that the parties never raised. In addition, modern courts have permitted third parties to use issue preclusion under the right circumstances.

Courts have various ways that they set out the elements of issue preclusion. Common elements used include:

- Nature of Judgment—The issue must be the subject of
  - a valid
  - final judgment
- On the same issue. Some courts use the term "identical issue."
- The issue was actually litigated and decided in the first lawsuit.
- The decision on the issue was necessary to the court's judgment.
- The parties are the same, in privity with the original parties, or the party against whom the earlier judgment is being used had a full and fair opportunity to litigate the issue in the first action. Many courts permit third parties to use issue preclusion if the party against whom they are asserting it had a full and fair opportunity to litigate the issue in the first lawsuit.

For comparison purposes, the Restatement (Second) of Judgments, Section 27, defines issue preclusion in this manner: "When an issue of fact or law is actually litigated and determined by a valid and final judgment, and the determination is essential to the judgment, the determination is conclusive in a subsequent action between the parties, whether on the same or a different claim." The elements are largely the same, with some slightly different terminology (e.g., "essential" to the judgment in the Restatement whereas we're using "necessary" in the elements above).

Parties can use issue preclusion both defensively and offensively. Thus, a plaintiff in a second lawsuit can use it offensively to prevent a defendant from relitigating an issue that was decided in the plaintiff's favor in the first lawsuit. In addition, a defendant that had an issue decided in its favor can use that judgment defensively to prevent relitigation of that issue in a subsequent lawsuit by the same plaintiff. Like claim preclusion, it's easier to understand issue preclusion by examining each element, including how issue preclusion differs from claim preclusion.

a. A Valid Final Judgment

Although this requirement looks the same as that applied in the claim preclusion context, courts have interpreted it slightly differently in the issue preclusion context. First, missing from this element for issue preclusion is that the judgment is "on the merits." If an issue that a party wants to avoid relitigating involves a procedural issue, the case need not be resolved on the merits of the underlying claims in the case for the judgment to be final for purposes of issue preclusion. An example helps illustrate this point. Assume that a breach of contract case is dismissed under Federal Rule of

Civil Procedure 12(b)(2) based on lack of personal jurisdiction over the defendant. If the plaintiff files the same case against the same defendant in the same jurisdiction, the defendant may raise the issue preclusive effect of the personal jurisdiction decision even though the first court never decided the underlying breach of contract claim on the merits. The first case was decided on the procedural issue and therefore has issue preclusive effect on that issue. *See, e.g., Transaero, Inc. v. La Fuerza Aerea Boliviana*, 162 F.3d 724, 731 (2d Cir. 1998). The plaintiff is still free to refile the case in an appropriate jurisdiction.

Second, some courts have been less stringent on the final judgment requirement for purposes of issue preclusion. In the context of claim preclusion, all that should remain in the case is execution of the judgment. In the issue preclusion context, the RESTATEMENT (SECOND) OF JUDGMENTS has acknowledged that "'[F]inal judgment' includes any prior adjudication of an issue in another action that is determined to be sufficiently firm to be accorded conclusive effect." *See* RESTATEMENT (SECOND) JUDGMENTS § 13 (1982); id. § 13, cmt. g, illus. 3; *see also Christo v. Padgett*, 223 F.3d 1324, 1339 (11th Cir. 2000) ("It is widely recognized that the finality requirement is less stringent for issue preclusion than for claim preclusion."); 18A CHARLES ALAN WRIGHT, FEDERAL PRACTICE AND PROCEDURE § 4434 (2d ed. 2002) ("Recent decisions have relaxed traditional views of the finality requirement by applying issue preclusion to matters resolved by preliminary rulings or to determinations of liability that have not yet been completed by an award of damages or other relief."). Why would the courts permit preliminary decisions to have issue preclusive effect in this manner?

The Supreme Court of the United States opined on the preclusive effect of administrative judgments in *B & B Hardware, Inc. v. Hargis Industries, Inc.*, ___ U.S. ___, 135 S. Ct. 1293 (2015). The Court held that a federal court should give issue preclusive effect to a decision by the Trademark Trial and Appeal Board ("TTAB") denying the registration of a trademark because it would cause confusion with an existing mark. The two actions, one in federal court and one before the TTAB, were pending at the same time. The TTAB action came to a final decision prior to the federal district court's ruling on the issue of likelihood of confusion. Justice Alito, for the majority, was clear that administrative decisions can have preclusive effect when an agency is acting in a judicial capacity, as provided for by Congress, so long as there is no evident indication of a statutory purpose to the contrary. *Id.* at 1303. Although the Eighth Circuit refused to give the TTAB's decision issue preclusive effect, reasoning that it used different factors to assess the likelihood of confusion than the TTAB, the Court opined that "'[m]inor variations in the application of what is in essence the same legal standard do not defeat preclusion.'" *Id.* at 1306 (quoting *Smith v. Bayer Corp.*, 564 U.S. 299, 312 n.9 (2011)).

b. Same Issue Was Actually Litigated

The issue resolved in the first lawsuit must be identical to the issue on which the party seeks preclusion in the second lawsuit for issue preclusion to apply. An example helps illustrate this. Suppose in a breach of contract action, the court held that there was a breach of contract and awarded the plaintiff damages for the breach. In a second action involving a new breach of the same contract, the same defendant raises for the first time that there was a failure of consideration for the contract. The defendant is not precluded from raising this issue in the second lawsuit because it was not litigated in the first lawsuit. On the other hand, if the defendant litigated the issue of failure of consideration in the first lawsuit, and the court rendered a judgment against the defendant on this issue, the defendant is precluded from raising it in the second lawsuit.

The "same issue" element is joined here for discussion purposes with the "actually litigated" element, because often both issues arise in the same case. Logically, if there is some question about whether an issue was determined in a case, this often is intermingled with the issue of whether the issue was actually litigated. An example of this is provided in the *O'Neal v. Remington Arms* case below.

Unlike claim preclusion, for issue preclusion to apply, the parties must have actually litigated the issue in order to be precluded from relitigating it. For claim preclusion to bar relitigation, it does not matter whether the parties raised the particular theory of liability in the first case. As long as the first case involved the same transaction or occurrence, claim preclusion applies.

So what does it mean to actually litigate an issue? Certainly, if the parties put on evidence as to an issue and the factfinder ultimately rules on that issue, the parties actually litigated that issue. However, what if a court enters a default judgment on the issue of liability? Have the parties actually litigated liability in the sense relevant for issue preclusion? In most courts the answer would be no. RESTATEMENT (SECOND) OF JUDGMENTS § 27, cmt. e ("In the case of a judgment entered by confession, consent, or default, none of the issues is actually litigated. Therefore, the rule of this Section [applicable to issue preclusion] does not apply with respect to any issue in a subsequent action. The judgment may be conclusive, however, with respect to one or more issues, if the parties have entered an agreement manifesting such an intention."); *but see In re Shiver*, 396 B.R. 110, 123–24 (Bankr. S.D.N.Y. 2008) (holding that Florida law gives issue preclusive effect to default judgments). Some courts have recognized an exception to the default rule where the court entered default as a sanction for deliberately delaying the resolution of a lawsuit by, for example, refusing to respond to discovery requests. *See, e.g., Wolstein v. Docteroff*, 133 F.3d 210, 214–15 (3d Cir. 1997).

Practice Pointer

You need to be alert for statements in cases that are dicta. Dicta is commentary in a court decision that is not necessary to the outcome of the case. Issue preclusion does not apply when the court's statement is merely dicta.

Exercise 13-5. *O'Neal v. Remington Arms*

As you read *O'Neal v. Remington Arms*, answer the following questions.

1. What law does the *O'Neal* court use to evaluate the issue preclusive effect of the prior judgments? Why does it use this law?

2. Why is each of the previous judgments insufficient for issue preclusion?

3. How do the inquiries regarding whether the case involves the "same issue" overlap with the "actually litigated" element of issue preclusion in this case?

O'Neal v. Remington Arms Company, LLC

No. Civ. 11-4182, 2014 WL 993020 (D.S.D. March. 13, 2014)

Order Denying Plaintiff's Motion for Partial Summary Judgment and
Granting Defendants' Motion for Summary Judgment

Karen E. Schreier, District Judge.

Plaintiff, Carol O'Neal, as personal representative of the estate of Lanny O'Neal, deceased, brought an action against defendants, Remington Arms Company, LLC, Sporting Goods Properties, Inc., and E.I. Dupont De Nemours and Company, alleging strict liability (product defect), strict liability (failure to warn), negligent design and manufacture, negligent failure to warn, and spoliation of evidence. O'Neal's spoliation of evidence claim was dismissed following a motion by defendants because it is not an independent cause of action.

Defendants previously moved for summary judgment while discovery was still occurring. The court denied defendants' motion at that time, in part because additional discovery may provide O'Neal sufficient facts to support her claims. Discovery has now concluded, and there are three motions pending before the court. O'Neal moves for partial summary judgment on the issue of product defect, arguing issue preclusion applies. Defendants ... also move for summary judgment on all of O'Neal's claims. For the following reasons, O'Neal's motion for partial summary judgment is denied, ... and defendants' motion for summary judgment is granted.

Background

The pertinent facts, viewed in the light most favorable to O'Neal, the nonmoving party, are as follows:

Carol O'Neal is the widow of Lanny O'Neal and is a resident of Brandon, South Dakota. Defendants are business entities registered in the state of Delaware and are in the business of selling firearms, one of which was the Remington Model 700, .243 caliber bolt action rifle that is at the center of this litigation.

On November 9, 2008, Lanny O'Neal was deer hunting with friends near Eagle Butte, South Dakota. Lanny loaned Mark Ritter, one of the hunters, a Remington Model 700 rifle to use hunting that day. The hunters were traveling in a pickup truck when they came across a deer. At the time, Ritter was sitting in the back seat of the truck and Lanny sat in the front seat. After the truck stopped, Ritter began exiting the truck so that he could shoot the deer. While Ritter was exiting, the rifle discharged when Ritter moved the safety from the "on" position to the "off" position, and Lanny was shot and killed. O'Neal alleges that the rifle was defective and that the defect was the reason the rifle discharged, causing the death of her husband.

The rifle was manufactured in 1971. Doug Swanson, Lanny's stepfather, acquired the rifle in the early-to-mid 1980s from the estate of his mother's boyfriend, Albert Mcilvenna. Swanson does not know when or how Mcilvenna acquired the rifle nor does he know whether the rifle was ever modified or altered prior to his acquisition of the rifle. Swanson would occasionally loan the rifle to others and loaned it to Lanny in approximately 2005 or 2006. Lanny remained in possession of the rifle until the day of the accident. The rifle was never altered or modified from the time Swanson acquired it until the day of the accident, and Swanson did not have a gunsmith examine the rifle while he owned it.

Following Lanny's death, Shawn O'Neal contacted the law firm of Robins, Kaplan, Miller & Ciresi, LLP (Robins Kaplan), in Minneapolis, Minnesota. In December 2008, Shawn and plaintiff, Carol O'Neal, met with attorney Chris Messerly of Robins Kaplan to discuss the circumstances of Lanny's death. After this meeting, Robins Kaplan acquired the rifle from the FBI but never had the rifle inspected. On March 26, 2010, plaintiff and her friend, Joe Weir, retrieved the rifle from Robins Kaplan after it was determined that no legal action would be taken by Robins Kaplan on behalf of plaintiff. O'Neal then asked Weir to destroy the rifle because she did not want the rifle that killed her husband to be in her house. Weir complied with O'Neal's request and destroyed the rifle.

O'Neal brought this product liability action against defendants on December 9, 2011, after hearing about a news report detailing certain problems with Remington rifles.

* * *

Discussion

I. O'Neal's Motion for Partial Summary Judgment

O'Neal moves for partial summary judgment on the issue of product defect, arguing that collateral estoppel (also known as issue preclusion) precludes defendants from relitigating the issue of whether their product — the Model 700 rifle — was defective.

The application of issue preclusion in diversity cases is determined according to state law. *Royal Ins. Co. of Am. v. Kirksville Coll. of Osteopathic Med., Inc.*, 304 F.3d 804, 807 (8th Cir. 2002). Under South Dakota law, "[i]ssue preclusion refers to the effect of a judgment in foreclosing relitigation of a matter that has been litigated and decided." *Nemec v. Goeman*, 810 N.W. 2d 443, 446 (S.D. 2012). "Issue preclusion only bars a point that was *actually and directly in issue* in a former action and was judicially passed upon and determined by a domestic court of competent jurisdiction." *Id.* For issue preclusion to apply, the following four elements must be met:

(1) The issue decided in the prior adjudication was identical with the one presented in the action in question;

(2) There was a final judgment on the merits;

(3) The party against whom issue preclusion is asserted was a party or in privity with a party to the prior adjudication; and

(4) The party against whom issue preclusion is asserted had a full and fair opportunity to litigate the issue in the prior adjudication.

SDDS, Inc. v. South Dakota, 569 N.W. 2d 289, 294 (S.D. 1997).

In support of her argument, O'Neal directs the court to three cases in which judgments were entered against defendant Remington Arms Company. The first, *Lewy v. Remington Arms Company, Inc.*, 836 F.2d 1104 (8th Cir. 1988), is a case from the Western District of Missouri. In *Lewy,* plaintiffs alleged claims for strict liability (design defect), strict liability (failure to warn), and negligent failure to warn after a Remington Model 700 bolt-action rifle discharged upon release of the safety. *Id.* at 1106. The jury returned a verdict in favor of plaintiffs on all three claims, and the district court entered judgment. The Eighth Circuit Court of Appeals, however, remanded the case for a new trial after it concluded that the district court erred in admitting evidence of similar incidents involving a Remington Model 600 rifle. Because the case was remanded for a new trial, the determination in *Lewy* was not a final judgment on the merits. Issue preclusion, therefore, does not apply.

Next, *Campbell v. Remington Arms Company*, 958 F.2d 376 (9th Cir. 1992) (unpublished), is a case from the District of Alaska. In *Campbell,* the jury found against Remington on plaintiff's product liability claim, in favor of Remington on plaintiff's negligence claim, and also found plaintiff was not comparatively negligent. *Id.* at * 1. To find in favor of plaintiff on the product liability claim, the court instructed the jury that the plaintiff was required to prove, among other things, that the product was defective. The court further instructed the jury that a product is defective if (1) the product failed to perform safely as an ordinary consumer would expect, or (2) the design of the product caused the injury, and the benefits of the design did not outweigh the risk of danger inherent in the design. The jury returned a special verdict, finding that the product made by Remington—a Model 700 barreled action—was defective, but the verdict form did not identify under which prong the finding was based. The jury could have found either that the specific rifle in that case had a manufacturing defect, i.e., a particular item in a line of products was defective, or a design defect, i.e., where an entire line of products all have the same defect. Because a manufacturing defect claim involves a specific product, issue preclusion would only apply in later litigation if the later suit involved the exact same product. Because the Model 700 rifle involved in this suit is a different rifle than the rifle in *Campbell*, the issue decided in *Campbell* is not identical to the one presented here, which bars application of issue preclusion. Additionally, South Dakota law recognizes the complete defense of post-sale modifications, alterations, and product misuses. The *Campbell* jury was not instructed on product misuse because the injury occurred before Alaska's Tort Reform Act took effect. *Campbell*, 958 F.2d 376, at *2. Therefore, the issue decided in *Campbell* was not identical to the one presented in this case.

The third case relied on by O'Neal is *Collins v. Remington Arms Company, Inc.*, No. 91-11-10856-CV (D. Maverick Cnty, Tex., 293d Jud. D. May 1, 1994), a state court case out of Texas. While the facts in *Collins* are not entirely clear, it appears the plaintiff alleged that the rifle discharged while it was being either loaded or unloaded and that the rifle was defective because it did not provide a safety feature that would prevent such a discharge. *Collins v. Remington Arms Co.*, JVR No. 161125, 1994 WL 866816 (Tex. Dist. 1994). Here, O'Neal claims the rifle is defective because it discharged when the safety was moved from on to off, not while the rifle was being loaded or unloaded. Therefore, the defect at issue here is different than the defect that was litigated in *Collins*. Issue preclusion, thus, does not apply.

O'Neal has the burden to prove that the specific Model 700 rifle at issue here is defective. O'Neal has not identified a final judgment that would allow her to meet her burden via issue preclusion. Simply put, the issues decided in *Lewy, Campbell,* and *Collins* are not identical to the issue presented here or there was not a final judgment on the merits, and thus, whether the particular Model 700 rifle in this case is defective was not *actually* litigated in previous cases. Therefore, issue preclusion does not preclude litigation of whether the Model 700 rifle involved in this case is defective, and O'Neal's motion for partial summary judgment is denied.

Exercise 13-6. Was the Same Issue Actually Litigated?

Given what you learned from the *O'Neal* case, assess whether the "same issue" was "actually litigated" in the first lawsuit for issue preclusion purposes.

1. A teacher files a lawsuit in state court against a school district, arguing that it had terminated her in violation of state teacher fair dismissal laws. The state court holds that the teacher was not terminated, but in fact resigned. The state court enters a judgment against the teacher. The teacher files a federal civil rights action alleging that she was terminated without due process of law. Will the defendant be successful arguing issue preclusion in the second action? *See Leslie v. Bolen*, 762 F.2d 663 (8th Cir. 1985) (issue preclusion prevents teacher from relitigating issue of resignation in subsequent lawsuit).

2. Plaintiff files a lawsuit for breach of contract in the federal court for the Southern District of New York. Defendant files a motion to dismiss for improper venue, which the court grants. Plaintiff refiles the lawsuit in the Northern District of California. Defendant once again moves to dismiss based on improper venue. Will the plaintiff be successful in arguing that issue preclusion applies to defendant's second motion to dismiss?

3. Plaintiff files a lawsuit for breach of contract, asserting that the plaintiff failed to make a payment pursuant to the contract. Defendant moves for summary judgment, supporting its motion with cancelled checks revealing that the payment was made. The court grants the defendant's motion. Three months later, the plaintiff files a second lawsuit, arguing that the defendant missed a subsequent payment. Will the defendant be able to use issue preclusion to avoid relitigating the payment issue?

c. Necessary to the Court's Judgment

The issue upon which a party seeks preclusion must also be necessary to the first court's judgment. Problems arise where there are multiple grounds for the first court's decision or where it is unclear why the first court ruled in the manner it did. A case helps illustrate this problem.

Exercise 13-7. *National Satellite Sports, Inc. v. Eliadis, Inc.*

As you read *National Satellite*, answer the following questions.

1. One of the issues in this case was whether the plaintiff had standing to sue. Look up this term in a legal dictionary. What does it mean?

2. The first case decided had alternative grounds for the court's ruling. What were these alternative grounds?

3. What are the varying approaches in the circuit courts to the issue preclusive effect of alternative grounds?

4. What are the competing policy concerns the court discusses in determining which courts to follow with respect to the preclusive effect of cases decided on alternative grounds?

5. The court in *National Satellite* decides that one ground of the first court's decision is primary and another ground is secondary. How does the court decide how to characterize each ground of the first court's decision?

National Satellite Sports, Inc. v. Elliadis, Inc.

253 F.3d 900 (6th Cir. 2001)

Gilman, Circuit Judge.

On the night of December 14, 1996, the Melody Lane Lounge, a commercial bar located in Massillon, Ohio, showed the live broadcast of a boxing match between Riddick Bowe and Andrew Golota (the event). National Satellite Sports, Inc. (NSS) had obtained the exclusive right to broadcast the event to commercial establishments in Ohio. Time Warner Entertainment Company, L.P. had obtained the exclusive right to broadcast the event on a pay-per-view basis to its Ohio residential customers. The Melody Lane Lounge, erroneously listed as a residential customer of Time Warner, ordered the event through Time Warner's service.

After learning that the Melody Lane Lounge had shown the event to its patrons on the night in question, NSS brought suit against Eliadis, Inc., the corporate owner of the bar. The suit also named Eliadis's two owners and Time Warner as defendants. NSS alleged that the showing of the event in a commercial establishment through Time Warner's residential service constituted a violation of the Federal Communications Act of 1934, which, among other things, prohibits the unauthorized divulgence of wire or radio communications.

Eliadis and its co-owners reached a prompt settlement with NSS. NSS and Time Warner then filed cross-motions for summary judgment against each other. The district court first granted summary judgment to NSS on the issue of liability, and subsequently entered a final judgment awarding NSS damages, costs, and attorney fees.

Time Warner appeals the district court's rulings, claiming that the court erred in failing to give preclusive effect to an adverse judgment against NSS in prior litigation between the parties on an allegedly controlling issue. In the alternative, Time Warner claims that NSS lacks standing to sue under the Communications Act and, in any event, that NSS has failed to establish a violation of that statute. For all of the reasons set forth below, we affirm the judgment of the district court.

I. Background

A. Factual background

NSS and Time Warner obtained their respective rights to broadcast the event through separate contracts....

NSS received its transmission of the telecast from a chain of distribution that traces back to the second satellite that received the initial signal from Main Events. [However,] the signals that NSS and Time Warner received in their respective Ohio facilities both originated from the same initial transmission sent by Main Events, and neither party disputes the right of the other to receive the signals in Ohio according to their separate contracts. Rather, the dispute centers on Time Warner allowing a commercial establishment to view the event on its residential-customer cable network.

Melody Lane Lounge's account was listed in the individual name of Gust Eliadis, a co-owner of Eliadis, Inc. In February of 1996, Ken Sovacool, a Time Warner employee, serviced Eliadis's cable account. Time Warner concedes that Sovacool should have recognized that the Melody Lane Lounge was a commercial establishment and not a residence. The structure of the building, an exterior identification sign, and neon beer signs in the window made this obvious. Nevertheless, having obtained residential-cable service, the Melody Lane Lounge had the capability to order pay-per-view programs.

Time Warner's account records show that Melody Lane Lounge had ordered one earlier program at the commercial rate. But Melody Lane Lounge ordered the event in question from Time Warner at the residential rate of $39.95. As a commercial establishment, Melody Lane Lounge should have paid NSS for the right to show the event, which would have cost it $987.50.

NSS hired investigators to visit various commercial establishments to monitor whether those showing the event had obtained the right to do so through NSS as the proper distribution channel. An investigator visited the Melody Lane Lounge on the night in question and ultimately determined that it was broadcasting the event through Time Warner's residential pay-per-view system. The Melody Lane Lounge claims that it would not have chosen to show the event had it been required to pay NSS's high commercial rate. Only 23 patrons were in the bar at the time the event was broadcast.

B. Procedural background and prior litigation between the parties

NSS commenced its action in the United States District Court for the Northern District of Ohio in November of 1997. Eliadis, Inc. and its co-owners soon settled with NSS, agreeing to the entry of judgment against them for violating 47 U.S.C. § 605, which is part of the Communications Act, and paying $250 in nominal damages. NSS's claim against Time Warner proceeded.

In July of 1999, the district court entered summary judgment in favor of NSS, finding that Time Warner had violated §605. A bench trial on the issue of damages was held several months later. The district court determined that Time Warner was liable for $4,500 in statutory damages. NSS further sought and was awarded attorney fees and costs pursuant to 47 U.S.C. §605(e)(3)(B)(iii), totaling $26,389.65, in March of 2000. Time Warner appeals the rulings of the district court, raising three alternative arguments.

First, Time Warner contends that the district court erred by failing to give preclusive effect to a separate district court judgment rendered in July of 1998 that arose from a substantially identical claim by NSS against Time Warner. NSS learned that a commercial establishment in Akron, Ohio called Lyndstalder, Inc., d/b/a Coach's Corner, had shown a boxing match between Evander Holyfield and Bobby Czyz that Coach's Corner obtained via residential-cable service from Time Warner in March of 1996. As in the case before us, Time Warner had obtained the exclusive right from the producer to distribute the match to residential customers in Ohio, while NSS received the exclusive license to sell the same program to Ohio's commercial establishments.

NSS commenced an action against Coach's Corner and its owner in the United States District Court for the Northern District of Ohio in August of 1997. When NSS learned of Time Warner's role in providing the broadcast to Coach's Corner, it added Time Warner as a defendant. In that suit, *National Satellite Sports, Inc. v. Lyndstalder, Inc. d/b/a/ Coach's Corner, et al.*, No. 5:97 CV 2039 (N.D.Ohio 1998), NSS alleged that both Coach's Corner and Time Warner had violated 47 U.S.C. §605. Coach's Corner settled with NSS. Time Warner then filed a motion for summary judgment, alleging that NSS had failed to establish either a contractual or a statutory claim against it.

The district court held a hearing on Time Warner's motion for summary judgment in July of 1998. It issued a bench ruling at that hearing, granting Time Warner's motion for summary judgment on the basis that NSS "failed to state a claim pursuant to the terms of the contracts [for distribution] at issue in this case as well as 47 U.S.C. §605." NSS did not appeal. Time Warner argues that the *Coach's Corner* decision precludes NSS from raising the identical §605 claim in the present case.

* * *

II. Analysis

* * *

B. NSS is not bound by the decision in *Coach's Corner*

NSS brought suit in both this case and in the *Coach's Corner* case under 47 U.S.C. §605. Section 605 defines what constitutes the unauthorized publication or use of electronic communications. It includes such prohibited practices as the divulgence of wire or radio communications by persons authorized to receive them to others who are not so authorized, and the interception of any radio communication by a person not authorized to receive that communication from the sender. According to §605, "[a]ny person aggrieved by any violation of subsection (a) of this section ... may bring a civil action in a United States district court or in any other court of competent jurisdiction." 47 U.S.C. §605(e)(3)(A). Furthermore, the statute directs that "the term 'any person aggrieved' shall include any person with proprietary rights in the intercepted communication by wire or radio, including wholesale or retail distributors of satellite cable programming." 47 U.S.C. §605(d)(6).

In its motion before the court in *Coach's Corner*, Time Warner argued that it was entitled to summary judgment because NSS was not a "person aggrieved" within the meaning of §605(d)(6), and could therefore not pursue a claim for an alleged violation of §605(a). NSS responded by arguing that standing to sue under §605 is not limited to those who meet the statutory definition of a "person aggrieved."

The district court granted Time Warner's motion for summary judgment in the *Coach's Corner* case. In articulating its reasoning from the bench on July 13, 1998, the court held that NSS had failed to state a claim under *both* the contracts at issue in that case *and* under 47 U.S.C. §605. The pertinent parts of the *Coach's Corner* ruling were as follows:

> With regard to the ruling, [NSS] has failed to state a claim pursuant to the terms of the contracts at issue in this case as well as 47 United States Code Section 605.
>
> ....
>
> Paragraph 14(e) of the Television Licensing Agreement provides for the enforcement of unauthorized display of the closed circuit television feed. That also provides that Joe Hand Promotions [the licensor of the event] could not assert any piracy claim without prior notice.
>
> [The agreement] provides that a sublicensee [NSS] has no rights to enforceability, quote, "It being understood that your sublicensee shall have no right to commence or settle any claim or litigation hereunder."
>
> The other relevant agreement is the March 12, 1996 Closed Circuit Television Agreement entered into between [the licensor] and [NSS].
>
> That agreement at paragraph 7 provides that there is no right to a piracy action to be pursued by [NSS].
>
> [NSS's] effort to overcome the language of the contract does not create a material fact for trial.

Time Warner now argues that the district court below should have given preclusive effect to the earlier ruling in *Coach's Corner*. It claims that *Coach's Corner* determined that when a commercial establishment shows a sporting event ordered through a residential-cable service rather than properly paying the fees exacted by the commercial distributor, the distributor does not have standing to sue the authorized residential-service provider under § 605. NSS obviously disagrees.

Our circuit has held that a prior decision shall have preclusive effect on an issue raised in a later case if four elements are met:

> (1) the precise issue raised in the present case must have been raised and actually litigated in the prior proceeding; (2) determination of the issue must have been necessary to the outcome of the prior proceeding; (3) the prior proceeding must have resulted in a final judgment on the merits; and (4) the party against whom estoppel is sought must have had a full and fair opportunity to litigate the issue in the prior proceeding.

Smith v. SEC, 129 F.3d 356, 362 (6th Cir. 1997) (en banc) (quoting Detroit Police *Officers Ass'n v. Young*, 824 F.2d 512, 515 (6th Cir. 1987).

In the present case, the district court concluded that Time Warner had failed to establish the second and fourth elements of this test....

* * *

2. Necessary to the outcome of the prior proceeding

The district court held that Time Warner failed to establish that NSS's lack of standing under § 605 was necessary to the grant of summary judgment for Time Warner in *Coach's Corner*. It determined that the *Coach's Corner* decision was instead primarily based on the conclusion that NSS was contractually barred from pursuing an action against Time Warner because of the particular language in the license agreements involved in that case. As such, it held that the alternative ground in *Coach's Corner* for granting Time Warner's motion for summary judgment—namely, that NSS was not a "person aggrieved" under § 605—was not necessary to that court's judgment.

Time Warner argues that the district court erred in reaching this conclusion. It notes that *Coach's Corner* is a case in which two alternative but independent grounds support the court's ultimate judgment. Time Warner claims that under the "weight of federal authority, a plaintiff is precluded from relitigating an issue actually decided against it in a prior case, even if the court in the prior case rested its judgment on alternative grounds." It cites the Second, Seventh, Ninth, and D.C. Circuits as upholding this general principle of issue preclusion.

This principle of issue preclusion, however, is counterbalanced by courts and commentaries that have adopted the opposite conclusion. For example, the American Law Institute (ALI) endorses NSS's position that "[i]f a judgment of a court of first instance is based on determinations of two issues, either of which standing independently would be sufficient to support the result, the judgment is not conclusive with respect to either issue standing alone." RESTATEMENT (SECOND) OF JUDGMENTS § 27 cmt. I (1980). Furthermore, one leading commentary describes the Restatement's view as the "new" and "modern" rule. *See* 18 JAMES WM. MOORE ET AL., MOORE'S FEDERAL PRACTICE ¶ 132.03[4][b] at 132-111 to 132-113 (3d ed. 1997). At least four circuits (the Third, Fourth, Eighth, and Tenth) have adopted this modern rule. In addition, the Seventh Circuit has embraced the modern rule in the context of the *Black Lung Benefits Act in Peabody Coal Co. v. Spese*, 117 F.3d 1001, 1008 (7th Cir. 1997 (en banc), without citing its contrary holding in [an earlier case].

The issue is a close one given the policy implications involved. Time Warner argues that by not recognizing *Coach's Corner* as precluding relitigation of whether NSS has standing to sue under § 605, NSS is free to relitigate the same issue again. NSS counters by arguing that because the *Coach's Corner* court decided that NSS was contractually barred from pursuing a claim against Time Warner, NSS had no incentive to appeal that court's secondary decision that NSS failed to state a claim under § 605.

We find NSS's point persuasive because, while it might have won the "battle" over § 605, NSS would almost surely have lost the "war" in being unable to overcome the contractual prohibition on commencing litigation against Time Warner. Furthermore, the district court's oral ruling in *Coach's Corner* transcribes into only a two-paragraph conclusory statement regarding NSS's claim under § 605, which was far overshadowed by the balance of its three-page discussion outlining the contractual obstacles that prevented NSS from suing Time Warner.

This circuit has not decided whether alternative grounds for a judgment are each "necessary to the outcome" for the purposes of issue preclusion in a subsequent case involving only one of the grounds. Based on the actual decision in *Coach's Corner*, we do not find it necessary to fully resolve this issue at the present time. We do hold, however, that where, as in *Coach's Corner*, one ground for the decision is clearly primary and the other only secondary, the secondary ground is not "necessary to the outcome" for the purposes of issue preclusion. *Coach's Corner*'s secondary holding that NSS failed to state a claim under § 605 was thus not necessary to the granting of Time Warner's motion for summary judgment.

d. Same Parties

Issue preclusion also requires that the second lawsuit involve the same parties or those in privity with the parties to the original lawsuit. However, third parties can use issue preclusion in some courts against parties who had a full and fair opportunity to litigate the issue in the first lawsuit. That is what Ms. O'Neal was attempting to do in the *Remington Arms Company* case.

Whether a third party can use issue preclusion depends on whether the courts in the particular jurisdiction follow the rule of mutuality of estoppel. Mutuality of estoppel means that party A can only use issue preclusion against party B if party B could have used issue preclusion against party A. Confused? Let's look at an example. Assume a plaintiff successfully sued a trucking company for injuries incurred when the defendant's driver was negligent resulting in an accident. The jury found that the driver was negligent. A second plaintiff who was a passenger in the car of the first plaintiff files a lawsuit regarding the same accident. The plaintiff in the second lawsuit would like to use that first judgment against the trucking company and avoid relitigating the issue of the driver's negligence. If the jurisdiction required mutuality, the second plaintiff could not use the judgment in the first suit, because the second plaintiff would not be bound by a judgment in the first lawsuit in the trucking company's favor. Having not had his day in court, the second plaintiff would relitigate the issue of negligence.

The doctrine of mutuality of estoppel came under attack in *Blonder-Tongue Laboratories, Inc. v. University of Illinois Foundation*, 402 U.S. 313 (1971). In *Blonder-Tongue*, the Court considered whether an earlier judgment holding a patent invalid in a patent infringement lawsuit brought by the University of Illinois Foundation had preclusive effect in a subsequent action brought by the University against a new defendant. The judge in the second lawsuit determined that he was not bound by the earlier judgment involving a different defendant and held the same patent valid based on the evidence before the court in spite of being aware that the earlier court had held the same patent invalid. An earlier Supreme Court case, *Triplett v. Lowell*, 297 U.S. 638 (1936), held that a court's determination that a patent was invalid did not have res judicata effect in a subsequent action by the patentee against a new purported infringer. The *Blonder-Tongue* Court reconsidered the ruling in *Triplett*.

In holding that mutuality was no longer necessary in the context of defensive use of issue preclusion, the Court began by noting that many courts had moved away from the requirement of mutuality. It also considered whether there might be special reasons to require mutuality in patent cases, given that a patent was a special right granted by the federal government. Rejecting arguments that patents were somehow special in this regard, the Court noted that patent infringement litigation is very costly to both the patentee and the defendant in such actions. It is especially costly for defendants, because a patentee enjoys the benefit of a presumption that its patent is valid. Thus, the burden of proving invalidity falls on the defendant. Because of this expense, many purported infringers simply choose to pay royalties rather than defend themselves in a patent infringement action. Based on this, the Court concluded:

When these judicial developments are considered in the light of our consistent view ... that the holder of a patent should not be insulated from the assertion of defenses and thus allowed to exact royalties for the use of an idea that is not in fact patentable or that is beyond the scope of the patent monopoly granted, it is apparent that the uncritical acceptance of the principle of mutuality of estoppel expressed in *Triplett v. Lowell* is today out of place. Thus, we conclude that *Triplett* should be overruled to the extent it forecloses a plea of estoppel by one facing a charge of infringement of a patent that has once been declared invalid.

402 U.S. at 349–50. While this case permitted defensive use of issue preclusion, it set the stage for the erosion of the mutuality requirement for issue preclusion in the federal court system. *Blonder-Tongue* left open the issue of whether a plaintiff in a second action could use issue preclusion offensively against a defendant who had lost on the same issue in a prior action. The following case addresses that issue.

Exercise 13-8. *Parklane Hosiery Co., Inc. v. Shore*

In this case, the Court refers to issue preclusion as collateral estoppel. As you read *Parklane*, answer the following questions.

1. *Parklane* involves offensive use of issue preclusion. What does that mean in the context of this case? How does it differ from defensive use of issue preclusion?

2. This case, like all issue preclusion cases, involves two lawsuits. Diagram the two lawsuits. Who sued whom for what in each case? What was the judgment of the first court?

3. What are the circumstances that the Court identifies in which it would be "unfair" to use issue preclusion against a defendant? Why do they not apply here?

4. How is the right to jury trial used by the parties to this action? What role does it play in the Court's decision in this case?

Parklane Hosiery Co., Inc. v. Shore
439 U.S. 322 (1979)

Mr. Justice Stewart delivered the opinion of the Court.

This case presents the question whether a party who has had issues of fact adjudicated adversely to it in an equitable action may be collaterally estopped from relitigating the same issues before a jury in a subsequent legal action brought against it by a new party.

The respondent brought this stockholder's class action against the petitioners in a Federal District Court. The complaint alleged that the petitioners, Parklane Hosiery Co., Inc. (Parklane), and 13 of its officers, directors, and stockholders, had issued a materially false and misleading proxy statement in connection with a merger. The proxy statement, according to the complaint, had violated [various section of the Securities Exchange Act of 1934] as well as various rules and regulations promulgated by the Securities and Exchange Commission (SEC). The complaint sought damages, rescission of the merger, and recovery of costs.

Before this action came to trial, the SEC filed suit against the same defendants in the Federal District Court, alleging that the proxy statement that had been issued by Parklane was materially false and misleading in essentially the same respects as those that had been alleged in the respondent's complaint. Injunctive relief was requested. After a 4-day trial, the District Court found that the proxy statement was materially false and misleading in the respects alleged, and entered a declaratory judgment to that effect. The Court of Appeals for the Second Circuit affirmed this judgment.

The respondent in the present case then moved for partial summary judgment against the petitioners, asserting that the petitioners were collaterally estopped from relitigating the issues that had been resolved against them in the action brought by the SEC. The District Court denied the motion on the ground that such an application of collateral estoppel would deny the petitioners their Seventh Amendment right to a jury trial. The Court of Appeals for the Second Circuit reversed, holding that a party who has had issues of fact determined against him after a full and fair opportunity to litigate in a nonjury trial is collaterally estopped from obtaining a subsequent jury trial of these same issues of fact. The appellate court concluded that "the Seventh Amendment preserves the right to jury trial only with respect to issues of fact, [and] once those issues have been fully and fairly adjudicated in a prior proceeding, nothing remains for trial, either with or without a jury." Because of an inter-circuit conflict, we granted certiorari.

I

The threshold question to be considered is whether, quite apart from the right to a jury trial under the Seventh Amendment, the petitioners can be precluded from relitigating facts resolved adversely to them in a prior equitable proceeding with another party under the general law of collateral estoppel. Specifically, we must determine whether a litigant who was not a party to a prior judgment may nevertheless use that judgment "offensively" to prevent a defendant from relitigating issues resolved in the earlier proceeding.

A

Collateral estoppel ... has the dual purpose of protecting litigants from the burden of relitigating an identical issue with the same party or his privy and of promoting judicial economy by preventing needless litigation.

Until relatively recently, however, the scope of collateral estoppel was limited by the doctrine of mutuality of parties. Under this mutuality doctrine, neither party could use a prior judgment as an estoppel against the other unless both parties were bound by the judgment. Based on the premise that it is somehow unfair to allow a party to use a prior judgment when he himself would not be so bound, the mutuality requirement provided a party who had litigated and lost in a previous action an opportunity to relitigate identical issues with new parties.

By failing to recognize the obvious difference in position between a party who has never litigated an issue and one who has fully litigated and lost, the mutuality requirement was criticized almost from its inception. Recognizing the validity of this criticism, the Court in *Blonder-Tongue Laboratories, Inc. v. University of Illinois Foundation*, abandoned the mutuality requirement, at least in cases where a patentee seeks to relitigate the validity of a patent after a federal court in a previous lawsuit has already declared it invalid. The "broader question" before the Court, however, was "whether it is any longer tenable to afford a litigant more than one full and fair opportunity for judicial resolution of the same issue." 402 U.S. at 328. The Court strongly suggested a negative answer to that question:

> "In any lawsuit where a defendant, because of the mutuality principle, is forced to present a complete defense on the merits to a claim which the plaintiff has fully litigated and lost in a prior action, there is an arguable misallocation of resources. To the extent the defendant in the second suit may not win by asserting, without contradiction, that the plaintiff had fully and fairly, but unsuccessfully, litigated the same claim in the prior suit, the defendant's time and money are diverted from alternative uses—productive or otherwise—to relitigation of a decided issue. And, still assuming that the issue was resolved correctly in the first suit, there is reason to be concerned about the plaintiff's allocation of resources. Permitting repeated litigation of the same issue as long as the supply of unrelated defendants holds out reflects either the aura of the gaming table or 'a lack of discipline and of disinterestedness on the part of the lower courts, hardly a worthy or wise basis for fashioning rules of procedure.' *Kerotest Mfg. Co. v. C-O-Two Co.*, 342 U.S. 180, 185 (1952). Although neither judges, the parties, nor the adversary system performs perfectly in all cases, the requirement of determining whether the party against whom an estoppel is asserted had a full and fair opportunity to litigate is a most significant safeguard." *Id.* at 329.

B

The *Blonder-Tongue* case involved defensive use of collateral estoppel—a plaintiff was estopped from asserting a claim that the plaintiff had previously litigated and lost against another defendant. The present case, by contrast, involves offensive use of collateral estoppel — a plaintiff is seeking to estop a defendant from relitigating the issues which the defendant previously litigated and lost against another plaintiff. In both the offensive and defensive use situations, the party against whom estoppel is asserted has litigated and lost in an earlier action. Nevertheless, several reasons have been advanced why the two situations should be treated differently.

First, offensive use of collateral estoppel does not promote judicial economy in the same manner as defensive use does. Defensive use of collateral estoppel precludes a plaintiff from relitigating identical issues by merely "switching adversaries." *Bernhard v. Bank of America Nat. Trust & Savings Assn.*, 19 Cal. 2d 807, 813 (1942). Thus defensive collateral estoppel gives a plaintiff a strong incentive to join all potential defendants in the first action if possible. Offensive use of collateral estoppel, on the other hand, creates precisely the opposite incentive. Since a plaintiff will be able to rely on a previous judgment against a defendant but will not be bound by that judgment if the defendant wins, the plaintiff has every incentive to adopt a "wait and see" attitude, in the hope that the first action by another plaintiff will result in a favorable judgment. Thus offensive use of collateral estoppel will likely increase rather than decrease the total amount of litigation, since potential plaintiffs will have everything to gain and nothing to lose by not intervening in the first action.

A second argument against offensive use of collateral estoppel is that it may be unfair to a defendant. If a defendant in the first action is sued for small or nominal damages, he may have little incentive to defend vigorously, particularly if future suits are not foreseeable. *The Evergreens v. Nunan*, 141 F.2d 927, 929 (2d Cir.), *cf. Bermer v. British Commonwealth Pac. Airlines*, 346 F.2d 532 (2d Cir.) (application of offensive collateral estoppel denied where defendant did not appeal an adverse judgment awarding damages of $35,000 and defendant was later sued for over $7 million). Allowing offensive collateral estoppel may also be unfair to a defendant if the judgment relied upon as a basis for the estoppel is itself inconsistent with one or more previous judgments in favor of the defendant. Still another situation where it might be unfair to apply offensive estoppel is where the second action affords the defendant procedural opportunities unavailable in the first action that could readily cause a different result.

C

We have concluded that the preferable approach for dealing with these problems in the federal courts is not to preclude the use of offensive collateral estoppel, but to grant trial courts broad discretion to determine when it should be applied. The general rule should be that in cases where a plaintiff could easily have joined in the earlier action or where, either for the reasons discussed above or for other reasons, the application of offensive estoppel would be unfair to a defendant, a trial judge should not allow the use of offensive collateral estoppel.

In the present case, however, none of the circumstances that might justify reluctance to allow the offensive use of collateral estoppel is present. The application of offensive collateral estoppel will not here reward a private plaintiff who could have joined in the previous action, since the respondent probably could not have joined in the injunctive action brought by the SEC even had he so desired. Similarly, there is no unfairness to the petitioners in applying offensive collateral estoppel in this case. First, in light of the serious allegations made in the SEC's complaint against the petitioners, as well as the foreseeability of subsequent private suits that typically follow a successful Government judgment, the petitioners had every incentive to litigate the SEC lawsuit fully and vigorously. Second, the judgment in the SEC action was not inconsistent with any previous decision. Finally, there will in the respondent's action be no procedural opportunities available to the petitioners that were unavailable in the first action of a kind that might be likely to cause a different result.

We conclude, therefore, that none of the considerations that would justify a refusal to allow the use of offensive collateral estoppel is present in this case. Since the petitioners received a "full and fair" opportunity to litigate their claims in the SEC action, the contemporary law of collateral estoppel leads inescapably to the conclusion that the petitioners are collaterally estopped from relitigating the question of whether the proxy statement was materially false and misleading.

II

The question that remains is whether, notwithstanding the law of collateral estoppel, the use of offensive collateral estoppel in this case would violate the petitioners' Seventh Amendment right to a jury trial.

[In Part A of the opinion, the Court describes cases suggesting that an equitable decision can have issue preclusive effect in a subsequent action at law.]

* * *

B

Despite the strong support to be found both in history and in the recent decisional law of this Court for the proposition that an equitable determination can have collateral-estoppel effect in a subsequent legal action, the petitioners argue that application of collateral estoppel in this case would nevertheless violate their Seventh Amendment right to a jury trial. The petitioners contend that since the scope of the Amendment must be determined by reference to the common law as it existed in 1791, and since the common law permitted collateral estoppel only where there was mutuality of parties, collateral estoppel cannot constitutionally be applied when such mutuality is absent.

The petitioners have advanced no persuasive reason, however, why the meaning of the Seventh Amendment should depend on whether or not mutuality of parties is present. A litigant who has lost because of adverse factual findings in an equity action is equally deprived of a jury trial whether he is estopped from relitigating the factual issues against the same party or a new party. In either case, the party against whom estoppel is asserted has litigated questions of fact, and has had the facts determined against him in an earlier proceeding. In either case there is no further factfinding function for the jury to perform, since the common factual issues have been resolved in the previous action.

The Seventh Amendment has never been interpreted in the rigid manner advocated by the petitioners. On the contrary, many procedural devices developed since 1791 that have diminished the civil jury's historic domain have been found not to be inconsistent with the Seventh Amendment....

The *Galloway [v. United States*, 319 U.S. 372 (1943)] case is particularly instructive. There the party against whom a directed verdict had been entered argued that the procedure was unconstitutional under the Seventh Amendment. In rejecting this claim, the Court said:

> "The Amendment did not bind the federal courts to the exact procedural incidents or details of jury trial according to the common law in 1791, any more than it tied them to the common-law system of pleading or the specific rules of evidence then prevailing. Nor were 'the rules of the common law' then prevalent, including those relating to the procedure by which the judge regulated the jury's role on questions of fact, crystalized in a fixed and immutable system....

> "The more logical conclusion, we think, and the one which both history and the previous decisions here support, is that the Amendment was designed to preserve the basic institution of jury trial in only its most fundamental elements, not the great mass of procedural forms and details, varying even then so widely among common-law jurisdictions." 319 U.S. at 390, 392 (footnote omitted).

The law of collateral estoppel, like the law in other procedural areas defining the scope of the jury's function, has evolved since 1791. Under the rationale of the *Galloway* case, these developments are not repugnant to the Seventh Amendment simply for the reason that they did not exist in 1791. Thus if, as we have held, the law of collateral estoppel forecloses the petitioners from relitigating the factual issues determined against them in the SEC action, nothing in the Seventh Amendment dictates a different result, even though because of lack of mutuality there would have been no collateral estoppel in 1791.

The judgment of the Court of Appeals is

Affirmed.

Mr. Justice Rehnquist, dissenting.

[In the first part of his dissent, Justice Rehnquist detailed the history of the jury trial right, concluding that the petitioners were denied the right to jury trial in this case.]

* * *

II

Even accepting, *arguendo*, the majority's position that there is no violation of the Seventh Amendment here, I nonetheless would not sanction the use of collateral estoppel in this case. The Court today holds:

> "The general rule should be that in cases where a plaintiff could easily have joined in the earlier action or where, either for the reasons discussed above or for other reasons, the application of offensive estoppel would be unfair to a defendant, a trial judge should not allow the use of offensive collateral estoppel." *Ante,* at 651.

In my view, it is "unfair" to apply offensive collateral estoppel where the party who is sought to be estopped has not had an opportunity to have the facts of his case determined by a jury. Since in this case petitioners were not entitled to a jury trial in the Securities and Exchange Commission (SEC) lawsuit, I would not estop them from relitigating the issues determined in the SEC suit before a jury in the private action. I believe that several factors militate in favor of this result.

* * *

Contrary to the majority's supposition, juries can make a difference, and our cases have, before today at least, recognized this obvious fact. Thus, in *Colgrove v. Battin*, 413 U.S. at 157, we stated that "the purpose of the jury trial in ... civil cases [is] to assure a fair and equitable resolution of factual issues, *Gasoline Products Co. v. Champlin Co.*, 283 U.S. 494, 498 (1931)...." And in *Byrd v. Blue Ridge Rural Electrical Cooperative*, 356 U.S. 525, 537 (1958), the Court conceded that "the nature of the tribunal which tries issues may be important in the enforcement of the parcel of rights making up a cause of action or defense.... It may well be that in the instant personal-injury case the outcome would be substantially affected by whether the issue of immunity is decided by a judge or a jury." See *Curtis v. Loether*, 415 U.S. at 198, cf. *Duncan v. Louisiana*, 391 U.S. 145, 156 (1968). Jurors bring to a case their common sense and community values; their "very inexperience is an asset because it secures a fresh perception of each trial, avoiding the stereotypes said to infect the judicial eye." H. Kalven & H. Zeisel, The American Jury 8 (1966).

The ultimate irony of today's decision is that its potential for significantly conserving the resources of either the litigants or the judiciary is doubtful at best. That being the case, I see absolutely no reason to frustrate so cavalierly the important federal policy favoring jury decisions of disputed fact questions. The instant case is an apt example of the minimal savings that will be accomplished by the Court's decision. As the Court admits, even if petitioners are collaterally estopped from relitigating whether the proxy was materially false and misleading, they are still entitled to have a jury determine whether respondent was injured by the alleged misstatements and the amount of damages, if any, sustained by respondent. Thus, a jury must be impaneled in this case in any event. The time saved by not trying the issue of whether the proxy was materially false and misleading before the jury is likely to be insubstantial. It is just as probable that today's decision will have the result of coercing defendants to agree to consent orders or settlements in agency enforcement actions in order to preserve their right to jury trial in the private actions. In that event, the Court, for no compelling reason, will have simply added a powerful club to the administrative agencies' arsenals that even Congress was unwilling to provide them.

Exercise 13-9. *Parklane Hosiery Co., Inc. v. Shore* and Applying the Elements of Issue Preclusion

Recall that issue preclusion consists of five elements: (1) a valid final judgment; (2) the same issue; (3) the issue was actually litigated and decided in the first lawsuit; (4) the decision on the issue was necessary to the judgment; and (5) the party against whom preclusion is being used had a full and fair opportunity to litigate the issue in the first lawsuit. Given these elements, should issue preclusion apply in the following cases?

1. Plaintiff, appearing pro se, files a class action against insurance company A, alleging that it discriminated against him based on race in violation of Title VII of the Civil Rights Act of 1964 by refusing to hire him in a position as a claims adjuster. Insurance company A moved for summary judgment on multiple grounds, including that the plaintiff had never applied for a job at the company and, in any event, was not qualified for the job alleged in the complaint. The trial court granted the defendant's motion for summary judgment, holding that the plaintiff had never submitted an employment application and therefore had never applied for a job. In addition, it held that the "plaintiff was so lacking in the elementary financial prudence, candor, stability, meaningful interest in the business world and definite career direction that no prudent insurance company

could reasonably employ him in a position of fiscal trust." The court entered judgment against the plaintiff, from which he did not appeal. Plaintiff filed another lawsuit against insurance company B, arguing that it refused to hire him based on his race in violation of Title VII. Can insurance company B use issue preclusion against the plaintiff in the second lawsuit? *See Stebbins v. Keystone Insurance Co.*, 481 F.2d 501 (D.C. Cir. 1973) (plaintiff can relitigate issue of employability).

2. Plaintiff was a truck driver for a large trucking company. He filed a workers' compensation action in state court against his employer when he injured his back while connecting two trailers together. He claimed he was violently pulled down by the weight of an improperly designed jiff lock axle. A jury rendered a verdict in favor of the employer, and the plaintiff did not appeal. The plaintiff filed a lawsuit based on diversity in federal court against the manufacturer of the jiff lock axle, alleging products liability. Plaintiff alleged that he injured his back due to the defectively designed jiff lock axle. Can the defendant in the second lawsuit use issue preclusion against the plaintiff?

3. Plaintiff entered into a contract with the United States to develop and run a concession at a federally owned recreation area that included a lake. During the term of the contract, which was renewed several times, the plaintiff made various improvements, including reconfiguring the area to add a resort, boat ramps, access roads, and parking lots. A year before the latest renewal of the contract was set to expire, the plaintiff brought an action in the federal court of claims, challenging the government's plan for soliciting new bids to run the facility. In particular, it argued that the government should require that new concessionaires provide compensation for the facilities the plaintiff built. The court held that federal law required the outgoing concessionaire to remove or abandon the facilities, unless the government "required" the facilities to remain, in which case the outgoing concessionaire would be compensated for those facilities. After the agreement expired, the plaintiff simply left the improvements on the property. Two years later, the plaintiff filed a second lawsuit, alleging that either the United States or its new concessionaire was using the facilities it built and therefore should pay plaintiff for them. Will either party be successful using issue preclusion in this second lawsuit? *See Laguna Hermosa Corp. v. United States*, 671 F.3d 1284 (Fed. Cir. 2012) (issues not adequately litigated or addressed in prior lawsuit).

4. Plaintiff SF sued AB Corporation for monopolization, attempted monopolization, and unfair competition. The lawsuit involved a competitive relationship between SF (a resistor manufacturer) and AB. SF contracted to purchase resistor chips from AB. After a trial on the merits, a jury returned a verdict for SF. After the parties settled, the trial judge dismissed the complaint with prejudice and vacated the verdict and judgment on

SF's claims. Plaintiff DF Corporation sued AB for unlawfully monopolizing and attempting to monopolize the market for resistors by procuring fraudulent patents and pursuing those who manufacture, sell, or distribute resistors with fraudulent patent rights claims. Will plaintiff DF be able to use issue preclusion in the second lawsuit? *See Angstrohm Precision, Inc. v. Vishay Intertechnology, Inc.*, 567 F. Supp. 537 (E.D.N.Y. 1982) (general verdict did not give rise to issue preclusion).

Exercise 13-10. Solving the Chapter Problem

Recall that in the chapter problem, Ms. Reyno once again was suing on behalf of the estate of one of the decedents in the Scotland plane crash. In the first case involving the first decedent, the court ruled against Ms. Reyno on a motion for summary judgment, holding that Piper could not be held liable for any design defects in the propeller. Will Piper be able to use preclusion in the second lawsuit?

5. Professional Development Reflection

Like other concepts coming out of civil procedure, preclusion often involves forum shopping by a party to a lawsuit. If you represent a client in a case in which preliminary motions suggest that the court is not viewing your client's case as you do, is it ethical or perhaps even ethically required that you refile the same suit in another jurisdiction in an effort to find a court that is more favorably disposed to your client's case? Note that when an attorney does so, it is a race to bring one of the cases to final judgment so that it will have preclusive effect in the second court. Is this the best use of the justice system? What alternatives do you have as an attorney when you believe a judge is predisposed against your client's position?

Chapter 14

Alternatives to Litigation

1. Chapter Problem

Surgery Gone Bad

Imagine that you have been diagnosed with a deviated septum, a sinus deformity that can prevent normal breathing and can lead to serious and chronic sinus infections. Luckily, your insurance company will cover the surgery that is necessary to correct the condition. Also luckily, it is a relatively simple outpatient procedure that involves few incisions and a short recovery time. All good news.

And then you actually get the surgery done. The first red flag is that, when you show up at your appointed time after starving yourself for 12 hours (required for anesthesia), you are told that your doctor has "another patient ahead of you." The doctor has double-booked your surgery time, even though you had to pre-pay the fee to secure your prompt attendance. So you wait in the waiting room for two hours while the doctor finishes the other surgery.

As he is nearing completion, the nurses begin to prep you. When you leave two hours later, you are groggy, and your head really hurts, but the staff tells you that this is normal, and they give you some pain killers. Two weeks later, your head still hurts quite a bit. Suddenly, you begin to gag, and this causes you to involuntarily throw up. Out comes a large (for someone's nose) sponge that seems to have been inadvertently left inside your head for two weeks since the surgery and was probably causing you all of that head pain. You make an appointment to discuss this with the surgeon, and he dismisses your concerns.

About six months later, you notice that your nose now looks "funny." Specifically, there is forming a deep depression right where the bridge of your nose used to be, making you look like a prize fighter. Again, you make an appointment with your surgeon, and he says that sometimes, minor cosmetic effects such as these can happen from any nasal surgery. Basically, he tells you to just live with it or get plastic surgery to fix it.

So you go to see a plastic surgeon, and she tells you after examining you that you have what is known as "saddle nose," a condition that involves the collapse of the superstructure of cartilage that is supposed to hold up the bottom part of your nose, where your tip and nostrils are. She says that if it is not corrected, it could lead to significant breathing problems

---

down the road. She also opines that it was the surgery, and a lack of care in that surgery, that caused the cartilage to collapse. She offers to fix the problem for $10,000.

Now you are furious at the surgeon. Not only did he leave a sponge inside your nose, causing you annoying headaches for two weeks, but he also has apparently ruined your nose cosmetically, and created the potential for future breathing problems. You resolve to contact an attorney and sue for compensation, including the $10,000 it will cost to correct the problem, and some reasonable amount for your pain and suffering before the sponge worked its way out of your head.

1. Leaving the substantive malpractice tort law of your jurisdiction to the side for the purposes of this problem (assume that it would allow you a remedy if you prove the facts above), what procedural difficulties do you foresee standing in the way of your seeking this relief?

2. How might you prefer to resolve this matter, other than through litigation in the federal or state courts?

3. In light of the procedural challenges you identify in response to question 1, what would be the advantages and/or disadvantages of resolving your dispute through non-judicial means?

2. Introduction

All of the preceding chapters have dealt with different aspects of the process of litigating a case in the federal courts. But as we pointed out in earlier chapters, over 90% of filed cases do not result in a verdict after a full trial, and many more disputes do not even make it past the earliest stages of litigation. Some are dismissed or decided through summary judgment. Prior chapters dealt with the mechanisms of these procedures.

Other disputes ultimately are resolved through methods not involving the courts, or are never resolved at all. First, due to the economics of legal practice, many genuine disputes are never even filed as legal proceedings, and are never resolved in any way. For example, in the Chapter problem, you find that it will cost $10,000 to fix your nose, and you determine that you have suffered about two weeks of moderate pain (basically, strong headaches) as a result of the surgeon's negligence. Will you be able to file and win a traditional lawsuit on this matter?

Assuming that the facts as laid out in the problem would justify a verdict in your favor, what else do you need? Well, you need a lawyer, first of all. No problem there, right? There are many, many lawyers in every state who specialize in personal injury law, and many of these further specialize in medical negligence and malpractice law, so you should be able to find one, right? Not so fast. Lawyers generally do not work for free, so you will have to find some way to pay your attorney. If you do not have the money to pay a retainer and regular, hourly bills that may run into the thousands of dollars very quickly, you will have to find an attorney willing to work on a contingent-fee basis. Most personal injury and malpractice attorneys who represent plaintiffs will agree to a contingent-fee arrangement, where the attorney will receive between 30 and 40% of your ultimate recovery. So, what will be your ultimate recovery? You have $10,000 of documentable compensatory damages, along with an unspecified amount of pain and suffering damages — let's say another $10,000. Forty percent of $20,000 is $8,000.

That potential recovery *might* convince a lawyer to take your case, but the fact that it will probably involve experts and insurance companies makes that pretty unlikely. So, even though you have what looks to be a meritorious claim, because it is not a very large claim, and because you do not have the funds to pay by the hour, you may not even be able to find someone to file it for you. This sort of result undoubtedly happens in thousands of cases a year — the claims just go unresolved.

Assuming that your pain and suffering damages are larger, or that you have some other basis for claiming a larger amount for damages, you might be able to file your claim in federal court, and if so, it may be resolved through the processes you have studied thus far, including pleading practice, motion practice, discovery, trial, and if necessary, appeal. But it might also be resolved through non-judicial means. The remainder of this chapter discusses the main non-judicial ways of resolving disputes that might otherwise be resolved through summary judgment or trial on the merits.

- Section 3 — Settlement and Offers of Judgment. This Section addresses the process of settling a case, as well as the procedural tools that the parties have to promote agreement.

- Section 4 — Mediation and Other Non-Adjudicatory Procedures. This Section introduces the primary non-adjudicatory and quasi-adjudicatory means of resolving a dispute, including mediation, early neutral evaluation, and mini-trial.

- Section 5 — Arbitration. This Section addresses fast-growing non-judicial adjudicatory means of resolving a dispute, including binding and non-binding arbitration.

- Section 6 — Professionalism in Alternative Dispute Resolution. This Section considers the professional and ethical issues that arise by virtue of resolving disputes without judicial adjudication.

3. Settlement and Offers of Judgment

The most basic way in which parties resolve their disputes without having to secure a litigated judgment in court is settlement. In the best-case scenario, a negotiated settlement provides each party with some measure of a "win"; the plaintiff might "win" a smaller recovery with certainty, while the defendant may "win" a limitation on damages with significant attendant savings of costs and attorneys' fees, not to mention time. In theory, both parties to any litigation should be interested in such a result, and in practice, most cases filed in the federal District Courts are resolved ultimately through settlement.

The remaining Sections of this Chapter focus on the main quasi-adjudicatory tools that the parties and the court can employ to help encourage the settlement of disputes. This Section focuses on the principal tool in the arsenal of the lawyer who seeks to settle, but who is not able to convince the opposing party to come to the table: the Offer of Judgment.

Under Rule 68, a defending party may, at any time up to 14 days before the trial, make an offer of judgment (basically, a formal settlement offer) to the plaintiff. The plaintiff then has 14 days during which to accept or reject the offer (silence constitutes rejection). If the offer is rejected, and the plaintiff fails to recover a judgment "more favorable" than the offer, then the plaintiff is liable to the defending party for the "costs" incurred since the date of the offer's rejection. Since Rule 68 was enacted, a recurring issue has been exactly what constitutes "costs," and a frequently litigated question is whether "costs" includes attorneys' fees, which can be far more substantial than even the monetary recovery in some cases. The following case analyzes this issue.

UMG Recordings, Inc. v. Shelter Capital Partners LLC
718 F.3d 1006 (9th Cir. 2013)

Before: Harry Pregerson, Raymond C. Fisher, and Marsha S. Bergon, Circuit Judges.

Fisher, Circuit Judge:

Veoh Networks (Veoh) operates a publicly accessible website that enables users to share videos with other users. Universal Music Group (UMG) is one of the world's largest recorded music and music publishing companies, and includes record labels such as Motown, Def Jam and Geffen. In addition to producing and distributing recorded music, UMG produces music videos. Although Veoh has implemented various procedures to prevent copyright infringement through its system, users of Veoh's service have in the past been able, without UMG's authorization, to download videos containing songs for which UMG owns the copyright. UMG responded by filing suit against Veoh for direct and secondary copyright infringement. The district court granted summary judgment to Veoh after determining that it was protected by the Digital Millennium Copyright Act (DMCA) "safe harbor" limiting service providers' liability for "infringement of copyright by reason of the storage at the direction of a user of material that resides on a system or network controlled or operated by or for the service provider." 17 U.S.C. §512(c). We agree, and accordingly affirm.

Background

* * *

Discussion

* * *

IV.

Veoh appeals the district court's refusal to grant it costs and attorney's fees under Federal Rule of Civil Procedure 68. "Under Rule 68, if a plaintiff rejects a defendant's offer of judgment, and the judgment finally obtained by plaintiff is not more favorable than the offer, the plaintiff must pay the costs incurred subsequent to the offer." "Rule 68 is designed to 'require plaintiffs to think very hard about whether continued litigation is worthwhile,'" and compensate defendants for costs they ought not have had to incur. *Champion Produce, Inc. v. Ruby Robinson Co.*, 342 F.3d 1016, 1032 (9th Cir.2003) (quoting *Marek v. Chesny*, 473 U.S. 1, 11 (1985)). In October 2008, Veoh offered UMG $100,000 to settle this lawsuit, pursuant to the procedures set forth in Rule 68. UMG declined the offer and ultimately failed to win any monetary relief. After the district court ruled that Veoh was entitled to §512(c) protection, the parties requested the entry of judgment and stipulated that Veoh "agree[d] to continue to disable access to the Allegedly Infringing Video Files and to continue to use hash filtering to prevent [infringing] video files ... from being accessed by users," and UMG "agree[d] that, even if it were to prevail on its remaining claims against Veoh..., it is entitled to no further relief."

Veoh contends that it was entitled to receive Rule 68 costs incurred from the time of its October 2008 settlement offer. It argues these costs should include attorney's fees because *Marek*, 473 U.S. at 9, held that, "where the underlying statute defines 'costs' to include attorney's fees, ... such fees are to be included as costs for purposes of Rule 68," and the Copyright Act, 17 U.S.C. §505, provides that a court "may ... award a reasonable attorney's fee to the prevailing party as part of the costs." ... [T]he district court declined to grant attorney's fees under Rule 68 because it had previously determined that fees were not "properly awardable" under §505. Veoh has not challenged the district court's decision with regard to §505, but argues on appeal that under Rule 68 an award of costs, including fees, was mandatory. We agree with the district court that, because it found that attorney's fees were not "properly awardable" under §505 in this case, fees could not be awarded under Rule 68. We remand to the district court to separately analyze whether Rule 68 costs, excluding attorney's fees, are warranted.

A.

In *Marek*, the Supreme Court held that "the term 'costs' in Rule 68 was intended to refer to all costs *properly awardable* under the relevant substantive statute." 473 U.S. at 9 (emphasis added). We have interpreted this to mean that attorney's fees may be awarded as Rule 68 costs only if those fees would have been properly awarded under the relevant substantive statute in that particular case. In [*United States v. Trident Seafoods Corp.*, 92 F.3d 855 (9th Cir.1996)] at 860, for example, the issue was the interplay between the Clean Air Act (CAA) and Rule 68. Under the CAA, fees may only be awarded if the action was "unreasonable." *Trident* held that "[t]he only interpretation that gives meaning to every word in both Rule 68 and the [CAA] is that 'costs' in Rule 68 include attorneys' fees only if the action was unreasonable." The fact that fees could have been awarded under the CAA, had its requirements been met, was insufficient to make them "properly awardable" within the meaning of *Marek* when the district court decided not to grant them in that case.

We confronted the same issue with regard to a different substantive statute in *Champion*. There, we considered whether Rule 68 "costs" included attorney's fees where Idaho Code § 12-120(3) permitted the award of fees to a "prevailing party," and the district court expressly held that the defendant had not prevailed within the meaning of that section. Relying on *Trident*, we held that "Rule 68 is not intended to expand the bases for a party's recovery of attorneys' fees," and thus,

> [j]ust as attorneys' fees are not "properly awardable" to a defendant in a Clean Air Act case unless "the court finds that such action was unreasonable," attorneys' fees are not "properly awardable" to a defendant in a case where the relevant statute awards attorneys' fees to a prevailing party unless the defendant is a prevailing party within the meaning of that statute.

Id. at 1031 (citing *Payne v. Milwaukee Cnty.*, 288 F.3d 1021, 1026 (7th Cir.2002) ("Briefly put, 'costs' cannot encompass more than the rules or other relevant statutes authorize.")). Although we have not yet confronted this question in a Copyright Act case, *Trident* and *Champion* make clear that in this context as well, because the district court determined that attorney's fees were not "properly awardable" to Veoh under § 505, they were not awardable under Rule 68 either.

B.

Even though Veoh is not entitled to attorney's fees under Rule 68, it may be entitled to its other costs. *See, e.g., Champion*, 342 F.3d at 1028 (holding that even though attorney's fees were not properly awardable under Rule 68, costs (excluding fees) were mandatory). The district court, however, did not analyze whether costs apart from fees were warranted.

Veoh has already been awarded some of its costs under Federal Rule of Civil Procedure 54(d), but it argues on appeal that it is entitled to all of its post-settlement offer costs under Rule 68. This may be true, if certain conditions are met. First, costs are awardable under Rule 68 where "the judgment that the offeree finally obtains is not more favorable than the unaccepted offer." Fed.R.Civ.P. 68(d). Veoh argues that "[b]ecause Veoh was already taking the measures set forth in the [stipulated] injunction, and UMG was primarily seeking monetary damages, the value of that stipulation was less than Veoh's Rule 68 Offer." Although this may prove true, the value of the stipulated injunction is not clear on this record.

Second, Veoh can recover Rule 68 costs only if it is not a prevailing defendant. In *Delta Air Lines, Inc. v. August*, 450 U.S. 346, 352 (1981), the Supreme Court held that Rule 68 "applies only to offers made by the defendant and only to judgments obtained by the plaintiff," and "therefore is simply inapplicable [where] it was the defendant that obtained the judgment." *See also Goldberg v. Pac. Indem. Co.*, 627 F.3d 752, 755 (9th Cir.2010) ("Rule 68 does not allow a defendant to recover costs when judgment is entered in the defendant's favor."). The Court observed that holding otherwise would create an odd system in which "any settlement offer, no matter how small, would apparently trigger the operation of the Rule," and "[t]hus any defendant, by performing the meaningless act of making a nominal settlement offer, could eliminate the trial judge's discretion under Rule 54(d)." *Delta*, 450 U.S. at 353. *Delta* rejected such an understanding of Rule 68:

> We cannot reasonably conclude that the drafters of the Federal Rules intended on the one hand affirmatively to grant the district judge discretion to deny costs to the prevailing party under Rule 54(d) and then on the other hand to give defendants—and only defendants—the power to take away that discretion by performing a token act.

Id.; see also MRO Commc'ns, Inc. v. Am. Tel. & Tel. Co., 197 F.3d 1276, 1280 (9th Cir.1999) ("Where a defendant prevails after making an offer of judgment, 'the trial judge retains his Rule 54(d) discretion.'").

Veoh argues that *Delta* does not apply because UMG "actually obtained certain relief" in the form of the parties' stipulation that Veoh would continue removing infringing content discovered by its hash filtering system, and thus UMG rather than Veoh "obtained the judgment." Although the district court determined that Veoh was "the prevailing party on the core issue in the litigation" for § 505 purposes, it did not clarify whether it also concluded that Veoh was a prevailing defendant under *Delta* for Rule 68 purposes. We therefore remand to the district court to consider in the first instance whether Veoh is eligible to receive Rule 68 costs under *Delta*, and, if so, whether "the judgment that the offeree finally obtain[ed] [wa]s not more favorable than the unaccepted offer." Fed.R.Civ.P. 68(d). If both conditions are met, then the district court should determine what remaining costs are due to Veoh.

Conclusion

We affirm the district court's determination on summary judgment that Veoh is entitled to § 512(c) safe harbor protection, and its dismissal of the claims of secondary liability against the Investor Defendants. We also affirm its determination that, in this case, attorney's fees may not be awarded under Rule 68. We remand for the district court to consider in the first instance whether Veoh is entitled to Rule 68 costs excluding attorney's fees.

The parties shall bear their own costs on appeal.

* * *

AFFIRMED in part and REMANDED in part.

Exercise 14-1. Rule 68 Offers and Safeguards

1. What is the court's basis for denying Veoh attorneys' fees as part of its post-offer "costs" in the case above? Is it that attorneys' fees can never be part of such costs, or is there a reason unique to this case that attorneys' fees cannot be awarded?

2. What obstacle will Veoh have to overcome on remand to recover its non-attorneys'-fee costs?

3. What is the purpose of allowing a defendant that loses, but ends up owing less in damages and other relief than it was offered in settlement, to recover its post-offer costs, but disallowing a defendant that wins a judgment from recovering its post-offer costs? Isn't a judgment in the defendant's favor inherently "less favorable" for the plaintiff than *any* settlement offer? What does the court see as the danger inherent in allowing Rule 68 costs awards in the scenario where the defendant actually wins the case?

---

4. Mediation and Other Non-Adjudicatory Procedures

Mediation is a process by which the parties attempt to work out a resolution of their dispute with the assistance of a neutral third party. Mediation as a formal means to helping the parties arrive at a settlement of their dispute is a relatively recent development in United States law. In recent decades, however, as court dockets have greatly increased, and as states and the federal government have sought ways of reducing costs, mediation has become a litigation staple.

No Federal Rule of Civil Procedure governs mediation specifically, but compulsory referrals to mediation in state-court cases are common. Some states even require mediation in minor criminal cases, hoping that the victim and the perpetrator can come to a non-judicial resolution that might avoid prosecution.

But this does not mean that mediation is not a part of what the federal courts do. Indeed, most (if not all) Local Rules of the District Courts specify procedures relating to settlement, and many authorize the court to refer the parties to mediation in any civil action. Below is one example of such a rule, Local Rule 16.3 for the United States District Court for the Northern District of Florida:

RULE 16.3 Mediation

(A) **Definition.** Mediation is an opportunity for the parties to negotiate their own settlement. Mediation is a supervised settlement conference presided over by a neutral mediator to promote conciliation, compromise and the ultimate settlement of a civil action. The mediator may be a mediator certified in accordance with these rules or any person mutually agreed upon by all parties. The mediator's role in the settlement of cases is to assist the parties in the identification of interests, suggest alternatives, analyze issues, question perceptions, conduct private caucuses, stimulate negotiations between opposing sides, and keep order. The mediation process does not allow for testimony of witnesses. The mediator does not review or rule upon questions of fact or law, or render any final decision in the case. Absent a settlement or consent of the parties, the mediator will only report to the presiding judge whether the case settled, was adjourned or continued for further mediation, or was terminated because settlement was not possible and the mediator declared an impasse.

(B) **Purpose.** Mediation is intended as an alternative method to resolve civil cases, thereby saving time and cost without sacrificing the quality of justice to be rendered or the right of the litigants to a full trial in the event of an impasse following mediation.

(C) **Qualifications of Mediators.** Any person who is certified and remains in good standing as a circuit court mediator under the rules adopted by the Supreme Court of Florida is qualified to serve as a mediator in this district. By mutual agreement and with court approval, any other person may be a mediator in a specific case.

(D) **Standards of Professional Conduct for Mediators.** All mediators, whether certified or not, who mediate in cases pending in this district shall be governed by standards of professional conduct and ethical rules adopted by the Supreme Court of Florida for circuit court mediators.

(E) **Disqualification of a Mediator.** After reasonable notice and hearing, and for good cause, the presiding judge shall have discretion and authority to disqualify any mediator from serving as mediator in a particular case. Good cause may include violation of the standards of professional conduct for mediators. Additionally, any person selected as a mediator may be disqualified for bias or prejudice as provided in 28 U.S.C. § 144, and shall be disqualified in any case in which such action would be required by a justice, district judge, or magistrate judge governed by 28 U.S.C. § 455.

(F) **Compensation of Mediators.** Absent agreement by all parties to the contrary, mediators shall be compensated and reimbursed for expenses at the rate set by the court. Further, absent agreement of the parties to the contrary or order of the court for good cause shown, the cost of the mediator's services shall be paid equally by the parties to the mediation conference.

(G) **Limitations on Acceptance of Compensation or Other Reimbursement.** Except as provided by these rules, no mediator shall charge or accept in connection with the mediation of any particular case, any compensation, fee, or any other thing of value from any other source without prior written approval of the court.

(H) **Mediators as Counsel in Other Cases.** Any member of the bar who is certified or selected as a mediator pursuant to these rules shall not, for that reason alone, be disqualified from appearing and acting as counsel in any other case pending in this district.

(I) **Referral to Mediation.** All litigants in civil cases not exempt under N.D. Fla. Loc. R. 26.1 shall consider the use of mediation as an alternative dispute resolution process at an appropriate stage in the litigation. Any pending civil case may be referred to mediation by the presiding judicial officer at such time as the judicial officer may determine to be in the interests of justice. The parties may request the court to submit any pending civil case to mediation at any time.

As you might surmise from the numbering of the Local Rule above, the Federal Rule of Civil procedure most closely associated with the mediation process is Rule 16.

Exercise 14-2. Reading Rule 16 for ADR Provisions

Read Federal Rule of Civil Procedure 16 carefully. Find all of the provisions of Rule 16 that seem to further the pursuit of alternative dispute resolution proceedings.

The "when authorized by statute or local rule" language of Rule 16(c)(2)(I) is satisfied by a number of federal statutes, as well as by local rules such as the one reprinted above. For example, Title 28 of the U.S. Code contains Chapter 44, titled "Alternative Dispute Resolution." Chapter 44 requires the United States Courts to draft local rules authorizing the use of any of the main forms of alternative dispute resolution to resolve disputes. *See* 28 U.S.C. §651 ("Each United States district court shall authorize, by local rule adopted under section 2071(a), the use of alternative dispute resolution processes in all civil actions, including adversary proceedings in bankruptcy, in accordance with this chapter, except that the use of arbitration may be authorized only as provided in section 654. Each United States district court shall devise and implement its own alternative dispute resolution program, by local rule adopted under section 2071 (a), to encourage and promote the use of alternative dispute resolution in its district."); 28 U.S.C. §652 ("Notwithstanding any provision of law to the contrary and except as provided in subsections (b) and (c), each district court shall, by local rule adopted under section 2071(a), require that litigants in all civil cases consider the use of an alternative dispute resolution process at an appropriate stage in the litigation. Each district court shall provide litigants in all civil cases with at least one alternative dispute resolution process, including, but not limited to, mediation, early neutral evaluation, minitrial, and arbitration as authorized in sections 654 through 658.").

Note that, in addition to mediation, Section 652 above mentions "early neutral evaluation, minitrial, and arbitration" as potential alternative dispute resolution mechanisms that a District may mandate that the parties consider. Arbitration will be treated in detail below, but early neutral evaluation and minitrial require only a brief explanation, as they each constitute an intermediary step between settlement and full trial.

Early Neutral Evaluation is a process through which the parties' attorneys each present a summary of the facts and legal arguments favoring their client's side of the case to a neutral intermediary (chosen either by the court or by the parties). There are no witnesses, few exhibits (if any), and no jury. The "Neutral," as the decision maker is called, is required to listen to the parties' arguments and render a non-binding, advisory opinion as to the strength or weakness of each party's case. It is hoped that, after such an opinion is issued, the parties will be more likely to settle the case.

Minitrial is a procedure that involves a trial of the case to a judicially appointed panel of "judges," sometimes including another judge of the District and two representative of the parties—in business cases, this might mean a high-level executive of each business. The panel hears argument from the parties' counsel and may hear testimony from one or more witnesses, including expert witnesses. Following these presentations, the panel might render an advisory opinion, or in some cases, the two panelists who are drawn from the disputing company parties may seek to settle the case, based on their new understanding of the strength or weakness of their positions.

Mediation, in contrast, does not necessarily involve the presentation of the case by the parties. The basic form of mediation involves the parties attempting to negotiate a settlement with the help of a neutral intermediary either appointed by the court or chosen by the parties. In most cases, this process involves either a mediated conference, with both parties speaking with the mediator at once, or a set of separate conferences, in which each party confers with the mediator separately from the other party(ies), while the mediator circulates from separate room to separate room to try to hone the dispute down to what will satisfy both parties.

A successful mediation may result in the drafting of a settlement agreement, a contract between the parties to end their dispute in court as long as each party fulfills the duties specified in the contract (which on the plaintiff's side might mean voluntarily dismissing the lawsuit, and on the defendant's side might mean paying over a sum of money or agreeing to do or stop doing something). In some cases, a settlement agreement will require court approval, but most settlement agreements do not. Also, in some cases, the parties are encouraged to provide the mediator with a "mediation brief," a mini-summary judgment brief that outlines the factual and legal arguments that each side of the dispute expects to make at summary judgment, and at trial if necessary.

Exercise 14-3. Local Rules Relating to Mediation and Settlement

Assume that you are counsel to the plaintiff in a lawsuit arising out of the facts related in the Chapter Problem. Obviously, it would be best for you and your client to settle the case as early in the proceedings as possible.

Assume that the events occurred either in the federal District where your law school sits, or (if your law school sits in the Northern District of Florida), any other federal District, such as the one where you grew up, the one in which you intend to live after graduation, etc. Research the Local Rules of your chosen District and determine:

1. Whether you *must* mediate your dispute.

2. Whether it is possible for you to obtain a court order forcing your opponent to mediate with you.

3. Whether any alternative dispute resolution options other than mediation are available to you to pursue a settlement of your dispute.

4. The procedures you must follow to make use of any alternative dispute resolution procedures available to you, including mediation.

Disputes over Mediation

Few disputes exist over mediation that rise to the level of requiring judicial intervention (and judges are none too pleased when such disputes arise). But ours is an adversarial system, and inevitably in such a system, there will be matters that cannot be resolved—even within an alternative dispute resolution process—without the intervention of a judge with the power to order the two sides to participate according to the law. Most commonly in the federal courts, these disputes involve the "authority" that a party's representative has to settle the case during a mediation. Below is an opinion resolving a typical such dispute.

Turner v. Young

205 F.R.D. 592 (D. Kan. 2002)

Memorandum & Order

O'Hara, United States Magistrate Judge.

I. Introduction.

This case comes before the court on the motion of plaintiff Tammy Turner for sanctions against defendant Stanhope Express, Inc. (Stanhope). The court has reviewed plaintiff's memorandum in support, Stanhope's memorandum in opposition, and plaintiff's reply. For the reasons explained below, plaintiff's motion is denied.

II. Background.

In compliance with the scheduling order entered in this case, the parties scheduled a mediation for December 13, 2001. On November 26, 2001, defense counsel sent a letter to plaintiff's counsel requesting permission to have the claims handler with settlement authority participate in the mediation by telephone. On November 27, 2001, plaintiff's counsel sent a response letter, objecting "vehemently" because he believed the mediation would be a "waste of time" if defendant did not send someone to the mediation with settlement authority. Plaintiff's counsel further stated: "If you insist on not participating fully, I would suggest that we contact the Court immediately so that this issue may be resolved well in advance of the mediation." Plaintiff's counsel heard nothing further from defense counsel about this issue.

On December 13, 2001, defense counsel came to the mediation and was accompanied by Scott Glow, a representative of defendant's liability insurance carrier, Carolina Casualty Insurance Company. Before the mediation, Carolina Casualty decided that it would give Glow authority to pay up to $25,000 to settle all of plaintiff's claims. When the mediation commenced, plaintiff's counsel communicated that the mediation was being conducted only to settle plaintiff's personal injury claims, but not the potential invasion of privacy claim plaintiff has not yet sued upon. Accordingly, Glow called Tony Sarchet, a representative in Carolina Casualty's home office, and Sarchet told Glow that he was authorized to pay only $20,000 if the settlement would not effect a release of plaintiff's invasion of privacy claim. Mediation proceeded, and the parties reached an impasse. Plaintiff's last demand was $32,500, and defendant's final offer was $20,000.

Plaintiff now seeks sanctions against defendant for its failure to send a representative to the mediation who had authority to settle plaintiff's claims.

III. Analysis.

Plaintiff argues that D. Kan. Rule 16.3 required Stanhope to send a representative with settlement authority to the mediation. It is unclear whether, by its terms, D. Kan. Rule 16.3 requires a party representative with settlement authority to participate in a mediation session facilitated by a private mediator. D. Kan. Rule 16.3 provides:

> Consistent with Fed.R.Civ.P. 16, the judge or magistrate judge to whom a case has been assigned will likely enter an order directing counsel and the parties, at the earliest appropriate opportunity, to attempt to resolve or settle their dispute using such extra-judicial proceedings as mediation, mini-trials, summary jury trials or other alternative dispute resolution programs. Any such order may set forth the terms of the extra-judicial proceedings. Pursuant to 28 U.S.C. § 652, as amended October 30, 1998, litigants in all civil cases are required to consider the use of an alternative dispute resolution process, including, but not limited to, mediation, settlement conferences, early neutral evaluation, mini trial, and arbitration as authorized in 28 U.S.C. §§ 654 and 658, at an appropriate stage in the litigation. Specific cases in which use of alternative dispute resolution would not be appropriate may be exempt from this requirement.

> Settlement conferences shall be conducted in such a way as to permit an informative discussion between counsel and the parties, and the judge, magistrate judge, or mediator of every possible aspect of the case bearing on its settlement, thus permitting the judge, magistrate judge, or mediator to privately express his or her views concerning the settlement of the case. *Attendance by a party representative with settlement authority at such conferences is mandatory, unless the court orders otherwise.* In cases where the United States is a party, attendance at the conference by the United States Attorney for the District of Kansas will satisfy this rule.

> Settlement conference statements or memoranda submitted to the court or any other communications which take place during the settlement conference shall not be used by any party in the trial of the case. The judge, magistrate judge, or mediator presiding over the settlement conference shall not communicate to the judge or magistrate judge trying the case the confidences of

the conference except to advise as to whether or not the case has been settled. If the conference is conducted by a mediator, the costs of the conference, including the reasonable fees of the mediator, shall be assessed to the parties in such proportions as shall be determined by the judge or magistrate judge.

D. Kan. Rule 16.3 (emphasis added). The emphasized language is at issue in this case.

Unfortunately, the present version of D. Kan. Rule 16.3 may not be a model of clarity in attempting to determine whether the emphasized language applies only when the court conducts a settlement conference, or whether it also applies when the parties hire a private mediator to facilitate a mediation session. Arguments can be made both ways. On the one hand, the third sentence in the first paragraph refers to "mediation" and "settlement conferences" as distinct forms of alternative dispute resolution, and the second and third paragraphs apply only to "settlement conferences," a term that refers to settlement conferences facilitated by a district judge or a magistrate judge, not to private mediation sessions. On the other hand, the second and third paragraphs repeatedly refer to a "judge," "magistrate judge," and "mediator" as distinct types of facilitators and, therefore, the term "mediator" undoubtedly refers to a private mediator.

In any event, to the extent the emphasized language might be read to apply only to require a party representative with settlement authority to attend settlement conferences facilitated by a district judge or a magistrate judge, the undersigned magistrate judge hereby expressly extends that requirement to mediation sessions facilitated by a private mediator. Thus, regardless of whether parties are attending a settlement conference or a private mediation session, "[a]ttendance by a party representative with settlement authority ... is mandatory." Of course, the court may enter an order alleviating this requirement. D. Kan. Rule 16.3 ("unless the court orders otherwise"). In addition, in the case of a private mediation session, a private mediator may alleviate this requirement if all parties are given reasonable notice before the scheduled mediation. That way, any party that believes mediation would be a "waste of time" in the absence of attendance by a party representative with settlement authority will have time to seek a court order alleviating that party of its obligation to participate in the mediation session.

The undersigned also wishes to clarify what, precisely, is meant by "[a]ttendance by a party representative with settlement authority." "Attendance" means to appear in person and participate directly, not to stand by or participate by telephone. "[S]ettlement authority" means full, meaningful, authority. A person with settlement authority does not need to pick up the phone to call anyone else to find out whether he or she can go higher or lower. A person with settlement authority is "the" decisionmaker. He or she is the person who has authority to meet the other party's demand, even if he or she chooses not to do so.

In this case, defendant argues that Glow had full authority to settle plaintiff's claims. Defendant provided an affidavit from Sarchet in which he states that Carolina Casualty decided, prior to the mediation, that the most Carolina Casualty was willing to offer to settle all of plaintiff's claims was $25,000, and that Carolina Casualty sent Glow to the mediation with "full authority" to settle plaintiff's claims accordingly. Glow is a paradigm example of the type of person who does not have the required settlement authority. At the beginning of the mediation, when plaintiff's counsel communicated that she was only willing to discuss settlement of plaintiff's personal injury claims, Glow called Sarchet to find out how high he could go to settle only those claim [*sic*]. Thus, Sarchet was the person with the required settlement authority, and defendant should have sent him to the mediation.

Nevertheless, when the court was presented with plaintiff's present motion, the court was struck by the absence of clear case law from this jurisdiction providing definitive guidance on this precise issue. Purely as a matter of common sense, courtesy, and good faith, this requirement seems clear to the court. However, because of the absence of precedent to alert Stanhope that it would be subject to sanctions for sending Grow instead of Sarchet, the court is reluctant to impose sanctions against Stanhope in this case.

In the future, however, this particular magistrate judge will expect all parties to be on notice that failure to abide by these guidelines will be regarded as exhibiting a lack of good faith, and could warrant sanctions under Fed.R.Civ.P. 16(f). *See generally, e.g., Nick v. Morgan's Foods, Inc.,* 270 F.3d 590 (8th Cir. 2001) (affirming a district court's order imposing sanctions against a party for its failure to participate in good faith in a court-ordered alternative dispute resolution); *St. Paul Fire & Marine Ins. Co. v. CEI Fla., Inc.,* 152 F.R.D. 95 (E.D. Mich. 1993) (imposing sanctions against a party for its lack of a good-faith attempt to comply with a local court rule and a pretrial order requiring a party representative with authority to settle the case to attend the final pretrial conference).

This opinion will be submitted for publication with the intent of ensuring that attorneys and litigants are aware that the undersigned expects party representatives with full, meaningful settlement authority to personally appear and directly participate in settlement conferences with a district judge or magistrate judge, as well as mediation sessions facilitated by a private mediator. Any party that devotes its time, resources, and efforts to send an authorized representative to a mediation session should be able to expect the same courtesy from all other parties. Of course, the court cannot, nor will it, force parties to settle. However, the court can ensure that, when appropriate, the parties put forth their best efforts to engage in meaningful settlement negotiations.

IV. Conclusion and Order.

In consideration of the foregoing,

IT IS HEREBY ORDERED:

1. Plaintiff's motion for sanctions against defendant Stanhope (doc. 23) is denied.

2. The clerk shall mail copies of this order to all counsel of record.

Exercise 14-4. *Turner v. Young*

1. Why, according to this Magistrate Judge, did Stanhope's representative (Glow) not have "full settlement authority"?

2. Would it have been proper for Sarchet to show up at the mediation and steadfastly refuse to budge above $20,000 once Plaintiff's counsel made it clear that settlement of the personal injury claim would not settle the potential invasion of privacy claim?

3. If Glow indeed did not have "full settlement authority," then why was Stanhope, the defendant company, not sanctioned?

4. If you represent Stanhope, and Sarchet is adamant that he wants to send Glow to the next mediation conference, how can you comply with Sarchet's wishes, while making sure that Stanhope is not sanctioned following this next conference?

---

5. Arbitration

Less formal than a trial but more formal than a mediation or an early neutral evaluation, while potentially more binding than a minitrial, arbitration is fast becoming the preferred means of dispute resolution in many areas of the law—particularly commercial and business law, including labor law, which almost always involves arbitration.

Arbitration takes on three main forms: (1) mandatory and binding; (2) mandatory but non-binding; and (3) voluntary and non-binding.

Mandatory, binding arbitration is typically required based on a contract between the parties executed before any problems arose between them giving rise to a legal dispute. Mandatory arbitration provisions have long been part of collective bargaining agreements between labor unions and employers, but over time, they have worked their way into securities agreements, insurance contracts, and even consumer contracts, such as cruise ship tickets, shrinkwrap agreements, and the ubiquitous "terms and conditions" agreements to which consumers must signify their assent before they may purchase software over the Internet.

Mandatory, binding arbitration contracts are enforced in federal courts through the Federal Arbitration Act (the "FAA"), codified at Title 9, United States Code. Two main provisions generate most of the litigation surrounding the FAA. The first simply declares that arbitration agreements are enforceable, but contains an important exception:

> A written provision in any maritime transaction or a contract evidencing a transaction involving commerce to settle by arbitration a controversy thereafter arising out of such contract or transaction, or the refusal to perform the whole or any part thereof, or an agreement in writing to submit to arbitration an existing controversy arising out of such a contract, transaction, or refusal, shall be valid, irrevocable, and enforceable, save upon such grounds as exist at law or in equity for the revocation of any contract.

9 U.S.C. § 2. The "save upon" clause at the end of this provision has generated a good deal of litigation as to the applicability of state-law defenses to contract enforcement, such as unconscionability.

The second of these major litigation-generating clauses is 9 U.S.C. § 4, which provides, in pertinent part:

> A party aggrieved by the alleged failure, neglect, or refusal of another to arbitrate under a written agreement for arbitration may petition any United States district court which, save for such agreement, would have jurisdiction under title 28, in a civil action or in admiralty of the subject matter of a suit arising out of the controversy between the parties, for an order directing that such arbitration proceed in the manner provided for in such agreement....

This provision allows a party to an arbitration agreement to petition the federal District Court that would otherwise have jurisdiction over the dispute to compel the parties to arbitrate. Often, this petition takes the form of a motion to compel arbitration, submitted in response to the service of a plaintiff's complaint in that very District Court.

For a number of years, these provisions were used only in certain substantive-law contexts, but in recent years, the Supreme Court has become quite active in applying the FAA to serve what it has called "a liberal federal policy favoring arbitration." *See Moses H. Cone Memorial Hospital v. Mercury Constr. Corp.*, 460 U.S. 1, 24 (1983) ("Section 2 is a congressional declaration of a liberal federal policy favoring arbitration agreements, notwithstanding any state substantive or procedural policies to the contrary. The effect of the section is to create a body of federal substantive law of arbitrability, applicable to any arbitration agreement within the coverage of the Act.") In practice, this interpretation of Section 2's enforceability provisions has tended to allow for state-law contract defenses that do not single out arbitration agreements for particularly negative treatment, but the issue nearly always comes up pursuant to a motion to compel arbitration under Section 4 (with the unenforceability argument set up in opposition to the motion). If factual issues must be resolved in determining whether the agreement is enforceable, or whether the issues involved in the pending lawsuit are issues that the parties agreed to arbitrate (i.e., "arbitrable issues"), then the party opposing enforcement may have the matter heard by summary jury trial (i.e., trial only of those facts). Parties seeking to arbitrate therefore have a strong financial incentive to fight very hard to see their agreements to arbitrate enforced.

Often, in cases evaluating arbitrability and enforceability, the decisions whether an issue is arbitrable and whether an arbitration agreement is enforceable are arguably issues themselves that the parties agreed to submit to arbitration. In such cases, courts are presented with the prospect of whether to vacate an arbitrator's decision. The standards for judicial review of an arbitrator's decision, codified at 9 U.S.C. §§ 10–11, greatly favor upholding arbitral awards. These standards can often frustrate parties who believe that their arbitrators did not decide the issues as competently as a court would have, but they can also work to preserve rulings that favor traditionally less powerful parties, as you will see below.

Below are three recent cases the Supreme Court has decided working through the questions of *enforceability*, or the validity of an agreement to arbitrate; *arbitrability*, or the question of whether a specific issue before the court is within the scope of issues which the parties agreed to arbitrate, and *judicial review of arbitral decisions*. In reading these decisions, try to determine how you might approach the negotiation and drafting of an arbitration clause within a larger contract if you were the attorney responsible for doing so.

Rent-A-Center, West, Inc. v. Jackson

561 U.S. 63 (2010)

Justice Scalia delivered the opinion of the Court.

We consider whether, under the Federal Arbitration Act (FAA or Act), 9 U.S.C. §§ 1–16, a district court may decide a claim that an arbitration agreement is unconscionable, where the agreement explicitly assigns that decision to the arbitrator.

I

On February 1, 2007, the respondent here, Antonio Jackson, filed an employment-discrimination suit under Rev. Stat. § 1977, 42 U.S.C. § 1981, against his former employer in the United States District Court for the District of Nevada. The defendant and petitioner here, Rent-A-Center,

West, Inc., filed a motion under the FAA to dismiss or stay the proceedings, 9 U.S.C. § 3, and to compel arbitration, § 4. Rent-A-Center argued that the Mutual Agreement to Arbitrate Claims (Agreement), which Jackson signed on February 24, 2003 as a condition of his employment there, precluded Jackson from pursuing his claims in court. The Agreement provided for arbitration of all "past, present or future" disputes arising out of Jackson's employment with Rent-A-Center, including "claims for discrimination" and "claims for violation of any federal ... law." It also provided that "[t]he Arbitrator, and not any federal, state, or local court or agency, shall have exclusive authority to resolve any dispute relating to the interpretation, applicability, enforceability or formation of this Agreement including, but not limited to any claim that all or any part of this Agreement is void or voidable."

Jackson opposed the motion on the ground that "the arbitration agreement in question is clearly unenforceable in that it is unconscionable" under Nevada law. Rent-A-Center responded that Jackson's unconscionability claim was not properly before the court because Jackson had expressly agreed that the arbitrator would have exclusive authority to resolve any dispute about the enforceability of the Agreement. It also disputed the merits of Jackson's unconscionability claims.

The District Court granted Rent-A-Center's motion to dismiss the proceedings and to compel arbitration. The court found that the Agreement "clearly and unmistakenly [sic]" gives the arbitrator exclusive authority to decide whether the Agreement is enforceable, and, because Jackson challenged the validity of the Agreement as a whole, the issue was for the arbitrator. The court noted that even if it were to examine the merits of Jackson's unconscionability claims, it would have rejected the claim that the agreement to split arbitration fees was substantively unconscionable under Nevada law. It did not address Jackson's procedural or other substantive unconscionability arguments.

Without oral argument, a divided panel of the Court of Appeals for the Ninth Circuit reversed in part, affirmed in part, and remanded. 581 F.3d 912 (2009). The court reversed on the question of who (the court or arbitrator) had the authority to decide whether the Agreement is enforceable. It noted that "Jackson does not dispute that the language of the Agreement clearly assigns the arbitrability determination to the arbitrator," but held that where "a party challenges an arbitration agreement as unconscionable, and thus asserts that he could not meaningfully assent to the agreement, the threshold question of unconscionability is for the court." The Ninth Circuit affirmed the District Court's alternative conclusion that the fee-sharing provision was not substantively unconscionable and remanded for consideration of Jackson's other unconscionability arguments. Judge Hall dissented on the ground that "the question of the arbitration agreement's validity should have gone to the arbitrator, as the parties 'clearly and unmistakably provide[d]' in their agreement."

We granted certiorari, 558 U.S. 1142 (2010).

II

A

The FAA reflects the fundamental principle that arbitration is a matter of contract. Section 2, the "primary substantive provision of the Act," *Moses H. Cone Memorial Hospital v. Mercury Constr. Corp.*, 460 U.S. 1, 24 (1983), provides:

> A written provision in ... a contract evidencing a transaction involving commerce to settle by arbitration a controversy thereafter arising out of such contract ... shall be valid, irrevocable, and enforceable, save upon such grounds as exist at law or in equity for the revocation of any contract. 9 U.S.C. § 2.

The FAA thereby places arbitration agreements on an equal footing with other contracts, and requires courts to enforce them according to their terms. Like other contracts, however, they may be invalidated by "generally applicable contract defenses, such as fraud, duress, or unconscionability."

The Act also establishes procedures by which federal courts implement § 2's substantive rule. Under § 3, a party may apply to a federal court for a stay of the trial of an action "upon any issue referable to arbitration under an agreement in writing for such arbitration." Under § 4, a party "aggrieved" by the failure of another party "to arbitrate under a written agreement for arbitration" may petition a federal court "for an order directing that such arbitration proceed in the manner provided for in such agreement." The court "shall" order arbitration "upon being satisfied that the making of the agreement for arbitration or the failure to comply therewith is not in issue."

The Agreement here contains multiple "written provision[s]" to "settle by arbitration a controversy," § 2. Two are relevant to our discussion. First, the section titled "Claims Covered By The Agreement" provides for arbitration of all "past, present or future" disputes arising out of Jackson's employment with Rent-A-Center. Second, the section titled "Arbitration Procedures" provides that "[t]he Arbitrator ... shall have exclusive authority to resolve any dispute relating to the ... enforceability ... of this Agreement including, but not limited to any claim that all or any part of this Agreement is void or voidable." The current "controversy" between the parties is whether the Agreement is unconscionable. It is the second provision, which delegates resolution of that controversy to the arbitrator, that Rent-A-Center seeks to enforce. Adopting the terminology used by the parties, we will refer to it as the delegation provision.

The delegation provision is an agreement to arbitrate threshold issues concerning the arbitration agreement. We have recognized that parties can agree to arbitrate "gateway" questions of "arbitrability," such as whether the parties have agreed to arbitrate or whether their agreement covers a particular controversy. This line of cases merely reflects the principle that arbitration is a matter of contract. An agreement to arbitrate a gateway issue is simply an additional, antecedent agreement the party seeking arbitration asks the federal court to enforce, and the FAA operates on this additional arbitration agreement just as it does on any other. The additional agreement is valid under §2 "save upon such grounds as exist at law or in equity for the revocation of any contract," and federal courts can enforce the agreement by staying federal litigation under §3 and compelling arbitration under §4. The question before us, then, is whether the delegation provision is valid under §2.

B

There are two types of validity challenges under §2: "One type challenges specifically the validity of the agreement to arbitrate," and "[t]he other challenges the contract as a whole, either on a ground that directly affects the entire agreement (e.g., the agreement was fraudulently induced), or on the ground that the illegality of one of the contract's provisions renders the whole contract invalid." In a line of cases neither party has asked us to overrule, we held that only the first type of challenge is relevant to a court's determination whether the arbitration agreement at issue is enforceable. *See Prima Paint Corp. v. Flood & Conklin Mfg. Co.,* 388 U.S. 395, 403–404 (1967). That is because §2 states that a "written provision" "to settle by arbitration a controversy" is "valid, irrevocable, and enforceable" without mention of the validity of the contract in which it is contained. Thus, a party's challenge to another provision of the contract, or to the contract as a whole, does not prevent a court from enforcing a specific agreement to arbitrate. "[A]s a matter of substantive federal arbitration law, an arbitration provision is severable from the remainder of the contract." *Buckeye Cash Checking, Inc. v. Cardegna,* 546 U.S. 440, 445 (2006).

But that agreements to arbitrate are severable does not mean that they are unassailable. If a party challenges the validity under §2 of the precise agreement to arbitrate at issue, the federal court must consider the challenge before ordering compliance with that agreement under §4. In *Prima Paint,* for example, if the claim had been "fraud in the inducement of the arbitration clause itself," then the court would have considered it. 388 U.S., at 403–404. "To immunize an arbitration agreement from judicial challenge on the ground of fraud in the inducement would be to elevate it over other forms of contract," *id.,* at 404, n. 12. In some cases the claimed basis of invalidity for the contract as a whole will be much easier to establish than the same basis as applied only to the severable agreement to arbitrate. Thus, in an employment contract many elements of alleged unconscionability applicable to the entire contract (outrageously low wages, for example) would not affect the agreement to arbitrate alone. But even where that is not the case—as in *Prima Paint* itself, where the alleged fraud that induced the whole contract equally induced the agreement to arbitrate which was part of that contract—we nonetheless require the basis of challenge to be directed specifically to the agreement to arbitrate before the court will intervene.

Here, the "written provision ... to settle by arbitration a controversy," 9 U.S.C. §2, that Rent-A-Center asks us to enforce is the delegation provision—the provision that gave the arbitrator "exclusive authority to resolve any dispute relating to the ... enforceability ... of this Agreement." The "remainder of the contract," is the rest of the agreement to arbitrate claims arising out of Jackson's employment with Rent-A-Center. To be sure this case differs from *Prima Paint*, *Buckeye*, and *Preston*, in that the arbitration provisions sought to be enforced in those cases were contained in contracts unrelated to arbitration—contracts for consulting services, see *Prima Paint*, *supra*, at 397, check-cashing services, see *Buckeye*, *supra*, at 442, and "personal management" or "talent agent" services, see *Preston*, *supra*, at 352. In this case, the underlying contract is itself an arbitration agreement. But that makes no difference. Application of the severability rule does not depend on the substance of the remainder of the contract. Section 2 operates on the specific "written provision" to "settle by arbitration a controversy" that the party seeks to enforce. Accordingly, unless Jackson challenged the delegation provision specifically, we must treat it as valid under §2, and must enforce it under §§3 and 4, leaving any challenge to the validity of the Agreement as a whole for the arbitrator.

C

The District Court correctly concluded that Jackson challenged only the validity of the contract as a whole. Nowhere in his opposition to Rent-A-Center's motion to compel arbitration did he even mention the delegation provision. Rent-A-Center noted this fact in its reply: "[Jackson's response] fails to rebut or otherwise address in any way [Rent-A-Center's] argument that the Arbitrator must decide [Jackson's] challenge to the enforceability of the Agreement. Thus, [Rent-A-Center's] argument is uncontested."

The arguments Jackson made in his response to Rent-A-Center's motion to compel arbitration support this conclusion. Jackson stated that "the entire agreement seems drawn to provide [Rent-A-Center] with undue advantages should an employment-related dispute arise." At one point, he argued that the limitations on discovery "further suppor[t][his] contention that the arbitration agreement as a whole is substantively unconscionable." And before this Court, Jackson describes his challenge in the District Court as follows: He "opposed the motion to compel on the ground that the entire arbitration agreement, including the delegation clause, was unconscionable." That is an accurate description of his filings.

As required to make out a claim of unconscionability under Nevada law, he contended that the Agreement was both procedurally and substantively unconscionable. It was procedurally unconscionable, he argued, because it "was imposed as a condition of employment and was non-negotiable." But we need not consider that claim because none of Jackson's substantive unconscionability challenges was specific to the delegation provision. First, he argued that the Agreement's coverage was one sided in that it required arbitration of claims an employee was likely to bring—contract, tort, discrimination, and statutory claims—but did not require arbitration of claims Rent-A-Center was likely to bring—intellectual property, unfair competition, and trade secrets claims. This one-sided-coverage argument clearly did not go to the validity of the delegation provision.

Jackson's other two substantive unconscionability arguments assailed arbitration procedures called for by the contract—the fee-splitting arrangement and the limitations on discovery—procedures that were to be used during arbitration under both the agreement to arbitrate employment-related disputes and the delegation provision. It may be that had Jackson challenged the delegation provision by arguing that these common procedures as applied to the delegation provision rendered that provision unconscionable, the challenge should have been considered by the court. To make such a claim based on the discovery procedures, Jackson would have had to argue that the limitation upon the number of depositions causes the arbitration of his claim that the Agreement is unenforceable to be unconscionable. That would be, of course, a much more difficult argument to sustain than the argument that the same limitation renders arbitration of his factbound employment-discrimination claim unconscionable. Likewise, the unfairness of the fee-splitting arrangement may be more difficult to establish for the arbitration of enforceability than for arbitration of more complex and fact-related aspects of the alleged employment discrimination. Jackson, however, did not make any arguments specific to the delegation provision; he argued that the fee-sharing and discovery procedures rendered the entire Agreement invalid.

Jackson's appeal to the Ninth Circuit confirms that he did not contest the validity of the delegation provision in particular. His brief noted the existence of the delegation provision, but his unconscionability arguments made no mention of it. He also repeated the arguments he had made before the District Court that the "entire agreement" favors Rent-A-Center and that the limitations on discovery further his "contention that the arbitration agreement as a whole is substantively unconscionable." Finally, he repeated the argument made in his District Court filings, that under state law the unconscionable clauses could not be severed from the arbitration agreement. The point of this argument, of course, is that the Agreement as a whole is unconscionable under state law.

Jackson repeated that argument before this Court. At oral argument, counsel stated: "There are certain elements of the arbitration agreement that are unconscionable and, under Nevada law, which would render the entire arbitration agreement unconscionable." And again, he stated, "we've got both certain provisions that are unconscionable, that under Nevada law render the entire agreement unconscionable..., and that's what the Court is to rely on."

In his brief to this Court, Jackson made the contention, not mentioned below, that the delegation provision itself is substantively unconscionable because the *quid pro quo* he was supposed to receive for it—that "in exchange for initially allowing an arbitrator to decide certain gateway questions," he would receive "plenary post-arbitration judicial review"—was eliminated by the Court's subsequent holding in *Hall Street Associates, L.L.C. v. Mattel, Inc.*, 552 U.S. 576 (2008), that the nonplenary grounds for judicial review in § 10 of the FAA are exclusive. He brought this challenge to the delegation provision too late, and we will not consider it.

* * *

We reverse the judgment of the Court of Appeals for the Ninth Circuit.

It is so ordered.

Justice Stevens dissented (opinion omitted).

Exercise 14-5. The "Substantive Federal Law of Arbitration"

Throughout this book, you have been exposed to procedural law. You have even been taught an elaborate means by which to distinguish procedural from substantive law when making choices between applying federal or state law to a dispute. Here, even though you are learning about a decidedly procedural mechanism for resolving disputes—arbitration—many of the cases depend on the acceptance of the rule that the federal common law interpreting the FAA is the "substantive federal law of arbitration."

1. What makes this body of law "substantive"?

2. If you were a judge presented with a dispute that required you to choose between application of the "substantive federal law of arbitration" that enforces arbitration agreements on their terms and a state-law doctrine disfavoring arbitration agreements in employment agreements on the basis of protecting the "substantive rights of employees to seek redress for workplace grievances," which one would you choose, based on the doctrines you learned about in Chapter 6 on choice of law?

3. Would your choice in such a situation (or the Supreme Court's declaration that the decisions interpreting the FAA constitute the "substantive law of arbitration") be in tension with any of the choice of law decisions?

AT&T Mobility LLC v. Concepcion
131 S. Ct. 1740 (2011)

Justice Scalia delivered the opinion of the Court.

Section 2 of the Federal Arbitration Act (FAA) makes agreements to arbitrate "valid, irrevocable, and enforceable, save upon such grounds as exist at law or in equity for the revocation of any contract." 9 U.S.C. §2. We consider whether the FAA prohibits States from conditioning the enforceability of certain arbitration agreements on the availability of classwide arbitration procedures.

I

In February 2002, Vincent and Liza Concepcion entered into an agreement for the sale and servicing of cellular telephones with AT&T Mobility LCC (AT&T). The contract provided for arbitration of all disputes between the parties, but required that claims be brought in the parties' "individual capacity, and not as a plaintiff or class member in any purported class or representative proceeding." The agreement authorized AT&T to make unilateral amendments, which it did to the arbitration provision on several occasions. The version at issue in this case reflects revisions made in December 2006, which the parties agree are controlling.

The revised agreement provides that customers may initiate dispute proceedings by completing a one-page Notice of Dispute form available on AT&T's Web site. AT&T may then offer to settle the claim; if it does not, or if the dispute is not resolved within 30 days, the customer may invoke arbitration by filing a separate Demand for Arbitration, also available on AT&T's Web site. In the event the parties proceed to arbitration, the agreement specifies that AT&T must pay all costs for nonfrivolous claims; that arbitration must take place in the county in which the customer is billed; that, for claims of $10,000 or less, the customer may choose whether the arbitration proceeds in person, by telephone, or based only on submissions; that either party may bring a claim in small claims court in lieu of arbitration; and that the arbitrator may award any form of individual relief, including injunctions and presumably punitive damages. The agreement, moreover, denies AT&T any ability to seek reimbursement of its attorney's fees, and, in the event that a customer receives an arbitration award greater than AT&T's last written settlement offer, requires AT&T to pay a $7,500 minimum recovery and twice the amount of the claimant's attorney's fees.

The Concepcions purchased AT&T service, which was advertised as including the provision of free phones; they were not charged for the phones, but they were charged $30.22 in sales tax based on the phones' retail value. In March 2006, the Concepcions filed a complaint against AT&T in the United States District Court for the Southern District of California. The complaint was later consolidated with a putative class action alleging, among other things, that AT&T had engaged in false advertising and fraud by charging sales tax on phones it advertised as free.

In March 2008, AT&T moved to compel arbitration under the terms of its contract with the Concepcions. The Concepcions opposed the motion, contending that the arbitration agreement was unconscionable and unlawfully exculpatory under California law because it disallowed classwide procedures. The District Court denied AT&T's motion. It described AT&T's arbitration agreement favorably, noting, for example, that the informal dispute-resolution process was "quick, easy to use" and likely to "promp[t] full or ... even excess payment to the customer without the need to arbitrate or litigate"; that the $7,500 premium functioned as "a substantial inducement for the consumer to pursue the claim in arbitration" if a dispute was not resolved informally; and that consumers who were members of a class would likely be worse off. Nevertheless, relying on the California Supreme Court's decision in *Discover Bank v. Superior Court*, 113 P.3d 1100 (2005), the court found that the arbitration provision was unconscionable because AT&T had not shown that bilateral arbitration adequately substituted for the deterrent effects of class actions.

The Ninth Circuit affirmed, also finding the provision unconscionable under California law as announced in *Discover Bank. Laster v. AT&T Mobility LLC*, 584 F.3d 849, 855 (2009). It also held that the *Discover Bank* rule was not preempted by the FAA because that rule was simply "a refinement of the unconscionability analysis applicable to contracts generally in California." In response to AT&T's argument that the Concepcions' interpretation of California law discriminated against arbitration, the Ninth Circuit rejected the contention that "class proceedings will reduce the efficiency and expeditiousness of arbitration" and noted that "*Discover Bank* placed arbitration agreements with class action waivers on the exact same footing as contracts that bar class action litigation outside the context of arbitration."

We granted certiorari.

II

The FAA was enacted in 1925 in response to widespread judicial hostility to arbitration agreements. Section 2, the "primary substantive provision of the Act," provides, in relevant part, as follows:

> A written provision in any maritime transaction or a contract evidencing a transaction involving commerce to settle by arbitration

a controversy thereafter arising out of such contract or transaction ... shall be valid, irrevocable, and enforceable, save upon such grounds as exist at law or in equity for the revocation of any contract. 9 U.S.C. § 2.

We have described this provision as reflecting both a "liberal federal policy favoring arbitration," and the "fundamental principle that arbitration is a matter of contract," *Rent-A-Center, West, Inc. v. Jackson*, 561 U.S. ___, ___, 130 S. Ct. 2772, 2776 (2010). In line with these principles, courts must place arbitration agreements on an equal footing with other contracts, and enforce them according to their terms.

The final phrase of § 2, however, permits arbitration agreements to be declared unenforceable "upon such grounds as exist at law or in equity for the revocation of any contract." This saving clause permits agreements to arbitrate to be invalidated by "generally applicable contract defenses, such as fraud, duress, or unconscionability," but not by defenses that apply only to arbitration or that derive their meaning from the fact that an agreement to arbitrate is at issue. *Doctors' Associates, Inc. v. Casarotto*, 517 U.S. 681, 687 (1986). The question in this case is whether § 2 preempts California's rule classifying most collective-arbitration waivers in consumer contracts as unconscionable. We refer to this rule as the *Discover Bank* rule.

Under California law, courts may refuse to enforce any contract found "to have been unconscionable at the time it was made," or may "limit the application of any unconscionable clause." Cal. Civ. Code Ann. § 1670.5(a) (West 1985). A finding of unconscionability requires a "procedural" and a "substantive" element, the former focusing on oppression or surprise due to unequal bargaining power, the latter on overly harsh or one-sided results.

In *Discover Bank*, the California Supreme Court applied this framework to class-action waivers in arbitration agreements and held as follows:

> "[W]hen the waiver is found in a consumer contract of adhesion in a setting in which disputes between the contracting parties predictably involve small amounts of damages, and when it is alleged that the party with the superior bargaining power has carried out a scheme to deliberately cheat large numbers of consumers out of individually small sums of money, then ... the waiver becomes in practice the exemption of the party 'from responsibility for [its] own fraud, or willful injury to the person or property of another.' Under these circumstances, such waivers are unconscionable under California law and should not be enforced."

California courts have frequently applied this rule to find arbitration agreements unconscionable.

III

A

The Concepcions argue that the *Discover Bank* rule, given its origins in California's unconscionability doctrine and California's policy against exculpation, is a ground that "exist[s] at law or in equity for the revocation of any contract" under FAA §2. Moreover, they argue that even if we construe the *Discover Bank* rule as a prohibition on collective-action waivers rather than simply an application of unconscionability, the rule would still be applicable to all dispute-resolution contracts, since California prohibits waivers of class litigation as well.

When state law prohibits outright the arbitration of a particular type of claim, the analysis is straightforward: The conflicting rule is displaced by the FAA. But the inquiry becomes more complex when a doctrine normally thought to be generally applicable, such as duress or, as relevant here, unconscionability, is alleged to have been applied in a fashion that disfavors arbitration. In *Perry v. Thomas*, 482 U.S. 483, (1987), for example, we noted that the FAA's preemptive effect might extend even to grounds traditionally thought to exist "at law or in equity for the revocation of any contract." We said that a court may not "rely on the uniqueness of an agreement to arbitrate as a basis for a state-law holding that enforcement would be unconscionable, for this would enable the court to effect what ... the state legislature cannot." *Id.* at 493, n.9.

An obvious illustration of this point would be a case finding unconscionable or unenforceable as against public policy consumer arbitration agreements that fail to provide for judicially monitored discovery. The rationalizations for such a holding are neither difficult to imagine nor different in kind from those articulated in *Discover Bank*. A court might reason that no consumer would knowingly waive his right to full discovery, as this would enable companies to hide their wrongdoing. Or the court might simply say that such agreements are exculpatory—restricting discovery would be of greater benefit to the company than the consumer, since the former is more likely to be sued than to sue. And, the reasoning would continue, because such a rule applies the general principle of unconscionability or public-policy disapproval of exculpatory agreements, it is applicable to "any" contract and thus preserved by §2 of the FAA. In practice, of course, the rule would have a disproportionate impact on arbitration agreements; but it would presumably apply to contracts purporting to restrict discovery in litigation as well.

Other examples are easy to imagine. The same argument might apply to a rule classifying as unconscionable arbitration agreements that fail to abide by the Federal Rules of Evidence, or that disallow an ultimate disposition by a jury (perhaps termed "a panel of twelve lay arbitrators" to help avoid preemption). Such examples are not fanciful, since the judicial hostility towards arbitration that prompted the FAA had manifested itself in "a great variety" of "devices and formulas" declaring arbitration against public policy. And although these statistics are not definitive, it is worth noting that California's courts have been more likely to hold contracts to arbitrate unconscionable than other contracts.

The Concepcions suggest that all this is just a parade of horribles, and no genuine worry. "Rules aimed at destroying arbitration" or "demanding procedures incompatible with arbitration," they concede, "would be pre-empted by the FAA because they cannot sensibly be reconciled with Section 2." The "grounds" available under § 2's saving clause, they admit, "should not be construed to include a State's mere preference for procedures that are incompatible with arbitration and 'would wholly eviscerate arbitration agreements.'"

We largely agree. Although § 2's saving clause preserves generally applicable contract defenses, nothing in it suggests an intent to preserve state-law rules that stand as an obstacle to the accomplishment of the FAA's objectives. As we have said, a federal statute's saving clause cannot in reason be construed as allowing a common law right, the continued existence of which would be absolutely inconsistent with the provisions of the act. In other words, the act cannot be held to destroy itself.

We differ with the Concepcions only in the application of this analysis to the matter before us. We do not agree that rules requiring judicially monitored discovery or adherence to the Federal Rules of Evidence are "a far cry from this case." The overarching purpose of the FAA, evident in the text of §§ 2, 3, and 4, is to ensure the enforcement of arbitration agreements according to their terms so as to facilitate streamlined proceedings. Requiring the availability of classwide arbitration interferes with fundamental attributes of arbitration and thus creates a scheme inconsistent with the FAA.

B

The principal purpose of the FAA is to ensure that private arbitration agreements are enforced according to their terms. This purpose is readily apparent from the FAA's text. Section 2 makes arbitration agreements "valid, irrevocable, and enforceable" as written (subject, of course, to the saving clause); § 3 requires courts to stay litigation of arbitral claims pending arbitration of those claims "in accordance with the terms of the agreement"; and § 4 requires courts to compel arbitration "in accordance with the terms of the agreement" upon the motion of either party to the agreement (assuming that the "making of the arbitration agreement or the failure ... to perform the same" is not at issue). In light of these provisions, we have held that parties may agree to limit the issues subject to arbitration, to arbitrate according to specific rules, and to limit with whom a party will arbitrate its disputes.

The point of affording parties discretion in designing arbitration processes is to allow for efficient, streamlined procedures tailored to the type of dispute. It can be specified, for example, that the decisionmaker be a specialist in the relevant field, or that proceedings be kept confidential to protect trade secrets. And the informality of arbitral proceedings is itself desirable, reducing the cost and increasing the speed of dispute resolution.

The dissent quotes *Dean Witter Reynolds Inc. v. Byrd*, 470 U.S. 213, 219 (1985), as "reject[ing] the suggestion that the overriding goal of the Arbitration Act was to promote the expeditious resolution of claims." That is greatly misleading. After saying (accurately enough) that "the overriding goal of the Arbitration Act was [not] to promote the expeditious resolution of claims," but to "ensure judicial enforcement of privately made agreements to arbitrate," *Dean Witter* went on to explain: "This is not to say that Congress was blind to the potential benefit of the legislation for expedited resolution of disputes. Far from it...." It then quotes a House Report saying that "the costliness and delays of litigation ... can be largely eliminated by agreements for arbitration." The concluding paragraph of this part of its discussion begins as follows:

> We therefore are not persuaded by the argument that the conflict between two goals of the Arbitration Act—enforcement of private agreements and encouragement of efficient and speedy dispute resolution—must be resolved in favor of the latter in order to realize the intent of the drafters. 470 U.S., at 221.

In the present case, of course, those "two goals" do not conflict—and it is the dissent's view that would frustrate both of them.

Contrary to the dissent's view, our cases place it beyond dispute that the FAA was designed to promote arbitration. They have repeatedly described the Act as embodying a national policy favoring arbitration, and a liberal federal policy favoring arbitration agreements, notwithstanding any state substantive or procedural policies to the contrary. Thus, in *Preston v. Ferrer*, holding preempted a state-law rule requiring exhaustion of administrative remedies before arbitration, we said: "A prime objective of an agreement to arbitrate is to achieve 'streamlined proceedings and expeditious results,'" which objective would be "frustrated" by requiring a dispute to be heard by an agency first. That rule, we said, would "at the least, hinder speedy resolution of the controversy." *Preston v. Ferrer*, 552 U.S. 346, 358 (2007).

California's *Discover Bank* rule similarly interferes with arbitration. Although the rule does not require classwide arbitration, it allows any party to a consumer contract to demand it *ex post*. The rule is limited to adhesion contracts, but the times in which consumer contracts were anything other than adhesive are long past. The rule also requires that damages be predictably small, and that the consumer allege a scheme to cheat consumers. The former requirement, however, is toothless and malleable (the Ninth Circuit has held that damages of $4,000 are sufficiently small), and the latter has no limiting effect, as all that is required is an allegation. Consumers remain free to bring and resolve their disputes on a bilateral basis under *Discover Bank*, and some may well do so; but there is little incentive for lawyers to arbitrate on behalf of individuals when they may do so for a class and reap far higher fees in the process. And faced with inevitable class arbitration, companies would have less incentive to continue resolving potentially duplicative claims on an individual basis.

Although we have had little occasion to examine classwide arbitration, our decision in *Stolt-Nielsen* is instructive. In that case we held that an arbitration panel exceeded its power under § 10(a)(4) of the FAA by imposing class procedures based on policy judgments rather than the arbitration agreement itself or some background principle of contract law that would affect its interpretation. 559 U.S. at ___, 130 S. Ct. at 1773–1776. We then held that the agreement at issue, which was silent on the question of class procedures, could not be interpreted to allow them because the "changes brought about by the shift from bilateral arbitration to class-action arbitration" are "fundamental." *Id.*, at ___, 130 S. Ct. at 1776. This is obvious as a structural matter: Classwide arbitration includes absent parties, necessitating additional and different procedures and involving higher stakes. Confidentiality becomes more difficult. And while it is theoretically possible to select an arbitrator with some expertise relevant to the class-certification question, arbitrators are not generally knowledgeable in the often-dominant procedural aspects of certification, such as the protection of absent parties. The conclusion follows that class arbitration, to the extent it is manufactured by *Discover Bank* rather than consensual, is inconsistent with the FAA.

First, the switch from bilateral to class arbitration sacrifices the principal advantage of arbitration—its informality—and makes the process slower, more costly, and more likely to generate procedural morass than final judgment. In bilateral arbitration, parties forgo the procedural rigor and appellate review of the courts in order to realize the benefits of private dispute resolution: lower costs, greater efficiency and speed, and the ability to choose expert adjudicators to resolve specialized disputes. But before an arbitrator may decide the merits of a claim in classwide procedures, he must first decide, for example, whether the class itself may be certified, whether the named parties are sufficiently representative and typical, and how discovery for the class should be conducted. A cursory comparison of bilateral and class arbitration illustrates the difference. According to the American Arbitration Association (AAA), the average consumer arbitration between January and August 2007 resulted in a disposition on the merits in six months, four months if the arbitration was conducted by documents only. AAA, Analysis of the AAA's Consumer Arbitration Caseload, online at http://www.adr.org/si.asp?id=5027. As of September 2009, the AAA had opened 283 class arbitrations. Of those, 121 remained active, and 162 had been settled, withdrawn, or dismissed. Not a single one, however, had resulted in a final award on the merits. For those cases that were no longer active, the median time from filing to settlement, withdrawal, or dismissal—not judgment on the merits—was 583 days, and the mean was 630 days.

Second, class arbitration requires procedural formality. The AAA's rules governing class arbitrations mimic the Federal Rules of Civil Procedure for class litigation. Compare AAA, Supplementary Rules for Class Arbitrations (effective Oct. 8, 2003), online at http://www.adr.org/sp.asp?id=21936, with Fed. Rule Civ. Proc. 23. And while parties can alter those procedures by contract, an alternative is not obvious. If procedures are too informal, absent class members would not be bound by the arbitration. For a class-action money judgment to bind absentees in litigation, class representatives must at all times adequately represent absent class members, and absent members must be afforded notice, an opportunity to be heard, and a right to opt out of the class. *Phillips Petroleum Co. v. Shutts*, 472 U.S. 797, 811–812 (1985). At least this amount of process would presumably be required for absent parties to be bound by the results of arbitration.

We find it unlikely that in passing the FAA Congress meant to leave the disposition of these procedural requirements to an arbitrator. Indeed, class arbitration was not even envisioned by Congress when it passed the FAA in 1925; as the California Supreme Court admitted in *Discover Bank*, class arbitration is a "relatively recent development." And it is at the very least odd to think that an arbitrator would be entrusted with ensuring that third parties' due process rights are satisfied.

Third, class arbitration greatly increases risks to defendants. Informal procedures do of course have a cost: The absence of multilayered review makes it more likely that errors will go uncorrected. Defendants are willing to accept the costs of these errors in arbitration, since their impact is limited to the size of individual disputes, and presumably outweighed by savings from avoiding the courts. But when damages allegedly owed to tens of thousands of potential claimants are aggregated and decided at once, the risk of an error will often become unacceptable. Faced with even a small chance of a devastating loss, defendants will be pressured into settling questionable claims. Other courts have noted the risk of "*in terrorem*" settlements that class actions entail, and class arbitration would be no different.

Arbitration is poorly suited to the higher stakes of class litigation. In litigation, a defendant may appeal a certification decision on an interlocutory basis and, if unsuccessful, may appeal from a final judgment as well. Questions of law are reviewed *de novo* and questions of fact for clear error. In contrast, 9 U.S.C. § 10 allows a court to vacate an arbitral award only where the award "was procured by corruption, fraud, or undue means"; "there was evident partiality or corruption in the arbitrators"; "the arbitrators were guilty of misconduct in refusing to postpone the hearing ... or in refusing to hear evidence pertinent and material to the controversy[,] or of any other misbehavior by which the rights of any party have been prejudiced"; or if the "arbitrators exceeded their powers, or so imperfectly executed them that a mutual, final, and definite award ... was not made." The AAA rules do authorize judicial review of certification decisions, but this review is unlikely to have much effect given these limitations; review under § 10 focuses on misconduct rather than mistake. And parties may not contractually expand the grounds or nature of judicial review. We find it hard to believe that defendants would bet the company with no effective means of review, and even harder to believe that Congress would have intended to allow state courts to force such a decision.

The Concepcions contend that because parties may and sometimes do agree to aggregation, class procedures are not necessarily incompatible with arbitration. But the same could be said about procedures that the Concepcions admit States may not superimpose on arbitration: Parties could agree to arbitrate pursuant to the Federal Rules of Civil Procedure, or pursuant to a discovery process rivaling that in litigation. Arbitration is a matter of contract, and the FAA requires courts to honor parties' expectations. But what the parties in the aforementioned examples would have agreed to is not arbitration as envisioned by the FAA, lacks its benefits, and therefore may not be required by state law.

The dissent claims that class proceedings are necessary to prosecute small-dollar claims that might otherwise slip through the legal system. But States cannot require a procedure that is inconsistent with the FAA, even if it is desirable for unrelated reasons. Moreover, the claim here was most unlikely to go unresolved. As noted earlier, the arbitration agreement provides that AT&T will pay claimants a minimum of $7,500 and twice their attorney's fees if they obtain an arbitration award greater than AT&T's last settlement offer. The District Court found this scheme sufficient to provide incentive for the individual prosecution of meritorious claims that are not immediately settled, and the Ninth Circuit admitted that aggrieved customers who filed claims would be "essentially guarantee[d]" to be made whole. Indeed, the District Court concluded that the Concepcions were better off under their arbitration agreement with AT&T than they would have been as participants in a class action, which "could take months, if not years, and which may merely yield an opportunity to submit a claim for recovery of a small percentage of a few dollars."

* * *

Because it stands as an obstacle to the accomplishment and execution of the full purposes and objectives of Congress, California's *Discover Bank* rule is preempted by the FAA. The judgment of the Ninth Circuit is reversed, and the case is remanded for further proceedings consistent with this opinion.

It is so ordered.

Justice Thomas, concurred (opinion omitted).

Justice Breyer dissented (opinion omitted).

Exercise 14-6. Negotiating an Arbitration Clause

Below is a sample basic arbitration clause, intended to be included in an overall employment agreement. You are attorneys involved in the negotiation of the executive employment agreement for the General Manager of a securities firm. Form groups of 2–4, with half of you taking the role of the employer and the other half taking the role of the employee. Thinking about what each party would likely want out of the deal, "mark up" (edit) the following arbitration clause to achieve your goals, while also complying with the legal standards reflected in the cases above.

Sample arbitration clause:

Employee and Employer agree that, in the event of any dispute or claim between them, either may elect to have that dispute or claim resolved by binding arbitration. This agreement to arbitrate is intended to be interpreted as broadly as the Federal Arbitration Act, Title IX, U.S. Code, allows.

Oxford Health Plans L.L.C. v. Sutter

133 S. Ct. 2064 (2013)

Justice Kagan delivered the opinion of the Court.

Class arbitration is a matter of consent: An arbitrator may employ class procedures only if the parties have authorized them. *See Stolt-Nielsen S.A. v. AnimalFeeds Int'l Corp.*, 559 U.S. 662, 684 (2010). In this case, an arbitrator found that the parties' contract provided for class arbitration. The question presented is whether in doing so he "exceeded [his] powers" under § 10(a)(4) of the Federal Arbitration Act (FAA or Act), 9 U.S.C. § 1 *et seq.* We conclude that the arbitrator's decision survives the limited judicial review § 10(a)(4) allows.

I

Respondent John Sutter, a pediatrician, entered into a contract with petitioner Oxford Health Plans, a health insurance company. Sutter agreed to provide medical care to members of Oxford's network, and Oxford agreed to pay for those services at prescribed rates. Several years later, Sutter filed suit against Oxford in New Jersey Superior Court on behalf of himself and a proposed class of other New Jersey physicians under contract with Oxford. The complaint alleged that Oxford had failed to make full and prompt payment to the doctors, in violation of their agreements and various state laws.

Oxford moved to compel arbitration of Sutter's claims, relying on the following clause in their contract:

> No civil action concerning any dispute arising under this Agreement shall be instituted before any court, and all such disputes shall be submitted to final and binding arbitration in New Jersey, pursuant to the rules of the American Arbitration Association with one arbitrator.

The state court granted Oxford's motion, thus referring the suit to arbitration.

The parties agreed that the arbitrator should decide whether their contract authorized class arbitration, and he determined that it did. Noting that the question turned on "construction of the parties' agreement," the arbitrator focused on the text of the arbitration clause quoted above. He reasoned that the clause sent to arbitration "the same universal class of disputes" that it barred the parties from bringing "as civil actions" in court: The "intent of the clause" was "to vest in the arbitration process everything that is prohibited from the court process." And a class action, the arbitrator continued, "is plainly one of the possible forms of civil action that could be brought in a court" absent the agreement. Accordingly, he concluded that "on its face, the arbitration clause ... expresses the parties' intent that class arbitration can be maintained."

Oxford filed a motion in federal court to vacate the arbitrator's decision on the ground that he had "exceeded [his] powers" under § 10(a)(4) of the FAA. The District Court denied the motion, and the Court of Appeals for the Third Circuit affirmed.

While the arbitration proceeded, this Court held in *Stolt-Nielsen* that "a party may not be compelled under the FAA to submit to class arbitration unless there is a contractual basis for concluding that the party agreed to do so." 559 U.S., at 684. The parties in *Stolt-Nielsen* had stipulated that they had never reached an agreement on class arbitration. Relying on

§ 10(a)(4), we vacated the arbitrators' decision approving class proceedings because, in the absence of such an agreement, the arbitrators had "simply ... imposed [their] own view of sound policy." *Id.*, at 672.

Oxford immediately asked the arbitrator to reconsider his decision on class arbitration in light of *Stolt-Nielsen*. The arbitrator issued a new opinion holding that *Stolt-Nielsen* had no effect on the case because this agreement authorized class arbitration. Unlike in *Stolt-Nielsen*, the arbitrator explained, the parties here disputed the meaning of their contract; he had therefore been required "to construe the arbitration clause in the ordinary way to glean the parties' intent." And in performing that task, the arbitrator continued, he had "found that the arbitration clause unambiguously evinced an intention to allow class arbitration." The arbitrator concluded by reconfirming his reasons for so construing the clause.

Oxford then returned to federal court, renewing its effort to vacate the arbitrator's decision under § 10(a)(4). Once again, the District Court denied the motion, and the Third Circuit affirmed. The Court of Appeals first underscored the limited scope of judicial review that § 10(a)(4) allows: So long as an arbitrator "makes a good faith attempt" to interpret a contract, "even serious errors of law or fact will not subject his award to vacatur." Oxford could not prevail under that standard, the court held, because the arbitrator had "endeavored to give effect to the parties' intent" and "articulate[d] a contractual basis for his decision." Oxford's objections to the ruling were "simply dressed-up arguments that the arbitrator interpreted its agreement erroneously."

We granted certiorari to address a circuit split on whether § 10(a)(4) allows a court to vacate an arbitral award in similar circumstances. Holding that it does not, we affirm the Court of Appeals.

II

Under the FAA, courts may vacate an arbitrator's decision only in very unusual circumstances. That limited judicial review, we have explained, maintains arbitration's essential virtue of resolving disputes straightaway. If parties could take full-bore legal and evidentiary appeals, arbitration would become merely a prelude to a more cumbersome and time-consuming judicial review process.

Here, Oxford invokes § 10(a)(4) of the Act, which authorizes a federal court to set aside an arbitral award "where the arbitrator[ ] exceeded [his] powers." A party seeking relief under that provision bears a heavy burden. "It is not enough ... to show that the [arbitrator] committed an error — or even a serious error." *Stolt-Nielsen*, 559 U.S., at 671. Because the parties bargained for the arbitrator's construction of their agreement, an arbitral decision even arguably construing or applying the contract must stand, regardless of a court's view of its (de)merits. Only if the arbitrator acts outside the scope of his contractually delegated authority — issuing an award that simply reflects his own notions of economic justice rather than drawing its essence from the contract — may a court overturn his determination. So the sole question for us is whether the arbitrator (even arguably) interpreted the parties' contract, not whether he got its meaning right or wrong.

And we have already all but answered that question just by summarizing the arbitrator's decisions; they are, through and through, interpretations of the parties' agreement. The arbitrator's first ruling recited the "question of construction" the parties had submitted to him: "whether [their] Agreement allows for class action arbitration." To resolve that matter, the arbitrator focused on the arbitration clause's text, analyzing (whether correctly or not makes no difference) the scope of both what it barred from court and what it sent to arbitration. The arbitrator concluded, based on that textual exegesis, that the clause "on its face ... expresses the parties' intent that class action arbitration can be maintained." When Oxford requested reconsideration in light of *Stolt-Nielsen*, the arbitrator explained that his prior decision was "concerned solely with the parties' intent as evidenced by the words of the arbitration clause itself." He then ran through his textual analysis again, and reiterated his conclusion: "[T]he text of the clause itself authorizes" class arbitration. Twice, then, the arbitrator did what the parties had asked: He considered their contract and decided whether it reflected an agreement to permit class proceedings. That suffices to show that the arbitrator did not "exceed[ ] [his] powers." § 10(a)(4).

Oxford's contrary view relies principally on *Stolt-Nielsen*. As noted earlier, we found there that an arbitration panel exceeded its powers under § 10(a)(4) when it ordered a party to submit to class arbitration. Oxford takes that decision to mean that "even the 'high hurdle' of Section 10(a)(4) review is overcome when an arbitrator imposes class arbitration without a sufficient contractual basis." Under *Stolt-Nielsen*, Oxford asserts, a court may thus vacate "as *ultra vires*" an arbitral decision like this one for misconstruing a contract to approve class proceedings.

But Oxford misreads *Stolt-Nielsen*: We overturned the arbitral decision there because it lacked any contractual basis for ordering class procedures, not because it lacked, in Oxford's terminology, a "sufficient" one. The parties in *Stolt-Nielsen* had entered into an unusual stipulation that they had never reached an agreement on class arbitration. In that circumstance, we noted, the panel's decision was not — indeed, could not have been — "based on a determination regarding the parties' intent." 559 U.S. at 673; *id.*, at 676. Nor, we continued, did the panel attempt to ascertain whether federal or state law established a "default rule" to take effect absent an agreement. *Id.*, at 673. Instead, "the panel simply imposed its own conception of sound policy" when it ordered class proceedings. *Id.*, at 675.

But "the task of an arbitrator," we stated, "is to interpret and enforce a contract, not to make public policy." *Id.*, at 672. In "impos[ing] its own policy choice," the panel "thus exceeded its powers." *Id.*, at 677.

The contrast with this case is stark. In *Stolt-Nielsen*, the arbitrators did not construe the parties' contract, and did not identify any agreement authorizing class proceedings. So in setting aside the arbitrators' decision, we found not that they had misinterpreted the contract, but that they had abandoned their interpretive role. Here, the arbitrator did construe the contract (focusing, per usual, on its language), and did find an agreement to permit class arbitration. So to overturn his decision, we would have to rely on a finding that he misapprehended the parties' intent. But § 10(a)(4) bars that course: It permits courts to vacate an arbitral decision only when the arbitrator strayed from his delegated task of interpreting a contract, not when he performed that task poorly. *Stolt-Nielsen* and this case thus fall on opposite sides of the line that § 10(a)(4) draws to delimit judicial review of arbitral decisions.

The remainder of Oxford's argument addresses merely the merits: The arbitrator, Oxford contends at length, badly misunderstood the contract's arbitration clause. The key text, again, goes as follows: "No civil action concerning any dispute arising under this Agreement shall be instituted before any court, and all such disputes shall be submitted to final and binding arbitration." The arbitrator thought that clause sent to arbitration all "civil action[s]" barred from court, and viewed class actions as falling within that category. But Oxford points out that the provision submits to arbitration not any "civil action[s]," but instead any "dispute arising under" the agreement. And in any event, Oxford claims, a class action is not a form of "civil action," as the arbitrator thought, but merely a procedural device that may be available in a court. At bottom, Oxford maintains, this is a garden-variety arbitration clause, lacking any of the terms or features that would indicate an agreement to use class procedures.

We reject this argument because, and only because, it is not properly addressed to a court. Nothing we say in this opinion should be taken to reflect any agreement with the arbitrator's contract interpretation, or any quarrel with Oxford's contrary reading. All we say is that convincing a court of an arbitrator's error — even his grave error — is not enough. So long as the arbitrator was "arguably construing" the contract — which this one was — a court may not correct his mistakes under § 10(a)(4). The potential for those mistakes is the price of agreeing to arbitration. As we have held before, we hold again: It is the arbitrator's construction of the contract which was bargained for; and so far as the arbitrator's decision concerns construction of the contract, the courts have no business overruling him because their interpretation of the contract is different from his. The arbitrator's construction holds, however good, bad, or ugly.

In sum, Oxford chose arbitration, and it must now live with that choice. Oxford agreed with Sutter that an arbitrator should determine what their contract meant, including whether its terms approved class arbitration. The arbitrator did what the parties requested: He provided an interpretation of the contract resolving that disputed issue. His interpretation went against Oxford, maybe mistakenly so. But still, Oxford does not get to rerun the matter in a court. Under § 10(a)(4), the question for a judge is not whether the arbitrator construed the parties' contract correctly, but whether he construed it at all. Because he did, and therefore did not "exceed his powers," we cannot give Oxford the relief it wants. We accordingly affirm the judgment of the Court of Appeals.

It is so ordered.

Justice Alito, with whom Justice Thomas joins, concurring.

As the Court explains, "[c]lass arbitration is a matter of consent," and petitioner consented to the arbitrator's authority by conceding that he should decide in the first instance whether the contract authorizes class arbitration. The Court accordingly refuses to set aside the arbitrator's ruling because he was "arguably construing ... the contract" when he allowed respondent to proceed on a classwide basis. Today's result follows directly from petitioner's concession and the narrow judicial review that federal law allows in arbitration cases. *See* 9 U.S.C. § 10(a).

But unlike petitioner, absent members of the plaintiff class never conceded that the contract authorizes the arbitrator to decide whether to conduct class arbitration. It doesn't. If we were reviewing the arbitrator's interpretation of the contract *de novo*, we would have little trouble concluding that he improperly inferred "[a]n implicit agreement to authorize class-action arbitration ... from the fact of the parties' agreement to arbitrate." *Stolt-Nielsen S.A. v. Animal Feeds Int'l Corp.*, 559 U.S. 662, 685 (2010).

With no reason to think that the absent class members ever agreed to class arbitration, it is far from clear that they will be bound by the arbitrator's ultimate resolution of this dispute. Arbitration "is a matter of consent, not coercion," and the absent members of the plaintiff class have not submitted themselves to this arbitrator's authority in any way. It is true that they signed contracts with arbitration clauses materially identical to those signed by the plaintiff who brought this suit. But an arbitrator's erroneous interpretation of contracts that do not authorize class arbitration cannot bind someone who has not authorized the arbitrator to make that determination. As the Court explains, "[a]n arbitrator may employ class procedures only if the parties have authorized them."

The distribution of opt-out notices does not cure this fundamental flaw in the class arbitration proceeding in this case. "[A]rbitration is simply a matter of contract between the parties," and an offeree's silence does not normally modify the terms of a contract, 1 RESTATEMENT (SECOND) OF CONTRACTS §69(1) (1979). Accordingly, at least where absent class members have not been required to opt in, it is difficult to see how an arbitrator's decision to conduct class proceedings could bind absent class members who have not authorized the arbitrator to decide on a classwide basis which arbitration procedures are to be used.

Class arbitrations that are vulnerable to collateral attack allow absent class members to unfairly claim the "benefit from a favorable judgment without subjecting themselves to the binding effect of an unfavorable one." In the absence of concessions like Oxford's, this possibility should give courts pause before concluding that the availability of class arbitration is a question the arbitrator should decide. But because that argument was not available to petitioner in light of its concession below, I join the opinion of the Court.

Exercise 14-7. Reviewing the Agreement and Defensive Drafting

After reading *Sutter*, what changes, if any would you make to your arbitration agreement? Are you confident that, absent any unwise stipulation on your part, your favorable provisions will be upheld and/or construed properly by the arbitrator? If not, how can you ensure that they will?

Exercise 14-8. Unintended Consequences

In most cases, arbitration favors the more powerful party, since that party can use the process to limit its expenses—expenses that the less powerful party often does not have to bear unless and until he prevails on the claim. However, in some cases, even the parties with more traditional power in a bilateral contract relationship can come to regret choosing arbitration.

What are some downsides to arbitration for traditionally powerful parties, such as corporations and employers, that might cause their attorneys to at least urge caution in selecting mandatory, binding arbitration of all their disputes?

Mandatory, non-binding arbitration might result from an agreement between the parties to pursue an advisory arbitral ruling to assist the resolution of their dispute. Where arbitration is "mandatory," it may be compelled, so this form of arbitration can often be the result of motion practice between the parties. The main difference between non-binding arbitration and binding arbitration is that any order from the arbitrator in non-binding arbitration will be reviewed in the District Court *de novo*, rather than under the very deferential standards of review discussed in the cases above.

Even where the parties have not agreed to arbitrate their dispute, and no local rule compels the parties to arbitrate before pursuing to a further stage of litigation in court, the court may still ask the parties to consider arbitrating. If they agree, then what results is **voluntary, non-binding arbitration**. *See* 28 U.S.C. §654 (authorizing federal courts to refer some cases to arbitration where the parties consent); 657(c) (authorizing parties to demand trial *de novo* in response to arbitral awards). This form of arbitration cannot be compelled through a judicial order, and any decision of the arbitrator will be reviewed in the District Court *de novo*. As you can readily see, as we move from one form of arbitration to another, the process begins to resemble trial less and less, and to resemble mediation, early neutral evaluation, and minitrial more and more.

Exercise 14-9. Contracting for Arbitration's Effect

1. Considering the discussion above, would you prefer to contract for binding or non-binding arbitration? Would your answer change depending on whom you represent?

2. Which features of binding versus non-binding arbitration might be beneficial to a traditionally powerful negotiating party, such as a corporation or employer. Which features might be detrimental?

3. How might these features be viewed by the traditionally less powerful parties, such as consumers or employees?

4. Are there any features of binding versus non-binding arbitration that both powerful and less powerful parties are likely to see as beneficial? Detrimental?

---

6. Professionalism and Alternative Dispute Resolution

The settlement of cases, as well as their resolution through non-traditional adjudicatory processes such as arbitration, presents a number of ethical issues. Settlement practices in particular present incentives to engage in undue pressuring of one's opponents and one's own clients, and a lawyer must take care to remember that the Rules of Professional Conduct admonish us to act at all times fairly with our opponents, and to pursue the best interests of our clients, even where those best interests do not necessarily reflect our own preferences. The final two exercises accordingly ask you to explore ethical issues particularly related to settlement.

Exercise 14-10. Mediation and Professionalism

Consider the *Young* case above once again. Should Stanhope's attorneys have been subjected to any professional discipline for bringing a party representative without "full settlement authority" to a mediation conference where each party was supposed to have such authority?

Research ABA Model Rules of Professional Conduct 1.2; 1.3; 1.6; and 1.13 (all available online, including explanatory comments) to assist you with your decision.

Exercise 14-11. Ethical Offers of Judgment

As outlined above, Rule 68 allows a party to force an opposing party to accept or reject an offer to settle the case for an amount, and the Rule imposes potentially very harsh penalties on parties that reject reasonable settlement offers, making them liable for attorneys' fees that may far exceed the recovery in the case, as long as the statute sued under defines "costs" to include attorneys' fees, and such fees are awardable under the statute in the particular case at bar.

The temptation for defense-side attorneys is obvious: Why not meet *every* complaint with an early offer of judgment offering an amount far below what your client is willing to pay to settle the suit, counting on the *in terrorem* effect of the potential penalties that will attach to any refusal of the offer to motivate risk-averse plaintiffs to settle for less than the claim is really worth?

Reasonable attorneys will disagree as to whether such a practice is ethical in the strictest sense, even though it appears compliant with Rule 68 itself, which places no restrictions on the timing or amount of an offer of judgment, other than that it must be presented more than 14 days before the trial.

If you were to partner with an attorney who followed a general practice of making low-ball offers of judgment to all parties, would you counsel your partner to abandon that practice or would you join in?

Chapter 15

Integration and Review

The purpose of this chapter is to integrate and review Civil Procedure concepts in the context of a hypothetical lawsuit. This chapter contains documents that typically arise in civil litigation, including pleadings, motions, and discovery, along with documents lawyers generate through interactions with their clients and other lawyers. Throughout the chapter, twenty-four exercises ask you to assume a variety of roles. The exercises address doctrine, analysis, strategy, and professionalism.

1. Client Interview — Plaintiffs

MEMORANDUM

To: Associate
From: Jan Fay (Partner)
Re: Poll, Beal, James

I met recently with three elderly residents of Spokane, Washington: Judy Poll (age 64), Norma Beal (age 73), and Edna James (age 68). Each of these women lives in her own home. One year ago, our three clients were each contacted by a door-to-door vacuum cleaner salesperson, Jack Darby.

Each client had a similar experience with Mr. Darby. Darby appeared at the client's home without any prior contact with the client. Darby was selling what he called "a revolutionary concept in fine carpet and furniture care." He asked the client if he could demonstrate the product, and the client agreed. Darby entered the client's house and sprinkled dirt on the client's carpet and furniture. Darby then demonstrated his product, a vacuum cleaner, for 15 minutes. During the demonstration, Darby enthusiastically pointed out the effectiveness and quality of the machine.

After the demonstration, Darby urged the client to purchase the vacuum cleaner. He told the client that she "should not miss this great opportunity," that the sale terms were "easy weekly payments," and that this offer was "for today only."

Each of the clients decided to purchase a vacuum from Darby while he was in her home. Darby's reply was, "Wise decision; now let's do the paperwork." Darby produced a form contract. (A copy of Ms. Beal's contract is attached; the other clients signed identical contracts.) Darby went over paragraph 1 with each client, filled in the blanks, and suggested that the

---

client review the remainder of the form. Each client signed the contract and made a $100 down payment.

Each of the clients is happy with the quality of the vacuum. However, each client is upset about the price she paid. One month ago, Ms. James discovered that vacuums similar, but not identical, to the one she bought from Darby were sold for $350 to $500 at several local department stores. She then calculated the total payments due under her contract: $100 down and $18 per week for 90 weeks, for a total of $1,720.

Ms. James is active in the Spokane Chapter of the Association for Retired Persons (ARP). At an ARP social event three weeks ago, she met Ms. Beal and Ms. Poll. After recounting their experiences with Mr. Darby, they all felt foolish and angry. The next day, the clients called Darby and complained about the sale terms. Darby asked whether they had complaints about their vacuums. They did not. They complained to Darby that he never informed them of the full price of the machine — $1,720. Darby said that they had signed valid contracts of their own free will and that the contracts were binding.

I met with our clients last week. They were quite upset. They heard at their ARP meeting that Darby is continuing to sell vacuums on similar terms to other elderly persons in Spokane. Our clients have each paid approximately $1000 to date for their vacuums. They would like to receive compensation for their overpayments. They also would like to teach Darby a lesson and protect others from being victimized by him.

Our paralegal has verified Darby's home and business address as the one on the contract. He checked with the Secretary of State and Department of Licensing to find out whether Elite Vacuum Sales is a corporation and is listed as the seller on the contract. It is. Its full name is Elite Vacuum Sales, Inc.

I think our clients are nice people who got ripped off. Let's do our best to help them.

CONDITIONAL SALES CONTRACT

Contract of Conditional Sale, made **April 6, [year]**, between **Norma Beal** (Buyer) and **Elite Vacuum Sales** (Seller).

1. Conditional Sale of Goods. The Seller hereby sells to Buyer, and the Buyer hereby accepts from the Seller, the goods **Elite Vacuum Model 4281 (Serial # 384J2614800M)** upon the following terms: **$100.00** upon the execution of this agreement and **$18.00** per week, due on Monday of each week, beginning **April 13, [year]** and ending **December 26, [next year]**.

2. Retention of Title. Title to the goods shall not pass to the Buyer, but shall remain in the Seller until such time as all payments hereunder have been made, and all other conditions fully performed. When all payments have been made and all conditions performed, the Seller shall execute and deliver to the Buyer an absolute bill of sale of the goods, and the obligations imposed upon the Buyer by this contract shall be of no further effect.

3. Location of Goods, Removal. The goods shall at all times be kept by the Buyer at the address below. The Buyer shall not remove the goods, or sell, mortgage, pledge, or otherwise dispose of his interest in, or part with possession of, the goods, or permit any lien to be acquired thereon, without the written consent of the Seller.

4. Risk of Loss. The risk of loss shall be upon the Buyer. The loss, injury, or destruction of the goods shall not release the Buyer of his obligation hereunder.

5. Insurance. The Buyer shall keep the goods insured against loss, injury, or destruction by fire, for no less than the total amount owing hereunder until such is fully paid. The Seller may place such insurance at the Buyer's expense. The proceeds of any insurance shall be applied toward the replacement of the goods or payment of this obligation, at the option of the Seller.

6. Expenses. The Buyer shall pay all charges which may accrue on the goods, and in the event of any default by the Buyer under this contract, the Buyer shall reimburse the Seller for legal and other expenses which the Seller may incur in enforcing its rights under this contract.

7. Acceleration. If the Buyer fails or neglects to comply with any term or condition of this contract, or to make any payment provided for herein, when due or payable, or violate any of the provisions hereof, or if the Seller should feel insecure or deem the goods in danger of misuse or confiscation, or if the Buyer makes any misrepresentation as to his name, address, or occupation, the Seller at its option and without notice to the Buyer may declare the whole amount unpaid hereunder immediately due and payable.

8. Repossession. In the event of default the Seller may, without notice to the Buyer, declare all of the Buyer's rights under this contract terminated, and without demand first made, and with or without legal process, immediately take possession of the goods, together with all additions, equipment, and accessories thereto, wherever the same may be found, using reasonable force if necessary, and hold the same, together with title thereto, and the Buyer waives all claims for damages due to or arising from, or connected with any such taking.

9. Sale. If the contract is terminated by the Seller repossessing the goods, the Seller may, if it so desires, sell the goods at public or private sale, with or without notice to the Buyer (if given, notice by mail to the Buyer's address as shown on this contract is sufficient), with or without having the goods at the place of sale, and upon the terms and in such manner as the Seller or its assigns may determine. The Seller or its assigns may bid at any such sale.

10. Proceeds of Sale. The net proceeds of any such sale shall be the remainder after deducting from the selling price all expenses for re-taking and conditioning, keeping, and selling the goods, including attorney's fees. In case the net proceeds from such sale, added to the payments theretofore made, do not cover the total payments required to be made by the Buyer hereunder, then the Buyer agrees to pay to the Seller, on demand, such difference, with interest thereon from the date of sale at the highest rate for which the parties may lawfully contract in the state in which this contract is executed.

11. Waiver. The Buyer hereby waives all statutes of limitation in any way affecting the time within which the Seller may enforce its rights hereunder and the defense thereof.

12. Entire Contract. This contract constitutes the entire contract and no waivers or modifications shall be valid unless written upon or attached to this contract, and the goods are accepted without any express or implied warranties unless written hereon at the date of purchase.

13. Receipt of Copy. The Buyer acknowledges receipt of a true executed copy of this contract.

Seller — Elite Vacuum Sales

By — *Jack Darby*

Address — 407 Northwest Blvd. Spokane, WA 99216

Phone — 509-345-6789

Buyer — Norma Beal

By — *Norma Beal*

Address — 1418 W. Pine Street, Spokane, WA, 99211

Phone — 509-222-3456

Exercise 15-1. Dispute Resolution Mechanisms

1. Advise Jan Fay about the relative advantages and disadvantages of civil litigation and mediation to resolve the dispute and to achieve the clients' goals.

2. Assume that the Conditional Sales Contract contains the following provision:

   "**Arbitration.** The Buyer and Seller agree to settle by arbitration all past, present, or future disputes arising out of or related in any way to this Conditional Sales Contract. The Arbitrator shall have exclusive authority to resolve any dispute relating to the enforceability of this Agreement including, but not limited to, any claim that all or any part of this Agreement is void or voidable."

Advise Jan Fay about the likelihood that a federal court would enforce the arbitration provision in the Conditional Sales Contract, forcing Poll, James, and Beal to resolve their dispute with Darby and Elite Vacuum Sales, Inc., through arbitration.

Exercise 15-2. Diversity Jurisdiction

In preparation for initiating a lawsuit on behalf of Poll, James, and Beal, Jan Fay asks you for advice about subject matter jurisdiction in state and federal court. What would you need to know about Poll, Beal, James, Darby, and Elite Vacuum Sales, Inc., to determine their citizenship for purposes of diversity jurisdiction?

2. Legal Research — Substantive Law

MEMORANDUM

To: Jan Fay
From: Law Clerk
Subject: Poll, Beal, and James Matter

At your request, I researched the substantive law relevant to this matter. First it appears that our clients may have claims under Washington common law fraud. The elements of fraud are: (1) defendant's false statement of material fact; (2) defendant's knowledge that the statement is untrue; (3) defendant's intent to deceive the victim; (4) the victim's justifiable reliance on the statement; and (5) injury to the victim.

Second, our clients may have claims under the Federal Consumer Solicitation Act (FCSA). The FCSA provides as follows:

§ 1. Purpose. This Act is intended to curb predatory sales practices of certain door-to-door solicitors who through fraudulent solicitations sell worthless goods to consumers or sell goods to consumers on credit at greatly inflated prices.

§ 2. Liability. It shall be unlawful for sellers of consumer goods to sell or to attempt to sell goods to consumers in their homes through fraudulent solicitation. The term "fraudulent solicitation" means that the seller intends to induce consumers to enter sales contracts through representations of the quality or price of goods, if the representations are misleading or untrue, and if the seller knows they are misleading or untrue.

§ 3. Limitations on Actions. Civil actions to prosecute violations of this act shall not be commenced more than two years after the violation has occurred.

§ 4. Defenses. All defenses to fraud, whether based on law or fact, shall constitute defenses to claims for violations of this Act.

§ 5. Remedies. Appropriate relief for violations of this act may include compensatory damages, punitive damages, and injunctions.

Third, I found the most recent Ninth Circuit case dealing with punitive damages and injunctions under the FCSA, *Bolt v. Nystrom*, decided in 2001. In *Bolt*, the court held that a plaintiff can recover punitive damages for an FCSA violation only if the defendant is guilty of malice. The court defined malice as conduct that evidences an evil mind. A plaintiff can establish malice by proving that the defendant intended to injure the plaintiff or that the defendant acted in reckless disregard of plaintiff's rights. The court listed the factors that a jury can consider in determining the amount of punitive damages: the reprehensibility of defendant's conduct, defendant's wealth, the amount defendant gained through the fraudulent conduct, and the amount needed to deter the defendant and others from engaging in similar conduct in the future. In *Bolt*, the court affirmed a jury award of $175,000 in punitive damages against a defendant who sold a mixture of vegetable oil and sawdust as a cancer cure. The court also held that a plaintiff can obtain an injunction if defendant's interaction with plaintiff violates the FCSA and if defendant is likely to continue to violate the FCSA if no injunction is issued.

Exercise 15-3. Subject Matter Jurisdiction

Your factual research reveals that Poll, Beal, James, and Darby are all citizens of the United States, domiciled in Washington state and Elite Vacuum Sales, Inc. is incorporated in Delaware with its headquarters and production facilities in Oregon. Jan Fay would like to assert two claims against both Darby and Elite Vacuum Sales, Inc. in the same lawsuit. One claim against both defendants would be based on Washington common law fraud and the other claim against both defendants would be based on the Federal Consumer Solicitation Act. Analyze subject matter jurisdiction over the lawsuit Jan Fay would like to initiate.

1. Would a federal court have diversity jurisdiction?

2. Would a federal court have arising under jurisdiction? Explain whether the *Grable* line of cases would apply.

3. Would a federal court have supplemental jurisdiction?

4. Would state courts have subject matter jurisdiction over the suit?

5. If Jan Fay initiated the suit in state court, would defendants be able to remove it to federal court?

Exercise 15-4. Personal Jurisdiction — Basis

Assume the same facts as Exercise 15-3. In addition, your research reveals the following.

Jack Darby rents his home and business in Spokane, Washington. Darby's full-time job appears to be retail vacuum sales for Elite Vacuum Sales, Inc. (Elite), in Washington. Darby owns a vacation home in Oregon. Darby lives in his Oregon home several weeks each year. The rest of the year, he rents the home, generating substantial annual income.

Elite does nearly all of its business through door-to-door retail sales in Oregon, California, and Washington. Elite employs approximately 10 sales people in Oregon and over 100 in California, where it generates over 90% of its sales. Elite expanded into the Washington market two years ago. Darby is Elite's only sales person in Washington.

1. Which states would have personal jurisdiction over Darby for the suit Jan Fay would like to bring?

2. Which states would have personal jurisdiction over Elite for the suit Jan Fay would like to bring?

Exercise 15-5. Venue

Assume the same facts as Exercise 15-3 and 15-4. Which federal courts would satisfy the venue requirements for the suit Jan Fay would like to initiate?

Exercise 15-6. Personal Jurisdiction — Service

If Jan Fay decides to file suit in the United States District Court for the Eastern District of Washington, explain the options for service of the summons and complaint on Darby and Elite.

3. Complaint

United States District Court for
the Eastern District of Washington

Judy Poll, Norma Beal,	)	
and Edna James, Plaintiffs	)	
	)	
v.	)	No. CV 2019-003
	)	
Jack Darby and Elite Vacuum Sales, Inc.,	)	
Defendants	)	

Complaint for Fraud under Washington Law and
the Federal Consumer Solicitation Act

JURISDICTION

1. This action arises under the Federal Consumer Solicitation Act (FCSA) and Washington law. Jurisdiction is based on 28 U.S.C. § 1331 and § 1367.

PARTIES

2. Plaintiffs Judy Poll (age 64), Norma Beal (age 73), and Edna James (age 68) are domiciled in Spokane, Washington.

3. Defendant Jack Darby is domiciled in Spokane, Washington.

4. Defendant Elite Vacuum Sales, Inc., is incorporated in Delaware with its principle place of business in Oregon.

CLAIMS FOR FRAUD AND VIOLATIONS OF FCSA

5. In April, [year], defendants sold a vacuum cleaner to each of the plaintiffs on credit in her home.

6. Defendants sold vacuums to each plaintiff at a greatly inflated price.

7. Defendants intended to induce each plaintiff to purchase a vacuum cleaner through representations that defendants knew were untrue or misleading, in violation of Washington law of fraud and the Federal Consumer Solicitation Act.

8. Defendants' course of dealing with each plaintiff constituted malice.

9. Defendants continue to engage in fraudulent solicitation of sales to elderly residents of Spokane, Washington.

REQUEST FOR RELIEF

Each plaintiff requests judgment as follows:

a.   Compensatory damages;

b.   An order enjoining defendant from engaging in fraudulent solicitation practices;

c.   Punitive damages; and

d.   The costs of this action, including attorneys' fees.

Dated: April 24, [year].

Jan Fay

Jan Fay
Attorney for Plaintiffs
622 Dakota Street
Spokane, WA 99204
509-555-1212
FayGroup@gmail.com

4. Responses to Complaint

Exercise 15-7. Default

After being served with the summons and complaint, both Defendants failed to forward those documents to their attorneys; consequently, no response to the Complaint was served or filed. What steps could Jan Fay take to obtain a judgment for Plaintiffs against Defendants?

Exercise 15-8. Motion to Dismiss

Ignore the facts of Exercise 15-7. Assume Defendants' first response to the Complaint was a motion to dismiss for failure to state a claim upon which relief can be granted, signed by attorney Fran Bell. Make Bell's best arguments in support of the motion.

Exercise 15-9. Waiver of Defenses

By making the motion to dismiss in Exercise 15-8 without joining other defenses, what defenses, if any, have Defendants waived?

Exercise 15-10. Voluntary Dismissal

While Defendants' motion to dismiss (Exercise 15-8) is pending, but not yet decided by the court, Jan Fay is thinking about voluntarily dismissing the suit and restarting it in another court. Explain Fay's options to achieve voluntary dismissal with the option of restarting the suit.

5. Amended Complaint

Exercise 15-11. Amended Pleadings

Assume that Defendants' Motion to Dismiss for Failure to State a Claim (Exercise 15-8) was served and filed on May 1. The court scheduled an oral argument on the motion for June 15. On June 1, Plaintiffs served and filed a motion for leave to serve and file the amended complaint below. In the role of law clerk, advise the judge about the following issues:

1. Do Plaintiffs have the right to serve and file the amended complaint, without prior approval of the court?

2. If the answer to the first question is "no," what standards govern the court's decision on whether to allow the amendment?

United States District Court for
the Eastern District of Washington

Judy Poll, Norma Beal, and Edna James, Plaintiffs))))	
v.)))	No. CV 2019-003
Jack Darby and Elite Vacuum Sales, Inc., Defendants))	

Amended Complaint for Fraud under Washington Law and
the Federal Consumer Solicitation Act

JURISDICTION AND VENUE

1. This action arises under the Federal Consumer Solicitation Act (FCSA) and Washington law. Jurisdiction is based on 28 U.S.C. § 1331 and § 1367. Venue is based on 28 U.S.C. § 1391(b)(2).

PARTIES

2. Plaintiffs Judy Poll (age 64), Norma Beal (age 73), and Edna James (age 68) are domiciled in Spokane, Washington.

3. Defendant Jack Darby is domiciled in Spokane, Washington.

4. Defendant Elite Vacuum Sales, Inc., is incorporated in Delaware with its principle place of business in Oregon.

CLAIMS FOR FRAUD AND VIOLATIONS OF FCSA

5. In April, [year], defendants sold a vacuum cleaner to each of the plaintiffs on credit in her home.

6. The retail, cash-sale value of each vacuum cleaner defendants sold to plaintiffs was between $350 and $500.

7. Each plaintiff purchased a vacuum from defendants through a written conditional sales contract that included these terms: $100 down and $18 per week for 97 weeks. A copy of the contract signed by Norma Beal is attached as Exhibit A.

8. The terms described in paragraph 7 of this Complaint would result in each plaintiff paying $1,720 for the vacuum.

9. During defendants' solicitation and sale to each plaintiff, defendant never revealed the information described in paragraphs 6 and 8 of this Amended Complaint.

10. Defendants told each plaintiff that she "should not miss this great opportunity" and that the offer was "for today only."

11. Defendants intended to induce each plaintiff to purchase a vacuum cleaner through representations that defendant knew were untrue or misleading, in violation of Washington common law of fraud and the Federal Consumer Solicitation Act § 2.

12. Each plaintiff has paid defendants $1000 under the terms of the conditional sales contract.

13. Defendants' course of dealing with each plaintiff constituted malice.

14. Defendants continue to engage in fraudulent solicitation of sales to elderly residents of Spokane.

REQUEST FOR RELIEF

Each plaintiff requests judgment as follows:

a. Compensatory damages of $1000.

b. An order enjoining defendant from engaging in fraudulent solicitation practices;

c. Punitive damages of $50,000; and

d. The costs of this action and attorneys' fees.

Dated: June 1, [year].

Jan Fay

Jan Fay
Attorney for Plaintiffs
622 Dakota Street
Spokane, WA 99204
509-555-1212
FayGroup@gmail.com

Exercise 15-12. Rule 11

Explain whether you would sign and file the Amended Complaint under Rule 11.

Exercise 15-13. Joinder of Claims and Parties

Apply the federal joinder rules to the Amended Complaint (ignore subject matter jurisdiction).

1. Explain whether Poll, Beal, and James *are able* to join together as plaintiffs.

2. Explain whether plaintiffs *are able* to join Darby and Elite as defendants.

3. Explain whether Poll, Beal, and James *must* join as plaintiffs and whether they *must* join both Darby and Elite as defendants.

4. Explain whether plaintiffs *are able* to assert two claims (fraud and FCSA) against the defendants in same suit.

5. What facts would Jan Fay need to ascertain in order to satisfy the prerequisites for a class action under Rule 23(a) and fit within one of the categories of class actions under Rule 23(b)?

6. Fran Bell's Notes of Initial Interviews with Defendants

Alex Hernandez

Alex is a senior vice-president of Elite Vacuum Sales, Inc. Alex has been with Elite from its founding in Oregon thirty years ago. Elite's business model is to produce high quality vacuum cleaners and accessories and to sell the products through door-to-door sales. Although some customers purchase Elite's products in cash, over 90% of the Elite's sales are through conditional sales contracts that allow customers to pay over time. The contract signed by Ms. Beal is a standard form contract provided by Elite to all sales personnel. Elite employs over 100 sales people in California, Oregon, and Washington. Most of those sales people work in California. Elite moved into the Washington market a couple years ago. All of Elite's sales people must complete a three-day training course. The course emphasizes the features of Elite's products and teaches sales people a standard door-to-door sales protocol. Because Elite produces excellent products and treats customers fairly, Elite rigorously enforces its contracts and vigorously defends lawsuits arising out of its sales. Each of the plaintiffs is currently delinquent on several weekly payments.

Jack Darby

Jack Darby became an Elite sales person two years ago, after completing the Elite training course. He follows the door-to-door sales protocol he learned in the course. That protocol has the following features:

- Target low to middle income neighborhoods, which Elite's research shows are the best sales territory for its products;

- Dress in business casual clothing and present a neat and clean appearance;

- Greet potential customers and ask for permission to enter the home to demonstrate Elite's "fantastic" products;

- Enthusiastically demonstrate the effectiveness of Elite's products on the potential customer's floor and furniture;

- Emphasize the quality of Elite's products and the easy weekly payment method of purchase;

- Create a sense of urgency by offering a time-sensitive incentive, such as a free accessory or discount;

- Review the first paragraph of the conditional sales contract with the customer word-by-word, filling in the blanks during the explanation;

- Invite the customer to review the rest of the contract;

- Secure the customer's signature on the contract;

- Immediately deliver the products to the customer; and,

- Provide the customer with contact information for Elite's customer assistance department.

Darby generally recalls his interactions with the plaintiffs, though not all of the details. He does not recall whether any of the plaintiffs asked the total price of the vacuums he sold them. His practice is to emphasize the advantages of the weekly payment plan and to discuss the total price if the customer asks directly. Darby is offended by the lawsuit. He believes that Elite sells excellent products and that its sales practices fully comply with the law.

7. Answer and Reply

United States District Court for
the Eastern District of Washington

Judy Poll, Norma Beal, and Edna James, Plaintiffs	)))	
v.	))	No. CV 2019-003
Jack Darby and Elite Vacuum Sales, Inc., Defendants	)))	

Defendants' Answer, Defense, and Counterclaims

DEFENDANTS' ANSWER

1. Defendants admit the allegations in paragraphs 1, 3, 4, 5, 7, and 8 of the Amended Complaint.

2. Defendants deny the allegations in paragraphs 6, 9, 10, 11, 12, 13, and 14 of the Complaint.

3. Regarding paragraph 2 of the Complaint, Defendants admit that each Plaintiff is domiciled in Spokane, Washington, but are without information sufficient to form a belief about the Plaintiffs' ages.

DEFENDANTS' DEFENSE

4. Plaintiffs' Amended Complaint fails to state a claim upon which relief can be granted.

COUNTERCLAIMS OF DEFENDANT ELITE VACUUM SALES

5. Plaintiffs are each in default for failing to make payments in accordance with the terms of the Conditional Sales Contract attached to Plaintiffs' Complaint.

6. Each Plaintiff is now liable for the remaining amount due under the terms of paragraph 7 of the Conditional Sales Contract.

7. Defendant Elite Vacuum Sales, Inc., has and will incur costs and attorneys' fees in this action.

8. Defendant Elite Vacuum Sales, Inc., is entitled to recover costs and attorneys' fees from Plaintiffs under the terms of paragraph 6 of the Conditional Sales Contract.

Defendants request:

a. An order dismissing the Amended Complaint on its merits;

b. Judgment for Defendant Elite Vacuum Sales, Inc., against Plaintiffs for the remaining amount due on each of their Conditional Sales Contracts;

c. Judgment for Defendant Elite Vacuum Sales, Inc., against Plaintiffs for the costs and attorneys' fees Defendants incurred in this action; and

d. Other relief that the court deems appropriate.

Dated: June 30, [year].

Fran Bell

Fran Bell
Attorney for Defendants
444 East 2nd Ave
Portland, OR 97204
(503) 444-5252
StongLaw@gmail.com

Exercise 15-14. Joinder by Defendant

Analyze the following:

1. Do the federal joinder rules *allow* Elite to make its counterclaim?

2. Do the federal joinder rules *require* Elite to make its counterclaim?

3. Does a federal court have subject matter jurisdiction over Elite's counterclaim?

United States District Court for
the Eastern District of Washington

Judy Poll, Norma Beal, and Edna James, Plaintiffs	)))	
v.	))	No. CV 2019-003
Jack Darby and Elite Vacuum Sales Inc., Defendants	))))	

Plaintiffs' Reply to Counterclaim of Elite Vacuum Sales Inc. (Elite)

REPLY

1. Plaintiffs deny paragraphs 5, 6, and 8 of Defendant Elite's Counterclaim.

2. Plaintiffs lack information sufficient to form a belief as to the truth of the allegations in paragraph 7 of Defendant Elite's Counterclaim.

AFFIRMATIVE DEFENSES

3. The Conditional Sales Contracts Plaintiffs entered with Defendants are unenforceable because they were procured through Defendants' fraud and duress.

REQUEST FOR RELIEF

Plaintiffs request that the court dismiss Defendant Elite's Counterclaim and award costs and other appropriate relief to Plaintiffs.

Dated: July 15, [year].

Jan Fay

Jan Fay
Attorney for Plaintiffs
622 Dakota Street
Spokane, WA 99204
509-555-1212
FayGroup@gmail.com

8. Right to a Jury

United States District Court for
the Eastern District of Washington

Judy Poll, Norma Beal, and Edna James, Plaintiffs	)))	
v.	))	No. CV 2019-003
Jack Darby and Elite Vacuum Sales, Inc., Defendants	))	

Demand for a Jury Trial

Under FRCP 38(b), Plaintiffs demand a jury trial on all issues triable of right by a jury.

Dated: July 20, [year].

Jan Fay

Jan Fay
Attorney for Plaintiffs
622 Dakota Street
Spokane, WA 99204
509-555-1212
FayGroup@gmail.com

Exercise 15-15. Right to a Jury

The judge asks her law clerk to brief the question of whether the Plaintiffs are entitled to a jury on the liability and remedy issues in the case. In the role of the judge's clerk, respond to the judge.

9. Discovery

Exercise 15-16. Initial Disclosures

Prepare plaintiffs' initial disclosures to defendants under Rule 26(a)(1).

United States District Court for the Eastern District of Washington

Judy Poll, Norma Beal, and Edna James, Plaintiffs	)))
v.	)) No. CV 2019-003)
Jack Darby and Elite Vacuum Sales, Inc., Defendants	))

Plaintiffs' First Request for Production of Documents from Defendant Elite Vacuum Sales, Inc.

Plaintiffs request that Defendant Elite Vacuum Sales, Inc., respond to the following requests for production of documents and electronically stored information within 30 days in accordance with Federal Rule of Civil Procedure 34. For purposes of these requests, Elite Vacuum Sales, Inc., is referred to as "Elite."

1. Forms for conditional sales contracts Elite provided to Jack Darby in [year].

2. Training material Elite provided to Jack Darby from [year] through [year + 2].

3. Records of door-to-door sales by Jack Darby of Elite products to customers in the State of Washington from [year]–[year + 2].

4. Customer complaints regarding vacuums sold by Elite.

5. Memoranda from Elite's corporate counsel to Elite's officers regarding compliance with the Federal Consumer Solicitation Act.

6. Memoranda of interviews of Elite's sales people conducted by Elite's insurer after June 1 [year].

Jan Fay

Jan Fay
Attorney for Plaintiffs
622 Dakota Street
Spokane, WA 99204
509-555-1212
FayGroup@gmail.com

Exercise 15-17. Requests for Production of Documents

Fran Bell is preparing Defendants' response to Plaintiffs' First Requests for Production of Documents from Defendants. Fran Bell intends to produce documents in response to requests 1, 2, and 3. Fran Bell would like your advice on what objections, if any, Defendants could assert to requests 4, 5, and 6.

Summaries of Deposition Testimony.

Fran Bell deposed Norma Beal, Judy Poll, and Edna James. Jan Fay deposed Jack Darby and Alex Hernandez. The substance of their deposition testimony follows.

Deposition of Norma Beal.

- Norma Beal is 74 years old.

- She lives in her own home in Spokane, Washington.

- In April, she was contacted by door-to-door vacuum cleaner salesperson, Jack Darby.

- Darby had not contacted her before knocking on her door on the day he sold her a vacuum.

- Darby was selling what he called "a revolutionary concept in fine carpet and furniture care."

- Darby asked if he could demonstrate the product. Ms. Beal agreed.

- Darby entered her house and sprinkled dirt on her carpet and furniture. He did this without asking her. It was upsetting.

- Darby demonstrated his product, a vacuum cleaner, for approximately 15 minutes. Darby aggressively pointed out the effectiveness and quality of the product.

- After the demonstration, Darby gave Ms. Beal "a high-pressure sales pitch," urging her to purchase the vacuum cleaner. Darby told her that she "should not miss this great opportunity," that the sale terms were "easy weekly payments," and that this offer was "for today only."

- Ms. Beal told Darby that she was unsure about whether to purchase the machine. She was hoping that he would pack up and leave her home.

- Instead, Darby again told her the she should "act now on this great opportunity." He took out a contract and began reading it to her. He filled in the blanks and told her that she would "only have to pay $100 today and $18 per week."

- Ms. Beal did not ask Darby the total price of the vacuum. She glimpsed at the contract before signing it but "did not understand much of what she was reading, so she just signed the contract."

- Ms. Beal gave Darby $100 in cash as a down payment.

- Ms. Beal made 50 weekly payments of $18 per payment, for a total of $900.

- Ms. Beal has not made a weekly payment for the past several months.
- Ms. Beal learned from Edna James that the Elite vacuums they purchased were worth less than $500.
- Ms. Beal thinks that the vacuum works OK but that she grossly overpaid.
- Ms. Beal called Darby and complained about the sale terms and the fact that Darby never informed her of the full price of the machine—$1,720.
- Darby said that she had signed valid contracts of her own free will and he intended to enforce the contracts.
- Ms. Beal knows other people from the Spokane Chapter of the Association for Retired Persons who purchased vacuums from Darby and regret it.
- Ms. Beal believes that Darby "preys on seniors with high-pressure misleading, sales practices."

Deposition of Judy Poll.

Except for the following, the substance of Judy Poll's deposition testimony is the same as the testimony of Norma Beal.

- Judy Poll is 65 years old.
- After Darby completed his demonstration of the vacuum, Ms. Poll asked Darby to leave. Instead of leaving, Darby began more demonstrations of the vacuum and told Ms. Poll that "she would be making a big mistake" if she did not "seize this one-time opportunity."
- Ms. Poll did not read any of the contract. She did not ask Darby the total price of the vacuum. She signed the contract because she thought it was the "only way to get Darby to leave."

Deposition of Edna James.

Except for the following, the substance of Edna James's deposition testimony is the same as the testimony of Norma Beal.

- Edna James is 69 years old.
- When Darby finished his demonstration, Ms. James asked Darby to compare the Elite vacuum to other brands. Darby told Ms. James that "no other manufacturer produces products that match the quality of Elite's vacuums and accessories" and that she "should not waste her time looking at inferior brands."
- When Darby filled in the blanks in the first paragraph of the contract, Ms. James asked Darby the total price of the vacuum. Darby "never gave a straight answer to the question." Instead Darby reemphasized the "easy weekly payments," assuring Ms. James that she could afford the $18 per week.

Deposition of Alex Hernandez.

- Alex Hernandez is a senior vice-president of Elite Vacuum Sales, Inc.
- Alex has been with Elite from its founding in Oregon thirty years ago.

- Elite's business model is to produce high quality vacuum cleaners and accessories and to sell the products through door-to-door sales.
- Although some customers purchase Elite's products in cash, over 90% of the Elite's sales are through conditional sales contracts that allow customers to pay over time.
- The contract signed by Ms. Beal is a standard form contract provided by Elite to all sales personnel.
- Elite employs over 100 sales people in California, Oregon, and Washington. Most of those sales people work in California. Elite moved into the Washington market a couple years ago.
- All of Elite's sales people must complete a three-day training course. The course emphasizes the features of Elite's products and teaches sales people a standard door-to-door sales protocol.
- Because Elite produces excellent products and treats customers fairly, Elite rigorously enforces its contracts and vigorously defends lawsuits arising out of its sales.
- Each of the plaintiffs is currently delinquent on her weekly payments under the contract.
- Elite receives complaints from approximately 25% of its customers. Most complaints concern the conditional sales contracts rather than Elite's products. Several complaints involve Jack Darby.
- Elite has been a defendant in approximately a dozen lawsuits under the Federal Consumer Solicitation Act and similar state laws. Elite settled most of those suits. One of those previous lawsuits involved Jack Darby.
- Elite has been a plaintiff in "numerous" lawsuits to enforce the provisions of its conditional sales contracts. Elite prevailed in most of those suits, usually by means of a default judgment.

Deposition of Jack Darby.

- Jack Darby became an Elite sales person two years ago, after completing the Elite training course. He follows the door-to-door sales protocol he learned in the course. That protocol has the following features:
  - Target low to middle income neighborhoods, which Elite's research shows are the best sales territory for its products;
  - Dress in business casual clothing and present a neat and clean appearance;
  - Greet potential customers and ask for permission to enter the home to demonstrate Elite's "fantastic" products;
  - Enthusiastically demonstrate the effectiveness of Elite's products on the potential customer's floor and furniture;
  - Emphasize the quality of Elite's products and the easy weekly payment method of purchase;
  - Create a sense of urgency by offering a time-sensitive incentive, such as a free accessory or discount;

- ○ Review the first paragraph of the conditional sales contract with the customer word-by-word, filling in the blanks during the explanation;
- ○ Invite the customer to review the rest of the contract;
- ○ Secure the customer's signature on the contract;
- ○ Immediately deliver the products to the customer; and
- ○ Provide the customer with contact information for Elite's customer assistance department.

- Darby recalls his interactions with the plaintiffs. On that day, he was offering a free "edging" accessory for customers who purchased vacuums.

- Each of the plaintiffs invited him into her home and none of the plaintiffs asked him to leave at any time.

- He does not believe any of the plaintiffs asked the total price of the vacuums he sold them. If they had asked, he would have followed his practice of emphasizing the advantages of the weekly payment plan and discussing the total price if the customer asks directly.

- He encouraged each of the plaintiffs to carefully read the conditional sales contract before signing it.

- Each of the plaintiffs seemed delighted with her purchase.

- Darby is offended by the lawsuit. He believes that Elite sells excellent products and that its sales practices fully comply with the law. His personal and business ethics are high. He would never engage in fraud.

Exercise 15-18. Experts

Jan Fay hired Dan and Inga, experts in the vacuum cleaner industry, to advise about the price and quality of Elite's vacuums. Dan and Inga each conducted research on the Elite Model 4281 and reported to Jan Fay their opinions on the price and quality of that vacuum. Dan concluded that the Elite Model 4281 had comparable features and was of comparable quality to vacuums from several other manufacturers, which were available for under $500 at many nationwide retailers. Inga concluded that the Elite 4281 was of significantly higher quality than the vacuums Elite's competitors sold for under $500. Jan Fay paid Inga, thanked her for her opinion, and told Inga that she would not testify at trial. Jan Fay and Dan agreed that for a fee, Dan would testify for the plaintiffs in the suit.

1. How, if at all, can Defendants learn about Dan's and Inga's opinions during discovery?

2. How does Jan Fay's retention of these experts affect the Plaintiffs' required disclosures to Defendants?

10. Motion for Summary Judgment

United States District Court for
the Eastern District of Washington

Judy Poll, Norma Beal, and Edna James, Plaintiffs	)))	
v.	))	No. CV 2019-003
Jack Darby and Elite Vacuum Sales, Inc., Defendants	)))	

Defendant Elite Vacuum Sales, Inc., Motion for Summary Judgment

Based on the Plaintiffs' testimony in their depositions, Defendant Elite Vacuum Sales, Inc., moves for summary judgment on its counterclaims. The grounds for the motion are that there is no genuine dispute of material fact and that Defendant Elite Vacuum Sales Inc., is entitled to judgment as a matter of law.

Fran Bell

Fran Bell
Attorney for Defendants
444 East 2nd Ave
Portland, OR 97204
(503) 444-5252
StongLaw@gmail.com

Exercise 15-19. Motion for Summary Judgment

In the role of law clerk for the judge assigned to the case, analyze how the court should rule on Elite's motion for summary judgment.

11. Trial

Plaintiffs' Case.

Each Plaintiff testified. Their testimony was substantially the same as their deposition testimony. In addition, each Plaintiff testified that she felt "duped by Darby" and "humiliated" that she "fell for Darby's high-pressure, misleading sales pitch," and signed the "outrageous" conditional sales contract agreeing to "grossly overpay" for the vacuum.

Dan Weld testified that the Elite Model 4281 had comparable features and was of comparable quality to vacuums from several other manufacturers, which were available for $400 to $500 at many nationwide retailers. He based his opinion on his testing of the Elite Model 4281 and his experience developed over 20 years in the retail vacuum business. Weld relied in part on documents setting out the technical specifications and features of the Elite Model 4281 and several comparable vacuums. Those documents were admitted into evidence.

Defendants' Case.

Alex Hernandez testified. His testimony was substantially the same as his deposition testimony. In addition, he testified that Dan Weld's conclusions were "simply wrong." Hernandez pointed out several differences between the Elite Model 4281 and the vacuums Weld analyzed from other manufacturers. Hernandez concluded that the Elite Model 4281 was "of substantially higher quality" than the other vacuums Weld analyzed.

Jack Darby testified. His testimony was substantially the same as his deposition testimony. In addition, Darby testified that although his demonstration of Elite's products to each Plaintiff was "thorough and enthusiastic," he "did not try to intimidate or mislead the Plaintiffs in any way."

Motions for Judgment as a Matter of Law.

At the close of all evidence, Plaintiffs and Defendants made motions for judgment as a matter of law. The judge denied those motions.

Jury Instructions.

Plaintiffs and Defendants submitted proposed jury instructions to the judge at the final pretrial conference. After discussing the proposed instructions with Jan Fay and Fran Bell, the judge drafted a final set of jury instructions. Neither Jan Fay nor Fran Bell objected to the final instructions. At the close of evidence, the judge read the final instructions to the jury. Key instructions defined the elements of Washington common law fraud, the elements of a claim under the Federal Consumer Solicitation Act, "malice," "compensatory damages," and "punitive damages." The instructions were consistent with the law in the law clerk's memo at the beginning of this chapter.

12. Jury Verdict

After several hours of deliberation, the jury returned a verdict.

United States District Court for
the Eastern District of Washington

Judy Poll, Norma Beal,	)	
and Edna James, Plaintiffs	)	
	)	
v.	)	No. CV 2019-003
	)	
Jack Darby and Elite Vacuum Sales, Inc.,	)	
Defendants	)	

QUESTION 1. Do you find by a preponderance of the evidence that Defendants are liable to the Plaintiffs under Washington common law fraud?

Answer: We do.

QUESTION 2. Do you find by a preponderance of the evidence that Defendants are liable to the Plaintiffs for violations of the Federal Consumer Solicitation Act?

Answer: We do.

QUESTION 3. If the answer to either QUESTION 1 or QUESTION 2 is "We do," what amount of compensatory damages, if any, are Plaintiffs entitled to recover?

Norma Beal	*$600*
Edna James	*$600*
Judy Poll	*$600*

QUESTION 4. If the answer to either QUESTION 1 or QUESTION 2 is "We do," do you find by a preponderance of the evidence that Defendants were guilty of malice?

Answer: We do not.

QUESTION 5. If the answer to QUESTION 4 is "We do," what amount of punitive damages, if any, are Plaintiffs entitled to recover?

Answer: Not applicable.

QUESTION 6. If the answer to both QUESTION 1 and QUESTION 2 is "We do not," how many weekly payments do you find by a preponderance of the evidence that each Plaintiff made to Defendant Elite Vacuum Sales,

Inc., under the terms of the conditional sales contract that each Plaintiff signed?

Norma Beal	*Not applicable.*
Edna James	*Not applicable.*
Judy Poll	*Not applicable.*

13. Post-Judgment Motions and Appeal

Based on the jury verdict, the court entered judgment in favor of the Plaintiffs and dismissed the counterclaims of Defendant Elite Vacuum Sales Inc., on the merits.

Exercise 15-20. Motions for a New Trial and for Judgment as a Matter of Law

Defendant served and filed timely motions for judgment as a matter of law and for a new trial on the ground that the evidence was insufficient to support the jury's answers to QUESTION 1 and QUESTION 2. Choose either party— make the party's arguments in support or in opposition to the motions.

Exercise 15-21. Appeal

Assume that the trial court denied Defendants' motion for judgment as a matter of law and granted Defendants' motion for a new trial.

1. Plaintiffs would like to immediately appeal the trial court's order granting the new trial. Explain to Jan Fay (a) whether Plaintiffs have the right to an immediate appeal and (b) whether the court of appeals is likely to exercise its discretion to allow an immediate appeal or grant a writ to review the trial court's order.

2. If the court of appeals decided to allow an immediate appeal of the trial court's order granting a new trial, explain to Jan Fay the standard of review that the court of appeals would apply.

Exercise 15-22. What Law Governs?

Assume that the trial court denied Defendants' new trial motion on two grounds:

(A) Washington state rules of procedure require defendants to move for a new trial within 10 days after entry of judgment, which Defendants failed to do. They served their new trial motion 20 days after the entry of judgment.

(B) Washington law applies the "scintilla" test to new trial motions (the motion should be denied if there is any evidence that supports the non-moving party), while federal law applies the "clear weight of the evidence" test (new trial motions should be denied unless the trial court concludes that the verdict is against the clear weight of the evidence). The trial court applied Washington law and found that Plaintiffs' evidence met the "scintilla" test.

Defendants appealed the denial of Defendants' new trial motion on the grounds that the trial court applied the wrong law when deciding Defendants' new trial motion. In the role of law clerk for the court of appeals, analyze for the court:

1. Whether the trial court applied the correct law on ground (A) above.

2. Whether the trial court applied the correct law on ground (B) above.

14. Preclusion

Assume that neither Plaintiffs nor Defendants filed post-judgment motions or appeals. Six months after the entry of judgment, a former employee of Elite Vacuum Sales Inc., Sam, approached Jan Fay. Assume that Sam was a second Elite sales person in Washington for the past two years. Sam attended Elite's training course two years ago. During the course, the trainers emphasized that that the weekly payment scheme was critical to Elite's strong profitability. Trainers cautioned that under no circumstances should the sales people reveal the total price of the vacuums to potential customers. According to the trainers, the key to successful sales was to emphasize the small amount of the weekly payment, to "take command" of the potential customer's home, to ignore customer's requests that the sales people leave the home, to discourage potential customers from reading the conditional sales contract, and to tell customers what they wanted to hear. Jan Fay confirmed Sam's statements in interviews with other former Elite employees, who told similar stories about Elite's training program and business practices. Norma Beal, Edna James, Judy Poll, and Jan Fay are convinced that the statements of Sam and other former Elite employees demonstrate that Elite was guilty of malice.

Exercise 15-23. Preclusion

1. Based on the former employees' statements, Judy Poll, Norma Beal, and Edna James again sue Jack Darby and Elite Vacuum Sales, Inc. for punitive damages under the Federal Consumer Solicitation Act. Defendants moved to dismiss the suit based on claim preclusion. Make arguments on behalf of Defendants in support of the motion.

2. Ignore the facts in question 1. Rather than bringing a second suit against Defendants, what post-judgment motion could Plaintiffs make to get before the court the former employees' statements and Plaintiffs' claims for punitive damages?

3. Ignore the facts in questions 1 and 2. Based on the former employees' statements, Jan Fay brings suit against Elite Vacuum Sales, Inc., and Jack Darby. The plaintiffs are other Washington residents who purchased Elite vacuums as a result of Darby's door-to-door solicitations. Explain why Defendants will not be able to use the jury's answer to QUESTION 4 in the verdict above to establish, via issue preclusion, that they are not guilty of malice.

15. Professionalism

Exercise 15-24. Agreeing to Represent Clients; Settlement

1. If potential plaintiffs with stories similar to the stories of Beal, Poll, and James asked you to represent them, what considerations would drive your decision?

2. If potential defendants with stories similar to Elite and Darby asked you to represent them, what considerations would drive your decision?

Assume plaintiffs brought the lawsuit described in Exercise 15-23.

3. Would you advise defendants to make a formal offer of judgment?

4. Would you advise plaintiffs to accept a favorable settlement offer from Defendants if the settlement agreement contained confidentiality and non-disclosure provisions designed to prevent plaintiffs from revealing anything about Defendants' actions?

Index